Number 59456   Tuesday 15 June 2010   http://www.london-gazette.co.uk   1

The London Gazette

Registered as a newspaper
Published by Authority
Established 1665

of Monday 14 June 2010
Supplement No. 2

List of Statutory Publications 2008

Contents

Preliminary Information	2
UK Legislation	**4**
Public general acts	4
Public general acts - explanatory notes	7
Local acts	8
Measures of the General Synod	8
Other statutory publications	8
Statutory Instruments, by subject heading	9
Statutory Instruments, by number	279
Subsidiary Numbers	319
Scottish Legislation	**325**
Acts of the Scottish Parliament	325
Acts of the Scottish Parliament - Explanatory notes	325
Other Scottish statutory publications	325
Scottish Statutory Instruments, by subject heading	326
Scottish Statutory Instruments, by number	367
Northern Ireland Legislation	373
Acts of the Northern Ireland Assembly	373
Acts of the Northern Ireland Assembly - explanatory notes	374
Other Northern Ireland statutory publications	374
Statutory Rules of Northern Ireland, by subject heading	375
Statutory Rules of Northern Ireland, by number	413
Alphabetical Index	**420**

Preface

Content and Layout

This list contains details of the statutory publications and accompanying Explanatory documents published during the year. It is arranged in three main sections that group the primary and delegated legislation of the United Kingdom, England & Wales, Scotland and Northern Ireland (Statutory Instruments made by the National Assembly for Wales are included within the UK section). Within each section the publications are listed in the same order:

- Acts and their Explanatory Notes;

- Statutory Instruments or Statutory Rules, arranged under subject headings. (Each entry includes, where available or appropriate: the enabling power; the date when the instrument was issued, made and laid and comes into force; a short note of any effect; territorial extent and classification; a note of the relevant EU legislation; pagination; ISBN and price);

- A numerical listing of the instruments, with their subject heading. This list also includes any subsidiary numbers in the series: C for commencement orders; L for instruments relating to court fees or procedure in England and Wales; NI for Orders in Council relating only to Northern Ireland; S for instruments relating only to Scotland, W for instruments made by the National Assembly for Wales;

There is a single alphabetical, subject index, which includes both subject headings and descriptive terms from the title. The index is cumulated throughout the year

Unpublished Statutory Instruments

Although the majority of Statutory Instruments are formally published, some SIs of limited, local application are unpublished. These are listed in this publication when they have been received and processed by the TSO Bibliographic Department.

Access to Documents

The full text of all legislation and delegated legislation (Statutory Instruments) is available from the OPSI website on the day of publication. The website contains legislation dating back to 1988 for Acts and 1987 for Statutory Instruments.

The relevant web addresses:

UK Acts and Statutory Instruments
www.opsi.gov.uk/legislation/uk.htm

Scottish Acts and Statutory Instruments
www.opsi.gov.uk/legislation/scotland/about.htm

Northern Ireland Acts and Statutory Rules
www.opsi.gov.uk/legislation/northernireland/ni_legislation.htm

Welsh Statutory Instruments
www.opsi.gov.uk/legislation/wales/wales_legislation.htm

The full text of the general statutory instruments and statutory rules are also published in the respective annual editions of: *Statutory Instruments, Scottish Statutory Instruments, Statutory Instruments made by the National Assembly for Wales* and *Statutory Rules of Northern Ireland.*

Copies of legislation and published delegated legislation can be purchased from the addresses on the back cover.

Copies of local instruments unobtainable from The Stationery Office may be obtained at prevailing prices from:

- The National Archives, Kew, Richmond, Surrey, TW9 4DU (from 1922 onwards – except for the years 1942, 1950, 1951 and up to SI no. 940 of 1952)

- Reader Information Services Department, The National Archives, Kew, Richmond, Surrey TW9 4DU (as before, up to 1960)

- British Library, Official Publications and Social Sciences Service, 96 Euston Road, London, NW1 2DB (as before, up to 1980)

Standing Orders

Standing orders can be set up to ensure the receipt of all statutory publications in a particular subject area, without the need to continually scan lists of new publications or place individual orders. The subject categories used can be either broad or very specific. For more information please contact the TSO Standing Orders department on 0870 600 5522, or fax: 0870 600 5533.

Copyright

Legislation from official sources is reproducible freely under waiver of copyright. Full details of which can be found at: http://www.nationalarchives.gov.uk/documents/reproduction-legislation.pdf

Most other TSO publications are Crown or Parliamentary copyright. Information about the licensing arrangements for Crown and Parliamentary copyright can be found on The National Archives' website at http://www.nationalarchives.gov.uk/information-management/our-services/click-use.htm.

Alternatively, you can apply for a licence by contacting the following address:

The National Archives
Kew, Richmond, Surrey
TW9 4DU

For any other use of this material please apply for a Click-Use PSI Licence atFor any other use of this material please apply for a Click-Use PSI Licence at

Http://www.opsi.gov.uk/click-use/system/online/pLogin.asp

or by writing to:

The National Archives
Kew, Richmond, Surrey
TW9 4DU

e-mail: psi@nationalarchives.gsi.gov.uk

List of Abbreviations

accord.	accordance
art(s).	article(s)
c.	chapter
C.	Commencement
CI.	Channel Islands
E.	England
EC	European Commission
EU	European Union
G.	Guernsey
GB.	Great Britain
GLA	Greater London Authority
IOM	Isle of Man
J.	Jersey
L.	Legal: fees or procedure in courts in E. & W.
NI.	Northern Ireland
para(s).	paragraph(s)
reg(s).	regulation(s)
s(s).	section(s)
S.	Scotland
sch(s).	schedule(s)
SI.	Statutory instrument(s)
SR.	Statutory rule(s) of Northern Ireland
SR & O.	Statutory rules and orders
SSI	Scottish Statutory Instrument
UK.	United Kingdom
W.	Wales

UK Legislation

Acts

Public General Acts 2008

Appropriation Act 2008: Chapter 3. - [1], 42p.: 30 cm. - Royal assent, 20th March 2008. An Act to authorise the use of resources for the service of the years ending with 31st March 2007 and 31st March 2008 and to apply certain sums out of the Consolidated Fund to the service of the year ending with 31st March 2008; and to appropriate the supply authorised in this Session of Parliament for the service of the years ending with 31st March 2007 and 31st March 2008. - 978-0-10-540308-1 £7.50

Appropriation (No. 2) Act 2008: Chapter 8. - 76p.: 30 cm. - Royal assent, 21st July 2008. An Act to authorise the use of resources for the service of the year ending with 31st March 2009 and to apply to certain sums out of the Consolidated Fund to the service of the year ending with 31st March 2009; to appropriate the supply authorised in this Session of Parliament for the service of the year ending 31st March 2009; and to repeal certain Consolidated Fund and Appropriation Acts. - 978-0-10-540808-6 £12.00

Appropriation (No. 3) Act 2008: Chapter 19. - [8]p.: 30 cm. - Royal assent, 16th October 2008. An Act to authorise the use of resources for the service of the year ending with 31st March 2009 and to apply a sum out of the Consolidated Fund to the service of that year; and to appropriate the supply authorised by this Act for the service of that year. - 978-0-10-541908-2 £4.00

Banking (Special Provisions) Act 2008: Chapter 2. - ii, 24p.: 30 cm. - Royal assent, 21st February 2008. An Act to make provision to enable the Treasury in certain circumstances to make an order relating to the transfer of securities issued by, or of property, rights or liabilities belonging to, an authorised deposit-taker; to make further provision in relation to building societies. Explanatory notes to assist in the understanding of the Act will be available separately. - 978-0-10-540208-4 £4.50

Channel Tunnel Rail Link (Supplementary Provisions) Act 2008: Chapter 5. - [2], 2p.: 30 cm. - Royal assent, 22nd May 2008. An Act to make provision amending, and supplementary to, the Channel Tunnel Rail Link Act 1996. Explanatory notes to assist in the understanding of the Act are available separately (ISBN 9780105604082). - 978-0-10-540508-5 £3.00

Child Maintenance and Other Payments Act 2008: Chapter 6. - iii, 85p.: 30 cm. - Royal assent, 5 June 2008. An Act to establish the Child Maintenance and Enforcement Commission; to amend the law relating to child support; to make provision about lump sum payments to or in respect of persons with diffuse mesothelioma. Explanatory notes to assist in the understanding of the Act are available (ISBN 9780105606086). With correction slip dated October 2008. - 978-0-10-540608-2 £13.50

Children and Young Persons Act 2008: Chapter 23. - iii, 44p.: 30 cm. - Royal assent, 13th November 2008. An Act to make provision about the delivery of local authority social work services for children and young persons; to amend parts 2 and 3 of the Children Act 1989; to make further provision about the functions of local authorities and others in relation to children and young persons; to make provision about the enforcement of care standards in relation to certain establishments or agencies connected with children; to make provision about the independent review of determinations relating to adoption. Explanatory notes to the Act are available separately (ISBN 9780105623083). - 978-0-10-542308-9 £9.00

Climate Change Act 2008: Chapter 27. - v, 103p.: 30 cm. - Royal assent, 26th November 2008. An Act to set a target for the year 2050 for the reduction of targeted greenhouse gas emissions; to provide for a system of carbon budgeting; to establish a Committee on Climate Change; to confer powers to establish trading schemes for the purpose of limiting greenhouse gas emissions or encouraging activities that reduce such emissions or remove greenhouse gas from the atmosphere; to make provision about adaptation to climate change; to confer powers to make schemes for providing financial incentives to produce less domestic waste and to recycle more of what is produced; to make provision about the collection of household waste; to confer powers to make provision about charging for single use carrier bags; to amend the provisions of the Energy Act 2004 about renewable transport fuel obligations; to make provision about carbon emissions reduction targets; to make other provision about climate change. Explanatory notes to the Act are available separately (ISBN 9780105627081). - 978-0-10-542708-7 £15.50

Consolidated Fund Act 2008: Chapter 33. - [8]p.: 30 cm. - Royal assent, 18th December 2008. An Act to authorise the use of resources for the service of the years ending with 31st March 2009 and 31st March 2010 and to apply certain sums out of the Consolidated Fund to the service of the years ending with 31st March 2009 and 31st March 2010. - 978-0-10-543308-8 £4.00

Counter-Terrorism Act 2008: Chapter 28. - vi, 113p.: 30 cm. - Royal assent, 26th November 2008. An Act to confer further powers to gather and share information for counter-terrorism and other purposes; to make further provision about the detention and questioning of terrorist suspects and the prosecution and punishment of terrorist offences; to impose notification requirements on persons convicted of such offences; to confer further powers to act against terrorist financing, money laundering and certain other activities; to provide for review of certain Treasury decisions and about evidence in, and other matters connected with, review proceedings; to amend the law relating to inquiries; to amend the definition of "terrorism"; to amend the enactments relating to terrorist offences, control orders and the forfeiture of terrorist cash; to provide for recovering the costs of policing at certain gas facilities; to amend provisions about the appointment of special advocates in Northern Ireland. Explanatory notes to the Act are available separately (ISBN 9780105628088). - 978-0-10-542808-4 £18.00

Criminal Evidence (Witness Anonymity) Act 2008: Chapter 15. - [2], 8p.: 30 cm. - Royal assent, 21st July 2008. An Act to make provision for the making of orders for securing the anonymity of witnesses in criminal proceedings. Explanatory notes to assist in the understanding of this Act are available separately (ISBN 9780105615088). - 978-0-10-541508-4 £3.00

Criminal Justice and Immigration Act 2008: Chapter 4. - ix, 326p.: 30 cm. - Royal assent, 8th May 2008. An Act to make further provision about criminal justice (including provision about the police) and dealing with offenders and defaulters; to make further provision about the management of offenders; to amend the criminal law; to make further provision for combatting crime and disorder; to make provision about the mutual recognition of financial penalties; to amend the Repatriation of Prisoners Act 1984; to make provision for a new immigration status in certain cases involving criminality; to make provision about the automatic deportation of prisoners under the UK Borders Act 2007; to amend section 127 of the Criminal Justice and Public Order Act 1994 and to confer power to suspend the operation of that section. Explanatory notes to assist in the understanding of the Act are available separately (ISBN 9780105605089). With correction slip dated July 2009. - 978-0-10-540408-8 £33.50

Crossrail Act 2008: Chapter 18. - iii, 250p.: 30 cm. - Royal assent, 22nd July 2008. An Act to to make provision for a railway transport system running from Maidenhead, in the County of Berkshire, and Heathrow Airport, in the London Borough of Hillingdon, through central London to Shenfield, in the County of Essex, and Abbey Wood, in the London Borough of Greenwich. Explanatory notes to assist in the understanding of this Act are available separately (ISBN 9780105618089). With correction slip dated November 2009. - 978-0-10-541808-5 £28.00

Dormant Bank and Building Society Accounts Act 2008: Chapter 31. - iii, 26p.: 30 cm. - Royal assent, 26th November 2008. An Act to make provision for, and in connection with, money from dormant bank and building society accounts for social or environmental purposes. With correction slip dated February 2009. Explanatory notes to the Act will be available separately. - 978-0-10-543108-4 £5.00

Education and Skills Act 2008: Chapter 25. - viii, 135p.: 30 cm. - Royal assent, 26th November 2008. An Act to make provision about education and training. Explanatory notes to the Act are available separately (ISBN 9780105625087). - 978-0-10-542508-3 £19.50

Employment Act 2008: Chapter 24. - [1], ii, 20p.: 30 cm. - Royal assent, 13th November 2008. An Act to make provision about the procedure for the resolution of employment disputes; to provide for compensation for financial loss in cases of unlawful underpayment or non-payment; to make provision about the enforcement of minimum wages legislation and the application of the national minimum wage to Cadet Force Adult Volunteers and voluntary workers; to make provision about the enforcement of offences under the Employment Agencies Act 1973; to make provision about the right of trade unions to expel or exclude members on the grounds of membership of a political party. Explanatory notes to the Act are available separately (ISBN 9780105624080). - 978-0-10-542408-6 £5.00

Energy Act 2008: Chapter 32. - vi, 154p.: 30 cm. - Royal assent, 26th November 2008. An Act to make provision relating to gas importation and storage; to make provision in relation to electricity generated from renewable sources; to make provision relating to electricity transmission; to make provision about payments to small-scale generators of low-carbon electricity; to make provision about the decommissioning of energy installations and wells; to make provision about the management and disposal of waste produced during the operation of nuclear installations; to make provision relating to petroleum licences; to make provision about third party access to oil and gas infrastructure and modifications of pipelines; to make provision about reports relating to energy matters; to make provision about the duties of the Gas and Electricity Markets Authority; to make provision about payments in respect of the renewable generation of heat; to make provision relating to gas meters and electricity meters and provision relating to electricity safety; to make provision about the security of equipment, software and information relating to nuclear matters. Explanatory notes to the Act are available separately (ISBN 9780105632085). - 978-0-10-543208-1 £22.00

European Communities (Finance) Act 2008: Chapter 1. - [4]p.: 30 cm. - Royal assent, 19th February 2008. An Act to amend the definition of "the Treaties" and "the Community Treaties" in section 1(2) of the European Communities Act 1972 so as to include the decision of 7th June 2007 of the Council on the Communities' own system of resources. Explanatory notes to assist in the understanding of the Act are available separately (ISBN 9780105601081). - 978-0-10-540108-7 £3.00

European Union (Amendment) Act 2008: Chapter 7. - [12]p.: 30 cm. - Royal assent, 19th June 2008. An Act to make provision in connection with the Treaty of Lisbon amending the Treaty on European Union and the Treaty establishing the European Community, signed at Lisbon on 13th December 2007. Explanatory notes to assist in the understanding of the Act are available separately (ISBN 9780105617083). - 978-0-10-540708-9 £3.00

Finance Act 2008: Chapter 9. - x, 451p.: 30 cm. - Royal assent, 21st July 2008. An Act to grant certain duties to alter other duties and to amend the law relating to the National Debt and the Public Revenue and to make further provision in connection with finance. - 978-0-10-540908-3 £41.30

Health and Safety (Offences) Act 2008: Chapter 20. - [16]p.: 30 cm. - Royal assent, 16th October 2008. An Act to revise the mode of trial and maximum penalties applicable to certain offences relating to health and safety. Explanatory notes to assist in the understanding of this Act are available separately (ISBN 9780105620082). - 978-0-10-542008-8 £5.00

Health and Social Care Act 2008: Chapter 14. - viii, 208p.: 30 cm. - Royal assent, 21st July 2008. An Act to establish and make provision in connection with a Care Quality Commission; to make provision about health care (including provision about the National Health Service) and about social care; to make provision about reviews and investigations under the Mental Health Act 1983; to establish and make provision in connection with an Office of the Health Professions Adjudicator and make other provision about the regulation of the health care professions; to confer power to modify the regulation of social care workers; to amend the Public Health (Control of Disease) Act 1984; to provide for the payment of a grant to women in connection with pregnancy; to amend the functions of the Health Protection Agency. Explanatory notes to assist in the understanding of this Act are available separately (ISBN 9780105614081). - 978-0-10-541408-7 £26.00

Housing and Regeneration Act 2008: Chapter 17. - xiii, 256p.: 30 cm. - Royal assent, 22nd July 2008. An Act to establish the Homes and Communities Agency and make provision about it; to abolish the Urban Regeneration Agency and the Commission for the New Towns and make provision in connection with their abolition; to regulate social housing; to enable the abolition of the Housing Corporation; to make provision about sustainability certificates, landlord and tenant matters, building regulations and mobile homes; to make further provision about housing. Explanatory notes to assist in the understanding of this Act are available separately (ISBN 9780105617082). - 978-0-10-541708-8 £31.00

Human Fertilisation and Embryology Act 2008: Chapter 22. - iv, 116p.: 30 cm. - Royal assent, 13th November 2008. An Act to amend the Human Fertilisation and Embryology Act 1990 and the Surrogate Arrangements Act 1985; to make provision about the persons who in certain circumstances are to be treated in law as the parents of a child. Explanatory notes to assist in the understanding of this Act are available separately (ISBN 9780105622086). - 978-0-10-542208-2 £18.00

Local Transport Act 2008: Chapter 26. - vii, 149p.: 30 cm. - Royal assent, 26th November 2008. An Act to make further provision in relation to local transport authorities, the provision and regulation of road transport services and the subsidising of passenger transport services; to amend sections 74, 75 and 79 of the Transport Act 1985; to make provision for or in relation to committees which represent the interests of users of public transport; to rename Passenger Transport Authorities as Integrated Transport Authorities and to make further provision in relation to them; to make further provision in relation to charging for the use of roads; to make provision about the meaning of "street works" and "street works licence" in Part 3 of the New Roads and Street Works Act 1991; to amend Part 6 of the Traffic Management Act 2004 and section 90F of the Road Traffic Offenders Act 1988; to make provision in relation to the acquisition, disclosure and use of information relating to vehicles registered outside the United Kingdom. Explanatory notes to the Act are available separately (ISBN 978010-5626084). - 978-0-10-542608-0 £22.00

National Insurance Contributions Act 2008: Chapter 16. - [2], 8p.: 30 cm. - Royal assent, 21st July 2008. An Act to make provision in connection with the upper earnings limit for national insurance contributions (including in particular provision about the upper accrual point). Explanatory notes to assist in the understanding of this Act are available separately (ISBN 9780105616085). - 978-0-10-541608-1 £3.00

Pensions Act 2008: Chapter 30. - viii, 147p.: 30 cm. - Royal assent, 26th November 2008. An Act to make provision relating to pensions. Explanatory notes to the Act will be available separately. With Correction Slip dated November 2009. - 978-0-10-543008-7 £22.00

Planning Act 2008: Chapter 29. - xi, 193p.: 30 cm. - Royal assent, 26th November 2008. An Act to establish the Infrastructure Planning Commission and make provision about its functions; to make provision about, and about matters ancillary to, the authorisation of projects for the development of nationally significant infrastructure; to make provision about town and country planning; to make provision about the imposition of a Community Infrastructure Levy. Explanatory notes to the Act are available separately (ISBN 9780105629085). - 978-0-10-542908-1 £26.00

Planning and Energy Act 2008: Chapter 21. - [8]p.: 30 cm. - Royal assent, 13th November 2008. An Act to enable local planning authorities to set requirements for energy use and energy efficiency in local plans. - 978-0-10-542108-5 £4.00

Regulatory Enforcement and Sanctions Act 2008: Chapter 13. - iv, 56p.: 30 cm. - Royal assent, 21st July 2008. An Act to make provision for the establishment of the Local Better Regulation Office; for the co-ordination of regulatory enforcement by local authorities; for the creation of civil sanctions in relation to regulatory offences; for the reduction and removal of regulatory burdens. Explanatory notes to assist in the understanding of the Act are available separately (ISBN 9780105613084). - 978-0-10-541308-0 £9.00

Sale of Student Loans Act 2008: Chapter 10. - [12]p.: 30 cm. - Royal assent, 21st July 2008. An Act to enable the sale of rights to repayments of student loans. Explanatory notes to assist in the understanding of this Act are available separately (ISBN 9780105610083). - 978-0-10-541008-9 £3.00

Special Educational Needs (Information) Act 2008: Chapter 11. - [8]p.: 30 cm. - Royal assent, 21st July 2008. An Act to amend the Education Act 1996 in relation to the provision and publication of information about children who have special educational needs. Explanatory notes to assist in the understanding of this Act will be available separately. - 978-0-10-541108-6 £3.00

Statute Law (Repeals) Act 2008: Chapter 12. - [1], 27p.: 30 cm. - Royal assent, 21st July 2008. An Act to promote the reform of the statute law by the repeal, in accordance with recommendations of the Law Commission and the Scottish Law Commission, of certain enactments which (except in so far as their effect is preserved) are no longer of practical utility, and to make other provision in connection with the repeal of those enactments. Explanatory notes to assist in the understanding of this Act will be available separately. - 978-0-10-541208-3 £5.00

Public General Acts - Explanatory Notes 2008

Channel Tunnel Rail Link (Supplementary Provisions) Act 2008: chapter 5: explanatory notes. - [8]p.: 30 cm. - These notes refer to the Channel Tunnel Rail Link (Supplementary Provisions) Act 2008 (c. 5) (ISBN 9780105405085) which received Royal Assent on 22 May 2008. - 978-0-10-560408-2 £3.00

Child Maintenance and Other Payments Act 2008: chapter 6: explanatory notes. - 79p.: 30 cm. - These notes refer to the Child Maintenance and Other Payments Act 2008 (c. 6) (ISBN 9780105406082) which received Royal Assent on 5 June 2008. - 978-0-10-560608-6 £12.00

Children and Young Persons Act 2008: Chapter 23: explanatory notes. - 35p.: 30 cm. - These notes refer to the Children and Young Persons Act 2008 (c. 23) (ISBN 9780105423089) which received Royal Assent on 13 November 2008. - 978-0-10-562308-3 £9.00

Climate Change Act 2008: Chapter 27: explanatory notes. - 81p.: 30 cm. - These notes refer to the Climate Change Act 2008 (c. 27) (ISBN 9780105427087) which received Royal Assent on 26th November 2008. - 978-0-10-562708-1 £13.00

Counter-Terrorism Act 2008: Chapter 28: explanatory notes. - 46p.: 30 cm. - These notes refer to the Counter-Terrorism Act 2008 (c. 28) (ISBN 9780105428084) which received Royal Assent on 26th November 2008. - 978-0-10-562808-8 £9.00

Criminal Evidence (Witness Anonymity) Act 2008: chapter 15: explanatory notes. - 9p.: 30 cm. - These notes refer to the Criminal Evidence (Witness Anonymity) Act 2008 (c. 15) (ISBN 9780105415084) which received Royal Assent on 21st July 2008. - 978-0-10-561508-8 £3.00

Criminal Justice and Immigration Act 2008: chapter 4: explanatory notes. - 141p.: 30 cm. - These notes refer to the Criminal Justice and Immigration Act 2008 (c. 4) (ISBN 9780105404088) which received Royal Assent on 8th May 2008. - 978-0-10-560508-9 £19.50

Crossrail Act 2008: chapter 18: explanatory notes. - 52p.: 30 cm. - These notes refer to the Crossrail Act 2008 (c. 18) (ISBN 9780105418085) which received Royal Assent on 22 July 2008. - 978-0-10-561808-9 £9.00

Education and Skills Act 2008: Chapter 25: explanatory notes. - 53p.: 30 cm. - These notes refer to the Education and Skills Act 2008 (c. 25) (ISBN 9780105425083) which received Royal Assent on 26 November 2008. - 978-0-10-562508-7 £9.00

Employment Act 2008: Chapter 24: explanatory notes. - 21p.: 30 cm. - These notes refer to the Employment Act 2008 (c. 24) (ISBN 9780105424086) which received Royal Assent on 13 November 2008. - 978-0-10-562408-0 £5.00

Energy Act 2008: Chapter 32: explanatory notes. - 116p.: 30 cm. - These notes refer to the Energy Act 2008 (c. 24) (ISBN 9780105432081) which received Royal Assent on 26 November 2008. - 978-0-10-563208-5 £18.00

European Communities (Finance) Act 2008: chapter 1: explanatory notes. - [8]p.: 30 cm. - These notes refer to the European Communities (Finance) Act 2008 (c. 1) (ISBN 9780105401087) which received Royal Assent on 19th February 2008. - 978-0-10-560108-1 £3.00

European Union (Amendment) Act 2008: chapter 7: explanatory notes. - 8p.: 30 cm. - These notes refer to the European Union (Amendment) Act 2008 (c. 7) (ISBN 9780105407089) which received Royal Assent on 19 July 2008. - 978-0-10-560708-3 £3.00

Health and Safety (Offences) Act 2008: Chapter 20: explanatory notes. - 13p.: 30 cm. - These note refer to the Health and Safety (Offences) Act 2008 c. 20 (ISBN 9780105420088) which received Royal assent on 16 October 2008. - 978-0-10-562008-2 £5.00

Health and Social Care Act 2008: chapter 14: explanatory notes. - 117p.: 30 cm. - These notes refer to the Health and Social Care Act 2008 (c. 14) (ISBN 9780105414087) which received Royal Assent on 21st July 2008. - 978-0-10-561408-1 £17.50

Housing and Regeneration Act 2008: chapter 17: explanatory notes. - 144p.: 30 cm. - These notes refer to the Housing and Regeneration Act 2008 (c. 17) (ISBN 9780105417088) which received Royal Assent on 22nd July 2008. - 978-0-10-561708-2 £19.50

Human Fertilisation and Embryology Act 2008: Chapter 22: explanatory notes. - 43p.: 30 cm. - These note refer to the Human Fertilisation and Embryology Act 2008 (c. 22, ISBN 9780105422082) which received Royal assent on 13 November 2008. - 978-0-10-562208-6 *£9.00*

Local Transport Act 2008: Chapter 26: explanatory notes. - 60p.: 30 cm. - These notes refer to the Local Transport Act 2008 (c. 26) (ISBN 9780105426080) which received Royal Assent on 26 November 2008. - 978-0-10-562608-4 *£9.00*

National Insurance Contributions Act 2008: chapter 16: explanatory notes. - 12p.: 30 cm. - These notes refer to the National Insurance Contributions Act 2008 (c. 16) (ISBN 9780105416081) which received Royal Assent on 21 July 2008. - 978-0-10-561608-5 *£3.00*

Planning Act 2008: Chapter 29: explanatory notes. - 61p.: 30 cm. - These notes refer to the Planning Act 2008 (c. 29) (ISBN 9780105429081) which received Royal Assent on 26 November 2008. - 978-0-10-562908-5 *£10.50*

Regulatory Enforcement and Sanctions Act 2008: chapter 13: explanatory notes. - 35p.: 30 cm. - These notes refer to the Regulatory Enforcement and Sanctions Act 2008 (c. 13) (ISBN 9780105413080) which received Royal Assent on 21 July 2008. - 978-0-10-561308-4 *£6.50*

Sale of Student Loans Act 2008: chapter 10: explanatory notes. - [1], 9p.: 30 cm. - These notes refer to the Sale of Student Loans Act 2008 (c. 10) (ISBN 97801054010089) which received Royal Assent on 21st July 2008. - 978-0-10-561008-3 *£3.00*

Local Acts 2008

London Local Authorities and Transport for London Act 2008: Elizabeth II. Chapter iii. - ii, 36p.: 30 cm. - Royal assent, 21st July 2008. An Act to confer further powers upon local authorities in London and upon Transport for London. - 978-0-10-531407-3 *£6.50*

St. Austell Market Act 2008: Chapter ii. - [12]p.: 30 cm. - Royal assent, 19th June 2008. An Act to provide for the vesting of the undertaking of the Commissioners of St. Austell Markets and Fairs in St. Austell Market House CIC and for the continuance of that undertaking; to repeal the St. Austell Market Act 1842. - 978-0-10-531307-6 *£3.00*

Transport for London Act 2008: Chapter i. - iii, 29p.: 30 cm. - Royal assent, 22nd May 2008. An Act to confer further powers upon Transport for London. - 978-0-10-531207-9 *£5.50*

MEASURES OF THE GENERAL SYNOD

Measures of the General Synod 2008

1   **Church of England Marriage Measure 2008**
- [2], 4p.: 30 cm. - Royal Assent, 22nd May 2008. A measure passed by the General Synod of the Church of England to enable persons to be married in a place of worship in a parish with which they have a qualifying connection. - 978-0-10-531107-2 *£3.00*

Other statutory publications

Cabinet Office.

Crown Proceedings Act 1947: list of authorised government departments and the names and addresses for service of the person who is, or is acting for the purposes of the act as, solicitor for such departments, published by the Minister for the Civil Service in pursuance of section 17 of the Crown Proceedings Act 1947. - [2009 ed.]. - [8]p.: 30 cm. - Supersedes list published on 31 August 2005 by the Treasury Solicitor. - 978-0-11-840464-8 *£5.50*

Her Majesty's Stationery Office.

Chronological table of the statutes [1235-2006]. - 2v. (xii, 1350; 1351-2689p.): hdbk: 25 cm. - 2 vols. not sold separately. Part 1: Covering the acts of the Parliaments of England, Great Britain and the United Kingdom from 1235 to the end of 1974; Part 2: Covering the acts of the Parliaments of the United Kingdom from 1975 to the end of 2006, the acts of the Parliaments of Scotland from 1424 to 1707, the acts of the Scottish Parliament from 1999 to the end of 2006, and the Church Assembly measures and General Synod measures from 1920 to the end of 2006. - 978-0-11-840441-9 *£355.00 per set*

Chronological table of the statutes [1235-2007]. - 2v. (xii, 1356; 1357-2733p.): hdbk: 25 cm. - 2 vols. not sold separately. Part 1: Covering the acts of the Parliaments of England, Great Britain and the United Kingdom from 1235 to the end of 1974; Part 2: Covering the acts of the Parliaments of the United Kingdom from 1975 to the end of 2007, the acts of the Parliaments of Scotland from 1424 to 1707, the acts of the Scottish Parliament from 1999 to the end of 2007, and the Church Assembly measures and General Synod measures from 1920 to the end of 2007. - 978-0-11-840449-5 *£400.00 per set*

The public general acts and General Synod measures 2006. - 6 v (a-l, 1-5959p.): hdbk: 31 cm. - 6 parts not sold separately. Contents: Chapters 1 - 55 & Measures 1 - 2 with tables & index. Includes alphabetical and chronological lists of Public General, Local, Personal Acts and General Synod Measures. - 978-0-11-840447-1 *£380.00 per set*

The public general acts and General Synod measures 2006: tables and index. - a-l, 1019p.: 30 cm. - 978-0-11-840448-8 *£80.00*

The public general acts and General Synod measures 2007. - 5v ([4155])p.: hdbk: 31 cm. - 5 parts not sold separately. Contents: Part 1: PGA chapters 1 - 3; Part 2: PGA chapters 4 - 14; Part 3: PGA chapters15 - 27; Part 4: PGA chapters 28 - 31, General Synod Measures 1; Part 5: Table V of Origins and Destinations (if applicable): Table VI - Effect of Legislation; General Index. - 978-0-11-840459-4 *£330.00 per set*

The public general acts and General Synod measures 2007: tables and index. - [851]p.: 30 cm. - 978-0-11-840460-0 *£60.00*

Statutory instruments 2006

Part 2: Section 1 nos. 1228 to 1468; Section 2 nos. 1469 to 1935; Section 3 nos. 1936 to 2356. 1st May to 31st August 2006. - 3v. (xix, p. 4677-8014): hdbk: 31 cm. - 3 vols. not sold separately. Includes: Guide to the edition; General statutory instruments issued in the period; selected local instruments; selected instruments not registered as statutory instruments; and Index to parts 1 and 2. - 978-0-11-840437-2 *£280.00 per set*

Part 3: Section 1 nos. 2362 to 2866; Section 2 nos. 2867 to 3236; Section 3 nos. 3237 to 3339; Section 4 nos. 3400 to 3511. 1st September to 31st December 2006. - 4v. (xx, p. 8015-12083): hdbk: 31 cm. - 4 vols. not sold separately. Includes: Guide to the edition; General statutory instruments issued in the period; selected local instruments; selected instruments not registered as statutory instruments; classified list of local statutory instruments; tables of effects to legislation; numerical and issue list; and Index to all parts. - 978-0-11-840438-9 *£400.00 per set*

Statutory instruments 2007

Part 1: Section 1 nos. 3 to 289; Section 2 nos. 290 to 698; Section 3 nos. 699 to 893; Section 4 nos. 901 to 1068; Section 5 nos. 1070 to 1367. 1st January to 30th April 2007. - 5v. (xxii, p. 1 - 5180): hdbk: 31 cm. - 5 vols. not sold separately. Includes: Guide to the edition; General statutory instruments issued in the period; selected local statutory instruments; index. - 978-0-11-840454-9 *£520.00 per set*

Part 2: Section 1 nos. 1368 to 1775; Section 2 nos. 1777 to 2142; Section 3 nos. 2143 to 2540. 1st May to 31st August 2007. - 3v. (xxii, p. 5181 - 8442): hdbk: 31 cm. - 3 vols. not sold separately. Includes: Guide to the edition; General statutory instruments issued in the period; selected local statutory instruments; selected instruments; index to parts 1 and 2. Part 1 published October 2008 (ISBN 9780118404549). - 978-0-11-840455-6 *£330.00 per set*

Statutory instruments made by the National Assembly for Wales 2007. - 3 v. (xxiv, 1-1002; iv, 1003-1968; iv, 1969-2803p.): hdbk: 31 cm. - 3 vols. not sold separately. Contain: contents of the edition; guide; lists of instruments; text of general WSIs 116 (W.7) to 3611 (W316); classified list of local statutory instruments registered during 2007; tables of effects; numerical and issue list 2007, and index. - 978-0-11-840458-7 *£290.00*

House of Commons

Official report (Hansard): House of Commons: centenary volume 1909-2009: an anthology of historic and memorable House of Commons speeches to celebrate the first 100 years. - Ian Church. - xxxi, 506p., col. ill.: hdbk: 30 cm. - An anthology of speeches from Hansard selected and introduced by politicians, commentators and academics. Foreword by Rt hon Michael J. Martin, Speaker of the House of Commons. On cover: Great speeches from 100 years. - 978-0-11-840463-1 *£35.00*

Statutory Instruments
Arranged by Subject Headings

Acquisition of land, England

The Home Loss Payments (Prescribed Amounts) (England) Regulations 2008 No. 2008/1598. - Enabling power: Land Compensation Act 1973, s. 30 (5). - Issued: 26.06.2008. Made: 19.06.2008. Laid: 26.06.2008. Coming into force: 01.09.2008. Effect: S.I. 2007/1750 revoked with savings. Territorial extent & classification: E. General. - 2p.: 30 cm. - 978-0-11-081893-1 *£3.00*

Acquisition of land, Wales

The Home Loss Payments (Prescribed Amounts) (Wales) Regulations 2008 No. 2008/2845 (W.255). - Enabling power: Land Compensation Act 1973, s. 30 (5). - Issued: 19.11.2008. Made: 02.11.2008. Laid before the National Assembly for Wales: 04.11.2008. Coming into force: 25.11.2008. Effect: S.I. 2007/2372 (W.195) revoked with savings. Territorial extent & classification: W. General. - In English and Welsh. Welsh title: Rheoliadau Taliadau Colli Cartref (Symiau Rhagnodedig) (Cymru) 2008. - 4p.: 30 cm. - 978-0-11-091866-2 £4.00

Administration of estates, England and Wales

The Intestate Succession (Interest and Capitalisation) (Amendment) Order 2008 No. 2008/3162. - Enabling power: Administration of Estates Act 1925, ss. 47A (3A) (3B). - Issued: 06.01.2009. Made: 09.12.2008. Laid: 11.12.2008. Coming into force: 01.02.2009. Effect: S.I. 1977/1491 amended. Territorial extent & classification: E/W. General. - 12p.: 30 cm. - 978-0-11-147190-6 £5.00

Aggregates levy

The Amusement Machine Licence Duty, etc (Amendments) Regulations 2008 No. 2008/2693. - Enabling power: Betting and Gaming Duties Act 1981, sch. 4, paras 5 (1), 12 & Finance Act 1994, ss. 54, 74 (7) (8) & Finance Act 1996, ss. 49, 71 (8) (9) & Finance Act 2000, sch. 6, paras. 41 (1) (2), 146 (7) & Finance Act 2001, ss. 25 (1) (2), 45 (5). - Issued: 15.10.2008. Made: 10.10.2008. Laid: 10.10.2008. Coming into force: 01/11/2008. Effect: S.I. 1994/1774; 1995/2631; 1996/1527; 2001/838; 2002/ 761 amended. Territorial extent & classification: E/W/S/NI. General. - 4p.: 30 cm. - 978-0-11-084575-3 £4.00

The Value Added Tax, etc (Correction of Errors, etc) Regulations 2008 No. 2008/1482. - Enabling power: Value Added Tax Act 1994, sch. 11, paras 2 (1) (10) (11) & Finance Act 1994, ss. 38 (1), 42 (2), 54, 74 (7) (8) & Finance Act 1996, ss. 49, 71 (8) (9) & Finance Act 2000, sch. 6, paras 41(1) (2), 146 (7) & Finance Act 2001, ss. 25 (1) (2), 45 (5). - Issued: 18.06.2008. Made: 09.06.2008. Laid: 10.06.2008. Coming into force: 01.07.2008. Effect: S.I. 1994/1738, 1774; 1995/2518; 1996/1527; 2001/838; 2002/761 amended. Territorial extent & classification: E/W/S/NI. General. - 12p.: 30 cm. - 978-0-11-081855-9 £3.00

Agriculture

The Agriculture and Horticulture Development Board Order 2008 No. 2008/576. - Enabling power: Natural Environment and Rural Communities Act 2006, ss. 87 to 91, 93, 96, 97(1) (2), sch. 8, paras 5 to 11, sch. 9, sch. 10. - Issued: 11.03.2008. Made: 28.02.2008. Coming into force: In accord. art. 1. Effect: 17 Acts and 7 statutory instruments amended and 2 Acts repealed and 16 statutory instruments revoked. Territorial extent & classification: E/W/S/NI. General. - Supersedes draft S.I. (ISBN 9780110789705) issued 20.11.2008. - 28p.: 30 cm. - 978-0-11-081120-8 £4.50

Agriculture: Livestock industries

The Scotland Act 1998 (Agency Arrangements) (Specification) Order 2008 No. 2008/1035. - Enabling power: Scotland Act 1998, ss. 93. - Issued: 15.04.2008. Made: 09.04.2008. Laid: 16.04.2008. Coming into force: 07.05.2008. Effect: None. Territorial extent & classification: GB. General. - 16p.: 30 cm. - 978-0-11-081605-0 £3.00

Agriculture, England

The Animals and Animal Products (Import and Export) (England) (Amendment) Regulations 2008 No. 2008/3203. - Enabling power: European Communities Act 1972, s. 2 (2), sch. 2, para. 1A. - Issued: 19.12.2008. Made: 15.12.2008. Laid: 19.12.2008. Coming into force: 15.01.2009. Effect: S.I. 2006/1471; 2007/3277 amended. Territorial extent & classification: E. General. - 12p.: 30 cm. - 978-0-11-147201-9 £5.00

The Beef and Veal Labelling Regulations 2008 No. 2008/3252. - Enabling power: European Communities Act 1972, s. 2 (2). - Issued: 23.12.2008. Made: 17.12.2008. Laid: 23.12.2008. Coming into force: 19.01.2009. Effect: S. I. 2000/3047; 2002/2315 revoked. Territorial extent & classification: E. General. - 8p.: 30 cm. - 978-0-11-147214-9 £5.00

The Common Agricultural Policy Single Payment and Support Schemes (Amendment) Regulations 2008 No. 2008/1139. - Enabling power: European Communities Act 1972, s. 2 (2). - Issued: 23.04.2008. Made: 18.04.2008. Laid: 22.04.2008. Coming into force: 14.05.2008. Effect: S.I. 2005/219 amended. Territorial extent & classification: E. General. - 2p.: 30 cm. - 978-0-11-081386-8 £3.00

The Common Agricultural Policy Single Payment and Support Schemes (Cross-compliance) (England) (Amendment) Regulations 2008 No. 2008/80. - Enabling power: European Communities Act 1972, s. 2 (2). - Issued: 21.01.2008. Made: 15.01.2008. Laid: 18.01.2008. Coming into force: 08.02.2008. Effect: S.I. 2005/3459 amended. Territorial extent & classification: E. General. - 2p.: 30 cm. - 978-0-11-080846-8 £3.00

The Feeding Stuffs (England) (Amendment) Regulations 2008 No. 2008/1523. - Enabling power: Agriculture Act 1970, ss. 66 (1), 68 (1), 74A, 84. - Issued: 18.06.2008. Made: 11.06.2008. Laid: 18.06.2008. Coming into force: 30.07.2008. Effect: S.I. 2005/3281 amended. Territorial extent & classification: E. General. - With correction slip dated September 2009.EC note: These Regulations provide for the implementation of Commission Directive 2008/4/EC amending Directive 94/39/EC as regards feedingstuffs intended for the reduction of the risk of milk fever. - 8p.: 30 cm. - 978-0-11-081849-8 *£3.00*

The Hill Farm Allowance Regulations 2008 No. 2008/51. - Enabling power: European Communities Act 1972, s. 2 (2). - Issued: 18.01.2007. Made: 12.01.2008. Laid: 16.01.2008. Coming into force: 07.02.2008. Effect: None. Territorial extent & classification: E. General. - EC note: These Regulations implement Council Regulation 1698/2005 on support for rural development by the European Agricultural Fund for Rural Development (EAFRD) and Council Regulation 1257/1999 on support for rural development from the European Agricultural Guidance and Guarantee Fund (EAGGF), in so far as those Regulations relate to less favoured areas. - 12p.: 30 cm. - 978-0-11-080838-3 *£3.00*

The Milk and Milk Products (Pupils in Educational Establishments) (England) Regulations 2008 No. 2008/2072. - Enabling power: European Communities Act 1972, s. 2 (2), sch. 2, para. 1A. - Issued: 04.08.2008. Made: 24.07.2008. Laid: 01.08.2008. Coming into force: 01.09.2008. Effect: S.I. 2001/994; 2007/3429 revoked. Territorial extent & classification: E. General. - EC note: These Regulations provide that references to Council Regulation (EC) No 1234/2007 establishing a common organisation of agricultural markets and on specific provisions for certain agricultural products (Single CMO Regulation) and to Commission Regulation (EC) No 657/2008 laying down detailed rules for applying Council Regulation (EC) No 1234/2007 as regards Community aid for supplying milk and certain milk products to pupils in educational establishments are references to these Regulations as amended from time to time. - 4p.: 30 cm. - 978-0-11-083656-0 *£3.00*

The Nitrate Pollution Prevention Regulations 2008 No. 2008/2349. - Enabling power: European Communities Act 1972, s. 2 (2). - Issued: 09.09.2008. Made: 01.09.2008. Laid: 04.09.2008. Coming into force: 01.01.2009 except reg. 22 (1) and Part 7; 01.01.2012 for reg. 22 (1) and Part 7, in accord. with reg. 3. Effect: S.I. 1994/1729; 1995/1708, 2095; 1996/888, 3105; 1997/990; 1998/79, 1202, 2138; 2002/744, 2614; 2003/562; 2006/1289 revoked in relation to England. Territorial extent & classification: E. General. - EC note: They continue to implement in England Council Directive 91/676/EEC concerning the protection of waters against pollution by nitrates from agricultural sources- 24p.: 30 cm. - 978-0-11-084012-3 *£5.00*

The Products of Animal Origin (Third Country Imports) (England) (Amendment) Regulations 2008 No. 2008/3230. - Enabling power: European Communities Act 1972, s. 2 (2), sch. 2, para. 1A. - Issued: 19.12.2008. Made: 15.12.2008. Laid: 19.12.2008. Coming into force: 15.01.2009. Effect: S.I. 2006/2841 amended. Territorial extent & classification: E. General. - 16p.: 30 cm. - 978-0-11-147200-2 *£5.00*

The Reporting of Prices of Milk Products (England) Regulations 2008 No. 2008/1428. - Enabling power: European Communities Act 1972, s. 2 (2), sch. 2, para. 1A. - Issued: 10.06.2008. Made: 03.06.2008. Laid: 09.06.2008. Coming into force: 01.07.2008. Effect: S.I. 2005/1441 revoked. Territorial extent & classification: E. General. - EC note: These Regulations implement in England article 6 of Commission Regulation No 562/2005 laying down rules for the implementation of Council Regulation No 1255/1999 as regards communications between the Member States and the Commission in the milk and milk products sector, as amended from time to time. - 4p.: 30 cm. - 978-0-11-081784-2 *£3.00*

The Rice Products from the United States of America (Restriction on First Placing on the Market) (England) Regulations 2008 No. 2008/622. - Enabling power: European Communities Act 1972 , s. 2 (2). - Issued: 13.03.2008. Made: 06.03.2008. Laid: 06.03.2008. Coming into force: 07.03.2008. Effect: S.I. 2006/2921 revoked. Territorial extent & classification: E. General. - EC note: These Regulations implement in relation to England Commission Decision 2006/601/EC on emergency measures regarding the non-authorised genetically modified organism "LL RICE 601" in rice products as last amended by Commission Decision 2008/162/EC. - 8p.: 30 cm. - 978-0-11-081126-0 *£3.00*

The Specified Products from China (Restriction on First Placing on the Market) (England) Regulations 2008 No. 2008/1079. - Enabling power: European Communities Act 1972 , s. 2 (2). - Issued: 17.04.2008. Made: 14.04.2008. Laid: 14.04.2008. Coming into force: 15.04.2008. Effect: None. Territorial extent & classification: E. General. - EC note: These Regulations implement, in England, Commission Decision 2008/289/EC on emergency measures regarding the unauthorised genetically modified organism 'Bt 63' in rice products. - 8p.: 30 cm. - 978-0-11-081373-8 *£3.00*

Agriculture, England and Wales

The Pesticides (Maximum Residue Levels) (England and Wales) Regulations 2008 No. 2008/2570. - Enabling power: European Communities Act 1972, s. 2 (2). - Issued: 07.10.2008. Made: 02.10.2008. Laid: 06.10.2008. Coming into force: 01.11.2008. Effect: S.I. 2005/3286; 2006/985, 1742, 2922; 2007/971, 2083, 2998, 3297; 2008/665 revoked. Territorial extent & classification: E/W. General. - EC note: These Regulations enforce the provisions of REG (EC) no. 396/2005 on maximum residue levels of pesticides in or on food and feed of plant and animal origin and amending Council Directive 91/414/EEC- 8p.: 30 cm. - 978-0-11-084363-6 *£5.00*

The Pesticides (Maximum Residue Levels in Crops, Food and Feeding Stuffs) (England and Wales) (Amendment) Regulations 2008 No. 2008/665. - Enabling power: European Communities Act 1972, s. 2 (2). - Issued: 27.03.2008. Made: 10.03.2008. Laid: 13.03.2008. Laid before the National Assembly of Wales: 13.03.2008. Coming into force: 09.04.2008 except for reg 4 (15.06.2008) and reg 5 (15.09.2008) in accord. with reg. 1(2). Effect: S.I. 2005/3286 amended. Territorial extent & classification: E/W. General. - Revoked by S.I. 2008/2570 (ISBN 9780110843636). EC note: These Regulations amend the Pesticides (Maximum Residue Levels in Crops, Food and Feeding Stuffs) (England and Wales) Regulations 2005 (S.I. 2005/3286) in order to transpose Commission Directive 2007/73/EC amending certain Annexes to Council Directives 86/362/EEC and 90/642/EEC as regards maximum residue levels for acetamiprid, atrazine, deltamethrin, imazalil, indoxacarb, pendimethalin, pymetrozine, pyraclostrobin, thiacloprid and trifloxystrobin- 24p.: 30 cm. - 978-0-11-081273-1 *£4.00*

Agriculture, Wales

The Common Agricultural Policy Single Payment and Support Schemes (Wales) (Amendment) Regulations 2008 No. 2008/2500 (W.218). - Enabling power: European Communities Act 1972, s. 2 (2). - Issued: 17.10.2008. Made: 22.09.2008. Laid before the National Assembly for Wales: 23.09.2008. Coming into force: 21.10.2008. Effect: S.I. 2005/360 (W. 29) amended. Territorial extent & classification: W. General. - In English and Welsh. Welsh title: Rheoliadau Cynllun Taliad Sengl a Chynlluniau Cymorth y Polisi Amaethyddol Cyffredin (Cymru) (Diwygio) 2007. - 8p.: 30 cm. - 978-0-11-091886-0 *£5.00*

The Feeding Stuffs (Wales) (Amendment) Regulations 2008 No. 2008/1806 (W.174). - Enabling power: Agriculture Act 1970, ss. 66 (1), 68 (1), 74A, 84. - Issued: 21.07.2008. Made: 07.07.2008. Laid before the National Assembly for Wales: 09.07.2008. Coming into force: 30.07.2008. Effect: S.I. 2006/116 (W.14) amended. Territorial extent & classification: W. General. - EC note: These Regulations provide for the implementation of Commission Directive 2008/4/EC amending Directive 94/39/EC as regards feeding stuffs intended for the reduction of the risk of milk fever. - In English and Welsh. Welsh title: Rheoliadau Bwydydd Anifeiliaid (Cymru) (Diwygio) 2008. - 8p.: 30 cm. - 978-0-11-091817-4 *£3.00*

The Nitrate Pollution Prevention (Wales) Regulations 2008 No. 2008/3143 (W.278). - Enabling power: European Communities Act 1972, s. 2 (2), sch. 2, para. 1A. - Issued: 31.12.2008. Made: 06.12.2008. Laid before the National Assembly for Wales: 09.12.2008. Coming into force: 01.01.2009 (other than reg. 22 (1) and part 7); 01.01.2012 for reg. 22 (1) and part 7, in accord. with reg. 3. Effect: S.I. 1996/888; 1998/1202; 2002/2297 (W. 226); 2006/1289 revoked insofar as they apply in relation to Wales. Territorial extent & classification: W. General. - In English and Welsh. Welsh title: Rheoliadau Atal Llygredd Nitradau (Cymru) 2008. - 40p.: 30 cm. - 978-0-11-091916-4 *£9.00*

The Rice Products from the United States of America (Restriction on First Placing on the Market) (Wales) (Amendment) Regulations 2008 No. 2008/1646 (W.159). - Enabling power: European Communities Act 1972, s. 2 (2). - Issued: 07.07.2008. Made: 23.06.2008. Laid before the National Assembly for Wales: 24.06.2008. Coming into force: 17.07.2008. Effect: S.I. 2008/781 (W.80) amended. Territorial extent & classification: W. General. - EC note: These Regulations amend S.I. 2008/781 (W.80) which implement in relation to Wales, Commission Decision 2006/601/EC on emergency measures regarding non-authorised genetically modified organism "LL RICE 601" in rice products as last amended by Commission Decision 2008/162/EC amending Decision 2006/601/EC. - In English and Welsh. Welsh title: Rheoliadau Cynhyrchion Reis o Unol Daleithiau America (Cyfyngiad ar eu Rhoi Gyntaf ar y Farchnad) (Cymru) (Diwygio) 2008. - 4p.: 30 cm. - 978-0-11-091838-9 *£3.00*

The Rice Products from the United States of America (Restriction on First Placing on the Market) (Wales) Regulations 2008 No. 2008/781 (W.80). - Enabling power: European Communities Act 1972, s. 2 (2). - Issued: 14.04.2008. Made: 18.03.2008. Laid before the National Assembly for Wales: 19.03.2008. Coming into force: 20.03.2008. Effect: S.I. 2006/2923 (W.260) revoked. Territorial extent & classification: W. General. - EC note: These Regulations implement in relation to Wales Commission Decision 2006/601/EC on emergency measures regarding non-authorised genetically modified organism "LL RICE 601" in rice products as last amended by Commission Decision 2008/162/EC amending Decision 2006/601/EC. - In English and Welsh. Welsh title: Rheoliadau Cynhyrchion Reis o Unol Daleithiau America (Cyfyngiad ar eu Rhoi Gyntaf ar y Farchnad) (Cymru) 2008. - 8p.: 30 cm. - 978-0-11-091753-5 *£3.00*

The School Milk (Wales) Regulations 2008 No. 2008/2141 (W.190). - Enabling power: European Communities Act 1972, s. 2 (2). - Issued: 21.08.2008. Made: 05.08.02008. Laid before the National Assembly for Wales: 11.08.2008. Coming into force: 01.09.2008. Effect: S.I. 2001/275 (W. 11) revoked. Territorial extent & classification: W. General. - EC note: These Regs implement measures in respect of art. 102 Council Reg no. 1234/2007 establishing a common organisation of agricultural markets and on specific provisions for certain agricultural products. Superseded by S.I. of same number and title (ISBN 9780110918532). - In English and Welsh. Welsh title: Rheoliadau Llaeth Ysgol (Cymru) 2008. - 8p.: 30 cm. - 978-0-11-091855-6 *£3.00*

The School Milk (Wales) Regulations 2008 No. 2008/2141 (W. 190). - Enabling power: European Communities Act 1972, s. 2 (2). - Issued: 02.09.2008. Made: 05.08.2008. Laid before the National Assembly for Wales: 11.08.2008. Coming into force: 01.09.2008. Effect: S.I. 2001/275 (W. 11) revoked. Territorial extent & classification: W. General. - In English and Welsh. Welsh title: Rheoliadau Llaeth Ysgol (Cymru) 2008. This Statutory Instrument has been printed in substitution of the SI of the same number (ISBN 9780110918556 published 21.08.2008) and is being issued free of charge to all known recipients of that Statutory Instrument. - EC note: Implements measures in respect of art. 102, Council Regulation (EC) no. 1234/2007 establishing a common organisation of agricultural markets and on specific provisions for certain agricultural products. - 8p.: 30 cm. - 978-0-11-091853-2 £3.00

The Welsh Levy Board Order 2008 No. 2008/420 (W.39). - Enabling power: Natural Environment and Rural Communities Act 2006, ss. 87 to 90, 97 (1) (2), sch. 8, paras 5 to 11, sch. 9, sch. 10 & Government of Wales Act 1998, s. 146A. - Issued: 31.03.2008. Made: 19.02.2008. Laid before the National Assembly for Wales: 10.03.2008. Coming into force: In accord. with art. 1. Effect: None. Territorial extent & classification: W. General. - In English and Welsh. Welsh title: Gorchymyn Bwrdd Ardollau Cymru 2008. - 16p.: 30 cm. - 978-0-11-091743-6 £3.00

Agriculture, Wales: Food, Wales

The Specified Products from China (Restriction on First Placing on the Market) (Wales) Regulations 2008 No. 2008/1080 (W.114). - Enabling power: European Communities Act 1972, s. 2 (2). - Issued: 28.04.2008. Made: 14.04.2008. Laid before the National Assembly for Wales: 14.04.2008. Coming into force: 15.04.2008. Effect: 1990 c. 16 modified. Territorial extent & classification: W. General. - EC note: These Regulations implement in relation to Wales Commission Decision 2008/289/EC on emergency measures regarding the unauthorised genetically modified organism "Bt 63" in rice products. - 8p.: 30 cm. - 978-0-11-091809-9 £3.00

Agriculture, Wales: Hill lands

The Heather and Grass etc. Burning (Wales) Regulations 2008 No. 2008/1081 (W.115). - Enabling power: Hill Farming Act 1946, s. 20 (1). - Issued: 28.04.2008. Made: 14.04.2008. Laid before the National Assembly for Wales: 15.04.2008. Coming into force: 06.05.2008. Effect: S.I. 2004/3280 (W.284) amended & S.I. 1986/428; 1987/1208 revoked in relation to Wales; 1990 c. 16 modified. Territorial extent & classification: W. General. - 12p.: 30 cm. - 978-0-11-091810-5 £3.00

Agriculture, Wales: Livestock industries

The Bovine Semen (Wales) Regulations 2008 No. 2008/1040 (W.110). - Enabling power: Animal Health and Welfare Act 1984, s. 10 & European Communities Act 1972, s. 2 (2), sch. 2, para. 1A. - Issued: 01.05.2008. Made: 07.04.02008. Laid before the National Assembly for Wales: 08.04.2008. Coming into force: 30.04.2008. Effect: S.I. 1987/390 amended in relation to Wales & S.I. 1984/1325; 1985/1861; 1987/904; 1992/671; 1993/1966; 1995/2549 revoked in relation to Wales & S.I. 2001/1539 (W.107); 2002/1131 (W.118) revoked. Territorial extent & classification: W. General. - In English and Welsh. Welsh title: Rheoliadau Semen Buchol (Cymru) 2008. - 48p.: 30 cm. - 978-0-11-091812-9 £7.50

Animals

The Cat and Dog Fur (Control of Import, Export and Placing on the Market) Regulations 2008 No. 2008/2795. - Enabling power: European Communities Act 1972, s. 2 (2). - Issued: 30.10.2008. Made: 26.10.2008. Laid: 28.10.2008. Coming into force: 31.12.2008. Effect: None. Territorial extent & classification: E/W/S/NI. General. - EC note: These Regulations implement in the UK Regulation (EC) No 1523/2007 which prohibits the import, export and placing on the market of cat and dog fur. - 8p.: 30 cm. - 978-0-11-084746-7 £5.00

Animals: Animal health

The Scotland Act 1998 (Agency Arrangements) (Specification) Order 2008 No. 2008/1035. - Enabling power: Scotland Act 1998, ss. 93. - Issued: 15.04.2008. Made: 09.04.2008. Laid: 16.04.2008. Coming into force: 07.05.2008. Effect: None. Territorial extent & classification: GB. General. - 16p.: 30 cm. - 978-0-11-081605-0 £3.00

Animals: Diseases of animals

The Scotland Act 1998 (Agency Arrangements) (Specification) Order 2008 No. 2008/1035. - Enabling power: Scotland Act 1998, ss. 93. - Issued: 15.04.2008. Made: 09.04.2008. Laid: 16.04.2008. Coming into force: 07.05.2008. Effect: None. Territorial extent & classification: GB. General. - 16p.: 30 cm. - 978-0-11-081605-0 £3.00

Animals, England: Animal health

The Bluetongue Regulations 2008 No. 2008/962. - Enabling power: European Communities Act 1972, s. 2 (2), sch. 2, para. 1A. - Issued: 07.04.2008. Made: 02.04.2008. Laid: 04.04.2008. Coming into force: 26.04.2008. Effect: S.I. 2007/3304 revoked exc. for art. 17. Territorial extent & classification: E. General. - 12p.: 30 cm. - 978-0-11-081341-7 £3.00

The Brucellosis (England) (Amendment) Order 2008 No. 2008/618. - Enabling power: Animal Health Act 1981, ss. 1, 8. - Issued: 13.03.2008. Made: 01.03.2008. Coming into force: 06.04.2008. Effect: S.I. 2000/2055 amended. Territorial extent & classification: E. General- This Statutory Instrument has been made in consequence of a defect in SI 2000/2055 and is being issued free of charge to all known recipients of that Statutory Instrument. EC note: This Order amends the 2000 Order which implements Council Directive 64/432 on animal health problems affecting intra- Community trade in bovine animals and swine and Council Directive 77/391/EEC introducing Community measures for the eradication of brucellosis, tuberculosis and leucosis in cattle- 2p.: 30 cm. - 978-0-11-081162-8 *£3.00*

The Disease Control (England) (Amendment) Order 2008 No. 2008/1066. - Enabling power: Animal Health Act 1981, ss. 1, 7, 8 (1). - Issued: 16.04.2008. Made: 09.04.2008. Coming into force: 12.05.2008. Effect: S.I. 2003/1729 amended. Territorial extent & classification: E. General. - This Statutory Instrument has been made in consequence of defects in S.I. 2003/1729 (ISBN 9780110470627) and is being issued free of charge to all known recipients of that Statutory Instrument. - 2p.: 30 cm. - 978-0-11-081370-7 *£3.00*

The Diseases of Animals (Approved Disinfectants) (Fees) (England) Order 2008 No. 2008/652. - Enabling power: Animal Health Act 1981, s. 84 (1). - Issued: 13.03.2008. Made: 05.12.2008. Laid: 12.03.2008. Coming into force: 06.04.2008. Effect: S.I. 2005/379 revoked. Territorial extent & classification: E. General. - Revoked by S.I. 2009/839 (ISBN 9780111477861). - 4p.: 30 cm. - 978-0-11-081170-3 *£3.00*

The Products of Animal Origin (Disease Control) (England) Regulations 2008 No. 2008/465. - Enabling power: European Communities Act 1972, s. 2 (2). - Issued: 28.02.2008. Made: 21.02.2008. Laid: 28.02.2008. Coming into force: 06.04.2008. Effect: None. Territorial extent & classification: E. General. - EC note: These regulations transpose in England Articles 3 and 4 of Council Directive 2002/99/EC laying down the animal health rules governing the production, processing, distribution and introduction of products of animal origin for human consumption which are also transposed by the Diseases of Poultry (England) Order 2003 (S.I. 2003/1078), the Foot-and-Mouth Disease (England) Order 2006 (S.I. 2006/182) and the Avian Influenza and Influenza of Avian Origin in Mammals (England) (No 2) Order 2006 (S.I. 2006/2702). These regulations also transpose, insofar as they apply to Newcastle Disease, Commission decision 2007/118/EC establishing an alternative health mark pursuant to Directive 2002/99/EC. - 12p.: 30 cm. - 978-0-11-081011-9 *£3.00*

The Specified Animal Pathogens Order 2008 No. 2008/944. - Enabling power: Animal Health Act 1981, ss. 1, 7, 35 (1), 87 (2) (5) (a), 88 (2) (4) (a). - Issued: 04.04.2008. Made: 01.04.2008. Coming into force: 28.04.2008. Effect: S.I. 1998/463 revoked in relation to England; S.I. 2006/1506 revoked. Territorial extent & classification: E. General. - 8p.: 30 cm. - 978-0-11-081328-8 *£3.00*

The Transmissible Spongiform Encephalopathies (England) (Amendment) Regulations 2008 No. 2008/3295. - Enabling power: European Communities Act 1972, s. 2 (2). - Issued: 31.12.2008. Made: 22.12.2008. Laid: 23.12.2008. Coming into force: 12.01.2009. Effect: S.I. 2008/1881 amended. Territorial extent & classification: E. General. - EC note: These Regulations take into account Commission Decision 2008/908/EC authorising certain Member States to revise their annual BSE monitoring programme. - 8p.: 30 cm. - 978-0-11-147238-5 *£5.00*

The Transmissible Spongiform Encephalopathies (England) Regulations 2008 No. 2008/1881. - Enabling power: European Communities Act 1972, s. 2 (2), sch. 2, para. 1A & Finance Act 1973, s. 56 (1) (2). - Issued: 22.07.2008. Made: 15.07.2008. Laid: 17.07.2008. Coming into force: 07.08.2008. Effect: S.I. 2005/3068; 2006/1228 revoked. Territorial extent & classification: E. General. - EC note: These Regulations, which apply in England, revoke and remake with amendments the Transmissible Spongiform Encephalopathies (No. 2) Regulations 2006 (S.I. 2006/1228), which enforced Regulation (EC) No 999/2001 laying down rules for the prevention, control and eradication of certain transmissible spongiform encephalopathies as amended (by Reg 727/2007 and as further amended). These Regulations now implement Commission Decision 2007/411 prohibiting the placing on the market of products derived from bovine animals born or reared within the United Kingdom before 1st August 1996 for any purpose and exempting such animals from certain control and eradication measures laid down in Regulation (EC) No. 999/2001 and repealing Decision 2005/598. - 48p.: 30 cm. - 978-0-11-083378-1 *£7.50*

The Transmissible Spongiform Encephalopathies (Fees) (England) Regulations 2008 No. 2008/2269. - Enabling power: Finance Act 1973, s. 56 (1) (2). - Issued: 03.09.2008. Made: 22.08.2008. Laid: 28.08.2008. Coming into force: 22.09.2008. Effect: S.I. 2008/1881 amended. Territorial extent & classification: E. General. - This Statutory Instrument has been made in consequence of a defect in S.I. 2008/1881 (ISBN 9780110833781) and is being issued free of charge to all known recipients of that Statutory Instrument. - 2p.: 30 cm. - 978-0-11-083872-4 *£4.00*

The Transmissible Spongiform Encephalopathies (No. 2) (Amendment) Regulations 2008 No. 2008/1180. - Enabling power: European Communities Act 1972, s. 2 (2). - Issued: 30.04.2008. Made: 24.04.2008. Laid: 25.04.2008. Coming into force: 26.04.2008. Effect: S.I. 2006/1228 amended and S.I. 1997/2959 revoked in relation to England. Territorial extent & classification: E. General. - EC note: These Regulations further amend the Transmissible Spongiform Encephalopathies (No. 2) Regulations 2006 (S.I. 2006/1228), which provide for the enforcement in England of Regulation (EC) No. 999/2001 laying down rules for the prevention, control and eradication of certain transmissible spongiform encephalopathies as amended. - 12p.: 30 cm. - 978-0-11-081409-4 *£3.00*

The Zoonoses and Animal By-Products (Fees) (England) (No. 2) Regulations 2008 No. 2008/3196. - Enabling power: Finance Act 1973, s. 56 (1) (2) & European Communities Act 1972, sch. 2, para 1A. - Issued: 19.12.2008. Made: 14.12.2008. Laid: 17.12.2008. Coming into force: 15.01.2009. Effect: S.I. 2008/2270 revoked. Territorial extent & classification: E. General. - Revoked by S.I. 2009/2043 (ISBN 9780111483688). - 4p.: 30 cm. - 978-0-11-147185-2 £4.00

The Zoonoses and Animal By-Products (Fees) (England) Regulations 2008 No. 2008/2270. - Enabling power: Finance Act 1973, s. 56 (1) (2). - Issued: 29.08.2008. Made: 22.08.2008. Laid: 29.08.2008. Coming into force: 01.10.2008. Effect: S.I. 2007/2074 revoked. Territorial extent & classification: E. General. - Revoked by S.I. 2008/3196 (ISBN 9780111471852). - 4p.: 30 cm. - 978-0-11-083864-9 £3.00

Animals, England: Animal welfare

The Mutilations (Permitted Procedures) (England) (Amendment) Regulations 2008 No. 2008/1426. - Enabling power: Animal Welfare Act 2006, s. 5 (4). - Issued: 09.06.2008. Made: 02.06.2008. Coming into force: 03.06.2008. Effect: S.I. 2007/1100 amended. Territorial extent & classification: E. General. - Supersedes draft S.I. (ISBN 9780110813929) issued 24.04.2008. EC note: In respect of tail docking and castration of pigs, these Regulations together with the 2007 Regulations (S.I. 2007/1100), implement paragraph 8 of Chapter I of the Annex to Council Directive 91/630/EEC as amended by Council Directive 2001/88/EC, Commission Directive 2001/93/EC and Council Regulation No. 806/2003. In respect of laying hens, these Regulations together with the 2007 Regulations implement paragraph 8 of the Annex to Council Directive 1999/74/EC as amended by Council Regulation No 806/2003. Superseded by S.I. 2008/1426 (ISBN 9780110817804). - 8p.: 30 cm. - 978-0-11-081780-4 £3.00

Animals, Wales: Animal health

The Bluetongue (Wales) (Amendment) Regulations 2008 No. 2008/1583 (W.158). - Enabling power: European Communities Act 1972, s, 2 (2). - Issued: 02.07.2008. Made: 18.06.2008. Laid before the National Assembly for Wales: 18.06.2008. Coming into force: 19.06.2008. Effect: S.I. 2008/1090 (W.116) amended. Territorial extent & classification: W. General. - 4p.: 30 cm. - 978-0-11-091837-2 £3.00

The Bluetongue (Wales) Regulations 2008 No. 2008/1090 (W.116). - Enabling power: European Communities Act 1972, s, 2 (2), sch. 2, para. 1A. - Issued: 28.04.2008. Made: 16.04.2008. Laid before the National Assembly for Wales: 17.04.2008. Coming into force: 26.04.2008. Effect: S.I. 2007/3309 (W.294) revoked with saving. Territorial extent & classification: W. General. - EC note: These Regulations implement Council Directive 2000/75/EC laying down specific provisions for the control and eradication of bluetongue and enforce Commission Regulation (EC) No. 1266/2007. - 16p.: 30 cm. - 978-0-11-091811-2 £3.00

The Control of Salmonella in Poultry (Wales) Order 2008 No. 2008/524 (W.50). - Enabling power: Animal Health Act 1981, ss. 1, 8. - Issued: 20.03.2008. Made: 26.02.2008. Coming into force: 25.03.2008. Effect: S.I. 2007/1708 (W.147) revoked. Territorial extent & classification: W. General. - EC note: This Order enforces Commission Regulation (EC) No. 1003/2005, Commission Regulation (EC) No. 1168/2006 and Commission Regulation (EC) No. 1177/2006. - In English and Welsh. Welsh title: Gorchymyn Rheoli Salmonela mewn Dofednod (Cymru) 2008. - 16p.: 30 cm. - 978-0-11-091765-8 £3.00

The Disease Control (Wales) (Amendment) Order 2008 No. 2008/1314 (W.136). - Enabling power: Animal Health Act 1981, ss. 1, 7, 8 (1). - Issued: 29.05.2008. Made: 14.05.2008. Coming into force: 06.06.2008. Effect: S.I. 2003/1966 (W.211) amended. Territorial extent & classification: W. General. - In English and Welsh. Welsh title: Gorchymyn Rheoli Clefydau (Cymru) (Diwygio) 2008. - 4p.: 30 cm. - 978-0-11-091786-3 £3.00

The Pigs (Records, Identification and Movement) (Wales) Order 2008 No. 2008/1742 (W.172). - Enabling power: Animal Health Act 1981, ss. 1, 8 (1). - Issued: 16.07.2008. Made: 02.07.2008. Coming into force: 24.07.2008. Effect: S.I. 2004/996 (W.104) revoked. Territorial extent & classification: W. General. - In English and Welsh. Welsh title: Gorchymyn Moch (Cofnodion, Adnabod a Symud) (Cymru) 2008. - 12p.: 30 cm. - 978-0-11-091849-5 £3.00

The Products of Animal Origin (Disease Control) (Wales) Regulations 2008 No. 2008/1275 (W.132). - Enabling power: European Communities Act 1972, s. 2 (2). - Issued: 23.05.2008. Made: 08.05.2008. Laid before the National Assembly for Wales: 09.05.2008. Coming into force: 03.06.2008. Effect: None. Territorial extent & classification: W. General. - EC notes: These Regulations transpose in Wales Articles 3 and 4 of Council Directive 2002/99/EC laying down the animal health rules governing the production, processing, distribution and introduction of products of animal origin for human consumption. - In English and Welsh. Welsh title: Rheoliadau Cynhyrchion sy'n Dod o Anifeiliaid (Rheoli Clefydau) (Cymru) 2008. - 20p.: 30 cm. - 978-0-11-091781-8 £3.50

The Sheep and Goats (Records, Identification and Movement) (Wales) Order 2008 No. 2008/130 (W.17). - Enabling power: Animal Health Act 1981, ss. 1, 8 (1), 83 (2). - Issued: 11.02.2008. Made: 21.01.2008. Coming into force: 22.01.2008. Effect: S.I. 2006/1036, 2926 revoked. Territorial extent & classification: W. General. - EC note: This Order makes provision for the administration and enforcement in Wales of Council Regulation No. 21/2004 (establishing a system for the identification and registration of ovine and caprine animals and amending Regulation No. 1782/2003 and Directives 92/102/EEC and 64/432/EEC). It revokes and replaces S.I. 2006/1036 (as amended by S.I. 2006/2926), changing the domestic identification requirements to reflect the fact that the UK will no longer take advantage of a derogation from the main double tagging regime under Council Regulation 21/2004. - In English and Welsh. Welsh title: Gorchymyn Defaid a Geifr (Cofnodion, Adnabod a Symud) (Cymru) 2008. - 36p.: 30 cm. - 978-0-11-091735-1 £6.50

The Specified Animal Pathogens (Wales) Order 2008 No. 2008/1270 (W.129). - Enabling power: Animal Health Act 1981, ss. 1, 7, 35 (1), 87 (2) (5) (a), 88 (2) (4) (a). - Issued: 23.05.2008. Made: 07.05.2008. Coming into force: 10.05.2008. Effect: S.I. 1998/463 (in relation to Wales); 2006/2981 (W.272) revoked. Territorial extent & classification: W. General. - In English and Welsh. Welsh title: Gorchymyn Pathogenau Anifeiliaid Penodedig (Cymru) 2008. - 12p.: 30 cm. - 978-0-11-091783-2 £3.00

The Transmissible Spongiform Encephalopathies (Wales) (Amendment) (No.2) Regulations 2008 No. 2008/3266 (W.288). - Enabling power: European Communities Act 1972, s. 2 (2). - Issued: 09.01.2009. Made: 19.12.2008. Laid before the National Assembly for Wales: 19.12.2008. Coming into force: 12.01.2009. Effect: S.I. 2008/3154 (W.282) amended. Territorial extent & classification: W. General. - EC note: These Regulations amend the Transmissible Spongiform Encephalopathies (Wales) Regulations 2008 (S.I. 2008/3154 (W.282)) which enforce Regulation (EC) No 999/2001 laying down rules for the prevention, control and eradication of certain transmissible spongiform encephalopathies. - In English & Welsh. Welsh title: Rheoliadau Enseffalopathïau Sbyngffurf Trosglwyddadwy (Cymru) (Diwygio) (Rhif 2) 2008. - 8p.: 30 cm. - 978-0-11-091919-5 £5.00

The Transmissible Spongiform Encephalopathies (Wales) (Amendment) Regulations 2008 No. 2008/1182 (W.119). - Enabling power: European Communities Act 1972, s. 2 (2). - Issued: 23.05.2008. Made: 25.04.2008. Laid before the National Assembly for Wales: 25.04.2008. Coming into force: 26.04.2008. Effect: S.I. 2006/1226 (W.117) amended & S.I. 1997/2959. revoked insofar as they apply to Wales. Territorial extent & classification: W. General. - EC note: These Regulations amend the 2006 Regulations (S.I. 2006/1226 (W.117)), as amended, which provide for the enforcement in relation to Wales of Regulation (EC) No. 999/2001,as amended, laying down rules for the prevention, control and eradication of certain transmissible spongiform encephalopathies. - In English & Welsh. Welsh title: Rheoliadau Enseffalopathïau Sbyngffurf Trosglwyddadwy (Cymru) (Diwygio) 2008. - 20p.: 30 cm. - 978-0-11-091780-1 £3.50

The Transmissible Spongiform Encephalopathies (Wales) Regulations 2008 No. 2008/3154 (W.282). - Enabling power: European Communities Act 1972, s. 2 (2). - Issued: 31.12.2008. Made: 09.12.2008. Laid before the National Assembly for Wales: 10.12.2008. Coming into force: 31.12.2008. Effect: S.I. 2005/3296 (W.254); 2006/1512 (W.148), 1513 (W.149), 1226 (W.117) revoked. Territorial extent & classification: W. General. - EC note: These Regulations, which apply in relation to Wales, revoke and remake with amendments the Transmissible Spongiform Encephalopathies (Wales) Regulations 2006 (S.I. 2006/1266 (W.117)), which enforced Regulation (EC) No 999/2001. These Regulations now implement Commission Decision 2007/411 prohibiting the placing on the market of products derived from bovine animals born or reared within the UK before 1 August 1996 for any purpose and exempting such animals from certain control and eradication measures laid down in Regulation (EC) No. 999/2001 and repealing Decision 2005/598. Commission Regulation (EC) No. 999/2001 was amended (amending Annex VII) by Commission Regulation (EC) No 727/2007. These Regulations implement those amendments with the exception of certain provisions that were suspended by a judgment of the European Court of First Instance on 28 September 2007 (points 2(3)(b)(iii), 2(3)(d) and 4 of Annex VII to Regulation (EC) No. 999/2001). - In English & Welsh. Welsh title: Rheoliadau Enseffalopathïau Sbyngffurf Trosglwyddadwy (Cymru) 2008. - 68p.: 30 cm. - 978-0-11-091915-7 £10.50

The Transport of Animals (Cleansing and Disinfection) (Wales) (No 3) (Amendment) Order 2008 No. 2008/789 (W.83). - Enabling power: Animal Health Act 1981, ss. 7, 37. - Issued: 14.04.2008. Made: 19.03.2008. Coming into force: 15.04.2008. Effect: S.I. 2003/1968 (W.213) amended. Territorial extent & classification: W. General. - In English and Welsh. Welsh title: Gorchymyn Cludo Anifeiliaid (Glanhau a Diheintio) (Cymru) (Rhif 3) (Diwygio) 2008. - 4p.: 30 cm. - 978-0-11-091751-1 £3.00

The Tuberculosis (Testing and Powers of Entry) (Wales) Order 2008 No. 2008/2774 (W.247). - Enabling power: Animal Health Act 1981, s. 62D. - Issued: 06.11.2008. Made: 21.10.2008. Coming into force: 22.10.2008. Effect: None. Territorial extent & classification: W. General. - In English and Welsh. Welsh title: Gorchymyn Twbercwlosis (Profi a Phwerau Mynediad) (Cymru) 2008. - 4p.: 30 cm. - 978-0-11-091863-1 £4.00

The Zoonoses and Animal By-Products (Fees) (Wales) (Amendment) Regulations 2008 No. 2008/3153 (W.281). - Enabling power: Finance Act 1973, s. 56 (1) (2) and European Communities Act 1972, sch. 2, para. 1A. - Issued: 30.12.2008. Made: 09.12.2008. Laid: 10.12.2008. Coming into force: 01.01.2009. Effect: S.I. 2008/2716 (W.245) amended. Territorial extent & classification: W. General. - EC note: These Regulations make provision for the Welsh Ministers to charge fees for conducting tests that farmers may request under Commission Regulation (EC) No 1237/2007. - In English and Welsh. Welsh title: Rheoliadau Milheintiau a Sgil-gynhyrchion Anifeilliad (Ffioedd) (Diwygio) 2008. - 4p.: 30 cm. - 978-0-11-091912-6 £4.00

Animals, Wales: Animal health

The Zoonoses and Animal By-Products (Fees) (Wales) Regulations 2008 No. 2008/2716 (W.245). - Enabling power: Finance Act 1973, s. 56 (1) (2). - Issued: 29.10.2008. Made: 16.10.2008. Laid before the National Assembly for Wales: 17.10.2008. Coming into force: 31.10.2008. Effect: S.I. 2007/2496 (W.215) revoked. Territorial extent & classification: W. General. - With correction slip dated December 2009/January 2010. EC note: These Regulations, make provision for the Welsh Ministers to charge fees for activities required under Commission Regulation (EC) No. 1003/2005, 1168/2006, 2160/2003 and the Animal By-Products (Wales) Regulations 2006. - In English and Welsh. Welsh title: Rheoliadau Milheintiau a Sgil-gynhyrchion Anifeiliad (Ffioedd) (Cymru) 2008. - 4p.: 30 cm. - 978-0-11-091862-4 £4.00

The Zootechnical Standards (Amendment) (Wales) Regulations 2008 No. 2008/1064 (W.113). - Enabling power: European Communities Act 1972, s. 2 (2). - Issued: 23.04.2008. Made: 09.04.2008. Laid before the National Assembly for Wales: 10.04.2008. Coming into force: 02.05.2008. Effect: S.I. 1992/2370 amended. Territorial extent & classification: W. General. - EC note: These Regulations amend the Zootechnical Standards Regulations 1992, S.I. 1992/2370 ("the 1992 Regulations"). The amendments give effect to the amendments to Council Directive 87/328/EEC on the acceptance for breeding purposes of pure-bred breeding animals of the bovine species made by Council Directive 2005/24/EC with regard to the use of ova and embryos and storage centres for semen from pure-bred breeding animals of the bovine species. - In English and Welsh. Welsh title: Rheoliadau Safonau Sootechnegol (Diwygio) (Cymru) 2008. - 4p.: 30 cm. - 978-0-11-091807-5 £3.00

Animals, Wales: Animal welfare

The Mutilations (Permitted Procedures) (Wales) (Amendment) Regulations 2008 No. 2008/3094 (W.273). - Enabling power: Animal Welfare Act 2006, s. 5 (4). - Issued: 23.12.2008. Made: 02.12.2008. Laid before the National Assembly for Wales: 29.10.2008. Coming into force: 03.12.2008. Effect: S.I. 2007/1029 (W. 96) amended. Territorial extent & classification: W. General. - EC note: In respect of tail docking and castration of pigs, these Regulations together with the 2007 Regulations implement paragraph 8 of Chapter I of the Annex to Council Directive 91/630/EEC laying down minimum standards for the protection of pigs, as amended by Council Directive 2001/88/EC (OJ No L316, 1.12.2001, p.1, Commission Directive 2001/93/EC and Council Regulation (EC) No. 806/2003. In respect of laying hens, these Regulations together with the 2007 Regulations implement paragraph 8 of the Annex to Council Directive 1999/74/EC laying down minimum standards for the protection of laying hens, as amended by Council Regulation (EC) No 806/2003. - In English and Welsh. Welsh language title: Rheoliadau Anffurfio (Triniaethau a Ganiateir) (Diwygio) (Cymru) 2008. - 8p.: 30 cm. - 978-0-11-091872-3 £5.00

Antarctica

The Antarctic (Amendment) Regulations 2008 No. 2008/3066. - Enabling power: Antarctic Act 1994, ss. 9 (1), 10 (1), 14 (1), 25 (1) (3), 32. - Issued: 15.01.2009. Made: 19.11.2008. Laid: 08.12.2008. Coming into force: 29.12.2008. Effect: S.I. 1995/490 amended. Territorial extent & classification: E/W/S/NI. General. - 36p., maps: 30 cm. - 978-0-11-147252-1 £9.00

Anti-Social behaviour, England and Wales

The Criminal Justice and Immigration Act 2008 (Commencement No. 3 and Transitional Provisions) Order 2008 No. 2008/2712 (C.118). - Enabling power: Criminal Justice and Immigration Act 2008, s. 153 (4) (7). Bringing into operation various provisions of the 2008 Act on 03.11.2008 in accord. with art. 2. - Issued: 20.10.2008. Made: 13.10.2008. Effect: None. Territorial extent & classification: E/W/NI [some aspects E/W only]. General. - 8p.: 30 cm. - 978-0-11-084677-4 £5.00

The Criminal Justice and Immigration Act 2008 (Commencement No. 4 and Saving Provision) Order 2008 No. 2008/2993 (C.128). - Enabling power: Criminal Justice and Immigration Act 2008, s. 153 (7). Bringing into operation various provisions of the 2008 Act on 01.12.2008, 26.01.2009 in accord. with art. 2 and subject to art. 3. - Issued: 21.11.2008. Made: 15.11.2008. Effect: None. Territorial extent & classification: E/W/NI (some aspects E/W only). General. - 8p.: 30 cm. - 978-0-11-147015-2 £5.00

Architects

The Architects (Recognition of European Qualifications etc and Saving and Transitional Provision) Regulations 2008 No. 2008/1331. - Enabling power: European Communities Act 1972, s. 2 (2). - Issued: 28.05.2008. Made: 19.05.2008. Laid: 27.05.2008. Coming into force: 20.06.2008. Effect: 1997 c. 22 amended. Territorial extent & classification: E/W/S/NI. General. - EC note: These Regulations implement, in part, Directive 2005/36/EC on the recognition of professional qualifications. It replaces Directive 85/384/EEC. - 20p.: 30 cm. - 978-0-11-081753-8 £3.50

Armorial bearings, ensigns and flags

The Lyon Court and Office Fees (Variation) Order 2008 No. 2008/1166. - Enabling power: Public Expenditure and Receipts Act 1968, s. 5. - Issued: 09.05.2008. Made: 28.04.2008. Laid: 30.04.2008. Coming into force: 23.05.2008. Effect: 1867 c. 17 amended. Territorial extent & classification: E/W/S/NI. General. - 8p.: 30 cm. - 978-0-11-081636-4 £3.00

Atomic energy and radioactive substances

The Transfrontier Shipment of Radioactive Waste and Spent Fuel Regulations 2008 No. 2008/3087. - Enabling power: European Communities Act 1972, s, 2 (2), sch. 2, para. 1A. - Issued: 08.12.2008. Made: 30.11.2008. Laid: 04.12.2008. Coming into force: 25.12.2008. Effect: S.I. 1993/3031 revoked. Territorial extent & classification: E/W/S/NI/Gib. General. - EC note: These Regulations revoke and replace the Transfrontier Shipment of Radioactive Waste Regulations 1993. They continue to implement Council Directive 96/29/Euratom laying down basic standards for the protection of the health of workers and the general public against the dangers arising from ionizing radiation, and implement Directive 2006/117/Euratom on the supervision and control of shipments of radioactive waste and spent fuel. - 12p.: 30 cm. - 978-0-11-147096-1 £5.00

Auditors

The Statutory Auditors and Third Country Auditors (Amendment) (No. 2) Regulations 2008 No. 2008/2639. - Enabling power: Companies Act 2006, ss. 1239 (1) (b) (2) (5) (d), 1246 (1), 1292 (1) (c)- Issued: 10.10.2008. Made: 06.10.2008. Laid: 07.10.2008. Coming into force: 31.10.2008. Effect: S.I. 2007/3494 amended. Territorial extent & classification: E/W/S/NI. General. - 8p.: 30 cm. - 978-0-11-084427-5 £5.00

The Statutory Auditors and Third Country Auditors (Amendment) Regulations 2008 No. 2008/499. - Enabling power: European Communities Act 1972, s. 2 (2) & Companies Act 2006, s. 1239. - Issued: 06.03.2008. Made: 26.02.2008. Laid: 03.03.2008. Coming into force: 05.04.2008. Effect: S.I. 2007/3494 amended. Territorial extent & classification: E/W/S/NI. General. - These Regulations have been made in consequence of defects in S.I. 2007/3494 (ISBN 9780110806099) and are being issued free of charge to all known recipients of those Regulations. - 4p.: 30 cm. - 978-0-11-081064-5 £3.00

Banks and banking

The Bank Accounts Directive (Miscellaneous Banks) Regulations 2008 No. 2008/567. - Enabling power: European Communities Act 1972, s. 2 (2). - Issued: 10.03.2008. Made: 26.02.2008. Laid: 05.03.2008. Coming into force: 06.04.2008. Effect: 2006 c. 46 & S.I. 2008/410 amended & S.I. 1991/2704 revoked with savings. Territorial extent & classification: E/W/S/NI. General. - EC note: These Regulations continue the implementation of Council Directive 86/635/EEC. They also implement in part, Directive 2006/43/EC. - 12p.: 30 cm. - 978-0-11-081094-2 £3.00

The Bradford & Bingley plc Compensation Scheme Order 2008 No. 2008/3249. - Enabling power: Banking (Special Provisions) Act 2008, ss. 5, 9, 12, 13 (2). - Issued: 23.12.2008. Made: 18.12.2008. Coming into force: 19.12.2008 in accord. with art. 1 (2). Effect: None. Territorial extent & classification: E/W/S/NI. General. - Supersedes draft S.I. (ISBN 9780111471180) issued 10.12.2008. - 12p.: 30 cm. - 978-0-11-147211-8 £5.00

The Bradford & Bingley plc Transfer of Securities and Property etc. Order 2008 No. 2008/2546. - Enabling power: Banking (Special Provisions) Act 2008, ss. 3, 4, 8, 12, 13 (2). - Issued: 29.09.2008. Made: 29.09.2008 at 7.40 am. Laid: 29.09.2008 at 11.00 am. Coming into force: 29.09.2008 at 8.00 am. Effect: 2000 c. 8 modified. Territorial extent & classification: E/W/S/NI. General. - With correction slip dated October 2009. - 24p.: 30 cm. - 978-0-11-084324-7 £5.00

The Cash Ratio Deposits (Value Bands and Ratios) Order 2008 No. 2008/1344. - Enabling power: Bank of England Act 1998, sch. 2, para. 5. - Issued: 29.05.2008. Made: 22.05.2008. Coming into force: 02.06.2008. Effect: S.I. 2004/1270 revoked. Territorial extent & classification: E/W/S/NI. General. - 2p.: 30 cm. - 978-0-11-081757-6 £3.00

The Heritable Bank plc (Determination of Compensation) Order 2008 No. 2008/3251. - Enabling power: Banking (Special Provisions) Act 2008, s. 7 (1) (a). - Issued: 23.12.2008. Made: 18.12.2008. Coming into force: 19.12.2008 in accord. with art. 1 (2). Effect: None. Territorial extent & classification: E/W/S/NI. General. - Supersedes draft S.I. (ISBN 9780111471135) issued 10.12.2008. - 2p.: 30 cm. - 978-0-11-147216-3 £4.00

The Heritable Bank plc Transfer of Certain Rights and Liabilities Order 2008 No. 2008/2644. - Enabling power: Banking (Special Provisions) Act 2008, ss. 6, 12, 13(2), sch. 2. - Issued: 13.10.2008. Made: 07.10.2008 at 9.27 am. Laid: 07.10.2008 at 12.30 pm. Coming into force: 07.10.2008 at 9.30 am. Effect: 2000 c. 8 modified. Territorial extent & classification: E/W/S/NI. General. - 16p.: 30 cm. - 978-0-11-084449-7 £5.00

The Kaupthing Singer & Friedlander Limited (Determination of Compensation) Order 2008 No. 2008/3250. - Enabling power: Banking (Special Provisions) Act 2008, s. 7 (1) (a). - Issued: 23.12.2008. Made: 18.12.2008. Coming into force: 19.12.2008 in accord. with art. 1 (2). Effect: None. Territorial extent & classification: E/W/S/NI. General. - Supersedes draft S.I. (ISBN 9780111471128) issued 10.12.2008. - 2p.: 30 cm. - 978-0-11-147215-6 £4.00

The Kaupthing Singer & Friedlander Limited Transfer of Certain Rights and Liabilities Order 2008 No. 2008/2674. - Enabling power: Banking (Special Provisions) Act 2008, ss. 6, 8, 12, 13 (2), sch. 2. - Issued: 08.10.2008. Made: 08.10.2008, at 12.05 pm. Laid: 08.10.2008, at 4.00 pm. Coming into force: 08.10.2008, at 12.15 pm. Effect: None. Territorial extent & classification: E/W/S/NI. General. - 16p.: 30 cm. - 978-0-11-084501-2 £5.00

The Landsbanki Freezing (Amendment) Order 2008 No. 2008/2766. - Enabling power: Anti-terrorism, Crime and Security Act 2001, ss. 4, 14, sch. 3. - Issued: 03.11.2008. Made: 20.10.2008. Laid: 20.10.2008. Coming into force: 21.10.2008. Effect: S.I. 2008/2668 amended. Territorial extent & classification: E/W/S/NI. General. - Revoked by S.I. 2009/1392 (ISBN 9780111480496). Approved by both Houses of Parliament. - 4p.: 30 cm. - 978-0-11-084765-8 £4.00

The Landsbanki Freezing (Amendment) Order 2008 No. 2008/2766. - Enabling power: Anti-terrorism, Crime and Security Act 2001, ss. 4, 14, sch. 3. - Issued: 27.10.2008. Made: 20.10.2008. Laid: 20.10.2008. Coming into force: 21.10.2008. Effect: S.I. 2008/2668 amended. Territorial extent & classification: E/W/S/NI. General. - Revoked by S.I. 2009/1392 (ISBN 9780111480496). For approval by each House before expiration of a period of 28 days beginning with the date on which the Order was made, no account to be taken of any time during which Parliament is dissolved or prorogued or during which both Houses are adjourned for more than 4 days. - 2p.: 30 cm. - 978-0-11-084713-9 £4.00

The Landsbanki Freezing Order 2008 No. 2008/2668. - Enabling power: Anti-terrorism, Crime and Security Act 2001, ss. 4, 14, sch. 3. - Issued: 05.11.2008. Made: 08.10.2008 at 10.00 am. Laid: 08.10.2008 at 12.00 pm. Coming into force: 08.10.2008 at 10.10 am. Effect: None. Territorial extent & classification: E/W/S/NI. General. - Approved by both Houses of Parliament. - 8p.: 30 cm. - 978-0-11-084835-8 £5.00

The Landsbanki Freezing Order 2008 No. 2008/2668. - Enabling power: Anti-terrorism, Crime and Security Act 2001, ss. 4, 14, sch. 3. - Issued: 08.10.2008. Made: 08.10.2008, at 10.00 am. Laid: 08.10.2008, at 12.00 pm. Coming into force: 08.10.2008, at 10.10 am. Effect: None. Territorial extent & classification: E/W/S/NI. General. - Revoked by S.I. 2009/1392 (ISBN 9780111480496). For approval by each House before expiration of a period of 28 days beginning with the date on which the Order was made, no account to be taken of any time during which Parliament is dissolved or prorogued or during which both Houses are adjourned for more than 4 days. With correction slip dated October 2009. - 8p.: 30 cm. - 978-0-11-084499-2 £5.00

The Northern Rock plc Compensation Scheme Order 2008 No. 2008/718. - Enabling power: Banking (Special Provisions) Act 2008, ss. 5, 9, 12, 13 (2). - Issued: 12.03.2008. Made: 12.03.2008. Coming into force: 13.03.2008 in accord. with art. 1 (2). Effect: 2000 c. 8; S.I. 2001/2476 modified. Territorial extent & classification: E/W/S/NI. General. - Supersedes draft (ISBN 9780110810058) issued 25.02.2008. - 12p.: 30 cm. - 978-0-11-081203-8 £3.00

The Northern Rock plc Transfer Order 2008 No. 2008/432. - Enabling power: Banking (Special Provisions) Act 2008, ss. 3, 4, 12, 13 (2). - Issued: 22.02.2008. Made: 21.02.2008. Laid: 21.02.2008. Coming into force: 22.02.2008. Effect: 2000 c. 8 modified. Territorial extent & classification: E/W/S/NI. General. - 12p.: 30 cm. - 978-0-11-081003-4 £3.00

The Takeover Code (Concert Parties) Regulations 2008 No. 2008/3073. - Enabling power: European Communities Act 1972, s. 2 (2). - Issued: 02.12.2008. Made: 28.11.2008 at 10.00 am. Laid: 28.11.2008 at 11.00 am. Coming into force: 28.11.208 at 12.00 pm. Effect: None. Territorial extent & classification: E/W/S/NI. General. - 2p.: 30 cm. - 978-0-11-147081-7 £4.00

The Transfer of Rights and Liabilities to ING Order 2008 No. 2008/2666. - Enabling power: Banking (Special Provisions) Act 2008, ss. 6, 8, 12, 13 (2), sch. 2. - Issued: 08.10.2008. Made: 08.10.2008, at 10.00 am. Laid: 08.10.2008, at 12.00 pm. Coming into force: 08.10.2008, at 10.10 am. Effect: 2000 c. 8 modified. Territorial extent & classification: E/W/S/NI. General. - 8p.: 30 cm. - 978-0-11-084470-1 £5.00

Betting, gaming and lotteries

The Categories of Casino Regulations 2008 No. 2008/1330. - Enabling power: Gambling Act 2005, ss. 7 (5) to (7), 355 (1). - Issued: 23.05.2008. Made: 19.05.2008. Coming into force: 20.05.2008 in accord. with art. 1. Effect: None. Territorial extent & classification: E/W/S. General. - Supersedes draft S.I. (ISBN 9780110810164) issued 28.02.2008. - 4p.: 30 cm. - 978-0-11-081494-0 £3.00

The Gambling Act 2005 (Advertising of Foreign Gambling) (Amendment) (No. 2) Regulations 2008 No. 2008/2829. - Enabling power: Gambling Act 2005, ss. 331 (4), 355 (1). - Issued: 04.11.2008. Made: 28.10.2008. Laid: 30.10.2008. Coming into force: 20.11.2008. Effect: S.I. 2007/2329 amended & S.I. 2008/19 revoked. Territorial extent & classification: E/W/S/NI. General. - 4p.: 30 cm. - 978-0-11-084823-5 £4.00

The Gambling Act 2005 (Advertising of Foreign Gambling) (Amendment) Regulations 2008 No. 2008/19. - Enabling power: Gambling Act 2005, ss. 331 (4), 355 (1). - Issued: 14.01.2008. Made: 08.01.2008. Laid: 10.01.2008. Coming into force: 31.01.2008. Effect: S.I. 2007/2329 amended. Territorial extent & classification: E/W/S/NI. General. - Revoked by S.I. 2008/2829 (ISBN 9780110848235). - 2p.: 30 cm. - 978-0-11-080825-3 £3.00

The Gambling Act 2005 (Commencement No. 8) Order 2008 No. 2008/1326 (C.59). - Enabling power: Gambling Act 2005, s. 358 (1) (2). Bringing various provisions of the 2005 Act into operation on 20.05.2008. - Issued: 23.05.2008. Made: 19.05.2008. Effect: None. Territorial extent & classification: E/W/S. General. - 8p.: 30 cm. - 978-0-11-081493-3 £3.00

The Gambling (Geographical Distribution of Large and Small Casino Premises Licences) Order 2008 No. 2008/1327. - Enabling power: Gambling Act 2005, ss. 175 (4), 355. - Issued: 19.05.2008. Made: 19.05.2008. Coming into force: 21.05.2008 in accord. with art. 1. Effect: None. Territorial extent & classification: E/W/S. General. - Supersedes draft S.I. (ISBN 97801108101570 issued 28.02.2008. - 4p.: 30 cm. - 978-0-11-081490-2 £3.00

The Gambling (Inviting Competing Applications for Large and Small Casino Premises Licences) Regulations 2008 No. 2008/469. - Enabling power: Gambling Act 2005, s. 355, sch. 9, para. 2. - Issued: 28.02.2008. Made: 25.02.2008. Laid: 26.02.2008. Coming into force: 18.03.2008. Effect: None. Territorial extent & classification: E/W/S. General. - 4p.: 30 cm. - 978-0-11-081013-3 £3.00

The Gambling (Operating Licence and Single-Machine Permit Fees) (Amendment) (No 2) Regulations 2008 No. 2008/3105. - Enabling power: Gambling Act 2005, ss. 69 (2) (g) (5), 100 (2) (3), 355 (1). - Issued: 10.12.2008. Made: 01.12.2008. Laid: 04.12.2008. Coming into force: 31.12.2008. Effect: S.I. 2006/3284 amended. Territorial extent & classification: E/W/S. General. - This Statutory Instrument has been made in consequence of a defect in S.I. 2008/1803 and is being issued free of charge to all known recipients of that Statutory Instrument. - 8p.: 30 cm. - 978-0-11-147116-6 £5.00

The Gambling (Operating Licence and Single-Machine Permit Fees) (Amendment) Regulations 2008 No. 2008/1803. - Enabling power: Gambling Act 2005, ss. 69 (2) (g) (5), 100 (2) (3), 103 (2), 104 (3) (4), 355 (1). - Issued: 14.08.2008. Made: 04.07.2008. Laid: 08.07.2008. Coming into force: 01.08.2008. Effect: S.I. 2006/3284 amended. Territorial extent & classification: E/W/S. General. - 20p.: 30 cm. - 978-0-11-081999-0 £3.50

British nationality

The British Citizenship (Designated Service) (Amendment) Order 2008 No. 2008/135. - Enabling power: British Nationality Act 1981, s. 2 (3). - Issued: 28.01.2008. Made: 21.01.2008. Laid: 24.01.2008. Coming into force: 14.02.2008. Effect: S.I. 2006/1390 amended. Territorial extent & classification: E/W/S/NI. General. - 2p.: 30 cm. - 978-0-11-080868-0 £3.00

The British Overseas Territories Citizenship (Designated Service) (Amendment) Order 2008 No. 2008/1240. - Enabling power: British Nationality Act 1981, s. 16 (3). - Issued: 07.05.2008. Made: 30.04.2008. Laid: 02.05.2008. Coming into force: 30.06.2008. Effect: S.I. 1982/1710 amended. Territorial extent & classification: E/W/S/NI & Overseas territories. General. - 2p.: 30 cm. - 978-0-11-081433-9 £3.00

Broadcasting

The Communications (Television Licensing) (Amendment) Regulations 2008 No. 2008/643. - Enabling power: Communications Act 2003, ss. 365 (1) (4), 402. - Issued: 13.03.2008. Made: 06.03.2008. Laid: 10.03.2008. Coming into force: 01.04.2008. Effect: S.I. 2004/692 amended. Territorial extent & classification: E/W/S/NI/IoM/Ch.Is. General. - With correction slip dated June 2008. - 8p.: 30 cm. - 978-0-11-081186-4 £3.00

The Digital Switchover (Disclosure of Information) Act 2007 (Prescription of Information) (Amendment) Order 2008 No. 2008/2557. - Enabling power: Digital Switchover (Disclosure of Information) Act 2007, s. 2. - Issued: 06.10.2008. Made: 29.09.2008. Laid: 01.10.2008. Coming into force: 27.10.2008. Effect: S.I. 2007/1768 amended. Territorial extent & classification: E/W/S/NI. General. - 2p.: 30 cm. - 978-0-11-084337-7 £4.00

The Multiplex Licence (Broadcasting of Programmes in Gaelic) Order 2008 No. 2008/1421. - Enabling power: Broadcasting Act 1996, s. 32 (1). - Issued: 13.06.2008. Made: 09.06.2008. Laid: 10.06.2008. Coming into force: 02.07.2008. Effect: S.I. 1996/2758 amended. Territorial extent & classification: E/W/S/NI. General. - 2p.: 30 cm. - 978-0-11-081828-3 £3.00

The S4C (Investment Activities) Approval Order 2008 No. 2008/693. - Enabling power: Communications Act 2003, s. 206 (2). - Issued: 17.03.2008. Made: 11.03.2008. Laid: 12.03.2008. Coming into force: 02.04.2008. Effect: None. Territorial extent & classification: E/W/S/NI. General. - 2p.: 30 cm. - 978-0-11-081204-5 £3.00

The Television Multiplex Services (Reservation of Digital Capacity) Order 2008 No. 2008/1420. - Enabling power: Communications Act 2003, s. 243 (1) (3), 402 (3). - Issued: 13.06.2008. Made: 09.06.2008. Laid: 10.06.2008. Coming into force: 02.07.2008. Effect: 1996 c.55 modified. Territorial extent & classification: E/W/S/NI/Ch.Is.& IoM. General. - 16p.: 30 cm. - 978-0-11-081829-0 £3.00

Building and buildings, England and Wales

The Building (Amendment) Regulations 2008 No. 2008/671. - Enabling power: Building Act 1984, ss. 1 (1), 35A (2), sch. 1, para. 4. - Issued: 13.03.2008. Made: 10.03.2008. Laid: 13.03.2008. Coming into force: 06.04.2008. Effect: S.I. 2000/2531 amended. Territorial extent & classification: E/W. General. - 2p.: 30 cm. - 978-0-11-081173-4 £3.00

The Building (Electronic Communications) Order 2008 No. 2008/2334. - Enabling power: Electronic Communications Act 2000, s. 8. - Issued: 04.09.2008. Made: 28.08.2008. Laid: 04.09.2008. Coming into force: 01.10.2008. Effect: 1984 c. 55; S.I. 2000/2531, 2532 amended. Territorial extent & classification: E/W. General. - 4p.: 30 cm. - With correction slip dated September 2009. - 978-0-11-083896-0 £4.00

The Energy Performance of Buildings (Certificates and Inspections) (England and Wales) (Amendment No. 2) Regulations 2008 No. 2008/2363. - Enabling power: European Communities Act 1972, s. 2 (2) & Building Act 1984, s. 1 (1), 35, 47, sch. 1, paras 1, 2, 4, 4A, 7, 8, 10. - Issued: 09.09.2008. Made: 04.09.2008. Laid: 09.09.2008. Coming into force: 01.10.2008. Effect: S.I. 2000/2531, 2532; 2007/991, 1667 amended. Territorial extent & classification: E/W. General. - 8p.: 30 cm. - 978-0-11-084094-9 £5.00

The Energy Performance of Buildings (Certificates and Inspections) (England and Wales) (Amendment) Regulations 2008 No. 2008/647. - Enabling power: European Communities Act 1972, s. 2 (2) & Building Act 1984, s. 1 (1), sch. 1, paras 8, 10. - Issued: 13.03.2008. Made: 06.03.2008. Laid: 13.03.2008. Coming into force: 06.04.2008. Effect: S.I. 2007/991 amended. Territorial extent & classification: E/W. General. - 4p.: 30 cm. - 978-0-11-081160-4 £3.00

Building societies

The Building Societies (Accounts and Related Provisions) (Amendment) Regulations 2008 No. 2008/1143. - Enabling power: Building Societies Act 1986, ss. 72C (1) (2), 72G (1) (2) (3), 76 (3). - Issued: 24.04.2008. Made: 21.04.2008. Laid: 21.04.2008. Coming into force: 29.06.2008. Effect: S.I. 1998/504 amended. Territorial extent & classification: E/W/S/NI. General. - EC note: These Regulations amend S.I. 1998/504 to implement in part Directive 2006/46/EC on the annual and consolidated accounts of certain types of companies, banks and other financial institutions. - 4p.: 30 cm. - 978-0-11-081390-5 £3.00

The Building Societies Act 1986 (Accounts, Audit and EEA State Amendments) Order 2008 No. 2008/1519. - Enabling power: Building Societies Act 1986, s. 104 (1) (3) (4) & European Communities Act 1972, s. 2 (2). - Issued: 19.06.2008. Made: 11.06.2008. Coming into force: 29.06.2008. Effect: 1986 c. 53 amended. Territorial extent & classification: E/W/S/NI. General. - Supersedes draft S.I. (ISBN 97890110813912) issued 24.04.2008. EC note: This Order amends the Building Societies Act 1986 to implement, in relation to building societies: parts of Directive 2006/43/EC on statutory audits of annual accounts and parts of Directive 2006/46/EC on the annual and consolidated accounts of certain types of companies, banks and other financial institutions. - 16p.: 30 cm. - 978-0-11-081872-6 £3.00

The Building Societies (Financial Assistance) Order 2008 No. 2008/1427. - Enabling power: Banking (Special Provisions) Act 2008, ss. 11, 12 (1) (2), 13 (2). - Issued: 09.06.2008. Made: 04.06.2008. Coming into force: 05.06.2008. Effect: 1986 c.53; S.I. 1999/2979 modified. Territorial extent & classification: E/W/S/NI. General. - Supersedes draft S.I. (ISBN 9780110813462) issued 08.04.2008. - 8p.: 30 cm. - 978-0-11-081783-5 £3.00

Capital gains tax

The Authorised Investment Funds (Tax) (Amendment No. 2) Regulations 2008 No. 2008/1463. - Enabling power: Finance (No. 2) Act 2005, ss. 17 (3), 18. - Issued: 11.06.2008. Made: 09.06.2008. Laid: 09.06.2008. Coming into force: 30.06.2008. Effect: S.I. 2006/964 amended. Territorial extent & classification: E/W/S/NI. General. - 4p.: 30 cm. - 978-0-11-081811-5 £3.00

The Authorised Investment Funds (Tax) (Amendment No. 3) Regulations 2008 No. 2008/3159. - Enabling power: Finance (No. 2) Act 2005, ss. 17 (3), 18. - Issued: 16.12.2008. Made: 10.12.2008. Laid: 11.12.2008. Coming into force: 01.01.2009. Effect: S.I. 2006/964 amended. Territorial extent & classification: E/W/S/NI. General. - 16p.: 30 cm. - With correction slip dated October 2009. - 978-0-11-147156-2 £5.00

The Authorised Investment Funds (Tax) (Amendment) Regulations 2008 No. 2008/705. - Enabling power: Finance (No. 2) Act 2005, ss. 17 (3), 18. - Issued: 12.03.2008. Made: 12.03.2008. Laid: 12.03.2008. Coming into force: 06.04.2008. Effect: S.I. 2006/964 amended. Territorial extent & classification: E/W/S/NI. General. - 34p.: 30 cm. - 978-0-11-081206-9 £6.50

The Capital Gains Tax (Annual Exempt Amount) Order 2008 No. 2008/708. - Enabling power: Taxation of Chargeable Gains Act 1992, s. 3 (4). - Issued: 12.03.2008. Made: 12.03.2008. Coming into force: 12.03.2008. Effect: None. Territorial extent & classification: E/W/S/NI. General. - 2p.: 30 cm. - 978-0-11-081205-2 £3.00

The Double Taxation Relief and International Tax Enforcement (Taxes on Income and Capital) (Moldova) Order 2008 No. 2008/1795. - Enabling power: Income and Corporation Taxes Act 1988, s. 788 (10) & Finance Act 2006, s. 173 (7). - Issued: 16.07.2008. Made: 09.07.2008. Coming into force: 09.07.2008. Effect: None. Territorial extent & classification: E/W/S/NI. General. - Supersedes draft S.I. (ISBN 9780110814803) issued 21.05.2008. - 20p.: 30 cm. - 978-0-11-083144-2 £3.50

The Double Taxation Relief and International Tax Enforcement (Taxes on Income and Capital) (New Zealand) Order 2008 No. 2008/1793. - Enabling power: Income and Corporation Taxes Act 1988, s. 788 (10) & Finance Act 2006, s. 173 (7). - Issued: 15.07.2008. Made: 09.07.2008. Coming into force: 09.07.2008. Effect: None. Territorial extent & classification: E/W/S/NI. General. - Supersedes draft S.I. (ISBN 9780110814537) issued 15.05.2008. - 8p.: 30 cm. - 978-0-11-083138-1 £3.00

The Double Taxation Relief and International Tax Enforcement (Taxes on Income and Capital) (Saudi Arabia) Order 2008 No. 2008/1770. - Enabling power: Income and Corporation Taxes Act 1988, s. 788 (10) & Finance Act 2006, s. 173 (7). - Issued: 16.07.2008. Made: 09.07.2008. Effect: None. Territorial extent & classification: E/W/S/NI. General. - Supersedes draft S.I. (ISBN 9780110814636) issued on 19.05.2008. - 20p.: 30 cm. - 978-0-11-083151-0 £3.50

The Double Taxation Relief and International Tax Enforcement (Taxes on Income and Capital) (Slovenia) Order 2008 No. 2008/1796. - Enabling power: Income and Corporation Taxes Act 1988, s. 788 (10) & Finance Act 2006, s. 173 (7). - Issued: 16.07.2008. Made: 09.07.2008. Coming into force: 09.07.2008. Effect: None. Territorial extent & classification: E/W/S/NI. General. - Supersedes draft S.I. (ISBN 9780110814544) issued 15.05.2008. - 24p.: 30 cm. - 978-0-11-083145-9 £4.00

The Taxation of Chargeable Gains (Gilt-edged Securities) Order 2008 No. 2008/1588. - Enabling power: Taxation of Chargeable Gains Act 1992, sch. 9, para. 1. - Issued: 24.06.2008. Made: 19.06.2008. Coming into force: 19.06.2008. Effect: None. Territorial extent & classification: E/W/S/NI. General. - 2p.: 30 cm. - 978-0-11-081881-8 £3.00

Caribbean and North Atlantic territories

The Cayman Islands (Constitution) (Amendment) Order 2008 No. 2008/3127. - Enabling power: West Indies Act 1962, ss. 5, 7. - Issued: 17.12.2008. Made: 10.12.2008. Laid: 17.12.2008. Coming into force: In accord. with art. 1 (4). Effect: S.I. 1972/1101 amended. Territorial extent & classification: E/W/S/NI. General. - 2p.: 30 cm. - 978-0-11-147152-4 £4.00

Channel Tunnel

The Channel Tunnel (International Arrangements) (Amendment) Order 2008 No. 2008/2366. - Enabling power: Channel Tunnel Act 1987, s. 11. - Issued: 12.09.2008. Made: 03.09.2008. Laid: 09.09.2008. Coming into force: 08.10.2008. Effect: S.I. 2005/3207 amended. Territorial extent & classification: E/W/S/NI. General. - 2p.: 30 cm. - 978-0-11-084114-4 £4.00

Charities

The Charities Act 2006 (Commencement No. 4, Transitional Provisions and Savings) Order 2008 No. 2008/945 (C.46). - Enabling power: Charities Act 2006, s. 79 (2) (3). Bringing into operation various provisions of the 2006 Act on 01.04.2008 & 01.04.2009, in accord. with arts. 2, 3. - Issued: 04.04.2008. Made: 31.03.2008. Effect: None. Territorial extent & classification: E/W/S/NI. General. - 8p.: 30 cm. - 978-0-11-081330-1 £3.00

Charities, England and Wales

The Charities (Accounts and Reports) Regulations 2008 No. 2008/629. - Enabling power: Charities Act 1993, ss. 42, 44, 45, 86 (3), sch. 5A, paras 3, 4, 6, 10, 15. - Issued: 10.03.2008. Made: 06.03.2008. Laid: 10.03.2008. Coming into force: 01.04.2008. Effect: S.I. 2005/572 revoked with savings. Territorial extent & classification: E/W. General. - 44p.: 30 cm. - 978-0-11-081132-1 £7.50

The Charities Act 1993 (Exception from Registration) Regulations 2008 No. 2008/3268. - Enabling power: Charities Act 1993, ss. 3A (2) (c), 86, 97 (1). - Issued: 07.01.2009. Made: 19.12.2008. Laid: 07.01.2009. Coming into force: 31.1.2009. Effect: None. Territorial extent & classification: E/W. General. - 2p.: 30 cm. - 978-0-11-147241-5 £4.00

The Charities Act 2006 (Charitable Companies Audit and Group Accounts Provisions) Order 2008 No. 2008/527. - Enabling power: Charities Act 2006, ss. 74 (2), 77. - Issued: 04.03.2008. Made: 27.02.2008. Coming into force: 01.04.2008. in acc.with art. 1. Effect: 1993 c.10 amended. Territorial extent & classification: E/W. General. - Supersedes draft S.I. (ISBN 9780110808703) issued 29.01.2008. - 8p.: 30 cm. - 978-0-11-081057-7 £3.00

The Charities Act 2006 (Commencement No. 3, Transitional Provisions and Savings) Order 2008 No. 2008/751 (C.32). - Enabling power: Charities Act 2006, s. 79 (2) (3). Bringing into operation various provisions of the 2006 Act on 18.03.2008, in accord. with arts. 3 to 12. - Issued: 20.03.2008. Made: 15.03.2008. Effect: 1969 c.22; 1987 c.15; 1993 c.41 amended. Territorial extent & classification: E/W. General. - 8p.: 30 cm. - 978-0-11-081262-5 £3.00

The Charities Act 2006 (Commencement No. 5, Transitional and Transitory Provisions and Savings) Order 2008 No. 2008/3267 (C.150). - Enabling power: Charities Act 2006, ss. 78 (6), 79 (2) (3)Bringing into operation various provisions of the 2006 Act on 31.01.2009 subject to provisions in arts. 3-17. - Issued: 29.12.2008. Made: 19.12.2008. Effect: None. Territorial extent & classification: E/W. General. - 12p.: 30 cm. - 978-0-11-147235-4 £5.00

Children and young persons, England

The Childcare Act 2006 (Commencement No. 4) Order 2008 No. 2008/785 (C.35). - Enabling power: Childcare Act 2006, s. 109 (2). Bringing into operation various provisions of the 2006 Act on 01.04.2008, in accord. with art. 2. - Issued: 31.03.2008. Made: 19.03.2008. Effect: None. Territorial extent & classification: E. General. - 4p.: 30 cm. - 978-0-11-081274-8 £3.00

The Childcare Act 2006 (Commencement No. 5 and Savings and Transitional Provisions) Order 2008 No. 2008/2261 (C.101). - Enabling power: Childcare Act 2006, ss. 104 (2), 109 (2). Bringing into operation various provisions of the 2006 Act on 01.09.2008, in accord. with art. 2. - Issued: 29.08.2008. Made: 19.08.2008. Effect: None. Territorial extent & classification: E. General. - 20p.: 30 cm. - 978-0-11-083856-4 £3.50

The Childcare (Disqualification) (Amendment) Regulations 2008 No. 2008/1740. - Enabling power: Childcare Act 2006, ss. 67, 75, 104. - Issued: 09.07.2008. Made: 02.07.2008. Laid: 09.07.2008. Coming into force: 01.09.2008. Effect: S.I. 2007/723 amended. Territorial extent & classification: E. General. - Revoked by S.I. 2009/1547 (ISBN 9780111481189). - 4p.: 30 cm. - 978-0-11-081955-6 £3.00

The Childcare (Early Years and General Childcare Registers) (Common Provisions) Regulations 2008 No. 2008/976. - Enabling power: Childcare Act 2006, ss. 37 (3), 56 (3), 64 (3), 69 (1) (2), 90 (2), 92 (3), 96 (6) (b), 104 (2). - Issued: 11.04.2008. Made: 31.03.2008. Laid: 11.04.2008. Coming into force: 01.09.2008. Effect: None. Territorial extent & classification: E. General. - With correction slip dated August 2008. - 8p.: 30 cm. - 978-0-11-081352-3 £3.00

The Childcare (Early Years Register) Regulations 2008 No. 2008/974. - Enabling power: Childcare Act 2006, ss. 35 (2) (a) (3) (b) (5), 36 (2) (a) (3) (b) (5), 104 (2). - Issued: 11.04.2008. Made: 31.03.2008. Laid: 11.04.2008. Coming into force: 01.09.2008. Effect: None. Territorial extent & classification: E. General. - 12p.: 30 cm. - 978-0-11-081350-9 £3.00

The Childcare (Exemptions from Registration) Order 2008 No. 2008/979. - Enabling power: Childcare Act 2006, ss. 33 (2) (3), 34 (3) (4), 52 (2) (3), 53 (3) (4), 104 (2) (a). - Issued: 11.04.2008. Made: 31.03.2008. Laid: 11.04.2008. Coming into force: 01.09.2008. Effect: None. Territorial extent & classification: E. General. - 4p.: 30 cm. - 978-0-11-081360-8 £3.00

The Childcare (Fees) Regulations 2008 No. 2008/1804. - Enabling power: Childcare Act 2006, ss. 35 (2) (c), 36 (2) (c), 37 (5), 54 (2) (c), 55 (2) (c), 56 (5), 62 (2) (c), 63 (2) (c), 64 (5), 89, 92 (5), 104 (2). - Issued: 11.07.2008. Made: 03.07.2008. Laid: 11.07.2008. Coming into force: 01.09.2008. Effect: None. Territorial extent & classification: E. General. - 8p.: 30 cm. - 978-0-11-082000-2 £3.00

The Childcare (General Childcare Register) Regulations 2008 No. 2008/975. - Enabling power: Childcare Act 2006, ss. 54 (2) (a) (3) (b) (5), 55 (2) (a) (3) (b) (5), 59, 62 (2) (a) (3) (b) (5), 63 (2) (a) (4) (b) (6), 67, 104 (2). - Issued: 11.04.2008. Made: 31.03.2008. Laid: 11.04.2008. Coming into force: 01.09.2008. Effect: S.I. 2007/730 revoked. Territorial extent & classification: E. General. - 28p.: 30 cm. - 978-0-11-081351-6 £4.50

The Childcare (Inspections) Regulations 2008 No. 2008/1729. - Enabling power: Childcare Act 2006, ss. 49, 50, 60, 61. - Issued: 09.07.2008. Made: 01.07.2008. Laid: 09.07.2008. Coming into force: 01.09.2008. Effect: None. Territorial extent & classification: E. General. - 8p.: 30 cm. - 978-0-11-081945-7 £3.00

The Childcare (Provision of Information About Young Children) (England) (Amendment) Regulations 2008 No. 2008/3071. - Enabling power: Childcare Act 2006, ss. 99 (1), 104 (2). - Issued: 04.12.2008. Made: 26.11.2008. Laid: 04.12.2008. Coming into force: 01.09.2008. Effect: S.I. 2008/1722 amended. Territorial extent & classification: E. General. - Revoked by S.I. 2009/1554 (ISBN 9780111481271). - 2p.: 30 cm. - 978-0-11-147077-0 £4.00

The Childcare (Provision of Information About Young Children) (England) Regulations 2008 No. 2008/1722. - Enabling power: Education Act 1996, s. 537A & Childcare Act 2006, ss. 99 (1), 104 (2). - Issued: 08.07.2008. Made: 30.06.2008. Laid: 08.07.2008. Coming into force: 01.09.2008. Effect: S.I. 1999/903; 2007/3224 amended & S.I. 2007/712, 3436 revoked. Territorial extent & classification: E. General. - Part revoked by S.I. 2009/1554 (ISBN 9780111481271). - 8p.: 30 cm. - 978-0-11-081941-9 £3.00

The Childcare (Supply and Disclosure of Information) (England) (Amendment) Regulations 2008 No. 2008/961. - Enabling power: Childcare Act 2006, ss. 83 (1) (2), 84 (1) (3). - Issued: 09.04.2008. Made: 31.03.2008. Laid: 09.04.2008. Coming into force: 01.09.2008. Effect: S.I. 2007/722 amended. Territorial extent & classification: E. General. - 4p.: 30 cm. - 978-0-11-081340-0 £3.00

The Childcare (Voluntary Registration) (Amendment) Regulations 2008 No. 2008/793. - Enabling power: Childcare Act 2006, s. 89 (1). - Issued: 28.03.2008. Made: 19.03.2008. Laid: 31.03.2008. Coming into force: 05.05.2008. Effect: S.I. 2007/730 amended. Territorial extent & classification: E. General. - With correction slip dated March 2008. The date Laid before Parliament should read 31st March 2008. - 2p.: 30 cm. - 978-0-11-081283-0 £3.00

The Children Act 1989 (Contact Activity Directions and Conditions: Financial Assistance) (England) Regulations 2008 No. 2008/2940. - Enabling power: Children Act 1989, ss. 11F (1) (6) (7), 104 (4). - Issued: 17.11.2008. Made: 13.11.2008. Laid: 17.11.2008. Coming into force: 08.12.2008. Effect: None. Territorial extent & classification: E. General. - 4p.: 30 cm. - 978-0-11-147001-5 £4.00

The Children Act 2004 (Commencement No. 9) Order 2008 No. 2008/752 (C.33). - Enabling power: Children Act 2004, s. 67 (2). Bringing into operation various provisions of the 2004 Act on 21.03.2008. - Issued: 25.03.2008. Made: 17.03.2008. Effect: None. Territorial extent & classification: E. General. - 4p.: 30 cm. - 978-0-11-081263-2 £3.00

The Early Years Foundation Stage (Exemptions from Learning and Development Requirements) Regulations 2008 No. 2008/1743. - Enabling power: Childcare Act 2006, ss. 46, 104 (2). - Issued: 09.07.2008. Made: 02.07.2008. Laid: 09.07.2008. Coming into force: 04.08.2008. Effect: None. Territorial extent & classification: E. General. - 4p.: 30 cm. - 978-0-11-081958-7 £3.00

The Early Years Foundation Stage (Learning and Development Requirements) (Amendment) Order 2008 No. 2008/1952. - Enabling power: Childcare Act 2006, ss. 39 (1) (a), 44 (1). - Issued: 25.07.2008. Made: 21.07.2008. Laid: 25.07.2008. Coming into force: 01.09.2008. Effect: S.I. 2007/1772 amended. Territorial extent & classification: E. General. - 2p.: 30 cm. - 978-0-11-083512-9 £3.00

The Early Years Foundation Stage (Welfare Requirements) (Amendment) Regulations 2008 No. 2008/1953. - Enabling power: Childcare Act 2006, ss. 39 (1) (b), 43 (3), 44 (1) (2), 104 (2). - Issued: 25.07.2008. Made: 17.07.2008. Laid: 25.07.2008. Coming into force: 01.09.2008. Effect: S.I. 2007/1771 amended. Territorial extent & classification: E. General. - 8p.: 30 cm. - 978-0-11-083514-3 £3.00

The Fostering Services (Amendment) Regulations 2008 No. 2008/640. - Enabling power: Care Standards Act 2000, ss. 22 (1), 118 (5). - Issued: 13.03.2008. Made: 06.03.2008. Laid: 10.03.2008. Coming into force: 31.03.2008. Effect: S.I. 2002/57 amended. Territorial extent & classification: E. General. - 2p.: 30 cm. - 978-0-11-081143-7 £3.00

The Inspectors of Education, Children's Services and Skills (No. 2) Order 2008 No. 2008/1484. - Enabling power: Education and Inspections Act 2006, s. 114 (1). - Issued: 18.06.2008. Made: 11.06.2008. Coming into force: 12.06.2008. Effect: None. Territorial extent & classification: E. General. - 2p.: 30 cm. - 978-0-11-081852-8 £3.00

The Inspectors of Education, Children's Services and Skills (No. 3) Order 2008 No. 2008/1784. - Enabling power: Education and Inspections Act 2006, s. 114 (1). - Issued: 16.07.2008. Made: 09.07.2008. Coming into force: 10.07.2008. Effect: None. Territorial extent & classification: E. General. - 2p.: 30 cm. - 978-0-11-083121-3 £3.00

The Inspectors of Education, Children's Services and Skills (No. 4) Order 2008 No. 2008/2563. - Enabling power: Education and Inspections Act 2006, s. 114 (1). - Issued: 16.10.2008. Made: 09.10.2008. Coming into force: 10.10.2008. Effect: None. Territorial extent & classification: E. General. - 2p.: 30 cm. - 978-0-11-084581-4 £4.00

The Inspectors of Education, Children's Services and Skills (No. 5) Order 2008 No. 2008/3126. - Enabling power: Education and Inspections Act 2006, s. 114 (1). - Issued: 17.12.2008. Made: 10.12.2008. Coming into force: 11.12.2008. Effect: None. Territorial extent & classification: E. General. - 2p.: 30 cm. - 978-0-11-147167-8 £4.00

The Inspectors of Education, Children's Services and Skills Order 2008 No. 2008/681. - Enabling power: Education and Inspections Act 2006, s. 114 (1). - Issued: 19.03.2008. Made: 12.03.2008. Coming into force: 13.03.2008. Effect: None. Territorial extent & classification: E. General. - 2p.: 30 cm. - 978-0-11-081227-4 £3.00

The Local Authority (Duty to Secure Early Years Provision Free of Charge) Regulations 2008 No. 2008/1724. - Enabling power: Childcare Act 2006 ss. 7, 104 (2). - Issued: 08.07.2008. Made: 30.06.2008. Laid: 08.07.2008. Coming into force: 01.09.2008. Effect: None. Territorial extent & classification: E. General. - 4p.: 30 cm. - 978-0-11-081950-1 £3.00

The Local Authority Targets (Well-Being of Young Children) (Amendment) Regulations 2008 No. 2008/1437. - Enabling power: Childcare Act 2006 s. 1 (3). - Issued: 11.06.2008. Made: 05.06.2008. Laid: 11.06.2008. Coming into force: 14.07.2008. Effect: S.I. 2007/1415 amended. Territorial extent & classification: E. General. - 2p.: 30 cm. - 978-0-11-081798-9 £3.00

The Qualifications and Curriculum Authority (Additional Functions) Order 2008 No. 2008/1744. - Enabling power: Education Act 1997, s. 23 (2ZA). - Issued: 09.07.2008. Made: 02.07.2008. Laid: 09.07.2008. Coming into force: 04.08.2008. Effect: None. Territorial extent & classification: E. General. - 4p.: 30 cm. - 978-0-11-081968-6 £3.00

The Safeguarding Vulnerable Groups Act 2006 (Commencement No. 1) (England) Order 2008 No. 2008/3204 (C.145). - Enabling power: Safeguarding Vulnerable Groups Act 2006, ss. 61 (5), 65. Bringing into operation various provisions of the 2006 Act on 19.05.2008. - Issued: 17.12.2008. Made: 16.12.2008. Effect: None. Territorial extent & classification: E. General. - 8p.: 30 cm. - 978-0-11-147192-0 £5.00

Children and young persons, England and Wales

The Adoptions with a Foreign Element (Special Restrictions on Adoptions from Abroad) Regulations 2008 No. 2008/1807. - Enabling power: Children and Adoption Act 2006, ss. 11 (3), 12 (1), 16 (4) (5). - Issued: 11.07.2008. Made: 08.07.2008. Laid: 11.07.2008. Coming into force: 01.08.2008. Effect: None. Territorial extent & classification: E/W/NI. General. - 4p.: 30 cm. - 978-0-11-082003-3 £3.00

The Children and Adoption Act 2006 (Commencement No. 2) Order 2008 No. 2008/1798 (C.76). - Enabling power: Children and Adoption Act 2006, s. 17 (2). Bringing into operation various provisions of the 2006 Act on 07.07.2008, 01.08.2008. - Issued: 11.07.2008. Made: 06.07.2007. Effect: None. Territorial extent & classification: E/W/NI. General. - 4p.: 30 cm. - 978-0-11-081994-5 £3.00

The Children and Adoption Act 2006 (Commencement No. 3) Order 2008 No. 2008/2870 (C.127). - Enabling power: Children and Adoption Act 2006, s. 17 (2). Bringing into operation various provisions of the 2006 Act on 07.11.2008, 08.12.2008. - Issued: 12.11.2008. Made: 05.11.2008. Effect: None. Territorial extent & classification: E/W. General. - 4p.: 30 cm. - 978-0-11-084984-3 £4.00

The Protection of Children and Vulnerable Adults and Care Standards Tribunal (Amendment) Regulations 2008 No. 2008/1802. - Enabling power: Protection of Children Act 1999, s. 9 (2) (g) (3) (3B). - Issued: 11.07.2008. Made: 03.07.2008. Laid: 08.07.2008. Coming into force: 01.09.2008. Effect: S.I. 2002/816 amended. Territorial extent & classification: E/W. General. - Revoked by S.I. 2008/2683 (ISBN 9780110846156). - 4p.: 30 cm. - 978-0-11-081998-3 £3.00

The Protection of Children and Vulnerable Adults and Care Standards Tribunal (Children's and Adults' Barred Lists) (Transitional Provisions) Regulations 2008 No. 2008/1497. - Enabling power: Safeguarding Vulnerable Groups Act 2006, ss. 4 (8), 61 (5), 64 (1). - Issued: 16.06.2008. Made: 09.06.2008. Laid: 11.06.2008. Coming into force: 02.07.2008. Effect: None. Territorial extent & classification: E/W. General. - Revoked by S.I. 2008/2683 (ISBN 9780110846156). - 16p.: 30 cm. - 978-0-11-081840-5 £3.00

The Safeguarding Vulnerable Groups Act 2006 (Barred List Prescribed Information) Regulations 2008 No. 2008/16. - Enabling power: Safeguarding Vulnerable Groups Act 2006, ss. 2 (5), 60 (1). - Issued: 14.01.2008. Made: 08.01.2008. Laid: 11.01.2008. Coming into force: 04.02.2008. Effect: None. Territorial extent & classification: E/W. General. - 4p.: 30 cm. - 978-0-11-080824-6 £3.00

The Safeguarding Vulnerable Groups Act 2006 (Barring Procedure) Regulations 2008 No. 2008/474. - Enabling power: Safeguarding Vulnerable Groups Act 2006, ss. 61 (5), 64 (1), sch. 3, paras 15 (1) (2), 18 (3) (b) (6). - Issued: 05.03.2008. Made: 28.02.2008. Laid: 05.03.2008. Coming into force: 07.04.2008. Effect: None. Territorial extent & classification: E/W. General. - 8p.: 30 cm. - 978-0-11-081062-1 £3.00

The Safeguarding Vulnerable Groups Act 2006 (Commencement No. 2) Order 2008 No. 2008/1320 (C.57). - Enabling power: Safeguarding Vulnerable Groups Act 2006, ss. 61 (5), 65. Bringing into operation various provisions of the 2006 Act on 19.05.2008. - Issued: 21.05.2008. Made: 14.05.2008. Effect: None. Territorial extent & classification: E/W (and UK in respect of the commencement of amendments to the Data Protection Act 1998). General. - 8p.: 30 cm. - 978-0-11-081479-7 £3.00

The Safeguarding Vulnerable Groups Act 2006 (Prescribed Criteria) (Foreign Offences) Order 2008 No. 2008/3050. - Enabling power: Safeguarding Vulnerable Groups Act 2006, s. 64 (1) (2) (a) (3). - Issued: 28.11.2008. Made: 12.11.2008. Coming into force: 13.11.2008 in accord. with art. 1. Effect: 2006 c.47 amended. Territorial extent & classification: E/W. General. - Supersedes draft S.I. (ISBN 9780110845623) issued 15.10.2008. - 4p.: 30 cm. - 978-0-11-147061-9 £4.00

The Safeguarding Vulnerable Groups Act 2006 (Prescribed Criteria) (Transitional Provisions) Regulations 2008 No. 2008/1062. - Enabling power: Safeguarding Vulnerable Groups Act 2006, ss. 61 (5), 64 (1), sch. 3, paras 1 (1), 7 (1), 24 (1) to (3). - Issued: 17.04.2008. Made: 03.04.2008. Coming into force: 07.04.2008. Effect: None. Territorial extent & classification: E/W. General. - Supersedes draft SI (ISBN 9780110810676) issued 05.03.2008. - 8p.: 30 cm. - 978-0-11-081362-2 £3.00

The Safeguarding Vulnerable Groups Act 2006 (Prescribed Information) Regulations 2008 No. 2008/3265. - Enabling power: Safeguarding Vulnerable Groups Act 2006, ss. 35 (1) (a) (b), 36 (1) (2) (3), 37 (2), 39 (1) (5), 40 (2), 41 (1) (5), 42 (2), 45 (1) (5), 46 (1) (a) (2), 61 (5), sch. 3, paras 19 (1) (b), 21. - Issued: 29.12.2008. Made: 18.12.2008. Laid: 29.12.2008. Coming into force: 20.01.2009 for regs 1, 2, 5, 7, 9, 11, 12, schedule & 12.10.2009 for remainder, in accord. with art. 1. Effect: None. Territorial extent & classification: E/W. General. - Supersedes draft S.I. (ISBN 9780110845623) issued 15.10.2008. - 8p.: 30 cm. - 978-0-11-147231-6 £5.00

The Safeguarding Vulnerable Groups Act 2006 (Transitional Provisions) Order 2008 No. 2008/473. - Enabling power: Safeguarding Vulnerable Groups Act 2006, ss. 61 (5), 64 (1), sch. 8, paras 2, 3. - Issued: 05.03.2008. Made: 28.02.2008. Laid: 05.03.2008. Coming into force: 07.04.2008. Effect: None. Territorial extent & classification: E/W. General. - 8p.: 30 cm. - 978-0-11-081061-4 £3.00

The Special Restrictions on Adoptions from Abroad (Cambodia) Order 2008 No. 2008/1808. - Enabling power: Children and Adoption Act 2006, s. 9 (4). - Issued: 11.07.2008. Made: 07.07.2008. Laid: 11.07.2008. Coming into force: 01.08.2008. Effect: None. Territorial extent & classification: E/W/NI. General. - 2p.: 30 cm. - 978-0-11-082002-6 £3.00

The Special Restrictions on Adoptions from Abroad (Guatemala) Order 2008 No. 2008/1809. - Enabling power: Children and Adoption Act 2006, s. 9 (4). - Issued: 11.07.2008. Made: 07.07.2008. Laid: 11.07.2008. Coming into force: 01.08.2008. Effect: None. Territorial extent & classification: E/W/NI. General. - 2p.: 30 cm. - 978-0-11-082004-0 £3.00

Children and young persons, Northern Ireland

The Adoptions with a Foreign Element (Special Restrictions on Adoptions from Abroad) Regulations 2008 No. 2008/1807. - Enabling power: Children and Adoption Act 2006, ss. 11 (3), 12 (1), 16 (4) (5). - Issued: 11.07.2008. Made: 08.07.2008. Laid: 11.07.2008. Coming into force: 01.08.2008. Effect: None. Territorial extent & classification: E/W/NI. General. - 4p.: 30 cm. - 978-0-11-082003-3 £3.00

The Children and Adoption Act 2006 (Commencement No. 2) Order 2008 No. 2008/1798 (C.76). - Enabling power: Children and Adoption Act 2006, s. 17 (2). Bringing into operation various provisions of the 2006 Act on 07.07.2008, 01.08.2008. - Issued: 11.07.2008. Made: 06.07.2007. Effect: None. Territorial extent & classification: E/W/NI. General. - 4p.: 30 cm. - 978-0-11-081994-5 £3.00

The Safeguarding Vulnerable Groups Act 2006 (Commencement No. 1) (Northern Ireland) Order 2008 No. 2008/930 (C.45). - Enabling power: Safeguarding Vulnerable Groups Act 2006, ss. 61 (5), 65. Bringing into operation various provisions of the 2006 Act on 31.03.2008. - Issued: 07.04.2008. Made: 27.03.2008. Effect: None. Territorial extent & classification: NI. General. - 4p.: 30 cm. - 978-0-11-081320-2 £3.00

The Special Restrictions on Adoptions from Abroad (Cambodia) Order 2008 No. 2008/1808. - Enabling power: Children and Adoption Act 2006, s. 9 (4). - Issued: 11.07.2008. Made: 07.07.2008. Laid: 11.07.2008. Coming into force: 01.08.2008. Effect: None. Territorial extent & classification: E/W/NI. General. - 2p.: 30 cm. - 978-0-11-082002-6 £3.00

The Special Restrictions on Adoptions from Abroad (Guatemala) Order 2008 No. 2008/1809. - Enabling power: Children and Adoption Act 2006, s. 9 (4). - Issued: 11.07.2008. Made: 07.07.2008. Laid: 11.07.2008. Coming into force: 01.08.2008. Effect: None. Territorial extent & classification: E/W/NI. General. - 2p.: 30 cm. - 978-0-11-082004-0 £3.00

Children and young persons, Wales

The Childcare Act 2006 (Commencement No. 1) (Wales) Order 2008 No. 2008/17 (W.6) (C.1). - Enabling power: Childcare Act 2006, s. 109 (2). Bringing into operation various provisions of the 2006 Act on 31.01.2008 & 01.04.2008 in accord. with arts 2 & 3. - Issued: 04.02.2008. Made: 08.01.2008. Effect: None. Territorial extent & classification: W. General. - In English and Welsh. Welsh language title: Gorchymyn Deddf Gofal Plant 2006 (Cychwyn Rhif 1) (Cymru) 2008. - 4p.: 30 cm. - 978-0-11-091732-0 £3.00

The Childcare Act 2006 (Local Authority Assessment) (Wales) Regulations 2008 No. 2008/169 (W.22). - Enabling power: Childcare Act 2006, s. 26. - Issued: 03.03.2008. Made: 28.01.2008. Laid before the National Assembly for Wales: 30.01.2008. Coming into force: 01.04.2008. Effect: None. Territorial extent & classification: W. General. - With correction slip dated March 2008. - In English and Welsh: Welsh title: Rheoliadau Deddf Gofal Plant 2006(Asesiadau Awdurdodau Lleol) (Cymru) 2008. - 8p.: 30 cm. - 978-0-11-091713-9 £3.00

The Childcare Act 2006 (Provision of Information) (Wales) (Amendment) Regulations 2008 No. 2008/1716 (W.163). - Enabling power: Childcare Act 2006, s. 27. - Issued: 16.07.2008. Made: 28.06.2008. Laid before the National Assembly for Wales: 01.07.2008. Coming into force: 31.07.2008. Effect: S.I. 2008/170 (W.23) amended. Territorial extent & classification: W. General. - With correction slip dated August 2008. - In English and Welsh. Welsh title: Rheoliadau Deddf Gofal Plant 2006 (Darparu Gwybodaeth) (Cymru) (Diwygio) 2008. - 4p.: 30 cm. - 978-0-11-091841-9 £3.00

The Childcare Act 2006 (Provision of Information) (Wales) Regulations 2008 No. 2008/170 (W.23). - Enabling power: Childcare Act 2006, s. 27. - Issued: 04.03.2008. Made: 28.01.2008. Laid: 30.01.2008. Coming into force: 01.04.2008. Effect: None. Territorial extent & classification: W. General. - In English and Welsh. Welsh title: Rheoliadau Deddf Gofal Plant 2006 (Darparu Gwybodaeth) (Cymru) 2008. - 8p.: 30 cm. - 978-0-11-091715-3 £3.00

The Children Act 1989 (Contact Activity Directions and Conditions: Financial Assistance) (Wales) Regulations 2008 No. 2008/2943 (W.260). - Enabling power: Children Act 1989, ss. 11F (3) (6) (7), 104 (4). - Issued: 05.12.2008. Made: 13.11.2008. Laid before the National Assembly for Wales: 14.11.2008. Coming into force: 08.12.2008. Effect: None. Territorial extent & classification: W. General. - In English and Welsh. Welsh title: Rheoliadau Deddf Plant 1989 (Cyfarwyddiadau ac Amodau Gweithgareddau Cyswllt: Cymorth Ariannol) (Cymru) 2008. - 4p.: 30 cm. - 978-0-11-091870-9 £4.00

The Children Act 2004 (Commencement No 8) (Wales) Order 2008 No. 2008/1904 (W.182)(C.85). - Enabling power: Children Act 2004, s. 67 (7) (e), sch. 5, parts, 1, 3, paras (b). Bringing into operation various provisions of the 2004 Act on 31.07.2008 in accord. with art 2. - Issued: 06.08.2008. Made: 16.07.2008. Effect: None. Territorial extent & classification: W. General. - In English and Welsh. Welsh title: Gorchymyn Deddf Plant 2004 (Cychwyn Rhif 8) (Cymru) 2008. - 8p.: 30 cm. - 978-0-11-091824-2 £3.00

The Disqualification from Caring for Children (Wales) (Amendment) Regulations 2008 No. 2008/2691 (W.239). - Enabling power: Children Act 1989, ss. 68 (1) (2), 79C (2) (3), 79M (1) (c), 104 (4), sch. 9A, para. 4. - Issued: 24.10.2008. Made: 08.10.2008. Laid before the National Assembly for Wales: 10.10.2008. Coming into force: 03.11.2008. Effect: S.I. 2004/2695 (W.235) revoked. Territorial extent & classification: W. General. - In English and Welsh. Welsh title: Rheoliadau Datgymhwyso rhag Gofalu am Blant (Cymru) (Diwygio) 2008. - 4p.: 30 cm. - 978-0-11-091861-7 £4.00

The Suspension of Day Care Providers and Child Minders (Wales) (Amendment) Regulations 2008 No. 2008/2689 (W.238). - Enabling power: Children Act 1989, ss. 79H (1) (2), 104 (4). - Issued: 24.10.2008. Made: 08.10.2008. Laid before the National Assembly for Wales: 10.10.2008. Coming into force: 03.11.2008. Effect: S.I. 2004/3282 amended. Territorial extent & classification: W. General. - In English and Welsh. Welsh title: Rheoliadau Atal Dros Dro Ddarparwyr Gofal Dydd a Gwarchodwyr Plant (Cymru) (Diwygio) 2008. - 4p.: 30 cm. - 978-0-11-091888-4 £4.00

Cinema and films

The Films Co-Production Agreements (Amendment) Order 2008 No. 2008/1783. - Enabling power: Films Act 1985, sch. 1, para. 4 (5). - Issued: 16.07.2008. Made: 09.07.2008. Coming into force: 01.08.2008. Effect: S.I. 1985/960 amended & S.I. 2007/2125 revoked. Territorial extent & classification: E/W/S/NI. General. - 2p.: 30 cm. - 978-0-11-083165-7 £3.00

Civil aviation

The Aerodromes (Designation) (Chargeable Air Services) (Amendment) Order 2008 No. 2008/518. - Enabling power: Transport Act 2000, s. 77 (4). - Issued: 07.03.2008. Made: 27.02.2008. Laid: 03.03.2008. Coming into force: 01.04.2008. Effect: S.I. 2001/354 amended. Territorial extent & classification: UK but, in practice, will only affect the aerodromes designated for the purposes of section 77(3) (b) of the Transport Act 2000 in England. General. - Revoked by S.I. 2009/189 (ISBN 9780111473443). - 2p.: 30 cm. - 978-0-11-081035-5 £3.00

The Air Navigation (Amendment) Order 2008 No. 2008/1782. - Enabling power: Civil Aviation Act 1982, ss. 60 (other than sub-section (3) (r)), 102, sch. 13. - Issued: 16.07.2008. Made: 09.07.2008. Laid: 16.07.2008. Coming into force: 06.08.2008. Effect: S.I. 2005/1970 amended. Territorial extent & classification: E/W/S/NI. General. - 2p.: 30 cm. - 978-0-11-083122-0 £3.00

The Air Navigation (Dangerous Goods) (Amendment) (No. 2) Regulations 2008 No. 2008/2429. - Enabling power: S.I. 2005/1970, art. 70 (1). - Issued: 18.09.2008. Made: 11.09.2008. Coming into force: 01.01.2009. Effect: S.I. 2002/2786 amended. Territorial extent & classification: E/W/S/NI. General. - Revoked by S.I. 2009/1492 (ISBN 9780111480786). - 2p.: 30 cm. - 978-0-11-084214-1 £4.00

The Air Navigation (Dangerous Goods) (Amendment) Regulations 2008 No. 2008/1943. - Enabling power: S.I. 2005/1970, art. 70 (1). - Issued: 28.07.2008. Made: 21.07.2008. Coming into force: 15.08.2008. Effect: S.I. 2002/2786 amended. Territorial extent & classification: E/W/S/NI. General. - Revoked by S.I. 2009/1492 (ISBN 9780111480786). - 2p.: 30 cm. - 978-0-11-083499-3 £3.00

The Air Navigation (Environmental Standards For Non-EASA Aircraft) Order 2008 No. 2008/3133. - Enabling power: Civil Aviation Act 1982, ss. 60 (1) (2) (a) (b) (3) (q) (r), 61 (1), 101 (1) (a), 102 (2), sch. 13. - Issued: 15.12.2008. Made: 10.12.2008. Coming into force: 21.12.2008 in accord. with art. 1. Effect: S.I. 2002/798 revoked. Territorial extent & classification: E/W/S/NI. General. - Supersedes draft S.I. (ISBN 9780110843773) issued 09.10.2008. - 20p.: 30 cm. - 978-0-11-147153-1 £5.00

The Air Navigation (Guernsey) (Revocation) Order 2008 No. 2008/3121. - Enabling power: Civil Aviation Act 1982, ss. 60 (other than subsection (3)(r)), 61 (1) (2), 77, 101, 102, sch. 13. - Issued: 17.12.2008. Made: 10.12.2008. Coming into force: In accord. with art. 1. Effect: S.I. 1981/1805 revoked with savings. Territorial extent & classification: Guernsey. General. - 2p.: 30 cm. - 978-0-11-147158-6 £4.00

The Air Navigation (Isle of Man) (Amendment) Order 2008 No. 2008/1487. - Enabling power: Civil Aviation Act 1982, ss. 60, 61. - Issued: 17.06.2008. Made: 11.06.2008. Coming into force: 01.07.2008. Effect: S.I. 2007/1115 amended. Territorial extent & classification: IoM. General. - 8p.: 30 cm. - 978-0-11-081847-4 £3.00

The Air Navigation (Jersey) Order 2008 No. 2008/2562. - Enabling power: Civil Aviation Act 1982, ss. 60 (other than subsection (3)(r)), 61 (1) (2), 77, 101, 102 (1) (2), sch. 13 & Airports Act 1986, s. 35. - Issued: 03.11.2008. Made: 09.10.2008. Coming into force: In accord. with art. 1. Effect: S.I. 2000/1346, 3246; 2002/1078 revoked. Territorial extent & classification: Jersey. General. - 28p.: 30 cm. - 978-0-11-084788-7 £5.00

The Air Navigation (Overseas Territories) (Amendment) Order 2008 No. 2008/3125. - Enabling power: Civil Aviation Act 1949, ss. 8, 41, 57, 58, 59, 61 & Civil Aviation Act 1982, s. 61. - Issued: 17.12.2008. Made: 10.12.2008. Laid: 17.12.2008. Coming into force: 07.01.2009. Effect: S.I. 2007/3468 amended. Territorial extent & classification: UK Overseas Territories with the exception of British Antarctic Territory and Gibraltar. General. - 4p.: 30 cm. - 978-0-11-147176-0 £4.00

The Air Navigation (Restriction of Flying) (Abingdon) Regulations 2008 No. 2008/181. - Enabling power: S.I. 2005/1970, art. 96. - Made: 19.01.2008. Coming into force: Forthwith. Effect: None. Territorial extent & classification: E. Local. - Revoked by S.I .2008/317 (Unpublished) *Unpublished*

The Air Navigation (Restriction of Flying) (Abingdon) (Revocation) Regulations 2008 No. 2008/317. - Enabling power: S.I. 2005/1970, art. 96. - Made: 21.01.2008. Coming into force: Forthwith. Effect: S.I. 2008/181 revoked. Territorial extent & classification: E. Local *Unpublished*

The Air Navigation (Restriction of Flying) (Bacton) Regulations 2008 No. 2008/808. - Enabling power: S.I. 2005/1970, art. 96. - Made: 28.02.2008. Coming into force: Forthwith. Effect: None. Territorial extent & classification: E. Local. - Revoked by S.I. 2008/809 (Unpublished) *Unpublished*

The Air Navigation (Restriction of Flying) (Bacton) (Revocation) Regulations 2008 No. 2008/809. - Enabling power: S.I. 2005/1970, art. 96. - Made: 29.02.2008. Coming into force: Forthwith. Effect: S.I. 2008/808 revoked. Territorial extent & classification: E. Local *Unpublished*

The Air Navigation (Restriction of Flying) (Biggin Hill) (Air Fair) (Amendment) Regulations 2008 No. 2008/1611. - Enabling power: S.I. 2005/1970, art. 96. - Made: 03.06.2008. Coming into force: 07.06.2008. Effect: S.I. 2008/810 amended. Territorial extent & classification: E. Local *Unpublished*

The Air Navigation (Restriction of Flying) (Biggin Hill) (Air Fair) Regulations 2008 No. 2008/810. - Enabling power: S.I. 2005/1970, art. 96. - Made: 29.02.2008. Coming into force: 07.06.2008. Effect: None. Territorial extent & classification: E. Local *Unpublished*

The Air Navigation (Restriction of Flying) (Bournemouth Air Festival) Regulations 2008 No. 2008/1855. - Enabling power: S.I. 2005/1970, art. 96. - Made: 26.06.2008. Coming into force: 28.08.2008. Effect: None. Territorial extent & classification: E. Local *Unpublished*

The Air Navigation (Restriction of Flying) (Bow, East London) (No. 2) Regulations 2008 No. 2008/1604. - Enabling power: S.I. 2005/1970, art. 96. - Made: 05.06.2008. Coming into force: Forthwith. Effect: None. Territorial extent & classification: E. Local. - Revoked by S.I. 2008/1605 *Unpublished*

The Air Navigation (Restriction of Flying) (Bow, East London) (No. 2) (Revocation) Regulations 2008 No. 2008/1605. - Enabling power: S.I. 2005/1970, art. 96. - Made: 05.06.2008. Coming into force: Forthwith. Effect: S.I. 2008/1604 revoked. Territorial extent & classification: E. Local *Unpublished*

The Air Navigation (Restriction of Flying) (Bow, East London) (No. 3) Regulations 2008 No. 2008/1606. - Enabling power: S.I. 2005/1970, art. 96. - Made: 06.06.2008. Coming into force: Forthwith. Effect: None. Territorial extent & classification: E. Local. - Revoked by S.I. 2008/1607 *Unpublished*

The Air Navigation (Restriction of Flying) (Bow, East London) (No. 3) (Revocation) Regulations 2008 No. 2008/1607. - Enabling power: S.I. 2005/1970, art. 96. - Made: 09.06.2008. Coming into force: Forthwith. Effect: S.I. 2008/1606 revoked. Territorial extent & classification: E. Local *Unpublished*

The Air Navigation (Restriction of Flying) (Bow, East London) Regulations 2008 No. 2008/1602. - Enabling power: S.I. 2005/1970, art. 96. - Made: 03.06.2008. Coming into force: Forthwith. Effect: None. Territorial extent & classification: E. Local. - Revoked by S.I. 2008/1603 *Unpublished*

The Air Navigation (Restriction of Flying) (Bow, East London) (Revocation) Regulations 2008 No. 2008/1603. - Enabling power: S.I. 2005/1970, art. 96. - Made: 03.06.2008. Coming into force: Forthwith. Effect: S.I. 2008/1602 revoked. Territorial extent & classification: E. Local *Unpublished*

The Air Navigation (Restriction of Flying) (Bruntingthorpe) Regulations 2008 No. 2008/1092. - Enabling power: S.I. 2005/1970, art. 96. - Made: 07.04.2008. Coming into force: 10.04.2008. Effect: None. Territorial extent & classification: E. Local *Unpublished*

The Air Navigation (Restriction of Flying) (Chelmsford Prison) Regulations 2008 No. 2008/1093. - Enabling power: S.I. 2005/1970, art. 96. - Made: 03.04.2008. Coming into force: Forthwith. Effect: None. Territorial extent & classification: E. Local. - Revoked by S.I. 2008/1094 (Unpublished) *Unpublished*

The Air Navigation (Restriction of Flying) (Chelmsford Prison) (Revocation) Regulations 2008 No. 2008/1094. - Enabling power: S.I. 2005/1970, art. 96. - Made: 04.04.2008. Coming into force: Forthwith. Effect: S.I. 2008/1093 revoked. Territorial extent & classification: E. Local *Unpublished*

The Air Navigation (Restriction of Flying) (Cheltenham) Regulations 2008 No. 2008/121. - Enabling power: S.I. 2005/1970, art. 96. - Made: 03.01.2008. Coming into force: 11.03.2008. Effect: None. Territorial extent & classification: E. Local *Unpublished*

The Air Navigation (Restriction of Flying) (Chilbolton) Regulations 2008 No. 2008/805. - Enabling power: S.I. 2005/1970, art. 96. - Made: 26.02.2008. Coming into force: 31.03.2008. Effect: None. Territorial extent & classification: E. Local *Unpublished*

The Air Navigation (Restriction of Flying) (City of Manchester Stadium) Regulations 2008 No. 2008/318. - Enabling power: S.I. 2005/1970, art. 96. - Made: 01.02.2008. Coming into force: 14.05.2008. Effect: None. Territorial extent & classification: E. Local *Unpublished*

The Air Navigation (Restriction of Flying) (Coombe Abbey) Regulations 2008 No. 2008/2257. - Enabling power: S.I. 2005/1970, art. 96. - Made: 18.08.2008. Coming into force: Forthwith. Effect: None. Territorial extent & classification: E. Local. - Revoked by S.I. 2008/2258 (Unpublished) *Unpublished*

The Air Navigation (Restriction of Flying) (Coombe Abbey) (Revocation) Regulations 2008 No. 2008/2258. - Enabling power: S.I. 2005/1970, art. 96. - Made: 19.08.2008. Coming into force: Forthwith. Effect: S.I. 2008/2257 revoked. Territorial extent & classification: E. Local *Unpublished*

The Air Navigation (Restriction of Flying) (Copdock) Regulations 2008 No. 2008/182. - Enabling power: S.I. 2005/1970, art. 96. - Made: 21.01.2008. Coming into force: Forthwith. Effect: None. Territorial extent & classification: E. Local. - Revoked by S.I. 2008/187 (Unpublished) *Unpublished*

The Air Navigation (Restriction of Flying) (Copdock) (Revocation) Regulations 2008 No. 2008/187. - Enabling power: S.I. 2005/1970, art. 96. - Made: 21.01.2008. Coming into force: Forthwith. Effect: S.I. 2008/182 revoked. Territorial extent & classification: E. Local *Unpublished*

The Air Navigation (Restriction of Flying) (Coventry) Regulations 2008 No. 2008/964. - Enabling power: S.I. 2005/1970, art. 96. - Made: 13.03.2008. Coming into force: Forthwith. Effect: None. Territorial extent & classification: E. Local. - Revoked by S.I. 2008/965 (Unpublished) *Unpublished*

The Air Navigation (Restriction of Flying) (Coventry) (Revocation) Regulations 2008 No. 2008/965. - Enabling power: S.I. 2005/1970, art. 96. - Made: 13.03.2008. Coming into force: Forthwith. Effect: S.I. 2008/964 revoked. Territorial extent & classification: E. Local *Unpublished*

The Air Navigation (Restriction of Flying) (Dover Straights) Regulations 2008 No. 2008/122. - Enabling power: S.I. 2005/1970, art. 96. - Made: 02.01.2008. Coming into force: Forthwith. Effect: None. Territorial extent & classification: E. Local. - Revoked by S.I. 2008/123 (Unpublished) *Unpublished*

The Air Navigation (Restriction of Flying) (Dover Straights) (Revocation) Regulations 2008 No. 2008/123. - Enabling power: S.I. 2005/1970, art. 96. - Made: 03.01.2008. Coming into force: Forthwith. Effect: S.I. 2008/122 revoked. Territorial extent & classification: E. Local *Unpublished*

The Air Navigation (Restriction of Flying) (Dunsfold) Regulations 2008 No. 2008/806. - Enabling power: S.I. 2005/1970, art. 96. - Made: 26.02.2008. Coming into force: 24.08.2008. Effect: None. Territorial extent & classification: E. Local *Unpublished*

The Air Navigation (Restriction of Flying) (Duxford) (No. 2) Regulations 2008 No. 2008/363. - Enabling power: S.I. 2005/1970, art. 96. - Made: 01.02.2008. Coming into force: 01.06.2008. Effect: None. Territorial extent & classification: E. Local *Unpublished*

The Air Navigation (Restriction of Flying) (Duxford) (No. 3) Regulations 2008 No. 2008/1853. - Enabling power: S.I. 2005/1970, art. 96. - Made: 26.06.2008. Coming into force: 12.07.2008. Effect: None. Territorial extent & classification: E. Local *Unpublished*

The Air Navigation (Restriction of Flying) (Duxford) (No. 4) Regulations 2008 No. 2008/2074. - Enabling power: S.I. 2005/1970, art. 96. - Made: 07.07.2008. Coming into force: 19.07.2008. Effect: None. Territorial extent & classification: E. Local *Unpublished*

The Air Navigation (Restriction of Flying) (Duxford) (No. 5) Regulations 2008 No. 2008/2303. - Enabling power: S.I. 2005/1970, art. 96. - Made: 27.08.2008. Coming into force: 06.09.2008. Effect: None. Territorial extent & classification: E. Local *Unpublished*

The Air Navigation (Restriction of Flying) (Duxford) Regulations 2008 No. 2008/362. - Enabling power: S.I. 2005/1970, art. 96. - Made: 01.02.2008. Coming into force: 18.05.2008. Effect: None. Territorial extent & classification: E. Local *Unpublished*

The Air Navigation (Restriction of Flying) (Eastbourne) Regulations 2008 No. 2008/966. - Enabling power: S.I. 2005/1970, art. 96. - Made: 12.03.2008. Coming into force: 14.08.2008. Effect: None. Territorial extent & classification: E. Local *Unpublished*

The Air Navigation (Restriction of Flying) (Enniskillen) Regulations 2008 No. 2008/2911. - Enabling power: S.I. 2005/1970, art. 96. - Made: 03.11.2008. Coming into force: 31.01.2009. Effect: None. Territorial extent & classification: E. Local *Unpublished*

The Air Navigation (Restriction of Flying) (Farnborough Airshow) Regulations 2008 No. 2008/1264. - Enabling power: S.I. 2005/1970, art. 96. - Made: 28.04.2008. Coming into force: 07.07.2008. Effect: None. Territorial extent & classification: E. Local *Unpublished*

The Air Navigation (Restriction of Flying) (Farnborough Flypast) Regulations 2008 No. 2008/2754. - Enabling power: S.I. 2005/1970, art. 96. - Made: 09.10.2008. Coming into force: 16.10.2008. Effect: None. Territorial extent & classification: E. Local *Unpublished*

The Air Navigation (Restriction of Flying) (Glastonbury Festival) Regulations 2008 No. 2008/120. - Enabling power: S.I. 2005/1970, art. 96. - Made: 10.01.2008. Coming into force: 25.06.2008. Effect: None. Territorial extent & classification: E. Local *Unpublished*

The Air Navigation (Restriction of Flying) (Her Majesty The Queen's 82nd Birthday Flypast) Regulations 2008 No. 2008/1411. - Enabling power: S.I. 2005/1970, art. 96. - Made: 06.05.2008. Coming into force: 11.06.2008. Effect: None. Territorial extent & classification: E. Local *Unpublished*

The Air Navigation (Restriction of Flying) (Ipswich) Regulations 2008 No. 2008/183. - Enabling power: S.I. 2005/1970, art. 96. - Made: 21.01.2008. Coming into force: Forthwith. Effect: None. Territorial extent & classification: E. Local. - Revoked by S.I. 2008/186 (Unpublished) *Unpublished*

The Air Navigation (Restriction of Flying) (Ipswich) (Revocation) Regulations 2008 No. 2008/186. - Enabling power: S.I. 2005/1970, art. 96. - Made: 21.01.2008. Coming into force: Forthwith. Effect: S.I. 2008/183 revoked. Territorial extent & classification: E. Local *Unpublished*

The Air Navigation (Restriction of Flying) (Jet Formation Display Teams) (Beaumaris) Regulations 2008 No. 2008/1417. - Enabling power: S.I. 2005/1970, art. 96. - Made: 21.05.2008. Coming into force: 23.05.2008. Effect: None. Territorial extent & classification: E. Local *Unpublished*

The Air Navigation (Restriction of Flying) (Jet Formation Display Teams) (No. 2) (Amendment) Regulations 2008 No. 2008/1416. - Enabling power: S.I. 2005/1970, art. 96. - Made: 21.05.2008. Coming into force: 25.05.2008. Effect: S.I. 2008/967 amended. Territorial extent & classification: E. Local *Unpublished*

The Air Navigation (Restriction of Flying) (Jet Formation Display Teams) (No. 2) Regulations 2008 No. 2008/967. - Enabling power: S.I. 2005/1970, art. 96. - Made: 12.03.2008. Coming into force: 25.05.2008. Effect: None. Territorial extent & classification: E. Local *Unpublished*

The Air Navigation (Restriction of Flying) (Jet Formation Display Teams) (No. 3) (Amendment) Regulations 2008 No. 2008/2259. - Enabling power: S.I. 2005/1970, art. 96. - Made: 18.08.2008. Coming into force: 25.08.2008. Effect: S.I. 2008/1856 amended. Territorial extent & classification: E. Local *Unpublished*

The Air Navigation (Restriction of Flying) (Jet Formation Display Teams) (No. 3) Regulations 2008 No. 2008/1856. - Enabling power: S.I. 2005/1970, art. 96. - Made: 26.06.2008. Coming into force: 07.08.2008. Effect: None. Territorial extent & classification: E. Local *Unpublished*

The Air Navigation (Restriction of Flying) (Jet Formation Display Teams) Regulations 2008 No. 2008/433. - Enabling power: S.I. 2005/1970, art. 96. - Made: 13.02.2008. Coming into force: 31.03.2008. Effect: None. Territorial extent & classification: E. Local *Unpublished*

The Air Navigation (Restriction of Flying) (Kemble) Regulations 2008 No. 2008/804. - Enabling power: S.I. 2005/1970, art. 96. - Made: 26.02.2008. Coming into force: 15.06.2008. Effect: None. Territorial extent & classification: E. Local *Unpublished*

The Air Navigation (Restriction of Flying) (Labour Party Conference Manchester) Regulations 2008 No. 2008/1854. - Enabling power: S.I. 2005/1970, art. 96. - Made: 26.06.2008. Coming into force: 19.09.2008. Effect: None. Territorial extent & classification: E. Local *Unpublished*

The Air Navigation (Restriction of Flying) (Lowestoft) Regulations 2008 No. 2008/320. - Enabling power: S.I. 2005/1970, art. 96. - Made: 28.01.2008. Coming into force: 24.07.2008. Effect: None. Territorial extent & classification: E. Local *Unpublished*

The Air Navigation (Restriction of Flying) (Nacton) Regulations 2008 No. 2008/184. - Enabling power: S.I. 2005/1970, art. 96. - Made: 21.01.2008. Coming into force: Forthwith. Effect: None. Territorial extent & classification: E. Local. - Revoked by S.I. 2008/185 (Unpublished) *Unpublished*

The Air Navigation (Restriction of Flying) (Nacton) (Revocation) Regulations 2008 No. 2008/185. - Enabling power: S.I. 2005/1970, art. 96. - Made: 21.01.2008. Coming into force: Forthwith. Effect: S.I. 2008/184 revoked. Territorial extent & classification: E. Local *Unpublished*

The Air Navigation (Restriction of Flying) (North Sea, Britannia Oil Rig) Regulations 2008 No. 2008/434. - Enabling power: S.I. 2005/1970, art. 96. - Made: 10.02.2008. Coming into force: Forthwith. Effect: None. Territorial extent & classification: E. Local. - Revoked by S.I. 2008/435 (Unpublished) *Unpublished*

The Air Navigation (Restriction of Flying) (North Sea, Britannia Oil Rig) (Revocation) Regulations 2008 No. 2008/435. - Enabling power: S.I. 2005/1970, art. 96. - Made: 10.02.2008. Coming into force: Forthwith. Effect: S.I. 2008/434 revoked. Territorial extent & classification: E. Local *Unpublished*

The Air Navigation (Restriction of Flying) (Nuclear Installations) (Amendment) Regulations 2008 No. 2008/3169. - Enabling power: S.I. 2005/1970, art. 96. - Issued: 19.12.2008. Made: 11.12.2008. Coming into force: 16.01.2009. Effect: S.I. 2007/1929 amended. Territorial extent & classification: E/W/S/NI. General. - 2p.: 30 cm. - 978-0-11-147177-7 £4.00

The Air Navigation (Restriction of Flying) (Orpington) Regulations 2008 No. 2008/1095. - Enabling power: S.I. 2005/1970, art. 96. - Made: 30.03.2008. Coming into force: Forthwith. Effect: None. Territorial extent & classification: E. Local. - Revoked by S.I. 2008/1096 (Unpublished) *Unpublished*

The Air Navigation (Restriction of Flying) (Orpington) (Revocation) Regulations 2008 No. 2008/1096. - Enabling power: S.I. 2005/1970, art. 96. - Made: 01.04.2008. Coming into force: Forthwith. Effect: S.I. 2008/1095 revoked. Territorial extent & classification: E. Local *Unpublished*

The Air Navigation (Restriction of Flying) (Remembrance Sunday) Regulations 2008 No. 2008/2305. - Enabling power: S.I. 2005/1970, art. 96. - Made: 27.08.2008. Coming into force: 09.11.2008. Effect: None. Territorial extent & classification: E. Local *Unpublished*

The Air Navigation (Restriction of Flying) (Royal Air Force 90th Anniversary Flypast) Regulations 2008 No. 2008/968. - Enabling power: S.I. 2005/1970, art. 96. - Made: 12.03.2008. Coming into force: 01.04.2008. Effect: None. Territorial extent & classification: E. Local *Unpublished*

The Air Navigation (Restriction of Flying) (Royal Air Force Colour Presentation) Regulations 2008 No. 2008/1851. - Enabling power: S.I. 2005/1970, art. 96. - Made: 20.06.2008. Coming into force: 07.07.2008. Effect: None. Territorial extent & classification: E. Local *Unpublished*

The Air Navigation (Restriction of Flying) (Royal Air Force Leuchars) Regulations 2008 No. 2008/1257. - Enabling power: S.I. 2005/1970, art. 96. - Made: 28.04.2008. Coming into force: 12.09.2008. Effect: None. Territorial extent & classification: E. Local *Unpublished*

The Air Navigation (Restriction of Flying) (Royal Air Force Role Demonstration) Regulations 2008 No. 2008/1245. - Enabling power: S.I. 2005/1970, art. 96. - Made: 29.04.2008. Coming into force: 06.05.2008. Effect: None. Territorial extent & classification: E. Local *Unpublished*

The Air Navigation (Restriction of Flying) (Royal Air Force Waddington) (No. 2) Regulations 2008 No. 2008/2796. - Enabling power: S.I. 2005/1970, art. 96. - Made: 24.10.2008. Coming into force: 30.10.2008. Effect: None. Territorial extent & classification: E. Local *Unpublished*

The Air Navigation (Restriction of Flying) (Royal Air Force Waddington) Regulations 2008 No. 2008/807. - Enabling power: S.I. 2005/1970, art. 96. - Made: 26.02.2008. Coming into force: 03.07.2008. Effect: None. Territorial extent & classification: E. Local *Unpublished*

The Air Navigation (Restriction of Flying) (Royal Albert Hall) Regulations 2008 No. 2008/2304. - Enabling power: S.I. 2005/1970, art. 96. - Made: 27.08.2008. Coming into force: 08.11.2008. Effect: None. Territorial extent & classification: E. Local *Unpublished*

The Air Navigation (Restriction of Flying) (Royal International Air Tattoo RAF Fairford) Regulations 2008 No. 2008/1857. - Enabling power: S.I. 2005/1970, art. 96. - Made: 25.06.2008. Coming into force: 07.07.2008. Effect: None. Territorial extent & classification: E. Local *Unpublished*

The Air Navigation (Restriction of Flying) (Rutland Water) Regulations 2008 No. 2008/436. - Enabling power: S.I. 2005/1970, art. 96. - Made: 13.02.2008. Coming into force: Forthwith. Effect: None. Territorial extent & classification: E. Local. - Revoked by S.I. 2008/437 (Unpublished) *Unpublished*

The Air Navigation (Restriction of Flying) (Rutland Water) (Revocation) Regulations 2008 No. 2008/437. - Enabling power: S.I. 2005/1970, art. 96. - Made: 14.02.2008. Coming into force: Forthwith. Effect: S.I. 2008/436 revoked. Territorial extent & classification: E. Local *Unpublished*

The Air Navigation (Restriction of Flying) (Scottish Highlands) Regulations 2008 No. 2008/1239. - Enabling power: S.I. 2005/1970, art. 96. - Issued: 06.05.2008. Made: 01.05.2008. Coming into force: 01.06.2008. Effect: S.I. 1981/1171 revoked. Territorial extent & classification: UK. General. - 4p.: 30 cm. - 978-0-11-081431-5 £3.00

The Air Navigation (Restriction of Flying) (Shenington, Oxfordshire) Regulations 2008 No. 2008/1608. - Enabling power: S.I. 2005/1970, art. 96. - Made: 03.06.2008. Coming into force: Forthwith. Effect: None. Territorial extent & classification: E. Local. - Revoked by S.I. 2008/1610 *Unpublished*

The Air Navigation (Restriction of Flying) (Shenington, Oxfordshire) (Revocation) Regulations 2008 No. 2008/1610. - Enabling power: S.I. 2005/1970, art. 96. - Made: 06.06.2008. Coming into force: Forthwith. Effect: S.I. 2008/1608 revoked. Territorial extent & classification: E. Local *Unpublished*

The Air Navigation (Restriction of Flying) (Silverstone and Turweston) Regulations 2008 No. 2008/1091. - Enabling power: S.I. 2005/1970, art. 96. - Made: 10.04.2008. Coming into force: 05.07.2008. Effect: None. Territorial extent & classification: E. Local *Unpublished*

The Air Navigation (Restriction of Flying) (Southend) Regulations 2008 No. 2008/321. - Enabling power: S.I. 2005/1970, art. 96. - Made: 01.02.2008. Coming into force: 25.05.2008. Effect: None. Territorial extent & classification: E. Local *Unpublished*

The Air Navigation (Restriction of Flying) (Southport) Regulations 2008 No. 2008/1412. - Enabling power: S.I. 2005/1970, art. 96. - Made: 06.05.2008. Coming into force: 06.09.2008. Effect: None. Territorial extent & classification: E. Local *Unpublished*

The Air Navigation (Restriction of Flying) (South Wales) Regulations 2008 No. 2008/2778. - Enabling power: S.I. 2005/1970, art. 96. - Made: 21.10.2008. Coming into force: 05.12.2008. Effect: None. Territorial extent & classification: E. Local *Unpublished*

The Air Navigation (Restriction of Flying) (State Opening of Parliament) Regulations 2008 No. 2008/2755. - Enabling power: S.I. 2005/1970, art. 96. - Made: 08.10.2008. Coming into force: 03.12.2008. Effect: None. Territorial extent & classification: E. Local *Unpublished*

The Air Navigation (Restriction of Flying) (Stonehenge) Regulations 2008 No. 2008/319. - Enabling power: S.I. 2005/1970, art. 96. - Made: 28.01.2008. Coming into force: 20.06.2008. Effect: None. Territorial extent & classification: E. Local *Unpublished*

The Air Navigation (Restriction of Flying) (Sunderland) Regulations 2008 No. 2008/1852. - Enabling power: S.I. 2005/1970, art. 96. - Made: 26.06.2008. Coming into force: 26.07.2008. Effect: None. Territorial extent & classification: E. Local *Unpublished*

The Air Navigation (Restriction of Flying) (Trooping of the Colour Ceremony) Regulations 2008 No. 2008/1413. - Enabling power: S.I. 2005/1970, art. 96. - Made: 23.05.2008. Coming into force: 14.06.2008. Effect: None. Territorial extent & classification: E. Local *Unpublished*

The Air Navigation (Restriction of Flying) (Usk Reservoir) Regulations 2008 No. 2008/2073. - Enabling power: S.I. 2005/1970, art. 96. - Made: 25.07.2008. Coming into force: 15.09.2008. Effect: None. Territorial extent & classification: E. Local *Unpublished*

The Air Navigation (Restriction of Flying) (Visit by the President of the United States of America) (No. 2) Regulations 2008 No. 2008/1601. - Enabling power: S.I. 2005/1970, art. 96. - Made: 13.06.2008. Coming into force: 16.06.2008. Effect: None. Territorial extent & classification: E. Local *Unpublished*

The Air Navigation (Restriction of Flying) (Visit by the President of the United States of America) Regulations 2008 No. 2008/1600. - Enabling power: S.I. 2005/1970, art. 96. - Made: 13.06.2008. Coming into force: 15.06.2008. Effect: None. Territorial extent & classification: E. Local *Unpublished*

The Air Navigation (Restriction of Flying) (Waddington) Regulations 2008 No. 2008/2912. - Enabling power: S.I. 2005/1970, art. 96. - Made: 06.11.2008. Coming into force: Forthwith. Effect: S.I. 2008/2796 amended. Territorial extent & classification: E. Local *Unpublished*

The Air Navigation (Restriction of Flying) (Walney Island) (Amendment) Regulations 2008 No. 2008/3299. - Enabling power: S.I. 2005/1970, art. 96. - Made: 18.12.2008. Coming into force: 22.12.2008. Effect: S.I. 2008/2075 amended. Territorial extent & classification: E. Local *Unpublished*

The Air Navigation (Restriction of Flying) (Walney Island) Regulations 2008 No. 2008/2075. - Enabling power: S.I. 2005/1970, art. 96. - Made: 09.07.2008. Coming into force: 24.09.2008. Effect: None. Territorial extent & classification: E. Local *Unpublished*

Civil aviation

The Air Navigation (Restriction of Flying) (Weston Park) Regulations 2008 No. 2008/1415. - Enabling power: S.I. 2005/1970, art. 96. - Made: 23.05.2008. Coming into force: 14.08.2008. Effect: None. Territorial extent & classification: E. Local *Unpublished*

The Air Navigation (Restriction of Flying) (Weston-super-Mare) Regulations 2008 No. 2008/970. - Enabling power: S.I. 2005/1970, art. 96. - Made: 26.03.2008. Coming into force: 23.07.2008. Effect: None. Territorial extent & classification: E. Local *Unpublished*

The Air Navigation (Restriction of Flying) (West Wales Airport) Regulations 2008 No. 2008/1414. - Enabling power: S.I. 2005/1970, art. 96. - Made: 23.05.2008. Coming into force: 30.06.2008. Effect: None. Territorial extent & classification: E. Local *Unpublished*

The Air Navigation (Restriction of Flying) (Whittlesey) (Amendment) Regulations 2008 No. 2008/802. - Enabling power: S.I. 2005/1970, art. 96. - Made: 25.02.2008. Coming into force: Forthwith. Effect: S.I. 2008/801 amended. Territorial extent & classification: E. Local *Unpublished*

The Air Navigation (Restriction of Flying) (Whittlesey) Regulations 2008 No. 2008/801. - Enabling power: S.I. 2005/1970, art. 96. - Made: 25.02.2008. Coming into force: Forthwith. Effect: None. Territorial extent & classification: E. Local. - Revoked by S.I. 2008/803 (Unpublished) *Unpublished*

The Air Navigation (Restriction of Flying) (Whittlesey) (Revocation) Regulations 2008 No. 2008/803. - Enabling power: S.I. 2005/1970, art. 96. - Made: 26.02.2008. Coming into force: Forthwith. Effect: S.I. 2008/801 revoked. Territorial extent & classification: E. Local *Unpublished*

The Air Navigation (Restriction of Flying) (Wycombe Air Park) (Aero Expo) Regulations 2008 No. 2008/811. - Enabling power: S.I. 2005/1970, art. 96. - Made: 29.02.2008. Coming into force: 13.06.2008. Effect: None. Territorial extent & classification: E. Local *Unpublished*

The Air Navigation (Restriction of Flying) (Yeovilton) Regulations 2008 No. 2008/322. - Enabling power: S.I. 2005/1970, art. 96. - Made: 01.02.2008. Coming into force: 05.07.2008. Effect: None. Territorial extent & classification: E. Local *Unpublished*

The Civil Aviation (Overseas Territories) (Gibraltar) (Revocations) (No. 2) Order 2008 No. 2008/3120. - Enabling power: Civil Aviation Act 1982, s. 108. - Issued: 17.12.2008. Made: 10.12.2008. Coming into force: In accord. with art. 1. Effect: S.I. 1969/592; 2001/3367 revoked insofar as they relate to Gibraltar; S.I. 1976/1912 already revoked in relation to other territories is now also revoked in relation to Gibraltar. Territorial extent & classification: Gibraltar. General. - 2p.: 30 cm. - 978-0-11-147163-0 *£4.00*

The Civil Aviation (Overseas Territories) (Gibraltar) (Revocations) Order 2008 No. 2008/3119. - Enabling power: Civil Aviation Act 1949, ss. 8, 41, 57, 58, 59, 61. - Issued: 17.12.2008. Made: 10.12.2008. Laid: 17.12.2008. Coming into force: In accord. with art. 1. Effect: S.I. 1989/2395; 1991/189, 1697; 1992/3198; 1995/2701; 1997/1746 which have been revoked in respect of their application to certain territories other than Gibraltar, are now also revoked in respect of their application to Gibraltar. Territorial extent & classification: Gibraltar. General. - 2p.: 30 cm. - 978-0-11-147169-2 *£4.00*

The Economic Regulation of Airports (Designation) Order (Amendment) Order 2008 No. 2008/2702. - Enabling power: Airports Act 1986, s. 40. - Issued: 20.10.2008. Made: 10.10.2008. Laid: 15.10.2008. Coming into force: 01.04.2009. Effect: S.I. 1986/1502 amended. Territorial extent & classification: E/W/S. General. - 2p.: 30 cm. - 978-0-11-084637-8 *£4.00*

The Rules of the Air (Amendment) Regulations 2008 No. 2008/669. - Enabling power: S.I. 2005/1970, art. 95 (1). - Issued: 17.03.2008. Made: 10.03.2008. Coming into force: 01.04.2008. Effect: S.I. 2007/734 amended. Territorial extent & classification: E/W/S/NI. General. - 2p.: 30 cm. - 978-0-11-081172-7 *£3.00*

Civil contingencies, England

The Civil Contingencies Act 2004 (Amendment of List of Responders) Order 2008 No. 2008/3012. - Enabling power: Civil Contingencies Act 2004, s. 13 (1) (3). - Issued: 26.11.2008. Made: 20.11.2008. Coming into force: 01.04.2009. Effect: 2004 c.36 amended. Territorial extent & classification: E. General. - Supersedes draft S.I. (ISBN 9780110847672) issued 31.10.2008. - 2p.: 30 cm. - 978-0-11-147033-6 *£4.00*

Clean air, England

The Smoke Control Areas (Authorised Fuels) (England) (Amendment) Regulations 2008 No. 2008/2342. - Enabling power: Clean Air Act 1993, s. 20 (6). - Issued: 09.09.2008. Made: 01.09.2008. Laid: 05.09.2008. Coming into force: 01.10.2008. Effect: S.I. 2008/514 amended. Territorial extent & classification: E. General. - 2p.: 30 cm. - 978-0-11-084062-8 *£4.00*

The Smoke Control Areas (Authorised Fuels) (England) Regulations 2008 No. 2008/514. - Enabling power: Clean Air Act 1993, s. 20 (6), 63 (1). - Issued: 04.03.2008. Made: 27.02.2008. Laid: 04.03.2008. Coming into force: 06.04.2008. Effect: S.I. 2001/3745; 2002/3046; 2005/2895; 2006/1869; 2007/2460 revoked. Territorial extent & classification: E. General. - 12p.: 30 cm. - 978-0-11-081046-1 *£3.00*

The Smoke Control Areas (Exempted Fireplaces) (England) (No. 2) Order 2008 No. 2008/2343. - Enabling power: Clean Air Act 1993, s. 21. - Issued: 09.09.2008. Made: 01.09.2008. Laid: 05.09.2008. Coming into force: 01.10.2008. Effect: S.I. 2008/515 revoked. Territorial extent & classification: E. General. - Revoked by S.I. 2009/449 (ISBN 9780111475089). - 16p.: 30 cm. - 978-0-11-084060-4 £5.00

The Smoke Control Areas (Exempted Fireplaces) (England) Order 2008 No. 2008/515. - Enabling power: Clean Air Act 1993, s. 21. - Issued: 04.03.2008. Made: 27.02.2008. Laid: 04.03.2008. Coming into force: 06.04.2008. Effect: S.I. 2007/2462 revoked. Territorial extent & classification: E. General. - Revoked by S.I. 2008/2343 (ISBN 9780110840604). - 12p.: 30 cm. - 978-0-11-081049-2 £3.00

Clean air, Wales

The Smoke Control Areas (Authorised Fuels) (Wales) Regulations 2008 No. 2008/3100 (W.274). - Enabling power: Clean Air Act 1993, ss. 20 (6), 63 (1). - Issued: 12.01.2009. Made: 03.12.2008. Laid before the National Assembly for Wales: 04.12.2008. Coming into force: 31.12.2008. Effect: S.I. 2006/2979 (W.270) revoked. Territorial extent & classification: W. General. - In English and Welsh. Welsh title: Rheoliadau Ardaloedd Rheoli Mwg (Tanwyddau Awdurdodedig) (Cymru) 2008. - 20p.: 30 cm. - 978-0-11-091918-8 £5.00

The Smoke Control Areas (Exempted Fireplaces) (Wales) Order 2008 No. 2008/3101 (W.275). - Enabling power: Clean Air Act 1993, s. 21. - Issued: 16.01.2009. Made: 03.12.2008. Laid before the National Assembly for Wales: 04.12.2008. Coming into force: 31.12.2008. Effect: S.I. 2006/2980 (W.271) revoked. Territorial extent & classification: W. General. - In English and Welsh. Welsh title: Gorchymyn Ardaloedd Rheoli Mwg (Lleoedd Tân Esempt) (Cymru) 2008. - 32p.: 30 cm. - 978-0-11-091923-2 £9.00

Clerk of the Crown in Chancery

The Crown Office Fees Order 2008 No. 2008/1977. - Enabling power: Great Seal (Offices) Act 1874, s. 9. - Issued: 29.07.2008. Made: 17.07.2008. Coming into force: 11.08.2008. Effect: S.I. 2003/92 revoked. Territorial extent & classification: E/W/S/NI. General. - 4p.: 30 cm. - 978-0-11-083630-0 £3.00

Climate change levy

The Amusement Machine Licence Duty, etc (Amendments) Regulations 2008 No. 2008/2693. - Enabling power: Betting and Gaming Duties Act 1981, sch. 4, paras 5 (1), 12 & Finance Act 1994, ss. 54, 74 (7) (8) & Finance Act 1996, ss. 49, 71 (8) (9) & Finance Act 2000, sch. 6, paras. 41 (1) (2), 146 (7) & Finance Act 2001, ss. 25 (1) (2), 45 (5). - Issued: 15.10.2008. Made: 10.10.2008. Laid: 10.10.2008. Coming into force: 01.11.2008. Effect: S.I. 1994/1774; 1995/2631; 1996/1527; 2001/838; 2002/ 761 amended. Territorial extent & classification: E/W/S/NI. General. - 4p.: 30 cm. - 978-0-11-084575-3 £4.00

The Value Added Tax, etc (Correction of Errors, etc) Regulations 2008 No. 2008/1482. - Enabling power: Value Added Tax Act 1994, sch. 11, paras 2 (1) (10) (11) & Finance Act 1994, ss. 38 (1), 42 (2), 54, 74 (7) (8) & Finance Act 1996, ss. 49, 71 (8) (9) & Finance Act 2000, sch. 6, paras 41(1) (2), 146 (7) & Finance Act 2001, ss. 25 (1) (2), 45 (5). - Issued: 18.06.2008. Made: 09.06.2008. Laid: 10.06.2008. Coming into force: 01.07.2008. Effect: S.I. 1994/1738, 1774; 1995/2518; 1996/1527; 2001/838; 2002/761 amended. Territorial extent & classification: E/W/S/NI. General. - 12p.: 30 cm. - 978-0-11-081855-9 £3.00

Commissioner for Older People in Wales

The Commissioner for Older People in Wales (Amendment) Regulations 2008 No. 2008/1512 (W.155). - Enabling power: Commissioner for Older People (Wales) Act 2006, ss. 5 (4) (b), 6 (5), 8 (1) (e), 10 (1) (5), 15 (1) (3), sch. 1, para. 8. - Issued: 15.07.2008. Made: 10.06.2008. Coming into force: 12.06.2008. Effect: S.I. 2007/398 (W.44) amended. Territorial extent & classification: W. General. - This Statutory Instrument has been printed in substitution of the SI of the same number (ISBN 9780110918365) and is being issued free of charge to all known recipients of that Statutory Instrument. - In English and Welsh. Welsh language title: Rheoliadau Comisiynydd Pobl Hyn Cymru (Diwygio) 2008. - 8p.: 30 cm. - 978-0-11-091840-2 £3.00

The Commissioner for Older People in Wales (Amendment) Regulations 2008 No. 2008/1512 (W.155). - Enabling power: Commissioner for Older People (Wales) Act 2006, ss. 5 (4) (b), 6 (5), 8 (1) (e), 10 (1) (5), 15 (1) (3), sch. 1, para. 8. - Issued: 27.06.2008. Made: 10.06.2008. Coming into force: 12.06.2008. Effect: S.I. 2007/398 (W.44) amended. Territorial extent & classification: W. General. - In English and Welsh. Welsh language title: Rheoliadau Comisiynydd Pobl Hyn Cymru (Diwygio) 2008. - 8p.: 30 cm. - 978-0-11-091836-5 £3.00

Commonhold, England and Wales

The Commonhold (Land Registration) (Amendment) Rules 2008 No. 2008/1920. - Enabling power: Commonhold and Leasehold Reform Act 2002, s. 65. - Issued: 24.07.2008. Made: 17.07.2008. Laid: 21.07.2008. Coming into force: 10.11.2008. Effect: S.I. 2004/1830 amended. Territorial extent & classification: E/W. General. - 12p.: 30 cm. - 978-0-11-083452-8 £3.00

Commons, England

The Commons Act 2006 (Commencement No. 4 and Savings) (England) Order 2008 No. 2008/1960 (C. 94). - Enabling power: Commons Act 2006, ss. 56 (1), 59 (1). Bringing into operation various provisions of the 2006 Act on 01.10.2008. - Issued: 28.07.2008. Made: 21.07.2008. Effect: None. Territorial extent & classification: E. General. - 4p.: 30 cm. - 978-0-11-083590-7 £3.00

The Commons Registration (England) Regulations 2008 No. 2008/1961. - Enabling power: Commons Act 2006, ss. 3 (5), 8 (1), 11 (5) (6), 14, 17 (3), 20, 21, 24 (1) to (3) (6) to (9), 59 (1), sch. 1, para. 1, sch. 2, paras 2 to 10, sch. 3, paras 2, 4, 5, 8 (2). - Issued: 04.08.2008. Made: 21.07.2008. Laid: 24.07.2008. Coming into force: 01.10.2008. Effect: S.I. 2007/457, 2585 cease to have effect in relation to the registration areas in England of the registration authorities specified in schedule 1. Territorial extent & classification: E. General. - 84.: 30 cm. - 978-0-11-083642-3 £12.00

The Dartmoor Commons (Authorised Severance) Order 2008 No. 2008/1962. - Enabling power: Commons Act 2006, sch. 1, para. 1 (5). - Issued: 28.07.2008. Made: 21.07.2008. Laid: 24.07.2008. Coming into force: 01.10.2008. Effect: None. Territorial extent & classification: E. General. - 2p.: 30 cm. - 978-0-11-083589-1 £3.00

Companies

The Accounting Standards (Prescribed Body) Regulations 2008 No. 2008/651. - Enabling power: Companies Act 2006, s. 464 (1) (3). - Issued: 13.03.2008. Made: 05.03.2008. Coming into force: 06.04.2008. Effect: S.R. 1990/338 & S.I. 2005/697 revoked. Territorial extent & classification: E/W/S/NI. General. - 2p.: 30 cm. - 978-0-11-081156-7 £3.00

The Companies Act 1985 (Annual Return) and Companies (Principal Business Activities) (Amendment) Regulations 2008 No. 2008/1659. - Enabling power: Companies Act 1985, ss. 364 (3), 365 (1). - Issued: 01.07.2008. Made: 24.06.2008. Laid: 27.06.2008. Coming into force: 01.10.2008. Effect: 1985 c. 6; S.I. 1990/1766 amended. Territorial extent & classification: E/W/S. General. - 4p.: 30 cm. - 978-0-11-081904-4 £3.00

The Companies Act 2006 (Amendment) (Accounts and Reports) Regulations 2008 No. 2008/393. - Enabling power: Companies Act 2006, ss. 468 (1) (2), 473 (2), 484, 1292 (1) (a) (c). - Issued: 25.02.2008. Made: 19.02.2008. Coming into force: 06.04.2008. Effect: 2006 c.46 amended. Territorial extent & classification: E/W/S/NI. General. - Supersedes draft S.I. (ISBN 9780110806228) issued 28.12.2007. - 8p.: 30 cm. - 978-0-11-080963-2 £3.00

The Companies Act 2006 (Annual Return and Service Addresses) Regulations 2008 No. 2008/3000. - Enabling power: Companies Act 2006, ss. 857, 1141, 1167, 1292 (1). - Issued: 24.11.2008. Made: 18.11.2008. Laid: 20.11.2008. Coming into force: 01.10.2009. Effect: 2006 c.46 amended. Territorial extent & classification: E/W/S/NI. General. - 8p.: 30 cm. - 978-0-11-147026-8 £5.00

The Companies Act 2006 (Commencement No. 6, Saving and Commencement Nos. 3 and 5 (Amendment)) Order 2008 No. 2008/674 (C. 26). - Enabling power: Companies Act 2006, ss. 1292 (1) (b), 1296 (1) (2), 1300 (2). Bringing into operation various provisions of the 2006 Act 01.04.2008 in accord. with art. 3. - Issued: 18.03.2008. Made: 07.03.2008. Laid: 11.03.2008. Coming into force: in accord. with art. 2. Effect: 1985 c.6; S.I. 2007/2194 (C. 84); 2007/3495 (C. 150) amended. Territorial extent & classification: E/W/S/NI. General. - Partially revoked by S.I. 2008/2860 (C.126) (ISBN 9780110849669) subject to any savings in sch. 2. This Order has been made partly in consequence of defects in S.I. 2007/2194 and 3495 and is being issued free of charge to all known recipients of those Orders. - 16p.: 30 cm. - 978-0-11-081182-6 £3.00

The Companies Act 2006 (Commencement No. 7, Transitional Provisions and Savings) Order 2008 No. 2008/1886 (C.83). - Enabling power: Companies Act 2006, ss. 1296 (2), 1300 (2). Bringing into operation various provisions of the 2006 Act on 11.08.2008 & 01.10.2008 in accord with art. 1 (2) (3). - Issued: 22.07.2008. Made: 16.07.2008. Laid: 17.07.2008. Coming into force: In accord. with art. 1 (2) (3). Effect: S.I. 2007/3495 (C. 150) amended (11.08.2008). Territorial extent & classification: E/W/S/NI. General. - Partially revoked by S.I. 2008/2860 (C.126) (ISBN 9780110849669) subject to any savings in sch. 2. - 8p.: 30 cm. - 978-0-11-083365-1 £3.00

The Companies Act 2006 (Commencement No. 8, Transitional Provisions and Savings) Order 2008 No. 2008/2860 (C.126). - Enabling power: Companies Act 2006, ss. 1292 (1), 1296 (1) (2), 1300 (2). Bringing into operation various provisions of the 2006 Act on 01.10.2009. - Issued: 12.11.2008. Made: 05.11.2008. Laid: 06.11.2008. Effect: S.I. 2006/3428 (C. 132). 2007/1093(C. 49), 2194 (C. 84), 3495 (C. 150); 2008/674 (C. 26), 2008/1886 (C. 83) partially revoked (subject to any savings specified in schedule 2). Territorial extent & classification: E/W/S/NI. General. - This S.I. has been corrected by S.I. 2009/2476 (ISBN 9780111485460) which is being issued free of charge to all known recipients of S.I. 2008/2860. - 36p.: 30 cm. - 978-0-11-084966-9 £9.00

The Companies Act 2006 (Consequential Amendments etc) Order 2008 No. 2008/948. - Enabling power: Companies Act 2006, ss. 1292, 1294, 1296. - Issued: 07.04.2008. Made: 01.04.2008. Coming into force: 06.04.2008 for arts 1 to 3, 5 to 12, schedules 1, 2; 01.10.2008 for art. 4,schedules 3, 4. Effect: 117 acts & 36 SI's amended. Territorial extent & classification: E/W/S/NI. General. - Supersedes draft SI (ISBN 9780110810683) issued 05.03.2008. - 76p.: 30 cm. - 978-0-11-081331-8 *£12.00*

The Companies Act 2006 (Extension of Takeover Panel Provisions) (Isle of Man) Order 2008 No. 2008/3122. - Enabling power: Companies Act 2006, s. 965. - Issued: 16.12.2008. Made: 10.12.2008. Coming into force: 01.03.2009. Effect: 2006 c.46 extended to IoM as modified. Territorial extent & classification: IoM. General. - Partially revoked by S.I. 2009/1378 (ISBN 9780111480632). - 8p.: 30 cm. - 978-0-11-147157-9 *£5.00*

The Companies (Authorised Minimum) Regulations 2008 No. 2008/729. - Enabling power: Companies Act 2006, ss. 763 (2), 766 (1) (a) (2), 1292 (1) (a) (b). - Issued: 18.03.2008. Made: 12.03.2008. Laid: 14.03.2008. Coming into force: 06.04.2008. Effect: None. Territorial extent & classification: E/W/S/NI. General. - Partially revoked by S.I. 2009/2425 (ISBN 9780111485149). - 8p.: 30 cm. - 978-0-11-081230-4 *£3.00*

The Companies (Company Records) Regulations 2008 No. 2008/3006. - Enabling power: Companies Act 2006, ss. 1136, 1137, and 1292 (1). - Issued: 27.11.2008. Made: 19.11.2008. Laid: 21.11.2008. Coming into force: 01.10.2009. Effect: S.I. 1991/1998; S.R. 1993/66 revoked with savings. Territorial extent & classification: E/W/S/NI. General. - 4p.: 30 cm. - 978-0-11-147031-2 *£4.00*

The Companies (Cross-Border Mergers) (Amendment) Regulations 2008 No. 2008/583. - Enabling power: European Communities Act 1972, s.2 (2). - Issued: 23.10.2007. Made: 28.02.2008. Laid: 06.03.2008. Coming into force: 06.04.2008. Effect: S.I. 2007/2974 amended. Territorial extent & classification: E/W/S/NI. General. - These Regulations have been made in consequence of a defect in S.I. 2007/2974 and are being issued free of charge to all known recipients of those Regulations. - 2p.: 30 cm. - 978-0-11-081105-5 *£3.00*

The Companies (Defective Accounts and Directors' Reports) (Authorised Person) and Supervision of Accounts and Reports (Prescribed Body) Order 2008 No. 2008/623. - Enabling power: Companies (Audit, Investigations and Community Enterprise) Act 2004, s. 14 (1) (5) (8) & Companies Act 2006, s. 457 (1) (2) (5) (6). - Issued: 12.03.2008. Made: 05.03.2008. Laid: 10.03.2008. Coming into force: 06.04.2008. Effect: S.R. 1991/269; S.I. 2005/699 revoked with savings. Territorial extent & classification: E/W/S/NI. General. - 4p.: 30 cm. - 978-0-11-081125-3 *£3.00*

The Companies (Disclosure of Auditor Remuneration and Liability Limitation Agreements) Regulations 2008 No. 2008/489. - Enabling power: European Communities Act 1972, s. 2 (2) (a) & Companies Act 2006, ss. 494, 538, 1292 (1) (a). - Issued: 29.02.2008. Made: 23.02.2008. Laid: 27.02.2008. Coming into force: 06.04.2008. Effect: S.I. 2005/2417 revoked with savings. Territorial extent & classification: E/W/S/NI. General. - 8p.: 30 cm. - 978-0-11-081014-0 *£3.00*

The Companies (Fees for Inspection of Company Records) Regulations 2008 No. 2008/3007. - Enabling power: Companies Act 2006, ss. 162 (5) (b), 275 (5) (b), 877 (4) (b), 892 (4) (b), 1137 (4), 1167, 1292 (1) (c). - Issued: 27.11.2008. Made: 19.11.2008. Laid: 21.11.2008. Coming into force: 01.10.2009. Effect: None. Territorial extent & classification: E/W/S/NI. General. - 2p.: 30 cm. - 978-0-11-147032-9 *£4.00*

The Companies (Forms) (Amendment) Regulations 2008 No. 2008/1861. - Enabling power: Companies Act 1985, s. 363(2) & Companies Act 2006, s. 1167. - Issued: 17.07.2008. Made: 03.07.2008. Coming into force: 01.10.2008. Effect: S.I. 1999/2356; 2002/691 amended. Territorial extent & classification: E/W/S. General. - 12p.: 30 cm. - 978-0-11-083203-6 *£3.00*

The Companies (Late Filing Penalties) and Limited Liability Partnerships (Filing Periods and Late Filing Penalties) Regulations 2008 No. 2008/497. - Enabling power: Companies Act 1985, s. 257 (1) (4) (a) (d) & Limited Liability Partnerships Act 2000, s. 15 (a) & Companies Act 2006, ss. 453, 1292 (1) (a) (c). - Issued: 29.02.2008. Made: 23.02.2008. Coming into force: 06.04.2008. Effect: 1985 c. 6; 2006 c.46; S.I. 2001/1090 amended. Territorial extent & classification: E/W/S/NI. General. - Supersedes draft S.I. (ISBN 9780110806181) issued 27.12.2008. - 8p.: 30 cm. - 978-0-11-081018-8 *£3.00*

The Companies (Mergers and Divisions of Public Companies) (Amendment) Regulations 2008 No. 2008/690. - Enabling power: European Communities Act 1972, s.2 (2). - Issued: 19.03.2008. Made: 07.03.2008. Laid: 13.03.2008. Coming into force: 06.04.2008. Effect: 2006 c.46 amended. Territorial extent & classification: E/W/S/NI. General. - EC note: These Regulations implement Directive 2007/63/EC amending Council Directives 78/855/EEC and 82/891/EEC as regards the requirement of an independent expert's report on the occasion of merger or division of public limited liability companies. They also amend the implementation in the Companies Act 2006 of Directive 78/855/EEC concerning mergers of public limited liability companies and Directive 82/891/EEC concerning the division of public limited liability companies. - 4p.: 30 cm. - 978-0-11-081188-8 *£3.00*

The Companies (Model Articles) Regulations 2008 No. 2008/3229. - Enabling power: Companies Act 2006, s. 19. - Issued: 23.12.2008. Made: 16.12.2008. Laid: 17.12.2008. Coming into force: 01.10.2009. Effect: None. Territorial extent & classification: E/W/S/NI. General. - 64p.: 30 cm. - 978-0-11-147196-8 *£10.50*

The Companies (Particulars of Company Charges) Regulations 2008 No. 2008/2996. - Enabling power: Companies Act 2006, ss. 860, 862, 878, 880, 1167. - Issued: 20.11.2008. Made: 17.11.2008. Coming into force: 01.10.2009. Effect: None. Territorial extent & classification: E/W/S/NI. General. - 2p.: 30 cm. - 978-0-11-147021-3 £4.00

The Companies (Reduction of Capital) (Creditor Protection) Regulations 2008 No. 2008/719. - Enabling power: European Communities Act 1972, s. 2 (2). - Issued: 19.03.2008. Made: 11.03.2008. Laid: 13.03.2008. Coming into force: 06.04.2008. Effect: 1985 c.6 amended & S.I. 1986/1032 (NI.6) amended. Territorial extent & classification: E/W/S/NI. General. - EC note: These Regulations implement the amendment made to Article 32(1) of Council Directive 77/91/EEC by Directive 2006/68/EC. A transposition note has been prepared which sets out how Directive 2006/68/EC is to be transposed into UK law. - 4p.: 30 cm. - 978-0-11-081215-1 £3.00

The Companies (Reduction of Share Capital) Order 2008 No. 2008/1915. - Enabling power: Companies Act 2006, ss. 643 (3), 654, 1167. - Issued: 24.07.2008. Made: 17.07.2008. Coming into force: 01.10.2008. Effect: None. Territorial extent & classification: E/W/S/NI. General. - Supersedes draft S.I. (ISBN 9780110818368) issued 16.06.2008. - 2p.: 30 cm. - 978-0-11-083451-1 £3.00

The Companies (Registration) Regulations 2008 No. 2008/3014. - Enabling power: Companies Act 2006, ss. 8 (2), 10 (3), 11 (2), 103 (2) (a), 110 (2) (a), 1167, 1292 (1) (a). - Issued: 27.11.2008. Made: 20.11.2008. Coming into force: 01.10.2009. Effect: None. Territorial extent & classification: E/W/S/NI. General. - 8p.: 30 cm. - 978-0-11-147038-1 £5.00

The Companies (Revision of Defective Accounts and Reports) Regulations 2008 No. 2008/373. - Enabling power: Companies Act 2006, ss. 454 (3) (4), 1292 (1) (a) (c). - Issued: 25.02.2008. Made: 19.02.2008. Laid: 20.02.2008. Coming into force: 06.04.2008. Effect: 2006 c.46 modified & S.I. 1990/2570 & S.R. 1991/268 revoked with savings. Territorial extent & classification: E/W/S/NI. General. - 16p.: 30 cm. - 978-0-11-080976-2 £3.00

The Companies (Summary Financial Statement) Regulations 2008 No. 2008/374. - Enabling power: Companies Act 2006, ss. 426 (1) (3), 427 (2) (5), 428 (2) (5), 1292 (1). - Issued: 25.02.2008. Made: 19.02.2008. Laid: 20.02.2008. Coming into force: 06.04.2008. Effect: S.I. 1995/2092 & S.R. 1996/179 revoked with savings (preserves them for financial years beginning before 6th April 2008). Territorial extent & classification: E/W/S/NI. General. - 24p.: 30 cm. - 978-0-11-080971-7 £4.00

The Companies (Tables A to F) (Amendment) Regulations 2008 No. 2008/739. - Enabling power: Companies Act 1985, s. 8 (4) (a) (c). - Issued: 20.03.2008. Made: 12.03.2008. Laid: 14.03.2008. Coming into force: 06.04.2008. Effect: S.I. 1985/805 amended. Territorial extent & classification: E/W/S. General. - 2p.: 30 cm. - 978-0-11-081242-7 £3.00

The Companies (Trading Disclosures) (Insolvency) Regulations 2008 No. 2008/1897. - Enabling power: European Communities Act 1972, s. 2 (2). - Issued: 23.07.2008. Made: 16.07.2008. Laid: 18.07.2008. Coming into force: 01.10.2008. Effect: S.I. 1986 c.45 amended. Territorial extent & classification: E/W/S/NI. General. - 4p.: 30 cm. - 978-0-11-083379-8 £3.00

The Companies (Trading Disclosures) Regulations 2008 No. 2008/495. - Enabling power: Companies Act 2006, ss. 82, 84, 1292 (1) (a), 1294. - Issued: 29.02.2008. Made: 23.02.2008. Coming into force: 01.10.2008. Effect: S.I. 2006/3429 amended. Territorial extent & classification: E/W/S/NI. General. - Supersedes draft S.I. (ISBN 9780110806570) issued 08.01.2008. - 8p.: 30 cm. - 978-0-11-081021-8 £3.00

The Company Names Adjudicator Rules 2008 No. 2008/1738. - Enabling power: Companies Act 2006, s. 71. - Issued: 07.07.2008. Made: 01.07.2008. Laid: 03.07.2008. Coming into force: 01.10.2008. Effect: None. Territorial extent & classification: E/W/S/NI. General. - 8p.: 30 cm. - 978-0-11-081954-9 £3.00

The Large and Medium-sized Companies and Groups (Accounts and Reports) Regulations 2008 No. 2008/410. - Enabling power: Companies Act 2006, ss. 396 (3), 404 (3), 409 (1) to (3), 412 (1) to (3), 416 (4), 421 (1) (2), 445 (3) (a) (b), 677 (3) (a), 712 (2) (b) (i), 831 (3) (a), 832 (4) (a), 836 (1) (b) (i), 1292 (1) (a) (c). - Issued: 27.02.2008. Made: 19.02.2008. Coming into force: 06.04.2008. Effect: None. Territorial extent & classification: E/W/S/NI. General. - Supersedes draft SI (ISBN9780110806303) issued 28.12.2007. EC note: The Regulations continue the implementation of the following Directives: Council Directive 78/660/EEC, Council Directive 83/349/EEC, Council Directive 86/635/EEC and Council Directive 91/674/EEC. - 156p.: 30 cm. - 978-0-11-080994-6 £22.00

The Small Companies and Groups (Accounts and Directors' Report) Regulations 2008 No. 2008/409. - Enabling power: Companies Act 2006, ss. 396 (3), 404 (3), 409 (1) to (3), 412 (1) to (3), 416 (4), 444 (3) (a) (b), 677 (3) (a), 712 (2) (b) (i), 836 (1) (b) (i), 1292 (1) (a) (c). - Issued: 25.02.2008. Made: 19.02.2008. Coming into force: 06.04.2008. Effect: None. Territorial extent & classification: E/W/S/NI. General. - EC note: The Regulations continue the implementation of the following Directives- Council Directive 78/660/EEC on the annual accounts of certain types of companies and Council Directive 83/349/EEC on consolidated accounts. They also implement article 1.5 of Directive 2006/46. - 64p.: 30 cm. - 978-0-11-080970-0 £10.50

The Statutory Auditors and Third Country Auditors (Amendment) (No. 2) Regulations 2008 No. 2008/2639. - Enabling power: Companies Act 2006, ss. 1239 (1) (b) (2) (5) (d), 1246 (1), 1292 (1) (c)- Issued: 10.10.2008. Made: 06.10.2008. Laid: 07.10.2008. Coming into force: 31.10.2008. Effect: S.I. 2007/3494 amended. Territorial extent & classification: E/W/S/NI. General. - 8p.: 30 cm. - 978-0-11-084427-5 £5.00

The Statutory Auditors and Third Country Auditors (Amendment) Regulations 2008 No. 2008/499. - Enabling power: European Communities Act 1972, s. 2 (2) & Companies Act 2006, s. 1239. - Issued: 06.03.2008. Made: 26.02.2008. Laid: 03.03.2008. Coming into force: 05.04.2008. Effect: S.I. 2007/3494 amended. Territorial extent & classification: E/W/S/NI. General. - These Regulations have been made in consequence of defects in S.I. 2007/3494 (ISBN 9780110806099) and are being issued free of charge to all known recipients of those Regulations. - 4p.: 30 cm. - 978-0-11-081064-5 £3.00

Companies: Auditors

The Statutory Auditors (Delegation of Functions etc) Order 2008 No. 2008/496. - Enabling power: Companies Act 1989, s. 46 (4) & Companies Act 2006, ss. 504 (1) (b) (ii), 1252 (1) (4) (a) (5) (8), 1253 (4), sch. 13, paras 7 (3), 11 (2) (3) (a). - Issued: 29.02.2008. Made: 23.02.2008. Coming into force: 01.03.2008; 06.04.2008; 29.06.2008 in accord. with art. 1. Effect: 2006 c. 46 modified & S.I. 2005/2337 revoked with savings(06.04.2008). Territorial extent & classification: E/W/S/NI. General- Supersedes draft S.I. (ISBN 9780110806075) issued 24.12.2008. EC note: These regs implement in part Article 32 (public oversight) of Directive 2006/43 EC on statutory audits of annual accounts and consolidated accounts, amending Council Directives 78/660/EEC and 83/349/EEC and repealing Council Directive 84/253/EEC. - 8p.: 30 cm. - 978-0-11-081019-5 £3.00

Companies, England and Wales

The Companies (Welsh Language Forms) (Amendment) Regulations 2008 No. 2008/1860. - Enabling power: Companies Act 1985, s. 363(2) & Companies Act 2006, s. 1167 as extended by the Welsh Language Act 1993, s. 26 (3). - Issued: 17.07.2008. Made: 03.07.2008. Coming into force: 01.10.2008. Effect: S.I. 1999/2357; 2000/2413; 2003/62 amended. Territorial extent & classification: E/W. General. - In English and Welsh. - 16p.: 30 cm. - 978-0-11-083202-9 £3.00

Compensation, England

The Home Loss Payments (Prescribed Amounts) (England) Regulations 2008 No. 2008/1598. - Enabling power: Land Compensation Act 1973, s. 30 (5). - Issued: 26.06.2008. Made: 19.06.2008. Laid: 26.06.2008. Coming into force: 01.09.2008. Effect: S.I. 2007/1750 revoked with savings. Territorial extent & classification: E. General. - 2p.: 30 cm. - 978-0-11-081893-1 £3.00

Competition

The Competition Act 1998 (Public Policy Exclusion) Order 2008 No. 2008/1820. - Enabling power: Competition Act 1998, sch. 3, para. 7 (1) (2). - Issued: 14.07.2008. Made: 08.07.2008. Laid: 10.07.2008. Coming into force: 01.09.2008. Effect: None. Territorial extent & classification: E/W/S/NI. General. - 4p.: 30 cm. - 978-0-11-083100-8 £3.00

The Enterprise Act 2002 (Bodies Designated to make Super-complaints) (Amendment) Order 2008 No. 2008/2161. - Enabling power: Enterprise Act 2002, s. 11. - Issued: 19.08.2008. Made: 07.08.2008. Laid: 14.08.2008. Coming into force: 01.10.2008. Effect: S.I. 2004/1517 amended. Territorial extent & classification: E/W/S/NI. General. - 4p.: 30 cm. - 978-0-11-083766-6 £3.00

The Enterprise Act 2002 (Specification of Additional Section 58 Consideration) Order 2008 No. 2008/2645. - Enabling power: Enterprise Act 2002, ss. 58 (3) (4), 124 (2) (4). - Issued: 10.10.2008. Made: 06.10.2008. Laid: 07.10.2008. Coming into force: 24.10.2008. Effect: 2002 c. 40 amended. Territorial extent & classification: E/W/S/NI. General. - For approval by resolution of each House of Parliament within twenty-eight days beginning with the day on which the Order was made, subject to extension for periods of dissolution, prorogation or adjournment for more than four days. - 4p.: 30 cm. - 978-0-11-084450-3 £4.00

Constitutional law

The Housing (Scotland) Act 2006 (Consequential Provisions) Order 2008 No. 2008/1889. - Enabling power: Scotland Act 1998, ss. 104, 112 (1), 113 (2) (3) (4) (5). - Issued: 21.07.2008. Made: 14.07.2008. Coming into force: 01.10.2008. Effect: 1975 c.24 modified. Territorial extent & classification: UK except for arts 2 & 3 which extend to S only. General. - 4p.: 30 cm. - 978-0-11-082019-4 £3.00

The National Assembly for Wales (Legislative Competence) (Education and Training) Order 2008 No. 2008/1036. - Enabling power: Government of Wales Act 2006, s. 95 (5). - Issued: 15.04.2008. Made: 09.04.2008. Coming into force: 10.04.2008 in accord. with art. 1. Effect: 2006 c. 32 amended. Territorial extent & classification: E/W. General. - 4p.: 30 cm. - 978-0-11-081367-7 £3.00

The National Assembly for Wales (Legislative Competence) (Social Welfare and Other Fields) Order 2008 No. 2008/3132. - Enabling power: Government of Wales Act 2006, s. 95 (1). - Issued: 14.01.2009. Made: 10.12.2008. Coming into force: 11.12.2008. In accord. with art. 1 (2). Effect: 2006 c. 32 amended. Territorial extent & classification: W. General. - This Statutory Instrument has been printed in substitution of the SI of the same number (different ISBN 9780111471616, issued 17.12.2008) and is being issued free of charge to all known recipients of that statutory instrument. - 8p.: 30 cm. - 978-0-11-147254-5 £5.00

The National Assembly for Wales (Legislative Competence) (Social Welfare and other Fields) Order 2008 No. 2008/3132. - Enabling power: Government of Wales Act 2006, s. 95 (1). - Issued: 17.12.2008. Made: 10.12.2008. Coming into force: In accord. with art. 1 (2) (3). Effect: 2006 c. 32 amended. Territorial extent & classification: W. General. - Supersedes draft S.I. (ISBN 9780110846620) issued 15.10.2008. Superseded by corrective reprint (ISBN 9780111472545). - 8p.: 30 cm. - 978-0-11-147161-6 £5.00

The National Assembly for Wales (Legislative Competence) (Social Welfare) Order 2008 No. 2008/1785. - Enabling power: Government of Wales Act 2006, s. 95 (1). - Issued: 16.07.2008. Made: 09.07.2008. Coming into force: 10.07.2008 in accord. with art. 1. Effect: 2006 c.32 amended. Territorial extent & classification: W. General. - Supersedes draft S.I. (ISBN 9780110819006) issued 25.06.2008. - 4p.: 30 cm. - 978-0-11-083132-9 £3.00

The Scotland Act 1998 (Agency Arrangements) (Specification) (No. 2) Order 2008 No. 2008/1788. - Enabling power: Scotland Act 1998, ss. 93 (3), 113 (2) (3). - Issued: 15.07.2008. Made: 09.07.2008. Laid: 16.07.2008. Laid before the Scottish Parliament: 16.07.2008. Coming into force: 03.10.2008. Effect: None. Territorial extent & classification: GB. General. - 8p.: 30 cm. - 978-0-11-082016-3 £3.00

The Scotland Act 1998 (Agency Arrangements) (Specification) Order 2008 No. 2008/1035. - Enabling power: Scotland Act 1998, ss. 93. - Issued: 15.04.2008. Made: 09.04.2008. Laid: 16.04.2008. Coming into force: 07.05.2008. Effect: None. Territorial extent & classification: GB. General. - 16p.: 30 cm. - 978-0-11-081605-0 £3.00

The Scotland Act 1998 (Transfer of Functions to the Scottish Ministers etc.) Order 2008 No. 2008/1776. - Enabling power: Scotland Act 1998, ss. 63 (1) (b), 113 (3) (4), 124 (2). - Issued: 16.07.2008. Made: 09.07.2008. Laid:-. Coming into force: 10.07.2008 in accord. with art. 1. Effect: None. Territorial extent & classification: E/W/S. General. - 4p.: 30 cm. - 978-0-11-082017-0 £3.00

The Scottish Parliament (Elections etc.) (Amendment) Order 2008 No. 2008/307 (S.3). - Enabling power: Scotland Act 1998, ss. 12 (1) (a), 113. - Issued: 14.02.2008. Made: 06.02.2008. Coming into force: 08.02.2008 in accord. with art. 1. Effect: S.I. 2007/937 amended. Territorial extent & classification: E/W/S/NI. General. - Supersedes draft SI (ISBN 9780110802275) issued 29.01.2008. - 32p.: 30 cm. - 978-0-11-081497-1 £5.50

The Welsh Ministers (Transfer of Functions) (Wales) Order 2008 No. 2008/1786. - Enabling power: Government of Wales Act 2006, s. 58, sch. 4, para. 2. - Issued: 15.07.2008. Made: 09.07.2008. Coming into force: 10.07.2008. Effect: None. Territorial extent & classification: W. General. - Supersedes draft S.I. (ISBN 9780110818993) issued 25.06.2008. - 4p.: 30 cm. - 978-0-11-083137-4 £3.00

Consumer credit

The Consumer Credit Act 2006 (Commencement No. 4 and Transitional Provisions) (Amendment) Order 2008 No. 2008/2444 (C.105). - Enabling power: Consumer Credit Act 2006, s. 71 (2). Bringing into operation various provisions of the 2006 Act on 31.10.2008. - Issued: 19.09.2008. Made: 15.09.2008. Effect: S.I. 2008/831 (C. 40) amended. Territorial extent & classification: E/W/S/NI. General. - This Statutory Instrument has been made in consequence of a defect in S.I. 2008/831 (C. 40) (ISBN 9780110812885) and is being issued free of charge to all known recipients of that Statutory Instrument. - 2p.: 30 cm. - 978-0-11-084238-7 £4.00

The Consumer Credit Act 2006 (Commencement No. 4 and Transitional Provisions) Order 2008 No. 2008/831 (C.40). - Enabling power: Consumer Credit Act 2006, ss. 69 (2), 71 (2). Bringing into operation various provisions of the 2006 Act on 06.04.2008, 01.10.2008, in accord. with art. 3. - Issued: 28.03.2008. Made: 20.03.2008. Effect: None. Territorial extent & classification: E/W/S/NI. General. - 8p.: 30 cm. - 978-0-11-081288-5 £3.00

The Consumer Credit (Exempt Agreements) (Amendment) Order 2008 No. 2008/645. - Enabling power: Consumer Credit Act 1974, ss. 16 (1) (4), 182 (4). - Issued: 14.03.2008. Made: 06.03.2008. Laid: 11.03.2008. Coming into force: 06.04.2008. Effect: S.I. 1989/869 amended. Territorial extent & classification: E/W/S/NI. General. - 2p.: 30 cm. - 978-0-11-081151-2 £3.00

The Consumer Credit (Information Requirements and Duration of Licences and Charges) (Amendment) Regulations 2008 No. 2008/1751. - Enabling power: Consumer Credit Act 1974, ss. 77A (2), 78 (4A), 86B (8), 130A (6), 182 (2) (4), 189 (1). - Issued: 09.07.2008. Made: 02.07.2008. Laid: 04.07.2008. Coming into force: 01.10.2008. Effect: S.I. 2007/1167 amended. Territorial extent & classification: E/W/S/NI. General. - This Statutory Instrument has been made to correct errors and clarify certain provisions in S.I. 2007/1167 (ISBN 9780110767598) and is being issued free of charge to all known recipients of that Statutory Instrument. - 4p.: 30 cm. - 978-0-11-081966-2 £3.00

Consumer protection

The Cancellation of Contracts made in a Consumer's Home or Place of Work etc. Regulations 2008 No. 2008/1816. - Enabling power: European Communities Act 1972, s. 2 (2) & Consumers, Estate Agents and Redress Act 2007, s. 59. - Issued: 16.07.2008. Made: 08.07.2008. Coming into force: 01.10.2008. Effect: 1974 c. 39 amended & S.I. 2001/3649; 2003/1374, 1376, 1400, 1633; 2006/3384; 2007/3544 amended & S.I. 1987/2117; 1988/958, 3050 revoked. Territorial extent & classification: E/W/S/NI. General. - These Regulations revoke the 1987 Regulations and re-implement Council Directive 85/577/EEC. Supersedes draft S.I. (ISBN 9780110818757) issued 23.06.2008. - 16p.: 30 cm. - 978-0-11-083101-5 £3.00

The Consumer Protection from Unfair Trading Regulations 2008 No. 2008/1277. - Enabling power: European Communities Act 1972, s. 2 (2). - Issued: 16.05.2008. Made: 08.05.2008. Coming into force: 26.05.2008. Effect: 46 Acts & 34 SIs amended; 5 Acts & 6 SIs revoked. Territorial extent & classification: E/W/S/NI. General. - Supersedes draft SI (ISBN 9780110811574) issued 13.03.2008. - 48p.: 30 cm. - 978-0-11-081462-9 *£7.50*

The Consumers, Estate Agents and Redress Act 2007 (Commencement No. 3 and Supplementary Provision) Order 2008 No. 2008/1262 (C.53). - Enabling power: Consumers, Estate Agents and Redress Act 2007, s. 63 (2) (3), 66 (2). Bringing into operation various provisions of the 2007 Act on 07.05.2008 in accord. with art. 3. - Issued: 09.05.2008. Made: 06.05.2008. Effect: None. Territorial extent & classification: E/W/S/NI General. - Supersedes draft SI (ISBN 9780110811543) issued 12.03.2008. - 4p.: 30 cm. - 978-0-11-081436-0 *£3.00*

The Consumers, Estate Agents and Redress Act 2007 (Commencement No. 4) Order 2008 No. 2008/905 (C.43). - Enabling power: Consumers, Estate Agents and Redress Act 2007, s. 66 (2). Bringing into operation various provisions of the 2007 Act on 01.04.2008; 01.10.2008 in accord. with art. 3. - Issued: 31.03.2008. Made: 26.03.2008. Effect: None. Territorial extent & classification: E/W/S/NI General. - 4p.: 30 cm. - 978-0-11-081303-5 *£3.00*

The Consumers, Estate Agents and Redress Act 2007 (Commencement No. 5 and Savings and Transitional Provisions) Order 2008 No. 2008/2550 (C. 111). - Enabling power: Consumers, Estate Agents and Redress Act 2007, s. 63 (2) (3), 66 (2). Bringing into operation various provisions of the 2007 Act on 01.10.2008 in accord. with arts. 2 & 3. - Issued: 01.10.2008. Made: 26.09.2008. Effect: None. Territorial extent & classification: E/W/S/NI General. - 8p.: 30 cm. - 978-0-11-084327-8 *£5.00*

The Cosmetic Products (Safety) (Amendment No. 2) Regulations 2008 No. 2008/2566. - Enabling power: Consumer Protection Act 1987, s. 11. - Issued: 08.10.2008. Made: 30.09.2008. Laid: 02.10.2008. Coming into force: 04.04.2009. Effect: S.I. 2008/1284 amended. Territorial extent & classification: E/W/S/NI. General. - EC note: These regs amend the Cosmetic Products (Safety) Regulations 2008 (S.I. 2008/1284) to give effect to Commission Directive 2008/42/EC. The Directive amends Council Directive 76/768/EEC on the approximation of the laws of the Member States on cosmetic products. - 20p.: 30 cm. - 978-0-11-084360-5 *£5.00*

The Cosmetic Products (Safety) (Amendment) Regulations 2008 No. 2008/2173. - Enabling power: Consumer Protection Act 1987, s. 11. - Issued: 19.08.2008. Made: 14.08.2008. Laid: 15.08.2008. Coming into force: 16.11.2008. Effect: S.I. 2008/1284 amended. Territorial extent & classification: E/W/S/NI. General. - This S.I. has been made in consequence of a defect in S.I. 2008/1284 (ISBN 9780110814835) and is being issued free of charge to all known recipients of that statutory instrument. EC note: These regs amend the Cosmetic Products (Safety) Regulations 2008 (S.I. 2008/1284) to give effect to Commission Directive 2008/14/EC which amends Council Directive 76/768/EEC on the approximation of the laws of the Member States on cosmetic products. - 4p.: 30 cm. - 978-0-11-083811-3 *£3.00*

The Cosmetic Products (Safety) Regulations 2008 No. 2008/1284. - Enabling power: Consumer Protection Act 1987, s. 11 & European Communities Act 1972, s. 2 (2). - Issued: 22.05.2008. Made: 13.05.2008. Laid: 13.05.2008. Coming into force: 18.06.2008. Effect: S.I. 2004/2152, 2361, 2988; 2005/1815, 3346; 2006/1198, 2231, 2907; 2007/1623, 2400, 3452 revoked. Territorial extent & classification: E/W/S/NI. General. - EC note: These regs revoke and re-enact the Cosmetic Products (Safety) Regulations 2004 (S.I. 2004/2152) which give effect to Council Directive 76/768/EEC on the approximation of the laws of the Member States relating to cosmetic products. These regs also give effect to the following Directives: 2007/22/EC; 2007/53/EC; 2007/54/EC all of which amend Directive 76/768/EEC. - 144p.: 30 cm. - 978-0-11-081483-4 *£19.50*

The Enterprise Act 2002 (Bodies Designated to make Super-complaints) (Amendment) Order 2008 No. 2008/2161. - Enabling power: Enterprise Act 2002, s. 11. - Issued: 19.08.2008. Made: 07.08.2008. Laid: 14.08.2008. Coming into force: 01.10.2008. Effect: S.I. 2004/1517 amended. Territorial extent & classification: E/W/S/NI. General. - 4p.: 30 cm. - 978-0-11-083766-6 *£3.00*

The Gas and Electricity Regulated Providers (Redress Scheme) Order 2008 No. 2008/2268. - Enabling power: Consumers, Estate Agents and Redress Act 2007, s. 47 (1) to (3). - Issued: 29.08.2008. Made: 16.08.2008. Laid: 27.08.2008. Coming into force: 01.10.2008. Effect: None. Territorial extent & classification: E/W/S. General. - 4p.: 30 cm. - 978-0-11-083863-2 *£3.00*

The Magnetic Toys (Safety) Regulations 2008 No. 2008/1654. - Enabling power: Consumer Protection Act 1987, s. 11. - Issued: 01.07.2008. Made: 24.06.2008. Laid: 26.06.2008. Coming into force: 21.07.2008. Effect: None. Territorial extent & classification: E/W/S/NI. General. - Revoked by S.I. 2009/1347 (ISBN 9780111480106). EC note: These Regulations give effect to Commission Decision 2008/239/EC requiring Member States to ensure that magnetic toys placed or made available on the market display a warning about the health and safety risks they pose. The Decision is made under Article 13 of Directive 2001/95/EC on general product safety. - 4p.: 30 cm. - 978-0-11-081921-1 *£3.00*

The Medical Devices (Amendment) Regulations 2008 No. 2008/2936. - Enabling power: European Communities Act 1972, s. 2 (2) & Consumer Protection 1987, s. 11. - Issued: 19.11.2008. Made: 12.11.2008. Laid: 19.11.2008. Coming into force: 21.03.2010. Effect: S.I. 2002/618 amended. Territorial extent & classification: E/W/S/NI. General. - EC note: These Regulations amend the Medical Devices Regulations 2002 to implement Directive 2007/47/EC. - 8p.: 30 cm. - 978-0-11-146999-6 *£5.00*

The Medicines (Products for Human Use-Fees) Regulations 2008 No. 2008/552. - Enabling power: Medicines Act 1971, s. 1 (1) (2) & European Communities Act 1972, s. 2 (2) & Finance Act 1973, s. 56 (1) (2). - Issued: 07.03.2008. Made: 28.02.2008. Laid: 07.03.2008. Coming into force: 01.04.2008. Effect: S.I. 1994/105 amended & S.I. 1998/574; 2000/592; 2001/795; 2002/236, 542; 2003/625; 2004/666; 2006/494, 2125; 2007/803 partially revoked & S.I. 1995/1116; 1996/683; 2000/3031; 2004/1157; 2005/1124, 2979 revoked. Territorial extent & classification: E/W/S/NI. General. - Revoked by S.I. 2009/389 (ISBN 9780111474969) with savings. With correction slip dated March 2008. - 64p.: 30 cm. - 978-0-11-081073-7 *£10.50*

The Postal Services Regulated Providers (Redress Scheme) Order 2008 No. 2008/2267. - Enabling power: Consumers, Estate Agents and Redress Act 2007, s. 47 (1) to (3). - Issued: 29.08.2008. Made: 16.08.2008. Laid: 27.08.2008. Coming into force: 01.10.2008. Effect: None. Territorial extent & classification: E/W/S/NI. General. - 4p.: 30 cm. - 978-0-11-083862-5 *£3.00*

The REACH Enforcement Regulations 2008 No. 2008/2852. - Enabling power: European Communities Act 1972, s. 2 (2). - Issued: 13.11.2008. Made: 01.11.2008. Laid: 10.11.2008. Coming into force: 01.12.2008. Effect: 9 SI's & 9 S.R's amended & S.I. 1993/3050; 1994/1806; 1996/1373; 2001/1055; 2002/2176; 2003/1511, 2650, 3310; 2004/2913; 2005/2001; 2006/2916, 3311; 2007/386, 1596, 3438 & S.R. 1994/6; 2003/36; 2004/76 revoked. Territorial extent & classification: E/W/S/NI. General. - EC note: These Regulations apply to the United Kingdom and provide for the enforcement of Regulation (EC) No. 1907/2006 concerning the Registration, Evaluation, Authorisation and Restriction of Chemicals (REACH). - 76p.: 30 cm. - 978-0-11-084991-1 *£13.00*

Consumer protection, England and Wales

The Compensation (Claims Management Services) (Amendment) Regulations 2008 No. 2008/1441. - Enabling power: Compensation Act 2006, ss. 8 (8), 9, 15, sch. - Issued: 11.06.2008. Made: 05.06.2008. Coming into force: 01.07.2008 except for regs 4 to 7; 01.08.2008 for regs 4 to 7 in accord. with reg. 1. Effect: S.I. 2006/3322 amended. Territorial extent & classification: E/W. - Supersedes draft S.I. (ISBN 9780110813936) issued 25.04.2008. - 4p.: 30 cm. - 978-0-11-081803-0 *£3.00*

Contracting out, England and Wales

The Contracting Out (Administrative and Other Court Staff) (Amendment) Order 2008 No. 2008/2791. - Enabling power: Courts Act 1971, s. 2 (6). - Issued: 31.10.2008. Made: 23.10.2008. Laid: 28.10.2008. Coming into force: 01.12.2008. Effect: S.I. 2001/3698 amended. Territorial extent & classification: E/W. General. - 2p.: 30 cm. - 978-0-11-084741-2 *£4.00*

Copyright

The Copyright and Performances (Application to Other Countries) Order 2008 No. 2008/677. - Enabling power: Copyright, Designs and Patents Act 1988, ss. 159, 208 & European Communities Act 1972, s. 2 (2). - Issued: 18.03.2008. Made: 12.03.2008. Laid: 13.03.2008. Coming into force: 06.04.2008. Effect: S.I. 2007/273 revoked. Territorial extent & classification: E/W/S/NI. General. - 16p.: 30 cm. - 978-0-11-081235-9 *£3.00*

The Copyright (Certification of Licensing Scheme for Educational Recording of Broadcasts) (Educational Recording Agency Limited) (Revocation and Amendment) Order 2008 No. 2008/211. - Enabling power: Copyright, Designs and Patents Act 1988, s. 143, sch. 2A. para. 16. - Issued: 08.02.2008. Made: 31.01.2008. Coming into force: 01.04.2008. Effect: S.I. 2007/266 amended & S.I. 2005/222 revoked. Territorial extent & classification: E/W/S/NI. General. - 4p.: 30 cm. - 978-0-11-080893-2 *£3.00*

Coroners, England and Wales

The Coroners (Amendment) Rules 2008 No. 2008/1652. - Enabling power: Coroners Act 1988, s. 32. - Issued: 01.07.2008. Made: 16.06.2008. Laid: 26.06.2008. Coming into force: 17.07.2008. Effect: S.I. 1984/552 amended. Territorial extent & classification: E/W. General. - 4p.: 30 cm. - 978-0-11-081911-2 *£3.00*

Corporation tax

The Authorised Investment Funds (Tax) (Amendment No. 2) Regulations 2008 No. 2008/1463. - Enabling power: Finance (No. 2) Act 2005, ss. 17 (3), 18. - Issued: 11.06.2008. Made: 09.06.2008. Laid: 09.06.2008. Coming into force: 30.06.2008. Effect: S.I. 2006/964 amended. Territorial extent & classification: E/W/S/NI. General. - 4p.: 30 cm. - 978-0-11-081811-5 *£3.00*

The Authorised Investment Funds (Tax) (Amendment No. 3) Regulations 2008 No. 2008/3159. - Enabling power: Finance (No. 2) Act 2005, ss. 17 (3), 18. - Issued: 16.12.2008. Made: 10.12.2008. Laid: 11.12.2008. Coming into force: 01.01.2009. Effect: S.I. 2006/964 amended. Territorial extent & classification: E/W/S/NI. General. - 16p.: 30 cm. - With correction slip dated October 2009. - 978-0-11-147156-2 *£5.00*

The Authorised Investment Funds (Tax) (Amendment) Regulations 2008 No. 2008/705. - Enabling power: Finance (No. 2) Act 2005, ss. 17 (3), 18. - Issued: 12.03.2008. Made: 12.03.2008. Laid: 12.03.2008. Coming into force: 06.04.2008. Effect: S.I. 2006/964 amended. Territorial extent & classification: E/W/S/NI. General. - 34p.: 30 cm. - 978-0-11-081206-9 £6.50

The Capital Allowances (Energy-saving Plant and Machinery) (Amendment) Order 2008 No. 2008/1916. - Enabling power: Capital Allowances Act 2001, ss. 45A (3) (4). - Issued: 23.07.2008. Made: 18.07.2008. Laid: 21.07.2008. Coming into force: 11.08.2007. Effect: S.I. 2001/2541 amended. Territorial extent & classification: E/W/S/NI. General. - 2p.: 30 cm. - 978-0-11-083442-9 £3.00

The Capital Allowances (Environmentally Beneficial Plant and Machinery) (Amendment) Order 2008 No. 2008/1917. - Enabling power: Capital Allowances Act 2001, ss. 45H (3) to (5), 45I. - Issued: 24.07.2008. Made: 18.07.2008. Laid: 21.07.2008. Coming into force: 11.08.2008. Effect: S.I. 2003/2076 amended. Territorial extent & classification: E/W/S/NI. General. - 4p.: 30 cm. - 978-0-11-083449-8 £3.00

The Community Investment Tax Relief (Accreditation of Community Development Finance Institutions) (Amendment) Regulations 2008 No. 2008/383. - Enabling power: Finance Act 2002, sch. 16, para. 4 (1) (2) & Income Tax Act 2007, ss. 340 (2) (b) (4) (5) (6), 341. - Issued: 25.02.2008. Made: 18.02.2008. Laid: 19.02.2008. Coming into force: 11.03.2008. Effect: S.I. 2003/96 amended. Territorial extent & classification: E/W/S/NI. General. - 8p.: 30 cm. - 978-0-11-080979-3 £3.00

The Corporation Tax (Implementation of the Mergers Directive) Regulations 2008 No. 2008/1579. - Enabling power: Finance Act 2007, s. 110. - Issued: 20.06.2008. Made: 16.06.2008. Laid: 17.06.2008. Coming into force: 08.07.2008. Effect: 1992 c. 12; 1996 c. 8; 2002 c. 23; S.I. 2007/3186 amended. Territorial extent & classification: E/W/S/NI. General. - EC note: These Regulations amend primary legislation to ensure that the United Kingdom's tax legislation is compliant with its obligations under Directive 90/434/EEC on cross-border mergers of limited liability companies as amended by Council Directive 2005/19/EC on the common system of taxation applicable to mergers, divisions, transfers of assets and exchanges of shares concerning companies of different member states. It should be read with the Corporation Tax (Implementation of the Mergers Directive) Regulations 2007 (S.I. 2007/3186)- 12p.: 30 cm. - 978-0-11-081864-1 £3.00

The Corporation Tax (Instalment Payments) (Amendment) Regulations 2008 No. 2008/2649. - Enabling power: Taxes Management Act 1970, s. 59E. - Issued: 10.10.2008. Made: 07.10.2008. Laid: 07.10.2008. Coming into force: 28.10.2008. Effect: S.I. 1998/3175 amended. Territorial extent & classification: E/W/S/NI. General. - 2p.: 30 cm. - 978-0-11-084452-7 £4.00

The Double Taxation Relief and International Tax Enforcement (Taxes on Income and Capital) (Moldova) Order 2008 No. 2008/1795. - Enabling power: Income and Corporation Taxes Act 1988, s. 788 (10) & Finance Act 2006, s. 173 (7). - Issued: 16.07.2008. Made: 09.07.2008. Coming into force: 09.07.2008. Effect: None. Territorial extent & classification: E/W/S/NI. General. - Supersedes draft S.I. (ISBN 9780110814803) issued 21.05.2008. - 20p.: 30 cm. - 978-0-11-083144-2 £3.50

The Double Taxation Relief and International Tax Enforcement (Taxes on Income and Capital) (New Zealand) Order 2008 No. 2008/1793. - Enabling power: Income and Corporation Taxes Act 1988, s. 788 (10) & Finance Act 2006, s. 173 (7). - Issued: 15.07.2008. Made: 09.07.2008. Coming into force: 09.07.2008. Effect: None. Territorial extent & classification: E/W/S/NI. General. - Supersedes draft S.I. (ISBN 9780110814537) issued 15.05.2008. - 8p.: 30 cm. - 978-0-11-083138-1 £3.00

The Double Taxation Relief and International Tax Enforcement (Taxes on Income and Capital) (Saudi Arabia) Order 2008 No. 2008/1770. - Enabling power: Income and Corporation Taxes Act 1988, s. 788 (10) & Finance Act 2006, s. 173 (7). - Issued: 16.07.2008. Made: 09.07.2008. Effect: None. Territorial extent & classification: E/W/S/NI. General. - Supersedes draft S.I. (ISBN 9780110814636) issued on 19.05.2008. - 20p.: 30 cm. - 978-0-11-083151-0 £3.50

The Double Taxation Relief and International Tax Enforcement (Taxes on Income and Capital) (Slovenia) Order 2008 No. 2008/1796. - Enabling power: Income and Corporation Taxes Act 1988, s. 788 (10) & Finance Act 2006, s. 173 (7). - Issued: 16.07.2008. Made: 09.07.2008. Coming into force: 09.07.2008. Effect: None. Territorial extent & classification: E/W/S/NI. General. - Supersedes draft S.I. (ISBN 9780110814544) issued 15.05.2008. - 24p.: 30 cm. - 978-0-11-083145-9 £4.00

The Energy-Saving Items (Corporation Tax) Regulations 2008 No. 2008/1520. - Enabling power: Income and Corporation Taxes Act 1988, ss. 31ZA, 31ZC. - Issued: 17.06.2008. Made: 11.06.2008. Laid: 12.06.2008. Coming into force: 07.07.2008. Effect: None. Territorial extent & classification: E/W/S/NI. General. - 4p.: 30 cm. - 978-0-11-081853-5 £3.00

The European Single Currency (Taxes) (Amendment) Regulations 2008 No. 2008/2647. - Enabling power: Finance Act 1998, s. 163. - Issued: 13.10.2008. Made: 07.10.2008. Laid: 07.10.2008. Coming into force: 28.10.2008. Effect: S.I. 1998/3177 amended. Territorial extent & classification: E/W/S/NI. General. - 2p.: 30 cm. - 978-0-11-084472-5 £4.00

The Finance Act 2007 (Schedule 9) Order 2008 No. 2008/379 (C. 14). - Enabling power: Finance Act 2007, sch. 9, para. 17 (2). - Issued: 22.02.2008. Made: 18.02.2008. Laid: 19.02.2008. Coming into force: 11.03.2008. Effect: None. Territorial extent & classification: E/W/S/NI. General. - 2p.: 30 cm. - 978-0-11-080962-5 £3.00

Corporation tax

The Finance Act 2007, Section 17(2) (Corporation Tax Deduction for Expenditure on Energy-Saving Items) (Appointed Day) Order 2008 No. 2008/1521 (C.68). - Enabling power: Finance Act 2007, s. 17 (2). Bringing into operation various provisions of the 2007 Act on 08.07.2008 in accord. with art. 2. - Issued: 17.06.2008. Made: 11.06.2008. Effect: None. Territorial extent & classification: E/W/S/NI. General. - 2p.: 30 cm. - 978-0-11-081851-1 £3.00

The Finance Act 2008, Section 26 (Appointed Day) Order 2008 No. 2008/1933 (C. 92). - Enabling power: Finance Act 2008, s. 26, sch. 8, paras 1 (4), 3(4). Bringing into force various provisions of the 2008 Act on 01.08.2008 in accord. with art. 2. - Issued: 25.07.2008. Made: 22.07.2008. Effect: None. Territorial extent & classification: E/W/S/NI. General. - 2p.: 30 cm. - 978-0-11-083549-5 £3.00

The Finance Act 2008, Section 27 (Appointed Day) Order 2008 No. 2008/1930 (C. 91). - Enabling power: Finance Act 2008, s. 27 (10). Bringing into force various provisions of the 2008 Act on 01.08.2008 in accord. with art. 2. - Issued: 25.07.2008. Made: 22.07.2008. Effect: None. Territorial extent & classification: E/W/S/NI. General. - 2p.: 30 cm. - 978-0-11-083567-9 £3.00

The Finance Act 2008, Section 28 (Appointed Day) Order 2008 No. 2008/1929 (C. 90). - Enabling power: Finance Act 2008, s. 28, sch. 9, par. 3. Bringing into force various provisions of the 2008 Act on 01.08.2008 in accord. with art. 2. - Issued: 25.07.2008. Made: 22.07.2008. Effect: None. Territorial extent & classification: E/W/S/NI. General. - 2p.: 30 cm. - 978-0-11-083565-5 £3.00

The Finance Act 2008, Section 29 (Appointed Day) Order 2008 No. 2008/1928 (C. 89). - Enabling power: Finance Act 2008, s. 29 (5). Bringing into force various provisions of the 2008 Act on 01.08.2008 in accord. with art. 2. - Issued: 25.07.2008. Made: 22.07.2008. Effect: None. Territorial extent & classification: E/W/S/NI. General. - 2p.: 30 cm. - 978-0-11-083566-2 £3.00

The Finance Act 2008, Section 30 (Appointed Day) Order 2008 No. 2008/1925 (C.88). - Enabling power: Finance Act 2008, s. 30 (2). Bringing into force various provisions of the 2008 Act on 01.08.2008 in accord. with art. 2. - Issued: 28.07.2008. Made: 22.07.2008. Effect: None. Territorial extent & classification: E/W/S/NI. General. - 2p.: 30 cm. - 978-0-11-083535-8 £3.00

The Financial Services and Markets Act 2000 (Consequential Amendments) (Taxes) Order 2008 No. 2008/2673. - Enabling power: Financial Services and Markets Act 2000, ss. 426, 428. - Issued: 14.10.2008. Made: 08.10.2008. Laid: 08.10.2008. Coming into force: 29.10.2008. Effect: 1988 c. 1 amended. Territorial extent & classification: E/W/S/NI. General. - With correction slip dated August 2009. - 2p.: 30 cm. - 978-0-11-084515-9 £4.00

The Financing-Arrangement-Funded Transfers to Shareholders Regulations 2008 No. 2008/1926. - Enabling power: Finance Act 1989, s. 83YE (1) (4). - Issued: 28.07.2008. Made: 22.07.2008. Laid: 22.07.2008. Coming into force: 12.08.2008. Effect: None. Territorial extent & classification: E/W/S/NI. General. - 8p.: 30 cm. - 978-0-11-083563-1 £3.00

The Friendly Societies (Modification of the Corporation Tax Acts) (Amendment) Regulations 2008 No. 2008/1937. - Enabling power: Income and Corporation Taxes Act 1988, s. 463. - Issued: 28.07.2008. Made: 22.07.2008. Laid: 22.07.2008. Coming into force: 12.08.2007. Effect: S.I. 2005/2014 amended. Territorial extent & classification: E/W/S/NI. General. - 8p.: 30 cm. - 978-0-11-083575-4 £3.00

The Friendly Societies (Transfers of Other Business) (Modification of the Corporation Tax Acts) Regulations 2008 No. 2008/1942. - Enabling power: Income and Corporation Taxes Act 1988, s. 461D (4) (5). - Issued: 28.07.2008. Made: 22.07.2008. Laid: 22.07.2008. Coming into force: 12.08.2008. Effect: 1988 c. 1; 2001 c. 2 modified. Territorial extent & classification: E/W/S/NI. General. - With 2 correction slips dated August 2008 & October 2009. - 8p.: 30 cm. - 978-0-11-083568-6 £3.00

The Group Relief for Overseas Losses (Modification of the Corporation Tax Acts for Non-resident Insurance Companies) Regulations 2008 No. 2008/2646. - Enabling power: Income and Corporation Taxes Act 1988, sch. 18A, para. 16 (2) to (4). - Issued: 10.10.2008. Made: 07.07.2008. Laid: 07.07.2008. Coming into force: 28.10.2008. Effect: 1988 c. 1; SI 1996/2991 modified & S.I. 2006/3389; 2007/2147 revoked. Territorial extent & classification: E/W/S/NI. General. - 4p.: 30 cm. - 978-0-11-084451-0 £4.00

The Insurance Business Transfer Schemes (Amendment of the Corporation Tax Acts) Order 2008 No. 2008/381. - Enabling power: Finance Act 2007, sch. 9, para. 16. - Issued: 27.02.2008. Made: 18.02.2008. Coming into force: 19.02.2008. Effect: 1988 c. 1; 1989 c.26; 1990 c.14; 1992 c.12; 2003 c.14; 2004 c.12; 2005 c.22; 2007 c.11 & S.I. 2001/3629 amended. Territorial extent & classification: E/W/S/NI. General. - Supersedes draft SI (ISBN 9780110805511) issued 20.12.2007. - 20p.: 30 cm. - 978-0-11-080964-9 £3.50

The Insurance Companies (Calculation of Profits: Policy Holders' Tax) (Amendment) Regulations 2008 No. 2008/1906. - Enabling power: Finance Act 1989, s. 82A. - Issued: 23.07.2008. Made: 17.07.2008. Laid: 18.07.2008. Coming into force: 08.08.2008. Effect: S.I. 2003/2082 amended. Territorial extent & classification: E/W/S/NI. General. - 2p.: 30 cm. - 978-0-11-083424-5 £3.00

The Insurance Companies (Corporation Tax Acts) (Amendment) (No. 2) Order 2008 No. 2008/3096. - Enabling power: Income and Corporation Taxes Act 1988, s. 431A (1) (6). - Issued: 08.12.2008. Made: 03.12.2008. Laid: 03.12.2008. Coming into force: 27.12.2008. Effect: 1988 c. 1; 1989 c. 26 amended. Territorial extent & classification: E/W/S/NI. General. - 4p.: 30 cm. - 978-0-11-147095-4 £4.00

The Insurance Companies (Corporation Tax Acts) (Amendment) Order 2008 No. 2008/1905. - Enabling power: Income and Corporation Taxes Act 1988, s. 431A (1) (6). - Issued: 22.07.2008. Made: 17.07.2008. Laid: 18.07.2008. Coming into force: 08.08.2008. Effect: 1989 c.26 amended. Territorial extent & classification: E/W/S/NI. General. - 2p.: 30 cm. - 978-0-11-083413-9 £3.00

The Insurance Companies (Overseas Life Assurance Business) (Compliance) (Amendment) Regulations 2008 No. 2008/2627. - Enabling power: Income and Corporation Taxes Act 1988, s. 431E. - Issued: 09.10.2008. Made: 06.10.2008. Laid: 06.10.2008. Coming into force: 27.10.2008. Effect: S.I. 1995/3237 amended. Territorial extent & classification: E/W/S/NI. General. - 4p.: 30 cm. - 978-0-11-084397-1 £4.00

The Insurance Companies (Overseas Life Assurance Business) (Excluded Business) (Amendment) Regulations 2008 No. 2008/2625. - Enabling power: Income and Corporation Taxes Act 1988, s. 431D. - Issued: 09.10.2008. Made: 06.10.2008. Laid: 06.10.2008. Coming into force: 27.10.2008. Effect: S.I. 2000/2089 amended. Territorial extent & classification: E/W/S/NI. General. - 2p.: 30 cm. - 978-0-11-084401-5 £4.00

The Insurance Companies (Reserves) (Tax) (Amendment) Regulations 2008 No. 2008/2679. - Enabling power: Income and Corporation Taxes Act 1988, s. 444BB (1) (3) (4) (5), 444BC, 444BD (1) (4) (5). - Issued: 14.10.2008. Made: 09.10.2008. Laid: 09.10.2008. Coming into force: 30.10.2008. Effect: S.I. 1996/2991 amended. Territorial extent & classification: E/W/S/NI. General. - 8p.: 30 cm. - 978-0-11-084550-0 £5.00

The Insurance Companies (Taxation of Insurance Special Purpose Vehicles) Order 2008 No. 2008/1923. - Enabling power: Income and Corporation Taxes Act 1988, s. 431A (2A). - Issued: 28.07.2008. Made: 22.07.2008. Laid: 22.07.2008. Coming into force: 12.08.2008. Effect: 1988 c. 1 amended. Territorial extent & classification: E/W/S/NI. General. - With correction slip dated September 2009. - 8p.: 30 cm. - 978-0-11-083534-1 £3.00

The Insurance Companies (Taxation of Reinsurance Business) (Amendment) (No. 2) Regulations 2008 No. 2008/2670. - Enabling power: Income and Corporation Taxes Act 1988, s. 442A (2) to (6). - Issued: 14.10.2008. Made: 06.10.2008. Laid: 08.10.2008. Coming into force: 29.10.2008. Effect: S.I. 1995/1730 amended. Territorial extent & classification: E/W/S/NI. General. - 2p.: 30 cm. - 978-0-11-084514-2 £4.00

The Insurance Companies (Taxation of Reinsurance Business) (Amendment) Regulations 2008 No. 2008/1944. - Enabling power: Income and Corporation Taxes Act 1988, s. 442A (2) to (6) & Finance Act 1995, sch. 8, para. 58. - Issued: 28.07.2008. Made: 22.07.2008. Laid: 22.07.2008. Coming into force: 12.08.2008. Effect: S.I. 1995/1730 amended. Territorial extent & classification: E/W/S/NI. General. - 4p.: 30 cm. - 978-0-11-083574-7 £3.00

The Loan Relationships and Derivative Contracts (Change of Accounting Practice) (Amendment) Regulations 2008 No. 2008/3237. - Enabling power: Finance Act 1996, ss. 85B (3) (5), sch. 9, para. 19B & Finance Act 2002, sch. 26, para. 17C & Finance Act 2005, sch. 4, para. 52 (1) (2). - Issued: 22.12.2008. Made: 17.12.2008. Laid: 17.12.2008. Coming into force: 07.01.2009. Effect: S.I. 2004/3271 amended. Territorial extent & classification: E/W/S/NI. General. - 4p.: 30 cm. - 978-0-11-147203-3 £4.00

The Non-resident Companies (General Insurance Business) (Amendment) Regulations 2008 No. 2008/2643. - Enabling power: Income and Corporation Taxes Act 1988, s. 755C. - Issued: 08.10.2008. Made: 06.10.2008. Laid: 07.10.2008. Coming into force: 27.10.2008. Effect: S.I. 1999/1408 amended. Territorial extent & classification: E/W/S/NI. General. - 2p.: 30 cm. - 978-0-11-084429-9 £4.00

The Overseas Life Insurance Companies (Amendment) Regulations 2008 No. 2008/1924. - Enabling power: Finance Act 2003, s. 156. - Issued: 28.07.2008. Made: 22.07.2008. Laid: 22.07.2008. Coming into force: 12.08.2008. Effect: S.I. 2006/3271 amended. Territorial extent & classification: E/W/S/NI. General. - With correction slip dated August 2008. - 8p.: 30 cm. - 978-0-11-083538-9 £3.00

The Taxation of Chargeable Gains (Gilt-edged Securities) Order 2008 No. 2008/1588. - Enabling power: Taxation of Chargeable Gains Act 1992, sch. 9, para. 1. - Issued: 24.06.2008. Made: 19.06.2008. Coming into force: 19.06.2008. Effect: None. Territorial extent & classification: E/W/S/NI. General. - 2p.: 30 cm. - 978-0-11-081881-8 £3.00

Council tax, England

The Council Tax and Non-Domestic Rating (Demand Notices) (England) (Amendment) (No. 2) Regulations 2008 No. 2008/3264. - Enabling power: Local Government Finance Act 1992, ss. 113 (1), 116 (1), sch. 2, paras 1, 2 (4) (e) (j). - Issued: 24.12.2008. Made: 18.12.2008. Laid: 22.12.2008. Coming into force: 20.01.2009. Effect: S.I. 2003/2613 amended. Territorial extent & classification: E. General. - 12p.: 30 cm. - 978-0-11-147230-9 £5.00

The Council Tax and Non-Domestic Rating (Demand Notices) (England) (Amendment) Regulations 2008 No. 2008/387. - Enabling power: Local Government Finance Act 1988, ss. 143 (1) (2), 146 (6), sch. 9, paras. 1, 2 (2) (ga) (h) & Local Government Finance Act 1992, ss. 113(1), 116 (1), sch. 2, paras 1, 2 (4) (e), 4 (4) (5), sch. 3, para. 6 (1) (2). - Issued: 26.02.2008. Made: 18.02.2008. Laid: 26.02.2008. Coming into force: 01.04.2008. Effect: S.I. 2003/2613 amended. Territorial extent & classification: E. General. - 16p.: 30 cm. - 978-0-11-080995-3 £3.00

The Council Tax (Electronic Communications) (England) Order 2008 No. 2008/316. - Enabling power: Electronic Communications Act 2000, s. 8. - Issued: 19.02.2008. Made: 12.02.2008. Laid: 19.02.2008. Coming into force: 01.04.2008. Effect: S.I. 1993/290 amended in relation to England. Territorial extent & classification: E. General. - 4p.: 30 cm. - 978-0-11-080944-1 £3.00

The Council Tax Limitation (Maximum Amounts) (England) Order 2008 No. 2008/1850. - Enabling power: Local Government Finance Act 1992, s. 52F (4) (7). - Issued: 16.07.2008. Made: 10.07.2008. Coming into force: 11.07.2008. Effect: None. Territorial extent & classification: E. General. - 4p.: 30 cm. - 978-0-11-083167-1 £3.00

The Council Tax (Valuations, Alteration of Lists and Appeals) (England) Regulations 2008 No. 2008/315. - Enabling power: Local Government Finance Act 1988, ss. 143 (1) (2), sch. 11, paras 1, 5 (1) (g), 8 and Local Government Finance Act 1992, ss. 21 (2), 24, 113 (1) (2). - Issued: 19.02.2008. Made: 12.02.2008. Laid: 19.02.2008. Coming into force: 01.04.2008. Effect: S.I. 1992/550; 1993/290 amended. Territorial extent & classification: E. General. - 16p.: 30 cm. - 978-0-11-080948-9 £3.00

The Local Government Finance (New Parishes) (England) Regulations 2008 No. 2008/626. - Enabling power: Local Government Finance Act 1992, s. 32 (9) & Local Government and Public Involvement in Health Act 2007, ss. 97, 98. - Issued: 11.03.2008. Made: 03.03.2008. Laid: 11.03.2008. Coming into force: 08.04.2008. Effect: None. Territorial extent & classification: E. General. - 4p.: 30 cm. - 978-0-11-081149-9 £3.00

Countryside, England

The Countryside and Rights of Way Act 2000 (Commencement No. 15) Order 2008 No. 2008/308 (C.8). - Enabling power: Countryside and Rights of Way Act 2000, s. 103 (3). Bringing into operation various provisions of the 2000 Act on 18.02.2008. - Issued: 14.02.2008. Made: 07.02.2008. Effect: None. Territorial extent & classification: E. General. - 4p.: 30 cm. - 978-0-11-080937-3 £3.00

Countryside, England and Wales

The Conservation (Natural Habitats, &c.) (Amendment) (England and Wales) Regulations 2008 No. 2008/2172. - Enabling power: European Communities Act 1972, s. 2 (2). - Issued: 20.08.2008. Made: 12.08.2008. Laid: 20.08.2008. Coming into force: 01.10.2008. Effect: 1981 c. 69 & S.I. 1994/2716 amended. Territorial extent & classification: E/W. General. - EC note: These Regulations amend the 1994 Regulations on the Conservation of Natural Habitats, which make provision implementing Council Directive 92/43/EEC on the conservation of natural habitats and of wild flora and fauna. - 4p.: 30 cm. - 978-0-11-083803-8 £3.00

County courts, England and Wales

The Civil Procedure (Amendment No.3) Rules 2008 No. 2008/3327 (L. 29). - Enabling power: Civil Procedure Act 1997, s. 2. - Issued: 09.01.2009. Made: 29.12.2008. Laid: 07.01.2009. Coming into force: 06.04.2009. Effect: S.I. 1998/3132 amended. Territorial extent & classification: E/W. General. - 8p.: 30 cm. - 978-0-11-147245-3 £5.00

The Civil Procedure (Amendment) Rules 2008 No. 2008/2178 (L.10). - Enabling power: Civil Procedure Act 1997, s. 2. - Issued: 19.08.2008. Made: 07.08.2008. Laid: 15.08.2008. Coming into force: In accord. with rule 1. Effect: S.I. 1998/3132 amended. Territorial extent & classification: E/W. General. - 44p.: 30 cm. - 978-0-11-083831-1 £6.50

The Civil Proceedings Fees (Amendment) Order 2008 No. 2008/2853 (L.19). - Enabling power: Courts Act 2003, s. 92. - Issued: 10.11.2008. Made: 04.11.2008. Laid: 05.11.2008. Coming into force: 26.11.2008. Effect: S.I. 2008/1053 amended. Territorial extent & classification: E/W. General. - 2p.: 30 cm. - 978-0-11-084949-2 £4.00

The Civil Proceedings Fees (Amendment) Order 2008 No. 2008/116 (L.2). - Enabling power: Courts Act 2003, s. 92. - Issued: 28.01.2008. Made: 21.01.2008. Laid: 21.01.2008. Coming into force: 11.02.2008. Effect: S.I. 2004/3121 amended. Territorial extent & classification: E/W. General. - Revoked by S.I. 2008/1053 (L.5) (ISBN 9780110813561). This Statutory Instrument has been made in consequence of defects in S.I. 2007/2176 (ISBN 9780110782829) and is being issued free of charge to all known recipients of that SI. - 2p.: 30 cm. - 978-0-11-080862-8 £3.00

The Civil Proceedings Fees Order 2008 No. 2008/1053 (L.5). - Enabling power: Courts Act 2003, s. 92 & Insolvency Act 1986, ss. 414, 415. - Issued: 11.04.2008. Made: 07.04.2008. Laid: 09.04.2008. Coming into force: 01.05.2008. Effect: S.I. 2004/3121; 2005/473, 3445; 2006/719; 2007/680, 2176, 2801; 2008/116 revoked. Territorial extent & classification: E/W. General. - 20p.: 30 cm. - 978-0-11-081356-1 £3.50

The Contracting Out (Administrative and Other Court Staff) (Amendment) Order 2008 No. 2008/2791. - Enabling power: Courts Act 1971, s. 2 (6). - Issued: 31.10.2008. Made: 23.10.2008. Laid: 28.10.2008. Coming into force: 01.12.2008. Effect: S.I. 2001/3698 amended. Territorial extent & classification: E/W. General. - 2p.: 30 cm. - 978-0-11-084741-2 £4.00

The Family Proceedings (Amendment) (No.2) Rules 2008 No. 2008/2861 (L.25). - Enabling power: Matrimonial and Family Proceedings Act 1984, s. 40 (1). - Issued: 12.11.2008. Made: 03.11.2008. Laid: 06.11.2008. Coming into force: 08.12.2008. Effect: S.I. 1991/1247 amended. Territorial extent & classification: E/W. General. - 60p.: 30 cm. - 978-0-11-084967-6 £9.00

The Family Proceedings (Amendment) Rules 2008 No. 2008/2446 (L.11). - Enabling power: Matrimonial and Family Proceedings Act 1984, s. 40 (1) (4) (aa). - Issued: 22.09.2008. Made: 16.09.2008. Laid: 18.09.2008. Coming into force: 03.11.2008 for rules 1, 2, 3(a), 5, 6, 10, 12; 25.11.2008 for remainder, in accord. with rule 1 (2). Effect: S.I. 1991/1247 amended. Territorial extent & classification: E/W. General. - 34p.: 30 cm. - 978-0-11-084250-9 £9.00

The Family Proceedings Fees (Amendment No. 2) Order 2008 No. 2008/3106 (L.27). - Enabling power: Courts Act 2003, s. 92. - Issued: 09.12.2008. Made: 03.12.2008. Laid: 04.12.2008. Coming into force: 05.12.2008. Effect: S.I. 2008/2856 (L.22) amended. Territorial extent & classification: E/W. General. - This Statutory Instrument is made in consequence of a defect in S.I. 2008/2856 and is being issued free of charge to all known recipients of that Statutory Instrument. - 2p.: 30 cm. - 978-0-11-147105-0 £4.00

The Family Proceedings Fees (Amendment) Order 2008 No. 2008/2856 (L.22). - Enabling power: Courts Act 2003, s. 92. - Issued: 10.11.2008. Made: 04.11.2008. Laid: 05.11.2008. Coming into force: 26.11.2008 except for art. 5; 08.12.2008 for art. 5. Effect: S.I. 2008/1054 (L.6) amended. Territorial extent & classification: E/W. General. - 4p.: 30 cm. - 978-0-11-084957-7 £4.00

The Family Proceedings Fees (Amendment) Order 2008 No. 2008/115 (L.1). - Enabling power: Courts Act 2003, s. 92. - Issued: 28.01.2008. Made: 21.01.2008. Laid: 21.01.2008. Coming into force: 11.02.2008. Effect: S.I. 2004/3114 amended. Territorial extent & classification: E/W. General. - Revoked by S.I. 2008/1054 (L.6) (ISBN 9780110813585). This Statutory Instrument has been made in consequence of defects in S.I. 2007/2175 (ISBN 9780110782836) and is being issued free of charge to all known recipients of that SI. - 2p.: 30 cm. - 978-0-11-080861-1 £3.00

The Family Proceedings Fees Order 2008 No. 2008/1054 (L.6). - Enabling power: Courts Act 2003, s. 92. - Issued: 14.04.2008. Made: 07.04.2008. Laid: 09.04.2008. Coming into force: 01.05.2008. Effect: S.I. 2004/3114; 2005/472, 3443; 2006/739; 2007/682, 2175, 2800; 2008/115 revoked. Territorial extent & classification: E/W. General. - 16p.: 30 cm. - 978-0-11-081358-5 £3.00

County courts, England and Wales: Jurisdiction

The High Court and County Courts Jurisdiction (Amendment) Order 2008 No. 2008/2934. - Enabling power: Courts and Legal Services Act 1990, ss. 1, 120. - Issued: 17.11.2008. Made: 11.11.2008. Laid: 13.11.2008. Coming into force: 12.12.2008; 01.01.2009; 06.04.2009 in accord. with art. 1. Effect: S.I. 1991/724 amended. Territorial extent & classification: E/W. General. - 4p.: 30 cm. - 978-0-11-146997-2 £4.00

Cremation, England and Wales

The Cremation (England and Wales) Regulations 2008 No. 2008/2841. - Enabling power: Cremation Act 1902, s. 7. - Issued: 05.11.2008. Made: 28.10.2008. Laid: 03.11.2008. Coming into force: 01.01.2009. Effect: S.R. & O. 1930/1016; S.I. 1952/1568; 1965/1146; 1979/1138; 1985/153; 2000/58; 2006/92 revoked. Territorial extent & classification: E/W. General. - 52p.: 30 cm. - 978-0-11-084852-5 £9.00

Criminal law

The Corporate Manslaughter and Corporate Homicide Act 2007 (Amendment of Schedule 1) Order 2008 No. 2008/396. - Enabling power: Corporate Manslaughter and Corporate Homicide Act 2007, s. 22 (1). - Issued: 25.02.2008. Made: 14.02.2008. Laid: 19.02.2008. Coming into force: 06.04.2008. Effect: 2007 c. 19 amended. Territorial extent & classification: E/W/S/NI. General. - 2p.: 30 cm. - 978-0-11-080980-9 £3.00

The Corporate Manslaughter and Corporate Homicide Act 2007 (Commencement No.1) Order 2008 No. 2008/401 (C.15). - Enabling power: Corporate Manslaughter and Corporate Homicide Act 2007, ss. 24 (4) (b), 27 (1). Bringing into operation various provisions of the 2007 Act on 06.04.2008. - Issued: 25.02.2008. Made: 14.02.2008. Effect: None. Territorial extent & classification: E/W/S/NI. General. - 2p.: 30 cm. - 978-0-11-080969-4 £3.00

The Crime (International Co-operation) Act 2003 (Commencement No. 4) Order 2008 No. 2008/3009 (C.130). - Enabling power: Crime (International Co-operation) Act 2003, s. 94 (1) (4). Bringing into operation various provisions of the 2003 Act on the date on which the convention on driving disqualifications applies to both the United Kingdom and Ireland and 17.12.2008 in accord. with arts. 2 & 3. - Issued: 26.11.2008. Made: 19.11.2008. Effect: None. Territorial extent & classification: E/W/S/NI. General. - 4p.: 30 cm. - 978-0-11-147037-4 £4.00

The Scotland Act 1998 (Agency Arrangements) (Specification) (No. 2) Order 2008 No. 2008/1788. - Enabling power: Scotland Act 1998, ss. 93 (3), 113 (2) (3). - Issued: 15.07.2008. Made: 09.07.2008. Laid: 16.07.2008. Laid before the Scottish Parliament: 16.07.2008. Coming into force: 03.10.2008. Effect: None. Territorial extent & classification: GB. General. - 8p.: 30 cm. - 978-0-11-082016-3 £3.00

Criminal law, England

The Criminal Justice and Immigration Act 2008 (Commencement No. 5) Order 2008 No. 2008/3260 (C.149). - Enabling power: Criminal Justice and Immigration Act 2008, s. 153 (5) (a) (7). Bringing into operation various provisions of the 2008 Act on 19.12.2008, 01.01.2009 in accord. with art. 2. - Issued: 23.12.2008. Made: 18.12.2008. Effect: None. Territorial extent & classification: E/W (some aspects E. only). General. - 4p.: 30 cm. - 978-0-11-147227-9 £4.00

Criminal law, England and Wales

The Bail (Electronic Monitoring of Requirements) (Responsible Officer) Order 2008 No. 2008/2713. - Enabling power: Bail Act 1976, s. 3AC (2). - Issued: 17.10.2008. Made: 13.10.2008. Coming into force: 03.11.2008. Effect: S.I. 2002/844 revoked. Territorial extent & classification: E/W. General. - 4p.: 30 cm. - 978-0-11-084663-7 £4.00

The Costs in Criminal Cases (General) (Amendment) Regulations 2008 No. 2008/2448. - Enabling power: Prosecution of Offences Act 1985, ss. 19 (1) (3) (5), 19B, 20 (1). - Issued: 22.09.2008. Made: 15.09.2008. Laid: 18.09.2008. Coming into force: 13.10.2008. Effect: S.I. 1986/1335 amended. Territorial extent & classification: E/W. General. - 4p.: 30 cm. - 978-0-11-084251-6 £4.00

The Crime and Disorder Act 1998 (Additional Authorities) Order 2008 No. 2008/78. - Enabling power: Crime and Disorder Act 1998, s. 17 (4). - Issued: 21.01.2008. Made: 14.01.2008. Coming into force: 15.02.2008. Effect: 1998 c. 37 amended. Territorial extent & classification: E/W [applies only to part of E.]. General. - Supersedes Draft SI (ISBN 9780110788937) issued 09.11.2008. - 2p.: 30 cm. - 978-0-11-080845-1 £3.00

The Crime and Disorder Act 1998 (Responsible Authorities) Order 2008 No. 2008/2163. - Enabling power: Crime and Disorder Act 1998, s. 5 (1A). - Issued: 19.08.2008. Made: 13.08.2008. Laid: 15.08.2008. Coming into force: 12.09.2008. Effect: None. Territorial extent & classification: E/W. General. - 2p.: 30 cm. - 978-0-11-083804-5 £3.00

The Crime and Disorder (Prescribed Information) (Amendment) Regulations 2008 No. 2008/1406. - Enabling power: Crime and Disorder Act 1998, ss. 17A (2), 114 (1) (2). - Issued: 04.06.2008. Made: 28.05.2008. Laid: 02.06.2008. Coming into force: 23.06.2008. Effect: S.I. 2007/1831 amended. Territorial extent & classification: E/W. General. - 2p.: 30 cm. - 978-0-11-081767-5 £3.00

The Crime (International Co-operation) Act 2003 (Designation of Participating Countries) (England, Wales and Northern Ireland) Order 2008 No. 2008/2156. - Enabling power: Crime (International Co-operation) Act 2003, s. 50 (5) (a). - Issued: 14.08.2008. Made: 07.08.2008. Coming into force: In accord. with art. 1. Effect: None. Territorial extent & classification: E/W/NI. General. - Supersedes draft S.I. (ISBN 9780110817798) issued on 06.06.2008. - 2p.: 30 cm. - 978-0-11-083748-2 £3.00

The Criminal Justice Act 1988 (Offensive Weapons) (Amendment No. 2) Order 2008 No. 2008/2039. - Enabling power: Criminal Justice Act 1988, s. 141 (11D). - Issued: 01.08.2008. Made: 25.07.2008. Coming into force: 01.08.2008. Effect: S.I. 1988/2019 amended. Territorial extent & classification: E/W/NI. General. - Supersedes draft S.I. (ISBN 9780110817774) issued 09.06.2008. - 2p.: 30 cm. - 978-0-11-083649-2 £3.00

The Criminal Justice Act 1988 (Offensive Weapons) (Amendment) Order 2008 No. 2008/973. - Enabling power: Criminal Justice Act 1988, s. 141 (2) (11D). - Issued: 09.04.2008. Made: 03.04.2008. Coming into force: 06.04.2008. Effect: S.I. 1988/2019 amended. Territorial extent & classification: E/W/NI. General. - Supersedes draft SI (ISBN 9780110810324) issued 03.03.2008. - 4p.: 30 cm. - 978-0-11-081344-8 £3.00

The Criminal Justice Act 2003 (Commencement No. 21) Order 2008 No. 2008/1424 (C. 63). - Enabling power: Criminal Justice Act 2003, s. 336 (3) (4). Bringing into operation various provisions of the 2003 Act on 09.06.2008 in accord. with art. 2. - Issued: 09.06.2008. Made: 03.06.2008. Effect: None. Territorial extent & classification: E/W. General. - 8p.: 30 cm. - 978-0-11-081776-7 £3.00

The Criminal Justice and Immigration Act 2008 (Commencement No. 2 and Transitional and Saving Provisions) Order 2008 No. 2008/1586 (C.69). - Enabling power: Criminal Justice and Immigration Act 2008, s. 153 (4) (7) (8). Bringing into operation various provisions of the 2008 Act on 14.07.2008 & 15.07.2008 in accord. with art. 2. - Issued: 25.06.2008. Made: 17.06.2008. Effect: None. Territorial extent & classification: E/W//NI. General. - 8p.: 30 cm. - 978-0-11-081886-3 £3.00

The Criminal Justice and Immigration Act 2008 (Commencement No. 3 and Transitional Provisions) Order 2008 No. 2008/2712 (C.118). - Enabling power: Criminal Justice and Immigration Act 2008, s. 153 (4) (7). Bringing into operation various provisions of the 2008 Act on 03.11.2008 in accord. with art. 2. - Issued: 20.10.2008. Made: 13.10.2008. Effect: None. Territorial extent & classification: E/W/NI [some aspects E/W only]. General. - 8p.: 30 cm. - 978-0-11-084677-4 £5.00

The Criminal Justice and Immigration Act 2008 (Commencement No. 4 and Saving Provision) Order 2008 No. 2008/2993 (C.128). - Enabling power: Criminal Justice and Immigration Act 2008, s. 153 (7). Bringing into operation various provisions of the 2008 Act on 01.12.2008, 26.01.2009 in accord. with art. 2 and subject to art. 3. - Issued: 21.11.2008. Made: 15.11.2008. Effect: None. Territorial extent & classification: E/W/NI (some aspects E/W only). General. - 8p.: 30 cm. - 978-0-11-147015-2 £5.00

The Criminal Justice and Immigration Act 2008 (Transitory Provisions) Order 2008 No. 2008/1587. - Enabling power: Criminal Justice and Immigration Act 2008, s. 148 (3) (4) (a). - Issued: 24.06.2008. Made: 17.06.2008. Laid: 19.06.2008. Coming into force: 14.07.2008. Effect: None. Territorial extent & classification: E/W/NI [part also incl. S]. General. - 4p.: 30 cm. - 978-0-11-081880-1 £3.00

The Criminal Justice (Sentencing) (Curfew Condition) Order 2008 No. 2008/2768. - Enabling power: Criminal Justice Act 1991, s. 37A (4) (5) (b) & Criminal Justice Act 2003, ss. 253 (5), 330 (3) (a). - Issued: 24.10.2008. Made: 18.10.2008. Coming into force: 20.10.2008. Effect: S.I. 1999/9; 2005/986 revoked. Territorial extent & classification: E/W. General. - 4p.: 30 cm. - 978-0-11-084697-2 £4.00

The Discharge of Fines by Unpaid Work (Pilot Schemes) (Amendment) Order 2008 No. 2008/621. - Enabling power: Courts Act 2003, s.97 (5). - Issued: 11.03.2008. Made: 06.03.2008. Laid: 06.03.2008. Coming into force: 30.03.2008. Effect: S.I. 2004/2198 amended. Territorial extent & classification: E/W. General. - 2p.: 30 cm. - 978-0-11-081127-7 £3.00

The Penalties for Disorderly Behaviour (Amount of Penalty) (Amendment) Order 2008 No. 2008/3297. - Enabling power: Criminal Justice and Police Act 2001, s. 3 (1) (1A). - Issued: 07.01.2009. Made: 29.12.2008. Laid: 02.01.2009. Coming into force: 26.01.2009. Effect: S.I. 2002/1837 amended & S.I. 2004/2468; 2005/581 revoked. Territorial extent & classification: E/W. General. - Revoked by S.I. 2009/83 (ISBN 9780111473160). - 8p.: 30 cm. - 978-0-11-147242-2 £5.00

The Remand on Bail (Disapplication of Credit Period) Rules 2008 No. 2008/2793. - Enabling power: Criminal Justice Act 2003, s. 240A (4) (a) (6) & Criminal Justice and Immigration Act 2008, sch. 6, para. 2 (4) (a) (6). - Issued: 31.10.2008. Made: 27.10.2008. Coming into force: 03.11.2008. Effect: None. Territorial extent & classification: E/W. General. - Supersedes draft S.I. (ISBN 9780110819907) issued 11.07.2008. - 4p.: 30 cm. - 978-0-11-084745-0 £4.00

The Serious Crime Act 2007 (Commencement No. 3) Order 2008 No. 2008/2504 (C. 108). - Enabling power: Serious Crime Act 2007, s. 94 (1). Bringing into operation various provisions of the 2007 Act on 01.10.2008. - Issued: 29.09.2008. Made: 24.09.2008. Effect: None. Territorial extent & classification: E/W/NI. General. - 4p.: 30 cm. - 978-0-11-084271-4 £4.00

The Violent Crime Reduction Act 2006 (Commencement No. 5) Order 2008 No. 2008/791 (C.38). - Enabling power: Violent Crime Reduction Act 2006, s. 66 (2). Bringing into operation various provisions of the 2006 Act on 01.04.2008, 06.04.2008 in accord. with arts 2 & 3. - Issued: 28.03.2008. Made: 20.03.2008. Effect: None. Territorial extent & classification: E/W/NI. General. - 4p.: 30 cm. - 978-0-11-081280-9 £3.00

The Violent Crime Reduction Act 2006 (Commencement No.6) Order 2008 No. 2008/1407 (C. 62). - Enabling power: Violent Crime Reduction Act 2006, s. 66 (2). Bringing into operation various provisions of the 2006 Act on 05.06.2008 in accord. with art. 2. - Issued: 04.06.2008. Made: 29.05.2008. Effect: None. Territorial extent & classification: E/W. General. - 4p.: 30 cm. - 978-0-11-081768-2 £3.00

The Youth Justice Board for England and Wales (Amendment) Order 2008 No. 2008/3155. - Enabling power: Crime and Disorder Act 1998, s. 41 (6) (b). - Issued: 15.12.2008. Made: 06.12.2008. Coming into force: 07.12.2008 in accord. with art. 1. Effect: S.I. 2000/1160, 3371 amended. Territorial extent & classification: E/W. General. - Supersedes draft S.I. (ISBN 9780110847092) issued 27.10.2008. - 8p.: 30 cm. - 978-0-11-147141-8 £5.00

Criminal law, Northern Ireland

The Crime (International Co-operation) Act 2003 (Designation of Participating Countries) (England, Wales and Northern Ireland) Order 2008 No. 2008/2156. - Enabling power: Crime (International Co-operation) Act 2003, s. 50 (5) (a). - Issued: 14.08.2008. Made: 07.08.2008. Coming into force: In accord. with art. 1. Effect: None. Territorial extent & classification: E/W/NI. General. - Supersedes draft S.I. (ISBN 9780110817798) issued on 06.06.2008. - 2p.: 30 cm. - 978-0-11-083748-2 £3.00

The Criminal Justice Act 1988 (Offensive Weapons) (Amendment No. 2) Order 2008 No. 2008/2039. - Enabling power: Criminal Justice Act 1988, s. 141 (11D). - Issued: 01.08.2008. Made: 25.07.2008. Coming into force: 01.08.2008. Effect: S.I. 1988/2019 amended. Territorial extent & classification: E/W/NI. General. - Supersedes draft S.I. (ISBN 9780110817774) issued 09.06.2008. - 2p.: 30 cm. - 978-0-11-083649-2 £3.00

The Criminal Justice Act 1988 (Offensive Weapons) (Amendment) Order 2008 No. 2008/973. - Enabling power: Criminal Justice Act 1988, s. 141 (2) (11D). - Issued: 09.04.2008. Made: 03.04.2008. Coming into force: 06.04.2008. Effect: S.I. 1988/2019 amended. Territorial extent & classification: E/W/NI. General. - Supersedes draft SI (ISBN 9780110810324) issued 03.03.2008. - 4p.: 30 cm. - 978-0-11-081344-8 £3.00

The Criminal Justice Act 2003 (Commencement No. 19) Order 2008 No. 2008/694 (C.28). - Enabling power: Criminal Justice Act 2003, s. 336 (3). Bringing into operation, for Northern Ireland, various provisions of the 2003 Act on 01.04.2008 in accord. with art. 2. - Issued: 03.04.2008. Made: 10.03.2008. Effect: None. Territorial extent & classification: NI. General. - 8p.: 30 cm. - 978-0-11-080090-5 £3.00

The Criminal Justice and Immigration Act 2008 (Commencement No. 2 and Transitional and Saving Provisions) Order 2008 No. 2008/1586 (C.69). - Enabling power: Criminal Justice and Immigration Act 2008, s. 153 (4) (7) (8). Bringing into operation various provisions of the 2008 Act on 14.07.2008 & 15.07.2008 in accord. with art. 2. - Issued: 25.06.2008. Made: 17.06.2008. Effect: None. Territorial extent & classification: E/W/NI. General. - 8p.: 30 cm. - 978-0-11-081886-3 £3.00

The Criminal Justice and Immigration Act 2008 (Commencement No. 3 and Transitional Provisions) Order 2008 No. 2008/2712 (C.118). - Enabling power: Criminal Justice and Immigration Act 2008, s. 153 (4) (7). Bringing into operation various provisions of the 2008 Act on 03.11.2008 in accord. with art. 2. - Issued: 20.10.2008. Made: 13.10.2008. Effect: None. Territorial extent & classification: E/W/NI [some aspects E/W only]. General. - 8p.: 30 cm. - 978-0-11-084677-4 £5.00

The Criminal Justice and Immigration Act 2008 (Commencement No. 4 and Saving Provision) Order 2008 No. 2008/2993 (C.128). - Enabling power: Criminal Justice and Immigration Act 2008, s. 153 (7). Bringing into operation various provisions of the 2008 Act on 01.12.2008, 26.01.2009 in accord. with art. 2 and subject to art. 3. - Issued: 21.11.2008. Made: 15.11.2008. Effect: None. Territorial extent & classification: E/W/NI (some aspects E/W only). General. - 8p.: 30 cm. - 978-0-11-147015-2 £5.00

The Criminal Justice and Immigration Act 2008 (Transitory Provisions) Order 2008 No. 2008/1587. - Enabling power: Criminal Justice and Immigration Act 2008, s. 148 (3) (4) (a). - Issued: 24.06.2008. Made: 17.06.2008. Laid: 19.06.2008. Coming into force: 14.07.2008. Effect: None. Territorial extent & classification: E/W/NI [part also incl. S]. General. - 4p.: 30 cm. - 978-0-11-081880-1 £3.00

The Domestic Violence, Crime and Victims Act 2004 (Commencement No. 10) Order 2008 No. 2008/3065 (C.131). - Enabling power: Domestic Violence, Crime and Victims Act 2004, s. 60. Bringing into operation, for Northern Ireland, various provisions of the 2004 Act on 14.12.2008 in accord. with art. 2. - Issued: 02.12.2008. Made: 17.03.2008. Effect: None. Territorial extent & classification: NI. General. - 2p.: 30 cm. - 978-0-11-081698-2 £4.00

The Police Act 1997 (Commencement No. 11) Order 2008 No. 2008/692 (C. 27). - Enabling power: Police Act 1997, s. 135. Bringing into operation for Northern Ireland various provisions of the 1997 Act on 01.04.2008. - Issued: 03.04.2008. Made: 10.03.2008. Effect: None. Territorial extent & classification: NI. General. - 4p.: 30 cm. - 978-0-11-080091-2 £3.00

The Police Act 1997 (Criminal Records)(Disclosure) Regulations (Northern Ireland) 2008 No. 2008/542. - Enabling power: Police Act 1997, ss. 112 (1) (a), 113B (9), 125 (1) (5). - Issued: 06.03.2008. Made: 27.02.2008. Laid: 05.03.2008. Coming into force: 01.04.2008. Effect: None. Territorial extent & classification: NI. General. - 16p.: 30 cm. - 978-0-11-080088-2 £3.00

The Serious Crime Act 2007 (Commencement No. 3) Order 2008 No. 2008/2504 (C. 108). - Enabling power: Serious Crime Act 2007, s. 94 (1). Bringing into operation various provisions of the 2007 Act on 01.10.2008. - Issued: 29.09.2008. Made: 24.09.2008. Effect: None. Territorial extent & classification: E/W/NI. General. - 4p.: 30 cm. - 978-0-11-084271-4 £4.00

The Serious Organised Crime and Police Act 2005 (Commencement No. 12) Order 2008 No. 2008/697 (C.29). - Enabling power: Serious Organised Crime and Police Act 2005, s. 178 (8) (9). Bringing into operation for Northern Ireland various provisions of the 2005 Act on 01.04.2008. - Issued: 03.04.2008. Made: 10.03.2008. Effect: None. Territorial extent & classification: NI. General. - 8p.: 30 cm. - 978-0-11-080092-9 £3.00

The Violent Crime Reduction Act 2006 (Commencement No. 5) Order 2008 No. 2008/791 (C.38). - Enabling power: Violent Crime Reduction Act 2006, s. 66 (2). Bringing into operation various provisions of the 2006 Act on 01.04.2008, 06.04.2008 in accord. with arts 2 & 3. - Issued: 28.03.2008. Made: 20.03.2008. Effect: None. Territorial extent & classification: E/W/NI. General. - 4p.: 30 cm. - 978-0-11-081280-9 £3.00

Criminal procedure, England and Wales

The Criminal Justice and Immigration Act 2008 (Commencement No. 2 and Transitional and Saving Provisions) Order 2008 No. 2008/1586 (C.69). - Enabling power: Criminal Justice and Immigration Act 2008, s. 153 (4) (7) (8). Bringing into operation various provisions of the 2008 Act on 14.07.2008 & 15.07.2008 in accord. with art. 2. - Issued: 25.06.2008. Made: 17.06.2008. Effect: None. Territorial extent & classification: E/W/NI. General. - 8p.: 30 cm. - 978-0-11-081886-3 £3.00

The Criminal Justice and Immigration Act 2008 (Commencement No. 3 and Transitional Provisions) Order 2008 No. 2008/2712 (C.118). - Enabling power: Criminal Justice and Immigration Act 2008, s. 153 (4) (7). Bringing into operation various provisions of the 2008 Act on 03.11.2008 in accord. with art. 2. - Issued: 20.10.2008. Made: 13.10.2008. Effect: None. Territorial extent & classification: E/W/NI [some aspects E/W only]. General. - 8p.: 30 cm. - 978-0-11-084677-4 £5.00

Criminal procedure, Northern Ireland

The Criminal Justice and Immigration Act 2008 (Commencement No. 2 and Transitional and Saving Provisions) Order 2008 No. 2008/1586 (C.69). - Enabling power: Criminal Justice and Immigration Act 2008, s. 153 (4) (7) (8). Bringing into operation various provisions of the 2008 Act on 14.07.2008 & 15.07.2008 in accord. with art. 2. - Issued: 25.06.2008. Made: 17.06.2008. Effect: None. Territorial extent & classification: E/W/NI. General. - 8p.: 30 cm. - 978-0-11-081886-3 *£3.00*

The Criminal Justice and Immigration Act 2008 (Commencement No. 3 and Transitional Provisions) Order 2008 No. 2008/2712 (C.118). - Enabling power: Criminal Justice and Immigration Act 2008, s. 153 (4) (7). Bringing into operation various provisions of the 2008 Act on 03.11.2008 in accord. with art. 2. - Issued: 20.10.2008. Made: 13.10.2008. Effect: None. Territorial extent & classification: E/W/NI [some aspects E/W only]. General. - 8p.: 30 cm. - 978-0-11-084677-4 *£5.00*

Cultural objects

The Protection of Cultural Objects on Loan (Publication and Provision of Information) Regulations 2008 No. 2008/1159. - Enabling power: Tribunals, Courts and Enforcement Act 2007, s. 134 (2) (e) (9) & Welsh Language Act 1993, s. 26. - Issued: 01.05.2008. Made: 21.04.2008. Laid: 23.04.2008. Coming into force: 20.05.2008. Effect: None. Territorial extent & classification: E/W/S/NI. General. - 8p.: 30 cm. - 978-0-11-081428-5 *£3.00*

Cultural objects, England and Wales

The Tribunals, Courts and Enforcement Act 2007 (Commencement No. 4) Order 2008 No. 2008/1158 (C.51). - Enabling power: Tribunals, Courts and Enforcement Act 2007, s. 148 (3). Bringing into operation, in relation to Wales & Northern Ireland, various provisions of the 2007 Act on 22.04.2008. - Issued: 28.04.2008. Made: 21.04.2008. Effect: None. Territorial extent & classification: E/W/NI. General. - 4p.: 30 cm. - 978-0-11-081402-5 *£3.00*

Cultural objects, Northern Ireland

The Tribunals, Courts and Enforcement Act 2007 (Commencement No. 4) Order 2008 No. 2008/1158 (C.51). - Enabling power: Tribunals, Courts and Enforcement Act 2007, s. 148 (3). Bringing into operation, in relation to Wales & Northern Ireland, various provisions of the 2007 Act on 22.04.2008. - Issued: 28.04.2008. Made: 21.04.2008. Effect: None. Territorial extent & classification: E/W/NI. General. - 4p.: 30 cm. - 978-0-11-081402-5 *£3.00*

Customs

The Cat and Dog Fur (Control of Import, Export and Placing on the Market) Regulations 2008 No. 2008/2795. - Enabling power: European Communities Act 1972, s. 2 (2). - Issued: 30.10.2008. Made: 26.10.2008. Laid: 28.10.2008. Coming into force: 31.12.2008. Effect: None. Territorial extent & classification: E/W/S/NI. General. - EC note: These Regulations implement in the UK Regulation (EC) No 1523/2007 which prohibits the import, export and placing on the market of cat and dog fur. - 8p.: 30 cm. - 978-0-11-084746-7 *£5.00*

The Export Control (Burma) Order 2008 No. 2008/1098. - Enabling power: European Communities Act 1972, s. 2 (2), sch. 2, para. 1A & Export Control Act 2002, ss. 1, 2, 3, 4, 5, 7. - Issued: 25.04.2008. Made: 21.04.2008. Laid: 22.04.2008. Coming into force: 23.04.2008. Effect: S.I. 2006/2682 revoked. Territorial extent & classification: E/W/S/NI. General. - EC note: This Order creates offences relating to the provisions of Council Regulation (EC) No 194/2008 ("the Regulation") that fall within the remit of the Department for Business, Enterprise and Regulatory Reform. The Regulation itself implements at European Community level the provisions of Common Position 2007/750/CFSP (amending Common Position 2006/318/CFSP) which strengthens the existing European Union sanctions and embargoes relating to Burma. It replaces Council Regulation (EC) No 817/2006 ("the previous regulation"). - 8p.: 30 cm. - 978-0-11-081384-4 *£3.00*

The Export Control (Democratic Republic of Congo) (Amendment) (No. 2) Order 2008 No. 2008/1964. - Enabling power: Export Control Act 2002, ss. 3, 4, 5, 7. - Issued: 30.07.2008. Made: 22.07.2008. Laid: 23.07.2008. Coming into force: 24.07.2008. Effect: S.I. 2005/1677 amended. Territorial extent & classification: E/W/S/NI. General. - EC note: This Order implements in part Council Regulation (EC) 666/2008 which amends Council Regulation (EC) 889/2005. - 2p.: 30 cm. - 978-0-11-083571-6 *£3.00*

The Export Control (Iran) (Amendment) Order 2008 No. 2008/3063. - Enabling power: European Communities Act 1972, s. 2 (2) & Export Control Act 2002, ss. 1, 2, 3, 4, 5, 7. - Issued: 01.12.2008. Made: 25.11.2008. Laid: 26.11.2008. Coming into force: 27.11.2008. Effect: S.I. 2007/1526 amended. Territorial extent & classification: E/W/S/NI. General. - 2p.: 30 cm. - 978-0-11-147067-1 *£4.00*

The Export Control Order 2008 No. 2008/3231. - Enabling power: European Communities Act 1972, s. 2 (2), sch. 2, para. 1A & Export Control Act 2002, ss. 1, 2, 3, 4, 5, 7. - Issued: 23.12.2008. Made: 15.12.2008. Laid: 17.12.2008. Coming into force: 06.04.2009. Effect: S.I. 2005/232, 3257; 2007/1334 amended & S.I. 2003/2764, 2765; 2004/318, 1049, 1050, 2561, 2741; 2005/443, 445, 468; 2006/300, 1331, 1696, 1719, 2271, 2683; 2007/1863; 2008/639, 1281, 1805, 3161 revoked. Territorial extent & classification: E/W/S/NI. General. - EC note: This Order is now where penalty and licensing provisions are to be found relating to Council Regulation (EC) No 1334/2000 (the "dual-use Regulation") and Council Regulation (EC) No 1236/2005 (the "torture Regulation"). These cover, respectively, goods, software and technology that can be used for both civil and military purposes and goods that can be used for capital punishment, torture or other cruel, inhuman or degrading treatment or punishment. Part 2 of the Order also supplements the directly applicable provisions of these Regulations by extending their controls, in particular to cover additional goods (see articles 4 and 5), intra-Community transfers and goods in transit (in the circumstances set out in 6, 7, 8 and 9) and different types of transfers of technology (see articles 10, 11 and 12). With correction slip dated August 2009. - 60p.: 30 cm. - 978-0-11-147206-4 £9.00

The Export Control (Security and Para-military Goods) Order 2008 No. 2008/639. - Enabling power: Export Control Act 2002, ss. 1, 2, 4, 5, 7. - Issued: 13.03.2008. Made: 06.03.2008. Laid: 10.03.2008. Coming into force: 06.04.2008. Effect: S.I. 2003/2764 amended. Territorial extent & classification: E/W/S/NI. General. - Revoked by S.I. 2008/3231 (ISBN 9780111472064). - 2p.: 30 cm. - 978-0-11-081141-3 £3.00

The Export of Goods, Transfer of Technology and Provision of Technical Assistance (Control) (Amendment) (No. 2) Order 2008 No. 2008/3161. - Enabling power: Export Control Act 2002, ss. 1, 2, 4, 5, 7. - Issued: 16.12.2008. Made: 10.12.2008. Laid: 12.12.2008. Coming into force: 02.01.2009. Effect: S.I. 2003/2764 amended. Territorial extent & classification: E/W/S/NI. General. - Revoked by S.I. 2008/3231 (ISBN 9780111472064). - 4p.: 30 cm. - 978-0-11-147149-4 £4.00

The Export of Goods, Transfer of Technology and Provision of Technical Assistance (Control) (Amendment) Order 2008 No. 2008/1281. - Enabling power: Export Control Act 2002, ss. 1, 2, 4, 5, 7. - Issued: 20.05.2008. Made: 10.05.2008. Laid: 13.05.2008. Coming into force: 03.06.2008. Effect: S.I. 2003/2764 amended. Territorial extent & classification: E/W/S/NI. General. - Revoked by S.I. 2008/3231 (ISBN 9780111472064). - 24p.: 30 cm. - 978-0-11-081461-2 £4.00

The Trade in Goods (Categories of Controlled Goods) Order 2008 No. 2008/1805. - Enabling power: Export Control Act 2002, ss. 4, 5, 7. - Issued: 14.07.2008. Made: 02.07.2008. Laid: 09.07.2008. Coming into force: 01.10.2008. Effect: S.I 2003/2765; 2004/318 amended. Territorial extent & classification: E/W/S/NI. General. - Revoked by S.I. 2008/3231 (ISBN 9780111472064). - 12p.: 30 cm. - 978-0-11-082001-9 £3.00

Customs and excise

The Export Control (Democratic Republic of Congo) (Amendment) Order 2008 No. 2008/131. - Enabling power: Export Control Act 2002, ss. 3, 4, 5, 7. - Issued: 25.01.2008. Made: 22.01.2008. Laid: 23.01.2008. Coming into force: 24.01.2008. Effect: S.I. 2005/1677 amended. Territorial extent & classification: E/W/S/NI. General. - EC note: This Order implements in part Council Regulation 1377/2007 which amends Council Regulation 889/2005. - 4p.: 30 cm. - 978-0-11-080864-2 £3.00

Dangerous drugs

The Controlled Drugs (Drug Precursors)(Community External Trade) Regulations 2008 No. 2008/296. - Enabling power: European Communities Act 1972, s. 2 (2). - Issued: 12.02.2008. Made: 07.02.2008. Laid: 11.02.2008. Coming into force: 07.03.2008. Effect: S.I. 1991/1285; 1992/2914 revoked with savings. Territorial extent & classification: E/W/S/NI. General. - With correction slip dated July 2009. EC note: These Regulations implement Council Regulation (EC) No. 111/2005 which imposes obligations on operators in respect of the documentation, recording and labelling of scheduled substances (substances useful for the manufacture of controlled drugs, known as drug precursors). It also requires operators engaged in the export or import or in intermediary activities involving scheduled substances to have a licence where those substances are in Category 1 of the Annex to the Community Regulation and to register where those substances are in Category 2 of that Annex. It requires operators to notify the competent authorities about their export, import or intermediary activities and about any circumstances which suggest that scheduled substances intended for import, export or intermediary activities might be diverted for the illicit manufacture of narcotic drugs or psychotropic substances. The Community Regulation also imposes obligations on operators to obtain an export authorisation prior to exporting scheduled substances that require a customs declaration and to obtain an import authorisation prior to importing scheduled substances in Category 1 of the Annex to the Community Regulation. - 8p.: 30 cm. - 978-0-11-080933-5 £3.00

The Controlled Drugs (Drug Precursors)(Intra-Community Trade) Regulations 2008 No. 2008/295. - Enabling power: European Communities Act 1972, s. 2 (2). - Issued: 12.02.2008. Made: 07.02.2008. Laid: 11.02.2008. Coming into force: 07.03.2008. Effect: S.I. 1993/2166; 2004/850 revoked with savings. Territorial extent & classification: E/W/S/NI. General. - With correction slip dated July 2009. EC note: These Regulations implement Council Regulation (EC) 273/2004 which requires operators who possess or place on the market a scheduled substance (substances useful for the manufacture of controlled drugs, known as drug precursors) to have a licence where that substance is in Category 1 of Annex I to the Community Regulation and to register where that substance is in Category 2 of Annex I to that Regulation. It permits such licences to be issued either for a specified duration or to be subject to a reporting requirement and permits Member States to operate a special system of licensing and registration for particular persons. The Community Regulation requires operators to appoint a responsible officer before placing on the market a scheduled substance in Category 1 or 2 of Annex I to the Community Regulation and imposes obligations on operators in respect of the documentation, recording and labelling of such substances. It also requires operators to inform the competent authorities of any circumstances which suggest that scheduled substances might be diverted for the illicit manufacture of narcotic drugs or psychotropic substances and to provide those competent authorities every 6 months with a summary of the transactions involving scheduled substances used and supplied in that period. - 8p.: 30 cm. - 978-0-11-080932-8 £3.00

The Misuse of Drugs Act 1971 (Amendment) Order 2008 No. 2008/3130. - Enabling power: Misuse of Drugs Act 1971, s. 2 (2) (4). - Issued: 17.12.2008. Made: 10.12.2008. Coming into force: 26.01.2009. Effect: 1971 c. 38 amended. Territorial extent & classification: E/W/S/NI. General. - Supersedes draft S.I. (ISBN 9780110846088) issued 15.10.2008. - 2p.: 30 cm. - 978-0-11-147160-9 £4.00

Dangerous drugs, Wales

The Controlled Drugs (Supervision of Management and Use) (Wales) Regulations 2008 No. 2008/3239 (W.286). - Enabling power: Health Act 2006, ss. 17, 18, 20 (3) (7), 79 (3). - Issued: 12.01.2009. Made: 16.12.2008. Laid before the National Assembly for Wales: 18.12.2008. Coming into force: 09.01.2009. Effect: None. Territorial extent & classification: W. General. - In English and Welsh. Welsh title: Rheoliadau Cyffuriau a Reolir (Goruchwylio Rheolaeth a Defnydd) (Cymru) 2008. - 32p.: 30 cm. - 978-0-11-091922-5 £9.00

Data protection

The Data Protection Act 1998 (Commencement No. 2) Order 2008 No. 2008/1592 (C.71). - Enabling power: Data Protection Act 1998, s. 75 (3). Bringing into operation various provisions of the 1998 Act on 07.07.2008. - Issued: 24.06.2008. Made: 19.06.2008. Effect: None. Territorial extent & classification: UK. General. - 4p.: 30 cm. - 978-0-11-081885-6 £3.00

The Safeguarding Vulnerable Groups Act 2006 (Commencement No. 2) Order 2008 No. 2008/1320 (C.57). - Enabling power: Safeguarding Vulnerable Groups Act 2006, ss. 61 (5), 65. Bringing into operation various provisions of the 2006 Act on 19.05.2008. - Issued: 21.05.2008. Made: 14.05.2008. Effect: None. Territorial extent & classification: E/W (and UK in respect of the commencement of amendments to the Data Protection Act 1998). General. - 8p.: 30 cm. - 978-0-11-081479-7 £3.00

Defence

The Air Force Act 1955 (Part 1) (Amendment) Regulations 2008 No. 2008/1585. - Enabling power: Air Force Act 1955, ss. 22, 23. - Issued: 24.06.2008. Made: 18.06.2008. Laid: 20.06.2008. Coming into force: 14.07.2008. Effect: S.I. 2007/651 amended. Territorial extent & classification: E/W/S/NI. General. - 12p.: 30 cm. - 978-0-11-081877-1 £3.00

The Armed Forces Act 2006 (Commencement No. 3) Order 2008 No. 2008/1650 (C.72). - Enabling power: Armed Forces Act 2006, s. 383 (2). Bringing into operation various provisions of the 2006 Act on 01.10.2008. - Issued: 30.06.2008. Made: 24.06.2008. Effect: None. Territorial extent & classification: E/W/S/NI. General. - 4p.: 30 cm. - 978-0-11-081909-9 £3.00

The Armed Forces (Alignment of Service Discipline Acts) (No. 2) Order 2008 No. 2008/3294. - Enabling power: Armed Forces Act 2006, s. 381 (1). - Issued: 30.12.2008. Made: 22.12.2008. Coming into force: 23.12.2008 in accord. with art.1. Effect: 1955 c.18, c.19; 1957 c.53 amended. Territorial extent & classification: E/W/S/NI. General. - Supersedes draft S.I. (ISBN 9780110846880) issued 24.10.2008. - 4p.: 30 cm. - 978-0-11-147239-2 £4.00

The Armed Forces (Alignment of Service Discipline Acts) Order 2008 No. 2008/1694. - Enabling power: Armed Forces Act 2006, s. 381 (1). - Issued: 03.07.2008. Made: 27.06.2008. Coming into force: 18.07.2008. Effect: 1955 c.18, c.19; 1957 c.53; 1976 c.52 amended. Territorial extent & classification: E/W/S/NI. General. - Supersedes draft S.I. (ISBN 9780110817507) issued 28.05.2008. - 20p.: 30 cm. - 978-0-11-081926-6 £3.50

The Armed Forces, Army, Air Force and Naval Discipline Acts (Continuation) Order 2008 No. 2008/1780. - Enabling power: Armed Forces Act 2006, s. 382 (3). - Issued: 16.07.2008. Made: 09.07.2008. Coming into force: 08.11.2008. Effect: None. Territorial extent & classification: E/W/S/NI. General. - Supersedes draft S.I. (ISBN 9780110817484) issued on 27.05.2008. - 2p.: 30 cm. - 978-0-11-083157-2 £3.00

The Armed Forces (Entry, Search and Seizure) (Amendment) Order 2008 No. 2008/1698. - Enabling power: Armed Forces Act 2001, ss. 10 (13), 11 (1), 31 (3). - Issued: 03.07.2008. Made: 27.06.2008. Laid: 01.07.2008. Coming into force: 21.07.2008. Effect: S.I. 2003/2273; 2006/3243 amended. Territorial extent & classification: E/W/S/NI. General. - 4p.: 30 cm. - 978-0-11-081929-7 £3.00

The Armed Forces (Service Complaints) (Consequential Amendments) Order 2008 No. 2008/1696. - Enabling power: Armed Forces Act 2006, s. 379 (1). - Issued: 03.07.2008. Made: 27.06.2008. Coming into force: 28.06.2008 in accord. with art. 1 (2). Effect: S.I. 1998/1833; 2000/1551; 2003/1660, 1661 amended. Territorial extent & classification: E/W/S/NI. General. - Supersedes draft S.I. (ISBN 9780110817491) issued 27.05.2008. - 4p.: 30 cm. - 978-0-11-081927-3 £3.00

The Armed Forces (Service Inquiries) Regulations 2008 No. 2008/1651. - Enabling power: Armed Forces Act 2006, s. 343. - Issued: 01.07.2008. Made: 25.06.2008. Laid: 27.06.2008. Coming into force: 01.10.2008. Effect: None. Territorial extent & classification: E/W/S/NI. General. - 16p.: 30 cm. - 978-0-11-081910-5 £3.00

The Army Terms of Service (Amendment etc.) Regulations 2008 No. 2008/1849. - Enabling power: Armed Forces Act 1966, s. 2. - Issued: 16.07.2008. Made: 10.07.2008. Laid: 15.07.2008. Coming into force: 06.08.2008. Effect: S.I. 2007/3382 amended & S.I. 1992/1366 revoked. Territorial extent & classification: E/W/S/NI. General. - 2p.: 30 cm. - 978-0-11-083169-5 £3.00

The Courts-Martial (Amendment) Rules 2008 No. 2008/1699. - Enabling power: Army Act 1955, s. 103; Air Force Act 1955, s. 103; and Naval Discipline Act 1957, s. 58. - Issued: 03.07.2008. Made: 27.06.2008. Laid: 01.07.2008. Coming into force: 21.07.2008. Effect: S.I. 2007/3442, 3443, 3444 amended. Territorial extent & classification: E/W/S/NI. General. - 2p.: 30 cm. - 978-0-11-081930-3 £3.00

The Criminal Procedure and Investigations Act 1996 (Application to the Armed Forces) Order 2008 No. 2008/635. - Enabling power: Criminal Procedure and Investigations Act 1996, ss. 78 (2) (a) (6) (a). - Issued: 13.03.2008. Made: 07.03.2008. Laid: 11.03.2008. Coming into force: 01.04.2008. Effect: None. Territorial extent & classification: E/W/S/NI. General. - Revoked by S.I. 2009/988 (ISBN 9780111478578) with saving. - 12p.: 30 cm. - 978-0-11-081153-6 £3.00

The Criminal Procedure and Investigations Act 1996 (Code of Practice) (Armed Forces) Order 2008 No. 2008/648. - Enabling power: Criminal Procedure and Investigations Act 1996, s. 78 (2) (b). - Issued: 17.03.2008. Made: 07.03.2008. Laid: 11.03.2008. Coming into force: 01.04.2008. Effect: None. Territorial extent & classification: E/W/S/NI. General. - Revoked by S.I. 2009/989 (ISBN 9780111478370) with saving. With correction slip dated March 2008. - 12p.: 30 cm. - 978-0-11-081220-5 £3.00

The Naval Medical Compassionate Fund (Amendment) Order 2008 No. 2008/1488. - Enabling power: Naval Medical Compassionate Fund Act 1915, s. 1. - Issued: 17.06.2008. Made: 11.06.2008. Coming into force: 12.06.2008. Effect: S.R. & O. 1915/769 amended. Territorial extent & classification: E/W/S/NI. General. - Revoked by S.I. 2008/3129 (ISBN 9780111471548). - 4p.: 30 cm. - 978-0-11-081848-1 £3.00

The Naval Medical Compassionate Fund Order 2008 No. 2008/3129. - Enabling power: Naval Medical Compassionate Fund Act 1915, s. 1. - Issued: 16.12.2008. Made: 10.12.2008. Coming into force: 11.12.2008. Effect: S.I. 1915/769; 1919/884; 1967/1484; 1977/819; 1988/1294; 1991/994; 1995/1965; 1996/3213; 2005/3185; 2008/1488 revoked. Territorial extent & classification: E/W/S/NI. General. - This Statutory Instrument has been made in consequence of defects in SI 2008/1488 and is being issued free of charge to all known recipients of that Statutory Instrument. - 4p.: 30 cm. - 978-0-11-147154-8 £4.00

The Protection of Military Remains Act 1986 (Designation of Vessels and Controlled Sites) Order 2008 No. 2008/950. - Enabling power: Protection of Military Remains Act 1986, s. 1 (2). - Issued: 04.04.2008. Made: 01.04.2008. Coming into force: 01.05.2008. Effect: S.I. 2006/2616 revoked. Territorial extent & classification: E/W/S/NI. General. - 4p.: 30 cm. - With correction slip. - 978-0-11-081332-5 £3.00

The Serious Organised Crime and Police Act 2005 (Commencement No. 13) Order 2008 No. 2008/1325 (C. 58). - Enabling power: Serious Organised Crime and Police Act 2005, s. 178 (8). Bringing into operation various provisions of the 2005 Act on 01.06.2008. - Issued: 23.05.2008. Made: 20.05.2008. Effect: None. Territorial extent & classification: E/W/S/NI. General. - 8p.: 30 cm. - 978-0-11-081489-6 £3.00

The Visiting Forces (Designation) Order 2008 No. 2008/299. - Enabling power: Visiting Forces Act 1952, ss. 1 (2), 15 (2). - Issued: 20.02.2008. Made: 12.02.2008. Laid: 19.02.2008. Coming into force: In accord. with art. 2. Effect: None. Territorial extent & classification: E/W/S/NI. General. - With correction slip dated February 2008. - 4p.: 30 cm. - 978-0-11-080957-1 £3.00

Dentists

The General Dental Council (Continuing Professional Development) (Dentists) Rules Order of Council 2008 No. 2008/1822. - Enabling power: Dentists Act 1984, ss. 34A (1) (4), 34B, 50A, 50C (5) (6). - Issued: 15.07.2008. Made: 04.07.2008. Coming into force: 01.08.2008. Effect: S.I. 2004/68 revoked. Territorial extent & classification: E/W/S/NI. General. - With Correction Slip dated January 2010. - 8p.: 30 cm. - 978-0-11-083119-0 £3.00

Designs

The Design Right (Semiconductor Topographies) (Amendment) (No.2) Regulations 2008 No. 2008/1434. - Enabling power: European Communities Act 1972, s. 2 (2). - Issued: 11.06.2008. Made: 05.06.2008. Laid: 06.06.2008. Coming into force: 01.07.2008. Effect: SI 1989/1100 amended. Territorial extent & classification: E/W/S/NI. General. - With correction slip dated August 2009. - 2p.: 30 cm. - 978-0-11-081797-2 £3.00

Devolution, Scotland

The Housing (Scotland) Act 2006 (Consequential Provisions) Order 2008 No. 2008/1889. - Enabling power: Scotland Act 1998, ss. 104, 112 (1), 113 (2) (3) (4) (5). - Issued: 21.07.2008. Made: 14.07.2008. Coming into force: 01.10.2008. Effect: 1975 c.24 modified. Territorial extent & classification: UK except for arts 2 & 3 which extent to S only. General. - 4p.: 30 cm. - 978-0-11-082019-4 £3.00

The Scotland Act 1998 (Agency Arrangements) (Specification) (No. 2) Order 2008 No. 2008/1788. - Enabling power: Scotland Act 1998, ss. 93 (3), 113 (2) (3). - Issued: 15.07.2008. Made: 09.07.2008. Laid: 16.07.2008. Laid before the Scottish Parliament: 16.07.2008. Coming into force: 03.10.2008. Effect: None. Territorial extent & classification: GB. General. - 8p.: 30 cm. - 978-0-11-082016-3 £3.00

The Scotland Act 1998 (Agency Arrangements) (Specification) Order 2008 No. 2008/1035. - Enabling power: Scotland Act 1998, ss. 93. - Issued: 15.04.2008. Made: 09.04.2008. Laid: 16.04.2008. Coming into force: 07.05.2008. Effect: None. Territorial extent & classification: GB. General. - 16p.: 30 cm. - 978-0-11-081605-0 £3.00

The Scotland Act 1998 (Transfer of Functions to the Scottish Ministers etc.) Order 2008 No. 2008/1776. - Enabling power: Scotland Act 1998, ss. 63 (1) (b), 113 (3) (4), 124 (2). - Issued: 16.07.2008. Made: 09.07.2008. Laid:-. Coming into force: 10.07.2008 in accord. with art. 1. Effect: None. Territorial extent & classification: E/W/S. General. - 4p.: 30 cm. - 978-0-11-082017-0 £3.00

The Scottish Parliament (Elections etc.) (Amendment) Order 2008 No. 2008/307 (S.3). - Enabling power: Scotland Act 1998, ss. 12 (1) (a), 113. - Issued: 14.02.2008. Made: 06.02.2008. Coming into force: 08.02.2008 in accord. with art. 1. Effect: S.I. 2007/937 amended. Territorial extent & classification: E/W/S/NI. General. - Supersedes draft SI (ISBN 9780110802275) issued 29.01.2008. - 32p.: 30 cm. - 978-0-11-081497-1 £5.50

Devolution, Wales

The National Assembly for Wales (Legislative Competence) (Education and Training) Order 2008 No. 2008/1036. - Enabling power: Government of Wales Act 2006, s. 95 (5). - Issued: 15.04.2008. Made: 09.04.2008. Coming into force: 10.04.2008 in accord. with art. 1. Effect: 2006 c. 32 amended. Territorial extent & classification: E/W. General. - 4p.: 30 cm. - 978-0-11-081367-7 £3.00

The National Assembly for Wales (Legislative Competence) (Social Welfare and Other Fields) Order 2008 No. 2008/3132. - Enabling power: Government of Wales Act 2006, s. 95 (1). - Issued: 14.01.2009. Made: 10.12.2008. Coming into force: 11.12.2008. In accord. with art. 1 (2). Effect: 2006 c. 32 amended. Territorial extent & classification: W. General. - This Statutory Instrument has been printed in substitution of the SI of the same number (different ISBN 9780111471616, issued 17.12.2008) and is being issued free of charge to all known recipients of that statutory instrument. - 8p.: 30 cm. - 978-0-11-147254-5 £5.00

The National Assembly for Wales (Legislative Competence) (Social Welfare and other Fields) Order 2008 No. 2008/3132. - Enabling power: Government of Wales Act 2006, s. 95 (1). - Issued: 17.12.2008. Made: 10.12.2008. Coming into force: In accord. with art. 1 (2) (3). Effect: 2006 c. 32 amended. Territorial extent & classification: W. General. - Supersedes draft S.I. (ISBN 9780110846620) issued 15.10.2008. Superseded by corrective reprint (ISBN 9780111472545). - 8p.: 30 cm. - 978-0-11-147161-6 £5.00

The National Assembly for Wales (Legislative Competence) (Social Welfare) Order 2008 No. 2008/1785. - Enabling power: Government of Wales Act 2006, s. 95 (1). - Issued: 16.07.2008. Made: 09.07.2008. Coming into force: 10.07.2008 in accord. with art. 1. Effect: 2006 c.32 amended. Territorial extent & classification: W. General. - Supersedes draft S.I. (ISBN 9780110819006) issued 25.06.2008. - 4p.: 30 cm. - 978-0-11-083132-9 £3.00

The Welsh Ministers (Transfer of Functions) (Wales) Order 2008 No. 2008/1786. - Enabling power: Government of Wales Act 2006, s. 58, sch. 4, para. 2. - Issued: 15.07.2008. Made: 09.07.2008. Coming into force: 10.07.2008. Effect: None. Territorial extent & classification: W. General. - Supersedes draft S.I. (ISBN 9780110818993) issued 25.06.2008. - 4p.: 30 cm. - 978-0-11-083137-4 £3.00

Diplomatic Service

The Consular Fees Order 2008 No. 2008/676. - Enabling power: Consular Fees Act 1980, s. 1 (1). - Issued: 18.03.2008. Made: 12.03.2008. Coming into force: 01.04.2008. Effect: S.I. 2007/649, 1680, 2124 revoked. Territorial extent & classification: E/W/S/NI. General. - Revoked by S.I. 2009/700 (ISBN 9780111477038). - 12p.: 30 cm. - 978-0-11-081228-1 £3.00

Disabled persons

The Disability Discrimination Code of Practice (Trade Organisations and Qualifications Bodies) (Revocation) Order 2008 No. 2008/1336. - Enabling power: Equality Act 2006, ss. 42 (3) (a) (5), 39 (2) (c). - Issued: 29.05.2008. Made: 22.05.2008. Laid: 29.05.2008. Coming into force: 23.06.2008. Effect: Disability Discrimination Act 1995 Code of Practice for Trade Organisations and Qualifications Bodies (ISBN 9780117034181) referred to in S.I. 2004/2302 is revoked. Territorial extent & classification: E/W/S. General- 2p.: 30 cm. - 978-0-11-081759-0 £3.00

The Disability Discrimination Code of Practice (Trade Organisations, Qualifications Bodies and General Qualifications Bodies) (Commencement) Order 2008 No. 2008/1335. - Enabling power: Equality Act 2006, ss. 14 (8) (b), 39 (2) (c). Bringing into operation the Disability Discrimination Act 1995 Code of Practice for Trade Organisations, Qualifications Bodies and General Qualifications Bodies (ISBN 9781842060490) on 23.06.2008 in accord. with art. 2. - Issued: 29.05.2008. Made: 22.05.2008. Effect: None. Territorial extent & classification: E/W/S. General- 2p.: 30 cm. - 978-0-11-081760-6 £3.00

The Disability Discrimination (General Qualifications Bodies) (Relevant Qualifications, Reasonable Steps and Physical Features) (Amendment) Regulations 2008 No. 2008/2159. - Enabling power: Disability Discrimination Act 1995, ss. 31AA (4), 31AD (6), 31AF. - Issued: 19.08.2008. Made: 11.08.2008. Laid: 19.08.2008. Coming into force: 24.10.2008. Effect: S.I. 2007/1764 amended. Territorial extent & classification: E/W/S. General. - 2p.: 30 cm. - 978-0-11-083847-2 £3.00

The Disability Discrimination (Public Authorities) (Statutory Duties) (Amendment) Regulations 2008 No. 2008/641. - Enabling power: Disability Discrimination Act 1995, ss. 49D (1) (2), 67 (2) (3). - Issued: 13.03.2008. Made: 05.03.2008. Laid: 13.03.2008. Coming into force: 06.04.2008. Effect: S.I.2005/2966 amended. Territorial extent & classification: E/W/S. General. - 4p.: 30 cm. - 978-0-11-081145-1 £3.00

The Public Service Vehicles Accessibility (Amendment) Regulations 2008 No. 2008/1459. - Enabling power: Disability Discrimination Act 1995, ss. 45 (1), 67. - Issued: 12.06.2008. Made: 05.06.2008. Laid: 12.06.2008. Coming into force: 13.07.2008. Effect: S.I. 2000/1970 amended. Territorial extent & classification: E/W/S/NI. General. - 4p.: 30 cm. - 978-0-11-081806-1 £3.00

The Rail Vehicle Accessibility (B2007 Vehicles) Exemption Order 2008 No. 2008/925. - Enabling power: Disability Discrimination Act 1995, ss. 47(1) (1A) (3) (4), 67 (2). - Issued: 03.04.2008. Made: 30.03.2008. Coming into force: 31.03.2008. Effect: None. Territorial extent & classification: E/W/S. General. - Supersedes draft SI (ISBN 9780110808970) issued 07.02.2008. - 8p.: 30 cm. - 978-0-11-081321-9 £3.00

The Rail Vehicle Accessibility Exemption Orders (Parliamentary Procedures) Regulations 2008 No. 2008/2975. - Enabling power: Disability Discrimination Act 1995, ss. 67 (2) (3) (b), 67A (3). - Issued: 24.11.2008. Made: 14.11.2008. Coming into force: 15.11.2008. Effect: None. Territorial extent & classification: E/W/S. General. - Supersedes draft S.I. (ISBN 9780110845821) issued 14.10.2008. - 4p.: 30 cm. - 978-0-11-147012-1 £4.00

The Rail Vehicle Accessibility (Interoperable Rail System) Regulations 2008 No. 2008/1746. - Enabling power: European Communities Act 1972, s. 2 (2) & Disability Discrimination Act 1995, s. 46 (1) & Transport Act 2000, s. 247. - Issued: 10.07.2008. Made: 02.07.2008. Coming into force: In accord. with reg. 1. Effect: 2005 c.13 & S.I. 1998/2456; 2006/397 amended. Territorial extent & classification: E/W/S/NI. General. - EC note: These Regulations pave the way for the introduction on the 1st July 2008 of European accessibility standards for passenger rail vehicles on the "interoperable rail system". Supersedes draft S.I. (ISBN 9780110817477) issued 28.05.2008. - 8p.: 30 cm. - 978-0-11-081967-9 £3.00

The Rail Vehicle Accessibility (London Underground Victoria Line 09TS Vehicles) Exemption Order 2008 No. 2008/2969. - Enabling power: Disability Discrimination Act 1995, ss. 47 (1) (1A) (3) (a) (4), 67 (2). - Issued: 24.11.2008. Made: 14.11.2008. Coming into force: 15.11.2008. Effect: None. Territorial extent & classification: E/W/S. General. - Supersedes draft S.I. (ISBN 9780110845579) issued 14.10.2008. - 4p.: 30 cm. - 978-0-11-147011-4 £4.00

Disclosure of information

The Serious Crime Act 2007 (Commencement No.1) Order 2008 No. 2008/219 (C.5). - Enabling power: Serious Crime Act 2007, s. 94 (1). Bringing into operation various provisions of the 2007 Act on 15.02.2008 & 01.03.2008. - Issued: 08.02.2008. Made: 05.02.2008. Effect: None. Territorial extent & classification: E/W/S/NI. General. - 4p.: 30 cm. - 978-0-11-080902-1 £3.00

The Serious Crime Act 2007 (Disclosure of Information by Revenue and Customs) Order 2008 No. 2008/403. - Enabling power: Serious Crime Act 2007, ss. 85 (7), 89 (1). - Issued: 22.02.2008. Made: 19.02.2008. Laid: 19.02.2008. Coming into force: 11.03.2008. Effect: None. Territorial extent & classification: E/W/S/NI. General. - 2p.: 30 cm. - 978-0-11-080966-3 £3.00

The Statistics and Registration Service Act 2007 (Commencement No. 2 and Transitional Provisions) Order 2008 No. 2008/839 (C.41). - Enabling power: Statistics and Registration Service Act 2007, s. 74. Bringing into operation various provisions of the 2007 Act on 01.04.2008. - Issued: 01.04.2008. Made: 20.03.2008. Effect: None. Territorial extent & classification: E/W/S/NI. General. - 2p.: 30 cm. - 978-0-11-081299-1 £3.00

The Statistics and Registration Service Act 2007 (Delegation of Functions) (Economic Statistics) Order 2008 No. 2008/792. - Enabling power: Statistics and Registration Service Act 2007, s. 24 (1) (4). - Issued: 28.03.2008. Made: 21.03.2008. Coming into force: 01.04.2008 in accord. with art. 1 (2). Effect: None. Territorial extent & classification: E/W/S/NI. General. - 2p.: 30 cm. - 978-0-11-081282-3 £3.00

Disclosure of information, England and Wales

The Serious Crime Act 2007 (Commencement No. 3) Order 2008 No. 2008/2504 (C. 108). - Enabling power: Serious Crime Act 2007, s. 94 (1). Bringing into operation various provisions of the 2007 Act on 01.10.2008. - Issued: 29.09.2008. Made: 24.09.2008. Effect: None. Territorial extent & classification: E/W/NI. General. - 4p.: 30 cm. - 978-0-11-084271-4 £4.00

The Serious Crime Act 2007 (Specified Anti-Fraud Organisations) Order 2008 No. 2008/2353. - Enabling power: Serious Crime Act 2007, s, 68 (8). - Issued: 09.09.2008. Made: 02.09.2008. Laid: 05.09.2008. Coming into force: 01.10.2008. Effect: None. Territorial extent & classification: E/W/NI. General. - 2p.: 30 cm. - 978-0-11-084059-8 £4.00

Disclosure of information, Northern Ireland

The Serious Crime Act 2007 (Commencement No. 3) Order 2008 No. 2008/2504 (C. 108). - Enabling power: Serious Crime Act 2007, s. 94 (1). Bringing into operation various provisions of the 2007 Act on 01.10.2008. - Issued: 29.09.2008. Made: 24.09.2008. Effect: None. Territorial extent & classification: E/W/NI. General. - 4p.: 30 cm. - 978-0-11-084271-4 £4.00

The Serious Crime Act 2007 (Specified Anti-Fraud Organisations) Order 2008 No. 2008/2353. - Enabling power: Serious Crime Act 2007, s, 68 (8). - Issued: 09.09.2008. Made: 02.09.2008. Laid: 05.09.2008. Coming into force: 01.10.2008. Effect: None. Territorial extent & classification: E/W/NI. General. - 2p.: 30 cm. - 978-0-11-084059-8 £4.00

Ecclesiastical law, England: Fees

The Parochial Fees Order 2008 No. 2008/2470. - Enabling power: Ecclesiastical Fees Measure 1986 no. 2, ss. 1, 2. - Issued: 03.10.2008. Laid before the General Synod in draft: 06.07.2008. Made (sealed by the Archbishop's Council): 18.09.2008. Laid before Parliament: 23.09.2008. Coming into force: 01.01.2009. Effect: S. I. 2007/2850 revoked. Territorial extent & classification: E. General. - 8p.: 30 cm. - 978-0-11-084264-6 £5.00

Ecclesiastical law, England and Wales

The Grants to the Churches Conservation Trust Order 2008 No. 2008/842. - Enabling power: Redundant Churches and other Religious Buildings Act 1969, s. 1. - Issued: 04.04.2008. Made: 19.03.2008. Coming into force: 20.03.2008. Effect: S.I. 2006/1008 revoked. Territorial extent & classification: E/W. General. - 2p.: 30 cm. - 978-0-11-081291-5 £3.00

The Payments to the Churches Conservation Trust Order 2008 No. 2008/1968. - Enabling power: Pastoral Measure 1983 (1983 no. 1), s. 53. - Issued: 04.08.2008. Made (Sealed by the Church Commissioners): 03.06.2008. Approved by the General Synod: 06.07.2008. Laid before Parliament: 24.07.2008. Coming into force: 01.04.2009. Effect: S.I. 2005/3202 revoked. Territorial extent & classification: E/W. General. - 4p.: 30 cm. - 978-0-11-083624-9 £3.00

Ecclesiastical law, England and Wales: Fees

The Ecclesiastical Judges, Legal Officers and Others (Fees) Order 2008 No. 2008/1970. - Enabling power: Ecclesiastical Fees Measure 1986, s. 6. - Issued: 04.08.2008. Made (approved by the General Synod): 04.07.2008. Laid: 24.07.2008. Coming into force: 01.01.2009. Effect: S.I. 2007/2340 revoked. Territorial extent & classification: E/W. General. - 12p.: 30 cm. - 978-0-11-083604-1 £3.00

The Legal Officers (Annual Fees) Order 2008 No. 2008/1969. - Enabling power: Ecclesiastical Fees Measure 1986, s. 5. - Issued: 04.08.2008. Made (approved by the General Synod) 04.07.2008. Laid: 24.07.2008. Coming into force: 01.01.2009. Effect: S.I. 2007/2336 revoked. Territorial extent & classification: E/W. General. - 12p.: 30 cm. - 978-0-11-083603-4 £3.00

Education

The Education (Student Loans) (Repayment) (Amendment) (No. 2) Regulations 2008 No. 2008/2715. - Enabling power: Teaching and Higher Education Act 1998, ss. 22, 42 & Sale of Student Loans Act 2008, ss. 5, 6 & Education (Scotland) Act 1980, ss. 73 (f), 73B. - Issued: 21.10.2008. Made: 12.10.2008. Laid: 21.10.2008. Coming into force: 14.11.2008. Effect: S.I. 2000/944 amended. Territorial extent & classification: E/W/S/NI. General. - Revoked by S.I. 2009/470 (ISBN 9780111475300). - 8p.: 30 cm. - 978-0-11-084678-1 £5.00

The Education (Student Loans) (Repayment) (Amendment) Regulations 2008 No. 2008/546. - Enabling power: Teaching and Higher Education Act 1998, ss. 22, 42 & Education (Scotland) Act 1980, ss. 73 (f), 73B. - Issued: 07.03.2008. Made: 28.02.2008. Laid: 07.03.2008. Coming into force: 01.04.2008. Effect: S.I. 2000/944 amended. Territorial extent & classification: UK in so far as they impose obligations on borrowers in relation to repayments of student loans granted in E/W/S. General. - Revoked by S.I. 2009/470 (ISBN 9780111475300). - 4p.: 30 cm. - 978-0-11-081078-2 £3.00

Education, England

The All Saints CE (Aided) Primary School (Designation as having a Religious Character) Order 2008 No. 2008/1875. - Enabling power: School Standards and Framework Act 1998, s. 69 (3) (4). - Issued: 22.07.2008. Made: 30.06.2008. Coming into force: 30.06.2008. Effect: None. Territorial extent & classification: E. Local. - 2p.: 30 cm. - 978-0-11-083291-3 £3.00

The All Saints CofE School (Designation as having a Religious Character) Order 2008 No. 2008/2092. - Enabling power: School Standards and Framework Act 1998, s. 69 (3) (4). - Issued: 07.08.2008. Made: 30.07.2008. Coming into force: 30.07.2008. Effect: None. Territorial extent & classification: E. Local. - 2p.: 30 cm. - 978-0-11-083700-0 £3.00

The Arnot St Mary CE Primary School (Designation as having a Religious Character) Order 2008 No. 2008/1874. - Enabling power: School Standards and Framework Act 1998, s. 69 (3) (4). - Issued: 22.07.2008. Made: 30.06.2008. Coming into force: 30.06.2008. Effect: None. Territorial extent & classification: E. Local. - 2p.: 30 cm. - 978-0-11-083249-4 £3.00

The Bede Sixth Form College, Billingham (Dissolution) Order 2008 No. 2008/812. - Enabling power: Further and Higher Education Act 1992, s. 27. - Issued: 02.04.2008. Made: 25.03.2008. Laid: 02.04.2008. Coming into force: 30.04.2008. Effect: None. Territorial extent & classification: E. General. - 2p.: 30 cm. - 978-0-11-081290-8 £3.00

The Bellefield Primary and Nursery School (Designation as having a Religious Character) Order 2008 No. 2008/1876. - Enabling power: School Standards and Framework Act 1998, s. 69 (3) (4). - Issued: 22.07.2008. Made: 30.06.2008. Coming into force: 30.06.2008. Effect: None. Territorial extent & classification: E. Local. - 2p.: 30 cm. - 978-0-11-083290-6 £3.00

The Canon Peter Hall CofE Primary School (Designation as having a Religious Character) Order 2008 No. 2008/2087. - Enabling power: School Standards and Framework Act 1998, s. 69 (3) (4). - Issued: 07.08.2008. Made: 30.07.2008. Coming into force: 30.07.2008. Effect: None. Territorial extent & classification: E. Local. - 2p.: 30 cm. - 978-0-11-083687-4 £3.00

The Canon Sharples Church of England Primary School and Nursery (Designation as having a Religious Character) Order 2008 No. 2008/2079. - Enabling power: School Standards and Framework Act 1998, s. 69 (3) (4). - Issued: 07.08.2008. Made: 30.07.2008. Coming into force: 30.07.2008. Effect: None. Territorial extent & classification: E. Local. - 2p.: 30 cm. - 978-0-11-083680-5 £3.00

The Christ the King Catholic and Church of England (VA) Centre for Learning (Designation as having a Religious Character) Order 2008 No. 2008/2078. - Enabling power: School Standards and Framework Act 1998, s. 69 (3) (4). - Issued: 07.08.2008. Made: 30.07.2008. Coming into force: 30.07.2008. Effect: None. Territorial extent & classification: E. Local. - 2p.: 30 cm. - 978-0-11-083679-9 £3.00

The Cleadon Village Church of England VA Primary School (Designation as having Religious Character) Order 2008 No. 2008/2080. - Enabling power: School Standards and Framework Act 1998, s. 69 (3) (4). - Issued: 07.08.2008. Made: 30.07.2008. Coming into force: 30.07.2008. Effect: None. Territorial extent & classification: E. Local. - 2p.: 30 cm. - 978-0-11-083676-8 £3.00

The Consistent Financial Reporting (England) (Amendment) Regulations 2008 No. 2008/46. - Enabling power: Education Act 2002, s. 44. - Issued: 17.01.2008. Made: 10.01.2008. Laid: 17.01.2008. Coming into force: 11.02.2008. Effect: S.I. 2003/373 amended. Territorial extent & classification: E. General. - 2p.: 30 cm. - 978-0-11-080832-1 £3.00

The Designation of Rural Primary Schools (England) Order 2008 No. 2008/2035. - Enabling power: Education and Inspections Act 2006, s. 15. - Issued: 31.07.2008. Made: 22.07.2008. Coming into force: 28.07.2008 in accord. with art. 1. Effect: S.I. 2007/817 revoked. Territorial extent & classification: E. General. - 2p.: 30 cm. - 978-0-11-083654-6 £3.00

The Designation of Schools having a Religious Character (England) (No. 2) Order 2008 No. 2008/3147. - Enabling power: School Standards and Framework Act 1998, ss. 69 (3) (4), 138 (7). - Issued: 15.12.2008. Made: 01.12.2008. Coming into force: 01.12.2008. Effect: None. Territorial extent & classification: E. General. - 8p.: 30 cm. - 978-0-11-147134-0 £5.00

The Designation of Schools Having a Religious Character (Independent Schools) (England) (No. 2) Order 2008 No. 2008/2340. - Enabling power: School Standards and Framework Act 1998, s. 69 (3). - Issued: 08.09.2008. Made: 29.08.2008. Coming into force: 29.08.2008. Effect: None. Territorial extent & classification: E. General. - 2p.: 30 cm. - 978-0-11-083995-0 £4.00

The Designation of Schools Having a Religious Character (Independent Schools) (England) Order 2008 No. 2008/783. - Enabling power: School Standards and Framework Act 1998, s. 69 (3). - Issued: 04.04.2008. Made: 17.03.2008. Coming into force: 17.03.2008. Effect: None. Territorial extent & classification: E. General. - 2p.: 30 cm. - 978-0-11-081272-4 £3.00

The Dewsbury College (Dissolution) Order 2008 No. 2008/1772. - Enabling power: Further and Higher Education Act 1992, s. 27. - Issued: 10.07.2008. Made: 03.07.2008. Laid: 10.07.2008. Coming into force: 01.08.2008. Effect: None. Territorial extent & classification: E. General. - 2p.: 30 cm. - 978-0-11-081987-7 £3.00

The Diocese of Carlisle (Educational Endowments) Order 2008 No. 2008/140. - Enabling power: Education Act 1996, ss. 554, 556. - Made: 24.01.2008. Coming into force: 28.01.2008. Effect: None. Territorial extent & classification: E. Local *Unpublished*

The Diocese of Chelmsford (Educational Endowments) Order 2008 No. 2008/1655. - Enabling power: Education Act 1996, ss. 554, 556. - Made: 25.06.2008. Coming into force: 16.07.2008. Effect: None. Territorial extent & classification: E. Local *Unpublished*

The Diocese of Chester (Educational Endowments) Order 2008 No. 2008/2948. - Enabling power: Education Act 1996, ss. 554, 556. - Made: 11.11.2008. Coming into force: 21.11.2008. Effect: None. Territorial extent & classification: E. Local *Unpublished*

The Diocese of Coventry (Educational Endowments) Order 2008 No. 2008/3005. - Enabling power: Education Act 1996, ss. 554, 556. - Made: 10.11.2008. Coming into force: 15.11.2008. Effect: None. Territorial extent & classification: E. Local *Unpublished*

The Diocese of Lichfield (Educational Endowments) Order 2008 No. 2008/1278. - Enabling power: Education Act 1996, ss. 554, 556. - Made: 12.05.2008. Coming into force: 28.05.2008. Effect: None. Territorial extent & classification: E. Local *Unpublished*

The East Devon College, Tiverton (Dissolution) Order 2008 No. 2008/1771. - Enabling power: Further and Higher Education Act 1992, s. 27. - Issued: 10.07.2008. Made: 03.07.2008. Laid: 10.07.2008. Coming into force: 01.08.2008. Effect: None. Territorial extent & classification: E. General. - 2p.: 30 cm. - 978-0-11-081986-0 *£3.00*

The Eccles College and Salford College (Dissolution) Order 2008 No. 2008/2773. - Enabling power: Further and Higher Education Act 1992, s. 27. - Issued: 27.10.2008. Made: 21.10.2008. Laid: 28.10.2008. Coming into force: 01.01.2009. Effect: None. Territorial extent & classification: E. General. - 2p.: 30 cm. - 978-0-11-084707-8 *£4.00*

The Education (Admissions Appeals Arrangements) (England) (Amendment) Regulations 2008 No. 2008/3092. - Enabling power: School Standards and Framework Act 1998, ss. 94 (5A), 95 (3A), 138 (7). - Issued: 11.12.2008. Made: 03.12.2008. Laid: 11.12.2008. Coming into force: 10.02.2009. Effect: S.I. 2002/2899 amended. Territorial extent & classification: E. General. - 8p.: 30 cm. - 978-0-11-147115-9 *£5.00*

The Education and Inspections Act 2006 (Commencement No. 1 and Saving Provisions) (Amendment) (England) Order 2008 No. 2008/54. - Enabling power: Education and Inspections Act 2006, ss. 181, 188. - Issued: 21.01.2008. Made: 14.01.2008. Coming into force: 17.01.2008. Effect: S.I. 2006/2990 (C.105) amended. Territorial extent & classification: E. General. - With Correction Slip dated February 2008. - 2p.: 30 cm. - 978-0-11-080841-3 *£3.00*

The Education and Inspections Act 2006 (Commencement No.7 and Transitional Provisions) Order 2008 No. 2008/1971 (C. 95). - Enabling power: Education and Inspections Act 2006, ss. 181 (2), 188 (3). - Issued: 29.07.2008. Made: 22.07.2008. Coming into force: 01.09.2008 in accord.with art. 2. Effect: None. Territorial extent & classification: E. General. - 8p.: 30 cm. - 978-0-11-083606-5 *£3.00*

The Education (Assisted Places) (Amendment) (England) Regulations 2008 No. 2008/1593. - Enabling power: Education (Schools) Act 1997, s. 3 (1) (2). - Issued: 26.06.2008. Made: 19.06.2008. Laid: 26.06.2008. Coming into force: 01.09.2008. Effect: S.I. 1997/1968 amended. Territorial extent & classification: E. General. - 4p.: 30 cm. - 978-0-11-081889-4 *£3.00*

The Education (Assisted Places) (Incidental Expenses) (Amendment) (England) Regulations 2008 No. 2008/1594. - Enabling power: Education (Schools) Act 1997, s. 3 (1) (3) (4). - Issued: 26.06.2008. Made: 19.06.2008. Laid: 26.06.2008. Coming into force: 01.09.2008. Effect: S.I. 1997/1969 amended. Territorial extent & classification: E. General. - 2p.: 30 cm. - 978-0-11-081890-0 *£3.00*

The Education (Budget Statements) (England) Regulations 2008 No. 2008/377. - Enabling power: School Standards and Framework Act 1998, ss. 52 (1) (1A) (3) (4), 138 (7). - Issued: 27.02.2008. Made: 15.02.2008. Laid: 27.02.2008. Coming into force: 20.03.2008. Effect: None. Territorial extent & classification: E. General. - 124p.: 30 cm. - With correction slip dated August 2008. - 978-0-11-080985-4 *£17.50*

The Education (Designated Institutions) (Amendment) (England) Order 2008 No. 2008/1643. - Enabling power: Education Reform Act 1988, s. 129 (1). - Issued: 02.07.2008. Made: 25.06.2008. Laid: 02.07.2008. Coming into force: 01.08.2008. Effect: S.I. 1989/282 amended. Territorial extent & classification: E. General. - 2p.: 30 cm. - 978-0-11-081913-6 *£3.00*

The Education (Hazardous Equipment and Materials in Schools) (Removal of Restrictions on Use) (England) Regulations 2008 No. 2008/1701. - Enabling power: Education Act 1996, ss. 347 (2), 546, 563. - Issued: 04.07.2008. Made: 26.06.2008. Laid: 04.07.2008. Coming into force: 01.09.2008. Effect: S.I. 1994/651 amended & S.I. 1989/351 revoked. Territorial extent & classification: E. General. - 2p.: 30 cm. - 978-0-11-081932-7 *£3.00*

The Education (Independent School Inspection Fees and Publication) (England) Regulations 2008 No. 2008/1801. - Enabling power: Education Act 2002, ss. 162A (3) (b), 162B (6), 210 (7). - Issued: 11.07.2008. Made: 07.07.2008. Laid: 11.07.2008. Coming into force: 01.09.2009. Effect: S.I. 2003/1926 revoked with savings. Territorial extent & classification: E. General. - Partially revoked by S.I. 2009/1607 (ISBN 9780111481899) with savings. - 4p.: 30 cm. - 978-0-11-081997-6 *£3.00*

The Education (Independent School Standards) (England) (Amendment) Regulations 2008 No. 2008/3253. - Enabling power: Education Act 2002, ss. 157 (1), 210 (7). - Issued: 29.12.2008. Made: 17.12.2008. Laid: 29.12.2008. Coming into force: 09.02.2009. Effect: S.I. 2003/1910 amended. Territorial extent & classification: E. General. - 8p.: 30 cm. - 978-0-11-147213-2 £5.00

The Education (Induction Arrangements for School Teachers) (England) Regulations 2008 No. 2008/657. - Enabling power: Teaching and Higher Education Act 1998, ss. 19, 42 (6). - Issued: 17.03.2008. Made: 07.03.2008. Laid: 17.03.2008. Coming into force: 01.09.2008. Effect: S.I. 2007/2782 amended & S.I. 2001/2897, 3938; 2002/2063; 2003/106, 2148; 2005/1740; 2007/172 revoked. Territorial extent & classification: E. General. - 20p.: 30 cm. - 978-0-11-081163-5 £3.50

The Education (Information About Individual Pupils) (England) (Amendment) Regulations 2008 No. 2008/3072. - Enabling power: Education Act 1996, ss. 537A (1), 569 (4). - Issued: 04.12.2008. Made: 26.11.2008. Laid: 04.12.2008. Coming into force: 01.09.2008. Effect: S.I. 2006/2601 amended. Territorial extent & classification: E. General. - 2p.: 30 cm. - 978-0-11-147078-7 £4.00

The Education (Listed Bodies) (England) (Amendment) Order 2008 No. 2008/2888. - Enabling power: Education Reform Act 1988, ss. 216 (2), 232 (5). - Issued: 13.11.2008. Made: 04.11.2008. Coming into force: 21.11.2008. Effect: S.I. 2007/2687 amended. Territorial extent & classification: E. General. - 4p.: 30 cm. - 978-0-11-084989-8 £4.00

The Education (National Curriculum) (Attainment Targets and Programme of Study in Art and Design in respect of the Third Key Stage) (England) Order 2008 No. 2008/1752. - Enabling power: Education Act 2002, ss. 87 (3) (a) (b) (5), 210 (7). - Issued: 10.07.2008 Made: 03.07.2008. Laid: 10.07.2008. Coming into force: 01.08.2008. Effect: S.I. 2000/1602 revoked with savings. Territorial extent & classification: E. General. - 4p.: 30 cm. - 978-0-11-081974-7 £3.00

The Education (National Curriculum) (Attainment Targets and Programme of Study in Design and Technology in respect of the Third Key Stage) (England) Order 2008 No. 2008/1754. - Enabling power: Education Act 2002, ss. 87 (3) (a) (b) (5), 210 (7). - Issued: 10.07.2008 Made: 03.07.2008. Laid: 10.07.2008. Coming into force: 01.08.2008. Effect: S.I. 2004/1794 revoked with savings. Territorial extent & classification: E. General. - 4p.: 30 cm. - 978-0-11-081977-8 £3.00

The Education (National Curriculum) (Attainment Targets and Programme of Study in Geography in respect of the Third Key Stage) (England) Order 2008 No. 2008/1756. - Enabling power: Education Act 2002, ss. 87 (3) (a) (b) (5), 210 (7). - Issued: 10.07.2008 Made: 03.07.2008. Laid: 10.07.2008. Coming into force: 01.08.2008. Effect: S.I. 2000/1605 revoked with savings. Territorial extent & classification: E. General. - 4p.: 30 cm. - 978-0-11-081978-5 £3.00

The Education (National Curriculum) (Attainment Targets and Programme of Study in History in respect of the Third Key Stage) (England) Order 2008 No. 2008/1757. - Enabling power: Education Act 2002, ss. 87 (3) (a) (b) (5), 210 (7). - Issued: 10.07.2008 Made: 03.07.2008. Laid: 10.07.2008. Coming into force: 01.08.2008. Effect: S.I. 2000/1606 revoked with savings. Territorial extent & classification: E. General. - 4p.: 30 cm. - 978-0-11-081980-8 £3.00

The Education (National Curriculum) (Attainment Targets and Programme of Study in Modern Foreign Languages in respect of the Third Key Stage) (England) Order 2008 No. 2008/1760. - Enabling power: Education Act 2002, ss. 87 (3) (a) (b) (5), 210 (7). - Issued: 10.07.2008 Made: 03.07.2008. Laid: 10.07.2008. Coming into force: 01.08.2008. Effect: S.I. 2004/1793 revoked with savings. Territorial extent & classification: E. General. - 4p.: 30 cm. - 978-0-11-081982-2 £3.00

The Education (National Curriculum) (Attainment Targets and Programme of Study in Music in respect of the Third Key Stage) (England) Order 2008 No. 2008/1761. - Enabling power: Education Act 2002, ss. 87 (3) (a) (b) (5), 210 (7). - Issued: 10.07.2008 Made: 03.07.2008. Laid: 10.07.2008. Coming into force: 01.08.2008. Effect: S.I. 2000/1597 revoked with savings. Territorial extent & classification: E. General. - 4p.: 30 cm. - 978-0-11-081983-9 £3.00

The Education (National Curriculum) (Attainment Targets and Programme of Study in Science in respect of the Third Key Stage) (England) Order 2008 No. 2008/1763. - Enabling power: Education Act 2002, ss. 87 (3) (a) (b) (5), 210 (7). - Issued: 10.07.2008 Made: 03.07.2008. Laid: 10.07.2008. Coming into force: 01.08.2008. Effect: S.I. 2004/1800 revoked with savings. Territorial extent & classification: E. General. - 4p.: 30 cm. - 978-0-11-081985-3 £3.00

The Education (National Curriculum) (Attainment Targets and Programmes of Study in Citizenship in respect of the Third and Fourth Key Stages) (England) Order 2008 No. 2008/1753. - Enabling power: Education Act 2002, ss. 87 (3) (a) (b) (5), 210 (7). - Issued: 10.07.2008 Made: 03.07.2008. Laid: 10.07.2008. Coming into force: 01.08.2008. Effect: S.I. 2000/1603 revoked with savings. Territorial extent & classification: E. General. - 4p.: 30 cm. - 978-0-11-081973-0 £3.00

The Education (National Curriculum) (Attainment Targets and Programmes of Study in English in respect of the Third and Fourth Key Stages) (England) Order 2008 No. 2008/1755. - Enabling power: Education Act 2002, ss. 87 (3) (a) (b) (5), 210 (7). - Issued: 10.07.2008 Made: 03.07.2008. Laid: 10.07.2008. Coming into force: 01.08.2008. Effect: S.I. 2000/1604 revoked with savings. Territorial extent & classification: E. General. - 4p.: 30 cm. - 978-0-11-081976-1 £3.00

The Education (National Curriculum) (Attainment Targets and Programmes of Study in Information and Communication Technology in respect of the Third and Fourth Key Stages) (England) Order 2008 No. 2008/1758. - Enabling power: Education Act 2002, ss. 87 (3) (a) (b) (5), 210 (7). - Issued: 10.07.2008. Made: 03.07.2008. Laid: 10.07.2008. Coming into force: 01.08.2008. Effect: S.I. 2000/1601 revoked with savings. Territorial extent & classification: E. General. - 4p.: 30 cm. - 978-0-11-081979-2 £3.00

The Education (National Curriculum) (Attainment Targets and Programmes of Study in Mathematics in respect of the Third and Fourth Key Stages) (England) Order 2008 No. 2008/1759. - Enabling power: Education Act 2002, ss. 87 (3) (a) (b) (5), 210 (7). - Issued: 10.07.2008 Made: 03.07.2008. Laid: 10.07.2008. Coming into force: 01.08.2008. Effect: S.I. 2000/1598 revoked with savings. Territorial extent & classification: E. General. - 4p.: 30 cm. - 978-0-11-081981-5 £3.00

The Education (National Curriculum) (Attainment Targets and Programmes of Study in Physical Education in respect of the Third and Fourth Key Stages) (England) Order 2008 No. 2008/1762. - Enabling power: Education Act 2002, ss. 87 (3) (a) (b) (5), 210 (7). - Issued: 10.07.2008 Made: 03.07.2008. Laid: 10.07.2008. Coming into force: 01.08.2008. Effect: S.I. 2000/1607 revoked with savings. Territorial extent & classification: E. General. - 4p.: 30 cm. - 978-0-11-081984-6 £3.00

The Education (National Curriculum) (Key Stage 3 Assessment Arrangements) (England) (Amendment) Order 2008 No. 2008/3081. - Enabling power: Education Act 2002, ss. 87 (3) (c) (7) (9) (10) (11), 210 (7). - Issued: 05.12.2008. Made: 01.12.2008. Coming into force: 02.12.2008 in accord. with art. 1. Effect: S.I. 2003/1039 amended. Territorial extent & classification: E. General. - 2p.: 30 cm. - 978-0-11-147088-6 £4.00

The Education (National Curriculum) (Modern Foreign Languages) (England) Order 2008 No. 2008/1766. - Enabling power: Education Act 2002, ss. 84 (4), 210 (7). - Issued: 10.07.2008. Made: 03.07.2008. Laid: 10.07.2008. Coming into force: 01.08.2008. Effect: S.I. 2004/260 revoked with savings. Territorial extent & classification: E. General. - 2p.: 30 cm. - 978-0-11-081971-6 £3.00

The Education (Nutritional Standards and Requirements for School Food) (England) (Amendment) Regulations 2008 No. 2008/1800. - Enabling power: School Standards and Framework Act 1998, ss. 114A, 138 (7) (8). - Issued: 11.07.2008. Made: 03.07.2008. Laid: 11.07.2008. Coming into force: 01.09.2008. Effect: S.I. 2007/2359 amended. Territorial extent & classification: E. General. - 8p.: 30 cm. - 978-0-11-081996-9 £3.00

The Education (Outturn Statements) (England) Regulations 2008 No. 2008/1575. - Enabling power: School Standards and Framework Act 1998, ss. 52 (2) (2B) (3), 138 (7). - Issued: 23.06.2008. Made: 15.06.2008. Laid: 25.06.2008. Coming into force: 24.07.2008. Effect: S.I. 2007/1720 revoked with saving. Territorial extent & classification: E. General. - Revoked by S.I. 2009/1586 (ISBN 9780111481561) with saving. - 16p.: 30 cm. - 978-0-11-081863-4 £3.00

The Education (Pupil Exclusions and Appeals) (Pupil Referral Units) (England) Regulations 2008 No. 2008/532. - Enabling power: Education Act 2002, ss. 52, 210 (7), 214. - Issued: 06.03.2008. Made: 26.02.2008. Laid: 06.03.2008. Coming into force: 01.04.2008. Effect: S.I. 2004/402; 2006/2189; 2007/1870 partially revoked & S.I. 2002/3179 revoked with savings. Territorial extent & classification: E. General. - 12p.: 30 cm. - 978-0-11-081052-2 £3.00

The Education (Pupil Information) (England) (Amendment) Regulations 2008 No. 2008/1747. - Enabling power: Education Act 1996, ss. 408, 563, 569 (4). - Issued: 09.07.2008. Made: 03.07.2008. Laid: 09.07.2008. Coming into force: 01.09.2008. Effect: S.I. 2005/1437 amended. Territorial extent & classification: E. General. - 8p.: 30 cm. - 978-0-11-081959-4 £3.00

The Education (Recognised Bodies) (England) (Amendment) Order 2008 No. 2008/2889. - Enabling power: Education Reform Act 1988, s. 216 (1). - Issued: 13.11.2008. Made: 06.11.2008. Coming into force: 21.11.2008. Effect: S.I. 2007/2688 amended. Territorial extent & classification: E. General. - 2p.: 30 cm. - 978-0-11-084990-4 £4.00

The Education (School and Local Education Authority Performance Targets) (England) (Amendment) Regulations 2008 No. 2008/3086. - Enabling power: Education Act 1997, ss. 19, 54 (3) & Education Act 2005, ss. 102, 120. - Issued: 08.12.2008. Made: 01.12.2008. Laid: 08.12.2008. Coming into force: 31.12.2008. Effect: S.I. 2004/2858; 2005/2450 amended. Territorial extent & classification: E. General. - 4p.: 30 cm. - 978-0-11-147092-3 £5.00

The Education (School Inspection etc.) (England) (Amendment) Regulations 2008 No. 2008/1723. - Enabling power: Education Act 2005, ss. 11A, 14 (4) (b), 16 (3) (b). - Issued: 07.07.2008. Made: 01.07.2008. Laid: 07.07.2008. Coming into force: 01.09.2008. Effect: S.I. 2005/2038; 2007/1089 amended. Territorial extent & classification: E. General. - 2p.: 30 cm. - 978-0-11-081942-6 £3.00

The Education (School Performance Information) (England) (Amendment) (No.2) Regulations 2008 No. 2008/1727. - Enabling power: Education Act 1996, ss. 408, 537, 537A, 569. - Issued: 08.07.2008. Made: 01.07.2008. Laid: 08.07.2008. Coming into force: 01.09.2008. Effect: S.I. 2007/2324 amended. Territorial extent & classification: E. General. - 4p.: 30 cm. - 978-0-11-081949-5 £3.00

The Education (School Performance Information) (England) (Amendment) Regulations 2008 No. 2008/364. - Enabling power: Education Act 1996, ss. 537, 537A, 569 (4). - Issued: 20.02.2008. Made: 13.02.2008. Laid: 20.02.2008. Coming into force: 01.04.2008. Effect: S.I. 2007/2324 amended. Territorial extent & classification: E. General. - 2p.: 30 cm. - 978-0-11-080953-3 *£3.00*

The Education (Special Educational Needs Co-ordinators) (England) Regulations 2008 No. 2008/2945. - Enabling power: Education Act 1996, s. 317 (3B). - Issued: 21.11.2008. Made: 13.11.2008. Laid: 21.11.2008. Coming into force: 01.09.2009. Effect: None. Territorial extent & classification: E. General. - 4p.: 30 cm. - 978-0-11-147005-3 *£4.00*

The Education (Specified Work and Registration) (England) (Amendment) Regulations 2008 No. 2008/1883. - Enabling power: Education Act 2002, ss. 134, 145, 210. - Issued: 22.07.2008. Made: 15.07.2008. Laid: 22.07.2008. Coming into force: 01.09.2008. Effect: S.I. 2003/1663 amended. Territorial extent & classification: E. General. - 4p.: 30 cm. - 978-0-11-083357-6 *£3.00*

The Education (Student Support) (Amendment) (No. 2) Regulations 2008 No. 2008/2094. - Enabling power: Teaching and Higher Education Act 1998, ss. 22, 42 (6). - Issued: 08.08.2008. Made: 31.07.2008. Laid: 08.08.2008. Coming into force: In accord. with reg. 1. Effect: S.I. 2008/529, 1582 amended. Territorial extent & classification: E. General. - This Statutory Instrument has been made to correct provisions in S.I. 2008/529 (ISBN 9780110810560) and 1582 (ISBN 9780110818733) and is being issued free of charge to all known recipients of those Statutory Instruments. With correction slip dated July 2009. - 12p.: 30 cm. - 978-0-11-083706-2 *£3.00*

The Education (Student Support) (Amendment) (No. 3) Regulations 2008 No. 2008/2939. - Enabling power: Teaching and Higher Education Act 1998, ss. 22, 42 (6). - Issued: 24.11.2008. Made: 13.11.2008. Laid: 25.11.2008. Coming into force: In accord. with reg. 1. Effect: S.I. 2008/529, 1582 amended. Territorial extent & classification: E. General. - 12p.: 30 cm. - 978-0-11-147000-8 *£5.00*

The Education (Student Support) (Amendment) Regulations 2008 No. 2008/235. - Enabling power: Teaching and Higher Education Act 1998, ss. 22, 42 (6). - Issued: 13.02.2008. Made: 06.02.2008. Laid: 07.02.2008. Coming into force: 28.02.2008. Effect: S.I. 2007/176 amended. Territorial extent & classification: E. General. - Revoked by S.I. 2008/1582 (ISBN 9780110818733). - 2p.: 30 cm. - 978-0-11-080925-0 *£3.00*

The Education (Student Support) (European Institutions) (Amendment) (No. 2) Regulations 2008 No. 2008/3054. - Enabling power: Teaching and Higher Education Act 1998, ss. 22, 42 (6), 43 (1). - Issued: 01.12.2008. Made: 24.11.2008. Laid: 01.12.2008. Coming into force: 01.01.2009. Effect: S.I. 2006/3156 amended. Territorial extent & classification: E. General. - 4p.: 30 cm. - 978-0-11-147065-7 *£4.00*

The Education (Student Support) (European Institutions) (Amendment) Regulations 2008 No. 2008/1478. - Enabling power: Teaching and Higher Education Act 1998, ss. 22, 42 (6), 43 (1). - Issued: 16.06.2008. Made: 09.06.2008. Laid: 16.06.2008. Coming into force: 18.07.2008. Effect: S.I. 2006/3156 amended. Territorial extent & classification: E. General. - 2p.: 30 cm. - 978-0-11-081830-6 *£3.00*

The Further Education and Training Act 2007 (Commencement No. 1) (England) Order 2008 No. 2008/313 (C.12). - Enabling power: Further Education and Training Act 2007, s. 32 (5). Bringing into operation various provisions of the 2007 Act on 21.02.2008 & 01.09.2008. - Issued: 18.02.2008. Made: 11.02.2008. Effect: None. Territorial extent & classification: E. General. - 4p.: 30 cm. - 978-0-11-080942-7 *£3.00*

The General Teaching Council for England (Disciplinary Functions) (Amendment) Regulations 2008 No. 2008/3256. - Enabling power: Teaching and Higher Education Act 1998, ss. 15, 15A. - Issued: 29.12.2008. Made: 17.12.2008. Laid: 29.12.2008. Coming into force: 20.01.2009. Effect: S.I. 2001/1268 amended. Territorial extent & classification: E. General. - 2p.: 30 cm. - 978-0-11-147219-4 *£4.00*

The General Teaching Council for England (Eligibility for Provisional Registration) Regulations 2008 No. 2008/1884. - Enabling power: Teaching and Higher Education Act 1998, s. 3 (3A). - Issued: 22.07.2008. Made: 15.07.2008 Laid: 22.07.2008. Coming into force: 01.09.2008. Effect: None. Territorial extent & classification: E. General. - 2p.: 30 cm. - 978-0-11-083358-3 *£3.00*

The Hackleton CofE Primary School (Designation as having a Religious Character) Order 2008 No. 2008/2081. - Enabling power: School Standards and Framework Act 1998, s. 69 (3) (4). - Issued: 07.08.2008. Made: 30.07.2008. Coming into force: 30.07.2008. Effect: None. Territorial extent & classification: E. Local. - 2p.: 30 cm. - 978-0-11-083677-5 *£3.00*

The Hawthorn Church of England Controlled First School (Designation as having a Religious Character) Order 2008 No. 2008/2082. - Enabling power: School Standards and Framework Act 1998, s. 69 (3) (4). - Issued: 07.08.2008. Made: 30.07.2008. Coming into force: 30.07.2008. Effect: None. Territorial extent & classification: E. Local. - 2p.: 30 cm. - 978-0-11-083678-2 *£3.00*

The Information as to Provision of Education (England) Regulations 2008 No. 2008/4. - Enabling power: Education Act 1996, ss. 29 (3), 569 (4). - Issued: 15.01.2008. Made: 07.01.2008. Laid: 15.01.2008. Coming into force: 14.02.2008. Effect: S.I. 1999/1066; 2003/190; 2005/346; 2006/1033 revoked. Territorial extent & classification: E. General. - 8p.: 30 cm. - 978-0-11-080802-4 *£3.00*

The Inspectors of Education, Children's Services and Skills (No. 2) Order 2008 No. 2008/1484. - Enabling power: Education and Inspections Act 2006, s. 114 (1). - Issued: 18.06.2008. Made: 11.06.2008. Coming into force: 12.06.2008. Effect: None. Territorial extent & classification: E. General. - 2p.: 30 cm. - 978-0-11-081852-8 £3.00

The Inspectors of Education, Children's Services and Skills (No. 3) Order 2008 No. 2008/1784. - Enabling power: Education and Inspections Act 2006, s. 114 (1). - Issued: 16.07.2008. Made: 09.07.2008. Coming into force: 10.07.2008. Effect: None. Territorial extent & classification: E. General. - 2p.: 30 cm. - 978-0-11-083121-3 £3.00

The Inspectors of Education, Children's Services and Skills (No. 4) Order 2008 No. 2008/2563. - Enabling power: Education and Inspections Act 2006, s. 114 (1). - Issued: 16.10.2008. Made: 09.10.2008. Coming into force: 10.10.2008. Effect: None. Territorial extent & classification: E. General. - 2p.: 30 cm. - 978-0-11-084581-4 £4.00

The Inspectors of Education, Children's Services and Skills (No. 5) Order 2008 No. 2008/3126. - Enabling power: Education and Inspections Act 2006, s. 114 (1). - Issued: 17.12.2008. Made: 10.12.2008. Coming into force: 11.12.2008. Effect: None. Territorial extent & classification: E. General. - 2p.: 30 cm. - 978-0-11-147167-8 £4.00

The Inspectors of Education, Children's Services and Skills Order 2008 No. 2008/681. - Enabling power: Education and Inspections Act 2006, s. 114 (1). - Issued: 19.03.2008. Made: 12.03.2008. Coming into force: 13.03.2008. Effect: None. Territorial extent & classification: E. General. - 2p.: 30 cm. - 978-0-11-081227-4 £3.00

The King's Stanley CofE Primary School (Designation as having a Religious Character) Order 2008 No. 2008/1867. - Enabling power: School Standards and Framework Act 1998, s. 69 (3) (4). - Issued: 22.07.2008. Made: 30.06.2008. Coming into force: 30.06.2008. Effect: None. Territorial extent & classification: E. Local. - 2p.: 30 cm. - 978-0-11-083221-0 £3.00

The Krishna-Avanti Primary School (Designation as having a Religious Character) Order 2008 No. 2008/1868. - Enabling power: School Standards and Framework Act 1998, s. 69 (3) (4). - Issued: 22.07.2008. Made: 30.06.2008. Coming into force: 30.06.2008. Effect: None. Territorial extent & classification: E. Local. - 2p.: 30 cm. - 978-0-11-083233-3 £3.00

The Leeds City College (Government) Regulations 2008 No. 2008/3084. - Enabling power: Further and Higher Education Act 1992, ss. 20 (2), 21 (1), sch. 4. - Issued: 08.12.2008. Made: 01.12.2008. Laid: 08.12.2008. Coming into force: 01.01.2009. Effect: None. Territorial extent & classification: E. General. - With Correction slip dated January 2010. - 20p.: 30 cm. - 978-0-11-147090-9 £5.00

The Leeds City College (Incorporation) Order 2008 No. 2008/3083. - Enabling power: Further and Higher Education Act 1992, ss. 16 (1) (a), 17. - Issued: 08.12.2008. Made: 01.12.2008. Laid: 08.12.2008. Coming into force: 01.01.2009. Effect: None. Territorial extent & classification: E. General. - 2p.: 30 cm. - 978-0-11-147089-3 £4.00

The London Skills and Employment Board (Establishment) Regulations 2008 No. 2008/118. - Enabling power: Learning and Skills Act 2000, s. 24B (1) (8). - Issued: 28.01.2008. Made: 21.01.2008. Laid: 28.01.2008. Coming into force: 25.02.2008. Effect: None. Territorial extent & classification: E. General. - 2p.: 30 cm. - 978-0-11-080859-8 £3.00

The London Skills and Employment Board (Specified Functions) Order 2008 No. 2008/119. - Enabling power: Learning and Skills Act 2000, s. 24B (3). - Issued: 28.01.2008. Made: 21.01.2008. Laid: 28.01.2008. Coming into force: 25.02.2008. Effect: None. Territorial extent & classification: E. General. - 2p.: 30 cm. - 978-0-11-080858-1 £3.00

The Manchester College (Government) Regulations 2008 No. 2008/50. - Enabling power: Further and Higher Education Act 1992, ss. 20 (2), 21 (1), sch. 4. - Issued: 21.01.2008. Made: 11.01.2008. Laid: 21.01.2008. Coming into force: 01.02.2008. Effect: None. Territorial extent & classification: E. General. - With correction slip dated February 2008. - 20p.: 30 cm. - 978-0-11-080837-6 £3.50

The Manchester College (Incorporation) Order 2008 No. 2008/49. - Enabling power: Further and Higher Education Act 1992, ss. 16 (1) (a), 17. - Issued: 21.01.2008. Made: 11.01.2008. Laid: 21.01.2008. Coming into force: 15.02.2008. Effect: None. Territorial extent & classification: E. General. - 2p.: 30 cm. - 978-0-11-080840-6 £3.00

The Manchester College of Arts and Technology and City College, Manchester (Dissolution) Order 2008 No. 2008/1418. - Enabling power: Further and Higher Education Act 1992, s. 27. - Issued: 09.06.2008. Made: 22.05.2008. Laid: 09.06.2008. Coming into force: 01.08.2008. Effect: None. Territorial extent & classification: E. General. - 2p.: 30 cm. - 978-0-11-081771-2 £3.00

The Manor CE VC Primary School (Designation as having a Religious Character) Order 2008 No. 2008/1869. - Enabling power: School Standards and Framework Act 1998, s. 69 (3) (4). - Issued: 22.07.2008. Made: 30.06.2008. Coming into force: 30.06.2008. Effect: None. Territorial extent & classification: E. Local. - 2p.: 30 cm. - 978-0-11-083234-0 £3.00

The Norham St Ceolwulfs CofE Controlled First School (Designation as having a Religious Character) Order 2008 No. 2008/1870. - Enabling power: School Standards and Framework Act 1998, s. 69 (3) (4). - Issued: 22.07.2008. Made: 30.06.2008. Coming into force: 30.06.2008. Effect: None. Territorial extent & classification: E. Local. - 2p.: 30 cm. - 978-0-11-083236-4 £3.00

The North Yorkshire County Council (School Meals) Order 2008 No. 2008/3016. - Enabling power: Education Act 2002, ss. 2 (1), 210. - Issued: 26.11.2008. Made: 20.11.2008. Laid: 26.11.2008. Coming into force: 19.12.2008. Effect: None. Territorial extent & classification: E. General. - 4p.: 30 cm. - 978-0-11-147040-4 £4.00

The Penwith College, Penzance (Dissolution) Order 2008 No. 2008/633. - Enabling power: Further and Higher Education Act 1992, s. 27. - Issued: 11.03.2008. Made: 06.03.2008. Laid: 11.03.2008. Coming into force: 01.04.2008. Effect: None. Territorial extent & classification: E. General. - 2p.: 30 cm. - 978-0-11-081138-3 £3.00

The Qualifications and Curriculum Authority (Additional Functions) Order 2008 No. 2008/1744. - Enabling power: Education Act 1997, s. 23 (2ZA). - Issued: 09.07.2008. Made: 02.07.2008. Laid: 09.07.2008. Coming into force: 04.08.2008. Effect: None. Territorial extent & classification: E. General. - 4p.: 30 cm. - 978-0-11-081968-6 £3.00

The Regional Learning and Skills Councils Regulations 2008 No. 2008/741. - Enabling power: Learning and Skills Act 2000, s. 18A (2). - Issued: 20.03.2008. Made: 12.03.2008. Coming into force: 19.03.2008. Effect: None. Territorial extent & classification: E. General. - 4p.: 30 cm. - 978-0-11-081245-8 £3.00

The Rochdale Sixth Form College (Government) Regulations 2008 No. 2008/1790. - Enabling power: Further and Higher Education Act 1992, ss. 20 (2), 21 (1), sch. 4. - Issued: 10.07.2008. Made: 03.07.2008. Laid: 10.07.2008. Coming into force: 01.08.2008. Effect: None. Territorial extent & classification: E. General. - With correction slip dated September 2009. - 20p.: 30 cm. - 978-0-11-081993-8 £3.50

The Rochdale Sixth Form College (Incorporation) Order 2008 No. 2008/1773. - Enabling power: Further and Higher Education Act 1992, ss. 16 (1) (a), 17. - Issued: 10.07.2008. Made: 03.07.2008. Laid: 10.07.2008. Coming into force: 01.08.2008. Effect: None. Territorial extent & classification: E. General. - 2p.: 30 cm. - 978-0-11-081988-4 £3.00

The Rodbaston College, Cannock Chase Technical College and Tamworth and Lichfield College (Dissolution) Order 2008 No. 2008/2992. - Enabling power: Further and Higher Education Act 1992, s. 27. - Issued: 25.11.2008. Made: 16.11.2008. Laid: 25.11.2008. Coming into force: 01.01.2009. Effect: None. Territorial extent & classification: E. General. - 2p.: 30 cm. - 978-0-11-147018-3 £4.00

The School Admission Appeals Code (Appointed Day) (England) Order 2008 No. 2008/53. - Enabling power: School Standards and Framework Act 1998, s. 85 (5). - Issued: 18.01.2008. Made: 14.01.2008. Coming into force: 17.01.2008. Effect: None. Territorial extent & classification: E. General. - 2p.: 30 cm. - 978-0-11-080835-2 £3.00

The School Admissions (Admission Arrangements) (England) Regulations 2008 No. 2008/3089. - Enabling power: School Standards and Framework Act 1998, ss. 1, 88B, 88C, 88D, 88E, 88F, 88G, 88H, 88I, 88K, 88L, 92, 100, 102, 138 (7) and Education Act 1996, s. 29 (3). - Issued: 10.12.2008. Made: 03.12.2008. Laid: 10.12.2008. Coming into force: 31.12.2008. Effect: S.I. 1998/1973, 2229; 1999/258; 2008/4 amended and S.I. 1999/126; 2002/2896; 2006/128, 3408; 2007/496, 497, 3009; 2008/1258 revoked with savings. Territorial extent & classification: E. General. - 20p.: 30 cm. - 978-0-11-147100-5 £5.00

The School Admissions (Alteration and Variation of, and Objections to, Arrangements) (England) (Amendment) Regulations 2008 No. 2008/1258. - Enabling power: School Standards and Framework Act 1998, s. 90 (9) (a). - Issued: 09.05.2008. Made: 06.05.2008. Laid: 06.05.2008. Coming into force: 28.05.2008. Effect: S.I. 2007/496 amended. Territorial extent & classification: E. General. - Revoked by S.I. 2008/3089 (ISBN 9780111471005) with savings. - 2p.: 30 cm. - 978-0-11-081435-3 £3.00

The School Admissions (Co-ordination of Admission Arrangements) (England) Regulations 2008 No. 2008/3090. - Enabling power: School Standards and Framework Act 1998, ss. 88M, 88N, 88O, 138 (7), 144 (1). - Issued: 12.12.2008. Made: 03.12.2008. Laid: 11.12.2008. Coming into force: 10.02.2009. Effect: S.I. 2007/194 revoked but does not have effect in relation to arrangements under which pupils are to be admitted to schools in England for academic years up to and including 2010 - 2011. Territorial extent & classification: E. General. - 12p.: 30 cm. - 978-0-11-147114-2 £5.00

The School Admissions (Local Authority Reports and Admission Forums) (England) Regulations 2008 No. 2008/3091. - Enabling power: School Standards and Framework Act 1998, ss. 85A, 85B, 88P, 88Q, 138(1) (7). - Issued: 11.12.2008. Made: 03.12.2008. Laid: 11.12.2008. Coming into force: 10.02.2009. Effect: S.I. 2002/2900; 2007/192 revoked. Territorial extent & classification: E. General. - 12p.: 30 cm. - 978-0-11-147108-1 £5.00

The School Finance (England) Regulations 2008 No. 2008/228. - Enabling power: School Standards and Framework Act 1998, ss. 45 (1B), 45A, 45AA, 47, 47A(4), 48(1) (2), 49 (2) (2A), 138 (7), sch. 14, para. 2B. - Issued: 14.02.2008. Made: 05.02.2008. Laid: 07.02.2008. Coming into force: 29.02.2008. Effect: S.I. 2004/3130, 3131; 2005/526 revoked (01.04.2008). Territorial extent & classification: E. General. - 40p.: 30 cm. - 978-0-11-080910-6 £6.50

The School Information (England) Regulations 2008 No. 2008/3093. - Enabling power: Education Act 1996, ss. 29 (5), 537, 569 (4) & School Standards and Framework Act 1998, s. 92. - Issued: 11.12.2008. Made: 03.12.2008. Laid: 11.12.2008. Coming into force: 10.02.2009. Effect: S.I. 2007/2979 partially revoked & S.I. 2002/2897; 2005/2152; 2007/1365 revoked. Territorial extent & classification: E. General. - With correction slip dated July 2009. - 12p.: 30 cm. - 978-0-11-147117-3 £5.00

The Schools Forums (England) (Amendment) Regulations 2008 No. 2008/47. - Enabling power: School Standards and Framework Act 1998, ss. 47A, 138 (7). - Issued: 17.01.2008. Made: 10.01.2008. Laid: 17.01.2008. Coming into force: 11.02.2008. Effect: S.I. 2002/2114 amended. Territorial extent & classification: E. General. - 4p.: 30 cm. - 978-0-11-080833-8 £3.00

The School Teachers' Incentive Payments (England) Order 2008 No. 2008/2099. - Enabling power: Education Act 2002, s. 123 (4) (a). - Issued: 11.08.2008. Made: 02.08.2008. Laid: 11.08.2008. Coming into force: 01.09.2008. Effect: None. Territorial extent & classification: E. General. - 2p.: 30 cm. - 978-0-11-083713-0 £3.00

The South Staffordshire College (Government) Regulations 2008 No. 2008/1734. - Enabling power: Further and Higher Education Act 1992, ss. 20 (2), 21 (1), sch. 4. - Issued: 10.07.2008. Made: 03.07.2008. Laid: 10.07.2008. Coming into force: 01.08.2008. Effect: None. Territorial extent & classification: E. General. - 20p.: 30 cm. - 978-0-11-081964-8 £3.50

The South Staffordshire College (Incorporation) Order 2008 No. 2008/1733. - Enabling power: Further and Higher Education Act 1992, ss. 16 (1) (a), 17. - Issued: 10.07.2008. Made: 02.07.2008. Laid: 10.07.2008. Coming into force: 01.08.2008. Effect: None. Territorial extent & classification: E. General. - 2p.: 30 cm. - 978-0-11-081965-5 £3.00

The Special Educational Needs (Information) Act 2008 (Commencement) Order 2008 No. 2008/2664 (C. 115). - Enabling power: Special Educational Needs (Information) Act 2008, s. 2 (3). Bringing into force various provisions of the Act on 01.01.2009, in accord. with reg. 1. - Issued: 13.10.2008. Made: 06.10.2008. Effect: None. Territorial extent & classification: E. General. - 2p.: 30 cm. - 978-0-11-084469-5 £4.00

The St Gregory's Catholic Primary School (Designation as having a Religious Character) Order 2008 No. 2008/2085. - Enabling power: School Standards and Framework Act 1998, s. 69 (3) (4). - Issued: 07.08.2008. Made: 30.07.2008. Coming into force: 30.07.2008. Effect: None. Territorial extent & classification: E. Local. - 2p.: 30 cm. - 978-0-11-083686-7 £3.00

The St Saviour's Catholic Primary School (Designation as having a Religious Character) Order 2008 No. 2008/1871. - Enabling power: School Standards and Framework Act 1998, s. 69 (3) (4). - Issued: 22.07.2008. Made: 30.06.2008. Coming into force: 30.06.2008. Effect: None. Territorial extent & classification: E. Local. - 2p.: 30 cm. - 978-0-11-083253-1 £3.00

The Student Fees (Amounts) (England) (Amendment) Regulations 2008 No. 2008/2507. - Enabling power: Higher Education Act 2004, ss. 24 (6), 47. - Issued: 02.10.2008. Made: 24.09.2008. Laid: 02.10.2008. Coming into force: 01.09.2009. Effect: S.I. 2004/1932 amended & S.I. 2007/1865 revoked. Territorial extent & classification: E. General. - 2p.: 30 cm. - 978-0-11-084282-0 £4.00

The Student Fees (Qualifying Courses and Persons) (England) (Amendment) Regulations 2008 No. 2008/1640. - Enabling power: Higher Education Act 2004, ss. 24 (6), 47. - Issued: 30.06.2008. Made: 23.06.2008. Laid: 30.06.2008. Coming into force: 01.09.2008. Effect: S.I. 2007/778 amended. Territorial extent & classification: E. General. - 2p.: 30 cm. - 978-0-11-081897-9 £3.00

The Thatcham Park Church of England Primary School (Designation as having a Religious Character) Order 2008 No. 2008/1872. - Enabling power: School Standards and Framework Act 1998, s. 69 (3) (4). - Issued: 22.07.2008. Made: 30.06.2008. Coming into force: 30.06.2008. Effect: None. Territorial extent & classification: E. Local. - 2p.: 30 cm. - 978-0-11-083242-5 £3.00

The Towcester CofE Primary School (Designation as having a Religious Character) Order 2008 No. 2008/1873. - Enabling power: School Standards and Framework Act 1998, s. 69 (3) (4). - Issued: 22.07.2008. Made: 30.06.2008. Coming into force: 30.06.2008. Effect: None. Territorial extent & classification: E. Local. - 2p.: 30 cm. - 978-0-11-083235-7 £3.00

The Trinity Anglican-Methodist Primary School (Designation as having a Religious Character) Order 2008 No. 2008/2083. - Enabling power: School Standards and Framework Act 1998, s. 69 (3) (4). - Issued: 07.08.2008. Made: 30.07.2008. Coming into force: 30.07.2008. Effect: None. Territorial extent & classification: E. Local. - 2p.: 30 cm. - 978-0-11-083681-2 £3.00

The William Parker School (Designation as having a Religious Character) Order 2008 No. 2008/100. - Enabling power: School Standards and Framework Act 1998, s. 69 (3) (4). - Issued: 30.01.2008. Made: 10.01.2008. Coming into force: 10.01.2008. Effect: None. Territorial extent & classification: E. Local. - 2p.: 30 cm. - 978-0-11-080875-8 £3.00

The Wylye Valley Church of England Voluntary Aided Primary School (Designation as having a Religious Character) Order 2008 No. 2008/2084. - Enabling power: School Standards and Framework Act 1998, s. 69 (3) (4). - Issued: 07.08.2008. Made: 30.07.2008. Coming into force: 30.07.2008. Effect: None. Territorial extent & classification: E. Local. - 2p.: 30 cm. - 978-0-11-083684-3 £3.00

Education, England and Wales

The Education and Skills Act 2008 (Commencement No. 1 and Savings) Order 2008 No. 2008/3077 (C.133). - Enabling power: Education and Skills Act 2008, s. 173. - Issued: 05.12.2008. Made: 01.12.2008. Coming into force: 02.12.2008; 26.01.2009. Effect: None. Territorial extent & classification: E/W. General. - 4p.: 30 cm. - 978-0-11-147085-5 £4.00

The Education (Mandatory Awards) (Amendment) Regulations 2008 No. 2008/1477. - Enabling power: Education Act 1962, ss. 1, 4 (2) & Education Act 1973, s. 3 (1) (2). - Issued: 16.06.2008. Made: 09.06.2008. Laid: 16.06.2008. Coming into force: 01.09.2008. Effect: S.I. 2003/1629; 2007/1629 amended. Territorial extent & classification: E/W. General. - 4p.: 30 cm. - 978-0-11-081826-9 *£3.00*

The Education (QCA Levy) (Revocation) Regulations 2008 No. 2008/923. - Enabling power: Education Act 1997, ss. 36, 54 (3). - Issued: 08.04.2008. Made: 25.03.2008. Laid: 08.04.2008. Coming into force: 30.09.2008. Effect: S.I. 2002/435, 1331 revoked. Territorial extent & classification: E/W/NI. General. - QCA = Qualifications and Curriculum Authority. - 2p.: 30 cm. - 978-0-11-081324-0 *£3.00*

The Education (School Teachers' Pay and Conditions) Order 2008 No. 2008/2155. - Enabling power: Education Act 2002, ss. 122 (1), 123, 124. - Issued: 13.08.2008. Made: 07.08.2008. Laid: 11.08.2008. Coming into force: 01.09.2008. Effect: S.I. 2007/2282 revoked. Territorial extent & classification: E/W. General. - Revoked by S.I. 2009/2132 (ISBN 9780111484326). - 2p.: 30 cm. - 978-0-11-083747-5 *£3.00*

The Education (Student Loans) (Amendment) (England and Wales) Regulations 2008 No. 2008/1479. - Enabling power: Education (Student Loans) Act 1990, ss. 1 (1) (2) (7), sch. 1, para. 1 (1). - Issued: 16.06.2008. Made: 09.06.2008. Laid: 16.06.2008. Coming into force: 01.08.2008. Effect: S.I. 2007/1630 amended. Territorial extent & classification: E/W. General. - 4p.: 30 cm. - 978-0-11-081831-3 *£3.00*

The Education (Student Support) (No.2) Regulations 2008 No. 2008/1582. - Enabling power: Teaching and Higher Education Act 1998, ss. 22, 42 (6). - Issued: 26.06.2008. Made: 17.06.2008. Laid: 26.06.2008. Coming into force: In accord. with reg. 1. Effect: S.I. 2008/529 amended then revoked with savings from 01.09.2009; S.I. 2008/235 revoked from 01.09.2009. Territorial extent & classification: E/W/NI. General. - With correction slip dated July 2009. - 128p.: 30 cm. - 978-0-11-081873-3 *£17.50*

The Education (Student Support) Regulations 2008 No. 2008/529. - Enabling power: Teaching and Higher Education Act 1998, ss. 22, 42 (6). - Issued: 07.03.2008. Made: 27.02.2008. Laid: 07.03.2008. Coming into force: 01.04.2008. Effect: S.I. 2007/1336, 2263 amended & S.I. 2007/176 revoked with savings. Territorial extent & classification: E/W/NI. General. - Revoked by S.I. 2008/1582 (ISBN 9780110818733) with savings. - 124p.: 30 cm. - 978-0-11-081056-0 *£17.50*

The Further Education and Training Act 2007 (Commencement No. 1) (England and Wales) Order 2008 No. 2008/1065 (C.49). - Enabling power: Further Education and Training Act 2007, s. 32 (5). Bringing into operation various provisions of the 2007 Act on 18.04.2008. - Issued: 16.04.2008. Made: 07.04.2008. Effect: None. Territorial extent & classification: E/W. General. - 2p.: 30 cm. - 978-0-11-081369-1 *£3.00*

The Teachers' Pensions (Miscellaneous Amendments) Regulations 2008 No. 2008/541. - Enabling power: Superannuation Act 1972, ss. 9, 12, sch. 3. - Issued: 07.03.2008. Made: 28.02.2008. Laid: 07.03.2008. Coming into force: 01.04.2008. Effect: S.I. 1994/2924; 1997/3001 amended. Territorial extent & classification: E/W. General. - 12p.: 30 cm. - 978-0-11-081066-9 *£3.00*

Education, Northern Ireland

The Education (QCA Levy) (Revocation) Regulations 2008 No. 2008/923. - Enabling power: Education Act 1997, ss. 36, 54 (3). - Issued: 08.04.2008. Made: 25.03.2008. Laid: 08.04.2008. Coming into force: 30.09.2008. Effect: S.I. 2002/435, 1331 revoked. Territorial extent & classification: E/W/NI. General. - QCA = Qualifications and Curriculum Authority. - 2p.: 30 cm. - 978-0-11-081324-0 *£3.00*

The Education (Student Support) (No.2) Regulations 2008 No. 2008/1582. - Enabling power: Teaching and Higher Education Act 1998, ss. 22, 42 (6). - Issued: 26.06.2008. Made: 17.06.2008. Laid: 26.06.2008. Coming into force: In accord. with reg. 1. Effect: S.I. 2008/529 amended then revoked with savings from 01.09.2009; S.I. 2008/235 revoked from 01.09.2009. Territorial extent & classification: E/W/NI. General. - With correction slip dated July 2009. - 128p.: 30 cm. - 978-0-11-081873-3 *£17.50*

The Education (Student Support) Regulations 2008 No. 2008/529. - Enabling power: Teaching and Higher Education Act 1998, ss. 22, 42 (6). - Issued: 07.03.2008. Made: 27.02.2008. Laid: 07.03.2008. Coming into force: 01.04.2008. Effect: S.I. 2007/1336, 2263 amended & S.I. 2007/176 revoked with savings. Territorial extent & classification: E/W/NI. General. - Revoked by S.I. 2008/1582 (ISBN 9780110818733) with savings. - 124p.: 30 cm. - 978-0-11-081056-0 *£17.50*

Education, Wales

The Assembly Learning Grant (Further Education) Regulations 2008 No. 2008/538 (W.51). - Enabling power: Teaching and Higher Education Act 1998, ss. 22, 42 (6). - Issued: 04.04.2008. Made: 26.02.2008. Laid before the National Assembly for Wales: 29.02.2008. Coming into force: 01.04.2008. Effect: None. Territorial extent & classification: W. General. - Revoked by W.S.I. 2009/2158 (W.182) (ISBN 9780348100532) with savings. - In English and Welsh. Welsh language title: Rheoliadau Grant Dysgu'r Cynulliad (Addysg Bellach) 2008. - 16p.: 30 cm. - 978-0-11-091750-4 *£3.00*

The Assembly Learning Grants and Loans (Higher Education) (Wales) (Amendment) Regulations 2008 No. 2008/2140 (W.189). - Enabling power: Teaching and Higher Education Act 1998, ss. 22, 42 (6), 43 (1). - Issued: 21.08.2008. Made: 05.08.2008. Laid before the National Assembly for Wales: 08.08.2008. Coming into force: In accord. with reg. 1. Effect: S.I. 2008/1273 (W. 130) amended. Territorial extent & classification: W. General. - Revoked by S.I. 2008/3170 (W.283) (ISBN 9780110919249) with savings. - In English and Welsh. Welsh title: Rheoliadau Grantiau a Benthyciadau Dysgu y Cynulliad (Addysg Uwch) (Cymru) (Diwygio) 2008. - 32p.: 30 cm. - 978-0-11-091854-9 £5.50

The Assembly Learning Grants and Loans (Higher Education) (Wales) (No.2) Regulations 2008 No. 2008/3170 (W.283). - Enabling power: Teaching and Higher Education Act 1998, ss. 22, 42 (6), 43 (1). - Issued: 26.01.2009. Made: 10.12.2008. Laid before the National Assembly for Wales: 15.12.2008. Coming into force: 09.01.2009. Effect: S.I. 2008/1273 (W. 130); 2140 (W.189) revoked, with savings, on 01.09.2009. Territorial extent & classification: W. General. - In English and Welsh. Welsh title: Rheoliadau Grantiau a Benthyciadau Dysgu y Cynulliad (Addysg Uwch) (Cymru) (Rhif 2) 2008. - 194p.: 30 cm. - 978-0-11-091924-9 £26.00

The Assembly Learning Grants and Loans (Higher Education) (Wales) Regulations 2008 No. 2008/1273 (W.130). - Enabling power: Teaching and Higher Education Act 1998, ss. 22, 42 (6), 43 (1). - Issued: 13.06.2008. Made: 07.05.2008. Laid before the National Assembly for Wales: 09.05.2008. Coming into force: 30.05.2008. Effect: S.I. 2007/1045 (W.104) revoked with savings (01.09.2008). Territorial extent & classification: W. General. - Revoked by S.I. 2008/3170 (W.283) (ISBN 9780110919249) with savings. - In English and Welsh. Welsh title: Rheoliadau Grantiau a Benthyciadau Dysgu y Cynulliad (Addysg Uwch) (Cymru) 2008. - 172p.: 30 cm. - 978-0-11-091792-4 £24.00

The Assembly Learning Grants (European Institutions) (Wales) (Amendment) (No. 2) Regulations 2008 No. 2008/3114 (W.276). - Enabling power: Teaching and Higher Education Act 1998, ss. 22, 42 (6), 43 (1). - Issued: 30.12.2008. Made: 05.12.2008. Laid before the National Assembly for Wales: 08.12.2008. Coming into force: 31.12.2008 except for regs 7, 8; 01.09.20098 for regs 7, 8 in accord. with reg. 1. Effect: S.I. 2008/18 (W. 7), 1324 (W.137) amended. Territorial extent & classification: W. General. - In English and Welsh. Welsh title: Rheoliadau Grantiau Dysgu'r Cynulliad (Sefydliadau Ewropeaidd) (Cymru) (Diwygio) (Rhif 2) 2008. - 8p.: 30 cm. - 978-0-11-091913-3 £5.00

The Assembly Learning Grants (European Institutions) (Wales) (Amendment) Regulations 2008 No. 2008/1324 (W.137). - Enabling power: Teaching and Higher Education Act 1998, ss. 22, 42 (6), 43 (1). - Issued: 09.06.2008. Made: 16.05.2008. Laid before the National Assembly for Wales: 20.05.2008. Coming into force: 13.06.2008. Effect: S.I. 2008/18 (W. 7) amended. Territorial extent & classification: W. General. - In English and Welsh. Welsh title: Rheoliadau Grantiau Dysgu'r Cynulliad (Sefydliadau Ewropeaidd) (Cymru) (Diwygio) 2008. - 4p.: 30 cm. - 978-0-11-091789-4 £3.00

The Assembly Learning Grants (European Institutions) (Wales) Regulations 2008 No. 2008/18 (W.7). - Enabling power: Teaching and Higher Education Act 1998, ss. 22, 42 (6) 43 (1). - Issued: 15.02.2008. Made: 08.01.2008. Laid before the National Assembly for Wales: 10.01.2008. Coming into force: 01.02.2008. Effect: S.I. 2007/2313 (W.184) amended & revoked with savings. Territorial extent & classification: W. General. - With correction slip dated March 2008. - In English and Welsh. Welsh title: Rheoliadau Grantiau Dysgu'r Cynulliad (Sefydliadau Ewropeaidd) (Cymru) 2008. - 48p.: 30 cm. - 978-0-11-091736-8 £7.50

The Collaboration Arrangements (Maintained Schools and Further Education Bodies) (Wales) Regulations 2008 No. 2008/3082 (W.271). - Enabling power: Education and Inspection Act 2006, s. 166. - Issued: 30.12.2008. Made: 28.11.2008. Laid before the National Assembly for Wales: 02.12.2008. Coming into force: 31.12.2008. Effect: None. Territorial extent & classification: W. General. - In English and Welsh. Welsh title: Rheoliadau Trefniadau Cydlafurio (Ysgolion a Gynhelir a ChyrffAddysg Bellach) (Cymru) 2008. - 16p.: 30 cm. - 978-0-11-091910-2 £5.00

The Collaboration Between Maintained Schools (Wales) Regulations 2008 No. 2008/168 (W.21). - Enabling power: Education Act 2002, ss. 19 (3), 23, 26, 210 (7). - Issued: 18.02.2008. Made: 28.01.2008. Laid before the National Assembly for Wales: 30.01.2008. Coming into force: 16.03.2008. Effect: None. Territorial extent & classification: W. General. - In English and Welsh. Welsh language title: Rheoliadau Cydweithio rhwng Ysgolion a Gynhelir (Cymru) 2008. - 16p.: 30 cm. - 978-0-11-091738-2 £3.00

The Control of School Premises (Wales) (Amendment) Regulations 2008 No. 2008/555 (W.55). - Enabling power: Education Act 2002, ss. 31, 210 (7). - Issued: 20.03.2008. Made: 29.02.2008. Laid before the National Assembly for Wales: 03.03.2008. Coming into force: 31.03.2008. Effect: S.I. 2008/136 (W.18) amended. Territorial extent & classification: W. General. - In English and Welsh. Rheoliadau Rheoli Mangreoedd Ysgol (Cymru) (Diwygio) 2008. - 4p.: 30 cm. - 978-0-11-091722-1 £3.00

The Control of School Premises (Wales) Regulations 2008 No. 2008/136 (W.18). - Enabling power: Education Act 2002, ss. 31, 210 (7). - Issued: 18.02.2008. Made: 23.01.2008. Laid before the National Assembly for Wales: 24.01.2008. Coming into force: 31.03.2008. Effect: None. Territorial extent & classification: W. General. - In English and Welsh. Rheoliadau Rheoli Mangreoedd Ysgol (Cymru) 2008. - 12p.: 30 cm. - 978-0-11-091740-5 £3.00

The Education Act 2002 (Commencement No. 12) (Wales) Order 2008 No. 2008/1728 (W.168) (C.75). - Enabling power: Education Act 2002, s. 216 (3) (4) (5). Bringing into force various provisions of the 2002 Act on 01.08.2008. - Issued: 16.07.2008. Made: 01.07.2008. Effect: None. Territorial extent & classification: W. General. - In English and Welsh. Welsh title: Gorchymyn Deddf Addysg 2002 (Cychwyn Rhif 12) (Cymru) 2008. - 16p.: 30 cm. - 978-0-11-091846-4 £3.00

The Education and Inspections Act 2006 (Commencement No. 1 and Saving Provisions) (Wales) Order 2008 No. 2008/1429 (W.148)(C.64). - Enabling power: Education and Inspections Act 2006, ss. 181, 188 (3). Bringing into force various provisions of the 2006 Act on 30.06.2008, 01.09.2008. - Issued: 19.06.2008. Made: 04.06.2008. Effect: None. Territorial extent & classification: W. General. - In English and Welsh. Welsh title: Gorchymyn Deddf Addysg ac Arolygiadau 2006 (Cychwyn Rhif 1 a Darpariaethau Arbed) (Cymru) 2008. - 8p.: 30 cm. - 978-0-11-091794-8 £3.00

The Education (Assisted Places) (Amendment) (Wales) Regulations 2008 No. 2008/509 (W.45). - Enabling power: Education (Schools) Act 1997, s. 3 (1) (2) (5) (9). - Issued: 20.03.2008. Made: 26.02.2008. Laid: 27.02.2008. Coming into force: 19.03.2008. Effect: S.I. 1997/1968 (in relation to Wales); 2006/3097 (W. 281) amended. Territorial extent & classification: W. General. - In English and Welsh. Welsh title: Rheoliadau Addysg (Cymorth Lleoedd) (Diwygio) (Cymru) 2008. - 8p.: 30 cm. - 978-0-11-091720-7 £3.00

The Education (Assisted Places) (Incidental Expenses) (Amendment) (Wales) Regulations 2008 No. 2008/510 (W.46). - Enabling power: Education (Schools) Act 1997, s. 3 (1) (3) (4) (5) (9). - Issued: 20.03.2008. Made: 26.02.2008. Laid: 27.02.2008. Coming into force: 19.03.2008. Effect: S.I. 1997/1969 (in relation to Wales); 2006/3098 (W.282) amended. Territorial extent & classification: W. General. - In English and Welsh. Welsh title: Rheoliadau Addysg (Lleoedd a Gynorthwyir) (Mân Dreuliau) (Diwygio) (Cymru) 2008. - 8p.: 30 cm. - 978-0-11-091721-4 £3.00

The Education (Disapplication of the National Curriculum for Wales at Key Stage 1) (Wales) Regulations 2008 No. 2008/1736 (W.170). - Enabling power: Education Act 2002, ss. 112, 210. - Issued: 16.07.2008. Made: 01.07.2008. Laid before the National Assembly for Wales: 03.07.2008. Coming into force: In accord. with reg. 1 (2). Effect: None. Territorial extent & classification: W. General. - In English and Welsh. Welsh title: Rheoliadau Addysg (Datgymhwyso Cwricwlwm Cenedlaethol Cymru yng Nghyfnod Allweddol 1) (Cymru) 2008. - 4p.: 30 cm. - 978-0-11-091845-7 £3.00

The Education (Fees and Awards) (Wales) (Amendment) Regulations 2008 No. 2008/1259 (W.126). - Enabling power: Education (Fees and Awards) Act 1983, ss. 1, 2. - Issued: 23.05.2008. Made: 05.05.2008. Laid before the National Assembly for Wales: 06.05.2008. Coming into force: 29.05.2008. Effect: S.I. 2007/2310 (W.181) amended. Territorial extent & classification: W. General. - In English and Welsh. Welsh title: Rheoliadau Addysg (Ffioedd a Dyfarniadau) (Cymru) (Diwygio) 2008. - 8p.: 30 cm. - 978-0-11-091784-9 £3.00

The Education (Inspectors of Education and Training in Wales) Order 2008 No. 2008/3118. - Enabling power: Education Act 2005, s. 19 (2). - Issued: 05.02.2009. Made: 10.12.2008. Coming into force: 11.12.2008. Effect: None. Territorial extent & classification: W. General. - 4p.: 30 cm. - 978-0-11-147356-6 £4.00

The Education (National Curriculum) (Attainment Targets and Programmes of Study) (Wales) (Amendment) Order 2008 No. 2008/1787 (W.173). - Enabling power: Education Act 2002, ss. 108 (3) (a) (b) (5), 210. - Issued: 21.07.2008. Made: 05.07.2008. Laid before the National Assembly for Wales: 08.07.2008. Coming into force: 01.08.2008. Effect: S.I. 2008/1409 (W.146) (Welsh language version only) amended. Territorial extent & classification: W. General. - In English and Welsh. Welsh title: Gorchymyn Addysg (Cwricwlwm Cenedlaethol) (Targedau Cyrhaeddiad a Rhaglenni Astudio) (Cymru) (Diwygio) 2008. - 4p.: 30 cm. - 978-0-11-091821-1 £3.00

The Education (National Curriculum) (Attainment Targets and Programmes of Study) (Wales) Order 2008 No. 2008/1409 (W.146). - Enabling power: Education Act 2002, ss. 108 (3) (a) (b) (5), 210. - Issued: 24.06.2008. Made: 30.05.2008. Laid before the National Assembly for Wales: 02.06.2008. Coming into force: 01.08.2008 except as provided for in arts 4 (1), 5 (1), 6 (1), 7 (1), 8 (1), 9 (1), 10 (1), 11 (1), 12 (1), 13 (1), 14 (1), 15 (1) (2). Effect: S.I. 2000/1098 (W.76), 1099 (W.77), 1100 (W.78), 1153 (W.84), 1154 (W.85), 1155 (W.86), 1156 (W.87), 1157 (W.88), 1158 (W.89), 1159 (W.90) revoked (01.08.2008). Territorial extent & classification: W. General. - In English and Welsh. Welsh title: Gorchymyn Addsg (Cwricwlwm Cenedlaethol) (Targedau Cyrhaeddiad a Rhaglenni Astudio) (Cymru) 2008. - 16p.: 30 cm. - 978-0-11-091797-9 £3.00

The Education (National Curriculum) (Foundation Stage) (Wales) (Amendment) Order 2008 No. 2008/2629 (W.229). - Enabling power: Education Act 2002, ss. 102, 108 (2), 210. - Issued: 24.10.2008. Made: 03.10.2008. Laid before the National Assembly for Wales: 07.10.2008. Coming into force: 28.10.2008. Effect: S.I. 2008/1732 (W.169) amended. Territorial extent & classification: W. General. - In English and Welsh. Welsh title: Gorchymyn Addysg (Y Cwricwlwm Cenedlaethol) (Y Cyfnod Sylfaen) (Cymru) (Diwygio) 2008. - 4p.: 30 cm. - 978-0-11-091859-4 £4.00

The Education (National Curriculum) (Foundation Stage) (Wales) Order 2008 No. 2008/1732 (W.169). - Enabling power: Education Act 2002, ss. 102, 108 (2), 210. - Issued: 16.07.2008. Made: 01.07.2008. Laid before the National Assembly for Wales: 03.07.2008. Coming into force: In accord. with art. 1 (2). Effect: None. Territorial extent & classification: W. General. - In English and Welsh. Welsh title: Gorchymyn Addysg (Y Cwricwlwm Cenedlaethol) (Y Cyfnod Sylfaen) (Cymru) 2008. - 4p.: 30 cm. - 978-0-11-091847-1 *£3.00*

The Education (National Curriculum) (Modern Foreign Languages) (Wales) Order 2008 No. 2008/1408 (W.145). - Enabling power: Education Act 2002, ss. 105 (4) (5), 210. - Issued: 24.06.2008. Made: 30.05.2008. Laid before the National Assembly for Wales: 02.06.2008. Coming into force: 01.08.2008. Effect: S.I. 2000/1980 (W.141) revoked. Territorial extent & classification: W. General. - In English and Welsh. Welsh title: Gorchymyn Addsg (Y Cwricwlwm Cenedlaethol) (Ieithoedd Tramor Modern) (Cymru) 2008. - 4p.: 30 cm. - 978-0-11-091835-8 *£3.00*

The Education (School Day and School Year) (Wales) (Amendment) Regulations 2008 No. 2008/1739 (W.171). - Enabling power: Education Act 1996, ss. 551, 569 (4) (5). - Issued: 16.07.2008. Made: 01.07.2008. Laid before the National Assembly for Wales: 03.07.2008. Coming into force: 01.08.2008. Effect: S.I. 2003/3231 (W.311) amended. Territorial extent & classification: W. General. - With correction slip dated August 2008. - In English and Welsh. Welsh title: Rheoliadau Addysg (Y Diwrnod Ysgol a'r Flwyddyn Ysgol) (Cymru) (Diwygio) 2008. - 8p.: 30 cm. - 978-0-11-091848-8 *£3.00*

The Education (School Teachers' Qualifications) (Amendment) (Wales) Regulations 2008 No. 2008/215 (W.26). - Enabling power: Education Act 2002, ss. 132, 145, 210 (7). - Issued: 20.02.2008. Made: 02.02.2008. Laid before the National Assembly for Wales: 05.02.2008. Coming into force: 01.09.2008. Effect: S.I. 2004/1729 (W. 173) amended. Territorial extent & classification: W. General. - In English and Welsh. Welsh language title: Rheoliadau Addysg (Cymwysterau Athrawon Ysgol) (Diwygio) (Cymru) 2008. - 4p.: 30 cm. - 978-0-11-091741-2 *£3.00*

The Further Education and Training Act 2007 (Commencement No. 2) (Wales) Order 2008 No. 2008/983 (W.108)(C.48). - Enabling power: Further Education and Training Act 2007, s. 32 (3). Bringing into force various provisions of the 2007 Act on 18.04.2008. - Issued: 01.05.2008. Made: 02.04.2008. Effect: None. Territorial extent & classification: W. General. - In English and Welsh. Welsh title: Gorchymyn Deddf Addysg Bellach a Hyffordiant 2007 (Cychwyn Rhif 2) (Cymru) 2008. - 4p.: 30 cm. - 978-0-11-091813-6 *£3.00*

The School Budget Shares (Prescribed Purposes and Consequential Amendments) (Wales) Regulations 2008 No. 2008/1866 (W.178). - Enabling power: School Standards and Framework Act 1998, ss. 47, 50 (3) (b). - Issued: 15.08.2008. Made: 11.07.2008. Laid before the National Assembly for Wales: 16.07.2008. Coming into force: 31.08.2008. Effect: S.I. 2004/2506 (W.224) amended. Territorial extent & classification: W. General. - In English and Welsh. Welsh title: Rheoliadau Cyfrannau Cyllideb Ysgolion (Dibenion Rhagnodedig a Diwygiadau Canlyniadol) (Cymru) 2008. - 4p.: 30 cm. - 978-0-11-091827-3 *£3.00*

The School Curriculum in Wales (Miscellaneous Amendments) Order 2008 No. 2008/1899 (W.181). - Enabling power: Education Act 2002, ss. 101 (3) (a), 105 (6),108 (3) (c) (7) (8) (9) (10) (11), 210 (7). - Issued: 15.08.2008. Made: 16.07.2008. Laid before the National Assembly for Wales: 04.06.2008. Coming into force: 01.08.2008. Effect: 2002 c.32; S.I. 2005/1394 (W.108) amended. Territorial extent & classification: W. General. - In English and Welsh. Welsh title: Gorchymyn y Cwricwlwm Ysgol yng Nghymru (Diwygiadau Amrywiol) 2008. - 4p.: 30 cm. - 978-0-11-091829-7 *£3.00*

Electricity

The Electricity and Gas (Billing) Regulations 2008 No. 2008/1163. - Enabling power: European Communities Act 1972, s. 2 (2). - Issued: 28.04.2008. Made: 23.04.2008. Laid: 24.04.2008. Coming into force: 17.05.2008. Effect: None. Territorial extent & classification: E/W/S. General. - EC note: These Regulations modify the standard conditions in electricity and gas supply licences in Great Britain. The modifications give effect to Article 13(3)(b) of Directive 2006/32/EC on energy end-use efficiency and energy services and repealing Council Directive 93/76/EEC. - 8p.: 30 cm. - 978-0-11-081401-8 *£3.00*

The Electricity and Gas (Carbon Emissions Reduction) Order 2008 No. 2008/188. - Enabling power: Gas Act 1986, 33BC & Electricity Act 1989, s. 41A & Utilities Act 2000, s. 103. - Issued: 05.02.2008. Made: 30.01.2008. Coming into force: 31.01.2008 in accord. with art. 1. Effect: None. Territorial extent & classification: E/W/S. General. - Supersedes draft SI (ISBN 9780110805306) issued 13.12.2007. - 16p.: 30 cm. - 978-0-11-080884-0 *£3.00*

The Electricity (Applications for Licences, Modifications of an Area and Extensions and Restrictions of Licences) Regulations 2008 No. 2008/2376. - Enabling power: Electricity Act 1989, ss. 6A (2) (3) (6), 60. - Issued: 15.09.2008. Made: 08.09.2008. Coming into force: 01.10.2008. Effect: S.I. 2007/1972 revoked. Territorial extent & classification: E/W/S. General- 12p.: 30 cm. - 978-0-11-084189-2 *£5.00*

The Gas and Electricity (Consumer Complaints Handling Standards) Regulations 2008 No. 2008/1898. - Enabling power: Consumers, Estate Agents and Redress Act 2007, ss, 43, 44, 46. - Issued: 23.07.2008. Made: 16.07.2008. Coming into force: 01.10.2008. Effect: None. Territorial extent & classification: E/W/S. General. - With correction slip dated August 2008. - 12p.: 30 cm. - 978-0-11-083411-5 £3.00

The Gas and Electricity Regulated Providers (Redress Scheme) Order 2008 No. 2008/2268. - Enabling power: Consumers, Estate Agents and Redress Act 2007, s. 47 (1) to (3). - Issued: 29.08.2008. Made: 16.08.2008. Laid: 27.08.2008. Coming into force: 01.10.2008. Effect: None. Territorial extent & classification: E/W/S. General. - 4p.: 30 cm. - 978-0-11-083863-2 £3.00

The Origin of Renewables Electricity (Power of Gas and Electricity Markets Authority to act for Northern Ireland Authority for Utility Regulation) Regulations 2008 No. 2008/1888. - Enabling power: European Communities Act 1972, s. 2 (2). - Issued: 22.07.2008. Made: 16.07.2008. Laid: 17.07.2008. Coming into force: 01.09.2008. Effect: 2004 c.20 amended. Territorial extent & classification: E/W/S/NI. General. - 2p.: 30 cm. - 978-0-11-083368-2 £3.00

Electricity, England

The River Humber (Upper Burcom Tidal Stream Generator) Order 2008 No. 2008/969. - Enabling power: Transport and Works Act 1992, ss. 3, 5 of, sch. 1, paras 1 to 5, 7, 8, 10, 11, 15 to 17. - Issued: 09.04.2008. Made: 02.04.2008. Coming into force: In accord. with art. 1. Effect: None. Territorial extent & classification: E. General. - 16p.: 30 cm. - 978-0-11-081348-6 £3.00

Electricity, England and Wales

The Electricity (Exemption from the Requirement for a Generation Licence) (Gunfleet Sands II) (England and Wales) Order 2008 No. 2008/3046. - Enabling power: Electricity Act 1989, s. 5. - Issued: 28.11.2008. Made: 22.11.2008. Laid: 25.11.2008. Coming into force: 22.12.2008. Effect: None. Territorial extent & classification: E/W. General. - 2p.: 30 cm. - 978-0-11-147050-3 £4.00

The Electricity (Exemption from the Requirement for a Generation Licence) (Little Cheyne Court) (England and Wales) Order 2008 No. 2008/3045. - Enabling power: Electricity Act 1989, s. 5. - Issued: 28.11.2008. Made: 22.11.2008. Laid: 25.11.2008. Coming into force: 22.12.2008. Effect: None. Territorial extent & classification: E/W. General. - 2p.: 30 cm. - 978-0-11-147059-6 £4.00

Electronic communications

The 3400-3800 MHz Frequency Band (Management) Regulations 2008 No. 2008/2794. - Enabling power: European Communities Act 1972, s. 2 (2). - Issued: 03.11.2008. Made: 27.10.2008. Laid: 29.10.2008. Coming into force: 20.11.2008. Effect: None. Territorial extent & classification: E/W/S/NI. General. - EC note: These Regulations implement in the UK Commission Decision 2008/411/EC on the harmonisation of the 3400-3800 MHz frequency band for terrestrial systems capable of providing electronic communications services in the Community- 4p.: 30 cm. - 978-0-11-084744-3 £4.00

The Communications (Television Licensing) (Amendment) Regulations 2008 No. 2008/643. - Enabling power: Communications Act 2003, ss. 365 (1) (4), 402. - Issued: 13.03.2008. Made: 06.03.2008. Laid: 10.03.2008. Coming into force: 01.04.2008. Effect: S.I. 2004/692 amended. Territorial extent & classification: E/W/S/NI/IoM/Ch.Is. General. - With correction slip dated June 2008. - 8p.: 30 cm. - 978-0-11-081186-4 £3.00

The Digital Switchover (Disclosure of Information) Act 2007 (Prescription of Information) (Amendment) Order 2008 No. 2008/2557. - Enabling power: Digital Switchover (Disclosure of Information) Act 2007, s. 2. - Issued: 06.10.2008. Made: 29.09.2008. Laid: 01.10.2008. Coming into force: 27.10.2008. Effect: S.I. 2007/1768 amended. Territorial extent & classification: E/W/S/NI. General. - 2p.: 30 cm. - 978-0-11-084337-7 £4.00

The Wireless Telegraphy (Automotive Short Range Radar) (Exemption) (No. 2) (Amendment) Regulations 2008 No. 2008/237. - Enabling power: Wireless Telegraphy Act 2006, s. 8 (3). - Issued: 18.02.2008. Made: 06.02.2008. Coming into force: 27.02.2008. Effect: S.I. 2005/1585 amended. Territorial extent & classification: E/W/S/NI/IoM/Ch.Is. General. - 4p.: 30 cm. - 978-0-11-080926-7 £3.00

The Wireless Telegraphy (Exemption) (Amendment) (No. 2) Regulations 2008 No. 2008/2426. - Enabling power: Wireless Telegraphy Act 2006, s. 8 (3). - Issued: 19.09.2008. Made: 10.09.2008. Coming into force: 01.10.2008. Effect: S.I. 2003/74 amended. Territorial extent & classification: E/W/S/NI/IoM/Ch.Is. General. - 4p.: 30 cm. - 978-0-11-084202-8 £4.00

The Wireless Telegraphy (Exemption) (Amendment) Regulations 2008 No. 2008/236. - Enabling power: Wireless Telegraphy Act 2006, s. 8 (3). - Issued: 18.02.2008. Made: 06.02.2008. Coming into force: 27.02.2008. Effect: S.I. 2003/74 amended. Territorial extent & classification: E/W/S/NI/IoM/Ch.Is. General. - 2p.: 30 cm. - 978-0-11-080924-3 £3.00

The Wireless Telegraphy (Licence Award) (Cardiff) Regulations 2008 No. 2008/3190. - Enabling power: Wireless Telegraphy Act 2006, ss. 14 (1) (2) (3) (4) (6) (7), 122 (7). - Issued: 22.12.2008. Made: 15.12.2008. Coming into force: 05.01.2009. Effect: None. Territorial extent & classification: E/W/S/NI [not CI or IoM]. General. - With correction slip dated October 2009. - 20p.: 30 cm. - 978-0-11-147180-7 £5.00

The Wireless Telegraphy (Licence Award) (Manchester) Regulations 2008 No. 2008/3191. - Enabling power: Wireless Telegraphy Act 2006, ss. 14 (1) (2) (3) (4) (6) (7), 122 (7). - Issued: 22.12.2008. Made: 15.12.2008. Coming into force: 05.01.2009. Effect: None. Territorial extent & classification: E/W/S/NI [not CI or IoM]. General. - With correction slip dated October 2009. - 20p.: 30 cm. - 978-0-11-147181-4 £5.00

The Wireless Telegraphy (Licence Award) Regulations 2008 No. 2008/686. - Enabling power: Wireless Telegraphy Act 2006, ss. 14 (1) (2) (3) (4) (6) (7), 122 (7). - Issued: 25.03.2008. Made: 12.03.2008. Coming into force: 02.04.2008. Effect: None. Territorial extent & classification: E/W/S/NI [not CI or IoM]. General. - 36p.: 30 cm. - 978-0-11-081217-5 £6.50

The Wireless Telegraphy (Licence Charges) (Amendment) (No. 2) Regulations 2008 No. 2008/2106. - Enabling power: Wireless Telegraphy Act 2006, ss. 12, 13 (2), 122 (7). - Issued: 11.08.2008. Made: 05.08.2008. Coming into force: 29.08.2008. Effect: S.I. 2005/1378 amended. Territorial extent & classification: E/W/S/NI. General. - 8p.: 30 cm. - 978-0-11-083745-1 £3.00

The Wireless Telegraphy (Licence Charges) (Amendment) Regulations 2008 No. 2008/139. - Enabling power: Wireless Telegraphy Act 2006, ss. 12, 13 (2), 122 (7). - Issued: 31.01.2008. Made: 23.01.2008. Coming into force: 13.02.2008. Effect: S.I. 2005/1378 amended. Territorial extent & classification: E/W/S/NI/IoM/Ch.Is. General. - 8p.: 30 cm. - 978-0-11-080871-0 £3.00

The Wireless Telegraphy (Limitation of Number of Spectrum Access Licences) (No. 2) Order 2008 No. 2008/3197. - Enabling power: Wireless Telegraphy Act 2006, s. 29 (1) to (3). - Issued: 22.12.2008. Made: 15.12.2008. Coming into force: 05.01.2009. Effect: None. Territorial extent & classification: E/W/S/NI [not CI or IoM]. General. - 4p.: 30 cm. - 978-0-11-147186-9 £4.00

The Wireless Telegraphy (Limitation of Number of Spectrum Access Licences) Order 2008 No. 2008/687. - Enabling power: Wireless Telegraphy Act 2006, s. 29 (1) to (3). - Issued: 19.03.2008. Made: 12.03.2008. Coming into force: 02.04.2008. Effect: None. Territorial extent & classification: E/W/S/NI [not CI or IoM]. General. - 2p.: 30 cm. - 978-0-11-081214-4 £3.00

The Wireless Telegraphy (Mobile Communication Services on Aircraft) (Exemption) Regulations 2008 No. 2008/2427. - Enabling power: Wireless Telegraphy Act 2006, s. 8 (3). - Issued: 19.09.2008. Made: 10.09.2008. Coming into force: 01.10.2008. Effect: None. Territorial extent & classification: E/W/S/NI. General. - EC note: These Regulations give effect to EU obligations of the UK contained in the Commission Decision of 7th April 2008 on harmonised conditions of spectrum use for the operation of mobile communication services on aircraft (MCA services) in the Community (OJ No L 98 10.4.2008, p. 19). - 4p.: 30 cm. - 978-0-11-084203-5 £4.00

The Wireless Telegraphy (Register) (Amendment) (No. 2) Regulations 2008 No. 2008/2104. - Enabling power: Wireless Telegraphy Act 2006, ss. 31 (1) (2), 122 (7). - Issued: 11.08.2008. Made: 05.08.2008. Coming into force: 29.08.2008. Effect: S.I. 2004/3155 amended. Territorial extent & classification: E/W/S/NI. General. - 4p.: 30 cm. - 978-0-11-083746-8 £3.00

The Wireless Telegraphy (Register) (Amendment) (No. 3) Regulations 2008 No. 2008/3193. - Enabling power: Wireless Telegraphy Act 2006, ss. 31 (1) (2), 122 (7). - Issued: 22.12.2008. Made: 15.12.2008. Coming into force: 05.01.2009. Effect: S.I. 2004/3155 amended. Territorial extent & classification: E/W/S/NI [not CI or IoM]. General. - 2p.: 30 cm. - 978-0-11-147182-1 £4.00

The Wireless Telegraphy (Register) (Amendment) Regulations 2008 No. 2008/689. - Enabling power: Wireless Telegraphy Act 2006, ss. 31 (1) (2), 122 (7). - Issued: 19.03.2008. Made: 12.03.2008. Coming into force: 02.04.2008. Effect: S.I. 2004/3155 amended. Territorial extent & classification: E/W/S/NI/IoM/CI. General. - 2p.: 30 cm. - 978-0-11-081218-2 £3.00

The Wireless Telegraphy (Spectrum Trading) (Amendment) (No. 2) Regulations 2008 No. 2008/2105. - Enabling power: Wireless Telegraphy Act 2006, ss. 30 (1) (3), 122 (7). - Issued: 11.08.2008. Made: 05.08.2008. Coming into force: 29.08.2008. Effect: S.I. 2004/3154 amended. Territorial extent & classification: E/W/S/NI. General. - 4p.: 30 cm. - 978-0-11-083744-4 £3.00

The Wireless Telegraphy (Spectrum Trading) (Amendment) (No. 3) Regulations 2008 No. 2008/3192. - Enabling power: Wireless Telegraphy Act 2006, ss. 30 (1) (3), 122 (7). - Issued: 22.12.2008. Made: 15.12.2008. Coming into force: 05.01.2009. Effect: S.I. 2004/3154 amended. Territorial extent & classification: E/W/S/NI [not CI or IoM]. General. - 2p.: 30 cm. - 978-0-11-147183-8 £4.00

The Wireless Telegraphy (Spectrum Trading) (Amendment) Regulations 2008 No. 2008/688. - Enabling power: Wireless Telegraphy Act 2006, ss. 30 (1) (3), 122 (7). - Issued: 19.03.2008. Made: 12.03.2008. Coming into force: 02.04.2008. Effect: S.I. 2004/3154 amended. Territorial extent & classification: E/W/S/NI/IoM/CI. General. - 2p.: 30 cm. - 978-0-11-081216-8 £3.00

Employment

The Employment Act 2008 (Commencement No. 1, Transitional Provisions and Savings) Order 2008 No. 2008/3232 (C.146). - Enabling power: Employment Act 2008, s. 22. Bringing into operation various provisions of the 2008 Act on 06.04.2009. - Issued: 23.12.2008. Made: 15.12.2008. Effect: None. Territorial extent & classification: E/W/S. General. - 8p.: 30 cm. - 978-0-11-147197-5 £5.00

The Gangmasters (Licensing Conditions) (No.2) (Amendment) Rules 2008 No. 2008/638. - Enabling power: Gangmasters (Licensing) Act 2004, ss. 8, 25 (2). - Issued: 13.03.2008. Made: 06.03.2008. Laid: 12.03.2008. Coming into force: 06.04.2008. Effect: S.I. 2006/2373 amended & S.I. 2007/401 revoked. Territorial extent & classification: E/W/S/NI. General. - Revoked by S.I. 2009/307 (ISBN 9780111474280). - 4p.: 30 cm. - 978-0-11-081140-6 £3.00

Employment and training

The Industrial Training Levy (Construction Industry Training Board) Order 2008 No. 2008/534. - Enabling power: Industrial Training Act 1982, ss. 11 (2), 12 (3) (4). - Issued: 07.03.2008. Made: 27.02.2008. Coming into force: 28.02.2008. Effect: None. Territorial extent & classification: E/W/S. General. - Supersedes draft S.I. (ISBN 9780110808178) issued 17.01.2008. - 8p.: 30 cm. - 978-0-11-081045-4 £3.00

The Industrial Training Levy (Engineering Construction Industry Training Board) Order 2008 No. 2008/535. - Enabling power: Industrial Training Act 1982, ss. 11 (2), 12 (3) (4). - Issued: 07.03.2008. Made: 27.02.2008. Coming into force: 28.02.2008. Effect: None. Territorial extent & classification: E/W/S. General. - Supersedes draft S.I. (ISBN 9780110808192) issued 26.01.2008. - 8p.: 30 cm. - 978-0-11-081054-6 £3.00

The Industrial Training Levy (Reasonable Steps) Regulations 2008 No. 2008/1639. - Enabling power: Industrial Training Act 1982, s. 11 (6B) (6C). - Issued: 27.06.2008. Made: 21.06.2008. Laid: 27.06.2008. Coming into force: 21.07.2008. Effect: None. Territorial extent & classification: E/W/S. General. - 4p.: 30 cm. - 978-0-11-081896-2 £3.00

Employment and training: Age discrimination

The Employment Equality (Age) Regulations 2006 (Amendment) Regulations 2008 No. 2008/573. - Enabling power: European Communities Act 1972, s. 2 (2). - Issued: 11.02.2008. Made: 02.03.2008. Laid: 06.03.2008. Coming into force: 06.04.2008. Effect: S.I. 2006/1031 amended. Territorial extent & classification: E/W/S. General. - 4p.: 30 cm. - 978-0-11-081102-4 £3.00

Employment tribunals

The Employment Tribunals (Constitution and Rules of Procedure) (Amendment) Regulations 2008 No. 2008/2771. - Enabling power: Employment Tribunals Act 1996, s. 1. - Issued: 23.10.2008. Made: 17.10.2008. Laid: 23.10.2008. Coming into force: 01.12.2008. Effect: S.I. 2004/1861 amended. Territorial extent & classification: E/W/S. General. - 2p.: 30 cm. - 978-0-11-084696-5 £4.00

The Employment Tribunals (Constitution and Rules of Procedure) (Amendment) Regulations 2008 No. 2008/3240. - Enabling power: Employment Tribunals Act 1996, ss. 1 (1), 4 (6), (6A), 7 (1) (3) (3ZA) (3A) (3AA) (3AB) (5), 9 (1) (4), 19, 41 (4). - Issued: 23.12.2008. Made: 15.12.2008. Laid: 17.12.2008. Coming into force: 06.04.2009. Effect: S.I. 2004/1861 amended. Territorial extent & classification: E/W/S. General. - With correction slip dated January 2010. - 12p.: 30 cm. - 978-0-11-147205-7 £5.00

Energy

The Climate Change and Sustainable Energy Act 2006 (Sources of Energy and Technologies) Order 2008 No. 2008/1767. - Enabling power: Climate Change and Sustainable Energy Act 2006, s. 26 (4). - Issued: 10.07.2008. Made: 03.07.2008. Coming into force: 23.07.2008. Effect: 2006 c.19 amended. Territorial extent & classification: E/W/S/NI. General. - Supersedes draft S.I. (ISBN 9780110814766) issued 20.05.2008. - 2p.: 30 cm. - 978-0-11-081969-3 £3.00

Environmental protection

The Batteries and Accumulators (Placing on the Market) Regulations 2008 No. 2008/2164. - Enabling power: European Communities Act 1972, s. 2 (2). - Issued: 21.08.2008. Made: 08.08.2008. Laid: 15.08.2008. Coming into force: 26.09.2008. Effect: S.I. 2004/693 amended & S.I. 1994/232; 2000/3097; 2001/2551 & S.R. 1995/122; 2002/300 revoked. Territorial extent & classification: E/W/S/NI. General. - EC note: These Regs partially implement Directive 2006/66/EC on batteries and accumulators and waste batteries and accumulators and repealing Council Directive 91/157/EEC. - 16p., ill.: 30 cm. - 978-0-11-083815-1 £3.00

The Environmental Protection (Controls on Ozone-Depleting Substances) (Amendment) Regulations 2008 No. 2008/91. - Enabling power: European Communities Act 1972, s 2 (2). - Issued: 22.01.2008. Made: 16.01.2008. Laid: 21.01.2008. Coming into force: 15.02.2008. Effect: S.I. 2002/528 amended. Territorial extent & classification: E/W/S including offshore installations, except in relation to importation where it will also apply to NI. General. - 12p.: 30 cm. - 978-0-11-080853-6 £3.00

The Fluorinated Greenhouse Gases Regulations 2008 No. 2008/41. - Enabling power: European Communities Act 1972, s. 2 (2). - Issued: 17.01.2008. Made: 10.01.2008. Laid: 15.01.2008. Coming into force: 15.02.2008. Effect: None. Territorial extent & classification: GB, including "offshore installations" as defined in Reg. 2, except in relation to importation, where the Regs will also apply in NI. General. - Revoked by S.I. 2009/261 (ISBN 9780111473870). EC note: These Regulations give effect to Regulation No 842/2006 on certain fluorinated greenhouse gases. The term "fluorinated greenhouse gases" is defined in Article 2(1) of the Council Regulation. - 20p.: 30 cm. - 978-0-11-080830-7 £3.50

The Non-Road Mobile Machinery (Emission of Gaseous and Particulate Pollutants) (Amendment) Regulations 2008 No. 2008/2011. - Enabling power: European Communities Act 1972, s. 2 (2). - Issued: 04.08.2008. Made: 23.07.2008. Laid: 28.07.2008. Coming into force: 08.09.2008. Effect: S.I. 1999/1053 amended. Territorial extent & classification: E/W/S/NI. General. - EC note: These regs implement the provision of Council Directive 2006/105/EC which amends Directive 97/68/EC on the approximation of the laws of the Member States relating to measures against the emission of gaseous and particulate pollutants from internal combustion engines to be installed in non-road mobile machinery, so as to have regard to the Treaty of Accession of Bulgaria and Romania. Council Directive 2006/105/EC amends Annex VIII of Council Directive 97/68/EC by including Bulgaria and Romania in the approval certificate numbering system. - 2p.: 30 cm. - 978-0-11-083637-9 £3.00

The Ozone Depleting Substances (Qualifications) (Amendment) Regulations 2008 No. 2008/97. - Enabling power: European Communities Act 1972, s 2 (2). - Issued: 22.01.2008. Made: 16.01.2008. Laid: 21.01.2008. Coming into force: 15.02.2008. Effect: S.I. 2006/1510 amended. Territorial extent & classification: E/W/S. General. - Revoked by S.I. 2009/216 (ISBN 9780111473801). - 2p.: 30 cm. - 978-0-11-080852-9 £3.00

The Producer Responsibility Obligations (Packaging Waste) (Amendment No. 2) Regulations 2008 No. 2008/1941. - Enabling power: Environment Act 1995, ss. 93 to 95. - Issued: 24.07.2008. Made: 18.07.2008. Coming into force: 19.07.2008. Effect: S.I. 2007/871 amended. Territorial extent & classification: E/W/S. General. - Supersedes draft S.I. (ISBN 9780110818795) issued on 24.06.2008. - 4p.: 30 cm. - 978-0-11-083488-7 £3.00

The Producer Responsibility Obligations (Packaging Waste) (Amendment) Regulations 2008 No. 2008/413. - Enabling power: Environment Act 1995, ss. 93 to 95. - Issued: 22.02.2008. Made: 19.02.2008. Laid: 21.02.2008. Coming into force: 14.03.2008. Effect: S.I. 2007/871 amended. Territorial extent & classification: E/W/S. General. - EC note: These regulations amend the 2007 Regulations which impose on producers the obligation to recover and recycle packaging waste, and related obligations, in order to attain the recovery and recycling targets set out in Article 6(1) of Council Directive 94/62/EC on packaging and packaging waste, as amended by Council Regulation (EC) No. 1882/2003, Council Directive 2004/12/EC and Council Directive 2005/20/EC. These Regulations change the recovery and recycling targets for 2008, 2009 and 2010. - 2p.: 30 cm. - 978-0-11-080975-5 £3.00

The REACH Enforcement Regulations 2008 No. 2008/2852. - Enabling power: European Communities Act 1972, s. 2 (2). - Issued: 13.11.2008. Made: 01.11.2008. Laid: 10.11.2008. Coming into force: 01.12.2008. Effect: 9 SI's & 9 S.R's amended & S.I. 1993/3050; 1994/1806; 1996/1373; 2001/1055; 2002/2176; 2003/1511, 2650, 3310; 2004/2913; 2005/2001; 2006/2916, 3311; 2007/386, 1596, 3438 & S.R. 1994/6; 2003/36; 2004/76 revoked. Territorial extent & classification: E/W/S/NI. General. - EC note: These Regulations apply to the United Kingdom and provide for the enforcement of Regulation (EC) No. 1907/2006 concerning the Registration, Evaluation, Authorisation and Restriction of Chemicals (REACH). - 76p.: 30 cm. - 978-0-11-084991-1 £13.00

The Restriction of the Use of Certain Hazardous Substances in Electrical and Electronic Equipment Regulations 2008 No. 2008/37. - Enabling power: European Communities Act 1972, s. 2 (2). - Issued: 15.01.2008. Made: 10.01.2008. Laid: 11.01.2008. Coming into force: 01.02.2008. Effect: S.I. 2004/693 amended & S.I. 2006/1463 revoked. Territorial extent & classification: E/W/S/NI. General. - EC note: These Regulations revoke and replace S.I. 2006/1463 which implemented Directive 2002/95/EC on the Restriction of the Use of Certain Hazardous Substances in Electrical and Electronic Equipment. The 2006 Regulations reflected the amendments made by Commission Decisions 2005/618/EC, 2005/717/EC, 2005/747/EC and 2006/310/EC. Since the 2006 Regulations were made, the Directive has been amended by a further three decisions: Commission Decision 2006/690/EC, Commission Decision 2006/691/EC and Commission Decision 2006/692/EC. All three decisions amend the list of exempt applications of lead, mercury, cadmium, hexavalent chromium, polybrominated biphenyls or polybrominated diphenyl ethers to which the Directive does not apply, which is set out in the Annex to the Directive- 16p.: 30 cm. - 978-0-11-080827-7 £3.00

The Scotland Act 1998 (Transfer of Functions to the Scottish Ministers etc.) Order 2008 No. 2008/1776. - Enabling power: Scotland Act 1998, ss. 63 (1) (b), 113 (3) (4), 124 (2). - Issued: 16.07.2008. Made: 09.07.2008. Laid:-. Coming into force: 10.07.2008 in accord. with art. 1. Effect: None. Territorial extent & classification: E/W/S. General. - 4p.: 30 cm. - 978-0-11-082017-0 £3.00

The Transfrontier Shipment of Waste (Amendment) Regulations 2008 No. 2008/9. - Enabling power: European Communities Act 1972, s. 2 (2). - Issued: 15.01.2008. Made: 07.01.2008. Laid: 11.01.2008. Coming into force: 05.02.2008. Effect: S.I. 2007/1711 amended. Territorial extent & classification: E/W/S/NI. General. - EC note: These Regulations amend the Transfrontier Shipment of Waste Regulations 2007. They insert regulation 23A which creates an offence for failure to comply with Commission Regulation (EC) No 1418/2007 which sets out the requirements for, and prohibitions that apply to, the export of waste listed in Annex III or IIIA to Regulation (EC) No 1013/2006 on shipments of waste that is destined for recovery in non-OECD Decision countries. They also insert regulation 23B which creates an offence for failure to comply with Article 37(5) of Regulation (EC) No 1013/2006 which applies the procedure of prior written notification and consent to the export of waste for recovery in countries to which the OECD Decision does not apply. Regulations 23A(4) and 23B(2)(b) create offences for failure to comply with Article 37(4) of Regulation (EC) No 1013/2006 which requires such waste to be sent to facilities that are authorised in the country of destination. - 4p.: 30 cm. - 978-0-11-080823-9 *£3.00*

Environmental protection: Emissions trading

The Community Emissions Trading Scheme (Allocation of Allowances for Payment) (Amendment) Regulations 2008 No. 2008/1939. - Enabling power: Finance Act 2007, s. 16 (2) (4) (6A). - Issued: 28.07.2008. Made: 22.07.2008. Laid: 22.07.2008. Coming into force: 12.08.2008. Effect: S.I. 2008/1825 amended. Territorial extent & classification: E/W/S/NI. General. - 8p.: 30 cm. - 978-0-11-083576-1 *£3.00*

The Community Emissions Trading Scheme (Allocation of Allowances for Payment) Regulations 2008 No. 2008/1825. - Enabling power: Finance Act 2007, s. 16 (2) (3) (4). - Issued: 15.07.2008. Made: 10.07.2008. Coming into force: 11.07.2008. Effect: None. Territorial extent & classification: E/W/S/NI. General. - Supersedes draft S.I. (ISBN 9780110817743) issued 05.06.2008. - 12p.: 30 cm. - 978-0-11-083103-9 *£3.00*

Environmental protection, England

The Environmental Noise (England) (Amendment) Regulations 2008 No. 2008/375. - Enabling power: European Communities Act 1972, s. 2 (2). - Issued: 25.02.2008. Made: 13.02.2008. Laid: 19.02.2008. Coming into force: 06.04.2008. Effect: S.I. 2006/2238 amended. Territorial extent & classification: E. General. - With correction slip dated June 2008. EC note: These Regulations amend the 2006 Regulations which implemented Directive 2002/49/EC relating to the assessment and management of environmental noise. - 2p.: 30 cm. - 978-0-11-080981-6 *£3.00*

The Genetically Modified Organisms (England) (Amendments) Regulations 2008 No. 2008/2598. - Enabling power: European Communities Act 1972, s. 2 (2). - Issued: 08.10.2008. Made: 02.10.2008. Laid: 08.10.2008. Coming into force: 14.11.2008. Effect: S.I. 2004/2412, 2692 amended. Territorial extent & classification: E. General. - This Statutory Instrument has been made in consequence of defects in S.I. 2004/2412 and S.I. 2004/2692, and is being issued free of charge to all known recipients of those Statutory Instruments. - 2p.: 30 cm. - 978-0-11-084376-6 *£4.00*

The Radioactive Contaminated Land (Modification of Enactments) (England) (Amendment) Regulations 2008 No. 2008/520. - Enabling power: Environmental Protection Act 1990, ss. 78A (9), 78YC. - Issued: 04.03.2008. Made: 25.02.2008. Laid: 03.03.2008. Coming into force: 06.04.2008. Effect: S.I. 2006/1379; 2007/3245 amended. Territorial extent & classification: E. General. - 4p.: 30 cm. - 978-0-11-081051-5 *£3.00*

The Site Waste Management Plans Regulations 2008 No. 2008/314. - Enabling power: Clean Neighbourhoods and Environment Act 2005, s. 54. - Issued: 18.02.2008. Made: 08.02.2008. Laid: 15.02.2008. Coming into force: 06.04.2008. Effect: None. Territorial extent & classification: E. General. - 8p.: 30 cm. - 978-0-11-080943-4 *£3.00*

Environmental protection, England and Wales

The Clean Neighbourhoods and Environment Act 2005 (Commencement No. 5) Order 2008 No. 2008/956 (C. 47). - Enabling power: Clean Neighbourhoods and Environment Act 2005, s. 108 (3) (e). Bringing into operation various provisions of the 2005 Act on 06.04.2008. - Issued: 07.04.2008. Made: 31.03.2008. Effect: None. Territorial extent & classification: E/W. General. - 8p.: 30 cm. - 978-0-11-081338-7 *£3.00*

The Financial Assistance for Environmental Purposes (England and Wales) Order 2008 No. 2008/3243. - Enabling power: Environmental Protection Act 1990, s. 153 (4). - Issued: 23.12.2008. Made: 17.12.2008. Laid: 23.12.2008. Coming into force: 23.01.2009. Effect: 1990 c. 43 varied. Territorial extent & classification: E/W. General. - 2p.: 30 cm. - 978-0-11-147208-8 *£4.00*

The Pollution Prevention and Control (Designation of Directives) (England and Wales) Order 2008 No. 2008/2549. - Enabling power: Pollution Prevention and Control Act 1999, sch. 1, para. 20 (2) (c) & European Communities Act 1972, sch. 2, para. 1A. - Issued: 07.10.2008. Made: 28.09.2008. Coming into force: 06.10.2008. Effect: None. Territorial extent & classification: E/W. General. - EC note: This Order designates Directives 2006/21/EC and 2008/1/EC as relevant directives for the purposes of sch. 1, para. 20 (2) (c) of the Pollution Prevention and Control Act 1999. - 4p.: 30 cm. - 978-0-11-084339-1 *£4.00*

Environmental protection, Wales

The Environmental Offences (Fixed Penalties) (Miscellaneous Provisions) (Wales) Regulations 2008 No. 2008/663 (W.71). - Enabling power: Refuse Disposal (Amenity) Act 1978, s. 11 (1); Control of Pollution (Amendment) Act 1989; s. 9 (1); Environmental Protection Act 1990, ss. 29 (1A) (b); 98 (1A) (b); Noise Act 1996, s. 11 (2A) (b); Anti-social Behaviour Act 2003, s. 47 (1); Clean Neighbourhoods and Environment Act 2005, ss. 9 (2), 66 (b), 67 (1), 81 (1). - Issued: 04.04.2008. Made: 09.03.2008. Laid before the National Assembly for Wales: 10.03.2008. Coming into force: 07.04.2008. Effect: S.I. 2007/739 (W. 67) amended. Territorial extent & classification: W. General. - In English and Welsh. Welsh title: Rheoliadau Tramgwyddau Amgylcheddol (Cosbau Penodedig) (Darpariaethau Amrywiol) (Cymru) 2008. - 8p.: 30 cm. - 978-0-11-091748-1 *£3.00*

The Radioactive Contaminated Land (Modification of Enactments) (Wales) (Amendment) Regulations 2008 No. 2008/521. - Enabling power: Environmental Protection Act 1990, ss. 78A (9), 78YC. - Issued: 04.03.2008. Made: 25.02.2008. Laid: 03.03.2008. Coming into force: 06.04.2008. Effect: S.I. 2006/2988 (W. 277); 2007/3250 amended. Territorial extent & classification: W. General. - 4p.: 30 cm. - 978-0-11-081041-6 *£3.00*

Estate agents

The Consumers, Estate Agents and Redress Act 2007 (Commencement No. 4) Order 2008 No. 2008/905 (C.43). - Enabling power: Consumers, Estate Agents and Redress Act 2007, s. 66 (2). Bringing into operation various provisions of the 2007 Act on 01.04.2008; 01.10.2008 in accord. with art. 3. - Issued: 31.03.2008. Made: 26.03.2008. Effect: None. Territorial extent & classification: E/W/S/NI General. - 4p.: 30 cm. - 978-0-11-081303-5 *£3.00*

The Estate Agents (Redress Scheme) Order 2008 No. 2008/1712. - Enabling power: Estate Agents Act 1979, s. 23A. - Issued: 03.07.2008. Made: 28.06.2008. Laid: 01.07.2008. Coming into force: 01.10.2008. Effect: None. Territorial extent & classification: E/W/S/NI General. - 2p.: 30 cm. - 978-0-11-081936-5 *£3.00*

The Estate Agents (Redress Scheme) (Penalty Charge) Regulations 2008 No. 2008/1713. - Enabling power: Estate Agents Act 1979, sch. 4, para. 2. - Issued: 03.07.2008. Made: 28.06.2008. Laid: 01.07.2008. Coming into force: 01.10.2008. Effect: None. Territorial extent & classification: E/W/S/NI General. - 2p.: 30 cm. - 978-0-11-081937-2 *£3.00*

European Communities

The European Communities (Definition of Treaties) (2006 International Tropical Timber Agreement) Order 2008 No. 2008/3116. - Enabling power: European Communities Act 1972, s. 1 (3). - Issued: 17.12.2008. Made: 10.12.2008. Coming into force: In accord with art. 1. Effect: None. Territorial extent & classification: E/W/S/NI. General. - 2p.: 30 cm. - 978-0-11-147164-7 *£4.00*

The European Communities (Definition of Treaties) (Agreement on Enlargement of the European Economic Area) Order 2008 No. 2008/297. - Enabling power: European Communities Act 1972, s. 1 (3). - Issued: 18.02.2008. Made: 12.02.2008. Coming into force: In accord with art. 1. Effect: None. Territorial extent & classification: E/W/S/NI. General. - Supersedes draft SI (ISBN 9780110789811) issued 21.11.2007. - 4p.: 30 cm. - 978-0-11-080949-6 *£3.00*

The European Communities (Designation) (No. 2) Order 2008 No. 2008/1792. - Enabling power: European Communities Act 1972, s. 2 (2). - Issued: 16.07.2008. Made: 09.07.2008. Laid: 16.07.2008. Coming into force: 06.08.2008. Effect: S.I. 2003/1246; 2007/1349 revoked. Territorial extent & classification: E/W/S/NI. General. - 4p.: 30 cm. - 978-0-11-083108-4 *£3.00*

The European Communities (Designation) (No. 3) Order 2008 No. 2008/2564. - Enabling power: European Communities Act 1972, s. 2 (2). - Issued: 15.10.2008. Made: 09.10.2008. Laid: 16.10.2008. Coming into force: 06.11.2008. Effect: None. Territorial extent & classification: E/W/S/NI. General. - 2p.: 30 cm. - 978-0-11-084576-0 *£4.00*

The European Communities (Designation) (No. 4) Order 2008 No. 2008/3117. - Enabling power: European Communities Act 1972, s. 2 (2). - Issued: 17.12.2008. Made: 10.12.2008. Laid: 17.12.2008. Coming into force: 07.01.2009. Effect: S.I. 2004/1110 revoked. Territorial extent & classification: E/W/S/NI. General. - 2p.: 30 cm. - 978-0-11-147159-3 *£4.00*

The European Communities (Designation) Order 2008 No. 2008/301. - Enabling power: European Communities Act 1972, s. 2 (2). - Issued: 19.02.2008. Made: 12.02.2008. Laid: 19.02.2008. Coming into force: 15.03.2008. Effect: S.I. 1984/353; 1985/956; 1988/2240 amended. Territorial extent & classification: E/W/S/NI. General. - 8p.: 30 cm. - 978-0-11-080945-8 *£3.00*

The European Grouping of Territorial Cooperation (Amendment) Regulations 2008 No. 2008/728. - Enabling power: European Communities Act 1972, s. 2 (2). - Issued: 20.03.2008. Made: 12.03.2008. Laid: 14.03.2008. Coming into force: 06.04.2008. Effect: S.I. 2007/ 1949 amended. Territorial extent & classification: E/W/S/NI. General. - EC note: These Regulations amend the European Grouping of Territorial Cooperation Regulations 2007 (S.I. 2007/1949), which make provision supplementing Regulation (EC) No 1082/2006 on a European grouping of territorial cooperation. - 4p.: 30 cm. - 978-0-11-081232-8 *£3.00*

The European Parliament (House of Lords Disqualification) Regulations 2008 No. 2008/1647. - Enabling power: European Communities Act 1972, s. 2 (2). - Issued: 27.06.2008. Made: 20.06.2008. Laid: 24.06.2008. Coming into force: 15.07.2008. Effect: None. Territorial extent & classification: E/W/S/NI. General. - EC note: By virtue of Council Decision 2002/772/EC, Euratom (implemented by S.I. 2004/304 and S.I. 2004/1374), the office of member of the European Parliament is incompatible with that of member of a national Parliament. Until the European Parliamentary elections in 2009, the UK has the benefit of a derogation. That derogation permits anyone who was a member of the House of Lords and who was also a member of the European Parliament at the time the Council Decision was introduced to continue to be permitted to have a dual mandate. - 2p.: 30 cm. - 978-0-11-081906-8 £3.00

European Communities, England

The European Regional Development Fund (London Operational Programme) (Implementation) Regulations 2008 No. 2008/1342. - Enabling power: European Communities Act 1972, s. 2 (2). - Issued: 28.05.2008. Made: 22.05.2008. Laid: 28.05.2008. Coming into force: 19.06.2008. Effect: None. Territorial extent & classification: E. General. - EC note: These Regulations implement Council Regulation (EC) No.1083/2006 laying down general provisions on the European Regional Development Fund, the European Social Fund and the Cohesion Fund and repealing Regulation (EC) No.1260/1999. The general provisions implemented by these Regulations relate to the European Regional Development Fund. - 8p.: 30 cm. - 978-0-11-081756-9 £3.00

Evidence, England and Wales

The Blood Tests (Evidence of Paternity) (Amendment) Regulations 2008 No. 2008/972. - Enabling power: Family Law Reform Act 1969, s. 22 (1). - Issued: 08.04.2008. Made: 03.04.2008. Laid: 03.04.2008. Coming into force: 25.04.2008. Effect: S.I. 1971/1861 amended. Territorial extent & classification: E/W. General. - 4p.: 30 cm. - 978-0-11-081343-1 £3.00

Excise

The Alcoholic Liquor Duties (Surcharges) and Tobacco Products Duty Order 2008 No. 2008/3026. - Enabling power: Excise Duties (Surcharges or Rebates) Act 1979, ss. 1 (1) (a) (2) (a) & Tobacco Products Duty Act 1979, s. 6 (1) (5) (a). - Issued: 23.01.2009. Made: 24.11.2008 at 1.00 pm. Laid: 24.11.2008. Coming into force: 24.11.2008 at 6.00pm for art. 3 & 01.12.2008 for art. 2. Effect: None. Territorial extent & classification: E/W/S/NI. General. - Approved by the House of Commons. - 4p.: 30 cm. - 978-0-11-147301-6 £4.00

The Alcoholic Liquor Duties (Surcharges) and Tobacco Products Duty Order 2008 No. 2008/3026. - Enabling power: Excise Duties (Surcharges or Rebates) Act 1979, ss. 1 (1) (a) (2) (a) and Tobacco Products Duty Act 1979, ss. 6 (1) (5) (a). - Issued: 25.11.2008. Made: 24.11.2008 at 1.00 pm. Laid: 24.11.2008. Coming into force: 24.11.2008 at 6.00pm for art. 3; 01.12.2008 for art. 2. Effect: None. Territorial extent & classification: E/W/S/NI. General. - For approval by the House of Commons within 28 days of the date on which it was made. - 2p.: 30 cm. - 978-0-11-147057-2 £4.00

The Alcoholic Liquor (Surcharge on Spirits Duty) Order 2008 No. 2008/3062. - Enabling power: Excise Duties (Surcharges or Rebates) Act 1979, ss. 1 (1) (a) (2) (a), 2 (3). - Issued: 26.01.2009. Made: 26.11.2008. Laid: 26.11.2008. Coming into force: 01.12.2008. Effect: S.I. 2008/3026 amended. Territorial extent & classification: E/W/S/NI. General. - Approved by the House of Commons. Supersedes SI of the same number (ISBN 9780111470930) issued 03.12.2008. - 2p.: 30 cm. - 978-0-11-147310-8 £4.00

The Alcoholic Liquor (Surcharge on Spirits Duty) Order 2008 No. 2008/3062. - Enabling power: Excise Duties (Surcharges or Rebates) Act 1979, ss. 1 (1) (a) (2) (a), 2 (3). - Issued: 03.12.2008. Made: 26.11.2008. Laid: 26.11.2008. Coming into force: 01.12.2008. Effect: S.I. 2008/3026 amended. Territorial extent & classification: E/W/S/NI. General. - For approval by the House of Commons within 28 days of the date on which it was made. - 2p.: 30 cm. - 978-0-11-147093-0 £4.00

The Amusement Machine Licence Duty, etc (Amendments) Regulations 2008 No. 2008/2693. - Enabling power: Betting and Gaming Duties Act 1981, sch. 4, paras 5 (1), 12 & Finance Act 1994, ss. 54, 74 (7) (8) & Finance Act 1996, ss. 49, 71 (8) (9) & Finance Act 2000, sch. 6, paras. 41 (1) (2), 146 (7) & Finance Act 2001, ss. 25 (1) (2), 45 (5). - Issued: 15.10.2008. Made: 10.10.2008. Laid: 10.10.2008. Coming into force: 01/11/2008. Effect: S.I. 1994/1774; 1995/2631; 1996/1527; 2001/838; 2002/ 761 amended. Territorial extent & classification: E/W/S/NI. General. - 4p.: 30 cm. - 978-0-11-084575-3 £4.00

The Beer, Cider and Perry and Wine and Made-wine (Amendment) Regulations 2008 No. 2008/1885. - Enabling power: Alcoholic Liquor Duties Act 1979, ss. 41A (7), 46 (1), 49 (1), 61 (1), 62 (5), 64 (1) & Finance (No. 2) Act 1992, ss. 1, 2. - Issued: 22.07.2008. Made: 16.07.2008. Laid: 17.07.2008. Coming into force: 01.09.2008. Effect: S.I. 1989/1355, 1356; 1993/1228; 1995/1046 amended. Territorial extent & classification: E/W/S/NI. General. - 8p.: 30 cm. - With correction slip dated August 2009. - 978-0-11-083364-4 £3.00

The Excise Duties (Road Fuel Gas) (Reliefs) Regulations 2008 No. 2008/2167. - Enabling power: Hydrocarbon Oil Duties Act 1979, ss. 20AA (1) (a) (2) (a) (b) (c) (h) (i). - Issued: 18.08.2008. Made: 13.08.2008. Laid: 14.08.2008. Coming into force: 01.10.2008. Effect: None. Territorial extent & classification: E/W/S/NI. General. - Revoked by S.I. 2008/3019 (ISBN 9780111470480). - 2p.: 30 cm. - 978-0-11-083793-2 £3.00

The Excise Duties (Road Fuel Gas) (Reliefs) (Revocation) Regulations 2008 No. 2008/3019. - Enabling power: Hydrocarbon Oil Duties Act 1979, ss. 20AA (1) (a) (2) (a) (b) (c) (h) (i). - Issued: 25.11.2008. Made: 24.11.2008. Laid: 24.11.2008. Coming into force: 01.12.2008. Effect: S.I. 2008/2167 revoked. Territorial extent & classification: E/W/S/NI. General. - 2p.: 30 cm. - 978-0-11-147048-0 *£4.00*

The Excise Duties (Surcharges or Rebates) (Hydrocarbon Oils etc.) Order 2008 No. 2008/2168. - Enabling power: Excise Duties (Surcharges or Rebates) Act 1979, ss. 1 (2), 2 (3). - Issued: 18.08.2008. Made: 13.08.2008. Laid: 14.08.2008. Coming into force: 01.10.2008. Effect: None. Territorial extent & classification: E/W/S/NI. General. - Revoked by S.I. 2008/3018 (ISBN 9780111473030). - 4p.: 30 cm. - 978-0-11-083771-0 *£3.00*

The Excise Duties (Surcharges or Rebates) (Hydrocarbon Oils etc.) (Revocation) Order 2008 No. 2008/3018. - Enabling power: Excise Duties (Surcharges or Rebates) Act 1979, ss. 1 (2), 2 (3). - Issued: 23.01.2009. Made: 24.11.2008. Laid: 24.11.2008. Coming into force: 01.12.2008. Effect: S.I. 2008/2168 revoked. Territorial extent & classification: E/W/S/NI. General. - Approved by the House of Commons. - 2p.: 30 cm. - 978-0-11-147303-0 *£4.00*

The Excise Duties (Surcharges or Rebates) (Hydrocarbon Oils etc.) (Revocation) Order 2008 No. 2008/3018. - Enabling power: Excise Duties (Surcharges or Rebates) Act 1979, ss. 1 (2), 2 (3). - Issued: 25.11.2008. Made: 24.11.2008. Laid: 24.11.2008. Coming into force: 01.12.2008. Effect: S.I. 2008/2168 revoked. Territorial extent & classification: E/W/S/NI. General. - For approval by resolution of that House within twenty-eight days, beginning with the day on which the Order was made, subject to extension for periods of dissolution, prorogation or adjournment for more than four days. - 2p.: 30 cm. - 978-0-11-147047-3 *£4.00*

The Excise Warehousing (Etc.) (Amendment) Regulations 2008 No. 2008/2832. - Enabling power: Customs and Excise Management Act 1979, s. 93 (1) (c) (e) (2) (a) (fa) (3). - Issued: 04.11.2008. Made: 30.10.2008. Laid: 31.10.2008. Coming into force: 01.12.2008. Effect: S.I. 1988/809 amended. Territorial extent & classification: E/W/S/NI. General. - 2p.: 30 cm. - 978-0-11-084826-6 *£4.00*

The Finance Act 1998, Schedule 2 (Assessments in Respect of Drawback) (Appointed Day) Order 2008 No. 2008/2302 (C. 102). - Enabling power: Finance Act 1998, sch. 2, para. 12. Bringing into operation various provisions of the 1998 Act on 01.09.2008 in accordance with art. 2. - Issued: 03.09.2008. Made: 29.08.2008. Effect: None. Territorial extent & classification: E/W/S/NI. General. - 2p.: 30 cm. - 978-0-11-083885-4 *£4.00*

The Gaming Duty (Amendment) Regulations 2008 No. 2008/1949. - Enabling power: Finance Act 1997, ss. 12 (4), 14 (1). - Issued: 25.07.2008. Made: 22.07.2008. Laid: 22.07.2008. Coming into force: 01.10.2008. Effect: S.I. 2006/1999 revoked. Territorial extent & classification: E/W/S/NI. General. - 2p.: 30 cm. - 978-0-11-083539-6 *£3.00*

The Hydrocarbon Oil and Bioblend (Private Pleasure-flying and Private Pleasure Craft) (Payment of Rebate etc.) Regulations 2008 No. 2008/2599. - Enabling power: Hydrocarbon Oil Duties Act 1979, ss. 13AC (3) (6) (7), 14E (3) (7) (8), 24 (1). - Issued: 09.10.2008. Made: 03.10.2008. Laid: 06.10.2008. Coming into force: 01.11.2008. Effect: None. Territorial extent & classification: E/W/S/NI. General. - EC note: The Regulations are part of the measures that implement Council Directive 2003/93/EC of 27 October 2003 on restructuring the Community framework for the taxation of energy products and electricity ("the Energy Products Directive"). A Transposition Note showing how the Energy Products Directive has been transposed is available at www.hmrc.gov.uk. - 4p.: 30 cm. - 978-0-11-084384-1 *£4.00*

The Hydrocarbon Oil, Biofuels and Other Fuel Substitutes (Determination of Composition of a Substance and Miscellaneous Amendments) Regulations 2008 No. 2008/753. - Enabling power: Customs and Excise Management Act 1979, ss. 100G(1), 100H(1)(b) (2) & Hydrocarbon Oil Duties Act 1979, ss. 6AC (1) (2) (4), 6AF (1) (2) (4), 20A (5) (6), 20AA (1) (a) (2) (3), 20AB (1) to (3), (5) (a) (12), 20AC, 21 (1) (a) (2), 23B, 24 (1), schedules 3, 4 & Finance (No.2) Act 1992, s. 1 & S.I. 2004/2063, reg. 3 & European Communities Act 1972, s. 2 (2). - Issued: 25.03.2008. Made: 19.03.2008. Laid: 19.03.2008. Coming into force: 01.04.2008 except for regs 3, 8 (3); 09.04.2008 for regs 3, 8 (3). Effect: S.I. 1973/1311; 1985/1450; 1996/2537; 2002/1773, 3057; 2004/2065; 2005/3320, 3472; 2006/3426; 2007/314 amended. Territorial extent & classification: E/W/S/NI. General. - Regulation 8(3) has been made in consequence of defects in S.I. 2007/1640 (ISBN 9780110773070) and 2007/3307 (ISBN 9780110801117) and this instrument is being issued free of charge to all known recipients of those Statutory Instruments. - 12p.: 30 cm. - 978-0-11-081268-7 *£3.00*

The Hydrocarbon Oil (Supply of Rebated Heavy Oil) (Payment of Rebate) Regulations 2008 No. 2008/2600. - Enabling power: Hydrocarbon Oil Duties Act 1979, ss. 13ZB (2) (5), 24 (1) (2). - Issued: 09.10.2008. Made: 03.10.2008. Laid: 06.10.2008. Coming into force: 01.11.2008. Effect: None. Territorial extent & classification: E/W/S/NI. General. - EC note: The Regulations are part of the measures that implement Council Directive 2003/93/EC of 27 October 2003 on restructuring the Community framework for the taxation of energy products and electricity ("the Energy Products Directive") which requires member States to tax heavy oil used as heating fuel or motor fuel. A Transposition Note showing how the Energy Products Directive has been transposed is available at www.hmrc.gov.uk. - 2p.: 30 cm. - 978-0-11-084385-8 *£4.00*

The Other Fuel Substitutes (Rates of Excise Duty etc.) (Amendment) Order 2008 No. 2008/754. - Enabling power: Hydrocarbon Oil Duties Act 1979, ss. 6A (3) (6) (9). - Issued: 25.03.2008. Made: 19.03.2008. Laid: 19.03.2008. Coming into force: 01.04.2008. Effect: S.I. 1995/2716 amended. Territorial extent & classification: E/W/S/NI. General. - 4p.: 30 cm. - 978-0-11-081270-0 £3.00

The Travellers' Allowances (Amendment) Order 2008 No. 2008/3058. - Enabling power: Customs and Excise Duties (General Reliefs) Act 1979, s. 13 (1) (3). - Issued: 23.01.2009. Made: 28.11.2008. Laid: 28.11.2008. Coming into force: 01.12.2008. Effect: S.I. 1994/955 amended & S.I. 1995/3044 revoked. Territorial extent & classification: E/W/S/NI. General. - Approved by the House of Commons- 4p.: 30 cm. - 978-0-11-147302-3 £4.00

The Travellers' Allowances (Amendment) Order 2008 No. 2008/3058. - Enabling power: Customs and Excise Duties (General Reliefs) Act 1979, s. 13 (1) (3). - Issued: 04.12.2008. Made: 28.11.2008. Laid: 28.11.2008. Coming into force: 01.12.2008. Effect: S.I. 1994/955 amended & S.I. 1995/3044 revoked. Territorial extent & classification: E/W/S/NI. General. - For approval by that House before the end of the period of 28 days beginning with the day on which it was made, no account being taken of any time during which Parliament is dissolved or prorogued or during which the House of Commons is adjourned for more than 4 days. - 4p.: 30 cm. - 978-0-11-147084-8 £4.00

The Value Added Tax, etc (Correction of Errors, etc) Regulations 2008 No. 2008/1482. - Enabling power: Value Added Tax Act 1994, sch. 11, paras 2 (1) (10) (11) & Finance Act 1994, ss. 38 (1), 42 (2), 54, 74 (7) (8) & Finance Act 1996, ss. 49, 71 (8) (9) & Finance Act 2000, sch. 6, paras 41(1) (2), 146 (7) & Finance Act 2001, ss. 25 (1) (2), 45 (5). - Issued: 18.06.2008. Made: 09.06.2008. Laid: 10.06.2008. Coming into force: 01.07.2008. Effect: S.I. 1994/1738, 1774; 1995/2518; 1996/1527; 2001/838; 2002/761 amended. Territorial extent & classification: E/W/S/NI. General. - 12p.: 30 cm. - 978-0-11-081855-9 £3.00

Extradition

The Extradition Act 2003 (Amendment to Designations) Order 2008 No. 2008/1589. - Enabling power: Extradition Act 2003, ss. 69 (1), 74 (11) (b). - Issued: 24.06.2008. Made: 19.06.2008. Coming into force: 27.06.2008 in accord. with art. 1. Effect: S.I. 2003/3334 amended. Territorial extent & classification: E/W/S/NI. General. - Supersedes draft S.I. (ISBN 9780110814322) issued 07.05.2008. - 2p.: 30 cm. - 978-0-11-081883-2 £3.00

Family law

The Child Maintenance and Other Payments Act 2008 (Commencement No.2) Order 2008 No. 2008/2033 (C.97). - Enabling power: Child Maintenance and Other Payments Act 2008, s. 62 (3). Bringing into operation various provisions of 2008 Act on 24.07.2008 & 05.08.2008 in accord. with art. 2. - Issued: 29.07.2008. Made: 23.07.2008. Effect: None. Territorial extent & classification: E/W/S. General. - 2p.: 30 cm. - 978-0-11-083638-6 £3.00

The Child Maintenance and Other Payments Act 2008 (Commencement No. 3 and Transitional and Savings Provisions) Order 2008 No. 2008/2548 (C.110). - Enabling power: Child Maintenance and Other Payments Act 2008, s. 62 (3) (4). Bringing into operation various provisions of 2008 Act on 26.09.2008 & 27.10.2008 in accord. with arts 2 & 3. - Issued: 01.10.2008. Made: 25.09.2008. Effect: None. Territorial extent & classification: E/W/S. General. - 4p.: 30 cm. - 978-0-11-084311-7 £4.00

The Child Support Information Regulations 2008 No. 2008/2551. - Enabling power: Child Support Act 1991, ss. 4 (4), 7 (5), 14 (1) (3), 50 (5), 51 (1), 52 (4), 54, 57 (1) (2), sch. 1, para. 16 (10). - Issued: 02.10.2008. Made: 26.09.2008. Laid: 02.10.2008. Coming into force: 27.10.2008. Effect: 1991 c. 48 modified & S.I. 1992/1812 revoked (with saving). Territorial extent & classification: E/W/S. General. - 12p.: 30 cm. - 978-0-11-084331-5 £5.00

Family law: Child support

The Child Maintenance and Other Payments Act 2008 (Commencement No. 4 and Transitional Provision) Order 2008 No. 2008/2675 (C.116). - Enabling power: Child Maintenance and Other Payments Act 2008, s. 62 (3) (4). Bringing into operation various provisions of 2008 Act on 01.11.2008 in accord. with arts 1, 2, 3, 4. - Issued: 01.10.2008. Made: 07.10.2008. Effect: None. Territorial extent & classification: E/W/S. General. - 4p.: 30 cm. - 978-0-11-084517-3 £4.00

The Child Maintenance and Other Payments Act 2008 (Commencement) Order 2008 No. 2008/1476 (C. 67). - Enabling power: Child Maintenance and Other Payments Act 2008, s. 62 (3) (4). Bringing into operation various provisions of 2008 Act are 10.06.2008, 14.07.2008 & 01.10.2008 in accord. with art. 2. - Issued: 13.06.2008. Made: 09.06.2008. Effect: -. Territorial extent & classification: E/W/S. General. - 4p.: 30 cm. - 978-0-11-081825-2 £3.00

The Child Support (Consequential Provisions) (No. 2) Regulations 2008 No. 2008/2656. - Enabling power: Child Maintenance and Other Payments Act 2008, s. 57 (2). - Issued: 10.10.2008. Made: 07.10.2008. Laid: 10.10.2008. Coming into force: 01.11.2008. Effect: 2002 c.22; 2003 c.42; S.I. 1991/991 amended. Territorial extent & classification: E/W/S. General. - 4p.: 30 cm. - 978-0-11-084455-8 £4.00

The Child Support (Consequential Provisions) Regulations 2008 No. 2008/2543. - Enabling power: Child Maintenance and Other Payments Act 2008, s. 57 (2). - Issued: 01.10.2008. Made: 26.09.2008. Laid: 01.10.2008. Coming into force: 27.10.2008. Effect: S.I. 1992/1813 amended. Territorial extent & classification: E/W/S. General. - 4p.: 30 cm. - 978-0-11-084309-4 *£4.00*

The Child Support (Miscellaneous Amendments) (No. 2) Regulations 2008 No. 2008/2544. - Enabling power: Child Support Act 1991, ss. 29 (2) (4) (6) (7), 32 (2) (bb), 51 (1) (2) (b), 52 (4), 54, sch. 1, paras 10 (1) (2), 11 & Child Support, Pensions and Social Security Act 2000, s. 29. - Issued: 01.10.2008. Made: 26.09.2008. Laid: 01.10.2008. Coming into force: 27.10.2008. Effect: S.I. 1992/1813, 1989; 1999/991; 2000/3186; 2001/155, 157 amended. Territorial extent & classification: E/W/S. General. - 8p.: 30 cm. - 978-0-11-084310-0 *£5.00*

The Child Support (Miscellaneous Amendments) Regulations 2008 No. 2008/536. - Enabling power: Child Support Act 1991, ss. 14 (1), 32 (1), (3) (a), (8) (9), 54. - Issued: 04.03.2008. Made: 27.02.2008. Laid: 04.03.2008. Coming into force: 06.04.2008. Effect: S.I. 1992/1812, 1989 amended. Territorial extent & classification: E/W/S. General. - 4p.: 30 cm. - 978-0-11-081050-8 *£3.00*

The Child Support, Pensions and Social Security Act 2000 (Commencement No. 14) Order 2008 No. 2008/2545 (C.109). - Enabling power: Child Support, Pensions and Social Security Act 2000, s. 86 (2). Bringing into operation various provisions of the 2000 Act on 26.09.2008 & 27.10.2008 in accord. with arts 2, 3, 4. - Issued: 01.10.2008. Made: 25.09.2008. Effect: None. Territorial extent & classification: E/W/S. General. - 8p.: 30 cm. - 978-0-11-084322-3 *£5.00*

Family law, England and Wales

The Allocation and Transfer of Proceedings Order 2008 No. 2008/2836 (L. 18). - Enabling power: Children Act 1989, s. 92 (9) (10), 94 (10), sch. 11, part 1 & Family Law Act 1996, ss. 57, 65 (2). - Issued: 04.11.2008. Made: 30.10.2008. Laid: 03.11.2008. Coming into force: In acord. with art. 1. Effect: S.I. 1991/1247; 2007/1898 amended & S.I. 1991/1677, 1801; 1993/624; 1994/2164, 3138; 1995/1649; 1997/1896, 1897; 1998/2166; 1999/524; 2000/2670; 2001/775, 1656; 2003/331; 2005/520, 2797, 2924; 2006/1541; 2007/1099 revoked (25.11.2008). Territorial extent & classification: E/W. General. - 20p.: 30 cm. - 978-0-11-084851-8 *£5.00*

The Forced Marriage (Civil Protection) Act 2007 (Commencement No.1) Order 2008 No. 2008/2779 (C.122). - Enabling power: Forced Marriage (Civil Protection) Act 2007, s. 4 (2). Bringing into operation various provisions of the 2007 Act on 25.11.2008. - Issued: 28.10.2008. Made: 20.10.2008. Effect: None. Territorial extent & classification: E/W. General. - 2p.: 30 cm. - 978-0-11-084719-1 *£4.00*

Family law, England and Wales: Child support

The Child Support Commissioners (Procedure) (Amendment) Regulations 2008 No. 2008/1955. - Enabling power: Child Support Act 1991, ss. 24 (6), 25 (2). - Issued: 08.08.2008. Made: 18.07.2008. Laid: 22.07.2008. Coming into force: 20.08.2008. Effect: S.I. 1999/1305 amended. Territorial extent & classification: E/W. General. - Revoked by S.I. 2008/2683 (ISBN 9780110846156). - 2p.: 30 cm. - 978-0-11-083730-7 *£3.00*

The Social Security and Child Support (Decisions and Appeals) (Amendment) Regulations 2008 No. 2008/1957. - Enabling power: Social Security Act 1998, s. 6 (3). - Issued: 25.07.2008. Made: 18.07.2008. Laid: 22.07.2008. Coming into force: 20.08.2008. Effect: S.I. 1999/991 amended. Territorial extent & classification: E/W. General. - Revoked by S.I. 2008/2683 (ISBN 9780110846156). - 2p.: 30 cm. - 978-0-11-083531-0 *£3.00*

Family proceedings, England and Wales

The Family Procedure (Adoption) (Amendment) Rules 2008 No. 2008/2447 (L. 12). - Enabling power: Courts Act 2003, ss. 75 (2) (4). - Issued: 18.09.2008. Made: 16.09.2008. Laid: 18.09.2008. Coming into force: 03.11.2008. Effect: S.I. 2005/2795 amended. Territorial extent & classification: E/W. General. - 2p.: 30 cm. - 978-0-11-084241-7 *£4.00*

The Family Proceedings (Amendment) (No.2) Rules 2008 No. 2008/2861 (L.25). - Enabling power: Matrimonial and Family Proceedings Act 1984, s. 40 (1). - Issued: 12.11.2008. Made: 03.11.2008. Laid: 06.11.2008. Coming into force: 08.12.2008. Effect: S.I. 1991/1247 amended. Territorial extent & classification: E/W. General. - 60p.: 30 cm. - 978-0-11-084967-6 *£9.00*

The Family Proceedings (Amendment) Rules 2008 No. 2008/2446 (L.11). - Enabling power: Matrimonial and Family Proceedings Act 1984, s. 40 (1) (4) (aa). - Issued: 22.090.2008. Made: 16.09.2008. Laid: 18.09.2008. Coming into force: 03.11.2008 for rules 1, 2, 3(a), 5, 6, 10, 12; 25.11.2008 for remainder, in accord. with rule 1 (2). Effect: S.I. 1991/1247 amended. Territorial extent & classification: E/W. General. - 34p.: 30 cm. - 978-0-11-084250-9 *£9.00*

The Family Proceedings Fees (Amendment No. 2) Order 2008 No. 2008/3106 (L.27). - Enabling power: Courts Act 2003, s. 92. - Issued: 09.12.2008. Made: 03.12.2008. Laid: 04.12.2008. Coming into force: 05.12.2008. Effect: S.I. 2008/2856 (L.22) amended. Territorial extent & classification: E/W. General. - This Statutory Instrument is made in consequence of a defect in S.I. 2008/2856 and is being issued free of charge to all known recipients of that Statutory Instrument. - 2p.: 30 cm. - 978-0-11-147105-0 *£4.00*

The Family Proceedings Fees (Amendment) Order 2008 No. 2008/2856 (L.22). - Enabling power: Courts Act 2003, s. 92. - Issued: 10.11.2008. Made: 04.11.2008. Laid: 05.11.2008. Coming into force: 26.11.2008 except for art. 5; 08.12.2008 for art. 5. Effect: S.I. 2008/1054 (L.6) amended. Territorial extent & classification: E/W. General. - 4p.: 30 cm. - 978-0-11-084957-7 £4.00

The Family Proceedings Fees (Amendment) Order 2008 No. 2008/115 (L.1). - Enabling power: Courts Act 2003, s. 92. - Issued: 28.01.2008. Made: 21.01.2008. Laid: 21.01.2008. Coming into force: 11.02.2008. Effect: S.I. 2004/3114 amended. Territorial extent & classification: E/W. General. - Revoked by S.I. 2008/1054 (L.6) (ISBN 9780110813585). This Statutory Instrument has been made in consequence of defects in S.I. 2007/2175 (ISBN 9780110782836) and is being issued free of charge to all known recipients of that SI. - 2p.: 30 cm. - 978-0-11-080861-1 £3.00

The Family Proceedings Fees Order 2008 No. 2008/1054 (L.6). - Enabling power: Courts Act 2003, s. 92. - Issued: 14.04.2008. Made: 07.04.2008. Laid: 09.04.2008. Coming into force: 01.05.2008. Effect: S.I. 2004/3114; 2005/472, 3443; 2006/739; 2007/682, 2175, 2800; 2008/115 revoked. Territorial extent & classification: E/W. General. - 16p.: 30 cm. - 978-0-11-081358-5 £3.00

Farriers

The Farriers' Qualifications (European Recognition) Regulations 2008 No. 2008/646. - Enabling power: European Communities Act 1972, s. 2 (2). - Issued: 13.03.2008. Made: 05.03.2008. Laid: 10.03.2008. Coming into force: 31.03.2008. Effect: 1975 c.35; 1977 c.31 amended. Territorial extent & classification: E/W/S. General. - EC note: These regs implement in part Directive 2005/36/EC. - 8p.: 30 cm. - 978-0-11-081150-5 £3.00

Fees: Insolvency practitioners

The Insolvency Practitioners and Insolvency Services Account (Fees) (Amendment) Order 2008 No. 2008/3. - Enabling power: Insolvency Act 1986, s.415A. - Issued: 10.01.2008. Made: 07.01.2008. Laid: 08.01.2008. Coming into force: 30.01.2008. Effect: S.I. 2003/3363 amended. Territorial extent & classification: E/W/S. General. - Revoked by S.I. 2009/487 (ISBN 9780111475409) in relation to England and Wales. - 4p.: 30 cm. - 978-0-11-080805-5 £3.00

Fees and charges

The Blood Safety and Quality (Fees Amendment) Regulations 2008 No. 2008/525. - Enabling power: European Communities Act 1972, s. 2 (2) & Finance Act 1973, s. 56 (1) (2). - Issued: 05.03.2008. Made: 27.02.2008. Laid: 05.03.2008. Coming into force: 01.04.2008. Effect: S.I. 2005/50 amended. Territorial extent & classification: E/W/S/NI. General. - These Regs further amend the 2005 Regs which implement Directive 2002/98/EC setting out the standards of quality and safety for the collection, testing, processing, storage and distribution of human blood and blood components and related Commission Directives. - 4p.: 30 cm. - 978-0-11-081038-6 £3.00

The Department for Transport (Driver Licensing and Vehicle Registration Fees) (Amendment) Order 2008 No. 2008/908. - Enabling power: Finance (No. 2) Act 1987, s. 102 (3) (4). - Issued: 03.04.2008. Made: 27.03.2008. Coming into force: 28.03.2008 in accord. with art. 1. Effect: S.I. 2003/2994 amended. Territorial extent & classification: E/W/S. General. - Supersedes draft SI (ISBN 9780110809687). With correction slip dated August 2009. - 4p.: 30 cm. - 978-0-11-081305-9 £3.00

The Measuring Instruments (EEC Requirements) (Fees) (Amendment) Regulations 2008 No. 2008/732. - Enabling power: Finance Act 1973, s. 56 (1) (2). - Issued: 20.03.2008. Made: 12.03.2008. Laid: 14.03.2008. Coming into force: 06.04.2008. Effect: S.I. 2004/1300 amended & S.I. 2006/604, 2679 partially revoked. Territorial extent & classification: E/W/S/NI. General. - 2p.: 30 cm. - 978-0-11-081240-3 £3.00

The Medical Devices (Fees Amendments) Regulations 2008 No. 2008/530. - Enabling power: European Communities Act 1972, s. 2 (2) & Finance Act 1973, s. 56 (1) (2). - Issued: 06.03.2008. Made: 27.02.2008. Laid: 06.03.2008. Coming into force: 01.04.2008. Effect: S.I. 1995/449; 2002/618 amended. Territorial extent & classification: E/W/S/NI. General. - 4p.: 30 cm. - 978-0-11-081043-0 £3.00

The Medicines (Products for Human Use-Fees) Regulations 2008 No. 2008/552. - Enabling power: Medicines Act 1971, s. 1 (1) (2) & European Communities Act 1972, s. 2 (2) & Finance Act 1973, s. 56 (1) (2). - Issued: 07.03.2008. Made: 28.02.2008. Laid: 07.03.2008. Coming into force: 01.04.2008. Effect: S.I. 1994/105 amended & S.I. 1998/574; 2000/592; 2001/795; 2002/236, 542; 2003/625; 2004/666; 2006/494, 2125; 2007/803 partially revoked & S.I. 1995/1116; 1996/683; 2000/3031; 2004/1157; 2005/1124, 2979 revoked. Territorial extent & classification: E/W/S/NI. General. - Revoked by S.I. 2009/389 (ISBN 9780111474969) with savings. With correction slip dated March 2008. - 64p.: 30 cm. - 978-0-11-081073-7 £10.50

Fees and charges, England and Wales

The Local Authorities (Alcohol Disorder Zones) Regulations 2008 No. 2008/1430. - Enabling power: Violent Crime Reduction Act 2006, ss. 15, 16 (7), 17 (6), 20 (5) & Local Government Act 2000, ss. 13, 105 (2). - Issued: 09.06.2008. Made: 04.06.2008. Coming into force: 05.06.2008. Effect: S.I. 2000/2853; 2007/399 amended. Territorial extent & classification: E/W. General. - Supersedes draft S.I. (ISBN 9780110813295) issued 04.04.2008. - 16p.: 30 cm. - 978-0-11-081787-3 £3.00

Financial services

The Definition of Financial Instrument Order 2008 No. 2008/3053. - Enabling power: European Communities Act 1972, s. 2 (2). - Issued: 02.12.2008. Made: 24.11.2008. Laid: 25.11.2008. Coming into force: 31.01.2009. Effect: 2000 c.8; S.I. 2001/996 amended. Territorial extent & classification: E/W/S/NI. General. - EC note: This Order amends the definition of "financial instrument" in Part 6 (Official Listing) of the Financial Services and Markets Act 2000 to give further implementation to Directive 2004/39/EC on markets in financial instruments. - 2p.: 30 cm. - 978-0-11-147074-9 £4.00

Financial services and markets

The Financial Services and Markets Act 2000 (Amendment of section 323) Regulations 2008 No. 2008/1469. - Enabling power: European Communities Act 1972, s. 2 (2). - Issued: 13.06.2008. Made: 09.06.2008. Laid: 09.06.2008. Coming into force: 30.06.2008. Effect: 2000 c.8 amended. Territorial extent & classification: E/W/S/NI. General. - 2p.: 30 cm. - 978-0-11-081819-1 £3.00

The Financial Services and Markets Act 2000 (Amendments to Part 7) Regulations 2008 No. 2008/1468. - Enabling power: Financial Services and Markets Act 2000, ss. 117 (b), 428 (3). - Issued: 13.06.2008. Made: 09.06.2008. Laid: 09.06.2008. Coming into force: 30.06.2008. Effect: 2000 c.8 amended. Territorial extent & classification: E/W/S/NI. General. - 2p.: 30 cm. - 978-0-11-081820-7 £3.00

The Financial Services and Markets Act 2000 (Collective Investment Schemes) (Amendment) (No. 2) Order 2008 No. 2008/1813. - Enabling power: Financial Services and Markets Act 2000, ss. 235 (5), 428 (3). - Issued: 14.07.2008. Made: 08.07.2008. Laid: 09.07.2008. Coming into force: 14.07.2008. Effect: S.I. 2008/1641 amended. Territorial extent & classification: E/W/S/NI. General. - This Statutory Instrument has been made in consequence of a defect in SI 2008/1641 (ISBN 9780110819013) and is being issued free of charge to all known recipients of that Statutory Instrument. - 4p.: 30 cm. - 978-0-11-083095-7 £3.00

The Financial Services and Markets Act 2000 (Collective Investment Schemes) (Amendment) Order 2008 No. 2008/1641. - Enabling power: Financial Services and Markets Act 2000, s. 426. - Issued: 27.06.2008. Made: 24.06.2008. Laid: 24.06.2008. Coming into force: 15.07.2008. Effect: S.I. 2001/1062 amended. Territorial extent & classification: E/W/S/NI. General. - With Correction Slip dated July 2008. - 4p.: 30 cm. - 978-0-11-081901-3 £3.00

The Financial Services and Markets Act 2000 (Consequential Amendments) Order 2008 No. 2008/733. - Enabling power: Financial Services and Markets Act 2000, s. 426. - Issued: 19.03.2008. Made: 13.03.2008. Laid: 14.03.2008. Coming into force: 06.04.2008. Effect: 1974 c.39 amended. Territorial extent & classification: E/W/S/NI. General. - 2p.: 30 cm. - 978-0-11-081231-1 £3.00

The Financial Services and Markets Act 2000 (Control of Business Transfers) (Requirements on Applicants) (Amendment) Regulations 2008 No. 2008/1467. - Enabling power: Financial Services and Markets Act 2000, ss. 108, 428 (3). - Issued: 12.06.2008. Made: 09.06.2008. Laid: 09.06.2008. Coming into force: 30.06.2008. Effect: S.I. 2001/3625 amended. Territorial extent & classification: E/W/S/NI. General. - 2p.: 30 cm. - 978-0-11-081815-3 £3.00

The Financial Services and Markets Act 2000 (Control of Transfers of Business Done at Lloyd's) (Amendment) Order 2008 No. 2008/1725. - Enabling power: Financial Services and Markets Act 2000, ss. 323, 428 (3). - Issued: 07.07.2008. Made: 01.07.2008. Laid: 02.07.2008. Coming into force: 23.07.2008. Effect: S.I. 2001/3626 amended. Territorial extent & classification: E/W/S/NI. General. - 2p.: 30 cm. - 978-0-11-081943-3 £3.00

The Financial Services and Markets Act 2000 (Exemption) (Amendment) Order 2008 No. 2008/682. - Enabling power: Financial Services and Markets Act 2000, ss. 38, 428 (3). - Issued: 14.03.2008. Made: 11.03.2008. Laid: 11.03.2008. Coming into force: 01.04.2008. Effect: S.I. 2001/1201 amended. Territorial extent & classification: E/W/S/NI. General. - 2p.: 30 cm. - 978-0-11-081202-1 £3.00

The Financial Services and Markets Act 2000 (Market Abuse) Regulations 2008 No. 2008/1439. - Enabling power: European Communities Act 1972, s. 2 (2). - Issued: 11.06.2008. Made: 05.06.2008. Laid: 06.06.2008. Coming into force: 30.06.2008. Effect: 2000 c.8 amended. Territorial extent & classification: E/W/S/NI. General. - 2p.: 30 cm. - 978-0-11-081804-7 £3.00

The Regulated Covered Bonds (Amendment) Regulations 2008 No. 2008/1714. - Enabling power: European Communities Act 1972, s. 2 (2). - Issued: 04.07.2008. Made: 30.06.2008. Laid: 01.07.2008. Coming into force: 22.07.2008. Effect: S.I. 2008/346 amended. Territorial extent & classification: E/W/S/NI. General. - 4p.: 30 cm. - 978-0-11-081938-9 £3.00

The Regulated Covered Bonds Regulations 2008 No. 2008/346. - Enabling power: European Communities Act 1972, s. 2 (2). - Issued: 19.02.2008. Made: 13.02.2008. Laid: 14.02.2008. Coming into force: 06.03.2008. Effect: 1985 c.6; 1986 c.45; 2000 c.8; 2006 c.46; S.I. 1986/1915 (S 139), 1925; 1989/2405 (N.I. 19). 2006/1030; S R. 1991/364; 2007/115 amended. Territorial extent & classification: E/W/S/NI. General. - 20p.: 30 cm. - 978-0-11-080950-2 £3.50

Fire and rescue services, England

The Fire and Rescue Services (National Framework) (England) Order 2008 No. 2008/1370. - Enabling power: Fire and Rescue Services Act 2004, s. 21 (6). - Issued: 03.06.2008. Made: 23.05.2008. Laid: 03.06.2008. Coming into force: 30.06.2008. Effect: None. Territorial extent & classification: E. General. - Article 2 of this Order, which applies in relation to fire and rescue authorities in England only, substitutes the 2008/11 Framework for the 2006/08 Framework. The 2008/11 Framework will have effect from 30th June 2008. - 2p.: 30 cm. - 978-0-11-081761-3 £3.00

The Firefighters' Pension Scheme (Amendment) (England) Order 2008 No. 2008/214. - Enabling power: Fire Services Act 1947, s. 26 (1) to (5) & Superannuation Act 1972, s. 12. - Issued: 07.02.2008. Made: 30.01.2008. Laid: 07.02.2008. Coming into force: 01.04.2007; 01.07.2007; 29.02.2008 in accord. with art. 1 (2). Effect: S.I. 1992/129 amended in relation to England. Territorial extent & classification: E. General. - 8p.: 30 cm. - 978-0-11-080900-7 £3.00

The Firefighters' Pension Scheme (England) (Amendment) Order 2008 No. 2008/213. - Enabling power: Fire and Rescue Services Act 2004, ss. 34, 60. - Issued: 07.02.2008. Made: 30.01.2008. Laid: 07.02.2008. Coming into force: in accord. with art. 1 (3) (4) (5). Effect: S.I. 2006/3432 amended. Territorial extent & classification: E. General. - 12p.: 30 cm. - 978-0-11-080890-1 £3.00

The Tyne and Wear Fire and Rescue Authority (Increase in Number of Members) Order 2008 No. 2008/566. - Enabling power: Local Government Act 1985, s. 29 (2). - Issued: 06.03.2008. Made: 27.02.2008. Laid: 06.03.2008. Coming into force: 01.05.2008. Effect: 1985 c.51 amended. Territorial extent & classification: E. General. - 2p.: 30 cm. - 978-0-11-081087-4 £3.00

Fire and rescue services, Wales

The Fire and Rescue Authorities (Best Value Performance Indicators) (Wales) Order 2008 No. 2008/450 (W.40). - Enabling power: Local Government Act 1999, ss. 4 (1) (a) (2), 29 (1). - Issued: 12.03.2008. Made: 19.02.2008. Laid before the National Assembly for Wales: 22.02.2008. Coming into force: 18.03.2008. Effect: None. Territorial extent & classification: W. General. - In English and Welsh. Welsh title: Gorchymyn Awdurdodau Tân ac Achub (Dangosyddion Perfformiad Gwerth Gorau) (Cymru) 2008. - 8p.: 30 cm. - 978-0-11-091718-4 £3.00

The Fire and Rescue Authorities (Improvement Plans) (Wales) Order 2008 No. 2008/199 (W.25). - Enabling power: Local Government Act 1999, ss. 6 (3), 7 (6), 29 (1). - Issued: 18.02.2008. Made: 30.01.2008. Laid before the National Assembly for Wales: 01.02.2008. Coming into force: 29.02.2008. Effect: None. Territorial extent & classification: W. General. - In English and Welsh. Welsh title: Gorchymyn yr Awdurdodau Tân ac Achub (Cynlluniau Gwella) (Cymru) 2008. - 4p.: 30 cm. - 978-0-11-091739-9 £3.00

The Fire and Rescue Services (National Framework) (Wales) Order 2008 No. 2008/2298 (W.197). - Enabling power: Fire and Rescue Services Act 2004, ss. 21 (6), 60, 62. - Issued: 15.09.2008. Made: 28.08.2008. Laid before the National Assembly for Wales: 01.09.2008. Coming into force: 22.09.2008. Effect: None. Territorial extent & classification: W. General. - In English and Welsh. Welsh title: Gorchymyn y Gwasanaethau Tân ac Achub (Fframwaith Cenedlaethol) (Cymru) 2008. - 4p.: 30 cm. - 978-0-11-091873-0 £4.00

Fish farming, England

The Fisheries and Aquaculture Structures (Grants) (England) (Amendment) Regulations 2008 No. 2008/1322. - Enabling power: European Communities Act 1972, s. 2 (2). - Issued: 22.05.2008. Made: 18.05.2008. Laid: 21.05.2008. Coming into force: 20.06.2008. Effect: S.I. 2001/1117 amended. Territorial extent & classification: E. General. - This Statutory Instrument has been made in consequence of a defect in S.I. 2001/1117 and is being issued free of charge to all known recipients of that Statutory Instrument. - 2p.: 30 cm. - 978-0-11-081484-1 £3.00

Food

The Charges for Residues Surveillance (Amendment) Regulations 2008 No. 2008/2999. - Enabling power: Food Safety Act 1990, ss. 6 (4), 45, 48 (1) (b). - Issued: 24.11.2008. Made: 15.11.2008. Laid: 21.11.2008. Coming into force: 12.12.2008. Effect: S.I. 2006/2285 amended & S.I. 2007/2439 revoked. Territorial extent & classification: E/W/S. General. - 4p.: 30 cm. - 978-0-11-147024-4 £4.00

The Dairy Produce Quotas (General Provisions) (Amendment) Regulations 2008 No. 2008/438. - Enabling power: European Communities Act 1972, s. 2 (2), sch. 2, para. 1 (A). - Issued: 27.02.2008. Made: 20.02.2008. Laid: 27.02.2008. Coming into force: 01.04.2008. Effect: S.I. 2002/458; 2007/477 amended & S.I. 2005/466 revoked. Territorial extent & classification: E/W/S/NI. General. - EC note: Council Regulation No 1788/2003, referred to in S.I. 2002/458, is repealed on 1st April 2008 and replaced by Articles 55(1)(a) and 55(2), in so far as it relates to milk and other milk products and Section III of Chapter III of Part II (Articles 65 to 84) of Council Regulation No. 1234/2007. These Regulations re-enact the definitions in regulation 2 of the 2002 Regulations accordingly. - 4p.: 30 cm. - 978-0-11-080999-1 £3.00

The Healthy Start Scheme and Welfare Food (Amendment) Regulations 2008 No. 2008/408. - Enabling power: Social Security Act 1988, s. 13 & Social Security Contributions and Benefits Act 1992, s. 175 (2) to (5). - Issued: 25.02.2008. Made: 18.02.2008. Laid: 25.02.2008. Coming into force: 06.04.2008. Effect: S.I. 2005/3262 amended. Territorial extent & classification: E/W/S. General. - 4p.: 30 cm. - 978-0-11-080967-0 *£3.00*

The Spirit Drinks Regulations 2008 No. 2008/3206. - Enabling power: European Communities Act 1972 , s. 2 (2), sch. 2, para. 1A. - Issued: 19.12.2008. Made: 15.12.2008. Laid: 18.12.2008. Coming into force: 16.01.2009. Effect: S.I. 1990/1179, 1196 (S. 136); 1995/484 (S. 33), 732 & S.R. 1990/219; 1995/105 revoked. Territorial extent & classification: E/W/S/NI. General. - EC note: These Regulations make provision for the enforcement of Regulation (EC) No 110/2008 on the definition, description, presentation, labelling and the protection of geographical indications of spirit drinks and repealing Council Regulation (EEC) No 1576/89, and give enforcement authorities new powers in relation to the enforcement of EC requirements relating to spirit drinks, including the power to give improvement notices and to impose monetary penalties by penalty notice. - 24p.: 30 cm. - 978-0-11-147191-3 *£5.00*

Food, England

The Condensed Milk and Dried Milk (England) (Amendment) Regulations 2008 No. 2008/85. - Enabling power: Food Safety Act 1990, ss. 16 (1) (e), 17 (1), 48 (1). - Issued: 22.01.2008. Made: 15.01.2008. Laid: 22.01.2008. Coming into force: 22.02.2008. Effect: S.I. 1995/3124, 3187 amended relation to England; S.I. 2003/1596 amended. Territorial extent & classification: E. General. - EC note: These regs. make provision for the implementation of Council Directive 2007/61/EC amending Directive 2001/114/EC relating to certain partly or wholly dehydrated preserved milk for human consumption. With correction slip dated June 2009. - 4p.: 30 cm. - 978-0-11-080851-2 *£3.00*

The Dairy Produce Quotas (Amendment) Regulations 2008 No. 2008/439. - Enabling power: European Communities Act 1972, s. 2 (2), sch. 2, para. 1 (A). - Issued: 27.02.2008. Made: 20.02.2008. Laid: 27.02.2008. Coming into force: 01.04.2008. Effect: S.I. 2005/465; 2007/106 amended. Territorial extent & classification: E. General. - EC note: These Regs amend S.E. 2005/465 which implement Council Regulation No 1788/2003 and Commission Regulation No 595/2004 laying down detailed rules for applying Council Regulation No 1788/2003. Council Regulation No 1788/2003 is repealed on 1st April 2008 and replaced by Articles 55(1)(a) and 55(2), in so far as it relates to milk and other milk products, and Section III of Chapter III of Part II (Articles 65 to 84) of Council Regulation No. 1234/2007. These Regulations replace the references in the 2005 Regulations accordingly. - 8p.: 30 cm. - 978-0-11-081000-3 *£3.00*

The Drinking Milk (England) Regulations 2008 No. 2008/1317. - Enabling power: European Communities Act 1972, sch. 2, para 1A & Food Safety Act 1990, ss. 6 (4), 16 (1), 17 (2), 26 (1) (3), 48 (1). - Issued: 20.05.2008. Made: 13.05.2008. Laid: 19.05.2008. Coming into force: 01.07.2008. Effect: S.I. 1996/1499 amended & S.I. 1998/2424; 2007/3428 revoked. Territorial extent & classification: E. General. - EC note: These regulations make provision for the enforcement of Article 114(2) of, and Annex XIII to, Council Regulation (EC) No 1234/2007 establishing a common organisation of agricultural markets and on specific provisions for certain agricultural products. - 8p.: 30 cm. - 978-0-11-081471-1 *£3.00*

The Eggs and Chicks (England) Regulations 2008 No. 2008/1718. - Enabling power: European Communities Act 1972, s. 2 (2), sch. 2, para. 1A & Food Safety Act 1990, ss. 6 (4), 16 (1), 17, 26 (2) (3), 48 (1). - Issued: 03.07.2008. Made: 30.06.2008. Laid: 01.07.2008. Coming into force: 02.07.2008. Effect: S.I. 2007/2245 revoked. Territorial extent & classification: E. General. - Revoked by S.I. 2009/2163 (ISBN 9780111484395). EC note: These Regulations revoke and remake, with modifications, the Eggs and Chicks (England) Regulations 2007 (S.I. 2007/2245) following the adoption of Council Regulation (EC) No 1234/2007 establishing a common organisation of agricultural markets and on specific provisions for certain agricultural products (Single CMO Regulation) and two Commission Regulations adopted under that Regulation, Commission Regulation (EC) No 617/2008 and Commission Regulation (EC) No 589/2008. - 24p.: 30 cm. - 978-0-11-081940-2 *£4.00*

The Food Labelling (Declaration of Allergens) (England) Regulations 2008 No. 2008/1188. - Enabling power: Food Safety Act 1990, ss. 16 (1) (e), 17 (1), 26 (1) (a), 48 (1). - Issued: 01.05.2008. Made: 24.04.2008. Laid: 01.05.2008. Coming into force: 31.05.2008. Effect: S.I. 1996/1499; 2004/2824 amended in relation to England & S.I. 2005/2057, 2969; 2007/3256 revoked. Territorial extent & classification: E. General. - Partially revoked by S.I. 2009/2801 (ISBN 9780111486757). EC note: 2. These Regulations implement in England Commission Directive No. 2007/68/EC amending Annex IIIa to Directive 2000/13/EC as regards certain food ingredients. The ingredients in question are those that are likely to cause an allergic reaction in some consumers. - 8p.: 30 cm. - 978-0-11-081413-1 *£3.00*

The Infant Formula and Follow-on Formula (England) (Amendment) Regulations 2008 No. 2008/2445. - Enabling power: Food Safety Act 1990, ss. 16 (1) (e), 17 (1), 26 (1) (a) (3), 48 (1). - Issued: 22.09.2008. Made: 16.09.2008. Laid: 22.09.2008. Coming into force: 29.10.2008. Effect: S.I. S.I. 2000/845; 2007/3521 amended. Territorial extent & classification: E. General. - EC note: These Regs amend the 2007 Regulations to comply with Commission Directive 2006/141/EC on infant formulae and follow-on formulae and amending Directive 1999/21/EC- 8p.: 30 cm. - 978-0-11-084242-4 *£5.00*

The Meat (Official Controls Charges) (England) Regulations 2008 No. 2008/447. - Enabling power: European Communities Act 1972, s. 2 (2), sch. 2, para. 1A. - Issued: 27.02.2008. Made: 20.02.2008. Laid: 27.02.2008. Coming into force: 31.03.2008. Effect: S.I. 2007/3385 revoked. Territorial extent & classification: E. General. - Revoked by S.I. 2009/1574 (ISBN 9780111481417). - 16p.: 30 cm. - 978-0-11-081001-0 £3.00

The Miscellaneous Food Additives (Amendment) (England) Regulations 2008 No. 2008/42. - Enabling power: Food Safety Act 1990, ss. 16 (1) (a), 17 (1), 48 (1), sch. 1, para. 1. - Issued: 17.01.2008. Made: 10.01.2008. Laid: 17.01.2008. Coming into force: 15.02.2008. Effect: S.I. 1995/3187 amended in relation to England. Territorial extent & classification: E. General. - This statutory instrument has been made in consequence of a defect in S.I. 2007/1778 (ISBN 9780110776439) and is being issued free of charge to all known recipients of that instrument. EC note: These Regs, which apply in relation to England only, further amend the 1995 Regs in order to rectify an error caused by a defect in S.I. 2007/1778. With correction slip dated June 2009. - 4p.: 30 cm. - 978-0-11-080831-4 £3.00

The Plastic Materials and Articles in Contact with Food (England) (Amendment) Regulations 2008 No. 2008/1642. - Enabling power: Food Safety Act 1990, ss. 16 (2), 17 (1) (2), 26 (1) (a), 48 (1). - Issued: 27.06.2008. Made: 23.06.2008. Laid: 24.06.2008. Coming into force: 30.06.2008 for the purpose of reg. 4; 01.07.2008 for all other purposes. Effect: S.I. 2007/2786, 2790; 2008/916 amended. Territorial extent & classification: E. General. - EC note: These Regs provide for the execution and enforcement in England of the Commission Regulation amending Commission Regulation (EC) No. 372/2007 laying down transitional migration limits for plasticisers in gaskets in lids intended to come into contact with foods, ("the new Commission Regulation"). The new Commission Regulation extends the relevant deadline for such materials and articles to 30th April 2009. - 4p.: 30 cm. - 978-0-11-081902-0 £3.00

The Plastic Materials and Articles in Contact with Food (England) Regulations 2008 No. 2008/916. - Enabling power: Food Safety Act 1990, ss. 16 (2), 17 (1) (2), 26 (1) (a) (2) (a) (3), 31, 48 (1). - Issued: 03.04.2008. Made: 31.03.2008. Laid: 03.04.2008. Coming into force: 01.05.2008 except for reg. 29 (c); 01.07.2008 for reg. 29 (c). Effect: S.I. 1990/2463; 2007/2790 amended & S.I. 2006/2687; 2007/2786 revoked. Territorial extent & classification: E. General. - Revoked by S.I. 2009/205 (ISBN 9780111473634). EC note: These Regs provide for the implementation of the further amendments made to Commission Directive 2002/72/EC and to Council Directive 85/572/EEC by Commission Directive 2007/19/EC (corrected version at OJ No. L 97, 12.4.2007, p.50). The principal Directives implemented by these Regulations are: Council Directive 82/711/EEC, as amended by Commission Directives 93/8/EEC and 97/48/EC; Council Directive 85/572/EEC, as amended by Directive 2007/19/EC ; Commission Directive 2002/72/EC, as amended by Commission Directives 2004/1/EC, 2004/19/EC and 2005/79/EC, and Directive 2007/19/EC. These regs also provide for the execution and enforcement of Regulation 1895/2005 on the restriction of use of certain epoxy derivatives in materials and articles intended to come into contact with food, which contains Community provisions relating to the epoxy derivatives known as BADGE, BFDGE and NOGE. With correction slip dated August 2009. - 36p.: 30 cm. - 978-0-11-081323-3 £6.50

The Rice Products from the United States of America (Restriction on First Placing on the Market) (England) Regulations 2008 No. 2008/622. - Enabling power: European Communities Act 1972 , s. 2 (2). - Issued: 13.03.2008. Made: 06.03.2008. Laid: 06.03.2008. Coming into force: 07.03.2008. Effect: S.I. 2006/2921 revoked. Territorial extent & classification: E. General. - EC note: These Regulations implement in relation to England Commission Decision 2006/601/EC on emergency measures regarding the non-authorised genetically modified organism "LL RICE 601" in rice products as last amended by Commission Decision 2008/162/EC. - 8p.: 30 cm. - 978-0-11-081126-0 £3.00

The Specified Products from China (Restriction on First Placing on the Market) (England) Regulations 2008 No. 2008/1079. - Enabling power: European Communities Act 1972 , s. 2 (2). - Issued: 17.04.2008. Made: 14.04.2008. Laid: 14.04.2008. Coming into force: 15.04.2008. Effect: None. Territorial extent & classification: E. General. - EC note: These Regulations implement, in England, Commission Decision 2008/289/EC on emergency measures regarding the unauthorised genetically modified organism 'Bt 63' in rice products. - 8p.: 30 cm. - 978-0-11-081373-8 £3.00

The Spreadable Fats (Marketing Standards) and the Milk and Milk Products (Protection of Designations) (England) Regulations 2008 No. 2008/1287. - Enabling power: Food Safety Act 1990, ss. 16 (1), 17 (2), 26 (1) (3), 48 (1). - Issued: 20.05.2008. Made: 13.05.2008. Laid: 20.05.2008. Coming into force: 01.07.2008. Effect: S.I. 1990/607 revoked in relation to England & S.I. 1999/2457; 2007/1615 revoked. Territorial extent & classification: E. General. - EC note: These Regulations provide for the execution and enforcement, in relation to England only, of certain provisions of Council Regulation 1234/2007 establishing a common organisation of agricultural markets and on specific provisions for certain agricultural products. - 8p.: 30 cm. - 978-0-11-081468-1 £3.00

Food, England: Composition and labelling

The Meat Products (England) (Amendment) Regulations 2008 No. 2008/517. - Enabling power: Food Safety Act 1990, ss. 16 (1) (e), 48 (1). - Issued: 05.03.2008. Made: 26.02.2008. Laid: 05.03.2008. Coming into force: 06.04.2008. Effect: S.I. 2003/2075 amended. Territorial extent & classification: E. General. - 4p.: 30 cm. - 978-0-11-081084-3 £3.00

Food, Wales

The Condensed Milk and Dried Milk (Wales) (Amendment) Regulations 2008 No. 2008/137 (W.19). - Enabling power: Food Safety Act 1990, ss. 16 (1) (e), 17 (1), 48 (1). - Issued: 27.02.2008. Made: 22.01.2008. Laid before the National Assembly for Wales: 24.01.2008. Coming into force: 22.02.2008. Effect: S.I. 1995/3124, 3187 amended in relation to Wales & S.I. 2003/3053 (W.291) amended. Territorial extent & classification: W. General. - EC note: These regs make provision for the implementation of Council Directive 2007/61/EC amending Directive 2001/114/EC relating to certain partly or wholly dehydrated preserved milk for human consumption. - In English and Welsh. Welsh title: Rheoliadau Llaeth Cyddwys a Llaeth Sych (Cymru) (Diwygio) 2008. - 8p.: 30 cm. - 978-0-11-091709-2 £3.00

The Dairy Produce Quotas (Wales) (Amendment) Regulations 2008 No. 2008/685 (W.72). - Enabling power: European Communities Act 1972, s. 2 (2). - Issued: 28.03.2008. Made: 10.03.2008. Laid before the National Assembly for Wales: 11.03.2008. Coming into force: 01.04.2008. Effect: S.I. 2005/537 (W.47); 2007/844 (W.76) amended. Territorial extent & classification: W. General. - EC note: These regs amend the 2005 regulations which implemented Council Regulation (EC) No. 1788/2003 establishing a levy in the milk and milk products sector and Commission Regulation (EC) No. 595/2004 laying down detailed rules for applying Council Regulation (EC) No. 1788/2003 establishing a levy in the milk and milk products sector. - In English and Welsh. Welsh title: Rheoliadau Cwotâu Cynnyrch Llaeth (Cymru) (Diwygio) 2007. - 12p.: 30 cm. - 978-0-11-091770-2 £3.00

The Food Labelling (Declaration of Allergens) (Wales) Regulations 2008 No. 2008/1268 (W.128). - Enabling power: Food Safety Act 1990, ss. 16 (1) (e), 17 (1), 26 (1) (a), 48 (1). - Issued: 23.05.2008. Made: 06.05.2008. Laid before the National Assembly for Wales: 08.05.2008. Coming into force: 31.05.2008. Effect: S.I. 1996/1499 amended in relation to Wales & S.I. 2004/3022 (W.261); 2005/2835 (W.200), 3626 (W.241); 2007/3379 (W.301) revoked. Territorial extent & classification: W. General. - EC note: These Regulations implement in Wales Commission Directive No. 2007/68/EC amending Annex IIIa to Directive 2000/13/EC as regards certain food ingredients. The ingredients in question are those likely to cause an allergic reaction in some consumers. - In English and Welsh. Welsh title: Rheoliadau Labelu Bwyd (Datgan Alergenau) (Cymru) 2008. - 8p.: 30 cm. - 978-0-11-091782-5 £3.00

The Honey (Wales) (Amendment) Regulations 2008 No. 2008/543 (W.53). - Enabling power: Food Safety Act 1990, ss. 16 (1) (e), 17 (1), 26 (1) (3), 48 (1). - Issued: 20.03.2008. Made: 28.02.2008. Laid before the National Assembly for Wales: 29.02.2008. Coming into force: 24.03.2008. Effect: S.I. 2003/3044 (W.288) amended. Territorial extent & classification: W. General. - EC note: These regs implement the Corrigendum to EC Directive 2001/110 which corrected an error to Annex II of that Directive. - In English and Welsh. Welsh title: Rheoliadau Mêl (Cymru) (Diwygio) 2008. - 4p.: 30 cm. - 978-0-11-091764-1 £3.00

The Infant Formula and Follow-on Formula (Amendment) (Wales) Regulations 2008 No. 2008/2602 (W.228). - Enabling power: Food Safety Act 1990, ss. 16 (1) (e), 17 (1), 26 (1) (a) (3), 48 (1). - Issued: 24.10.2008. Made: 01.10.2008. Laid before the National Assembly for Wales: 06.10.2008. Coming into force: 29.10.2008. Effect: S.I. 2000/1866 (W.125); 2007/3573 (W.316) amended. Territorial extent & classification: W. General. - In English and Welsh. Welsh title: Rheoliadau Fformiwla Fabanod a Fformiwla Ddilynol (Diwygio) (Cymru) 2008. - 8p.: 30 cm. - 978-0-11-091860-0 £5.00

The Meat (Official Controls Charges) (Wales) Regulations 2008 No. 2008/601 (W.63). - Enabling power: European Communities Act 1972, s. 2 (2), sch. 2, para. 1A. - Issued: 04.04.2008. Made: 04.03.2008. Laid before the National Assembly for Wales: 06.03.2008. Coming into force: 31.03.2008. Effect: S.I. 2007/3461 (W.306) revoked. Territorial extent & classification: W. General. - Revoked by W.S.I. 2009/1557 (W.152) (ISBN 9780348100495). EC note: These Regulations provide for the execution and enforcement in relation to Wales of Articles 26 and 27 of Regulation (EC) No. 882/2004 on official controls performed to ensure the verification of compliance with feed and food law, animal health and animal welfare rules. The revised text of Regulation (EC) No. 882/2004 is now set out in a Corrigendum, OJ No. L191, 28.5.2004, p.1, which should be read with a further Corrigendum, OJ No.L204, 4.8.2007, p.29). - In English and Welsh. Welsh language title: Rheoliadau Cig (Ffioedd Rheolaethau Swyddogol) (Cymru) 2008. - 24p.: 30 cm. - 978-0-11-091749-8 £4.00

The Miscellaneous Food Additives and the Sweeteners in Food (Amendment) (Wales) Regulations 2008 No. 2008/138 (W.20). - Enabling power: Food Safety Act 1990, ss. 16 (1) (a), 17 (1), 26 (1) (3), 48 (1), sch. 1, para. 1. - Issued: 19.02.2008. Made: 22.01.2008. Laid before the National Assembly for Wales: 24.01.2008. Coming into force: 15.02.2008. Effect: S.I. 1995/3123, 3187 amended. Territorial extent & classification: W. General. - These regs provide for the implementation of Directive 2006/52/EC amending Directive 95/2/EC on food additives other than colours and sweeteners and Directive 94/35/EC on sweeteners for use in foodstuffs as corrected by a Corrigendum and Commission Directive 2006/129/EC amending and correcting Directive 96/77/EC laying down specific purity criteria on food additives other than colours or sweeteners. - In English and Welsh. Rheoliadau Ychwanegion Bwyd Amrywiol a Melysyddion mewn Bwyd (Diwygio) (Cymru) 2008. - 20p.: 30 cm. - 978-0-11-091737-5 *£3.50*

The Plastic Materials and Articles in Contact with Food (Lid Gaskets) (Wales) Regulations 2008 No. 2008/56 (W.11). - Enabling power: Food Safety Act 1990, ss. 16 (2) (c), 17 (2), 26 (1) (a) (3), 48 (1). - Issued: 08.02.2008. Made: 14.01.2008. Laid before the National Assembly for Wales: 16.01.2008. Coming into force: 08.02.2008. Effect: S.I. 1990/2463 amended in relation to Wales. Territorial extent & classification: W. General. - Revoked by W.S.I. 2008/1237 (W.124) (ISBN 9780110917795). EC note: These Regulations, which apply in relation to Wales, provide for the execution and enforcement of Commission Regulation No 372/2007 laying down transitional migration limits for plasticisers in gaskets in lids intended to come into contact with foods. - In English and Welsh. Welsh title: Rheoliadau Defnyddiau ac Eitemau Plastig mewn Cyffyrddiad â Bwyd (Gasgedi mewn Caeadau) (Cymru) 2008. - 12p.: 30 cm. - 978-0-11-091734-4 *£3.00*

The Plastic Materials and Articles in Contact with Food (Wales) (No.2) Regulations 2008 No. 2008/1682 (W.162). - Enabling power: Food Safety Act 1990, ss. 16 (2), 17 (1) (2), 26 (1) (a) (2) (a) (3), 31, 48 (1). - Issued: 21.07.2008. Made: 27.06.2008. Laid before the National Assembly for Wales: 27.06.2008. Coming into force: 30.06.2008 for reg. 30 (a) & 01.07.2008 for all other purposes. Effect: S.I. 1990/2463; 2007/3252 (W.287); S.I. 2008/56 (W.11) amended & S.I. 2008/1237 (W.124) partially revoked (30.06.2008) and then fully revoked (01.07.2008). Territorial extent & classification: W. General. - Revoked by W.S.I. 2009/481 (W.162) (ISBN 9780110918228). EC note: These regs revoke the Plastic Materials and Articles in Contact with Food (Wales) Regulations 2008, (S.I. 2008/1237 (W.124)), and re-enact those Regulations with certain changes. The main change is to provide for the execution and enforcement in Wales of Commission Regulation (EC) No. 597/2008 amending Commission Regulation (EC) No. 372/2007 laying down transitional migration limits for plasticisers in gaskets in lids intended to come into contact with foods, (the new Commission Regulation). The new Commission Regulation extends the relevant deadline for such materials and articles to 30 April 2009. These Regulations provide for the execution and enforcement of the new Commission Regulation in regulations 22(3)(a) and 30(a). - In English and Welsh. Welsh title: Rheoliadau Deunyddiau ac Eitemau Plastig mewn Cyffyrddiad a Bywd (Cymru) (Rhif 2) 2008. - 68p.: 30 cm. - 978-0-11-091822-8 *£10.50*

The Plastic Materials and Articles in Contact with Food (Wales) Regulations 2008 No. 2008/1237 (W.124). - Enabling power: Food Safety Act 1990, ss. 16 (2), 17 (1) (2), 26 (1) (a) (2) (a) (3), 31, 48 (1). - Issued: 19.05.2008. Made: 30.04.2008. Laid before the National Assembly for Wales: 30.04.2008. Coming into force: 01.05.2008 except for reg. 29 (c) & 01.07.2008 for reg 29 (c). Effect: S.I. 1990/2463; 2007/3252 (W.287) amended & S.I. 2006/2982 (W.273); 2008/56 (W.11) revoked. Territorial extent & classification: W. General. - Revoked by W.S.I. 2008/1682 (W.162) (ISBN 9780110918228). EC note: These regs implement further amendments made to Commission Directive 2002/72/EC and to Council Directive 85/572/EEC by Commission Directive 2007/19/EC (corrected version at OJ No. L 97, 12.4.2007, p.50). They also implement: Council Directive 82/711/EEC, as amended by Commission Directives 93/8/EEC and 97/48/EC; Council Directive 85/572/EEC, as amended by the new Commission Directive; Commission Directive 2002/72/EC, as amended by Commission Directives 2004/1/EC, 2004/19/EC and 2005/79/EC, and 2007/19/EC. - 36p.: 30 cm. - 978-0-11-091779-5 *£6.50*

The Rice Products from the United States of America (Restriction on First Placing on the Market) (Wales) (Amendment) Regulations 2008 No. 2008/1646 (W.159). - Enabling power: European Communities Act 1972, s. 2 (2). - Issued: 07.07.2008. Made: 23.06.2008. Laid before the National Assembly for Wales: 24.06.2008. Coming into force: 17.07.2008. Effect: S.I. 2008/781 (W.80) amended. Territorial extent & classification: W. General. - EC note: These Regulations amend S.I. 2008/781 (W.80) which implement in relation to Wales, Commission Decision 2006/601/EC on emergency measures regarding non-authorised genetically modified organism "LL RICE 601" in rice products as last amended by Commission Decision 2008/162/EC amending Decision 2006/601/EC. - In English and Welsh. Welsh title: Rheoliadau Cynhyrchion Reis o Unol Daleithiau America (Cyfyngiad ar eu Rhoi Gyntaf ar y Farchnad) (Cymru) (Diwygio) 2008. - 4p.: 30 cm. - 978-0-11-091838-9 £3.00

The Rice Products from the United States of America (Restriction on First Placing on the Market) (Wales) Regulations 2008 No. 2008/781 (W.80). - Enabling power: European Communities Act 1972, s. 2 (2). - Issued: 14.04.2008. Made: 18.03.2008. Laid before the National Assembly for Wales: 19.03.2008. Coming into force: 20.03.2008. Effect: S.I. 2006/2923 (W.260) revoked. Territorial extent & classification: W. General. - EC note: These Regulations implement in relation to Wales Commission Decision 2006/601/EC on emergency measures regarding non-authorised genetically modified organism "LL RICE 601" in rice products as last amended by Commission Decision 2008/162/EC amending Decision 2006/601/EC. - In English and Welsh. Welsh title: Rheoliadau Cynhyrchion Reis o Unol Daleithiau America (Cyfyngiad ar eu Rhoi Gyntaf ar y Farchnad) (Cymru) 2008. - 8p.: 30 cm. - 978-0-11-091753-5 £3.00

The Spreadable Fats (Marketing Standards) and the Milk and Milk Products (Protection of Designations) (Wales) Regulations 2008 No. 2008/1341 (W.141). - Enabling power: Food Safety Act 1990, ss. 16 (1), 17 (2), 26 (1) (3), 48 (1). - Issued: 09.06.2008. Made: 21.05.2008. Laid before the National Assembly for Wales: 22.05.2008. Coming into force: 01.07.2008. Effect: S.I. 1990/607 revoked in relation to Wales; S.I. 2001/1361 (W.89), 2007/1905 (W.163) revoked. Territorial extent & classification: W. General. - EC note: These Regulations provide for the execution and enforcement, in relation to Wales, of certain provisions of Council Regulation (EC) No. 1234/2007 establishing a common organisation of agricultural markets and on specific provisions for certain agricultural products. - In English and Welsh. Welsh title: Rheoliadau Brasterau Taenadwy (Safonau Marchnata) a Llaeth a Chynhyrchion Llaeth (Diogelu Dynodiadau) (Cymru) 2008. - 8p.: 30 cm. - 978-0-11-091791-7 £3.00

Food, Wales: Composition and labelling

The Meat Products (Wales) (Amendment) Regulations 2008 No. 2008/713 (W.74). - Enabling power: Food Safety Act 1990, ss. 16 (1) (e), 48 (1). - Issued: 28.03.2008. Made: 11.03.2008. Laid before the National Assembly for Wales: 12.03.2008. Coming into force: 06.04.2008. Effect: S.I. 2004/1396 (W.141) amended. Territorial extent & classification: W. General. - EC note: Following the repeal of Council Directive 77/99/EEC, these Regulations remove a requirement in S.I. 1996/1449 (as amended) concerning food labelling. - In English and Welsh. Welsh title: Rheoliadau Cynhyrchion Cig (Cymru) (Diwygio) 2008. - 4p.: 30 cm. - 978-0-11-091769-6 £3.00

Freedom of information

The Freedom of Information (Additional Public Authorities) Order 2008 No. 2008/1271. - Enabling power: Freedom of Information Act 2000, s. 4 (1) (6). - Issued: 12.05.2008. Made: 08.05.2008. Laid: 08.05.2008. Coming into force: 02.06.2008. Effect: 2000 c. 36 amended. Territorial extent & classification: E/W/S/NI. General. - 2p.: 30 cm. - 978-0-11-081447-6 £3.00

The Freedom of Information (Parliament and National Assembly for Wales) Order 2008 No. 2008/1967. - Enabling power: Freedom of Information Act 2000, s. 7 (3) (a). - Issued: 28.07.2008. Made: 22.07.2008. Coming into force: 23.07.2008. Effect: 2000 c. 36 amended. Territorial extent & classification: E/W/S/NI. General. - Supersedes draft S.I. (ISBN 9780110833385) issued 21.07.2008. - 4p.: 30 cm. - 978-0-11-083599-0 £3.00

Friendly societies

The Friendly Societies (Accounts and Related Provisions) (Amendment) Regulations 2008 No. 2008/1144. - Enabling power: Friendly Societies Act 1992, ss. 69C (1) (2) (3), 69G (1) (2) (3), 121 (3). - Issued: 24.04.2008. Made: 21.04.2005. Laid: 21.04.2008. Coming into force: 29.06.2008. Effect: S.I. 1994/1983 amended. Territorial extent & classification: E/W/S/NI. General. - EC note: These Regulations amend S.I. 1994/1983 to implement in part Directive 2006/46/EC on the annual and consolidated accounts of certain types of companies, banks and other financial institutions. - 4p.: 30 cm. - 978-0-11-081389-9 £3.00

The Friendly Societies (Accounts, Audit and EEA State Amendments) Order 2008 No. 2008/1140. - Enabling power: Friendly Societies Act 1992, s. 102 (1) (3) (4) & European Communities Act 1972, s. 2 (2). - Issued: 24.04.2008. Made: 21.04.2008. Laid: 21.04.2008. Coming into force: 29.06.2008. Effect: 1992 c. 40 modified. Territorial extent & classification: E/W/S/NI. General. - EC note: This Order amends the Friendly Societies Act 1992 to implement, in relation to friendly societies, parts of Directive 2006/43/EC on statutory audits of annual accounts and parts of Directive 2006/46/EC on the annual and consolidated accounts of certain types of companies, banks and other financial institutions. With correction slip dated July 2009. - 16p.: 30 cm. - 978-0-11-081387-5 £3.00

Gas

The Electricity and Gas (Billing) Regulations 2008 No. 2008/1163. - Enabling power: European Communities Act 1972, s. 2 (2). - Issued: 28.04.2008. Made: 23.04.2008. Laid: 24.04.2008. Coming into force: 17.05.2008. Effect: None. Territorial extent & classification: E/W/S. General. - EC note: These Regulations modify the standard conditions in electricity and gas supply licences in Great Britain. The modifications give effect to Article 13(3)(b) of Directive 2006/32/EC on energy end-use efficiency and energy services and repealing Council Directive 93/76/EEC. - 8p.: 30 cm. - 978-0-11-081401-8 £3.00

The Electricity and Gas (Carbon Emissions Reduction) Order 2008 No. 2008/188. - Enabling power: Gas Act 1986, 33BC & Electricity Act 1989, s. 41A & Utilities Act 2000, s. 103. - Issued: 05.02.2008. Made: 30.01.2008. Coming into force: 31.01.208 in accord. with art. 1. Effect: None. Territorial extent & classification: E/W/S. General. - Supersedes draft SI (ISBN 9780110805306) issued 13.12.2007. - 16p.: 30 cm. - 978-0-11-080884-0 £3.00

The Gas and Electricity (Consumer Complaints Handling Standards) Regulations 2008 No. 2008/1898. - Enabling power: Consumers, Estate Agents and Redress Act 2007, ss, 43, 44, 46. - Issued: 23.07.2008. Made: 16.07.2008. Coming into force: 01.10.2008. Effect: None. Territorial extent & classification: E/W/S. General. - With correction slip dated August 2008. - 12p.: 30 cm. - 978-0-11-083411-5 £3.00

The Gas and Electricity Regulated Providers (Redress Scheme) Order 2008 No. 2008/2268. - Enabling power: Consumers, Estate Agents and Redress Act 2007, s. 47 (1) to (3). - Issued: 29.08.2008. Made: 16.08.2008. Laid: 27.08.2008. Coming into force: 01.10.2008. Effect: None. Territorial extent & classification: E/W/S. General. - 4p.: 30 cm. - 978-0-11-083863-2 £3.00

The Gas (Applications for Licences and Extensions and Restrictions of Licences) Regulations 2008 No. 2008/2375. - Enabling power: Gas Act 1986, ss. 7B (1) (2) (11), 47. - Issued: 15.09.2008. Made: 08.09.2008. Coming into force: 01.10.2008. Effect: S.I. 2007/1971 revoked. Territorial extent & classification: E/W/S. General. - 12p.: 30 cm. - 978-0-11-084182-3 £5.00

The Gas (Standards of Performance) (Amendment) Regulations 2008 No. 2008/696. - Enabling power: Gas Act 1986, ss. 33A, 33AA, 33D, 47. - Issued: 14.03.2008. Made: 10.03.2008. Coming into force: 01.04.2008. Effect: S.I. 2005/1135 amended. Territorial extent & classification: E/W/S/NI. General. - 12p.: 30 cm. - 978-0-11-081190-1 £3.00

Gender recognition

The Gender Recognition (Application Fees) (Amendment) Order 2008 No. 2008/715. - Enabling power: Gender Recognition Act 2004, ss. 7 (2), 24 (1). - Issued: 17.03.2008. Made: 07.03.2008. Laid: 12.03.2008. Coming into force: 06.04.2008. Effect: S.I. 2006/758 amended. Territorial extent & classification: E/W/S/NI. General. - 2p.: 30 cm. - 978-0-11-081200-7 £3.00

Government resources and accounts

The Government Resources and Accounts Act 2000 (Audit of Public Bodies) Order 2008 No. 2008/817. - Enabling power: Government Resources and Accounts Act 2000, s. 25 (6) (7). - Issued: 31.03.2008. Made: 25.03.2008. Coming into force: 26.03.2008 in accord. with art. 1. Effect: 1993 c.48; 1998 c.18; 2004 c.35; 2006 c.41; S.R. 2002/260 amended. Territorial extent & classification: E/W/S/NI. General. - Supersedes draft S.I. (ISBN 9780110810300) issued 04.03.2008. - 4p.: 30 cm. - 978-0-11-081289-2 £3.00

The Whole of Government Accounts (Designation of Bodies) (No. 2) Order 2008 No. 2008/1907. - Enabling power: Government Resources and Accounts Act 2000, s. 10 (1). - Issued: 23.07.2008. Made: 17.07.2008. Laid: 18.07.2008. Coming into force: 08.08.2008. Effect: S.I. 2008/1440 revoked. Territorial extent & classification: E/W/S/NI. General. - 28p.: 30 cm. - 978-0-11-083426-9 £4.50

The Whole of Government Accounts (Designation of Bodies) Order 2008 No. 2008/1440. - Enabling power: Government Resources and Accounts Act 2000, s. 25 (6) (7). - Issued: 12.06.2008. Made: 05.06.2008. Laid: 06.06.2008. Coming into force: 27.06.2008. Effect: None. Territorial extent & classification: E/W/S/NI. General. - Revoked by S.I. 2008/1907 (ISBN 9780110834269). - 28p.: 30 cm. - 978-0-11-081805-4 £4.50

Government trading funds

The Defence Aviation Repair Agency Trading Fund (Amendment) Order 2008 No. 2008/628. - Enabling power: Government Trading Funds Act 1973, ss. 1, 2 (7), 2AA (1), 2A (1), 6 (1). - Issued: 13.03.2008. Made: 05.03.2008. Laid: 10.03.2008. Coming into force: 01.04.2008. Effect: S.I. 2001/1165 amended. Territorial extent & classification: E/W/S/NI. General. - 4p.: 30 cm. - 978-0-11-081137-6 £3.00

The Defence Aviation Repair Agency Trading Fund (Revocation) Order 2008 No. 2008/1208. - Enabling power: Government Trading Funds Act 1973, ss. 1, 6 (1). - Issued: 06.05.2008. Made: 28.04.2008. Laid: 01.05.2008. Coming into force: 23.05.2008. Effect: S.I. 2001/1165 revoked. Territorial extent & classification: E/W/S/NI. General. - 2p.: 30 cm. - 978-0-11-081426-1 *£3.00*

The Defence Support Group Trading Fund Order 2008 No. 2008/563. - Enabling power: Government Trading Funds Act 1973, ss. 1, 2 (1), 2 (7), 2AA (1), 2A (1), 2C (1), 6 (1). - Issued: 06.03.2008. Made: 27.02.2008. Coming into force: 01.04.2008. Effect: S.I. 2002/719 revoked. Territorial extent & classification: E/W/S/NI. General. - Supersedes draft S.I. (ISBN 9780110808420) issued on 18.01.2008. - 4p.: 30 cm. - 978-0-11-081082-9 *£3.00*

The FCO Services Trading Fund Order 2008 No. 2008/590. - Enabling power: Government Trading Funds Act 1973, ss. 1, 2, 2AA (1) (2), 2A (1), 2C (1). - Issued: 11.03.2008. Made: 03.03.2008. Coming into force: 01.04.2008. Effect: None. Territorial extent & classification: E/W/S/NI. General. - 4p.: 30 cm. - 978-0-11-081117-8 *£3.00*

Harbours, docks, piers and ferries

The Harwich Haven Harbour Revision Order 2008 No. 2008/2359. - Enabling power: Harbours Act 1964, s. 14 (7). - Issued: 10.09.2008. Made: 02.09.2008. Coming into force: 08.09.2008. Effect: 1974 c. i; 1988 c. xxxiv; S.I. 1985/1803 partially repealed/revoked. Territorial extent & classification: E. Local. - 4p.: 30 cm. - 978-0-11-084076-5 *£4.00*

The London Gateway Port Harbour Empowerment Order 2008 No. 2008/1261. - Enabling power: Harbours Act 1964, s. 16 (1). - Issued: 14.05.2008. Made: 02.05.2008. Coming into force: 16.05.2008. Effect: None. Territorial extent & classification: E/W/S/NI. General. - With correction slip dated June 2008. - 92p.: 30 cm. - 978-0-11-081448-3 *£13.50*

The Port of Tyne Harbour Revision Order 2008 No. 2008/1817. - Enabling power: Harbours Act 1964, s. 14 (7). - Issued: 15.07.2008. Made: 08.07.2008. Coming into force: 14.07.2008. Effect: None. Territorial extent & classification: E. Local. - 2p.: 30 cm. - 978-0-11-083102-2 *£3.00*

The Port of Weston Harbour Revision Order 2008 No. 2008/230. - Enabling power: Harbours Act 1964, s. 14 (7). - Issued: 13.02.2008. Made: 06.02.2008. Coming into force: 27.02.2008. Effect: None. Territorial extent & classification: E. Local. - 8p.: 30 cm. - 978-0-11-080915-1 *£3.00*

The Teesport Harbour Revision Order 2008 No. 2008/1160. - Enabling power: Harbours Act 1964, s. 14. - Issued: 28.04.2008. Made: 18.04.2008. Coming into force: 08.05.2008. Effect: None. Territorial extent & classification: E. Local. - 12p.: 30 cm. - 978-0-11-081398-1 *£3.00*

Health and personal social services, Northern Ireland

The Health Service Branded Medicines (Control of Prices and Supply of Information) (No. 2) Regulations 2008 No. 2008/3258. - Enabling power: National Health Service Act 2006, ss. 261 (7), 262 (1), 263 to 265, 266 (1) (2), 272 (7) (8). - Issued: 23.12.2008. Made: 17.12.2008. Laid: 23.12.2008. Coming into force: 01.02.2009. Effect: S.I. 2007/1320 amended & S.I. 2008/1938 revoked. Territorial extent & classification: E/W/S/NI. General. - 8p.: 30 cm. - 978-0-11-147224-8 *£5.00*

The Health Service Branded Medicines (Control of Prices and Supply of Information) Regulations 2008 No. 2008/1938. - Enabling power: National Health Service Act 2006, ss. 261 (7), 262 (1), 263 to 265, 266 (1) (2), 272 (7) (8). - Issued: 24.07.2008. Made: 19.07.2008. Laid: 21.07.2008. Coming into force: 01.09.2008. Effect: S.I. 2007/1320 amended. Territorial extent & classification: E/W/S/NI. General. - Revoked by S.I. 2008/3258 (ISBN 9780111472248). - 8p.: 30 cm. - 978-0-11-083521-1 *£3.00*

Health and safety

The Adventure Activities Licensing (Amendment) Regulations 2008 No. 2008/1973. - Enabling power: Activity Centres (Young Persons' Safety) Act 1995, s. 1 (4) (f). - Issued: 25.07.2008. Made: 16.07.2008. Laid: 25.07.2008. Coming into force: 01.10.2008. Effect: S.I. 2004/1309 amended. Territorial extent & classification: E/W/S. General. - 4p.: 30 cm. - 978-0-11-083609-6 *£3.00*

The Blood Safety and Quality (Fees Amendment) Regulations 2008 No. 2008/525. - Enabling power: European Communities Act 1972, s. 2 (2) & Finance Act 1973, s. 56 (1) (2). - Issued: 05.03.2008. Made: 27.02.2008. Laid: 05.03.2008. Coming into force: 01.04.2008. Effect: S.I. 2005/50 amended. Territorial extent & classification: E/W/S/NI. General. - These Regs further amend the 2005 Regs which implement Directive 2002/98/EC setting out the standards of quality and safety for the collection, testing, processing, storage and distribution of human blood and blood components and related Commission Directives. - 4p.: 30 cm. - 978-0-11-081038-6 *£3.00*

The Chemicals (Hazard Information and Packaging for Supply) (Amendment) Regulations 2008 No. 2008/2337. - Enabling power: European Communities Act 1972, s. 2 (2) & Health and Safety at Work etc. Act 1974, ss. 15 (1) (2) (3) (a) (c) (4) (a) (b), sch. 3, paras. 1 (1) (b) (4), 3 (2). - Issued: 05.09.2008. Made: 01.09.2008. Laid: 05.09.2008. Coming into force: 01.10.2008. Effect: S.I. 1999/743; 2002/1689; 2005/2571 amended. Territorial extent & classification: E/W/S. General. - Revoked by S.I. 2009/716 (ISBN 9780111476741) in accord. with Sch. 6 and 7. EC note: Transposes provisions of Directive 1992/32/EEC and 1999/45/EC; amends Regulations in accordance with Directive 2006/8. - 12p.: 30 cm. - With correction slip dated September 2009. - 978-0-11-083984-4 *£5.00*

The Control of Major Accident Hazard (Amendment) Regulations 2008 No. 2008/1087. - Enabling power: Health and Safety at Work etc. Act 1974, ss. 43 (2) (4) (5) (6), 82 (3) (a). - Issued: 23.04.2008. Made: 16.04.2008. Laid: 17.04.2008. Coming into force: 18.04.2008. Effect: S.I. 1999/743 amended. Territorial extent & classification: E/W/S. General. - This Statutory Instrument has been made in consequence of a defect in S.I. 2008/736 and is being issued free of charge to all known recipients of that Statutory Instrument. - 2p.: 30 cm. - 978-0-11-081379-0 *£3.00*

The Export and Import of Dangerous Chemicals Regulations 2008 No. 2008/2108. - Enabling power: European Communities Act 1972, s. 2 (2), sch. 2, para. 1A. - Issued: 08.08.2008. Made: 05.08.2008. Laid: 08.08.2008. Coming into force: 03.09.2008. Effect: S.I. 1993/3050; 2002/1689 & S.R. 1994/6; 2002/301 amended & S.I. 2005/928; S.R. 1992/460; 1999/127 revoked. Territorial extent & classification: E/W/S/NI. General. - With correction slip dated August 2009. EC note: These Regulations make provision for the operation of Regulation 689/2008 concerning the export and import of dangerous chemicals. The 2005 Regulations (revoked and replaced by these regulations) made provision in Great Britain for the operation of Regulation No 304/2003 as amended by Commission Regulation No 1213/2003 and Commission Regulation No 775/2004. These EC Regulations implemented within the European Community the Rotterdam Convention on the prior informed consent (PIC) procedure for certain hazardous chemicals and pesticides in international trade signed by the Community on 11th September 1998. Regulation No 304/2003 was annulled and replaced with amendments by (EC) No 689/2008. - 8p.: 30 cm. - 978-0-11-083715-4 *£3.00*

The Health and Safety (Enforcing Authority for Railways and Other Guided Transport Systems) (Amendment) Regulations 2008 No. 2008/2323. - Enabling power: Health and Safety at Work etc. Act 1974, ss. 15 (1) (3) (c), 82 (3) (a). - Issued: 04.09.2008. Made: 27.08.2008. Laid: 02.09.2008. Coming into force: 01.10.2008. Effect: S.I. 2006/557 amended. Territorial extent & classification: E/W/S. General. - 8p.: 30 cm. - 978-0-11-083894-6 *£5.00*

The Health and Safety (Fees) Regulations 2008 No. 2008/736. - Enabling power: European Communities Act 1972, s. 2 (2) & Health and Safety at Work etc. Act 1974, ss. 43 (2) (4) (5) (6), 82 (3) (a). - Issued: 19.03.2008. Made: 11.03.2008. Laid: 14.03.2008. Coming into force: 06.04.2008. Effect: S.I. 1999/743 amended & S.I. 2007/813, 1672 revoked. Territorial extent & classification: E/W/S. General. - 56p.: 30 cm. - 978-0-11-081241-0 *£9.00*

The Legislative Reform (Health and Safety Executive) Order 2008 No. 2008/960. - Enabling power: Legislative and Regulatory Reform Act 2006, s. 2. - Issued: 07.04.2008. Made: 31.03.2008. Coming into force: 01.04.2008. Effect: 36 acts and 33 SIs amended. Territorial extent & classification: E/W/S. General. - Supersedes draft SI (ISBN 9780110809526) issued 18.02.2008. - 24p.: 30 cm. - 978-0-11-081339-4 *£4.00*

The REACH Enforcement Regulations 2008 No. 2008/2852. - Enabling power: European Communities Act 1972, s. 2 (2). - Issued: 13.11.2008. Made: 01.11.2008. Laid: 10.11.2008. Coming into force: 01.12.2008. Effect: 9 SI's & 9 S.R's amended & S.I. 1993/3050; 1994/1806; 1996/1373; 2001/1055; 2002/2176; 2003/1511, 2650, 3310; 2004/2913; 2005/2001; 2006/2916, 3311; 2007/386, 1596, 3438 & S.R. 1994/6; 2003/36; 2004/76 revoked. Territorial extent & classification: E/W/S/NI. General. - EC note: These Regulations apply to the United Kingdom and provide for the enforcement of Regulation (EC) No. 1907/2006 concerning the Registration, Evaluation, Authorisation and Restriction of Chemicals (REACH). - 76p.: 30 cm. - 978-0-11-084991-1 *£13.00*

The Supply of Machinery (Safety) Regulations 2008 No. 2008/1597. - Enabling power: European Communities Act 1972, s. 2 (2). - Issued: 30.06.2008. Made: 19.04.2008. Laid: 23.06.2008. Coming into force: 29.12.2009. Effect: S.I. 1989/2288; 1997/831; 1998/2306, 2307; 1999/2001; 2001/1701; 2004/693; 2006/2183; 2007/3544 amended & S.I. 1992/3073; 1994/2063; 2005/831 revoked. Territorial extent & classification: E/W/S/NI. General. - EC note: These Regulations implement Directive 2006/42/EC on machinery, and amending Directive 95/16/EC (the Machinery Directive). The Machinery Directive revokes and replaces Directive 98/37/EC on the approximation of the laws of the Member States relating to machinery with effect from 29 December 2009. Directive 98/37/EC was implemented in the United Kingdom by the Supply of Machinery (Safety) Regulations 1992 (S.I. 1992/3073), as amended, which these Regulations revoke with effect from the same date. - 80p.: 30 cm. - 978-0-11-081892-4 *£12.00*

Health care and associated professions

The Council for Healthcare Regulatory Excellence (Appointment, Procedure etc.) Regulations 2008 No. 2008/2927. - Enabling power: National Health Service Reform and Health Care Professions Act 2002, s. 38 (5) (7), sch. 7, para. 6. - Issued: 14.11.2008. Made: 10.11.2008. Laid: 14.11.2008. Coming into force: 01.01.2009. Effect: S.I. 2002/2376 revoked. Territorial extent & classification: E/W/S/NI. General. - 8p.: 30 cm. - 978-0-11-084996-6 *£5.00*

The European Qualifications (Health and Social Care Professions) (Amendment) Regulations 2008 No. 2008/462. - Enabling power: European Communities Act 1972, s. 2 (2). - Issued: 28.02.2008. Made: 20.02.2008. Laid: 28.02.2008. Coming into force: 31.03.2008. Effect: S.I. 2007/3101 amended. Territorial extent & classification: E/W/S/NI. General. - 2p.: 30 cm. - 978-0-11-081006-5 *£3.00*

The General Dental Council (Continuing Professional Development) (Dentists) Rules Order of Council 2008 No. 2008/1822. - Enabling power: Dentists Act 1984, ss. 34A (1) (4), 34B, 50A, 50C (5) (6). - Issued: 15.07.2008. Made: 04.07.2008. Coming into force: 01.08.2008. Effect: S.I. 2004/68 revoked. Territorial extent & classification: E/W/S/NI. General. - With Correction Slip dated January 2010. - 8p.: 30 cm. - 978-0-11-083119-0 *£3.00*

The General Dental Council (Continuing Professional Development) (Professions Complementary to Dentistry) Rules Order of Council 2008 No. 2008/1823. - Enabling power: Dentists Act 1984, ss. 36Z1 (1) (4), 36Z2, 50A, 50C (5) (6). - Issued: 15.07.2008. Made: 04.07.2008. Coming into force: 01.08.2008. Effect: None. Territorial extent & classification: E/W/S/NI. General. - With Correction Slip dated January 2010. - 8p.: 30 cm. - 978-0-11-083118-3 £3.00

The General Optical Council (Therapeutics and Contact Lens Specialties) Rules Order of Council 2008 No. 2008/1940. - Enabling power: Opticians Act 1989, ss. 10 (1) (1A), 11A, 11B (6), 25 (3), 31A. - Issued: 24.07.2008. Made: 21.07.2008. Coming into force: 11.08.2008. Effect: S.I. 1988/1305; 2005/1473, 1478 amended. Territorial extent & classification: E/W/S/NI. General. - 8p.: 30 cm. - 978-0-11-083480-1 £3.00

The Health and Social Care Act 2008 (Commencement No. 1) Order 2008 No. 2008/2214 (C.100). - Enabling power: Health and Social Care Act 2008, s. 170 (3) (4). Bringing into operation various provisions of the 2008 Act on 25.08.2008, in accord. with art 2. - Issued: 21.08.2008. Made: 15.08.2008. Effect: None. Territorial extent & classification: E/WS/NI. General. - 2p.: 30 cm. - 978-0-11-083833-5 £3.00

The Health and Social Care Act 2008 (Commencement No.2) Order 2008 No. 2008/2497 (C.106). - Enabling power: Health and Social Care Act 2008, s. 170 (3) (4). Bringing into operation various provisions of the 2008 Act on 01.10.2008; 01.01.2009. - Issued: 25.09.2008. Made: 19.09.2008. Effect: None. Territorial extent & classification: E/WS/NI [parts E or E/W only]. General. - 4p.: 30 cm. - 978-0-11-084265-3 £4.00

The Health and Social Care Act 2008 (Commencement No. 3) Order 2008 No. 2008/2717 (C.120). - Enabling power: Health and Social Care Act 2008, s. 170 (3) (4). Bringing into operation various provisions of the 2008 Act on 03.11.2008. - Issued: 21.10.2008. Made: 16.10.2008. Effect: None. Territorial extent & classification: E/WS/NI. General. - 4p.: 30 cm. - 978-0-11-084679-8 £4.00

The Health Care and Associated Professions (Miscellaneous Amendments) Order 2008 No. 2008/1774. - Enabling power: Health Act 1999, ss. 60, 62 (4), sch. 3. - Issued: 16.07.2008. Made: 09.07.2008. Coming into force: In accord. with art. 1 (2) to (5). Effect: 1983 c.54; 1984 c.24; 1989 c.44; 1993 c.21; 1994 c.17 amended & S.I. 1998/1019, 3117; 1999/1537; 2001/3057; 2002/827, 1263, 3136; 2005/1474; 2007/616 revoked. Territorial extent & classification: E/W/S/NI. General. - Supersedes draft S.I. (ISBN 9780110818160) issued 11.06.2008. - 32p.: 30 cm. - 978-0-11-083150-3 £5.50

The Health Care and Associated Professions (Miscellaneous Amendments) Order 2008 (Commencement No. 1) Order of Council 2008 No. 2008/2556 (C.112). - Enabling power: Health Care and Associated Professions (Miscellaneous Amendments) Order 2008, ss. 1 (5), 6 (1). Bringing into force various provisions of this Order on 03.11.2008, 01.01.2009 in accord with reg. 2. - Issued: 06.10.2008. Made: 29.09.2008. Effect: None. Territorial extent & classification: E/W/S/NI. General. - 2p.: 30 cm. - 978-0-11-084341-4 £4.00

The Health Care and Associated Professions (Miscellaneous Amendments) Order 2008 (Commencement No. 2) Order of Council 2008 No. 2008/3150 (C.138). - Enabling power: S.I. 2008/1774, art. 1 (5). Bringing into force various provisions of the Order on 01.01.2009, 09.02.2009, 01.04.2009 in accord with art. 2. - Issued: 11.12.2008. Made: 09.12.2008. Effect: None. Territorial extent & classification: E/W/S/NI. General. - 4p.: 30 cm. - 978-0-11-147135-7 £4.00

The Medical Profession (Miscellaneous Amendments) Order 2008 No. 2008/3131. - Enabling power: Health Act 1999, ss. 60, 62 (4), sch. 3. - Issued: 17.12.2008. Made: 10.12.2008. Coming into force: In accord. with art. 1(2) to (4). Effect: 1983 c. 54 & S.I. 2003/1250 amended. Territorial extent & classification: E/W/S/NI. General. - Supersedes draft S.I. (ISBN 9780110846361) issued 16.10.2008. - 12p.: 30 cm. - 978-0-11-147166-1 £5.00

Health care and associated professions: Chiropractors

The General Chiropractic Council (Constitution) Order 2008 No. 2008/3047. - Enabling power: Chiropractors Act 1994, s. 1 (4), sch. 1, para. 1B. - Issued: 01.12.2008. Made: 20.11.2008. Laid: 01.12.2008. Coming into force: In accord. with art. 1 (1). Effect: None. Territorial extent & classification: E/W/S/NI. General. - 12p.: 30 cm. - 978-0-11-147051-0 £5.00

Health care and associated professions: Dentists

The General Dental Council (Constitution) (Amendment) Order of Council 2008 No. 2008/3238. - Enabling power: Dentists Act 1984, s. 1 (2A) (2B). - Issued: 23.12.2008. Made: 16.12.2008. Laid: 17.12.2008. Coming into force: 19.01.2009. Effect: S.I. 2006/1666 amended. Territorial extent & classification: E/W/S/NI. General. - 2p.: 30 cm. - 978-0-11-147202-6 £4.00

Health care and associated professions: Doctors

The General Medical Council (Constitution) Order 2008 No. 2008/2554. - Enabling power: Medical Act 1983, s. 1 (2), sch. 1, para. 1B. - Issued: 06.10.2008. Made: 29.09.2008. Laid: 06.10.2008. Coming into force: In accord. with art. 1 (1). Effect: None. Territorial extent & classification: E/W/S/NI. General. - 12p.: 30 cm. - 978-0-11-084335-3 *£5.00*

The General Medical Council (Fitness to Practise) (Amendment in Relation to Standard of Proof) Rules Order of Council 2008 No. 2008/1256. - Enabling power: Medical Act 1983, s. 43, sch. 4, para. 1 (1). - Issued: 08.05.2008. Made: 01.05.2008. Laid: 08.05.2008. Coming into force: 31.05.2008. Effect: S.I. 2004/2608 amended. Territorial extent & classification: E/W/S/NI. General. - 4p: 30 cm. - 978-0-11-081434-6 *£3.00*

The Medical Act 1983 (Qualifying Examinations) Order 2008 No. 2008/1037. - Enabling power: Medical Act 1983, s. 8 (2). - Issued: 15.04.2008. Made: 09.04.2008. Coming into force: 14.05.2008. Effect: 1983 c.54 amended. Territorial extent & classification: E/W/S/NI. General. - 2p.: 30 cm. - 978-0-11-081364-6 *£3.00*

The Postgraduate Medical Education and Training Board (Fees) Rules Order 2008 No. 2008/554. - Enabling power: S.I. 2003/1250, arts 24, 25 (1). - Issued: 07.03.2008. Made: 28.02.2008. Laid: 07.03.2008. Coming into force: 01.04.2008. Effect: S.I. 2007/565 revoked. Territorial extent & classification: E/W/S/NI. General. - Revoked by S.I. 2009/385 (ISBN 9780111474662). - 8p.: 30 cm. - 978-0-11-081077-5 *£3.00*

Health care and associated professions: Nurses and midwives

The Nursing and Midwifery Council (Constitution) Order 2008 No. 2008/2553. - Enabling power: S.I. 2002/253, art. 3 (7A), sch. 1, para. 1B. - Issued: 06.10.2008. Made: 29.09.2008. Laid: 06.10.2008. Coming into force: In accord. with art. 1 (1). Effect: None. Territorial extent & classification: E/W/S/NI. General. - 12p.: 30 cm. - 978-0-11-084332-2 *£5.00*

The Nursing and Midwifery Council (Midwifery and Practice Committees) (Constitution) Rules Order of Council 2008 No. 2008/3148. - Enabling power: S.I. 2002/253, art. 22 (4), 26 (3) (4), 30 (9), 32, 33 (4), 47 (2), sch.1, paras 16, 17. - Issued: 12.12.2008. Made: 09.12.2008. Laid: 11.12.2008. Coming into force: 05.01.2009. Effect: S.I. 2004/1761 amended. Territorial extent & classification: E/W/S/NI. General. - 12p.: 30 cm. - 978-0-11-147138-8 *£5.00*

The Nursing and Midwifery (Amendment) Order 2008 No. 2008/1485. - Enabling power: Health Act 1999, ss. 60, 62 (4), sch. 3. - Issued: 18.06.2008. Made: 11.06.2008. Coming into force: In accord. with art. 1 (2) to (5). Effect: S.I. 2002/253, 2004/1767 amended & S.I. 2005/2250; 2006/1199; 2007/3134 revoked. Territorial extent & classification: E/W/S/NI. General. - Supersedes draft S.I. (ISBN 9780110813837) issued 21.04.2008. - 12p.: 30 cm. - 978-0-11-081844-3 *£3.00*

Health care and associated professions: Opticians

The General Optical Council (Committee Constitution) (Amendment) Rules Order of Council 2008 No. 2008/3113. - Enabling power: Opticians Act 1989, ss. 2 (2), 3 (2), 4 (3), 5 (2), 5A (3), 5B (2), 5C (3), 5D (5) and 31A, sch. 1, para. 12A. - Issued: 11.12.2008. Made: 01.12.2008. Laid: 11.12.2008. Coming into force: 05.01.2009. Effect: S.I. 2005/1474 amended. Territorial extent & classification: E/W/S/NI. General. - 16p.: 30 cm. - 978-0-11-147123-4 *£5.00*

The General Optical Council (Fitness to Practise) (Amendment in Relation to Standard of Proof) Rules Order of Council 2008 No. 2008/2690. - Enabling power: Opticians Act 1989, ss. 23C, 31A. - Issued: 14.10.2008. Made: 06.10.2008. Coming into force: 03.11.2008. Effect: S.I. 2005/1475 amended. Territorial extent & classification: E/W/S/NI. General. - 4p.: 30 cm. - 978-0-11-084563-0 *£4.00*

Health care and associated professions: Pharmacists

The Royal Pharmaceutical Society of Great Britain (Registration Amendment Rules) Order of Council 2008 No. 2008/1553. - Enabling power: S.I. 2007/289, arts 17 (1), 40 (1), 66 (1). - Issued: 18.06.2008. Made: 12.06.2008. Laid: 17.06.2008. Coming into force: 21.07.2008. Effect: S.I. 2007/441 amended. Territorial extent & classification: E/W/S. General. - 4p.: 30 cm. - 978-0-11-081857-3 *£3.00*

Healthcare and associated professions: Professions complementary to dentistry

The General Dental Council (Constitution) (Amendment) Order of Council 2008 No. 2008/3238. - Enabling power: Dentists Act 1984, s. 1 (2A) (2B). - Issued: 23.12.2008. Made: 16.12.2008. Laid: 17.12.2008. Coming into force: 19.01.2009. Effect: S.I. 2006/1666 amended. Territorial extent & classification: E/W/S/NI. General. - 2p.: 30 cm. - 978-0-11-147202-6 *£4.00*

Hearing Aid Council

The Health and Social Care Act 2008 (Commencement No.2) Order 2008 No. 2008/2497 (C.106). - Enabling power: Health and Social Care Act 2008, s. 170 (3) (4). Bringing into operation various provisions of the 2008 Act on 01.10.2008; 01.01.2009. - Issued: 25.09.2008. Made: 19.09.2008. Effect: None. Territorial extent & classification: E/WS/NI [parts E or E/W only]. General. - 4p.: 30 cm. - 978-0-11-084265-3 £4.00

Highways, England

The A1 Motorway (Dishforth to Barton Section and Connecting Roads) Scheme 2008 No. 2008/2253. - Enabling power: Highways Act 1980,ss. 16, 17, 19. - Issued: 03.09.2008. Made: 18.08.2008. Coming into force: 25.09.2008. Effect: S.I. 1996/1830 revoked. Territorial extent & classification: E. Local. - 4p.: 30 cm. - 978-0-11-083880-9 £4.00

The A1 Trunk Road (Dishforth to Barton) (Detrunking) Order 2008 No. 2008/2254. - Enabling power: Highways Act 1980, ss. 10, 12. - Issued: 05.09.2008. Made: 18.08.2008. Coming into force: 25.09.2008. Effect: SI. 1996/1831revoked. Territorial extent & classification: E. Local. - 4p.: 30 cm. - 978-0-11-083882-3 £4.00

The A4 Trunk Road (Bath to Bristol) (Detrunking) Order 2008 No. 2008/342. - Enabling power: Highways Act 1980, ss. 10, 12. - Issued: 22.02.2008. Made: 11.02.2008. Coming into force: 01.04.2008. Effect: None. Territorial extent & classification: E. Local. - 2p.: 30 cm. - 978-0-11-080951-9 £3.00

The A38 Trunk Road (Langley Mill, Warwickshire/Birmingham) (Detrunking) Order 2008 No. 2008/3292. - Enabling power: Highways Act 1980, ss. 10, 12. - Issued: 29.12.2008. Made: 17.12.2008. Coming into force: 26.02.2009. Effect: None. Territorial extent & classification: E. Local. - 2p.: 30 cm. - 978-0-11-147237-8 £4.00

The A38 Trunk Road (Weeford, Staffordshire to Minworth, Birmingham) (Detrunking) Order 2008 No. 2008/3291. - Enabling power: Highways Act 1980, ss. 10, 12. - Issued: 29.12.2008. Made: 17.12.2008. Coming into force: 26.02.2009. Effect: None. Territorial extent & classification: E. Local. - 2p.: 30 cm. - 978-0-11-147236-1 £4.00

The A65 Trunk Road (From M6 Junction 36 to the Roundabout Junction with the A59) (Detrunking) Order 2008 No. 2008/3199. - Enabling power: Highways Act 1980, ss. 20, 12. - Issued: 19.01.2009. Made: 08.12.2008. Coming into force: 31.01.2009 & 01.04.2009. Effect: None. Territorial extent & classification: E. Local. - This statutory instrument has been printed in substitution of the the SI of the same number and ISBN (issued 19.01.2009) and is being issued free of charge to all known recipients of that statutory instrument. - 2p.: 30 cm. - 978-0-11-147259-0 £4.00

The A282 Trunk Road (Dartford-Thurrock Crossing Charging Scheme) Order 2008 No. 2008/1951. - Enabling power: Transport Act 2000, ss. 167, 168, 171, 172 (2). - Issued: 28.07.2008. Made: 21.07.2008. Coming into force: 15.11.2008. Effect: S.I. 2002/1040 revoked. Territorial extent & classification: E. General. - 8p.: 30 cm. - 978-0-11-083591-4 £3.00

The A421 Trunk Road (M1 Junction 13 Improvements) Order 2008 No. 2008/2109. - Enabling power: Highways Act 1980, ss. 10, 12, 41. - Issued: 12.08.2008. Made: 29.07.2008. Coming into force: 31.07.2008. Effect: None. Territorial extent & classification: E. Local. - 2p.: 30 cm. - 978-0-11-083732-1 £3.00

The A421 Trunk Road (M1 Junction 13 to Bedford Improvements and Detrunking) Order 2008 No. 2008/2107. - Enabling power: Highways Act 1980, ss. 10, 12, 41. - Issued: 11.08.2008. Made: 29.07.2008. Coming into force: 31.07.2008. Effect: None. Territorial extent & classification: E. Local. - 4p.: 30 cm. - 978-0-11-083731-4 £3.00

The A456 Trunk Road (Detrunking) Order 2008 No. 2008/585. - Enabling power: Highways Act 1980, ss. 10, 12. - Issued: 01.04.2008. Made: 03.03.2008. Coming into force: 28.04.2008. Effect: None. Territorial extent & classification: E. Local. - 2p.: 30 cm. - 978-0-11-081285-4 £3.00

The A465 Trunk Road (Llangua Bridge to A49/A465 Belmont Roundabout) (Detrunking) Order 2008 No. 2008/2350. - Enabling power: Highways Act 1980, ss. 10, 12. - Issued: 08.09.2008. Made: 26.08.2008. Coming into force: 29.10.2008. Effect: None. Territorial extent & classification: E. Local. - 2p.: 30 cm. - 978-0-11-084068-0 £4.00

The A556(M) Motorway (M6 to M56 Link) and Connecting Roads Scheme 1996 (Revocation) Order 2008 No. 2008/231. - Enabling power: Highways Act 1980, ss. 16, 17, 19. - Issued: 07.03.2008. Made: 30.01.2008. Coming into force: 07.03.2008. Effect: S.I. 1996/1648 revoked. Territorial extent & classification: E. Local. - 2p.: 30 cm. - 978-0-11-080919-9 £3.00

The A556(M) Motorway (M6 to M56 Link) Supplementary Connecting Roads Scheme 1996 (Revocation) Order 2008 No. 2008/232. - Enabling power: Highways Act 1980, ss. 16, 17, 19. - Issued: 07.03.2008. Made: 30.01.2008. Coming into force: 07.03.2008. Effect: S.I. 1996/1649 revoked. Territorial extent & classification: E. Local. - 2p.: 30 cm. - 978-0-11-080920-5 £3.00

The A556 Trunk Road (Church Farm-Turnpike Wood, Over Tabley) Order 1996 (Revocation) Order 2008 No. 2008/233. - Enabling power: Highways Act 1980, s. 10. - Issued: 07.03.2008. Made: 30.01.2008. Coming into force: 07.03.2008. Effect: S.I. 1996/1650 revoked. Territorial extent & classification: E. Local. - 2p.: 30 cm. - 978-0-11-080921-2 £3.00

The A556 Trunk Road (Turnpike Wood, Over Tabley-A56 Bowden Roundabout) (Detrunking) Order 1996 (Revocation) Order 2008 No. 2008/234. - Enabling power: Highways Act 1980, ss. 10, 12. - Issued: 07.03.2008. Made: 30.01.2008. Coming into force: 07.03.2008. Effect: S.I. 1996/1651 revoked. Territorial extent & classification: E. Local. - 2p.: 30 cm. - 978-0-11-080922-9 £3.00

The A570 Trunk Road (Lancashire County Boundary to Kew Roundabout) (Detrunking) Order 2008 No. 2008/2511. - Enabling power: Highways Act 1980, ss. 10, 12. - Issued: 30.09.2008. Made: 04.09.2008. Coming into force: 01.10.2008. Effect: None. Territorial extent & classification: E. Local. - 4p., 1 map: 30 cm. - 978-0-11-084293-6 £4.00

The A570 Trunk Road (North of M58 to the Lancashire County Boundary) (Detrunking) Order 2008 No. 2008/2510. - Enabling power: Highways Act 1980, ss. 10, 12. - Issued: 30.09.2008. Made: 04.09.2008. Coming into force: 01.10.2008. Effect: None. Territorial extent & classification: E. Local. - 4p.: 30 cm. - 978-0-11-084292-9 £4.00

The A4123 Trunk Road (Sandwell and Dudley) (Detrunking) Order 2008 No. 2008/2502. - Enabling power: Highways Act 1980, ss. 10, 12. - Issued: 29.09.2008. Made: 22.09.2008. Coming into force: 13.11.2008. Effect: None. Territorial extent & classification: E. Local. - 2p.: 30 cm. - 978-0-11-084281-3 £4.00

The Council to the City of Wakefield (Wakefield Waterfront Hepworth Gallery Footbridge) Scheme 2008 Confirmation Instrument 2008 No. 2008/2988. - Enabling power: Highways Act 1980, s. 106 (3). - Issued: 26.11.2008. Made: 13.11.2008. Coming into force: In accord. with art. 1. Effect: None. Territorial extent & classification: E. Local. - 4p., plans: 30 cm. - 978-0-11-147019-0 £4.00

The Dartford - Thurrock Crossing (Amendment) Regulations 2008 No. 2008/2171. - Enabling power: Dartford - Thurrock Crossing Act 1988, s. 25 (1) (b). - Issued: 21.08.2008. Made: 13.08.2008. Laid: 18.08.2008. Coming into force: 12.09.2008. Effect: S.I. 1998/1908 amended. Territorial extent & classification: E. General. - 2p.: 30 cm. - 978-0-11-083800-7 £3.00

The Dartmouth-Kingswear Floating Bridge (Vehicle Classifications & Revision of Charges) Order 2008 No. 2008/2102. - Enabling power: Transport Charges & c. (Miscellaneous Provisions) Act 1954, s. 6. - Issued: 11.08.2008. Made: 04.08.2008. Coming into force: 13.08.2008. Effect: S.I. 2008/1910 revoked [before publishing]. Territorial extent & classification: E. Local. - 2p.: 30 cm. - 978-0-11-083717-8 £3.00

The Dartmouth-Kingswear Floating Bridge (Vehicle Classifications & Revision of Charges) Order 2008 No. 2008/1910. - Enabling power: Transport Charges & c. (Miscellaneous Provisions) Act 1954, s. 6. - Issued: 28.07.2008. Made: 16.07.2008. Coming into force: 23.07.2008. Effect: S.I. 2001/3772 revoked. Territorial extent & classification: E. Local. - Revoked before publishing. Revoked by S.I. 2008/2102 (ISBN 9780110837178). - 2p.: 30 cm. - 978-0-11-083592-1 £3.00

The Kent County Council (Milton Creek Bridge) (No. 2) Scheme 2007 Confirmation Instrument 2008 No. 2008/3298. - Enabling power: Highways Act 1980, s. 106 (3). - Issued: 08.01.2009. Made: 23.12.2008. Coming into force: In accord. with art. 1. Effect: None. Territorial extent & classification: E. Local. - 8p., plans: 30 cm. - 978-0-11-147243-9 £5.00

The Kingston upon Hull City Council (Scale Lane Bridge) Scheme 2008 Confirmation Instrument 2008 No. 2008/1373. - Enabling power: Highways Act 1980, s. 106 (3). - Issued: 03.06.2008. Made: 20.05.2008. Coming into force: In accord. with art. 1. Effect: None. Territorial extent & classification: E. Local. - 8p., plans: 30 cm. - 978-0-11-081764-4 £3.00

The Knowsley Metropolitan Borough Council (M62 Motorway, Junction 6 Improvements) Scheme 2008 Confirmation Instrument 2008 No. 2008/3325. - Enabling power: Highways Act 1980, s. 16. - Issued: 09.01.2009. Made: 30.12.2008. Coming into force: In accord with art. 1. Effect: None. Territorial extent & classification: E. Local. - 8p.: 30 cm. - 978-0-11-147246-0 £4.00

The M1 Motorway (Junction 13 and Connecting Roads) Order 2008 No. 2008/2110. - Enabling power: Highways Act 1980, ss. 16, 17, 19. - Issued: 11.08.2008. Made: 29.07.2008. Coming into force: 31.07.2008. Effect: None. Territorial extent & classification: E. Local. - 2p.: 30 cm. - 978-0-11-083734-5 £3.00

The Public Rights of Way (Combined Orders) (England) Regulations 2008 No. 2008/442. - Enabling power: Wildlife and Countryside Act 1981, ss. 53A (1) (a), 56 (3A), 57 (1) (2) (6A). - Issued: 06.03.2008. Made: 19.02.2008. Laid: 25.02.2008. Coming into force: 06.04.2008. Effect: Applies to section 53A of the Wildlife and Countryside Act 1981 (c. 69) to the types of Order listed in regulation 3. Territorial extent & classification: E. General. - 8p.: 30 cm. - 978-0-11-080998-4 £3.00

The Severn Bridges Tolls Order 2008 No. 2008/3263. - Enabling power: Severn Bridges Act 1992, s. 9 (1) (2) (b) (3) (b) (4) (6). - Issued: 30.12.2008. Made: 18.12.2008. Coming into force: 01.01.2009. Effect: S.I. 2007/3496 revoked. Territorial extent & classification: E. Local. - 2p.: 30 cm. - 978-0-11-147234-7 £4.00

The Street Works (Inspection Fees) (England) (Amendment) Regulations 2008 No. 2008/589. - Enabling power: New Roads and Street Works Act 1991, ss. 75, 104 (1). - Issued: 11.03.2008. Made: 28.02.2008. Laid: 06.03.2008. Coming into force: 01.04.2008. Effect: S.I. 2002/2092 amended. Territorial extent & classification: E. General. - 2p.: 30 cm. - 978-0-11-081122-2 £3.00

Highways, England: Trunk roads

The M1-A1 Link Road Junction 45 East Leeds Link Road Connecting Roads Scheme 2008 No. 2008/2374. - Enabling power: Highways Act 1980, s. 16. - Made: 29.08.2008. Coming into force: 30.08.2008. Effect: None. Territorial extent & classification: E. Local *Unpublished*

The M1-A1 Link Road Junction 45 East Leeds Link Road (Trunking) Order 2008 No. 2008/2373. - Enabling power: Highways Act 1980, s. 10. - Made: 29.08.2008. Coming into force: 30.08.2008. Effect: None. Territorial extent & classification: E. Local *Unpublished*

Highways, Wales

The Cardiff to Glan Conwy Trunk Road (A470) (Penloyn to Tan Lan Improvement) Order 2008 No. 2008/2701 (W.241). - Enabling power: Highways Act 1980, s. 10. - Issued: 24.10.2008. Made: 10.10.2008. Coming into force: 30.10.2008. Effect: None. Territorial extent & classification: W. General. - In English and Welsh. Welsh language title: Gorchymyn Cefnffordd Caerdydd i Lan Conwy (yr A470) (Gwelliant Penloyn i Dan Lan) 2008. - 4p.: 30 cm. - 978-0-11-091889-1 £4.00

The Civil Enforcement of Parking Contraventions (City and County of Swansea) Designation Order 2008 No. 2008/1896 (W.180). - Enabling power: Traffic Management Act 2004, sch. 8, para. 8 (1), sch. 10, para. 3 (1). - Issued: 15.08.2008. Made: 15.07.2008. Laid before the National Assembly for Wales: 17.07.2008. Coming into force: 01.09.2008. Effect: None. Territorial extent & classification: W. General. - In English and Welsh. Welsh language title: Gorchymyn Dynodi Gorfodi Sifil ar Dramgwyddau Parcio (Dinas a Sir Abertawe) 2008. - 4p.: 30 cm. - 978-0-11-091826-6 £3.00

The London To Fishguard Trunk Road (A40) (Penblewin To Slebech Park Improvement) Order 2008 No. 2008/3138 (W.277). - Enabling power: Highways Act 1980, ss. 10, 12, 106. - Issued: 09.01.2009. Made: 08.12.2008. Coming into force: 17.12.2008. Effect: None. Territorial extent & classification: W. General. - In English and Welsh. Welsh title: Gorchymyn Cefnffordd Llundain I Abergwaun (YR A40) (Gwelliant Penblewin I Barc Slebets) 2008. - 8p., plans: 30 cm. - 978-0-11-091917-1 £5.00

The Street Works (Fixed Penalty) (Wales) (Amendment) Regulations 2008 No. 2008/466 (W.41). - Enabling power: New Roads and Street Works Act 1991, ss. 48 (2), 95A (5), 97, 104 (1), sch. 4B, paras 2, 4 (1), 5 (2), 8 (a), 9 (b). - Issued: 20.03.2008. Made: 22.02.2008. Laid before the National Assembly for Wales: 25.02.2008. Coming into force: 12.05.2008. Effect: SI 2008/102 (W.15) amended. Territorial extent & classification: W. General. - In English and Welsh. Welsh language title: Rheoliadau Gwaith Stryd (Cosbau Penodedig) (Cymru) (Diwygio) 2008. - 4p.: 30 cm. - 978-0-11-091762-7 £3.00

The Street Works (Fixed Penalty) (Wales) Regulations 2008 No. 2008/102 (W.15). - Enabling power: New Roads and Street Works Act 1991, ss. 48 (2), 95A (5), 97, 104 (1), sch. 4B, paras 2, 4 (1), 5 (2), 8 (a), 9 (b). - Issued: 27.02.2008. Made: 17.01.2008. Laid before the National Assembly for Wales: 18.01.2008. Coming into force: 12.05.2008. Effect: 1991 c.22 amended. Territorial extent & classification: W. General. - In English and Welsh. Welsh title: Rheoliadau Gwaith Stryd (Cosbau Penodedig) (Cymru) 2008. - 16p.: 30 cm. - 978-0-11-091707-8 £3.00

The Street Works (Inspection Fees) (Wales) (Amendment) (No. 2) Regulations 2008 No. 2008/1213 (W.121). - Enabling power: New Roads and Street Works Act 1991, ss. 75, 104 (1). - Issued: 14.05.2008. Made: 29.04.2008. Laid before the National Assembly for Wales: 30.04.2008. Coming into force: 22.05.2008. Effect: S.I. 2006/1532 (W.150) amended & S.I. 2008/600 (W.62) revoked. Territorial extent & classification: W. General. - In English and Welsh. Welsh title: Rheoliadau Gwaith Stryd (Ffioedd Arolygu) (Cymru) (Diwygio) (Rhif 2) 2008. - 4p.: 30 cm. - 978-0-11-091816-7 £3.00

The Street Works (Inspection Fees) (Wales) (Amendment) Regulations 2008 No. 2008/600 (W.62). - Enabling power: New Roads and Street Works Act 1991, ss. 75, 104 (1). - Issued: 20.03.2008. Made: 05.03.2008. Laid before the National Assembly for Wales: 06.03.2008. Coming into force: 01.04.2008. Effect: S.I. 2006/1532 (W.150) amended. Territorial extent & classification: W. General. - Revoked by W.S.I. 2008/1213 (W.121) (ISBN 9780110918167). - In English and Welsh. Welsh title: Rheoliadau Gwaith Stryd (Ffioedd Arolygu) (Cymru) (Diwygio) 2008. - 4p.: 30 cm. - 978-0-11-091761-0 £3.00

The Street Works (Registers, Notices, Directions and Designations) (Wales) (No 2) Regulations 2008 No. 2008/540 (W.52). - Enabling power: New Roads and Street Works Act 1991, ss. 48 (2), 49 (5), 53 (1) (2) (3) (6), 54 (1) (2) (3) (4) (4A) (4B), 55 (1) (2) (3) (7) (8), 56 (2), 56A (4), 57 (2) (3), 58 (1) (2) (3) (4) (5) (7) (7A), 58A, 62 (1), 63 (2), 64 (1) (2), 70 (3) (b) (4A) (4B), 97, 104 (1) (3), sch. 3A, paras 1 (2), 2 (2) (3) (4) (f) (5), 3 (5) (b), 4 (4) (5), 5 (2) (c) (3) (4). - Issued: 15.04.2008. Made: 28.02.2008. Laid before the National Assembly for Wales: 29.02.2008. Coming into force: 01.04.2008. Effect: S.I. 1992/2985 amended & S.I. 2008/101 (W.14). revoked. Territorial extent & classification: W. General. - In English and Welsh. Welsh language title: Rheoliadau Gwaith Stryd (Cofrestrau, Hysbysiadau, Cyfarwyddiadau a Dynodiadau) (Cymru) (Rhif 2) 2008. - 32p.: 30 cm. - 978-0-11-091754-2 £5.50

The Street Works (Registers, Notices, Directions and Designations) (Wales) Regulations 2008 No. 2008/101 (W.14). - Enabling power: New Roads and Street Works Act 1991, ss. 48 (2), 49 (5), 53 (1) (2) (3) (6), 54 (1) (2) (3) (4) (4A) (4B), 55 (1) (2) (3) (7) (8), 56 (2), 56A (4), 57 (2) (3), 58 (1) (2) (3) (4) (5) (7) (7A), 58A, 62 (1), 63 (2), 64 (1) (2), 70 (3) (b) (4A) (4B), 97, 104 (1) (3), sch. 3A, paras 1 (2), 2 (2) (3) (4) (f) (5), 3 (5) (b), 4 (4) (5), 5 (2) (c) (3) (4). - Issued: 28.02.2008. Made: 17.01.2008. Laid before the National Assembly for Wales: 18.01.2008. Coming into force: 01.04.2008. Effect: 1991 c.22 modified; S.I. 1992/2985 amended. Territorial extent & classification: W. General. - Revoked by S.I. 2008/540 (W.52) (ISBN 9780110917542). With correction slip dated March 2008. - In English and Welsh. Welsh language title: Rheoliadau Gwaith Stryd (Cofrestrau, Hysbysiadau, Cyfarwyddiadau a Dynodiadau) (Cymru) 2008. - 36p.: 30 cm. - 978-0-11-091712-2 £5.50

Housing

The Housing (Scotland) Act 2006 (Consequential Provisions) Order 2008 No. 2008/1889. - Enabling power: Scotland Act 1998, ss. 104, 112 (1), 113 (2) (3) (4) (5). - Issued: 21.07.2008. Made: 14.07.2008. Coming into force: 01.10.2008. Effect: 1975 c.24 modified. Territorial extent & classification: UK except for arts 2 & 3 which extent to S only. General. - 4p.: 30 cm. - 978-0-11-082019-4 £3.00

The Rent Officers (Housing Benefit Functions) Amendment (No. 2) Order 2008 No. 2008/3156. - Enabling power: Housing Act 1996, s. 122 (1) (6). - Issued: 15.12.2008. Made: 09.12.2008. Laid: 15.12.2008. Coming into force: 05.01.2009. Effect: S.I. 1997/1984, 1995 amended. Territorial extent & classification: E/W/S. General. - 4p.: 30 cm. - 978-0-11-147142-5 £4.00

Housing, England

The Allocation of Housing (England) (Amendment) (Family Intervention Tenancies) Regulations 2008 No. 2008/3015. - Enabling power: Housing Act 1996, ss. 160 (4). - Issued: 26.11.2008. Made: 19.11.2008. Laid: 26.11.2008. Coming into force: 01.01.2009. Effect: S.I. 2002/3264 amended. Territorial extent & classification: E. General. - 2p.: 30 cm. - 978-0-11-147039-8 £4.00

The Disabled Facilities Grants (Maximum Amounts and Additional Purposes) (England) Order 2008 No. 2008/1189. - Enabling power: Housing Grants, Construction and Regeneration Act 1996, ss. 23 (1) (l), 33, 146. - Issued: 07.05.2008. Made: 28.04.2008. Laid: 30.04.2008. Coming into force: 22.05.2008. Effect: S.I. 1996/2888 amended. Territorial extent & classification: E. General. - 4p.: 30 cm. - 978-0-11-081414-8 £3.00

The Family Intervention Tenancies (Review of Local Authority Decisions) (England) Regulations 2008 No. 2008/3111. - Enabling power: Housing and Regeneration Act 2008, s. 298 (5). - Issued: 11.12.2008. Made: 04.12.2008. Laid: 11.12.2008. Coming into force: 05.01.2009. Effect: None. Territorial extent & classification: E. General. - 8p.: 30 cm. - 978-0-11-147121-0 £5.00

The Houses in Multiple Occupation (Specified Educational Establishments) (England) Regulations 2008 No. 2008/2346. - Enabling power: Housing Act 2004, sch. 14, para. 4 (2). - Issued: 08.09.2008. Made: 02.09.2008. Laid: 08.09.2008. Coming into force: 01.10.2008. Effect: 2004 c.34 amended & S.I. 2007/2601 revoked. Territorial extent & classification: E. General. - Revoked by S.I. 2009/2298 (ISBN 9780111484777). With correction slip dated September 2008. - 8p.: 30 cm. - 978-0-11-084058-1 £5.00

The Housing and Regeneration Act 2008 (Commencement No. 1 and Transitional Provision) Order 2008 No. 2008/2358 (C. 103). - Enabling power: Housing and Regeneration Act 2008, ss. 320, 322, 325. Bringing in operation various provisions of the 2008 Act on 08.09.2008, 22.09.2008. - Issued: 08.09.2008. Made: 02.09.2008. Effect: None. Territorial extent & classification: E/W but applies to England only. General. - 4p.: 30 cm. - 978-0-11-084077-2 £4.00

The Housing (Approval of a Code of Management Practice) (Student Accommodation) (England) Order 2008 No. 2008/2345. - Enabling power: Housing Act 2004, ss. 233 (1) (3) (4). - Issued: 10.09.2008. Made: 02.09.2008. Laid: 08.09.2008. Coming into force: 01.10.2008. Effect: S.I. 2006/646 amended. Territorial extent & classification: E. General. - With correction slip dated September 2008. - 2p.: 30 cm. - 978-0-11-084016-1 £3.00

The Housing Renewal Grants (Amendment) (England) Regulations 2008 No. 2008/1190. - Enabling power: Housing Grants, Construction and Regeneration Act 1996, ss. 30, 146. - Issued: 07.05.2008. Made: 28.04.2008. Laid: 30.04.2008. Coming into force: 22.05.2008. Effect: S.I. 1996/2890 amended. Territorial extent & classification: E. General. - 8p.: 30 cm. - 978-0-11-081415-5 £3.00

The Housing Renewal Grants (Amendment) (No. 2) (England) Regulations 2008 No. 2008/3104. - Enabling power: Housing Grants, Construction and Regeneration Act 1996, ss. 30, 146. - Issued: 09.12.2008. Made: 03.12.2008. Laid: 09.12.2008. Coming into force: 31.12.2008. Effect: S.I. 1996/2890 modified. Territorial extent & classification: E. General. - 4p.: 30 cm. - 978-0-11-147104-3 £4.00

The Housing (Right to Buy) (Service Charges) (Amendment) (England) Order 2008 No. 2008/533. - Enabling power: Housing Act 1985, sch. 6, part 3, para. 16D. - Issued: 06.03.2008. Made: 27.02.2008. Laid: 06.03.2008. Coming into force: 06.04.2008. Effect: S.I. 1986/2195 amended in relation to England. Territorial extent & classification: E. General. - 2p.: 30 cm. - 978-0-11-081048-5 £3.00

The Housing (Right to Manage) (England) Regulations 2008 No. 2008/2361. - Enabling power: Housing Act 1985, ss. 27 (4) (17), 27AB. - Issued: 10.09.2008. Made: 04.09.2008. Laid: 10.09.2008. Coming into force: 01.10.2008. Effect: S.I. 1994/627 partially revoked. Territorial extent & classification: E. General. - With correction slip dated September 2009. - 12p.: 30 cm. - 978-0-11-084100-7 £5.00

The Local Authorities (England) (Charges for Property Searches) (Disapplication) Order 2008 No. 2008/2909. - Enabling power: Local Government Act 2003, s. 94. - Issued: 13.11.2008. Made: 10.11.2008. Laid: 13.11.2008. Coming into force: In accord. with art. 1 (2). Effect: None. Territorial extent & classification: E. General. - 4p.: 30 cm. - 978-0-11-084993-5 £4.00

The Local Authorities (England) (Charges for Property Searches) Regulations 2008 No. 2008/3248. - Enabling power: Local Government and Housing Act 1989, s. 150. - Issued: 29.12.2008. Made: 16.12.2008. Coming into force: In accord. with art. 1 (2). Effect: S.I. 1994/1885 revoked (with savings) in relation to England. Territorial extent & classification: E. General. - Supersedes draft S.I. (ISBN 9780110849942) issued 13.11.2008. - 8p.: 30 cm. - 978-0-11-147210-1 £5.00

The Persons subject to Immigration Control (Housing Authority Accommodation and Homelessness) (Amendment) Order 2008 No. 2008/1768. - Enabling power: Immigration and Asylum Act 1999, ss. 118, 119, 166 (3). - Issued: 09.07.2008. Made: 03.07.2008. Laid: 08.07.2008. Coming into force: 07.08.2008. Effect: S.I. 2000/706 amended. Territorial extent & classification: E/S/NI. General. - With correction slip dated July 2009. - 4p.: 30 cm. - 978-0-11-081975-4 £3.00

Housing, England and Wales

The Home Information Pack (Amendment) (No. 2) Regulations 2008 No. 2008/1266. - Enabling power: Housing Act 2004, ss. 163, 250 (2). - Issued: 14.05.2008. Made: 06.05.2008. Laid: 08.05.2008. Coming into force: 01.06.2008. Effect: S.I. 2007/1667 amended. Territorial extent & classification: E/W. General. - 2p.: 30 cm. - 978-0-11-081440-7 £3.00

The Home Information Pack (Amendment) (No. 3) Regulations 2008 No. 2008/3107. - Enabling power: Housing Act 2004, ss. 163, 250 (2). - Issued: 08.12.2008. Made: 04.12.2008. Laid: 08.12.2008. Coming into force: 01.01.2009 for regs 1 to 7 & 06.04.2009 for regs 8 - 12. Effect: S.I. 2007/1667 amended. Territorial extent & classification: E/W. General. - With correction slip dated September 2009. - This Statutory Instrument has been corrected by SI 2009/34 (ISBN 9780111472743) which is being issued free of charge to all known recipients of 2008/3107. - 16p.: 30 cm. - 978-0-11-147106-7 £5.00

The Home Information Pack (Amendment) Regulations 2008 No. 2008/572. - Enabling power: Housing Act 2004, ss. 163, 250 (2). - Issued: 06.03.2008. Made: 27.02.2008. Laid: 06.03.2008. Coming into force: 31.03.2008. Effect: S.I. 2007/1667 amended. Territorial extent & classification: E/W. General. - With correction slip dated March 2008. - 8p.: 30 cm. - 978-0-11-081101-7 £3.00

The Housing Act 2004 (Commencement No. 11) (England and Wales) Order 2008 No. 2008/898 (C.42). - Enabling power: Housing Act 2004, s. 270 (6) (8). Bringing into operation various provisions of the 2004 Act on 06.04.2008. - Issued: 03.04.2008. Made: 13.03.2008. Effect: None. Territorial extent & classification: E/W. General. - 4p.: 30 cm. - 978-0-11-081307-3 £3.00

The Housing and Regeneration Act 2008 (Commencement No. 2 and Transitional, Saving and Transitory Provisions) Order 2008 No. 2008/3068 (C.132). - Enabling power: Housing and Regeneration Act 2008, ss. 322, 325. Bringing in operation various provisions of the 2008 Act on 01.12.2008. - Issued: 01.12.2008. Made: 26.11.2008. Effect: 21 acts; 3 SIs amended & S.I. 2002/367 revoked. Territorial extent & classification: E/W. General. - 12p.: 30 cm. - 978-0-11-147076-3 £5.00

The Housing and Regeneration Act 2008 (Consequential Provisions) (No. 2) Order 2008 No. 2008/2831. - Enabling power: Housing and Regeneration Act 2008, ss. 320, 321. - Issued: 03.11.2008. Made: 30.10.2008. Laid: 03.11.2008. Coming into force: In accord. with art. 1 (2). Effect: 25 S.I.s amended. Territorial extent & classification: E/W. General. - This Statutory Instrument has been printed in substitution of the SI of the same number and is being issued free of charge to all known recipients of that SI (ISBN 9780110848242). - 12p.: 30 cm. - 978-0-11-147002-2 £5.00

The Housing and Regeneration Act 2008 (Consequential Provisions) (No. 2) Order 2008 No. 2008/2831. - Enabling power: Housing and Regeneration Act 2008, ss. 320, 321. - Issued: 03.11.2008. Made: 30.10.2008. Laid: 03.11.2008. Coming into force: In accord. with art. 1 (2). Effect: 26 S.I.s amended. Territorial extent & classification: E/W. General. - Superseded by S.I. of same no. and title (ISBN 9780111470022). - 12p.: 30 cm. - 978-0-11-084824-2 £5.00

The Housing and Regeneration Act 2008 (Consequential Provisions) Order 2008 No. 2008/3002. - Enabling power: Housing and Regeneration Act 2008, ss. 320, 321. - Issued: 26.11.2008. Made: 18.11.2008. Coming into force: In accord. with art. 1. Effect: 13 Acts amended. Territorial extent & classification: E/W but E/W/NI in so far as it relates to section 16 of the Consumer Credit Act 1974. General. - 16p.: 30 cm. - 978-0-11-147027-5 £5.00

Transfer of Housing Corporation Functions (Modifications and Transitional Provisions) Order 2008 No. 2008/2839. - Enabling power: Housing and Regeneration Act 2008, ss. 67, 320. - Issued: 06.11.2008. Made: 30.10.2008. Laid: 03.11.2008. Coming into force: In accord. with art. 1 (1). Effect: 1985 c. 68, c. 69; 1988 c. 50; 1996 c. 52; 1999 c. 29 modification of enactments. Territorial extent & classification: E/W. General. - 12p.: 30 cm. - With correction slip dated September 2009. - 978-0-11-084857-0 *£5.00*

Housing, Northern Ireland

The Housing and Regeneration Act 2008 (Consequential Provisions) Order 2008 No. 2008/3002. - Enabling power: Housing and Regeneration Act 2008, ss. 320, 321. - Issued: 26.11.2008. Made: 18.11.2008. Coming into force: In accord. with art. 1. Effect: 13 Acts amended. Territorial extent & classification: E/W but E/W/NI in so far as it relates to section 16 of the Consumer Credit Act 1974. General. - 16p.: 30 cm. - 978-0-11-147027-5 *£5.00*

The Persons subject to Immigration Control (Housing Authority Accommodation and Homelessness) (Amendment) Order 2008 No. 2008/1768. - Enabling power: Immigration and Asylum Act 1999, ss. 118, 119, 166 (3). - Issued: 09.07.2008. Made: 03.07.2008. Laid: 08.07.2008. Coming into force: 07.08.2008. Effect: S.I. 2000/706 amended. Territorial extent & classification: E/S/NI. General. - With correction slip dated July 2009. - 4p.: 30 cm. - 978-0-11-081975-4 *£3.00*

Housing, Scotland

The Persons subject to Immigration Control (Housing Authority Accommodation and Homelessness) (Amendment) Order 2008 No. 2008/1768. - Enabling power: Immigration and Asylum Act 1999, ss. 118, 119, 166 (3). - Issued: 09.07.2008. Made: 03.07.2008. Laid: 08.07.2008. Coming into force: 07.08.2008. Effect: S.I. 2000/706 amended. Territorial extent & classification: E/S/NI. General. - With correction slip dated July 2009. - 4p.: 30 cm. - 978-0-11-081975-4 *£3.00*

Housing, Wales

The Disabled Facilities Grants (Maximum Amounts and Additional Purposes) (Wales) Order 2008 No. 2008/2370 (W.205). - Enabling power: Housing Grants, Construction and Regeneration Act 1996, ss. 23 (1) (l), 33, 146. - Issued: 24.09.2008. Made: 06.09.2008. Laid before the National Assembly for Wales: 09.08.2008. Coming into force: 02.10.2008. Effect: None. Territorial extent & classification: W. General. - In English and Welsh. Welsh title: Gorchymyn Grantiau Cyfleusterau i'r Anabl (Uchafsymiau a Dibenion Ychwanegol) (Cymru) 2008. - 4p.: 30 cm. - 978-0-11-091876-1 *£4.00*

The Housing Renewal Grants (Amendment) (Wales) Regulations 2008 No. 2008/2377 (W.206). - Enabling power: Housing Grants, Construction and Regeneration Act 1996, ss. 30, 146. - Issued: 24.09.2008. Made: 06.09.2008. Laid before the National Assembly for Wales: 09.08.2008. Coming into force: 02.10.2008. Effect: S.I. 1996/2890 amended in relation to Wales. Territorial extent & classification: W. General. - In English and Welsh. Welsh title: Rheoliadau Grantiau Adnewyddu Tai (Diwygio) (Cymru) 2008. - 12p.: 30 cm. - 978-0-11-091875-4 *£5.00*

The Housing (Right to Buy) (Priority of Charges) (Wales) Order 2008 No. 2008/371 (W.37). - Enabling power: Housing Act 1985, s. 156 (4). - Issued: 03.03.2008. Made: 14.02.2008. Coming into force: 28.02.2008. Effect: None. Territorial extent & classification: W. General. - In English and Welsh: Welsh title: Gorchymyn Tai (Hawl i Brynu) (Blaenoriaeth Arwystlon) (Cymru) 2008. - 4p.: 30 cm. - 978-0-11-091714-6 *£3.00*

The Rent Repayment Orders (Supplementary Provisions) (Wales) Regulations 2008 No. 2008/254 (W.30). - Enabling power: Housing Act 2004, ss. 74 (15), 97 (15). - Issued: 27.02.2008. Made: 06.02.2008. Laid before the National Assembly for Wales: 07.02.2008. Coming into force: 04.03.2008. Effect: None. Territorial extent & classification: W. General. - In English and Welsh. Welsh title: Rheoliadau Gorchmynion Ad-dalu Rhent (Darpariaethau Atodol) (Cymru) 2008. - 8p.: 30 cm. - 978-0-11-091708-5 *£3.00*

Human rights

The Health and Social Care Act 2008 (Commencement No. 4) Order 2008 No. 2008/2994 (C.129). - Enabling power: Health and Social Care Act 2008, s. 170 (3) (4). Bringing into operation various provisions of the 2008 Act on 01.12.2008, 01.04.2009 in accord. with art. 3. - Issued: 21.11.2008. Made: 15.11.2008. Effect: None. Territorial extent & classification: E/WS/NI (parts E or E/W only). General. - 4p.: 30 cm. - 978-0-11-147028-2 *£4.00*

Human tissue, England and Wales

The Human Tissue Act 2004 (Ethical Approval, Exceptions from Licensing and Supply of Information about Transplants) (Amendment) Regulations 2008 No. 2008/3067. - Enabling power: Human Tissue Act 2004, ss. 16 (3), 52 (1). - Issued: 02.12.2008. Made: 26.11.2008. Laid: 02.12.2008. Coming into force: 29.12.2008. Effect: S.I. 2006/1260 amended. Territorial extent & classification: E/W/NI. General. - This Statutory Instrument has been made in consequence of a defect in SI 2006/1260 and is being issued free of charge to all known recipients of that Statutory Instrument. - 2p.: 30 cm. - 978-0-11-147075-6 *£4.00*

Human tissue, Northern Ireland

The Human Tissue Act 2004 (Ethical Approval, Exceptions from Licensing and Supply of Information about Transplants) (Amendment) Regulations 2008 No. 2008/3067. - Enabling power: Human Tissue Act 2004, ss. 16 (3), 52 (1). - Issued: 02.12.2008. Made: 26.11.2008. Laid: 02.12.2008. Coming into force: 29.12.2008. Effect: S.I. 2006/1260 amended. Territorial extent & classification: E/W/NI. General. - This Statutory Instrument has been made in consequence of a defect in SI 2006/1260 and is being issued free of charge to all known recipients of that Statutory Instrument. - 2p.: 30 cm. - 978-0-11-147075-6 £4.00

Immigration

The Asylum and Immigration Tribunal (Fast Track Procedure) (Amendment) Rules 2008 No. 2008/1089 (L.8). - Enabling power: Nationality, Immigration and Asylum Act 2002, ss. 106 (1) to (3), 112 (3) & British Nationality Act 1981, s. 40A (3). - Issued: 21.04.2008. Made: 11.04.2008. Laid: 21.04.2008. Coming into force: 12.05.2008. Effect: S.I. 2005/560 amended. Territorial extent & classification: E/W/S/NI. General. - 2p.: 30 cm. - 978-0-11-081382-0 £3.00

The Asylum and Immigration Tribunal (Procedure) (Amendment) Rules 2008 No. 2008/1088 (L.7). - Enabling power: Nationality, Immigration and Asylum Act 2002, ss. 106 (1) to (3), 112 (3) & British Nationality Act 1981, s. 40A (3). - Issued: 21.04.2008. Made: 11.04.2008. Laid: 21.04.2008. Coming into force: 12.05.2008. Effect: S.I. 2005/230 amended. Territorial extent & classification: E/W/S/NI. General. - 4p.: 30 cm. - 978-0-11-081381-3 £3.00

The Asylum Support (Amendment) Regulations 2008 No. 2008/760. - Enabling power: Immigration and Asylum Act 1999, s. 166 (3), sch. 8, paras 1, 3 (a). - Issued: 26.03.2008. Made: 18.03.2008. Laid: 19.03.2008. Coming into force: 14.03.2008. Effect: S.I. 2000/704 amended. Territorial extent & classification: E/W/S/NI. General. - Revoked by S.I. 2009/1388 (ISBN 9780111480458). - 2p.: 30 cm. - 978-0-11-081266-3 £3.00

The Immigration and Nationality (Cost Recovery Fees) (Amendment No.2) Regulations 2008 No. 2008/1337. - Enabling power: Immigration, Asylum and Nationality Act 2006, ss. 51 (3), 52 (3). - Issued: 28.05.2008. Made: 20.05.2008. Laid: 22.05.2008. Coming into force: 30.05.2008. Effect: S.I. 2007/936 amended. Territorial extent & classification: E/W/S/NI. General. - Revoked by S.I. 2009/421 (ISBN 9780111475904). - 8p.: 30 cm. - 978-0-11-081752-1 £3.00

The Immigration and Nationality (Cost Recovery Fees) (Amendment No. 3) Regulations 2008 No. 2008/2790. - Enabling power: Immigration, Asylum and Nationality Act 2006, ss. 51 (3), 52 (3). - Issued: 30.10.2008. Made: 22.10.2008. Laid: 28.10.2008. Coming into force: 27.11.2008 & 01.02.2009 in accord. with reg. 2. Effect: S.I. 2007/936 amended. Territorial extent & classification: E/W/S/NI. General. - Revoked by S.I. 2009/421 (ISBN 9780111475904). - 4p.: 30 cm. - 978-0-11-084740-5 £4.00

The Immigration and Nationality (Cost Recovery Fees) (Amendment) Regulations 2008 No. 2008/218. - Enabling power: Immigration, Asylum and Nationality Act 2006, ss. 51 (3), 52 (3). - Issued: 08.02.2008. Made: 04.02.2008. Laid: 06.02.2008. Coming into force: 29.02.2008 except for reg. 2 (4) (6); 01.04.2008 for reg. 2 (4) (6). Effect: S.I. 2007/936 amended. Territorial extent & classification: E/W/S/NI. General. - Revoked by S.I. 2009/421 (ISBN 9780111475904). - 8p.: 30 cm. - 978-0-11-080901-4 £3.00

The Immigration and Nationality (Fees) (Amendment No. 2) Regulations 2008 No. 2008/1695. - Enabling power: Immigration, Asylum and Nationality Act 2006, ss. 51 (3), 52 (3) & Asylum and Immigration (Treatment of Claimants, etc.) Act 2004, s. 42 (1) (2A). - Issued: 01.07.2008. Made: 26.06.2008. Coming into force: 30.06.2008. Effect: S.I. 2007/1158 amended. Territorial extent & classification: E/W/S/NI. General. - Revoked by S.I. 2009/816 (ISBN 9780111477694). - Supersedes draft S.I. (ISBN 9780110814582) issued 15.05.2008. - 8p.: 30 cm. - 978-0-11-081924-2 £3.00

The Immigration and Nationality (Fees) (Amendment No. 3) Regulations 2008 No. 2008/3017. - Enabling power: Immigration, Asylum and Nationality Act 2006, ss. 51 (3), 52 (3) & Asylum and Immigration (Treatment of Claimants, etc.) Act 2004, s. 42 (1) (2A). - Issued: 26.11.2008. Made: 19.11.2008. Coming into force: 27.11.2008. Effect: S.I. 2007/1158 amended. Territorial extent & classification: E/W/S/NI. General. - Revoked by S.I. 2009/816 (ISBN 9780111477694). - Supersedes draft S.I. (ISBN 9780110843674) issued 06.10.2008. - 4p.: 30 cm. - 978-0-11-147041-1 £4.00

The Immigration and Nationality (Fees) (Amendment) Order 2008 No. 2008/166. - Enabling power: Immigration, Asylum and Nationality Act 2006, s. 51 (1) (2) (b). - Issued: 04.02.2008. Made: 28.01.2008. Coming into force: 29.01.2008. Effect: S.I. 2007/807 amended. Territorial extent & classification: E/W/S/NI. General. - Supersedes draft published 26.11.2007 (ISBN 9780110797786). - 4p.: 30 cm. - 978-0-11-080880-2 £3.00

The Immigration and Nationality (Fees)(Amendment) Regulations 2008 No. 2008/544. - Enabling power: Immigration, Asylum and Nationality Act 2006, ss. 51 (3), 52 (3). - Issued: 04.03.2008. Made: 28.02.2008. Coming into force: 29.02.2008, 01.04.2008 in accord. with reg. 1 (2) (3). Effect: S.I. 2007/1158 amended. Territorial extent & classification: E/W/S/NI. General. - Revoked by S.I. 2009/816 (ISBN 9780111477694). - 8p.: 30 cm. - 978-0-11-081070-6 £3.00

The Immigration and Police (Passenger, Crew and Service Information) Order 2008 No. 2008/5. - Enabling power: Immigration Act 1971, sch. 2, paras 27, 27B & Immigration, Asylum and Nationality Act 2006, s. 32. - Issued: 11.01.2008. Made: 03.01.2008. Laid: 10.01.2008. Coming into force: 01.03.2008. Effect: S.I. 1972/1667; 1975/980; 2000/912 revoked. Territorial extent & classification: E/W/S/NI. General. - 12p.: 30 cm. - 978-0-11-080801-7 £3.00

The Immigration, Asylum and Nationality Act 2006 (Commencement No. 8 and Transitional and Saving Provisions) Order 2008 No. 2008/310 (C.10). - Enabling power: Immigration, Asylum and Nationality Act 2006, s. 62. Bringing into operation various provisions of the 2006 Act on 29.02.2008; 01.04.2008. - Issued: 14.02.2008. Made: 08.02.2008. Effect: None. Territorial extent & classification: E/W/S/NI. General. - 8p.: 30 cm. - 978-0-11-080939-7 £3.00

The Immigration, Asylum and Nationality Act 2006 (Data Sharing Code of Practice) Order 2008 No. 2008/8. - Enabling power: Immigration, Asylum and Nationality Act 2006, s. 37 (2). - Issued: 11.01.2008. Made: 08.01.2008. Laid: 10.01.2008. Coming into force: 01.03.2008. Effect: None. Territorial extent & classification: E/W/S/NI. General. - 2p.: 30 cm. - 978-0-11-080807-9 £3.00

The Immigration, Asylum and Nationality Act 2006 (Duty to Share Information and Disclosure of Information for Security Purposes) Order 2008 No. 2008/539. - Enabling power: Immigration, Asylum and Nationality Act 2006, ss. 36 (4), 38 (4). - Issued: 04.03.2008. Made: 28.02.20008. Coming into force: 01.03.2008. Effect: None. Territorial extent & classification: E/W/S/NI. General. - 8p.: 30 cm. - 978-0-11-081055-3 £3.00

The Immigration (Biometric Registration) (Civil Penalty Code of Practice) Order 2008 No. 2008/3049. - Enabling power: UK Borders Act 2007, ss. 13 (6), 14. - Issued: 27.11.2008. Made: 24.11.2008. Coming into force: 25.11.2008. Effect: None. Territorial extent & classification: E/W/S/NI. General. - 2p.: 30 cm. - 978-0-11-147060-2 £4.00

The Immigration (Biometric Registration) (Objection to Civil Penalty) Order 2008 No. 2008/2830. - Enabling power: UK Borders Act 2007, ss. 10, 14. - Issued: 07.11.2008. Made: 29.10.2008. Laid: 31.10.2008. Coming into force: 25.11.2008. Effect: None. Territorial extent & classification: E/W/S/NI. General. - 8p.: 30 cm. - 978-0-11-084917-1 £5.00

The Immigration (Biometric Registration) (Pilot) Regulations 2008 No. 2008/1183. - Enabling power: UK Borders Act 2007, ss. 5, 6 (3), 6 (6), 7, 8, 15 (1) (g). - Issued: 30.04.2008. Made: 25.04.2008. Coming into force: 26.04.2008. Effect: None. Territorial extent & classification: E/W/S/NI. General. - Revoked by S.I. 2008/3048 (ISBN 9780110470589) with saving. - 8p.: 30 cm. - 978-0-11-081410-0 £3.00

The Immigration (Biometric Registration) Regulations 2008 No. 2008/3048. - Enabling power: UK Borders Act 2007, ss. 5, 6 (3) (6), 7, 8, 15 (1) (g). - Issued: 27.11.2008. Made: 24.11.2008. Coming into force: 25.11.2008. Effect: SI 2008/1183 revoked with savings. Territorial extent & classification: E/W/S/NI. General. - 8p.: 30 cm. - 978-0-11-147058-9 £5.00

The Immigration (Designation of Travel Bans) (Amendment) Order 2008 No. 2008/3052. - Enabling power: Immigration Act 1971, 8B (5). - Issued: 27.11.2008. Made: 20.11.2008. Laid: 26.11.2008. Coming into force: 17.12.2008. Effect: S.I. 2000/2724 amended & S.I. 2007/3440 revoked. Territorial extent & classification: E/W/S/NI. General. - 8p.: 30 cm. - 978-0-11-147064-0 £5.00

The Immigration (Disposal of Property) Regulations 2008 No. 2008/786. - Enabling power: UK Borders Act 2007, s. 26 (5) (6). - Issued: 31.03.2008. Made: 20.03.2008. Laid: 26.03.2008. Coming into force: 17.04.2008. Effect: None. Territorial extent & classification: E/W/S/NI. General. - 4p.: 30 cm. - 978-0-11-081275-5 £3.00

The Immigration (Employment of Adults Subject to Immigration Control) (Maximum Penalty) Order 2008 No. 2008/132. - Enabling power: Immigration, Asylum and Nationality Act 2006, s. 15 (2). - Issued: 28.01.2008. Made: 22.01.2008. Coming into force: 29.02.2008. Effect: None. Territorial extent & classification: E/W/S/NI. General. - 2p.: 30 cm. - 978-0-11-080866-6 £3.00

The Immigration (Isle of Man) Order 2008 No. 2008/680. - Enabling power: Immigration Act 1971, s. 36 & Criminal Justice Act 1982, s. 81 (11) (12) & Asylum and Immigration Act 1996, s. 13 (5) & Immigration and Asylum Act 1999, s. 170 (7) & Nationality, Immigration and Asylum Act 2002, s. 163 (4) & Asylum and Immigration (Treatment of Claimants, etc.) Act 2004, s. 49 (3) & Immigration, Asylum and Nationality Act 2006, s. 63 (3). - Issued: 25.04.2008. Made: 12.03.2008. Coming into force: 13.03.2008 & 01.05.2008 in accord. with art. 1 (2). Effect: 1971 c.77; 1981 c.61; 1982 c.48; 1988 c.14; 1996 c.49; 1999 c.33; 2002 c.41; 2004 c.19; 2006 c.13 extended to IoM & S.I. 1991/2630; 1997/275 revoked. Territorial extent & classification: Extends UK immigration legislation to IoM. General. - 160p.: 30 cm. - 978-0-11-081249-6 £22.00

The Immigration (Notices) (Amendment) (No.2) Regulations 2008 No. 2008/1819. - Enabling power: Nationality, Immigration and Asylum Act 2002, s. 105. - Issued: 15.07.2008. Made: 08.07.2008. Laid: 10.07.2008. Coming into force: 01.08.2008. Effect: S.I. 2003/658 amended. Territorial extent & classification: E/W/S/NI. General. - 2p.: 30 cm. - 978-0-11-083098-8 £3.00

The Immigration (Notices) (Amendment) Regulations 2008 No. 2008/684. - Enabling power: Nationality, Immigration and Asylum Act 2002, ss. 105, 112 (2). - Issued: 14.03.2008. Made: 10.03.2008. Laid: 11.03.2008. Coming into force: 01.04.2008. Effect: S.I. 2003/658 amended. Territorial extent & classification: E/W/S/NI. General. - With correction slip dated September 2009. - 2p.: 30 cm. - 978-0-11-081185-7 £3.00

The Immigration (Registration Card) Order 2008 No. 2008/1693. - Enabling power: Immigration Act 1971, s. 26A (7) (a). - Issued: 01.07.2008. Made: 26.06.2008. Coming into force: 27.06.2008. Effect: 1971 c. 77 amended. Territorial extent & classification: E/W/S/NI. General. - Supersedes draft S.I. (ISBN 9780110810690) issued 07.03.2008. - 2p.: 30 cm. - 978-0-11-081923-5 £3.00

The Immigration Services Commissioner (Designated Professional Body) (Fees) Order 2008 No. 2008/505. - Enabling power: Immigration and Asylum Act 1999, s. 86 (10) (12). - Issued: 29.02.2008. Made: 21.02.2008. Laid: 27.02.2008. Coming into force: 21.03.2008. Effect: None. Territorial extent & classification: E/W/S/NI. General. - 2p.: 30 cm. - 978-0-11-081022-5 £3.00

The Immigration (Supply of Information to the Secretary of State for Immigration Purposes) Order 2008 No. 2008/2077. - Enabling power: Immigration and Asylum Act 1999, ss. 20 (1) (f) (3) (e) (5). - Issued: 04.08.2008. Made: 30.07.2008. Coming into force: 31.07.2008. Effect: None. Territorial extent & classification: E/W/S/NI. General. - Supersedes Draft SI (ISBN 9780110818764). - 2p.: 30 cm. - 978-0-11-083659-1 £3.00

The Persons subject to Immigration Control (Housing Authority Accommodation and Homelessness) (Amendment) Order 2008 No. 2008/1768. - Enabling power: Immigration and Asylum Act 1999, ss. 118, 119, 166 (3). - Issued: 09.07.2008. Made: 03.07.2008. Laid: 08.07.2008. Coming into force: 07.08.2008. Effect: S.I. 2000/706 amended. Territorial extent & classification: E/S/NI. General. - With correction slip dated July 2009. - 4p.: 30 cm. - 978-0-11-081975-4 £3.00

The UK Borders Act 2007 (Code of Practice on Children) Order 2008 No. 2008/3158. - Enabling power: UK Borders Act 2007, s. 21 (3). - Issued: 16.12.2008. Made: 05.12.2008. Laid: 12.12.2008. Coming into force: 06.01.2009. Effect: None. Territorial extent & classification: E/W/S/NI. General. - 2p.: 30 cm. - 978-0-11-147143-2 £4.00

The UK Borders Act 2007 (Commencement No. 1 and Transitional Provisions) Order 2008 No. 2008/99 (C.2). - Enabling power: UK Borders Act 2007, s. 59 (2) to (4). Bringing into force various provisions of the 2007 Act on 31.01.2008. - Issued: 23.01.2008. Made: 17.01.2008. Effect: None. Territorial extent & classification: E/W/S/NI. General. - 2p.: 30 cm. - 978-0-11-080854-3 £3.00

The UK Borders Act 2007 (Commencement No. 2 and Transitional Provisions) Order 2008 No. 2008/309 (C.9). - Enabling power: UK Borders Act 2007, s. 59 (2) to (4). Bringing into force various provisions of the 2007 Act on 29.02.2008; 31.03.2008; 01.04.2008. - Issued: 14.02.2008. Made: 08.02.2008. Effect: None. Territorial extent & classification: E/W/S/NI. General. - 4p.: 30 cm. - 978-0-11-080941-0 £3.00

The UK Borders Act 2007 (Commencement No. 3 and Transitional Provisions) Order 2008 No. 2008/1818 (C.77). - Enabling power: UK Borders Act 2007, s. 59 (2) to (4). Bringing into force various provisions of the 2007 Act on 01.08.2008. - Issued: 14.07.2008. Made: 08.07.2008. Effect: None. Territorial extent & classification: E/W/S/NI. General. - 4p.: 30 cm. - 978-0-11-083096-4 £3.00

The UK Borders Act 2007 (Commencement No. 4) Order 2008 No. 2008/2822 (C.125). - Enabling power: UK Borders Act 2007, s. 59 (2) (3). Bringing into force various provisions of the 2007 Act on 25.11.2008. - Issued: 03.11.2008. Made: 29.10.2008. Effect: None. Territorial extent & classification: E/W/S/NI. General. - 4p.: 30 cm. - 978-0-11-084776-4 £4.00

The UK Borders Act 2007 (Commencement No. 5) Order 2008 No. 2008/3136 (C.135). - Enabling power: UK Borders Act 2007, s. 59 (2) (3) (a). Bringing into force various provisions of the 2007 Act on 06.01.2009. - Issued: 10.12.2008. Made: 05.12.2008. Effect: None. Territorial extent & classification: E/W/S/NI. General. - 4p.: 30 cm. - 978-0-11-147124-1 £4.00

Immigration, England and Wales

The Independent Police Complaints Commission (Immigration and Asylum Enforcement Functions) Regulations 2008 No. 2008/212. - Enabling power: Police and Justice Act 2006, s. 41. - Issued: 08.02.2008. Made: 31.01.2008. Laid: 04.02.2008. Coming into force: 25.02.2008. Effect: 2002 c.30 modified & S.I. 2004/643, 660 modified. Territorial extent & classification: E/W. General. - Revoked by S.I. 2009/2133 (ISBN 9780111484340) with savings. - 24p.: 30 cm. - 978-0-11-080889-5 £4.00

Income tax

The Alternative Finance Arrangements (Community Investment Tax Relief) Order 2008 No. 2008/1821. - Enabling power: Finance Act 2006, s. 98. - Issued: 15.07.2008. Made: 09.07.2008. Coming into force: 10.07.2008. Effect: 2005 c.7 amended. Territorial extent & classification: E/W/S/NI. General. - Supersedes draft S.I. (ISBN 9780110814858) issued 22.05.2008. - 4p.: 30 cm. - 978-0-11-083120-6 £3.00

The Authorised Investment Funds (Tax) (Amendment No. 2) Regulations 2008 No. 2008/1463. - Enabling power: Finance (No. 2) Act 2005, ss. 17 (3), 18. - Issued: 11.06.2008. Made: 09.06.2008. Laid: 09.06.2008. Coming into force: 30.06.2008. Effect: S.I. 2006/964 amended. Territorial extent & classification: E/W/S/NI. General. - 4p.: 30 cm. - 978-0-11-081811-5 £3.00

The Authorised Investment Funds (Tax) (Amendment No. 3) Regulations 2008 No. 2008/3159. - Enabling power: Finance (No. 2) Act 2005, ss. 17 (3), 18. - Issued: 16.12.2008. Made: 10.12.2008. Laid: 11.12.2008. Coming into force: 01.01.2009. Effect: S.I. 2006/964 amended. Territorial extent & classification: E/W/S/NI. General. - 16p.: 30 cm. - With correction slip dated October 2009. - 978-0-11-147156-2 £5.00

The Authorised Investment Funds (Tax) (Amendment) Regulations 2008 No. 2008/705. - Enabling power: Finance (No. 2) Act 2005, ss. 17 (3), 18. - Issued: 12.03.2008. Made: 12.03.2008. Laid: 12.03.2008. Coming into force: 06.04.2008. Effect: S.I. 2006/964 amended. Territorial extent & classification: E/W/S/NI. General. - 34p.: 30 cm. - 978-0-11-081206-9 £6.50

The Capital Allowances (Energy-saving Plant and Machinery) (Amendment) Order 2008 No. 2008/1916. - Enabling power: Capital Allowances Act 2001, ss. 45A (3) (4). - Issued: 23.07.2008. Made: 18.07.2008. Laid: 21.07.2008. Coming into force: 11.08.2007. Effect: S.I. 2001/2541 amended. Territorial extent & classification: E/W/S/NI. General. - 2p.: 30 cm. - 978-0-11-083442-9 £3.00

The Capital Allowances (Environmentally Beneficial Plant and Machinery) (Amendment) Order 2008 No. 2008/1917. - Enabling power: Capital Allowances Act 2001, ss. 45H (3) to (5), 45I- Issued: 24.07.2008. Made: 18.07.2008. Laid: 21.07.2008. Coming into force: 11.08.2008. Effect: S.I. 2003/2076 amended. Territorial extent & classification: E/W/S/NI. General. - 4p.: 30 cm. - 978-0-11-083449-8 £3.00

The Car Fuel Benefit Order 2008 No. 2008/511. - Enabling power: Income Tax (Earnings and Pensions) Act 2003, s. 170 (5) (6). - Issued: 03.03.2008. Made: 26.02.2008. Laid: 27.02.2008. Coming into force: 19.03.2008. Effect: 2003 c.1 amended. Territorial extent & classification: E/W/S/NI. General. - 2p.: 30 cm. - 978-0-11-081029-4 £3.00

The Community Investment Tax Relief (Accreditation of Community Development Finance Institutions) (Amendment) Regulations 2008 No. 2008/383. - Enabling power: Finance Act 2002, sch. 16, para. 4 (1) (2) & Income Tax Act 2007, ss. 340 (2) (b) (4) (5) (6), 341. - Issued: 25.02.2008. Made: 18.02.2008. Laid: 19.02.2008. Coming into force: 11.03.2008. Effect: S.I. 2003/96 amended. Territorial extent & classification: E/W/S/NI. General. - 8p.: 30 cm. - 978-0-11-080979-3 £3.00

The Double Taxation Relief and International Tax Enforcement (Taxes on Income and Capital) (Moldova) Order 2008 No. 2008/1795. - Enabling power: Income and Corporation Taxes Act 1988, s. 788 (10) & Finance Act 2006, s. 173 (7). - Issued: 16.07.2008. Made: 09.07.2008. Coming into force: 09.07.2008. Effect: None. Territorial extent & classification: E/W/S/NI. General. - Supersedes draft S.I. (ISBN 9780110814803) issued 21.05.2008. - 20p.: 30 cm. - 978-0-11-083144-2 £3.50

The Double Taxation Relief and International Tax Enforcement (Taxes on Income and Capital) (New Zealand) Order 2008 No. 2008/1793. - Enabling power: Income and Corporation Taxes Act 1988, s. 788 (10) & Finance Act 2006, s. 173 (7). - Issued: 15.07.2008. Made: 09.07.2008. Coming into force: 09.07.2008. Effect: None. Territorial extent & classification: E/W/S/NI. General. - Supersedes draft S.I. (ISBN 9780110814537) issued 15.05.2008. - 8p.: 30 cm. - 978-0-11-083138-1 £3.00

The Double Taxation Relief and International Tax Enforcement (Taxes on Income and Capital) (Saudi Arabia) Order 2008 No. 2008/1770. - Enabling power: Income and Corporation Taxes Act 1988, s. 788 (10) & Finance Act 2006, s. 173 (7). - Issued: 16.07.2008. Made: 09.07.2008. Effect: None. Territorial extent & classification: E/W/S/NI. General. - Supersedes draft S.I. (ISBN 9780110814636) issued on 19.05.2008. - 20p.: 30 cm. - 978-0-11-083151-0 £3.50

The Double Taxation Relief and International Tax Enforcement (Taxes on Income and Capital) (Slovenia) Order 2008 No. 2008/1796. - Enabling power: Income and Corporation Taxes Act 1988, s. 788 (10) & Finance Act 2006, s. 173 (7). - Issued: 16.07.2008. Made: 09.07.2008. Coming into force: 09.07.2008. Effect: None. Territorial extent & classification: E/W/S/NI. General. - Supersedes draft S.I. (ISBN 9780110814544) issued 15.05.2008. - 24p.: 30 cm. - 978-0-11-083145-9 £4.00

The Double Taxation Relief (Surrender of Relievable Tax Within a Group) (Amendment) Regulations 2008 No. 2008/2681. - Enabling power: Income and Corporation Taxes Act 1988, s. 806H. - Issued: 14.10.2008. Made: 09.10.2008. Laid: 09.10.2008. Coming into force: 30.10.2008. Effect: S.I. 2001/1163 amended. Territorial extent & classification: E/W/S/NI. General. - 2p.: 30 cm. - 978-0-11-084555-5 £4.00

The Finance Act 2006, Section 28 (Appointed Day) Order 2008 No. 2008/1878 (C. 80). - Enabling power: Finance Act 2006, s. 28 (5). Bringing into force various provisions of the 2006 Act on 01.08.2008 in accord. with art. 2. - Issued: 21.07.2008. Made: 16.07.2008. Effect: None. Territorial extent & classification: E/W/S/NI. General. - With correction slip dated July 2008. - 2p.: 30 cm. - 978-0-11-083312-5 £3.00

The Finance Act 2007 Section 46 (Commencement) Order 2008 No. 2008/561 (C.19). - Enabling power: Finance Act 2007, s. 46 (9). Bringing into operation various provisions of the 2007 Act on 06.04.2008 in accord. with art. 2. - Issued: 13.03.2008. Made: 04.03.2008. Effect: None. Territorial extent & classification: E/W/S/NI. General. - This Statutory Instrument has been printed in substitution of the SI of the same number (issued 07.03.2008) and is being issued free of charge to all known recipients of that Statutory Instrument. - 2p.: 30 cm. - 978-0-11-081103-1 £3.00

Income tax

The Finance Act 2007, Section 50 (Appointed Day) Order 2008 No. 2008/1880 (C. 81). - Enabling power: Finance Act 2007, s. 50 (7). Bringing into force various provisions of the 2007 Act on 01.08.2008 in accord. with art. 2. - Issued: 21.07.2008. Made: 16.07.2008. Effect: None. Territorial extent & classification: E/W/S/NI. General. - With Correction Slip dated July 2008. - 2p.: 30 cm. - 978-0-11-083313-2 £3.00

The Finance Act 2008, Section 31 (Specified Tax Year) Order 2008 No. 2008/3165 (C. 141). - Enabling power: Finance Act 2008, s. 31 (2) (3). - Issued: 16.12.2008. Made: 10.12.2008. Coming into force: 10.12.2008. Effect: None. Territorial extent & classification: E/W/S/NI. General. - 2p.: 30 cm. - 978-0-11-147172-2 £4.00

The Income Tax (Construction Industry Scheme) (Amendment No. 2) Regulations 2008 No. 2008/1282. - Enabling power: Finance Act 2004, sch. 11, paras. 4 (3), 8 (2), 12 (2). - Issued: 21.05.2008. Made: 12.05.2008. Laid: 13.05.2008. Coming into force: 03.06.2008. Effect: S.I. 2005/2045 amended. Territorial extent & classification: E/W/S/NI. General. - 2p.: 30 cm. - 978-0-11-081482-7 £3.00

The Income Tax (Construction Industry Scheme) (Amendment) Regulations 2008 No. 2008/740. - Enabling power: Finance Act 2004, s. 71. - Issued: 19.03.2008. Made: 13.03.2008. Laid: 14.03.2008. Coming into force: 06.04.2008. Effect: S.I. 2005/2045 amended. Territorial extent & classification: E/W/S/NI. General. - 4p.: 30 cm. - 978-0-11-081243-4 £3.00

The Income Tax (Deposit-takers and Building Societies) (Interest Payments) Regulations 2008 No. 2008/2682. - Enabling power: Income Tax Act 2007, ss. 852, 871. - Issued: 15.10.2008. Made: 09.10.2008. Laid: 10.10.2008. Coming into force: 31.10.2008. Effect: S.I. 2003/3297 amended & S.I. 1990/2231, 2232; 1992/10, 11, 12, 13, 14, 2915; 1994/295, 296; 1995/1184; 1996/223; 2001/404, 406; 2005/3474 revoked. Territorial extent & classification: UK. General. - 16p.: 30 cm. - 978-0-11-084556-2 £5.00

The Income Tax (Indexation) (No. 2) Order 2008 No. 2008/709. - Enabling power: Income Tax Act 2007, s. 21 (5). - Issued: 12.03.2008. Made: 12.03.2008. Coming into force: 12.03.2008. Effect: None. Territorial extent & classification: E/W/S/NI. General. - 2p.: 30 cm. - 978-0-11-081207-6 £3.00

The Income Tax (Indexation) (No. 3) Order 2008 No. 2008/3023. - Enabling power: Income Tax Act 2007, ss. 21 (5), 57 (6). - Issued: 25.11.2008. Made: 24.11.2008. Coming into force: 24.11.2008. Effect: 2007 c. 3 amended. Territorial extent & classification: E/W/S/NI. General. - 4p.: 30 cm. - 978-0-11-147054-1 £4.00

The Income Tax (Indexation) (No. 4) Order 2008 No. 2008/3024. - Enabling power: Income and Corporation Taxes Act 1988, ss. 257C (3), 265 (1A). - Issued: 25.11.2008. Made: 24.11.2008. Laid: 24.11.2008. Coming into force: 06.04.2009. Effect: 1988 c. 1 amended. Territorial extent & classification: E/W/S/NI. General. - 4p.: 30 cm. - 978-0-11-147055-8 £4.00

The Income Tax (Indexation) Order 2008 No. 2008/673. - Enabling power: Income and Corporation Taxes Act 1988, ss. 257C (3), 265 (1A), - Issued: 13.03.2008. Made: 10.03.2008. Laid: 11.03.2008. Coming into force: 06.04.2008. Effect: None. Territorial extent & classification: E/W/S/NI. General. - 4p.: 30 cm. - 978-0-11-081174-1 £3.00

The Income Tax (Interest Payments) (Information Powers) (Amendment) Regulations 2008 No. 2008/2688. - Enabling power: Taxes Management Act 1970, ss. 17 (5) (6), 18 (3B) (3C). - Issued: 15.10.2008. Made: 09.10.2008. Laid: 10.10.2008. Coming into force: 31.10.2008. Effect: S.I. 1992/15 amended. Territorial extent & classification: E/W/S/NI. General. - 4p.: 30 cm. - 978-0-11-084597-5 £4.00

The Income Tax (Limits for Enterprise Management Incentives) Order 2008 No. 2008/706. - Enabling power: Income Tax (Earnings and Pensions) Act 2003, sch. 5, para. 54 (1) (b) (i) (2). - Issued: 13.03.2008. Made: 12.03.2008. Laid: 13.03.2008. Coming into force: 06.04.2008. Effect: 2003 c.1 amended. Territorial extent & classification: E/W/S/NI. General. - 2p.: 30 cm. - 978-0-11-081212-0 £3.00

The Income Tax (Pay As You Earn) (Amendment) (No.2) Regulations 2008 No. 2008/2601. - Enabling power: Income Tax (Earnings and Pensions) Act 2003, s. 684. - Issued: 09.10.2008. Made: 03.10.2008. Laid: 06.10.2008. Coming into force: 27.10.2008. Effect: S.I. 2003/2682 amended. Territorial extent & classification: E/W/S/NI. General. - 12p.: 30 cm. - 978-0-11-084383-4 £5.00

The Income Tax (Pay As You Earn) (Amendment) Regulations 2008 No. 2008/782. - Enabling power: Income Tax (Earnings and Pensions) Act 2003, s. 684 (1) (2). - Issued: 28.03.2008. Made: 20.03.2008. Laid: 20.03.2008. Coming into force: 06.04.2008. Effect: S.I. 2003/2682 amended. Territorial extent & classification: E/W/S/NI. General. - 8p.: 30 cm. - 978-0-11-081276-2 £3.00

The Income Tax (Payments on Account) (Amendment) Regulations 2008 No. 2008/838. - Enabling power: Taxes Management Act 1970, s. 59A (1). - Issued: 01.04.2008. Made: 26.03.2008. Laid: 27.03.2008. Coming into force: 06.04.2009. Effect: S.I. 1996/1654 amended. Territorial extent & classification: E/W/S/NI. General. - 2p.: 30 cm. - 978-0-11-081297-7 £3.00

The Income Tax (Professional Fees) Order 2008 No. 2008/836. - Enabling power: Income Tax (Earnings and Pensions) Act 2003, s. 343 (3) (4). - Issued: 01.04.2008. Made: 26.03.2008. Coming into force: 06.04.2008. Effect: 2003 c.1 amended. Territorial extent & classification: E/W/S/NI. General. - 2p.: 30 cm. - 978-0-11-081296-0 £3.00

The Income Tax (Purchased Life Annuities) (Amendment) Regulations 2008 No. 2008/1481. - Enabling power: Income and Corporation Taxes Act 1988, s. 658 (3) & Income Tax (Trading and Other Income) Act 2005, s. 724. - Issued: 16.06.2008. Made: 09.06.2008. Laid: 10.06.2008. Coming into force: 01.07.2008. Effect: S.I. 2008/562 amended. Territorial extent & classification: E/W/S/NI. General. - This Statutory Instrument has been printed in consequence of a defect in SI 2008/562 and is being issued free of charge to all known recipients of that Statutory Instrument. - 2p.: 30 cm. - 978-0-11-081837-5 *£3.00*

The Income Tax (Purchased Life Annuities) Regulations 2008 No. 2008/562. - Enabling power: Income and Corporation Taxes Act 1988, s. 658 (3) & Income Tax (Trading and Other Income) Act 2005, s. 724. - Issued: 11.03.2008. Made: 05.03.2008. Laid: 05.03.2008. Coming into force: 06.04.2008. Effect: 1970 c.9 amended & S.I. 1956/1230; 1960/2308; 1990/626; 1991/2808 revoked. Territorial extent & classification: E/W/S/NI. General. - With correction slips dated March 2008 and August 2009. - 16p.: 30 cm. - 978-0-11-081109-3 *£3.00*

The Income Tax (Qualifying Child Care) Regulations 2008 No. 2008/2170. - Enabling power: Income Tax (Earnings and Pensions) Act 2003, s. 318D (2). - Issued: 18.08.2008. Made: 13.08.2008. Laid: 14.08.2008. Coming into force: 01.09.2008. Effect: 2003 c. 1 amended. Territorial extent & classification: E/W/S/NI. General. - 4p.: 30 cm. - 978-0-11-083792-5 *£3.00*

The Individual Savings Account (Amendment No. 2) Regulations 2008 No. 2008/1934. - Enabling power: Income Tax (Trading and Other Income) Act 2005, ss. 694 to 701 & Taxation of Chargeable Gains Act 1992, s. 151. - Issued: 25.07.2008. Made: 22.07.2008. Laid: 22.07.2008. Coming into force: 12.08.2008. Effect: S.I. 1998/1870 amended. Territorial extent & classification: E/W/S/NI. General. - 4p.: 30 cm. - 978-0-11-083551-8 *£3.00*

The Individual Savings Account (Amendment No. 3) Regulations 2008 No. 2008/3025. - Enabling power: Income Tax (Trading and Other Income) Act 2005, ss. 694 to 701 & Taxation of Chargeable Gains Act 1992, s. 151. - Issued: 25.11.2008. Made: 24.11.2008. Laid: 24.11.2008. Coming into force: 16.12.2008. Effect: S.I. 1998/1870 amended. Territorial extent & classification: E/W/S/NI. General. - 2p.: 30 cm. - 978-0-11-147056-5 *£4.00*

The Individual Savings Account (Amendment) Regulations 2008 No. 2008/704. - Enabling power: Income Tax (Trading and Other Income) Act 2005, ss. 694 to 701 & Taxation of Chargeable Gains Act 1992, s. 151. - Issued: 13.03.2008. Made: 12.03.2008. Laid: 13.03.2008. Coming into force: 06.04.2008. Effect: S.I. 1998/1870 amended. Territorial extent & classification: E/W/S/NI. General. - 8p.: 30 cm. - With correction dated June 2008. - 978-0-11-081213-7 *£3.00*

The Life Assurance and Other Policies (Keeping of Information and Duties of Insurers) (Amendment) Regulations 2008 No. 2008/2628. - Enabling power: Income and Corporation Taxes Act 1988, s. 552ZA (6) to (8). - Issued: 09.10.2008. Made: 06.10.2008. Laid: 06.10.2008. Coming into force: 27.10.2008. Effect: S.I. 1997/265 amended. Territorial extent & classification: E/W/S/NI. General. - 2p.: 30 cm. - 978-0-11-084396-4 *£4.00*

The Overseas Insurers (Tax Representatives) (Amendment) Regulations 2008 No. 2008/2626. - Enabling power: Income and Corporation Taxes Act 1988, s. 552A (7) (9) (10). - Issued: 09.10.2008. Made: 06.10.2008. Laid: 06.10.2008. Coming into force: 27.10.2008. Effect: S.I. 1999/881 amended. Territorial extent & classification: E/W/S/NI. General. - 4p.: 30 cm. - 978-0-11-084398-8 *£4.00*

The Registered Pension Schemes (Provision of Information) (Amendment) Regulations 2008 No. 2008/720. - Enabling power: Finance Act 2004, s. 251 (1) (a) (b) (4) (a) (b) (5). - Issued: 19.03.2008. Made: 12.03.2008. Laid: 13.03.2008. Coming into force: 06.04.2008. Effect: S.I. 2006/567 amended. Territorial extent & classification: E/W/S/NI. General. - 8p.: 30 cm. - 978-0-11-081257-1 *£3.00*

The Registered Pension Schemes (Transfer of Sums and Assets) (Amendment) Regulations 2008 No. 2008/1946. - Enabling power: Finance Act 2004, sch. 28, paras. 3 (2B) (2C) (2CA), 17 (3) (4) (4A). - Issued: 28.07.2008. Made: 22.07.2008. Laid: 22.07.2008. Coming into force: 01.11.2008. Effect: S.I. 2006/499 amended. Territorial extent & classification: E/W/S/NI. General. - 4p.: 30 cm. - 978-0-11-083578-5 *£3.00*

The Taxation of Benefits under Government Pilot Schemes (Better off in Work Credit) Order 2008 No. 2008/2603. - Enabling power: Finance Act 1996, s. 151 (1) (a) (7) (a). - Issued: 09.10.2008. Made: 06.10.2008 Laid: 06.10.2008. Coming into force: 27.10.2008. Effect: None. Territorial extent & classification: E/W/S/NI. General. - 2p.: 30 cm. - 978-0-11-084386-5 *£4.00*

The Taxation of Benefits under Government Pilot Schemes (Up-Front Childcare Fund) Order 2008 No. 2008/1464. - Enabling power: Finance Act 1996, s. 151 (1) (a) (7) (a). - Issued: 12.06.2008. Made: 09.06.2008. Laid: 09.06.2008. Coming into force: 01.07.2008. Effect: None. Territorial extent & classification: E/W/S/NI. General. - 2p.: 30 cm. - 978-0-11-081812-2 *£3.00*

The Taxation of Pension Schemes (Transitional Provisions) (Amendment) Order 2008 No. 2008/2990. - Enabling power: Finance Act 2004, s. 283 (2) (3A) (3C). - Issued: 21.11.2008. Made: 17.11.2008. Laid: 18.11.02008. Coming into force: 01.01.2009. Effect: S.I. 2006/572 amended. Territorial extent & classification: E/W/S/NI. General. - 4p.: 30 cm. - 978-0-11-147016-9 *£4.00*

The Venture Capital Trust (Amendment) Regulations 2008 No. 2008/1893. - Enabling power: Income Tax Act 2007, ss. 272 (2) (3), 284. - Issued: 23.07.2008. Made: 17.07.2008. Laid: 17.07.2008. Coming into force: 01.09.2008. Effect: S.I. 1995/1979 amended. Territorial extent & classification: E/W/S/NI. General. - 12p.: 30 cm. - 978-0-11-083388-0 £3.00

Industrial development

The Financial Assistance for Industry (Increase of Limit) Order 2008 No. 2008/1272. - Enabling power: Industrial Development Act 1982, s. 8 (5). - Issued: 12.05.2008. Made: 07.05.2008. Coming into force: 08.05.2008. Effect: 1982 c. 52 amended. Territorial extent & classification: E/W/S/NI. General. - Supersedes draft SI (ISBN 9780110774763) issued 25.06.2008. - 2p.: 30 cm. - 978-0-11-081446-9 £3.00

Industrial organisation and development

The Wool Textile Industry (Export Promotion Levy) (Revocation) Order 2008 No. 2008/2932. - Enabling power: Industrial Organisation and Development Act 1947, s. 9 (7). - Issued: 14.11.2008. Made: 11.11.2008. Coming into force: 12.11.2008. Effect: S.I. 1970/348; 1971/880; 1982/485 revoked. Territorial extent & classification: E/W/S. General. - Supersedes draft S.I. (ISBN 9780110844282) issued 02.10.2008. - 4p.: 30 cm. - 978-0-11-146996-5 £4.00

Inheritance tax

The Inheritance Tax (Delivery of Accounts) (Excepted Settlements) Regulations 2008 No. 2008/606. - Enabling power: Inheritance Tax Act 1984, s. 256 (1) (a). - Issued: 12.03.2008. Made: 06.03.2008. Laid: 06.03.2008. Coming into force: 06.04.2008. Effect: S. I. 2002/1732 revoked in relation to an occasion of a chargeable event on or after 6th April 2007. Territorial extent & classification: E/W/S/NI. General- With correction slip dated August 2009. - 8p.: 30 cm. - 978-0-11-081123-9 £3.00

The Inheritance Tax (Delivery of Accounts) (Excepted Transfers and Excepted Terminations) Regulations 2008 No. 2008/605. - Enabling power: Inheritance Tax Act 1984, s. 256 (1) (a). - Issued: 18.03.2008. Made: 06.03.2008. Laid: 06.03.2008. Coming into force: 06.04.2008. Effect: S. I. 2002/1731 revoked in relation to any excepted transfer or excepted termination made on or after 06.04.2008. Territorial extent & classification: E/W/S/NI. General. - With correction slip dated August 2009. - 8p.: 30 cm. - 978-0-11-081253-3 £3.00

Insolvency: Fees

The Insolvency Practitioners and Insolvency Services Account (Fees) (Amendment) (No. 2) Order 2008 No. 2008/672. - Enabling power: Insolvency Act 1986, s.415A. - Issued: 18.03.2008. Made: 09.03.2008. Laid: 12.03.2008. Coming into force: 06.04.2008. Effect: S.I. 2003/3363 amended. Territorial extent & classification: E/W/S. General. - 4p.: 30 cm. - 978-0-11-081179-6 £3.00

Insolvency: Insolvency practitioners

The Insolvency Practitioners and Insolvency Services Account (Fees) (Amendment) (No. 2) Order 2008 No. 2008/672. - Enabling power: Insolvency Act 1986, s.415A. - Issued: 18.03.2008. Made: 09.03.2008. Laid: 12.03.2008. Coming into force: 06.04.2008. Effect: S.I. 2003/3363 amended. Territorial extent & classification: E/W/S. General. - 4p.: 30 cm. - 978-0-11-081179-6 £3.00

The Insolvency Practitioners and Insolvency Services Account (Fees) (Amendment) Order 2008 No. 2008/3. - Enabling power: Insolvency Act 1986, s.415A. - Issued: 10.01.2008. Made: 07.01.2008. Laid: 08.01.2008. Coming into force: 30.01.2008. Effect: S.I. 2003/3363 amended. Territorial extent & classification: E/W/S. General. - Revoked by S.I. 2009/487 (ISBN 9780111475409) in relation to England and Wales. - 4p.: 30 cm. - 978-0-11-080805-5 £3.00

Insolvency, England and Wales: Companies

The Insolvency (Amendment) Regulations 2008 No. 2008/670. - Enabling power: S.I. 1986/1925, rule 12.1 & Insolvency Act 1986, s. 411, sch.8, para. 27. - Issued: 18.03.2008. Made: 09.03.2009. Laid: 12.03.2008. Coming into force: 06.04.2008. Effect: S.I. 1994/2507 amended. Territorial extent & classification: E/W. General. - 4p.: 30 cm. - 978-0-11-081175-8 £3.00

The Insolvency (Amendment) Rules 2008 No. 2008/737. - Enabling power: Insolvency Act 1986, s. 411. - Issued: 20.03.2008. Made: 13.03.2008. Laid: 14.03.2008. Coming into force: 06.04.2008. Effect: S.I. 1986/1925 amended. Territorial extent & classification: E/W. General. - 12p.: 30 cm. - 978-0-11-081238-0 £3.00

Insolvency, England and Wales: Fees

The Insolvency Proceedings (Fees) (Amendment) Order 2008 No. 2008/714. - Enabling power: Insolvency Act 1986, ss. 414, 415. - Issued: 18.03.2008. Made: 10.03.2008. Laid: 13.03.2008. Coming into force: 06.04.2008. Effect: S.I. 2004/593 amended. Territorial extent & classification: E/W. General. - 4p.: 30 cm. - 978-0-11-081199-4 £3.00

Insolvency, Scotland: Companies

The Insolvency (Scotland) Amendment Rules 2008 No. 2008/662 (S.4). - Enabling power: Insolvency Act 1986, s. 411. - Issued: 14.03.2008. Made: 09.03.2008. Laid before the Scottish Parliament: 12.03.2008. Coming into force: 06.04.2008. Effect: 1986 c.45 amended. Territorial extent & classification: S. General. - 4p.: 30 cm. - 978-0-11-081576-3 £3.00

Insurance

The Employers' Liability (Compulsory Insurance) (Amendment) Regulations 2008 No. 2008/1765. - Enabling power: Employers Liability (Compulsory Insurance) Act 1969, ss. 4 (2), 6. - Issued: 10.07.2008. Made: 04.07.2008. Laid: 04.07.2008. Coming into force: 01.10.2008. Effect: S.I. 1998/2573 amended. Territorial extent & classification: E/W/S. General. - 2p.: 30 cm. - 978-0-11-081970-9 £3.00

The Insurance Accounts Directive (Lloyd's Syndicate and Aggregate Accounts) Regulations 2008 No. 2008/1950. - Enabling power: European Communities Act 1972, s. 2 (2). - Issued: 28.07.2008. Made: 22.07.2008. Laid: 22.07.2008. Coming into force: 15.08.2007. Effect: 2006 c. 46 amended & S.I. 2004/3219 revoked with savings. Territorial extent & classification: E/W/S/NI. General. - With correction slip dated September 2009. These Regulations update the implementation of Council Directive 91/674/EEC on the annual accounts and consolidated accounts of insurance undertakings as amended by Directive 2003/51/EC in relation to Lloyd's. They also implement, in part, Directive 2006/43/EC on statutory audits of annual accounts and consolidated accounts, and Directive 2006/46/EC amending Council Directives 78/660 on the annual accounts of certain types of companies, 83/349/EEC on consolidated accounts, 86/635/EEC on the annual accounts and consolidated accounts of banks and other financial institutions and 91/674/EEC on the annual accounts and consolidated accounts of insurance undertakings. - 32p.: 30 cm. - 978-0-11-083587-7 £5.50

The Insurance Accounts Directive (Miscellaneous Insurance Undertakings) Regulations 2008 No. 2008/565. - Enabling power: European Communities Act 1972, s. 2 (2). - Issued: 10.03.2008. Made: 26.02.2008. Laid: 05.03.2008. Coming into force: 06.04.2008. Effect: 2006 c. 46 amended & 1965 c.12; 1968 c.55; 1969 c.24 (N.I.) modified & S.I. 1993/3245 & S.R. 1994/429 revoked with savings. Territorial extent & classification: E/W/S/NI. General. - EC note: The Regulations continue the implementation of Council Directive 91/674/EEC. They also implement, in part, Directive 2006/43/EC ("the Audit Directive"). - 20p.: 30 cm. - 978-0-11-081095-9 £3.50

Insurance premium tax

The Amusement Machine Licence Duty, etc (Amendments) Regulations 2008 No. 2008/2693. - Enabling power: Betting and Gaming Duties Act 1981, sch. 4, paras 5 (1), 12 & Finance Act 1994, ss. 54, 74 (7) (8) & Finance Act 1996, ss. 49, 71 (8) (9) & Finance Act 2000, sch. 6, paras. 41 (1) (2), 146 (7) & Finance Act 2001, ss. 25 (1) (2), 45 (5). - Issued: 15.10.2008. Made: 10.10.2008. Laid: 10.10.2008. Coming into force: 01/11/2008. Effect: S.I. 1994/1774; 1995/2631; 1996/1527; 2001/838; 2002/ 761 amended. Territorial extent & classification: E/W/S/NI. General. - 4p.: 30 cm. - 978-0-11-084575-3 £4.00

The Insurance Premium Tax (Amendment) Regulations 2008 No. 2008/1945. - Enabling power: Finance Act 1994, ss. 53 (6), 65 (1), 74 (8). - Issued: 25.07.2008. Made: 22.07.2008. Laid: 22.07.2008. Coming into force: 01.09.2008. Effect: S.I. 1994/1774 amended. Territorial extent & classification: E/W/S/NI. General. - 8p.: 30 cm. - 978-0-11-083562-4 £3.00

The Value Added Tax, etc (Correction of Errors, etc) Regulations 2008 No. 2008/1482. - Enabling power: Value Added Tax Act 1994, sch. 11, paras 2 (1) (10) (11) & Finance Act 1994, ss. 38 (1), 42 (2), 54, 74 (7) (8) & Finance Act 1996, ss. 49, 71 (8) (9) & Finance Act 2000, sch. 6, paras 41(1) (2), 146 (7) & Finance Act 2001, ss. 25 (1) (2), 45 (5). - Issued: 18.06.2008. Made: 09.06.2008. Laid: 10.06.2008. Coming into force: 01.07.2008. Effect: S.I. 1994/1738, 1774; 1995/2518; 1996/1527; 2001/838; 2002/761 amended. Territorial extent & classification: E/W/S/NI. General. - 12p.: 30 cm. - 978-0-11-081855-9 £3.00

International criminal court

The International Criminal Court (Remand Time) Order 2008 No. 2008/3135. - Enabling power: International Criminal Court Act 2001, s. 4 (4), sch. 1, para. 3. - Issued: 17.12.2008. Made: 10.12.2008. Coming into force: 17.12.2008 in accord. with art. 1. Effect: None. Territorial extent & classification: E/W/S/NI. General. - Supersedes draft S.I. (ISBN 9780110843612) issued 07.10.2008. - 2p.: 30 cm. - 978-0-11-147162-3 £4.00

International development

The African Development Bank (Eleventh Replenishment of the African Development Fund) Order 2008 No. 2008/2088. - Enabling power: International Development Act 2002, s. 11. - Issued: 06.08.2008. Made: 17.07.2008. Coming into force: 18.07.2008 in accord. with art. 1. Effect: None. Territorial extent & classification: E/W/S/NI. General. - Supersedes draft S.I. (ISBN 9780110817903) issued 10.06.2008. - 4p.: 30 cm. - 978-0-11-083709-3 £3.00

The African Development Fund (Multilateral Debt Relief Initiative) (Amendment) Order 2008 No. 2008/2089. - Enabling power: International Development Act 2002, s. 11. - Issued: 06.08.2008. Made: 17.07.2008. Coming into force: 18.07.2008 in accord. with art. 1. Effect: S.I. 2006/2321 amended. Territorial extent & classification: E/W/S/NI. General. - Supersedes draft S.I. (ISBN 9780110817866) issued 10.06.2008. - 2p.: 30 cm. - 978-0-11-083695-9 *£3.00*

The Crown Agents Holding and Realisation Board (Prescribed Day) Order 2008 No. 2008/921. - Enabling power: Crown Agents Act 1979, sch. 5, para. 23 (1). - Issued: 02.04.2008. Made: 26.03.2008. Coming into force: 28.03.2008. Effect: None. Territorial extent & classification: E/W/S/NI. General. - Supersedes draft SI (ISBN 9780110808956) issued 06.02.2008. - 2p.: 30 cm. - 978-0-11-081316-5 *£3.00*

The International Development Association (Fifteenth Replenishment) Order 2008 No. 2008/2090. - Enabling power: International Development Act 2002, s. 11. - Issued: 06.08.2008. Made: 17.07.2008. Coming into force: 18.07.2008 in accord. with art. 1. Effect: None. Territorial extent & classification: E/W/S/NI. General. - Supersedes draft S.I. (ISBN 9780110817910) issued 10.06.2008. - 4p.: 30 cm. - 978-0-11-083696-6 *£3.00*

The International Development Association (Multilateral Debt Relief Initiative) (Amendment) Order 2008 No. 2008/2086. - Enabling power: International Development Act 2002, s. 11. - Issued: 06.08.2008. Made: 17.07.2008. Coming into force: 18.07.2008 in accord. with art. 1. Effect: S.I. 2006/2323 amended. Territorial extent & classification: E/W/S/NI. General. - Supersedes draft SI (ISBN 9780110817934). - 2p.: 30 cm. - 978-0-11-083694-2 *£3.00*

International immunities and privileges

The International Organization for Migration (Immunities and Privileges) Order 2008 No. 2008/3124. - Enabling power: International Organisations Act 1968, s. 1. - Issued: 14.01.2009. Made: 10.12.2008. Coming into force: 11.12.2008. Effect: None. Territorial extent & classification: E/W/S/NI. General. - Supersedes draft S.I. (ISBN 9780110848532) issued 05.11.2008. - 4p.: 30 cm. - 978-0-11-147221-7 *£4.00*

Investigatory powers

The Serious Crime Act 2007 (Commencement No.1) Order 2008 No. 2008/219 (C.5). - Enabling power: Serious Crime Act 2007, s. 94 (1). Bringing into operation various provisions of the 2007 Act on 15.02.2008 & 01.03.2008. - Issued: 08.02.2008. Made: 05.02.2008. Effect: None. Territorial extent & classification: E/W/S/NI. General. - 4p.: 30 cm. - 978-0-11-080902-1 *£3.00*

Judges

The Discipline of Judges (Designation) Order 2008 No. 2008/2700. - Enabling power: Constitutional Reform Act 2005, s. 118 (2). - Issued: 15.10.2008. Made: 07.10.2008. Laid: 13.10.2008. Coming into force: 03.11.2008. Effect: None. Territorial extent & classification: E/W/S/NI. General. - Revoked by S.I. 2009/590 (ISBN 9780111476277). - 2p.: 30 cm. - 978-0-11-084634-7 *£4.00*

Judicial appointments and discipline

The Judicial Appointments Order 2008 No. 2008/2995. - Enabling power: Tribunals, Courts and Enforcement Act 2007, s. 51 & Social Security Act 1998, s. 7 (6A) (6B). - Issued: 21.11.2008. Made: 17.11.2008. Coming into force: 18.11.2008 except for art. 7 (b); 30.11.2010 for art. 7 (b) in accord. with art. 1 (2). Effect: None. Territorial extent & classification: E/W/S/NI. General. - Supersedes draft S.I. (ISBN 9780110843360) issued 06.10.2008. - 4p.: 30 cm. - 978-0-11-147020-6 *£4.00*

The Judicial Discipline (Prescribed Procedures) (Amendment) Regulations 2008 No. 2008/2098. - Enabling power: Constitutional Reform Act 2005, ss. 115, 120, 121. - Issued: 21.08.2008. Made: 17.07.2008. Laid: 05.08.2008. Coming into force: 28.08.2008. Effect: S.I. 2006/676 amended. Territorial extent & classification: E/W/S/NI. General. - 8p.: 30 cm. - 978-0-11-083846-5 *£3.00*

The Tribunals, Courts and Enforcement Act 2007 (Commencement No. 5 and Transitional Provisions) Order 2008 No. 2008/1653 (C.73). - Enabling power: Tribunals, Courts and Enforcement Act 2007, s. 145, 148 (5). Bringing into operation various provisions of the 2007 Act on 21.07.2008. - Issued: 01.07.2008. Made: 23.06.2008. Laid: 26.06.2008. Effect: None. Territorial extent & classification: E/W/S/NI. General. - 4p.: 30 cm. - 978-0-11-081912-9 *£3.00*

The Tribunals, Courts and Enforcement Act 2007 (Commencement No. 6 and Transitional Provisions) Order 2008 No. 2008/2696 (C.117). - Enabling power: Tribunals, Courts and Enforcement Act 2007, ss. 31 (9), 148 (5). Bringing into operation various provisions of the 2007 Act on 03.11.2008 & 01.04.2009 in accord. with art. 2. - Issued: 20.10.2008. Made: 09.10.2008. Laid: 15.10.2008. Effect: None. Territorial extent & classification: E/W/S/NI. General. - 8p.: 30 cm. - 978-0-11-084610-1 *£5.00*

Judicial appointments and discipline, England and Wales

The Constitutional Reform Act 2005 (Commencement No. 10) Order 2008 No. 2008/2597 (C.114). - Enabling power: Constitutional Reform Act 2005, s. 148. Bringing into operation various provisions of the 2005 Act on 02.10.2008, in accord. with art. 2. - Issued: 08.10.2008. Made: 02.10.2008. Effect: None. Territorial extent & classification: E/W. General. - 4p.: 30 cm. - 978-0-11-084375-9 £4.00

Judicial Committee

The Judicial Committee (General Appellate Jurisdiction) Rules (Amendment) Order 2008 No. 2008/300. - Enabling power: Judicial Committee Act 1833, s. 24 & Judicial Committee Act 1844, s. 1. - Issued: 18.02.2008. Made: 12.02.2008. Coming into force: 04.03.2008. Effect: S.I. 1982/1676 amended. Territorial extent & classification: E/W/S/NI. General. - With correction slip dated August 2008. Revoked by S.I. 2009/224 (ISBN 9780111474037). - 4p.: 30 cm. - 978-0-11-080947-2 £3.00

Land drainage, England

The East Suffolk Internal Drainage Board Order 2008 No. 2008/750. - Enabling power: Land Drainage Act 1991, s. 3 (5) (7). - Issued: 25.03.2008. Made: 10.01.2008. Coming into force: In accord with art. 1. Effect: None. Territorial extent & classification: E. Local. - 12p.: 30 cm. - 978-0-11-081261-8 £3.00

The Reconstitution of the Black Sluice Internal Drainage Board Order 2008 No. 2008/1423. - Enabling power: Land Drainage Act 1991, s. 3 (5) (7). - Issued: 09.06.2008. Made: 25.03.2008. Coming into force: In accord with art. 1. Effect: None. Territorial extent & classification: E. Local. - 4p.: 30 cm. - 978-0-11-081778-1 £3.00

The Reconstitution of the Welland and Deepings Internal Drainage Board Order 2008 No. 2008/1422. - Enabling power: Land Drainage Act 1991, s. 3 (5) (7). - Issued: 09.06.2008. Made: 25.03.2008. Coming into force: In accord with art. 1. Effect: None. Territorial extent & classification: E. Local. - 4p.: 30 cm. - 978-0-11-081775-0 £3.00

Landfill tax

The Amusement Machine Licence Duty, etc (Amendments) Regulations 2008 No. 2008/2693. - Enabling power: Betting and Gaming Duties Act 1981, sch. 4, paras 5 (1), 12 & Finance Act 1994, ss. 54, 74 (7) (8) & Finance Act 1996, ss. 49, 71 (8) (9) & Finance Act 2000, sch. 6, paras. 41 (1) (2), 146 (7) & Finance Act 2001, ss. 25 (1) (2), 45 (5). - Issued: 15.10.2008. Made: 10.10.2008. Laid: 10.10.2008. Coming into force: 01/11/2008. Effect: S.I. 1994/1774; 1995/2631; 1996/1527; 2001/838; 2002/ 761 amended. Territorial extent & classification: E/W/S/NI. General. - 4p.: 30 cm. - 978-0-11-084575-3 £4.00

The Landfill Tax (Amendment) Regulations 2008 No. 2008/770. - Enabling power: Finance Act 1996, ss. 51 (1), 53 (1) (4) (a) (c) (d). - Issued: 25.03.2008. Made: 19.03.2008. Laid: 19.03.2008. Coming into force: 01.04.2008. Effect: S.I. 1996/1527 amended. Territorial extent & classification: E/W/S/NI. General. - 2p.: 30 cm. - 978-0-11-081267-0 £3.00

The Landfill Tax (Material from Contaminated Land) (Phasing out of Exemption) Order 2008 No. 2008/2669. - Enabling power: Finance Act 1996, ss. 46, 71 (1) (9). - Issued: 13.10.2008. Made: 08.10.2008. Laid: 08.10.2008. Coming into force: 15.11.2008, for the purposes of arts. 1 and 2; 01.12.2008, for the purposes of art. 3; 01.04.2012, for the purposes of art. 4. Effect: 1996 c. 8 amended. Territorial extent & classification: E/W/S/NI. General. - For approval by that House before the expiration of a period of 28 days beginning with the date on which the Order was made, no account to be taken of any time during which Parliament is dissolved or prorogued or during which the House of Commons is adjourned for more than 4 days. - 4p.: 30 cm. - 978-0-11-084502-9 £4.00

The Landfill Tax (Material from Contaminated Land) (Phasing out of Exemption) Order 2008 No. 2008/2669. - Enabling power: Finance Act 1996, ss. 46, 71 (1) (9). - Issued: 03.11.2008. Made: 08.10.2008. Laid: 08.10.2008. Coming into force: 15.11.2008, for the purposes of arts. 1 and 2; 01.12.2008, for the purposes of art. 3 & 01.04.2012, for the purposes of art. 4. Effect: 1996 c. 8 amended. Territorial extent & classification: E/W/S/NI. General. - Approved by the House of Commons. - 4p.: 30 cm. - 978-0-11-084766-5 £4.00

The Value Added Tax, etc (Correction of Errors, etc) Regulations 2008 No. 2008/1482. - Enabling power: Value Added Tax Act 1994, sch. 11, paras 2 (1) (10) (11) & Finance Act 1994, ss. 38 (1), 42 (2), 54, 74 (7) (8) & Finance Act 1996, ss. 49, 71 (8) (9) & Finance Act 2000, sch. 6, paras 41(1) (2), 146 (7) & Finance Act 2001, ss. 25 (1) (2), 45 (5). - Issued: 18.06.2008. Made: 09.06.2008. Laid: 10.06.2008. Coming into force: 01.07.2008. Effect: S.I. 1994/1738, 1774; 1995/2518; 1996/1527; 2001/838; 2002/761 amended. Territorial extent & classification: E/W/S/NI. General. - 12p.: 30 cm. - 978-0-11-081855-9 £3.00

Landlord and tenant, England

The Agricultural Holdings (Units of Production) (England) Order 2008 No. 2008/2708. - Enabling power: Agricultural Holdings Act 1986, sch. 6, para. 4. - Issued: 17.10.2008. Made: 13.10.2008. Laid: 16.10.2008. Coming into force: 07.11.2008. Effect: S.I. 2007/2968 revoked. Territorial extent & classification: E. General. - 8p.: 30 cm. - 978-0-11-084659-0 £5.00

Landlord and tenant, Wales

The Agricultural Holdings (Units of Production) (Wales) (No.2) Order 2008 No. 2008/3200 (W.285). - Enabling power: Agricultural Holdings Act 1986, sch. 6, para. 4. - Issued: 09.01.2009. Made: 15.12.2008. Laid: 16.12.2008. Coming into force: 08.01.2009. Effect: S.I. 2008/253 (W.29) revoked. Territorial extent & classification: W. General. - In English and Welsh: Welsh title: Gorchymyn Daliadau Amaethyddol (Unedau Cynhyrchu) (Cymru) (Rhif 2) 2008. - 12p.: 30 cm. - 978-0-11-091920-1 £5.00

The Agricultural Holdings (Units of Production) (Wales) Order 2008 No. 2008/253 (W.29). - Enabling power: Agricultural Holdings Act 1986, sch. 6, para. 4. - Issued: 04.03.2008. Made: 06.02.2008. Laid: 07.02.2008. Coming into force: 03.03.2008. Effect: S.I. 2007/2398 (W.199) revoked. Territorial extent & classification: W. General. - Revoked by W.S.I. 2008/3200 (W.285) (ISBN 9780110919201). - In English and Welsh: Welsh title: Gorchymyn Daliadau Amaethyddol (Unedau Cynhyrchu) (Cymru) 2008. - 12p.: 30 cm. - 978-0-11-091716-0 £3.00

Land registration, England and Wales

The Adjudicator to Her Majesty's Land Registry (Practice and Procedure) (Amendment) Rules 2008 No. 2008/1731. - Enabling power: Land Registration Act 2002, ss. 109 (2) (3), 110 (2) (3), 114, 128 (1). - Issued: 07.07.2008. Made: 27.06.2008. Laid: 03.07.2008. Coming into force: 25.07.2008. Effect: S.I. 2003/2171 amended. Territorial extent & classification: E/W. General. - With correction slip dated August 2008. - 12p.: 30 cm. - 978-0-11-081948-8 £3.00

The Land Registration Act 2002 (Amendment) Order 2008 No. 2008/2872. - Enabling power: Land Registration Act 2002, s. 5 (1). - Issued: 12.11.2008. Made: 06.11.2008. Laid: 10.11.2008. Coming into force: 06.04.2009. Effect: 2002 c. 9 amended. Territorial extent & classification: E/W. General. - 2p.: 30 cm. - 978-0-11-084987-4 £4.00

The Land Registration (Amendment) Rules 2008 No. 2008/1919. - Enabling power: Land Registration Act 2002, ss. 1 (2), 13 (a), 14 (a) (b), 21 (2) (a) (b) (c), 22, 25 (1), 27 (6), 36 (4), 43 (2) (a) (c) (d), 47, 60 (3), 66 (2), 67 (3), 70, 73 (2) (3) (4), 88, 126, 127 (1), 128 (1), 134 (2) sch. 2, paras 2 (2), 7 (3), sch. 4, para. 7 (b) (c) (d), sch. 6, paras 2 (1) (e), 10 (4), 15, sch. 8, para. 9, sch. 10, paras 3 (a), 5 (2) (a), 6 (a) (b), 8, sch. 12, para. 2 (4). - Issued: 29.07.2008. Made: 17.07.2008. Laid: 21.07.2008. Coming into force: 10.11.2008 in accord.with rule 2. Effect: S.I. 2003/1417 amended. Territorial extent & classification: E/W. General. - 244p.: 30 cm. - With correction slip dated August 2008. - 978-0-11-083498-6 £28.00

The Land Registration (Electronic Conveyancing) Rules 2008 No. 2008/1750. - Enabling power: Land Registration Act 2002, ss. 1 (2), 25 (1), 66 (2), 67 (3), 71, 73 (4), 91 (2), 91 (3) (d), 92 (2), 95 (b), 126, 128 (1), sch. 5, para. 5, sch. 10, paras 6 (a) (b) (c), 8. - Issued: 08.07.2008. Made: 02.07.2008. Laid: 04.07.2008. Coming into force: 04.08.2008. Effect: S.I. 2003/1417 amended. Territorial extent & classification: E/W. General. - 8p.: 30 cm. - 978-0-11-081963-1 £3.00

The Land Registration (Network Access) Rules 2008 No. 2008/1748. - Enabling power: Land Registration Act 2002, ss. 92 (2), 128 (1), sch. 5, paras 1 (4), 2, 3, 11. - Issued: 10.03.2008. Made: -. Coming into force: In accord. with rule 1. Effect: None. Territorial extent & classification: E/W. General. - Supersedes draft (ISBN 9780110810799). - 16p.: 30 cm. - 978-0-11-081962-4 £3.00

The Land Registration (Proper Office) (Amendment) Order 2008 No. 2008/1921. - Enabling power: Land Registration Act 2002, ss. 100 (3). - Issued: 24.07.2008. Made: 17.07.2008. Laid: 21.07.2008. Coming into force: 10.11.2008. Effect: S.I. 2007/3517 amended. Territorial extent & classification: E/W. General. - Revoked by S.I. 2008/3201 (ISBN 9780111471944). - 2p.: 30 cm. - 978-0-11-083465-8 £3.00

The Land Registration (Proper Office) Order 2008 No. 2008/3201. - Enabling power: Land Registration Act 2002, s. 100 (3). - Issued: 19.12.2008. Made: 15.12.2008. Laid: 16.12.2008. Coming into force: 01.04.2009. Effect: S.I. 2007/3517; 2008/1921 revoked. Territorial extent & classification: E/W. General. - Revoked by S.I. 2009/1393 (ISBN 9780111480519). - 8p.: 30 cm. - 978-0-11-147194-4 £5.00

The Network Access Appeal Rules 2008 No. 2008/1730. - Enabling power: Land Registration Act 2002, ss. 109, 114, sch. 5, para. 4 (3). - Issued: 07.07.2008. Made: 30.06.2008. Laid: 03.07.2008. Coming into force: 25.07.2008. Effect: None. Territorial extent & classification: E/W. General. - 16p.: 30 cm. - 978-0-11-081946-4 £3.00

Legal profession, England and Wales

The European Communities (Lawyer's Practice and Services of Lawyers) (Amendment) Regulations 2008 No. 2008/81. - Enabling power: European Communities Act 1972, s. 2 (2). - Issued: 21.01.2008. Made: 15.01.2008. Laid: 16.01.2008. Coming into force: 11.02.2008. Effect: S.I. 1978/1910; 2000/1119 amended. Territorial extent & classification: E/W/NI. General. - EC note: The amendments made in these Regulations are made in consequence of the Treaty concerning the accession of Bulgaria and Romania to the European Union, signed at Luxembourg on 25th April 2005. These Regulations implement the adaptations to Article 1(2) of the Services Directive made by Council Directive 2006/100/EC. With correction slip dated June 2009. - 4p.: 30 cm. - 978-0-11-080847-5 £3.00

Legal profession, Northern Ireland

The European Communities (Lawyer's Practice and Services of Lawyers) (Amendment) Regulations 2008 No. 2008/81. - Enabling power: European Communities Act 1972, s. 2 (2). - Issued: 21.01.2008. Made: 15.01.2008. Laid: 16.01.2008. Coming into force: 11.02.2008. Effect: S.I. 1978/1910; 2000/1119 amended. Territorial extent & classification: E/W/NI. General. - EC note: The amendments made in these Regulations are made in consequence of the Treaty concerning the accession of Bulgaria and Romania to the European Union, signed at Luxembourg on 25th April 2005. These Regulations implement the adaptations to Article 1(2) of the Services Directive made by Council Directive 2006/100/EC. With correction slip dated June 2009. - 4p.: 30 cm. - 978-0-11-080847-5 £3.00

Legal Services Commission, England and Wales

The Community Legal Service (Financial) (Amendment No. 2) Regulations 2008 No. 2008/2703. - Enabling power: Access to Justice Act 1999, s. 7. - Issued: 20.10.2008. Made: 13.10.2008. Laid: 15.10.2008. Coming into force: 03.11.2008. Effect: S.I. 2000/627 amended. Territorial extent & classification: E/W. General. - 2p.: 30 cm. - 978-0-11-084658-3 £4.00

The Community Legal Service (Financial) (Amendment) Regulations 2008 No. 2008/658. - Enabling power: Access to Justice Act 1999, ss. 7, 10. - Issued: 13.03.2008. Made: 07.03.2008. Laid: 11.03.2008. Coming into force: 07.04.2008. Effect: S.I. 2000/516 amended. Territorial extent & classification: E/W. General. - 4p.: 30 cm. - 978-0-11-081168-0 £3.00

The Community Legal Service (Funding) (Amendment No. 2) Order 2008 No. 2008/2704. - Enabling power: Access to Justice Act 1999, s. 6 (4). - Issued: 20.10.2008. Made: 13.10.2008. Laid: 15.10.2008. Coming into force: 03.11.2008. Effect: S.I. 2000/627 amended. Territorial extent & classification: E/W. General. - 4p.: 30 cm. - 978-0-11-084641-5 £4.00

The Community Legal Service (Funding) (Amendment) Order 2008 No. 2008/1328. - Enabling power: Access to Justice Act 1999, s. 6 (4). - Issued: 27.05.2008. Made: 20.05.2008. Laid: 20.05.2008. Coming into force: 01.07.2008. Effect: S.I. 2007/2441 amended. Territorial extent & classification: E/W. General. - 12p.: 30 cm. - 978-0-11-081792-7 £3.00

The Criminal Defence Service (Financial Eligibility) (Amendment) Regulations 2008 No. 2008/723. - Enabling power: Access to Justice Act 1999, sch. 3, para. 3B (1). - Issued: 18.03.2008. Made: 12.03.2008. Laid: 13.03.2008. Coming into force: 07.04.2008. Effect: S.I. 2006/2492 amended. Territorial extent & classification: E/W. General. - 2p.: 30 cm. - 978-0-11-081223-6 £3.00

The Criminal Defence Service (Funding) (Amendment No. 2) Order 2008 No. 2008/2930. - Enabling power: Access to Justice Act 1999, s. 14 (3). - Issued: 17.11.2008. Made: 11.11.2008. Laid: 12.11.2008. Coming into force: 13.11.2008. Effect: S.I. 2007/1174 amended. Territorial extent & classification: E/W. General. - 4p.: 30 cm. - 978-0-11-084999-7 £4.00

The Criminal Defence Service (Funding) (Amendment) Order 2008 No. 2008/957. - Enabling power: Access to Justice Act 1999, s. 14 (3). - Issued: 04.04.2008. Made: 02.04.2008. Laid: 02.04.2008. Coming into force: 24.04.2008. Effect: S.I. 2007/1174 amended. Territorial extent & classification: E/W. General. - 4p.: 30 cm. - 978-0-11-081336-3 £3.00

The Criminal Defence Service (General) (No. 2) (Amendment) Regulations 2008 No. 2008/725. - Enabling power: Access to Justice Act 1999, ss. 12 (2) (g), 13 (1). - Issued: 18.03.2008. Made: 12.03.2008. Laid: 13.03.2008. Coming into force: 06.04.2008 for regs 1, 2; 07.04.2008 for reg. 3 in accord. with reg. 1. Effect: S.I. 2001/1437 amended. Territorial extent & classification: E/W. General. - 2p.: 30 cm. - 978-0-11-081225-0 £3.00

The Criminal Defence Service (Recovery of Defence Costs Orders) (Amendment) Regulations 2008 No. 2008/2430. - Enabling power: Access to Justice Act 1999, s. 17 (3). - Issued: 17.09.2008. Made: 09.09.2008. Laid: 15.09.2008. Coming into force: 06.10.2008. Effect: S.I. 2001/856 amended. Territorial extent & classification: E/W. General. - 4p.: 30 cm. - 978-0-11-084216-5 £4.00

The Criminal Defence Service (Very High Cost Cases) Regulations 2008 No. 2008/40. - Enabling power: Access to Justice Act 1999, s. 15 (5). - Issued: 16.01.2008. Made: 11.01.2008. Coming into force: 12.01.2008 in accord.with reg. 1. Effect: S.I. 2001/1169 revoked. Territorial extent & classification: E/W. General. - Supersedes draft SI (ISBN 9780110779355) issued 24.07.2008. - 4p.: 30 cm. - 978-0-11-080829-1 £3.00

The Criminal Justice and Immigration Act 2008 (Commencement No. 2 and Transitional and Saving Provisions) Order 2008 No. 2008/1586 (C.69). - Enabling power: Criminal Justice and Immigration Act 2008, s. 153 (4) (7) (8). Bringing into operation various provisions of the 2008 Act on 14.07.2008 & 15.07.2008 in accord. with art. 2. - Issued: 25.06.2008. Made: 17.06.2008. Effect: None. Territorial extent & classification: E/W/NI. General. - 8p.: 30 cm. - 978-0-11-081886-3 £3.00

Legal services, England and Wales

The Community Legal Service (Funding) (Counsel in Family Proceedings) (Amendment) Order 2008 No. 2008/666. - Enabling power: Access to Justice Act 1999, s. 6 (4). - Issued: 14.03.2008. Made: 10.03.2008. Laid: 11.03.2008. Coming into force: 01.04.2008. Effect: S.I. 2001/1077 amended. Territorial extent & classification: E/W. General. - Superseded by S.I. of same no. (ISBN 9780110834351). - 4p.: 30 cm. - 978-0-11-081177-2 £3.00

The Community Legal Service (Funding) (Counsel in Family Proceedings) (Amendment) Order 2008 No. 2008/666. - Enabling power: Access to Justice Act 1999, s. 6 (4). - Issued: 23.07.2008. Made: 10.03.2008. Laid: 18.07.2008. Coming into force: 01.04.2008. Effect: S.I. 2001/1077 amended. Territorial extent & classification: E/W. General. - Supersedes SI of same number (ISBN 9780110811772) issued 14.03.2008. This Statutory Instrument is being re-laid before Parliament in consequence of a defect in the original instrument and is being issued free of charge to all known recipients of that Statutory Instrument. - 4p.: 30 cm. - 978-0-11-083435-1 £3.00

The Courts and Legal Services Act 1990 (Modification of Power to Make Rules about Licensed Conveyancers) Order 2008 No. 2008/537. - Enabling power: Courts and Legal Services Act 1990, s. 53 (8). - Issued: 04.03.2008. Made: 28.02.2008. Laid: 28.02.2008. Coming into force: 28.03.2008. Effect: 1985 c.61 amended. Territorial extent & classification: E/W. General. - 2p.: 30 cm. - 978-0-11-081047-8 £3.00

The Legal Services Act 2007 (Commencement No.1 and Transitory Provisions) Order 2008 No. 2008/222 (C.6). - Enabling power: Legal Services Act 2007, ss. 208 (2) (4), 211. Bringing into operation various provisions of the 2007 Act on 07.03.2008. - Issued: 08.02.2008. Made: 04.02.2008. Laid: 05.02.2008. Effect: 2007 c.29 modified. Territorial extent & classification: E/W. General. - 8p.: 30 cm. - 978-0-11-080904-5 £3.00

The Legal Services Act 2007 (Commencement No. 2 and Transitory Provisions) (Amendment) Order 2008 No. 2008/1591 (C.70). - Enabling power: Legal Services Act 2007, s. 211 (2). - Issued: 24.06.2008. Made: 18.06.2008. Coming into force: 18.06.2008. Effect: S.I. 2008/1436 (C. 65) amended. Territorial extent & classification: E/W. General. - This Statutory Instrument has been printed in consequence of a defect in S.I. 2008/1436 (C. 65) (ISBN 9780110817941) and is being issued free of charge to all known recipients of that Statutory Instrument. - 2p.: 30 cm. - 978-0-11-081891-7 £3.00

The Legal Services Act 2007 (Commencement No. 2 and Transitory Provisions) Order 2008 No. 2008/1436 (C.65). - Enabling power: Legal Services Act 2007, ss. 204, 208 (2) (4), 211 (2). Bringing into operation various provisions of the 2007 Act on 30.06.2008. - Issued: 10.06.2008. Made: 05.06.2008. Laid: 05.06.2008. Coming into force: 30.06.2008. Effect: None. Territorial extent & classification: E/W. General. - 8p.: 30 cm. - 978-0-11-081794-1 £3.00

The Legal Services Act 2007 (Commencement No. 3 and Transitory Provisions) Order 2008 No. 2008/3149 (C.137). - Enabling power: Legal Services Act 2007, ss. 204, 208 (2) (4), 211 (2). Bringing into operation various provisions of the 2007 Act on 01.01.2009. - Issued: 15.12.2008. Made: 06.12.2008. Laid: 10.12.2008. Effect: None. Territorial extent & classification: E/W. General. - 8p.: 30 cm. - 978-0-11-147133-3 £5.00

The Legal Services Act 2007 (Functions of a Designated Regulator) Order 2008 No. 2008/3074. - Enabling power: Legal Services Act 2007, sch. 22, para. 2. - Issued: 02.12.2008. Made: 26.11.2008. Coming into force: 27.11.2008 in accord. with art. 1. Effect: 1985 c. 61 amended. Territorial extent & classification: E/W. General. - Supersedes draft S.I. (ISBN 9780110847061) issued 27.10.2008. - 4p.: 30 cm. - 978-0-11-147082-4 £4.00

The Legal Services Act 2007 (Prescribed Charity) Order 2008 No. 2008/2680. - Enabling power: Legal Services Act 2007, s. 194 (8). - Issued: 14.10.2008. Made: 07.10.2008. Laid: 09.10.2008. Coming into force: 03.11.2008. Effect: None. Territorial extent & classification: E/W. General. - 2p.: 30 cm. - 978-0-11-084554-8 £4.00

The Legal Services Act 2007 (Transitory Provision) Order 2008 No. 2008/1799. - Enabling power: Legal Services Act 2007, s. 208 (2). - Issued: 11.07.2008. Made: 03.07.2008. Laid: 08.07.2008. Coming into force: 31.07.2008. Effect: None. Territorial extent & classification: E/W. General. - 2p.: 30 cm. - 978-0-11-081995-2 £3.00

The Probate Services (Approved Bodies) Order 2008 No. 2008/1865. - Enabling power: Courts and Legal Services Act 1990, s. 55 (3), sch. 9, para. 4. - Issued: 18.07.2008. Made: 10.07.2008. Coming into force: 01.08.2008. Effect: None. Territorial extent & classification: E/W. General. - Supersedes draft S.I. (ISBN 9780110817996) issued 09.06.2008. - 2p.: 30 cm. - 978-0-11-083212-8 £3.00

Legal services, Scotland

The Legal Services Act 2007 (Transitional, Savings and Consequential Provisions) (Scotland) Order 2008 No. 2008/2341. - Enabling power: Legal Services Act 2007, s. 208 (2). - Issued: 05.09.2008. Made: 29.08.2008. Laid: 03.09.2008. Coming into force: 01.10.2008. Effect: None. Territorial extent & classification: S. General. - 4p.: 30 cm. - 978-0-11-084008-6 £4.00

Limited liability partnerships

The Large and Medium-sized Limited Liability Partnerships (Accounts) Regulations 2008 No. 2008/1913. - Enabling power: Limited Liability Partnerships Act 2000, ss. 15, 17. - Issued: 25.07.2008. Made: 17.07.2008. Coming into force: 01.10.2008. Effect: S.I. 2008/410 modified. Territorial extent & classification: E/W/S/NI. General. - Supersedes draft S.I. (ISBN 9780110818351) issued 16.06.2008. - 48p.: 30 cm. - 978-0-11-083503-7 £7.50

The Limited Liability Partnerships (Accounts and Audit) (Application of Companies Act 2006) Regulations 2008 No. 2008/1911. - Enabling power: Limited Liability Partnerships Act 2000, ss. 15, 17 & Companies Act 2006, ss. 1210 (1) (h), 1292 (2). - Issued: 25.07.2008. Made: 17.07.2008. Coming into force: 01.10.2008. Effect: S.I. 2001/1090; S.R. 2004/307 revoked with saving. Territorial extent & classification: E/W/S/NI. General. - Supersedes draft S.I. (ISBN 9780110818337) issued 16.06.2008. - 76p.: 30 cm. - 978-0-11-083500-6 £12.00

The Small Limited Liability Partnerships (Accounts) Regulations 2008 No. 2008/1912. - Enabling power: Limited Liability Partnerships Act 2000, ss. 15, 17. - Issued: 25.07.2008. Made: 17.07.2008. Coming into force: 01.10.2008. Effect: S.I. 2008/409 modified. Territorial extent & classification: E/W/S/NI. General. - Supersedes draft S.I. (ISBN 9780110818344) issued 16.06.2008. - 48p.: 30 cm. - 978-0-11-083519-8 £7.50

Local government, England

The Alnwick (Parishes) Order 2008 No. 2008/1573. - Enabling power: Local Government and Rating Act 1997, ss. 14, 23. - Made: 13.06.2008. Coming into force: In accord. with art. 1 (2). Effect: None. Territorial extent & classification: E. Local *Unpublished*

The Bedfordshire (Structural Changes) Order 2008 No. 2008/907. - Enabling power: Local Government and Public Involvement in Health Act 2007, ss. 7, 11, 12, 13. - Issued: 03.04.2008. Made: 27.03.2008. Laid: 10.03.2008. Coming into force: In accord. with art. 1. Effect: S.I. 2001/4066, 4067, 4068 amended. Territorial extent & classification: E. General. - Supersedes draft SI (ISBN 9780110811833). - 24p.: 30 cm. - 978-0-11-081308-0 £4.00

The Berwick-upon-Tweed (Parishes) Order 2008 No. 2008/290. - Enabling power: Local Government and Rating Act 1997, ss. 14, 23. - Made: 07.02.2008. Coming into force: In accord. with art. 1 (2). Effect: None. Territorial extent & classification: E. Local *Unpublished*

The Borough of Barrow-in-Furness (Electoral Changes) Order 2008 No. 2008/427. - Enabling power: Local Government Act 1992, ss. 17, 26. - Issued: 25.02.2008. Made: 20.02.2008. Coming into force: In accord. with art. 1 (2) (3). Effect: S.I. 1998/2571 partially revoked. Territorial extent & classification: E. Local. - 8p.: 30 cm. - 978-0-11-080993-9 £3.00

The Borough of Basingstoke and Deane (Electoral Changes) Order 2008 No. 2008/425. - Enabling power: Local Government Act 1992, ss. 17, 26. - Issued: 25.02.2008. Made: 20.02.2008. Coming into force: In accord. with art. 1 (2) (3). Effect: S.I. 2001/1019 partially revoked. Territorial extent & classification: E. Local. - 8p.: 30 cm. - 978-0-11-080988-5 £3.00

The Borough of Berwick-upon-Tweed (Parish Electoral Arrangements and Electoral Changes) Order 2008 No. 2008/747. - Enabling power: Local Government and Rating Act 1997, ss. 14, 23. - Made: 03.03.2008. Coming into force: In accordance with art. 1 (2). Effect: None. Territorial extent & classification: E. Local *Unpublished*

The Borough of Tewkesbury (Parish Electoral Arrangements) Order 2008 No. 2008/951. - Enabling power: Local Government and Rating Act 1997, ss. 14, 23. - Made: 03.03.2008. Coming into force: In accordance with art. 1 (2). Effect: S.I. 2001/3881 partially revoked. Territorial extent & classification: E. Local *Unpublished*

The Borough of Welwyn Hatfield (Electoral Changes) Order 2008 No. 2008/424. - Enabling power: Local Government Act 1992, ss. 17, 26. - Issued: 25.02.2008. Made: 20.02.2008. Coming into force: In accord. with art. 1 (2). Effect: S.I. 1998/2560 partially revoked. Territorial extent & classification: E. Local. - 8p.: 30 cm. - 978-0-11-080986-1 £3.00

The Bradford (Electoral Changes) Order 2008 No. 2008/173. - Enabling power: Local Government and Rating Act 1997, ss. 14, 23. - Made: 25.01.2008. Coming into force: In accordance with art. 1 (2). Effect: None. Territorial extent & classification: E. Local *Unpublished*

The Case Tribunals (England) Regulations 2008 No. 2008/2938. - Enabling power: Local Government Act 2000, ss. 64 (7), 65 (4A), 77 (2) (6), 78A (4) (5) (7) (8), 105 (2). - Issued: 18.11.2008. Made: 13.11.2008. Laid: 18.11.2008. Coming into force: 12.12.2008. Effect: None. Territorial extent & classification: E. General. - 4p.: 30 cm. - 978-0-11-147009-1 £4.00

The Cheshire (Structural Changes) Order 2008 No. 2008/634. - Enabling power: Local Government and Public Involvement in Health Act 2007, ss. 7, 11, 12, 13. - Issued: 19.03.2008. Made: 04.03.2008. Coming into force: 05.03.2008 in accord. with art. 1. Effect: S.I. 1998/2843, 2845, 2847, 2866 amended. Territorial extent & classification: E. General. - Supersedes draft S.I (ISBN 9780110808871) issued 08.02.2008. - 20p.: 30 cm. - 978-0-11-081256-4 £3.50

The Cornwall (Structural Change) Order 2008 No. 2008/491. - Enabling power: Local Government and Public Involvement in Health Act 2007, ss. 7, 11, 12, 13. - Issued: 04.03.2008. Made: 25.02.2008. Coming into force: 26.02.2008 in accord. with art. 1. Effect: S.I. 2002/2593 amended. Territorial extent & classification: E. General. - Supersedes draft S.I. (ISBN 9780110808147) issued 15.01.2008. - 12p.: 30 cm. - 978-0-11-081025-6 *£3.00*

The Cotswold (Parishes) Order 2008 No. 2008/304. - Enabling power: Local Government and Rating Act 1997, ss. 14, 23. - Made: 07.02.2008. Coming into force: In accord. with art. 1 (2). Effect: None. Territorial extent & classification: E. Local *Unpublished*

The County Durham (Structural Change) Order 2008 No. 2008/493. - Enabling power: Local Government and Public Involvement in Health Act 2007, ss. 7, 11, 12, 13. - Issued: 03.03.2008. Made: 25.02.2008. Coming into force: 26.02.2008. Effect: None. Territorial extent & classification: E. General. - Supersedes draft S.I. (ISBN 9780110808154) issued 15.01.2008. - 12p.: 30 cm. - 978-0-11-081027-0 *£3.00*

The Daventry (Parishes) Order 2008 No. 2008/2739. - Enabling power: Local Government and Rating Act 1997, ss. 14, 23. - Made: 16.10.2008. Coming into force: In accord. with art. 1 (2). Effect: None. Territorial extent & classification: E. Local *Unpublished*

The Derwentside (Parish Electoral Arrangements) Order 2008 No. 2008/746. - Enabling power: Local Government and Rating Act 1997, ss. 14, 23. - Made: 27.02.2008. Coming into force: In accordance with art. 1 (2). Effect: None. Territorial extent & classification: E. Local *Unpublished*

The District of South Lakeland (Electoral Changes) Order 2008 No. 2008/423. - Enabling power: Local Government Act 1992, ss. 17, 26. - Issued: 26.02.2008. Made: 20.02.2008. Coming into force: In accord. with art. 1 (2) (3) (4). Effect: S.I. 1998/2548 partially revoked. Territorial extent & classification: E. Local. - 12p.: 30 cm. - 978-0-11-080987-8 *£3.00*

The Ellesmere Port and Neston (Parish) (Amendment) Order 2008 No. 2008/980. - Enabling power: Local Government and Rating Act 1997, ss. 14, 23. - Made: 28.03.2008. Coming into force: In accord. with art. 1 (2). Effect: S.I. 2007/3578 amended. Territorial extent & classification: E. Local *Unpublished*

The Halton (Parish Electoral Arrangements) Order 2008 No. 2008/174. - Enabling power: Local Government and Rating Act 1997, ss. 14, 23. - Made: 25.01.2008. Coming into force: In accordance with art. 1 (2). Effect: None. Territorial extent & classification: E. Local *Unpublished*

The Hertmere (Parish) Order 2008 No. 2008/43. - Enabling power: Local Government and Rating Act 1997, ss. 14, 23. - Made: 10.01.2008. Coming into force: In accord. with art. 1 (2). Effect: None. Territorial extent & classification: E. Local *Unpublished*

The Hertsmere (Parish Electoral Arrangements) Order 2008 No. 2008/175. - Enabling power: Local Government and Rating Act 1997, ss. 14, 23. - Made: 25.01.2008. Coming into force: In accordance with art. 1 (2). Effect: None. Territorial extent & classification: E. Local *Unpublished*

The High Peak (Parishes) Order 2008 No. 2008/303. - Enabling power: Local Government and Rating Act 1997, ss. 14, 23. - Made: 07.02.2008. Coming into force: In accord. with art. 1 (2). Effect: None. Territorial extent & classification: E. Local *Unpublished*

The Isle of Wight (Electoral Changes) Order 2008 No. 2008/2435. - Enabling power: Local Government Act 1992, ss. 17, 26. - Issued: 22.09.2008. Made: 16.09.2008. Coming into force: In accord. with art. 1 (2) (3). Effect: None. Territorial extent & classification: E. Local. - 8p.: 30 cm. - 978-0-11-084220-2 *£5.00*

The Isle of Wight (Parishes) Order 2008 No. 2008/376. - Enabling power: Local Government and Rating Act 1997, ss. 14, 23. - Made: 12.02.2008. Coming into force: In accord. with art. 1 (2). Effect: None. Territorial extent & classification: E. Local *Unpublished*

The Kettering (Parishes) Order 2008 No. 2008/602. - Enabling power: Local Government and Rating Act 1997, ss. 14, 23. - Made: 04.03.2008. Coming into force: In accord. with art. 1 (1). Effect: None. Territorial extent & classification: E. Local *Unpublished*

The Leeds (Parish) Order 2008 No. 2008/421. - Enabling power: Local Government and Rating Act 1997, ss. 14, 23. - Made: 18.02.2008. Coming into force: In accord. with art. 1 (2). Effect: None. Territorial extent & classification: E. Local *Unpublished*

The Lichfield (Parishes) Order 2008 No. 2008/2740. - Enabling power: Local Government and Rating Act 1997, ss. 14, 23. - Made: 16.10.2008. Coming into force: In accord. with art. 1 (2). Effect: None. Territorial extent & classification: E. Local *Unpublished*

The Local Authorities (Capital Finance and Accounting) (England) (Amendment) Regulations 2008 No. 2008/414. - Enabling power: Local Government Act 2003, ss. 9 (3), 21 (1), 123 (1). - Issued: 26.02.2008. Made: 18.02.2008. Laid: 26.02.2008. Coming into force: 31.03.2008. Effect: S.I. 2003/3146 amended. Territorial extent & classification: E. General. - 4p.: 30 cm. - 978-0-11-080982-3 *£3.00*

The Local Authorities (Elected Mayors) (England) Regulations 2008 No. 2008/3112. - Enabling power: Local Government Act 2000, ss. 39 (5B). - Issued: 11.12.2008. Made: 03.12.2008. Laid: 09.12.2008. Coming into force: 31.12.2008. Effect: None. Territorial extent & classification: E. General. - With correction slip dated October 2009. - 2p.: 30 cm. - 978-0-11-147120-3 *£4.00*

The Local Authorities (Functions and Responsibilities) (England) (Amendment No. 2) Regulations 2008 No. 2008/744. - Enabling power: Local Government Act 2000, ss. 13, 105. - Issued: 18.03.2008. Made: 11.03.2008. Laid: 18.03.2008. Coming into force: 01.04.2008. Effect: S.I. 2000/2853 amended. Territorial extent & classification: E. General. - This Statutory Instrument has been made in consequence of a defect in S.I. 2008/516 (ISBN 9780110810423) and is being issued free of charge to all known recipients of that statutory instrument. - 2p.: 30 cm. - 978-0-11-081247-2 £3.00

The Local Authorities (Functions and Responsibilities) (England) (Amendment No. 3) Regulations 2008 No. 2008/2787. - Enabling power: Local Government Act 2000, ss. 13, 105. - Issued: 30.10.2008. Made: 23.10.2008. Laid: 30.10.2008. Coming into force: 28.11.2008. Effect: S.I. 2000/2853; 2008/516 amended. Territorial extent & classification: E. General. - 4p.: 30 cm. - 978-0-11-084734-4 £4.00

The Local Authorities (Functions and Responsibilities) (England) (Amendment) Regulations 2008 No. 2008/516. - Enabling power: Local Government Act 2000, ss. 13, 105. - Issued: 03.03.2008. Made: 26.02.2008. Laid: 03.03.2008. Coming into force: 31.03.2008 for regs 1 to 6, 7 (b); 01.04.2008 for reg. 7 (a). Effect: S.I. 2000/2853 amended. Territorial extent & classification: E. General. - 8p.: 30 cm. - With correction slip dated September 2009. - 978-0-11-081042-3 £3.00

The Local Elections (Ordinary Day of Elections in 2009) Order 2008 No. 2008/2857. - Enabling power: Representation of the People Act 1983, s. 37A. - Issued: 10.11.2008. Made: 04.11.2008 at 8.45 p.m. Coming into force: 05.11.2008 in accord. with art. 1 (1). Effect: None. Territorial extent & classification: E. General. - Supersedes draft S.I. (ISBN 9780110843513) issued 07.10.2008. - 4p.: 30 cm. - 978-0-11-084958-4 £4.00

The Local Government and Public Involvement in Health Act 2007 (Commencement No. 2 and Savings) Order 2008 No. 2008/172 (C.4). - Enabling power: Local Government and Public Involvement in Health Act 2007, s. 245 (5) (6). Bringing into operation various provisions of the 2007 Act on 31.01.2008, 31.03.2008 & 01.04.2008. - Issued: 04.02.2008. Made: 30.01.2008. Effect: None. Territorial extent & classification: E. General. - With correction slip dated February 2008. - 8p.: 30 cm. - 978-0-11-080885-7 £3.00

The Local Government and Public Involvement in Health Act 2007 (Commencement No. 3, Transitional and Saving Provisions and Commencement No. 2 (Amendment)) Order 2008 No. 2008/337 (C.13). - Enabling power: Local Government and Public Involvement in Health Act 2007, s. 245. Bringing into operation various provisions of the 2007 Act on 13.02.2008. - Issued: 21.02.2008. Made: 12.02.2008. Effect: S.I. 2008/172 (C.4) amended. Territorial extent & classification: E. General. - With correction slip dated March 2008. - 12p.: 30 cm. - 978-0-11-080958-8 £3.00

The Local Government Finance (New Parishes) (England) Regulations 2008 No. 2008/626. - Enabling power: Local Government Finance Act 1992, s. 32 (9) & Local Government and Public Involvement in Health Act 2007, ss. 97, 98. - Issued: 11.03.2008. Made: 03.03.2008. Laid: 11.03.2008. Coming into force: 08.04.2008. Effect: None. Territorial extent & classification: E. General. - 4p.: 30 cm. - 978-0-11-081149-9 £3.00

The Local Government (Parishes and Parish Councils) (England) Regulations 2008 No. 2008/625. - Enabling power: Local Government and Public Involvement in Health Act 2007, ss. 97, 98. - Issued: 11.03.2008. Made: 03.03.2008. Laid: 11.03.2008. Coming into force: 08.04.2008. Effect: None. Territorial extent & classification: E. General. - 8p.: 30 cm. - 978-0-11-081144-4 £3.00

The Local Government (Structural and Boundary Changes) (Staffing) Regulations 2008 No. 2008/1419. - Enabling power: Local Government and Public Involvement in Health Act 2007, ss. 14, 240 (10). - Issued: 10.06.2008. Made: 02.06.2008. Laid: 05.06.2008. Coming into force: 28.06.2008. Effect: None. Territorial extent & classification: E. General. - With correction slip dated August 2009. - 8p.: 30 cm. - 978-0-11-081773-6 £3.00

The Local Government (Structural Changes) (Transfer of Functions, Property, Rights and Liabilities) Regulations 2008 No. 2008/2176. - Enabling power: Local Government and Public Involvement in Health Act 2007, ss. 14, 240 (10). - Issued: 18.08.2008. Made: 14.08.2008. Laid: 18.08.2008. Coming into force: 08.09.2008. Effect: None. Territorial extent & classification: E. General. - 16p.: 30 cm. - 978-0-11-083823-6 £3.00

The Local Government (Structural Changes) (Transitional Arrangements) (No.2) Regulations 2008 No. 2008/2867. - Enabling power: Local Government and Public Involvement in Health Act 2007, ss. 14, 240 (10). - Issued: 10.11.2008. Made: 05.11.2008. Laid: 06.11.2008. Coming into force: 28.11.2008. Effect: 1972 c.70; 1989 c.42; 2002 c.7; 2004 c.5 modified & S.I. 1994/867 amended. Territorial extent & classification: E. General. - 28p.: 30 cm. - 978-0-11-084971-3 £5.00

The Local Government (Structural Changes) (Transitional Arrangements) Regulations 2008 No. 2008/2113. - Enabling power: Local Government and Public Involvement in Health Act 2007, s. 14. - Issued: 07.08.2008. Made: 04.08.2008. Laid: 07.08.2008. Coming into force: 29.08.2008. Effect: 2007 c.28; S.I. 2000/2853 modified. Territorial extent & classification: E. General. - 8p.: 30 cm. - 978-0-11-083728-4 £3.00

The Maidstone (Electoral Changes) Order 2008 No. 2008/176. - Enabling power: Local Government and Rating Act 1997, ss. 14, 23. - Made: 25.01.2008. Coming into force: In accordance with art. 1 (2) (3). Effect: None. Territorial extent & classification: E. Local *Unpublished*

The Newark and Sherwood Forest (Parish Electoral Arrangements) Order 2008 No. 2008/426. - Enabling power: Local Government and Rating Act 1997, ss. 14, 23. - Made: 20.02.2008. Coming into force: In accordance with art. 1 (2). Effect: None. Territorial extent & classification: E. Local *Unpublished*

The Newark and Sherwood (Parish) Order 2008 No. 2008/179. - Enabling power: Local Government and Rating Act 1997, ss. 14, 23. - Made: 25.01.2008. Coming into force: In accord. with art. 1 (2). Effect: None. Territorial extent & classification: E. Local *Unpublished*

The North Dorset (Parishes) Order 2008 No. 2008/3142. - Enabling power: Local Government and Rating Act 1997, ss. 14, 23. - Made: 05.12.2008. Coming into force: In accord. with art. 1 (2). Effect: None. Territorial extent & classification: E. Local *Unpublished*

The North Norfolk (Parishes) Order 2008 No. 2008/180. - Enabling power: Local Government and Rating Act 1997, ss. 14, 23. - Made: 25.01.2008. Coming into force: In accord. with art. 1 (2). Effect: None. Territorial extent & classification: E. Local *Unpublished*

The Northumberland (Structural Change) Order 2008 No. 2008/494. - Enabling power: Local Government and Public Involvement in Health Act 2007, ss. 7, 11, 12, 13. - Issued: 03.03.2008. Made: 25.02.2008. Coming into force: 26.02.2008. Effect: None. Territorial extent & classification: E. General. - Supersedes draft S.I. (ISBN 9780110808123) issued 15.01.2008. - 12p.: 30 cm. - 978-0-11-081017-1 £3.00

The North Wiltshire (Parishes) Order 2008 No. 2008/3141. - Enabling power: Local Government and Rating Act 1997, ss. 14, 23. - Made: 05.12.2008. Coming into force: In accord. with art. 1 (2). Effect: None. Territorial extent & classification: E. Local *Unpublished*

The Overview and Scrutiny (Reference by Councillors) (Excluded Matters) (England) Order 2008 No. 2008/3261. - Enabling power: Local Government Act 2000, s. 21A(11). - Issued: 30.12.2008. Made: 18.12.2008. Laid: 30.12.2008. Coming into force: 01.04.2009. Effect: None. Territorial extent & classification: E. General. - 4p.: 30 cm. - 978-0-11-147228-6 £4.00

The Oxford (Parish Electoral Arrangements) Order 2008 No. 2008/501. - Enabling power: Local Government and Rating Act 1997, ss. 14, 23. - Made: 25.02.2008. Coming into force: In accordance with art. 1 (2). Effect: None. Territorial extent & classification: E. Local *Unpublished*

The Oxford (Parishes) Order 2008 No. 2008/372. - Enabling power: Local Government and Rating Act 1997, ss. 14, 23. - Made: 12.02.2008. Coming into force: In accord. with art. 1 (2). Effect: None. Territorial extent & classification: E. Local *Unpublished*

The Parish Councils (Power to Promote Well-being) (Prescribed Conditions) Order 2008 No. 2008/3095. - Enabling power: Local Government Act 2000, ss. 1 (2), 105. - Issued: 09.12.2008. Made: 02.12.2008. Laid: 09.12.2008. Coming into force: 31.12.2008. Effect: None. Territorial extent & classification: E. General. - 4p.: 30 cm. - 978-0-11-147094-7 £4.00

The Pendle (Parishes) Order 2008 No. 2008/549. - Enabling power: Local Government and Rating Act 1997, ss. 14, 23. - Made: 28.02.2008. Coming into force: In accord. with art. 1 (2). Effect: None. Territorial extent & classification: E. Local *Unpublished*

The Recreation Grounds (Revocation of Parish Council Byelaws) Order 2008 No. 2008/1285. - Enabling power: Local Government Act 1972, s. 262 (8) (d). - Issued: 20.05.2008. Made: 08.05.2008. Laid: 20.05.2008. Coming into force: 18.06.2008. Effect: Revokes byelaws relating to recreation grounds as specified in the schedule. Territorial extent & classification: E. General. - 2p.: 30 cm. - 978-0-11-081465-0 £3.00

The Restormel (Parishes) Order 2008 No. 2008/1313. - Enabling power: Local Government and Rating Act 1997, ss. 14, 23. - Made: 13.05.2008. Coming into force: In accord. with art. 1 (2). Effect: None. Territorial extent & classification: E. Local *Unpublished*

The Salisbury (Parishes) Order 2008 No. 2008/1283. - Enabling power: Local Government and Rating Act 1997, ss. 14, 23. - Made: 12.05.2008. Coming into force: In accord. with art. 1 (2). Effect: None. Territorial extent & classification: E. Local *Unpublished*

The Sevenoaks (Parish Electoral Arrangements) Order 2008 No. 2008/500. - Enabling power: Local Government and Rating Act 1997, ss. 14, 23. - Made: 25.02.2008. Coming into force: In accordance with art. 1 (2). Effect: None. Territorial extent & classification: E. Local *Unpublished*

The Sevenoaks (Parishes) Order 2008 No. 2008/422. - Enabling power: Local Government and Rating Act 1997, ss. 14, 23. - Made: 18.02.2008. Coming into force: In accord. with art. 1 (2). Effect: None. Territorial extent & classification: E. Local *Unpublished*

The Shrewsbury and Atcham (Parish) Order 2008 No. 2008/1321. - Enabling power: Local Government and Rating Act 1997, ss. 14, 23. - Made: 13.05.2008. Coming into force: In accord. with art. 1 (2). Effect: None. Territorial extent & classification: E. Local *Unpublished*

The Shropshire (Structural Change) Order 2008 No. 2008/492. - Enabling power: Local Government and Public Involvement in Health Act 2007, ss. 7, 11, 12, 13. - Issued: 03.03.2008. Made: 25.02.2008. Coming into force: 26.02.2008. Effect: S.I. 2008/1725 amended. Territorial extent & classification: E. General. - Supersedes draft S.I. (ISBN 9780110808116) issued 15.01.2008. - 12p.: 30 cm. - 978-0-11-081026-3 £3.00

The South Cambridgeshire (Electoral Changes) Order 2008 No. 2008/177. - Enabling power: Local Government and Rating Act 1997, ss. 14, 23. - Made: 25.01.2008. Coming into force: In accordance with art. 1 (2) (3). Effect: None. Territorial extent & classification: E. Local *Unpublished*

The Standards Committee (England) Regulations 2008 No. 2008/1085. - Enabling power: Local Government Act 2000, ss. 53 (6) (12), 54 (4), 54A (4), 55 (8), 57C (7), 66 (1) to (4A), 73 (1) (6), 105. - Issued: 21.04.2008. Made: 14.04.2008. Laid: 17.04.2008. Coming into force: 08.05.2008. Effect: S.I. 2001/2812; 2003/1483 amended. Territorial extent & classification: E. General. - 24p.: 30 cm. - With correction slip dated July 2008. - 978-0-11-081377-6 £4.00

The St Helens (Parish) Order 2008 No. 2008/603. - Enabling power: Local Government and Rating Act 1997, ss. 14, 23. - Made: 04.03.2008. Coming into force: In accord. with art. 1 (2). Effect: None. Territorial extent & classification: E. Local *Unpublished*

The Stratford-on-Avon (Parish Electoral Arrangements and Electoral Changes) Order 2008 No. 2008/748. - Enabling power: Local Government and Rating Act 1997, ss. 14, 23. - Made: 03.03.2008. Coming into force: In accordance with art. 1 (2) (3) (4) (5). Effect: None. Territorial extent & classification: E. Local *Unpublished*

The Stroud (Parish Electoral Arrangements and Electoral Changes) Order 2008 No. 2008/756. - Enabling power: Local Government and Rating Act 1997, ss. 14, 23. - Made: 29.02.2008. Coming into force: In accordance with art. 1 (2) (3) (4). Effect: None. Territorial extent & classification: E. Local *Unpublished*

The Sustainable Communities Regulations 2008 No. 2008/2694. - Enabling power: Sustainable Communities Act 2007, s. 5- Issued: 13.10.2008. Made: 09.10.2008. Laid: 13.10.2008. Coming into force: 03.11.2008. Effect: None. Territorial extent & classification: E. General. - 4p.: 30 cm. - 978-0-11-084580-7 £4.00

The Uttlesford (Electoral Changes) Order 2008 No. 2008/178. - Enabling power: Local Government and Rating Act 1997, ss. 14, 23. - Made: 25.01.2008. Coming into force: In accordance with art. 1 (2) (3). Effect: None. Territorial extent & classification: E. Local *Unpublished*

The Wiltshire (Structural Change) Order 2008 No. 2008/490. - Enabling power: Local Government and Public Involvement in Health Act 2007, ss. 7, 11, 12, 13. - Issued: 04.03.2008. Made: 25.02.2008. Coming into force: 26.02.2008 in accord. with art. 1. Effect: None. Territorial extent & classification: E. General. - Supersedes draft S.I. (ISBN 9780110808130) issued 15.01.2008. - 8p.: 30 cm. - 978-0-11-081024-9 £3.00

Local government, England: Finance

The Local Authorities (Alteration of Requisite Calculations) (England) Regulations 2008 No. 2008/227. - Enabling power: Local Government Finance Act 1992, ss. 32 (9), 33 (4), 43 (7), 44 (4), 113 (2) & Greater London Authority Act 1999, ss. 86 (5), 88 (8), 89 (9), 420 (1). - Issued: 11.02.2008. Made: 05.02.2008. Laid: 11.02.2008. Coming into force: 12.02.2008. Effect: S.I. 1992 c.14; 1999 c.29 amended. Territorial extent & classification: E. General. - 8p.: 30 cm. - 978-0-11-080908-3 £3.00

The Local Government (Structural Changes) (Finance) Regulations 2008 No. 2008/3022. - Enabling power: Local Government and Public Involvement in Health Act 2007, ss. 14, 240 (10). - Issued: 26.11.2008. Made: 20.11.2008. Laid: 26.11.2008. Coming into force: 24.12.2008. Effect: 1992 c.14 & S.I. 1992/612, 2904 amended. Territorial extent & classification: E. General. - 20p.: 30 cm. - 978-0-11-147042-8 £5.00

Local government, England and Wales

The Legislative Reform (Local Authority Consent Requirements) (England and Wales) Order 2008 No. 2008/2840. - Enabling power: Legislative and Regulatory Reform Act 2006, s. 1. - Issued: 04.11.2008. Made: 29.10.2008. Coming into force: 30.10.2008. Effect: 1939 c. 13; 1972 c. 70; 1993 c. 25; 1996 c. 56 amended. Territorial extent & classification: E/W. General. - Supersedes draft S.I. (ISBN 9780110818948) issued 26.06.2008. - 4p.: 30 cm. - 978-0-11-084850-1 £4.00

The Local Authorities (Alcohol Disorder Zones) Regulations 2008 No. 2008/1430. - Enabling power: Violent Crime Reduction Act 2006, ss. 15, 16 (7), 17 (6), 20 (5) & Local Government Act 2000, ss. 13, 105 (2). - Issued: 09.06.2008. Made: 04.06.2008. Coming into force: 05.06.2008. Effect: S.I. 2000/2853; 2007/399 amended. Territorial extent & classification: E/W. General. - Supersedes draft S.I. (ISBN 9780110813295) issued 04.04.2008. - 16p.: 30 cm. - 978-0-11-081787-3 £3.00

The Local Government and Public Involvement in Health Act 2007 (Commencement No. 5 and Transitional, Saving and Transitory Provision) Order 2008 No. 2008/917 (C.44). - Enabling power: Local Government and Public Involvement in Health Act 2007, s. 245 (5) (6). Bringing into operation various provisions of the 2007 Act on 01.04.2008 & 01.04.2009 in accord. with arts 2, 3. - Issued: 01.04.2008. Made: 27.03.2008. Effect: None. Territorial extent & classification: E/W. General. - 8p.: 30 cm. - 978-0-11-081310-3 £3.00

The Local Government and Public Involvement in Health Act 2007 (Commencement No. 6 and Transitional and Saving Provision) Order 2008 No. 2008/1265 (C.54). - Enabling power: Local Government and Public Involvement in Health Act 2007, s. 245 (5) (6). Bringing into operation various provisions of the 2007 Act on 08.05.2008 in accord. with art. 2. - Issued: 14.05.2008. Made: 06.05.2008. Effect: None. Territorial extent & classification: E/W. General. - 4p.: 30 cm. - 978-0-11-081439-1 £3.00

The Local Government and Public Involvement in Health Act 2007 (Commencement No. 8) Order 2008 No. 2008/3110 (C.134). - Enabling power: Local Government and Public Involvement in Health Act 2007, s. 245 (5) (6). Bringing into operation various provisions of the 2007 Act on 12.12.2008; 31.12.2008; 01.04.2009; 01.08.2009; 01.10.2009. - Issued: 11.12.2008. Made: 03.12.2008. Effect: None. Territorial extent & classification: E/W. General. - 8p.: 30 cm. - 978-0-11-147107-4 £5.00

The Police Authorities (Best Value) Performance Indicators Order 2008 No. 2008/659. - Enabling power: Local Government Act 1999, s. 4 (1) (a). - Issued: 14.03.2008. Made: 10.03.2008. Laid: 11.03.2008. Coming into force: 01.04.2008. Effect: S.I. 2005/470; 2006/620 revoked. Territorial extent & classification: E/W. General. - 4p.: 30 cm. - 978-0-11-081167-3 £3.00

Local government finance, England

The Local Government Finance (England) (Substitution of Penalties) Order 2008 No. 2008/981. - Enabling power: Local Government Finance Act 1992, ss. 14 (2), 113 , sch. 3, para. 5. - Issued: 08.04.2008. Made: 03.04.2008. Laid: 04.04.2008. Coming into force: 01.05.2008. Effect: 1992 c.14 amended. Territorial extent & classification: E. General. - 2p.: 30 cm. - 978-0-11-081349-3 £3.00

Local government, Wales

The Local Authorities (Capital Finance and Accounting) (Wales) (Amendment) Regulations 2008 No. 2008/588 (W.59). - Enabling power: Local Government Act 2003, ss. 9 (3), 21 (1), 24, 123 (1). - Issued: 20.03.2008. Made: 03.03.2008. Laid before the National Assembly for Wales: 05.03.2008. Coming into force: 31.03.2008. Effect: S.I. 2003/3239 (W.319) amended. Territorial extent & classification: W. General. - In English and Welsh. Welsh title: Rheoliadau Awdurdodau Lleol (Cyllid Cyfalaf a Chyfrifyddu) (Cymru) (Diwygio) 2008. - 8p.: 30 cm. - With correction slip dated June 2008. - 978-0-11-091723-8 £3.00

The Local Authorities (Conduct of Referendums) (Wales) Regulations 2008 No. 2008/1848 (W.177). - Enabling power: Welsh Language Act 1993, s. 26 & Local Government 2000, ss. 45, 105, 106 (1). - Issued: 06.08.2008. Made: 09.07.2008. Coming into force: 23.07.2008 in accord. with reg. 1. Effect: 1983 c. 2; 2000 c. 2, c.41; 2006 c. 22 & S.I. 1960/543; 2001/341 modified & S.I. 2004/870 (W.85) revoked. Territorial extent & classification: W. General. - In English and Welsh. Welsh language title: Rheoliadau Awdurdodau Lleol (Cynnal Refferenda) (Cymru) 2008. - 124p.: 30 cm. - 978-0-11-091823-5 £17.50

The Local Authorities (Model Code of Conduct) (Wales) Order 2008 No. 2008/788 (W.82). - Enabling power: Local Government Act 2000, ss. 50 (2) (3) (4) (4E), 81 (2) (3), 105. - Issued: 14.04.2008. Made: 20.03.2008. Laid before the National Assembly for Wales: 25.03.2008. Coming into force: 18.04.2008. Effect: S.I. 2001/2289 (W.177); 2004/163 (W.18), 1510 (W.159) revoked. Territorial extent & classification: W. General. - In English and Welsh. Welsh title: Gorchymyn Awdurdodau Lleol (Cod Ymddygiad Enghreifftiol) (Cymru) 2008. - 20p.: 30 cm. - 978-0-11-091752-8 £3.50

The Local Government and Public Involvement in Health Act 2007 (Commencement) (Wales) Order 2008 No. 2008/591 (W.60)(C.22). - Enabling power: Local Government and Public Involvement in Health Act 2007, s. 245 (4). Bringing various provisions of the 2007 Act into operation on 01.04.2008. - Issued: 31.03.2008. Made: 03.03.2008. Effect: None. Territorial extent & classification: W. General. - In English and Welsh. Welsh title: Gorchymyn Deddf Llywodraeth Leol a Chynnwys y Cyhoedd mewn Iechyd 2007 (Cychwyn) (Cymru) 2008. - 4p.: 30 cm. - 978-0-11-091776-4 £3.00

The Local Government (Best Value Performance Indicators) (Wales) Order 2005 No. 2008/503 (W.44). - Enabling power: Local Government Act 1999, ss. 4 (1) (a) (2), 29 (1). - Issued: 08.03.2008. Made: 23.02.2008. Laid before the National Assembly for Wales: 26.02.2008. Coming into force: 01.04.2008. Effect: S.I. 2005/665 (W.55) revoked. Territorial extent & classification: W. General. - In English and Welsh. Welsh title: Gorchymyn Llywodraeth Leol (Dangosyddion Perfformiad Gwerth Gorau) (Cymru) 2008. - 12p.: 30 cm. - 978-0-11-091719-1 £3.00

The Local Government (Politically Restricted Posts) (Wales) Regulations 2008 No. 2008/220 (W.27). - Enabling power: Local Government and Housing Act 1989, ss. 2 (2) (a), 190 (1). - Issued: 20.02.2008. Made: 03.02.2008. Laid before the National Assembly for Wales: 05.02.2008. Coming into force: 29.02.2008. Effect: S.I. 1990/1447 revoked in relation to Wales. Territorial extent & classification: W. General. - In English and Welsh. Welsh language title: Rheoliadau Llywrodraeth Leol (Swyddi dan Gyfyngiadau Gwleidyddol) (Cymru) 2008. - 4p.: 30 cm. - 978-0-11-091705-4 £3.00

The Powys (Communities) Order 2008 No. 2008/584 (W.58). - Enabling power: Local Government Act 1972, ss. 58 (2), 67 (4) (5). - Issued: 27.03.2008. Made: 02.03.2008. Coming into force: In accord. with art. 1 (2) (3). Effect: None. Territorial extent & classification: W. General. - In English and Welsh. Welsh title: Gorchymyn Powys (Cymunedau) 2008. - 40p.: 30 cm. - 978-0-11-091767-2 £6.50

The Relevant Authorities (Code of Conduct) (Prescribed Period for Undertakings) (Wales) Order 2008 No. 2008/929. - Enabling power: Local Government and Public Involvement in Health Act 2007, ss. 183 (6) (11), 240 (10). - Issued: 08.04.2008. Made: 27.03.2008. Laid: 08.04.2008. Coming into force: 30.04.2008. Effect: None. Territorial extent & classification: W. General. - 2p.: 30 cm. - 978-0-11-081322-6 £3.00

The Rhondda Cynon Taf (Llanharan, Llanharry, Llantrisant and Pont-y-clun Communities) Order 2008 No. 2008/3152 (W.280). - Enabling power: Local Government Act 1972, s. 58 (2). - Issued: 30.12.2008. Made: 08.12.2008. Coming into force: In accord. with art. 1 (2) to (4). Effect: None. Territorial extent & classification: W. General. - In English and Welsh. Welsh title: Gorchymyn Rhondda Cynon Taf (Cymunedau Llanharan, Llanhari,Llantrisant a Phont-y-clun) 2008. - 12p.: 30 cm. - 978-0-11-091911-9 £5.00

Local government, Wales: Finance

The Local Authorities (Alteration of Requisite Calculations) (Wales) Regulations 2008 No. 2008/476 (W.42). - Enabling power: Local Government Finance Act 1992, ss. 32 (9), 33 (4), 43 (7), 44 (4), 113 (2). - Issued: 10.03.2008. Made: 22.02.2008. Laid before the National Assembly for Wales: 25.02.2008. Coming into force: 27.02.2008. Effect: 1992 c.14 amended. Territorial extent & classification: W. General. - In English and Welsh. Welsh title: Rheoliadau Awdurdodau Lleol (Addasu Cyfrifiadau Angenrheidiol) (Cymru) 2008. - 8p.: 30 cm. - 978-0-11-091717-7 £3.00

Local loans

The Local Loans (Increase of Limit) Order 2008 No. 2008/3004. - Enabling power: National Loans Act 1968, s. 4 (1). - Issued: 25.11.2008. Made: 19.11.2008. Coming into force: 20.11.2008. Effect: None. Territorial extent & classification: E/W/S/NI. General. - Supersedes draft S.I. (ISBN 9780110846767) issued 21.10.2008. - 2p.: 30 cm. - 978-0-11-147029-9 £4.00

London government

The Greater London Authority Act 2007 (Commencement No. 2) Order 2008 No. 2008/113 (C.3). - Enabling power: Greater London Authority Act 2007, s. 59 (7) (9). Bringing into force various provisions of the 2007 Act on 21.01.2008. - Issued: 25.01.2008. Made: 16.01.2008. Effect: None. Territorial extent & classification: E/W. General. - 4p.: 30 cm. - 978-0-11-080855-0 £3.00

The Greater London Authority Act 2007 (Commencement No. 3) Order 2008 No. 2008/582 (C.21). - Enabling power: Greater London Authority Act 2007, s. 59 (7) (9). Bringing into force various provisions of the 2007 Act on 06.04.2008, in accord. with art. 2. - Issued: 11.03.2008. Made: 04.03.2008. Effect: None. Territorial extent & classification: E. General. - 2p.: 30 cm. - 978-0-11-081096-6 £3.00

The Greater London Authority Act 2007 (Commencement No. 4 and Saving) Order 2008 No. 2008/1372 (C.61). - Enabling power: Greater London Authority Act 2007, ss. 53 (1), 59 (7) (9). Bringing into force various provisions of the 2007 Act on 27.06.2008, in accord. with art. 2. - Issued: 02.06.2008. Made: 19.05.2008. Laid: -. Coming into force: -. Effect: None. Territorial extent & classification: E/W. General. - 2p.: 30 cm. - 978-0-11-081763-7 £3.00

The Greater London Authority Act 2007 (Commencement No.5) Order 2008 No. 2008/2037 (C.98). - Enabling power: Greater London Authority Act 2007, s. 59 (7) (9). Bringing into force various provisions of the 2007 Act on 24.07.2008, in accord. with art. 2. - Issued: 31.07.2008. Made: 23.07.2008. Laid: -. Coming into force: -. Effect: None. Territorial extent & classification: E. General. - 2p.: 30 cm. - 978-0-11-083648-5 £3.00

The Greater London Authority Elections (Election Addresses) (Amendment) Order 2008 No. 2008/507. - Enabling power: Greater London Authority Act 1999, s. 17A (3). - Issued: 29.02.2008. Made: 25.02.2008. Coming into force: 26.02.2008. Effect: S.I. 2003/1907 amended. Territorial extent & classification: E. General. - Supersedes draft S.I. (ISBN 9780110808185) issued 14.01.2008. - 4p.: 30 cm. - 978-0-11-081028-7 £3.00

The Greater London Authority (Limitation of Salaries) (Amendment) Order 2008 No. 2008/724. - Enabling power: Greater London Authority Act 1999, ss. 25, 420 (1). - Issued: 19.03.2008. Made: 11.03.2008. Laid: 19.03.2008. Coming into force: 01.05.2008. Effect: S.I. 2000/1032 amended. Territorial extent & classification: E. General. - 2p.: 30 cm. - 978-0-11-081224-3 £3.00

The Greater London Authority (Mayor of London Appointments) Order 2008 No. 2008/701. - Enabling power: Greater London Authority Act 1999, s. 377A(5). - Issued: 18.03.2008. Made: 10.03.2008. Laid: 12.03.2008. Coming into force: 06.04.2008. Effect: None. Territorial extent & classification: E. General. - 2p.: 30 cm. - 978-0-11-081222-9 £3.00

The London Waste and Recycling Board Order 2008 No. 2008/2038. - Enabling power: Greater London Authority Act 1999, ss. 60A (5), 356B (1), 405 (1). - Issued: 01.08.2008. Made: 23.07.2008. Coming into force: 24.07.2008 in accord. with art. 1. Effect: 1998 c. 18; 1999 c.29 amended. Territorial extent & classification: E. General. - Supersedes draft S.I. (ISBN 9780110818504) issued 17.6.2008. - 12p.: 30 cm. - 978-0-11-083657-7 £3.00

The Road User Charging (Enforcement and Adjudication) (London) (Amendment) Regulations 2008 No. 2008/1956. - Enabling power: Greater London Authority Act 1999, sch. 23, paras. 12 (3), 28. - Issued: 24.07.2008. Made: 18.07.2008. Laid: 22.07.2008. Coming into force: 20.08.2008. Effect: S.I. 2001/2313 amended. Territorial extent & classification: E. General. - 2p.: 30 cm. - 978-0-11-083522-8 £3.00

Lord Chancellor

The Discipline of Judges (Designation) Order 2008 No. 2008/2700. - Enabling power: Constitutional Reform Act 2005, s. 118 (2). - Issued: 15.10.2008. Made: 07.10.2008. Laid: 13.10.2008. Coming into force: 03.11.2008. Effect: None. Territorial extent & classification: E/W/S/NI. General. - Revoked by S.I. 2009/590 (ISBN 9780111476277). - 2p.: 30 cm. - 978-0-11-084634-7 £4.00

Lord Chief Justice

The Discipline of Judges (Designation) Order 2008 No. 2008/2700. - Enabling power: Constitutional Reform Act 2005, s. 118 (2). - Issued: 15.10.2008. Made: 07.10.2008. Laid: 13.10.2008. Coming into force: 03.11.2008. Effect: None. Territorial extent & classification: E/W/S/NI. General. - Revoked by S.I. 2009/590 (ISBN 9780111476277). - 2p.: 30 cm. - 978-0-11-084634-7 £4.00

The Judicial Discipline (Prescribed Procedures) (Amendment) Regulations 2008 No. 2008/2098. - Enabling power: Constitutional Reform Act 2005, ss. 115, 120, 121. - Issued: 21.08.2008. Made: 17.07.2008. Laid: 05.08.2008. Coming into force: 28.08.2008. Effect: S.I. 2006/676 amended. Territorial extent & classification: E/W/S/NI. General. - 8p.: 30 cm. - 978-0-11-083846-5 £3.00

Magistrates' courts, England and Wales

The Contracting Out (Administrative and Other Court Staff) (Amendment) Order 2008 No. 2008/2791. - Enabling power: Courts Act 1971, s. 2 (6). - Issued: 31.10.2008. Made: 23.10.2008. Laid: 28.10.2008. Coming into force: 01.12.2008. Effect: S.I. 2001/3698 amended. Territorial extent & classification: E/W. General. - 2p.: 30 cm. - 978-0-11-084741-2 £4.00

The Criminal Justice and Immigration Act 2008 (Commencement No. 3 and Transitional Provisions) Order 2008 No. 2008/2712 (C.118). - Enabling power: Criminal Justice and Immigration Act 2008, s. 153 (4) (7). Bringing into operation various provisions of the 2008 Act on 03.11.2008 in accord. with art. 2. - Issued: 20.10.2008. Made: 13.10.2008. Effect: None. Territorial extent & classification: E/W/NI [some aspects E/W only]. General. - 8p.: 30 cm. - 978-0-11-084677-4 £5.00

The Criminal Procedure (Amendment No. 2) Rules 2008 No. 2008/3269 (L.28). - Enabling power: Courts Act 2003, s. 69. - Issued: 24.12.2008. Made: 14.12.2008. Laid: 19.12.2008. Coming into force: 06.04.2009. Effect: S.I. 2005/384 amended. Territorial extent and classification: E/W. General. - 24p.: 30 cm. - 978-0-11-147233-0 £5.00

The Criminal Procedure (Amendment) Rules 2008 No. 2008/2076 (L.9). - Enabling power: Courts Act 2003, s. 69. - Issued: 06.08.2008. Made: 21.07.2008. Laid: 31.07.2008. Coming into force: 06.10.2008. Effect: S.I. 2005/384 amended. Territorial extent and classification: E/W. General. - 20p.: 30 cm. - 978-0-11-083658-4 £3.50

The Family Proceedings Courts (Children Act 1989) (Amendment) Rules 2008 No. 2008/2858 (L.23). - Enabling power: Magistrates' Courts Act 1980, s. 144. - Issued: 11.11.2008. Made: 03.11.2008. Laid: 06.11.2008. Coming into force: 08.12.2008. Effect: S.I. 1991/1395 amended. Territorial extent & classification: E/W. General. - 28p.: 30 cm. - 978-0-11-084959-1 £5.00

The Fines Collection (Disclosure of Information) (Prescribed Benefits) Regulations 2008 No. 2008/3242. - Enabling power: Courts Act 2003, sch. 5, para. 9C. - Issued: 23.12.2008. Made: 16.12.2008. Laid: 18.12.2008. Coming into force: 12.01.2009. Effect: None. Territorial extent & classification: E/W. General. - 2p.: 30 cm. - 978-0-11-147207-1 £4.00

The Magistrates' Courts (Enforcement of Children Act 1989 Contact Orders) Rules 2008 No. 2008/2859 (L.24). - Enabling power: Magistrates' Courts Act 1980, s. 144. - Issued: 11.11.2008. Made: 03.11.2008. Laid: 06.11.2008. Coming into force: 08.12.2008. Effect: S.I. 1991/1395 modified. Territorial extent & classification: E/W. General. - 36p.: 30 cm. - 978-0-11-084960-7 £9.00

The Magistrates' Courts Fees (Amendment) Order 2008 No. 2008/117 (L.3). - Enabling power: Courts Act 2003, s. 92. - Issued: 28.01.2007. Made: 21.01.2008. Laid: 21.01.2008. Coming into force: 11.02.2008. Effect: S.I. 2005/3444 amended. Territorial extent & classification: E/W. General. - Revoked by S.I. 2008/1052 (L.4) (ISBN 9780110813554). This Statutory Instrument has been made in consequence of defects in S.I. 2007/2619 (ISBN 9780110787572) and is being issued free of charge to all known recipients of that SI. - 2p.: 30 cm. - 978-0-11-080860-4 £3.00

The Magistrates' Courts Fees (Amendment) Order 2008 No. 2008/2855 (L.21). - Enabling power: Courts Act 2003, s. 92. - Issued: 10.11.2008. Made: 04.11.2008. Laid: 05.11.2008. Coming into force: 26.11.2008 except for arts 3, 6; 08.12.2008 for arts 3, 6. Effect: S.I. 2008/1052 amended. Territorial extent & classification: E/W. General. - 4p.: 30 cm. - 978-0-11-084956-0 £4.00

The Magistrates' Courts Fees (Amendment) Order 2008 (Correction Slip) No. 2008/2855 (L.21) COR. - Correction slip to SI 2008/2855 (L.21) (ISBN 9780110849560). - 1 sheet: 30 cm. *Free*

The Magistrates' Courts Fees Order 2008 No. 2008/1052 (L.4). - Enabling power: Courts Act 2003, s. 92. - Issued: 11.04.2008. Made: 07.04.2008. Laid: 09.04.2008. Coming into force: 01.05.2008. Effect: S.I. 2005/3444; 2006/715; 2007/2619; 2008/117 revoked. Territorial extent & classification: E/W. General. - 12p.: 30 cm. - 978-0-11-081355-4 £3.00

Maintenance of dependants

The Reciprocal Enforcement of Maintenance Orders (Designation of Reciprocating Countries) Order 2008 No. 2008/1202. - Enabling power: Maintenance Orders (Reciprocal Enforcement) Act 1972, ss. 1, 24. - Issued: 14.05.2008. Made: 07.05.2008. Laid: 14.05.2008. Coming into force: 19.06.2008. Effect: None. Territorial extent & classification: E/W/S/NI. General. - 4p.: 30 cm. - 978-0-11-081442-1 £3.00

Maintenance of dependants, England and Wales

The Maintenance Orders (Facilities for Enforcement) (Revocation) Order 2008 No. 2008/1203. - Enabling power: Maintenance Orders Act 1958, s. 19. - Issued: 13.05.2008. Made: 07.05.2008. Coming into force: 19.05.2008. Effect: S.I. 1959/377 amended. Territorial extent & classification: E/W/NI. General. - 2p.: 30 cm. - 978-0-11-081444-5 £3.00

Maintenance of dependants, Northern Ireland

The Maintenance Orders (Facilities for Enforcement) (Revocation) Order 2008 No. 2008/1203. - Enabling power: Maintenance Orders Act 1958, s. 19. - Issued: 13.05.2008. Made: 07.05.2008. Coming into force: 19.05.2008. Effect: S.I. 1959/377 amended. Territorial extent & classification: E/W/NI. General. - 2p.: 30 cm. - 978-0-11-081444-5 £3.00

Marine pollution

The Merchant Shipping (Prevention of Air Pollution from Ships) Regulations 2008 No. 2008/2924. - Enabling power: S.I. 1996/282, art. 2 & S.I. 2006/1248, arts 2, 3 & Merchant Shipping Act 1995, s. 128 (5) (6). - Issued: 19.11.2008. Made: 12.11.2008. Laid: 14.11.2008. Coming into force: 08.12.2008. Effect: None. Territorial extent & classification: E/W/S/NI. General. - 32p.: 30 cm. - With correction slip dated September 2009. 978-0-11-147008-4 £9.00

The Merchant Shipping (Prevention of Pollution by Sewage and Garbage from Ships) Regulations 2008 No. 2008/3257. - Enabling power: Merchant Shipping Act 1995, s. 128 (5) (6); S.I. 1996/282, art. 2; S.I. 2006/2950, arts 3, 4, 5. - Issued: 30.12.2008. Made: 18.12.2008. Laid: 22.12.2008. Coming into force: 01.02.2009. Effect: S.I. 1998/1377 revoked. Territorial extent & classification: E/W/S/NI. General. - 32p.: 30 cm. - 978-0-11-147223-1 £9.00

Medical profession, England

The Abortion (Amendment) Regulations 2008 No. 2008/735. - Enabling power: Abortion Act 1967, s.2. - Issued: 19.03.2008. Made: 13.03.2008. Laid: 19.03.2008. Coming into force: 21.03.2008. Effect: S.I. 1991/499 amended. Territorial extent & classification: E. General. - 2p.: 30 cm. - 978-0-11-081250-2 £3.00

Medical profession, Wales

The Abortion (Amendment) (Wales) Regulations 2008 No. 2008/1338 (W.140). - Enabling power: Abortion Act 1967, s. 2. - Issued: 09.06.2008. Made: 21.05.2008. Laid before the National Assembly for Wales: 22.05.2008. Coming into force: 17.06.2008. Effect: S.I. 1991/499 amended. Territorial extent & classification: W. General. - In English and Welsh. Welsh title: Rheoliadau Erthylu (Diwygio) (Cymru) 2008. - 4p.: 30 cm. - 978-0-11-091790-0 £3.00

Medicines

The Health Act 2006 (Commencement No. 6) Order 2008 No. 2008/2714 (C.119). - Enabling power: Health Act 2006, s. 83 (7) (8). Bringing into operation various provisions of the 2006 Act on 01.10.2009. - Issued: 20.10.2008. Made: 14.10.2008. Effect: None. Territorial extent & classification: E/W/S/NI. General. - 4p.: 30 cm. - 978-0-11-084670-5 £4.00

The Medicines for Human Use (Clinical Trials) and Blood Safety and Quality (Amendment) Regulations 2008 No. 2008/941. - Enabling power: European Communities Act 1972, s. 2 (2). - Issued: 07.04.2008. Made: 31.03.2008. Laid: 07.04.2008. Coming into force: 01.05.2008. Effect: S.I. 2004/1031; 2005/50 amended. Territorial extent & classification: E/W/S/NI. General. - EC note: These Regulations amend the Medicines for Human Use (Clinical Trials) Regulations 2004 (the Clinical Trials Regulations) which implement Directive 2001/20/EC on the approximation of the laws, regulations and administrative provisions of the Member States relating to the implementation of good clinical practice in the conduct of clinical trials on medicinal products for human use. This includes updating the definition of the Clinical Trials Directive and Directive 2001/83/EC respectively to take account of the subsequent amendment of those Directives by Community Regulations. - 8p.: 30 cm. - 978-0-11-081325-7 £3.00

The Medicines for Human Use (Marketing Authorisations Etc.) Amendment Regulations 2008 No. 2008/3097. - Enabling power: European Communities Act 1972, s. 2 (2). - Issued: 08.12.2008. Made: 03.12.2008. Laid: 08.12.2008. Coming into force: 29.12.2008. Effect: 1968 c. 67 & S.I. 1994/3144; 2008/1692 amended. Territorial extent & classification: E/W/S/NI. General. - EC note: These Regulations give effect in the United Kingdom to Regulation No 1901/2006 on medicinal products for paediatric use and amending Regulation No 1768/92, Directive 2001/20/EC, Directive 2001/83/EC and Regulation No 726/2004, as amended by Regulation No 1902/2006 amending Regulation 1901/2006 on medicinal products for paediatric use (the Paediatric Regulation). - 8p.: 30 cm. - 978-0-11-147097-8 £5.00

The Medicines for Human Use (Prescribing by EEA Practitioners) Regulations 2008 No. 2008/1692. - Enabling power: European Communities Act 1972, s. 2 (2). - Issued: 02.07.2008. Made: 26.06.2008. Laid: 02.07.2008. Coming into force: 03.11.2008. Effect: None. Territorial extent & classification: E/W/S/NI. General. - 4p.: 30 cm. - 978-0-11-081922-8 £3.00

The Medicines for Human Use (Prescribing) (Miscellaneous Amendments) Order 2008 No. 2008/1161. - Enabling power: Medicines Act 1968, ss. 57 (1) (2), 58 (1) (1A) (4) (5), 129 (4). - Issued: 29.04.2008. Made: 22.04.2008. Laid: 29.04.2008. Coming into force: 04.06.2008. Effect: S.I. 1997/1830; 1980/1924 amended. Territorial extent & classification: E/W/S/NI. General. - 4p.: 30 cm. - 978-0-11-081399-8 £3.00

The Medicines for Human Use (Prohibition) (Senecio and Miscellaneous Amendments) Order 2008 No. 2008/548. - Enabling power: Medicines Act 1968, ss. 62 (1) (a) (2), 129 (4). - Issued: 06.03.2008. Made: 28.02.2008. Laid: 06.03.2008. Coming into force: 01.04.2008. Effect: S.I. 1977/670; 2001/1841; 2002/3170 amended. Territorial extent & classification: E/W/S/NI. General. - 8p.: 30 cm. - 978-0-11-081071-3 £3.00

The Medicines (Pharmacies) (Applications for Registration and Fees) Amendment Regulations 2008 No. 2008/2946. - Enabling power: Medicines Act 1968, ss. 75 (1), 76 (1) (2), 129 (1) (5). - Issued: 19.11.2008. Made: 12.11.2008. Laid: 19.11.2008. Coming into force: 01.01.2009. Effect: S.I. 1973/1822 amended. Territorial extent & classification: E/W/S. General. - 4p.: 30 cm. - 978-0-11-147006-0 £4.00

The Medicines (Pharmacies) (Responsible Pharmacist) Regulations 2008 No. 2008/2789. - Enabling power: Medicines Act 1968, ss. 72A (4) (b) (5) (b) (6) (7) (b) (e) (f), 129 (1) (5). - Issued: 29.10.2008. Made: 24.10.2008. Laid: 29.10.2008. Coming into force: 01.10.2009. Effect: None. Territorial extent & classification: E/W/S/NI. General. - 8p.: 30 cm. - 978-0-11-084736-8 £5.00

The Medicines (Products for Human Use-Fees) Regulations 2008 No. 2008/552. - Enabling power: Medicines Act 1971, s. 1 (1) (2) & European Communities Act 1972, s. 2 (2) & Finance Act 1973, s. 56 (1) (2). - Issued: 07.03.2008. Made: 28.02.2008. Laid: 07.03.2008. Coming into force: 01.04.2008. Effect: S.I. 1994/105 amended & S.I. 1998/574; 2000/592; 2001/795; 2002/236, 542; 2003/625; 2004/666; 2006/494, 2125; 2007/803 partially revoked & S.I. 1995/1116; 1996/683; 2000/3031; 2004/1157; 2005/1124, 2979 revoked. Territorial extent & classification: E/W/S/NI. General. - Revoked by S.I. 2009/389 (ISBN 9780111474969) with savings. With correction slip dated March 2008. - 64p.: 30 cm. - 978-0-11-081073-7 £10.50

The Medicines (Sale or Supply) (Miscellaneous Amendments) Regulations 2008 No. 2008/1162. - Enabling power: Medicines Act 1968, ss. 66 (1), 87 (1), 91 (2), 129 (1) (5). - Issued: 29.04.2008. Made: 22.04.2008. Laid: 29.04.2008. Coming into force: 04.06.2008. Effect: S.I. 1980/1923; 2003/2317 amended. Territorial extent & classification: E/W/S/NI. General. - 4p.: 30 cm. - 978-0-11-081400-1 £3.00

The Prescription Only Medicines (Human Use) Amendment Order 2008 No. 2008/464. - Enabling power: Medicines Act 1968, ss. 58 (1) (1A) (4) (4A), (4B) (5), 129 (4). - Issued: 29.02.2008. Made: 20.02.2008. Laid: 29.02.2008. Coming into force: 01.04.2008. Effect: S.I. 1997/1830 amended. Territorial extent & classification: E/W/S/NI. General. - 4p.: 30 cm. - 978-0-11-081009-6 £3.00

The Veterinary Medicines (Amendment) Regulations 2008 No. 2008/2648. - Enabling power: European Communities Act 1972, s. 2 (2). - Issued: 10.10.2008. Made: 03.10.2008. Laid: 08.10.2008. Coming into force: 01.11.2008. Effect: S.I. 2008/2297 amended. Territorial extent & classification: E/W/S/NI. General. - This Statutory Instrument has been made in consequence of a defect in S.I. 2008/2297 and is being issued free of charge to all known recipients of that Statutory Instrument. - 2p.: 30 cm. - 978-0-11-084454-1 £4.00

The Veterinary Medicines Regulations 2008 No. 2008/2297. - Enabling power: European Communities Act 1972, s. 2 (2) & Finance Act 1973, s. 56 (1). - Issued: 03.09.2008. Made: 26.08.2008. Laid: 01.09.2008. Coming into force: 01.10.2008. Effect: 1971 c.69 amended & S.I. 1988/1586; 2007/2539 revoked. Territorial extent & classification: E/W/S/NI. General. - Revoked by S.I. 2009/2297 (ISBN 9780111484760) with savings. EC note: These Regulations implement Directives 2001/82/EC and 90/167, and enforce Regulations (EC) nos 178/2002, 1831/2003, 882/2004, 183/2005. - 116p.: 30 cm. - 978-0-11-083870-0 £15.50

Mental capacity, England

The Mental Capacity (Deprivation of Liberty: Appointment of Relevant Person's Representative) (Amendment) Regulations 2008 No. 2008/2368. - Enabling power: Mental Capacity Act 2005, s. 65 (1), sch. A1, paras. 138 (1), 143, 144. - Issued: 12.09.2008. Made: 05.09.2008. Laid: 12.09.2008. Coming into force: 03.11.2008. Effect: S.I. 2008/1315 amended. Territorial extent & classification: E. General. - This Statutory Instrument has been made in consequence of a defect in SI 2008/1315 (ISBN 9780110814704) and is being issued free of charge to all known recipients of that Statutory Instrument. - 2p.: 30 cm. - 978-0-11-084149-6 £4.00

The Mental Capacity (Deprivation of Liberty: Appointment of Relevant Person's Representative) Regulations 2008 No. 2008/1315. - Enabling power: Mental Capacity Act 2005, s. 65 (1), sch. A1, paras. 138 (1), 142 to 145, 148, 149, 151. - Issued: 20.05.2008. Made: 14.05.2008. Laid: 20.05.2008. Coming into force: 03.11.2008. Effect: None. Territorial extent & classification: E. General. - 8p.: 30 cm. - 978-0-11-081470-4 £3.00

The Mental Capacity (Deprivation of Liberty: Standard Authorisations, Assessments and Ordinary Residence) Regulations 2008 No. 2008/1858. - Enabling power: Mental Capacity Act 2005, s. 65 (1), sch. A1, paras. 31, 33 (4), 47, 70, 129 (3), 130, 183 (6) (7). - Issued: 17.07.2008. Made: 09.07.2008. Coming into force: 03.11.2008. Effect: None. Territorial extent & classification: E. General. - Supersedes draft S.I. (ISBN 9780110814773) issued on 20.05.2008. - 12p.: 30 cm. - 978-0-11-083168-8 £3.00

Mental capacity, England and Wales

The Contracting Out (Administrative and Other Court Staff) (Amendment) Order 2008 No. 2008/2791. - Enabling power: Courts Act 1971, s. 2 (6). - Issued: 31.10.2008. Made: 23.10.2008. Laid: 28.10.2008. Coming into force: 01.12.2008. Effect: S.I. 2001/3698 amended. Territorial extent & classification: E/W. General. - 2p.: 30 cm. - 978-0-11-084741-2 £4.00

Mental health

The Mental Health Act 2007 (Consequential Amendments) Order 2008 No. 2008/2828. - Enabling power: Mental Health Act 2007, s. 54 (1) (2). - Issued: 04.11.2008. Made: 28.10.2008. Coming into force: 03.11.2008 except for arts 11, 12, 13, 14, 17 (b), 18 (b), 19 (b); 04.05.2009 for 11, 12, 13, 14, 17 (b), 18 (b), 19 (b), in accord. with art. 1. Effect: 4 acts & 11 S.I.'s & 1 S.S.I amended & S.I. 1996/295; 2001/3712 revoked (03.11.2008). Territorial extent & classification: E/W/S/NI in accord. with art. 2. General. - Supersedes draft S.I. (ISBN 9780110819600) issued 08.08.2008. - 8p.: 30 cm. - 978-0-11-084815-0 £5.00

Mental health, England

The Mental Health Act 1983 (Independent Mental Health Advocates) (England) Regulations 2008 No. 2008/3166. - Enabling power: Mental Health Act 1983, s. 130A & National Health Service Act 2006, ss. 7, 8, 14, 19, 75, 272 (7) (8), 273 (4). - Issued: 16.12.2008. Made: 09.12.2008. Laid: 16.12.2008. Coming into force: 01.04.2009. Effect: S.I.2000/617; 2002/2375 amended. Territorial extent & classification: E. General. - 4p.: 30 cm. - 978-0-11-147171-5 £4.00

The Mental Health (Approved Mental Health Professionals) (Approval) (England) Regulations 2008 No. 2008/1206. - Enabling power: Mental Health Act 1983, s. 114. - Issued: 07.05.2008. Made: 28.04.2008. Laid: 07.05.2008. Coming into force: 03.11.2008. Effect: None. Territorial extent & classification: E. General. - 8p.: 30 cm. - 978-0-11-081418-6 £3.00

The Mental Health (Conflicts of Interest) (England) Regulations 2008 No. 2008/1205. - Enabling power: Mental Health Act 1983, s. 12A. - Issued: 07.05.2008. Made: 28.04.2008. Laid: 07.05.2008. Coming into force: 03.11.2008. Effect: None. Territorial extent & classification: E. General. - 4p.: 30 cm. - 978-0-11-081417-9 £3.00

The Mental Health (Hospital, Guardianship and Treatment) (England) (Amendment) Regulations 2008 No. 2008/2560. - Enabling power: Mental Health Act 1983, ss. 19A (1), 32 (1) (2). - Issued: 06.10.2008. Made: 30.09.2008. Laid: 06.10.2008. Coming into force: 03.11.2008, in accord. with reg. 1 (2). Effect: S.I. 2008/1184 amended. Territorial extent & classification: E. General. - With correction slip dated October 2009. - This Statutory Instrument has been published in substitution of the SI of the same number (ISBN 9780110843506, published 06.10.2008) and is being issued free of charge to all known recipients of that version. - 4p.: 30 cm. - 978-0-11-084446-6 £4.00

The Mental Health (Hospital, Guardianship and Treatment) (England) (Amendment) Regulations 2008 No. 2008/2560. - Enabling power: Mental Health Act 1983, ss. 19A (1), 32 (1) (2). - Issued: 06.10.2008. Made: 30.09.2008. Laid: 06.10.2008. Coming into force: 03.11.2008, in accord. with reg. 1 (2). Effect: S.I. 2008/1184 amended. Territorial extent & classification: E. General. - With correction slip dated October 2009. - Superseded by S.I. of same number (ISBN 9780110844466). - 4p.: 30 cm. - 978-0-11-084350-6 £4.00

The Mental Health (Hospital, Guardianship and Treatment) (England) Regulations 2008 No. 2008/1184. - Enabling power: Mental Health Act 1983, ss. 9, 17F (2), 19 (1) (4), 19A (1), 32 (1) (2) (3), 57 (1) (b), 58A (1) (b), 64 (2), 64H (2), 134 (3A) (a), 134(8). - Issued: 07.05.2008. Made: 28.04.2008. Laid: 07.05.2008. Coming into force: 03.11.2008. Effect: S.I. 1983/893: 1993/2156: 1996/540: 1997/801: 1998/2624: 2003/2042 revoked. Territorial extent & classification: E. General. - 92p.: 30 cm. - 978-0-11-081421-6 £13.50

The Mental Health (Nurses) (England) Order 2008 No. 2008/1207. - Enabling power: Mental Health Act 1983, s. 5 (4) (7). - Issued: 07.05.2008. Made: 28.04.2008. Coming into force: 03.11.2008 in accord. with art. 1 (2). Effect: S.I. 1998/2625 revoked in relation to England. Territorial extent & classification: E. General. - 2p.: 30 cm. - 978-0-11-081419-3 £3.00

Mental health, England and Wales

The Mental Health Act 2007 (Commencement No. 4) Order 2008 No. 2008/745 (C.30). - Enabling power: Mental Health Act 2007, s. 56 (1) (2). Bringing into operation various provisions of the 2007 Act on 01.04.2008, in accord. with art. 2. - Issued: 19.03.2008. Made: 13.03.2008. Effect: None. Territorial extent & classification: E/W. General. - 4p.: 30 cm. - 978-0-11-081252-6 £3.00

The Mental Health Act 2007 (Commencement No. 5 and Transitional Provisions) Order 2008 No. 2008/800 (C.39). - Enabling power: Mental Health Act 2007, s. 56 (1) (4) (b). Bringing into operation various provisions of the 2007 Act on 30.04.2008, in accord. with art. 2. - Issued: 01.04.2008. Made: 19.03.2008. Laid: 01.04.2008. Effect: None. Territorial extent and classification: E/W. General. - 4p.: 30 cm. - 978-0-11-081286-1 £3.00

The Mental Health Act 2007 (Commencement No. 6 and Aftercare under Supervision: Savings, Modifications and Transitional Provisions) Order 2008 No. 2008/1210 (C.52). - Enabling power: Mental Health Act 2007, ss. 54 (1) (2), 56 (1) (4), 57. Bringing into operation various provisions of the 2007 Act on 03.11.2008; 04.05.2009, in accord. with art. 1. - Issued: 07.05.2008. Made: 28.04.2008. Laid: 07.05.2008. Effect: 1983 c.20 modified & S.I. 1996/294 revoked. Territorial extent & classification: E/W. General. - 12p.: 30 cm. - 978-0-11-081429-2 £3.00

The Mental Health Act 2007 (Commencement No. 7 and Transitional Provisions) Order 2008 No. 2008/1900 (C.84). - Enabling power: Mental Health Act 2007, s. 56 (1) (2) (4) (b) (5). Bringing into operation various provisions of the 2007 Act on 03.11.2008 in accord. with art. 1 (1). - Issued: 22.07.2008. Made: 17.07.2008. Laid: 22.07.2008. Coming into force: In accord. with art. 1. Effect: None. Territorial extent & classification: E/W. General. - With correction slip dated October 2009. - 8p.: 30 cm. - 978-0-11-083385-9 £3.00

The Mental Health Act 2007 (Commencement No. 8 and Transitional Provisions) Order 2008 No. 2008/2561 (C.113). - Enabling power: Mental Health Act 2007, s. 56 (1) (2) (4) (b) (5). Bringing into operation various provisions of the 2007 Act on 03.11.2008. - Issued: 06.10.2008. Made: 30.097.2008. Laid: 06.10.2008. Effect: None. Territorial extent & classification: E/W. General. - 4p.: 30 cm. - 978-0-11-084352-0 £4.00

The Mental Health Act 2007 (Commencement No. 9) Order 2008 No. 2008/2788 (C.124). - Enabling power: Mental Health Act 2007, s. 56 (1). Bringing into operation various provisions of the 2007 Act on 28.10.2008. - Issued: 28.10.2008. Made: 22.10.2008. Effect: None. Territorial extent & classification: E/W. General. - 4p.: 30 cm. - 978-0-11-084735-1 £4.00

The Mental Health (Mutual Recognition) Regulations 2008 No. 2008/1204. - Enabling power: Mental Health Act 1983, s. 142A. - Issued: 07.05.2008. Made: 28.04.2008. Laid: 07.05.2008. Laid before the National Assembly for Wales: 07.05.2008. Coming into force: 03.11.2008. Effect: None. Territorial extent & classification: E/W. General. - 4p.: 30 cm. - 978-0-11-081416-2 £3.00

Mental health, Wales

The Mental Health (Approval of Persons to be Approved Mental Health Professionals) (Wales) Regulations 2008 No. 2008/2436 (W.209). - Enabling power: Mental Health Act 1983, s. 114. - Issued: 10.10.2008. Made: 15.09.2008. Laid before the National Assembly for Wales: 17.09.2008. Coming into force: 03.11.2008. Effect: None. Territorial extent & classification: W. General. - In English and Welsh. Welsh title: Rheoliadau Iechyd Meddwl (Cymeradwyo Personau i fod yn Weithwyr Proffesiynol Iechyd Meddwl Cymeradwy) (Cymru) 2008. - 12p.: 30 cm. - 978-0-11-091883-9 £5.00

The Mental Health (Conflicts of Interest) (Wales) Regulations 2008 No. 2008/2440 (W.213). - Enabling power: Mental Health Act 1983, s. 12A. - Issued: 10.10.2008. Made: 15.09.2008. Laid before the National Assembly for Wales: 17.09.2008. Coming into force: 03.11.2008. Effect: None. Territorial extent & classification: W. General. - In English and Welsh. Welsh title: Rheoliadau Iechyd Meddwl (Gwrthdrawiad Buddiannau) (Cymru) 2008. - 8p.: 30 cm. - 978-0-11-091884-6 £5.00

The Mental Health (Hospital, Guardianship, Community Treatment and Consent to Treatment) (Wales) Regulations 2008 No. 2008/2439 (W.212). - Enabling power: Mental Health Act 1983, ss. 9, 17F (2), 19 (1) (4), 19A, 32 (1) (2) (3), 57 (1) (b), 58A (1) (b), 64 (2), 64H (2), 134 (3A) (a) (8). - Issued: 10.10.2008. Made: 15.09.2008. Laid before the National Assembly for Wales: 17.09.2008. Coming into force: 03.11.2008. Effect: S.I. 1983/893; 1993/2156; 1996/540; 1997/801; 1998/2624 revoked in relation to Wales. Territorial extent & classification: W. General. - In English and Welsh. Welsh title: Rheoliadau Iechyd Meddwl (Ysbyty, Gwarcheidiaeth, Triniaeth Gymunedol a Chydsynio i Driniaeth) (Cymru) 2008. - 100p.: 30 cm. - 978-0-11-091885-3 £13.50

The Mental Health (Independent Mental Health Advocates) (Wales) Regulations 2008 No. 2008/2437 (W.210). - Enabling power: Mental Health Act 1983, s. 130A & National Health Service (Wales) Act 2006, ss. 12, 204. - Issued: 10.10.2008. Made: 15.09.2008. Laid before the National Assembly for Wales: 17.09.2008. Coming into force: 03.11.2008. Effect: None. Territorial extent & classification: W. General. - In English and Welsh. Welsh title: Rheoliadau Iechyd Meddwl (Eiriolwyr Annibynnol Iechyd Meddwl) (Cymru) 2008. - 8p.: 30 cm. - 978-0-11-091880-8 £5.00

The Mental Health (Nurses) (Wales) Order 2008 No. 2008/2441 (W.214). - Enabling power: Mental Health Act 1983, ss. 5 (4) (7), 143. - Issued: 10.10.2008. Made: 15.09.2008. Coming into force: 03.11.2008. Effect: S.I. 1998/2625 revoked in relation to Wales. Territorial extent & classification: W. General. - In English and Welsh. Welsh title: Gorchymyn Iechyd Meddwl (Nyrsys) (Cymru) 2008. - 4p.: 30 cm. - 978-0-11-091882-2 £4.00

Merchant shipping

The Merchant Shipping and Fishing Vessels (Lifting Operations and Lifting Equipment) (Amendment) Regulations 2008 No. 2008/2166. - Enabling power: European Communities Act 1972, s. 2 (2) & Merchant Shipping Act 1995, ss. 85 (1) (a) (b) (3), 86 (1). - Issued: 19.08.2008. Made: 11.08.2008. Laid: 15.08.2008. Coming into force: 08.09.2008. Effect: S.I. 2006/2184 amended. Territorial extent & classification: E/W/S/NI. General. - With correction slip dated August 2009. This Statutory Instrument has been made in consequence of defects in SI 2006/2184 and is being issued free of charge to all known recipients of that Statutory Instrument. - 2p.: 30 cm. - 978-0-11-083768-0 £3.00

The Merchant Shipping and Fishing Vessels (Provision and Use of Work Equipment) (Amendment) Regulations 2008 No. 2008/2165. - Enabling power: European Communities Act 1972, s. 2 (2) & Merchant Shipping Act 1995, ss. 85 (1) (a) (b) (3), 86 (1). - Issued: 19.08.2008. Made: 11.08.2008. Laid: 15.08.2008. Coming into force: 08.09.2008. Effect: S.I. 2006/2183 amended. Territorial extent & classification: E/W/S/NI. General. - With correction slip dated August 2009. This Statutory Instrument has been made in consequence of defects in SI 2006/2183 and is being issued free of charge to all known recipients of that Statutory Instrument. - 2p.: 30 cm. - 978-0-11-083770-3 £3.00

The Merchant Shipping (Categorisation of Registries of Relevant British Possessions) (Amendment) Order 2008 No. 2008/1243. - Enabling power: Merchant Shipping Act 1995. s. 18. - Issued: 14.05.2008. Made: 07.05.2008 Laid: 14.05.2008. Coming into force: 04.06.2008. Effect: S.I. 2003/1248 amended. Territorial extent & classification: E/W/S/NI/Anguilla, Bermuda, British Virgin Islands, Cayman Islands, Falkland Islands, Gibraltar, Montserrat, St Helena and the Turks and Caicos Islands; and IoM, Jersey and Guernsey. General. - 2p.: 30 cm. - 978-0-11-081445-2 £3.00

The Merchant Shipping (Liner Conferences) Act 1982 (Repeal) Regulations 2008 No. 2008/163. - Enabling power: European Communities Act 1972, s. 2 (2). - Issued: 30.01.2008. Made: 23.01.2008. Laid: 28.01.2008. Coming into force: 26.02.2008 & 18.10.2008 in accord. with reg. 1 (2) (3) (4). Effect: 1982 c.37 & S.I. 1985/405, 406 repealed in part. Territorial extent & classification: E/W/S/NI. General. - EC note: Council Regulation (EC) No. 1419/2006 repealed Council Regulation (EEC) No. 4056/86 and thereby removed the block exemption from Arts 81 and 82 of the EC Treaty granted to liner shipping conferences, subject to a transitional period of two years for conferences which complied with the requirements of Regulation 4056/86 on 18th October 2006. As a consequence, Council Regulation (EEC) No. 954/79 which gave effect to the Code within the European Union, has become inapplicable. The present Regulations repeal the provisions giving effect to Regulation 954/79. - 4p.: 30 cm. - 978-0-11-080877-2 £3.00

The Merchant Shipping (Vessel Traffic Monitoring and Reporting Requirements) (Amendment) Regulations 2008 No. 2008/3145. - Enabling power: European Communities Act 1972, s. 2 (2) & Merchant Shipping Act 1995, ss. 85, 86. - Issued: 12.12.2008. Made: 05.12.2008. Laid: 11.12.2008. Coming into force: 02.01.2009. Effect: S.I. 1995/2498; 2004/2110 amended. Territorial extent & classification: E/W/S/NI. General. - With correction slip dated January 2010, inserting EC note. EC note: These Regulations implement art. 2.2(b) of Directive 2002/59/EC. - 4p.: 30 cm. - 978-0-11-147132-6 £4.00

Merchant shipping: Masters and seamen

The Merchant Shipping (Training and Certification) (Amendment) Regulations 2008 No. 2008/2851. - Enabling power: Merchant Shipping Act 1995, ss. 47 (1) (3), 85 (1) (3) (5) & European Communities Act 1972, s. 2 (2). - Issued: 12.11.2008. Made: 04.11.2008. Laid: 07.11.2008. Coming into force: 02.12.2008. Effect: S.I. 1997/348 amended. Territorial extent & classification: E/W/S/NI. General. - EC note: These Regulations give effect to Directive 2005/45/EC on the mutual recognition of seafarers' certificates and amending Directive 2001/25/EC. - 4p.: 30 cm. - 978-0-11-084947-8 £4.00

Merchant shipping: Overseas territories

The Merchant Shipping (Liner Conferences) (Gibraltar) (Repeal) Order 2008 No. 2008/1794. - Enabling power: Merchant Shipping (Liner Conferences) Act 1982, s. 15 (4). - Issued: 16.07.2008. Made: 09.07.2008. Coming into force: 30.07.2008 & 18.10.2008 in accord. with art. 1 (2) (3) (4). Effect: 1982 c.37 & S.I. 1985/405, 406 repealed in part. Territorial extent & classification: Gibraltar. General. - 2p.: 30 cm. - 978-0-11-083131-2 £3.00

Ministers of the Crown

The Transfer of Functions (Miscellaneous) Order 2008 No. 2008/1034. - Enabling power: Ministers of the Crown Act 1975, ss. 1, 2. - Issued: 16.04.2008. Made: 09.04.2008. Laid: 16.04.2008. Coming into force: 07.05.2008. Effect: 1970 c. lxxvi; 1972 c. xl; 1984 c. 21 amended. Territorial extent & classification: E/W/S. General. - 8p.: 30 cm. - 978-0-11-081368-4 £3.00

Ministers of the Crown, England

The Transfer of Functions (Administration of Rent Officer Service in England) Order 2008 No. 2008/3134. - Enabling power: Ministers of the Crown Act 1975, ss. 1, 5A. - Issued: 17.12.2008. Made: 10.12.2008. Laid: 17.12.2008. Coming into force: 01.04.2009. Effect: 1977 c. 42 & S.I. 1999/2403 amended. Territorial extent & classification: E. General. - 4p.: 30 cm. - 978-0-11-147168-5 £4.00

Ministers of the Crown, England and Wales

The Transfer of Functions (Registration) Order 2008 No. 2008/678. - Enabling power: Ministers of the Crown Act 1975, s. 1. - Issued: 18.03.2008. Made: 12.03.2008. Laid: 13.03.2008. Coming into force: 03.04.2008. Effect: 15 acts amended. Territorial extent & classification: E/W. General. - 8p.: 30 cm. - 978-0-11-081234-2 £3.00

Museums and galleries

The Tate Gallery Board (Additional Members) Order 2008 No. 2008/919. - Enabling power: Museums and Galleries Act 1992, sch. 2, para. 2 (12) (a). - Issued: 04.04.2008. Made: 20.03.2008. Coming into force: 21.03.2008. Effect: 1992 c. 44 amended. Territorial extent & classification: E/W/S. General. - 2p.: 30 cm. - 978-0-11-081318-9 £3.00

National assistance services, England

The National Assistance (Sums for Personal Requirements and Assessment of Resources) Amendment (England) Regulations 2008 No. 2008/593. - Enabling power: National Assistance Act 1948, s. 22 (4). - Issued: 11.03.2008. Made: 05.03.2008. Laid: 11.03.2008. Coming into force: 07.04.2008. Effect: S.I. 1992/2977; 2003/628 amended. Territorial extent & classification: E. General. - 4p.: 30 cm. - 978-0-11-081108-6 £3.00

National assistance, Wales

The National Assistance (Assessment of Resources and Sums for Personal Requirements) (Amendment) (Wales) Regulations 2008 No. 2008/743 (W.78). - Enabling power: National Assistance Act 1948, s. 22 (4) (5). - Issued: 04.04.2008. Made: 12.03.2008. Laid: 14.03.2008. Coming into force: 07.04.2008. Effect: S.I. 1992/2977 amended & 2007/1041 partially revoked. Territorial extent & classification: W. General. - Partially revoked by W.S.I. 2009/632 (W.58) (ISBN 9780110919553). - In English & Welsh. Welsh title: Rheoliadau Cymorth Gwladol (Asesu Adnoddau a Symiau at Anghenion Personol) (Diwygio) (Cymru) 2008. - 4p.: 30 cm. - 978-0-11-091747-4 £3.00

National Health Service

The Health and Social Care Act 2008 (Consequential Amendments and Transitory Provisions) Order 2008 No. 2008/2250. - Enabling power: Health and Social Care Act 2008, s. 167. - Issued: 28.08.2008. Made: 20.08.2008. Laid: 28.08.2008. Coming into force: 01.10.2008. Effect: 1952 c. 52; 1996 c.16; 1998 c.18; 1999 c. 27; 2000 c.10; c. 43; 2003 c. 39; 2004 c. 23; 2006 c. 40, c. 41 modified & S.I. 1999/260, 2277; 2000/89; 2003/3060; 2005/408, 1447; 2415, 2531; 2006/2380, 3335 amended. Territorial extent & classification: E/W/S/NI. General. - 8p.: 30 cm. - 978-0-11-083849-6 £3.00

National Health Service, England

The Appointments Commission (Amendment) Regulations 2008 No. 2008/2792. - Enabling power: Health Act 2006, sch. 4, para. 2 (b) (d). - Issued: 31.10.2008. Made: 26.10.2008. Laid: 31.10.2008. Coming into force: 08.12.2008. Effect: S.I. 2006/2380 amended. Territorial extent & classification: E/W/S/NI [some aspects E. only]. General. - 2p.: 30 cm. - 978-0-11-084743-6 £4.00

The Bradford District Care Trust (Transfer of Trust Property) Order 2008 No. 2008/2786. - Enabling power: National Health Service Act 2006, ss. 213, 217 (2), 272 (8). - Issued: 29.10.2008. Made: 23.10.008. Laid: 29.10.2008. Coming into force: 01.12.2008. Effect: None. Territorial extent & classification: E. General. - 2p.: 30 cm. - 978-0-11-084733-7 £4.00

The Cambridgeshire and Peterborough Mental Health Partnership National Health Service Trust (Transfer of Trust Property) Order 2008 No. 2008/1323. - Enabling power: National Health Service Act 2006, ss. 213, 217 (2), 272 (8). - Issued: 23.05.2008. Made: 19.05.2008. Laid: 23.05.2008. Coming into force: 01.07.2008. Effect: None. Territorial extent & classification: E. General. - 2p.: 30 cm. - 978-0-11-081487-2 £3.00

The Cardiothoracic Centre-Liverpool National Health Service Trust (Change of Name) (Establishment) Amendment Order 2008 No. 2008/1471. - Enabling power: National Health Service Act 2006, ss. 25 (1), 272 (8), 273 (1), sch. 4, para. 5 (1). - Issued: 12.06.2008. Made: 05.06.2008. Coming into force: 01.07.2008. Effect: S.I. 1990/2404 amended. Territorial extent & classification: E. General. - 2p.: 30 cm. - 978-0-11-081824-5 £3.00

The Care Quality Commission (Membership) Regulations 2008 No. 2008/2252. - Enabling power: Health and Social Care Act 2008, s. 161 (3) (4), sch. 1, para. 3 (3). - Issued: 03.09.2008. Made: 20.08.2008. Laid: 03.09.2008. Coming into force: 01.10.2008. Effect: None. Territorial extent & classification: E. General. - With correction slip dated September 2009. - 8p.: 30 cm. - 978-0-11-083851-9 £3.00

The Cornwall Partnership National Health Service Trust (Transfer of Trust Property) Order 2008 No. 2008/430. - Enabling power: National Health Service Act 2006, ss. 213, 217 (2), 272 (8). - Issued: 27.02.2008. Made: 19.02.2008. Laid: 27.02.2008. Coming into force: 01.04.2008. Effect: None. Territorial extent & classification: E. General. - 2p.: 30 cm. - 978-0-11-080992-2 £3.00

The Dorset Primary Care Trust (Transfer of Trust Property) Order 2008 No. 2008/416. - Enabling power: National Health Service Act 2006, ss. 213, 217 (2), 272 (8). - Issued: 26.02.2008. Made: 19.02.2008. Laid: 26.02.2008. Coming into force: 01.04.2008. Effect: None. Territorial extent & classification: E. General. - 2p.: 30 cm. - 978-0-11-080977-9 £3.00

The Dudley and Walsall Mental Health Partnership National Health Service Trust (Establishment) Order 2008 No. 2008/2431. - Enabling power: National Health Service Act 2006, ss. 25 (1), 272 (7), sch. 4, para. 5. - Issued: 17.09.2008. Made: 11.09.2008. Coming into force: 01.10.2008. Effect: None. Territorial extent & classification: E. General. - 2p.: 30 cm. - 978-0-11-084217-2 £4.00

The East Kent Hospitals National Health Service Trust (Change of Name) (Establishment) Amendment Order 2008 No. 2008/1859. - Enabling power: National Health Service Act 2006, ss. 25 (1), 272 (8), 273 (1), sch. 4, para. 5 (1). - Issued: 17.07.2008. Made: 10.07.2008. Coming into force: 01.08.2008. Effect: S.I. 1999/896 amended. Territorial extent & classification: E. General. - 4p.: 30 cm. - 978-0-11-083170-1 £3.00

The East Kent Hospitals National Health Service Trust (Transfer of Trust Property) Order 2008 No. 2008/83. - Enabling power: National Health Service Act 2006, ss. 213, 217 (2), 272 (8). - Issued: 22.01.2008. Made: 15.01.2008. Laid: 22.01.2008. Coming into force: 18.02.2008. Effect: None. Territorial extent & classification: E. General. - 2p.: 30 cm. - 978-0-11-080850-5 £3.00

The General Ophthalmic Services Contracts Regulations 2008 No. 2008/1185. - Enabling power: National Health Service Act 1977, ss. 28WB, 28WC, 28WE, 28WF and 126(4) & National Health Service Act 2006, s. 9 (8). - Issued: 06.05.2008. Made: 28.04.2008. Laid: 06.05.2008. Coming into force: 01.08.2008. Effect: None. Territorial extent & classification: E. General. - 40p.: 30 cm. - 978-0-11-081422-3 £6.50

The Health Act 2006 (Commencement No. 4) Order 2008 No. 2008/1147 (C.50). - Enabling power: Health Act 2006, s. 83 (7) (8). Bringing into operation various provisions of the 2006 Act on 22.04.2008; 28.04.2008; 01.05.2008. - Issued: 25.04.2008. Made: 21.04.2008. Effect: None. Territorial extent & classification: E/S [parts E. only]. General. - 4p.: 30 cm. - 978-0-11-081396-7 £3.00

The Health Act 2006 (Commencement No. 5) Order 2008 No. 2008/1972 (C. 96). - Enabling power: Health Act 2006, s. 83 (7) (8). Bringing into operation various provisions of the 2006 Act on 01.08.2008. - Issued: 28.07.2008. Made: 22.07.2008. Effect: None. Territorial extent & classification: E. General. - 4p.: 30 cm. - 978-0-11-083625-6 £3.00

The Health and Social Care Act 2008 (Commencement No.2) Order 2008 No. 2008/2497 (C.106). - Enabling power: Health and Social Care Act 2008, s. 170 (3) (4). Bringing into operation various provisions of the 2008 Act on 01.10.2008; 01.01.2009. - Issued: 25.09.2008. Made: 19.09.2008. Effect: None. Territorial extent & classification: E/WS/NI [parts E or E/W only]. General. - 4p.: 30 cm. - 978-0-11-084265-3 £4.00

The Health and Social Care Act 2008 (Commencement No. 4) Order 2008 No. 2008/2994 (C.129). - Enabling power: Health and Social Care Act 2008, s. 170 (3) (4). Bringing into operation various provisions of the 2008 Act on 01.12.2008, 01.04.2009 in accord. with art. 3. - Issued: 21.11.2008. Made: 15.11.2008. Effect: None. Territorial extent & classification: E/WS/NI [parts E or E/W only]. General. - 4p.: 30 cm. - 978-0-11-147028-2 £4.00

The Health and Social Care Act 2008 (Commencement No.6, Transitory and Transitional Provisions) Order 2008 No. 2008/3168 (C.143). - Enabling power: Health and Social Care Act 2008, ss. 161 (3) (4), 167, 170 (3) (4). Bringing into operation various provisions of the 2008 Act on 12.01.2009 in accord. with art. 2. - Issued: 17.12.2008. Made: 11.12.2008. Laid: 17.12.2008. Effect: None. Territorial extent & classification: E/W but has affect in E only. General. - 8p.: 30 cm. - 978-0-11-147174-6 £5.00

The Health and Social Care Information Centre (Transfer of Staff, Property and Liabilities) Order 2008 No. 2008/519. - Enabling power: National Health Service Act 2006, ss. 28 (2) (4), 272 (7) (8). - Issued: 04.03.2008. Made: 27.02.2008. Laid: 04.03.2008. Coming into force: 01.04.2008. Effect: None. Territorial extent & classification: E. General. - 4p.: 30 cm. - 978-0-11-081036-2 £3.00

The Imperial College Healthcare National Health Service Trust (Trust Funds: Appointment of Trustees) Order 2008 No. 2008/79. - Enabling power: National Health Service Act 2006, sch. 4, para. 10 (1) (2). - Issued: 21.01.2008. Made: 15.01.2008. Coming into force: 01.02.2008. Effect: None. Territorial extent & classification: E. General. - 2p.: 30 cm. - 978-0-11-080844-4 £3.00

The Local Government and Public Involvement in Health Act 2007 (Commencement No. 4) Order 2008 No. 2008/461 (C.17). - Enabling power: Local Government and Public Involvement in Health Act 2007, s. 245 (5) (6). Bringing into operation various provisions of the 2007 Act on 21.02.2008; 10.03.2008; 01.04.2008; 30.06.2008 in accord. with art. 2. - Issued: 28.02.2008. Made: 19.02.2008. Effect: None. Territorial extent & classification: E. General. - 4p.: 30 cm. - 978-0-11-081004-1 £3.00

The Local Government and Public Involvement in Health Act 2007 (Commencement No. 7) Order 2008 No. 2008/2434 (C. 105). - Enabling power: Local Government and Public Involvement in Health Act 2007, s. 245 (5) (6). Bringing into operation various provisions of the 2007 Act on 26.09.2008 & 03.11.2008 in accord. with art. 2. - Issued: 18.09.2008. Made: 11.09.2008. Effect: None. Territorial extent & classification: E. General. - 4p.: 30 cm. - 978-0-11-084218-9 £4.00

The Local Government and Public Involvement in Health Act 2007 Consequential Provisions Order 2008 No. 2008/526. - Enabling power: Local Government and Public Involvement in Health Act 2007, s. 243 (1). - Issued: 05.03.2008. Made: 25.02.2008. Laid: 05.03.2008. Coming into force: 30.06.2008. Effect: S.I. 2003/3006, 2005/2966 amended. Territorial extent & classification: E. General. - 2p.: 30 cm. - 978-0-11-081039-3 £3.00

The Local Involvement Networks (Amendment) Regulations 2008 No. 2008/1877. - Enabling power: Local Government and Public Involvement in Health Act 2007, s. 228 (3). - Issued: 18.07.2008. Made: 11.07.2008. Laid: 18.07.2008. Coming into force: 01.09.2008. Effect: S.I. 2008/528 amended. Territorial extent & classification: E. General. - 2p.: 30 cm. - 978-0-11-083292-0 £3.00

The Local Involvement Networks (Duty of Services-Providers to Allow Entry) Regulations 2008 No. 2008/915. - Enabling power: Local Government and Public Involvement in Health Act 2007, ss. 225 (1) to (3) (7), 229 (2). - Issued: 02.04.2008. Made: 27.03.2008. Coming into force: 01.04.2008. Effect: None. Territorial extent & classification: E. General. - Supersedes draft SI (ISBN 9780110809311) issued 18.02.2008. - 4p.: 30 cm. - 978-0-11-081313-4 £3.00

The Local Involvement Networks (Miscellaneous Amendments) Regulations 2008 No. 2008/1514. - Enabling power: National Health Service Act 2006, ss. 89 (1) (2), 94 (1), 104 (1) (2), 109 (1), 121 (1) (2), 126 (1) (2), 272 (7) (8), sch. 12, para. 3. - Issued: 17.06.2008. Made: 11.06.2008. Laid: 16.06.2008. Coming into force: 14.07.2008. Effect: S.I. 1986/975; 2004/291, 627; 2005/64, 3361, 3373; 2006/552 amended. Territorial extent & classification: E. General. - 4p.: 30 cm. - 978-0-11-081843-6 £3.00

The Local Involvement Networks Regulations 2008 No. 2008/528. - Enabling power: Health and Social Care (Community Health and Standards) Act 2003, ss. 113 (1), 175 (1) (2) & National Health Service Act 2006, ss. 13 (4), 89 (1), 94 (1), 104 (1), 109 (1), 121 (1), 126 (2), 243 (8) to (10), 244 (2), 272 (7) (8), sch. 12, paras 2, 3 & Local Government and Public Involvement in Health Act 2007, ss. 223, 224 (1), 226 (6), 228 (3) (4) (5), 229 (2), 240 (10). - Issued: 05.03.2008. Made: 25.02.2008. Laid: 05.03.2008. Coming into force: 01.04.2008. Effect: S.I. 1986/975; 2002/3007, 3038, 3048; 2003/1617, 3006; 2004/291, 627, 1768; 2005/641, 3361, 3373; 2006/552 amended. Territorial extent & classification: E. General. - 20p.: 30 cm. - With correction slip dated August 2008. - 978-0-11-081040-9 £3.50

The National Child Measurement Programme Regulations 2008 No. 2008/3080. - Enabling power: National Health Service Act 2006, ss. 7, 8, 19, 272, 273 (4), sch. 1, para. 7B. - Issued: 04.12.2008. Made: 27.11.2008. Laid: 04.12.2008. Coming into force: 05.01.2009. Effect: None. Territorial extent & classification: E. General. - 4p.: 30 cm. - 978-0-11-147087-9 £4.00

The National Health Service (Charges for Drugs and Appliances) Amendment Regulations 2008 No. 2008/2593. - Enabling power: National Health Service Act 2006, ss. 172, 182, 184, 272 (7). - Issued: 08.10.2008. Made: 02.10.2008. Laid: 08.10.2008. Coming into force: 03.11.2008. Effect: S.I. 2000/620 amended. Territorial extent & classification: E. General. - 2p.: 30 cm. - 978-0-11-084374-2 £4.00

The National Health Service (Charges for Drugs and Appliances) and (Travel Expenses and Remission of Charges) Amendment (No.2) Regulations 2008 No. 2008/1697. - Enabling power: National Health Service Act 2006, ss. 172, 182, 183, 184, 272 (7) (8). - Issued: 03.07.2008. Made: 26.06.2008. Laid: 03.07.2008. Coming into force: 01.08.2008 for regs, 1, 2, 5; 27.10.2008 for regs 3, 4. Effect: S.I. 1987/1967; 2000/620; 2003/2382 amended. Territorial extent & classification: E. General. - 4p.: 30 cm. - 978-0-11-081928-0 £3.00

The National Health Service (Charges for Drugs and Appliances) and (Travel Expenses and Remission of Charges) Amendment Regulations 2008 No. 2008/571. - Enabling power: National Health Service Act 2006, ss. 172, 174, 182, 183, 184, 272 (7) (8). - Issued: 10.03.2008. Made: 03.03.2008. Laid: 10.03.2008. Coming into force: 01.04.2008. Effect: S.I. 2000/620; 2003/2382 amended. Territorial extent & classification: E. General. - 8p.: 30 cm. - 978-0-11-081085-0 £3.00

The National Health Service (Charges to Overseas Visitors) (Amendment) Regulations 2008 No. 2008/2251. - Enabling power: National Health Service Act 2006, ss. 175, 272 (8). - Issued: 27.08.2008. Made: 20.08.2008. Laid: 27.08.2008. Coming into force: 06.10.2008. Effect: S.I. 1989/306 amended. Territorial extent & classification: E. General. - 2p.: 30 cm. - 978-0-11-083850-2 £3.00

The National Health Service Delegation of Functions to the NHS Business Services Authority (Awdurdod Gwasanaethau Busnes y GIG) (Counter Fraud and Security Management) Regulations 2008 No. 2008/1148. - Enabling power: National Health Service Act 2006, ss. 7 (1), 199 (2) to (5), 209 (4), 273 (4). - Issued: 25.04.2008. Made: 21.04.2008. Laid: 25.04.2008. Coming into force: 26.05.2008. Effect: None. Territorial extent & classification: E. General. - 8p.: 30 cm. - 978-0-11-081394-3 £3.00

The National Health Service (Dental Charges) Amendment Regulations 2008 No. 2008/547. - Enabling power: National Health Service Act 2006, ss. 176, 272 (7). - Issued: 06.03.2008. Made: 27.02.2008. Laid: 06.03.2008. Coming into force: 01.04.2008. Effect: S.I. 2005/3477 amended. Territorial extent & classification: E. General. - 2p.: 30 cm. - 978-0-11-081074-4 £3.00

The National Health Service (Directions by Strategic Health Authorities to Primary Care Trusts Regarding Arrangements for Involvement) (No. 2) Regulations 2008 No. 2008/2677. - Enabling power: National Health Service Act 2006, ss. 7 (1), 8 (1), 242B, 272 (7), 273 (4). - Issued: 23.10.2008. Made: 08.10.2008. Laid: 10.10.2008. Coming into force: 13.10.2008 for purposes of reg. 7; 03.11.2008 for all other purposes. Effect: S.I. 2002/2375 amended & 2008/2496 revoked (13.10.2008). Territorial extent & classification: E. General. - This Statutory Instrument has been made in consequence of a defect in SI 2008/2496 (ISBN 9780110842554) and is being issued free of charge to all known recipients of that Statutory Instrument. This S.I. is a corrected reprint and replaces all previous copies. - 8p.: 30 cm. - 978-0-11-084542-5 £5.00

The National Health Service (Directions by Strategic Health Authorities to Primary Care Trusts Regarding Arrangements for Involvement) Regulations 2008 No. 2008/2496. - Enabling power: National Health Service Act 2006, ss. 7 (1), 8 (1), 242B, 272 (7), 273 (4). - Issued: 23.09.2008. Made: 14.09.2008. Laid: 23.09.2008. Coming into force: 03.11.2008. Effect: S.I. 2002/2375 amended. Territorial extent & classification: E. General. - Revoked by S.I. 2008/2677 (ISBN 9780110845425). - 4p.: 30 cm. - 978-0-11-084255-4 £4.00

The National Health Service (Functions of Strategic Health Authorities and Primary Care Trusts and Administration Arrangements) (England) (Amendment) Regulations 2008 No. 2008/224. - Enabling power: National Health Service Act 2006, ss. 7 (1), 8, 272 (7), 273 (1) (4). - Issued: 11.02.2008. Made: 04.02.2008. Laid: 11.02.2008. Coming into force: 01.04.2008. Effect: S.I. 2002/2375 amended. Territorial extent & classification: E. General. - 2p.: 30 cm. - 978-0-11-080906-9 £3.00

The National Health Service (Optical Charges and Payments) Amendment (No. 2) Regulations 2008 No. 2008/1657. - Enabling power: National Health Service Act 1977, s. 126 (4), sch. 12, paras 2A, 2B. - Issued: 01.07.2008. Made: 26.06.2008. Laid: 01.07.2008. Coming into force: 01.08.2008. Effect: S.I. 1997/818 amended. Territorial extent & classification: E. General. - 8p.: 30 cm. - 978-0-11-081915-0 £3.00

The National Health Service (Optical Charges and Payments) Amendment Regulations 2008 No. 2008/553. - Enabling power: National Health Service Act 1977, s. 126 (4), sch. 12, para. 2A. - Issued: 06.03.2008. Made: 27.02.2008. Laid: 06.03.2008. Coming into force: 01.04.2008. Effect: S.I. 1997/818 amended. Territorial extent & classification: E. General. - 4p.: 30 cm. - 978-0-11-081076-8 £3.00

The National Health Service (Performers Lists) Amendment and Transitional Provisions Regulations 2008 No. 2008/1187. - Enabling power: National Health Service Act 1977, ss. 28X, 126 (4). - Issued: 08.05.2008. Made: 28.04.2008. Laid: 06.05.2008. Coming into force: 01.08.2006. Effect: S.I. 2004/585 amended. Territorial extent & classification: E. General. - Revoked by S.I. 2009/462 (C.31) (ISBN 9780111475218). - 12p.: 30 cm. - 978-0-11-081427-8 £3.00

The National Health Service (Pharmaceutical Services) (Amendment) Regulations 2008 No. 2008/683. - Enabling power: National Health Service Act 2006, ss. 126, 129, 164 (6) (7), 272 (7) (8). - Issued: 14.03.2008. Made: 06.03.2008. Laid: 14.03.2008. Coming into force: 21.04.2008. Effect: S.I. 2005/641 amended. Territorial extent & classification: E. General. - 4p.: 30 cm. - 978-0-11-081184-0 £3.00

The National Health Service (Travel Expenses and Remission of Charges) Amendment (No. 2) Regulations 2008 No. 2008/2868. - Enabling power: National Health Service Act 2006, ss. 182, 183, 184, 272 (7). - Issued: 10.11.2008. Made: 05.11.2008. Laid: 10.11.2008. Coming into force: 01.12.2008. Effect: S.I. 2003/2382 modified. Territorial extent & classification: E. General. - 8p.: 30 cm. - 978-0-11-084973-7 £5.00

The National Health Service (Travel Expenses and Remission of Charges) Amendment Regulations 2008 No. 2008/843. - Enabling power: National Health Service Act 2006, ss. 182, 183 (a), 184 (1) (2), 272 (7). - Issued: 02.04.2008. Made: 26.03.2008. Laid: 02.04.2008. Coming into force: 01.05.2008. Effect: S.I. 2003/2382 modified. Territorial extent & classification: E. General. - 2p.: 30 cm. - 978-0-11-081292-2 £3.00

The National Health Service Trusts (Originating Capital) Order 2008 No. 2008/727. - Enabling power: National Health Service Act 2006, sch. 5, para. 1 (1). - Issued: 18.03.2008. Made: 12.03.2008. Coming into force: 31.03.2008. Effect: None. Territorial extent & classification: E. General. - 2p.: 30 cm. - 978-0-11-081236-6 £3.00

The National Information Governance Board for Health and Social Care Regulations 2008 No. 2008/2558. - Enabling power: National Health Service Act 2006, ss. 250C, 272 (7) (8). - Issued: 06.10.2008. Made: 30.09.2008. Laid: 06.10.2008. Coming into force: 27.10.2008. Effect: None. Territorial extent & classification: E. General. - With correction slip dated October 2009 correcting the title and other passages. - 8p.: 30 cm. - 978-0-11-084338-4 £5.00

The NHS Direct National Health Service Trust (Establishment) Amendment Order 2008 No. 2008/2769. - Enabling power: National Health Service Act 2006, ss. 25 (1), 272 (8), 273 (1), sch. 4, para. 5 (1). - Issued: 23.10.2008. Made: 20.10.2008. Coming into force: 31.10.2008. Effect: S.I. 2007/478 amended. Territorial extent & classification: E. General. - 2p.: 30 cm. - 978-0-11-084693-4 £4.00

The NHS Foundation Trusts (Trust Funds: Appointment of Trustees) Amendment Order 2008 No. 2008/1902. - Enabling power: National Health Service Act 2006, ss. 51 (1) (2), 64 (5) (6), 273 (1). - Issued: 21.07.2008. Made: 17.07.2008. Coming into force: 01.08.2008. Effect: S.I. 2000/212; 2007/1766 amended. Territorial extent & classification: E. General. - 2p.: 30 cm. - 978-0-11-083399-6 £3.00

The NHS Professionals Special Health Authority (Establishment and Constitution) (Amendment) Order 2008 No. 2008/558. - Enabling power: National Health Service Act 2006, ss. 28 (1) (2) (4), 272 (7), 273 (1). - Issued: 07.03.2008. Made: 28.02.2008. Laid: 07.03.2008. Coming into force: 01.04.2008. Effect: S.I. 2003/3059 amended. Territorial extent & classification: E. General. - 2p.: 30 cm. - 978-0-11-081081-2 £3.00

The North Bristol National Health Service Trust (Transfer of Trust Property) Order 2008 No. 2008/440. - Enabling power: National Health Service Act 2006, ss. 213, 217 (2), 272 (8). - Issued: 27.02.2008. Made: 19.02.2008. Laid: 27.02.2008. Coming into force: 01.04.2008. Effect: None. Territorial extent & classification: E. General. - 2p.: 30 cm. - 978-0-11-080996-0 £3.00

The North Cumbria Acute Hospitals National Health Service Trust (Change of Name) (Establishment) Amendment Order 2008 No. 2008/1775. - Enabling power: National Health Service Act 2006, ss. 25 (1), 272 (8), 273 (1), sch. 4, para. 5 (1). - Issued: 10.07.2008. Made: 03.07.2008. Coming into force: 01.08.2008. Effect: S.I. 2001/656 amended. Territorial extent & classification: E. General. - 4p.: 30 cm. - 978-0-11-081989-1 £3.00

The North Tees Teaching Primary Care Trust (Change of Name) Order 2008 No. 2008/1812. - Enabling power: National Health Service Act 2006, ss. 18 (2), 272 (7) (8), 273 (1), sch. 3, para. 13 (1). - Issued: 14.07.2008. Made: 08.07.2008. Coming into force: 01.08.2008. Effect: S.I. 2001/500 amended. Territorial extent & classification: E. General. - 2p.: 30 cm. - 978-0-11-083093-3 £3.00

The Northumberland, Tyne and Wear National Health Service Trust (Transfer of Trust Property) Order 2008 No. 2008/412. - Enabling power: National Health Service Act 2006, ss. 213, 217 (2), 272 (8). - Issued: 26.02.2008. Made: 19.02.2008. Laid: 26.02.2008. Coming into force: 31.03.2008. Effect: None. Territorial extent & classification: E. General. - 2p.: 30 cm. - 978-0-11-080974-8 £3.00

The Primary Care Trusts and National Health Service Trusts (Membership and Procedure) Amendment Regulations 2008 No. 2008/1269. - Enabling power: National Health Service Act 2006, s. 272 (7) (8), sch. 3, para. 4 (1), sch. 4, para 4 (1). - Issued: 13.05.2008. Made: 06.05.2008. Laid: 13.05.2008. Coming into force: 16.06.2008. Effect: S.I. 1990/2024; 2000/89 amended. Territorial extent & classification: E. General. - 8p.: 30 cm. - 978-0-11-081441-4 £3.00

The Primary Ophthalmic Services Amendment, Transitional and Consequential Provisions Regulations 2008 No. 2008/1700. - Enabling power: National Health Service Act 1977, ss. 16CD, 28WE, 28X (2A). - Issued: 03.07.2008. Made: 28.06.2008. Laid: 03.07.2008. Coming into force: 01.08.2008. Effect: 18 SIs amended and S.I. 1986/975; 1988/486; 1989/395, 1175; 1990/1051; 1995/558; 1999/2714; 2005/3491 revoked. Territorial extent & classification: E. General. - 16p.: 30 cm. - 978-0-11-081931-0 £3.00

The Primary Ophthalmic Services and National Health Service (Optical Charges and Payments) Amendment Regulations 2008 No. 2008/2449. - Enabling power: National Health Service Act 2006, ss. 115 (2), 116 (2), 180 (1) (2) (5). - Issued: 22.09.2008. Made: 16.09.2008. Laid: 22.09.2008. Coming into force: 27.10.2008. Effect: S.I. 1997/818; 2008/1186 amended. Territorial extent & classification: E. General. - 4p.: 30 cm. - 978-0-11-084253-0 £4.00

The Primary Ophthalmic Services Regulations 2008 No. 2008/1186. - Enabling power: National Health Service Act 1977, ss. 16CD (1) (2) (3), 16CE, 126 (4). - Issued: 06.05.2008. Made: 28.04.2008. Laid: 06.05.2008. Coming into force: 01.08.2008. Effect: None. Territorial extent & classification: E. General. - 8p.: 30 cm. - 978-0-11-081425-4 £3.00

The Primary Ophthalmic Services Transitional Provisions Regulations 2008 No. 2008/1209. - Enabling power: Health Act 2006, ss. 43, 79 (3). - Issued: 06.05.2008. Made: 28.04.2008. Laid: 06.05.2008. Coming into force: 03.06.2008. Effect: None. Territorial extent & classification: E. General. - 4p.: 30 cm. - 978-0-11-081420-9 £3.00

The South Devon Healthcare NHS Foundation Trust (Transfer of Trust Property) Order 2008 No. 2008/2784. - Enabling power: National Health Service Act 2006, ss. 213, 217 (2), 272 (8). - Issued: 28.10.2008. Made: 23.10.2008. Laid: 28.10.2008. Coming into force: 01.12.2008. Effect: None. Territorial extent & classification: E. General. - 2p.: 30 cm. - 978-0-11-084731-3 £4.00

The Surrey Primary Care Trust (Transfer of Trust Property) Order 2008 No. 2008/415. - Enabling power: National Health Service Act 2006, ss. 213, 217 (2), 272 (8). - Issued: 26.02.2008. Made: 19.02.2008. Laid: 26.02.2008. Coming into force: 31.03.2008. Effect: None. Territorial extent & classification: E. General. - 2p.: 30 cm. - 978-0-11-080973-1 £3.00

The Trustees for the Hammersmith Hospitals National Health Service Trust (Transfer of Trust Property) Order 2008 No. 2008/895. - Enabling power: National Health Service Act 2006, ss. 213, 217 (2), 272 (8). - Issued: 02.04.2008. Made: 26.03.2008. Laid: 02.04.2008. Coming into force: 01.05.2008. Effect: None. Territorial extent & classification: E. General. - 2p.: 30 cm. - 978-0-11-081304-2 £3.00

The Trustees for the St Mary's National Health Service Trust (Transfer of Trust Property) Order 2008 No. 2008/894. - Enabling power: National Health Service Act 2006, ss. 213, 217 (2), 272 (8). - Issued: 02.04.2008. Made: 26.03.2008. Laid: 02.04.2008. Coming into force: 01.05.2008. Effect: None. Territorial extent & classification: E. General. - 2p.: 30 cm. - 978-0-11-081301-1 £3.00

National Health Service, England and Wales

The Health Service Branded Medicines (Control of Prices and Supply of Information) (No. 2) Regulations 2008 No. 2008/3258. - Enabling power: National Health Service Act 2006, ss. 261 (7), 262 (1), 263 to 265, 266 (1) (2), 272 (7) (8). - Issued: 23.12.2008. Made: 17.12.2008. Laid: 23.12.2008. Coming into force: 01.02.2009. Effect: S.I. 2007/1320 amended & S.I. 2008/1938 revoked. Territorial extent & classification: E/W/S/NI. General. - 8p.: 30 cm. - 978-0-11-147224-8 £5.00

The Health Service Branded Medicines (Control of Prices and Supply of Information) Regulations 2008 No. 2008/1938. - Enabling power: National Health Service Act 2006, ss. 261 (7), 262 (1), 263 to 265, 266 (1) (2), 272 (7) (8). - Issued: 24.07.2008. Made: 19.07.2008. Laid: 21.07.2008. Coming into force: 01.09.2008. Effect: S.I. 2007/1320 amended. Territorial extent & classification: E/W/S/NI. General. - Revoked by S.I. 2008/3258 (ISBN 9780111472248). - 8p.: 30 cm. - 978-0-11-083521-1 £3.00

The National Health Service Pension Scheme (Additional Voluntary Contributions) and National Health Service (Injury Benefits and Compensation for Premature Retirement) Amendment Regulations 2008 No. 2008/655. - Enabling power: Superannuation Act 1972, ss. 10 (1) (2), 12 (1) (2), 24 (1) (3) (4), sch. 3. - Issued: 27.03.2008. Made: 11.03.2008. Laid: 11.03.2008. Coming into force: 01.04.2008. Effect: S.I. 1995/866; 2000/619, 2002/1311 amended. Territorial extent & classification: E/W. General. - 12p.: 30 cm. - 978-0-11-081244-1 £3.00

The National Health Service Pension Scheme (Amendment) Regulations 2008 No. 2008/654. - Enabling power: Superannuation Act 1972, ss. 10 (1) (2), 12 (1) (2), sch. 3. - Issued: 27.03.2008. Made: 11.03.2008. Laid: 11.03.2008. Coming into force: 01.04.2008. Effect: S.I. 1995/300 amended. Territorial extent & classification: E/W. General. - 64p.: 30 cm. - 978-0-11-081246-5 £10.50

The National Health Service Pension Scheme and Injury Benefits (Amendment) Regulations 2008 No. 2008/2263. - Enabling power: Superannuation Act 1972, ss. 10 (1) (2), 12 (1) (2) (4), sch. 3. - Issued: 03.09.2008. Made: 22.08.2008. Laid: 03.09.2008. Coming into force: In accord. with reg. 1 (2). Effect: S.I. 1995/300, 866; 2008/653 amended. Territorial extent & classification: E/W. General. - 44p.: 30 cm. - 978-0-11-083858-8 £7.50

The National Health Service Pension Scheme (Correction to Amendment) Regulations 2008 No. 2008/906. - Enabling power: Superannuation Act 1972, ss. 10 (1) (2), 12 (1) (2), sch. 3. - Issued: 02.04.2008. Made: 26.03.2008. Laid: 27.03.2008. Coming into force: 31.03.2008. Effect: S.I. 2008/654 amended. Territorial extent & classification: E/W. General. - This Statutory Instrument has been made in consequence of a defect in S.I. 2008/654 and is being issued free of charge to all known recipients of that Statutory Instrument. - 2p.: 30 cm. - 978-0-11-081302-8 £3.00

The National Health Service Pension Scheme Regulations 2008 No. 2008/653. - Enabling power: Superannuation Act 1972, ss. 10 (1) (2), 12 (1) (2), sch. 3. - Issued: 27.03.2008. Made: 11.03.2008. Laid: 11.03.2008. Coming into force: 01.04.2008. Effect: None. Territorial extent & classification: E/W. General. - 208p.: 30 cm. - 978-0-11-081248-9 £26.00

The Personal Injuries (NHS Charges) (Amounts) Amendment Regulations 2008 No. 2008/252. - Enabling power: Health and Social Care (Community Health and Standards) Act 2003, ss. 153 (2) (5), 195 (1) (2). - Issued: 13.02.2008. Made: 06.02.2008. Laid: 13.02.2008. Coming into force: 01.04.2008. Effect: S.I. 2007/115 amended. Territorial extent & classification: E/W. General. - 2p.: 30 cm. - 978-0-11-080927-4 £3.00

National Health Service, Scotland

The Health Act 2006 (Commencement No. 4) Order 2008 No. 2008/1147 (C.50). - Enabling power: Health Act 2006, s. 83 (7) (8). Bringing into operation various provisions of the 2006 Act on 22.04.2008; 28.04.2008; 01.05.2008. - Issued: 25.04.2008. Made: 21.04.2008. Effect: None. Territorial extent & classification: E/S [parts E. only]. General. - 4p.: 30 cm. - 978-0-11-081396-7 £3.00

The Health Service Branded Medicines (Control of Prices and Supply of Information) (No. 2) Regulations 2008 No. 2008/3258. - Enabling power: National Health Service Act 2006, ss. 261 (7), 262 (1), 263 to 265, 266 (1) (2), 272 (7) (8). - Issued: 23.12.2008. Made: 17.12.2008. Laid: 23.12.2008. Coming into force: 01.02.2009. Effect: S.I. 2007/1320 amended & S.I. 2008/1938 revoked. Territorial extent & classification: E/W/S/NI. General. - 8p.: 30 cm. - 978-0-11-147224-8 £5.00

The Health Service Branded Medicines (Control of Prices and Supply of Information) Regulations 2008 No. 2008/1938. - Enabling power: National Health Service Act 2006, ss. 261 (7), 262 (1), 263 to 265, 266 (1) (2), 272 (7) (8). - Issued: 24.07.2008. Made: 19.07.2008. Laid: 21.07.2008. Coming into force: 01.09.2008. Effect: S.I. 2007/1320 amended. Territorial extent & classification: E/W/S/NI. General. - Revoked by S.I. 2008/3258 (ISBN 9780111472248). - 8p.: 30 cm. - 978-0-11-083521-1 £3.00

National Health Service, Wales

The Abertawe Bro Morgannwg University National Health Service Trust (Establishment) Order 2008 No. 2008/716 (W.75). - Enabling power: National Health Service (Wales) Act 2006, s. 18 (1) (2), sch. 3, paras 5, 7 & Welsh Language Act 1993, s. 25. - Issued: 28.03.2008. Made: 11.03.2008. Coming into force: 12.03.2008. Effect: None. Territorial extent & classification: W. General. - Revoked by W.S.I. 2009/1306 (W.117) (ISBN 9780110919966). - In English and Welsh. Welsh title: Gorchymyn Ymddiriedolaeth Brifysgol Gwasanaeth Iechyd Gwladol Abertawe Bro Morgannwg (Sefydlu) 2008. - 4p.: 30 cm. - 978-0-11-091773-3 £3.00

The Abertawe Bro Morgannwg University National Health Service Trust (Transfer of Property, Rights and Liabilities) Order 2008 No. 2008/2438 (W.211). - Enabling power: National Health Service (Wales) Act 2006, s. 203 (9) (10), sch. 3, para 9 (1). - Issued: 01.10.2008. Made: 15.09.2008. Coming into force: 16.09.2008. Effect: None. Territorial extent & classification: W. General. - In English and Welsh. Welsh title: Gorchymyn Ymddiriedolaeth Gwasanaeth Iechyd Gwladol Prifysgol Abertawe Bro Morgannwg (Trosglwyddo Eiddo, Hawliau a Rhwymedigaethau) 2008. - 4p.: 30 cm. - 978-0-11-091879-2 £4.00

The Bro Morgannwg National Health Service Trust (Dissolution) Order 2008 No. 2008/939 (W.99). - Enabling power: National Health Service (Wales) Act 2006, s. 204 (1), sch. 3, para. 28 (1). - Issued: 22.04.2008. Made: 28.03.2008. Coming into force: 01.04.2008. Effect: S.I. 2000/1076 (W.70) revoked. Territorial extent & classification: W. General. - In English and Welsh. Welsh title: Gorchymyn Ymddiriedolaeth Gwasanaeth Iechyd Gwladol Bro Morgannwg (Diddymu) 2008. - 4p.: 30 cm. - 978-0-11-091756-6 £3.00

The Bro Morgannwg National Health Service Trust (Transfer of Staff, Property, Rights and Liabilities) Order 2008 No. 2008/927 (W.90). - Enabling power: National Health Service (Wales) Act 2006, s. 203 (9) (10), sch. 3, para. 29. - Issued: 22.04.2008. Made: 28.03.2008. Coming into force: 01.04.2008. Effect: None. Territorial extent & classification: W. General. - In English and Welsh. Welsh title: Gorchymyn Ymddiriedolaeth Gwasanaeth Iechyd Gwladol Bro Morgannwg (Trosglwyddo Staff, Eiddo, Hawliau a Rhwymedigaethau) 2008. - 8p.: 30 cm. - 978-0-11-091805-1 £3.00

The Carmarthenshire National Health Service Trust (Dissolution) Order 2008 No. 2008/933 (W.93). - Enabling power: National Health Service (Wales) Act 2006, s. 204 (1), sch. 3, para. 28 (1). - Issued: 28.04.2008. Made: 28.03.2008. Coming into force: 01.04.2008. Effect: S.I. 1998/3316 revoked. Territorial extent & classification: W. General. - In English and Welsh. Welsh title: Gorchymyn Ymddiriedolaeth Gwasanaeth Iechyd Gwladol Sir Gaerfyrddin (Diddymu) 2008. - 4p.: 30 cm. - 978-0-11-091808-2 £3.00

The Carmarthenshire National Health Service Trust (Transfer of Staff, Property, Rights and Liabilities) Order 2008 No. 2008/931 (W.91). - Enabling power: National Health Service (Wales) Act 2006, s. 203 (9) (10), sch. 3, para 29. - Issued: 22.04.2008. Made: 28.03.2008. Coming into force: 01.04.2008. Effect: None. Territorial extent & classification: W. General. - In English and Welsh. Welsh title: Gorchymyn Ymddiriedolaeth Gwasanaeth Iechyd Gwladol Sir Gaerfyrddin (Trosglwyddo Staff, Eiddo, Hawliau a Rhwymedigaethau) 2008. - 8p.: 30 cm. - 978-0-11-091801-3 £3.00

The Ceredigion and Mid Wales National Health Service Trust (Dissolution) Order 2008 No. 2008/934 (W.94). - Enabling power: National Health Service (Wales) Act 2006, s. 204 (1), sch. 3, para. 28 (1). - Issued: 22.04.2008. Made: 28.03.2008. Coming into force: 01.04.2008. Effect: S.I. 1992/2735 revoked. Territorial extent & classification: W. General. - In English and Welsh. Welsh title: Gorchymyn Ymddiriedolaeth Gwasanaeth Iechyd Gwladol Ceredigion a Chanolbarth Cymru (Diddymu) 2008. - 4p.: 30 cm. - 978-0-11-091759-7 £3.00

The Ceredigion and Mid Wales National Health Service Trust (Transfer of Staff, Property, Rights and Liabilities) Order 2008 No. 2008/935 (W.95). - Enabling power: National Health Service (Wales) Act 2006, s. 203 (9) (10), sch. 3, para. 29. - Issued: 22.04.2008. Made: 28.03.2008. Coming into force: 01.04.2008. Effect: None. Territorial extent & classification: W. General. - In English and Welsh. Welsh title: Gorchymyn Ymddiriedolaeth Gwasanaeth Iechyd Gwladol Ceredigion a Chanolbarth Cymru (Trosglwyddo Staff, Eiddo, Hawliau a Rhwymedigaethau) 2008. - 8p.: 30 cm. - 978-0-11-091800-6 £3.00

The Conwy and Denbighshire National Health Service Trust (Dissolution) Order 2008 No. 2008/1719 (W.165). - Enabling power: National Health Service (Wales) Act 2006, s. 204 (1), sch. 3, para 28 (1). - Issued: 16.07.2008. Made: 30.06.2008. Coming into force: 01.07.2008. Effect: S.I. 1998/3317 revoked. Territorial extent & classification: W. General. - In English and Welsh. Welsh title: Gorchymyn Ymddiriedolaeth Gwasanaeth Iechyd Gwladol Conwy a Sir Ddinbych (Diddymu) 2008. - 4p.: 30 cm. - 978-0-11-091852-5 £3.00

The Conwy and Denbighshire National Health Service Trust (Transfer of Staff, Property, Rights and Liabilities) Order 2008 No. 2008/1720 (W.166). - Enabling power: National Health Service (Wales) Act 2006, s. 203 (9) (10), sch. 3, para 29. - Issued: 21.07.2008. Made: 30.06.2008. Coming into force: 01.07.2008. Effect: None. Territorial extent & classification: W. General. - In English and Welsh. Welsh title: Gorchymyn Ymddiriedolaeth Gwasanaeth Iechyd Gwladol Conwy a Sir Ddinbych (Trosglwyddo Staff, Eiddo, Hawliau a Rhwymedigaethau) 2008. - 8p.: 30 cm. - 978-0-11-091820-4 £3.00

The Cwm Taf National Health Service Trust (Establishment) Order 2008 No. 2008/717 (W.76). - Enabling power: National Health Service (Wales) Act 2006, s. 18 (1) (2), sch. 3, paras 5, 7 & Welsh Language Act 1993, s. 25. - Issued: 28.03.2008. Made: 11.03.2008. Coming into force: 12.03.2008. Effect: None. Territorial extent & classification: W. General. - Revoked by W.S.I. 2009/1306 (W.117) (ISBN 9780110919966). - In English and Welsh. Welsh title: Gorchymyn Ymddiriedolaeth Gwasanaeth Iechyd Gwladol Cwm Taf (Sefydlu) 2008. - 4p.: 30 cm. - 978-0-11-091771-9 £3.00

The Health Act 2006 (Commencement No. 2) (Wales) Order 2008 No. 2008/3171 (W.284) (C.144). - Enabling power: Health Act 2006, s. 83 (5) (a). Bringing into operation various provisions of the 2006 Act on 13.12.2008. - Issued: 09.01.2009. Made: 12.12.2008. Effect: None. Territorial extent & classification: W. General. - In English and Welsh. Welsh title: Gorchymyn Deddf Iechyd 2006 (Cychwyn Rhif 2) (Cymru) 2008. - 12p.: 30 cm. - 978-0-11-091921-8 £5.00

The Hywel Dda National Health Service Trust (Establishment) Order 2008 No. 2008/712 (W.73). - Enabling power: National Health Service (Wales) Act 2006, s. 18 (1) (2), sch. 3, paras 5, 7 and Welsh Language Act 1993, s. 25. - Issued: 28.03.2008. Made: 11.03.2008. Coming into force: 12.03.2008. Effect: None. Territorial extent & classification: W. General. - Revoked by W.S.I. 2009/1306 (W.117) (ISBN 9780110919966). - In English and Welsh. Welsh title: Gorchymyn Ymddiriedolaeth Gwasanaeth Iechyd Gwladol Cwm Taf (Sefydlu) 2008. - 4p.: 30 cm. - 978-0-11-091772-6 £3.00

The National Health Service (Charges to Overseas Visitors) (Amendment) (Wales) Regulations 2008 No. 2008/2364 (W.203). - Enabling power: National Health Service (Wales) Act 2006, ss. 124, 203 (10). - Issued: 19.09.2008. Made: 04.09.2008. Laid before the National Assembly for Wales: 08.09.2008. Coming into force: 01.10.2008. Effect: S.I. 1989/306 amended in relation to Wales. Territorial extent & classification: W. General. - In English and Welsh. Welsh title: Rheoliadau Gwasanaeth Iechyd Gwladol (Ffioedd Ymwelwyr Tramor) (Diwygio) (Cymru) 2008. - 4p.: 30 cm. - 978-0-11-091874-7 £4.00

The National Health Service (General Medical Services Contracts) (Wales) (Amendment) Regulations 2008 No. 2008/1329 (W.138). - Enabling power: National Health Service (Wales) Act 2006, ss. 47 (1), 203 (9) (10). - Issued: 09.06.2008. Made: 19.05.2008. Laid before the National Assembly for Wales: 21.05.2008. Coming into force: 16.06.2008. Effect: S.I. 2004/478 (W.48) amended. Territorial extent & classification: W. General. - In English and Welsh. Welsh title: Rheoliadau'r Gwasanaeth Iechyd Gwladol (Contractau Gwasanaethau Meddygol Cyffredinol) (Cymru) (Diwygio) 2008. - 4p.: 30 cm. - 978-0-11-091788-7 £3.00

The National Health Service (General Ophthalmic Services) and (Optical Charges and Payments) (Amendment) (Wales) Regulations 2008 No. 2008/2552 (W. 222). - Enabling power: National Health Service (Wales) Act 2006, ss. 71, 128, 129, 203 (9) (10). - Issued: 17.10.2008. Made: 29.09.2008. Laid before the National Assembly for Wales: 30.09.2008. Coming into force: 27.10.2008. Effect: S.I. 1986/975; 1997/818 amended in relation to Wales. Territorial extent & classification: W. General. - In English and Welsh. Welsh title: Rheoliadau'r Gwasanaeth Iechyd Gwladol (Gwasanaethau Offthalmig Cyffredinol) a (Ffioedd a Thaliadau Optegol) (Diwygio) (Cymru) 2008. - 8p.: 30 cm. - 978-0-11-091887-7 £5.00

The National Health Service (Optical Charges and Payments) (Amendment) (Wales) Regulations 2008 No. 2008/660 (W.70). - Enabling power: National Health Service (Wales) Act 2006, ss. 129, 203 (9) (10). - Issued: 31.03.2008. Made: 10.03.2008. Laid before the National Assembly for Wales: 11.03.2008. Coming into force: 01.04.2008. Effect: S.I. 1997/818 amended in relation to Wales. Territorial extent & classification: W. General. - In English and Welsh. Welsh title: Rheoliadau'r Gwasanaeth Iechyd Gwladol (Ffioedd a Thaliadau Optegol) (Diwygio) (Cymru) 2008. - 8p.: 30 cm. - 978-0-11-091742-9 £3.00

The National Health Service (Optical Charges and Payments) and (General Ophthalmic Services) (Amendment) (Wales) Regulations 2008 No. 2008/577 (W.56). - Enabling power: National Health Service (Wales) Act 2006, ss. 71, 76, 77, 128, 129, 203 (9) (10). - Issued: 26.03.2008. Made: 03.03.2008. Laid before the National Assembly for Wales: 04.03.2008. Coming into force: 28.03.2007. Effect: S.I. 1986/975; 1997/818 amended in relation to Wales. Territorial extent & classification: W. General. - In English and Welsh. Welsh title: Rheoliadau'r Gwasanaeth Iechyd Gwladol (Ffioedd a Thaliadau Optegol) a (Gwasanaethau Offthalmig Cyffredinol) (Diwygio) (Cymru) 2008. - 4p.: 30 cm. - 978-0-11-091766-5 £3.00

The National Health Service (Primary Medical Services) and (Performers Lists) (Miscellaneous Amendments) (Wales) Regulations 2008 No. 2008/1425 (W.147). - Enabling power: National Health Service (Wales) Act 2006, ss. 47, 49, 63, 203 (9) (10). - Issued: 19.06.2008. Made: 03.06.2008. Laid before the National Assembly for Wales: 04.06.2008. Coming into force: 01.07.2008. Effect: S.I. 2004/478 (W.48), 1020 (W.117) amended. Territorial extent & classification: W. General. - In English and Welsh. Welsh title: Rheoliadau'r Gwasanaeth Iechyd Gwladol (Gwasanaethau Meddygol Sylfaenol) a (Rhestri Cyflawnwyr) (Diwygiadau Amrywiol) (Cymru) 2008. - 12p.: 30 cm. - 978-0-11-091795-5 £3.00

The National Health Service (Travelling Expenses and Remission of Charges) (Wales) (Amendment) (No. 2) Regulations 2008 No. 2008/2568 (W.226). - Enabling power: National Health Service (Wales) Act 2006, ss. 130, 131, 132, 203 (9) (10). - Issued: 24.10.2008. Made: 01.10.2008. Laid before the National Assembly for Wales: 02.10.2008. Coming into force: 27.10.2008. Effect: S.I. 2007/1104 (W.116) amended. Territorial extent & classification: W. General. - In English and Welsh. Welsh title: Rheoliadau'r Gwasanaeth Iechyd Gwladol (Treuliau Teithio a Pheidio â Chodi Tâl) (Cymru) (Diwygio) (Rhif 2) 2008. - 8p.: 30 cm. - 978-0-11-091858-7 £5.00

National Health Service, Wales

The National Health Service (Travelling Expenses and Remission of Charges) (Wales) (Amendment) Regulations 2008 No. 2008/1480 (W.153). - Enabling power: National Health Service (Wales) Act 2006, ss. 130, 131, 132, 203 (9) (10). - Issued: 23.06.2008. Made: 09.06.2008. Laid before the National Assembly for Wales: 10.06.2008. Coming into force: 01.07.2008. Effect: S.I. 2007/1104 (W.116) amended. Territorial extent & classification: W. General. - In English and Welsh. Welsh title: Rheoliadau'r Gwasanaeth Iechyd Gwladol (Treuliau Teithio a Pheidio â Chodi Tâl) (Cymru) (Diwygio) 2008. - 8p.: 30 cm. - 978-0-11-091796-2 £3.00

The North East Wales National Health Service Trust (Dissolution) Order 2008 No. 2008/1717 (W.164). - Enabling power: National Health Service (Wales) Act 2006, s. 204 (1), sch. 3, para. 28 (1). - Issued: 16.07.2008. Made: 30.06.2008. Coming into force: 01.07.2008. Effect: S.I 1998/3320 revoked. Territorial extent & classification: W. General. - In English and Welsh. Welsh title: Gorchymyn Ymddiriedolaeth Gwasanaeth Iechyd Gwladol Gogledd-ddwyrain Cymru (Diddymu) 2008. - 4p.: 30 cm. - 978-0-11-091851-8 £3.00

The North East Wales National Health Service Trust (Transfer of Staff, Property, Rights and Liabilities) Order 2008 No. 2008/1721 (W.167). - Enabling power: National Health Service (Wales) Act 2006, s. 203 (9) (10), sch. 3, para 29. - Issued: 16.07.2008. Made: 30.06.2008. Coming into force: 01.07.2008. Effect: None. Territorial extent & classification: W. General. - In English and Welsh. Welsh title: Gorchymyn Ymddiriedolaeth Gwasanaeth Iechyd Gwladol Gogledd-ddwyrain Cymru (Trosglwyddo Staff, Eiddo, Hawliau a Rhwymedigaethau) 2008. - 12p.: 30 cm. - 978-0-11-091850-1 £3.00

The North Glamorgan National Health Service Trust (Dissolution) Order 2008 No. 2008/940 (W.100). - Enabling power: National Health Service (Wales) Act 2006, s. 204 (1), sch. 3, para. 28 (1). - Issued: 22.04.2008. Made: 28.03.2008. Coming into force: 01.04.2008. Effect: S.I 1996/259 revoked. Territorial extent & classification: W. General. - In English and Welsh. Welsh title: Gorchymyn Ymddiriedolaeth Gwasanaeth Iechyd Gwladol Gogledd Morgannwg (Diddymu) 2008. - 4p.: 30 cm. - 978-0-11-091755-9 £3.00

The North Glamorgan National Health Service Trust (Transfer of Staff, Property, Rights and Liabilities) Order 2008 No. 2008/922 (W.87). - Enabling power: National Health Service (Wales) Act 2006, s. 203 (9) (10), sch. 3, para. 29. - Issued: 22.04.2008. Made: 28.03.2008. Coming into force: 01.04.2008. Effect: None. Territorial extent & classification: W. General. - In English and Welsh. Welsh title: Gorchymyn Ymddiriedolaeth Gwasanaeth Iechyd Gwladol Gogledd Morgannwg (Trosglwyddo Staff, Eiddo, Hawliau a Rhwymedigaethau) 2008. - 8p.: 30 cm. - 978-0-11-091802-0 £3.00

The North Wales National Health Service Trust (Establishment) Order 2008 No. 2008/1648 (W.160). - Enabling power: National Health Service (Wales) Act 2006, s. 18 (1) (2), sch. 3, paras 5, 7 & Welsh Language Act 1993, s. 25. - Issued: 07.07.2008. Made: 24.06.2008. Coming into force: 25.06.2008. Effect: None. Territorial extent & classification: W. General. - Revoked by W.S.I. 2009/1306 (W.117) (ISBN 9780110919966). - In English and Welsh. Welsh title: Gorchymyn Ymddiriedolaeth Gwasanaeth Iechyd Gwladol Gogledd Cymru (Sefydlu) 2008. - 4p.: 30 cm. - 978-0-11-091839-6 £3.00

The North Wales National Health Service Trust (Transfer of Property, Rights and Liabilities) Order 2008 No. 2008/2443 (W.215). - Enabling power: National Health Service (Wales) Act 2006, s. 203 (9) (10), sch. 3, para. 9 (1). - Issued: 01.10.2008. Made: 15.09.2008. Coming into force: 16.09.2008. Effect: None. Territorial extent & classification: W. General. - In English and Welsh. Welsh title: Gorchymyn Ymddiriedolaeth Gwasanaeth Iechyd Gwladol Gogledd Cymru (Trosglwyddo Eiddo, Hawliau a Rhwymedigaethau) 2008. - 4p.: 30 cm. - 978-0-11-091878-5 £4.00

The Pembrokeshire and Derwen National Health Service Trust (Dissolution) Order 2008 No. 2008/937 (W.97). - Enabling power: National Health Service (Wales) Act 2006, s. 204 (1), sch. 3, para. 28 (1). - Issued: 22.04.2008. Made: 28.03.2008. Coming into force: 01.04.2008. Effect: S.I. 1997/876 revoked. Territorial extent & classification: W. General. - In English and Welsh. Welsh title: Gorchymyn Ymddiriedolaeth Gwasanaeth Iechyd Gwladol Sir Benfro a Derwen (Diddymu) 2008. - 4p.: 30 cm. - 978-0-11-091758-0 £3.00

The Pembrokeshire and Derwen National Health Service Trust (Transfer of Staff, Property, Rights and Liabilities) Order 2008 No. 2008/936 (W.96). - Enabling power: National Health Service (Wales) Act 2006, s. 203 (9) (10), sch. 3, para 29. - Issued: 22.04.2008. Made: 28.03.2008. Coming into force: 01.04.2008. Effect: None. Territorial extent & classification: W. General. - In English and Welsh. Welsh title: Gorchymyn Ymddiriedolaeth Gwasanaeth Iechyd Gwladol Sir Benfro a Derwen (Trosglwyddo Staff, Eiddo, Hawliau a Rhwymedigaethau) 2008. - 8p.: 30 cm. - 978-0-11-091799-3 £3.00

The Pontypridd and Rhondda National Health Service Trust (Dissolution) Order 2008 No. 2008/932 (W.92). - Enabling power: National Health Service (Wales) Act 2006, s. 204 (1), sch. 3, para. 28 (1). - Issued: 22.04.2008. Made: 28.03.2008. Coming into force: 01.04.2008. Effect: S.I 1998/3318 revoked. Territorial extent & classification: W. General. - In English and Welsh. Welsh title: Gorchymyn Ymddiriedolaeth Gwasanaeth Iechyd Gwladol Pontypridd a Rhondda (Diddymu) 2008. - 4p.: 30 cm. - 978-0-11-091760-3 £3.00

The Pontypridd and Rhondda National Health Service Trust (Transfer of Staff, Property, Rights and Liabilities) Order 2008 No. 2008/924 (W.88). - Enabling power: National Health Service (Wales) Act 2006, s. 203 (9) (10), sch. 3, para. 29. - Issued: 22.04.2008. Made: 28.03.2008. Coming into force: 01.04.2008. Effect: None. Territorial extent & classification: W. General. - In English and Welsh. Welsh title: Gorchymyn Ymddiriedolaeth Gwasanaeth Iechyd Gwladol Pontypridd a Rhondda (Trosglwyddo Staff, Eiddo, Hawliau a Rhwymedigaethau) 2008. - 8p.: 30 cm. - 978-0-11-091803-7 £3.00

The Swansea National Health Service Trust (Dissolution) Order 2008 No. 2008/938 (W.98). - Enabling power: National Health Service (Wales) Act 2006, s. 204 (1), sch. 3, para. 28 (1). - Issued: 22.04.2008. Made: 28.03.2008. Coming into force: 01.04.2008. Effect: S.I. 1998/3315; 1999/1321 revoked. Territorial extent & classification: W. General. - In English and Welsh. Welsh title: Gorchymyn Ymddiriedolaeth Gwasanaeth Iechyd Gwladol Abertawe (Diddymu) 2008. - 4p.: 30 cm. - 978-0-11-091757-3 £3.00

The Swansea National Health Service Trust (Transfer of Staff, Property, Rights and Liabilities) Order 2008 No. 2008/926 (W.89). - Enabling power: National Health Service (Wales) Act 2006, s. 203 (9) (10), sch. 3, para. 29. - Issued: 22.04.2008. Made: 28.03.2008. Coming into force: 01.04.2008. Effect: None. Territorial extent & classification: W. General. - In English and Welsh. Welsh title: Gorchymyn Ymddiriedolaeth Gwasanaeth Iechyd Gwladol Abertawe (Trosglwyddo Staff, Eiddo, Hawliau a Rhwymedigaethau) 2008. - 8p.: 30 cm. - 978-0-11-091804-4 £3.00

Nationality

The Immigration and Nationality (Cost Recovery Fees) (Amendment No.2) Regulations 2008 No. 2008/1337. - Enabling power: Immigration, Asylum and Nationality Act 2006, ss. 51 (3), 52 (3). - Issued: 28.05.2008. Made: 20.05.2008. Laid: 22.05.2008. Coming into force: 30.05.2008. Effect: S.I. 2007/936 amended. Territorial extent & classification: E/W/S/NI. General. - Revoked by S.I. 2009/421 (ISBN 9780111475904). - 8p.: 30 cm. - 978-0-11-081752-1 £3.00

The Immigration and Nationality (Cost Recovery Fees) (Amendment No. 3) Regulations 2008 No. 2008/2790. - Enabling power: Immigration, Asylum and Nationality Act 2006, ss. 51 (3), 52 (3). - Issued: 30.10.2008. Made: 22.10.2008. Laid: 28.10.2008. Coming into force: 27.11.2008 & 01.02.2009 in accord. with reg. 2. Effect: S.I. 2007/936 amended. Territorial extent & classification: E/W/S/NI. General. - Revoked by S.I. 2009/421 (ISBN 9780111475904). - 4p.: 30 cm. - 978-0-11-084740-5 £4.00

The Immigration and Nationality (Cost Recovery Fees) (Amendment) Regulations 2008 No. 2008/218. - Enabling power: Immigration, Asylum and Nationality Act 2006, ss. 51 (3), 52 (3). - Issued: 08.02.2008. Made: 04.02.2008. Laid: 06.02.2008. Coming into force: 29.02.2008 except for reg. 2 (4) (6); 01.04.2008 for reg. 2 (4) (6). Effect: S.I. 2007/936 amended. Territorial extent & classification: E/W/S/NI. General. - Revoked by S.I. 2009/421 (ISBN 9780111475904). - 8p.: 30 cm. - 978-0-11-080901-4 £3.00

The Immigration and Nationality (Fees) (Amendment No. 2) Regulations 2008 No. 2008/1695. - Enabling power: Immigration, Asylum and Nationality Act 2006, ss. 51 (3), 52 (3) & Asylum and Immigration (Treatment of Claimants, etc.) Act 2004, s. 42 (1) (2A). - Issued: 01.07.2008. Made: 26.06.2008. Coming into force: 30.06.2008. Effect: S.I. 2007/1158 amended. Territorial extent & classification: E/W/S/NI. General. - Revoked by S.I. 2009/816 (ISBN 9780111477694). - Supersedes draft S.I. (ISBN 9780110814582) issued 15.05.2008. - 8p.: 30 cm. - 978-0-11-081924-2 £3.00

The Immigration and Nationality (Fees) (Amendment No. 3) Regulations 2008 No. 2008/3017. - Enabling power: Immigration, Asylum and Nationality Act 2006, ss. 51 (3), 52 (3) & Asylum and Immigration (Treatment of Claimants, etc.) Act 2004, s. 42 (1) (2A). - Issued: 26.11.2008. Made: 19.11.2008. Coming into force: 27.11.2008. Effect: S.I. 2007/1158 amended. Territorial extent & classification: E/W/S/NI. General. - Revoked by S.I. 2009/816 (ISBN 9780111477694). - Supersedes draft S.I. (ISBN 9780110843674) issued 06.10.2008. - 4p.: 30 cm. - 978-0-11-147041-1 £4.00

The Immigration and Nationality (Fees)(Amendment) Regulations 2008 No. 2008/544. - Enabling power: Immigration, Asylum and Nationality Act 2006, ss. 51 (3), 52 (3). - Issued: 04.03.2008. Made: 28.02.2008. Coming into force: 29.02.2008, 01.04.2008 in accord. with reg. 1 (2) (3). Effect: S.I. 2007/1158 amended. Territorial extent & classification: E/W/S/NI. General. - Revoked by S.I. 2009/816 (ISBN 9780111477694). - 8p.: 30 cm. - 978-0-11-081070-6 £3.00

National lottery

The Payments into the Olympic Lottery Distribution Fund etc. Order 2008 No. 2008/255. - Enabling power: National Lottery etc. Act 1993, s. 29A & Horserace Betting and Olympic Lottery Act 2004, ss. 25, 36. - Issued: 11.02.2008. Made: 02.02.2008. Coming into force: 03.02.2008. Effect: None. Territorial extent & classification: E/W/S/NI. General. - Supersedes draft SI (ISBN 9780110788982) issued 31.10.2007. - 8p.: 30 cm. - 978-0-11-080923-6 £3.00

National lottery, England

The Parks for People (England) Joint Scheme (Authorisation) Order 2008 No. 2008/3103. - Enabling power: National Lottery etc. Act 1993, sch. 3A, paras. 2 (1), 3, 6 (1). - Issued: 09.12.2008. Made: 03.12.2008. Laid: 04.12.2008. Coming into force: 01.01.2009. Effect: S.I. 2005/3274 revoked. Territorial extent & classification: E. General. - 4p.: 30 cm. - 978-0-11-147103-6 £4.00

Northern Ireland

The Criminal Justice (Northern Ireland Consequential Amendments) Order 2008 No. 2008/1241. - Enabling power: Northern Ireland Act 1998, s. 84 (2). - Issued: 21.05.2008. Made: -. Coming into force: In accord. with art. 1 (2). Effect: 1975 c. 24; 1997 c. 43; 2000 c. 36; 2001 c. 17 amended. Territorial extent & classification: E/W/S/NI. General. - 2p.: 30 cm. - 978-0-11-081481-0 £3.00

The Criminal Justice (Northern Ireland) Order 2008 No. 2008/1216 (NI.1). - Enabling power: Northern Ireland Act 1998, s. 85. - Issued: 16.05.2008. Made: 07.05.2008. Coming into force: In accord. with arts 1 (2) to (4). Effect: 15 Acts & 19 orders amended or partially repealed & S.I. 1976/226 (N.I. 4) repealed. Territorial extent & classification: NI. General. - 100p.: 30 cm. - 978-0-11-081695-1 £15.50

The Electoral Administration Act 2006 (Commencement No.1 and Transitional Provisions) (Northern Ireland) Order 2008 No. 2008/1656 (C. 74). - Enabling power: Electoral Administration Act 2006, ss. 77 (2) (4). Bringing into operation various provisions of the 2006 Act, so far as they extend to Northern Ireland, on 01.07.2008. - Issued: 01.07.2008. Made: 25.06.2008. Effect: None. Territorial extent & classification: NI. General. - 8p.: 30 cm. - 978-0-11-081914-3 £3.00

The Northern Ireland Arms Decommissioning Act 1997 (Amnesty Period) Order 2008 No. 2008/378. - Enabling power: Northern Ireland Arms Decommissioning Act 1997, s. 2 (2) (b). - Issued: 21.02.2008. Made: 18.02.2008. Coming into force: 19.02.2008. Effect: S.I. 2007/715 revoked. Territorial extent & classification: NI. General. - Revoked by S.I. 2009/281 (ISBN 9780111474143). Supersedes draft S.I. (ISBN 9780110805092) issued 07.12.2007. - 2p.: 30 cm. - 978-0-11-080961-8 £3.00

The Northern Ireland (Miscellaneous Provisions) Act 2006 (Commencement No. 4) Order 2008 No. 2008/1318 (C.56). - Enabling power: Northern Ireland (Miscellaneous Provisions) Act 2006, s. 31 (3). Bringing into operation various provisions of the 2006 Act on 14.05.2008. - Issued: 21.05.2008. Made: 13.05.2008. Effect: None. Territorial extent & classification: NI. General. - 2p.: 30 cm. - 978-0-11-081472-8 £3.00

The Sexual Offences (Northern Ireland Consequential Amendments) Order 2008 No. 2008/1779. - Enabling power: Northern Ireland Act 1998, s. 84 (2). - Issued: 22.07.2008. Made: 09.07.2008. Coming into force: In accord. with art. 2. Effect: 1994 c. 33; 2003 c. 42, 44 amended. Territorial extent & classification: NI. General. - Supersedes draft S.I. (ISBN 9780110800950) issued 30.04.2008. - 12p.: 30 cm. - 978-0-11-081697-5 £3.00

The Sexual Offences (Northern Ireland) Order 2008 No. 2008/1769 (NI. 2). - Enabling power: Northern Ireland Act 1998, s. 85. - Issued: 22.07.2008. Made: 09.07.2008. Coming into force: In accord. with art. 1 (2) (3). Effect: 21 Acts and 17 SIs amended. Territorial extent & classification: NI. General. - Supersedes draft S.I. (ISBN 978011080036) issued 30.04.2008. - 56p.: 30 cm. - 978-0-11-081696-8 £9.00

Northern Ireland: Pensions

The Northern Ireland Act 1998 (Modification) Order 2008 No. 2008/1242. - Enabling power: Northern Ireland Act 1998, s. 87 (7). - Issued: 14.05.2008. Made: 07.05.2008. Laid: 14.05.2008. Coming into force: 18.06.2008. Effect: 1998 c. 47 modified. Territorial extent & classification: E/W/S/NI. General. - 2p.: 30 cm. - 978-0-11-081443-8 £3.00

Northern Ireland: Social security

The Northern Ireland Act 1998 (Modification) Order 2008 No. 2008/1242. - Enabling power: Northern Ireland Act 1998, s. 87 (7). - Issued: 14.05.2008. Made: 07.05.2008. Laid: 14.05.2008. Coming into force: 18.06.2008. Effect: 1998 c. 47 modified. Territorial extent & classification: E/W/S/NI. General. - 2p.: 30 cm. - 978-0-11-081443-8 £3.00

Official statistics

The Official Statistics Order 2008 No. 2008/928. - Enabling power: Statistics and Registration Service Act 2007, s. 6 (1) (b) (2). - Issued: 03.04.2008. Made: 31.03.2008. Coming into force: 01.04.2008 in accord. with art. 1 (2). Effect: None. Territorial extent & classification: E/W/S/NI. General. - Revoked by S.I. 2009/753 (ISBN 9780111477120). Supersedes draft SI (ISBN 9780110810027) issued 26.02.2008. - 4p.: 30 cm. - 978-0-11-081319-6 £3.00

The Pre-release Access to Official Statistics Order 2008 No. 2008/2998. - Enabling power: Statistics and Registration Service Act 2007, s. 11(2) (4) (5) (6). - Issued: 21.11.2008. Made: 18.11.2008. Coming into force: 01.12.2008. Effect: None. Territorial extent & classification: E/W/S/NI. General. - 8p.: 30 cm. - 978-0-11-147023-7 £5.00

The Statistics and Registration Service Act 2007 (Commencement No. 2 and Transitional Provisions) Order 2008 No. 2008/839 (C.41). - Enabling power: Statistics and Registration Service Act 2007, s. 74. Bringing into operation various provisions of the 2007 Act on 01.04.2008. - Issued: 01.04.2008. Made: 20.03.2008. Effect: None. Territorial extent & classification: E/W/S/NI. General. - 2p.: 30 cm. - 978-0-11-081299-1 *£3.00*

Offshore installations

The Offshore Installations (Safety Zones) (No. 2) Order 2008 No. 2008/2157. - Enabling power: Petroleum Act 1987, s. 22 (1) (2). - Issued: 14.08.2008. Made: 11.08.2008. Coming into force: 01.09.2008. Effect: None. Territorial extent & classification: E/W/S. General. - 2p.: 30 cm. - 978-0-11-083760-4 *£3.00*

The Offshore Installations (Safety Zones) (No. 3) Order 2008 No. 2008/2454. - Enabling power: Petroleum Act 1987, s. 22 (1) (2). - Issued: 24.09.2008. Made: 18.09.2008. Coming into force: 17.10.2008. Effect: None. Territorial extent & classification: E/W/S. General. - 2p.: 30 cm. - 978-0-11-084254-7 *£4.00*

The Offshore Installations (Safety Zones) (No. 4) Order 2008 No. 2008/3011. - Enabling power: Petroleum Act 1987, s. 22 (1) (2). - Issued: 25.11.2008. Made: 19.11.2008. Coming into force: 10.12.2008. Effect: None. Territorial extent & classification: E/W/S. General. - 2p.: 30 cm. - 978-0-11-147035-0 *£4.00*

The Offshore Installations (Safety Zones) Order 2008 No. 2008/1522. - Enabling power: Petroleum Act 1987, s. 22 (1) (2). - Issued: 17.06.2008. Made: 10.06.2008. Coming into force: 01.07.2008. Effect: None. Territorial extent & classification: E/W/S. General. - 2p.: 30 cm. - 978-0-11-081846-7 *£3.00*

Offshore installations, England

The River Humber (Upper Burcom Tidal Stream Generator) Order 2008 No. 2008/969. - Enabling power: Transport and Works Act 1992, ss. 3, 5 of, sch. 1, paras 1 to 5, 7, 8, 10, 11, 15 to 17. - Issued: 09.04.2008. Made: 02.04.2008. Coming into force: In accord. with art. 1. Effect: None. Territorial extent & classification: E. General. - 16p.: 30 cm. - 978-0-11-081348-6 *£3.00*

Olympic games and paralympic games

The Payments into the Olympic Lottery Distribution Fund etc. Order 2008 No. 2008/255. - Enabling power: National Lottery etc. Act 1993, s. 29A & Horserace Betting and Olympic Lottery Act 2004, ss. 25, 36. - Issued: 11.02.2008. Made: 02.02.2008. Coming into force: 03.02.2008. Effect: None. Territorial extent & classification: E/W/S/NI. General. - Supersedes draft SI (ISBN 9780110788982) issued 31.10.2007. - 8p.: 30 cm. - 978-0-11-080923-6 *£3.00*

Opticians

The General Optical Council (Therapeutics and Contact Lens Specialties) Rules Order of Council 2008 No. 2008/1940. - Enabling power: Opticians Act 1989, ss. 10 (1) (1A), 11A, 11B (6), 25 (3), 31A. - Issued: 24.07.2008. Made: 21.07.2008. Coming into force: 11.08.2008. Effect: S.I. 1988/1305; 2005/1473, 1478 amended. Territorial extent & classification: E/W/S/NI. General. - 8p.: 30 cm. - 978-0-11-083480-1 *£3.00*

Parliament

The Ministerial and other Salaries Order 2008 No. 2008/1781. - Enabling power: Ministerial and other Salaries Act 1975, s. 1B. - Issued: 16.07.2008. Made: 09.07.2008. Coming into force: 10.07.2008. Effect: None. Territorial extent & classification: E/W/S/NI. General. - Supersedes draft S.I. (ISBN 9780110817699) issued on 04.06.2008. - 4p.: 30 cm. - 978-0-11-083156-5 *£3.00*

Parliamentary Commissioner

The Parliamentary Commissioner Order 2008 No. 2008/3115. - Enabling power: Parliamentary Commissioner Act 1967, ss. 4 (2), 5 (4) (9). - Issued: 17.12.2008. Made: 10.12.2008. Laid: 17.12.2008. Coming into force: 13.02.2009. Effect: 1967 c.13 amended. Territorial extent & classification: E/W/S/NI. General. - 16p.: 30 cm. - 978-0-11-147155-5 *£5.00*

Partnership

The Partnerships (Accounts) Regulations 2008 No. 2008/569. - Enabling power: European Communities Act 1972, s. 2 (2) & Companies Act 2006, ss. 1210 (1) (h), 1292 (2). - Issued: 10.03.2008. Made: 26.02.2008. Laid: 05.03.2008. Coming into force: 06.04.2008. Effect: S.I. 2008/409, 410 amended & S.I. 1993/1820 & S.R. 1994/133 revoked with savings. Territorial extent & classification: E/W/S/NI. General. - EC note: These Regulations continue the implementation of Council Directive 90/605/EEC amending Directive 78/660/EEC on annual accounts and Directive 83/349/EEC on consolidated accounts. They also implement, in part, Directive 2006/43/EC. - 16p.: 30 cm. - 978-0-11-081093-5 *£3.00*

Pensions

The Armed Forces and Reserve Forces (Compensation Scheme) (Amendment No. 2) Order 2008 No. 2008/2160. - Enabling power: Armed Forces (Pensions and Compensation) Act 2004, ss. 1 (2), 10 (2) (3). - Issued: 18.08.2008. Made: 12.08.2008. Laid: 14.08.2008. Coming into force: 16.09.2008. Effect: S.I. 2005/439 amended. Territorial extent & classification: E/W/S/NI. General. - 24p.: 30 cm. - 978-0-11-083761-1 *£4.00*

The Armed Forces and Reserve Forces (Compensation Scheme) (Amendment No. 3) Order 2008 No. 2008/2942. - Enabling power: Armed Forces (Pensions and Compensation) Act 2004, ss. 1 (2), 10 (2) (3). - Issued: 19.11.2008. Made: 13.11.2008. Laid: 18.11.2008. Coming into force: 15.12.2008. Effect: S.I. 2005/439 amended. Territorial extent & classification: E/W/S/NI. General. - 8p.: 30 cm. - 978-0-11-147004-6 £5.00

The Armed Forces and Reserve Forces (Compensation Scheme) (Amendment) Order 2008 No. 2008/39. - Enabling power: Armed Forces (Pensions and Compensation) Act 2004, ss. 1 (2), 10 (2) (3). - Issued: 16.01.2008. Made: 11.01.2008. Laid: 16.01.2008. Coming into force: 08.02.2008. Effect: S.I. 2005/439 amended. Territorial extent & classification: E/W/S/NI. General. - 8p.: 30 cm. - 978-0-11-080828-4 £3.00

The Armed Forces (Gurkha Pensions) (Amendment) Order 2008 No. 2008/229. - Enabling power: Armed Forces (Pensions and Compensation) Act 2004, s. 1 (1) (a). - Issued: 11.02.2008. Made: 06.02.2008. Laid: 07.02.2008. Coming into force: 29.02.2008. Effect: S.I. 2005/437, 438 amended. Territorial extent & classification: E/W/S/NI. General. - 2p.: 30 cm. - 978-0-11-080914-4 £3.00

The Financial Assistance Scheme (Amendment) Regulations 2008 No. 2008/3069. - Enabling power: Pensions Act 2004, ss. 286 (2) (b), 315(5), 318(1). - Issued: 02.12.2008. Made: 27.11.2008. Laid: 02.12.2008. Coming into force: 23.12.2008. Effect: S.I. 2005/1986 amended. Territorial extent & classification: E/W/S/NI. General. - 4p.: 30 cm. - 978-0-11-147079-4 £4.00

The Financial Assistance Scheme (Miscellaneous Amendments) Regulations 2008 No. 2008/1903. - Enabling power: Pension Schemes Act 1993, s. 181 (1), sch. 2, para. 5 (3B) & Pension Schemes (Northern Ireland) Act 1993, sch. 1, para. 5 (3B) (4A) & Pensions Act 2004, ss. 286, 315 (2) (4), 318 (1). - Issued: 23.07.2008. Made: 16.07.2008. Coming into force: 17.07.2008 in accord. with reg 1. Effect: S.I. 1996/1172; 2005/1986, 1994, 2189, 3273 & S.R. 1996/493 amended. Territorial extent & classification: E/W/S/NI. General. - Supersedes draft S.I. (ISBN 9780110818788) issued 25.06.2008. - 20p.: 30 cm. - 978-0-11-083400-9 £3.50

The Financial Assistance Scheme (Miscellaneous Provisions) Regulations 2008 No. 2008/1432. - Enabling power: Pensions Act 2004, ss. 286, 315 (2) (4), 318 (1) & Pensions Act 2007, ss. 18 (9), 25 (2). - Issued: 10.06.2008. Made: 03.06.2008. Coming into force: 04.06.2008 in accord. with reg 1. Effect: 2007 c.22 & S.I. 2005/1986 amended. Territorial extent & classification: E/W/S/NI. General. - Supersedes draft S.I. (ISBN 9780110814063) issued 29.04.2008. - 8p.: 30 cm. - 978-0-11-081795-8 £3.00

The Guaranteed Minimum Pensions Increase Order 2008 No. 2008/581. - Enabling power: Pension Schemes Act 1993, s. 109 (4). - Issued: 13.03.2008. Made: 04.03.2008. Coming into force: 06.04.2008. Effect: None. Territorial extent & classification: E/W/S. General. - Supersedes draft S.I. (ISBN 9780110808574) issued 23.01.2008. - 2p.: 30 cm. - 978-0-11-081158-1 £3.00

The Judicial Pensions and Retirement Act 1993 (Addition of Qualifying Judicial Offices) Order 2008 No. 2008/171. - Enabling power: Judicial Pensions and Retirement Act 1993, ss. 1 (8), 29 (3), 30 (1). - Issued: 04.02.2008. Made: 30.01.2008. Laid: 30.01.2008. Coming into force: 25.02.2008. Effect: 1993 c. 8 amended. Territorial extent & classification: E/W/S/NI. General. - 2p.: 30 cm. - 978-0-11-080883-3 £3.00

The Naval, Military and Air Forces Etc. (Disablement and Death) Service Pensions (Amendment) Order 2008 No. 2008/679. - Enabling power: Social Security (Miscellaneous Provisions) Act 1977, ss. 12 (1), 24 (3). - Issued: 19.03.2008. Made: 12.03.2008. Laid: 13.03.2008. Coming into force: In accord. with art. 2. Effect: S.I. 2006/606 amended. Territorial extent & classification: E/W/S/NI. General. - 16p.: 30 cm. - 978-0-11-081233-5 £3.00

The Occupational and Personal Pension Schemes (General Levy) (Amendment) Regulations 2008 No. 2008/661. - Enabling power: Pension Schemes Act 1993, ss. 175, 181 (1), 182 (2). - Issued: 14.03.2008. Made: 09.03.2008. Laid: 11.03.2008. Coming into force: 01.04.2008. Effect: S.I. 2005/626 amended. Territorial extent & classification: E/W/S. General. - 2p.: 30 cm. - 978-0-11-081166-6 £3.00

The Occupational and Personal Pension Schemes (Levy Ceiling) Order 2008 No. 2008/911. - Enabling power: Pensions Act 2004, ss. 178 (1), 315 (2) (5). - Issued: 02.04.2008. Made: 27.03.2008. Coming into force: In accord. with art. 1 (2), 31.03.2008; 01.04.2008. Effect: S.I. 2007/1012 revoked. Territorial extent & classification: E/W/S. General. - Revoked by S.I. 2009/794 (ISBN 9780110477403). - 2p.: 30 cm. - 978-0-11-081311-0 £3.00

The Occupational and Personal Pension Schemes (Transfer Values) (Amendment) Regulations 2008 No. 2008/2450. - Enabling power: Pension Schemes Act 1993, ss. 97 (1) (2) (b), 101AF (1) (3) (b) (4) (b), 181 (1), 182 (2) (3), 183. - Issued: 22.09.2008. Made: 18.09.2008. Laid: 22.09.2008. Coming into force: 13.10.2008. Effect: S.I. 1987/1112; 1996/1847; 2006/33 amended. Territorial extent & classification: E/W/S. General. - 4p.: 30 cm. - 978-0-11-084252-3 £4.00

The Occupational Pension Schemes (Employer Debt and Miscellaneous Amendments) Regulations 2008 No. 2008/731. - Enabling power: Pensions Act 1995, ss. 68 (2) (e), 75 (1) (b) (5) (10), 75A (1) to (8), 118 (1) (a) (b), 119, 124 (1), 125 (3) (a), 174 (2) (3) & Pensions Act 2004, ss. 69 (2) (a) (3) (a), 93 (2) (q), 126 (5), 232, 307 (1) (b), 315 (2) to (5), 318 (1) (4) (a), sch. 1, para. 21 (e). - Issued: 18.08.2009. Made: 12.03.2008. Laid: 14.03.2008. Coming into force: 06.04.2008. Effect: S.I 2005/441, 590, 678, 2188, 3377 amended. Territorial extent & classification: E/W/S. General. - This SI has been printed in substitution of the SI of the same number (published on 19.03.2008) and is being issued free of charge to all known recipients of that Statutory Instrument. It has also been corrected by S.I. 2008/1068 (ISBN 9780110813721) which was also sent free of charge to known recipients of the original SI 2009/731. - 32p.: 30 cm. - 978-0-11-081255-7 £9.50

The Occupational Pension Schemes (Employer Debt - Apportionment Arrangements) (Amendment) Regulations 2008 No. 2008/1068. - Enabling power: Pensions Act 1995, ss. 68 (2) (e), 75 (5), 75A (1) to (8), 124 (1), 174 (2) (3). - Issued: 16.04.2008. Made: 11.04.2008. Laid: 14.04.2008. Coming into force: 15.04.2008. Effect: S.I. 2005/678 amended. Territorial extent & classification: E/W/S. General. - This Statutory Instrument has been printed to correct errors in SI 2008/731 (ISBN 9780110812557) and is being issued free of charge to all known recipients of that Statutory Instrument. - 4p.: 30 cm. - 978-0-11-081372-1 £3.00

The Occupational Pension Schemes (Internal Dispute Resolution Procedures Consequential and Miscellaneous Amendments) Regulations 2008 No. 2008/649. - Enabling power: Pension Schemes Act 1993, ss. 113 (1) (d), 181 (1), 182 (2) (3) & Pensions Act 1995, ss. 50 (8) (c) (9) (c), 124 (1), 174 (2) (3). - Issued: 13.03.2008. Made: 05.03.2008. Laid: 13.03.2008. Coming into force: 06.04.2008. Effect: S.I. 1996/1655, 2475; 2000/1403 amended and S.I. 1996/1270 revoked. Territorial extent & classification: E/W/S. General. - With correction slip dated August 2008. - 4p.: 30 cm. - 978-0-11-081155-0 £3.00

The Occupational Pension Schemes (Levies) (Amendment) Regulations 2008 No. 2008/910. - Enabling power: Pensions Act 2004, ss. 117 (1) (3), 315 (2), 318 (1). - Issued: 02.04.2008. Made: 27.03.2008. Coming into force: 31.03.2008. Effect: S.I. 2005/842 amended. Territorial extent & classification: E/W/S. General. - Supersedes draft S.I. (ISBN 9780110810928) issued on 7th March 2008- 2p.: 30 cm. - 978-0-11-081315-8 £3.00

The Occupational Pension Schemes (Levy Ceiling - Earnings Percentage Increase) Order 2008 No. 2008/217. - Enabling power: Pensions Act 2004, s. 178 (6). - Issued: 08.02.2008. Made: 05.02.2008. Laid: 08.02.2008. Coming into force: 04.03.2008. Effect: None. Territorial extent & classification: E/W/S. General. - 2p.: 30 cm. - 978-0-11-080912-0 £3.00

The Occupational Pension Schemes (Non-European Schemes Exemption) Regulations 2008 No. 2008/624. - Enabling power: Pensions Act 2004, ss. 253 (5), 315 (2), 318 (1). - Issued: 11.03.2008. Made: 04.03.2008. Laid: 11.03.2008. Coming into force: 06.04.2008. Effect: None. Territorial extent & classification: E/W/S. General. - 2p.: 30 cm. - 978-0-11-081124-6 £3.00

The Occupational Pension Schemes (Transfer Values) (Amendment) Regulations 2008 No. 2008/1050. - Enabling power: Pension Schemes Act 1993, ss. 27 (3), 93A (2), 95 (2) (d), 97 (1) (2) (b) (3) (c) (4), 101AC (2) (a), 101AF (1) (3) (b) (4) (b) (5) (a), 101H (2) (3), 101I, 101L, 113 (1) (3), 181 (1), 182 (2) (3), 183 & Pensions Act 1995, ss. 67D (4), 124 (1), 174 (2) (3) & Welfare Reform and Pensions Act 1999, ss. 23 (1) (b), 26 (1), 30, 41 (1) (2), 83 (4) (6), sch. 5, para. 5 (b), 8 (1) (2). - Issued: 11.04.2008. Made: 03.04.2008. Laid: 11.04.2008. Coming into force: 01.10.2008. Effect: S.I. 1987/1112; 1996/1537, 1847; 2000/1048, 1049, 1052, 1053, 1054; 2006/33, 759 amended. Territorial extent & classification: E/W/S. General. - 24p.: 30 cm. - 978-0-11-081363-9 £4.00

The Occupational Pensions (Revaluation) Order 2008 No. 2008/3070. - Enabling power: Pension Schemes Act 1993, sch. 3, para. 2 (1). - Issued: 02.12.2008. Made: 27.11.2008. Laid: 02.12.2008. Coming into force: 01.01.2009. Effect: None. Territorial extent & classification: E/W/S. General. - 2p.: 30 cm. - 978-0-11-147080-0 £4.00

The Pension Protection Fund (Entry Rules) Amendment Regulations 2008 No. 2008/1810. - Enabling power: Pensions Act 2004, ss. 126 (3), 315 (2), 318 (1). - Issued: 11.07.2008. Made: 07.07.2008. Laid: 11.07.2008. Coming into force: 02.08.2008. Effect: S.I. 2005/590 amended. Territorial extent & classification: E/W/S. General. - 2p.: 30 cm. - 978-0-11-082005-7 £3.00

The Pension Protection Fund (Pension Compensation Cap) Order 2008 No. 2008/909. - Enabling power: Pensions Act 2004, s. 315 (5), sch. 7, paras 26 (7), 27 (2) (3). - Issued: 02.04.2008. Made: 27.03.2008. Coming into force: 01.04.2008. Effect: S.I. 2007/989 revoked. Territorial extent & classification: E/W/S. General. - Revoked by S.I. 2009/795 (ISBN 9780110477397). Supersedes draft SI (ISBN 0110810074). - 2p.: 30 cm. - 978-0-11-081309-7 £3.00

The Pension Protection Fund (Prescribed Payments) Regulations 2008 No. 2008/664. - Enabling power: Pensions Act 2004, as. 173 (3) (k), 315 (2) (4), 318 (1). - Issued: 14.03.2008. Made: 09.03.2008. Laid: 11.03.2008. Coming into force: 01.04.2008. Effect: None. Territorial extent & classification: E/W/S. General. - 2p.: 30 cm. - 978-0-11-081165-9 £3.00

The Pensions Act 2004 (Code of Practice) (Dispute Resolution) Appointed Day Order 2008 No. 2008/1882 (C.82). - Enabling power: Pensions Act 2004, s. 91 (9). Bringing into effect the Pensions Regulator Code of Practice No. 11: Dispute resolution - reasonable periods on 28.07.2008. - Issued: 18.07.2008. Made: 16.07.2008. Effect: None. Territorial extent & classification: E/W/S. General. - 2p.: 30 cm. - 978-0-11-083314-9 £3.00

The Pensions Act 2004 (Commencement No. 11) Order 2008 No. 2008/627 (C.25). - Enabling power: Pension Act 2004, ss. 315 (2), 322 (1). Bringing into operation various provisions of the 2004 Act on 05.03.2008; 06.04.2008 in accord. with reg. 2. - Issued: 11.03.2008. Made: 04.03.2008. Effect: None. Territorial extent & classification: E/W/S. General. - 16p.: 30 cm. - 978-0-11-081133-8 £3.00

The Pensions Act 2007 (Acturial Guidance) (Consequential Provisions) Order 2008 No. 2008/2301. - Enabling power: Pensions Act 2007, s. 27 (1). - Issued: 02.09.2008. Made: 28.08.2008. Laid: 02.09.2008. Coming into force: 01.09.2008. Effect: S.I. 1987/1110; 1996/1655; 2000/1403; 1996/1172, 3126, 3128; 2005/3377 amended. Territorial extent & classification: E/W/S. General. - 4p.: 30 cm. - 978-0-11-083879-3 £4.00

The Pensions Act 2008 (Commencement No. 1 and Consequential Provision) Order 2008 No. 2008/3241 (C.147). - Enabling power: Pensions Act 2008, ss. 144 (2) (4), 149 (1). Bringing into operation various provisions of the 2008 Act on 19.12.2008. - Issued: 22.12.2008. Made: 16.12.2008. Effect: S.I. 2005/1986 amended. Territorial extent & classification: E/W/S. General. - 2p.: 30 cm. - 978-0-11-147204-0 £4.00

The Pensions Increase (Review) Order 2008 No. 2008/711. - Enabling power: Social Security Pensions Act 1975, s. 59 (1) (2) (5) (5ZA). - Issued: 13.03.2008. Made: 12.03.2008. Laid: 13.03.2008. Coming into force: 07.04.2008. Effect: None. Territorial extent & classification: E/W/S/NI. General. - 8p.: 30 cm. - 978-0-11-081226-7 £3.00

The Personal and Occupational Pension Schemes (Amendment) Regulations 2008 No. 2008/1979. - Enabling power: Pension Schemes Act 1993, ss. 9 (5) (a), 26, 28 (5), 181 (1), 182 (2) (3). - Issued: 29.07.2008. Made: 23.07.2008. Laid: 29.07.2008. Coming into force: 01.10.2008. Effect: S.I. 1996/1537; 1997/470 amended & S.I. 2001/943 partially revoked & S.I. 2006/147 revoked. Territorial extent & classification: E/W/S. General. - 4p.: 30 cm. - 978-0-11-083633-1 £3.00

The Personal Injuries (Civilians) (Amendment) Scheme 2008 No. 2008/592. - Enabling power: Personal Injuries (Emergency Provisions) Act 1939, ss. 1, 2. - Issued: 11.03.2008. Made: 03.03.2008. Laid: 07.03.2008. Coming into force: 07.04.2008. Effect: S.I. 1983/686 amended. Territorial extent & classification: E/W/S/NI. General. - 8p.: 30 cm. - 978-0-11-081110-9 £3.00

The Superannuation (Admission to Schedule 1 to the Superannuation Act 1972) Order 2008 No. 2008/1891. - Enabling power: Superannuation Act 1972, s. 1 (5) (a) (b) (c) (8) (a). - Issued: 22.07.2008. Made: 16.07.2008. Laid: 22.07.2008. Coming into force: 01.09.2008. Effect: 1972 c.11 amended. Territorial extent & classification: E/W/S/NI. General. - 4p.: 30 cm. - 978-0-11-083377-4 £3.00

Pensions, England

The Firefighters' Pension Scheme (Amendment) (England) Order 2008 No. 2008/214. - Enabling power: Fire Services Act 1947, s. 26 (1) to (5) & Superannuation Act 1972, s. 12. - Issued: 07.02.2008. Made: 30.01.2008. Laid: 07.02.2008. Coming into force: 01.04.2007; 01.07.2007; 29.02.2008 in accord. with art. 1 (2). Effect: S.I. 1992/129 amended in relation to England. Territorial extent & classification: E. General. - 8p.: 30 cm. - 978-0-11-080900-7 £3.00

The Firefighters' Pension Scheme (England) (Amendment) Order 2008 No. 2008/213. - Enabling power: Fire and Rescue Services Act 2004, ss. 34, 60. - Issued: 07.02.2008. Made: 30.01.2008. Laid: 07.02.2008. Coming into force: in accord. with art. 1 (3) (4) (5). Effect: S.I. 2006/3432 amended. Territorial extent & classification: E. General. - 12p.: 30 cm. - 978-0-11-080890-1 £3.00

The Judicial Pensions and Retirement Act 1993 (Addition of Qualifying Judicial Offices) (No.2) Order 2008 No. 2008/2947. - Enabling power: Judicial Pensions and Retirement Act 1993, s. 1 (8). - Issued: 19.11.2008. Made: 13.11.2008. Laid: 19.11.2008. Coming into force: 12.12.2008. Effect: 1993 c. 8 amended. Territorial extent & classification: E/W/S/NI but applies to E. only. General. - 2p.: 30 cm. - 978-0-11-147007-7 £4.00

Pensions, England and Wales

The Judicial Pensions and Retirement Act 1993 (Addition of Qualifying Judicial Offices) (No. 3) Order 2008 No. 2008/3139. - Enabling power: Judicial Pensions and Retirement Act 1993, ss. 1 (8), 26 (9) (a), 30 (1)- Issued: 11.12.2008. Made: 08.12.2008. Laid: 09.12.2008. Coming into force: 02.01.2009. Effect: 1993 c. 8 amended. Territorial extent & classification: E/W. General. - 2p.: 30 cm. - 978-0-11-147128-9 £4.00

The Local Government Pension Scheme (Administration) (Amendment) Regulations 2008 No. 2008/3245. - Enabling power: Superannuation Act 1972, ss. 7, 12. - Issued: 23.12.2008. Made: 16.12.2008. Laid: 23.12.2008. Coming into force: 01.04.2009. Effect: S.I. 2008/239 amended. Territorial extent & classification: E/W. General. - 4p.: 30 cm. - 978-0-11-147212-5 £4.00

The Local Government Pension Scheme (Administration) Regulations 2008 No. 2008/239. - Enabling power: Superannuation Act 1972, s. 7. - Issued: 14.02.2008. Made: 06.02.2008. Laid: 14.02.2008. Coming into force: 01.04.2008. Effect: None. Territorial extent & classification: E/W. General. - 60p.: 30 cm. - With correction slip dated July 2009. - 978-0-11-080928-1 £9.00

The Local Government Pension Scheme (Amendment) (No. 2) Regulations 2008 No. 2008/2989. - Enabling power: Superannuation Act 1972, ss. 7, 12. - Issued: 24.11.2008. Made: 17.11.2008. Laid: 24.11.2008. Coming into force: 16.12.2008, having effect from 01.12.2008 except for reg. 3 which comes into force 01.04.2009. Effect: S.I. 2008/239 amended. Territorial extent & classification: E/W. General. - 4p.: 30 cm. - 978-0-11-147014-5 £4.00

The Local Government Pension Scheme (Amendment) Regulations 2008 No. 2008/1083. - Enabling power: Superannuation Act 1972, ss. 7, 12. - Issued: 22.04.2008. Made: 14.04.2008. Laid: 16.04.2008. Coming into force: 07.05.2008. Effect: S.I. 2007/1166; 2008/238, 239 amended. Territorial extent & classification: E/W. General. - 12p.: 30 cm. - With correction slip dated September 2009. - 978-0-11-081380-6 £3.00

The Local Government Pension Scheme (Miscellaneous) Regulations 2008 No. 2008/2425. - Enabling power: Superannuation Act 1972, ss. 7, 12. - Issued: 17.09.2008. Made: 09.09.2008. Laid: 17.09.2008. Coming into force: 17.10.2008 in accord. with art. 1 (3). Effect: S.I. 1997/1612; 1998/1831; 2007/1166; 2008/238, 239 amended. Territorial extent & classification: E/W. General. - 8p.: 30 cm. - With correction slip dated September 2009. - 978-0-11-084201-1 *£5.00*

The Local Government Pension Scheme (Transitional Provisions) Regulations 2008 No. 2008/238. - Enabling power: Superannuation Act 1972, ss. 7, 12. - Issued: 14.02.2008. Made: 06.02.2008. Laid: 14.02.2008. Coming into force: 10.03.2008 for reg. 8; 01.04.2008 for remainder in accord. with art. 1(3). Effect: S.I. 1997/1612; 2000/3025; 2005/2004 partially revoked & 30 instruments revoked. Territorial extent & classification: E/W. General. - 8p.: 30 cm. - 978-0-11-080930-4 *£3.00*

The Police Pensions (Amendment) Regulations 2008 No. 2008/1887. - Enabling power: Police Pensions Act 1976, s. 1. - Issued: 21.07.2008. Made: 15.07.2008. Laid: 17.07.2008. Coming into force: 08.08.2008 but has effect in accord. with reg. 1 (2) (3). Effect: S.I. 1987/257, 2215; 2006/932, 3415; 2007/1932 amended. Territorial extent & classification: E/W. General. - 12p.: 30 cm. - 978-0-11-083366-8 *£3.00*

Pesticides, England and Wales

The Pesticides (Maximum Residue Levels) (England and Wales) Regulations 2008 No. 2008/2570. - Enabling power: European Communities Act 1972, s. 2 (2). - Issued: 07.10.2008. Made: 02.10.2008. Laid: 06.10.2008. Coming into force: 01.11.2008. Effect: S.I. 2005/3286; 2006/985, 1742, 2922; 2007/971, 2083, 2998, 3297; 2008/665 revoked. Territorial extent & classification: E/W. General. - EC note: These Regulations enforce the provisions of REG (EC) no. 396/2005 on maximum residue levels of pesticides in or on food and feed of plant and animal origin and amending Council Directive 91/414/EEC- 8p.: 30 cm. - 978-0-11-084363-6 *£5.00*

The Pesticides (Maximum Residue Levels in Crops, Food and Feeding Stuffs) (England and Wales) (Amendment) Regulations 2008 No. 2008/665. - Enabling power: European Communities Act 1972, s. 2 (2). - Issued: 27.03.2008. Made: 10.03.2008. Laid: 13.03.2008. Laid before the National Assembly of Wales: 13.03.2008. Coming into force: 09.04.2008 except for reg 4 (15.06.2008) and reg 5 (15.09.2008) in accord. with reg. 1(2). Effect: S.I. 2005/3286 amended. Territorial extent & classification: E/W. General. - Revoked by S.I. 2008/2570 (ISBN 9780110843636). EC note: These Regulations amend S.I. 2005/3286 in order to transpose Commission Directive 2007/73/EC amending certain Annexes to Council Directives 86/362/EEC and 90/642/EEC as regards maximum residue levels for acetamiprid, atrazine, deltamethrin, imazalil, indoxacarb, pendimethalin, pymetrozine, pyraclostrobin, thiacloprid and trifloxystrobin- 24p.: 30 cm. - 978-0-11-081273-1 *£4.00*

Petroleum

The Petroleum Licensing (Production) (Seaward Areas) Regulations 2008 No. 2008/225. - Enabling power: Petroleum Act 1998, s. 4. - Issued: 11.02.2008. Made: 05.02.2008. Laid: 06.02.2008. Coming into force: 06.04.2008. Effect: None. Territorial extent & classification: E/W/S/NI. General. - 28p.: 30 cm. - 978-0-11-080905-2 *£4.50*

Plant health

The Plant Health (Fees) (Forestry) (Amendment) Regulations 2008 No. 2008/702. - Enabling power: European Communities Act 1972, s. 2 (2). - Issued: 14.03.2008. Made: 07.03.2008. Laid: 14.03.2008. Coming into force: 06.04.2008. Effect: S.I. 2006/2697 amended. Territorial extent & classification: E/W/S. General. - EC note: These regs implement Article 13d(2) of Council Directive 2000/29/EC on protective measures against the introduction into the Community of organisms harmful to plants or plant products and against their spread within the Community. Articles 13a(2), 13d(2) and 18(2) of the Directive provide for reduced plant health check fees to be charged for imports of certain consignments of wood, such fees being levied whether or not the consignments are subject to a plant health check. The fees, and the consignments to which they apply, are specified in Schedule 3A to the principal Regulations, as inserted by these Regulations. - 4p.: 30 cm. - 978-0-11-081194-9 *£3.00*

The Plant Health (Forestry) (Amendment) Order 2008 No. 2008/644. - Enabling power: Plant Health Act 1967, ss. 2, 3 (1) & European Communities Act 1972, sch. 2, para. 1A. - Issued: 17.03.2008. Made: 07.03.2008. Laid: 10.03.2008. Coming into force: 31.03.2008. Effect: S.I. 2005/2517 amended. Territorial extent & classification: E/W/S. General. - EC note: This Order amends S.I. 2005/2517 (principal order) so as to implement Commission Directive 2007/433/EC, as amended from time to time. - 4p.: 30 cm. - 978-0-11-081152-9 *£3.00*

Plant health, England

The Plant Health (England) (Amendment) (No. 2) Order 2008 No. 2008/2765. - Enabling power: Plant Health Act 1967, ss. 2, 3 (1). - Issued: 23.10.2008. Made: 19.10.2008. Laid: 20.10.2008. Coming into force: 10.11.2008. Effect: S.I. 2005/2530 amended. Territorial extent & classification: E. General. - 4p.: 30 cm. - 978-0-11-084685-9 *£4.00*

The Plant Health (England) (Amendment) Order 2008 No. 2008/2411. - Enabling power: Plant Health Act 1967, ss. 2, 3 (1) (2) (4) & European Communities Act 1972, sch. 2, para. 1A. - Issued: 15.09.2008. Made: 09.09.2008. Laid: 10.09.2008. Coming into force: 01.10.2008. Effect: S.I. 2005/2530 amended & S.I. 2001/3194; 2004/1452; 2005/279 revoked. Territorial extent & classification: E. General. - EC note: These regs implement: Commission Directive 2008/64/EC amending Annexes I to IV to Council Directive 2000/29/EC; Commission Directive 2008/61/EC; and Commission Decision 2008/86/EC. - 4p.: 30 cm. - 978-0-11-084191-5 £4.00

The Plant Health (Import Inspection Fees) (England) (Amendment) Regulations 2008 No. 2008/3233. - Enabling power: Finance Act 1973, s. 56 (1). - Issued: 22.12.2008. Made: 16.12.2008. Laid: 17.12.2008. Coming into force: 07.01.2009. Effect: S.I. 2006/1879 amended. Territorial extent & classification: E. General. - 8p.: 30 cm. - 978-0-11-147199-9 £5.00

The Seed Potatoes (England) (Amendment) Regulations 2008 No. 2008/560. - Enabling power: Plant Varieties and Seeds Act 1964, s. 16 (1). - Issued: 06.03.2008. Made: 25.02.2008. Laid: 05.03.2008. Coming into force: 06.04.2008. Effect: S.I. 2006/1161 amended. Territorial extent & classification: Extends to E/W but applies only to E. General. - 2p.: 30 cm. - 978-0-11-081083-6 £3.00

Plant health, Wales

The Plant Health (Wales) (Amendment) (No. 2) Order 2008 No. 2008/2913 (W.257). - Enabling power: Plant Health Act 1967, ss. 2, 3 (1). - Issued: 26.11.2008. Made: 09.11.2008. Laid before the National Assembly for Wales: 11.11.2008. Coming into force: 10.12.2008. Effect: S.I. 2006/1643 (W.158) amended. Territorial extent & classification: W. General. - In English and Welsh. Welsh title: Gorchymyn Iechyd Planhigion (Cymru) (Diwygio) (Rhif 2) 2008. - 8p.: 30 cm. - 978-0-11-091869-3 £5.00

The Plant Health (Wales) (Amendment) Order 2008 No. 2008/2781 (W.248). - Enabling power: Plant Health Act 1967, ss. 2, 3 (1) (2) (4) & European Communities Act 1972, sch. 2, para. 1A. - Issued: 13.11.2008. Made: 22.10.2008. Laid before the National Assembly for Wales: 23.10.2008. Coming into force: 17.11.2008. Effect: S.I. 2006/1643 (W.158) amended & S.I. 2001/3541 (W.288); 2004/2697 (W.236); 2005/1162 (W.77) revoked. Territorial extent & classification: W. General. - EC note: This Order amends S.I. 2006/1643 (W.158) so as to implement: Commission Directive 2008/64/EC amending Annexes I to IV to Council Directive 2000/29/EC; Commission Directive 2008/61/EC; Commission Decision 2008/86/EC, being Decision No. 1/2008 of the Joint Committee on Agriculture set up by the Agreement between the European Community and the Swiss Confederation on Trade in Agricultural Products, which makes changes to the list of relevant material originating in Switzerland which may be landed in or moved within Wales if accompanied by a Swiss plant passport (article 2(13)). - In English and Welsh. Welsh title: Gorchymyn Iechyd Planhigion (Cymru) (Diwygio) 2008. - 8p.: 30 cm. - 978-0-11-091865-5 £5.00

The Seed Potatoes (Wales) (Amendment) Regulations 2008 No. 2008/1063 (W.112). - Enabling power: Plant Varieties and Seeds Act 1964, s. 16 (1). - Issued: 23.04.2008. Made: 09.04.2008. Laid before the National Assembly for Wales: 10.04.2008. Coming into force: 06.05.2008. Effect: S.I. 2006/2929 (W. 264) amended. Territorial extent & classification: W. General. - In English and Welsh. Welsh title: Rheoliadau Tatws Hadyd (Cymru) (Diwygio) 2008. - 4p.: 30 cm. - 978-0-11-091806-8 £3.00

Police

The Immigration and Police (Passenger, Crew and Service Information) Order 2008 No. 2008/5. - Enabling power: Immigration Act 1971, sch. 2, paras 27, 27B & Immigration, Asylum and Nationality Act 2006, s. 32. - Issued: 11.01.2008. Made: 03.01.2008. Laid: 10.01.2008. Coming into force: 01.03.2008. Effect: S.I. 1972/1667; 1975/980; 2000/912 revoked. Territorial extent & classification: E/W/S/NI. General. - 12p.: 30 cm. - 978-0-11-080801-7 £3.00

The Immigration, Asylum and Nationality Act 2006 (Data Sharing Code of Practice) Order 2008 No. 2008/8. - Enabling power: Immigration, Asylum and Nationality Act 2006, s. 37 (2). - Issued: 11.01.2008. Made: 08.01.2008. Laid: 10.01.2008. Coming into force: 01.03.2008. Effect: None. Territorial extent & classification: E/W/S/NI. General. - 2p.: 30 cm. - 978-0-11-080807-9 £3.00

The Immigration, Asylum and Nationality Act 2006 (Duty to Share Information and Disclosure of Information for Security Purposes) Order 2008 No. 2008/539. - Enabling power: Immigration, Asylum and Nationality Act 2006, ss. 36 (4), 38 (4). - Issued: 04.03.2008. Made: 28.02.2008. Coming into force: 01.03.2008. Effect: None. Territorial extent & classification: E/W/S/NI. General. - 8p.: 30 cm. - 978-0-11-081055-3 £3.00

The Ministry of Defence Police Appeal Tribunals (Amendment) Regulations 2008 No. 2008/2059. - Enabling power: Ministry of Defence Police Act 1987, s. 4A (3). - Issued: 01.08.2008. Made: 29.07.2008. Laid: 30.07.2008. Coming into force: 20.08.2008. Effect: S.I. 2004/652 amended. Territorial extent & classification: E/W/S. General. - 2p.: 30 cm. - 978-0-11-083655-3 £3.00

Police, England and Wales

The Criminal Justice and Immigration Act 2008 (Commencement No. 2 and Transitional and Saving Provisions) Order 2008 No. 2008/1586 (C.69). - Enabling power: Criminal Justice and Immigration Act 2008, s. 153 (4) (7) (8). Bringing into operation various provisions of the 2008 Act on 14.07.2008 & 15.07.2008 in accord. with art. 2. - Issued: 25.06.2008. Made: 17.06.2008. Effect: None. Territorial extent & classification: E/W/NI. General. - 8p.: 30 cm. - 978-0-11-081886-3 £3.00

The Criminal Justice and Immigration Act 2008 (Commencement No. 3 and Transitional Provisions) Order 2008 No. 2008/2712 (C.118). - Enabling power: Criminal Justice and Immigration Act 2008, s. 153 (4) (7). Bringing into operation various provisions of the 2008 Act on 03.11.2008 in accord. with art. 2. - Issued: 20.10.2008. Made: 13.10.2008. Effect: None. Territorial extent & classification: E/W/NI [some aspects E/W only]. General. - 8p.: 30 cm. - 978-0-11-084677-4 £5.00

The Criminal Justice and Immigration Act 2008 (Commencement No. 4 and Saving Provision) Order 2008 No. 2008/2993 (C.128). - Enabling power: Criminal Justice and Immigration Act 2008, s. 153 (7). Bringing into operation various provisions of the 2008 Act on 01.12.2008, 26.01.2009 in accord. with art. 2 and subject to art. 3. - Issued: 21.11.2008. Made: 15.11.2008. Effect: None. Territorial extent & classification: E/W/NI (some aspects E/W only). General. - 8p.: 30 cm. - 978-0-11-147015-2 £5.00

The Criminal Justice and Immigration Act 2008 (Commencement No. 5) Order 2008 No. 2008/3260 (C.149). - Enabling power: Criminal Justice and Immigration Act 2008, s. 153 (5) (a) (7). Bringing into operation various provisions of the 2008 Act on 19.12.2008, 01.01.2009 in accord. with art. 2. - Issued: 23.12.2008. Made: 18.12.2008. Effect: None. Territorial extent & classification: E/W (some aspects E. only). General. - 4p.: 30 cm. - 978-0-11-147227-9 £4.00

The Local Authorities (Alcohol Disorder Zones) Regulations 2008 No. 2008/1430. - Enabling power: Violent Crime Reduction Act 2006, ss. 15, 16 (7), 17 (6), 20 (5) & Local Government Act 2000, ss. 13, 105 (2). - Issued: 09.06.2008. Made: 04.06.2008. Coming into force: 05.06.2008. Effect: S.I. 2000/2853; 2007/399 amended. Territorial extent & classification: E/W. General. - Supersedes draft S.I. (ISBN 9780110813295) issued 04.04.2008. - 16p.: 30 cm. - 978-0-11-081787-3 £3.00

The Metropolitan Police Authority Regulations 2008 No. 2008/631. - Enabling power: Police Act 1996, sch. 2A, paras 1, 7. - Issued: 12.03.2008. Made: 06.03.2008. Laid: 07.03.2008. Coming into force: 01.04.2008. Effect: None. Territorial extent & classification: E/W. General. - 12p.: 30 cm. - 978-0-11-081134-5 £3.00

The Penalties for Disorderly Behaviour (Amount of Penalty) (Amendment) Order 2008 No. 2008/3297. - Enabling power: Criminal Justice and Police Act 2001, s. 3 (1) (1A). - Issued: 07.01.2009. Made: 29.12.2008. Laid: 02.01.2009. Coming into force: 26.01.2009. Effect: S.I. 2002/1837 amended & S.I. 2004/2468; 2005/581 revoked. Territorial extent & classification: E/W. General. - Revoked by S.I. 2009/83 (ISBN 9780111473160). - 8p.: 30 cm. - 978-0-11-147242-2 £5.00

The Police Act 1997 (Criminal Records) (Amendment) Regulations 2008 No. 2008/2143. - Enabling power: Police Act 1997, s. 113B (2) (b), 113D (4) (d), 125. - Issued: 13.08.2008. Made: 07.08.2008. Laid: 11.08.2008. Coming into force: 01.09.2008. Effect: S.I. 2002/233 amended. Territorial extent & classification: E/W. General. - 2p.: 30 cm. - 978-0-11-083740-6 £3.00

The Police (Amendment) Regulations 2008 No. 2008/2865. - Enabling power: Police Act 1996, s. 50. - Issued: 11.11.2008. Made: 05.11.2008. Laid: 07.11.2008. Coming into force: 01.12.2008. Effect: S.I. 2003/527 amended. Territorial extent & classification: E/W. General. - 4p.: 30 cm. - 978-0-11-084985-0 £4.00

The Police and Criminal Evidence Act 1984 (Codes of Practice) Order 2008 No. 2008/167. - Enabling power: Police and Criminal Evidence Act 1984, ss. 60 (1) (a), 66 (1) (a) to (d). - Issued: 04.02.2008. Made: 29.01.2008. Coming into force: 01.02.2008. Effect: None. Territorial extent & classification: E/W. General. - Supersedes draft S.I. (ISBN 9780110805849) issued 20.12.2007. - 2p.: 30 cm. - 978-0-11-080882-6 £3.00

The Police and Criminal Evidence Act 1984 (Codes of Practice) (Revisions to Code A) (No. 2) Order 2008 No. 2008/3146. - Enabling power: Police and Criminal Evidence Act 1984, s. 67 (5). - Issued: 17.12.2008. Made: 08.12.2008. Laid: 10.12.2008. Coming into force: 01.01.2009. Effect: Brings into operation the revision of PACE Code A (the Police and Criminal Evidence Act 1984 Code of Practice on stop and search) which was laid before Parliament on 10.12.2008. Territorial extent & classification: E/W. General. - This is a corrected reprint replacing the SI of the same number (ISBN 9780111471371) issued 12.12.2008, and is being issued free of charge to all known recipients of the original version. - 2p.: 30 cm. - 978-0-11-147179-1 £4.00

The Police and Criminal Evidence Act 1984 (Codes of Practice) (Revisions to Code A) (No. 2) Order 2008 No. 2008/3146. - Enabling power: Police and Criminal Evidence Act 1984, s. 67 (5). - Issued: 12.12.2008. Made: 08.12.2008. Laid: 10.12.2008. Coming into force: 01.01.2009. Effect: Brings into operation the revision of PACE Code A (the Police and Criminal Evidence Act 1984 Code of Practice on stop and search) which was laid before Parliament on 10.12.2008. Territorial extent & classification: E/W. General. - Superseded by S.I. of same no. and title (ISBN 9780111471791). - 2p.: 30 cm. - 978-0-11-147137-1 £4.00

The Police and Criminal Evidence Act 1984 (Codes of Practice) (Revisions to Code A) Order 2008 No. 2008/2638. - Enabling power: Police and Criminal Evidence Act 1984, s. 67 (5). - Issued: 09.10.2008. Made: 06.10.2008. Laid: 06.10.2008. Coming into force: 27.10.2008. Effect: Brings into operation the revision of para. 4 of PACE Code A (the Police and Criminal Evidence Act 1984 Code of Practice on stop and search) which was laid before Parliament on 06.10.2008. Territorial extent & classification: E/W. General. - 2p.: 30 cm. - 978-0-11-084402-2 £4.00

The Police and Justice Act 2006 (Commencement No.1, Transitional and Saving Provisions) (Amendment) Order 2008 No. 2008/617 (C. 24). - Enabling power: Police and Justice Act 2006, ss. 49 (3) (c), 53 (1). - Issued: 12.03.2008. Made: 06.03.2008. Coming into force: 30.03.2008. Effect: S.I. 2006/3364 (C. 123) amended. Territorial extent & classification: E/W. General. - With correction slip dated March 2008. - 2p.: 30 cm. - 978-0-11-081130-7 £3.00

The Police and Justice Act 2006 (Commencement No. 7 and Savings Provision) Order 2008 No. 2008/311 (C.11). - Enabling power: Police and Justice Act 2006, ss. 49 (3) (c), 53 (1). Bringing into operation various provisions of the 2006 Act on 14.03.2008. - Issued: 14.02.2008. Made: 11.02.2008. Effect: None. Territorial extent & classification: E/W. General. - With correction slip dated April 2008. - 4p.: 30 cm. - 978-0-11-080938-0 £3.00

The Police and Justice Act 2006 (Commencement No. 8) Order 2008 No. 2008/790 (C.37). - Enabling power: Police and Justice Act 2006, s. 53 (1). Bringing into operation various provisions of the 2006 Act on 01.04.2008. - Issued: 28.03.2008. Made: 18.03.2008. Effect: None. Territorial extent & classification: E/W/NI. General. - 4p.: 30 cm. - 978-0-11-081279-3 £3.00

The Police and Justice Act 2006 (Commencement No. 9) Order 2008 No. 2008/2503 (C.107). - Enabling power: Police and Justice Act 2006, s. 53 (1). Bringing into operation various provisions of the 2006 Act on 01.10.2008. - Issued: 29.09.2008. Made: 24.09.2008. Effect: None. Territorial extent & classification: E/W/NI. General. - 8p.: 30 cm. - 978-0-11-084270-7 £5.00

The Police and Justice Act 2006 (Commencement No. 10) Order 2008 No. 2008/2785 (C.123). - Enabling power: Police and Justice Act 2006, ss. 49 (3), 53 (1). Bringing into operation various provisions of the 2006 Act on 14.11.2008. - Issued: 28.10.2008. Made: 24.10.2008. Effect: None. Territorial extent & classification: E/W. General. - 4p.: 30 cm. - 978-0-11-084732-0 £4.00

The Police and Justice Act 2006 (Supplementary and Transitional Provisions) (Amendment) Order 2008 No. 2008/619. - Enabling power: Police and Justice Act 2006, s. 51. - Issued: 12.03.2008. Made: 06.03.2008. Laid: 07.03.2008. Coming into force: 30.03.2008. Effect: S.I. 2006/3365 amended. Territorial extent & classification: E/W. General. - 2p.: 30 cm. - 978-0-11-081129-1 £3.00

The Police Appeals Tribunals Rules 2008 No. 2008/2863. - Enabling power: Police Act 1996, s. 85. - Issued: 11.11.2008. Made: 05.11.2008. Coming into force: 01.12.2008. Effect: S.I. 2006/594 amended & S.I. 1999/818 revoked. Territorial extent & classification: E/W. General. - Supersedes draft S.I. (ISBN 9780110835150) issued 24.07.2008. - 12p.: 30 cm. - 978-0-11-084982-9 £5.00

The Police Authorities (Best Value) Performance Indicators Order 2008 No. 2008/659. - Enabling power: Local Government Act 1999, s. 4 (1) (a). - Issued: 14.03.2008. Made: 10.03.2008. Laid: 11.03.2008. Coming into force: 01.04.2008. Effect: S.I. 2005/470; 2006/620 revoked. Territorial extent & classification: E/W. General. - 4p.: 30 cm. - 978-0-11-081167-3 £3.00

The Police Authorities (Particular Functions and Transitional Provisions) Order 2008 No. 2008/82. - Enabling power: Police Act 1996, s. 6ZA, Police and Justice Act 2006, s. 51. - Issued: 21.01.2008. Made: 03.01.2008. Laid: 18.01.2008. Coming into force: 14.03.2008. Effect: None. Territorial extent & classification: E/W. General. - 2p.: 30 cm. - 978-0-11-080848-2 £3.00

The Police Authority Regulations 2008 No. 2008/630. - Enabling power: Police Act 1996, s. 4 (2), sch. 2, paras 1, 7. - Issued: 12.03.2008. Made: 06.03.2008. Laid: 07.03.2008. Coming into force: 01.04.2008, 01.10.2008 in accord. with reg. 1. Effect: S.I. 1994/2023 revoked. Territorial extent & classification: E/W. General. - 12p.: 30 cm. - 978-0-11-081136-9 £3.00

The Police (Complaints and Misconduct) (Amendment) Regulations 2008 No. 2008/2866. - Enabling power: Police Reform Act 2002, ss. 13, 23 (1) (2) (g) (r), 105 (4), sch. 3, paras 19B (7) (10), 19C (2) (b), 19D, 22 (7), 29. - Issued: 11.11.2008. Made: 05.11.2008. Laid: 07.11.2008. Coming into force: 01.12.2008. Effect: S.I. 2004/643 amended. Territorial extent & classification: E/W. General. - 8p.: 30 cm. - 978-0-11-084986-7 £5.00

The Police (Conduct) Regulations 2008 No. 2008/2864. - Enabling power: Police Act 1996, ss. 50, 51, 84. - Issued: 12.11.2008. Made: 05.11.2008. Coming into force: 01.12.2008. Effect: S.I. 2004/645 revoked with saving. Territorial extent & classification: E/W. General. - Supersedes draft S.I. (ISBN 9780110845265) issued 10.10.2008. - 40p.: 30 cm. - 978-0-11-084983-6 £9.00

Police, England and Wales

The Police Pensions (Amendment) Regulations 2008 No. 2008/1887. - Enabling power: Police Pensions Act 1976, s. 1. - Issued: 21.07.2008. Made: 15.07.2008. Laid: 17.07.2008. Coming into force: 08.08.2008 but has effect in accord. with reg. 1 (2) (3). Effect: S.I. 1987/257, 2215; 2006/932, 3415; 2007/1932 amended. Territorial extent & classification: E/W. General. - 12p.: 30 cm. - 978-0-11-083366-8 £3.00

The Police (Performance) Regulations 2008 No. 2008/2862. - Enabling power: Police Act 1996, ss. 50, 51, 84. - Issued: 11.11.2008. Made: 05.11.2008. Coming into force: 01.12.2008. Effect: S.I. 1999/732; 2003/528, 2600 revoked with savings. Territorial extent & classification: E/W. General. - Supersedes draft S.I. (ISBN 9780110835181) issued 24.07.2008. - 32p.: 30 cm. - 978-0-11-084981-2 £9.00

The Police (Promotion) (Amendment) Regulations 2008 No. 2008/273. - Enabling power: Police Act 1996, s. 50. - Issued: 12.02.2008. Made: 07.02.2008. Laid: 11.02.2008. Coming into force: 07.03.2008. Effect: S.I. 1996/1685 amended. Territorial extent & classification: E/W. General. - 2p.: 30 cm. - 978-0-11-080929-8 £3.00

The Police (Retention and Disposal of Motor Vehicles) (Amendment) Regulations 2008 No. 2008/2096. - Enabling power: Police Reform Act 2002, ss. 60, 105 (4). - Issued: 07.08.2008. Made: 28.07.2008. Laid: 05.08.2008. Coming into force: 01.10.2008. Effect: S.I. 2002/3049 amended. Territorial extent & classification: E/W. General. - 4p.: 30 cm. - 978-0-11-083702-4 £3.00

The Policing Plan Regulations 2008 No. 2008/312. - Enabling power: Police Act 1996, s. 6ZB (5) (6) (7) and Police and Justice Act 2006, s. 51. - Issued: 14.02.2008. Made: 11.02.2008. Laid: 12.02.2008. Coming into force: 14.03.2008. Effect: None. Territorial extent & classification: E/W. General. - 4p.: 30 cm. - 978-0-11-080940-3 £3.00

The Serious Crime Act 2007 (Commencement No. 2 and Transitional and Transitory Provisions and Savings) Order 2008 No. 2008/755 (C.34). - Enabling power: Serious Crime Act 2007, ss. 91 (2), 94 (1). Bringing into operation various provisions of the 2007 Act on 01.04.2008 & 06.04.2008. - Issued: 25.03.2008. Made: 17.03.2008. Effect: None. Territorial extent & classification: E/W/S/NI [part E/W only]. General. - 12p.: 30 cm. - 978-0-11-081264-9 £3.00

The Serious Organised Crime and Police Act 2005 (Commencement No. 12) Order 2008 No. 2008/306 (C.7). - Enabling power: Serious Organised Crime and Police Act 2005, s. 178 (8) (9). Bringing into operation, for England & Wales, various provisions of the 2005 Act on 29.02.2008. - Issued: 13.02.2008. Made: 07.02.2008. Effect: None. Territorial extent & classification: E/W. General. - 8p.: 30 cm. - 978-0-11-080934-2 £3.00

The Supply of Information (Register of Deaths) (England and Wales) Order 2008 No. 2008/570. - Enabling power: Police and Justice Act 2006, s. 13 (1) (d). - Issued: 19.03.2008. Made: 03.03.2008. Laid: 04.03.2008. Coming into force: 25.03.2008. Effect: S.I. 2007/3460 revoked. Territorial extent & classification: E/W. General. - This Statutory Instrument has been made in consequence of a defect in Statutory Instrument 2007/3460 (ISBN 9780110806358) and is being issued free of charge to all known recipients of that Statutory Instrument. - 4p.: 30 cm. - 978-0-11-081259-5 £3.00

Police, Northern Ireland

The Police and Justice Act 2006 (Commencement No. 8) Order 2008 No. 2008/790 (C.37). - Enabling power: Police and Justice Act 2006, s. 53 (1). Bringing into operation various provisions of the 2006 Act on 01.04.2008. - Issued: 28.03.2008. Made: 18.03.2008. Effect: None. Territorial extent & classification: E/W/NI. General. - 4p.: 30 cm. - 978-0-11-081279-3 £3.00

The Police and Justice Act 2006 (Commencement No. 9) Order 2008 No. 2008/2503 (C.107). - Enabling power: Police and Justice Act 2006, s. 53 (1). Bringing into operation various provisions of the 2006 Act on 01.10.2008. - Issued: 29.09.2008. Made: 24.09.2008. Effect: None. Territorial extent & classification: E/W/NI. General. - 8p.: 30 cm. - 978-0-11-084270-7 £5.00

The Supply of Information (Register of Deaths) (Northern Ireland) Order 2008 No. 2008/700. - Enabling power: Police and Justice Act 2006, ss. 13 (1) (d), 49. - Issued: 19.03.2008. Made: 08.03.2008. Laid: 17.03.2008. Coming into force: 08.04.2008. Effect: S.I. 2007/3390 revoked. Territorial extent & classification: NI. General. - This Statutory Instrument has been made in consequence of a defect in S.I. 2007/3390 (ISBN 9780110800868) and is being issued free of charge to all known recipients of that statutory instrument. - 4p.: 30 cm. - 978-0-11-080089-9 £3.00

Political parties

The Electoral Administration Act 2006 (Commencement No.1 and Transitional Provisions) (Northern Ireland) Order 2008 No. 2008/1656 (C. 74). - Enabling power: Electoral Administration Act 2006, ss. 77 (2) (4). Bringing into operation various provisions of the 2006 Act, so far as they extend to Northern Ireland, on 01.07.2008. - Issued: 01.07.2008. Made: 25.06.2008. Effect: None. Territorial extent & classification: NI. General. - 8p.: 30 cm. - 978-0-11-081914-3 £3.00

The Electoral Administration Act 2006 (Regulation of Loans etc: Northern Ireland) Order 2008 No. 2008/1319. - Enabling power: Electoral Administration Act 2006, s. 63 (1) (3) (a) (b) (c) (e). - Issued: 20.05.2008. Made: 14.05.2008. Coming into force: 15.05.2008 for arts 1, 2, 6; 01.07.2008 for remainder- in accord. with art. 1 (2). Effect: 2000 c.41 amended. Territorial extent & classification: NI. General. - Supersedes draft SI (ISBN 9780110811956) issued 18.03.2008. - 8p.: 30 cm. - 978-0-11-081474-2 £3.00

The Political Parties, Elections and Referendums Act 2000 (Northern Ireland Political Parties) Order 2008 No. 2008/1737. - Enabling power: S.I. 2008/1319, art. 6 (1) (2) (a) & Political Parties, Elections and Referendums Act 2000, ss. 71Z1 (1) (a) (b), 71Z3 (1), 71Z4 (2) (b) (4), 156 (5). - Issued: 07.07.2008. Made: 30.06.2008. Coming into force: 01.07.2008. Effect: 2000 c. 41 amended. Territorial extent & classification: NI. General. - Supersedes draft S.I. (ISBN 9780110814780) published on 22.05.2008. - 8p.: 30 cm. - 978-0-11-081953-2 £3.00

Political parties: Donations

The Political Donations and Regulated Transactions (Anonymous Electors) Regulations 2008 No. 2008/2869. - Enabling power: Political Parties, Elections and Referendums Act 2000, s. 65 (2A), sch. 6, paras 2 (3B) (3C), 3 (2) (3), sch 6A, para. 2 (3), sch. 7, para. 10 (4A), sch. 11, para. 10 (4), sch. 15, 10 (4). - Issued: 11.11.2008. Made: 04.11.2008. Laid: 06.11.2008. Coming into force: 01.12.2008. Effect: S.I. 2006/2974 revoked. Territorial extent & classification: E/W/S. General. - 2p.: 30 cm. - 978-0-11-084979-9 £4.00

Postal services

The Postal Services (Consumer Complaints Handling Standards) Regulations 2008 No. 2008/2355. - Enabling power: Consumers, Estate Agents and Redress Act 2007, ss. 43, 44, 46. - Issued: 08.09.2008. Made: 03.09.2008. Coming into force: 01.10.2008. Effect: None. Territorial extent & classification: E/W/S/NI. General. - 8p.: 30 cm. - 978-0-11-084067-3 £5.00

The Postal Services Regulated Providers (Redress Scheme) Order 2008 No. 2008/2267. - Enabling power: Consumers, Estate Agents and Redress Act 2007, s. 47 (1) to (3). - Issued: 29.08.2008. Made: 16.08.2008. Laid: 27.08.2008. Coming into force: 01.10.2008. Effect: None. Territorial extent & classification: E/W/S/NI. General. - 4p.: 30 cm. - 978-0-11-083862-5 £3.00

Poultry

The Scotland Act 1998 (Agency Arrangements) (Specification) Order 2008 No. 2008/1035. - Enabling power: Scotland Act 1998, ss. 93. - Issued: 15.04.2008. Made: 09.04.2008. Laid: 16.04.2008. Coming into force: 07.05.2008. Effect: None. Territorial extent & classification: GB. General. - 16p.: 30 cm. - 978-0-11-081605-0 £3.00

Prevention and suppression of terrorism

The Counter-Terrorism Act 2008 (Commencement No. 1) Order 2008 No. 2008/3296 (C.151). - Enabling power: Counter-Terrorism Act 2008, s. 100 (5). Bringing into operation various provisions of the 2008 Act on 24.12.2008. - Issued: 30.12.2008. Made: 23.12.2008. Effect: None. Territorial extent & classification: E/W/S/NI. General. - With correction slip dated August 2009. - 2p.: 30 cm. - 978-0-11-147240-8 £4.00

The Prevention of Terrorism Act 2005 (Continuance in force of sections 1 to 9) Order 2008 No. 2008/559. - Enabling power: Prevention of Terrorism Act 2005, s. 13 (2) (c). - Issued: 05.03.2008. Made: 03.03.2008. Coming into force: 11.03.2008. Effect: None. Territorial extent & classification: E/W/S/NI. General. - Supersedes draft SI (ISBN 9780110808819) issued 01.02.2008. - 2p.: 30 cm. - 978-0-11-081080-5 £3.00

The Terrorism Act 2000 (Proscribed Organisations) (Amendment) (No. 2) Order 2008 No. 2008/1931. - Enabling power: Terrorism Act 2000, s. 3 (3). - Issued: 23.07.2008. Made: 17.07.2008. Coming into force: 18.07.2008 in accord. with art. 1. Effect: 2000 c. 11 amended. Territorial extent & classification: E/W/S/NI. General. - Supersedes draft S.I. (ISBN 9780110819525) issued 07.07.2008. - 2p.: 30 cm. - 978-0-11-083479-5 £3.00

The Terrorism Act 2000 (Proscribed Organisations) (Amendment) Order 2008 No. 2008/1645. - Enabling power: Terrorism Act 2000, s. 3 (3) (b). - Issued: 26.06.2008. Made: 23.06.2008. Coming into force: 24.06.2008 in accord. with art. 1. Effect: 2000 c. 11 amended. Territorial extent & classification: E/W/S/NI. General. - Supersedes draft S.I. (ISBN 9780110814957) issued 23.05.2008. - 2p.: 30 cm. - 978-0-11-081903-7 £3.00

The Terrorism Act 2006 (Disapplication of Section 25) Order 2008 No. 2008/1745. - Enabling power: Terrorism Act 2006, s. 25 (2). - Issued: 23.05.2008. Made: 03.07.2008. Coming into force: 25.07.2008. Effect: None. Territorial extent & classification: E/W/S/NI. General. - Supersedes draft (ISBN 9780110814889). - 2p.: 30 cm. - 978-0-11-081957-0 £3.00

Prisons

The Criminal Justice and Immigration Act 2008 (Transitory Provisions) Order 2008 No. 2008/1587. - Enabling power: Criminal Justice and Immigration Act 2008, s. 148 (3) (4) (a). - Issued: 24.06.2008. Made: 17.06.2008. Laid: 19.06.2008. Coming into force: 14.07.2008. Effect: None. Territorial extent & classification: E/W/NI [part also incl. S]. General. - 4p.: 30 cm. - 978-0-11-081880-1 *£3.00*

Prisons, England and Wales

The Criminal Justice and Immigration Act 2008 (Commencement No. 1 and Transitional Provisions) Order 2008 No. 2008/1466 (C. 66). - Enabling power: Criminal Justice and Immigration Act 2008, s. 153 (7) (8) (b). Bringing into operation various provisions of the 2008 Act on 09.06.2008 in accord. with art. 2. - Issued: 11.06.2008. Made: 07.06.2008. Effect: None. Territorial extent & classification: E/W. General. - 4p.: 30 cm. - 978-0-11-081814-6 *£3.00*

The Early Removal of Fixed-Term Prisoners (Amendment of Eligibility Period) Order 2008 No. 2008/978. - Enabling power: Criminal Justice Act 2003, s. 260 (6) (a). - Issued: 08.04.2008. Made: 02.04.2008. Coming into force: 07.04.2008. Effect: 2003 c.44 amended. Territorial extent & classification: E/W. General. - Supersedes draft SI (ISBN 9780110811970) issued 14.03.2008. - 2p.: 30 cm. - 978-0-11-081345-5 *£3.00*

The Early Removal of Short-Term and Long-Term Prisoners (Amendment of Requisite Period) Order 2008 No. 2008/977. - Enabling power: Criminal Justice Act 1991, s. 46A (6) (a). - Issued: 08.04.2008. Made: 02.04.2008. Coming into force: 07.04.2008. Effect: 1991 c.53 amended. Territorial extent & classification: E/W. General. - Supersedes draft SI (ISBN 9780110811987) issued 14.03.2008. - 2p.: 30 cm. - 978-0-11-081342-4 *£3.00*

The Offender Management Act 2007 (Commencement No. 2 and Transitional Provision) Order 2008 No. 2008/504 (C.18). - Enabling power: Offender Management Act 2007, s. 41. Bringing into operation various provisions of the 2007 Act on 01.03.2008; 01.04.2008. - Issued: 29.02.2008. Made: 25.02.2008. Effect: None. Territorial extent & classification: E/W. General. - 4p.: 30 cm. - 978-0-11-081020-1 *£3.00*

The Prison (Amendment) Rules 2008 No. 2008/597. - Enabling power: Prison Act 1952, s. 47. - Issued: 18.03.2008. Made: 04.03.2008. Laid: 05.03.2008. Coming into force: 01.04.2008. Effect: S.I. 1999/728 amended. Territorial extent & classification: E/W. General. - 4p.: 30 cm. - 978-0-11-081254-0 *£3.00*

Prisons, England and Wales: Repatriation

The Criminal Justice and Immigration Act 2008 (Commencement No. 2 and Transitional and Saving Provisions) Order 2008 No. 2008/1586 (C.69). - Enabling power: Criminal Justice and Immigration Act 2008, s. 153 (4) (7) (8). Bringing into operation various provisions of the 2008 Act on 14.07.2008 & 15.07.2008 in accord. with art. 2. - Issued: 25.06.2008. Made: 17.06.2008. Effect: None. Territorial extent & classification: E/W/NI. General. - 8p.: 30 cm. - 978-0-11-081886-3 *£3.00*

Prisons, Northern Ireland

The Northern Ireland (Sentences) Act 1998 (Specified Organisations) Order 2008 No. 2008/1975. - Enabling power: Northern Ireland (Sentences) Act 1998, s. 3 (8). - Issued: 28.07.2008. Made: 22.07.2008. Coming into force: 23.07.2008. Effect: S.I. 2005/2558 revoked. Territorial extent & classification: NI. General. - 2p.: 30 cm. - 978-0-11-083626-3 *£3.00*

Prisons, Northern Ireland: Repatriation

The Criminal Justice and Immigration Act 2008 (Commencement No. 2 and Transitional and Saving Provisions) Order 2008 No. 2008/1586 (C.69). - Enabling power: Criminal Justice and Immigration Act 2008, s. 153 (4) (7) (8). Bringing into operation various provisions of the 2008 Act on 14.07.2008 & 15.07.2008 in accord. with art. 2. - Issued: 25.06.2008. Made: 17.06.2008. Effect: None. Territorial extent & classification: E/W/NI. General. - 8p.: 30 cm. - 978-0-11-081886-3 *£3.00*

Private international law, England and Wales

The Law Applicable to Non-Contractual Obligations (England and Wales and Northern Ireland) Regulations 2008 No. 2008/2986. - Enabling power: European Communities Act 1972, s. 2 (2). - Issued: 25.11.2008. Made: 12.11.2008. Laid: 18.11.2008. Coming into force: 11.01.2009. Effect: 1984 c. 16; 1995 c. 42; S.I. 1985/754 (N.I. 5) amended. Territorial extent & classification: E/W/NI. General. - With correction slip dated September 2009. - 4p.: 30 cm. - 978-0-11-147046-6 *£4.00*

Private international law, Northern Ireland

The Law Applicable to Non-Contractual Obligations (England and Wales and Northern Ireland) Regulations 2008 No. 2008/2986. - Enabling power: European Communities Act 1972, s. 2 (2). - Issued: 25.11.2008. Made: 12.11.2008. Laid: 18.11.2008. Coming into force: 11.01.2009. Effect: 1984 c. 16; 1995 c. 42; S.I. 1985/754 (N.I. 5) amended. Territorial extent & classification: E/W/NI. General. - With correction slip dated September 2009. - 4p.: 30 cm. - 978-0-11-147046-6 *£4.00*

Probation

The Offender Management Act 2007 (Consequential Amendments) Order 2008 No. 2008/912. - Enabling power: Offender Management Act 2007, s. 38 (1) (a) (2) (a). - Issued: 03.04.2008. Made: 27.03.2008. Laid: 06.02.2008. Coming into force: 01.04.2008. Effect: 34 acts & 15 SIs amended. Territorial extent & classification: E/W/S/NI. General. - With correction slip dated June 2008. - 28p.: 30 cm. - 978-0-11-081306-6 £4.50

Probation, England and Wales

The Offender Management Act 2007 (Approved Premises) Regulations 2008 No. 2008/1263. - Enabling power: Offender Management Act 2007, s. 13 (2). - Issued: 12.05.2008. Made: 06.05.2008. Laid: 07.05.2008. Coming into force: 01.06.2008. Effect: S.I. 2001/850 revoked. Territorial extent & classification: E/W. General. - 8p.: 30 cm. - 978-0-11-081437-7 £3.00

The Offender Management Act 2007 (Commencement No. 2 and Transitional Provision) Order 2008 No. 2008/504 (C.18). - Enabling power: Offender Management Act 2007, s. 41. Bringing into operation various provisions of the 2007 Act on 01.03.2008; 01.04.2008. - Issued: 29.02.2008. Made: 25.02.2008. Effect: None. Territorial extent & classification: E/W. General. - 4p.: 30 cm. - 978-0-11-081020-1 £3.00

The Offender Management Act 2007 (Establishment of Probation Trusts) Order 2008 No. 2008/598. - Enabling power: Offender Management Act 2007, s. 5 (1). - Issued: 11.03.2008. Made: 05.03.2008. Laid: 05.03.2008. Coming into force: 01.04.2008. Effect: None. Territorial extent & classification: E/W. General. - 2p.: 30 cm. - 978-0-11-081114-7 £3.00

Proceeds of crime

The Proceeds of Crime Act 2002 (Cash Searches: Code of Practice) Order 2008 No. 2008/947. - Enabling power: Proceeds of Crime Act 2002, ss. 292 (4) (5), 459 (2) (b). - Issued: 04.04.2008. Made: 31.03.2008. Coming into force: 06.04.2008. Effect: None. Territorial extent & classification: E/W/S/NI. General. - 4p.: 30 cm. - 978-0-11-081327-1 £3.00

The Proceeds of Crime Act 2002 (Disclosure of Information) Order 2008 No. 2008/1909. - Enabling power: Proceeds of Crime Act 2002, ss. 436 (6), 438 (9). - Issued: 22.07.2008. Made: 17.07.2008. Coming into force: 23.07.2008. Effect: S.I. 2003/335 revoked. Territorial extent & classification: E/W/S/NI. General. - Supersedes draft S.I. (ISBN 9780110814506) issued 13.05.2008. - 4p.: 30 cm. - 978-0-11-083418-4 £3.00

The Proceeds of Crime Act 2002 (External Requests and Orders) (Amendment) Order 2008 No. 2008/302. - Enabling power: Proceeds of Crime Act 2002, s. 444. - Issued: 19.02.2008. Made: 12.02.2008. Laid: 19.02.2008. Coming into force: 01.04.2008 except for art. 3; 06.04.2008 for art. 3 in accord. with art. 1. Effect: 1980 c.58; S.I. 1989/1339 (N.I. 11); 2005/3181 amended. Territorial extent & classification: E/W/S/NI. General. - 8p.: 30 cm. - 978-0-11-080946-5 £3.00

The Proceeds of Crime Act 2002 (Investigations in different parts of the United Kingdom) (Amendment) Order 2008 No. 2008/298. - Enabling power: Proceeds of Crime Act 2002, ss. 443 (1) (d) (e) (3) (4). - Issued: 19.02.2008. Made: 12.02.2008. Laid: 19.02.2008. Coming into force: 01.04.2008 except for art 2 (3) (6), 06.04.2008 for art 2 (3) (6). Effect: S.I. 2003/425 amended. Territorial extent & classification: E/W/S/NI. General. - 4p.: 30 cm. - 978-0-11-080956-4 £3.00

The Proceeds of Crime Act 2002 (Investigations in England, Wales and Northern Ireland: Code of Practice) Order 2008 No. 2008/946. - Enabling power: Proceeds of Crime Act 2002, ss. 377 (4) (8), 459 (2) (b). - Issued: 04.04.2008. Made: 31.03.2008. Coming into force: 01.04.2008. Effect: None. Territorial extent & classification: E/W/S/NI. General. - 2p.: 30 cm. - 978-0-11-081326-4 £3.00

The Serious Crime Act 2007 (Amendment of the Proceeds of Crime Act 2002) Order 2008 No. 2008/949. - Enabling power: Serious Crime Act 2007, s, 90 (1). - Issued: 04.04.2008. Made: 31.03.2008. Coming into force: 01.04.2008 in accord. with art. 1. Effect: 2002 c. 29 amended. Territorial extent & classification: E/W/S/NI. General. - Supersedes draft SI (ISBN 9780110809656) issued 22.02.2008. - 2p.: 30 cm. - 978-0-11-081333-2 £3.00

The Serious Crime Act 2007 (Commencement No.1) Order 2008 No. 2008/219 (C.5). - Enabling power: Serious Crime Act 2007, s. 94 (1). Bringing into operation various provisions of the 2007 Act on 15.02.2008 & 01.03.2008. - Issued: 08.02.2008. Made: 05.02.2008. Effect: None. Territorial extent & classification: E/WS/NI. General. - 4p.: 30 cm. - z£3.00

The Serious Crime Act 2007 (Commencement No. 2 and Transitional and Transitory Provisions and Savings) Order 2008 No. 2008/755 (C.34). - Enabling power: Serious Crime Act 2007, ss. 91 (2), 94 (1). Bringing into operation various provisions of the 2007 Act on 01.04.2008 & 06.04.2008. - Issued: 25.03.2008. Made: 17.03.2008. Effect: None. Territorial extent & classification: E/W/S/NI [part E/W only]. General. - 12p.: 30 cm. - 978-0-11-081264-9 £3.00

The Serious Organised Crime and Police Act 2005 and Serious Crime Act 2007 (Consequential and Supplementary Amendments to Secondary Legislation) Order 2008 No. 2008/574. - Enabling power: Serious Organised Crime and Police Act 2005, s. 173 (1) & Serious Crime Act 2007, s. 90 (1). - Issued: 07.03.2008. Made: 04.03.2008. Laid: 06.03.2008. Coming into force: 01.04.2008. Effect: S.R. 1979/90; 2003/122; 2004/246; S.I. 1994/1811; 1996/1299 (N.I. 9); 2003/1417; 2007/3544 amended. Territorial extent & classification: E/W/S/NI [This Order amends several instruments the extent of which varies. The majority of the instruments amended only effect England and Wales or Northern Ireland. Insofar as any of the instruments amended effect Scotland the amendments are not within the legislative competence of the Scottish Parliament]. General. - With correction slip dated August 2009. - 8p.: 30 cm. - 978-0-11-081086-7 £3.00

Proceeds of crime, England and Wales

The Assets Recovery Agency (Abolition) Order 2008 No. 2008/575. - Enabling power: Serious Crime Act 2007, s. 74 (1). - Issued: 07.03.2008. Made: 04.03.2008. Coming into force: 01.04.2008. Effect: None. Territorial extent & classification: E/W/NI. General. - 2p.: 30 cm. - 978-0-11-081091-1 £3.00

The Proceeds of Crime Act 2002 (Investigative Powers of Prosecutors in England, Wales and Northern Ireland: Code of Practice) Order 2008 No. 2008/1978. - Enabling power: Proceeds of Crime Act 2002, s. 377A (5). - Issued: 29.07.2008. Made: 21.07.2008. Coming into force. 22.07.2008 in accord. with art. 1. Effect: None. Territorial extent & classification: E/W/NI. General. - Supersedes draft S.I. (ISBN 9780110818986) issued 27.06.2008. - 2p.: 30 cm. - 978-0-11-083631-7 £3.00

The Proceeds of Crime Act 2002 (Legal Expenses in Civil Recovery Proceedings) (Amendment) Regulations 2008 No. 2008/523. - Enabling power: Proceeds of Crime Act 2002, ss. 286A, 286B, 459 (2) & S.I. 2005/3181, arts 5 (2), 198, 199. - Issued: 03.03.2008. Made: 27.02.2008. Laid: 27.02.2008. Coming into force: 01.04.2008. Effect: S.I. 2005/3382 amended. Territorial extent & classification: E/W/NI. General. - 4p.: 30 cm. - 978-0-11-081034-8 £3.00

Proceeds of crime, Northern Ireland

The Assets Recovery Agency (Abolition) Order 2008 No. 2008/575. - Enabling power: Serious Crime Act 2007, s. 74 (1). - Issued: 07.03.2008. Made: 04.03.2008. Coming into force: 01.04.2008. Effect: None. Territorial extent & classification: E/W/NI. General. - 2p.: 30 cm. - 978-0-11-081091-1 £3.00

The Proceeds of Crime Act 2002 (Investigative Powers of Prosecutors in England, Wales and Northern Ireland: Code of Practice) Order 2008 No. 2008/1978. - Enabling power: Proceeds of Crime Act 2002, s. 377A (5). - Issued: 29.07.2008. Made: 21.07.2008. Coming into for. 22.07.2008 in accord. with art. 1. Effect: None. Territorial extent & classification: E/W/NI. General. - Supersedes draft S.I. (ISBN 9780110818986) issued 27.06.2008. - 2p.: 30 cm. - 978-0-11-083631-7 £3.00

The Proceeds of Crime Act 2002 (Legal Expenses in Civil Recovery Proceedings) (Amendment) Regulations 2008 No. 2008/523. - Enabling power: Proceeds of Crime Act 2002, ss. 286A, 286B, 459 (2) & S.I. 2005/3181, arts 5 (2), 198, 199. - Issued: 03.03.2008. Made: 27.02.2008. Laid: 27.02.2008. Coming into force: 01.04.2008. Effect: S.I. 2005/3382 amended. Territorial extent & classification: E/W/NI. General. - 4p.: 30 cm. - 978-0-11-081034-8 £3.00

Professions complementary to dentistry

The General Dental Council (Continuing Professional Development) (Professions Complementary to Dentistry) Rules Order of Council 2008 No. 2008/1823. - Enabling power: Dentists Act 1984, ss. 36Z1 (1) (4), 36Z2, 50A, 50C (5) (6). - Issued: 15.07.2008. Made: 04.07.2008. Coming into force: 01.08.2008. Effect: None. Territorial extent & classification: E/W/S/NI. General. - With Correction Slip dated January 2010. - 8p.: 30 cm. - 978-0-11-083118-3 £3.00

Protection of vulnerable adults, England

The Safeguarding Vulnerable Groups Act 2006 (Commencement No. 1) (England) Order 2008 No. 2008/3204 (C.145). - Enabling power: Safeguarding Vulnerable Groups Act 2006, ss. 61 (5), 65. Bringing into operation various provisions of the 2006 Act on 19.05.2008. - Issued: 17.12.2008. Made: 16.12.2008. Effect: None. Territorial extent & classification: E. General. - 8p.: 30 cm. - 978-0-11-147192-0 £5.00

Protection of vulnerable adults, England and Wales

The Protection of Children and Vulnerable Adults and Care Standards Tribunal (Children's and Adults' Barred Lists) (Transitional Provisions) Regulations 2008 No. 2008/1497. - Enabling power: Safeguarding Vulnerable Groups Act 2006, ss. 4 (8), 61 (5), 64 (1). - Issued: 16.06.2008. Made: 09.06.2008. Laid: 11.06.2008. Coming into force: 02.07.2008. Effect: None. Territorial extent & classification: E/W. General. - Revoked by S.I. 2008/2683 (ISBN 9780110846156). - 16p.: 30 cm. - 978-0-11-081840-5 £3.00

The Safeguarding Vulnerable Groups Act 2006 (Barred List Prescribed Information) Regulations 2008 No. 2008/16. - Enabling power: Safeguarding Vulnerable Groups Act 2006, ss. 2 (5), 60 (1). - Issued: 14.01.2008. Made: 08.01.2008. Laid: 11.01.2008. Coming into force: 04.02.2008. Effect: None. Territorial extent & classification: E/W. General. - 4p.: 30 cm. - 978-0-11-080824-6 £3.00

The Safeguarding Vulnerable Groups Act 2006 (Barring Procedure) Regulations 2008 No. 2008/474. - Enabling power: Safeguarding Vulnerable Groups Act 2006, ss. 61 (5), 64 (1), sch. 3, paras 15 (1) (2), 18 (3) (b) (6). - Issued: 05.03.2008. Made: 28.02.2008. Laid: 05.03.2008. Coming into force: 07.04.2008. Effect: None. Territorial extent & classification: E/W. General. - 8p.: 30 cm. - 978-0-11-081062-1 £3.00

The Safeguarding Vulnerable Groups Act 2006 (Commencement No. 2) Order 2008 No. 2008/1320 (C.57). - Enabling power: Safeguarding Vulnerable Groups Act 2006, ss. 61 (5), 65. Bringing into operation various provisions of the 2006 Act on 19.05.2008. - Issued: 21.05.2008. Made: 14.05.2008. Effect: None. Territorial extent & classification: E/W (and UK in respect of the commencement of amendments to the Data Protection Act 1998). General. - 8p.: 30 cm. - 978-0-11-081479-7 £3.00

The Safeguarding Vulnerable Groups Act 2006 (Prescribed Criteria) (Foreign Offences) Order 2008 No. 2008/3050. - Enabling power: Safeguarding Vulnerable Groups Act 2006, s. 64 (1) (2) (a) (3). - Issued: 28.11.2008. Made: 12.11.2008. Coming into force: 13.11.2008 in accord. with art. 1. Effect: 2006 c.47 amended. Territorial extent & classification: E/W. General. - Supersedes draft S.I. (ISBN 9780110845623) issued 15.10.2008. - 4p.: 30 cm. - 978-0-11-147061-9 £4.00

The Safeguarding Vulnerable Groups Act 2006 (Prescribed Criteria) (Transitional Provisions) Regulations 2008 No. 2008/1062. - Enabling power: Safeguarding Vulnerable Groups Act 2006, ss. 61 (5), 64 (1), sch. 3, paras 1 (1), 7 (1), 24 (1) to (3). - Issued: 17.04.2008. Made: 03.04.2008. Coming into force: 07.04.2008. Effect: None. Territorial extent & classification: E/W. General. - Supersedes draft SI (ISBN 9780110810676) issued 05.03.2008. - 8p.: 30 cm. - 978-0-11-081362-2 £3.00

The Safeguarding Vulnerable Groups Act 2006 (Prescribed Information) Regulations 2008 No. 2008/3265. - Enabling power: Safeguarding Vulnerable Groups Act 2006, ss. 35 (1) (a) (b), 36 (1) (2) (3), 37 (2), 39 (1) (5), 40 (2), 41 (1) (5), 42 (2), 45 (1) (5), 46 (1) (a) (2), 61 (5), sch. 3, paras 19 (1) (b), 21. - Issued: 29.12.2008. Made: 18.12.2008. Laid: 29.12.2008. Coming into force: 20.01.2009 for regs 1, 2, 5, 7, 9, 11, 12, schedule & 12.10.2009 for remainder, in accord. with art. 1. Effect: None. Territorial extent & classification: E/W. General. - Supersedes draft S.I. (ISBN 9780110845623) issued 15.10.2008. - 8p.: 30 cm. - 978-0-11-147231-6 £5.00

The Safeguarding Vulnerable Groups Act 2006 (Transitional Provisions) Order 2008 No. 2008/473. - Enabling power: Safeguarding Vulnerable Groups Act 2006, ss. 61 (5), 64 (1), sch. 8, paras 2, 3. - Issued: 05.03.2008. Made: 28.02.2008. Laid: 05.03.2008. Coming into force: 07.04.2008. Effect: None. Territorial extent & classification: E/W. General. - 8p.: 30 cm. - 978-0-11-081061-4 £3.00

Protection of vulnerable adults, Northern Ireland

The Safeguarding Vulnerable Groups Act 2006 (Commencement No. 1) (Northern Ireland) Order 2008 No. 2008/930 (C.45). - Enabling power: Safeguarding Vulnerable Groups Act 2006, ss. 61 (5), 65. Bringing into operation various provisions of the 2006 Act on 31.03.2008. - Issued: 07.04.2008. Made: 27.03.2008. Effect: None. Territorial extent & classification: NI. General. - 4p.: 30 cm. - 978-0-11-081320-2 £3.00

Protection of wrecks, England

The Protection of Wrecks (Designation) (England) Order 2008 No. 2008/2775. - Enabling power: Protection of Wrecks Act 1973, s. 1 (1) (2) (4). - Issued: 27.10.2008. Made: 21.10.2008. Laid: 23.10.2008. Coming into force: 24.10.2008. Effect: None. Territorial extent & classification: E. General. - 2p.: 30 cm. - 978-0-11-084712-2 £4.00

Public audit

The Serious Crime Act 2007 (Commencement No.1) Order 2008 No. 2008/219 (C.5). - Enabling power: Serious Crime Act 2007, s. 94 (1). Bringing into operation various provisions of the 2007 Act on 15.02.2008 & 01.03.2008. - Issued: 08.02.2008. Made: 05.02.2008. Effect: None. Territorial extent & classification: E/W/S/NI. General. - 4p.: 30 cm. - 978-0-11-080902-1 £3.00

The Serious Crime Act 2007 (Commencement No. 2 and Transitional and Transitory Provisions and Savings) Order 2008 No. 2008/755 (C.34). - Enabling power: Serious Crime Act 2007, ss. 91 (2), 94 (1). Bringing into operation various provisions of the 2007 Act on 01.04.2008 & 06.04.2008. - Issued: 25.03.2008. Made: 17.03.2008. Effect: None. Territorial extent & classification: E/W/S/NI [part E/W only]. General. - 12p.: 30 cm. - 978-0-11-081264-9 £3.00

Public health

The Appointments Commission (Amendment) Regulations 2008 No. 2008/2792. - Enabling power: Health Act 2006, sch. 4, para. 2 (b) (d). - Issued: 31.10.2008. Made: 26.10.2008. Laid: 31.10.2008. Coming into force: 08.12.2008. Effect: S.I. 2006/2380 amended. Territorial extent & classification: E/W/S/NI [some aspects E. only]. General. - 2p.: 30 cm. - 978-0-11-084743-6 £4.00

The Commission for Healthcare Audit and Inspection (Defence Medical Services) Regulations 2008 No. 2008/1181. - Enabling power: Health and Social Care (Community Health and Standards) Act 2003, ss. 124 (1), 195 (1) (2). - Issued: 01.05.2008. Made: 24.04.2008. Laid: 01.05.2008. Coming into force: 02.06.2008. Effect: None. Territorial extent & classification: E/W/S/NI. General. - Revoked by S.I. 2009/462 (C.31) (ISBN 9780111478547). - 2p.: 30 cm. - 978-0-11-081408-7 £3.00

The Health and Social Care Act 2008 (Consequential Amendments and Transitory Provisions) Order 2008 No. 2008/2250. - Enabling power: Health and Social Care Act 2008, s. 167. - Issued: 28.08.2008. Made: 20.08.2008. Laid: 28.08.2008. Coming into force: 01.10.2008. Effect: 1952 c. 52; 1996 c.16; 1998 c.18; 1999 c. 27; 2000 c.10; c. 43; 2003 c. 39; 2004 c. 23; 2006 c. 40, c. 41 modified & S.I. 1999/260, 2277; 2000/89; 2003/3060; 2005/408, 1447; 2415, 2531; 2006/2380, 3335 amended. Territorial extent & classification: E/W/S/NI. General. - 8p.: 30 cm. - 978-0-11-083849-6 £3.00

The Vaccine Damage Payments (Specified Disease) Order 2008 No. 2008/2103. - Enabling power: Vaccine Damage Payments Act 1979, ss. 1 (2) (i), 2 (2). - Issued: 08.08.2008. Made: 05.08.2008. Laid: 08.08.2008. Coming into force: 01.09.2008. Effect: 1979 c. 17 modified. Territorial extent & classification: E/W/S/NI/IoM. General. - 2p.: 30 cm. - 978-0-11-083716-1 £3.00

Public health, England

The Care Quality Commission (Membership) Regulations 2008 No. 2008/2252. - Enabling power: Health and Social Care Act 2008, s. 161 (3) (4), sch. 1, para. 3 (3). - Issued: 03.09.2008. Made: 20.08.2008. Laid: 03.09.2008. Coming into force: 01.10.2008. Effect: None. Territorial extent & classification: E. General. - With correction slip dated September 2009. - 8p.: 30 cm. - 978-0-11-083851-9 £3.00

The Health and Social Care Act 2008 (Commencement No.2) Order 2008 No. 2008/2497 (C.106). - Enabling power: Health and Social Care Act 2008, s. 170 (3) (4). Bringing into operation various provisions of the 2008 Act on 01.10.2008; 01.01.2009. - Issued: 25.09.2008. Made: 19.09.2008. Effect: None. Territorial extent & classification: E/WS/NI [parts E or E/W only]. General. - 4p.: 30 cm. - 978-0-11-084265-3 £4.00

The Health and Social Care Act 2008 (Commencement No. 4) Order 2008 No. 2008/2994 (C.129). - Enabling power: Health and Social Care Act 2008, s. 170 (3) (4). Bringing into operation various provisions of the 2008 Act on 01.12.2008, 01.04.2009 in accord. with art. 3. - Issued: 21.11.2008. Made: 15.11.2008. Effect: None. Territorial extent & classification: E/WS/NI (parts E or E/W only). General. - 4p.: 30 cm. - 978-0-11-147028-2 £4.00

The Private and Voluntary Health Care (England) Amendment Regulations 2008 No. 2008/2352. - Enabling power: Care Standards Act 2000, ss. 2 (4) (7) (8), 22 (1) (2), 118 (5) to (7). - Issued: 08.09.2008. Made: 03.09.2008. Laid: 08.09.2008. Coming into force: 01.10.2008. Effect: S.I. 2001/3968 amended. Territorial extent & classification: E. General. - 4p.: 30 cm. - 978-0-11-084015-4 £4.00

Public health, Northern Ireland

The Health and Social Care (Community Health and Standards) Act 2003 (Commencement No. 12) Order 2008 No. 2008/1334 (C.60). - Enabling power: Health and Social Care (Community Health and Standards) Act 2003, s. 199 (1). Bringing into operation various provisions of the 2003 Act on 02.06.2008, in accord. with art 2. - Issued: 29.05.2008. Made: 21.05.2008. Effect: None. Territorial extent & classification: S/NI. General. - 8p.: 30 cm. - 978-0-11-081751-4 £3.00

Public health, Scotland

The Health and Social Care (Community Health and Standards) Act 2003 (Commencement No. 12) Order 2008 No. 2008/1334 (C.60). - Enabling power: Health and Social Care (Community Health and Standards) Act 2003, s. 199 (1). Bringing into operation various provisions of the 2003 Act on 02.06.2008, in accord. with art 2. - Issued: 29.05.2008. Made: 21.05.2008. Effect: None. Territorial extent & classification: S/NI. General. - 8p.: 30 cm. - 978-0-11-081751-4 £3.00

Public health, Wales

The Private Dentistry (Wales) Regulations 2008 No. 2008/1976 (W.185). - Enabling power: Care Standards Act 2000, ss. 12 (2), 14 (1) (d), 15 (3), 16 (1) (3), 22 (1), 22 (2) (a) (c) (d), 25 (1), 42 (1), 118 (5) to (7). - Issued: 15.08.2008. Made: 23.07.2008. Laid before the National Assembly for Wales: 24.07.2008. Coming into force: 01.01.2009. Effect: 2000 c.14 modified; S.I. 2002/919 (W.107); 2006/878 (W.83) amended. Territorial extent & classification: W. General. - In English and Welsh. Welsh title: Rheoliadau Deintyddiaeth Breifat (Cymru) 2008. - 20p.: 30 cm. - 978-0-11-091825-9 £3.50

Public passenger transport

The Community Bus (Amendment) Regulations 2008 No. 2008/1465. - Enabling power: Public Passenger Vehicles Act 1981, ss. 52 (1) (a), 60 (1) (e) & Transport Act 1985, ss. 126 (1), 134. - Issued: 13.06.2008. Made: 05.06.2008. Laid: 12.06.2008. Coming into force: 01.08.2008. Effect: S.I. 1986/1245 amended. Territorial extent & classification: E/W/S. General. - Revoked by S.I. 2009/366 (ISBN 9780111474600). - 2p.: 30 cm. - 978-0-11-081813-9 £3.00

The Public Service Vehicles (Conditions of Fitness, Equipment, Use and Certification) (Amendment) Regulations 2008 No. 2008/1458. - Enabling power: Public Passenger Vehicles Act 1981, ss. 10 (1), 52 (1), 60. - Issued: 12.06.2008. Made: 05.06.2008. Laid: 12.06.2008. Coming into force: 13.07.2008. Effect: S.I. 1981/257 amended. Territorial extent & classification: E/W/S. General. - 4p.: 30 cm. - 978-0-11-081807-8 £3.00

The Public Service Vehicles (Operators' Licences) (Fees) (Amendment) Regulations 2008 No. 2008/1473. - Enabling power: Public Passenger Vehicles Act 1981, ss. 52 (1) (a), 60 (1) (e) (1A). - Issued: 12.06.2008. Made: 05.06.2008. Laid: 12.06.2008. Coming into force: 01.08.2008. Effect: S.I. 1995/2909 amended. Territorial extent & classification: E/W/S. General. - 4p.: 30 cm. - 978-0-11-081822-1 £3.00

The Road Transport (International Passenger Services) (Amendment) Regulations 2008 No. 2008/1577. - Enabling power: Finance Act 1973, s. 56 (1) (2). - Issued: 23.06.2008. Made: 13.06.2008. Laid: 17.06.2008. Coming into force: 01.08.2008. Effect: S.I. 1984/748 amended. Territorial extent & classification: E/W/S. General. - 2p.: 30 cm. - 978-0-11-081867-2 £3.00

Public passenger transport, England

The Concessionary Bus Travel (Permits) (England) (Amendment) Regulations 2008 No. 2008/2091. - Enabling power: Greater London Authority Act 1999, s. 243 (7) & Transport Act 2000, ss. 145A (5). - Issued: 06.08.2008. Made: 30.07.2008. Laid: 04.08.2008. Coming into force: 01.09.2008. Effect: S.I. 2008/417 amended. Territorial extent & classification: E. General. - 2p.: 30 cm. - 978-0-11-083699-7 £3.00

The Concessionary Bus Travel (Permits)(England) Regulations 2008 No. 2008/417. - Enabling power: Greater London Authority Act 1999, ss. 243 (7), 420 (1) & Transport Act 2000, ss. 145A (5), 160. - Issued: 27.02.2008. Made: 20.02.2008. Laid: 21.02.2008. Coming into force: 21.03.2008. Effect: None. Territorial extent & classification: E. General. - 12p., ill.: 30 cm. - 978-0-11-080978-6 £4.00

Public passenger transport, England and Wales

The Public Service Vehicles (Registration of Local Services) (Amendment) (England and Wales) Regulations 2008 No. 2008/1470. - Enabling power: Public Passenger Vehicles Act 1981, ss. 52 (1) (a), 60 (1) (e) (1A) & Transport Act 1985, ss. 126 (1), 134. - Issued: 12.06.2008. Made: 05.06.2008. Laid: 12.06.2008. Coming into force: 01.08.2008. Effect: S.I. 1986/1671 amended. Territorial extent & classification: E/W. General. - 4p.: 30 cm. - 978-0-11-081823-8 £3.00

Public procurement, England and Wales

The Public Contracts and Utilities Contracts (CPV Code Amendments) Regulations 2008 No. 2008/2256. - Enabling power: European Communities Act 1972, s. 2 (2). - Issued: 27.08.2008. Made: 22.08.2008. Laid: 22.08.2008. Coming into force: 15.09.2008. Effect: S.I. 2006/5, 6 amended. Territorial extent & classification: E/W/NI. General. - With correction slip dated September 2008. EC note: These regulations amend the 2006 regulations to reflect the amendments made by Commission Regulation (EC) 213/2008 to Directives 2004/17/EC and 2004/18/EC. - 12p.: 30 cm. - 978-0-11-083855-7 £3.00

The Public Contracts and Utilities Contracts (Postal Services Amendments) Regulations 2008 No. 2008/2848. - Enabling power: European Communities Act 1972, s. 2 (2). - Issued: 07.11.2008. Made: 03.11.2008. Laid: 04.11.2008. Coming into force: 01.12.2008. Effect: S.I. 2006/5, 6 amended. Territorial extent & classification: E/W/NI. General. - EC note: Implements article 6 of Council Directive 2004/17/EC concerning the co-ordination of procurement procedures of entities operating in the water, energy, transport and postal service sectors. - 4p.: 30 cm. - 978-0-11-084916-4 £4.00

Public procurement, Northern Ireland

The Public Contracts and Utilities Contracts (CPV Code Amendments) Regulations 2008 No. 2008/2256. - Enabling power: European Communities Act 1972, s. 2 (2). - Issued: 27.08.2008. Made: 22.08.2008. Laid: 22.08.2008. Coming into force: 15.09.2008. Effect: S.I. 2006/5, 6 amended. Territorial extent & classification: E/W/NI. General. - With correction slip dated September 2008. EC note: These regulations amend the 2006 regulations to reflect the amendments made by Commission Regulation (EC) 213/2008 to Directives 2004/17/EC and 2004/18/EC. - 12p.: 30 cm. - 978-0-11-083855-7 £3.00

The Public Contracts and Utilities Contracts (Postal Services Amendments) Regulations 2008 No. 2008/2848. - Enabling power: European Communities Act 1972, s. 2 (2). - Issued: 07.11.2008. Made: 03.11.2008. Laid: 04.11.2008. Coming into force: 01.12.2008. Effect: S.I. 2006/5, 6 amended. Territorial extent & classification: E/W/NI. General. - EC note: Implements article 6 of Council Directive 2004/17/EC concerning the co-ordination of procurement procedures of entities operating in the water, energy, transport and postal service sectors. - 4p.: 30 cm. - 978-0-11-084916-4 £4.00

Race relations

The Race Relations Act 1976 (Amendment) Regulations 2008 No. 2008/3008. - Enabling power: European Communities Act 1972, s. 2 (2). - Issued: 25.11.2008. Made: 19.11.2008. Laid: 25.11.2008. Coming into force: 22.12.2008. Effect: 1976 c.74 amended. Territorial extent & classification: E/W/S. General. - 2p.: 30 cm. - 978-0-11-147030-5 £4.00

Rating and valuation, England

The Central Rating List (England) (Amendment) Regulations 2008 No. 2008/429. - Enabling power: Local Government Finance Act 1988, ss. 53 (1) (2) (4), 64 (3), 65 (4), 143 (1) (2), 146 (6). - Issued: 28.02.2008. Made: 20.02.2008. Laid: 28.02.2008. Coming into force: 01.04.2008. Effect: S.I. 2005/551 amended. Territorial extent & classification: E. General. - 2p.: 30 cm. - 978-0-11-080991-5 £3.00

The Council Tax and Non-Domestic Rating (Demand Notices) (England) (Amendment) (No. 2) Regulations 2008 No. 2008/3264. - Enabling power: Local Government Finance Act 1992, ss. 113 (1), 116 (1), sch. 2, paras 1, 2 (4) (e) (j)- Issued: 24.12.2008. Made: 18.12.2008. Laid: 22.12.2008. Coming into force: 20.01.2009. Effect: S.I. 2003/2613 amended. Territorial extent & classification: E. General. - 12p.: 30 cm. - 978-0-11-147230-9 £5.00

The Council Tax and Non-Domestic Rating (Demand Notices) (England) (Amendment) Regulations 2008 No. 2008/387. - Enabling power: Local Government Finance Act 1988, ss. 143 (1) (2), 146 (6), sch. 9, paras. 1, 2 (2) (ga) (h) & Local Government Finance Act 1992, ss. 113(1), 116 (1), sch. 2, paras 1, 2 (4) (e), 4 (4) (5), sch. 3, para. 6 (1) (2). - Issued: 26.02.2008. Made: 18.02.2008. Laid: 26.02.2008. Coming into force: 01.04.2008. Effect: S.I. 2003/2613 amended. Territorial extent & classification: E. General. - 16p.: 30 cm. - 978-0-11-080995-3 £3.00

The Local Government (Non-Domestic Rating) (Consequential Amendments) (England) Order 2008 No. 2008/428. - Enabling power: Local Government Act 2003, s. 127 (3) & Rating (Empty Properties) Act 2007, sch. 1, para. 8 (1). - Issued: 27.02.2008. Made: 20.02.2008. Laid: 27.02.2008. Coming into force: 24.03.2008. Effect: S.I. 1989/1058; 1990/145; 2004/3387 amended. Territorial extent & classification: E. General. - 4p.: 30 cm. - 978-0-11-080990-8 £3.00

The Non-Domestic Rating (Communications Hereditaments) (Valuation, Alteration of Lists and Appeals and Material Day) (England) Regulations 2008 No. 2008/2333. - Enabling power: Local Government Finance Act 1988, ss. 55 (2) (4) (6), 143 (1) (2), 146 (6), sch. 6, para. 2 (6A) (8). - Issued: 04.09.2008. Made: 28.08.2008. Laid: 04.09.2008. Coming into force: 01.10.2008. Effect: S.I. 1992/556; 2005/551 modified. Territorial extent & classification: E. General. - 4p.: 30 cm. - 978-0-11-083901-1 £4.00

The Non-Domestic Rating Contributions (England) (Amendment) Regulations 2008 No. 2008/3078. - Enabling power: Local Government Finance Act 1988, ss. 143 (1) (2), sch. 8, paras 4, 6. - Issued: 04.12.2008. Made: 27.11.2008. Laid: 04.12.2008. Coming into force: 31.12.2008. Effect: S.I. 1992/3082 amended. Territorial extent & classification: E. General. - 4p.: 30 cm. - 978-0-11-147086-2 £4.00

The Non-Domestic Rating (Unoccupied Property) (England) Regulations 2008 No. 2008/386. - Enabling power: Local Government Finance Act 1988, ss. 45 (1) (d) (9) (10), 143 (2), 146 (6). - Issued: 26.02.2008. Made: 18.02.2008. Laid: 26.02.2008. Coming into force: 01.04.2008. Effect: S.I. 1989/2261 revoked in relation to England, with savings. Territorial extent & classification: E. General. - 4p.: 30 cm. - 978-0-11-080972-4 £3.00

The Rating Lists (Valuation Date) (England) Order 2008 No. 2008/216. - Enabling power: Local Government Finance Act 1988, s. 143 (1), sch. 6, para. 2 (3) (b). - Issued: 06.02.2008. Made: 30.01.2008. Laid: 06.02.2008. Coming into force: 31.03.2008. Effect: S.I. 2003/329 revoked. Territorial extent & classification: E. General. - 2p.: 30 cm. - 978-0-11-080899-4 £3.00

The Valuation for Rating (Plant and Machinery) (England) (Amendment) Regulations 2008 No. 2008/2332. - Enabling power: Local Government Finance Act 1988, ss. 143 (2), sch. 6, para. 2 (8). - Issued: 04.09.2008. Made: 28.08.2008. Laid: 04.09.2008. Coming into force: 01.10.2008. Effect: S.I. 2000/540 amended. Territorial extent & classification: E. General. - 4p.: 30 cm. - 978-0-11-083908-0 £4.00

Rating and valuation, Wales

The Central Rating List (Wales) (Amendment) Regulations 2008 No. 2008/2672 (W.236). - Enabling power: Local Government Finance Act 1988, ss. 53 (1) (2) (4) (4A), 64 (3), 65 (4), 143 (1) (2), 146 (6). - Issued: 24.10.2008. Made: 06.10.2008. Laid before the National Assembly for Wales: 08.10.2008. Coming into force: 30.10.2008. Effect: S.I. 2005/422 (W.40) amended. Territorial extent & classification: W. General. - In English and Welsh. Welsh title: Rheoliadau Rhestr Ardrethu Canolog (Cymru) (Diwygio) 2008. - 8p.: 30 cm. - 978-0-11-091857-0 £5.00

The Non-Domestic Rating (Communications Hereditaments) (Valuation, Alteration of Lists and Appeals and Material Day) (Wales) Regulations 2008 No. 2008/2671 (W.235). - Enabling power: Local Government Finance Act 1988, ss. 55 (2) (4) (6), 143 (1) (2), 146 (6), sch. 6, para. 2 (6A) (8). - Issued: 24.10.2008. Made: 06.10.2008. Laid before the National Assembly for Wales: 08.10.2008. Coming into force: 31.10.2008. Effect: None. Territorial extent & classification: W. General. - In English and Welsh: Welsh title: Rheoliadau Ardrethu Annomestig (Hereditamentau Cyfathrebu) (Prisio, Newid Rhestri ac Apelau a Diwrnod Perthnasol) (Cymru) 2008. - 8p.: 30 cm. - 978-0-11-091856-3 £5.00

The Non-Domestic Rating Contributions (Wales) (Amendment) (No. 2) Regulations 2008 No. 2008/2929 (W.258). - Enabling power: Local Government Finance Act 1988, ss. 60, 140 (4), 143 (1), sch. 8, paras 4, 6. - Issued: 26.11.2008. Made: 10.11.2008. Laid before the National Assembly for Wales: 12.11.2008. Coming into force: 31.12.2008. Effect: S.I. 1992/3238 amended & S.I. 2008/2838 (W.252) revoked. Territorial extent & classification: W. General. - In English and Welsh: Welsh title: Rheoliadau Cyfraniadau Ardrethu Annomestig (Cymru) (Diwygio) (Rhif 2) 2008. - 8p.: 30 cm. - 978-0-11-091868-6 £5.00

The Non-Domestic Rating Contributions (Wales) (Amendment) Regulations 2008 No. 2008/2838 (W.252). - Enabling power: Local Government Finance Act 1988, ss. 60, 140 (4), 143 (1), sch. 8, paras 4, 6. - Issued: 19.11.2008. Made: 28.10.2008. Laid before the National Assembly for Wales: 31.10.2008. Coming into force: 31.12.2008. Effect: S.I. 1992/3238 amended. Territorial extent & classification: W. General. - Revoked by W.S.I. 2008/2929 (W.258) (ISBN 9780110918686). - In English and Welsh: Welsh title: Rheoliadau Cyfraniadau Ardredthu Annomestig (Cymru) (Diwygio) 2008. - 8p.: 30 cm. - 978-0-11-091867-9 £5.00

The Non-Domestic Rating (Demand Notices) (Wales) (Amendment No. 2) Regulations 2008 No. 2008/3075 (W.269). - Enabling power: Local Government Finance Act 1988, ss. 62, 143 (2), 146 (6), sch. 9, paras 1, 2 (2) & Welsh Language Act 1993, s. 26 (3). - Issued: 23.12.2008. Made: 26.11.2008. Laid before the National Assembly for Wales: 28.11.2008. Coming into force: 01.01.2009. Effect: S.I. 1993/252 amended. Territorial extent & classification: W. General. - In English and Welsh: Welsh title: Rheoliadau Ardrethu Annomestig (Hysbysiadau Galw am Dalu) (Cymru) (Diwygio Rhif 2) 2008. - 8p.: 30 cm. - 978-0-11-091909-6 £5.00

The Non-Domestic Rating (Demand Notices) (Wales) (Amendment) Regulations 2008 No. 2008/7 (W.3). - Enabling power: Local Government Finance Act 1988, ss. 62, 143 (3) (4A), 146 (6), sch. 9, paras 1, 2 (2) & Welsh Language Act 1993, s. 26 (3). - Issued: 28.01.2008. Made: 07.01.2008. Laid before the National Assembly for Wales: 08.01.2008. Coming into force: 02.02.2008. Effect: S.I. 1993/252 amended. Territorial extent & classification: W. General. - In English and Welsh: Welsh title: Rheoliadau Ardrethu Annomestig (Hysbysiadau Galw am Dalu) (Cymru) (Diwygio) 2008. - 4p.: 30 cm. - 978-0-11-091731-3 £3.00

The Non-Domestic Rating (Miscellaneous Provisions) (Amendment) (Wales) Regulations 2008 No. 2008/2997 (W.262). - Enabling power: Local Government Finance Act 1988, s. 143 (1), sch. 6, para. 2 (8). - Issued: 05.12.2008. Made: 17.11.2008. Laid before the National Assembly for Wales: 19.11.2008. Coming into force: 11.12.2008. Effect: S.I. 1989/2303 amended. Territorial extent & classification: W. General. - In English and Welsh: Welsh title: Rheoliadau Ardrethu Annomestig (Darpariaethau Amrywiol) (Diwygio) (Cymru) 2008. - 4p.: 30 cm. - 978-0-11-091871-6 £4.00

The Non-Domestic Rating (Small Business Relief) (Wales) Order 2008 No. 2008/2770 (W.246). - Enabling power: Local Government Finance Act 1988, ss. 43 (4B) (b), 44 (9), 143 (1) (2), 146 (6). - Issued: 13.11.2008. Made: 18.10.2008. Laid before the National Assembly for Wales: 22.10.2008. Coming into force: 01.12.2008 [but has effect from 01.04.2008]. Effect: S.I. 2006/3345 (W.306) revoked with savings. Territorial extent & classification: W. General. - In English and Welsh: Welsh title: Gorchymyn Ardrethu Annomestig (Rhyddhad Ardrethi i Fusnesau Bach) (Cymru) 2008. - 16p.: 30 cm. - 978-0-11-091864-8 £5.00

The Non-Domestic Rating (Unoccupied Property) (Wales) Regulations 2008 No. 2008/2499 (W.217). - Enabling power: Local Government Finance Act 1988, ss. 45 (1) (d) (9) (10), 143 (2), 146 (6). - Issued: 10.10.2008. Made: 20.09.2008. Laid before the National Assembly for Wales: 23.09.2008. Coming into force: 01.11.2008. Effect: S.I. 1989/2261 revoked in relation to Wales. Territorial extent & classification: W. General. - In English and Welsh. Welsh title: Rheoliadau Ardrethu Annomestig (Eiddo Heb ei Feddiannu) (Cymru) 2008. - 8p.: 30 cm. - 978-0-11-091881-5 £5.00

Recovery of taxes

The Recovery of Taxes etc Due in Other Member States (Amendment of Section 134 of the Finance Act 2002) Regulations 2008 No. 2008/2871. - Enabling power: European Communities Act 1972, s. 2 (2). - Issued: 12.11.2008. Made: 07.11.2008. Laid: 07.11.2008. Coming into force: 28.11.2008. Effect: 2002 c. 23 amended & S.I. 2005/1479 revoked. Territorial extent & classification: E/W/S/NI. General. - EC note: Council Directive 2008/55/EC repeals earlier legislation, most notably, Council Directive 76/308/EEC. These Regulations amend the definition of the "Mutual Assistance Recovery Directive" in section 134(2) of the Finance Act 2002 so that the definition refers to the Directive currently in force. These Regulations also apply transitional provisions so that requests for assistance made under the 1976 Directive are to be treated as if they had been made under the 2008 Directive. - 2p.: 30 cm. - 978-0-11-084988-1 £4.00

Registration of births, deaths and marriages, etc.

The Statistics and Registration Service Act 2007 (Commencement No. 2 and Transitional Provisions) Order 2008 No. 2008/839 (C.41). - Enabling power: Statistics and Registration Service Act 2007, s. 74. Bringing into operation various provisions of the 2007 Act on 01.04.2008. - Issued: 01.04.2008. Made: 20.03.2008. Effect: None. Territorial extent & classification: E/W/S/NI. General. - 2p.: 30 cm. - 978-0-11-081299-1 £3.00

Registration of births, deaths and marriages, etc., England & Wales

The Supply of Information (Register of Deaths) (England and Wales) Order 2008 No. 2008/570. - Enabling power: Police and Justice Act 2006, s. 13 (1) (d). - Issued: 19.03.2008. Made: 03.03.2008. Laid: 04.03.2008. Coming into force: 25.03.2008. Effect: S.I. 2007/3460 revoked. Territorial extent & classification: E/W. General. - This Statutory Instrument has been made in consequence of a defect in Statutory Instrument 2007/3460 (ISBN 9780110806358) and is being issued free of charge to all known recipients of that Statutory Instrument. - 4p.: 30 cm. - 978-0-11-081259-5 £3.00

Registration of births, deaths and marriages, etc., Northern Ireland

The Supply of Information (Register of Deaths) (Northern Ireland) Order 2008 No. 2008/700. - Enabling power: Police and Justice Act 2006, ss. 13 (1) (d), 49. - Issued: 19.03.2008. Made: 08.03.2008. Laid: 17.03.2008. Coming into force: 08.04.2008. Effect: S.I. 2007/3390 revoked. Territorial extent & classification: NI. General. - This Statutory Instrument has been made in consequence of a defect in S.I. 2007/3390 (ISBN 9780110800868) and is being issued free of charge to all known recipients of that statutory instrument. - 4p.: 30 cm. - 978-0-11-080089-9 £3.00

Regulatory reform

The Legislative Reform (Consumer Credit) Order 2008 No. 2008/2826. - Enabling power: Legislative and Regulatory Reform Act 2006, s. 1. - Issued: 04.11.2008. Made: 30.10.2008. Coming into force: 31.10.2008. Effect: 1974 c. 39; 2006 c. 14 amended & S.I. 2007/1167 partially revoked. Territorial extent & classification: E/W/S/NI. General. - Supersedes draft S.I. (ISBN 9780110818542) issued 20.06.2008. - 8p.: 30 cm. - 978-0-11-084774-0 £5.00

The Legislative Reform (Health and Safety Executive) Order 2008 No. 2008/960. - Enabling power: Legislative and Regulatory Reform Act 2006, s. 2. - Issued: 07.04.2008. Made: 31.03.2008. Coming into force: 01.04.2008. Effect: 36 acts and 33 SIs amended. Territorial extent & classification: E/W/S. General. - Supersedes draft SI (ISBN 9780110809526) issued 18.02.2008. - 24p.: 30 cm. - 978-0-11-081339-4 £4.00

The Legislative Reform (Lloyd's) Order 2008 No. 2008/3001. - Enabling power: Legislative and Regulatory Reform Act 2006, s. 1. - Issued: 24.11.2008. Made: 18.11.2008. Coming into force: 19.11.2008. Effect: 1982 c. xiv amended. Territorial extent & classification: E/W/S/NI. General. - Supersedes draft S.I. (ISBN 9780110834504) issued 24.07.2008. - 8p.: 30 cm. - 978-0-11-147025-1 £5.00

The Legislative Reform (Local Authority Consent Requirements) (England and Wales) Order 2008 No. 2008/2840. - Enabling power: Legislative and Regulatory Reform Act 2006, s. 1. - Issued: 04.11.2008. Made: 29.10.2008. Coming into force: 30.10.2008. Effect: 1939 c. 13; 1972 c. 70; 1993 c. 25; 1996 c. 56 amended. Territorial extent & classification: E/W. General. - Supersedes draft S.I. (ISBN 9780110818948) issued 26.06.2008. - 4p.: 30 cm. - 978-0-11-084850-1 £4.00

The Legislative Reform (Verification of Weighing and Measuring Equipment) Order 2008 No. 2008/3262. - Enabling power: Legislative and Regulatory Reform Act 2006, s. 1. - Issued: 23.12.2008. Made: 18.12.2008. Coming into force: 19.12.2008. Effect: 1985 c. 72 amended. Territorial extent & classification: E/W/S. General. - Supersedes draft S.I. (ISBN 9780110846873) issued 23.10.2008. - 2p.: 30 cm. - 978-0-11-147229-3 £4.00

The Regulatory Enforcement and Sanctions Act 2008 (Commencement No 1) Order 2008 No. 2008/2371 (C.104). - Enabling power: Regulatory Enforcement and Sanctions Act 2008, s. 76 (1). Bringing into operation various provisions of the 2008 Act on 01.10.2008. - Issued: 11.09.2008. Made: 08.09.2008. Effect: None. Territorial extent & classification: E/W/S/NI. General. - 2p.: 30 cm. - 978-0-11-084165-6 £4.00

Rehabilitation of offenders, England and Wales

The Criminal Justice and Immigration Act 2008 (Commencement No. 5) Order 2008 No. 2008/3260 (C.149). - Enabling power: Criminal Justice and Immigration Act 2008, s. 153 (5) (a) (7). Bringing into operation various provisions of the 2008 Act on 19.12.2008, 01.01.2009 in accord. with art. 2. - Issued: 23.12.2008. Made: 18.12.2008. Effect: None. Territorial extent & classification: E/W (some aspects E. only). General. - 4p.: 30 cm. - 978-0-11-147227-9 £4.00

The Rehabilitation of Offenders Act 1974 (Exceptions) (Amendment) (England and Wales) Order 2008 No. 2008/3259. - Enabling power: Rehabilitation of Offenders Act 1974, ss. 4 (4), 7 (4), 10 (1), sch. 2, paras 4, 6 (4). - Issued: 23.12.2008. Made: 17.12.2008. Coming into force: 18.12.2008. Effect: S.I. 1975/1023 amended. Territorial extent & classification: E/W. General. - Supersedes draft S.I. (ISBN 9780110847535) issued 03.11.2008. - 4p.: 30 cm. - 978-0-11-147226-2 £4.00

Representation of the people

The Absent Voting (Transitional Provisions) (Scotland) Regulations 2008 No. 2008/48 (S.1). - Enabling power: Electoral Administration Act 2006, s. 14 (5) (7). - Issued: 17.01.2008. Made: 11.01.2008. Laid: 16.01.2008. Coming into force: 08.02.2008. Effect: None. Territorial extent & classification: S. General. - 4p.: 30 cm. - 978-0-11-080209-1 £3.00

The Electoral Administration Act 2006 (Commencement No.6) Order 2008 No. 2008/610 (C.23). - Enabling power: Electoral Administration Act 2006, s. 77 (2). Bringing into operation various provisions of the 2006 Act on 10.03.2008 in accord. with art 2. - Issued: 11.03.2008. Made: 05.03.2008. Effect: None. Territorial extent & classification: E/W/S/NI. General. - 4p.: 30 cm. - 978-0-11-081159-8 £3.00

The Electoral Administration Act 2006 (Commencement No.7) Order 2008 No. 2008/1316 (C.55). - Enabling power: Electoral Administration Act 2006, s. 77 (2) (3). Bringing into operation various provisions of the 2006 Act on 14.05.2008 & 01.07.2008 in relation to NI in accord. with art 2. - Issued: 20.05.2008. Made: 13.05.2008. Effect: None. Territorial extent & classification: E/W/S/NI. General. - 8p.: 30 cm. - 978-0-11-081475-9 £3.00

The European Parliamentary Elections (Appointed Day of Poll) Order 2008 No. 2008/3102. - Enabling power: European Parliamentary Elections Act 2002, s. 4. - Issued: 09.12.2008. Made: 03.12.2008. Laid: 04.12.2008. Coming into force: 08.12.2008. Effect: None. Territorial extent & classification: E/W/S/NI & Gibraltar. General. - 2p.: 30 cm. - 978-0-11-147102-9 £4.00

The European Parliamentary Elections (Returning Officers) Order 2008 No. 2008/1914. - Enabling power: European Parliamentary Elections Act 2002, s. 6 (2) (b) (3) (b). - Issued: 23.07.2008. Made: 15.07.2008. Coming into force: 16.07.2008 in accord. with art. 1. Effect: S.I. 2004/1056 revoked. Territorial extent & classification: E/W/S. General. - 4p.: 30 cm. - 978-0-11-083441-2 £3.00

The European Parliament (Number of MEPs and Distribution between Electoral Regions) (United Kingdom and Gibraltar) Order 2008 No. 2008/1954. - Enabling power: European Parliament (Representation) Act 2003, ss. 5 (1), 6 (3). - Issued: 25.07.2008. Made: 17.07.2008. Coming into force: 18.07.2008 in accord. with art. 1. Effect: 2002 c. 24 amended & S.I. 2004/1245 revoked. Territorial extent & classification: E/W/S/NI/Gibraltar. General. - Supersedes draft S.I. (ISBN 9780110818023) issued 11.06.2008. - 4p.: 30 cm. - 978-0-11-083513-6 £3.00

The Parliamentary Constituencies and Assembly Electoral Regions (Wales) (Amendment) Order 2008 No. 2008/1791. - Enabling power: Parliamentary Constituencies Act 1986, s. 4 (5). - Issued: 16.07.2008. Made: 09.07.2008. Coming into force: 10.07.2008 in accord. with art. 1 (2). Effect: S.I. 2006/1041 amended. Territorial extent & classification: W. General. - Supersedes draft S.I. (ISBN 9780110818177) issued 11.06.2008. - 4p.: 30 cm. - 978-0-11-083130-5 £3.00

The Representation of the People (Amendment) Regulations 2008 No. 2008/1901. - Enabling power: Electoral Administration Act 2006, s. 42 (4) (b) & Representation of the People Act 1983, sch. 1, rule 57 (6) (b). - Issued: 23.07.2008. Made: 17.07.2008. Coming into force: 18.07.2008 in accord. with reg. 1. Effect: S.I. 2001/341, 497 amended. Territorial extent & classification: E/W/S. General. - Supersedes draft S.I. (ISBN 9780110818399) issued 13.06.2008. - 4p.: 30 cm. - 978-0-11-083396-5 £3.00

The Representation of the People (Northern Ireland) Regulations 2008 No. 2008/1741. - Enabling power: Representation of the People Act 1983, ss. 4 (4), 7 (3) (aa), 7A (3) (aa),7C (2) (aa), 9 (2), 10A (1) (3) (5) (b) (7) (9), 13 (3), 13A (1) (a) (2) (6), 13BA, 13 (C) (2), 14 (1), 15 (2) (aa), 16, 53, 58 (2) (a) (b) (6) (a), 75 (3), 89 (1), 201 (1) (3), sch. 1, rules 19A, 24, 28 (3), 29 (3A), 32 (3), 37 (1F), 57, sch. 2 & Representation of the People Act 1985, ss. 2 (2) (aa) (3), 3 (5) (6) (7), 6 (1) (5), 7 (1) (3), 8 (6) (7), 9 (4) (7) (8), 15 (5) & European Communities Act 1972, s. 2 (2) & European Parliamentary Elections Act 2002, s. 7 (3) (4) & Electoral Administration Act 2006, s. 42. - Issued: 08.07.2008. Made: 30.06.2008. Coming into force: 01.07.2008. Effect: 1983 c. 2 & S.I. 2002/881; 2003/1557, 3075; 2004/1771; 2005/2114 amended & S.I. 2001/400, 1877; 2002/1873; 2003/1942; 2007/1612 revoked. Territorial extent & classification: NI. General. - Supersedes draft S.I. (ISBN 9780110814674) published on 23.05.2008. - 84p.: 30 cm. - 978-0-11-081956-3 £12.00

The Representation of the People (Scotland) (Amendment) Regulations 2008 No. 2008/305 (S.2). - Enabling power: Representation of the People Act 1983, ss. 53, 89 (1), sch. 2, paras. 5A, 12; sch. 1, rules 24, 28 (3) (3A), 31A, 45 (1B) & Representation of the People Act 2000, sch. 4, paras 3 (1) (b) (2) (c), 4 (1) (b) (2) (c) (4) (a), 6 (7) (8), 7 (5) (c). - Issued: 14.02.2008. Made: 06.02.2008. Coming into force: 08.02.2008 in accord. with reg.1. Effect: S.I. 2001/497 amended. Territorial extent & classification: S. General. - Supersedes draft S.I. (ISBN 9780110802121) issued 22.01.2008. - 24p.: 30 cm. - 978-0-11-081496-4 £4.00

The Service Voters' Registration Period (Northern Ireland) Order 2008 No. 2008/1726. - Enabling power: Representation of the People Act 1983, s. 15 (9). - Issued: 07.07.2008. Made: 30.06.2008. Laid: -. Coming into force: 01.07.2008. Effect: None. Territorial extent & classification: NI. General. - Supersedes draft S.I. (ISBN 9780110814575) issued 16.05.2008. - 2p.: 30 cm. - 978-0-11-081944-0 £3.00

Representation of the people: Redistribution of seats and review of election arrangements

The Parliamentary Constituencies (Northern Ireland) Order 2008 No. 2008/1486. - Enabling power: Parliamentary Constituencies Act 1986, s. 4. - Issued: 18.06.2008. Made: 11.06.2008. Coming into force: 12.06.2008 in accord. with art. 1. Effect: None. Territorial extent & classification: NI. General. - Supersedes draft S.I. (ISBN 9780110813172) issued 03.04.2008. - 8p.: 30 cm. - 978-0-11-081861-0 £3.00

Revenue and customs

The Finance Act 2007, Schedule 24 (Commencement and Transitional Provisions) Order 2008 No. 2008/568 (C.20). - Enabling power: Finance Act 2007, s. 97. Bringing into operation various provisions of the 2007 Act on 01.04.2008; 01.07.2008; 01.01.2009; 01.04.2009 in accord. with art. 2. - Issued: 07.03.2008. Made: 03.03.2008. Effect: None. Territorial extent & classification: E/W/S/NI. General. - 4p.: 30 cm. - 978-0-11-081088-1 £3.00

The Finance Act 2008 Section 135 (Disaster or Emergency) Order 2008 No. 2008/1936. - Enabling power: Finance Act 2008, s. 135. - Issued: 25.07.2008. Made: 22.07.2008. Laid: 22.07.2008. Coming into force: 13.08.2008. Effect: None. Territorial extent & classification: E/W/S/NI. General. - 2p.: 30 cm. - With correction slip dated September 2009. - 978-0-11-083555-6 £3.00

The Immigration, Asylum and Nationality Act 2006 (Data Sharing Code of Practice) Order 2008 No. 2008/8. - Enabling power: Immigration, Asylum and Nationality Act 2006, s. 37 (2). - Issued: 11.01.2008. Made: 08.01.2008. Laid: 10.01.2008. Coming into force: 01.03.2008. Effect: None. Territorial extent & classification: E/W/S/NI. General. - 2p.: 30 cm. - 978-0-11-080807-9 £3.00

The Immigration, Asylum and Nationality Act 2006 (Duty to Share Information and Disclosure of Information for Security Purposes) Order 2008 No. 2008/539. - Enabling power: Immigration, Asylum and Nationality Act 2006, ss. 36 (4), 38 (4). - Issued: 04.03.2008. Made: 28.02.20008. Coming into force: 01.03.2008. Effect: None. Territorial extent & classification: E/W/S/NI. General. - 8p.: 30 cm. - 978-0-11-081055-3 £3.00

The Serious Crime Act 2007 (Commencement No.1) Order 2008 No. 2008/219 (C.5). - Enabling power: Serious Crime Act 2007, s. 94 (1). Bringing into operation various provisions of the 2007 Act on 15.02.2008 & 01.03.2008. - Issued: 08.02.2008. Made: 05.02.2008. Effect: None. Territorial extent & classification: E/W/S/NI. General. - 4p.: 30 cm. - 978-0-11-080902-1 £3.00

The Serious Crime Act 2007 (Disclosure of Information by Revenue and Customs) Order 2008 No. 2008/403. - Enabling power: Serious Crime Act 2007, ss. 85 (7), 89 (1). - Issued: 22.02.2008. Made: 19.02.2008. Laid: 19.02.2008. Coming into force: 11.03.2008. Effect: None. Territorial extent & classification: E/W/S/NI. General. - 2p.: 30 cm. - 978-0-11-080966-3 £3.00

The Taxes and Duties (Interest Rate) (Amendment) Regulations 2008 No. 2008/3234. - Enabling power: Finance Act 1989, s. 178 (1) to (3) & Finance Act 1996, s. 197. - Issued: 22.12.2008. Made: 16.12.2008. Laid: 17.12.2008. Coming into force: 07.01.2009. Effect: S.I. 1989/1297; 1998/1461 amended. Territorial extent & classification: E/W/S/NI. General. - 4p.: 30 cm. - 978-0-11-147195-1 £4.00

Rights in performances

The Copyright and Performances (Application to Other Countries) Order 2008 No. 2008/677. - Enabling power: Copyright, Designs and Patents Act 1988, ss. 159, 208 & European Communities Act 1972, s. 2 (2). - Issued: 18.03.2008. Made: 12.03.2008. Laid: 13.03.2008. Coming into force: 06.04.2008. Effect: S.I. 2007/273 revoked. Territorial extent & classification: E/W/S/NI. General. - 16p.: 30 cm. - 978-0-11-081235-9 £3.00

Road traffic

The Crime (International Co-operation) Act 2003 (Commencement No. 4) Order 2008 No. 2008/3009 (C.130). - Enabling power: Crime (International Co-operation) Act 2003, s. 94 (1) (4). Bringing into operation various provisions of the 2003 Act on the date on which the convention on driving disqualifications applies to both the United Kingdom and Ireland and 17.12.2008 in accord. with arts. 2 & 3. - Issued: 26.11.2008. Made: 19.11.2008. Effect: None. Territorial extent & classification: E/W/S/NI. General. - 4p.: 30 cm. - 978-0-11-147037-4 £4.00

The Goods Vehicles (Authorisation of International Journeys) (Fees) (Amendment) Regulations 2008 No. 2008/1576. - Enabling power: Finance Act 1973, s. 56 (1) (2). - Issued: 07.07.2008. Made: 13.06.2008. Laid: 17.06.2008. Coming into force: 01.08.2008. Effect: S.I. 2001/3606 amended. Territorial extent & classification: E/W/S. General. - 2p.: 30 cm. - 978-0-11-081871-9 £3.00

The Goods Vehicles (Licensing of Operators) (Fees) (Amendment) Regulations 2008 No. 2008/1474. - Enabling power: Goods Vehicles (Licensing of Operators) Act 1995, ss. 45 (1), 57 (1) (2) (7). - Issued: 16.06.2008. Made: 05.06.2008. Laid: 12.06.2008. Coming into force: 01.08.2008. Effect: S.I. 1995/3000 amended. Territorial extent & classification: E/W/S. General. - 4p.: 30 cm. - 978-0-11-081842-9 £3.00

The Goods Vehicles (Plating and Testing) (Amendment) Regulations 2008 No. 2008/1460. - Enabling power: Road Traffic Act 1988, ss. 49, 51 (1). - Issued: 12.06.2008. Made: 05.06.2008. Laid: 12.06.2008. Coming into force: 13.07.2008. Effect: S.I. 1988/1478 amended. Territorial extent & classification: E/W/S. General. - 8p.: 30 cm. - 978-0-11-081808-5 £3.00

The International Carriage of Dangerous Goods by Road (Fees) (Amendment) Regulations 2008 No. 2008/1578. - Enabling power: Finance Act 1973, s. 56 (1) (2). - Issued: 23.06.2008. Made: 13.06.2008. Laid: 17.06.2008. Coming into force: 13.07.2008. Effect: S.I. 1988/370 amended. Territorial extent & classification: E/W/S/NI. General. - 4p.: 30 cm. - 978-0-11-081870-2 £3.00

The International Transport of Goods under Cover of TIR Carnets (Fees) (Amendment) Regulations 2008 No. 2008/1580. - Enabling power: Finance Act 1973, s. 56 (1) (2). - Issued: 23.06.2008. Made: 13.06.2008. Laid: 17.06.2008. Coming into force: 13.07.2008. Effect: S.I. 1988/371 amended. Territorial extent & classification: E/W/S/NI. General. - 4p.: 30 cm. - 978-0-11-081865-8 £3.00

The Motor Cars (Driving Instruction) (Amendment) Regulations 2008 No. 2008/419. - Enabling power: Road Traffic Act 1988, ss. 123 (2), 125 (3), 125A (5), 127 (2), 129 (5), 132 (2) (b), 141. - Issued: 27.02.2008. Made: 20.02.2008. Laid: 22.02.2008. Coming into force: 01.04.2008. Effect: S.I. 2005/1902 amended. Territorial extent & classification: E/W/S. General. - 2p.: 30 cm. - 978-0-11-080983-0 £3.00

The Motor Cycles Etc. (Single Vehicle Approval) (Fees) (Amendment) Regulations 2008 No. 2008/1462. - Enabling power: Road Traffic Act 1988, s. 61 (1) (2). - Issued: 13.06.2008. Made: 05.06.2008. Laid: 12.06.2008. Coming into force: 13.07.2008. Effect: S.I. 2003/1960 amended. Territorial extent & classification: E/W/S. General. - 4p.: 30 cm. - 978-0-11-081810-8 £3.00

The Motor Vehicles (Approval) (Fees) (Amendment) Regulations 2008 No. 2008/1443. - Enabling power: Road Traffic Act 1988, s. 61 (1) (2) & Finance Act 1990, s. 128. - Issued: 12.06.2008. Made: 05.06.2008. Laid: 12.06.2008. Coming into force: 13.07.2008. Effect: S.I. 2001/2486 amended. Territorial extent & classification: E/W/S. General. - 4p.: 30 cm. - 978-0-11-081801-6 £3.00

The Motor Vehicles (Driving Licences) (Amendment No. 2) Regulations 2008 No. 2008/1038. - Enabling power: Road Traffic Act 1988, ss. 97 (1), 105 (1) (4). - Issued: 14.04.2008. Made: 01.04.2008. Laid: 08.04.2008. Coming into force: 16.05.2008. Effect: S.I. 1999/2864 amended. Territorial extent & classification: E/W/S. General. - Revoked by S.I. 2008/1312 (ISBN 9780110814698). - 4p.: 30 cm. - 978-0-11-081361-5 £3.00

The Motor Vehicles (Driving Licences) (Amendment No. 3) Regulations 2008 No. 2008/1312. - Enabling power: Road Traffic Act 1988, ss. 97 (1), 99 (7ZA), 105 (1) (2) (4). - Issued: 22.05.2008. Made: 14.05.2008. Laid: 15.05.2008. Coming into force: 15.05.2008 at 11.59 pm for reg. 2; 16.05.2008 for remainder. Effect: S.I. 1999/2864 amended & S.I. 2008/1038 revoked (15.05.2008, 11.59pm). Territorial extent & classification: E/W/S. General. - This Statutory Instrument has been made in consequence of a defect in SI 2008/1038 and is being issued free of charge to all known recipients of that Statutory Instrument. - 4p.: 30 cm. - 978-0-11-081469-8 £3.00

The Motor Vehicles (Driving Licences) (Amendment) (No. 4) Regulations 2008 No. 2008/1435. - Enabling power: Road Traffic Act 1988, ss. 89 (3) (4) (5) (5ZA), 105 (1) (2) (3) (4). - Issued: 13.06.2008. Made: 04.06.2008. Laid: 10.06.2008. Coming into force: 07.07.2008. Effect: S.I. 1999/2864 amended. Territorial extent & classification: E/W/S. General. - 16p.: 30 cm. - 978-0-11-081827-6 £3.00

The Motor Vehicles (Driving Licences) (Amendment) (No. 5) Regulations 2008 No. 2008/2508. - Enabling power: Road Traffic Act 1988, ss. 89 (3) (a), 105 (1) (3). - Issued: 02.10.2008. Made: 25.09.2008. Laid: 26.09.2008. Coming into force: 29.09.2008. Effect: S.I. 1999/2864 amended. Territorial extent & classification: E/W/S. General. - 2p.: 30 cm. - 978-0-11-084283-7 £4.00

The Motor Vehicles (Driving Licences) (Amendment) Regulations 2008 No. 2008/508. - Enabling power: Road Traffic Act 1988, ss. 89 (3) (4) (5), 97 (1), 105 (1) (2) (3) (4). - Issued: 06.03.2008. Made: 25.02.2008. Laid: 27.02.2008. Coming into force: 01.04.2008 for all regs other than regs 7 (a) (b), 12 & 29.09.2008 for regs 7 (a) (b), 12. Effect: S.I. 1999/2864 amended. Territorial extent & classification: E/W/S. General. - 12p.: 30 cm. - 978-0-11-081075-1 £3.00

The Motor Vehicles (EC Type Approval) (Amendment) Regulations 2008 No. 2008/2844. - Enabling power: European Communities Act 1972, s. 2 (2). - Issued: 10.11.2008. Made: 31.10.2008. Laid: 05.11.2008. Coming into force: 10.12.1008 except for reg 4 (7); 02.01.2013 for reg 4 (7). Effect: S.I. 1998/2051 amended. Territorial extent & classification: E/W/S/NI. General. - Revoked by S.I. 2009/717 (ISBN 9780111477298). EC note: These Regulations implement, for the purposes of the EC type approval of light passenger vehicles: Commission Directive 2007/34/EC; Commission Directive 2007/35/EC; Directive 2007/37/EC (amends Directive 70/156/EEC); Regulation (EC) 706/2007 and Regulation (EC) No. 715/2007. - 4p.: 30 cm. - 978-0-11-084856-3 £4.00

The Motor Vehicles (Tests) (Amendment) (No. 2) Regulations 2008 No. 2008/1461. - Enabling power: Road Traffic Act 1988, ss. 45, 46. - Issued: 16.06.2008. Made: 05.06.2008. Laid: 12.06.2008. Coming into force: 13.07.2008. Effect: S.I. 1981/1694 amended. Territorial extent & classification: E/W/S. General. - 4p.: 30 cm. - 978-0-11-081809-2 £3.00

The Motor Vehicles (Tests) (Amendment) Regulations 2008 No. 2008/1402. - Enabling power: Road Traffic Act 1988, ss. 45 (2) (7), 46 (1) (f). - Issued: 05.06.2008. Made: 28.05.2008. Laid: 03.06.2008. Coming into force: 30.06.2008. Effect: S.I. 1981/1694 amended. Territorial extent & classification: E/W/S. General. - 4p.: 30 cm. - 978-0-11-081765-1 £3.00

The Mutual Recognition of Driving Disqualifications (Great Britain and Ireland) Regulations 2008 No. 2008/3010. - Enabling power: Crime (International Co-operation) Act 2003, ss. 57 (2) (b) (4) (b), 72 (3). - Issued: 26.11.2008. Made: 19.11.2008. Laid: 25.11.2008. Coming into force: In accord. with reg. 1. Effect: None. Territorial extent & classification: E/W/S/NI. General. - 2p.: 30 cm. - 978-0-11-147034-3 £4.00

The Passenger and Goods Vehicles (Recording Equipment) (Approval of Fitters and Workshops) (Fees) (Amendment) Regulations 2008 No. 2008/1581. - Enabling power: Finance Act 1973, s. 56 (1) (2). - Issued: 23.06.2008. Made: 13.06.2008. Laid: 17.06.2008. Coming into force: 13.07.2008. Effect: S.I. 1986/2128 amended. Territorial extent & classification: E/W/S. General. - 2p.: 30 cm. - 978-0-11-081866-5 £3.00

The Passenger and Goods Vehicles (Recording Equipment) (Downloading and Retention of Data) Regulations 2008 No. 2008/198. - Enabling power: Transport Act 1968, ss. 95 (1) (1A), 101 (2) & European Communities Act 1972, s. 2 (2). - Issued: 06.02.2008. Made: 29.01.2008. Coming into force: In accord. with reg. 1 (1). Effect: 1968 c. 73 amended. Territorial extent & classification: E/W/S. General. - Supersedes draft SI (ISBN 9780110801155) issued 04.12.2008. EC note: These regs implement certain provisions of Regulation (EC) 561/2006 on the harmonisation of certain social legislation relating to road transport and amending Council Regulations (EEC) No 3821/85 and (EC) No 2135/98 and repealing Council Regulation (EEC) No 3820/85) which have not previously been implemented. - 12p.: 30 cm. - 978-0-11-080894-9 £3.00

The Retention of Registration Marks (Amendment) Regulations 2008 No. 2008/2850. - Enabling power: Vehicle Excise and Registration Act 1994, ss. 26, 57 (2). - Issued: 11.11.2008. Made: 04.11.2008. Laid: 06.11.2008. Coming into force: 01.12.2008. Effect: S.I. 1993/987 amended. Territorial extent & classification: E/W/S/NI. General. - 4p.: 30 cm. - 978-0-11-084918-8 £4.00

The Road Safety Act 2006 (Commencement No. 3) Order 2008 No. 2008/1864 (C. 79). - Enabling power: Road Safety Act 2006, s. 61. Bringing into operation various provisions of the 2006 Act on 31.07.2008. - Issued: 21.08.2008. Made: 14.07.2008. Effect: None. Territorial extent & classification: E/W/S/NI. General. - 4p.: 30 cm. - 978-0-11-083204-3 £3.00

The Road Safety Act 2006 (Commencement No. 4) Order 2008 No. 2008/1918 (C.86). - Enabling power: Road Safety Act 2006, s. 61. Bringing into operation various provisions of the 2006 Act on 18.08.2008. - Issued: 24.07.2008. Made: 17.07.2008. Effect: None. Territorial extent & classification: E/W/S/NI. General. - 4p.: 30 cm. - 978-0-11-083502-0 £3.00

The Road Safety Act 2006 (Commencement No. 5) Order 2008 No. 2008/3164 (C.140). - Enabling power: Road Safety Act 2006, s. 61. Bringing into operation various provisions of the 2006 Act on 05.01.2009; 31.03.2009; 01.04.2009. - Issued: 15.12.2008. Made: 08.12.2008. Effect: None. Territorial extent & classification: E/W/S/NI. General. - 4p.: 30 cm. - 978-0-11-147170-8 £4.00

The Road Traffic Act 1988 (Retention and Disposal of Seized Motor Vehicles) (Amendment) Regulations 2008 No. 2008/2097. - Enabling power: Road Traffic Act 1988, s. 165B. - Issued: 07.08.2008. Made: 28.07.2008. Laid: 05.08.2008. Coming into force: 01.10.2008. Effect: S.I. 2005/1606 amended. Territorial extent & classification: E/W/S. General. - 4p.: 30 cm. - 978-0-11-083701-7 £3.00

The Road Traffic Offenders (Prescribed Devices) Order 2008 No. 2008/1332. - Enabling power: Road Traffic Offenders Act 1988, s. 20 (9). - Issued: 23.05.2008. Made: 20.05.2008. Laid: 22.05.2008. Coming into force: 16.06.2008. Effect: None. Territorial extent & classification: E/W/S. General. - 2p.: 30 cm. - 978-0-11-081746-0 £3.00

The Road Vehicles (Construction and Use) (Amendment) Regulations 2008 No. 2008/1702. - Enabling power: Road Traffic Act 1988, s. 41 (1) (2) (5). - Issued: 03.07.2008. Made: 30.06.2008. Laid: 03.07.2008. Coming into force: 01.08.2008. Effect: S.I. 1986/1078 amended. Territorial extent & classification: E/W/S. General. - 2p.: 30 cm. - 978-0-11-081933-4 £3.00

The Road Vehicles (Registration and Licensing) (Amendment) (No. 2) Regulations 2008 No. 2008/1444. - Enabling power: Vehicle Excise and Registration Act 1994, ss. 22 (1) (h), 22A (2) (a), 22A (3) (d), 57, 61B. - Issued: 16.06.2008. Made: 05.06.2008. Laid: 12.06.2008. Coming into force: 13.07.2008. Effect: S.I. 2002/2742 amended. Territorial extent & classification: E/W/S. General. - 4p.: 30 cm. - 978-0-11-081800-9 £3.00

The Road Vehicles (Registration and Licensing) (Amendment No. 3) Regulations 2008 No. 2008/2849. - Enabling power: Vehicle Excise and Registration Act 1994, ss. 22 (1) (c). - Issued: 12.11.2008. Made: 03.11.2008. Laid: 06.11.2008. Coming into force: 15.12.2008. Effect: S.I. 2002/2742 amended. Territorial extent & classification: E/W/S. General. - 2p.: 30 cm. - 978-0-11-084946-1 £4.00

The Road Vehicles (Registration and Licensing) (Amendment) Regulations 2008 No. 2008/642. - Enabling power: Vehicle Excise and Registration Act 1994, s. 21(3). - Issued: 14.03.2008. Made: 07.03.2008. Laid: 10.03.2008. Coming into force: 01.04.2008. Effect: S.I. 2002/2742 amended. Territorial extent & classification: E/W/S/NI. General. - 2p.: 30 cm. - 978-0-11-081146-8 £3.00

The Sale of Registration Marks (Amendment) Regulations 2008 No. 2008/2372. - Enabling power: Vehicle Excise and Registration Act 1994, ss. 27, 57 (2). - Issued: 16.09.2008. Made: 09.09.2008. Laid: 12.09.2008. Coming into force: 06.10.2008. Effect: S.I. 1995/2880 amended. Territorial extent & classification: E/W/S/NI. General. - 4p.: 30 cm. - 978-0-11-084181-6 £4.00

The Tractor etc (EC Type-Approval) (Amendment) Regulations 2008 No. 2008/1980. - Enabling power: European Communities Act 1972, s. 2 (2). - Issued: 04.08.2008. Made: 23.07.2008. Laid: 28.07.2008. Coming into force: 08.09.2008. Effect: S.I. 2005/390 amended Territorial extent & classification: E/W/S/NI. General. - EC note: The principal Regulations transposed Directive 2003/37/EC ; they also transpose Directive 2008/2/EC on the field of vision and windscreen wipers for wheeled agricultural or forestry tractors as last amended by Directive 97/54/EC. - 4p.: 30 cm. - 978-0-11-083634-8 £3.00

The Traffic Signs (Amendment) Regulations and General Directions 2008 No. 2008/2177. - Enabling power: Road Traffic Regulation Act 1984, ss. 64 (1) (2) (3), 85 (2). - Issued: 04.09.2008. Made: 12.08.2008. Laid: 18.08.2008. Coming into force: 15.09.2008. Effect: S.I. 2002/3113 amended. Territorial extent & classification: E/W/S. General. - This statutory instrument has been printed in substitution of the the SI of the same number (ISBN 9780110838328, published 19.08.2008) and is being issued free of charge to all known recipients of that instrument. - 8p., col. ill.: 30 cm. - 978-0-11-083866-3 £3.50

The Traffic Signs (Amendment) Regulations and General Directions 2008 No. 2008/2177. - Enabling power: Road Traffic Regulation Act 1984, ss. 64 (1) (2) (3), 85 (2). - Issued: 19.08.2008. Made: 12.08.2008. Laid: 18.08.2008. Coming into force: 15.09.2008. Effect: S.I. 2002/3113 amended. Territorial extent & classification: E/W/S. General. - Replaced by corrected version (ISBN 9780110838663) issued on 04.09.2008 and issued free of charge to all known recipients of the original version. - 8p., col. ill.: 30 cm. - 978-0-11-083832-8 £3.00

The Vehicle Drivers (Certificates of Professional Competence) (Amendment) (No. 2) Regulations 2008 No. 2008/1965. - Enabling power: European Communities Act 1972, s. 2 (2) & Finance Act 1973, s. 56 (1) (2) & Criminal Justice and Court Services Act 2000, s. 71 (2). - Issued: 01.08.2008. Made: 21.07.2008. Laid: 25.07.2008. Coming into force: 01.09.2008. Effect: S.I. 2001/3343; 2007/605 amended. Territorial extent & classification: E/W/S/NI. General. - 12p.: 30 cm. - 978-0-11-083588-4 £3.00

The Vehicle Drivers (Certificates of Professional Competence) (Amendment) Regulations 2008 No. 2008/506. - Enabling power: Finance Act 1973, s. 56 (1) (2). - Issued: 04.03.2008. Made: 25.02.2008. Laid: 27.02.2008. Coming into force: 01.04.2008. Effect: S.I. 2007/605 amended. Territorial extent & classification: E/W/S/NI. General. - EC note: These Regs amend S.I. 2007/605 which implemented Council Directive 2003/59/EC on the initial qualification and periodic training of drivers of certain road vehicles for the carriage of goods or passengers- 2p.: 30 cm. - 978-0-11-081023-2 £3.00

The Vehicle Excise Duty (Immobilisation, Removal and Disposal of Vehicles) (Amendment) Regulations 2008 No. 2008/2266. - Enabling power: Vehicle Excise and Registration Act 1994, S. 32A, sch. 2A. - Issued: 02.09.2008. Made: 20.08.2008. Laid: 27.08.2008. Coming into force: 01.10.2008. Effect: S.I. 1997/2439 amended. Territorial extent & classification: E/W/S/NI. General. - [8]p.: 30 cm. - 978-0-11-083865-6 £3.00

The Vehicles Crime (Registration of Registration Plate Suppliers) Regulations 2008 No. 2008/1715. - Enabling power: Vehicles (Crime) Act 2001, ss. 17 (3), 18 (2), 19 (1), 24 (1) (3), 25 (1) (2), 41 (2). - Issued: 08.07.2008. Made: 30.06.2008. Laid: 03.07.2008. Coming into force: 01.08.2008. Effect: S.I. 2002/2977; 2003/228; 2005/2981 revoked. Territorial extent & classification: E/W/S/NI. General. - 8p.: 30 cm. - 978-0-11-081939-6 £3.00

Road traffic: Speed limits

The A5 Trunk Road (M42 Junction 10 to Grendon, Warwickshire) (40 Miles Per Hour and 50 Miles Per Hour Speed Limit) Order 2008 No. 2008/1024. - Enabling power: Road Traffic Regulation Act 1984, s. 84 (1) (a) (2), sch. 9, para. 27 (1). - Made: 17.03.2008. Coming into force: 31.03.2008. Effect: S.I. 1971/1996 revoked. Territorial extent & classification: E. Local *Unpublished*

The A5 Trunk Road (Nesscliffe Bypass, Shropshire) (Derestriction) Order 2008 No. 2008/291. - Enabling power: Road Traffic Regulation Act 1984, ss. 82 (1), 83 (1), sch. 9, para. 27 (1). - Made: 24.01.2008. Coming into force: 07.02.2008. Effect: None. Territorial extent & classification: E. Local *Unpublished*

The A5 Trunk Road (Witherley to M69 Junction 1) (40 Miles Per Hour and 50 Miles Per Hour Speed Limit) Order 2008 No. 2008/1032. - Enabling power: Road Traffic Regulation Act 1984, s. 84 (1) (a) (2), sch. 9, para. 27 (1). - Made: 17.03.2008. Coming into force: 31.03.2008. Effect: None. Territorial extent & classification: E. Local *Unpublished*

The A13 and A1089 Trunk Roads (Wennington Interchange to Tilbury Docks) (Derestriction) (No 1) Order 2008 No. 2008/771. - Enabling power: Road Traffic Regulation Act 1984, ss. 82 (2), 83 (1). - Made: 25.02.2008. Coming into force: 10.03.2008. Effect: None. Territorial extent & classification: E. Local *Unpublished*

The A19 Trunk Road (Moor Farm Roundabout, Cramlington) (40 Miles Per Hour Speed Limit) Order 2008 No. 2008/405. - Enabling power: Road Traffic Regulation Act 1984, ss. 82 (2), 83 (1), 84 (1) (a) (2), sch. 9, para. 27 (1). - Made: 13.02.2008. Coming into force: 24.02.2008. Effect: None. Territorial extent & classification: E. Local *Unpublished*

The A40 Trunk Road (Pencraig, Herefordshire) (50 Miles Per Hour Speed Limit) Order 2005 Variation Order 2008 No. 2008/288. - Enabling power: Road Traffic Regulation Act 1984, s. 84 (1) (a) (2), sch. 9, para. 27 (1). - Made: 24.01.2008. Coming into force: 07.02.2008. Effect: S.I. 2005/1706 varied. Territorial extent & classification: E. Local *Unpublished*

The A43 Trunk Road (Swan Valley Way Link Roads, Rothersthorpe, Northamptonshire) (40 Miles Per Hour Speed Limit) Order 2008 No. 2008/1383. - Enabling power: Road Traffic Regulation Act 1984, s. 84 (1) (a) (2). - Made: 15.05.2008. Coming into force: 02.06.2008. Effect: None. Territorial extent & classification: E. Local *Unpublished*

The A49 Trunk Road (Ludlow Bypass, Shropshire) (Derestriction) Order 2008 No. 2008/289. - Enabling power: Road Traffic Regulation Act 1984, ss. 82 (2), 83 (1), sch. 9, para. 27 (1). - Made: 24.01.2008. Coming into force: 07.02.2008. Effect: None. Territorial extent & classification: E. Local *Unpublished*

The A49 Trunk Road (Moreton, Herefordshire) (Derestriction) Order 2008 No. 2008/1099. - Enabling power: Road Traffic Regulation Act 1984, ss. 82 (2), 83 (1). - Made: 03.04.2008. Coming into force: 17.04.2008. Effect: None. Territorial extent & classification: E. Local *Unpublished*

The A49 Trunk Road (Much Birch, Herefordshire) (40 Miles Per Hour and 50 Miles Per Hour Speed Limit) Order 2005 Variation Order 2008 No. 2008/2472. - Enabling power: Road Traffic Regulation Act 1984, s. 84 (1) (a) (2), sch. 9, para. 27 (1). - Made: 07.08.2008. Coming into force: 21.08.2008. Effect: S.I. 2005/1557 varied. Territorial extent & classification: E. Local *Unpublished*

The A49 Trunk Road (North of Hope under Dinmore, Herefordshire) (Derestriction) Order 2008 No. 2008/2728. - Enabling power: Road Traffic Regulation Act 1984, ss. 82 (2), 83 (1), sch. 9, para. 27 (1). - Made: 02.10.2008. Coming into force: 16.10.2008. Effect: None. Territorial extent & classification: E. Local *Unpublished*

The A64 Trunk Road (Staxton Crossroads) (40 Miles Per Hour Speed Limit) Order 2008 No. 2008/402. - Enabling power: Road Traffic Regulation Act 1984, s. 84 (1) (a) (2), sch. 9, para. 27 (1). - Made: 12.02.2008. Coming into force: 22.02.2008. Effect: None. Territorial extent & classification: E. Local *Unpublished*

The A65 Trunk Road (Hellifield) (40 Miles Per Hour Speed Limit) Order 2008 No. 2008/1374. - Enabling power: Road Traffic Regulation Act 1984, s. 84 (1) (a) (2). - Made: 19.05.2008. Coming into force: 06.06.2008. Effect: None. Territorial extent & classification: E. Local *Unpublished*

The A65 Trunk Road (Hornsbarrow) (40 Miles Per Hour Speed Limit) Order 2008 No. 2008/206. - Enabling power: Road Traffic Regulation Act 1984, s. 84 (1) (2). - Made: 22.01.2008. Coming into force: 04.02.2008. Effect: None. Territorial extent & classification: E. Local *Unpublished*

The A65 Trunk Road (Long Preston) (30 Miles Per Hour Speed Limit) Order 2008 No. 2008/1533. - Enabling power: Road Traffic Regulation Act 1984, ss. 84 (1) (a) (2). - Made: 02.06.2008. Coming into force: 16.06.2008. Effect: None. Territorial extent & classification: E. Local *Unpublished*

The A69 Trunk Road (Denton Burn Interchange to West Denton Interchange) (50 Miles Per Hour Speed Restriction) Order 2008 No. 2008/2915. - Enabling power: Road Traffic Regulation Act 1984, s. 84 (1) (a) (2), sch. 9, para. 27 (1). - Made: 03.11.2008. Coming into force: 14.11.2008. Effect: S.I. 1980/1597 revoked. Territorial extent & classification: E. Local *Unpublished*

The A282 Trunk Road (Dartford - Thurrock Crossing and Approach Roads) (Speed Limits) Order 2008 No. 2008/1503. - Enabling power: Road Traffic Regulation Act 1984, s. 84 (1) (a) (2), 126. - Made: 02.06.2008. Coming into force: 16.06.2008. Effect: None. Territorial extent & classification: E. Local *Unpublished*

The A419 Trunk Road (Commonhead Junction, Swindon) (40 Miles Per Hour Speed Limit) Order 2008 No. 2008/3346. - Enabling power: Road Traffic Regulation Act 1984, s. 84 (1) (a) (2). - Made: 22.12.2008. Coming into force: 05.01.2009. Effect: None. Territorial extent & classification: E. Local *Unpublished*

The A494 and the A550 Trunk Roads (Deeside Park Junction) (De-Restriction) Order 2008 No. 2008/3332. - Enabling power: Road Traffic Regulation Act 1984, ss. 82 (2) (a), 83 (1). - Made: 08.12.2008. Coming into force: 19.12.2008. Effect: None. Territorial extent & classification: E. Local *Unpublished*

The A550 and A494 Trunk Roads (Woodbank Junction) (50 Miles Per Hour Speed Limit) Order 2008 No. 2008/3333. - Enabling power: Road Traffic Regulation Act 1984, s. 84 (1) (a) (2). - Made: 08.12.2008. Coming into force: 19.12.2008. Effect: None. Territorial extent & classification: E. Local *Unpublished*

The A556 Trunk Road (Millington) (50 Miles Per Hour Speed Limit) Order 2008 No. 2008/2797. - Enabling power: Road Traffic Regulation Act 1984, s. 84 (1) (a) (2). - Made: 06.10.2008. Coming into force: 17.10.2008. Effect: None. Territorial extent & classification: E. Local *Unpublished*

The A595 Trunk Road (Bigrigg) (40 Miles Per Hour Speed Limit) Order 2008 No. 2008/2415. - Enabling power: Road Traffic Regulation Act 1984, s. 84 (1) (a) (2). - Made: 29.08.2008. Coming into force: 12.09.2008. Effect: None. Territorial extent & classification: E. Local *Unpublished*

The A595 Trunk Road (Parton to Lillyhall Improvement) (Howgate 40 Miles Per Hour Speed Limit) Order 2008 No. 2008/3320. - Enabling power: Road Traffic Regulation Act 1984, ss. 84 (1) (a) (2), 122 (A). - Made: 01.12.2008. Coming into force: 17.12.2008. Effect: None. Territorial extent & classification: E. Local *Unpublished*

Road traffic: Traffic regulation

The A1 and the A47 Trunk Roads (Wanstead, Peterborough) (Slip Roads) (Temporary Prohibition of Traffic) Order 2008 No. 2008/146. - Enabling power: Road Traffic Regulation Act 1984, s. 14 (1) (a). - Made: 14.01.2008. Coming into force: 21.01.2008. Effect: None. Territorial extent & classification: E. Local *Unpublished*

The A1(M) and A1 Trunk Road (A1(M) Junction 17 to Water Newton, Cambridgeshire) (Temporary Prohibition of Traffic) Order 2008 No. 2008/1154. - Enabling power: Road Traffic Regulation Act 1984, s. 14 (1) (a). - Made: 11.04.2008. Coming into force: 18.04.2008. Effect: None. Territorial extent & classification: E. Local *Unpublished*

The A1(M) and A1 Trunk Road (Between Blyth and Ranby, Nottinghamshire) (Temporary Prohibition of Traffic) Order 2008 No. 2008/2223. - Enabling power: Road Traffic Regulation Act 1984, s. 14 (1) (a). - Made: 04.08.2008. Coming into force: 11.08.2008. Effect: None. Territorial extent & classification: E. Local *Unpublished*

The A1(M) Motorway (Alconbury to Spittals Interchange, Cambridgeshire) (Temporary Prohibition of Traffic) Order 2008 No. 2008/2139. - Enabling power: Road Traffic Regulation Act 1984, s. 14 (1) (a). - Made: 29.07.2008. Coming into force: 05.08.2008. Effect: None. Territorial extent & classification: E. Local *Unpublished*

The A1(M) Motorway and the A1 Trunk Road (Blyth, Nottinghamshire) (Temporary Restriction and Prohibition of Traffic) Order 2008 No. 2008/1002. - Enabling power: Road Traffic Regulation Act 1984, ss. 14 (1) (a) 7, 122A. - Made: 07.03.2008. Coming into force: 14.03.2008. Effect: None. Territorial extent & classification: E. Local *Unpublished*

The A1(M) Motorway and the A1 Trunk Road (Junction 56, Barton Interchange) (Temporary Restriction and Prohibition of Traffic) Order 2008 No. 2008/884. - Enabling power: Road Traffic Regulation Act 1984, ss. 14 (1) (a) (7). - Made: 03.03.2008. Coming into force: 14.03.2008. Effect: None. Territorial extent & classification: E. Local *Unpublished*

The A1(M) Motorway and the A1 Trunk Road (Junction 63 to Eighton Lodge) and the A194(M) Motorway (Birtley to Havnnah) (Temporary Restriction and Prohibition of Traffic) Order 2008 No. 2008/480. - Enabling power: Road Traffic Regulation Act 1984, s. 14 (1) (a) (7). - Made: 18.02.2008. Coming into force: 02.03.2008. Effect: None. Territorial extent & classification: E. Local *Unpublished*

The A1(M) Motorway and the A167 Trunk Road (Junction 63, Blind Lane Interchange) (Temporary Restriction and Prohibition of Traffic) Order 2008 No. 2008/2004. - Enabling power: Road Traffic Regulation Act 1984, s. 14 (1) (a). - Made: 07.07.2008. Coming into force: 20.07.2008. Effect: None. Territorial extent & classification: E. Local *Unpublished*

The A1(M) Motorway (Hatfield Tunnel) (Temporary Prohibition of Traffic) Order 2008 No. 2008/3275. - Enabling power: Road Traffic Regulation Act 1984, s. 14 (1) (a). - Made: 08.12.2008. Coming into force: 01.01.2009. Effect: None. Territorial extent & classification: E. Local *Unpublished*

The A1(M) Motorway (Junction 1 - 4, Northbound) (Temporary Restriction and Prohibition of Traffic) Order 2008 No. 2008/1681. - Enabling power: Road Traffic Regulation Act 1984, s. 14 (1) (a) (7). - Made: 23.06.2008. Coming into force: 28.06.2008. Effect: None. Territorial extent & classification: E. Local *Unpublished*

The A1(M) Motorway (Junction 6, Southbound Entry Slip Road) (Temporary Prohibition of Traffic) Order 2008 No. 2008/868. - Enabling power: Road Traffic Regulation Act 1984, s. 14 (1) (a). - Made: 10.03.2008. Coming into force: 15.03.2008. Effect: None. Territorial extent & classification: E. Local *Unpublished*

The A1(M) Motorway (Junction 6, Welwyn to Junction 7 Stevenage, Hertfordshire) (Temporary Restriction and Prohibition of Traffic) Order 2008 No. 2008/1023. - Enabling power: Road Traffic Regulation Act 1984, s. 14 (1) (a) (7). - Made: 18.03.2008. Coming into force: 25.03.2008. Effect: None. Territorial extent & classification: E. Local *Unpublished*

The A1(M) Motorway (Junction 15, Sawtry, Cambridgeshire) (Temporary Restriction and Prohibition of Traffic) Order 2008 No. 2008/2274. - Enabling power: Road Traffic Regulation Act 1984, s. 14 (1) (a). - Made: 18.08.2008. Coming into force: 26.08.2008. Effect: None. Territorial extent & classification: E. Local *Unpublished*

The A1(M) Motorway (Junction 16, Norman Cross, Cambridgeshire) (Temporary Prohibition of Traffic) Order 2008 No. 2008/2128. - Enabling power: Road Traffic Regulation Act 1984, s. 14 (1) (a). - Made: 28.07.2008. Coming into force: 04.08.2008. Effect: None. Territorial extent & classification: E. Local *Unpublished*

The A1(M) Motorway (Junction 34 Blyth Roundabout to Junction 35 Wadworth) (Temporary Restriction and Prohibition of Traffic) Order 2008 No. 2008/2245. - Enabling power: Road Traffic Regulation Act 1984, s. 14 (1) (a) (7). - Made: 13.08.2008. Coming into force: 25.08.2008. Effect: None. Territorial extent & classification: E. Local *Unpublished*

The A1(M) Motorway (Junction 35 to Junction 37) (Temporary Prohibition of Traffic) (No. 2) Order 2008 No. 2008/2916. - Enabling power: Road Traffic Regulation Act 1984, s. 14 (1) (a). - Made: 03.11.2008. Coming into force: 16.11.2008. Effect: None. Territorial extent & classification: E. Local *Unpublished*

The A1(M) Motorway (Junction 35 to Junction 37) (Temporary Prohibition of Traffic) Order 2008 No. 2008/2135. - Enabling power: Road Traffic Regulation Act 1984, s. 14 (1) (a). - Made: 28.07.2008. Coming into force: 10.08.2008. Effect: None. Territorial extent & classification: E. Local *Unpublished*

The A1(M) Motorway (Junction 36 to the A1 Trunk Road Blyth Roundabout) (Temporary Prohibition of Traffic) Order 2008 No. 2008/1690. - Enabling power: Road Traffic Regulation Act 1984, s. 14 (1) (a). - Made: 23.06.2008. Coming into force: 06.07.2008. Effect: None. Territorial extent & classification: E. Local *Unpublished*

The A1(M) Motorway (Junction 37, Marr Interchange) (Temporary Prohibition of Traffic) Order 2008 No. 2008/1026. - Enabling power: Road Traffic Regulation Act 1984, s. 14 (1) (a). - Made: 17.03.2008. Coming into force: 30.03.2008. Effect: None. Territorial extent & classification: E. Local *Unpublished*

The A1(M) Motorway (Junction 42 to Junction 44) (Temporary Prohibition of Traffic) (No. 2) Order 2008 No. 2008/1570. - Enabling power: Road Traffic Regulation Act 1984, s. 14 (1) (a). - Made: 09.06.2008. Coming into force: 22.06.2008. Effect: None. Territorial extent & classification: E. Local *Unpublished*

The A1(M) Motorway (Junction 44 Hook Moor to Junction 45 Bramham Crossroads) (Temporary Restriction and Prohibition of Traffic) Order 2008 No. 2008/2009. - Enabling power: Road Traffic Regulation Act 1984, s. 14 (1) (a). - Made: 08.07.2008. Coming into force: 20.07.2008. Effect: None. Territorial extent & classification: E. Local *Unpublished*

The A1(M) Motorway (Junction 44) (Temporary Prohibition of Traffic) Order 2008 No. 2008/768. - Enabling power: Road Traffic Regulation Act 1984, s. 14 (1) (a). - Made: 25.02.2008. Coming into force: 09.03.2008. Effect: None. Territorial extent & classification: E. Local *Unpublished*

The A1(M) Motorway (Junction 45, Bramham Crossroads) (Temporary Prohibition of Traffic) Order 2008 No. 2008/1250. - Enabling power: Road Traffic Regulation Act 1984, s. 14 (1) (a). - Made: 28.04.2008. Coming into force: 11.05.2008. Effect: None. Territorial extent & classification: E. Local *Unpublished*

The A1(M) Motorway (Junction 49 to Walshford) (Temporary Restriction and Prohibition of Traffic) Order 2008 No. 2008/1387. - Enabling power: Road Traffic Regulation Act 1984, s. 14 (1) (a) (7). - Made: 20.05.2008. Coming into force: 01.06.2008. Effect: None. Territorial extent & classification: E. Local *Unpublished*

The A1(M) Motorway (Junction 56 to Junction 57) and the A66(M) Motorway (Temporary Restriction and Prohibition of Traffic) Order 2008 No. 2008/1122. - Enabling power: Road Traffic Regulation Act 1984, s. 14 (1) (a) (7). - Made: 04.04.2008. Coming into force: 13.04.2008. Effect: None. Territorial extent & classification: E. Local *Unpublished*

The A1(M) Motorway (Junction 58 to Junction 59) and the A167 Trunk Road (Coatham Interchange) (Temporary Restriction and Prohibition of Traffic) Order 2008 No. 2008/107. - Enabling power: Road Traffic Regulation Act 1984, s. 14 (1) (a) (7). - Made: 14.01.2008. Coming into force: 27.01.2008. Effect: None. Territorial extent & classification: E. Local *Unpublished*

The A1(M) Motorway (Junction 60, Bradbury Interchange) (Temporary 50 Miles Per Hour Speed Restriction) Order 2008 No. 2008/262. - Enabling power: Road Traffic Regulation Act 1984, s. 14 (1) (a). - Made: 28.01.2008. Coming into force: 10.02.2008. Effect: None. Territorial extent & classification: E. Local *Unpublished*

The A1(M) Motorway (Junction 60 to Junction 59) (Temporary Restriction and Prohibition of Traffic) Order 2008 No. 2008/2001. - Enabling power: Road Traffic Regulation Act 1984, s. 14 (1) (a). - Made: 07.07.2008. Coming into force: 20.07.2008. Effect: None. Territorial extent & classification: E. Local *Unpublished*

The A1(M) Motorway (Junction 61, Bowburn Interchange) (Temporary 50 Miles Per Hour Speed Restriction) Order 2008 No. 2008/2208. - Enabling power: Road Traffic Regulation Act 1984, s. 14 (1) (a). - Made: 07.08.2008. Coming into force: 17.08.2008. Effect: None. Territorial extent & classification: E. Local *Unpublished*

The A1(M) Motorway (Junction 61, Bowburn Interchange) (Temporary Restriction and Prohibition of Traffic) Order 2008 No. 2008/2050. - Enabling power: Road Traffic Regulation Act 1984, ss. 14 (1) (a). - Made: 14.07.2008. Coming into force: 27.07.2008. Effect: None. Territorial extent & classification: E. Local *Unpublished*

The A1(M) Motorway (Junction 61, Bowburn) (Temporary Restriction and Prohibition of Traffic) Order 2008 No. 2008/1121. - Enabling power: Road Traffic Regulation Act 1984, s. 14 (1) (a). - Made: 04.04.2008. Coming into force: 16.04.2008. Effect: None. Territorial extent & classification: E. Local *Unpublished*

The A1(M) Motorway (Junction 61 to Junction 62) (Temporary Restriction and Prohibition of Traffic) Order 2008 No. 2008/1447. - Enabling power: Road Traffic Regulation Act 1984, s. 14 (1) (a) (7). - Made: 23.05.2008. Coming into force: 08.06.2008. Effect: None. Territorial extent & classification: E. Local *Unpublished*

The A1(M) Motorway (Junction 62, Carrville Interchange) (Temporary Restriction and Prohibition of Traffic) Order 2008 No. 2008/1128. - Enabling power: Road Traffic Regulation Act 1984, s. 14 (1) (a). - Made: 04.04.2008. Coming into force: 13.04.2008. Effect: None. Territorial extent & classification: E. Local *Unpublished*

The A1(M) Motorway (Junction 62 to Junction 63) (Temporary Restriction of Traffic) Order 2008 No. 2008/338. - Enabling power: Road Traffic Regulation Act 1984, s. 14 (1) (a) (7). - Made: 04.02.2008. Coming into force: 17.02.2008. Effect: None. Territorial extent & classification: E. Local *Unpublished*

Road traffic: Traffic regulation

The A1(M) Motorway (Junction 63 Blind Lane Interchange) to the A194(M) (Havannah Interchange) (Temporary Restriction and Prohibition of Traffic) Order 2008 No. 2008/2763. - Enabling power: Road Traffic Regulation Act 1984, s. 14 (1) (a). - Made: 13.10.2008. Coming into force: 26.10.2008. Effect: None. Territorial extent & classification: E. Local *Unpublished*

The A1(M) Motorway (Junction 63 to Junction 64) (Temporary Restriction and Prohibition of Traffic) Order 2008 No. 2008/1131. - Enabling power: Road Traffic Regulation Act 1984, s. 14 (1) (a). - Made: 14.04.2008. Coming into force: 27.04.2008. Effect: None. Territorial extent & classification: E. Local *Unpublished*

The A1(M) Motorway (Junctions 2 and 3, Slip Roads) (Temporary Prohibition of Traffic) Order 2008 No. 2008/1626. - Enabling power: Road Traffic Regulation Act 1984, ss. 14 (1) (a). - Made: 16.06.2008. Coming into force: 21.06.2008. Effect: None. Territorial extent & classification: E. Local *Unpublished*

The A1(M) Motorway (Junctions 3 - 1, Southbound) (Temporary Prohibition of Traffic) Order 2008 No. 2008/2520. - Enabling power: Road Traffic Regulation Act 1984, s. 14 (1) (a) (7). - Made: 15.09.2008. Coming into force: 20.09.2008. Effect: None. Territorial extent & classification: E. Local *Unpublished*

The A1(M) Motorway (Junctions 3 and 4, Slip Roads) (Temporary Prohibition of Traffic) Order 2008 No. 2008/454. - Enabling power: Road Traffic Regulation Act 1984, s. 14 (1) (a). - Made: 18.02.2008. Coming into force: 23.02.2008. Effect: None. Territorial extent & classification: E. Local *Unpublished*

The A1(M) Motorway (Junctions 15 and 17, Cambridgeshire) (Temporary Prohibition of Traffic) Order 2008 No. 2008/2199. - Enabling power: Road Traffic Regulation Act 1984, s. 14 (1) (a). - Made: 04.08.2008. Coming into force: 11.08.2008. Effect: None. Territorial extent & classification: E. Local *Unpublished*

The A1(M) Motorway (South of Junction 5 - Junction 6, Northbound) (Temporary Restriction and Prohibition of Traffic) Order 2008 No. 2008/2891. - Enabling power: Road Traffic Regulation Act 1984, s. 14 (1) (a) (7). - Made: 27.10.2008. Coming into force: 01.11.2008. Effect: None. Territorial extent & classification: E. Local *Unpublished*

The A1 Trunk Road (A1(M) Junction 17, Peterborough) (Temporary Prohibition of Traffic) Order 2008 No. 2008/1292. - Enabling power: Road Traffic Regulation Act 1984, s. 14 (1) (a). - Made: 25.04.2008. Coming into force: 02.05.2008. Effect: None. Territorial extent & classification: E. Local *Unpublished*

The A1 Trunk Road (Adderstone) (Temporary Restriction and Prohibition of Traffic) Order 2008 No. 2008/394. - Enabling power: Road Traffic Regulation Act 1984, s. 14 (1) (a). - Made: 12.02.2008. Coming into force: 24.02.2008. Effect: None. Territorial extent & classification: E. Local *Unpublished*

The A1 Trunk Road (Ainderby Quernhow to Middleton Quernhow) (Temporary 10 Miles Per Hour and 40 Miles Per Hour Speed Restriction) Order 2008 No. 2008/2623. - Enabling power: Road Traffic Regulation Act 1984, s. 14 (1) (a). - Made: 29.09.2008. Coming into force: 10.10.2008. Effect: None. Territorial extent & classification: E. Local *Unpublished*

The A1 Trunk Road (Alnwick to Berwick upon Tweed) (Temporary Restriction and Prohibition of Traffic) Order 2008 No. 2008/158. - Enabling power: Road Traffic Regulation Act 1984, s. 14 (1) (a). - Made: 21.01.2008. Coming into force: 03.02.2008. Effect: None. Territorial extent & classification: E. Local *Unpublished*

The A1 Trunk Road (Alnwick to Rashercap) (Temporary Restriction and Prohibition of Traffic) Order 2008 No. 2008/391. - Enabling power: Road Traffic Regulation Act 1984, s. 14 (1) (a). - Made: 12.02.2008. Coming into force: 24.02.2008. Effect: None. Territorial extent & classification: E. Local *Unpublished*

The A1 Trunk Road (Alnwick to Scottish Border) (Temporary Restriction and Prohibition of Traffic) Order 2008 No. 2008/1629. - Enabling power: Road Traffic Regulation Act 1984, s. 14 (1) (a). - Made: 16.06.2008. Coming into force: 29.06.2008. Effect: None. Territorial extent & classification: E. Local *Unpublished*

The A1 Trunk Road and the A1(M) Motorway (A5135 Junction - Junction 6) (Temporary Prohibition of Traffic) Order 2008 No. 2008/2726. - Enabling power: Road Traffic Regulation Act 1984, s. 14 (1) (a). - Made: 06.10.2008. Coming into force: 14.10.2008. Effect: None. Territorial extent & classification: E. Local *Unpublished*

The A1 Trunk Road and the A1(M) Motorway (Eighton Lodge to Junction 64) and the A194(M) Motorway (Havannah to Birtley) (Temporary Restriction and Prohibition of Traffic) Order 2008 No. 2008/886. - Enabling power: Road Traffic Regulation Act 1984, s. 14 (1) (a). - Made: 03.03.2008. Coming into force: 14.03.2008. Effect: None. Territorial extent & classification: E. Local *Unpublished*

The A1 Trunk Road and the A1(M) Motorway (Scotch Corner to Junction 56, Barton) (Temporary Restriction and Prohibition of Traffic) Order 2008 No. 2008/1030. - Enabling power: Road Traffic Regulation Act 1984, s. 14 (1) (a) (7). - Made: 14.03.2008. Coming into force: 25.03.2008. Effect: None. Territorial extent & classification: E. Local *Unpublished*

The A1 Trunk Road and the A1(M) Motorway (Scotch Corner to Junction 57) and the A66 Trunk Road (Scotch Corner to Sedbury Lodge) (Temporary Restriction and Prohibition of Traffic) Order 2008 No. 2008/1130. - Enabling power: Road Traffic Regulation Act 1984, s. 14 (1) (a) (7). - Made: 31.03.2008. Coming into force: 06.04.2008. Effect: None. Territorial extent & classification: E. Local *Unpublished*

The A1 Trunk Road and the A66 Trunk Road (Scotch Corner Interchange) (Temporary Restriction and Prohibition of Traffic) Order 2008 No. 2008/63. - Enabling power: Road Traffic Regulation Act 1984, s. 14 (1) (a). - Made: 07.01.2008. Coming into force: 20.01.2008. Effect: None. Territorial extent & classification: E. Local *Unpublished*

The A1 Trunk Road (Apleyhead, Nottinghamshire) (Temporary Prohibition of Traffic) Order 2008 No. 2008/1151. - Enabling power: Road Traffic Regulation Act 1984, s. 14 (1) (a). - Made: 14.04.2008. Coming into force: 21.04.2008. Effect: None. Territorial extent & classification: E. Local *Unpublished*

The A1 Trunk Road (Apleyhead to Newark on Trent, Nottinghamshire) (Temporary Prohibition of Traffic) (No. 2) Order 2008 No. 2008/1361. - Enabling power: Road Traffic Regulation Act 1984, s. 14 (1) (a). - Made: 09.05.2008. Coming into force: 16.05.2008. Effect: None. Territorial extent & classification: E. Local *Unpublished*

The A1 Trunk Road (Apleyhead to Newark on Trent, Nottinghamshire) (Temporary Prohibition of Traffic) Order 2008 No. 2008/816. - Enabling power: Road Traffic Regulation Act 1984, s. 14 (1) (a). - Made: 25.02.2008. Coming into force: 03.03.2008. Effect: None. Territorial extent & classification: E. Local *Unpublished*

The A1 Trunk Road (Balderton, Nottinghamshire) (Slip Road) (Temporary Prohibition of Traffic) Order 2008 No. 2008/389. - Enabling power: Road Traffic Regulation Act 1984, s. 14 (1) (a). - Made: 11.02.2008. Coming into force: 18.02.2008. Effect: None. Territorial extent & classification: E. Local *Unpublished*

The A1 Trunk Road (Barrowby to Long Bennington, Lincolnshire) (Temporary Prohibition of Traffic) Order 2008 No. 2008/2798. - Enabling power: Road Traffic Regulation Act 1984, s. 14 (1) (a). - Made: 13.10.2008. Coming into force: 20.10.2008. Effect: None. Territorial extent & classification: E. Local *Unpublished*

The A1 Trunk Road (Belford to Scottish Border) (Temporary 40 Miles Per Hour and 50 Miles Per Hour Speed Restriction) Order 2008 No. 2008/3040. - Enabling power: Road Traffic Regulation Act 1984, s. 14 (1) (a). - Made: 18.11.2008. Coming into force: 30.11.2008. Effect: None. Territorial extent & classification: E. Local *Unpublished*

The A1 Trunk Road (Biggleswade North Roundabout to Black Cat Roundabout, Bedfordshire) (Temporary Prohibition of Traffic) Order 2008 No. 2008/2017. - Enabling power: Road Traffic Regulation Act 1984, s. 14 (1) (a). - Made: 08.07.2008. Coming into force: 15.07.2008. Effect: None. Territorial extent & classification: E. Local *Unpublished*

The A1 Trunk Road (Birtley Interchange to Lobley Hill Interchange) (Temporary Restriction and Prohibition of Traffic) Order 2008 No. 2008/2288. - Enabling power: Road Traffic Regulation Act 1984, s. 14 (1) (a) (7). - Made: 19.08.2008. Coming into force: 28.08.2008. Effect: None. Territorial extent & classification: E. Local *Unpublished*

The A1 Trunk Road (Birtley Interchange to Seaton Burn Interchange) (Temporary Restriction and Prohibition of Traffic) Order 2008 No. 2008/2191. - Enabling power: Road Traffic Regulation Act 1984, s. 14 (1) (a). - Made: 04.08.2008. Coming into force: 17.08.2008. Effect: None. Territorial extent & classification: E. Local *Unpublished*

The A1 Trunk Road (Birtley to Consett Route) (Temporary Restriction and Prohibition of Traffic) Order 2008 No. 2008/61. - Enabling power: Road Traffic Regulation Act 1984, s. 14 (1) (a). - Made: 07.01.2008. Coming into force: 20.01.2008. Effect: None. Territorial extent & classification: E. Local *Unpublished*

The A1 Trunk Road (Black Cat Roundabout to Sandy Roundabout, Bedfordshire) (Temporary Restriction and Prohibition of Traffic) Order 2008 No. 2008/485. - Enabling power: Road Traffic Regulation Act 1984, s. 14 (1) (a). - Made: 18.02.2008. Coming into force: 25.02.2008. Effect: None. Territorial extent & classification: E. Local *Unpublished*

The A1 Trunk Road (Blaydon Interchange to Seaton Burn Interchange) (Temporary Restriction and Prohibition of Traffic) Order 2008 No. 2008/2762. - Enabling power: Road Traffic Regulation Act 1984, s. 14 (1) (a). - Made: 13.10.2008. Coming into force: 26.10.2008. Effect: None. Territorial extent & classification: E. Local *Unpublished*

The A1 Trunk Road (Borehamwood Junction, Northbound Lay-by) (Temporary Prohibition of Traffic) Order 2008 No. 2008/2187. - Enabling power: Road Traffic Regulation Act 1984, s. 14 (1) (a). - Made: 04.08.2008. Coming into force: 09.08.2008. Effect: None. Territorial extent & classification: E. Local *Unpublished*

The A1 Trunk Road (Catterick North Interchange to Scotch Corner Interchange) (Temporary Restriction and Prohibition of Traffic) Order 2008 No. 2008/3218. - Enabling power: Road Traffic Regulation Act 1984, s. 14 (1) (a). - Made: 24.11.2008. Coming into force: 07.12.2008. Effect: None. Territorial extent & classification: E. Local *Unpublished*

The A1 Trunk Road (Causey Park Junction to Denwick) (Temporary Restriction and Prohibition of Traffic) Order 2008 No. 2008/2974. - Enabling power: Road Traffic Regulation Act 1984, s. 14 (1) (a). - Made: 10.11.2008. Coming into force: 23.11.2008. Effect: None. Territorial extent & classification: E. Local *Unpublished*

The A1 Trunk Road (Charlton Mires to Belford) (Temporary Restriction and Prohibition of Traffic) Order 2008 No. 2008/1689. - Enabling power: Road Traffic Regulation Act 1984, s. 14 (1) (a). - Made: 24.06.2008. Coming into force: 06.07.2008. Effect: None. Territorial extent & classification: E. Local *Unpublished*

The A1 Trunk Road (Crosshall Bridge, Eaton Ford, Cambridgeshire) (Temporary Prohibition of Traffic) Order 2008 No. 2008/2151. - Enabling power: Road Traffic Regulation Act 1984, s. 14 (1) (a). - Made: 22.07.2008. Coming into force: 29.07.2008. Effect: None. Territorial extent & classification: E. Local *Unpublished*

Road traffic: Traffic regulation

The A1 Trunk Road (Deanmoor to Charlton Mires) (Temporary Restriction and Prohibition of Traffic) Order 2008 No. 2008/2227. - Enabling power: Road Traffic Regulation Act 1984, s. 14 (1) (a). - Made: 12.08.2008. Coming into force: 25.08.2008. Effect: None. Territorial extent & classification: E. Local *Unpublished*

The A1 Trunk Road (Ducketts Hill Layby, Kneeton) (Temporary Prohibition of Traffic) Order 2008 No. 2008/3041. - Enabling power: Road Traffic Regulation Act 1984, s. 14 (1) (a). - Made: 18.11.2008. Coming into force: 30.11.2008. Effect: None. Territorial extent & classification: E. Local *Unpublished*

The A1 Trunk Road (Dunston Interchange to Metro Centre) (Temporary Restriction and Prohibition of Traffic) (No. 2) Order 2008 No. 2008/1304. - Enabling power: Road Traffic Regulation Act 1984, s. 14 (1) (a). - Made: 06.05.2008. Coming into force: 18.05.2008. Effect: None. Territorial extent & classification: E. Local *Unpublished*

The A1 Trunk Road (Dunston Interchange to Metro Centre) (Temporary Restriction and Prohibition of Traffic) Order 2008 No. 2008/395. - Enabling power: Road Traffic Regulation Act 1984, s. 14 (1) (a). - Made: 12.02.2008. Coming into force: 24.02.2008. Effect: None. Territorial extent & classification: E. Local *Unpublished*

The A1 Trunk Road (Dunston Interchange to the A694 Blaydon Interchange) (Temporary Prohibition of Traffic) (No. 2) Order 2008 No. 2008/3348. - Enabling power: Road Traffic Regulation Act 1984, s. 14 (1) (a). - Made: 22.12.2008. Coming into force: 01.01.2009. Effect: None. Territorial extent & classification: E. Local *Unpublished*

The A1 Trunk Road (Dunston Interchange to the A694 Blaydon Interchange) (Temporary Prohibition of Traffic) Order 2008 No. 2008/2295. - Enabling power: Road Traffic Regulation Act 1984, s. 14 (1) (a). - Made: 18.08.2008. Coming into force: 31.08.2008. Effect: None. Territorial extent & classification: E. Local *Unpublished*

The A1 Trunk Road (Edworth, Biggleswade, Bedfordshire) (Temporary Restriction of Traffic) Order 2008 No. 2008/2209. - Enabling power: Road Traffic Regulation Act 1984, s. 14 (1) (a). - Made: 11.08.2008. Coming into force: 18.08.2008. Effect: None. Territorial extent & classification: E. Local *Unpublished*

The A1 Trunk Road (Eighton Lodge Interchange & Kingsway Interchange) (Temporary Prohibition of Traffic) Order 2008 No. 2008/2630. - Enabling power: Road Traffic Regulation Act 1984, s. 14 (1) (a). - Made: 29.09.2008. Coming into force: 12.10.2008. Effect: None. Territorial extent & classification: E. Local *Unpublished*

The A1 Trunk Road (Eighton Lodge Interchange to Birtley Interchange) (Temporary 50 Miles Per Hour Speed Restriction) Order 2008 No. 2008/1126. - Enabling power: Road Traffic Regulation Act 1984, s. 14 (1) (a). - Made: 04.04.2008. Coming into force: 10.04.2008. Effect: None. Territorial extent & classification: E. Local *Unpublished*

The A1 Trunk Road (Elkesley, Nottinghamshire) (Temporary Prohibition of Traffic) Order 2008 No. 2008/3181. - Enabling power: Road Traffic Regulation Act 1984, s. 14 (1) (b). - Made: 28.11.2008. Coming into force: 05.12.2008. Effect: None. Territorial extent & classification: E. Local *Unpublished*

The A1 Trunk Road (Fair Moor to Hebron Junction) (Temporary Restriction and Prohibition of Traffic) Order 2008 No. 2008/2983. - Enabling power: Road Traffic Regulation Act 1984, s. 14 (1) (a). - Made: 12.11.2008. Coming into force: 23.11.2008. Effect: None. Territorial extent & classification: E. Local *Unpublished*

The A1 Trunk Road (Felton Bypass) (Temporary Restriction and Prohibition of Traffic) Order 2008 No. 2008/865. - Enabling power: Road Traffic Regulation Act 1984, s. 14 (1) (a). - Made: 25.02.2008. Coming into force: 09.03.2008. Effect: None. Territorial extent & classification: E. Local *Unpublished*

The A1 Trunk Road (Fenwick to Haggerston) (Temporary Restriction and Prohibition of Traffic) Order 2008 No. 2008/264. - Enabling power: Road Traffic Regulation Act 1984, s. 14 (1) (a). - Made: 29.01.2008. Coming into force: 11.02.2008. Effect: None. Territorial extent & classification: E. Local *Unpublished*

The A1 Trunk Road (Gatenby Interchange) (Temporary Restriction and Prohibition of Traffic) Order 2008 No. 2008/2229. - Enabling power: Road Traffic Regulation Act 1984, s. 14 (1) (a). - Made: 11.08.2008. Coming into force: 26.08.2008. Effect: None. Territorial extent & classification: E. Local *Unpublished*

The A1 Trunk Road (Gonerby Moor, Lincolnshire) (Temporary Prohibition of Traffic) Order 2008 No. 2008/1638. - Enabling power: Road Traffic Regulation Act 1984, s. 14 (1) (a). - Made: 23.05.2008. Coming into force: 30.05.2008. Effect: None. Territorial extent & classification: E. Local *Unpublished*

The A1 Trunk Road (Grantham, Lincolnshire) (Temporary Prohibition of Traffic in Layby) Order 2008 No. 2008/3034. - Enabling power: Road Traffic Regulation Act 1984, s. 14 (1) (a). - Made: 07.11.2008. Coming into force: 14.11.2008. Effect: None. Territorial extent & classification: E. Local *Unpublished*

The A1 Trunk Road (Great Ponton, Lincolnshire) (Temporary Prohibition of Traffic) Order 2008 No. 2008/2614. - Enabling power: Road Traffic Regulation Act 1984, s. 14 (1) (a). - Made: 19.09.2008. Coming into force: 26.09.2008. Effect: None. Territorial extent & classification: E. Local *Unpublished*

The A1 Trunk Road (Hitchcroft to Hampeth) (Temporary Restriction and Prohibition of Traffic) Order 2008 No. 2008/2477. - Enabling power: Road Traffic Regulation Act 1984, s. 14 (1) (a). - Made: 09.09.2008. Coming into force: 23.09.2008. Effect: None. Territorial extent & classification: E. Local *Unpublished*

The A1 Trunk Road (Junction 38, Redhouse) (Temporary Prohibition of Traffic) Order 2008 No. 2008/1248. - Enabling power: Road Traffic Regulation Act 1984, s. 14 (1) (a). - Made: 28.04.2008. Coming into force: 11.05.2008. Effect: None. Territorial extent & classification: E. Local *Unpublished*

The A1 Trunk Road (Junction 49, Dishforth) (Temporary Prohibition of Traffic) Order 2008 No. 2008/1249. - Enabling power: Road Traffic Regulation Act 1984, s. 14 (1) (a). - Made: 28.04.2008. Coming into force: 11.05.2008. Effect: None. Territorial extent & classification: E. Local *Unpublished*

The A1 Trunk Road (Junction with the A606, near Stamford) (Temporary Prohibition of Traffic) Order 2008 No. 2008/3031. - Enabling power: Road Traffic Regulation Act 1984, s. 14 (1) (a). - Made: 07.11.2008. Coming into force: 14.11.2008. Effect: None. Territorial extent & classification: E. Local *Unpublished*

The A1Trunk Road (Kingsway Interchange to Eighton Lodge Interchange) (Temporary Restriction and Prohibition of Traffic) Order 2008 No. 2008/2533. - Enabling power: Road Traffic Regulation Act 1984, s. 14 (1) (a). - Made: 15.09.2008. Coming into force: 21.09.2008. Effect: None. Territorial extent & classification: E. Local *Unpublished*

The A1 Trunk Road (Layby North of Junction 38, Redhouse) (Temporary Prohibition of Traffic) Order 2008 No. 2008/1495. - Enabling power: Road Traffic Regulation Act 1984, s. 14 (1) (a). - Made: 22.05.2008. Coming into force: 30.05.2008. Effect: None. Territorial extent & classification: E. Local *Unpublished*

The A1 Trunk Road (Leases Hall to Londonderry Interchange) (Temporary Restriction and Prohibition of Traffic) Order 2008 No. 2008/3345. - Enabling power: Road Traffic Regulation Act 1984, s. 14 (1) (a). - Made: 22.12.2008. Coming into force: 04.01.2009. Effect: None. Territorial extent & classification: E. Local *Unpublished*

The A1 Trunk Road (Little Holtby to Thornbrough) (Temporary Restriction and Prohibition of Traffic) Order 2008 No. 2008/2982. - Enabling power: Road Traffic Regulation Act 1984, s. 14 (1) (a). - Made: 10.11.2008. Coming into force: 23.11.2008. Effect: None. Territorial extent & classification: E. Local *Unpublished*

The A1 Trunk Road (Little Ponton, Lincolnshire) (Temporary Prohibition of Traffic) Order 2008 No. 2008/3224. - Enabling power: Road Traffic Regulation Act 1984, s. 14 (1) (a). - Made: 21.11.2008. Coming into force: 28.11.2008. Effect: None. Territorial extent & classification: E. Local *Unpublished*

The A1 Trunk Road (Londonderry to Leeming Bar) (Temporary Prohibition of Traffic) Order 2008 No. 2008/1613. - Enabling power: Road Traffic Regulation Act 1984, s. 14 (1) (a). - Made: 11.06.2008. Coming into force: 20.06.2009. Effect: None. Territorial extent & classification: E. Local *Unpublished*

The A1 Trunk Road (Low Espley to Causey Park) (Temporary 40 Miles Per Hour Speed Restriction) Order 2008 No. 2008/2051. - Enabling power: Road Traffic Regulation Act 1984, s. 14 (1) (a). - Made: 14.07.2008. Coming into force: 27.07.2008. Effect: None. Territorial extent & classification: E. Local *Unpublished*

The A1 Trunk Road (Low Lynn Junction) (Temporary 10 Miles Per Hour Speed Restriction) Order 2008 No. 2008/2937. - Enabling power: Road Traffic Regulation Act 1984, s. 14 (1) (a). - Made: 05.11.2008. Coming into force: 09.11.2008. Effect: None. Territorial extent & classification: E. Local *Unpublished*

The A1 Trunk Road (Markham Moor, Nottinghamshire) (Temporary Prohibition and Restriction of Traffic) Order 2008 No. 2008/2386. - Enabling power: Road Traffic Regulation Act 1984, ss. 14 (1) (a), 122A. - Made: 19.08.2008. Coming into force: 26.08.2008. Effect: None. Territorial extent & classification: E. Local *Unpublished*

The A1 Trunk Road (Markham Moor, Nottinghamshire) (Temporary Prohibition of Traffic) Order 2008 No. 2008/2225. - Enabling power: Road Traffic Regulation Act 1984, s. 14 (1) (a). - Made: 01.08.2008. Coming into force: 08.08.2008. Effect: None. Territorial extent & classification: E. Local *Unpublished*

The A1 Trunk Road (Markham Moor, Nottinghamshire) (Temporary Restriction of Traffic) Order 2008 No. 2008/3182. - Enabling power: Road Traffic Regulation Act 1984, s. 14 (1) (a). - Made: 28.11.2008. Coming into force: 05.12.2008. Effect: None. Territorial extent & classification: E. Local *Unpublished*

The A1 Trunk Road (Markham Moor to Apleyhead, Nottinghamshire) (Temporary Prohibition of Traffic) Order 2008 No. 2008/822. - Enabling power: Road Traffic Regulation Act 1984, s. 14 (1) (a). - Made: 22.02.2008. Coming into force: 29.02.2008. Effect: None. Territorial extent & classification: E. Local *Unpublished*

The A1 Trunk Road (Mitford to Hemelspeth Junction) (Temporary Restriction and Prohibition of Traffic) Order 2008 No. 2008/2973. - Enabling power: Road Traffic Regulation Act 1984, s. 14 (1) (a). - Made: 10.11.2008. Coming into force: 23.11.2008. Effect: None. Territorial extent & classification: E. Local *Unpublished*

The A1 Trunk Road (Morpeth Bypass) (Temporary Restriction and Prohibition of Traffic) Order 2008 No. 2008/1059. - Enabling power: Road Traffic Regulation Act 1984, s. 14 (1) (a). - Made: 18.03.2008. Coming into force: 31.03.2008. Effect: None. Territorial extent & classification: E. Local *Unpublished*

The A1 Trunk Road (Near Easton, Lincolnshire) (Temporary Restriction and Prohibition of Traffic) Order 2008 No. 2008/2487. - Enabling power: Road Traffic Regulation Act 1984, s. 14 (1) (a). - Made: 29.08.2008. Coming into force: 05.09.2008. Effect: None. Territorial extent & classification: E. Local *Unpublished*

Road traffic: Traffic regulation

The A1 Trunk Road (Near Gonerby Moor, Lincolnshire) (Temporary Prohibition of Traffic) Order 2008 No. 2008/1000. - Enabling power: Road Traffic Regulation Act 1984, s. 14 (1) (a). - Made: 07.03.2008. Coming into force: 14.03.2008. Effect: None. Territorial extent & classification: E. Local *Unpublished*

The A1 Trunk Road (Near Tuxford, Nottinghamshire) (Temporary Restriction and Prohibition of Traffic) Order 2008 No. 2008/3359. - Enabling power: Road Traffic Regulation Act 1984, s. 14 (1) (a). - Made: 22.12.2008. Coming into force: 29.12.2008. Effect: None. Territorial extent & classification: E. Local *Unpublished*

The A1 Trunk Road (Newark on Trent to Apleyhead, Nottinghamshire) (Temporary Prohibition of Traffic) Order 2008 No. 2008/1073. - Enabling power: Road Traffic Regulation Act 1984, s. 14 (1) (a). - Made: 24.03.2008. Coming into force: 31.03.2008. Effect: None. Territorial extent & classification: E. Local *Unpublished*

The A1 Trunk Road (Newark on Trent to Gonerby Moor) (Temporary Prohibition of Traffic) Order 2008 No. 2008/1538. - Enabling power: Road Traffic Regulation Act 1984, s. 14 (1) (a). - Made: 27.05.2008. Coming into force: 03.06.2008. Effect: None. Territorial extent & classification: E. Local *Unpublished*

The A1 Trunk Road (Newark on Trent to Markham Moor, Nottinghamshire) (Temporary Prohibition of Traffic) Order 2008 No. 2008/350. - Enabling power: Road Traffic Regulation Act 1984, s. 14 (1) (a). - Made: 01.02.2008. Coming into force: 08.02.2008. Effect: None. Territorial extent & classification: E. Local *Unpublished*

The A1 Trunk Road (Northbound Exit Slip Road to Darrington) (Temporary Prohibition of Traffic) Order 2008 No. 2008/2631. - Enabling power: Road Traffic Regulation Act 1984, s. 14 (1) (a). - Made: 22.09.2008. Coming into force: 05.10.2008. Effect: None. Territorial extent & classification: E. Local *Unpublished*

The A1 Trunk Road (North Brunton to Stannington) and the A19 Trunk Road (Seaton Burn, Killingworth and Silverlink Interchanges) (Temporary Restriction and Prohibition of Traffic) Order 2008 No. 2008/263. - Enabling power: Road Traffic Regulation Act 1984, s. 14 (1) (a). - Made: 28.01.2008. Coming into force: 03.02.2008. Effect: None. Territorial extent & classification: E. Local *Unpublished*

The A1 Trunk Road (North of Markham Moor, Nottinghamshire) (Temporary Prohibition of Traffic) Order 2008 No. 2008/1365. - Enabling power: Road Traffic Regulation Act 1984, s. 14 (1) (a). - Made: 13.05.2008. Coming into force: 20.05.2008. Effect: None. Territorial extent & classification: E. Local *Unpublished*

The A1 Trunk Road (Rainton to Pickhill) (Temporary Restriction and Prohibition of Traffic) Order 2008 No. 2008/2972. - Enabling power: Road Traffic Regulation Act 1984, s. 14 (1) (a). - Made: 03.11.2008. Coming into force: 16.11.2008. Effect: None. Territorial extent & classification: E. Local *Unpublished*

The A1 Trunk Road (Ranby to Blyth, Nottinghamshire) (Temporary Prohibition of Traffic) Order 2008 No. 2008/1537. - Enabling power: Road Traffic Regulation Act 1984, s. 14 (1) (a). - Made: 02.06.2008. Coming into force: 09.06.2008. Effect: None. Territorial extent & classification: E. Local *Unpublished*

The A1 Trunk Road (Rashercap to Shilbottle) (Temporary Restriction and Prohibition of Traffic) Order 2008 No. 2008/2817. - Enabling power: Road Traffic Regulation Act 1984, s. 14 (1) (a). - Made: 20.10.2008. Coming into force: 02.11.2008. Effect: None. Territorial extent & classification: E. Local *Unpublished*

The A1 Trunk Road (Scotch Corner Interchange) (Temporary Prohibition of Traffic) Order 2008 No. 2008/2054. - Enabling power: Road Traffic Regulation Act 1984, s. 14 (1) (a). - Made: 14.07.2008. Coming into force: 25.07.2008. Effect: None. Territorial extent & classification: E. Local *Unpublished*

The A1 Trunk Road (Scotswood Interchange) (Temporary Prohibition of Traffic) Order 2008 No. 2008/159. - Enabling power: Road Traffic Regulation Act 1984, s. 14 (1) (a). - Made: 21.01.2008. Coming into force: 03.02.2008. Effect: None. Territorial extent & classification: E. Local *Unpublished*

The A1 Trunk Road (Seaton Burn to Stannington) (Temporary Restriction and Prohibition of Traffic) Order 2008 No. 2008/2296. - Enabling power: Road Traffic Regulation Act 1984, s. 14 (1) (a). - Made: 18.08.2008. Coming into force: 31.08.2008. Effect: None. Territorial extent & classification: E. Local *Unpublished*

The A1 Trunk Road (Sinderby Interchange to Gatenby Interchange) (Temporary Restriction and Prohibition of Traffic) Order 2008 No. 2008/3039. - Enabling power: Road Traffic Regulation Act 1984, s. 14 (1) (a). - Made: 18.11.2008. Coming into force: 30.11.2008. Effect: None. Territorial extent & classification: E. Local *Unpublished*

The A1 Trunk Road (Skeeby) (Temporary 10 Miles Per Hour and 40 Miles Per Hour Speed Restriction) Order 2008 No. 2008/2131. - Enabling power: Road Traffic Regulation Act 1984, s. 14 (1) (a). - Made: 28.07.2008. Coming into force: 08.08.2008. Effect: None. Territorial extent & classification: E. Local *Unpublished*

The A1 Trunk Road (Stamford to Grantham) (Temporary Prohibition of Traffic) (No. 2) Order 2008 No. 2008/1631. - Enabling power: Road Traffic Regulation Act 1984, s. 14 (1) (a). - Made: 02.06.2008. Coming into force: 09.06.2008. Effect: None. Territorial extent & classification: E. Local *Unpublished*

The A1 Trunk Road (Stamford to Grantham) (Temporary Prohibition of Traffic) Order 2008 No. 2008/2579. - Enabling power: Road Traffic Regulation Act 1984, s. 14 (1) (a). - Made: 12.09.2008. Coming into force: 19.09.2008. Effect: None. Territorial extent & classification: E. Local *Unpublished*

The A1 Trunk Road (Stamford to Grantham) (Temporary Prohibition of Traffic) Order 2008 No. 2008/1366. - Enabling power: Road Traffic Regulation Act 1984, s. 14 (1) (a). - Made: 05.05.2008. Coming into force: 12.05.2008. Effect: None. Territorial extent & classification: E. Local *Unpublished*

The A1 Trunk Road (Stannington Bypass Southbound Layby) (Temporary Prohibition of Traffic) Order 2008 No. 2008/887. - Enabling power: Road Traffic Regulation Act 1984, s. 14 (1) (a). - Made: 10.03.2008. Coming into force: 24.03.2008. Effect: None. Territorial extent & classification: E. Local *Unpublished*

The A1 Trunk Road (Stannington Vale Bridge) (Temporary Restriction and Prohibition of Traffic and Pedestrians) Order 2008 No. 2008/1389. - Enabling power: Road Traffic Regulation Act 1984, s. 14 (1) (a). - Made: 19.05.2008. Coming into force: 01.06.2008. Effect: None. Territorial extent & classification: E. Local *Unpublished*

The A1 Trunk Road (St Neots to Brampton Hut Interchange, Cambridgeshire) (Temporary Prohibition of Traffic) Order 2008 No. 2008/1547. - Enabling power: Road Traffic Regulation Act 1984, s. 14 (1) (a). - Made: 02.06.2008. Coming into force: 09.06.2008. Effect: None. Territorial extent & classification: E. Local *Unpublished*

The A1 Trunk Road (Stoke Rochford, Lincolnshire) (Temporary Prohibition of Traffic) Order 2008 No. 2008/3032. - Enabling power: Road Traffic Regulation Act 1984, s. 14 (1) (a). - Made: 07.11.2008. Coming into force: 14.11.2008. Effect: None. Territorial extent & classification: E. Local *Unpublished*

The A1 Trunk Road (Swalwell Interchange to Dunston Interchange) (Temporary Restriction and Prohibition of Traffic) Order 2008 No. 2008/2132. - Enabling power: Road Traffic Regulation Act 1984, s. 14 (1). - Made: 28.07.2008. Coming into force: 07.08.2008. Effect: None. Territorial extent & classification: E. Local *Unpublished*

The A1 Trunk Road (The A58 Walton Road, Wetherby & the A659 Grange Moor Junctions) (Temporary Prohibition of Traffic) Order 2008 No. 2008/1499. - Enabling power: Road Traffic Regulation Act 1984, s. 14 (1) (a). - Made: 03.06.2008. Coming into force: 15.06.2008. Effect: None. Territorial extent & classification: E. Local *Unpublished*

The A1 Trunk Road (The A184 Consett Route Interchange) (Temporary Prohibition of Traffic) Order 2008 No. 2008/1835. - Enabling power: Road Traffic Regulation Act 1984, s. 14 (1) (a). - Made: 01.07.2008. Coming into force: 14.07.2008. Effect: None. Territorial extent & classification: E. Local *Unpublished*

The A1 Trunk Road (The A184 Consett Route Interchange) (Temporary Restriction and Prohibition of Traffic and Pedestrians) Order 2008 No. 2008/2292. - Enabling power: Road Traffic Regulation Act 1984, s. 14 (1) (a). - Made: 18.08.2008. Coming into force: 28.08.2008. Effect: None. Territorial extent & classification: E. Local *Unpublished*

The A1 Trunk Road (The A184 Consett Route Interchange) (Temporary Restriction and Prohibition of Traffic and Pedestrians) Order 2008 (Amendment) Order 2008 No. 2008/2950. - Enabling power: Road Traffic Regulation Act 1984, s. 14 (1) (a). - Made: 05.11.2008. Coming into force: 10.11.2008. Effect: S.I. 2008/2292 amended. Territorial extent & classification: E. Local *Unpublished*

The A1 Trunk Road (The A659 Grange Moor Interchange) (Temporary Prohibition of Traffic) Order 2008 No. 2008/2904. - Enabling power: Road Traffic Regulation Act 1984, s. 14 (1) (a). - Made: 28.10.2008. Coming into force: 10.11.2008. Effect: None. Territorial extent & classification: E. Local *Unpublished*

The A1 Trunk Road (The A659 Grange Moor Interchange to the B1224 York Road Bridge) (Temporary Prohibition of Traffic) Order 2008 No. 2008/1132. - Enabling power: Road Traffic Regulation Act 1984, s. 14 (1) (b) (7). - Made: 14.04.2008. Coming into force: 26.04.2008. Effect: None. Territorial extent & classification: E. Local *Unpublished*

The A1 Trunk Road (The A659 Grange Moor Interchange to the B1224 York Road Bridge) (Temporary Prohibition of Traffic) Order 2008 (Amendment) Order 2008 No. 2008/3176. - Enabling power: Road Traffic Regulation Act 1984, s. 14 (1) (b) (7). - Made: 27.11.2008. Coming into force: 29.11.2008. Effect: S.I. 2008/1132 amended. Territorial extent & classification: E. Local *Unpublished*

The A1 Trunk Road (The A697 Warreners House Junction to Felton) (Temporary Restriction and Prohibition of Traffic and Pedestrians) Order 2008 No. 2008/2380. - Enabling power: Road Traffic Regulation Act 1984, s. 14 (1) (a). - Made: 26.08.2008. Coming into force: 07.09.2008. Effect: None. Territorial extent & classification: E. Local *Unpublished*

The A1 Trunk Road (The A1056 North Brunton Interchange) (Temporary Prohibition of Traffic) Order 2008 No. 2008/2378. - Enabling power: Road Traffic Regulation Act 1984, s. 14 (1) (a). - Made: 26.08.2008. Coming into force: 29.08.2008. Effect: None. Territorial extent & classification: E. Local *Unpublished*

The A1 Trunk Road (The B6317 Swalwell Interchange) (Temporary Prohibition of Traffic) Order 2008 No. 2008/2246. - Enabling power: Road Traffic Regulation Act 1984, s. 14 (1) (a). - Made: 14.08.2008. Coming into force: 26.08.2008. Effect: None. Territorial extent & classification: E. Local *Unpublished*

The A1 Trunk Road (The Consett Route Interchange to Kingsway Interchange) (Temporary Restriction and Prohibition of Traffic) Order 2008 No. 2008/2068. - Enabling power: Road Traffic Regulation Act 1984, s. 14 (1) (a). - Made: 22.07.2008. Coming into force: 03.08.2008. Effect: None. Territorial extent & classification: E. Local *Unpublished*

The A1 Trunk Road (Tinwell, Near Stamford) (Slip Road) (Temporary Prohibition of Traffic) Order 2008 No. 2008/2956. - Enabling power: Road Traffic Regulation Act 1984, s. 14 (1) (a). - Made: 31.10.2008. Coming into force: 07.11.2008. Effect: None. Territorial extent & classification: E. Local *Unpublished*

The A1 Trunk Road (Tinwell to Carpenter's Lodge Roundabout) (Temporary Prohibition of Traffic) Order 2008 No. 2008/819. - Enabling power: Road Traffic Regulation Act 1984, s. 14 (1) (a). - Made: 22.02.2008. Coming into force: 29.02.2008. Effect: None. Territorial extent & classification: E. Local *Unpublished*

The A1 Trunk Road (Wansford, Peterborough) (Slip Road) (Temporary Prohibition of Traffic) Order 2008 No. 2008/246. - Enabling power: Road Traffic Regulation Act 1984, s. 14 (1) (a). - Made: 28.01.2008. Coming into force: 04.02.2008. Effect: None. Territorial extent & classification: E. Local *Unpublished*

The A1 Trunk Road (Winthorpe to North Muskham, Nottinghamshire) (Temporary Restriction and Prohibition of Traffic) Order 2008 No. 2008/824. - Enabling power: Road Traffic Regulation Act 1984, s. 14 (1) (a). - Made: 25.02.2008. Coming into force: 03.03.2008. Effect: None. Territorial extent & classification: E. Local *Unpublished*

The A1 Trunk Road (Wittering, Peterborough) (Temporary Prohibition of Traffic in Layby) Order 2008 No. 2008/2961. - Enabling power: Road Traffic Regulation Act 1984, s. 14 (1) (a). - Made: 24.10.2008. Coming into force: 31.10.2008. Effect: None. Territorial extent & classification: E. Local *Unpublished*

The A1 Trunk Road (Wothorpe to Thornhaugh) (Temporary Prohibition of Traffic) Order 2008 No. 2008/243. - Enabling power: Road Traffic Regulation Act 1984, s. 14 (1) (a). - Made: 25.01.2008. Coming into force: 01.02.2008. Effect: None. Territorial extent & classification: E. Local *Unpublished*

The A1 Trunk Road (Wothorpe to Wansford) (Temporary Prohibition and Restriction of Traffic) (No. 3) Order 2008 No. 2008/3185. - Enabling power: Road Traffic Regulation Act 1984, s. 14 (1) (a). - Made: 28.11.2008. Coming into force: 05.12.2008. Effect: None. Territorial extent & classification: E. Local *Unpublished*

The A1 Trunk Road (Wothorpe to Wansford) (Temporary Prohibition and Restriction of Traffic) Order 2008 No. 2008/2488. - Enabling power: Road Traffic Regulation Act 1984, s. 14 (1) (a). - Made: 02.09.2008. Coming into force: 09.09.2008. Effect: None. Territorial extent & classification: E. Local *Unpublished*

The A1 Trunk Road (Wothorpe to Wansford) (Temporary Prohibition of Traffic) Order 2008 No. 2008/2387. - Enabling power: Road Traffic Regulation Act 1984, s. 14 (1) (a). - Made: 19.08.2008. Coming into force: 26.08.2008. Effect: None. Territorial extent & classification: E. Local *Unpublished*

The A1 Trunk Road (Wothorpe to Wansford) (Temporary Restriction of Traffic) (No. 2) Order 2008 No. 2008/3033. - Enabling power: Road Traffic Regulation Act 1984, s. 14 (1) (a). - Made: 07.11.2008. Coming into force: 14.11.2008. Effect: None. Territorial extent & classification: E. Local *Unpublished*

The A1 Trunk Road (Wyboston, Bedfordshire to Eaton Socon, Cambridgeshire) (Temporary Prohibition of Traffic) Order 2008 No. 2008/1661. - Enabling power: Road Traffic Regulation Act 1984, s. 14 (1) (a). - Made: 04.06.2008. Coming into force: 11.06.2008. Effect: None. Territorial extent & classification: E. Local *Unpublished*

The A2 Trunk Road (A2018 Junction, Westbound Exit Slip Road) (Temporary Prohibition of Traffic) Order 2008 No. 2008/1168. - Enabling power: Road Traffic Regulation Act 1984, s. 14 (1) (a). - Made: 21.04.2008. Coming into force: 26.04.2008. Effect: None. Territorial extent & classification: E. Local *Unpublished*

The A2 Trunk Road and the M2 Motorway (Bean - Junction 2) (Temporary Restriction and Prohibition of Traffic) Order 2008 No. 2008/279. - Enabling power: Road Traffic Regulation Act 1984, s. 14 (1) (a). - Made: 28.01.2008. Coming into force: 04.02.2008. Effect: None. Territorial extent & classification: E. Local *Unpublished*

The A2 Trunk Road and the M2 Motorway (Junctions 1 - 4, Slip Roads) (Temporary Prohibition of Traffic) Order 2008 No. 2008/1114. - Enabling power: Road Traffic Regulation Act 1984, s. 14 (1) (a). - Made: 07.04.2008. Coming into force: 16.04.2008. Effect: None. Territorial extent & classification: E. Local *Unpublished*

The A2 Trunk Road (Boughton Hill) (Temporary Speed Restriction) Order 2008 No. 2008/2484. - Enabling power: Road Traffic Regulation Act 1984, s. 14 (1) (a). - Made: 08.09.2008. Coming into force: 13.09.2008. Effect: None. Territorial extent & classification: E. Local *Unpublished*

The A2 Trunk Road (Boughton, Londonbound) (Temporary Restriction and Prohibition of Traffic) Order 2008 No. 2008/1350. - Enabling power: Road Traffic Regulation Act 1984, s. 14 (1) (a). - Made: 12.05.2008. Coming into force: 17.05.2008. Effect: None. Territorial extent & classification: E. Local *Unpublished*

The A2 Trunk Road (Boughton, Londonbound) (Temporary Speed Restriction) Order 2008 No. 2008/773. - Enabling power: Road Traffic Regulation Act 1984, s. 14 (1) (a). - Made: 25.02.2008. Coming into force: 01.03.2008. Effect: None. Territorial extent & classification: E. Local *Unpublished*

The A2 Trunk Road (Brenley Corner - Harbledon) (Temporary Resstriction and Prohibition of Traffic) Order 2008 No. 2008/2324. - Enabling power: Road Traffic Regulation Act 1984, s. 14 (1) (a). - Made: 26.08.2008. Coming into force: 30.08.2008. Effect: None. Territorial extent & classification: E. Local *Unpublished*

The A2 Trunk Road (Canterbury - Dover) (Temporary Restriction and Prohibition of Traffic) Order 2008 No. 2008/1840. - Enabling power: Road Traffic Regulation Act 1984, s. 14 (1) (a). - Made: 30.06.2008. Coming into force: 05.07.2008. Effect: None. Territorial extent & classification: E. Local *Unpublished*

The A2 Trunk Road (Coxhill - Wootton Lane) (Temporary 50 Miles Per Hour Speed Restriction) Order 2008 No. 2008/3173. - Enabling power: Road Traffic Regulation Act 1984, s. 14 (1) (a). - Made: 01.12.2008. Coming into force: 03.01.2009. Effect: None. Territorial extent & classification: E. Local *Unpublished*

The A2 Trunk Road (Dartford Heath, Eastbound Exit Slip Road) (Temporary Prohibition of Traffic) Order 2008 No. 2008/2721. - Enabling power: Road Traffic Regulation Act 1984, s. 14 (1) (a). - Made: 06.10.2008. Coming into force: 11.10.2008. Effect: None. Territorial extent & classification: E. Local *Unpublished*

The A2 Trunk Road (Dartford Heath-M25 Junction 2) (Temporary Restriction and Prohibition of Traffic) Order 2008 No. 2008/2279. - Enabling power: Road Traffic Regulation Act 1984, s. 14 (1) (a). - Made: 18.08.2008. Coming into force: 23.08.2008. Effect: None. Territorial extent & classification: E. Local *Unpublished*

The A2 Trunk Road (Dartford Heath, Slip Roads) (Temporary Prohibition of Traffic) Order 2008 No. 2008/1687. - Enabling power: Road Traffic Regulation Act 1984, s. 14 (1) (a). - Made: 23.06.2008. Coming into force: 30.06.2008. Effect: None. Territorial extent & classification: E. Local *Unpublished*

The A2 Trunk Road (Dover Road, Londonbound) (Temporary Restriction and Prohibition of Traffic) Order 2008 No. 2008/1843. - Enabling power: Road Traffic Regulation Act 1984, s. 14 (1) (a). - Made: 30.06.2008. Coming into force: 05.07.2008. Effect: None. Territorial extent & classification: E. Local *Unpublished*

The A2 Trunk Road (Ebbsfleet) (Temporary Restriction and Prohibition of Traffic) Order 2008 No. 2008/2538. - Enabling power: Road Traffic Regulation Act 1984, s. 14 (1) (a). - Made: 22.09.2008. Coming into force: 27.09.2008. Effect: None. Territorial extent & classification: E. Local. - Revoked by S.I. 2009/2072 (Unpublished) *Unpublished*

The A2 Trunk Road (Guston Roundabout - Dover, Coastbound Carriageway) (Temporary Prohibition of Traffic) Order 2008 No. 2008/2514. - Enabling power: Road Traffic Regulation Act 1984, s. 14 (1) (a). - Made: 15.09.2008. Coming into force: 20.09.2008. Effect: None. Territorial extent & classification: E. Local. - Revoked by S.I. 2009/1530 (Unpublished) *Unpublished*

The A2 Trunk Road (Jubilee Way, Coastbound Carriageway) (Temporary Prohibition of Traffic) Order 2008 No. 2008/2539. - Enabling power: Road Traffic Regulation Act 1984, s. 14 (1) (a). - Made: 22.09.2008. Coming into force: 01.10.2008. Effect: None. Territorial extent & classification: E. Local *Unpublished*

The A2 Trunk Road (Near Whitfield) (Temporary 40 Miles Per Hour Speed Restriction) Order 2008 No. 2008/94. - Enabling power: Road Traffic Regulation Act 1984, s. 14 (1) (a), sch. 9, para. 27 (1). - Made: 14.01.2008. Coming into force: 19.01.2008. Effect: S.I. 2007/2683 revoked. Territorial extent & classification: E. Local *Unpublished*

The A2 Trunk Road (Patrixbourne and Bishopsbourne) (Temporary Restriction and Prohibition of Traffic) Order 2008 No. 2008/3210. - Enabling power: Road Traffic Regulation Act 1984, s. 14 (1) (a), sch. 9, para. 27 (1). - Made: 24.11.2008. Coming into force: 29.11.2008. Effect: S.I. 2007/2033 revoked. Territorial extent & classification: E. Local *Unpublished*

The A2 Trunk Road (Pepper Hill, Londonbound Entry Slip Road) (Temporary Prohibition of Traffic) Order 2008 No. 2008/90. - Enabling power: Road Traffic Regulation Act 1984, s. 14 (1) (a). - Made: 14.01.2008. Coming into force: 16.01.2008. Effect: None. Territorial extent & classification: E. Local *Unpublished*

The A2 Trunk Road (Thanington) (Temporary Restriction and Prohibition of Traffic) Order 2008 No. 2008/1346. - Enabling power: Road Traffic Regulation Act 1984, s. 14 (1) (a). - Made: 12.05.2008. Coming into force: 17.05.2008. Effect: None. Territorial extent & classification: E. Local *Unpublished*

The A2 Trunk Road (Upper Harbledown - Whitfield, Slip Roads) (Temporary Prohibition of Traffic) Order 2008 No. 2008/3280. - Enabling power: Road Traffic Regulation Act 1984, s. 14 (1) (a). - Made: 08.12.2008. Coming into force: 17.12.2008. Effect: None. Territorial extent & classification: E. Local *Unpublished*

The A2 Trunk Road (Whitfield Roundabout - Duke of York Roundabout) (Temporary 50 Miles Per Hour Speed Restriction) Order 2008 No. 2008/385. - Enabling power: Road Traffic Regulation Act 1984, s. 14 (1) (a). - Made: 11.02.2008. Coming into force: 16.02.2008. Effect: None. Territorial extent & classification: E. Local *Unpublished*

The A2 Trunk Road (Whitfield Roundabout) (Temporary Restriction and Prohibition of Traffic) Order 2008 No. 2008/2519. - Enabling power: Road Traffic Regulation Act 1984, s. 14 (1) (a). - Made: 15.09.2008. Coming into force: 20.09.2008. Effect: None. Territorial extent & classification: E. Local *Unpublished*

The A2 Trunk Road (Wootton Lane Junction, Near Shepherswell) (Closure in Gap in the Central Reservation) Order 2008 No. 2008/2968. - Enabling power: Road Traffic Regulation Act 1984, ss. 1 (1), 2 (1) (2). - Made: 10.11.2008. Coming into force: 25.01.2009. Effect: None. Territorial extent & classification: E. Local *Unpublished*

The A3 Trunk Road (Bramshott Chase - Hindhead) (Temporary Restriction and Prohibition of Traffic) Order 2008 No. 2008/384. - Enabling power: Road Traffic Regulation Act 1984, s. 14 (1) (a). - Made: 11.02.2008. Coming into force: 18.02.2008. Effect: None. Territorial extent & classification: E. Local. - Revoked by S.I. 2009/901 (Unpublished) *Unpublished*

The A3 Trunk Road (Bramshott Chase - Liphook) (Temporary Restriction and Prohibition of Traffic) Order 2008 No. 2008/2723. - Enabling power: Road Traffic Regulation Act 1984, s. 14 (1) (a). - Made: 06.10.2008. Coming into force: 16.10.2008. Effect: None. Territorial extent & classification: E. Local. - Revoked by S.I. 2009/901 (Unpublished) *Unpublished*

The A3 Trunk Road (Chalton Junction, Southbound) (Temporary Restriction and Prohibition of Traffic) Order 2008 No. 2008/149. - Enabling power: Road Traffic Regulation Act 1984, s. 14 (1) (a). - Made: 21.01.2008. Coming into force: 26.01.2008. Effect: None. Territorial extent & classification: E. Local *Unpublished*

The A3 Trunk Road (Chalton Lane, Northbound Exit Slip Road) (Temporary Prohibition of Traffic) Order 2008 No. 2008/1623. - Enabling power: Road Traffic Regulation Act 1984, s. 14 (1) (a). - Made: 16.06.2008. Coming into force: 21.06.2008. Effect: None. Territorial extent & classification: E. Local *Unpublished*

The A3 Trunk Road (Compton Interchange - Hog's Back Interchange) (Temporary Restriction and Prohibition of Traffic) Order 2008 No. 2008/88. - Enabling power: Road Traffic Regulation Act 1984, s. 14 (1) (a). - Made: 14.01.2008. Coming into force: 19.01.2008. Effect: None. Territorial extent & classification: E. Local *Unpublished*

The A3 Trunk Road (Esher Common Junction Slip Roads) (Temporary Prohibition of Traffic) Order 2008 No. 2008/1174. - Enabling power: Road Traffic Regulation Act 1984, s. 14 (1) (a). - Made: 21.04.2008. Coming into force: 26.04.2008. Effect: None. Territorial extent & classification: E. Local *Unpublished*

The A3 Trunk Road (Esher - Ockham Slip Roads) (Temporary Prohibition of Traffic) (No. 2) Order 2008 No. 2008/3315. - Enabling power: Road Traffic Regulation Act 1984, s. 14 (1) (a). - Made: 15.12.2008. Coming into force: 15.01.2009. Effect: None. Territorial extent & classification: E. Local *Unpublished*

The A3 Trunk Road (Esher - Ockham, Slip Roads) (Temporary Prohibition of Traffic) Order 2008 No. 2008/32. - Enabling power: Road Traffic Regulation Act 1984, s. 14 (1) (a). - Made: 07.01.2008. Coming into force: 15.01.2008 (shall apply for a period of 12 months). Effect: None. Territorial extent & classification: E. Local *Unpublished*

The A3 Trunk Road (Hog's Back Interchange - Abbotswood) (Temporary Prohibition of Traffic) Order 2008 No. 2008/1490. - Enabling power: Road Traffic Regulation Act 1984, s. 14 (1) (a), sch. 9, para. 27 (1). - Made: 27.05.2008. Coming into force: 31.05.2008. Effect: S.I. 2007/3602 revoked. Territorial extent & classification: E. Local *Unpublished*

The A3 Trunk Road (Hog's Back Interchange - Abbotswood) (Temporary Prohibition of Traffic) Order 2008 No. 2008/455. - Enabling power: Road Traffic Regulation Act 1984, s. 14 (1) (a). - Made: 18.02.2008. Coming into force: 23.02.2008. Effect: None. Territorial extent & classification: E. Local *Unpublished*

The A3 Trunk Road (Milford - Hog's Back) (Temporary Restriction and Prohibition of Traffic) Order 2008 No. 2008/3276. - Enabling power: Road Traffic Regulation Act 1984, s. 14 (1) (a). - Made: 08.12.2008. Coming into force: 29.12.2008. Effect: None. Territorial extent & classification: E. Local *Unpublished*

The A3 Trunk Road (Milford Interchange) (Temporary Prohibition of Traffic) Order 2008 No. 2008/1236. - Enabling power: Road Traffic Regulation Act 1984, s. 14 (1) (a). - Made: 29.04.2008. Coming into force: 04.05.2008. Effect: None. Territorial extent & classification: E. Local *Unpublished*

The A3 Trunk Road (Thursley - Hindhead) (Temporary Restriction and Prohibition of Traffic) Order 2008 No. 2008/2537. - Enabling power: Road Traffic Regulation Act 1984, ss. 14 (1) (a), 15 (2). - Made: 22.09.2008. Coming into force: 01.10.2008. Effect: None. Territorial extent & classification: E. Local *Unpublished*

The A3 Trunk Road (Wisley Interchange, Carriageways) (Temporary Prohibition of Traffic) Order 2008 No. 2008/1844. - Enabling power: Road Traffic Regulation Act 1984, s. 14 (1) (a). - Made: 30.06.2008. Coming into force: 05.07.2008. Effect: None. Territorial extent & classification: E. Local *Unpublished*

The A3 Trunk Road (Wisley - Painshill) (Temporary Restriction and Prohibition of Traffic) Order 2008 No. 2008/380. - Enabling power: Road Traffic Regulation Act 1984, s. 14 (1) (a). - Made: 11.02.2008. Coming into force: 16.02.2008. Effect: None. Territorial extent & classification: E. Local *Unpublished*

The A4 Trunk Road and A46 Trunk Road (London Road Junction, Bath) (Temporary Prohibition of Traffic) Order 2008 No. 2008/1194. - Enabling power: Road Traffic Regulation Act 1984, s. 14 (1) (a). - Made: 23.04.2008. Coming into force: 26.04.2008. Effect: None. Territorial extent & classification: E. Local *Unpublished*

The A4 Trunk Road (Avonmouth Way West, Bristol) (Temporary Prohibition of Traffic) Order 2008 No. 2008/103. - Enabling power: Road Traffic Regulation Act 1984, s. 14 (1) (a) (7). - Made: 15.01.2008. Coming into force: 18.01.2008. Effect: None. Territorial extent & classification: E. Local *Unpublished*

The A4 Trunk Road (Layby at Bath Road, Saltford) (Prohibition of Waiting) Order 2008 No. 2008/1031. - Enabling power: Road Traffic Regulation Act 1984, s. 1 (1), 2 (1) (2), 4 (1). - Made: 28.03.2008. Coming into force: 05.04.2008. Effect: None. Territorial extent & classification: E. Local *Unpublished*

The A4 Trunk Road (St Andrews Gate Roundabout to St Brendans Roundabout, Avonmouth) (Temporary Prohibition of Traffic) Order 2008 No. 2008/64. - Enabling power: Road Traffic Regulation Act 1984, s. 14 (1) (a). - Made: 09.01.2008. Coming into force: 12.01.2008. Effect: None. Territorial extent & classification: E. Local *Unpublished*

The A5 and A49 Trunk Roads (Bayleys Roundabout, Shrewsbury, Shropshire) (Temporary Restriction and Prohibition of Traffic) Order 2008 No. 2008/883. - Enabling power: Road Traffic Regulation Act 1984, s. 14 (1) (a), sch. 9, para. 27 (1). - Made: 15.02.2008. Coming into force: 22.02.2008. Effect: S.I. 2007/3686 revoked. Territorial extent & classification: E. Local *Unpublished*

The A5 Trunk Road (A4146 Bletcham Way, Caldecote, Milton Keynes) (Temporary Prohibition of Traffic) Order 2008 No. 2008/2129. - Enabling power: Road Traffic Regulation Act 1984, s. 14 (1) (a). - Made: 28.07.2008. Coming into force: 04.08.2008. Effect: None. Territorial extent & classification: E. Local *Unpublished*

The A5 Trunk Road (A4146 Bletcham Way Interchange, Milton Keynes) (Temporary Prohibition of Traffic) Order 2008 No. 2008/850. - Enabling power: Road Traffic Regulation Act 1984, s. 14 (1) (a). - Made: 03.03.2008. Coming into force: 10.03.2008. Effect: None. Territorial extent & classification: E. Local *Unpublished*

The A5 Trunk Road (Atherstone, Warwickshire) (Temporary Restriction and Prohibition of Traffic) Order 2008 No. 2008/2457. - Enabling power: Road Traffic Regulation Act 1984, s. 14 (1) (a). - Made: 01.09.2008. Coming into force: 08.09.2008. Effect: None. Territorial extent & classification: E. Local *Unpublished*

The A5 Trunk Road (Between Cannock and Brownhills, Staffordshire) (Temporary Restriction and Prohibition of Traffic) Order 2008 No. 2008/1830. - Enabling power: Road Traffic Regulation Act 1984, s. 14 (1) (a). - Made: 23.06.2008. Coming into force: 30.06.2008. Effect: None. Territorial extent & classification: E. Local *Unpublished*

The A5 Trunk Road (Between M69 Junction 1 and Smockington) (Temporary Restriction and Prohibition of Traffic) Order 2008 No. 2008/2121. - Enabling power: Road Traffic Regulation Act 1984, s. 14 (1) (a). - Made: 21.07.2008. Coming into force: 28.07.2008. Effect: None. Territorial extent & classification: E. Local *Unpublished*

The A5 Trunk Road (Brockhall, Welton and Kilsby Railway Bridges, Northamptonshire) (Temporary Restriction and Prohibition of Traffic) Order 2008 No. 2008/406. - Enabling power: Road Traffic Regulation Act 1984, s. 14 (1) (a). - Made: 11.02.2008. Coming into force: 18.02.2008. Effect: None. Territorial extent & classification: E. Local *Unpublished*

The A5 Trunk Road (Cross in Hand Roundabout to Wibtoft) (Temporary Restriction and Prohibition of Traffic) Order 2008 No. 2008/1635. - Enabling power: Road Traffic Regulation Act 1984, s. 14 (1) (a). - Made: 09.06.2008. Coming into force: 16.06.2008. Effect: None. Territorial extent & classification: E. Local *Unpublished*

The A5 Trunk Road (Dordon, Warwickshire) (Temporary Prohibition and Restriction of Traffic) Order 2008 No. 2008/2388. - Enabling power: Road Traffic Regulation Act 1984, s. 14 (1) (a). - Made: 18.08.2008. Coming into force: 25.08.2008. Effect: None. Territorial extent & classification: E. Local *Unpublished*

The A5 Trunk Road (Dunstable, Bedfordshire) (Temporary Restriction and Prohibition of Traffic) Order 2008 No. 2008/1008. - Enabling power: Road Traffic Regulation Act 1984, s. 14 (1) (a). - Made: 20.03.2008. Coming into force: 28.03.2008. Effect: None. Territorial extent & classification: E. Local *Unpublished*

The A5 Trunk Road (Dunstable, Bedfordshire) (Temporary Restriction and Prohibition of Traffic) Order 2008 No. 2008/1847. - Enabling power: Road Traffic Regulation Act 1984, s. 14 (1) (a). - Made: 25.06.2008. Coming into force: 02.07.2008. Effect: None. Territorial extent & classification: E. Local *Unpublished*

The A5 Trunk Road (Dunstable, Bedfordshire) (Temporary Restriction and Prohibition of Traffic) Order 2008 (Revocation) Order 2008 No. 2008/1524. - Enabling power: Road Traffic Regulation Act 1984, s. 14 (1) (a), sch. 9, para. 27 (1). - Made: 27.05.2008. Coming into force: 03.06.2008. Effect: S.I. 2008/294 revoked. Territorial extent & classification: E. Local *Unpublished*

The A5 Trunk Road (Emstrey, Shropshire) (Temporary Restriction and Prohibition of Traffic) Order 2008 No. 2008/2957. - Enabling power: Road Traffic Regulation Act 1984, s. 14 (1) (a). - Made: 31.10.2008. Coming into force: 07.11.2008. Effect: None. Territorial extent & classification: E. Local *Unpublished*

The A5 Trunk Road (Gailey, Staffordshire) (Temporary Restriction and Prohibition of Traffic) Order 2008 No. 2008/996. - Enabling power: Road Traffic Regulation Act 1984, s. 14 (1) (a). - Made: 11.03.2008. Coming into force: 18.03.2008. Effect: None. Territorial extent & classification: E. Local *Unpublished*

The A5 Trunk Road (Grendon to Atherstone, Warwickshire) (Temporary Restriction and Prohibition of Traffic) Order 2008 No. 2008/111. - Enabling power: Road Traffic Regulation Act 1984, s. 14 (1) (a). - Made: 04.01.2008. Coming into force: 11.01.2008. Effect: None. Territorial extent & classification: E. Local *Unpublished*

The A5 Trunk Road (Houghton Regis to Dunstable, Bedfordshire) (Temporary Prohibition of Traffic) Order 2008 No. 2008/1546. - Enabling power: Road Traffic Regulation Act 1984, s. 14 (1) (a). - Made: 02.06.2008. Coming into force: 09.06.2008. Effect: None. Territorial extent & classification: E. Local *Unpublished*

The A5 Trunk Road (London Road, Dunstable, Bedfordshire) (Temporary Restriction of Traffic) Order 2007 (Revocation) Order 2008 No. 2008/294. - Enabling power: Road Traffic Regulation Act 1984, s. 14 (1) (a), sch. 9, para. 27 (1). - Made: 28.01.2008. Coming into force: 04.02.2008. Effect: S.I. 2007/3366 revoked. Territorial extent & classification: E. Local. - Revoked by S.I. 2008/1524 (Unpublished) *Unpublished*

The A5 Trunk Road (Long Buckby Wharf to Watford, Northamptonshire) (Temporary Prohibition of Traffic) Order 2008 No. 2008/1567. - Enabling power: Road Traffic Regulation Act 1984, s. 14 (1) (a). - Made: 09.06.2008. Coming into force: 16.06.2008. Effect: None. Territorial extent & classification: E. Local *Unpublished*

Road traffic: Traffic regulation

The A5 Trunk Road (Markyate, Hertfordshire) (Temporary Restriction and Prohibition of Traffic) Order 2008 No. 2008/1303. - Enabling power: Road Traffic Regulation Act 1984, s. 14 (1) (a). - Made: 02.05.2008. Coming into force: 09.05.2008. Effect: None. Territorial extent & classification: E. Local *Unpublished*

The A5 Trunk Road (Mile Oak, Staffordshire) (Temporary 50 Miles Per Hour Speed Restriction) Order 2008 No. 2008/251. - Enabling power: Road Traffic Regulation Act 1984, s. 14 (1) (a). - Made: 21.01.2008. Coming into force: 28.01.2008. Effect: None. Territorial extent & classification: E. Local *Unpublished*

The A5 Trunk Road (Mile Oak to Marlborough Way, Tamworth) (Temporary Prohibition of Traffic) Order 2008 No. 2008/1676. - Enabling power: Road Traffic Regulation Act 1984, s. 14 (1) (a). - Made: 13.06.2008. Coming into force: 20.06.2008. Effect: None. Territorial extent & classification: E. Local *Unpublished*

The A5 Trunk Road (Milton Keynes Bypass) (Temporary Restriction and Prohibition of Traffic) Order 2008 No. 2008/2887. - Enabling power: Road Traffic Regulation Act 1984, s. 14 (1) (a). - Made: 20.10.2008. Coming into force: 27.10.2008. Effect: None. Territorial extent & classification: E. Local *Unpublished*

The A5 Trunk Road (Near Crick, Northamptonshire) (Temporary Prohibition of Traffic) Order 2008 No. 2008/834. - Enabling power: Road Traffic Regulation Act 1984, s. 14 (1) (a). - Made: 25.02.2008. Coming into force: 03.03.2008. Effect: None. Territorial extent & classification: E. Local *Unpublished*

The A5 Trunk Road (Near Shawell, Warwickshire) (Temporary Restriction and Prohibition of Traffic) Order 2008 No. 2008/820. - Enabling power: Road Traffic Regulation Act 1984, s. 14 (1) (a). - Made: 25.02.2008. Coming into force: 03.03.2008. Effect: None. Territorial extent & classification: E. Local *Unpublished*

The A5 Trunk Road (Near Witherley, Warwickshire) (Temporary Prohibition of Traffic in Layby) Order 2008 No. 2008/2967. - Enabling power: Road Traffic Regulation Act 1984, s. 14 (1) (a). - Made: 31.10.2008. Coming into force: 07.11.2008. Effect: None. Territorial extent & classification: E. Local *Unpublished*

The A5 Trunk Road (Old Stratford Roundabout, Northamptonshire to A5/A509 Interchange, Milton Keynes Bypass, Milton Keynes) (Temporary Prohibition of Traffic) Order 2008 No. 2008/1111. - Enabling power: Road Traffic Regulation Act 1984, s. 14 (1) (a). - Made: 07.04.2008. Coming into force: 14.04.2008. Effect: None. Territorial extent & classification: E. Local *Unpublished*

The A5 Trunk Road (Redmoor Roundabout, Milton Keynes) (Temporary Prohibition of Traffic) Order 2008 No. 2008/833. - Enabling power: Road Traffic Regulation Act 1984, s. 14 (1) (a). - Made: 25.02.2008. Coming into force: 03.03.2008. Effect: None. Territorial extent & classification: E. Local *Unpublished*

The A5 Trunk Road (Sheep Lane/Wobun Road Roundabout to Sandhouse Lane, Near Heath and Reach, Bedfordshire) (Temporary Restriction and Prohibition of Traffic) Order 2008 No. 2008/2198. - Enabling power: Road Traffic Regulation Act 1984, s. 14 (1) (a). - Made: 04.08.2008. Coming into force: 11.08.2008. Effect: None. Territorial extent & classification: E. Local *Unpublished*

The A5 Trunk Road (Stowehill Tunnel, Near Church Stowe, Northamptonshire) (Temporary Prohibition of Traffic) Order 2008 No. 2008/3342. - Enabling power: Road Traffic Regulation Act 1984, s. 14 (1) (a). - Made: 29.12.2008. Coming into force: 05.01.2009. Effect: None. Territorial extent & classification: E. Local *Unpublished*

The A5 Trunk Road (Tamworth Bypass, Staffordshire) (Temporary Restriction and Prohibition of Traffic) Order 2008 No. 2008/3356. - Enabling power: Road Traffic Regulation Act 1984, s. 14 (1) (a). - Made: 29.12.2008. Coming into force: 05.01.2009. Effect: None. Territorial extent & classification: E. Local *Unpublished*

The A5 Trunk Road (Towcester, Northamptonshire) (Temporary Prohibition of Traffic and Pedestrians) Order 2008 No. 2008/2976. - Enabling power: Road Traffic Regulation Act 1984, s. 14 (1) (a). - Made: 10.11.2008. Coming into force: 17.11.2008. Effect: None. Territorial extent & classification: E. Local *Unpublished*

The A5 Trunk Road (Ventura Park, Tamworth, Staffordshire) (Slip Road) (Temporary Prohibition of Traffic) Order 2008 No. 2008/1828. - Enabling power: Road Traffic Regulation Act 1984, s. 14 (1) (a). - Made: 23.06.2008. Coming into force: 30.06.2008. Effect: None. Territorial extent & classification: E. Local *Unpublished*

The A5 Trunk Road (Watling Street, Towcester, Northamptonshire) (Prohibition and Restriction of Waiting) Order 2008 No. 2008/483. - Enabling power: Road Traffic Regulation Act 1984, s. 1 (1), 2 (1) (2), sch. 9, para. 27 (1). - Made: 18.02.2008. Coming into force: 03.03.2008. Effect: S.I. 2000/202 varied Territorial extent & classification: E. Local *Unpublished*

The A5 Trunk Road (Weeford Island to Wall Island, Staffordshire) (Temporary Restriction and Prohibition of Traffic) Order 2008 No. 2008/998. - Enabling power: Road Traffic Regulation Act 1984, s. 14 (1) (a). - Made: 11.03.2008. Coming into force: 18.03.2008. Effect: None. Territorial extent & classification: E. Local *Unpublished*

The A11 Trunk Road (Besthorpe to A11/A47 Thickthorn Roundabout, Norfolk) (Temporary Restriction and Prohibition of Traffic) Order 2008 No. 2008/258. - Enabling power: Road Traffic Regulation Act 1984, s. 14 (1) (a). - Made: 25.01.2008. Coming into force: 01.02.2008. Effect: None. Territorial extent & classification: E. Local *Unpublished*

The A11 Trunk Road (Elveden, Suffolk) (Temporary 10 Miles Per Hour and 40 Miles Per Hour Speed Restriction) Order 2008 No. 2008/330. - Enabling power: Road Traffic Regulation Act 1984, s. 14 (1) (a). - Made: 01.02.2008. Coming into force: 08.02.2008. Effect: None. Territorial extent & classification: E. Local *Unpublished*

The A11 Trunk Road (Five Ways Roundabout Barton Mills to B1106 Junction Elveden, Suffolk) (Temporary Prohibition of Traffic) Order 2008 No. 2008/3305. - Enabling power: Road Traffic Regulation Act 1984, s. 14 (1) (a). - Made: 15.12.2008. Coming into force: 22.12.2008. Effect: None. Territorial extent & classification: E. Local *Unpublished*

The A11 Trunk Road (Six Mile Bottom, Cambridgeshire) (Temporary Restriction and Prohibition of Traffic) Order 2008 No. 2008/900. - Enabling power: Road Traffic Regulation Act 1984, s. 14 (1) (a). - Made: 29.02.2008. Coming into force: 07.03.2008. Effect: None. Territorial extent & classification: E. Local *Unpublished*

The A11 Trunk Road (Six Mile Bottom to Nine Mile Hill Interchange, Cambridgeshire) (Temporary Restriction and Prohibition of Traffic) Order 2008 No. 2008/257. - Enabling power: Road Traffic Regulation Act 1984, s. 14 (1) (a). - Made: 25.01.2008. Coming into force: 01.02.2008. Effect: None. Territorial extent & classification: E. Local *Unpublished*

The A11 Trunk Road (Spooner Row Interchange and Besthorpe Interchange, Norfolk) (Temporary Prohibition of Traffic) Order 2008 No. 2008/3186. - Enabling power: Road Traffic Regulation Act 1984, s. 14 (1) (a). - Made: 02.12.2008. Coming into force: 09.12.2008. Effect: None. Territorial extent & classification: E. Local *Unpublished*

The A11 Trunk Road (Thetford Bypass, Norfolk) (Temporary 10 Miles Per Hour, 40 Miles Per Hour and 50 Miles Per Hour Speed Restriction) Order 2008 No. 2008/328. - Enabling power: Road Traffic Regulation Act 1984, s. 14 (1) (a). - Made: 01.02.2008. Coming into force: 08.02.2008. Effect: None. Territorial extent & classification: E. Local *Unpublished*

The A11 Trunk Road (Wymondham Bypass, Norfolk) (Temporary Restriction and Prohibition of Traffic) Order 2008 No. 2008/1515. - Enabling power: Road Traffic Regulation Act 1984, s. 14 (1) (a). - Made: 27.05.2008. Coming into force: 02.06.2008. Effect: None. Territorial extent & classification: E. Local *Unpublished*

The A12 and A120 Trunk Roads (Eight Ash Green Interchange, Junction 26 to Hare Green Interchange, Colchester, Essex) (Temporary Prohibition of Traffic) Order 2008 No. 2008/1027. - Enabling power: Road Traffic Regulation Act 1984, s. 14 (1) (a). - Made: 28.03.2008. Coming into force: 04.04.2008. Effect: None. Territorial extent & classification: E. Local *Unpublished*

The A12 Trunk Road (Bascule Bridge, Lowestoft, Suffolk) (Temporary Prohibition of Traffic) Order 2007 Variation Order 2008 No. 2008/143. - Enabling power: Road Traffic Regulation Act 1984, s. 14 (1) (a), sch. 9, para, 27 (1). - Made: 11.01.2008. Coming into force: 18.01.2008. Effect: None. Territorial extent & classification: E. Local *Unpublished*

The A12 Trunk Road (Battery Green Road, Lowestoft, Suffolk) (Temporary Restriction and Prohibition of Traffic) Order 2008 No. 2008/2874. - Enabling power: Road Traffic Regulation Act 1984, s. 14 (1) (a). - Made: 21.10.2008. Coming into force: 28.10.2008. Effect: None. Territorial extent & classification: E. Local *Unpublished*

The A12 Trunk Road (Breydon Bridge, Great Yarmouth Western Bypass, Norfolk) (Temporary Prohibition of Traffic) Order 2008 No. 2008/899. - Enabling power: Road Traffic Regulation Act 1984, s. 14 (1) (a) (7). - Made: 29.02.2008. Coming into force: 07.03.2008. Effect: None. Territorial extent & classification: E. Local *Unpublished*

The A12 Trunk Road (Coleman's Interchange to Kelvedon North Interchange, Essex) (Temporary Restriction and Prohibition of Traffic) Order 2008 No. 2008/2604. - Enabling power: Road Traffic Regulation Act 1984, s. 14 (1) (a). - Made: 23.09.2008. Coming into force: 30.09.2008. Effect: None. Territorial extent & classification: E. Local *Unpublished*

The A12 Trunk Road (Crown Interchange, Colchester, Essex) (Temporary Prohibition of Traffic) Order 2008 No. 2008/3303. - Enabling power: Road Traffic Regulation Act 1984, s. 14 (1) (a). - Made: 15.12.2008. Coming into force: 22.12.2008. Effect: None. Territorial extent & classification: E. Local *Unpublished*

The A12 Trunk Road (Crown Interchange, Junction 29, Colchester, Essex) (Temporary Prohibition of Traffic) Order 2008 No. 2008/1707. - Enabling power: Road Traffic Regulation Act 1984, s. 14 (1) (a). - Made: 23.06.2008. Coming into force: 30.06.2008. Effect: None. Territorial extent & classification: E. Local *Unpublished*

The A12 Trunk Road (East Bergholt, Suffolk to Langham, Essex) (Temporary Restriction and Prohibition of Traffic) Order 2008 No. 2008/3306. - Enabling power: Road Traffic Regulation Act 1984, s. 14 (1) (a). - Made: 15.12.2008. Coming into force: 22.12.2008. Effect: None. Territorial extent & classification: E. Local *Unpublished*

The A12 Trunk Road (Foxbourrow Hill and Yarmouth Road, Lowestoft, Suffolk) (Temporary 10 Miles Per Hour Speed Restriction) Order 2008 No. 2008/292. - Enabling power: Road Traffic Regulation Act 1984, s. 14 (1) (a). - Made: 28.01.2008. Coming into force: 04.02.2008. Effect: None. Territorial extent & classification: E. Local *Unpublished*

The A12 Trunk Road (Great Yarmouth Western Bypass, Norfolk) (Temporary Prohibition of Traffic) Order 2008 No. 2008/2978. - Enabling power: Road Traffic Regulation Act 1984, s. 14 (1) (a). - Made: 11.11.2008. Coming into force: 18.11.2008. Effect: None. Territorial extent & classification: E. Local *Unpublished*

The A12 Trunk Road (Junction 17, Howe Green, Essex) (Temporary Prohibition of Traffic) Order 2008 No. 2008/1566. - Enabling power: Road Traffic Regulation Act 1984, s. 14 (1) (a). - Made: 09.06.2008. Coming into force: 16.06.2008. Effect: None. Territorial extent & classification: E. Local *Unpublished*

Road traffic: Traffic regulation

The A12 Trunk Road (Kelvedon, Essex) (Temporary Prohibition of Traffic) Order 2008 No. 2008/1012. - Enabling power: Road Traffic Regulation Act 1984, s. 14 (1) (a). - Made: 20.03.2008. Coming into force: 28.03.2008. Effect: None. Territorial extent & classification: E. Local *Unpublished*

The A12 Trunk Road (Lowestoft, Suffolk) (Prohibition and Restriction of Waiting) Order 2008 No. 2008/2532. - Enabling power: Road Traffic Regulation Act 1984, ss. 1 (1), 2 (1) (2), 4 (1) (2). - Made: 11.09.2008. Coming into force: 25.09.2008. Effect: None. Territorial extent & classification: E. Local *Unpublished*

The A12 Trunk Road (Lowestoft, Suffolk) (Prohibition of Various Traffic Movements) Order 2008 No. 2008/2531. - Enabling power: Road Traffic Regulation Act 1984, ss. 1 (1), 2 (1) (2). - Made: 11.09.2008. Coming into force: 25.09.2008. Effect: None. Territorial extent & classification: E. Local *Unpublished*

The A12 Trunk Road (Spring Lane Interchange, Junction 27, Colchester, Essex) (Temporary Prohibition of Traffic) Order 2008 No. 2008/2875. - Enabling power: Road Traffic Regulation Act 1984, s. 14 (1) (a). - Made: 21.10.2008. Coming into force: 28.10.2008. Effect: None. Territorial extent & classification: E. Local *Unpublished*

The A12 Trunk Road (Stratford St Mary, Essex to Capel St Mary, Suffolk) (Temporary Restriction and Prohibition of Traffic) Order 2008 No. 2008/2542. - Enabling power: Road Traffic Regulation Act 1984, s. 14 (1) (a). - Made: 22.09.2008. Coming into force: 29.09.2008. Effect: None. Territorial extent & classification: E. Local *Unpublished*

The A12 Trunk Road (Vauxhall Roundabout to Gapton Hall Roundabout, Great Yarmouth, Norfolk) (Temporary Prohibition of Traffic) Order 2008 No. 2008/293. - Enabling power: Road Traffic Regulation Act 1984, s. 14 (1) (a). - Made: 28.01.2008. Coming into force: 04.02.2008. Effect: None. Territorial extent & classification: E. Local *Unpublished*

The A13 and A1089 Trunk Roads (Wennington Interchange - Marshfoot Interchange) (Temporary Prohibition of Traffic) Order 2008 No. 2008/2926. - Enabling power: Road Traffic Regulation Act 1984, s. 14 (1) (a), sch. 9, para. 27 (1). - Made: 03.11.2008. Coming into force: 14.11.2008. Effect: S.I. 2008/1560 revoked. Territorial extent & classification: E. Local *Unpublished*

The A13 and A1089 Trunk Roads (Wennington Interchange to Tilbury Docks) (24 Hours Clearway) Order 2008 No. 2008/775. - Enabling power: Road Traffic Regulation Act 1984, ss. 1 (1), 2 (1) (2), 4 (1). - Made: 25.02.2008. Coming into force: 10.03.2008. Effect: None. Territorial extent & classification: E. Local *Unpublished*

The A13 Trunk Road and the A1089 Trunk Road (Grays) (Temporary Prohibition of Traffic) Order 2008 No. 2008/3208. - Enabling power: Road Traffic Regulation Act 1984, s. 14 (1) (a). - Made: 24.11.2008. Coming into force: 29.11.2008. Effect: None. Territorial extent & classification: E. Local *Unpublished*

The A13 Trunk Road (East of Mar Dyke Interchange) (Temporary Speed Restriction) Order 2008 No. 2008/845. - Enabling power: Road Traffic Regulation Act 1984, s. 14 (1) (a). - Made: 03.03.2008. Coming into force: 08.03.2008. Effect: None. Territorial extent & classification: E. Local *Unpublished*

The A13 Trunk Road (Near Grays) (Temporary Speed Restriction) Order 2008 No. 2008/844. - Enabling power: Road Traffic Regulation Act 1984, s. 14 (1) (a). - Made: 03.03.2008. Coming into force: 08.03.2008. Effect: None. Territorial extent & classification: E. Local *Unpublished*

The A13 Trunk Road (Wennington - A1089, Slip Roads) (Temporary Prohibition of Traffic) Order 2008 No. 2008/1560. - Enabling power: Road Traffic Regulation Act 1984, s. 14 (1) (a). - Made: 09.06.2008. Coming into force: 16.06.2008. Effect: None. Territorial extent & classification: E. Local. - Revoked by S.I. 2009/2926 (Unpublished) *Unpublished*

The A14 and A12 Trunk Roads (Beacon Hill Interchange to Copdock Interchange, Ipswich, Suffolk) (Temporary Restriction and Prohibition of Traffic) Order 2008 No. 2008/3304. - Enabling power: Road Traffic Regulation Act 1984, s. 14 (1) (a). - Made: 15.12.2008. Coming into force: 22.12.2008. Effect: None. Territorial extent & classification: E. Local *Unpublished*

The A14 Trunk Road (Bythorn, Junction 15 - Swavesey/Boxworth, Junction 28) (Prohibition of Entry) Order 2008 No. 2008/1010. - Enabling power: Road Traffic Regulation Act 1984, s. 1 (1), 2 (1) (2), 4. - Made: 20.03.2008. Coming into force: 04.04.2008. Effect: None. Territorial extent & classification: E. Local *Unpublished*

The A14 Trunk Road (Catworth to Brampton Hut, Huntingdon, Cambridgeshire) (Temporary Prohibition of Traffic) Order 2008 No. 2008/2897. - Enabling power: Road Traffic Regulation Act 1984, s. 14 (1) (a). - Made: 27.10.2008. Coming into force: 03.11.2008. Effect: None. Territorial extent & classification: E. Local *Unpublished*

The A14 Trunk Road (Cold Ashby, Junction 1 to Cranford St. John, Junction 11, Northamptonshire) (Temporary Restriction and Prohibition of Traffic) Order 2008 No. 2008/242. - Enabling power: Road Traffic Regulation Act 1984, s. 14 (1) (a). - Made: 21.01.2008. Coming into force: 28.01.2008. Effect: None. Territorial extent & classification: E. Local *Unpublished*

The A14 Trunk Road (Dock Gate No. 2, Felixstowe, Suffolk) (Temporary Prohibition of Traffic) Order 2008 No. 2008/329. - Enabling power: Road Traffic Regulation Act 1984, s. 14 (1) (a), 5 (b) (7). - Made: 01.02.2008. Coming into force: 08.02.2008. Effect: None. Territorial extent & classification: E. Local *Unpublished*

The A14 Trunk Road (Exning Interchange, Newmarket, Suffolk) (Temporary Prohibition of Traffic) Order 2008 No. 2008/3188. - Enabling power: Road Traffic Regulation Act 1984, s. 14 (1) (a). - Made: 02.12.2008. Coming into force: 09.12.2008. Effect: None. Territorial extent & classification: E. Local *Unpublished*

The A14 Trunk Road (Felixstowe South Interchange to Dock Gate No.1 Roundabout, Suffolk) (Temporary Prohibition of Traffic) Order 2008 No. 2008/3038. - Enabling power: Road Traffic Regulation Act 1984, s. 14 (1) (a). - Made: 18.11.2008. Coming into force: 25.11.2008. Effect: None. Territorial extent & classification: E. Local *Unpublished*

The A14 Trunk Road (Galley Hill Interchange to Hemingford Abbots Interchange, Huntingdon, Cambridgeshire) (Temporary Restriction and Prohibition of Traffic) Order 2008 No. 2008/66. - Enabling power: Road Traffic Regulation Act 1984, s. 14 (1) (a). - Made: 07.01.2008. Coming into force: 10.01.2008. Effect: None. Territorial extent & classification: E. Local *Unpublished*

The A14 Trunk Road (Haughley New Street to Stowmarket Improvement) (Prohibition of Various Traffic Movements) Order 2008 No. 2008/3271. - Enabling power: Road Traffic Regulation Act 1984, s. 1 (1), 2 (1) (2). - Made: 01.12.2008. Coming into force: 15.12.2008. Effect: None. Territorial extent & classification: E. Local, plans *Unpublished*

The A14 Trunk Road (Haughley New Street to Stowmarket, Suffolk) (Temporary Restriction and Prohibition of Traffic) Order 2008 No. 2008/2019. - Enabling power: Road Traffic Regulation Act 1984, s. 14 (1) (a). - Made: 04.07.2008. Coming into force: 11.07.2008. Effect: None. Territorial extent & classification: E. Local *Unpublished*

The A14 Trunk Road (Huntingdon Railway Viaduct, Cambridgeshire) (Temporary Restriction and Prohibition of Traffic) Order 2008 No. 2008/190. - Enabling power: Road Traffic Regulation Act 1984, s. 14 (1) (a). - Made: 21.01.2008. Coming into force: 29.01.2008. Effect: None. Territorial extent & classification: E. Local *Unpublished*

The A14 Trunk Road (Huntingdon Road/Robins Lane Junction, Lolworth, Cambridgeshire) (Prohibition of Traffic) Order 2008 No. 2008/2880. - Enabling power: Road Traffic Regulation Act 1984, ss. 1 (1), 2 (1) (2). - Made: 23.10.2008. Coming into force: 08.11.2008. Effect: None. Territorial extent & classification: E. Local *Unpublished*

The A14 Trunk Road (Junction 18, Spaldwick, Cambridgeshire) (Temporary Prohibition of Traffic) Order 2008 No. 2008/2328. - Enabling power: Road Traffic Regulation Act 1984, s. 14 (1) (a). - Made: 26.08.2008. Coming into force: 02.09.2008. Effect: None. Territorial extent & classification: E. Local *Unpublished*

The A14 Trunk Road (Junction 33, Milton Interchange, Cambridgeshire) (Temporary Prohibition of Traffic) Order 2008 No. 2008/2540. - Enabling power: Road Traffic Regulation Act 1984, s. 14 (1) (b). - Made: 22.09.2008. Coming into force: 29.09.2008. Effect: None. Territorial extent & classification: E. Local *Unpublished*

The A14 Trunk Road (Junction 50-49, Newton Road Bridge, Stowmarket, Suffolk) (Temporary Restriction and Prohibition of Traffic) Order 2008 No. 2008/484. - Enabling power: Road Traffic Regulation Act 1984, s. 14 (1) (a). - Made: 18.02.2008. Coming into force: 25.02.2008. Effect: None. Territorial extent & classification: E. Local *Unpublished*

The A14 Trunk Road (Leighton Bromswold, Junction 17 - Easton, Junction 19, Cambridgeshire) (Temporary Restriction and Prohibition of Traffic) Order 2008 No. 2008/69. - Enabling power: Road Traffic Regulation Act 1984, s. 14 (1) (a). - Made: 07.01.2008. Coming into force: 14.01.2008. Effect: None. Territorial extent & classification: E. Local *Unpublished*

The A14 Trunk Road (Lolworth, Cambridgeshire) (Temporary Restriction and Prohibition of Traffic) Order 2008 No. 2008/2919. - Enabling power: Road Traffic Regulation Act 1984, s. 14 (1) (a). - Made: 03.11.2008. Coming into force: 10.11.2008. Effect: None. Territorial extent & classification: E. Local *Unpublished*

The A14 Trunk Road (Nacton Interchange, Ipswich, Suffolk) (Temporary Prohibition of Traffic) Order 2008 No. 2008/2030. - Enabling power: Road Traffic Regulation Act 1984, s. 14 (1) (a). - Made: 08.07.2008. Coming into force: 15.07.2008. Effect: None. Territorial extent & classification: E. Local *Unpublished*

The A14 Trunk Road (Near M1 Junction 19, Leicestershire to Kettering, Northamptonshire) (Temporary Restriction and Prohibition of Traffic) Order 2008 No. 2008/2396. - Enabling power: Road Traffic Regulation Act 1984, s. 14 (1) (a). - Made: 01.09.2008. Coming into force: 08.09.2008. Effect: None. Territorial extent & classification: E. Local *Unpublished*

The A14 Trunk Road (North of Girton Interchange, Cambridgeshire) (Temporary Prohibition of Traffic) Order 2008 No. 2008/68. - Enabling power: Road Traffic Regulation Act 1984, s. 14 (1) (c). - Made: 07.01.2008. Coming into force: 14.01.2008. Effect: None. Territorial extent & classification: E. Local *Unpublished*

The A14 Trunk Road (Orwell Crossing Lorry Park, Ipswich, Suffolk) (Temporary Prohibition of Traffic) Order 2008 No. 2008/896. - Enabling power: Road Traffic Regulation Act 1984, s. 14 (1) (a). - Made: 29.02.2008. Coming into force: 07.03.2008. Effect: None. Territorial extent & classification: E. Local *Unpublished*

The A14 Trunk Road (Risby, Near Bury St Edmunds, Suffolk) (Temporary 40 Miles Per Hour Speed Restriction) Order 2008 No. 2008/2055. - Enabling power: Road Traffic Regulation Act 1984, s. 14 (1) (a). - Made: 14.07.2008. Coming into force: 21.07.2008. Effect: None. Territorial extent & classification: E. Local *Unpublished*

The A14 Trunk Road (Spaldwick to Ellington, Cambridgeshire) (Temporary 50 Miles Per Hour Speed Restriction) Order 2008 No. 2008/1199. - Enabling power: Road Traffic Regulation Act 1984, s. 14 (1) (a). - Made: 21.04.2008. Coming into force: 28.04.2008. Effect: None. Territorial extent & classification: E. Local *Unpublished*

The A14 Trunk Road (Stukeley Interchange to Spittals Interchange, Cambridgeshire) (Temporary Restriction and Prohibition of Traffic) Order 2008 No. 2008/1621. - Enabling power: Road Traffic Regulation Act 1984, s. 14 (1) (a). - Made: 09.06.2008. Coming into force: 16.06.2008. Effect: None. Territorial extent & classification: E. Local *Unpublished*

The A14 Trunk Road (Thrapston, Northamptonshire to Lolworth, Cambridgeshire) (Temporary Restriction and Prohibition of Traffic) Order 2008 No. 2008/325. - Enabling power: Road Traffic Regulation Act 1984, s. 14 (1) (a). - Made: 01.02.2008. Coming into force: 08.02.2008. Effect: None. Territorial extent & classification: E. Local *Unpublished*

The A14 Trunk Road (Various Laybys, Catthorpe Interchange to Girton Interchange, Cambridgeshire and Leicestershire) (Temporary Prohibition of Traffic) Order 2008 No. 2008/2012. - Enabling power: Road Traffic Regulation Act 1984, s. 14 (1) (a). - Made: 02.07.2008. Coming into force: 09.07.2008. Effect: None. Territorial extent & classification: E. Local *Unpublished*

The A14 Trunk Road (Welford - Kelmarsh, Northamptonshire) (Prohibition of Heavy Commercial Vehicles) Order 2008 No. 2008/2605. - Enabling power: Road Traffic Regulation Act 1984, ss. 1 (1), 2 (1) (2). - Made: 18.09.2008. Coming into force: 02.10.2008. Effect: None. Territorial extent & classification: E. Local *Unpublished*

The A14 Trunk Road (Whitehouse Interchange and Sproughton Interchange, Ipswich and Bucklesham Junction, Trimley St. Martin, Suffolk) (Temporary Prohibition of Traffic) Order 2008 No. 2008/3187. - Enabling power: Road Traffic Regulation Act 1984, s. 14 (1) (a). - Made: 02.12.2008. Coming into force: 09.12.2008. Effect: None. Territorial extent & classification: E. Local *Unpublished*

The A14 Trunk Road (Woolpit Interchange, Junction 47, Suffolk) (Temporary Prohibition of Traffic) (No. 2) Order 2008 No. 2008/1113. - Enabling power: Road Traffic Regulation Act 1984, s. 14 (1) (a). - Made: 07.04.2008. Coming into force: 14.04.2008. Effect: None. Territorial extent & classification: E. Local *Unpublished*

The A14 Trunk Road (Woolpit Interchange, Junction 47, Suffolk) (Temporary Prohibition of Traffic) Order 2008 No. 2008/897. - Enabling power: Road Traffic Regulation Act 1984, s. 14 (1) (a), 5 (b) (7). - Made: 29.02.2008. Coming into force: 07.03.2008. Effect: None. Territorial extent & classification: E. Local *Unpublished*

The A19 Trunk Road (A1068 Seaton Burn Roundabout to the A1058 Coast Road Roundabout) (Temporary Restriction and Prohibition of Traffic) Order 2008 No. 2008/2190. - Enabling power: Road Traffic Regulation Act 1984, s. 14 (1) (a). - Made: 04.08.2008. Coming into force: 17.08.2008. Effect: None. Territorial extent & classification: E. Local *Unpublished*

The A19 Trunk Road and the A66 Trunk Road (Stockton Road Interchange) (Temporary Prohibition of Traffic) Order 2008 No. 2008/24. - Enabling power: Road Traffic Regulation Act 1984, s. 14 (1) (a). - Made: 03.01.2008. Coming into force: 13.01.2008. Effect: None. Territorial extent & classification: E. Local *Unpublished*

The A19 Trunk Road and the A66 Trunk Road (Stockton Road Interchange to Portrack Interchange) (Temporary Prohibition of Traffic) Order 2008 No. 2008/1571. - Enabling power: Road Traffic Regulation Act 1984, s. 14 (1) (a). - Made: 09.06.2008. Coming into force: 22.06.2008. Effect: None. Territorial extent & classification: E. Local *Unpublished*

The A19 Trunk Road (Black Swan Crossroads) (Temporary 50 Miles Per Hour Speed Restriction) Order 2008 No. 2008/1138. - Enabling power: Road Traffic Regulation Act 1984, s. 14 (1) (a). - Made: 31.03.2008. Coming into force: 06.04.2008. Effect: None. Territorial extent & classification: E. Local *Unpublished*

The A19 Trunk Road (Crathorne Interchange) (Temporary Restriction and Prohibition of Traffic) Order 2008 No. 2008/1077. - Enabling power: Road Traffic Regulation Act 1984, s. 14 (1) (a). - Made: 18.03.2008. Coming into force: 29.04.2008. Effect: None. Territorial extent & classification: E. Local *Unpublished*

The A19 Trunk Road (Lindisfarne Roundabout to Silverlink Roundabout) (Temporary Restriction and Prohibition of Traffic) Order 2008 No. 2008/1388. - Enabling power: Road Traffic Regulation Act 1984, ss. 14 (1) (a), 15 (2). - Made: 19.05.2008. Coming into force: 01.06.2008. Effect: None. Territorial extent & classification: E. Local *Unpublished*

The A19 Trunk Road (Mandale Interchange) (Temporary Prohibition of Traffic) Order 2008 No. 2008/157. - Enabling power: Road Traffic Regulation Act 1984, s. 14 (1) (a). - Made: 21.01.2008. Coming into force: 03.02.2008. Effect: None. Territorial extent & classification: E. Local *Unpublished*

The A19 Trunk Road (Moor Farm Roundabout) (Temporary Restriction and Prohibition of Traffic) Order 2008 No. 2008/160. - Enabling power: Road Traffic Regulation Act 1984, s. 14 (1) (a) (7). - Made: 21.01.2008. Coming into force: 03.02.2008. Effect: None. Territorial extent & classification: E. Local *Unpublished*

The A19 Trunk Road (Moor Farm Roundabout to Seaton Burn Interchange) and the A1 Trunk Road (Seaton Burn Interchange) (Temporary Restriction and Prohibition of Traffic) Order 2008 No. 2008/3178. - Enabling power: Road Traffic Regulation Act 1984, s. 14 (1) (a). - Made: 01.12.2008. Coming into force: 14.12.2008. Effect: None. Territorial extent & classification: E. Local *Unpublished*

The A19 Trunk Road (Northbound Layby Between Holystone Interchange and Killingworth Interchange) (Temporary Prohibition of Traffic) Order 2008 No. 2008/397. - Enabling power: Road Traffic Regulation Act 1984, s. 14 (1) (a). - Made: 12.02.2008. Coming into force: 15.02.2008. Effect: None. Territorial extent & classification: E. Local *Unpublished*

Road traffic: Traffic regulation

The A19 Trunk Road (Portrack Interchange to Stockton Ring Road Interchange) (Temporary Prohibition of Traffic) Order 2008 No. 2008/1504. - Enabling power: Road Traffic Regulation Act 1984, s. 14 (1) (a). - Made: 02.06.2008. Coming into force: 13.06.2008. Effect: None. Territorial extent & classification: E. Local *Unpublished*

The A19 Trunk Road (Ryhope Spur Interchange to Durham Road Interchange) (Temporary Restriction and Prohibition of Traffic) Order 2008 No. 2008/1305. - Enabling power: Road Traffic Regulation Act 1984, s. 14 (1) (a). - Made: 06.05.2008. Coming into force: 18.05.2008. Effect: None. Territorial extent & classification: E. Local *Unpublished*

The A19 Trunk Road (South Kilvington to Nether Silton) (Temporary Restriction and Prohibition of Traffic) Order 2008 No. 2008/1105. - Enabling power: Road Traffic Regulation Act 1984, s. 14 (1) (a) (7). - Made: 10.04.2008. Coming into force: 13.04.2008. Effect: None. Territorial extent & classification: E. Local *Unpublished*

The A19 Trunk Road (Stockton Ring Road to Dalton Piercy) (Temporary Restriction and Prohibition of Traffic) Order 2008 No. 2008/404. - Enabling power: Road Traffic Regulation Act 1984, s. 14 (1) (a). - Made: 11.02.2008. Coming into force: 24.02.2008. Effect: None. Territorial extent & classification: E. Local *Unpublished*

The A19 Trunk Road (The A139 Norton Interchange to Dalton Piercy Junction) (Temporary Restriction and Prohibition of Traffic) Order 2008 No. 2008/3180. - Enabling power: Road Traffic Regulation Act 1984, s. 14 (1) (a). - Made: 01.12.2008. Coming into force: 14.12.2008. Effect: None. Territorial extent & classification: E. Local *Unpublished*

The A19 Trunk Road (The A179 Sheraton Interchange) (Temporary Prohibition of Traffic) Order 2008 No. 2008/2228. - Enabling power: Road Traffic Regulation Act 1984, s. 14 (1) (a). - Made: 11.08.2008. Coming into force: 25.08.2008. Effect: None. Territorial extent & classification: E. Local *Unpublished*

The A19 Trunk Road (The A182, Cold Hesledon Interchange) (Temporary 40 Miles Per Hour Speed Restriction) Order 2008 No. 2008/1025. - Enabling power: Road Traffic Regulation Act 1984, s. 14 (1) (a). - Made: 18.03.2008. Coming into force: 24.03.2008. Effect: None. Territorial extent & classification: E. Local *Unpublished*

The A19 Trunk Road (The A194 Lindisfarne Roundabout Interchange) (Temporary Prohibition of Traffic) Order 2008 No. 2008/2381. - Enabling power: Road Traffic Regulation Act 1984, s. 14 (1) (a). - Made: 26.08.2008. Coming into force: 07.09.2008. Effect: None. Territorial extent & classification: E. Local *Unpublished*

The A19 Trunk Road (The A684 Osmotherley Interchange) (Temporary Restriction and Prohibition of Traffic) Order 2008 No. 2008/2917. - Enabling power: Road Traffic Regulation Act 1984, s. 14 (1) (a). - Made: 03.11.2008. Coming into force: 16.11.2008. Effect: None. Territorial extent & classification: E. Local *Unpublished*

The A19 Trunk Road (The A1058 Coast Road Interchange to the A191 Holystone Interchange) (Temporary Restriction and Prohibition of Traffic) Order 2008 No. 2008/2192. - Enabling power: Road Traffic Regulation Act 1984, s. 14 (1) (a). - Made: 01.08.2008. Coming into force: 10.08.2008. Effect: None. Territorial extent & classification: E. Local *Unpublished*

The A19 Trunk Road (Tontine Interchange) (Temporary Prohibition of Traffic) Order 2008 No. 2008/1137. - Enabling power: Road Traffic Regulation Act 1984, s. 14 (1) (a). - Made: 31.03.2008. Coming into force: 06.04.2008. Effect: None. Territorial extent & classification: E. Local *Unpublished*

The A19 Trunk Road (Tontine Interchange to Parkway Interchange) (Temporary Prohibition of Traffic) Order 2008 No. 2008/1999. - Enabling power: Road Traffic Regulation Act 1984, s. 14 (1) (a). - Made: 07.07.2008. Coming into force: 18.07.2008. Effect: None. Territorial extent & classification: E. Local *Unpublished*

The A19 Trunk Road (Tyne Tunnel Roundabout to Holystone Interchange) (Temporary Restriction and Prohibition of Traffic) Order 2008 No. 2008/392. - Enabling power: Road Traffic Regulation Act 1984, s. 14 (1) (a). - Made: 12.02.2008. Coming into force: 24.02.2008. Effect: None. Territorial extent & classification: E. Local *Unpublished*

The A19 Trunk Road (Wellfield Interchange to Easington Interchange) (Temporary Restriction and Prohibition of Traffic) Order 2008 No. 2008/1135. - Enabling power: Road Traffic Regulation Act 1984, s. 14 (1) (a). - Made: 15.04.2008. Coming into force: 26.04.2008. Effect: None. Territorial extent & classification: E. Local *Unpublished*

The A20 Trunk Road (Alkham Valley Interchange and Courtwood Interchange, Slip Roads) (Temporary Prohibition of Traffic) Order 2008 No. 2008/93. - Enabling power: Road Traffic Regulation Act 1984, s. 14 (1) (a). - Made: 14.01.2008. Coming into force: 21.01.2008. Effect: None. Territorial extent & classification: E. Local *Unpublished*

The A20 Trunk Road and the M20 Motorway (Junctions 9 - 13, Slip Roads) (Temporary Prohibition of Traffic) Order 2008 No. 2008/1116. - Enabling power: Road Traffic Regulation Act 1984, s. 14 (1) (a). - Made: 07.04.2008. Coming into force: 16.04.2008. Effect: None. Territorial extent & classification: E. Local *Unpublished*

The A20 Trunk Road (Dover Bus Lay-bys) (Temporary Prohibition of Traffic) Order 2008 No. 2008/3312. - Enabling power: Road Traffic Regulation Act 1984, s. 14 (1) (a). - Made: 15.12.2008. Coming into force: 03.01.2009. Effect: None. Territorial extent & classification: E. Local *Unpublished*

The A20 Trunk Road (M25 Motorway Junction 3) (Temporary Prohibition of Traffic) Order 2008 No. 2008/3037. - Enabling power: Road Traffic Regulation Act 1984, s. 14 (1) (a). - Made: 17.11.2008. Coming into force: 22.11.2008. Effect: None. Territorial extent & classification: E. Local *Unpublished*

The A20 Trunk Road (Petham Court Bridge, Lay-by) (Temporary Prohibition of Traffic) Order 2008 No. 2008/1838. - Enabling power: Road Traffic Regulation Act 1984, s. 14 (1) (a). - Made: 30.06.2008. Coming into force: 09.07.2008. Effect: None. Territorial extent & classification: E. Local *Unpublished*

The A20 Trunk Road (Roundhill Tunnel) (Temporary Prohibition of Traffic) Order 2008 No. 2008/1013. - Enabling power: Road Traffic Regulation Act 1984, s. 14 (1) (a). - Made: 17.03.2008. Coming into force: 22.03.2008. Effect: None. Territorial extent & classification: E. Local *Unpublished*

The A20 Trunk Road (Roundhill Tunnel) (Temporary Restriction and Prohibition of Traffic) Order 2008 No. 2008/2322. - Enabling power: Road Traffic Regulation Act 1984, s. 14 (1) (a). - Made: 26.08.2008. Coming into force: 30.08.2008. Effect: None. Territorial extent & classification: E. Local *Unpublished*

The A21 Trunk Road (Flimwell - Hurst Green) (Temporary Restriction and Prohibition of Traffic) Order 2008 No. 2008/2285. - Enabling power: Road Traffic Regulation Act 1984, s. 14 (1) (a). - Made: 18.08.2008. Coming into force: 23.08.2008. Effect: None. Territorial extent & classification: E. Local *Unpublished*

The A21 Trunk Road (Kipping's Cross Roundabout - Cryals Road) (Temporary Speed Restrictions) Order 2008 No. 2008/456. - Enabling power: Road Traffic Regulation Act 1984, s. 14 (1) (a). - Made: 18.02.2008. Coming into force: 23.02.2008. Effect: None. Territorial extent & classification: E. Local *Unpublished*

The A21 Trunk Road (Lamberhurst - Flimwell) (Temporary Speed Restrictions) Order 2008 No. 2008/776. - Enabling power: Road Traffic Regulation Act 1984, s. 14 (1) (a), sch. 9, para. 27 (1). - Made: 25.02.2008. Coming into force: 01.03.2008. Effect: S.I. 2007/2816 revoked. Territorial extent & classification: E. Local *Unpublished*

The A21 Trunk Road (Morley's Interchange - Pembury Road Interchange, Slip Roads) (Temporary Prohibition of Traffic) Order 2008 No. 2008/283. - Enabling power: Road Traffic Regulation Act 1984, s. 14 (1) (a). - Made: 28.01.2008. Coming into force: 04.02.2008. Effect: None. Territorial extent & classification: E. Local *Unpublished*

The A21 Trunk Road (Northbridge Street Roundabout) (Temporary Prohibition of Traffic) Order 2008 No. 2008/2896. - Enabling power: Road Traffic Regulation Act 1984, s. 16A (2) (a). - Made: 27.10.2008. Coming into force: 01.11.2008. Effect: None. Territorial extent & classification: E. Local *Unpublished*

The A21 Trunk Road (Tonbridge Bypass) (Temporary Restriction and Prohibition of Traffic) Order 2008 No. 2008/1104. - Enabling power: Road Traffic Regulation Act 1984, s. 14 (1) (a). - Made: 07.04.2008. Coming into force: 12.04.2008. Effect: None. Territorial extent & classification: E. Local *Unpublished*

The A21 Trunk Road (Woodmans Green Gateway) (Temporary Speed Restrictions) Order 2008 No. 2008/3212. - Enabling power: Road Traffic Regulation Act 1984, s. 14 (1) (a). - Made: 24.11.2008. Coming into force: 29.11.2008. Effect: None. Territorial extent & classification: E. Local *Unpublished*

The A21 Trunk Road (Woodmans Green - Kent Street, Near Sedlescombe) (Temporary 40 Miles Per Hour Speed Restriction) Order 2008 No. 2008/903. - Enabling power: Road Traffic Regulation Act 1984, s. 14 (1) (a). - Made: 03.03.2008. Coming into force: 08.03.2008. Effect: None. Territorial extent & classification: E. Local *Unpublished*

The A23 Trunk Road and the A27 Trunk Road (Patcham Junction, Link Roads) (Temporary Prohibition of Traffic) Order 2008 No. 2008/95. - Enabling power: Road Traffic Regulation Act 1984, s. 14 (1) (a). - Made: 14.01.2008. Coming into force: 21.01.2008. Effect: None. Territorial extent & classification: E. Local *Unpublished*

The A23 Trunk Road and the M23 Motorway (Junctions 9 - 11, Slip Roads) (Temporary Prohibition of Traffic) Order 2008 No. 2008/148. - Enabling power: Road Traffic Regulation Act 1984, s. 14 (1) (a). - Made: 21.01.2008. Coming into force: 28.01.2008. Effect: None. Territorial extent & classification: E. Local *Unpublished*

The A23 Trunk Road (Bolney Interchange - Hickstead Interchange, Southbound) (Temporary Restriction and Prohibition of Traffic) Order 2008 No. 2008/2725. - Enabling power: Road Traffic Regulation Act 1984, s. 14 (1) (a). - Made: 06.10.2008. Coming into force: 11.10.2008. Effect: None. Territorial extent & classification: E. Local. - Revoked by S.I. 2009/251 (Unpublished) *Unpublished*

The A23 Trunk Road (Bolney - Pease Pottage) (Temporary Prohibition of Traffic) Order 2008 No. 2008/2764. - Enabling power: Road Traffic Regulation Act 1984, s. 14 (1) (a). - Made: 13.10.2008. Coming into force: 18.10.2008. Effect: None. Territorial extent & classification: E. Local *Unpublished*

The A23 Trunk Road (Bolney - Pyecombe, Southbound) (Temporary Restriction and Prohibition of Traffic) Order 2008 No. 2008/2392. - Enabling power: Road Traffic Regulation Act 1984, s. 14 (1) (a). - Made: 18.08.2008. Coming into force: 23.08.2008. Effect: None. Territorial extent & classification: E. Local *Unpublished*

The A23 Trunk Road (Dale Hill Junction, Southbound) (Temporary Restriction and Prohibition of Traffic) Order 2008 No. 2008/2281. - Enabling power: Road Traffic Regulation Act 1984, s. 14 (1) (a). - Made: 18.08.2008. Coming into force: 23.08.2008. Effect: None. Territorial extent & classification: E. Local *Unpublished*

The A23 Trunk Road (Hickstead, Northbound) (Temporary Restriction and Prohibition of Traffic) Order 2008 No. 2008/904. - Enabling power: Road Traffic Regulation Act 1984, s. 14 (1) (a). - Made: 03.03.2008. Coming into force: 08.03.2008. Effect: None. Territorial extent & classification: E. Local *Unpublished*

The A23 Trunk Road (Hooley, Lay-By) (Temporary Prohibition of Traffic) Order 2008 No. 2008/1454. - Enabling power: Road Traffic Regulation Act 1984, s. 14 (1) (a). - Made: 27.05.2008. Coming into force: 31.05.2008. Effect: None. Territorial extent & classification: E. Local *Unpublished*

The A23 Trunk Road (Warninglid Interchange - Hickstead Interchange, Slip Roads) (Temporary Prohibition of Traffic) Order 2008 No. 2008/92. - Enabling power: Road Traffic Regulation Act 1984, s. 14 (1) (a). - Made: 14.01.2008. Coming into force: 21.01.2008. Effect: None. Territorial extent & classification: E. Local *Unpublished*

The A23 Trunk Road (Warninglid - Sayers Common) (Temporary Restriction and Prohibition of Traffic) Order 2008 No. 2008/3310. - Enabling power: Road Traffic Regulation Act 1984, s. 14 (1) (a). - Made: 15.12.2008. Coming into force: 03.01.2009. Effect: None. Territorial extent & classification: E. Local *Unpublished*

The A27 Trunk Road (A280 Junction - Poling) (Temporary Restriction and Prohibition of Traffic) Order 2008 No. 2008/349. - Enabling power: Road Traffic Regulation Act 1984, s. 14 (1) (a). - Made: 04.02.2008. Coming into force: 09.02.2008. Effect: None. Territorial extent & classification: E. Local *Unpublished*

The A27 Trunk Road (Binsted Lane - Ford Road Roundabout, Near Arundel) (Temporary Prohibition of Traffic) Order 2008 No. 2008/96. - Enabling power: Road Traffic Regulation Act 1984, s. 14 (1) (a). - Made: 14.01.2008. Coming into force: 19.01.2008. Effect: None. Territorial extent & classification: E. Local *Unpublished*

The A27 Trunk Road (Burgh Lane) (Temporary Speed Restriction) Order 2008 No. 2008/861. - Enabling power: Road Traffic Regulation Act 1984, s. 14 (1) (a). - Made: 10.03.2008. Coming into force: 15.03.2008. Effect: None. Territorial extent & classification: E. Local *Unpublished*

The A27 Trunk Road (Causeway Roundabout - Crossbush Interchange) (Temporary Prohibition of Pedestrians and Traffic) Order 2008 No. 2008/2394. - Enabling power: Road Traffic Regulation Act 1984, s. 14 (1) (a). - Made: 01.09.2008. Coming into force: 06.09.2008. Effect: None. Territorial extent & classification: E. Local *Unpublished*

The A27 Trunk Road (Chichester - Fontwell) (Temporary 50 Miles Per Hour Speed Restriction) Order 2007 Variation Order 2008 No. 2008/1385. - Enabling power: Road Traffic Regulation Act 1984, s. 14 (1) (a), sch. 9, para. 27 (1). - Made: 19.05.2008. Coming into force: 27.05.2008. Effect: S.I. 2007/3416 varied. Territorial extent & classification: E. Local *Unpublished*

The A27 Trunk Road (Cop Hall Roundabout, Dedicated Link Road) (Temporary Prohibition of Traffic) Order 2008 No. 2008/153. - Enabling power: Road Traffic Regulation Act 1984, s. 14 (1) (a). - Made: 21.01.2008. Coming into force: 28.01.2008. Effect: None. Territorial extent & classification: E. Local *Unpublished*

The A27 Trunk Road (Fontwell Avenue Roundabout - Fairmile Bottom Roundabout) (Temporary 50 Miles Per Hour Speed Restriction) Order 2008 No. 2008/3036. - Enabling power: Road Traffic Regulation Act 1984, s. 14 (1) (a). - Made: 17.11.2008. Coming into force: 22.11.2008. Effect: None. Territorial extent & classification: E. Local *Unpublished*

The A27 Trunk Road (Glynde) (Temporary Prohibition of Traffic) Order 2008 No. 2008/987. - Enabling power: Road Traffic Regulation Act 1984, s. 14 (1) (a). - Made: 25.03.2008. Coming into force: 29.03.2008. Effect: None. Territorial extent & classification: E. Local *Unpublished*

The A27 Trunk Road (Holmbush Interchange to Hangleton) (Temporary Prohibition of Traffic) Order 2008 No. 2008/990. - Enabling power: Road Traffic Regulation Act 1984, s. 14 (1) (a). - Made: 25.03.2008. Coming into force: 01.04.2008. Effect: None. Territorial extent & classification: E. Local *Unpublished*

The A27 Trunk Road (Lewes Bypass, Eastbound) (Temporary Restriction and Prohibition of Traffic) Order 2008 No. 2008/2483. - Enabling power: Road Traffic Regulation Act 1984, s. 14 (1) (a). - Made: 08.09.2008. Coming into force: 13.09.2008. Effect: None. Territorial extent & classification: E. Local *Unpublished*

The A27 Trunk Road (Near Chichester) (Temporary 50 Miles Per Hour Speed Restriction) Order 2008 No. 2008/1230. - Enabling power: Road Traffic Regulation Act 1984, s. 14 (1) (a). - Made: 28.04.2008. Coming into force: 03.05.2008. Effect: None. Territorial extent & classification: E. Local *Unpublished*

The A27 Trunk Road (Near Chichester) (Temporary Speed Restrictions) Order 2008 No. 2008/2517. - Enabling power: Road Traffic Regulation Act 1984, s. 14 (1) (a). - Made: 15.09.2008. Coming into force: 20.09.2008. Effect: None. Territorial extent & classification: E. Local. - Revoked by S.I. 2009/561 (Unpublished) *Unpublished*

The A27 Trunk Road (Old Shoreham Road and Shoreham Bypass) (Temporary Restriction and Prohibition of Traffic) Order 2008 No. 2008/2280. - Enabling power: Road Traffic Regulation Act 1984, s. 14 (1) (b). - Made: 18.08.2008. Coming into force: 23.08.2008. Effect: None. Territorial extent & classification: E. Local *Unpublished*

The A27 Trunk Road (Patcham Interchange, Westbound) (Temporary Restriction and Prohibition of Traffic) Order 2008 No. 2008/2724. - Enabling power: Road Traffic Regulation Act 1984, s. 14 (1) (a). - Made: 06.10.2008. Coming into force: 11.10.2008. Effect: None. Territorial extent & classification: E. Local *Unpublished*

The A27 Trunk Road (Patcham Viaduct, Westbound) (Temporary Restriction and Prohibition of Traffic) Order 2008 No. 2008/3213. - Enabling power: Road Traffic Regulation Act 1984, s. 14 (1) (a), sch. 9, para. 27 (1). - Made: 24.11.2008. Coming into force: 29.11.2008. Effect: S.I. 2007/2026 revoked. Territorial extent & classification: E. Local *Unpublished*

The A27 Trunk Road (Pook Lane Footbridge) (Temporary Restriction and Prohibition of Traffic) Order 2008 No. 2008/1624. - Enabling power: Road Traffic Regulation Act 1984, s. 14 (1) (a). - Made: 16.06.2008. Coming into force: 21.06.2008. Effect: None. Territorial extent & classification: E. Local *Unpublished*

The A27 Trunk Road (Tangmere) (Temporary Restriction and Prohibition of Traffic) Order 2008 No. 2008/155. - Enabling power: Road Traffic Regulation Act 1984, s. 14 (1) (a). - Made: 21.01.2008. Coming into force: 01.02.2008. Effect: None. Territorial extent & classification: E. Local *Unpublished*

The A27 Trunk Road (Tangmere) (Temporary Restriction and Prohibition of Traffic) Order 2008 Variation Order 2008 No. 2008/1011. - Enabling power: Road Traffic Regulation Act 1984, s. 14 (1) (a), sch. 9, para. 27 (1). - Made: 17.03.2008. Coming into force: 25.03.2008. Effect: S.I. 2008/155 varied. Territorial extent & classification: E. Local *Unpublished*

The A27 Trunk Road (Warblington Interchange - Falmer Interchange, Slip Roads) (Temporary Prohibition of Traffic) Order 2008 No. 2008/154. - Enabling power: Road Traffic Regulation Act 1984, s. 14 (1) (a). - Made: 21.01.2008. Coming into force: 28.01.2008. Effect: None. Territorial extent & classification: E. Local *Unpublished*

The A27 Trunk Road (West of Manor Road Roundabout) (Temporary Prohibition of Traffic) Order 2008 No. 2008/3324. - Enabling power: Road Traffic Regulation Act 1984, s. 14 (1) (a). - Made: 15.12.2008. Coming into force: 10.01.2009. Effect: None. Territorial extent & classification: E. Local *Unpublished*

The A30 and A303 Trunk Roads (Honiton to Southfields Roundabout, Ilminster) (Temporary Prohibition of Traffic) Order 2008 No. 2008/1446. - Enabling power: Road Traffic Regulation Act 1984, s. 14 (1) (a). - Made: 28.05.2008. Coming into force: 30.05.2008. Effect: None. Territorial extent & classification: E. Local *Unpublished*

The A30 Trunk Road (Alphington Interchange to Pearces Hill Interchange, Exeter) and M5 Motorway (Junction 31) (Temporary Prohibition and Restriction of Traffic) Order 2008 No. 2008/23. - Enabling power: Road Traffic Regulation Act 1984, s. 14 (1) (a). - Made: 03.01.2008. Coming into force: 05.01.2008. Effect: None. Territorial extent & classification: E. Local *Unpublished*

The A30 Trunk Road (Alphington to Whiddon Down, Devon) (Temporary Restriction of Traffic) (Number 2) Order 2008 No. 2008/2873. - Enabling power: Road Traffic Regulation Act 1984, s. 14 (1) (a). - Made: 23.10.2008. Coming into force: 26.10.2008. Effect: None. Territorial extent & classification: E. Local *Unpublished*

The A30 Trunk Road (Alphington to Whiddon Down, Devon) (Temporary Restriction of Traffic) Order 2008 No. 2008/1703. - Enabling power: Road Traffic Regulation Act 1984, s. 14 (1) (a). - Made: 25.06.2008. Coming into force: 28.06.2008. Effect: None. Territorial extent & classification: E. Local *Unpublished*

The A30 Trunk Road and the M25 Motorway (Junction 13) (Temporary Prohibition of Traffic) Order 2008 No. 2008/2482. - Enabling power: Road Traffic Regulation Act 1984, s. 14 (1) (a). - Made: 08.09.2008. Coming into force: 13.09.2008. Effect: None. Territorial extent & classification: E. Local *Unpublished*

The A30 Trunk Road (Camborne Bypass, Cornwall) (Temporary Restriction of Traffic) Order 2008 No. 2008/2902. - Enabling power: Road Traffic Regulation Act 1984, s. 14 (1) (a). - Made: 28.10.2008. Coming into force: 31.10.2008. Effect: None. Territorial extent & classification: E. Local *Unpublished*

The A30 Trunk Road (Carland Cross Roundabout, Cornwall) (Temporary Prohibition of Traffic) Order 2008 No. 2008/2589. - Enabling power: Road Traffic Regulation Act 1984, s. 14 (1) (a). - Made: 23.09.2008. Coming into force: 26.09.2008. Effect: None. Territorial extent & classification: E. Local *Unpublished*

The A30 Trunk Road (Dunheved Bridge Layby, Launceston) (Temporary Prohibition of Traffic) Order 2008 No. 2008/259. - Enabling power: Road Traffic Regulation Act 1984, s. 14 (1) (a). - Made: 29.01.2008. Coming into force: 02.02.2008. Effect: None. Territorial extent & classification: E. Local *Unpublished*

The A30 Trunk Road (Fatherford Cutting Layby, Near Okehampton) (Temporary Prohibition of Traffic) Order 2008 No. 2008/827. - Enabling power: Road Traffic Regulation Act 1984, s. 14 (1) (a). - Made: 27.02.2008. Coming into force: 01.03.2008. Effect: None. Territorial extent & classification: E. Local *Unpublished*

The A30 Trunk Road (Fingle Glen Junction, Devon) (Temporary Restriction of Traffic) Order 2008 No. 2008/2663. - Enabling power: Road Traffic Regulation Act 1984, s. 14 (1) (a). - Made: 01.10.2008. Coming into force: 07.10.2008. Effect: None. Territorial extent & classification: E. Local *Unpublished*

The A30 Trunk Road (Helland Junction to Carminnow Junction, Bodmin) (Temporary Restriction and Prohibition of Traffic) Order 2008 No. 2008/333. - Enabling power: Road Traffic Regulation Act 1984, s. 14 (1) (a). - Made: 05.02.2008. Coming into force: 09.02.2008. Effect: None. Territorial extent & classification: E. Local *Unpublished*

The A30 Trunk Road (Honiton Bypass, Devon) (Temporary Prohibition of Traffic) Order 2008 No. 2008/2058. - Enabling power: Road Traffic Regulation Act 1984, s. 14 (1) (a) (5) (b) (7). - Made: 16.07.2008. Coming into force: 21.07.2008. Effect: None. Territorial extent & classification: E. Local *Unpublished*

The A30 Trunk Road (Innis Downs to Bodmin, Cornwall) (Temporary Restriction of Traffic) Order 2008 No. 2008/2474. - Enabling power: Road Traffic Regulation Act 1984, s. 14 (1) (a). - Made: 09.09.2008. Coming into force: 12.09.2008. Effect: None. Territorial extent & classification: E. Local *Unpublished*

The A30 Trunk Road (Kennards House Junction to Bolventor, Cornwall) (Temporary Prohibition and Restriction of Traffic) (Number 2) Order 2008 No. 2008/1006. - Enabling power: Road Traffic Regulation Act 1984, s. 14 (1) (a), sch. 9, para. 27 (1). - Made: 26.03.2008. Coming into force: 29.03.2008. Effect: S.I. 2008/324 revoked. Territorial extent & classification: E. Local *Unpublished*

The A30 Trunk Road (Kennards House Junction to Bolventor, Cornwall) (Temporary Prohibition and Restriction of Traffic) Order 2008 No. 2008/324. - Enabling power: Road Traffic Regulation Act 1984, s. 14 (1) (a). - Made: 05.02.2008. Coming into force: 08.02.2008. Effect: None. Territorial extent & classification: E. Local. - Revoked by S.I. 2008/1006 (Unpublished) *Unpublished*

The A30 Trunk Road (Liftondown to Sourton Cross, near Okehampton) (Temporary Prohibition of Traffic) Order 2008 No. 2008/2662. - Enabling power: Road Traffic Regulation Act 1984, s. 14 (1) (a). - Made: 01.10.2008. Coming into force: 04.10.2008. Effect: None. Territorial extent & classification: E. Local *Unpublished*

The A30 Trunk Road (London Road, Near Ashford) (Temporary 10 Miles Per Hour Speed Restriction) Order 2008 No. 2008/2481. - Enabling power: Road Traffic Regulation Act 1984, s. 14 (1) (a). - Made: 08.09.2008. Coming into force: 13.09.2008. Effect: None. Territorial extent & classification: E. Local *Unpublished*

The A30 Trunk Road (London Road, Near Ashford) (Temporary 10 Miles Per Hour Speed Restriction) Order 2008 No. 2008/2211. - Enabling power: Road Traffic Regulation Act 1984, s. 14 (1) (a). - Made: 11.08.2008. Coming into force: 16.08.2008. Effect: None. Territorial extent & classification: E. Local *Unpublished*

The A30 Trunk Road (M25 Junction 13, Link Road) (Temporary Prohibition of Traffic) Order 2008 No. 2008/1014. - Enabling power: Road Traffic Regulation Act 1984, s. 14 (1) (a). - Made: 25.03.2008. Coming into force: 02.04.2008. Effect: None. Territorial extent & classification: E. Local *Unpublished*

The A30 Trunk Road (M25 Junction 13, Westbound Exit Slip Road) (Temporary Prohibition of Traffic) Order 2008 No. 2008/780. - Enabling power: Road Traffic Regulation Act 1984, s. 14 (1) (a). - Made: 25.02.2008. Coming into force: 01.03.2008. Effect: None. Territorial extent & classification: E. Local *Unpublished*

The A30 Trunk Road (Minzies Downs Layby, Devon) (Temporary Prohibition of Traffic) Order 2008 No. 2008/2587. - Enabling power: Road Traffic Regulation Act 1984, s. 14 (1) (a). - Made: 23.09.2008. Coming into force: 27.09.2008. Effect: None. Territorial extent & classification: E. Local *Unpublished*

The A30 Trunk Road (Newtown Roundabout to CHy-An-Mor Roundabout, Longrock near Penzance) (Temporary Prohibition of Traffic) (Number 2) Order 2008 No. 2008/2654. - Enabling power: Road Traffic Regulation Act 1984, s. 14 (1) (a). - Made: 30.09.2008. Coming into force: 03.10.2008. Effect: None. Territorial extent & classification: E. Local *Unpublished*

The A30 Trunk Road (Newtown Roundabout to Chy-An-Mor Roundabout, Longrock near Penzance) (Temporary Prohibition of Traffic) Order 2008 No. 2008/21. - Enabling power: Road Traffic Regulation Act 1984, s. 14 (1) (a). - Made: 02.01.2008. Coming into force: 05.01.2008. Effect: None. Territorial extent & classification: E. Local *Unpublished*

The A30 Trunk Road (Pounds Conce Right Turn Ban) (Temporary Prohibition of Traffic) Order 2008 No. 2008/1452. - Enabling power: Road Traffic Regulation Act 1984, s. 14 (1) (b). - Made: 27.05.2008. Coming into force: 30.05.2008. Effect: None. Territorial extent & classification: E. Local *Unpublished*

The A30 Trunk Road (Pounds Conce / Temple Fishery Junction, near Bodmin) (Temporary Prohibition and Restriction of Traffic) Order 2008 No. 2008/1529. - Enabling power: Road Traffic Regulation Act 1984, s. 14 (1) (a), sch. 9, para. 27 (1). - Made: 03.06.2008. Coming into force: 07.06.2008. Effect: S.I. 2008/22 revoked. Territorial extent & classification: E. Local *Unpublished*

The A30 Trunk Road (Pounds Conce / Temple Fishery Junction, near Bodmin) (Temporary Restriction of Traffic) Order 2008 No. 2008/22. - Enabling power: Road Traffic Regulation Act 1984, s. 14 (1) (a). - Made: 02.01.2008. Coming into force: 05.01.2008. Effect: None. Territorial extent & classification: E. Local. - Revoked by S.I. 2008/1529 (Unpublished) *Unpublished*

The A30 Trunk Road (Shallow Water, Near Bolventor, Cornwall) (Temporary Prohibition and Restriction of Traffic) Order 2008 No. 2008/2592. - Enabling power: Road Traffic Regulation Act 1984, s. 14 (1) (a). - Made: 23.09.2008. Coming into force: 27.09.2008. Effect: None. Territorial extent & classification: E. Local *Unpublished*

The A30 Trunk Road (St Erth Roundabout to Newtown Roundabout, Near Hayle, Cornwall) (Temporary Prohibition of Traffic) Order 2008 No. 2008/1704. - Enabling power: Road Traffic Regulation Act 1984, s. 14 (1) (a). - Made: 24.06.2008. Coming into force: 27.06.2008. Effect: None. Territorial extent & classification: E. Local *Unpublished*

The A30 Trunk Road (Stowford Cross to Sourton Cross, near Okehampton) (Temporary Prohibition of Traffic) Order 2008 No. 2008/880. - Enabling power: Road Traffic Regulation Act 1984, s. 14 (1) (a). - Made: 16.01.2008. Coming into force: 19.01.2008. Effect: None. Territorial extent & classification: E. Local *Unpublished*

The A30 Trunk Road (Tolvaddon Interchange, Camborne to Avers Interchange, Redruth) (Temporary Prohibition and Restriction of Traffic) (Number 2) Order 2008 No. 2008/2609. - Enabling power: Road Traffic Regulation Act 1984, s. 14 (1) (a). - Made: 24.09.2008. Coming into force: 27.09.2008. Effect: None. Territorial extent & classification: E. Local *Unpublished*

Road traffic: Traffic regulation

The A30 Trunk Road (Tolvaddon Interchange, Camborne to Avers Interchange, Redruth) (Temporary Prohibition and Restriction of Traffic) Order 2008 No. 2008/20. - Enabling power: Road Traffic Regulation Act 1984, s. 14 (1) (a). - Made: 02.01.2008. Coming into force: 04.01.2008. Effect: None. Territorial extent & classification: E. Local *Unpublished*

The A30 Trunk Road (Tongue End Junction, Near Okehampton) (Temporary Prohibition of Traffic) Order 2008 No. 2008/1670. - Enabling power: Road Traffic Regulation Act 1984, s. 14 (1) (a). - Made: 18.06.2008. Coming into force: 21.06.2008. Effect: None. Territorial extent & classification: E. Local *Unpublished*

The A30 Trunk Road (Tregoss Moor, Roche, Cornwall) (Prohibition of Right Turn) Order 2004 (Revocation) Order 2008 No. 2008/1176. - Enabling power: Road Traffic Regulation Act 1984, ss. 1 (1) (2), 2 (1), sch. 9, para. 27 (1). - Made: 22.04.2008. Coming into force: 01.05.2008. Effect: S.I. 2004/1638 revoked. Territorial extent & classification: E. Local *Unpublished*

The A30 Trunk Road (Whiddon Down Junction, Devon) (Temporary Prohibition of Traffic) Order 2008 No. 2008/1018. - Enabling power: Road Traffic Regulation Act 1984, s. 14 (1) (a). - Made: 27.03.2008. Coming into force: 31.03.2008. Effect: None. Territorial extent & classification: E. Local *Unpublished*

The A30 Trunk Road (Woodleigh Junction, Devon) (Temporary Restriction of Traffic) Order 2008 No. 2008/2727. - Enabling power: Road Traffic Regulation Act 1984, s. 14 (1) (a). - Made: 01.10.2008. Coming into force: 06.10.2008. Effect: None. Territorial extent & classification: E. Local *Unpublished*

The A30 Trunk Road (Woodleigh Junction to Whiddon Down Junction, Devon) (Temporary Prohibition of Traffic) Order 2008 No. 2008/2738. - Enabling power: Road Traffic Regulation Act 1984, s. 14 (1) (a). - Made: 08.10.2008. Coming into force: 11.10.2008. Effect: None. Territorial extent & classification: E. Local *Unpublished*

The A31 Trunk Road (Picket Post Interchange, Westbound Exit Slip Road) (Temporary Prohibition of Traffic) Order 2008 No. 2008/1685. - Enabling power: Road Traffic Regulation Act 1984, s. 14 (1) (a). - Made: 23.06.2008. Coming into force: 28.06.2008. Effect: None. Territorial extent & classification: E. Local *Unpublished*

The A31 Trunk Road (Wimborne Minster - Stoney Cross) (Temporary Restriction and Prohibition of Traffic) Order 2008 No. 2008/2637. - Enabling power: Road Traffic Regulation Act 1984, s. 14 (1) (a). - Made: 29.09.2008. Coming into force: 04.10.2008. Effect: None. Territorial extent & classification: E. Local *Unpublished*

The A34 Trunk Road (Beacon Hill - Bullington Cross) (Temporary Speed Restrictions) Order 2008 No. 2008/1384. - Enabling power: Road Traffic Regulation Act 1984, s. 14 (1) (a). - Made: 19.05.2008. Coming into force: 24.05.2008. Effect: None. Territorial extent & classification: E. Local *Unpublished*

The A34 Trunk Road (Beacon Hill - Tot Hill, Northbound) (Temporary Prohibition of Traffic) Order 2008 No. 2008/2218. - Enabling power: Road Traffic Regulation Act 1984, s. 14 (1) (a). - Made: 21.07.2008. Coming into force: 26.07.2008. Effect: None. Territorial extent & classification: E. Local *Unpublished*

The A34 Trunk Road (Beacon Hill - Tot Hill) (Temporary Restriction and Prohibition of Traffic) Order 2008 No. 2008/1489. - Enabling power: Road Traffic Regulation Act 1984, s. 14 (1) (a). - Made: 27.05.2008. Coming into force: 31.05.2008. Effect: None. Territorial extent & classification: E. Local *Unpublished*

The A34 Trunk Road (Beedon - Chieveley, Southbound) (Temporary Restriction and Prohibition of Traffic) Order 2008 No. 2008/1508. - Enabling power: Road Traffic Regulation Act 1984, s. 14 (1) (a). - Made: 02.06.2008. Coming into force: 07.06.2008. Effect: None. Territorial extent & classification: E. Local *Unpublished*

The A34 Trunk Road (Beedon - Hinksey Hill) (Temporary Prohibition of Traffic) Order 2008 No. 2008/345. - Enabling power: Road Traffic Regulation Act 1984, s. 14 (1) (a). - Made: 04.02.2008. Coming into force: 19.02.2008. Effect: None. Territorial extent & classification: E. Local *Unpublished*

The A34 Trunk Road (Beedon - West Ilsley) (Temporary Prohibition of Traffic) Order 2008 No. 2008/1455. - Enabling power: Road Traffic Regulation Act 1984, s. 14 (1) (a). - Made: 27.05.2008. Coming into force: 31.05.2008. Effect: None. Territorial extent & classification: E. Local *Unpublished*

The A34 Trunk Road (Botley - Hinksey Hill) (Temporary Restriction and Prohibition of Traffic) Order 2008 No. 2008/1347. - Enabling power: Road Traffic Regulation Act 1984, s. 14 (1) (a). - Made: 12.05.2008. Coming into force: 17.05.2008. Effect: None. Territorial extent & classification: E. Local *Unpublished*

The A34 Trunk Road (Botley Interchange Peartree Interchange) (Temporary Restriction and Prohibition of Traffic) Order 2008 No. 2008/1352. - Enabling power: Road Traffic Regulation Act 1984, s. 14 (1) (a). - Made: 12.05.2008. Coming into force: 17.05.2008. Effect: None. Territorial extent & classification: E. Local *Unpublished*

The A34 Trunk Road (Botley - Kidlington) (Temporary Restriction and Prohibition of Traffic) Order 2008 No. 2008/901. - Enabling power: Road Traffic Regulation Act 1984, ss. 14 (1) (a), 15 (2). - Made: 03.03.2008. Coming into force: 17.05.2008. Effect: None. Territorial extent & classification: E. Local *Unpublished*

The A34 Trunk Road (Bullington Cross Interchange - Kings Worthy Interchange) (Temporary Prohibition of Traffic) Order 2008 No. 2008/1228. - Enabling power: Road Traffic Regulation Act 1984, s. 14 (1) (a). - Made: 28.04.2008. Coming into force: 03.05.2008. Effect: None. Territorial extent & classification: E. Local *Unpublished*

The A34 Trunk Road (Chilton, Northbound) (Temporary Restriction of Traffic) Order 2008 No. 2008/2283. - Enabling power: Road Traffic Regulation Act 1984, s. 14 (1) (a). - Made: 18.08.2008. Coming into force: 23.08.2008. Effect: None. Territorial extent & classification: E. Local *Unpublished*

The A34 Trunk Road (Harwell - Milton Interchange) (Temporary Restriction and Prohibition of Traffic) Order 2008 No. 2008/1492. - Enabling power: Road Traffic Regulation Act 1984, s. 14 (1) (a). - Made: 27.05.2008. Coming into force: 31.05.2008. Effect: None. Territorial extent & classification: E. Local *Unpublished*

The A34 Trunk Road (Hinksey Hill Interchange - Marcham Interchange) (Temporary Prohibition of Traffic) Order 2008 No. 2008/1510. - Enabling power: Road Traffic Regulation Act 1984, s. 14 (1) (a). - Made: 02.06.2008. Coming into force: 07.06.2008. Effect: None. Territorial extent & classification: E. Local *Unpublished*

The A34 Trunk Road (Kings Worthy - M3 Junction 9) (Temporary Speed Restrictions) Order 2008 No. 2008/1511. - Enabling power: Road Traffic Regulation Act 1984, s. 14 (1) (a). - Made: 02.06.2008. Coming into force: 07.06.2008. Effect: None. Territorial extent & classification: E. Local *Unpublished*

The A34 Trunk Road (Lichfield, Southbound) (Temporary Restriction and Prohibition of Traffic) Order 2008 No. 2008/1506. - Enabling power: Road Traffic Regulation Act 1984, s. 14 (1) (a). - Made: 02.06.2008. Coming into force: 07.06.2008. Effect: None. Territorial extent & classification: E. Local *Unpublished*

The A34 Trunk Road (M4 Motorway Junction 13) (Temporary Prohibition of Traffic) Order 2008 No. 2008/3318. - Enabling power: Road Traffic Regulation Act 1984, s. 14 (1) (a). - Made: 15.12.2008. Coming into force: 12.01.2009. Effect: None. Territorial extent & classification: E. Local *Unpublished*

The A34 Trunk Road (Milton Interchange) (Temporary Restriction and Prohibition of Traffic) Order 2008 No. 2008/2045. - Enabling power: Road Traffic Regulation Act 1984, s. 14 (1) (a). - Made: 14.07.2008. Coming into force: 19.07.2008. Effect: None. Territorial extent & classification: E. Local *Unpublished*

The A34 Trunk Road (North of Chieveley Interchange - South of Tot Hill Interchange) (Temporary Speed Restrictions) Order 2008 No. 2008/2325. - Enabling power: Road Traffic Regulation Act 1984, s. 14 (1) (a). - Made: 26.08.2008. Coming into force: 30.08.2008. Effect: None. Territorial extent & classification: E. Local *Unpublished*

The A34 Trunk Road (Tot Hill - Beacon Hill Interchange, Southbound) (Temporary Prohibition of Traffic) Order 2008 No. 2008/1351. - Enabling power: Road Traffic Regulation Act 1984, s. 14 (1) (a). - Made: 12.05.2008. Coming into force: 17.05.2008. Effect: None. Territorial extent & classification: E. Local *Unpublished*

The A34 Trunk Road (West Ilsley - Beedon) (Temporary Restriction and Prohibition of Traffic) Order 2008 No. 2008/1500. - Enabling power: Road Traffic Regulation Act 1984, s. 14 (1) (a). - Made: 02.06.2008. Coming into force: 07.06.2008. Effect: None. Territorial extent & classification: E. Local *Unpublished*

The A34 Trunk Road (Weston-on-the-Green - M40 Junction 9) (Temporary Restriction and Prohibition of Traffic) Order 2008 No. 2008/1562. - Enabling power: Road Traffic Regulation Act 1984, s. 14 (1) (a). - Made: 09.06.2008. Coming into force: 14.06.2008. Effect: None. Territorial extent & classification: E. Local *Unpublished*

The A34 Trunk Road (Whitchurch Interchange, Northbound Exit Slip Road) (Temporary Prohibition of Traffic) Order 2008 No. 2008/1842. - Enabling power: Road Traffic Regulation Act 1984, s. 14 (1) (a). - Made: 30.06.2008. Coming into force: 05.07.2008. Effect: None. Territorial extent & classification: E. Local *Unpublished*

The A35 Trunk Road (Berne Lane, Charmouth to Tizard's Knap, Morcombelake, Dorset) (Temporary Restriction of Traffic) Order 2008 No. 2008/2145. - Enabling power: Road Traffic Regulation Act 1984, s. 14 (1) (a). - Made: 30.07.2008. Coming into force: 02.08.2008. Effect: None. Territorial extent & classification: E. Local *Unpublished*

The A35 Trunk Road (East Road Bridport) (Temporary Restriction of Traffic) Order 2008 No. 2008/2148. - Enabling power: Road Traffic Regulation Act 1984, s. 14 (1) (a). - Made: 30.07.2008. Coming into force: 02.08.2008. Effect: None. Territorial extent & classification: E. Local *Unpublished*

The A35 Trunk Road (Melplash Show, Bridport, Dorset) (Temporary Prohibition of Traffic) Order 2008 No. 2008/2232. - Enabling power: Road Traffic Regulation Act 1984, s. 14 (1) (b). - Made: 13.08.2008. Coming into force: 19.08.2008. Effect: None. Territorial extent & classification: E. Local *Unpublished*

The A35 Trunk Road (Raymonds Hill to Penn Duals, Between Axminser and Charmouth) (Temporary Restriction of Traffic) Order 2008 No. 2008/2149. - Enabling power: Road Traffic Regulation Act 1984, s. 14 (1) (a). - Made: 30.07.2008. Coming into force: 02.08.2008. Effect: None. Territorial extent & classification: E. Local *Unpublished*

The A35 Trunk Road (Tilly Whim Lane to Monkey Jump Roundabout, Near Dorchester) (Temporary Restriction of Traffic) Order 2008 No. 2008/2146. - Enabling power: Road Traffic Regulation Act 1984, s. 14 (1) (a). - Made: 30.07.2008. Coming into force: 02.08.2008. Effect: None. Territorial extent & classification: E. Local *Unpublished*

The A35 Trunk Road (Walditch to Winterbourne Abbas) (Temporary Restriction of Traffic) Order 2008 No. 2008/2147. - Enabling power: Road Traffic Regulation Act 1984, s. 14 (1) (a). - Made: 30.07.2008. Coming into force: 02.08.2008. Effect: None. Territorial extent & classification: E. Local *Unpublished*

Road traffic: Traffic regulation

The A36 Trunk Road (A3090 Roundabout to M27 Junction 2) (Temporary Prohibition and Restriction of Traffic) Order 2008 No. 2008/87. - Enabling power: Road Traffic Regulation Act 1984, s. 14 (1) (a). - Made: 09.01.2008. Coming into force: 12.01.2008. Effect: None. Territorial extent & classification: E. Local *Unpublished*

The A36 Trunk Road (Bathampton to Beckington) (Temporary Prohibition of Traffic) Order 2008 No. 2008/1003. - Enabling power: Road Traffic Regulation Act 1984, s. 14 (1) (a). - Made: 26.03.2008. Coming into force: 29.03.2008. Effect: None. Territorial extent & classification: E. Local *Unpublished*

The A36 Trunk Road (Black Dog Hill, near Westbury) (Temporary Prohibition and Restriction of Traffic) Order 2008 No. 2008/1895. - Enabling power: Road Traffic Regulation Act 1984, s. 14 (1) (a). - Made: 02.07.2008. Coming into force: 05.07.2008. Effect: None. Territorial extent & classification: E. Local *Unpublished*

The A36 Trunk Road (College Roundabout, Salisbury, to the A3090 Romsey Roundabout) (Temporary Prohibition of Traffic) Order 2008 No. 2008/287. - Enabling power: Road Traffic Regulation Act 1984, s. 14 (1) (a). - Made: 30.01.2008. Coming into force: 02.02.2008. Effect: None. Territorial extent & classification: E. Local *Unpublished*

The A36 Trunk Road (Fisherton de la Mere to Wylye, Wiltshire) (Temporary Restriction of Traffic) Order 2008 No. 2008/2473. - Enabling power: Road Traffic Regulation Act 1984, s. 14 (1) (a). - Made: 09.09.2008. Coming into force: 13.09.2008. Effect: None. Territorial extent & classification: E. Local *Unpublished*

The A36 Trunk Road (Warminster Bypass, Wiltshire) (Temporary Prohibition and Restriction of Traffic) Order 2008 No. 2008/1981. - Enabling power: Road Traffic Regulation Act 1984, s. 14 (1) (a). - Made: 02.07.2008. Coming into force: 05.07.2008. Effect: None. Territorial extent & classification: E. Local *Unpublished*

The A36 Trunk Road (Warminster Road, Bathampton) (Prohibition of Waiting) Order 2008 No. 2008/2029. - Enabling power: Road Traffic Regulation Act 1984, ss. 1 (1), 2 (1), 4 (1) (2). - Made: 11.07.2008. Coming into force: 21.07.2008. Effect: None. Territorial extent & classification: E. Local *Unpublished*

The A36 Trunk Road (Wylye to Wilton, Near Salisbury) (Temporary Prohibition of Traffic) Order 2008 No. 2008/2315. - Enabling power: Road Traffic Regulation Act 1984, s. 14 (1) (a). - Made: 26.08.2008. Coming into force: 30.08.2008. Effect: None. Territorial extent & classification: E. Local *Unpublished*

The A38 Trunk Road (Alfreton, Derbyshire) (Temporary Prohibition of Traffic) Order 2008 No. 2008/1831. - Enabling power: Road Traffic Regulation Act 1984, s. 14 (1) (a). - Made: 23.06.2008. Coming into force: 30.06.2008. Effect: None. Territorial extent & classification: E. Local *Unpublished*

The A38 Trunk Road (Alfreton) (Temporary Prohibition of Traffic) Order 2008 No. 2008/2382. - Enabling power: Road Traffic Regulation Act 1984, s. 14 (1) (a). - Made: 26.08.2008. Coming into force: 02.09.2008. Effect: None. Territorial extent & classification: E. Local *Unpublished*

The A38 Trunk Road (Barton-under-Needwood) (Temporary Restriction and Prohibition of Traffic) Order 2008 No. 2008/2492. - Enabling power: Road Traffic Regulation Act 1984, s. 14 (1) (a). - Made: 29.08.2008. Coming into force: 05.09.2008. Effect: None. Territorial extent & classification: E. Local *Unpublished*

The A38 Trunk Road (Branston, Staffordshire) (Temporary Restriction and Prohibition of Traffic) Order 2008 No. 2008/353. - Enabling power: Road Traffic Regulation Act 1984, s. 14 (1) (a). - Made: 25.01.2008. Coming into force: 01.02.2008. Effect: None. Territorial extent & classification: E. Local *Unpublished*

The A38 Trunk Road (Chudleigh to Splatford Junction, Devon) (Temporary Prohibition and Restriction of Traffic) Order 2008 No. 2008/1254. - Enabling power: Road Traffic Regulation Act 1984, s. 14 (1) (a). - Made: 30.04.2008. Coming into force: 03.05.2008. Effect: None. Territorial extent & classification: E. Local *Unpublished*

The A38 Trunk Road (Clay Mills to Egginton) (Temporary Restriction and Prohibition of Traffic) Order 2008 No. 2008/2741. - Enabling power: Road Traffic Regulation Act 1984, s. 14 (1) (a). - Made: 03.10.2008. Coming into force: 10.10.2008. Effect: None. Territorial extent & classification: E. Local *Unpublished*

The A38 Trunk Road (Cornwall Layby Closures - Various Sities) (Temporary Prohibition of Traffic) Order 2008 No. 2008/2591. - Enabling power: Road Traffic Regulation Act 1984, s. 14 (1) (a). - Made: 23.09.2008. Coming into force: 27.09.2008. Effect: None. Territorial extent & classification: E. Local *Unpublished*

The A38 Trunk Road (Deep Lane Junction, Near Plymouth, Devon) (Temporary Prohibition of Traffic) Order 2008 No. 2008/2406. - Enabling power: Road Traffic Regulation Act 1984, s. 14 (1) (a). - Made: 03.09.2008. Coming into force: 09.09.2008. Effect: None. Territorial extent & classification: E. Local *Unpublished*

The A38 Trunk Road (Devon Layby Closures - Various Sities) (Temporary Prohibition of Traffic) Order 2008 No. 2008/2590. - Enabling power: Road Traffic Regulation Act 1984, s. 14 (1) (a). - Made: 23.09.2008. Coming into force: 27.09.2008. Effect: None. Territorial extent & classification: E. Local *Unpublished*

The A38 Trunk Road (Dobwalls Bypass Westbound Entry Slip Road, Liskeard) (Temporary Prohibition and Restriction of Traffic) Order 2008 No. 2008/2461. - Enabling power: Road Traffic Regulation Act 1984, s. 14 (1) (a). - Made: 10.09.2008. Coming into force: 13.09.2008. Effect: None. Territorial extent & classification: E. Local *Unpublished*

The A38 Trunk Road (Dobwalls, Liskeard, Cornwall) (Temporary Prohibition and Restriction of Traffic) (Number 2) Order 2008 No. 2008/2057. - Enabling power: Road Traffic Regulation Act 1984, ss. 14 (1) (a), 122A. - Made: 16.07.2008. Coming into force: 21.07.2008. Effect: None. Territorial extent & classification: E. Local *Unpublished*

The A38 Trunk Road (Dobwalls, Liskeard, Cornwall) (Temporary Prohibition and Restriction of Traffic) Order 2008 No. 2008/1155. - Enabling power: Road Traffic Regulation Act 1984, ss. 14 (1) (a), 122A. - Made: 16.04.2008. Coming into force: 19.04.2008. Effect: None. Territorial extent & classification: E. Local *Unpublished*

The A38 Trunk Road (Drybridge Junction, Near South Brent, Devon) (Temporary Prohibition and Restriction of Traffic) Order 2008 No. 2008/1671. - Enabling power: Road Traffic Regulation Act 1984, s. 14 (1) (a). - Made: 18.06.2008. Coming into force: 21.06.2008. Effect: None. Territorial extent & classification: E. Local *Unpublished*

The A38 Trunk Road (Findern Interchange, Derbyshire) (Temporary Prohibition of Traffic) Order 2008 No. 2008/1987. - Enabling power: Road Traffic Regulation Act 1984, s. 14 (1) (a). - Made: 02.07.2008. Coming into force: 09.07.2008. Effect: None. Territorial extent & classification: E. Local *Unpublished*

The A38 Trunk Road (Goodstone to Drumbridges, Near Newton Abbot, Devon) (Temporary Prohibition and Restriction of Traffic) Order 2008 No. 2008/2150. - Enabling power: Road Traffic Regulation Act 1984, s. 14 (1) (a). - Made: 30.07.2008. Coming into force: 02.08.2008. Effect: None. Territorial extent & classification: E. Local *Unpublished*

The A38 Trunk Road (Goodstone to Whistley Hill, Near Ashburton, Devon) (Temporary Prohibition and Restriction of Traffic) Order 2008 No. 2008/2530. - Enabling power: Road Traffic Regulation Act 1984, s. 14 (1) (a). - Made: 17.09.2008. Coming into force: 20.09.2008. Effect: None. Territorial extent & classification: E. Local *Unpublished*

The A38 Trunk Road (Holbrook to Little Eaton, Derbyshire) (Temporary Restriction and Prohibition of Traffic) Order 2008 No. 2008/869. - Enabling power: Road Traffic Regulation Act 1984, s. 14 (1) (a). - Made: 29.02.2008. Coming into force: 07.03.2008. Effect: None. Territorial extent & classification: E. Local *Unpublished*

The A38 Trunk Road (Kingsteignton Over Bridge, Chudleigh Knighton, Devon) (Temporary Prohibition and Restriction of Traffic) Order 2008 No. 2008/2405. - Enabling power: Road Traffic Regulation Act 1984, s. 14 (1) (a). - Made: 03.09.2008. Coming into force: 06.09.2008. Effect: None. Territorial extent & classification: E. Local *Unpublished*

The A38 Trunk Road (Lee Mill Eastbound Exit Slip Road, near Ivybridge, Devon) (Temporary Prohibition of Traffic) Order 2008 No. 2008/477. - Enabling power: Road Traffic Regulation Act 1984, s. 14 (1) (a). - Made: 20.02.2008. Coming into force: 23.02.2008. Effect: None. Territorial extent & classification: E. Local *Unpublished*

The A38 Trunk Road (Lee Mill, Near Ivybridge, Devon to Merafield Road Overbridge, Plympton, Plymouth) (Temporary Prohibition of Traffic) Order 2008 No. 2008/3370. - Enabling power: Road Traffic Regulation Act 1984, s. 14 (1) (a). - Made: 30.12.2008. Coming into force: 03.01.2009. Effect: None. Territorial extent & classification: E. Local *Unpublished*

The A38 Trunk Road (Lower Dean Layby Closure, Devon) (Temporary Prohibition of Traffic) Order 2008 No. 2008/104. - Enabling power: Road Traffic Regulation Act 1984, s. 14 (1) (a). - Made: 15.01.2008. Coming into force: 18.01.2008. Effect: None. Territorial extent & classification: E. Local *Unpublished*

The A38 Trunk Road (Marley Head Junction, Near South Brent, Devon) (Temporary Prohibition of Traffic) Order 2008 No. 2008/2407. - Enabling power: Road Traffic Regulation Act 1984, s. 14 (1) (a). - Made: 03.09.2008. Coming into force: 08.09.2008. Effect: None. Territorial extent & classification: E. Local *Unpublished*

The A38 Trunk Road (Marley Head to South Brent, near Ivybridge, Devon) (Temporary Prohibition of Traffic) Order 2008 No. 2008/826. - Enabling power: Road Traffic Regulation Act 1984, s. 14 (1) (a). - Made: 26.02.2008. Coming into force: 01.03.2008. Effect: None. Territorial extent & classification: E. Local *Unpublished*

The A38 Trunk Road (Menheniot, Near Liskeard, Cornwall) (Temporary Prohibition and Restriction of Traffic) Order 2008 No. 2008/828. - Enabling power: Road Traffic Regulation Act 1984, ss. 14 (1) (a). - Made: 27.02.2008. Coming into force: 01.03.2008. Effect: None. Territorial extent & classification: E. Local *Unpublished*

The A38 Trunk Road (Minworth to Derby) and the M6 Toll Motorway (Temporary Restriction and Prohibition of Traffic) Order 2008 No. 2008/1985. - Enabling power: Road Traffic Regulation Act 1984, s. 14 (1) (a). - Made: 03.07.2008. Coming into force: 10.07.2008. Effect: None. Territorial extent & classification: E. Local *Unpublished*

The A38 Trunk Road (Notter Bridge to Landrake, Cornwall) (Temporary Prohibition and Restriction of Traffic) Order 2008 No. 2008/2460. - Enabling power: Road Traffic Regulation Act 1984, s. 14 (1) (a) (7). - Made: 10.09.2008. Coming into force: 13.09.2008. Effect: None. Territorial extent & classification: E. Local *Unpublished*

The A38 Trunk Road (Ripley, Derbyshire) (Temporary Prohibition of Traffic) Order 2008 No. 2008/2886. - Enabling power: Road Traffic Regulation Act 1984, s. 14 (1) (a). - Made: 20.10.2008. Coming into force: 27.10.2008. Effect: None. Territorial extent & classification: E. Local *Unpublished*

The A38 Trunk Road (Streethay, Near Lichfield, Staffordshire) (Temporary Prohibition and Restriction of Traffic) Order 2008 No. 2008/2965. - Enabling power: Road Traffic Regulation Act 1984, s. 14 (1) (a). - Made: 24.10.2008. Coming into force: 31.10.2008. Effect: None. Territorial extent & classification: E. Local *Unpublished*

The A38 Trunk Road (Streethay, Staffordshire) (Temporary Prohibition of Traffic) Order 2008 No. 2008/2123. - Enabling power: Road Traffic Regulation Act 1984, s. 14 (1) (a). - Made: 22.07.2008. Coming into force: 29.07.2008. Effect: None. Territorial extent & classification: E. Local *Unpublished*

The A38 Trunk Road (Swinfen Island to Weeford Island, Staffordshire) (Temporary Restriction and Prohibition of Traffic) Order 2008 No. 2008/1827. - Enabling power: Road Traffic Regulation Act 1984, s. 14 (1) (a). - Made: 20.06.2008. Coming into force: 27.06.2008. Effect: None. Territorial extent & classification: E. Local *Unpublished*

The A38 Trunk Road (Swinfen, Staffordshire) (Closure of Gap in the Central Reservation) Order 2008 No. 2008/2804. - Enabling power: Road Traffic Regulation Act 1984, ss. 1 (1), 2 (1) (2). - Made: 10.10.2008. Coming into force: 24.10.2008. Effect: None. Territorial extent & classification: E. Local *Unpublished*

The A38 Trunk Road (Swinfen, Staffordshire) (Closure of Gap in the Central Reservation, Prohibition of Entry and One Way) Order 2008 No. 2008/2803. - Enabling power: Road Traffic Regulation Act 1984, ss. 1 (1), 2 (1) (2). - Made: 10.10.2008. Coming into force: 24.10.2008. Effect: None. Territorial extent & classification: E. Local *Unpublished*

The A38 Trunk Road (Swinfen, Staffordshire) (Temporary Restriction and Prohibition of Traffic) Order 2008 No. 2008/354. - Enabling power: Road Traffic Regulation Act 1984, s. 14 (1) (a). - Made: 28.01.2008. Coming into force: 04.02.2008. Effect: None. Territorial extent & classification: E. Local *Unpublished*

The A38 Trunk Road (Toyota Interchange, Derbyshire) (Slip Road) (Temporary Prohibition of Traffic) Order 2008 No. 2008/1542. - Enabling power: Road Traffic Regulation Act 1984, s. 14 (1) (a). - Made: 02.06.2008. Coming into force: 09.06.2008. Effect: None. Territorial extent & classification: E. Local *Unpublished*

The A38 Trunk Road (Trerulefoot to Heskyn Mill, Tideford, Cornwall) (Temporary Prohibition of Traffic) Order 2008 No. 2008/1834. - Enabling power: Road Traffic Regulation Act 1984, s. 14 (1) (a). - Made: 01.07.2008. Coming into force: 03.07.2008. Effect: None. Territorial extent & classification: E. Local *Unpublished*

The A38 Trunk Road (Trethawle Railway Bridge, Liskeard) (Temporary Restriction of Traffic) Order 2008 No. 2008/3371. - Enabling power: Road Traffic Regulation Act 1984, s. 14 (1) (a). - Made: 30.12.2008. Coming into force: 03.01.2009. Effect: None. Territorial extent & classification: E. Local *Unpublished*

The A38 Trunk Road (Turfdown Roundabout to Twelvewoods Roundabout, Near Bodmin) (Temporary Prohibition and Restriction of Traffic) Order 2008 No. 2008/2925. - Enabling power: Road Traffic Regulation Act 1984, s. 14 (1) (a). - Made: 04.11.2008. Coming into force: 08.11.2008. Effect: None. Territorial extent & classification: E. Local *Unpublished*

The A38 Trunk Road (Twelvewoods Roundabout to Dobwalls, Cornwall) (Temporary Prohibition and Restriction of Traffic) Order 2008 No. 2008/2287. - Enabling power: Road Traffic Regulation Act 1984, s. 14 (1) (a). - Made: 19.08.2008. Coming into force: 23.08.2008. Effect: None. Territorial extent & classification: E. Local. - Revoked by S.I. 2008/3321 (Unpublished) *Unpublished*

The A38 Trunk Road (Twelvewoods Roundabout to Dobwalls, Cornwall) (Temporary Prohibition and Restriction of Traffic) Order 2008 No. 2008/3321. - Enabling power: Road Traffic Regulation Act 1984, s. 14 (1) (a), sch. 9, para. 27 (1). - Made: 16.12.2008. Coming into force: 02.01.2009. Effect: S.I. 2008/2287 revoked. Territorial extent & classification: E. Local *Unpublished*

The A38 Trunk Road (Voss Farm Interchange, Near Plympton, Devon) (Slip Road Closure) (Experimental) Order 2008 No. 2008/2984. - Enabling power: Road Traffic Regulation Act 1984, ss. 9 (1) (3), 10 (1) (2), 14 (1), sch. 9, para. 27 (1). - Made: 13.11.2008. Coming into force: 04.12.2008. Effect: S.I. 2007/1692 revoked. Territorial extent & classification: E. Local *Unpublished*

The A38 Trunk Road (Watchorn Interchange, Alfreton, Derbyshire) (Temporary Prohibition of Traffic) Order 2008 No. 2008/2249. - Enabling power: Road Traffic Regulation Act 1984, s. 14 (1) (a). - Made: 12.08.2008. Coming into force: 19.08.2008. Effect: None. Territorial extent & classification: E. Local *Unpublished*

The A38 Trunk Road (Weeford Roundabout to Swinfen Roundabout) and the A5148 Trunk Road (Swinfen Roundabout to Wall Roundabout) (Temporary Prohibition of Traffic) Order 2008 No. 2008/2582. - Enabling power: Road Traffic Regulation Act 1984, s. 14 (1) (a). - Made: 12.09.2008. Coming into force: 19.09.2008. Effect: None. Territorial extent & classification: E. Local *Unpublished*

The A38 Trunk Road (Weeford, Staffordshire) (Closure of Gap in the Central Reservation and Prohibition of U-Turns) Order 2008 No. 2008/3347. - Enabling power: Road Traffic Regulation Act 1984, s. 1 (1), 2 (1) (2). - Made: 23.12.2008. Coming into force: 07.01.2009. Effect: S.I. 2002/449 revoked. Territorial extent & classification: E. Local *Unpublished*

The A38 Trunk Road (Weeford, Staffordshire) (Temporary Restriction and Prohibition of Traffic) Order 2008 No. 2008/3353. - Enabling power: Road Traffic Regulation Act 1984, s. 14 (1) (a). - Made: 22.12.2008. Coming into force: 29.12.2008. Effect: None. Territorial extent & classification: E. Local *Unpublished*

The A38 Trunk Road (Weeford to Bassetts Pole, Staffordshire) (Temporary Prohibition of Traffic) Order 2008 No. 2008/2573. - Enabling power: Road Traffic Regulation Act 1984, s. 14 (1) (a). - Made: 15.09.2008. Coming into force: 22.09.2008. Effect: None. Territorial extent & classification: E. Local *Unpublished*

The A38 Trunk Road (Wobbly Wheel Interchange to Haldon Hill, Devon) (Temporary Restriction of Traffic) Order 2008 No. 2008/2408. - Enabling power: Road Traffic Regulation Act 1984, s. 14 (1) (a). - Made: 03.09.2008. Coming into force: 06.09.2008. Effect: None. Territorial extent & classification: E. Local *Unpublished*

The A40 and A49 Trunk Roads (Ross-on-Wye, Herefordshire) (Temporary Restriction and Prohibition of Traffic) (No. 2) Order 2008 No. 2008/3343. - Enabling power: Road Traffic Regulation Act 1984, s. 14 (1) (a). - Made: 22.12.2008. Coming into force: 29.12.2008. Effect: None. Territorial extent & classification: E. Local *Unpublished*

The A40 and A49 Trunk Roads (Ross-on-Wye, Herefordshire) (Temporary Restriction and Prohibition of Traffic) Order 2008 No. 2008/2578. - Enabling power: Road Traffic Regulation Act 1984, s. 14 (1) (a). - Made: 12.09.2008. Coming into force: 19.09.2008. Effect: None. Territorial extent & classification: E. Local *Unpublished*

The A40 Trunk Road (Denham Roundabout) (Temporary Prohibition of Traffic) Order 2008 No. 2008/2065. - Enabling power: Road Traffic Regulation Act 1984, s. 14 (1) (a), sch. 9, para. 27 (1). - Made: 21.07.2009. Coming into force: 01.08.2009. Effect: S.I. 2007/2450 revoked. Territorial extent & classification: E. Local *Unpublished*

The A40 Trunk Road (Overross Industrial Estate to Hildersley Roundabout, Ross-on-Wye) (Temporary Prohibition of Traffic) Order 2008 No. 2008/1392. - Enabling power: Road Traffic Regulation Act 1984, s. 14 (1) (a). - Made: 20.05.2008. Coming into force: 23.05.2008. Effect: None. Territorial extent & classification: E. Local *Unpublished*

The A40 Trunk Road (Over Roundabout to Higham Roundabout, Bus Lane, Gloucestershire) (Temporary Prohibition of Traffic) Order 2008 No. 2008/2907. - Enabling power: Road Traffic Regulation Act 1984, s. 14 (1) (b). - Made: 28.10.2008. Coming into force: 31.10.2008. Effect: None. Territorial extent & classification: E. Local *Unpublished*

The A40 Trunk Road (Over Roundabout to Highnam Roundabout, Gloucestershire) (Number 2) (Temporary Prohibition of Traffic) Order 2008 No. 2008/1675. - Enabling power: Road Traffic Regulation Act 1984, s. 14 (1) (a) (7). - Made: 18.06.2008. Coming into force: 21.06.2008. Effect: None. Territorial extent & classification: E. Local *Unpublished*

The A40 Trunk Road (Over Roundabout to Highnam Roundabout, Gloucestershire) (Temporary Prohibition and Restriction of Traffic) Order 2008 No. 2008/1001. - Enabling power: Road Traffic Regulation Act 1984, s. 14 (1) (a). - Made: 26.03.2008. Coming into force: 29.03.2008. Effect: None. Territorial extent & classification: E. Local *Unpublished*

The A40 Trunk Road (Ross-On-Wye, Herefordshire) (Temporary 40 Miles Per Hour Speed Restriction) Order 2008 No. 2008/2661. - Enabling power: Road Traffic Regulation Act 1984, s. 14 (1) (a). - Made: 26.09.2008. Coming into force: 03.10.2008. Effect: None. Territorial extent & classification: E. Local *Unpublished*

The A40 Trunk Road (Ross-on-Wye, Herefordshire) (Temporary Restriction of Traffic) Order 2008 No. 2008/2491. - Enabling power: Road Traffic Regulation Act 1984, s. 14 (1) (a). - Made: 01.09.2008. Coming into force: 08.09.2008. Effect: None. Territorial extent & classification: E. Local *Unpublished*

The A40 Trunk Road (Ross-on-Wye, Hertfordshire) (Temporary Restriction and Prohibition of Traffic) Order 2008 No. 2008/2455. - Enabling power: Road Traffic Regulation Act 1984, s. 14 (1) (a). - Made: 01.09.2008. Coming into force: 08.09.2008. Effect: None. Territorial extent & classification: E. Local *Unpublished*

The A43 Trunk Road (Baynards Green Roundabout, Cherwell, Oxfordshire to Barley Mow Roundabout, South of Brackley, Northamptonshire) (Temporary Prohibition of Traffic) Order 2008 No. 2008/2606. - Enabling power: Road Traffic Regulation Act 1984, s. 14 (1) (a). - Made: 23.09.2008. Coming into force: 30.09.2008. Effect: None. Territorial extent & classification: E. Local. - Revoked by S.I. 2009/327 *Unpublished*

The A43 Trunk Road (Renault World Series Event, Silverstone, Northamptonshire) (Temporary Restriction and Prohibition of Traffic) Order 2008 No. 2008/1517. - Enabling power: Road Traffic Regulation Act 1984, s. 14 (1) (b). - Made: 27.05.2008. Coming into force: 03.06.2008. Effect: None. Territorial extent & classification: E. Local *Unpublished*

The A43 Trunk Road (Silverstone British Grand Prix, Brackley to Towcester, Northamptonshire) (Temporary Restriction and Prohibition of Traffic) Order 2008 No. 2008/1667. - Enabling power: Road Traffic Regulation Act 1984, s. 14 (1) (b). - Made: 16.06.2008. Coming into force: 23.06.2008. Effect: None. Territorial extent & classification: E. Local *Unpublished*

The A43 Trunk Road (Various Laybys, Baynards Green, Oxfordshire to Tiffield, Northamptonshire) (Temporary Prohibition of Traffic) Order 2008 No. 2008/2048. - Enabling power: Road Traffic Regulation Act 1984, s. 14 (1) (a). - Made: 15.07.2008. Coming into force: 22.07.2008. Effect: None. Territorial extent & classification: E. Local *Unpublished*

The A45 and A46 Trunk Roads (Festival Island) (Temporary Prohibition of Traffic) Order 2008 No. 2008/1637. - Enabling power: Road Traffic Regulation Act 1984, s. 14 (1) (a). - Made: 09.06.2008. Coming into force: 16.06.2008. Effect: None. Territorial extent & classification: E. Local *Unpublished*

The A45 Trunk Road (A508 Queen Eleanor
Interchange, Northamptonshire) (Temporary
Prohibition of Traffic) Order 2008 No. 2008/1401. -
Enabling power: Road Traffic Regulation Act 1984, s. 14
(1) (a). - Made: 19.05.2008. Coming into force:
27.05.2008. Effect: None. Territorial extent &
classification: E. Local *Unpublished*

The A45 Trunk Road (A509 Little Irchester
Interchange, Northamptonshire) (Temporary
Prohibition of Traffic) Order 2008 No. 2008/830. -
Enabling power: Road Traffic Regulation Act 1984, s. 14
(1) (a). - Made: 25.02.2008. Coming into force:
03.03.2008. Effect: None. Territorial extent &
classification: E. Local *Unpublished*

The A45 Trunk Road (A509 Turnells Mill Interchange,
Wellingborough, Northamptonshire) (Temporary
Prohibition of Traffic) Order 2008 No. 2008/2277. -
Enabling power: Road Traffic Regulation Act 1984, s. 14
(1) (a). - Made: 19.08.2008. Coming into force:
26.08.2008. Effect: None. Territorial extent &
classification: E. Local *Unpublished*

The A45 Trunk Road (Brackmills Interchange,
Northamptonshire) (Temporary Restriction and
Prohibition of Traffic) Order 2008 No. 2008/2130. -
Enabling power: Road Traffic Regulation Act 1984, s. 14
(1) (a). - Made: 28.07.2008. Coming into force:
04.08.2008. Effect: None. Territorial extent &
classification: E. Local *Unpublished*

The A45 Trunk Road (Higham Ferrers to Stanwick,
Northamptonshire) (Temporary Prohibition of Traffic)
Order 2008 No. 2008/486. - Enabling power: Road Traffic
Regulation Act 1984, s. 14 (1) (a). - Made: 18.02.2008.
Coming into force: 25.02.2008. Effect: None. Territorial
extent & classification: E. Local *Unpublished*

The A45 Trunk Road (London Road, Warwickshire)
(Temporary Restriction of Traffic) Order 2008 No.
2008/142. - Enabling power: Road Traffic Regulation Act
1984, s. 14 (1) (a). - Made: 02.01.2008. Coming into force:
09.01.2008. Effect: None. Territorial extent &
classification: E. Local *Unpublished*

The A45 Trunk Road (Ryton-on-Dunsmore to Tollbar
End, Warwickshire) (Temporary Prohibition of
Traffic) Order 2008 No. 2008/2458. - Enabling power:
Road Traffic Regulation Act 1984, s. 14 (1) (a). - Made:
02.09.2008. Coming into force: 09.09.2008. Effect: None.
Territorial extent & classification: E. Local *Unpublished*

The A45 Trunk Road (Stretton-on-Dunsmore to
Festival Island, Coventry) (Temporary Prohibition and
Restriction of Traffic) Order 2008 No. 2008/2744. -
Enabling power: Road Traffic Regulation Act 1984, s. 14
(1) (a). - Made: 03.10.2008. Coming into force:
10.10.2008. Effect: None. Territorial extent &
classification: E. Local *Unpublished*

The A45 Trunk Road (Stretton-on-Dunsmore to
Ryton-on-Dunsmore, Warwickshire) (Temporary
Prohibition of Traffic) Order 2008 No. 2008/145. -
Enabling power: Road Traffic Regulation Act 1984, s. 14
(1) (a). - Made: 11.01.2008. Coming into force:
18.01.2008. Effect: None. Territorial extent &
classification: E. Local *Unpublished*

The A45 Trunk Road (Thurlaston to
Ryton-on-Dunsmore) (Temporary Restriction and
Prohibition of Traffic) Order 2008 No. 2008/2459. -
Enabling power: Road Traffic Regulation Act 1984, s. 14
(1) (a). - Made: 29.08.2008. Coming into force:
05.09.2008. Effect: None. Territorial extent &
classification: E. Local *Unpublished*

The A45 Trunk Road (Wellingborough Interchange,
Northamptonshire) Westbound Exit Slip Road
(Temporary Restriction and Prohibition of Traffic)
Order 2008 No. 2008/2729. - Enabling power: Road
Traffic Regulation Act 1984, s. 14 (1) (a). - Made:
06.10.2008. Coming into force: 13.10.2008. Effect: None.
Territorial extent & classification: E. Local *Unpublished*

The A45 Trunk Road (Weston Favell to Earls Barton,
Northamptonshire) (Temporary Restriction and
Prohibition of Traffic) Order 2008 No. 2008/1217. -
Enabling power: Road Traffic Regulation Act 1984, s. 14
(1) (a). - Made: 21.04.2008. Coming into force:
28.04.2008. Effect: None. Territorial extent &
classification: E. Local *Unpublished*

The A46 and A52 Trunk Roads (Radcliffe on Trent to
Farndon, Nottinghamshire) (Temporary Restriction of
Traffic) Order 2008 No. 2008/1291. - Enabling power:
Road Traffic Regulation Act 1984, s. 14 (1) (a). - Made:
21.04.2008. Coming into force: 28.04.2008. Effect: None.
Territorial extent & classification: E. Local *Unpublished*

The A46 and A435 Trunk Roads (Oversley
Roundabout, Warwickshire) (Temporary Restriction of
Traffic) Order 2008 No. 2008/60. - Enabling power: Road
Traffic Regulation Act 1984, s. 14 (1) (a). - Made:
07.01.2008. Coming into force: 14.01.2008. Effect: None.
Territorial extent & classification: E. Local *Unpublished*

The A46 Trunk Road and M69 Motorway (Near
Coventry) (Temporary Prohibition and Restriction of
Traffic) Order 2008 No. 2008/2883. - Enabling power:
Road Traffic Regulation Act 1984, s. 14 (1) (a) (7). -
Made: 20.10.2008. Coming into force: 27.10.2008. Effect:
None. Territorial extent & classification: E. Local
Unpublished

The A46 Trunk Road (Ashton under Hill to Hinton
Cross, Worcestershire) (Temporary Restriction and
Prohibition of Traffic) Order 2008 No. 2008/2585. -
Enabling power: Road Traffic Regulation Act 1984, s. 14
(1) (a). - Made: 17.09.2008. Coming into force:
24.09.2008. Effect: None. Territorial extent &
classification: E. Local *Unpublished*

The A46 Trunk Road (Beckford, Worcestershire) (Temporary Restriction of Traffic) Order 2008 No. 2008/2005. - Enabling power: Road Traffic Regulation Act 1984, s. 14 (1) (a). - Made: 07.07.2008. Coming into force: 14.07.2008. Effect: None. Territorial extent & classification: E. Local *Unpublished*

The A46 Trunk Road (Between Skellingthorpe Roundabout and Riseholme Roundabout, Lincolnshire) (Temporary Prohibition of Traffic) Order 2008 No. 2008/1679. - Enabling power: Road Traffic Regulation Act 1984, s. 14 (1) (a). - Made: 16.06.2008. Coming into force: 23.06.2008. Effect: None. Territorial extent & classification: E. Local *Unpublished*

The A46 Trunk Road (Bishopton, Warwickshire) (Temporary Restriction of Traffic) Order 2008 No. 2008/193. - Enabling power: Road Traffic Regulation Act 1984, s. 14 (1) (a). - Made: 21.01.2008. Coming into force: 28.01.2008. Effect: None. Territorial extent & classification: E. Local *Unpublished*

The A46 Trunk Road (Charmy Down Layby, near Bath) (Temporary Prohibition of Traffic) Order 2008 No. 2008/2653. - Enabling power: Road Traffic Regulation Act 1984, s. 14 (1) (b). - Made: 30.09.2008. Coming into force: 03.10.2008. Effect: None. Territorial extent & classification: E. Local *Unpublished*

The A46 Trunk Road (Charmy Down, Near Bath) (Layby Closure) Order 2008 No. 2008/3366. - Enabling power: Road Traffic Regulation Act 1984, ss. 1 (1), 2 (1) (2), 4 (1). - Made: 29.12.2008. Coming into force: 12.01.2009. Effect: None. Territorial extent & classification: E. Local *Unpublished*

The A46 Trunk Road (Cold Ashton Roundabout to Hall Lane, near Tadwick) (Temporary Prohibition of Traffic) Order 2008 No. 2008/1399. - Enabling power: Road Traffic Regulation Act 1984, s. 14 (1) (a). - Made: 21.05.2008. Coming into force: 24.05.2008. Effect: None. Territorial extent & classification: E. Local *Unpublished*

The A46 Trunk Road (Cold Ashton Roundabout to M4 Junction 18) (Temporary Prohibition of Traffic) Order 2008 No. 2008/1393. - Enabling power: Road Traffic Regulation Act 1984, s. 14 (1) (a). - Made: 20.05.2008. Coming into force: 23.05.2008. Effect: None. Territorial extent & classification: E. Local *Unpublished*

The A46 Trunk Road (Junction with A6, Wanlip, Leicestershire) (Slip Roads) (Temporary Prohibition of Traffic) Order 2008 No. 2008/1362. - Enabling power: Road Traffic Regulation Act 1984, s. 14 (1) (a). - Made: 06.05.2008. Coming into force: 13.05.2008. Effect: None. Territorial extent & classification: E. Local *Unpublished*

The A46 Trunk Road (Leek Wooton to Warwick) (Temporary Restriction and Prohibition of Traffic) Order 2008 No. 2008/332. - Enabling power: Road Traffic Regulation Act 1984, s. 14 (1) (a). - Made: 01.02.2008. Coming into force: 08.02.2008. Effect: None. Territorial extent & classification: E. Local *Unpublished*

The A46 Trunk Road (Near Thrussington, Leicestershire) (Temporary Prohibition of Traffic) Order 2008 No. 2008/3350. - Enabling power: Road Traffic Regulation Act 1984, s. 14 (1) (a). - Made: 29.12.2008. Coming into force: 05.01.2009. Effect: None. Territorial extent & classification: E. Local *Unpublished*

The A46 Trunk Road (Near Widmerpool, Nottinghamshire) (Temporary Prohibition of Traffic in Layby) Order 2008 No. 2008/2385. - Enabling power: Road Traffic Regulation Act 1984, s. 14 (1) (a). - Made: 19.08.2008. Coming into force: 26.08.2008. Effect: None. Territorial extent & classification: E. Local *Unpublished*

The A46 Trunk Road (North of Six Hills, Leicestershire) (Slip Road) (Temporary Prohibition of Traffic) (No. 2) Order 2008 No. 2008/2248. - Enabling power: Road Traffic Regulation Act 1984, s. 14 (1) (a). - Made: 12.08.2008. Coming into force: 19.08.2008. Effect: None. Territorial extent & classification: E. Local *Unpublished*

The A46 Trunk Road (North of Six Hills, Leicestershire) (Slip Road) (Temporary Prohibition of Traffic) Order 2008 No. 2008/1297. - Enabling power: Road Traffic Regulation Act 1984, s. 14 (1) (a). - Made: 25.04.2008. Coming into force: 02.05.2008. Effect: None. Territorial extent & classification: E. Local *Unpublished*

The A46 Trunk Road (Oversley, Near Alcester, Warwickshire) (Temporary Restriction and Prohibition of Traffic) Order 2008 No. 2008/1153. - Enabling power: Road Traffic Regulation Act 1984, s. 14 (1) (a). - Made: 11.04.2008. Coming into force: 18.04.2008. Effect: None. Territorial extent & classification: E. Local *Unpublished*

The A46 Trunk Road (Salford Priors) (Temporary Restriction of Traffic) Order 2008 No. 2008/2003. - Enabling power: Road Traffic Regulation Act 1984, s. 14 (1) (a). - Made: 30.06.2008. Coming into force: 07.07.2008. Effect: None. Territorial extent & classification: E. Local *Unpublished*

The A46 Trunk Road (Salford Priors, Warwickshire) (Temporary Restriction of Traffic) Order 2008 No. 2008/2116. - Enabling power: Road Traffic Regulation Act 1984, s. 14 (1) (a). - Made: 21.07.2008. Coming into force: 28.07.2008. Effect: None. Territorial extent & classification: E. Local *Unpublished*

The A46 Trunk Road (Saxondale to Newark-on-Trent, Nottinghamshire) (Temporary Restriction and Prohibition of Traffic) Order 2008 No. 2008/2885. - Enabling power: Road Traffic Regulation Act 1984, s. 14 (1) (a). - Made: 20.10.2008. Coming into force: 27.10.2008. Effect: None. Territorial extent & classification: E. Local *Unpublished*

The A46 Trunk Road (Six Hills to Ratcliffe on the Wreake) (Temporary Restriction and Prohibition of Traffic) Order 2008 No. 2008/351. - Enabling power: Road Traffic Regulation Act 1984, s. 14 (1) (a). - Made: 01.02.2008. Coming into force: 08.02.2008. Effect: None. Territorial extent & classification: E. Local *Unpublished*

Road traffic: Traffic regulation

The A46 Trunk Road (South of Coventry) (Temporary Restriction and Prohibition of Traffic) Order 2008 No. 2008/2882. - Enabling power: Road Traffic Regulation Act 1984, ss. 3 (2), 14 (1) (a) (5) (b) (6). - Made: 17.10.2008. Coming into force: 24.10.2008. Effect: None. Territorial extent & classification: E. Local *Unpublished*

The A46 Trunk Road (Stratford Northern Bypass, Warwickshire) (Temporary 40 Miles Per Hour Speed Restriction) Order 2008 No. 2008/2391. - Enabling power: Road Traffic Regulation Act 1984, s. 14 (1) (a). - Made: 19.08.2008. Coming into force: 26.08.2008. Effect: None. Territorial extent & classification: E. Local *Unpublished*

The A46 Trunk Road (Syston, Leicestershire) (Temporary Restriction and Prohibition of Traffic) Order 2008 No. 2008/3044. - Enabling power: Road Traffic Regulation Act 1984, s. 14 (1) (a). - Made: 07.11.2008. Coming into force: 14.11.2008. Effect: None. Territorial extent & classification: E. Local *Unpublished*

The A46 Trunk Road (Teddington Hands, Gloucestershire) (Temporary Restriction of Traffic) Order 2008 No. 2008/388. - Enabling power: Road Traffic Regulation Act 1984, s. 14 (1) (a). - Made: 11.02.2008. Coming into force: 18.02.2008. Effect: None. Territorial extent & classification: E. Local *Unpublished*

The A46 Trunk Road (Vicarage Lane, Warwickshire) (Temporary Prohibition of Traffic) Order 2008 No. 2008/2222. - Enabling power: Road Traffic Regulation Act 1984, s. 14 (1) (a). - Made: 04.08.2008. Coming into force: 11.08.2008. Effect: None. Territorial extent & classification: E. Local *Unpublished*

The A46 Trunk Road (Warwick Bypass) (Temporary Restriction and Prohibition of Traffic) (No. 2) Order 2008 No. 2008/3228. - Enabling power: Road Traffic Regulation Act 1984, s. 14 (1) (a). - Made: 14.11.2008. Coming into force: 21.11.2008. Effect: None. Territorial extent & classification: E. Local *Unpublished*

The A46 Trunk Road (Warwick Bypass) (Temporary Restriction and Prohibition of Traffic) Order 2008 No. 2008/2118. - Enabling power: Road Traffic Regulation Act 1984, s. 14 (1) (a). - Made: 21.07.2008. Coming into force: 28.07.2008. Effect: None. Territorial extent & classification: E. Local *Unpublished*

The A46 Trunk Road (Widmerpool, Nottinghamshire) (Temporary Prohibition of Traffic) Order 2008 No. 2008/110. - Enabling power: Road Traffic Regulation Act 1984, s. 14 (1) (a). - Made: 07.01.2008. Coming into force: 14.01.2008. Effect: None. Territorial extent & classification: E. Local *Unpublished*

The A46 Trunk Road (Widmerpool, Nottinghamshire) (Temporary Restriction of Traffic) Order 2008 No. 2008/57. - Enabling power: Road Traffic Regulation Act 1984, s. 14 (1) (a). - Made: 07.01.2008. Coming into force: 14.01.2008. Effect: None. Territorial extent & classification: E. Local *Unpublished*

The A46 Trunk Road (Widmerpool to Saxondale, Nottinghamshire) (Temporary Prohibition of Traffic) Order 2008 No. 2008/2960. - Enabling power: Road Traffic Regulation Act 1984, s. 14 (1) (a). - Made: 24.10.2008. Coming into force: 31.10.2008. Effect: None. Territorial extent & classification: E. Local *Unpublished*

The A46 Trunk Road (Willoughby Fields and Six Hills, Leicestershire) (Slip Roads) (Temporary Prohibition of Traffic) Order 2008 No. 2008/3349. - Enabling power: Road Traffic Regulation Act 1984, s. 14 (1) (a). - Made: 29.12.2008. Coming into force: 05.01.2009. Effect: None. Territorial extent & classification: E. Local *Unpublished*

The A47 Trunk Road (A47/A15 Interchange, Junction 18 to Bretton Gate Interchange, Junction 16, City of Peterborough) (Temporary Restriction and Prohibition of Traffic) Order 2008 No. 2008/852. - Enabling power: Road Traffic Regulation Act 1984, s. 14 (1) (a). - Made: 03.03.2008. Coming into force: 10.03.2008. Effect: None. Territorial extent & classification: E. Local *Unpublished*

The A47 Trunk Road (Bawburgh to Easton, Norfolk) (Temporary Restriction and Prohibition of Traffic) Order 2008 No. 2008/326. - Enabling power: Road Traffic Regulation Act 1984, s. 14 (1) (a). - Made: 01.02.2008. Coming into force: 08.02.2008. Effect: None. Territorial extent & classification: E. Local *Unpublished*

The A47 Trunk Road (Brundall to Acle, Norfolk) (Temporary Restriction and Prohibition of Traffic) Order 2008 No. 2008/327. - Enabling power: Road Traffic Regulation Act 1984, s. 14 (1) (a). - Made: 01.02.2008. Coming into force: 08.02.2008. Effect: None. Territorial extent & classification: E. Local *Unpublished*

The A47 Trunk Road (C539 Mattishall Road Junction, Honingham, Norfolk) (Temporary Restriction and Prohibition of Traffic) Order 2008 No. 2008/2329. - Enabling power: Road Traffic Regulation Act 1984, s. 14 (1) (a). - Made: 26.08.2008. Coming into force: 02.09.2008. Effect: None. Territorial extent & classification: E. Local *Unpublished*

The A47 Trunk Road (Dereham, Norfolk) (Temporary Restriction and Prohibition of Traffic) Order 2008 No. 2008/2423. - Enabling power: Road Traffic Regulation Act 1984, s. 14 (1) (a). - Made: 02.09.2008. Coming into force: 09.09.2008. Effect: None. Territorial extent & classification: E. Local. - Revoked by S.I. 2009/681 (Unpublished) *Unpublished*

The A47 Trunk Road (Eye Green Bypass, City of Peterborough) (Temporary Restriction and Prohibition of Traffic) Order 2008 No. 2008/3272. - Enabling power: Road Traffic Regulation Act 1984, s. 14 (1) (a). - Made: 21.11.2008. Coming into force: 28.11.2008. Effect: None. Territorial extent & classification: E. Local *Unpublished*

The A47 Trunk Road (Guyhirn, Cambridgeshire) (Temporary Restriction of Traffic) Order 2008 No. 2008/2881. - Enabling power: Road Traffic Regulation Act 1984, s. 14 (1) (a). - Made: 23.10.2008. Coming into force: 30.10.2008. Effect: None. Territorial extent & classification: E. Local *Unpublished*

The A47 Trunk Road (Kings Lynn Southern Bypass, Norfolk) (Temporary Restriction and Prohibition of Traffic) Order 2008 No. 2008/2272. - Enabling power: Road Traffic Regulation Act 1984, s. 14 (1) (a). - Made: 18.08.2008. Coming into force: 29.08.2008. Effect: None. Territorial extent & classification: E. Local *Unpublished*

The A47 Trunk Road (Norwich Southern Bypass, Norfolk) (Temporary Restriction and Prohibition of Traffic) Order 2008 No. 2008/2273. - Enabling power: Road Traffic Regulation Act 1984, s. 14 (1) (a). - Made: 18.08.2008. Coming into force: 26.08.2008. Effect: None. Territorial extent & classification: E. Local. - Revoked by S.I. 2009/102 (Unpublished) *Unpublished*

The A47 Trunk Road (Reedham Road Interchange, Acle, Great Yarmouth, Norfolk) (Temporary Prohibition of Traffic) Order 2008 No. 2008/3189. - Enabling power: Road Traffic Regulation Act 1984, s. 14 (1) (a). - Made: 02.12.2008. Coming into force: 09.12.2008. Effect: None. Territorial extent & classification: E. Local *Unpublished*

The A47 Trunk Road (Scarning, Norfolk) (Temporary Restriction and Prohibition of Traffic) Order 2008 No. 2008/1528. - Enabling power: Road Traffic Regulation Act 1984, s. 14 (1) (a). - Made: 27.05.2008. Coming into force: 03.06.2008. Effect: None. Territorial extent & classification: E. Local *Unpublished*

The A47 Trunk Road (Soke Parkway Interchange, City of Peterborough) (Temporary Restriction and Prohibition of Traffic) Order 2008 No. 2008/1496. - Enabling power: Road Traffic Regulation Act 1984, ss. 14 (1) (a), 15 (2). - Made: 23.05.2008. Coming into force: 30.05.2008. Effect: None. Territorial extent & classification: E. Local *Unpublished*

The A47 Trunk Road (Soke Parkway Interchange, City of Peterborough) (Temporary Restriction and Prohibition of Traffic) Order 2008 Variation Order 2008 No. 2008/2397. - Enabling power: Road Traffic Regulation Act 1984, ss. 14 (1) (a), 15 (2), sch. 9, para. 27 (1). - Made: 01.09.2008. Coming into force: 08.09.2008. Effect: S.I. 2008/1496 varied. Territorial extent & classification: E. Local *Unpublished*

The A47 Trunk Road (Soke Parkway to Wansford, City of Peterborough) (Temporary Restriction and Prohibition of Traffic) Order 2008 No. 2008/2657. - Enabling power: Road Traffic Regulation Act 1984, s. 14 (1) (a). - Made: 29.09.2008. Coming into force: 06.10.2008. Effect: None. Territorial extent & classification: E. Local *Unpublished*

The A47 Trunk Road (Sutton to Bretton Way/Nene Parkway Interchange, Junction 15, City of Peterborough) (Temporary Restriction and Prohibition of Traffic) Order 2008 No. 2008/1156. - Enabling power: Road Traffic Regulation Act 1984, s. 14 (1) (a). - Made: 14.04.2008. Coming into force: 21.04.2008. Effect: None. Territorial extent & classification: E. Local *Unpublished*

The A47 Trunk Road (Thomas Cook Interchange, City of Peterborough) (Temporary Restriction and Prohibition of Traffic) Order 2008 No. 2008/2918. - Enabling power: Road Traffic Regulation Act 1984, s. 14 (1) (a). - Made: 03.11.2008. Coming into force: 10.11.2008. Effect: None. Territorial extent & classification: E. Local *Unpublished*

The A47 Trunk Road (Wansford, City of Peterborough) (Temporary Prohibition of Traffic) Order 2008 No. 2008/2475. - Enabling power: Road Traffic Regulation Act 1984, s. 14 (1) (a). - Made: 08.09.2008. Coming into force: 15.09.2008. Effect: None. Territorial extent & classification: E. Local *Unpublished*

The A47 Trunk Road (Wansford, City of Peterborough) (Temporary Prohibition of Traffic) Order 2008 No. 2008/2905. - Enabling power: Road Traffic Regulation Act 1984, s. 14 (1) (a). - Made: 28.10.2008. Coming into force: 04.11.2008. Effect: None. Territorial extent & classification: E. Local *Unpublished*

The A47 Trunk Road (Wisbech Bypass, Norfolk and Redmoor, Cambridgeshire) (Temporary Restriction and Prohibition of Traffic) Order 2008 No. 2008/3307. - Enabling power: Road Traffic Regulation Act 1984, s. 14 (1) (a). - Made: 15.12.2008. Coming into force: 22.12.2008. Effect: None. Territorial extent & classification: E. Local *Unpublished*

The A49 Trunk Road (Between Bromfield and Craven Arms, Shropshire) (Temporary Prohibition of Traffic) Order 2008 No. 2008/1994. - Enabling power: Road Traffic Regulation Act 1984, s. 14 (1) (a). - Made: 07.07.2008. Coming into force: 14.07.2008. Effect: None. Territorial extent & classification: E. Local *Unpublished*

The A50 Trunk Road (Blythe Bridge to Uttoxeter Bypass) (Temporary Prohibition of Traffic) Order 2008 No. 2008/1534. - Enabling power: Road Traffic Regulation Act 1984, s. 14 (1) (a). - Made: 23.05.2008. Coming into force: 30.05.2008. Effect: None. Territorial extent & classification: E. Local *Unpublished*

The A50 Trunk Road (Doveridge Bypass) (Temporary 50 Miles Per Hour Speed Restriction) Order 2008 No. 2008/134. - Enabling power: Road Traffic Regulation Act 1984, s. 14 (1) (a). - Made: 04.01.2008. Coming into force: 11.01.2008. Effect: None. Territorial extent & classification: E. Local *Unpublished*

The A50 Trunk Road (Doveridge Bypass) (Temporary Prohibition of Traffic) Order 2008 No. 2008/867. - Enabling power: Road Traffic Regulation Act 1984, s. 14 (1) (a). - Made: 29.02.2008. Coming into force: 07.03.2008. Effect: None. Territorial extent & classification: E. Local *Unpublished*

The A50 Trunk Road (Foston to Sudbury, Derbyshire) (Temporary Restriction and Prohibition of Traffic) Order 2008 No. 2008/1539. - Enabling power: Road Traffic Regulation Act 1984, s. 14 (1) (a). - Made: 27.05.2008. Coming into force: 03.06.2008. Effect: None. Territorial extent & classification: E. Local *Unpublished*

The A50 Trunk Road (Grindley Interchange, Staffordshire) (Temporary Prohibition of Traffic) Order 2008 No. 2008/1678. - Enabling power: Road Traffic Regulation Act 1984, s. 14 (1) (a). - Made: 16.06.2008. Coming into force: 23.06.2008. Effect: None. Territorial extent & classification: E. Local *Unpublished*

The A50 Trunk Road (Heron Cross, Stoke-on-Trent) (Temporary Prohibition of Traffic) Order 2008 No. 2008/2489. - Enabling power: Road Traffic Regulation Act 1984, s. 14 (1) (b). - Made: 29.08.2008. Coming into force: 05.09.2008. Effect: None. Territorial extent & classification: E. Local *Unpublished*

The A50 Trunk Road (Heron Cross to Sideway, Stoke-on-Trent) (Temporary Restriction and Prohibition of Traffic) Order 2008 No. 2008/3220. - Enabling power: Road Traffic Regulation Act 1984, s. 14 (1) (a). - Made: 21.11.2008. Coming into force: 28.11.2008. Effect: Non. Territorial extent & classification: E. Local *Unpublished*

The A50 Trunk Road (Junction with Blurton Road, Stokeon Trent) (Temporary Prohibition of Traffic) Order 2008 No. 2008/1294. - Enabling power: Road Traffic Regulation Act 1984, s. 14 (1) (a). - Made: 28.04.2008. Coming into force: 05.05.2008. Effect: None. Territorial extent & classification: E. Local *Unpublished*

The A50 Trunk Road (Junction with the A6, near Chellaston) (Temporary Prohibition of Traffic) Order 2008 No. 2008/1369. - Enabling power: Road Traffic Regulation Act 1984, s. 14 (1) (a). - Made: 05.05.2008. Coming into force: 12.05.2008. Effect: None. Territorial extent & classification: E. Local *Unpublished*

The A50 Trunk Road (Junction with the A6, near Thulston, Derbyshire) (Temporary Prohibition of Traffic) Order 2008 No. 2008/2572. - Enabling power: Road Traffic Regulation Act 1984, s. 14 (1) (a). - Made: 15.09.2008. Coming into force: 22.09.2008. Effect: None. Territorial extent & classification: E. Local *Unpublished*

The A50 Trunk Road (Junction with the A511, near Scropton, Derbyshire) (Temporary Prohibition of Traffic) Order 2008 No. 2008/993. - Enabling power: Road Traffic Regulation Act 1984, s. 14 (1) (a). - Made: 14.03.2008. Coming into force: 21.03.2008. Effect: None. Territorial extent & classification: E. Local *Unpublished*

The A50 Trunk Road (Junction with the A522, Uttoxeter, Staffordshire) (Temporary Restriction and Prohibition of Traffic) Order 2008 No. 2008/2615. - Enabling power: Road Traffic Regulation Act 1984, s. 14 (1) (a). - Made: 19.09.2008. Coming into force: 26.09.2008. Effect: None. Territorial extent & classification: E. Local *Unpublished*

The A50 Trunk Road (Meir, Staffordshire) (Prohibition and Restriction of Waiting in Layby) Order 2008 No. 2008/2806. - Enabling power: Road Traffic Regulation Act 1984, ss. 1 (1), 2 (1) (2), 4 (1) (2). - Made: 16.10.2008. Coming into force: 30.10.2008. Effect: None. Territorial extent & classification: E. Local *Unpublished*

The A50 Trunk Road (Meir, Stoke on Trent) (Temporary Prohibition of Traffic) Order 2008 No. 2008/250. - Enabling power: Road Traffic Regulation Act 1984, s. 14 (1) (a). - Made: 21.01.2008. Coming into force: 28.01.2008. Effect: None. Territorial extent & classification: E. Local *Unpublished*

The A50 Trunk Road (Meir Tunnel, Stoke-On-Trent) (Temporary Prohibition of Traffic) (No. 2) Order 2008 No. 2008/1543. - Enabling power: Road Traffic Regulation Act 1984, s. 14 (1) (a). - Made: 02.06.2008. Coming into force: 09.06.2008. Effect: None. Territorial extent & classification: E. Local *Unpublished*

The A50 Trunk Road (Meir Tunnel, Stoke-on-Trent) (Temporary Prohibition of Traffic) Order 2008 No. 2008/109. - Enabling power: Road Traffic Regulation Act 1984, s. 14 (1) (a). - Made: 07.01.2008. Coming into force: 14.01.2008. Effect: None. Territorial extent & classification: E. Local *Unpublished*

The A50 Trunk Road (Near Chellaston, Derbyshire) (Temporary Prohibition of Traffic) Order 2008 No. 2008/1075. - Enabling power: Road Traffic Regulation Act 1984, s. 14 (1) (a). - Made: 28.03.2008. Coming into force: 04.04.2008. Effect: None. Territorial extent & classification: E. Local *Unpublished*

The A50 Trunk Road (North of Castle Donnington, Leicestershire) (Temporary Restriction and Prohibition of Traffic) Order 2008 No. 2008/2226. - Enabling power: Road Traffic Regulation Act 1984, s. 14 (1) (a). - Made: 01.08.2008. Coming into force: 08.08.2008. Effect: None. Territorial extent & classification: E. Local *Unpublished*

The A50 Trunk Road (Service Area near Aston-on-Trent, Derbyshire) (Slip Road) (Temporary Prohibition of Traffic) Order 2008 No. 2008/2486. - Enabling power: Road Traffic Regulation Act 1984, s. 14 (1) (a). - Made: 29.08.2008. Coming into force: 05.09.2008. Effect: None. Territorial extent & classification: E. Local *Unpublished*

The A50 Trunk Road (Stoke-on-Trent, Staffordshire) (Temporary Restriction and Prohibition of Traffic) Order 2008 No. 2008/875. - Enabling power: Road Traffic Regulation Act 1984, s. 14 (1) (a). - Made: 03.03.2008. Coming into force: 10.03.2008. Effect: None. Territorial extent & classification: E. Local *Unpublished*

The A50 Trunk Road (Stoke-on-Trent) (Temporary Prohibition of Traffic) Order 2008 No. 2008/876. - Enabling power: Road Traffic Regulation Act 1984, s. 14 (1) (a). - Made: 03.03.2008. Coming into force: 10.03.2008. Effect: None. Territorial extent & classification: E. Local *Unpublished*

The A50 Trunk Road (Trentham Lakes to Normacot, Stoke-on-Trent) (Temporary Prohibition of Traffic) Order 2008 No. 2008/2617. - Enabling power: Road Traffic Regulation Act 1984, s. 14 (1) (a). - Made: 19.09.2008. Coming into force: 26.09.2008. Effect: None. Territorial extent & classification: E. Local *Unpublished*

The A50 Trunk Road (Uttoexeter, Staffordshire) (Temporary Prohibition of Traffic) Order 2008 No. 2008/2042. - Enabling power: Road Traffic Regulation Act 1984, s. 14 (1) (a). - Made: 14.07.2008. Coming into force: 21.07.2008. Effect: None. Territorial extent & classification: E. Local *Unpublished*

The A50 Trunk Road (Willington, Derbyshire) (Temporary Prohibition of Traffic) Order 2008 No. 2008/3285. - Enabling power: Road Traffic Regulation Act 1984, s. 14 (1) (a). - Made: 05.12.2008. Coming into force: 12.12.2008. Effect: None. Territorial extent & classification: E. Local *Unpublished*

The A52 Trunk Road and the A5111 Trunk Road (Derbyshire) (Slip Road) (Temporary Prohibition of Traffic) Order 2008 No. 2008/352. - Enabling power: Road Traffic Regulation Act 1984, s. 14 (1) (a). - Made: 04.02.2008. Coming into force: 11.02.2008. Effect: None. Territorial extent & classification: E. Local *Unpublished*

The A52 Trunk Road (Bingham to Barrowby) (Temporary Restriction and Prohibition of Traffic) Order 2008 No. 2008/141. - Enabling power: Road Traffic Regulation Act 1984, s. 14 (1) (a). - Made: 04.01.2008. Coming into force: 11.01.2008. Effect: None. Territorial extent & classification: E. Local *Unpublished*

The A52 Trunk Road (Bingham to Barrowby) (Temporary Restriction and Prohibition of Traffic) Order 2008 No. 2008/1680. - Enabling power: Road Traffic Regulation Act 1984, s. 14 (1) (a). - Made: 13.06.2008. Coming into force: 20.06.2008. Effect: None. Territorial extent & classification: E. Local *Unpublished*

The A52 Trunk Road (Borrowash Bypass, Derbyshire) (Temporary Prohibition of Traffic) Order 2008 No. 2008/192. - Enabling power: Road Traffic Regulation Act 1984, s. 14 (1) (a). - Made: 18.01.2008. Coming into force: 25.01.2008. Effect: None. Territorial extent & classification: E. Local *Unpublished*

The A52 Trunk Road (Clifton Boulevard, Nottingham) (Slip Road) (Temporary Prohibition of Traffic) Order 2008 No. 2008/2580. - Enabling power: Road Traffic Regulation Act 1984, s. 14 (1) (a). - Made: 12.09.2008. Coming into force: 19.09.2008. Effect: None. Territorial extent & classification: E. Local *Unpublished*

The A52 Trunk Road (Derby Road, Nottingham) (Footway) (Temporary Prohibition of Traffic) Order 2008 No. 2008/2746. - Enabling power: Road Traffic Regulation Act 1984, s. 14 (1) (a). - Made: 06.10.2008. Coming into force: 13.10.2008. Effect: None. Territorial extent & classification: E. Local *Unpublished*

The A52 Trunk Road (Gamston to Holme House, Nottinghamshire) (Temporary Prohibition of Traffic) Order 2008 No. 2008/1536. - Enabling power: Road Traffic Regulation Act 1984, s. 14 (1) (a). - Made: 30.05.2008. Coming into force: 06.06.2008. Effect: None. Territorial extent & classification: E. Local *Unpublished*

The A52 Trunk Road (Holme House Junction, Nottinghamshire) (Temporary Prohibition of Traffic) Order 2008 No. 2008/1293. - Enabling power: Road Traffic Regulation Act 1984, s. 14 (1) (b). - Made: 25.04.2008. Coming into force: 02.05.2008. Effect: None. Territorial extent & classification: E. Local *Unpublished*

The A52 Trunk Road (Near Saxondale, Nottinghamshire) (Temporary Prohibition of Traffic in Layby) Order 2008 No. 2008/818. - Enabling power: Road Traffic Regulation Act 1984, s. 14 (1) (a). - Made: 19.02.2008. Coming into force: 26.02.2008. Effect: None. Territorial extent & classification: E. Local *Unpublished*

The A52 Trunk Road (Near Stapleford, Nottinghamshire) (Temporary Prohibition of Traffic) Order 2008 No. 2008/1367. - Enabling power: Road Traffic Regulation Act 1984, s. 14 (1) (a). - Made: 02.05.2008. Coming into force: 09.05.2008. Effect: None. Territorial extent & classification: E. Local *Unpublished*

The A52 Trunk Road (Priory Roundabout to Bardills Roundabout, Nottinghamshire) (Temporary Prohibition of Traffic) Order 2008 No. 2008/1677. - Enabling power: Road Traffic Regulation Act 1984, s. 14 (1) (a). - Made: 16.06.2008. Coming into force: 23.06.2008. Effect: None. Territorial extent & classification: E. Local *Unpublished*

The A52 Trunk Road (QMC Hospital, Nottingham) (Temporary Prohibition of Traffic) Order 2008 No. 2008/823. - Enabling power: Road Traffic Regulation Act 1984, s. 14 (1) (a). - Made: 22.02.2008. Coming into force: 29.02.2008. Effect: None. Territorial extent & classification: E. Local *Unpublished*

The A52 Trunk Road (Spondon - Long Eaton, Derbyshire) (Temporary Prohibition of Traffic) Order 2008 No. 2008/2658. - Enabling power: Road Traffic Regulation Act 1984, s. 14 (1) (a). - Made: 26.09.2008. Coming into force: 03.10.2008. Effect: None. Territorial extent & classification: E. Local *Unpublished*

The A52 Trunk Road (Wheatcroft Roundabout, West Bridgford, Nottinghamshire) (Temporary Restriction of Traffic) Order 2008 No. 2008/3030. - Enabling power: Road Traffic Regulation Act 1984, s. 14 (1) (a). - Made: 07.11.2008. Coming into force: 14.11.2008. Effect: None. Territorial extent & classification: E. Local *Unpublished*

The A55 Trunk Road (Junctions with A51 and A483 and Westbound and Eastbound Entry and Exit Slip Roads) (Temporary Prohibition of Traffic) Order 2008 No. 2008/2024. - Enabling power: Road Traffic Regulation Act 1984, s. 14 (1) (a). - Made: 23.06.2008. Coming into force: 17.07.2008. Effect: None. Territorial extent & classification: E. Local *Unpublished*

The A55 Trunk Road (Junctions with A51 and M53 (Junction 12) and Eastbound Exit and Entry Slip Roads to and from the A51) (Temporary Prohibition of Traffic) Order 2008 No. 2008/1532. - Enabling power: Road Traffic Regulation Act 1984, s. 14 (1) (a). - Made: 27.05.2008. Coming into force: 05.06.2008. Effect: None. Territorial extent & classification: E. Local *Unpublished*

Road traffic: Traffic regulation

The A56 Trunk Road (Bent Gate) (Temporary Restriction of Traffic) Order 2008 No. 2008/2718. - Enabling power: Road Traffic Regulation Act 1984, s. 14 (1) (b). - Made: 17.09.2008. Coming into force: 21.09.2008. Effect: None. Territorial extent & classification: E. Local *Unpublished*

The A56 Trunk Road (Huncoat) and the M65 Motorway (Junction 8 Eastbound Entry Slip Road) (Temporary Prohibition and Restriction of Traffic) Order 2008 No. 2008/1060. - Enabling power: Road Traffic Regulation Act 1984, s. 14 (1) (a). - Made: 18.03.2008. Coming into force: 24.03.2008. Effect: None. Territorial extent & classification: E. Local *Unpublished*

The A56 Trunk Road (Huncoat) (Temporary Prohibition of Traffic) Order 2008 No. 2008/874. - Enabling power: Road Traffic Regulation Act 1984, s. 14 (1) (a). - Made: 27.02.2008. Coming into force: 02.03.2008. Effect: None. Territorial extent & classification: E. Local *Unpublished*

The A56 Trunk Road (Northbound Exit and Southbound Entry Slip Roads at Bent Gate) (Temporary Prohibition of Traffic) Order 2008 No. 2008/3336. - Enabling power: Road Traffic Regulation Act 1984, s. 14 (1) (a). - Made: 30.12.2008. Coming into force: 25.01.2009. Effect: S.I. 2008/2287 revoked. Territorial extent & classification: E. Local *Unpublished*

The A56 Trunk Road (Northbound Exit Slip Road to the A679) (Temporary Prohibition of Traffic) Order 2008 No. 2008/3289. - Enabling power: Road Traffic Regulation Act 1984, s. 14 (1) (a). - Made: 09.12.2008. Coming into force: 06.01.2009. Effect: None. Territorial extent & classification: E. Local *Unpublished*

The A56 Trunk Road (Rising Bridge to Bent Gate) (50 Miles Per Hour and 'U' Turn Ban) (Temporary Prohibition and Restriction of Traffic) Order 2008 No. 2008/1997. - Enabling power: Road Traffic Regulation Act 1984, s. 14 (1) (b). - Made: 23.06.2008. Coming into force: 20.07.2008. Effect: None. Territorial extent & classification: E. Local *Unpublished*

The A56 Trunk Road (Rising Bridge to the A679) (Temporary Prohibition of Traffic) Order 2008 No. 2008/2521. - Enabling power: Road Traffic Regulation Act 1984, s. 14 (1) (a). - Made: 02.09.2008. Coming into force: 25.09.2008. Effect: None. Territorial extent & classification: E. Local *Unpublished*

The A57 Trunk Road (Gun Inn Junction to Back Moor Road) (Temporary 10 Miles Per Hour Speed Restriction) Order 2008 No. 2008/3217. - Enabling power: Road Traffic Regulation Act 1984, s. 14 (1) (a). - Made: 24.11.2008. Coming into force: 07.12.2008. Effect: None. Territorial extent & classification: E. Local *Unpublished*

The A62 Trunk Road (Gildersome Interchange Northern Roundabout) (Temporary Prohibition of Traffic) Order 2008 No. 2008/860. - Enabling power: Road Traffic Regulation Act 1984, s. 14 (1) (a). - Made: 28.02.2008. Coming into force: 09.03.2008. Effect: None. Territorial extent & classification: E. Local *Unpublished*

The A62 Trunk Road (Gildersome Interchange Northern Roundabout to Southern Roundabout) (Temporary Restriction and Prohibition of Traffic) Order 2008 No. 2008/2732. - Enabling power: Road Traffic Regulation Act 1984, s. 14 (1) (a) (7). - Made: 07.10.2008. Coming into force: 12.10.2008. Effect: None. Territorial extent & classification: E. Local *Unpublished*

The A63 Trunk Road (Brighton Street Interchange to Daltry Street Flyover) (Temporary Prohibition of Traffic) Order 2008 No. 2008/2134. - Enabling power: Road Traffic Regulation Act 1984, s. 14 (1) (a). - Made: 29.07.2008. Coming into force: 10.08.2008. Effect: None. Territorial extent & classification: E. Local *Unpublished*

The A63 Trunk Road (Daltry Street Flyover to Garrison Road Roundabout) (Temporary Prohibition of Traffic) Order 2008 No. 2008/1157. - Enabling power: Road Traffic Regulation Act 1984, s. 14 (1) (a). - Made: 16.04.2008. Coming into force: 27.04.2008. Effect: None. Territorial extent & classification: E. Local *Unpublished*

The A63 Trunk Road (Garrison Road, Hull) (Temporary Prohibition of Traffic and Pedestrians) Order 2008 No. 2008/1118. - Enabling power: Road Traffic Regulation Act 1984, s. 14 (1) (a). - Made: 07.04.2008. Coming into force: 19.04.2008. Effect: None. Territorial extent & classification: E. Local *Unpublished*

The A63 Trunk Road (Garrison Road Roundabout) (Temporary Restriction and Prohibition of Traffic) Order 2008 No. 2008/2293. - Enabling power: Road Traffic Regulation Act 1984, s. 14 (1) (a) (7). - Made: 18.08.2008. Coming into force: 31.08.2008. Effect: None. Territorial extent & classification: E. Local *Unpublished*

The A63 Trunk Road (Hambleton Village) (Temporary Restriction and Prohibition of Traffic) Order 2008 No. 2008/274. - Enabling power: Road Traffic Regulation Act 1984, s. 14 (1) (a). - Made: 21.01.2008. Coming into force: 03.02.2008. Effect: None. Territorial extent & classification: E. Local *Unpublished*

The A63 Trunk Road (Junction of Poolbank Lane Welton) (Prohibition of Traffic) Order 2008 No. 2008/2400. - Enabling power: Road Traffic Regulation Act 1984, s. 1 (1), 2 (1) (2). - Made: 01.09.2008. Coming into force: 15.09.2008. Effect: None. Territorial extent & classification: E. Local *Unpublished*

The A63 Trunk Road (Junction of Poolbank Lane Welton) (Temporary Prohibition of Traffic) Order 2008 No. 2008/479. - Enabling power: Road Traffic Regulation Act 1984, s. 14 (1) (a). - Made: 18.02.2008. Coming into force: 27.02.2008. Effect: None. Territorial extent & classification: E. Local *Unpublished*

The A63 Trunk Road (Market Place Junction to Garrison Road Roundabout) (Temporary Prohibition of Traffic) Order 2008 No. 2008/2403. - Enabling power: Road Traffic Regulation Act 1984, s. 14 (1) (b). - Made: 01.09.2008. Coming into force: 11.09.2008. Effect: None. Territorial extent & classification: E. Local *Unpublished*

Road traffic: Traffic regulation

The A63 Trunk Road (Monk Fryston to Hambleton) (Temporary Restriction and Prohibition of Traffic) Order 2008 No. 2008/2294. - Enabling power: Road Traffic Regulation Act 1984, s. 14 (1) (a). - Made: 18.08.2008. Coming into force: 31.08.2008. Effect: None. Territorial extent & classification: E. Local *Unpublished*

The A63 Trunk Road (Selby Bypass) (Temporary Restriction and Prohibition of Traffic) Order 2008 No. 2008/2632. - Enabling power: Road Traffic Regulation Act 1984, s. 14 (1). - Made: 23.09.2008. Coming into force: 05.10.2008. Effect: None. Territorial extent & classification: E. Local *Unpublished*

The A63 Trunk Road (Selby Bypass: the A1041 Bawtry Road to the A19 Riccall/Barlby Roundabout) (Temporary Prohibition of Traffic) Order 2008 No. 2008/2451. - Enabling power: Road Traffic Regulation Act 1984, s. 14 (1) (a). - Made: 08.09.2008. Coming into force: 20.09.2008. Effect: None. Territorial extent & classification: E. Local *Unpublished*

The A63 Trunk Road (Selby Bypass: the A1041 to the A19) (Temporary Prohibition of Traffic) Order 2008 No. 2008/265. - Enabling power: Road Traffic Regulation Act 1984, s. 14 (1). - Made: 29.01.2008. Coming into force: 09.02.2008. Effect: None. Territorial extent & classification: E. Local *Unpublished*

The A63 Trunk Road (Welton Junction to South Cave Junction) (Temporary Prohibition of Traffic) Order 2008 No. 2008/266. - Enabling power: Road Traffic Regulation Act 1984, s. 14 (1) (a). - Made: 28.01.2008. Coming into force: 10.02.2008. Effect: None. Territorial extent & classification: E. Local *Unpublished*

The A63 Trunk Road (Western Interchange) (Temporary Prohibition of Traffic) Order 2008 No. 2008/1247. - Enabling power: Road Traffic Regulation Act 1984, s. 14 (1) (a). - Made: 28.04.2008. Coming into force: 11.05.2008. Effect: None. Territorial extent & classification: E. Local *Unpublished*

The A63 Trunk Road (Western Interchange to North Cave Interchange) and the M62 Motorway (North Cave Interchange) (Temporary Prohibition of Traffic) Order 2008 No. 2008/2289. - Enabling power: Road Traffic Regulation Act 1984, s. 14 (1) (a). - Made: 19.08.2008. Coming into force: 31.08.2008. Effect: None. Territorial extent & classification: E. Local *Unpublished*

The A64 Trunk Road (A1036 Bond Hill Interchange to the A1036 Hopgrove Interchange) (Temporary Prohibition of Traffic) Order 2008 No. 2008/2049. - Enabling power: Road Traffic Regulation Act 1984, s. 14 (1) (a). - Made: 15.07.2008. Coming into force: 27.07.2008. Effect: None. Territorial extent & classification: E. Local *Unpublished*

The A64 Trunk Road (Askham Bryan Interchange) (Temporary Prohibition of Traffic) Order 2008 No. 2008/1502. - Enabling power: Road Traffic Regulation Act 1984, s. 14 (1) (a). - Made: 02.06.2008. Coming into force: 15.06.2008. Effect: None. Territorial extent & classification: E. Local *Unpublished*

The A64 Trunk Road (Bramham Crossroads) (Temporary Restriction and Prohibition of Traffic) Order 2008 No. 2008/3179. - Enabling power: Road Traffic Regulation Act 1984, s. 14 (1) (a). - Made: 01.12.2008. Coming into force: 09.12.2008. Effect: None. Territorial extent & classification: E. Local *Unpublished*

The A64 Trunk Road (Fourth Milestone Layby) (Temporary Prohibition of Traffic) Order 2008 No. 2008/108. - Enabling power: Road Traffic Regulation Act 1984, s. 14 (1). - Made: 14.01.2008. Coming into force: 27.01.2008. Effect: None. Territorial extent & classification: E. Local *Unpublished*

The A64 Trunk Road (Fulford Interchange) (Temporary Prohibition of Traffic) Order 2008 No. 2008/106. - Enabling power: Road Traffic Regulation Act 1984, s. 14 (1). - Made: 16.01.2008. Coming into force: 20.01.2008. Effect: None. Territorial extent & classification: E. Local *Unpublished*

The A64 Trunk Road (Hopgrove Roundabout) (Temporary Restriction and Prohibition of Traffic) Order 2008 No. 2008/2981. - Enabling power: Road Traffic Regulation Act 1984, s. 14 (1) (a). - Made: 12.11.2008. Coming into force: 16.11.2008. Effect: None. Territorial extent & classification: E. Local *Unpublished*

The A64 Trunk Road (Layby at Potter Brompton) (Temporary Prohibition of Traffic) Order 2008 No. 2008/26. - Enabling power: Road Traffic Regulation Act 1984, s. 14 (1). - Made: 03.01.2008. Coming into force: 13.01.2008. Effect: None. Territorial extent & classification: E. Local *Unpublished*

The A64 Trunk Road (Pickering Interchange) (Temporary Prohibition of Traffic) Order 2008 No. 2008/1376. - Enabling power: Road Traffic Regulation Act 1984, s. 14 (1). - Made: 12.05.2008. Coming into force: 26.05.2008. Effect: None. Territorial extent & classification: E. Local *Unpublished*

The A64 Trunk Road (Rillington to East Knapton) (Temporary Restriction and Prohibition of Traffic) Order 2008 No. 2008/2633. - Enabling power: Road Traffic Regulation Act 1984, s. 14 (1). - Made: 22.09.2008. Coming into force: 05.10.2008. Effect: None. Territorial extent & classification: E. Local *Unpublished*

The A64 Trunk Road (Scagglethorpe to Rillington) (Temporary Restriction and Prohibition of Traffic) Order 2008 No. 2008/3042. - Enabling power: Road Traffic Regulation Act 1984, s. 14 (1) (a) (7). - Made: 17.11.2008. Coming into force: 30.11.2008. Effect: None. Territorial extent & classification: E. Local *Unpublished*

The A64 Trunk Road (Spital Beck to Crambeck) (Temporary Restriction and Prohibition of Traffic) Order 2008 No. 2008/275. - Enabling power: Road Traffic Regulation Act 1984, s. 14 (1). - Made: 21.01.2008. Coming into force: 03.02.2008. Effect: None. Territorial extent & classification: E. Local *Unpublished*

Road traffic: Traffic regulation

The A64 Trunk Road (Staxton Crossroads) (Temporary 10 Miles Per Hour and 40 Miles Per Hour Speed Restriction) Order 2008 No. 2008/25. - Enabling power: Road Traffic Regulation Act 1984, s. 14 (1). - Made: 02.01.2008. Coming into force: 06.01.2008. Effect: None. Territorial extent & classification: E. Local *Unpublished*

The A64 Trunk Road (Tadcaster to Willerby) (Temporary Restriction and Prohibition of Traffic) Order 2008 No. 2008/2819. - Enabling power: Road Traffic Regulation Act 1984, s. 14 (1) (a). - Made: 20.10.2008. Coming into force: 26.10.2008. Effect: None. Territorial extent & classification: E. Local *Unpublished*

The A65 Trunk Road (Crooklands to Kirkby Lonsdale) (Temporary Restriction and Prohibition of Traffic) Order 2008 No. 2008/2417. - Enabling power: Road Traffic Regulation Act 1984, s. 14 (1) (a). - Made: 26.08.2008. Coming into force: 21.09.2008. Effect: None. Territorial extent & classification: E. Local *Unpublished*

The A65 Trunk Road (Farleton to Kirkby Lonsdale) (Temporary Restriction and Prohibition of Traffic) Order 2008 No. 2008/1103. - Enabling power: Road Traffic Regulation Act 1984, s. 14 (1) (a). - Made: 07.04.2008. Coming into force: 05.05.2008. Effect: None. Territorial extent & classification: E. Local *Unpublished*

The A65 Trunk Road (Gargrave to Woomber Bridge) (Temporary Restriction and Prohibition of Traffic) Order 2008 No. 2008/3035. - Enabling power: Road Traffic Regulation Act 1984, s. 14 (1) (a). - Made: 12.11.2008. Coming into force: 17.11.2008. Effect: None. Territorial extent & classification: E. Local *Unpublished*

The A65 Trunk Road (Hipping Hall to Newby) (Temporary Restriction and Prohibition of Traffic) Order 2008 No. 2008/1223. - Enabling power: Road Traffic Regulation Act 1984, s. 14 (1) (a). - Made: 21.04.2008. Coming into force: 11.05.2008. Effect: None. Territorial extent & classification: E. Local *Unpublished*

The A65 Trunk Road (Hutton Roof to Spital Farm, Kirkby Lonsdale Resurfacing) (Temporary Prohibition of Traffic) Order 2008 No. 2008/77. - Enabling power: Road Traffic Regulation Act 1984, s. 14 (1) (a). - Made: 08.01.2008. Coming into force: 03.02.2008. Effect: None. Territorial extent & classification: E. Local *Unpublished*

The A65 Trunk Road (Katies Well to Coniston Cold) (Temporary Restriction and Prohibition of Traffic) Order 2008 No. 2008/335. - Enabling power: Road Traffic Regulation Act 1984, s. 14 (1) (a). - Made: 05.02.2008. Coming into force: 02.03.2008. Effect: None. Territorial extent & classification: E. Local *Unpublished*

The A65 Trunk Road (Long Preston to Hellifield) (Temporary Restriction and Prohibition of Traffic) Order 2008 No. 2008/1288. - Enabling power: Road Traffic Regulation Act 1984, s. 14 (1) (a). - Made: 28.04.2008. Coming into force: 15.05.2008. Effect: None. Territorial extent & classification: E. Local *Unpublished*

The A65 Trunk Road (M6 Junction 36 to Kirkby Lonsdale) (Temporary Restriction and Prohibition of Traffic) Order 2008 No. 2008/1551. - Enabling power: Road Traffic Regulation Act 1984, s. 14 (1) (a). - Made: 04.06.2008. Coming into force: 08.06.2008. Effect: None. Territorial extent & classification: E. Local *Unpublished*

The A65 Trunk Road (Newby to Clapham) (Temporary Restriction and Prohibition of Traffic) Order 2008 No. 2008/444. - Enabling power: Road Traffic Regulation Act 1984, s. 14 (1) (a). - Made: 18.02.2008. Coming into force: 17.03.2008. Effect: None. Territorial extent & classification: E. Local *Unpublished*

The A65 Trunk Road (Skipton Roundabout to Newby Moor) (Temporary Restriction and Prohibition of Traffic) Order 2008 No. 2008/2182. - Enabling power: Road Traffic Regulation Act 1984, s. 14 (1) (a). - Made: 04.08.2008. Coming into force: 31.08.2008. Effect: None. Territorial extent & classification: E. Local *Unpublished*

The A66(M) Motorway (The A1(M) Motorway Junction 57 to Blackwell Roundabout) (Temporary Prohibition of Traffic) Order 2008 No. 2008/3368. - Enabling power: Road Traffic Regulation Act 1984, s. 14 (1) (a). - Made: 30.12.2008. Coming into force: 07.01.2009. Effect: None. Territorial extent & classification: E. Local *Unpublished*

The A66 Trunk Road and the A66(M) Motorway (Blands Corner Roundabout to the A1(M) Motorway) (Temporary Restriction of Traffic) Order 2008 No. 2008/1507. - Enabling power: Road Traffic Regulation Act 1984, s. 14 (1) (a) (7). - Made: 03.06.2008. Coming into force: 15.06.2008. Effect: None. Territorial extent & classification: E. Local *Unpublished*

The A66 Trunk Road (Appleby Bypass) (Temporary Prohibition and Restriction of Traffic) Order 2008 No. 2008/3365. - Enabling power: Road Traffic Regulation Act 1984, s. 14 (1) (a). - Made: 31.12.2008. Coming into force: 25.01.2009. Effect: None. Territorial extent & classification: E. Local *Unpublished*

The A66 Trunk Road (B6277 Cross Lane to Bowes) (Temporary Restriction and Prohibition of Traffic) Order 2008 No. 2008/1837. - Enabling power: Road Traffic Regulation Act 1984, s. 14 (1) (a). - Made: 01.07.2008. Coming into force: 13.07.2008. Effect: None. Territorial extent & classification: E. Local *Unpublished*

The A66 Trunk Road (Bassenthwaite Lake) (Temporary Restriction and Prohibition of Traffic) Order 2008 No. 2008/2878. - Enabling power: Road Traffic Regulation Act 1984, s. 14 (1) (a). - Made: 15.10.2008. Coming into force: 18.10.2008. Effect: None. Territorial extent & classification: E. Local *Unpublished*

The A66 Trunk Road (Blands Corner Roundabout) (Temporary Restriction and Prohibition of Traffic) Order 2008 No. 2008/1836. - Enabling power: Road Traffic Regulation Act 1984, s. 14 (1) (a). - Made: 01.07.2008. Coming into force: 13.07.2008. Effect: None. Territorial textent & classification: E. Local *Unpublished*

Road traffic: Traffic regulation

The A66 Trunk Road (Boathouse Lane Interchange and Thornaby Road Interchange) (Temporary Prohibition of Traffic) Order 2008 No. 2008/2306. - Enabling power: Road Traffic Regulation Act 1984, s. 14 (1) (a). - Made: 18.08.2008. Coming into force: 31.08.2008. Effect: None. Territorial extent & classification: E. Local *Unpublished*

The A66 Trunk Road (Bowes Bypass) (Temporary Restriction and Prohibition of Traffic) Order 2008 No. 2008/161. - Enabling power: Road Traffic Regulation Act 1984, s. 14 (1) (a). - Made: 21.01.2008. Coming into force: 03.02.2008. Effect: None. Territorial extent & classification: E. Local *Unpublished*

The A66 Trunk Road (Carleton Underpass) (Temporary Restriction and Prohibition of Traffic) Order 2008 No. 2008/445. - Enabling power: Road Traffic Regulation Act 1984, s. 14 (1) (a). - Made: 11.02.2008. Coming into force: 09.03.2008. Effect: None. Territorial extent & classification: E. Local *Unpublished*

The A66 Trunk Road (Crackenthorpe) (Temporary Restriction and Prohibition of Traffic) Order 2008 No. 2008/2494. - Enabling power: Road Traffic Regulation Act 1984, s. 14 (1) (a). - Made: 03.09.2008. Coming into force: 28.09.2008. Effect: None. Territorial extent & classification: E. Local *Unpublished*

The A66 Trunk Road (Cross Lanes) (Temporary 50 Miles Per Hour, 40 Miles Per Hour and 10 Miles Per Hour Speed Restriction) Order 2008 No. 2008/3216. - Enabling power: Road Traffic Regulation Act 1984, s. 14 (1) (a). - Made: 25.11.2008. Coming into force: 30.11.2008. Effect: None. Territorial extent & classification: E. Local *Unpublished*

The A66 Trunk Road (Crossthwaite to Briery Interchange, Keswick) (Temporary Prohibition and Restriction of Traffic) Order 2008 No. 2008/125. - Enabling power: Road Traffic Regulation Act 1984, s. 14 (1) (a). - Made: 15.01.2008. Coming into force: 09.02.2008. Effect: None. Territorial extent & classification: E. Local *Unpublished*

The A66 Trunk Road (Dacre Junction to Newbiggin Junction) (Temporary Restriction and Prohibition of Traffic) Order 2008 No. 2008/2276. - Enabling power: Road Traffic Regulation Act 1984, s. 14 (1) (a). - Made: 12.08.2008. Coming into force: 07.09.2008. Effect: None. Territorial extent & classification: E. Local *Unpublished*

The A66 Trunk Road (Dubwath Resurfacing) (Temporary Prohibition and Restriction of Traffic) Order 2008 No. 2008/2307. - Enabling power: Road Traffic Regulation Act 1984, s. 14 (1) (a). - Made: 19.08.2008. Coming into force: 14.09.2008. Effect: None. Territorial extent & classification: E. Local *Unpublished*

The A66 Trunk Road (Green Brough to Bowes Cross Farm) (Temporary Restriction and Prohibition of Traffic) Order 2008 No. 2008/2291. - Enabling power: Road Traffic Regulation Act 1984, s. 14 (1) (a) (7). - Made: 18.08.2008. Coming into force: 31.08.2008. Effect: None. Territorial extent & classification: E. Local *Unpublished*

The A66 Trunk Road (Kemplay to Brougham) (Temporary Restriction and Prohibition of Traffic) Order 2008 No. 2008/1101. - Enabling power: Road Traffic Regulation Act 1984, s. 14 (1) (a). - Made: 07.04.2008. Coming into force: 05.05.2008. Effect: None. Territorial extent & classification: E. Local *Unpublished*

The A66 Trunk Road (Lake Bassenthwaite) (Temporary Restriction and Prohibition of Traffic) Order 2008 No. 2008/446. - Enabling power: Road Traffic Regulation Act 1984, s. 14 (1) (a). - Made: 12.02.2008. Coming into force: 08.03.2008. Effect: None. Territorial extent & classification: E. Local *Unpublished*

The A66 Trunk Road (Lambfoot to Embleton) (Temporary Prohibition and Restriction of Traffic) Order 2008 No. 2008/1381. - Enabling power: Road Traffic Regulation Act 1984, s. 14 (1) (a). - Made: 14.05.2008. Coming into force: 18.05.2008. Effect: None. Territorial extent & classification: E. Local *Unpublished*

The A66 Trunk Road (Layby Closures) (Temporary Prohibition of Traffic) Order 2008 No. 2008/1709. - Enabling power: Road Traffic Regulation Act 1984, s. 14 (1) (a). - Made: 23.06.2008. Coming into force: 17.07.2008. Effect: None. Territorial extent & classification: E. Local *Unpublished*

The A66 Trunk Road (Little Burdon, Darlington) (Prohibition of Use of Gaps in the Central Reservation) Order 2008 No. 2008/2060. - Enabling power: Road Traffic Regulation Act 1984, s. 1 (1), 2 (1) (2). - Made: 21.07.2008. Coming into force: 31.07.2008. Effect: None. Territorial extent & classification: E. Local *Unpublished*

The A66 Trunk Road (Little Burdon Roundabout to Morton Palms Roundabout) (Temporary Prohibition of Traffic) Order 2008 No. 2008/390. - Enabling power: Road Traffic Regulation Act 1984, s. 14 (1) (a). - Made: 12.02.2008. Coming into force: 24.02.2008. Effect: None. Territorial extent & classification: E. Local *Unpublished*

The A66 Trunk Road (Little Burdon to Elton) (Temporary Restriction and Prohibition of Traffic) Order 2008 No. 2008/62. - Enabling power: Road Traffic Regulation Act 1984, s. 14 (1) (a). - Made: 10.01.2008. Coming into force: 22.01.2008. Effect: None. Territorial extent & classification: E. Local *Unpublished*

The A66 Trunk Road (Long Newton Grade Separated Junction) (Temporary Restriction and Prohibition of Traffic) Order 2008 No. 2008/482. - Enabling power: Road Traffic Regulation Act 1984, s. 14 (1) (a). - Made: 18.02.2008. Coming into force: 02.03.2008. Effect: None. Territorial extent & classification: E. Local *Unpublished*

The A66 Trunk Road (Long Newton to Elton) (Prohibition of Use of Gaps in the Central Reservation) Order 2008 No. 2008/2061. - Enabling power: Road Traffic Regulation Act 1984, s. 1 (1), 2 (1) (2). - Made: 21.07.2008. Coming into force: 31.07.2008. Effect: None. Territorial extent & classification: E. Local *Unpublished*

The A66 Trunk Road (Long Newton to Thornaby Road Interchange) (Temporary Restriction and Prohibition of Traffic and Pedestrians) Order 2008 No. 2008/2622. - Enabling power: Road Traffic Regulation Act 1984, s. 14 (1) (a) (7). - Made: 29.09.2008. Coming into force: 09.10.2008. Effect: None. Territorial extent & classification: E. Local *Unpublished*

The A66 Trunk Road (Lorton Embankment, Cockermouth) (Temporary Prohibition of Traffic) Order 2008 No. 2008/2418. - Enabling power: Road Traffic Regulation Act 1984, s. 14 (1) (a). - Made: 02.09.2008. Coming into force: 28.09.2008. Effect: None. Territorial extent & classification: E. Local *Unpublished*

The A66 Trunk Road (Lowside) (Temporary Prohibition and Restriction of Traffic) Order 2008 No. 2008/1995. - Enabling power: Road Traffic Regulation Act 1984, s. 14 (1) (a). - Made: 30.06.2008. Coming into force: 27.07.2008. Effect: None. Territorial extent & classification: E. Local *Unpublished*

The A66 Trunk Road (M6 Motorway Junction 40 to Kemplay Roundabout) (Temporary Restriction and Prohibition of Traffic) Order 2008 No. 2008/209. - Enabling power: Road Traffic Regulation Act 1984, s. 14 (1) (a). - Made: 22.01.2008. Coming into force: 17.02.2008. Effect: None. Territorial extent & classification: E. Local *Unpublished*

The A66 Trunk Road (Morton Palms Roundabout to Sadberge West Junction) (Temporary Prohibition of Traffic) Order 2008 No. 2008/2401. - Enabling power: Road Traffic Regulation Act 1984, s. 14 (1) (b). - Made: 01.09.2008. Coming into force: 12.09.2008. Effect: None. Territorial extent & classification: E. Local *Unpublished*

The A66 Trunk Road (Neasham Road Roundabout, Darlington) (Temporary Restriction and Prohibition of Traffic) (No. 2) Order 2008 No. 2008/1691. - Enabling power: Road Traffic Regulation Act 1984, s. 14 (1) (a). - Made: 18.06.2008. Coming into force: 29.06.2008. Effect: None. Territorial extent & classification: E. Local *Unpublished*

The A66 Trunk Road (Neasham Road Roundabout, Darlington) (Temporary Restriction and Prohibition of Traffic) Order 2008 No. 2008/1377. - Enabling power: Road Traffic Regulation Act 1984, s. 14 (1) (a). - Made: 13.05.2008. Coming into force: 26.05.2008. Effect: None. Territorial extent & classification: E. Local *Unpublished*

The A66 Trunk Road (Rheged to Penruddock) (Temporary Prohibition and Restriction of Traffic) Order 2008 No. 2008/1047. - Enabling power: Road Traffic Regulation Act 1984, s. 14 (1) (a). - Made: 18.03.2008. Coming into force: 13.04.2008. Effect: None. Territorial extent & classification: E. Local *Unpublished*

The A66 Trunk Road (Roger Head to Coupland Beck) (Temporary Restriction and Prohibition of Traffic) Order 2008 No. 2008/1127. - Enabling power: Road Traffic Regulation Act 1984, s. 14 (1) (a). - Made: 14.04.2008. Coming into force: 12.05.2008. Effect: None. Territorial extent & classification: E. Local *Unpublished*

The A66 Trunk Road (Scales to Troutbeck) (Temporary Prohibition and Restriction of Traffic) Order 2008 No. 2008/1309. - Enabling power: Road Traffic Regulation Act 1984, s. 14 (1) (a). - Made: 06.05.2008. Coming into force: 01.06.2008. Effect: None. Territorial extent & classification: E. Local *Unpublished*

The A66 Trunk Road (Scotch Corner to Sedbury Lodge) (Prohibition of U-Turns) Order 2008 No. 2008/2807. - Enabling power: Road Traffic Regulation Act 1984, ss. 1 (1), 2 (1) (2). - Made: 01.10.2008. Coming into force: 10.10.2008. Effect: None. Territorial extent & classification: E. Local *Unpublished*

The A66 Trunk Road (Sedbury Layby) (Temporary Prohibition of Traffic) (No. 2) Order 2008 No. 2008/1124. - Enabling power: Road Traffic Regulation Act 1984, s. 14 (1) (a). - Made: 04.04.2008. Coming into force: 08.04.2008. Effect: None. Territorial extent & classification: E. Local *Unpublished*

The A66 Trunk Road (Sedbury Layby) (Temporary Prohibition of Traffic) Order 2008 No. 2008/878. - Enabling power: Road Traffic Regulation Act 1984, s. 14 (1) (a). - Made: 03.03.2008. Coming into force: 16.03.2008. Effect: None. Territorial extent & classification: E. Local *Unpublished*

The A66 Trunk Road (Spital Bridge to East Pasture End) (Temporary Restriction and Prohibition of Traffic) Order 2008 No. 2008/2734. - Enabling power: Road Traffic Regulation Act 1984, s. 14 (1) (a). - Made: 06.10.2008. Coming into force: 19.10.2008. Effect: None. Territorial extent & classification: E. Local *Unpublished*

The A66 Trunk Road (Spittal Ings Layby) (Temporary Restriction and Prohibition of Traffic) Order 2008 No. 2008/460. - Enabling power: Road Traffic Regulation Act 1984, s. 14 (1) (a). - Made: 30.01.2008. Coming into force: 24.02.2008. Effect: None. Territorial extent & classification: E. Local *Unpublished*

The A66 Trunk Road (Stainburn to Chapel Brow) (Temporary Prohibition and Restriction of Traffic) Order 2008 No. 2008/2525. - Enabling power: Road Traffic Regulation Act 1984, s. 14 (1) (a). - Made: 10.09.2008. Coming into force: 05.10.2008. Effect: None. Territorial extent & classification: E. Local *Unpublished*

The A66 Trunk Road (Stockton and Thornaby Bypass) (Temporary Restriction and Prohibition of Traffic) Order 2006 (Revocation) Order 2008 No. 2008/2133. - Enabling power: Road Traffic Regulation Act 1984, ss. 14 (1) (a), 15 (2). - Made: 21.07.2008. Coming into force: 25.07.2008. Effect: S.I. 2006/67 revoked. Territorial extent & classification: E. Local *Unpublished*

The A66 Trunk Road (Teeside Park Interchange) (Temporary Prohibition of Traffic) Order 2008 No. 2008/2479. - Enabling power: Road Traffic Regulation Act 1984, s. 14 (1) (a). - Made: 09.09.2008. Coming into force: 21.09.2008. Effect: None. Territorial extent & classification: E. Local *Unpublished*

The A66 Trunk Road (Temple Sowerby to Crackenthorpe) (Temporary Prohibition and Restriction of Traffic) Order 2008 No. 2008/356. - Enabling power: Road Traffic Regulation Act 1984, s. 14 (1) (a). - Made: 06.02.2008. Coming into force: 10.02.2008. Effect: None. Territorial extent & classification: E. Local *Unpublished*

The A66 Trunk Road (The B6277, Cross Lanes Junction) (Temporary Restriction and Prohibition of Traffic) Order 2008 No. 2008/885. - Enabling power: Road Traffic Regulation Act 1984, s. 14 (1) (a). - Made: 10.03.2008. Coming into force: 24.03.2008. Effect: None. Territorial extent & classification: E. Local *Unpublished*

The A66 Trunk Road (Threlkeld to Castlerigg) (Temporary Restriction and Prohibition of Traffic) Order 2008 No. 2008/1102. - Enabling power: Road Traffic Regulation Act 1984, s. 14 (1) (a). - Made: 07.04.2008. Coming into force: 05.05.2008. Effect: None. Territorial extent & classification: E. Local *Unpublished*

The A66 Trunk Road (Troutbeck Layby) (Temporary Prohibition and Restriction of Traffic) Order 2008 No. 2008/3319. - Enabling power: Road Traffic Regulation Act 1984, s. 14 (1) (a). - Made: 16.12.2008. Coming into force: 11.01.2009. Effect: None. Territorial extent & classification: E. Local *Unpublished*

The A68 Trunk Road (Burtree Interchange) (Temporary Restriction and Prohibition of Traffic) Order 2008 No. 2008/858. - Enabling power: Road Traffic Regulation Act 1984, s. 14 (1) (a) (7). - Made: 06.03.2008. Coming into force: 07.03.2008. Effect: None. Territorial extent & classification: E. Local *Unpublished*

The A69 Trunk Road (Bardon Mill to Ridley Bridge) (Temporary Restriction and Prohibition of Traffic) Order 2008 No. 2008/1498. - Enabling power: Road Traffic Regulation Act 1984, s. 14 (1) (a). - Made: 02.06.2008. Coming into force: 15.06.2008. Effect: None. Territorial extent & classification: E. Local *Unpublished*

The A69 Trunk Road (Haltwhistle Bypass) (Temporary Restriction and Prohibition of Traffic) Order 2008 No. 2008/1134. - Enabling power: Road Traffic Regulation Act 1984, s. 14 (1) (a). - Made: 04.04.2008. Coming into force: 17.04.2008. Effect: None. Territorial extent & classification: E. Local *Unpublished*

The A69 Trunk Road (Haydon Bridge Bypass) (No. 2) (Temporary Prohibition and Restriction of Traffic) Order 2008 No. 2008/2954. - Enabling power: Road Traffic Regulation Act 1984, ss. 14 (1) (a), 122 (a). - Made: 04.11.2008. Coming into force: 30.11.2008. Effect: None. Territorial extent & classification: E. Local *Unpublished*

The A69 Trunk Road (Haydon Bridge Bypass) (Temporary Prohibition and Restriction of Traffic) Order 2008 No. 2008/2810. - Enabling power: Road Traffic Regulation Act 1984, s. 14 (1) (a). - Made: 15.10.2008. Coming into force: 19.10.2008. Effect: None. Territorial extent & classification: E. Local *Unpublished*

The A69 Trunk Road (Haydon Bridge) (Temporary Prohibition and Restriction of Traffic) Order 2008 No. 2008/468. - Enabling power: Road Traffic Regulation Act 1984, s. 14 (1) (a). - Made: 18.02.2008. Coming into force: 22.02.2008. Effect: None. Territorial extent & classification: E. Local *Unpublished*

The A69 Trunk Road (Newcastle upon Tyne to Carlisle) (Temporary Restriction and Prohibition of Traffic) Order 2008 No. 2008/1136. - Enabling power: Road Traffic Regulation Act 1984, s. 14 (1) (a) (7). - Made: 04.04.2008. Coming into force: 17.04.2008. Effect: None. Territorial extent & classification: E. Local *Unpublished*

The A69 Trunk Road (Smallburn to Redpeth Junction) (Temporary Restriction and Prohibition of Traffic) Order 2008 No. 2008/2478. - Enabling power: Road Traffic Regulation Act 1984, s. 14 (1) (a). - Made: 08.09.2008. Coming into force: 18.09.2008. Effect: None. Territorial extent & classification: E. Local *Unpublished*

The A69 Trunk Road (Throckley Interchange) (Temporary Restriction and Prohibition of Traffic) Order 2008 No. 2008/1494. - Enabling power: Road Traffic Regulation Act 1984, s. 14 (1) (a). - Made: 23.05.2008. Coming into force: 08.06.2008. Effect: None. Territorial extent & classification: E. Local *Unpublished*

The A120 Trunk Road (Braintree to Marks Tey, Essex) (Temporary Restriction and Prohibition of Traffic) Order 2008 No. 2008/488. - Enabling power: Road Traffic Regulation Act 1984, s. 14 (1) (a). - Made: 18.02.2008. Coming into force: 25.02.2008. Effect: None. Territorial extent & classification: E. Local *Unpublished*

The A120 Trunk Road (Little Bentley, Tendring, Essex) (Temporary Restriction and Prohibition of Traffic) Order 2008 No. 2008/2541. - Enabling power: Road Traffic Regulation Act 1984, s. 14 (1) (a). - Made: 22.09.2008. Coming into force: 29.09.2008. Effect: None. Territorial extent & classification: E. Local *Unpublished*

The A120 Trunk Road (Marks Farm to A131 Panners Interchange, Braintree, Essex) (Temporary Restriction and Prohibition of Traffic) Order 2008 No. 2008/835. - Enabling power: Road Traffic Regulation Act 1984, s. 14 (1) (a). - Made: 25.02.2008. Coming into force: 03.03.2008. Effect: None. Territorial extent & classification: E. Local *Unpublished*

The A160 Trunk Road and the A180 Trunk Road (Brocklesby Interchange) (Temporary Prohibition of Traffic) Order 2008 No. 2008/1345. - Enabling power: Road Traffic Regulation Act 1984, s. 14 (1) (a). - Made: 07.05.2008. Coming into force: 18.05.2008. Effect: None. Territorial extent & classification: E. Local *Unpublished*

The A160 Trunk Road (Haborough Roundabout to Manby Road Roundabout) (Temporary Restriction and Prohibition of Traffic) Order 2008 No. 2008/400. - Enabling power: Road Traffic Regulation Act 1984, s. 14 (1) (a). - Made: 11.02.2008. Coming into force: 24.02.2008. Effect: None. Territorial extent & classification: E. Local *Unpublished*

Road traffic: Traffic regulation

The A160 Trunk Road (The A1077 Ucleby Road to Top Road Roundabout) (Temporary Prohibition of Traffic) Order 2008 No. 2008/1311. - Enabling power: Road Traffic Regulation Act 1984, s. 14 (1) (a). - Made: 07.05.2008. Coming into force: 11.05.2008. Effect: None. Territorial extent & classification: E. Local *Unpublished*

The A168 Trunk Road (Asenby Interchange to Topcliffe Interchange) (Temporary Restriction and Prohibition of Traffic) Order 2008 No. 2008/2124. - Enabling power: Road Traffic Regulation Act 1984, s. 14 (1) (a) (7). - Made: 14.07.2008. Coming into force: 25.07.2008. Effect: None. Territorial extent & classification: E. Local *Unpublished*

The A174 Trunk Road (Blue Bell Interchange to Stokesley Road Interchange) (Temporary Restriction and Prohibition of Traffic) Order 2008 No. 2008/1501. - Enabling power: Road Traffic Regulation Act 1984, s. 14 (1) (a). - Made: 03.06.2008. Coming into force: 14.06.2008. Effect: None. Territorial extent & classification: E. Local *Unpublished*

The A180 Trunk Road and the A160 Trunk Road (Brocklesby Interchange) (Temporary Prohibition of Traffic) Order 2008 No. 2008/2818. - Enabling power: Road Traffic Regulation Act 1984, s. 14 (1) (a). - Made: 20.10.2008. Coming into force: 02.11.2008. Effect: None. Territorial extent & classification: E. Local *Unpublished*

The A180 Trunk Road (Barnetby Interchange to Brocklesby Interchange) (Temporary Restriction and Prohibition of Traffic) Order 2008 No. 2008/3341. - Enabling power: Road Traffic Regulation Act 1984, s. 14 (1) (a) (7). - Made: 23.12.2008. Coming into force: 07.01.2009. Effect: None. Territorial extent & classification: E. Local *Unpublished*

The A180 Trunk Road (Brocklesby Interchange) (Temporary Prohibition of Traffic) Order 2008 No. 2008/1375. - Enabling power: Road Traffic Regulation Act 1984, s. 14 (1) (a). - Made: 12.05.2008. Coming into force: 26.05.2008. Effect: None. Territorial extent & classification: E. Local *Unpublished*

The A184 Trunk Road (Whitemare Pool Interchange to Testos Roundabout) (Temporary Restriction and Prohibition of Traffic) Order 2008 No. 2008/162. - Enabling power: Road Traffic Regulation Act 1984, s. 14 (1) (a). - Made: 21.01.2008. Coming into force: 03.02.2008. Effect: None. Territorial extent & classification: E. Local *Unpublished*

The A194(M) Motorway (Birtley Interchange to Whitemare Pool Interchange) (Temporary Restriction and Prohibition of Traffic) Order 2008 No. 2008/2069. - Enabling power: Road Traffic Regulation Act 1984, s. 14 (1) (a). - Made: 21.07.2008. Coming into force: 01.08.2008. Effect: None. Territorial extent & classification: E. Local *Unpublished*

The A194(M) Motorway (Follingsby Interchange to Havannah Interchange) (Temporary Restriction and Prohibition of Traffic) Order 2008 No. 2008/1129. - Enabling power: Road Traffic Regulation Act 1984, s. 14 (1) (a) (7). - Made: 14.04.2008. Coming into force: 27.04.2008. Effect: None. Territorial extent & classification: E. Local *Unpublished*

The A249 Trunk Road (Key Street - Cowstead Roundabout) (Temporary Prohibition of Traffic) Order 2008 No. 2008/89. - Enabling power: Road Traffic Regulation Act 1984, s. 14 (1) (a). - Made: 14.01.2008. Coming into force: 21.01.2008. Effect: None. Territorial extent & classification: E. Local *Unpublished*

The A249 Trunk Road (Kingsferry Bridge) (Temporary Prohibition of Traffic) Order 2008 No. 2008/1563. - Enabling power: Road Traffic Regulation Act 1984, s. 14 (1) (a). - Made: 09.06.2008. Coming into force: 20.06.2008. Effect: None. Territorial extent & classification: E. Local *Unpublished*

The A249 Trunk Road (Whiteway - Queensborough) (Temporary Prohibition of Traffic) Order 2008 No. 2008/150. - Enabling power: Road Traffic Regulation Act 1984, s. 14 (1) (a). - Made: 21.01.2008. Coming into force: 28.01.2008. Effect: None. Territorial extent & classification: E. Local *Unpublished*

The A259 Trunk Road (Camber Bend) (Temporary Speed Restrictions) Order 2008 No. 2008/2516. - Enabling power: Road Traffic Regulation Act 1984, s. 14 (1) (a). - Made: 15.09.2008. Coming into force: 20.09.2008. Effect: None. Territorial extent & classification: E. Local *Unpublished*

The A259 Trunk Road (Guldeford Lane Corner - Woolpack Corner) (Temporary 10 Miles Per Hour Speed Restriction) Order 2008 No. 2008/1173. - Enabling power: Road Traffic Regulation Act 1984, s. 14 (1) (a). - Made: 21.04.2008. Coming into force: 26.04.2008. Effect: None. Territorial extent & classification: E. Local *Unpublished*

The A259 Trunk Road (Icklesham) (Temporary Restriction and Prohibtion of Traffic) Order 2008 No. 2008/2720. - Enabling power: Road Traffic Regulation Act 1984, s. 14 (1) (a). - Made: 06.10.2008. Coming into force: 11.10.2008. Effect: None. Territorial extent & classification: E. Local *Unpublished*

The A259 Trunk Road (King Offa Way) (Temporary Prohibition of Traffic) Order 2008 No. 2008/1172. - Enabling power: Road Traffic Regulation Act 1984, s. 14 (1) (a). - Made: 21.04.2008. Coming into force: 26.04.2008. Effect: None. Territorial extent & classification: E. Local *Unpublished*

The A259 Trunk Road (Little Common Road, Bexhill) (Temporary Prohibition of Traffic) Order 2008 No. 2008/2894. - Enabling power: Road Traffic Regulation Act 1984, s. 16A (2) (a). - Made: 27.10.2008. Coming into force: 01.11.2008. Effect: None. Territorial extent & classification: E. Local *Unpublished*

The A259 Trunk Road (Various Roads, Rye) (Temporary Restriction and Prohibition of Traffic) Order 2008 No. 2008/2892. - Enabling power: Road Traffic Regulation Act 1984, s. 16A (2) (a). - Made: 27.10.2008. Coming into force: 01.11.2008. Effect: None. Territorial extent & classification: E. Local *Unpublished*

The A282 Trunk Road (Junction 1A) (Temporary Prohibition of Traffic) Order 2008 No. 2008/3316. - Enabling power: Road Traffic Regulation Act 1984, s. 14 (1) (a). - Made: 15.12.2008. Coming into force: 03.01.2009. Effect: None. Territorial extent & classification: E. Local *Unpublished*

The A303 Trunk Road (A345 Countess Roundabout to A338 Parkhouse Junction) (Temporary Prohibition of Traffic) Order 2008 No. 2008/2409. - Enabling power: Road Traffic Regulation Act 1984, s. 14 (1) (a). - Made: 03.09.2008. Coming into force: 05.09.2008. Effect: None. Territorial extent & classification: E. Local *Unpublished*

The A303 Trunk Road (A356 Prophets Lane to Hayes End Roundabout, South Petherton, Somerset) (Temporary Prohibition of Traffic) Order 2008 No. 2008/1449. - Enabling power: Road Traffic Regulation Act 1984, s. 14 (1) (a). - Made: 28.05.2008. Coming into force: 30.05.2008. Effect: None. Territorial extent & classification: E. Local *Unpublished*

The A303 Trunk Road (Barton Stacey Junction, Slip Roads) (Temporary Prohibition of Traffic) Order 2008 No. 2008/846. - Enabling power: Road Traffic Regulation Act 1984, s. 14 (1) (a). - Made: 03.03.2008. Coming into force: 08.03.2008. Effect: None. Territorial extent & classification: E. Local *Unpublished*

The A303 Trunk Road (Bearley Lane, near Tintinhull) (Temporary Prohibition of Traffic) Order 2008 No. 2008/1357. - Enabling power: Road Traffic Regulation Act 1984, s. 14 (1) (b). - Made: 14.05.2008. Coming into force: 21.05.2008. Effect: None. Territorial extent & classification: E. Local *Unpublished*

The A303 Trunk Road (Bullington Cross - Bransbury) (Temporary Restriction and Prohibition of Traffic) Order 2008 No. 2008/1839. - Enabling power: Road Traffic Regulation Act 1984, s. 14 (1) (a). - Made: 30.06.2008. Coming into force: 05.07.2008. Effect: None. Territorial extent & classification: E. Local *Unpublished*

The A303 Trunk Road (Cartgate Roundabout to A356 Prophets Lane, near Martock, Somerset) (Temporary Prohibition of Traffic) Order 2008 No. 2008/1451. - Enabling power: Road Traffic Regulation Act 1984, s. 14 (1) (a). - Made: 28.05.2008. Coming into force: 30.05.2008. Effect: None. Territorial extent & classification: E. Local *Unpublished*

The A303 Trunk Road (Cartgate Roundabout to Ilchester Road Junction , Somerset) (Temporary Prohibition of Traffic) Order 2008 No. 2008/2398. - Enabling power: Road Traffic Regulation Act 1984, s. 14 (1) (a). - Made: 02.09.2008. Coming into force: 05.09.2008. Effect: None. Territorial extent & classification: E. Local *Unpublished*

The A303 Trunk Road (Chicklade, Wiltshire) (Temporary Restriction of Traffic) Order 2008 No. 2008/3323. - Enabling power: Road Traffic Regulation Act 1984, s. 14 (1) (a). - Made: 17.12.2008. Coming into force: 30.12.2008. Effect: None. Territorial extent & classification: E. Local *Unpublished*

The A303 Trunk Road (Ilminster to South Petherton, Somerset) (Temporary Prohibition and Restriction of Traffic) Order 2008 No. 2008/2906. - Enabling power: Road Traffic Regulation Act 1984, s. 14 (1) (a). - Made: 28.10.2008. Coming into force: 31.10.2008. Effect: None. Territorial extent & classification: E. Local *Unpublished*

The A303 Trunk Road (Mere to Hindon, Wiltshire) (Temporary Prohibition and Restriction of Traffic) Order 2008 No. 2008/3322. - Enabling power: Road Traffic Regulation Act 1984, s. 14 (1) (a). - Made: 17.12.2008. Coming into force: 31.12.2008. Effect: None. Territorial extent & classification: E. Local *Unpublished*

The A303 Trunk Road (Mere to Junction with the A350 Near Hindon, Wiltshire) (Temporary Prohibition of Traffic) Order 2008 No. 2008/112. - Enabling power: Road Traffic Regulation Act 1984, s. 14 (1) (a). - Made: 16.01.2008. Coming into force: 19.01.2008. Effect: None. Territorial extent & classification: E. Local *Unpublished*

The A303 Trunk Road (Salisbury Road Interchange - Hundred Acre Interchange) (Temporary Retriction and Prohibition of Traffic) Order 2008 No. 2008/2321. - Enabling power: Road Traffic Regulation Act 1984, s. 14 (1) (a). - Made: 26.08.2008. Coming into force: 30.08.2008. Effect: None. Territorial extent & classification: E. Local *Unpublished*

The A303 Trunk Road (Southfields Roundabout to Horton, Somerset) (Temporary Prohibition of Traffic) Order 2008 No. 2008/1493. - Enabling power: Road Traffic Regulation Act 1984, s. 14 (1) (a). - Made: 27.05.2008. Coming into force: 30.05.2008. Effect: None. Territorial extent & classification: E. Local *Unpublished*

The A303 Trunk Road (Stonehenge Summer Solstice) (Temporary Restriction of Traffic) Order 2008 No. 2008/1620. - Enabling power: Road Traffic Regulation Act 1984, s. 14 (1) (b). - Made: 13.06.2008. Coming into force: 18.06.2008. Effect: None. Territorial extent & classification: E. Local *Unpublished*

The A303 Trunk Road (Tinkers Hill Junction, near Mere to Countess Roundabout, near Amesbury, Wiltshire) (Temporary Prohibition of Traffic) Order 2008 No. 2008/2399. - Enabling power: Road Traffic Regulation Act 1984, s. 14 (1) (a). - Made: 02.09.2008. Coming into force: 05.09.2008. Effect: None. Territorial extent & classification: E. Local *Unpublished*

The A303 Trunk Road (West of Andover - Salisbury Road) (Temporary Restriction and Prohibition of Traffic) Order 2008 No. 2008/280. - Enabling power: Road Traffic Regulation Act 1984, s. 14 (1) (a). - Made: 28.01.2008. Coming into force: 02.02.2008. Effect: None. Territorial extent & classification: E. Local *Unpublished*

The A404(M) Motorway (Junction 9A, Northbound Exit Slip Road) (Temporary Prohibition of Traffic) Order 2008 No. 2008/1298. - Enabling power: Road Traffic Regulation Act 1984, s. 14 (1) (a). - Made: 06.05.2008. Coming into force: 10.05.2008. Effect: None. Territorial extent & classification: E. Local *Unpublished*

The A404 Trunk Road (Bisham - Marlow) (Temporary Speed Restrictions) Order 2008 No. 2008/147. - Enabling power: Road Traffic Regulation Act 1984, s. 14 (1) (a). - Made: 21.01.2008. Coming into force: 26.01.2008. Effect: None. Territorial extent & classification: E. Local *Unpublished*

The A404 Trunk Road (Marlow - Handy Cross, Northbound) (Temporary Prohibition of Traffic) Order 2008 No. 2008/1009. - Enabling power: Road Traffic Regulation Act 1984, s. 14 (1) (a). - Made: 17.03.2008. Coming into force: 22.03.2008. Effect: None. Territorial extent & classification: E. Local *Unpublished*

The A404 Trunk Road (Marlow Interchange and Bisham Roundabout) (Temporary Restriction and Prohibition of Traffic) Order 2008 No. 2008/1058. - Enabling power: Road Traffic Regulation Act 1984, s. 14 (1) (a). - Made: 25.02.2008. Coming into force: 01.03.2008. Effect: None. Territorial extent & classification: E. Local *Unpublished*

The A405 Trunk Road (M1 Junction 6) (Temporary Prohibition of Traffic) Order 2008 No. 2008/1232. - Enabling power: Road Traffic Regulation Act 1984, s. 14 (1) (a). - Made: 28.04.2008. Coming into force: 04.05.2008. Effect: None. Territorial extent & classification: E. Local *Unpublished*

The A417 & A419 Trunk Roads (Swindon and Gloucestershire Layby Closures - Various Sites) (Temporary Prohibition of Traffic) Order 2008 No. 2008/2588. - Enabling power: Road Traffic Regulation Act 1984, s. 14 (1) (a). - Made: 23.09.2008. Coming into force: 29.09.2008. Effect: None. Territorial extent & classification: E. Local *Unpublished*

The A417 Trunk Road (Burford Road Junction to Air Balloon Roundabout, Gloucestershire) (Temporary Prohibition and Restriction of Traffic) Order 2008 No. 2008/2031. - Enabling power: Road Traffic Regulation Act 1984, s. 14 (1) (a). - Made: 09.07.2008. Coming into force: 16.07.2008. Effect: None. Territorial extent & classification: E. Local *Unpublished*

The A419 Trunk Road (A420 White Hart Roundabout to Commonhead Junction, Swindon) (Temporary Prohibition of Traffic) Order 2008 No. 2008/2801. - Enabling power: Road Traffic Regulation Act 1984, s. 14 (1) (a). - Made: 14.10.2008. Coming into force: 21.10.2008. Effect: None. Territorial extent & classification: E. Local *Unpublished*

The A419 Trunk Road (Castle Eaton and Kingshill Junctions, Near Cricklade) (Temporary Prohibition of Traffic) Order 2008 No. 2008/1989. - Enabling power: Road Traffic Regulation Act 1984, s. 14 (1) (b). - Made: 08.07.2008. Coming into force: 11.07.2008. Effect: None. Territorial extent & classification: E. Local *Unpublished*

The A419 Trunk Road (Commonhead Junction to Turnpike Junction, Swindon) (Temporary Prohibition of Traffic) Order 2008 No. 2008/2802. - Enabling power: Road Traffic Regulation Act 1984, s. 14 (1) (a). - Made: 14.10.2008. Coming into force: 22.10.2008. Effect: None. Territorial extent & classification: E. Local *Unpublished*

The A419 Trunk Road (Commonhead Roundabout to A420 White Hart Roundabout, Swindon) (Temporary Prohibition of Traffic) Order 2008 No. 2008/2314. - Enabling power: Road Traffic Regulation Act 1984, s. 14 (1) (a). - Made: 26.08.2008. Coming into force: 03.09.2008. Effect: None. Territorial extent & classification: E. Local *Unpublished*

The A419 Trunk Road (South Cerney to Cricklade, Wiltshire) (Temporary Prohibition of Traffic) Order 2008 No. 2008/2800. - Enabling power: Road Traffic Regulation Act 1984, s. 14 (1) (a). - Made: 14.10.2008. Coming into force: 22.10.2008. Effect: None. Territorial extent & classification: E. Local *Unpublished*

The A419 Trunk Road (Turnpike Roundabout to Blunsdon Hill) (Temporary Prohibition and Restriction of Traffic) Order 2008 No. 2008/1302. - Enabling power: Road Traffic Regulation Act 1984, ss. 14 (1) (a), 122A. - Made: 06.05.2008. Coming into force: 09.05.2008. Effect: None. Territorial extent & classification: E. Local *Unpublished*

The A421 Trunk Road (A421/A6 Interchange, Bedford Southern Bypass, Elstow, Bedfordshire) (Temporary Prohibition of Traffic) (No. 2) Order 2008 No. 2008/189. - Enabling power: Road Traffic Regulation Act 1984, s. 14 (1) (a). - Made: 21.01.2008. Coming into force: 28.01.2008. Effect: None. Territorial extent & classification: E. Local *Unpublished*

The A421 Trunk Road (A421/A6 Interchange, Bedford Southern Bypass, Elstow, Bedfordshire) (Temporary Prohibition of Traffic) Order 2008 No. 2008/1527. - Enabling power: Road Traffic Regulation Act 1984, s. 14 (1) (a). - Made: 27.05.2008. Coming into force: 03.06.2008. Effect: None. Territorial extent & classification: E. Local *Unpublished*

The A421 Trunk Road (A421/A6 Interchange, Bedford Southern Bypass, Elstow, Bedfordshire) (Temporary Prohibition of Traffic) Order 2008 No. 2008/65. - Enabling power: Road Traffic Regulation Act 1984, s. 14 (1) (a). - Made: 04.01.2008. Coming into force: 11.01.2008. Effect: None. Territorial extent & classification: E. Local *Unpublished*

The A421 Trunk Road (Bedford Southern Bypass, Bedfordshire) (Temporary Prohibition of Traffic) (No. 3) Order 2008 No. 2008/1022. - Enabling power: Road Traffic Regulation Act 1984, s. 14 (1) (a). - Made: 25.03.2008. Coming into force: 31.03.2008. Effect: None. Territorial extent & classification: E. Local *Unpublished*

The A421 Trunk Road (Kempston, Bedfordshire) (Temporary 40 Miles Per Hour Speed Restriction) Order 2008 No. 2008/991. - Enabling power: Road Traffic Regulation Act 1984, s. 14 (1) (a). - Made: 11.03.2008. Coming into force: 18.03.2008. Effect: None. Territorial extent & classification: E. Local *Unpublished*

The A421 Trunk Road (Marsh Leys Interchange, Kempston, Bedfordshire) (Temporary Restriction of Traffic) Order 2008 No. 2008/2231. - Enabling power: Road Traffic Regulation Act 1984, s. 14 (1) (a). - Made: 12.08.2008. Coming into force: 19.08.2008. Effect: None. Territorial extent & classification: E. Local *Unpublished*

The A428 Trunk Road (Eltisley, Cambridgeshire) (Temporary Restriction and Prohibition of Traffic) Order 2008 No. 2008/1708. - Enabling power: Road Traffic Regulation Act 1984, s. 14 (1) (a). - Made: 23.06.2008. Coming into force: 30.06.2008. Effect: None. Territorial extent & classification: E. Local *Unpublished*

The A428 Trunk Road (St. Neots Bypass, Cambridgeshire) (Temporary Prohibition of Traffic) Order 2008 No. 2008/1306. - Enabling power: Road Traffic Regulation Act 1984, s. 14 (1) (a). - Made: 06.05.2008. Coming into force: 12.05.2008. Effect: None. Territorial extent & classification: E. Local *Unpublished*

The A449 Trunk Road (Gailey to Four Ashes, Staffordshire) (Temporary 10 mph Speed Limits) Order 2008 No. 2008/761. - Enabling power: Road Traffic Regulation Act 1984, s. 14 (1) (a). - Made: 18.02.2008. Coming into force: 25.02.2008. Effect: None. Territorial extent & classification: E. Local *Unpublished*

The A453 Trunk Road (Kegworth to Nottingham) (Temporary Prohibition of Traffic) Order 2008 No. 2008/3351. - Enabling power: Road Traffic Regulation Act 1984, s. 14 (1) (a). - Made: 29.12.2008. Coming into force: 05.01.2009. Effect: None. Territorial extent & classification: E. Local *Unpublished*

The A453 Trunk Road (Ratcliffe on Soar) (Temporary Prohibition and Restriction of Traffic) Order 2008 No. 2008/191. - Enabling power: Road Traffic Regulation Act 1984, s. 14 (1) (a). - Made: 18.01.2008. Coming into force: 25.01.2008. Effect: None. Territorial extent & classification: E. Local. - Revoked by S.I .2008/3219 (Unpublished) *Unpublished*

The A453 Trunk Road (Ratcliffe on Soar) (Temporary Prohibition of Traffic) Order 2008 No. 2008/2799. - Enabling power: Road Traffic Regulation Act 1984, s. 14 (1) (a). - Made: 10.10.2008. Coming into force: 17.10.2008. Effect: None. Territorial extent & classification: E. Local *Unpublished*

The A453 Trunk Road (Ratcliffe on Soar) (Temporary Restriction and Prohibition of Traffic) Order 2008 No. 2008/3219. - Enabling power: Road Traffic Regulation Act 1984, s. 14 (1) (a), sch. 9, para. 27 (1). - Made: 21.11.2008. Coming into force: 28.11.2008. Effect: S.I. 2008/191 revoked. Territorial extent & classification: E. Local *Unpublished*

The A456 Trunk Road (Kidderminster to Blakedown, Worcestershire) (Temporary Restriction of Traffic) Order 2008 No. 2008/821. - Enabling power: Road Traffic Regulation Act 1984, s. 14 (1) (a). - Made: 25.02.2008. Coming into force: 03.03.2008. Effect: None. Territorial extent & classification: E. Local *Unpublished*

The A483 Trunk Road (A55 Posthouse Roundabout to Pulford Brook) (Temporary Prohibition of Traffic) Order 2008 No. 2008/3207. - Enabling power: Road Traffic Regulation Act 1984, s. 14 (1) (a). - Made: 11.11.2008. Coming into force: 04.12.2008. Effect: None. Territorial extent & classification: E. Local *Unpublished*

The A483 Trunk Road (Llanymynech, Shropshire) (Temporary Prohibition of Traffic) Order 2008 No. 2008/1049. - Enabling power: Road Traffic Regulation Act 1984, s. 14 (1) (a). - Made: 22.02.2008. Coming into force: 29.02.2008. Effect: None. Territorial extent & classification: E. Local *Unpublished*

The A483 Trunk Road (Llynclys, Shropshire) (Temporary Restriction of Traffic) Order 2008 No. 2008/448. - Enabling power: Road Traffic Regulation Act 1984, s. 14 (1) (a). - Made: 15.02.2008. Coming into force: 22.02.2008. Effect: None. Territorial extent & classification: E. Local *Unpublished*

The A483 Trunk Road (Posthouse Roundabout Resurfacing) (Temporary Prohibition of Traffic) Order 2008 No. 2008/1614. - Enabling power: Road Traffic Regulation Act 1984, s. 14 (1) (a). - Made: 11.06.2008. Coming into force: 15.06.2008. Effect: None. Territorial extent & classification: E. Local *Unpublished*

The A500 Trunk Road and M6 Motorway (Near Stoke-on-Trent, Staffordshire) (Temporary Restriction and Prohibition of Traffic) Order 2008 No. 2008/2659. - Enabling power: Road Traffic Regulation Act 1984, s. 14 (1) (a). - Made: 26.09.2008. Coming into force: 03.10.2008. Effect: None. Territorial extent & classification: E. Local *Unpublished*

The A500 Trunk Road (Hanford, Staffordshire) (Temporary Prohibition of Traffic) Order 2008 No. 2008/248. - Enabling power: Road Traffic Regulation Act 1984, s. 14 (1) (a). - Made: 21.01.2008. Coming into force: 28.01.2008. Effect: None. Territorial extent & classification: E. Local *Unpublished*

The A500 Trunk Road (Junction with the A53 Etruria Road) (Slip Road) (Temporary Prohibition of Traffic) Order 2008 No. 2008/2120. - Enabling power: Road Traffic Regulation Act 1984, s. 14 (1) (a). - Made: 21.07.2008. Coming into force: 28.07.2008. Effect: None. Territorial extent & classification: E. Local *Unpublished*

The A500 Trunk Road (Junction with the A53 Etruria Road) (Southbound Exit Slip Road) (Temporary Prohibition of Traffic) Order 2008 No. 2008/3355. - Enabling power: Road Traffic Regulation Act 1984, s. 14 (1) (a). - Made: 29.12.2008. Coming into force: 05.01.2009. Effect: None. Territorial extent & classification: E. Local *Unpublished*

The A500 Trunk Road (Near Tunstall, Staffordshire) (Temporary Prohibition of Traffic in Layby) Order 2008 No. 2008/1295. - Enabling power: Road Traffic Regulation Act 1984, s. 14 (1) (a). - Made: 25.04.2008. Coming into force: 02.05.2008. Effect: None. Territorial extent & classification: E. Local *Unpublished*

The A500 Trunk Road (Porthill Interchange, Staffordshire) (Temporary Prohibition of Traffic) Order 2008 No. 2008/1998. - Enabling power: Road Traffic Regulation Act 1984, s. 14 (1) (a). - Made: 07.07.2008. Coming into force: 14.07.2008. Effect: None. Territorial extent & classification: E. Local *Unpublished*

The A500 Trunk Road (Queensway, Stoke-on-Trent) (Temporary Prohibition of Traffic) Order 2008 No. 2008/3284. - Enabling power: Road Traffic Regulation Act 1984, s. 14 (1) (a). - Made: 05.12.2008. Coming into force: 12.12.2008. Effect: None. Territorial extent & classification: E. Local *Unpublished*

The A500 Trunk Road (Stoke-on-Trent and Newcastle-under-Lyme) (Temporary Restriction and Prohibition of Traffic) Order 2008 No. 2008/2195. - Enabling power: Road Traffic Regulation Act 1984, s. 14 (1) (a). - Made: 28.07.2008. Coming into force: 04.08.2008. Effect: None. Territorial extent & classification: E. Local *Unpublished*

The A500 Trunk Road (Stoke-on-Trent) (Temporary Prohibition of Traffic) Order 2008 No. 2008/3283. - Enabling power: Road Traffic Regulation Act 1984, s. 14 (1) (a). - Made: 05.12.2008. Coming into force: 12.12.2008. Effect: None. Territorial extent & classification: E. Local *Unpublished*

The A500 Trunk Road (Talke Roundabout, Staffordshire) (Temporary Restriction and Prohibition of Traffic) Order 2008 No. 2008/2581. - Enabling power: Road Traffic Regulation Act 1984, s. 14 (1) (a). - Made: 12.09.2008. Coming into force: 19.09.2008. Effect: None. Territorial extent & classification: E. Local *Unpublished*

The A500 Trunk Road (Tunstall Junction, Staffordshire) (Temporary Prohibition of Traffic) Order 2008 No. 2008/986. - Enabling power: Road Traffic Regulation Act 1984, s. 14 (1) (a). - Made: 14.03.2008. Coming into force: 21.03.2008. Effect: None. Territorial extent & classification: E. Local *Unpublished*

The A550 Trunk Road (Between the A5117 at Shotwick and the A540 at Two Mills) (Temporary Prohibition of Traffic) Order 2008 No. 2008/2421. - Enabling power: Road Traffic Regulation Act 1984, s. 14 (1) (a). - Made: 19.08.2008. Coming into force: 14.09.2008. Effect: None. Territorial extent & classification: E. Local *Unpublished*

The A550 Trunk Road (Woodbank Junction) (Prohibition of Left and Right Turns) Order 2008 No. 2008/3334. - Enabling power: Road Traffic Regulation Act 1984, ss. 1 (1), 2 (1)(2). - Made: 08.12.2008. Coming into force: 19.12.2008. Effect: None. Territorial extent & classification: E. Local *Unpublished*

The A556 Trunk Road (Millington) (50 Miles Per Hour Speed Limit) Experimental Traffic Order 2008 No. 2008/881. - Enabling power: Road Traffic Regulation Act 1984, ss. 9 (1) (3) (4), 10 (1) (2). - Made: 25.02.2008. Coming into force: 06.03.2008. Effect: None. Territorial extent & classification: E. Local *Unpublished*

The A556 Trunk Road (RHS Flower Show) (Temporary Prohibition of Right Turns) Order 2008 No. 2008/1982. - Enabling power: Road Traffic Regulation Act 1984, s. 14 (1) (b). - Made: 27.06.2008. Coming into force: 22.07.2008. Effect: None. Territorial extent & classification: E. Local *Unpublished*

The A570 Trunk Road (Liverpool Road to Scarth Hill Lane) (Temporary Prohibition of Traffic) Order 2008 No. 2008/127. - Enabling power: Road Traffic Regulation Act 1984, s. 14 (1) (a). - Made: 14.01.2008. Coming into force: 10.02.2008. Effect: None. Territorial extent & classification: E. Local *Unpublished*

The A570 Trunk Road (Scarisbrick Brick, Scarisbrick) (Temporary Prohibition of Traffic) Order 2008 No. 2008/459. - Enabling power: Road Traffic Regulation Act 1984, s. 14 (1) (a). - Made: 11.02.2008. Coming into force: 06.03.2008. Effect: None. Territorial extent & classification: E. Local *Unpublished*

The A585 Trunk Road (Left Turn Lane into West Drive, Thornton-Cleveleys) (Temporary Prohibition of Pedestrians and Traffic) Order 2008 No. 2008/2595. - Enabling power: Road Traffic Regulation Act 1984, s. 14 (1) (a). - Made: 22.09.2008. Coming into force: 19.10.2008. Effect: None. Territorial extent & classification: E. Local *Unpublished*

The A585 Trunk Road (Thornton Roundabout to Norcross Roundabout) (Temporary Restriction and Prohibition of Traffic) Amendment Order 2008 No. 2008/2613. - Enabling power: Road Traffic Regulation Act 1984, s. 14 (1) (a). - Made: 26.08.2008. Coming into force: 21.09.2008. Effect: None. Territorial extent & classification: E. Local *Unpublished*

The A585 Trunk Road (Thornton Roundabout to Norcross Roundabout) (Temporary Restriction and Prohibition of Traffic) Order 2008 No. 2008/2021. - Enabling power: Road Traffic Regulation Act 1984, s. 14 (1) (a). - Made: 07.07.2008. Coming into force: 03.08.2008. Effect: None. Territorial extent & classification: E. Local *Unpublished*

The A590 Trunk Road (Arrad Foot Resurfacing) (Temporary Prohibition and Restriction of Traffic) Order 2008 No. 2008/2416. - Enabling power: Road Traffic Regulation Act 1984, s. 14 (1) (a). - Made: 26.08.2008. Coming into force: 21.09.2008. Effect: None. Territorial extent & classification: E. Local *Unpublished*

The A590 Trunk Road (Arrad Foot to Greenodd) (Temporary Prohibition and Restriction of Traffic) Order 2008 No. 2008/2016. - Enabling power: Road Traffic Regulation Act 1984, s. 14 (1) (a). - Made: 07.07.2008. Coming into force: 03.08.2008. Effect: None. Territorial extent & classification: E. Local *Unpublished*

The A590 Trunk Road (Booths Roundabout to Tank Square Roundabout, Ulverston) (Temporary Restriction and Prohibition of Traffic) Order 2008 No. 2008/1619. - Enabling power: Road Traffic Regulation Act 1984, s. 14 (1) (a). - Made: 09.06.2008. Coming into force: 06.07.2008. Effect: None. Territorial extent & classification: E. Local *Unpublished*

The A590 Trunk Road (Brettargh Holt Roundabout) (Temporary Prohibition and Restriction of Traffic) Order No. 2 2008 No. 2008/2413. - Enabling power: Road Traffic Regulation Act 1984, s. 14 (1) (a). - Made: 02.09.2008. Coming into force: 28.09.2008. Effect: None. Territorial extent & classification: E. Local *Unpublished*

The A590 Trunk Road (Brettargh Holt Roundabout) (Temporary Prohibition of Traffic) Order 2008 No. 2008/2620. - Enabling power: Road Traffic Regulation Act 1984, s. 14 (1) (a). - Made: 24.09.2008. Coming into force: 29.09.2008. Effect: None. Territorial extent & classification: E. Local *Unpublished*

The A590 Trunk Road (Brettargh Holt) (Temporary Restriction of Traffic) Order 2008 No. 2008/849. - Enabling power: Road Traffic Regulation Act 1984, s. 14 (1) (a). - Made: 27.02.2008. Coming into force: 09.03.2008. Effect: None. Territorial extent & classification: E. Local *Unpublished*

The A590 Trunk Road (Brettargh Holt to Milton) (Temporary Prohibition and Restriction of Traffic) Order 2008 No. 2008/2234. - Enabling power: Road Traffic Regulation Act 1984, s. 14 (1) (a). - Made: 11.08.2008. Coming into force: 06.09.2008. Effect: None. Territorial extent & classification: E. Local *Unpublished*

The A590 Trunk Road (Gilpin Bridge to Witherslack) (Temporary Prohibition and Restriction of Traffic) Order 2008 No. 2008/1710. - Enabling power: Road Traffic Regulation Act 1984, s. 14 (1) (a). - Made: 23.06.2008. Coming into force: 20.07.2008. Effect: None. Territorial extent & classification: E. Local *Unpublished*

The A590 Trunk Road (Greenodd to Ulverston) (Temporary Prohibition and Restriction of Traffic) Order 2008 No. 2008/2020. - Enabling power: Road Traffic Regulation Act 1984, s. 14 (1) (a). - Made: 07.07.2008. Coming into force: 03.08.2008. Effect: None. Territorial extent & classification: E. Local *Unpublished*

The A590 Trunk Road (High and Low Newton Bypass) (Temporary Restriction and Prohibition of Traffic) Order 2008 No. 2008/848. - Enabling power: Road Traffic Regulation Act 1984, s. 14 (1) (a). - Made: 27.02.2008. Coming into force: 02.03.2008. Effect: None. Territorial extent & classification: E. Local *Unpublished*

The A590 Trunk Road (High and Low Newton Bypass) (Temporary Restriction of Traffic) Order 2008 No. 2008/1016. - Enabling power: Road Traffic Regulation Act 1984, s. 14 (1) (a). - Made: 25.03.2008. Coming into force: 30.03.2008. Effect: None. Territorial extent & classification: E. Local *Unpublished*

The A590 Trunk Road (High and Low Newton) (Cartmel Lane Junction) (Temporary Prohibition and Restriction of Traffic) Order 2008 No. 2008/407. - Enabling power: Road Traffic Regulation Act 1984, s. 14 (1) (a). - Made: 16.01.2008. Coming into force: 20.01.2008. Effect: None. Territorial extent & classification: E. Local *Unpublished*

The A590 Trunk Road (High and Low Newton) (Clearway) (Temporary Prohibition of Traffic) Order 2008 No. 2008/284. - Enabling power: Road Traffic Regulation Act 1984, s. 14 (1) (b). - Made: 29.01.2008. Coming into force: 24.02.2008. Effect: None. Territorial extent & classification: E. Local *Unpublished*

The A590 Trunk Road (High and Low Newton) (Near Oak Head Junction) (Temporary Prohibition of Traffic) Order 2008 No. 2008/1070. - Enabling power: Road Traffic Regulation Act 1984, s. 14 (1) (a). - Made: 02.04.2008. Coming into force: 06.04.2008. Effect: None. Territorial extent & classification: E. Local *Unpublished*

The A590 Trunk Road (High and Low Newton) (Oak Head Road Junction) (Temporary Prohibition and Restriction of Traffic) Order 2008 No. 2008/144. - Enabling power: Road Traffic Regulation Act 1984, s. 14 (1) (a). - Made: 15.01.2008. Coming into force: 10.02.2008. Effect: None. Territorial extent & classification: E. Local *Unpublished*

The A590 Trunk Road (Levens Easbound Layby) (Temporary Prohibition and Restriction of Traffic) Order 2008 No. 2008/70. - Enabling power: Road Traffic Regulation Act 1984, s. 14 (1) (a). - Made: 08.01.2008. Coming into force: 03.02.2008. Effect: None. Territorial extent & classification: E. Local *Unpublished*

The A590 Trunk Road (Levens Westbound Carriageway Resurfacing) (Temporary Prohibition and Restriction of Traffic) Order 2008 No. 2008/2495. - Enabling power: Road Traffic Regulation Act 1984, s. 14 (1) (a). - Made: 08.09.2008. Coming into force: 05.10.2008. Effect: None. Territorial extent & classification: E. Local *Unpublished*

The A590 Trunk Road (Meathop) (Closure of Gap in the Central Reservation) Order 2008 No. 2008/331. - Enabling power: Road Traffic Regulation Act 1984, s. 1 (1), 2 (1) (2). - Made: 29.01.2008. Coming into force: 14.02.2008. Effect: None. Territorial extent & classification: E. Local *Unpublished*

The A590 Trunk Road (Meathop Roundabout to Witherslack Junction) (Temporary Prohibition and Restriction of Traffic) Order 2008 No. 2008/2757. - Enabling power: Road Traffic Regulation Act 1984, s. 14 (1) (a). - Made: 07.10.2008. Coming into force: 02.11.2008. Effect: None. Territorial extent & classification: E. Local *Unpublished*

The A590 Trunk Road (Newby Bridge) (Temporary Restriction of Traffic) Order 2008 No. 2008/240. - Enabling power: Road Traffic Regulation Act 1984, s. 14 (1) (a). - Made: 22.01.2008. Coming into force: 03.02.2008. Effect: None. Territorial extent & classification: E. Local *Unpublished*

The A590 Trunk Road (Old Blackbarrow to Fiddler Hall, Newby Bridge) (Temporary Restriction and Prohibition of Traffic) Order 2008 No. 2008/2529. - Enabling power: Road Traffic Regulation Act 1984, s. 14 (1) (a). - Made: 15.09.2008. Coming into force: 12.10.2008. Effect: None. Territorial extent & classification: E. Local *Unpublished*

The A590 Trunk Road (Ulpha Cattle Grid) (Temporary Prohibition of Traffic) Order 2008 No. 2008/2412. - Enabling power: Road Traffic Regulation Act 1984, s. 14 (1) (a). - Made: 26.08.2008. Coming into force: 21.09.2008. Effect: None. Territorial extent & classification: E. Local *Unpublished*

The A595 Trunk Road (Crossbarrow to Winscales Resurfacing) (No. 2) (Temporary Restriction and Prohibition of Traffic) Order 2008 No. 2008/2183. - Enabling power: Road Traffic Regulation Act 1984, s. 14 (1) (a). - Made: 05.08.2008. Coming into force: 31.08.2008. Effect: None. Territorial extent & classification: E. Local *Unpublished*

The A595 Trunk Road (Crossbarrow to Winscales Resurfacing) (Temporary Restriction and Prohibition of Traffic) Order 2008 No. 2008/124. - Enabling power: Road Traffic Regulation Act 1984, s. 14 (1) (a). - Made: 15.01.2008. Coming into force: 10.02.2008. Effect: None. Territorial extent & classification: E. Local *Unpublished*

The A595 Trunk Road (Mirehouse to Westlakes) (Temporary Prohibition and Restriction of Traffic) Order 2008 No. 2008/2308. - Enabling power: Road Traffic Regulation Act 1984, s. 14 (1) (a). - Made: 19.08.2008. Coming into force: 14.09.2008. Effect: None. Territorial extent & classification: E. Local *Unpublished*

The A616 Trunk Road (Midhopestones) (Temporary 10 Miles Per Hour Speed Restriction) Order 2008 No. 2008/2404. - Enabling power: Road Traffic Regulation Act 1984, s. 14 (1) (a). - Made: 02.09.2008. Coming into force: 16.09.2008. Effect: None. Territorial extent & classification: E. Local *Unpublished*

The A616 Trunk Road (Westwood Roundabout to Newton Chambers Roundabout) and the M1 Motorway (Junction 35A) (Temporary Prohibition of Traffic) Order 2008 No. 2008/2379. - Enabling power: Road Traffic Regulation Act 1984, s. 14 (1) (a) (7). - Made: 26.08.2008. Coming into force: 07.09.2008. Effect: None. Territorial extent & classification: E. Local *Unpublished*

The A616 Trunk Road (Wortley Interchange) (Temporary Prohibition of Traffic) Order 2008 No. 2008/2971. - Enabling power: Road Traffic Regulation Act 1984, s. 14 (1) (a). - Made: 10.11.2008. Coming into force: 25.11.2008. Effect: None. Territorial extent & classification: E. Local *Unpublished*

The A616 Trunk Road (Wortley Junction to Newton Chambers Roundabout) (Temporary Prohibition of Traffic) Order 2008 No. 2008/1673. - Enabling power: Road Traffic Regulation Act 1984, s. 14 (1) (a). - Made: 19.06.2008. Coming into force: 02.07.2008. Effect: None. Territorial extent & classification: E. Local *Unpublished*

The A627(M) Motorway (Junction 2 to Junction 1 Southbound Carriageway, Junction 1 Southbound Exit Slip Road and Junction 2 Southbound Entry Slip Road) (Temporary Prohibition of Traffic) Order 2008 No. 2008/1382. - Enabling power: Road Traffic Regulation Act 1984, s. 14 (1) (a). - Made: 12.05.2008. Coming into force: 15.05.2008. Effect: None. Territorial extent & classification: E. Local *Unpublished*

The A627(M) Motorway (Northbound Link Road to the A664 Edinburgh Way) (Temporary Prohibition of Traffic) Order 2008 No. 2008/361. - Enabling power: Road Traffic Regulation Act 1984, s. 14 (1) (a). - Made: 04.02.2008. Coming into force: 14.02.2008. Effect: None. Territorial extent & classification: E. Local *Unpublished*

The A628 Trunk Road (Woodhead Pass Layby - Enterclough Retaining Wall) (Temporary Prohibition of Traffic) Order 2008 No. 2008/2476. - Enabling power: Road Traffic Regulation Act 1984, s. 14 (1) (b). - Made: 01.09.2008. Coming into force: 09.09.2008. Effect: None. Territorial extent & classification: E. Local *Unpublished*

The A628 Trunk Road (Woodhead to Salter's Brook) (Temporary Restriction and Prohibition of Traffic) (No. 2) Order 2008 No. 2008/1628. - Enabling power: Road Traffic Regulation Act 1984, s. 14 (1) (a). - Made: 16.06.2008. Coming into force: 29.06.2008. Effect: None. Territorial extent & classification: E. Local *Unpublished*

The A628 Trunk Road (Woodhead to Salter's Brook) (Temporary Restriction and Prohibition of Traffic) Order 2008 No. 2008/1028. - Enabling power: Road Traffic Regulation Act 1984, s. 14 (1) (a). - Made: 17.03.2008. Coming into force: 30.03.2008. Effect: None. Territorial extent & classification: E. Local *Unpublished*

The A631 Trunk Road (Tinsley Viaduct Lower Deck) (Temporary Prohibition of Traffic) (No. 2) Order 2008 No. 2008/1246. - Enabling power: Road Traffic Regulation Act 1984, s. 14 (1) (a). - Made: 28.04.2008. Coming into force: 11.05.2008. Effect: None. Territorial extent & classification: E. Local *Unpublished*

The A631 Trunk Road (Tinsley Viaduct Lower Deck) (Temporary Prohibition of Traffic) Order 2008 No. 2008/272. - Enabling power: Road Traffic Regulation Act 1984, s. 14 (1) (a). - Made: 21.01.2008. Coming into force: 21.01.2008. Effect: None. Territorial extent & classification: E. Local *Unpublished*

The A663 Trunk Road (Broadway, Chadderton) (Temporary Prohibition of Traffic) Order 2008 No. 2008/1662. - Enabling power: Road Traffic Regulation Act 1984, s. 14 (1) (a). - Made: 18.06.2008. Coming into force: 22.06.2008. Effect: None. Territorial extent & classification: E. Local *Unpublished*

The A1089 Trunk Road (Asda Roundabout) (Temporary Restriction and Prohibition of Traffic) Order 2008 No. 2008/2515. - Enabling power: Road Traffic Regulation Act 1984, s. 14 (1) (a). - Made: 15.09.2008. Coming into force: 20.09.2008. Effect: None. Territorial extent & classification: E. Local *Unpublished*

The A1089 Trunk Road (Asda Roundabout - Tilbury Docks) (Temporary Restriction and Prohibition of Traffic) Order 2008 No. 2008/348. - Enabling power: Road Traffic Regulation Act 1984, s. 14 (1) (a). - Made: 04.02.2008. Coming into force: 09.02.2008. Effect: None. Territorial extent & classification: E. Local *Unpublished*

The A1089 Trunk Road (ASDA Roundabout - Tilbury Docks) (Temporary Restriction and Prohibition of Traffic) Order 2008 Variation Order 2008 No. 2008/1120. - Enabling power: Road Traffic Regulation Act 1984, s. 14 (1) (a), sch. 9, para. 27 (1). - Made: 14.04.2008. Coming into force: 28.04.2008. Effect: S.I. 2008/348 varied. Territorial extent & classification: E. Local *Unpublished*

The A1089 Trunk Road (Orsett Heath, Lay-By) (Temporary Prohibition of Traffic) Order 2008 No. 2008/2812. - Enabling power: Road Traffic Regulation Act 1984, s. 14 (1) (a). - Made: 20.10.2008. Coming into force: 25.10.2008. Effect: None. Territorial extent & classification: E. Local *Unpublished*

The A2070 Trunk Road (A2042 Junction, Slip Roads) (Temporary Prohibition of Traffic) Order 2008 No. 2008/3279. - Enabling power: Road Traffic Regulation Act 1984, s. 14 (1) (a). - Made: 08.12.2008. Coming into force: 17.12.2008. Effect: None. Territorial extent & classification: E. Local *Unpublished*

The A2070 Trunk Road (Sheepfold Lane - Brenzett) (Temporary Speed Restriction) Order 2008 No. 2008/1057. - Enabling power: Road Traffic Regulation Act 1984, s. 14 (1) (a). - Made: 25.02.2008. Coming into force: 01.03.2008. Effect: None. Territorial extent & classification: E. Local *Unpublished*

The A4123 Trunk Road and the M5 Motorway (Junction 2, Oldbury) (Temporary Prohibition of Traffic) Order 2008 No. 2008/2584. - Enabling power: Road Traffic Regulation Act 1984, s. 14 (1) (a). - Made: 19.09.2008. Coming into force: 26.09.2008. Effect: None. Territorial extent & classification: E. Local *Unpublished*

The A4123 Trunk Road (Junction with Causeway Green Road) (Temporary Prohibition of Traffic) Order 2008 No. 2008/2576. - Enabling power: Road Traffic Regulation Act 1984, s. 14 (1) (a). - Made: 12.09.2008. Coming into force: 19.09.2008. Effect: None. Territorial extent & classification: E. Local *Unpublished*

The A4123 Trunk Road (Temporary Restriction and Prohibition of Traffic) Order 2008 No. 2008/2221. - Enabling power: Road Traffic Regulation Act 1984, s. 14 (1) (a). - Made: 08.08.2008. Coming into force: 15.08.2008. Effect: None. Territorial extent & classification: E. Local *Unpublished*

The A5006 Trunk Road (Sideway, Stoke-on-Trent) (Temporary Prohibition of Traffic) Order 2008 No. 2008/2219. - Enabling power: Road Traffic Regulation Act 1984, s. 14 (1) (a). - Made: 01.08.2008. Coming into force: 08.08.2008. Effect: None. Territorial extent & classification: E. Local *Unpublished*

The A5036 Trunk Road (Switch Island to A565 Crosby Road) (Temporary Prohibition and Restriction of Traffic) Order 2008 No. 2008/2596. - Enabling power: Road Traffic Regulation Act 1984, s. 14 (1) (a). - Made: 15.09.2008. Coming into force: 10.10.2008. Effect: None. Territorial extent & classification: E. Local *Unpublished*

The A5036 Trunk Road (Westbound from Princess Way Roundabout to Rawson Road) (Temporary Prohibition of Traffic) Order 2008 No. 2008/2655. - Enabling power: Road Traffic Regulation Act 1984, s. 14 (1) (a). - Made: 22.09.2008. Coming into force: 26.09.2008. Effect: None. Territorial extent & classification: E. Local *Unpublished*

The A5103 Trunk Road (And Southbound Entry Slip Road from the B5167) (Temporary Prohibition of Traffic) Order 2008 No. 2008/3340. - Enabling power: Road Traffic Regulation Act 1984, s. 14 (1) (a). - Made: 29.12.2008. Coming into force: 05.01.2009. Effect: None. Territorial extent & classification: E. Local *Unpublished*

The A5117 Trunk Road (Deeside Park Junction Improvement) (Temporary Prohibition of Traffic) Order 2008 No. 2008/2749. - Enabling power: Road Traffic Regulation Act 1984, s. 14 (1) (a). - Made: 07.10.2008. Coming into force: 12.10.2008. Effect: None. Territorial extent & classification: E. Local *Unpublished*

The A5117 Trunk Road (Deeside Park) (No. 2) (Temporary Prohibition of Traffic) Order 2008 No. 2008/3282. - Enabling power: Road Traffic Regulation Act 1984, s. 14 (1) (a). - Made: 01.12.2008. Coming into force: 07.12.2008. Effect: None. Territorial extent & classification: E. Local *Unpublished*

The A5117 Trunk Road (Deeside Park) (No.2) (Temporary Restriction of Traffic) Order 2008 No. 2008/854. - Enabling power: Road Traffic Regulation Act 1984, s. 14 (1) (b). - Made: 25.02.2008. Coming into force: 20.03.2008. Effect: None. Territorial extent & classification: E. Local *Unpublished*

The A5117 Trunk Road (Deeside Park) (Temporary Prohibition of Traffic) Order 2008 No. 2008/2420. - Enabling power: Road Traffic Regulation Act 1984, s. 14 (1) (a). - Made: 18.08.2008. Coming into force: 11.09.2008. Effect: None. Territorial extent & classification: E. Local *Unpublished*

The M1 (Junction 19) and M6 Motorways (Northamptonshire, Warwickshire and Leicestershire) (Temporary Restriction and Prohibition of Traffic) Order 2008 No. 2008/2144. - Enabling power: Road Traffic Regulation Act 1984, s. 14 (1) (a) (7). - Made: 29.07.2008. Coming into force: 05.08.2008. Effect: S.I. 1982/1163 partially suspended. Territorial extent & classification: E. Local *Unpublished*

The M1 Motorway and A42 and A453 Trunk Roads (Junction 23a, Leicestershire) (Temporary Restriction and Prohibition of Traffic) Order 2008 No. 2008/2119. - Enabling power: Road Traffic Regulation Act 1984, ss. 3 (2), 14 (1) (a) (5) (b) (6). - Made: 21.07.2008. Coming into force: 28.07.2008. Effect: None. Territorial extent & classification: E. Local *Unpublished*

The M1 Motorway and A42 Trunk Road (M1 Junction 23A, Leicestershire) (Slip Road) (Temporary Prohibition of Traffic) Order 2008 No. 2008/249. - Enabling power: Road Traffic Regulation Act 1984, s. 14 (1) (a). - Made: 18.01.2008. Coming into force: 25.01.2008. Effect: None. Territorial extent & classification: E. Local *Unpublished*

Road traffic: Traffic regulation

The M1 Motorway and the M10 Motorway (Junctions 6 - 8 and M10 Junction 1) (Temporary Prohibition of Traffic) Order 2008 No. 2008/2066. - Enabling power: Road Traffic Regulation Act 1984, s. 14 (1) (a). - Made: 21.07.2008. Coming into force: 01.08.2008. Effect: None. Territorial extent & classification: E. Local *Unpublished*

The M1 Motorway and the M62 Motorway (Lofthouse Interchange) (Temporary Prohibition of Traffic) (No. 2) Order 2008 No. 2008/2070. - Enabling power: Road Traffic Regulation Act 1984, s. 14 (1) (a). - Made: 21.07.2008. Coming into force: 03.08.2008. Effect: None. Territorial extent & classification: E. Local *Unpublished*

The M1 Motorway and the M62 Motorway (Lofthouse Interchange) (Temporary Prohibition of Traffic) (No. 3) Order 2008 No. 2008/2010. - Enabling power: Road Traffic Regulation Act 1984, s. 14 (1) (a). - Made: 07.07.2008. Coming into force: 19.07.2008. Effect: None. Territorial extent & classification: E. Local *Unpublished*

The M1 Motorway and the M62 Motorway (Lofthouse Interchange) (Temporary Prohibition of Traffic) Order 2008 No. 2008/892. - Enabling power: Road Traffic Regulation Act 1984, s. 14 (1) (a). - Made: 03.03.2008. Coming into force: 16.03.2008. Effect: None. Territorial extent & classification: E. Local *Unpublished*

The M1 Motorway (Junction 5, Northbound Entry Slip Road) (Temporary Prohibition of Traffic) Order 2008 No. 2008/1219. - Enabling power: Road Traffic Regulation Act 1984, s. 14 (1) (a). - Made: 21.04.2008. Coming into force: 26.04.2008. Effect: None. Territorial extent & classification: E. Local *Unpublished*

The M1 Motorway (Junction 11) Northbound Entry Slip Road (Temporary Prohibition of Traffic) Order 2008 No. 2008/339. - Enabling power: Road Traffic Regulation Act 1984, s. 14 (1) (a). - Made: 04.02.2008. Coming into force: 11.02.2008. Effect: None. Territorial extent & classification: E. Local *Unpublished*

The M1 Motorway (Junction 13) and the A421 Trunk Road (Brogborough, Bedfordshire) (Temporary Restriction and Prohibition of Traffic) Order 2008 No. 2008/341. - Enabling power: Road Traffic Regulation Act 1984, s. 14 (1) (a) 7. - Made: 04.02.2008. Coming into force: 11.02.2008. Effect: None. Territorial extent & classification: E. Local *Unpublished*

The M1 Motorway (Junction 14, Milton Keynes) (Temporary Restriction and Prohibition of Traffic) Order 2008 No. 2008/2179. - Enabling power: Road Traffic Regulation Act 1984, s. 14 (1) (a) (7). - Made: 29.07.2009. Coming into force: 05.08.2008. Effect: None. Territorial extent & classification: E. Local *Unpublished*

The M1 Motorway (Junction 16, Weedon, Northamptonshire) (Temporary Prohibition of Traffic) Order 2008 No. 2008/2462. - Enabling power: Road Traffic Regulation Act 1984, s. 14 (1) (a). - Made: 09.09.2008. Coming into force: 16.09.2008. Effect: None. Territorial extent & classification: E. Local *Unpublished*

The M1 Motorway (Junction 18 to Watford Gap Service Area, Northamptonshire) (Temporary Restriction and Prohibition of Traffic) Order 2008 No. 2008/1526. - Enabling power: Road Traffic Regulation Act 1984, s. 14 (1) (a) (7). - Made: 27.05.2008. Coming into force: 03.06.2008. Effect: None. Territorial extent & classification: E. Local *Unpublished*

The M1 Motorway (Junction 20, Lutterworth, Leicestershire) (Slip Road) (Temporary Prohibition of Traffic) Order 2008 No. 2008/3227. - Enabling power: Road Traffic Regulation Act 1984, s. 14 (1) (a). - Made: 14.11.2008. Coming into force: 21.11.2008. Effect: None. Territorial extent & classification: E. Local *Unpublished*

The M1 Motorway (Junction 21a to 21) (Southbound Carriageway) (Temporary Restriction of Traffic) Order 2008 No. 2008/323. - Enabling power: Road Traffic Regulation Act 1984, s. 14 (1) (a) 7. - Made: 21.01.2008. Coming into force: 28.01.2008. Effect: None. Territorial extent & classification: E. Local *Unpublished*

The M1 Motorway (Junction 23) (Slip Roads) (Temporary Prohibition of Traffic) Order 2008 No. 2008/1829. - Enabling power: Road Traffic Regulation Act 1984, s. 14 (1) (a). - Made: 20.06.2008. Coming into force: 27.06.2008. Effect: None. Territorial extent & classification: E. Local *Unpublished*

The M1 Motorway (Junction 24A, Leicestershire) (Temporary Restriction and Prohibition of Traffic) Order 2008 No. 2008/3360. - Enabling power: Road Traffic Regulation Act 1984, s. 14 (1) (a) (7). - Made: 22.12.2008. Coming into force: 29.12.2008. Effect: None. Territorial extent & classification: E. Local *Unpublished*

The M1 Motorway (Junction 24A) (Southbound Exit Slip Road) (Temporary Prohibition of Traffic) Order 2008 No. 2008/2959. - Enabling power: Road Traffic Regulation Act 1984, s. 14 (1) (a). - Made: 31.10.2008. Coming into force: 07.11.2008. Effect: None. Territorial extent & classification: E. Local *Unpublished*

The M1 Motorway (Junction 24 - Junction 29) (Slip Roads) (Temporary Prohibition of Traffic) Order 2008 No. 2008/247. - Enabling power: Road Traffic Regulation Act 1984, s. 14 (1) (a). - Made: 25.01.2008. Coming into force: 01.02.2008. Effect: None. Territorial extent & classification: E. Local *Unpublished*

The M1 Motorway (Junction 24, Near Kegworth, Leicestershire) (Temporary Restriction and Prohibition of Traffic) Order 2008 No. 2008/2383. - Enabling power: Road Traffic Regulation Act 1984, s. 14 (1) (a) (7). - Made: 22.08.2009. Coming into force: 29.08.2008. Effect: None. Territorial extent & classification: E. Local *Unpublished*

The M1 Motorway (Junction 29A) (Slip Road) (Temporary Prohibition of Traffic) Order 2008 No. 2008/2742. - Enabling power: Road Traffic Regulation Act 1984, s. 14 (1) (a). - Made: 03.10.2008. Coming into force: 10.10.2008. Effect: None. Territorial extent & classification: E. Local *Unpublished*

The M1 Motorway (Junction 30, Barlborough) (Temporary Prohibition of Traffic) Order 2008 No. 2008/767. - Enabling power: Road Traffic Regulation Act 1984, s. 14 (1) (a). - Made: 21.02.2008. Coming into force: 22.02.2008. Effect: None. Territorial extent & classification: E. Local *Unpublished*

The M1 Motorway (Junction 30 to Junction 31) (Temporary Restriction of Traffic) Order 2008 No. 2008/2137. - Enabling power: Road Traffic Regulation Act 1984, s. 14 (1) (a) (7). - Made: 29.07.2008. Coming into force: 08.08.2008. Effect: None. Territorial extent & classification: E. Local *Unpublished*

The M1 Motorway (Junction 31, Aston Interchange) (Temporary Prohibition of Traffic) Order 2008 No. 2008/3369. - Enabling power: Road Traffic Regulation Act 1984, s. 14 (1) (a). - Made: 30.12.2008. Coming into force: 11.01.2009. Effect: None. Territorial extent & classification: E. Local *Unpublished*

The M1 Motorway (Junction 34, Tinsley Viaduct) (Temporary Prohibition of Traffic) (No. 2) Order 2008 No. 2008/3043. - Enabling power: Road Traffic Regulation Act 1984, s. 14 (1) (a). - Made: 17.11.2008. Coming into force: 28.11.2008. Effect: None. Territorial extent & classification: E. Local *Unpublished*

The M1 Motorway (Junction 34, Tinsley Viaduct) (Temporary Prohibition of Traffic) Order 2008 No. 2008/766. - Enabling power: Road Traffic Regulation Act 1984, s. 14 (1) (a). - Made: 21.02.2008. Coming into force: 22.02.2008. Effect: None. Territorial extent & classification: E. Local *Unpublished*

The M1 Motorway (Junction 35A, Stocksbridge) (Temporary Prohibition of Traffic) Order 2008 No. 2008/1627. - Enabling power: Road Traffic Regulation Act 1984, s. 14 (1) (a). - Made: 16.06.2008. Coming into force: 18.06.2008. Effect: None. Territorial extent & classification: E. Local *Unpublished*

The M1 Motorway (Junction 36 to Junction 37) (Temporary Prohibition of Traffic) Order 2008 No. 2008/891. - Enabling power: Road Traffic Regulation Act 1984, s. 14 (1) (a). - Made: 03.03.2008. Coming into force: 16.03.2008. Effect: None. Territorial extent & classification: E. Local *Unpublished*

The M1 Motorway (Junction 38, Haigh) (Temporary Prohibition of Traffic) Order 2008 No. 2008/2053. - Enabling power: Road Traffic Regulation Act 1984, s. 14 (1) (a). - Made: 15.07.2008. Coming into force: 27.07.2008. Effect: None. Territorial extent & classification: E. Local *Unpublished*

The M1 Motorway (Junction 40 to Junction 41) (Temporary Restriction and Prohibition of Traffic) Order 2008 No. 2008/2067. - Enabling power: Road Traffic Regulation Act 1984, s. 14 (1) (a) (7). - Made: 22.07.2008. Coming into force: 03.08.2008. Effect: None. Territorial extent & classification: E. Local *Unpublished*

The M1 Motorway (Junction 42 to Junction 44 and Junction 47) (Temporary Restriction and Prohibition of Traffic) Order 2008 No. 2008/2204. - Enabling power: Road Traffic Regulation Act 1984, s. 14 (1) (a). - Made: 05.08.2008. Coming into force: 14.08.2008. Effect: None. Territorial extent & classification: E. Local *Unpublished*

The M1 Motorway (Junction 42 to Junction 44) and the M62 Motorway (Lofthouse Interchange) (Temporary Prohibition of Traffic) Order 2008 No. 2008/893. - Enabling power: Road Traffic Regulation Act 1984, s. 14 (1) (a). - Made: 04.03.2008. Coming into force: 17.03.2008. Effect: None. Territorial extent & classification: E. Local *Unpublished*

The M1 Motorway (Junction 44, Rothwell Haigh) (Temporary 50 Miles Per Hour Speed Restriction) (No. 2) Order 2008 No. 2008/1251. - Enabling power: Road Traffic Regulation Act 1984, s. 14 (1) (b). - Made: 28.04.2008. Coming into force: 05.05.2008. Effect: None. Territorial extent & classification: E. Local *Unpublished*

The M1 Motorway (Junction 44, Rothwell Haigh) (Temporary Prohibition of Traffic) Order 2008 No. 2008/1252. - Enabling power: Road Traffic Regulation Act 1984, s. 14 (1) (a). - Made: 28.04.2008. Coming into force: 12.05.2008. Effect: None. Territorial extent & classification: E. Local *Unpublished*

The M1 Motorway (Junction 44 Rothwell Haigh) (Temporary Restriction and Prohibition of Traffic) Order 2008 No. 2008/1569. - Enabling power: Road Traffic Regulation Act 1984, s. 14 (1) (a) (7). - Made: 09.06.2008. Coming into force: 23.06.2008. Effect: None. Territorial extent & classification: E. Local *Unpublished*

The M1 Motorway (Junction45 to Junction 48) and the A1(M) Motorway (Junction 45, Bramham Crossroads) (Temporary Restriction and Prohibition of Traffic) Order 2008 No. 2008/2635. - Enabling power: Road Traffic Regulation Act 1984, s. 14 (1) (a) (7). - Made: 29.09.2008. Coming into force: 12.10.2008. Effect: None. Territorial extent & classification: E. Local *Unpublished*

The M1 Motorway (Junction 47 to Junction 48) (Temporary Prohibition of Traffic) Order 2008 No. 2008/890. - Enabling power: Road Traffic Regulation Act 1984, s. 14 (1) (a). - Made: 10.03.2008. Coming into force: 25.03.2008. Effect: None. Territorial extent & classification: E. Local *Unpublished*

The M1 Motorway (Junctions 1 - 4, Slip Roads) (Temporary Prohibition of Traffic) Order 2008 No. 2008/994. - Enabling power: Road Traffic Regulation Act 1984, s. 14 (1) (a). - Made: 25.03.2008. Coming into force: 01.04.2008. Effect: None. Territorial extent & classification: E. Local *Unpublished*

The M1 Motorway (Junctions 1 - 4) (Temporary Prohibition of Traffic) Order 2008 No. 2008/2985. - Enabling power: Road Traffic Regulation Act 1984, s. 14 (1) (a). - Made: 10.11.2008. Coming into force: 15.11.2008. Effect: None. Territorial extent & classification: E. Local *Unpublished*

Road traffic: Traffic regulation

The M1 Motorway (Junctions 3 - 5, Northbound) (Temporary Restriction and Prohibition of Traffic) Order 2008 No. 2008/3278. - Enabling power: Road Traffic Regulation Act 1984, s. 14 (1) (a) (7). - Made: 08.12.2008. Coming into force: 29.12.2008. Effect: None. Territorial extent & classification: E. Local *Unpublished*

The M1 Motorway (Junctions 13 to 15, Bedfordshire and Buckinghamshire) (Temporary Restriction and Prohibition of Traffic) Order 2008 No. 2008/2196. - Enabling power: Road Traffic Regulation Act 1984, s. 14 (1) (a) (7). - Made: 04.08.2008. Coming into force: 11.08.2008. Effect: None. Territorial extent & classification: E. Local *Unpublished*

The M1 Motorway (Junctions 13 to 15, Bedfordshire and Buckinghamshire) (Temporary Restriction and Prohibition of Traffic) Order 2008 No. 2008/1516. - Enabling power: Road Traffic Regulation Act 1984, s. 14 (1) (a) (7). - Made: 27.05.2008. Coming into force: 02.06.2008. Effect: None. Territorial extent & classification: E. Local *Unpublished*

The M1 Motorway (Junctions 20 - 21, Leicestershire) (Temporary Restriction and Prohibition of Traffic) Order 2008 No. 2008/2747. - Enabling power: Road Traffic Regulation Act 1984, s. 14 (1) (a) (7). - Made: 03.10.2008. Coming into force: 10.10.2008. Effect: None. Territorial extent & classification: E. Local *Unpublished*

The M1 Motorway Junctions 20 - 24 and A46 Trunk Road Leicestershire) (Temporary Restriction and Prohibition of Traffic) Order 2008 No. 2008/1544. - Enabling power: Road Traffic Regulation Act 1984, s. 14 (1) (a) 7. - Made: 16.05.2008. Coming into force: 23.05.2008. Effect: None. Territorial extent & classification: E. Local *Unpublished*

The M1 Motorway (Junctions 25-24A, Near Long Eaton) (Temporary Restriction and Prohibition of Traffic) Order 2008 No. 2008/3223. - Enabling power: Road Traffic Regulation Act 1984, s. 14 (1) (a) (7). - Made: 17.11.2008. Coming into force: 24.11.2008. Effect: None. Territorial extent & classification: E. Local *Unpublished*

The M1 Motorway (Junctions 29-28, Derbyshire) (Temporary Restriction and Prohibition of Traffic) Order 2008 No. 2008/3028. - Enabling power: Road Traffic Regulation Act 1984, s. 14 (1) (a) (7). - Made: 07.11.2008. Coming into force: 14.11.2008. Effect: None. Territorial extent & classification: E. Local *Unpublished*

The M1 Motorway (Junctions 29 - 30, Derbyshire) (Temporary Restriction and Prohibition of Traffic) Order 2008 No. 2008/2574. - Enabling power: Road Traffic Regulation Act 1984, s. 14 (1) (a) (7). - Made: 15.09.2008. Coming into force: 22.09.2008. Effect: None. Territorial extent & classification: E. Local *Unpublished*

The M1 Motorway (Junctions 41 Carr Gate) (Temporary Prohibition of Traffic) Order 2008 No. 2008/2731. - Enabling power: Road Traffic Regulation Act 1984, s. 14 (1) (a). - Made: 06.10.2008. Coming into force: 15.10.2008. Effect: None. Territorial extent & classification: E. Local *Unpublished*

The M2 Motorway and the A2 Trunk Road (M2 Junction 6 - Brenley Corner) (Temporary Restriction and Prohibition of Traffic) Order 2008 No. 2008/3311. - Enabling power: Road Traffic Regulation Act 1984, s. 14 (1) (a). - Made: 15.12.2008. Coming into force: 03.01.2009. Effect: None. Territorial extent & classification: E. Local *Unpublished*

The M2 Motorway (Junction 4, Slip Roads) (Temporary Prohibition of Traffic) Order 2008 No. 2008/1505. - Enabling power: Road Traffic Regulation Act 1984, s. 14 (1) (a). - Made: 02.06.2008. Coming into force: 07.06.2008. Effect: None. Territorial extent & classification: E. Local *Unpublished*

The M2 Motorway (Junctions 4 - 6) (Temporary Restriction of Traffic) Order 2008 No. 2008/866. - Enabling power: Road Traffic Regulation Act 1984, s. 14 (1) (a). - Made: 10.03.2008. Coming into force: 15.03.2008. Effect: None. Territorial extent & classification: E. Local *Unpublished*

The M2 Motorway (Junctions 5 - 6) (Temporary Restriction and Prohibition of Traffic) Order 2008 No. 2008/3277. - Enabling power: Road Traffic Regulation Act 1984, s. 14 (1) (a) (7). - Made: 08.12.2008. Coming into force: 03.01.2009. Effect: None. Territorial extent & classification: E. Local *Unpublished*

The M2 Motorway (Junctions 5 - 7, Slip Roads) (Temporary Prohibition of Traffic) Order 2008 No. 2008/1108. - Enabling power: Road Traffic Regulation Act 1984, s. 14 (1) (a). - Made: 07.04.2008. Coming into force: 16.04.2008. Effect: None. Territorial extent & classification: E. Local *Unpublished*

The M2 Motorway (Junctions 5 - 7) (Temporary Restriction and Prohibition of Traffic) Order 2008 No. 2008/2393. - Enabling power: Road Traffic Regulation Act 1984, s. 14 (1) (a) (7). - Made: 04.08.2008. Coming into force: 09.08.2008. Effect: None. Territorial extent & classification: E. Local *Unpublished*

The M2 Motorway (Medway Service Area, Londonbound Exit Slip Road) (Temporary Prohibition of Traffic) Order 2008 No. 2008/2188. - Enabling power: Road Traffic Regulation Act 1984, s. 14 (1) (a). - Made: 04.08.2008. Coming into force: 09.08.2008. Effect: None. Territorial extent & classification: E. Local *Unpublished*

The M3 Motorway and the A316 Trunk Road (Junction 1, Eastbound) (Temporary Restriction of Traffic) Order 2008 No. 2008/382. - Enabling power: Road Traffic Regulation Act 1984, s. 14 (1) (a). - Made: 11.02.2008. Coming into force: 16.02.2008. Effect: None. Territorial extent & classification: E. Local *Unpublished*

The M3 Motorway and the A316 Trunk Road (Junction 1, Slip Roads) (Temporary Prohibition of Traffic) (No. 2) Order 2008 No. 2008/3317. - Enabling power: Road Traffic Regulation Act 1984, s. 14 (1) (a). - Made: 15.12.2008. Coming into force: 15.01.2009. Effect: None. Territorial extent & classification: E. Local *Unpublished*

Road traffic: Traffic regulation

The M3 Motorway and the A316 Trunk Road (Junction 1, Slip Roads) (Temporary Prohibition of Traffic) Order 2008 No. 2008/33. - Enabling power: Road Traffic Regulation Act 1984, s. 14 (1) (a). - Made: 07.01.2008. Coming into force: 15.01.2008. Effect: None. Territorial extent & classification: E. Local *Unpublished*

The M3 Motorway and the M25 Motorway (Thorpe Interchange) (Temporary Restriction and Prohibition of Traffic) Order 2008 No. 2008/777. - Enabling power: Road Traffic Regulation Act 1984, s. 14 (1) (a) (7). - Made: 25.02.2008. Coming into force: 01.03.2008. Effect: None. Territorial extent & classification: E. Local *Unpublished*

The M3 Motorway (Junction 6, Westbound Entry Slip Road) (Temporary Prohibition of Traffic) Order 2008 No. 2008/1007. - Enabling power: Road Traffic Regulation Act 1984, s. 14 (1) (a). - Made: 17.03.2008. Coming into force: 22.03.2008. Effect: None. Territorial extent & classification: E. Local *Unpublished*

The M3 Motorway (Junction 7, Slip Roads) (Temporary Prohibition of Traffic) Order 2008 No. 2008/1354. - Enabling power: Road Traffic Regulation Act 1984, s. 14 (1) (a). - Made: 12.05.2008. Coming into force: 17.05.2008. Effect: None. Territorial extent & classification: E. Local *Unpublished*

The M3 Motorway (Junction 9, Slip Roads) (Temporary Prohibition of Traffic) Order 2008 No. 2008/1355. - Enabling power: Road Traffic Regulation Act 1984, s. 14 (1) (a). - Made: 12.05.2008. Coming into force: 17.05.2008. Effect: None. Territorial extent & classification: E. Local *Unpublished*

The M3 Motorway (Junctions 1 - 2, Westbound) (Temporary Prohibition of Traffic) Order 2008 No. 2008/1106. - Enabling power: Road Traffic Regulation Act 1984, s. 14 (1) (a). - Made: 07.04.2008. Coming into force: 12.04.2008. Effect: None. Territorial extent & classification: E. Local *Unpublished*

The M3 Motorway (Junctions 3 - 2, Eastbound) (Temporary Restriction of Traffic) Order 2008 No. 2008/3329. - Enabling power: Road Traffic Regulation Act 1984, s. 14 (1) (a). - Made: 24.11.2008. Coming into force: 29.11.2008. Effect: None. Territorial extent & classification: E. Local *Unpublished*

The M3 Motorway (Junctions 3 - 4) (Temporary Restriction and Prohibition of Traffic) Order 2008 No. 2008/3274. - Enabling power: Road Traffic Regulation Act 1984, s. 14 (1) (a) (7). - Made: 08.12.2008. Coming into force: 29.12.2008. Effect: None. Territorial extent & classification: E. Local *Unpublished*

The M3 Motorway (Junctions 7 - 9) (Temporary Prohibition of Traffic) Order 2008 No. 2008/1015. - Enabling power: Road Traffic Regulation Act 1984, s. 14 (1) (a). - Made: 17.03.2008. Coming into force: 22.03.2008. Effect: None. Territorial extent & classification: E. Local *Unpublished*

The M3 Motorway (Junctions 11 and 12, Slip Roads) (Temporary Prohibition of Traffic) Order 2008 No. 2008/1353. - Enabling power: Road Traffic Regulation Act 1984, s. 14 (1) (a). - Made: 12.05.2008. Coming into force: 17.05.2008. Effect: None. Territorial extent & classification: E. Local *Unpublished*

The M4 Motorway (East of Junction 6) (Temporary Restriction of Traffic) Order 2008 No. 2008/2189. - Enabling power: Road Traffic Regulation Act 1984, s. 14 (1) (a) (7). - Made: 04.08.2008. Coming into force: 09.08.2008. Effect: None. Territorial extent & classification: E. Local *Unpublished*

The M4 Motorway (Junction 4B, Link Road) (Temporary Prohibition of Traffic) Order 2008 No. 2008/3313. - Enabling power: Road Traffic Regulation Act 1984, s. 14 (1) (a). - Made: 15.12.2008. Coming into force: 03.01.2009. Effect: None. Territorial extent & classification: E. Local *Unpublished*

The M4 Motorway (Junction 4, Eastbound) (Temporary Prohibition of Traffic) Order 2008 No. 2008/30. - Enabling power: Road Traffic Regulation Act 1984, s. 14 (1) (a). - Made: 07.01.2008. Coming into force: 12.01.2008. Effect: None. Territorial extent & classification: E. Local *Unpublished*

The M4 Motorway (Junction 4 - Heathrow Spur) (Temporary Prohibition of Traffic) Order 2008 No. 2008/3314. - Enabling power: Road Traffic Regulation Act 1984, s. 14 (1) (a) (7). - Made: 15.12.2008. Coming into force: 10.01.2009. Effect: None. Territorial extent & classification: E. Local *Unpublished*

The M4 Motorway (Junction 4, Link Road) (Temporary Prohibition of Traffic) Order 2008 No. 2008/34. - Enabling power: Road Traffic Regulation Act 1984, s. 14 (1) (a). - Made: 07.01.2008. Coming into force: 14.01.2008. Effect: None. Territorial extent & classification: E. Local. - Revoked by S.I. 2008/2126 *Unpublished*

The M4 Motorway (Junction 4, Slip/Link Roads) (Temporary Prohibition of Traffic) Order 2008 No. 2008/2480. - Enabling power: Road Traffic Regulation Act 1984, s. 14 (1) (a). - Made: 08.09.2008. Coming into force: 13.09.2008. Effect: None. Territorial extent & classification: E. Local *Unpublished*

The M4 Motorway (Junction 5, Westbound Carriageway) (Temporary Prohibition of Traffic) Order 2008 No. 2008/2047. - Enabling power: Road Traffic Regulation Act 1984, s. 14 (1) (a) (7). - Made: 14.07.2008. Coming into force: 19.07.2008. Effect: None. Territorial extent & classification: E. Local *Unpublished*

The M4 Motorway (Junction 6, Exit Slip Roads) (Temporary Prohibition of Traffic) Order 2008 No. 2008/1457. - Enabling power: Road Traffic Regulation Act 1984, s. 14 (1) (a). - Made: 27.05.2008. Coming into force: 31.05.2008. Effect: None. Territorial extent & classification: E. Local *Unpublished*

The M4 Motorway (Junction 10, Eastbound Link Road) (Temporary Prohibition of Traffic) Order 2008 No. 2008/1170. - Enabling power: Road Traffic Regulation Act 1984, s. 14 (1) (a). - Made: 21.04.2008. Coming into force: 26.04.2008. Effect: None. Territorial extent & classification: E. Local *Unpublished*

The M4 Motorway (Junction 11) (Temporary Restriction and Prohibition of Traffic) Order 2008 No. 2008/2719. - Enabling power: Road Traffic Regulation Act 1984, s. 14 (1) (a) (7). - Made: 06.10.2008. Coming into force: 11.10.2008. Effect: None. Territorial extent & classification: E. Local *Unpublished*

The M4 Motorway (Junction 12, Theale Interchange) (Temporary Restriction and Prohibition of Traffic) Order 2008 No. 2008/2813. - Enabling power: Road Traffic Regulation Act 1984, s. 14 (1) (a) (7). - Made: 20.10.2008. Coming into force: 25.10.2008. Effect: None. Territorial extent & classification: E. Local *Unpublished*

The M4 Motorway (Junction 13, Chieveley Interchange) (Temporary 40 Miles Per Hour Speed Restriction) Order 2008 No. 2008/1100. - Enabling power: Road Traffic Regulation Act 1984, s. 14 (1) (a). - Made: 07.04.2008. Coming into force: 14.04.2008. Effect: None. Territorial extent & classification: E. Local *Unpublished*

The M4 Motorway (Junction 14) (Temporary Restriction of Traffic) Order 2008 No. 2008/36. - Enabling power: Road Traffic Regulation Act 1984, s. 14 (1) (a) (7). - Made: 07.01.2008. Coming into force: 12.01.2008. Effect: None. Territorial extent & classification: E. Local *Unpublished*

The M4 Motorway (Junction 16-17) (Temporary Prohibition of Traffic) (Number 2) Order 2008 No. 2008/856. - Enabling power: Road Traffic Regulation Act 1984, s. 14 (1) (a). - Made: 05.03.2008. Coming into force: 12.03.2008. Effect: None. Territorial extent & classification: E. Local *Unpublished*

The M4 Motorway (Junction 17) (Temporary Prohibition of Traffic) Order 2008 No. 2008/1548. - Enabling power: Road Traffic Regulation Act 1984, s. 14 (1) (a). - Made: 03.06.2008. Coming into force: 07.06.2008. Effect: None. Territorial extent & classification: E. Local *Unpublished*

The M4 Motorway (Junction 18) (Temporary Prohibition of Traffic) Order 2008 No. 2008/1391. - Enabling power: Road Traffic Regulation Act 1984, s. 14 (1) (a). - Made: 20.05.2008. Coming into force: 24.05.2008. Effect: None. Territorial extent & classification: E. Local *Unpublished*

The M4 Motorway (Junction 19) and M32 Motorway (Junction 1) (Temporary Prohibition and Restriction of Traffic) Order 2008 No. 2008/2901. - Enabling power: Road Traffic Regulation Act 1984, s. 14 (1) (a). - Made: 29.10.2008. Coming into force: 01.11.2008. Effect: None. Territorial extent & classification: E. Local *Unpublished*

The M4 Motorway (Junction 19) (Temporary Prohibition of Traffic) Order 2008 No. 2008/1192. - Enabling power: Road Traffic Regulation Act 1984, s. 14 (1) (a). - Made: 23.04.2008. Coming into force: 26.04.2008. Effect: None. Territorial extent & classification: E. Local *Unpublished*

The M4 Motorway (Junction 20) (Almondsbury Interchange) (Temporary Prohibition of Traffic) Order 2008 No. 2008/1396. - Enabling power: Road Traffic Regulation Act 1984, s. 14 (1) (a). - Made: 21.05.2008. Coming into force: 24.05.2008. Effect: None. Territorial extent & classification: E. Local *Unpublished*

The M4 Motorway (Junction 22 Slip Roads) (Temporary Prohibition of Traffic) Order 2008 No. 2008/1197. - Enabling power: Road Traffic Regulation Act 1984, s. 14 (1) (a). - Made: 23.04.2008. Coming into force: 26.04.2008. Effect: None. Territorial extent & classification: E. Local *Unpublished*

The M4 Motorway (Junctions 1 - 3) (Temporary Prohibition of Traffic) (No. 2) Order 2008 No. 2008/3337. - Enabling power: Road Traffic Regulation Act 1984, s. 14 (1) (a). - Made: 15.12.2008. Coming into force: 03.01.2009. Effect: None. Territorial extent & classification: E. Local *Unpublished*

The M4 Motorway (Junctions 1 - 3) (Temporary Prohibition of Traffic) Order 2008 No. 2008/997. - Enabling power: Road Traffic Regulation Act 1984, s. 14 (1) (a). - Made: 25.03.2008. Coming into force: 01.04.2008. Effect: None. Territorial extent & classification: E. Local *Unpublished*

The M4 Motorway (Junctions 3 - 5, Link and Slip Roads) (Temporary Prohibition of Traffic) Order 2008 No. 2008/2126. - Enabling power: Road Traffic Regulation Act 1984, s. 14 (1) (a). - Made: 28.07.2008. Coming into force: 02.08.2008. Effect: S.I. 2008/34 revoked. Territorial extent & classification: E. Local *Unpublished*

The M4 Motorway (Junctions 5 - 8/9, Slip Roads) (Temporary Restriction and Prohibition of Traffic) Order 2008 No. 2008/453. - Enabling power: Road Traffic Regulation Act 1984, s. 14 (1) (a) (7). - Made: 18.02.2008. Coming into force: 23.02.2008. Effect: None. Territorial extent & classification: E. Local *Unpublished*

The M4 Motorway (Junctions 10 - 12) (Temporary Restriction and Prohibition of Traffic) Order 2008 No. 2008/156. - Enabling power: Road Traffic Regulation Act 1984, s. 14 (1) (a) (7). - Made: 21.01.2008. Coming into force: 26.01.2008. Effect: None. Territorial extent & classification: E. Local *Unpublished*

The M4 Motorway (Junctions 12 and 13, Slip Roads) (Temporary Prohibition of Traffic) Order 2008 No. 2008/1559. - Enabling power: Road Traffic Regulation Act 1984, s. 14 (1) (a). - Made: 09.06.2008. Coming into force: 14.06.2008. Effect: None. Territorial extent & classification: E. Local *Unpublished*

The M4 Motorway (Junctions 13 - 14) (Temporary Restriction and Prohibition of Traffic) Order 2008 No. 2008/2282. - Enabling power: Road Traffic Regulation Act 1984, s. 14 (1) (a) (7). - Made: 18.08.2008. Coming into force: 23.08.2008. Effect: None. Territorial extent & classification: E. Local *Unpublished*

The M4 Motorway (Junctions 13, Carriageays) (Temporary Restriction of Traffic) Order 2008 No. 2008/2327. - Enabling power: Road Traffic Regulation Act 1984, s. 14 (1) (a) (7). - Made: 26.08.2008. Coming into force: 30.08.2008. Effect: None. Territorial extent & classification: E. Local *Unpublished*

The M4 Motorway (Junctions 14, Slip Roads) (Temporary Prohibition of Traffic) Order 2008 No. 2008/1561. - Enabling power: Road Traffic Regulation Act 1984, s. 14 (1) (a). - Made: 09.06.2008. Coming into force: 14.06.2008. Effect: None. Territorial extent & classification: E. Local *Unpublished*

The M4 Motorway (Junctions 15-16) (Temporary Prohibition and Restriction of Traffic) Order 2008 No. 2008/2330. - Enabling power: Road Traffic Regulation Act 1984, s. 14 (1) (a) (7). - Made: 27.08.2008. Coming into force: 30.08.2008. Effect: None. Territorial extent & classification: E. Local *Unpublished*

The M4 Motorway (Junctions 15-16) (Temporary Prohibition of Traffic) Order 2008 No. 2008/1253. - Enabling power: Road Traffic Regulation Act 1984, s. 14 (1) (a). - Made: 29.04.2008. Coming into force: 07.05.2008. Effect: None. Territorial extent & classification: E. Local *Unpublished*

The M4 Motorway (Junctions 15-17) (Temporary Prohibition and Restriction of Traffic) Order 2008 No. 2008/3364. - Enabling power: Road Traffic Regulation Act 1984, s. 14 (1) (a) (7). - Made: 31.12.2008. Coming into force: 03.01.2009. Effect: None. Territorial extent & classification: E. Local *Unpublished*

The M4 Motorway (Junctions 17 - 18) (Temporary Prohibition and Restriction of Traffic) Order 2008 No. 2008/813. - Enabling power: Road Traffic Regulation Act 1984, s. 14 (1) (a) (7). - Made: 20.02.2008. Coming into force: 26.02.2008. Effect: None. Territorial extent & classification: E. Local *Unpublished*

The M4 Motorway (Junctions 19 - 18) (Temporary Restriction of Traffic) Order 2008 No. 2008/2286. - Enabling power: Road Traffic Regulation Act 1984, s. 14 (1) (a) (7). - Made: 20.08.2008. Coming into force: 23.08.2008. Effect: None. Territorial extent & classification: E. Local *Unpublished*

The M4 Motorway (Rogiet Toll Plaza) (Temporary 50 mph Speed Restriction) Order 2008 No. 2008/1231. - Enabling power: Road Traffic Regulation Act 1984, s. 14 (1) (b). - Made: 25.04.2008. Coming into force: 29.04.2008. Effect: None. Territorial extent & classification: E. Local *Unpublished*

The M5 and M42 Motorways (M5 North of Junction 4 to South of Junction 4A, Worcestershire) (Temporary Restriction and Prohibition of Traffic) Order 2008 No. 2008/3361. - Enabling power: Road Traffic Regulation Act 1984, s. 14 (1) (a) (7). - Made: 22.12.2008. Coming into force: 29.12.2008. Effect: None. Territorial extent & classification: E. Local *Unpublished*

The M5 Motorway (Junction 1 - Junction 5) (Slip Roads) (Temporary Prohibition of Traffic) Order 2008 No. 2008/3222. - Enabling power: Road Traffic Regulation Act 1984, s. 14 (1) (a). - Made: 21.11.2008. Coming into force: 28.11.2008. Effect: None. Territorial extent & classification: E. Local *Unpublished*

The M5 Motorway (Junction 1, Sandwell) (Southbound Entry Slip Road) (Temporary Prohibition of Traffic) Order 2008 No. 2008/3027. - Enabling power: Road Traffic Regulation Act 1984, s. 14 (1) (a). - Made: 10.11.2008. Coming into force: 17.11.2008. Effect: None. Territorial extent & classification: E. Local *Unpublished*

The M5 Motorway (Junction 2, Sandwell) (Southbound Entry Slip Road) (Temporary Prohibition of Traffic) Order 2008 No. 2008/1117. - Enabling power: Road Traffic Regulation Act 1984, s. 14 (1) (a). - Made: 09.04.2008. Coming into force: 16.04.2008. Effect: None. Territorial extent & classification: E. Local *Unpublished*

The M5 Motorway (Junction 4a - 4) (Temporary Restriction and Prohibition of Traffic) Order 2008 No. 2008/873. - Enabling power: Road Traffic Regulation Act 1984, s. 14 (1) (a) (7). - Made: 29.02.2008. Coming into force: 07.03.2008. Effect: None. Territorial extent & classification: E. Local *Unpublished*

The M5 Motorway (Junction 4, Worcestershire) (Slip Road) (Temporary Prohibition of Traffic) Order 2008 No. 2008/2271. - Enabling power: Road Traffic Regulation Act 1984, s. 14 (1) (a). - Made: 24.06.2008. Coming into force: 01.07.2008. Effect: None. Territorial extent & classification: E. Local *Unpublished*

The M5 Motorway (Junction 5) (Slip Roads) and the A38 Trunk Road (Temporary Prohibition and Restriction of Traffic) Order 2008 No. 2008/3338. - Enabling power: Road Traffic Regulation Act 1984, s. 14 (1) (a). - Made: 22.12.2008. Coming into force: 29.12.2008. Effect: None. Territorial extent & classification: E. Local *Unpublished*

The M5 Motorway (Junction 6, Worcestershire) (Southbound Carriageway) (Temporary Prohibition of Traffic) Order 2008 No. 2008/2194. - Enabling power: Road Traffic Regulation Act 1984, s. 14 (1) (a). - Made: 28.07.2008. Coming into force: 04.08.2008. Effect: None. Territorial extent & classification: E. Local *Unpublished*

The M5 Motorway (Junction 6, Worcestershire) (Southbound Exit Slip Road) (Temporary Prohibition of Traffic) Order 2008 No. 2008/1540. - Enabling power: Road Traffic Regulation Act 1984, s. 14 (1) (a). - Made: 26.05.2008. Coming into force: 02.06.2008. Effect: None. Territorial extent & classification: E. Local *Unpublished*

The M5 Motorway (Junction 7, Worcestershire) (Slip Road) (Temporary Prohibition of Traffic) Order 2008 No. 2008/3225. - Enabling power: Road Traffic Regulation Act 1984, s. 14 (1) (a). - Made: 17.11.2008. Coming into force: 24.11.2008. Effect: None. Territorial extent & classification: E. Local *Unpublished*

The M5 Motorway (Junction 8, Worcestershire) (Northbound Entry and Exit Slip Roads to Strensham Services) (Temporary Prohibition of Traffic) Order 2008 No. 2008/1634. - Enabling power: Road Traffic Regulation Act 1984, s. 14 (1) (a). - Made: 02.06.2008. Coming into force: 09.06.2008. Effect: None. Territorial extent & classification: E. Local *Unpublished*

The M5 Motorway (Junction 8, Worcestershire) (Temporary Restriction and Prohibition of Traffic) Order 2008 No. 2008/59. - Enabling power: Road Traffic Regulation Act 1984, s. 14 (1) (a) (7). - Made: 04.01.2008. Coming into force: 11.01.2008. Effect: None. Territorial extent & classification: E. Local *Unpublished*

The M5 Motorway (Junction 9) (Temporary Restriction and Prohibition of Traffic) Order 2008 No. 2008/3367. - Enabling power: Road Traffic Regulation Act 1984, s. 14 (1) (a) (7). - Made: 29.12.2008. Coming into force: 05.01.2009. Effect: None. Territorial extent & classification: E. Local *Unpublished*

The M5 Motorway (Junction 10) (Temporary Prohibition of Traffic) Order 2008 No. 2008/1196. - Enabling power: Road Traffic Regulation Act 1984, s. 14 (1) (a). - Made: 23.04.2008. Coming into force: 26.04.2008. Effect: None. Territorial extent & classification: E. Local *Unpublished*

The M5 Motorway (Junction 11 Slip Roads) (Temporary Prohibition of Traffic) Order 2008 No. 2008/2612. - Enabling power: Road Traffic Regulation Act 1984, s. 14 (1) (a). - Made: 24.09.2008. Coming into force: 29.09.2008. Effect: None. Territorial extent & classification: E. Local *Unpublished*

The M5 Motorway (Junction 11 Southbound Exit Slip Road) and A40 Trunk Road (Eastbound Exit Slip Road) (Temporary Prohibition of Traffic) Order 2008 No. 2008/1833. - Enabling power: Road Traffic Regulation Act 1984, s. 14 (1) (a). - Made: 01.07.2008. Coming into force: 03.07.2008. Effect: None. Territorial extent & classification: E. Local *Unpublished*

The M5 Motorway (Junction 11) (Temporary Prohibition of Traffic) Order 2008 No. 2008/1109. - Enabling power: Road Traffic Regulation Act 1984, s. 14 (1) (a). - Made: 09.04.2008. Coming into force: 12.04.2008. Effect: None. Territorial extent & classification: E. Local *Unpublished*

The M5 Motorway (Junction 15) and M4 Motorway (Junction 20) (Almondsbury Interchange) (Temporary Prohibition of Traffic) Order 2008 No. 2008/1235. - Enabling power: Road Traffic Regulation Act 1984, s. 14 (1) (a). - Made: 25.04.2008. Coming into force: 29.04.2008. Effect: None. Territorial extent & classification: E. Local *Unpublished*

The M5 Motorway (Junction 18A) and A4 Trunk Road (Crowley Way, Avonmouth) (Temporary Prohibition of Traffic) Order 2008 No. 2008/2230. - Enabling power: Road Traffic Regulation Act 1984, s. 14 (1) (a). - Made: 12.08.2008. Coming into force: 14.08.2008. Effect: None. Territorial extent & classification: E. Local *Unpublished*

The M5 Motorway (Junction 18 Link Road to Portway Roundabout, Avonmouth) (Temporary Prohibition of Traffic) Order 2008 No. 2008/1397. - Enabling power: Road Traffic Regulation Act 1984, s. 14 (1) (a). - Made: 21.05.2008. Coming into force: 24.05.2008. Effect: None. Territorial extent & classification: E. Local *Unpublished*

The M5 Motorway (Junction 18) (Temporary Prohibition of Traffic) Order 2008 No. 2008/2977. - Enabling power: Road Traffic Regulation Act 1984, s. 14 (1) (a). - Made: 12.11.2008. Coming into force: 15.11.2008. Effect: None. Territorial extent & classification: E. Local *Unpublished*

The M5 Motorway (Junction 21 and Junction 23) (Temporary Prohibition of Traffic) Order 2008 No. 2008/2608. - Enabling power: Road Traffic Regulation Act 1984, s. 14 (1) (a). - Made: 24.09.2008. Coming into force: 27.09.2008. Effect: None. Territorial extent & classification: E. Local *Unpublished*

The M5 Motorway (Junction 23) (Temporary Prohibition of Traffic) Order 2008 No. 2008/1557. - Enabling power: Road Traffic Regulation Act 1984, s. 14 (1) (a). - Made: 09.06.2008. Coming into force: 13.06.2008. Effect: None. Territorial extent & classification: E. Local *Unpublished*

The M5 Motorway (Junction 24) (Temporary Prohibition of Traffic) Order 2008 No. 2008/1020. - Enabling power: Road Traffic Regulation Act 1984, s. 14 (1) (a). - Made: 31.03.2008. Coming into force: 04.04.2008. Effect: None. Territorial extent & classification: E. Local *Unpublished*

The M5 Motorway (Junction 27 Northbound Entry Slip Road) (Temporary Prohibition of Traffic) Order 2008 No. 2008/1300. - Enabling power: Road Traffic Regulation Act 1984, s. 14 (1) (a). - Made: 06.05.2008. Coming into force: 10.05.2008. Effect: None. Territorial extent & classification: E. Local *Unpublished*

The M5 Motorway (Junction 27 Slip Roads) (Temporary Prohibition of Traffic) Order 2008 No. 2008/825. - Enabling power: Road Traffic Regulation Act 1984, s. 14 (1) (a) (5) (b) (7). - Made: 26.02.2008. Coming into force: 29.02.2008. Effect: None. Territorial extent & classification: E. Local *Unpublished*

The M5 Motorway (Junction 28) (Temporary Prohibition and Restriction of Traffic) Order 2008 No. 2008/1177. - Enabling power: Road Traffic Regulation Act 1984, s. 14 (1) (a) (7). - Made: 22.04.2008. Coming into force: 26.04.2008. Effect: None. Territorial extent & classification: E. Local *Unpublished*

Road traffic: Traffic regulation

The M5 Motorway (Junction 28) (Temporary Prohibition of Traffic) Order 2008 No. 2008/1568. - Enabling power: Road Traffic Regulation Act 1984, s. 14 (1) (a). - Made: 11.06.2008. Coming into force: 14.06.2008. Effect: None. Territorial extent & classification: E. Local *Unpublished*

The M5 Motorway (Junction 29) (Temporary Prohibition and Restriction of Traffic) Order 2008 No. 2008/1220. - Enabling power: Road Traffic Regulation Act 1984, s. 14 (1) (a) (7). - Made: 25.04.2008. Coming into force: 29.04.2008. Effect: None. Territorial extent & classification: E. Local *Unpublished*

The M5 Motorway (Junction 30) (Temporary Restriction of Traffic) Order 2008 No. 2008/2410. - Enabling power: Road Traffic Regulation Act 1984, s. 14 (1) (a) (7). - Made: 03.09.2008. Coming into force: 05.09.2008. Effect: None. Territorial extent & classification: E. Local *Unpublished*

The M5 Motorway (Junctions 1 - 2) (Temporary 50 Miles Per Hour Speed Restriction) Order 2008 No. 2008/2884. - Enabling power: Road Traffic Regulation Act 1984, s. 14 (1) (a). - Made: 20.10.2008. Coming into force: 27.10.2008. Effect: None. Territorial extent & classification: E. Local *Unpublished*

The M5 Motorway (Junctions 9 and 10) (Temporary Prohibition of Traffic) Order 2008 No. 2008/1394. - Enabling power: Road Traffic Regulation Act 1984, s. 14 (1) (a). - Made: 20.05.2008. Coming into force: 24.05.2008. Effect: None. Territorial extent & classification: E. Local *Unpublished*

The M5 Motorway (Junctions 10-11A) (Temporary Restriction of Traffic) Order 2008 No. 2008/2903. - Enabling power: Road Traffic Regulation Act 1984, s. 14 (1) (a) (7). - Made: 28.10.2008. Coming into force: 31.10.2008. Effect: None. Territorial extent & classification: E. Local *Unpublished*

The M5 Motorway (Junctions 10 -11A) (Temporary Restriction of Traffic) Order 2008 No. 2008/2331. - Enabling power: Road Traffic Regulation Act 1984, s. 14 (1) (a). - Made: 27.08.2008. Coming into force: 30.08.2008. Effect: None. Territorial extent & classification: E. Local *Unpublished*

The M5 Motorway (Junctions 11-9) (Temporary Prohibition and Restriction of Traffic) Order 2008 No. 2008/2811. - Enabling power: Road Traffic Regulation Act 1984, s. 14 (1) (a). - Made: 21.10.2008. Coming into force: 24.10.2008. Effect: None. Territorial extent & classification: E. Local *Unpublished*

The M5 Motorway (Junctions 11A-12) (Temporary Prohibition of Traffic) Order 2008 No. 2008/1255. - Enabling power: Road Traffic Regulation Act 1984, s. 14 (1) (a). - Made: 30.04.2008. Coming into force: 03.05.2008. Effect: None. Territorial extent & classification: E. Local *Unpublished*

The M5 Motorway (Junctions 11A - 14) (Temporary Restriction of Traffic) Order 2008 No. 2008/1017. - Enabling power: Road Traffic Regulation Act 1984, s. 14 (1) (a). - Made: 19.03.2008. Coming into force: 22.03.2008. Effect: None. Territorial extent & classification: E. Local *Unpublished*

The M5 Motorway (Junctions 13-14, Gloucestershire) (Temporary Restriction of Traffic) Order 2008 No. 2008/2610. - Enabling power: Road Traffic Regulation Act 1984, s. 14 (1) (a). - Made: 24.09.2008. Coming into force: 27.09.2008. Effect: None. Territorial extent & classification: E. Local *Unpublished*

The M5 Motorway (Junctions 13 - 14) (Temporary Restriction of Traffic) Order 2008 No. 2008/1669. - Enabling power: Road Traffic Regulation Act 1984, s. 14 (1) (a) (7). - Made: 18.06.2008. Coming into force: 21.06.2008. Effect: S.I. 2008/285 revoked. Territorial extent & classification: E. Local *Unpublished*

The M5 Motorway (Junctions 13 - 14) (Temporary Restriction of Traffic) Order 2008 No. 2008/285. - Enabling power: Road Traffic Regulation Act 1984, s. 14 (1) (a) (7). - Made: 30.01.2008. Coming into force: 02.02.2008. Effect: None. Territorial extent & classification: E. Local. - Revoked by S.I. 2008/1669 *Unpublished*

The M5 Motorway (Junctions 13 - 14) (Temporary Restriction of Traffic) Order 2008 No. 2008/2071. - Enabling power: Road Traffic Regulation Act 1984, s. 14 (1) (a) (7). - Made: 22.07.2008. Coming into force: 26.07.2008. Effect: None. Territorial extent & classification: E. Local. - Revoked by S.I. 2008/1669 *Unpublished*

The M5 Motorway (Junctions 14-16) (Temporary Prohibition and Restriction of Traffic) Order 2008 No. 2008/1400. - Enabling power: Road Traffic Regulation Act 1984, s. 14 (1) (a). - Made: 21.05.2008. Coming into force: 24.05.2008. Effect: None. Territorial extent & classification: E. Local *Unpublished*

The M5 Motorway (Junctions 15-14) (Temporary Prohibition and Restriction of Traffic) Order 2008 No. 2008/1390. - Enabling power: Road Traffic Regulation Act 1984, s. 14 (1) (a) (7). - Made: 20.05.2008. Coming into force: 24.05.2008. Effect: None. Territorial extent & classification: E. Local *Unpublished*

The M5 Motorway (Junctions 15 - 16 including Almondsbury Interchange Slip Roads) (Temporary Prohibition and Restriction of Traffic) Order 2008 No. 2008/28. - Enabling power: Road Traffic Regulation Act 1984, s. 14 (1) (a). - Made: 04.01.2008. Coming into force: 08.01.2008. Effect: None. Territorial extent & classification: E. Local *Unpublished*

The M5 Motorway (Junctions 15 - 16) (Temporary Prohibition of Traffic) Order 2008 No. 2008/1233. - Enabling power: Road Traffic Regulation Act 1984, s. 14 (1) (a). - Made: 25.04.2008. Coming into force: 29.04.2008. Effect: None. Territorial extent & classification: E. Local *Unpublished*

The M5 Motorway (Junctions 18 & 18A) (Temporary Prohibition of Traffic) Order 2008 No. 2008/1672. - Enabling power: Road Traffic Regulation Act 1984, s. 14 (1) (a). - Made: 18.06.2008. Coming into force: 21.06.2008. Effect: None. Territorial extent & classification: E. Local *Unpublished*

The M5 Motorway (Junctions 18 - 18A) (Temporary Restriction of Traffic) (Number 2) Order 2008 No. 2008/1195. - Enabling power: Road Traffic Regulation Act 1984, s. 14 (1) (a) (7). - Made: 23.04.2008. Coming into force: 26.04.2008. Effect: None. Territorial extent & classification: E. Local *Unpublished*

The M5 Motorway (Junctions 18 - 18A) (Temporary Restriction of Traffic) Order 2008 No. 2008/241. - Enabling power: Road Traffic Regulation Act 1984, s. 14 (1) (a) (7). - Made: 23.01.2008. Coming into force: 30.01.2008. Effect: None. Territorial extent & classification: E. Local *Unpublished*

The M5 Motorway (Junctions 18-19 Avonmouth Bridge), M49 Motorway and the A4 Trunk Road (Temporary Prohibition and Restriction of Traffic) Order 2008 No. 2008/2180. - Enabling power: Road Traffic Regulation Act 1984, s. 14 (1) (a) (7). - Made: 06.08.2008. Coming into force: 09.08.2008. Effect: None. Territorial extent & classification: E. Local *Unpublished*

The M5 Motorway (Junctions 19 and 20) (Temporary Prohibition of Traffic) Order 2008 No. 2008/2611. - Enabling power: Road Traffic Regulation Act 1984, s. 14 (1) (a). - Made: 24.09.2008. Coming into force: 27.09.2008. Effect: None. Territorial extent & classification: E. Local *Unpublished*

The M5 Motorway (Junctions 20-19) (Temporary Restriction of Traffic) Order 2008 No. 2008/882. - Enabling power: Road Traffic Regulation Act 1984, s. 14 (1) (a). - Made: 12.03.2008. Coming into force: 15.03.2008. Effect: None. Territorial extent & classification: E. Local *Unpublished*

The M5 Motorway (Junctions 21-22 Slip Roads) (Temporary Restriction of Traffic) (Number 2) Order 2008 No. 2008/1193. - Enabling power: Road Traffic Regulation Act 1984, s. 14 (1) (a) (7). - Made: 23.04.2008. Coming into force: 26.04.2008. Effect: None. Territorial extent & classification: E. Local *Unpublished*

The M5 Motorway (Junctions 21-22 Slip Roads) (Temporary Restriction of Traffic) Order 2008 No. 2008/210. - Enabling power: Road Traffic Regulation Act 1984, s. 14 (1) (a) (7). - Made: 23.01.2008. Coming into force: 30.01.2008. Effect: None. Territorial extent & classification: E. Local *Unpublished*

The M5 Motorway (Strensham, Worcestershire) (Temporary Restriction and Prohibition of Traffic) Order 2008 No. 2008/2964. - Enabling power: Road Traffic Regulation Act 1984, s. 14 (1) (a). - Made: 24.10.2008. Coming into force: 31.10.2008. Effect: None. Territorial extent & classification: E. Local *Unpublished*

The M6 and M42 Motorways (M6 Junctions 4 - 5) (Temporary Restriction and Prohibition of Traffic) Order 2008 No. 2008/1119. - Enabling power: Road Traffic Regulation Act 1984, s. 14 (1) (a) 7. - Made: 07.04.2008. Coming into force: 14.04.2008. Effect: None. Territorial extent & classification: E. Local *Unpublished*

The M6, M6 Toll and M42 Motorways (M42 Junctions 7 - 9) (Temporary Restriction and Prohibition of Traffic) Order 2007 Variation Order 2008 No. 2008/244. - Enabling power: Road Traffic Regulation Act 1984, s. 14 (1) (a), sch. 9, para. 27 (1). - Made: 25.01.2008. Coming into force: 01.02.2008. Effect: S.I. 2007/3666 varied. Territorial extent & classification: E. Local *Unpublished*

The M6, M6 Toll, M42 and M69 Motorways (M6 Junctions 1 - 4) and the A46 Trunk Road (Temporary Restriction and Prohibition of Traffic) Order 2008 No. 2008/2002. - Enabling power: Road Traffic Regulation Act 1984, s. 14 (1) (a) 7. - Made: 04.07.2008. Coming into force: 11.07.2008. Effect: None. Territorial extent & classification: E. Local *Unpublished*

The M6, M40, M42 and M6 Toll Motorways (Temporary Restriction and Prohibition of Traffic) (No. 2) Order 2008 No. 2008/3286. - Enabling power: Road Traffic Regulation Act 1984, ss. 14 (1) (a) (7), 15 (2), sch. 9, para. 27 (1). - Made: 05.12.2008. Coming into force: 12.12.2008. Effect: S.I. 2008/2395 revoked. Territorial extent & classification: E. Local *Unpublished*

The M6, M40, M42 and M6 Toll Motorways (Temporary Restriction and Prohibition of Traffic) Order 2008 No. 2008/2395. - Enabling power: Road Traffic Regulation Act 1984, ss. 14 (1) (a) (7), 15 (2). - Made: 15.08.2008. Coming into force: 22.08.2008. Effect: None. Territorial extent & classification: E. Local. - Revoked by S.I. 2008/3286 (Unpublished) *Unpublished*

The M6, M42 and M6 Toll Motorways (M42 Junction 9 - Junction 11) and the A42 Trunk Road (Temporary Restriction and Prohibition of Traffic) (No. 2) Order 2008 No. 2008/2966. - Enabling power: Road Traffic Regulation Act 1984, s. 14 (1) (a) (7), sch, 9, para. 27 (1). - Made: 30.10.2008. Coming into force: 06.11.2008. Effect: S.I. 2008/2117 revoked. Territorial extent & classification: E. Local *Unpublished*

The M6, M42 and M6 Toll Motorways (M42 Junction 9 - Junction 11) and the A42 Trunk Road (Temporary Restriction and Prohibition of Traffic) Order 2008 No. 2008/2117. - Enabling power: Road Traffic Regulation Act 1984, s. 14 (1) (a). - Made: 21.07.2008. Coming into force: 28.07.2008. Effect: None. Territorial extent & classification: E. Local. - Revoked by S.I. 2008/2966 (Unpublished) *Unpublished*

The M6, M54 and M6 Toll Motorways (Staffordshire) (Temporary Restriction and Prohibition of Traffic) Order 2008 No. 2008/2958. - Enabling power: Road Traffic Regulation Act 1984, s. 14 (1) (a) (7). - Made: 24.10.2008. Coming into force: 31.10.2008. Effect: None. Territorial extent & classification: E. Local *Unpublished*

The M6 Motorway (Junction 3, Bedworth, Warwickshire) (Temporary Prohibition and Restriction of Traffic) Order 2008 No. 2008/2389. - Enabling power: Road Traffic Regulation Act 1984, s. 14 (1) (a). - Made: 19.09.2008. Coming into force: 26.09.2008. Effect: None. Territorial extent & classification: E. Local *Unpublished*

The M6 Motorway (Junction 3, Bedworth) (Slip Road) (Temporary Prohibition of Traffic) Order 2008 No. 2008/2217. - Enabling power: Road Traffic Regulation Act 1984, s. 14 (1) (a). - Made: 11.08.2008. Coming into force: 18.08.2008. Effect: None. Territorial extent & classification: E. Local *Unpublished*

The M6 Motorway (Junction 3, Warwickshire) (Southbound Entry Slip Road) (Temporary Prohibition of Traffic) Order 2008 No. 2008/3352. - Enabling power: Road Traffic Regulation Act 1984, s. 14 (1) (a). - Made: 22.12.2008. Coming into force: 29.12.2008. Effect: None. Territorial extent & classification: E. Local *Unpublished*

The M6 Motorway (Junction 4a - Junction 6) (Temporary Restriction and Prohibition of Traffic) Order 2008 No. 2008/1364. - Enabling power: Road Traffic Regulation Act 1984, s. 14 (1) (a) (7). - Made: 13.05.2008. Coming into force: 20.05.2008. Effect: None. Territorial extent & classification: E. Local *Unpublished*

The M6 Motorway (Junction 4 - Junction 3) (Temporary 50 Miles Per Hour Speed Restriction) Order 2008 No. 2008/3358. - Enabling power: Road Traffic Regulation Act 1984, s. 14 (1) (a). - Made: 29.12.2008. Coming into force: 05.01.2009. Effect: None. Territorial extent & classification: E. Local *Unpublished*

The M6 Motorway (Junction 4) (Temporary Restriction of Traffic) Order 2008 No. 2008/1632. - Enabling power: Road Traffic Regulation Act 1984, s. 14 (1) (a). - Made: 30.05.2008. Coming into force: 06.06.2008. Effect: None. Territorial extent & classification: E. Local *Unpublished*

The M6 Motorway (Junction 5, Birmingham) (Southbound Entry Slip Road) (Temporary Prohibition of Traffic) Order 2008 No. 2008/3226. - Enabling power: Road Traffic Regulation Act 1984, s. 14 (1) (a). - Made: 17.11.2008. Coming into force: 24.11.2008. Effect: None. Territorial extent & classification: E. Local *Unpublished*

The M6 Motorway (Junction 5, Birmingham) (Southbound Entry Slip Road) (Temporary Prohibition of Traffic) Order 2008 No. 2008/1071. - Enabling power: Road Traffic Regulation Act 1984, s. 14 (1) (a). - Made: 01.04.2008. Coming into force: 08.04.2008. Effect: None. Territorial extent & classification: E. Local *Unpublished*

The M6 Motorway (Junction 6, Birmingham) (Slip Roads) (Temporary Prohibition of Traffic) Order 2008 No. 2008/1368. - Enabling power: Road Traffic Regulation Act 1984, s. 14 (1) (a). - Made: 06.05.2008. Coming into force: 13.05.2008. Effect: None. Territorial extent & classification: E. Local *Unpublished*

The M6 Motorway (Junction 6, Birmingham) (Temporary Prohibition of Traffic) Order 2008 No. 2008/2583. - Enabling power: Road Traffic Regulation Act 1984, s. 14 (1) (a). - Made: 19.09.2008. Coming into force: 26.09.2008. Effect: None. Territorial extent & classification: E. Local *Unpublished*

The M6 Motorway (Junction 6) (Slip Roads) (Temporary Prohibition of Traffic) (No. 2) Order 2008 No. 2008/1832. - Enabling power: Road Traffic Regulation Act 1984, s. 14 (1) (a). - Made: 23.06.2008. Coming into force: 30.06.2008. Effect: None. Territorial extent & classification: E. Local *Unpublished*

The M6 Motorway (Junction 6) (Slip Roads) (Temporary Prohibition of Traffic) Order 2008 No. 2008/1152. - Enabling power: Road Traffic Regulation Act 1984, s. 14 (1) (a). - Made: 14.04.2008. Coming into force: 21.04.2008. Effect: None. Territorial extent & classification: E. Local *Unpublished*

The M6 Motorway (Junction 6) (Slip Road) (Temporary Prohibition of Traffic) Order 2008 No. 2008/2193. - Enabling power: Road Traffic Regulation Act 1984, s. 14 (1) (a). - Made: 28.07.2008. Coming into force: 04.08.2008. Effect: None. Territorial extent & classification: E. Local *Unpublished*

The M6 Motorway (Junction 6) (Southbound Exit Slip Road) (Temporary Prohibition of Traffic) Order 2008 No. 2008/449. - Enabling power: Road Traffic Regulation Act 1984, s. 14 (1) (a). - Made: 15.02.2008. Coming into force: 22.02.2008. Effect: None. Territorial extent & classification: E. Local *Unpublished*

The M6 Motorway (Junction 7) (Link Road) (Temporary Prohibition of Traffic) Order 2008 No. 2008/2115. - Enabling power: Road Traffic Regulation Act 1984, s. 14 (1) (a). - Made: 21.07.2008. Coming into force: 28.07.2008. Effect: None. Territorial extent & classification: E. Local *Unpublished*

The M6 Motorway (Junction 7) (Slip Roads) (Temporary Prohibition of Traffic) Order 2008 No. 2008/2384. - Enabling power: Road Traffic Regulation Act 1984, s. 14 (1) (a). - Made: 21.07.2008. Coming into force: 28.07.2008. Effect: None. Territorial extent & classification: E. Local *Unpublished*

The M6 Motorway (Junction 7) (Slip Road) (Temporary Prohibition of Traffic) Order 2008 No. 2008/3184. - Enabling power: Road Traffic Regulation Act 1984, s. 14 (1) (a). - Made: 28.11.2008. Coming into force: 05.12.2008. Effect: None. Territorial extent & classification: E. Local *Unpublished*

The M6 Motorway (Junction 7) (Southbound Entry Slip Road) (Temporary Prohibition of Traffic) Order 2008 No. 2008/194. - Enabling power: Road Traffic Regulation Act 1984, s. 14 (1) (a). - Made: 21.01.2008. Coming into force: 28.01.2008. Effect: None. Territorial extent & classification: E. Local *Unpublished*

The M6 Motorway (Junction 8) (Temporary Prohibition of Traffic) Order 2008 No. 2008/985. - Enabling power: Road Traffic Regulation Act 1984, s. 14 (1) (a). - Made: 18.03.2008. Coming into force: 25.03.2008. Effect: None. Territorial extent & classification: E. Local *Unpublished*

The M6 Motorway (Junction 9, Walsall) (Slip Roads) (Temporary Prohibition of Traffic) Order 2008 No. 2008/2469. - Enabling power: Road Traffic Regulation Act 1984, s. 14 (1) (a). - Made: 05.09.2008. Coming into force: 12.09.2008. Effect: None. Territorial extent & classification: E. Local *Unpublished*

The M6 Motorway (Junction 9, Walsall) (Slip Road) (Temporary Prohibition of Traffic) Order 2008 No. 2008/847. - Enabling power: Road Traffic Regulation Act 1984, s. 14 (1) (a). - Made: 05.03.2008. Coming into force: 12.03.2008. Effect: None. Territorial extent & classification: E. Local *Unpublished*

The M6 Motorway (Junction 9, Walsall) (Temporary Prohibition of Traffic) Order 2008 No. 2008/3362. - Enabling power: Road Traffic Regulation Act 1984, s. 14 (1) (a). - Made: 23.12.2008. Coming into force: 30.12.2008. Effect: None. Territorial extent & classification: E. Local *Unpublished*

The M6 Motorway (Junction 12 - Junction 11) and the M6 Toll Motorway (Junction 11A) (Temporary Prohibition of Traffic) Order 2008 No. 2008/2660. - Enabling power: Road Traffic Regulation Act 1984, s. 14 (1) (a). - Made: 26.09.2008. Coming into force: 03.10.2008. Effect: None. Territorial extent & classification: E. Local *Unpublished*

The M6 Motorway (Junction 12) (Slip Road) (Temporary Prohibition of Traffic) Order 2008 No. 2008/3183. - Enabling power: Road Traffic Regulation Act 1984, s. 14 (1) (a). - Made: 28.11.2008. Coming into force: 05.12.2008. Effect: None. Territorial extent & classification: E. Local *Unpublished*

The M6 Motorway (Junction 12), the M54 Motorway (Junctions 2 - 3) and the A5 Trunk Road (Temporary Prohibition of Traffic) Order 2008 No. 2008/2224. - Enabling power: Road Traffic Regulation Act 1984, s. 14 (1) (b) (7). - Made: 04.08.2008. Coming into force: 11.08.2008. Effect: None. Territorial extent & classification: E. Local *Unpublished*

The M6 Motorway (Junction 14) (Northbound Entry Slip Road) (Temporary Prohibition of Traffic) Order 2008 No. 2008/2452. - Enabling power: Road Traffic Regulation Act 1984, s. 14 (1) (a). - Made: 02.09.2008. Coming into force: 09.09.2008. Effect: None. Territorial extent & classification: E. Local *Unpublished*

The M6 Motorway (Junction 16, Northbound Entry Slip Road) (Temporary Prohibition of Traffic) Order 2008 No. 2008/205. - Enabling power: Road Traffic Regulation Act 1984, s. 14 (1) (a). - Made: 15.01.2008. Coming into force: 20.01.2008. Effect: None. Territorial extent & classification: E. Local *Unpublished*

The M6 Motorway (Junction 17, Northbound and Southbound Exit Slip Roads) (Temporary Prohibition of Traffic) Order 2008 No. 2008/3290. - Enabling power: Road Traffic Regulation Act 1984, s. 14 (1) (a). - Made: 05.12.2008. Coming into force: 04.01.2009. Effect: None. Territorial extent & classification: E. Local *Unpublished*

The M6 Motorway (Junction 17, Northbound Entry Slip Road) (Temporary Prohibition of Traffic) Order 2008 No. 2008/204. - Enabling power: Road Traffic Regulation Act 1984, s. 14 (1) (a). - Made: 15.01.2008. Coming into force: 21.01.2008. Effect: None. Territorial extent & classification: E. Local *Unpublished*

The M6 Motorway (Junction 17, Southbound Entry Slip Road) (Temporary Prohibition of Traffic) Order 2008 No. 2008/343. - Enabling power: Road Traffic Regulation Act 1984, s. 14 (1) (a). - Made: 22.01.2008. Coming into force: 28.01.2008. Effect: None. Territorial extent & classification: E. Local *Unpublished*

The M6 Motorway (Junction 18, Northbound and Southbound Exit Slip Roads) (Temporary Prohibition of Traffic) Order 2008 No. 2008/2200. - Enabling power: Road Traffic Regulation Act 1984, s. 14 (1) (a). - Made: 04.08.2008. Coming into force: 31.08.2008. Effect: None. Territorial extent & classification: E. Local *Unpublished*

The M6 Motorway (Junction 18, Southbound Carriageway) (Temporary Prohibition of Traffic) Order 2008 No. 2008/879. - Enabling power: Road Traffic Regulation Act 1984, s. 14 (1) (a). - Made: 25.02.2008. Coming into force: 05.03.2008. Effect: None. Territorial extent & classification: E. Local *Unpublished*

The M6 Motorway (Junction 18, Southbound Entry Slip Road) (Temporary Prohibition of Traffic) (No. 2) Order 2008 No. 2008/2751. - Enabling power: Road Traffic Regulation Act 1984, s. 14 (1) (a). - Made: 06.10.2008. Coming into force: 02.11.2008. Effect: None. Territorial extent & classification: E. Local *Unpublished*

The M6 Motorway (Junction 18, Southbound Entry Slip Road) (Temporary Prohibition of Traffic) Order 2008 No. 2008/195. - Enabling power: Road Traffic Regulation Act 1984, s. 14 (1) (a). - Made: 22.01.2008. Coming into force: 27.01.2008. Effect: None. Territorial extent & classification: E. Local *Unpublished*

The M6 Motorway (Junction 19, Northbound Entry Slip Road) (Temporary Prohibition of Traffic) Order 2008 No. 2008/203. - Enabling power: Road Traffic Regulation Act 1984, s. 14 (1) (a). - Made: 15.01.2008. Coming into force: 22.01.2008. Effect: None. Territorial extent & classification: E. Local *Unpublished*

The M6 Motorway (Junction 19, Southbound Entry Slip Road) (Temporary Prohibition of Traffic) Order 2008 No. 2008/202. - Enabling power: Road Traffic Regulation Act 1984, s. 14 (1) (a). - Made: 15.01.2008. Coming into force: 24.01.2008. Effect: None. Territorial extent & classification: E. Local *Unpublished*

The M6 Motorway (Junction 20 Northbound Carriageway and Northbound Exit Slip Road) (Temporary Prohibition and Restriction of Traffic) Order 2008 No. 2008/128. - Enabling power: Road Traffic Regulation Act 1984, s. 14 (1) (a) (7). - Made: 07.01.2008. Coming into force: 16.01.2008. Effect: None. Territorial extent & classification: E. Local *Unpublished*

The M6 Motorway (Junction 20, Northbound Entry Slip Road) (Temporary Prohibition of Traffic) Order 2008 No. 2008/105. - Enabling power: Road Traffic Regulation Act 1984, s. 14 (1) (a). - Made: 15.01.2008. Coming into force: 22.01.2008. Effect: None. Territorial extent & classification: E. Local *Unpublished*

The M6 Motorway (Junction 20 Slip Roads and Link Roads) (Temporary Prohibition of Traffic) Order 2008 No. 2008/2278. - Enabling power: Road Traffic Regulation Act 1984, s. 14 (1) (a). - Made: 11.08.2008. Coming into force: 02.09.2008. Effect: None. Territorial extent & classification: E. Local *Unpublished*

The M6 Motorway (Junction 21A) (M62 Motorway Eastbound and Westbound Link Roads to the M6 Northbound) (Temporary Prohibition and Restriction of Traffic) Order 2008 No. 2008/75. - Enabling power: Road Traffic Regulation Act 1984, s. 14 (1) (a) (7). - Made: 0401.2008. Coming into force: 31.01.2008. Effect: None. Territorial extent & classification: E. Local *Unpublished*

The M6 Motorway (Junction 21A Southbound Link Road to the M62 Motorway Westbound) and the M62 Motorway (Junction 10 Westbound Carriageway) (Temporary Prohibition and Restriction of Traffic) Order 2008 No. 2008/2935. - Enabling power: Road Traffic Regulation Act 1984, s. 14 (1) (a) (7). - Made: 20.10.2008. Coming into force: 16.11.2008. Effect: None. Territorial extent & classification: E. Local *Unpublished*

The M6 Motorway (Junction 21, Northbound Entry Slip Road) (Temporary Prohibition of Traffic) Order 2008 No. 2008/472. - Enabling power: Road Traffic Regulation Act 1984, s. 14 (1) (a). - Made: 15.02.2008. Coming into force: 13.03.2008. Effect: None. Territorial extent & classification: E. Local *Unpublished*

The M6 Motorway (Junction 25 Northbound and Southbound Carriageways and Junction 28 Southbound Entry Slip Road) (Temporary Prohibition and Restriction of Traffic) Order 2008 No. 2008/2513. - Enabling power: Road Traffic Regulation Act 1984, s. 14 (1) (a) (7). - Made: 02.09.2008. Coming into force: 11.09.2008. Effect: None. Territorial extent & classification: E. Local *Unpublished*

The M6 Motorway (Junction 25 Southbound Carriageway and Junction 25 Southbound Entry Slip Road) (Temporary Prohibition and Restriction of Traffic) Order 2008 No. 2008/2493. - Enabling power: Road Traffic Regulation Act 1984, s. 14 (1) (a) (7). - Made: 26.08.2008. Coming into force: 21.09.2008. Effect: None. Territorial extent & classification: E. Local *Unpublished*

The M6 Motorway (Junction 26 Northbound Carriageway and Junction 26 Northbound Entry Slip Road) (Temporary Prohibition and Restriction of Traffic) Order 2008 No. 2008/1992. - Enabling power: Road Traffic Regulation Act 1984, s. 14 (1) (a) (7). - Made: 30.06.2008. Coming into force: 29.07.2008. Effect: None. Territorial extent & classification: E. Local *Unpublished*

The M6 Motorway (Junction 26 Southbound Carriageway and Junction 26 Southbound Entry Slip Road) (Temporary Prohibition and Restriction of Traffic) Order 2008 No. 2008/2203. - Enabling power: Road Traffic Regulation Act 1984, s. 14 (1) (a) (7). - Made: 04.08.2008. Coming into force: 31.08.2008. Effect: None. Territorial extent & classification: E. Local *Unpublished*

The M6 Motorway (Junction 31A Northbound Exit and Southbound Entry Slip Roads) (Temporary Prohibition and Restriction of Traffic) Order 2008 No. 2008/2018. - Enabling power: Road Traffic Regulation Act 1984, s. 14 (1) (a). - Made: 08.07.2008. Coming into force: 03.08.2008. Effect: None. Territorial extent & classification: E. Local *Unpublished*

The M6 Motorway (Junction 32-33, Northbound and Southbound Carriageways) (Temporary Prohibition of Traffic) Order 2008 No. 2008/1308. - Enabling power: Road Traffic Regulation Act 1984, s. 14 (1) (b). - Made: 06.05.2008. Coming into force: 10.05.2008. Effect: None. Territorial extent & classification: E. Local *Unpublished*

The M6 Motorway (Junction 32) (Link Roads to the M55 Motorway) (Temporary Prohibition and Restriction of Traffic) Order 2008 No. 2008/74. - Enabling power: Road Traffic Regulation Act 1984, s. 14 (1) (a). - Made: 08.01.2008. Coming into force: 01.02.2008. Effect: None. Territorial extent & classification: E. Local *Unpublished*

The M6 Motorway (Junction 32 Northbound and Southbound Carriageways and Link Roads to the M55 Motorway) and M55 Motorway (Temporary Prohibition and Restriction of Traffic) Order 2008 No. 2008/2275. - Enabling power: Road Traffic Regulation Act 1984, s. 14 (1) (a). - Made: 13.08.2008. Coming into force: 17.08.2008. Effect: None. Territorial extent & classification: E. Local *Unpublished*

The M6 Motorway (Junction 32, Northbound and Southbound Main Carriageways) (Temporary Restriction of Traffic) Order 2008 No. 2008/208. - Enabling power: Road Traffic Regulation Act 1984, s. 14 (1) (a) (7). - Made: 22.01.2008. Coming into force: 17.02.2008. Effect: None. Territorial extent & classification: E. Local *Unpublished*

The M6 Motorway (Junction 33-34, Northbound and Southbound Carriageways) (Temporary Prohibition of Traffic) Order 2008 No. 2008/1378. - Enabling power: Road Traffic Regulation Act 1984, s. 14 (1) (b). - Made: 13.05.2008. Coming into force: 16.05.2008. Effect: None. Territorial extent & classification: E. Local *Unpublished*

The M6 Motorway (Junction 33 Northbound Carriageway and Junction 33 Northbound Entry Slip Road) (Temporary Prohibition and Restriction of Traffic) Order 2008 No. 2008/2621. - Enabling power: Road Traffic Regulation Act 1984, s. 14 (1) (a). - Made: 23.09.2008. Coming into force: 29.09.2008. Effect: None. Territorial extent & classification: E. Local *Unpublished*

The M6 Motorway (Junction 35 Northbound and Southbound Carriageways and Junction 35 Northbound Exit and Southbound Entry Slip Roads) (Temporary Prohibition and Restriction of Traffic) Order 2008 No. 2008/2419. - Enabling power: Road Traffic Regulation Act 1984, s. 14 (1) (a). - Made: 26.08.2008. Coming into force: 20.09.2008. Effect: None. Territorial extent & classification: E. Local *Unpublished*

The M6 Motorway (Junction 36 to 38, Northbound Carriageway) (Temporary Restriction of Traffic) Order 2008 No. 2008/1445. - Enabling power: Road Traffic Regulation Act 1984, s. 14 (1) (a). - Made: 19.05.2008. Coming into force: 15.06.2008. Effect: None. Territorial extent & classification: E. Local *Unpublished*

The M6 Motorway (Junction 37 to 38 Northbound and Southbound Carriageways) (Temporary Restriction of Traffic) Order 2008 No. 2008/1617. - Enabling power: Road Traffic Regulation Act 1984, s. 14 (1) (a). - Made: 09.06.2008. Coming into force: 06.07.2008. Effect: None. Territorial extent & classification: E. Local *Unpublished*

The M6 Motorway (Junction 38, Northbound and Southbound Carriageways, Northbound Entry and Exit Slip Roads and Southbound Exit Slip Road) (Temporary Prohibition and Restriction of Traffic) Order 2008 No. 2008/72. - Enabling power: Road Traffic Regulation Act 1984, s. 14 (1) (a). - Made: 08.01.2008. Coming into force: 03.02.2008. Effect: None. Territorial extent & classification: E. Local *Unpublished*

The M6 Motorway (Junction 39, Northbound Carriageway) (Temporary Prohibition and Restriction of Traffic) Order 2008 No. 2008/207. - Enabling power: Road Traffic Regulation Act 1984, s. 14 (1) (a) (7). - Made: 22.01.2008. Coming into force: 15.02.2008. Effect: None. Territorial extent & classification: E. Local *Unpublished*

The M6 Motorway (Junction 39 to 40, Northbound and Southbound Carriageways and Junction 39 Southbound Exit Slip Road) (Temporary Restriction of Traffic) Order 2008 No. 2008/2138. - Enabling power: Road Traffic Regulation Act 1984, s. 14 (1) (a). - Made: 28.07.2008. Coming into force: 25.08.2008. Effect: None. Territorial extent & classification: E. Local *Unpublished*

The M6 Motorway (Junction 39 to 40, Northbound and Southbound Carriageways and Junction 40, Northbound Entry Slip Road) (Temporary Restriction of Traffic) Order 2008 No. 2008/2181. - Enabling power: Road Traffic Regulation Act 1984, s. 14 (1) (a). - Made: 04.08.2008. Coming into force: 31.08.2008. Effect: None. Territorial extent & classification: E. Local *Unpublished*

The M6 Motorway (Junction 39 to 40, Northbound and Southbound Carriageways) (Temporary Restriction of Traffic) Order 2008 No. 2008/71. - Enabling power: Road Traffic Regulation Act 1984, s. 14 (1) (a). - Made: 08.01.2008. Coming into force: 03.02.2008. Effect: None. Territorial extent & classification: E. Local *Unpublished*

The M6 Motorway (Junction 39 to 41, Northbound Carriageway and Junction 40, Northbound Entry Slip Road) (Temporary Restriction of Traffic) Order 2008 No. 2008/1618. - Enabling power: Road Traffic Regulation Act 1984, s. 14 (1) (a). - Made: 09.06.2008. Coming into force: 06.07.2008. Effect: None. Territorial extent & classification: E. Local *Unpublished*

The M6 Motorway (Junction 39 to 42, Northbound Carriageway and Junctions 40 and 41, Northbound Entry Slip Roads) (Temporary Restriction of Traffic) Order 2008 No. 2008/1307. - Enabling power: Road Traffic Regulation Act 1984, s. 14 (1) (a). - Made: 06.05.2008. Coming into force: 01.06.2008. Effect: None. Territorial extent & classification: E. Local *Unpublished*

The M6 Motorway (Junction 40 to 41 Northbound and Southbound Carriageways) (Temporary Restriction of Traffic) Order 2008 No. 2008/2528. - Enabling power: Road Traffic Regulation Act 1984, s. 14 (1) (a). - Made: 09.09.2008. Coming into force: 04.10.2008. Effect: None. Territorial extent & classification: E. Local *Unpublished*

The M6 Motorway (Junction 41, Northbound Carriageway) (Catterlen Interchange) (Temporary Restriction of Traffic) Order 2008 No. 2008/334. - Enabling power: Road Traffic Regulation Act 1984, s. 14 (1) (a). - Made: 05.02.2008. Coming into force: 02.03.2008. Effect: None. Territorial extent & classification: E. Local *Unpublished*

The M6 Motorway (Junction 41 to 42, Northbound and Southbound Carriageway) (Temporary Restriction of Traffic) Order 2008 No. 2008/763. - Enabling power: Road Traffic Regulation Act 1984, s. 14 (1) (a). - Made: 19.02.2008. Coming into force: 24.02.2008. Effect: None. Territorial extent & classification: E. Local *Unpublished*

The M6 Motorway (Junction 42, Northbound and Southbound Entry and Exit Slip Roads) (Temporary Prohibition and Restriction of Traffic) Order 2008 No. 2008/3205. - Enabling power: Road Traffic Regulation Act 1984, s. 14 (1) (a). - Made: 18.11.2008. Coming into force: 23.11.2008. Effect: None. Territorial extent & classification: E. Local *Unpublished*

The M6 Motorway (Junction 42 to 40, Southbound Carriageway) (Temporary Restriction of Traffic) Order 2008 No. 2008/1201. - Enabling power: Road Traffic Regulation Act 1984, s. 14 (1) (a). - Made: 15.04.2008. Coming into force: 11.05.2008. Effect: None. Territorial extent & classification: E. Local *Unpublished*

The M6 Motorway (Junction 42 to 43, Northbound and Southbound Carriageway) (Temporary Restriction of Traffic) Order 2008 No. 2008/1227. - Enabling power: Road Traffic Regulation Act 1984, s. 14 (1) (a). - Made: 21.04.2008. Coming into force: 18.05.2008. Effect: None. Territorial extent & classification: E. Local *Unpublished*

The M6 Motorway (Junction 42 to 43, Northbound and Southbound Carriageway) (Temporary Restriction of Traffic) Order 2008 No. 2008/762. - Enabling power: Road Traffic Regulation Act 1984, s. 14 (1) (a). - Made: 19.02.2008. Coming into force: 16.03.2008. Effect: None. Territorial extent & classification: E. Local *Unpublished*

The M6 Motorway (Junctions 1-2, Warwickshire) (Temporary Prohibition of Traffic) Order 2008 No. 2008/2962. - Enabling power: Road Traffic Regulation Act 1984, s. 14 (1) (a) (7). - Made: 24.10.2008. Coming into force: 31.10.2008. Effect: None. Territorial extent & classification: E. Local *Unpublished*

The M6 Motorway (Junctions 2 to 3) (Temporary Prohibition and Restriction of Traffic) Order 2008 No. 2008/2000. - Enabling power: Road Traffic Regulation Act 1984, s. 14 (1) (a) 7. - Made: 07.07.2008. Coming into force: 14.07.2008. Effect: None. Territorial extent & classification: E. Local *Unpublished*

The M6 Motorway (Junctions 5 - 6, Birmingham) (Temporary Prohibition of Traffic) Order 2008 No. 2008/3363. - Enabling power: Road Traffic Regulation Act 1984, s. 14 (1) (a). - Made: 29.12.2008. Coming into force: 05.01.2009. Effect: None. Territorial extent & classification: E. Local *Unpublished*

The M6 Motorway (Junctions 7 - 9) (Temporary Prohibition and Restriction of Traffic) Order 2008 No. 2008/2616. - Enabling power: Road Traffic Regulation Act 1984, s. 14 (1) (a) 7. - Made: 19.09.2008. Coming into force: 26.09.2008. Effect: None. Territorial extent & classification: E. Local *Unpublished*

The M6 Motorway (Junctions 9 - 10A) (Temporary Restriction and Prohibition of Traffic) Order 2008 No. 2008/1633. - Enabling power: Road Traffic Regulation Act 1984, s. 14 (1) (a) (7). - Made: 02.06.2008. Coming into force: 09.06.2008. Effect: None. Territorial extent & classification: E. Local *Unpublished*

The M6 Motorway (Junctions 10 - 9) (Temporary Prohibition and Restriction of Traffic) Order 2008 No. 2008/2586. - Enabling power: Road Traffic Regulation Act 1984, s. 14 (1) (a) (7). - Made: 19.09.2008. Coming into force: 26.09.2008. Effect: None. Territorial extent & classification: E. Local *Unpublished*

The M6 Motorway (Junctions 12-11, Staffordshire) (Temporary Prohibition of Traffic) Order 2008 No. 2008/1636. - Enabling power: Road Traffic Regulation Act 1984, s. 14 (1) (a). - Made: 02.06.2008. Coming into force: 09.06.2008. Effect: None. Territorial extent & classification: E. Local *Unpublished*

The M6 Motorway (Junctions 13 - 16) (Temporary Restriction and Prohibition of Traffic) Order 2008 No. 2008/1535. - Enabling power: Road Traffic Regulation Act 1984, s. 14 (1) (a) 7. - Made: 23.05.2008. Coming into force: 30.05.2008. Effect: None. Territorial extent & classification: E. Local *Unpublished*

The M6 Motorway (Junctions 14 - 15, Staffordshire) (Temporary Restriction and Prohibition of Traffic) Order 2008 No. 2008/3354. - Enabling power: Road Traffic Regulation Act 1984, s. 14 (1) (a) (7). - Made: 29.12.2008. Coming into force: 05.01.2009. Effect: None. Territorial extent & classification: E. Local *Unpublished*

The M6 Motorway (Junctions 15-14) (Temporary Prohibition of Traffic) Order 2008 No. 2008/2453. - Enabling power: Road Traffic Regulation Act 1984, s. 14 (1) (a) (7). - Made: 01.09.2008. Coming into force: 08.09.2008. Effect: None. Territorial extent & classification: E. Local *Unpublished*

The M6 Motorway (Junctions 18-19, Northbound Carriageway) (Temporary Prohibition and Restriction of Traffic) Order 2008 No. 2008/851. - Enabling power: Road Traffic Regulation Act 1984, s. 14 (1) (a) (7). - Made: 25.02.2008. Coming into force: 29.02.2008. Effect: None. Territorial extent & classification: E. Local *Unpublished*

The M6 Motorway (Junctions 21A Southbound Carriageway and Southbound Link Roads to the M62 Motorway Eastbound and Westbound) (Temporary Prohibition and Restriction of Traffic) Order 2008 No. 2008/260. - Enabling power: Road Traffic Regulation Act 1984, s. 14 (1) (a) (7). - Made: 25.01.2008. Coming into force: 21.02.2008. Effect: None. Territorial extent & classification: E. Local *Unpublished*

The M6 Motorway (Junctions 23 - 33, Northbound and Southbound Carriageways) (Temporary Prohibition of Traffic) (No. 2) Order 2008 No. 2008/1665. - Enabling power: Road Traffic Regulation Act 1984, s. 14 (1) (b). - Made: 16.06.2008. Coming into force: 12.07.2008. Effect: None. Territorial extent & classification: E. Local *Unpublished*

The M6 Motorway (Junctions 24 to 26, Northbound Carriageway) (Temporary Prohibition and Restriction of Traffic) Order 2008 No. 2008/1226. - Enabling power: Road Traffic Regulation Act 1984, s. 14 (1) (a) (7). - Made: 21.04.2008. Coming into force: 15.05.2008. Effect: None. Territorial extent & classification: E. Local *Unpublished*

The M6 Motorway (Junctions 27 - 28, Northbound and Southbound Carriageways and Junction 28 Southbound Entry Slip Road) (Temporary Prohibition and Restriction of Traffic) Order 2008 No. 2008/2594. - Enabling power: Road Traffic Regulation Act 1984, s. 14 (1) (a) (7). - Made: 15.09.2008. Coming into force: 10.10.2008. Effect: None. Territorial extent & classification: E. Local *Unpublished*

The M6 Motorway (Junctions 29-30, Southbound Main Carriageway) (Temporary Prohibition and Restriction of Traffic) Order 2008 No. 2008/1615. - Enabling power: Road Traffic Regulation Act 1984, s. 14 (1) (a) (7). - Made: 09.06.2008. Coming into force: 03.07.2008. Effect: None. Territorial extent & classification: E. Local *Unpublished*

The M6 Motorway (Junctions 31-34, Northbound and Southbound Carriageways and Slip Roads) and the M55 Motorway (Eastbound Link Road to the M6 Northbound) (Temporary Prohibition and Restriction of Traffic) Order 2008 No. 2008/2955. - Enabling power: Road Traffic Regulation Act 1984, s. 14 (1) (a). - Made: 04.11.2008. Coming into force: 28.11.2008. Effect: None. Territorial extent & classification: E. Local *Unpublished*

The M6 Motorway (Junctions 32-33, Barton Lane Bridge and Three Stiles Footbridge) (Temporary Prohibition and Restriction of Traffic) Order 2008 No. 2008/2233. - Enabling power: Road Traffic Regulation Act 1984, s. 14 (1) (a) (7). - Made: 11.08.2008. Coming into force: 05.09.2008. Effect: None. Territorial extent & classification: E. Local *Unpublished*

The M6 Motorway (Junctions 32-33, Keepers and Woodacre Great Wood Footbridges) (Temporary Prohibition and Restriction of Traffic) Order 2008 No. 2008/764. - Enabling power: Road Traffic Regulation Act 1984, s. 14 (1) (a). - Made: 19.02.2008. Coming into force: 14.03.2008. Effect: None. Territorial extent & classification: E. Local *Unpublished*

The M6 Motorway (Junctions 32 - 33, Northbound and Southbound Carriageways) (Temporary Restriction of Traffic) (No. 2) Order 2008 No. 2008/2922. - Enabling power: Road Traffic Regulation Act 1984, s. 14 (1) (a). - Made: 28.10.2008. Coming into force: 22.11.2008. Effect: None. Territorial extent & classification: E. Local *Unpublished*

The M6 Motorway (Junctions 32-33, Northbound and Southbound Carriageways) (Temporary Restriction of Traffic) Order 2008 No. 2008/2953. - Enabling power: Road Traffic Regulation Act 1984, s. 14 (1) (a). - Made: 04.11.2008. Coming into force: 30.11.2008. Effect: None. Territorial extent & classification: E. Local *Unpublished*

The M6 Motorway (Junctions 32-33, Northbound and Southbound Carriageways) (Temporary Restriction of Traffic) Order 2008 No. 2008/1616. - Enabling power: Road Traffic Regulation Act 1984, s. 14 (1) (a). - Made: 09.06.2008. Coming into force: 06.07.2008. Effect: None. Territorial extent & classification: E. Local *Unpublished*

The M6 Motorway (Junctions 32-33, Northbound and Southbound) (Temporary Restriction of Traffic) (No. 3) Order 2008 No. 2008/3301. - Enabling power: Road Traffic Regulation Act 1984, s. 14 (1) (a) (7). - Made: 09.12.2008. Coming into force: 02.01.2009. Effect: None. Territorial extent & classification: E. Local *Unpublished*

The M6 Motorway (Junctions 32-33 Southbound Carriageway) (Temporary Restriction of Traffic) Order 2008 No. 2008/2153. - Enabling power: Road Traffic Regulation Act 1984, s. 14 (1) (a). - Made: 21.07.2008. Coming into force: 17.08.2008. Effect: None. Territorial extent & classification: E. Local *Unpublished*

The M6 Motorway (Junctions 33-34, Northbound and Southbound Carriageways and Junction 34 Northbound and Southbound Entry and Exit Slip Roads) (Temporary Prohibition and Restriction of Traffic) Order 2008 No. 2008/2805. - Enabling power: Road Traffic Regulation Act 1984, s. 14 (1) (a). - Made: 14.10.2008. Coming into force: 19.10.2008. Effect: None. Territorial extent & classification: E. Local *Unpublished*

The M6 Motorway (Junctions 33-34, Northbound and Southbound Carriageways) (Temporary Restriction of Traffic) Order 2008 No. 2008/2758. - Enabling power: Road Traffic Regulation Act 1984, s. 14 (1) (a). - Made: 07.10.2008. Coming into force: 02.11.2008. Effect: None. Territorial extent & classification: E. Local *Unpublished*

The M6 Motorway (Junctions 34-36 Northbound and Southbound Carriageways and Junction 35 Northbound Entry and Southbound Exit Slip Roads) (Temporary Prohibition and Restriction of Traffic) Order 2008 No. 2008/1991. - Enabling power: Road Traffic Regulation Act 1984, s. 14 (1) (a). - Made: 30.06.2008. Coming into force: 25.07.2008. Effect: None. Territorial extent & classification: E. Local *Unpublished*

The M6 Motorway (Junctions 35-36, Northbound and Southbound Carriageways) (Temporary Restriction of Traffic) Order 2008 No. 2008/2825. - Enabling power: Road Traffic Regulation Act 1984, s. 14 (1) (a). - Made: 07.10.2008. Coming into force: 02.11.2008. Effect: None. Territorial extent & classification: E. Local *Unpublished*

The M6 Motorway (Junctions 35-36 Southbound Carriageway and Junction 35 Southbound Exit Slip Road) (Temporary Prohibition and Restriction of Traffic) Order 2008 No. 2008/336. - Enabling power: Road Traffic Regulation Act 1984, s. 14 (1) (a). - Made: 05.02.2008. Coming into force: 02.03.2008. Effect: None. Territorial extent & classification: E. Local *Unpublished*

The M6 Motorway (Junctions 38 to 39, Northbound Carriageway) (Temporary Restriction of Traffic) Order 2008 No. 2008/2184. - Enabling power: Road Traffic Regulation Act 1984, s. 14 (1) (a). - Made: 06.08.2008. Coming into force: 31.08.2008. Effect: None. Territorial extent & classification: E. Local *Unpublished*

The M6 Motorway (Junctions 41-42 Northbound Carriageway) (Temporary Prohibition and Restriction of Traffic) Order 2008 No. 2008/2524. - Enabling power: Road Traffic Regulation Act 1984, s. 14 (1) (a) (7). - Made: 15.09.2008. Coming into force: 11.10.2008. Effect: None. Territorial extent & classification: E. Local *Unpublished*

The M6 Motorway (North and South of Junction 13, Staffordshire) (Temporary Restriction and Prohibition of Traffic) Order 2008 No. 2008/2390. - Enabling power: Road Traffic Regulation Act 1984, s. 14 (1) (a) (7). - Made: 19.09.2008. Coming into force: 26.09.2008. Effect: None. Territorial extent & classification: E. Local *Unpublished*

The M6 Toll Motorway (Junctions T1 - T4) (Temporary Prohibition of Traffic) Order 2008 No. 2008/1179. - Enabling power: Road Traffic Regulation Act 1984, s. 14 (1) (a) (7). - Made: 18.04.2008. Coming into force: 25.04.2008. Effect: None. Territorial extent & classification: E. Local *Unpublished*

The M6 Toll Motorway (Junction T3 Langley Mill) (Temporary Prohibition of Traffic) (No. 2) Order 2008 No. 2008/1363. - Enabling power: Road Traffic Regulation Act 1984, s. 14 (1) (a) (7). - Made: 02.05.2008. Coming into force: 09.05.2008. Effect: None. Territorial extent & classification: E. Local *Unpublished*

The M6 Toll Motorway (Junction T3 Langley Mill) (Temporary Prohibition of Traffic) Order 2008 No. 2008/1296. - Enabling power: Road Traffic Regulation Act 1984, s. 14 (1) (a) (7). - Made: 25.04.2008. Coming into force: 02.05.2008. Effect: None. Territorial extent & classification: E. Local *Unpublished*

The M6 Toll Motorway (Norton Canes Service Area, Staffordshire) (Temporary Prohibition of Traffic) Order 2008 No. 2008/1386. - Enabling power: Road Traffic Regulation Act 1984, s. 14 (1) (a) (7). - Made: 16.05.2008. Coming into force: 23.05.2008. Effect: None. Territorial extent & classification: E. Local *Unpublished*

The M6 Toll Motorway (South of Junction T6, Staffordshire) (Temporary Prohibition of Traffic) Order 2008 No. 2008/1360. - Enabling power: Road Traffic Regulation Act 1984, s. 14 (1) (a) (7). - Made: 12.05.2008. Coming into force: 19.05.2008. Effect: None. Territorial extent & classification: E. Local *Unpublished*

The M6 Toll Motorway (South of Junction T6) (Temporary Prohibition of Traffic) Order 2008 No. 2008/1178. - Enabling power: Road Traffic Regulation Act 1984, s. 14 (1) (a) (7). - Made: 17.04.2008. Coming into force: 24.04.2008. Effect: None. Territorial extent & classification: E. Local *Unpublished*

The M11 Motorway, A14 Trunk Road and A1307 (Girton Interchange, Cambridgeshire) (Temporary Prohibition of Traffic) Order 2008 No. 2008/2027. - Enabling power: Road Traffic Regulation Act 1984, s. 14 (1) (a). - Made: 07.07.2008. Coming into force: 14.07.2008. Effect: None. Territorial extent & classification: E. Local *Unpublished*

The M11 Motorway and the A120 Trunk Road (Stansted, Essex) Slip Roads (Temporary Prohibition of Traffic) Order 2008 No. 2008/1029. - Enabling power: Road Traffic Regulation Act 1984, s. 14 (1) (a). - Made: 28.03.2008. Coming into force: 04.04.2008. Effect: None. Territorial extent & classification: E. Local *Unpublished*

The M11 Motorway (Chigwell Police Control Centre, Slip Road) (Temporary Suspension of a Statutory Provision) Order 2008 No. 2008/2890. - Enabling power: Road Traffic Regulation Act 1984, ss. 14 (1) (a), 15 (2). - Made: 27.10.2008. Coming into force: 03.11.2008. Effect: None. Territorial extent & classification: E. Local *Unpublished*

The M11 Motorway (Junction 8) and the A120 Trunk Road (Thremhall Avenue, Esses) (Temporary Restriction and Prohibition of Traffic) Order 2008 No. 2008/1358. - Enabling power: Road Traffic Regulation Act 1984, s. 14 (1) (a). - Made: 12.05.2008. Coming into force: 19.05.2008. Effect: None. Territorial extent & classification: E. Local *Unpublished*

The M11 Motorway (Junction 11) Northbound Entry Slip Road (Temporary Prohibition of Traffic) Order 2008 No. 2008/2056. - Enabling power: Road Traffic Regulation Act 1984, s. 14 (1) (a). - Made: 14.07.2008. Coming into force: 21.07.2008. Effect: None. Territorial extent & classification: E. Local *Unpublished*

The M11 Motorway (Junction 12) Southbound Exit Slip Road (Temporary Prohibition of Traffic) Order 2008 No. 2008/1289. - Enabling power: Road Traffic Regulation Act 1984, s. 14 (1) (a). - Made: 28.04.2008. Coming into force: 05.05.2008. Effect: None. Territorial extent & classification: E. Local *Unpublished*

The M11 Motorway (Junction 12) Southbound Exit Slip Road (Temporary Prohibition of Traffic) Order 2008 No. 2008/2197. - Enabling power: Road Traffic Regulation Act 1984, s. 14 (1) (a), sch. 9, para. 27 (1). - Made: 04.08.2008. Coming into force: 11.08.2008. Effect: None. Territorial extent & classification: E. Local *Unpublished*

The M11 Motorway (Junction13) and A14 Trunk Road (Spittals Interchange, Junction 23 to Girton Interchange, Junction 31, Cambridgeshire) (Temporary Prohibition of Traffic) Order 2008 No. 2008/458. - Enabling power: Road Traffic Regulation Act 1984, s. 14 (1) (a). - Made: 15.02.2008. Coming into force: 22.02.2008. Effect: None. Territorial extent & classification: E. Local *Unpublished*

The M11 Motorway (Junctions 4 - 6) (Temporary Restriction and Prohibition of Traffic) Order 2008 No. 2008/457. - Enabling power: Road Traffic Regulation Act 1984, s. 14 (1) (a) (7). - Made: 18.02.2008. Coming into force: 23.02.2008. Effect: None. Territorial extent & classification: E. Local *Unpublished*

The M11 Motorway (Junctions 4 - 7) (Temporary Prohibition of Traffic) Order 2008 No. 2008/2186. - Enabling power: Road Traffic Regulation Act 1984, s. 14 (1) (a). - Made: 04.08.2008. Coming into force: 14.08.2008. Effect: None. Territorial extent & classification: E. Local *Unpublished*

The M11 Motorway (Junctions 5 - 4) (Temporary Restriction of Traffic) (No. 2) Order 2008 No. 2008/2127. - Enabling power: Road Traffic Regulation Act 1984, s. 14 (1) (a) (7). - Made: 28.07.2008. Coming into force: 02.08.2008. Effect: S.I. 2008/347 revoked. Territorial extent & classification: E. Local *Unpublished*

The M11 Motorway (Junctions 5 - 4) (Temporary Restriction of Traffic) Order 2008 No. 2008/347. - Enabling power: Road Traffic Regulation Act 1984, s. 14 (1) (a) (7). - Made: 04.02.2008. Coming into force: 09.02.2008. Effect: None. Territorial extent & classification: E. Local. - Revoked by S.I. 2008/2127 *Unpublished*

The M11 Motorway (Junctions 8 to 9, Essex) (Temporary Restriction and Prohibition of Traffic) Order 2008 No. 2008/1115. - Enabling power: Road Traffic Regulation Act 1984, s. 14 (1) (a) 7. - Made: 07.04.2008. Coming into force: 14.04.2008. Effect: None. Territorial extent & classification: E. Local *Unpublished*

The M11 Motorway (Junctions 8 to 11, Cambridgeshire) (Temporary 50 Miles Per Hour Speed Restriction) Order 2008 No. 2008/2022. - Enabling power: Road Traffic Regulation Act 1984, s. 14 (1) (a). - Made: 07.07.2008. Coming into force: 14.07.2008. Effect: None. Territorial extent & classification: E. Local *Unpublished*

The M11 Motorway (Junctions 9 - 9a, Cambridgeshire) (Temporary Prohibition of Traffic) Order 2008 No. 2008/1668. - Enabling power: Road Traffic Regulation Act 1984, s. 14 (1) (a). - Made: 16.06.2008. Coming into force: 23.06.2008. Effect: None. Territorial extent & classification: E. Local *Unpublished*

The M11 Motorway (Junctions 9 to 9A, Cambridgeshire) (Temporary 50 Miles Per Hour Speed Restriction) Order 2008 No. 2008/487. - Enabling power: Road Traffic Regulation Act 1984, s. 14 (1) (a). - Made: 18.02.2008. Coming into force: 25.02.2008. Effect: None. Territorial extent & classification: E. Local *Unpublished*

The M11 Motorway (Junctions 10 to 12, Cambridgeshire) (Temporary Prohibition of Traffic) Order 2008 No. 2008/1705. - Enabling power: Road Traffic Regulation Act 1984, s. 14 (1) (a). - Made: 23.06.2008. Coming into force: 30.06.2008. Effect: None. Territorial extent & classification: E. Local *Unpublished*

The M11 Motorway (Junctions 14 to 12, Cambridgeshire) (Temporary Prohibition of Traffic) Order 2008 No. 2008/832. - Enabling power: Road Traffic Regulation Act 1984, s. 14 (1) (a). - Made: 25.02.2008. Coming into force: 03.03.2008. Effect: None. Territorial extent & classification: E. Local *Unpublished*

The M11 Motorway (Junctions 14 to 13, Cambridgeshire) (Temporary Prohibition of Traffic) Order 2008 No. 2008/67. - Enabling power: Road Traffic Regulation Act 1984, s. 14 (1) (a). - Made: 07.01.2008. Coming into force: 14.01.2008. Effect: None. Territorial extent & classification: E. Local *Unpublished*

The M18/M180 Motorways (North Ings Interchange) (Temporary Prohibition of Traffic) Order 2008 No. 2008/815. - Enabling power: Road Traffic Regulation Act 1984, s. 14 (1) (a). - Made: 2502.2008. Coming into force: 09.03.2008. Effect: None. Territorial extent & classification: E. Local *Unpublished*

The M18 Motorway (Junction 2 to Junction 3) (Temporary Prohibition of Traffic) Order 2008 No. 2008/267. - Enabling power: Road Traffic Regulation Act 1984, s. 14 (1) (a) (7). - Made: 28.01.2008. Coming into force: 03.02.2008. Effect: None. Territorial extent & classification: E. Local *Unpublished*

The M18 Motorway (Junction 2 Wadworth) (Temporary Prohibition of Traffic) Order 2008 No. 2008/2733. - Enabling power: Road Traffic Regulation Act 1984, s. 14 (1) (a). - Made: 06.10.2008. Coming into force: 19.10.2008. Effect: None. Territorial extent & classification: E. Local *Unpublished*

The M18 Motorway (Junction 3 to Junction 3) (Temporary Restriction and Prohibition of Traffic) Order 2008 No. 2008/3344. - Enabling power: Road Traffic Regulation Act 1984, s. 14 (1) (a) (7). - Made: 22.12.2008. Coming into force: 04.01.2009. Effect: None. Territorial extent & classification: E. Local *Unpublished*

The M18 Motorway (Junction 5, North Ings) (Temporary Prohibition of Traffic) Order 2008 No. 2008/481. - Enabling power: Road Traffic Regulation Act 1984, s. 14 (1) (a). - Made: 18.02.2008. Coming into force: 28.02.2008. Effect: None. Territorial extent & classification: E. Local *Unpublished*

The M20 Motorway and the A20 Trunk Road (Folkestone - Dover) (Temporary Restriction and Prohibition of Traffic) Order 2008 No. 2008/769. - Enabling power: Road Traffic Regulation Act 1984, s. 14 (1) (a). - Made: 25.02.2008. Coming into force: 01.03.2008. Effect: None. Territorial extent & classification: E. Local *Unpublished*

The M20 Motorway and the A20 Trunk Road (Junctions 1- 2, Slip Roads) (Temporary Prohibition of Traffic) Order 2008 No. 2008/2125. - Enabling power: Road Traffic Regulation Act 1984, s. 14 (1) (a). - Made: 28.07.2008. Coming into force: 02.08.2008. Effect: None. Territorial extent & classification: E. Local *Unpublished*

The M20 Motorway and the A20 Trunk Road (Roundhill Tunnels) (Temporary Restriction and Prohibition of Traffic) Order 2008 No. 2008/3172. - Enabling power: Road Traffic Regulation Act 1984, s. 14 (1) (a). - Made: 01.12.2008. Coming into force: 06.12.2008. Effect: None. Territorial extent & classification: E. Local *Unpublished*

The M20 Motorway and the A20 Trunk Road (Southeast of Junction 10 - Capel-le-Ferne) (Temporary Restriction and Prohibition of Traffic) (No. 2) Order 2008 No. 2008/2319. - Enabling power: Road Traffic Regulation Act 1984, s. 14 (1) (a) (b) (7). - Made: 26.08.2008. Coming into force: 01.09.2008. Effect: None. Territorial extent & classification: E. Local. - Revoked by S.I. 2008/2893 (Unpublished) *Unpublished*

The M20 Motorway and the A20 Trunk Road (Southeast of Junction 10 - Capel-le-Ferne) (Temporary Restriction and Prohibition of Traffic) (No. 3) Order 2008 No. 2008/2893. - Enabling power: Road Traffic Regulation Act 1984, s. 14 (1) (a) (b) (7), sch. 9, para. 27 (1). - Made: 27.10.2008. Coming into force: 01.11.2008. Effect: S.I. 2008/2319 revoked. Territorial extent & classification: E. Local *Unpublished*

The M20 Motorway and the A20 Trunk Road
(Southeast of Junction 10 - Capel-le-Ferne) (Temporary
Restriction and Prohibition of Traffic) Order 2008 No.
2008/779. - Enabling power: Road Traffic Regulation Act
1984, s. 14 (1) (a) (7). - Made: 25.02.2008. Coming into
force: 01.03.2008. Effect: None. Territorial extent &
classification: E. Local *Unpublished*

The M20 Motorway and the A20 Trunk Road
(Southeast of Junction 10 - Capel-le-Ferne) (Temporary
Restriction and Prohibition of Traffic) Order 2008
Variation Order 2008 No. 2008/2064. - Enabling power:
Road Traffic Regulation Act 1984, s. 14 (1) (a) (7), sch. 9,
para. 27 (1). - Made: 21.07.2008. Coming into force:
01.08.2008. Effect: S.I. 2008/779 varied. Territorial extent
& classification: E. Local *Unpublished*

The M20 Motorway and the M40 Motorway (M25
Junction 16 and M40 Junction 1A) (Temporary
Prohibition of Traffic) Order 2008 No. 2008/3174. -
Enabling power: Road Traffic Regulation Act 1984, s. 14
(1) (a). - Made: 01.12.2008. Coming into force:
06.12.2008. Effect: None. Territorial extent &
classification: E. Local *Unpublished*

The M20 Motorway (Junction 1, Carriageways)
(Temporary Prohibition of Traffic) Order 2008 No.
2008/3308. - Enabling power: Road Traffic Regulation Act
1984, s. 14 (1) (a). - Made: 15.12.2008. Coming into force:
03.01.2009. Effect: None. Territorial extent &
classification: E. Local *Unpublished*

The M20 Motorway (Junction 1, Link Road)
(Temporary Prohibition of Traffic) Order 2008 No.
2008/2320. - Enabling power: Road Traffic Regulation Act
1984, s. 14 (1) (a). - Made: 26.08.2008. Coming into force:
30.08.2008. Effect: None. Territorial extent &
classification: E. Local *Unpublished*

The M20 Motorway (Junction 6, Coastbound
Distributor Road) (Temporary Prohibition of Traffic)
Order 2008 No. 2008/2212. - Enabling power: Road
Traffic Regulation Act 1984, s. 14 (1) (a). - Made:
11.08.2008. Coming into force: 18.08.2008. Effect: None.
Territorial extent & classification: E. Local *Unpublished*

The M20 Motorway (Junction 7, Londonbound
Carriageway) (Temporary Prohibition of Traffic)
Order 2008 No. 2008/1841. - Enabling power: Road
Traffic Regulation Act 1984, s. 14 (1) (a). - Made:
30.06.2008. Coming into force: 05.07.2008. Effect: None.
Territorial extent & classification: E. Local *Unpublished*

The M20 Motorway (Junctions 3 - 7) (Temporary
Restriction and Prohibition of Traffic) Order 2008 No.
2008/2015. - Enabling power: Road Traffic Regulation Act
1984, s. 14 (1) (a) (7). - Made: 07.07.2008. Coming into
force: 14.07.2008. Effect: S.I. 2007/522 revoked.
Territorial extent & classification: E. Local *Unpublished*

The M20 Motorway (Junctions 3 - 8) (Temporary 50
Miles Per Hour Speed Restriction) Order 2008 No.
2008/864. - Enabling power: Road Traffic Regulation Act
1984, s. 14 (1) (a). - Made: 10.03.2008. Coming into force:
15.03.2008. Effect: None. Territorial extent &
classification: E. Local *Unpublished*

The M20 Motorway (Junctions 4 - 7) (Temporary
Prohibition of Traffic) Order 2008 No. 2008/3309. -
Enabling power: Road Traffic Regulation Act 1984, s. 14
(1) (a). - Made: 15.12.2008. Coming into force:
03.01.2009. Effect: None. Territorial extent &
classification: E. Local *Unpublished*

The M20 Motorway (Junctions 4 - 8) (Temporary
Prohibition of Traffic) Order 2008 No. 2008/992. -
Enabling power: Road Traffic Regulation Act 1984, s. 14
(1) (a). - Made: 25.03.2008. Coming into force:
02.04.2008. Effect: None. Territorial extent &
classification: E. Local *Unpublished*

The M20 Motorway (Junctions 5 - 8) (Temporary
Restriction and Prohibition of Traffic) Order 2008 No.
2008/3209. - Enabling power: Road Traffic Regulation Act
1984, s. 14 (1) (a) (7), sch. 9, para. 27 (1). - Made:
24.11.2008. Coming into force: 29.11.2008. Effect: S.I.
2007/1927 revoked. Territorial extent & classification: E.
Local *Unpublished*

The M20 Motorway (Junctions 7 - 11) (Temporary
Restriction of Traffic) Order 2008 No. 2008/151. -
Enabling power: Road Traffic Regulation Act 1984, s. 14
(1) (a) (7). - Made: 21.01.2008. Coming into force:
26.01.2008. Effect: None. Territorial extent &
classification: E. Local *Unpublished*

The M20 Motorway (Junctions 8 - 7, Londonbound)
(Temporary Restriction of Traffic) Order 2008 No.
2008/2921. - Enabling power: Road Traffic Regulation Act
1984, s. 14 (1) (a). - Made: 03.11.2008. Coming into force:
04.11.2008. Effect: None. Territorial extent &
classification: E. Local *Unpublished*

The M20 Motorway (Junctions 9 - 10) (Temporary
Restriction of Traffic) Order 2008 No. 2008/3211. -
Enabling power: Road Traffic Regulation Act 1984, s. 14
(1) (a) (7), sch. 9, para. 27 (1). - Made: 24.11.2008.
Coming into force: 29.11.2008. Effect: S.I. 2007/2031
revoked. Territorial extent & classification: E. Local
Unpublished

The M20 Motorway (Junctions 11 and 12, Slip Roads)
(Temporary Prohibition of Traffic) Order 2008 No.
2008/1033. - Enabling power: Road Traffic Regulation Act
1984, s. 14 (1) (a). - Made: 31.03.2008. Coming into force:
05.04.2008. Effect: None. Territorial extent &
classification: E. Local *Unpublished*

The M23 Motorway and the M25 Motorway (Junctions
7 and 8) (Temporary Restriction and Prohibition of
Traffic) Order 2008 No. 2008/2722. - Enabling power:
Road Traffic Regulation Act 1984, s. 14 (1) (a) (7). -
Made: 06.10.2008. Coming into force: 11.10.2008. Effect:
None. Territorial extent & classification: E. Local
Unpublished

The M23 Motorway (Junctions 9 - 10A) (Temporary
Restriction and Prohibition of Traffic) Order 2008 No.
2008/282. - Enabling power: Road Traffic Regulation Act
1984, s. 14 (1) (a) (7). - Made: 28.01.2008. Coming into
force: 02.02.2008. Effect: None. Territorial extent &
classification: E. Local *Unpublished*

The M23 Motorway (Junctions 9-10, Southbound) (Temporary Restriction and Prohibition of Traffic) Order 2008 No. 2008/2815. - Enabling power: Road Traffic Regulation Act 1984, s. 14 (1) (a) (7). - Made: 20.10.2008. Coming into force: 25.10.2008. Effect: None. Territorial extent & classification: E. Local. - Revoked by S.I. 2009/298 *Unpublished*

The M23 Motorway (Junctions 10A - 11) (Temporary Restriction of Traffic) Order 2008 No. 2008/1169. - Enabling power: Road Traffic Regulation Act 1984, s. 14 (1) (a) (7). - Made: 21.04.2008. Coming into force: 26.04.2008. Effect: None. Territorial extent & classification: E. Local *Unpublished*

The M23 Motorway (North of Junction 9, Northbound Carriageway) (Temporary Speed Restriction) Order 2008 No. 2008/1299. - Enabling power: Road Traffic Regulation Act 1984, s. 14 (1) (a). - Made: 06.05.2008. Coming into force: 10.05.2008. Effect: None. Territorial extent & classification: E. Local *Unpublished*

The M25 and M20 Motorways and the A20 Trunk Road (Swanley Interchange) (Temporary Prohibition of Traffic) Order 2008 No. 2008/1453. - Enabling power: Road Traffic Regulation Act 1984, s. 14 (1) (a). - Made: 27.05.2008. Coming into force: 01.06.2008. Effect: None. Territorial extent & classification: E. Local *Unpublished*

The M25 and M26 Motorways (Junctions 4 and 5) (Temporary Prohibition of Traffic) Order 2008 No. 2008/1125. - Enabling power: Road Traffic Regulation Act 1984, s. 14 (1) (a). - Made: 14.04.2008. Coming into force: 23.04.2008. Effect: None. Territorial extent & classification: E. Local *Unpublished*

The M25 Motorway and the A2 and A282 Trunk Roads (Junctions 1B - 5) (Temporary Prohibition of Traffic) Order 2008 No. 2008/1004. - Enabling power: Road Traffic Regulation Act 1984, s. 14 (1) (a). - Made: 17.03.2008. Coming into force: 22.03.2008. Effect: None. Territorial extent & classification: E. Local *Unpublished*

The M25 Motorway and the A2 and the A282 Trunk Roads (Junction 2) (Temporary Prohibition of Traffic) Order 2008 No. 2008/1123. - Enabling power: Road Traffic Regulation Act 1984, s. 14 (1) (a). - Made: 14.04.2008. Coming into force: 21.04.2008. Effect: None. Territorial extent & classification: E. Local *Unpublished*

The M25 Motorway and the A3 Trunk Road (Junction 10, Wisley Interchange) (Temporary Prohibition of Traffic) Order 2008 No. 2008/1456. - Enabling power: Road Traffic Regulation Act 1984, s. 14 (1) (a). - Made: 27.05.2008. Coming into force: 01.06.2008. Effect: None. Territorial extent & classification: E. Local *Unpublished*

The M25 Motorway and the A21 Trunk Road (Sevenoaks - Kipping's Cross) (Temporary Restriction and Prohibition of Traffic) Order 2008 No. 2008/2317. - Enabling power: Road Traffic Regulation Act 1984, s. 14 (1) (a). - Made: 26.08.2008. Coming into force: 30.08.2008. Effect: None. Territorial extent & classification: E. Local *Unpublished*

The M25 Motorway and the A282 Trunk Road (Junctions 26 - 31) (Temporary Prohibition of Traffic) Order 2008 No. 2008/2816. - Enabling power: Road Traffic Regulation Act 1984, s. 14 (1) (a), sch. 9, para. 27 (1). - Made: 20.10.2008. Coming into force: 01.11.2008. Effect: S.I. 2008/902 revoked. Territorial extent & classification: E. Local *Unpublished*

The M25 Motorway and the A282 Trunk Road (Junctions 28 and 30) (Temporary Restriction and Prohibition of Traffic) Order 2008 No. 2008/2534. - Enabling power: Road Traffic Regulation Act 1984, s. 14 (1) (a) (7). - Made: 22.09.2008. Coming into force: 27.09.2008. Effect: None. Territorial extent & classification: E. Local *Unpublished*

The M25 Motorway and the M4 Motorway (Thorney Interchange, Link Roads) (Temporary Prohibition of Traffic) Order 2008 No. 2008/862. - Enabling power: Road Traffic Regulation Act 1984, s. 14 (1) (a). - Made: 10.03.2008. Coming into force: 15.03.2008. Effect: None. Territorial extent & classification: E. Local *Unpublished*

The M25 Motorway and the M11 Motorway (Junctions 26 - 27) (Temporary Restriction and Prohibition of Traffic) Order 2008 No. 2008/2326. - Enabling power: Road Traffic Regulation Act 1984, s. 14 (1) (a) (7). - Made: 26.08.2008. Coming into force: 01.09.2008. Effect: None. Territorial extent & classification: E. Local *Unpublished*

The M25 Motorway and the M11 Motorway (Theydon Interchange Link Roads) (Temporary Prohibition of Traffic) Order 2008 No. 2008/2210. - Enabling power: Road Traffic Regulation Act 1984, s. 14 (1) (a). - Made: 11.08.2008. Coming into force: 18.08.2008. Effect: None. Territorial extent & classification: E. Local *Unpublished*

The M25 Motorway (Bell Common Tunnel) (Temporary Restriction and Prohibition of Traffic) Order 2008 No. 2008/1491. - Enabling power: Road Traffic Regulation Act 1984, s. 14 (1) (a) (7). - Made: 27.05.2008. Coming into force: 04.06.2008. Effect: None. Territorial extent & classification: E. Local *Unpublished*

The M25 Motorway (Holmesdale Tunnel) (Temporary Restriction and Prohibition of Traffic) Order 2008 No. 2008/2062. - Enabling power: Road Traffic Regulation Act 1984, s. 14 (1) (a) (7). - Made: 21.07.2008. Coming into force: 01.08.2008. Effect: None. Territorial extent & classification: E. Local *Unpublished*

The M25 Motorway (Junction 3, Clockwise Carriageway) (Temporary Prohibition of Traffic) Order 2008 No. 2008/1686. - Enabling power: Road Traffic Regulation Act 1984, s. 14 (1) (a). - Made: 23.06.2008. Coming into force: 28.06.2008. Effect: None. Territorial extent & classification: E. Local *Unpublished*

The M25 Motorway (Junction 4) (Temporary Restriction and Prohibition of Traffic) Order 2008 No. 2008/772. - Enabling power: Road Traffic Regulation Act 1984, s. 14 (1) (a) (7). - Made: 25.02.2008. Coming into force: 01.03.2008. Effect: None. Territorial extent & classification: E. Local *Unpublished*

The M25 Motorway (Junction 6, Anti-clockwise) (Temporary Restriction of Traffic) Order 2008 No. 2008/3214. - Enabling power: Road Traffic Regulation Act 1984, s. 14 (1) (a) (7). - Made: 24.11.2008. Coming into force: 29.11.2008. Effect: None. Territorial extent & classification: E. Local *Unpublished*

The M25 Motorway (Junction 7, Clockwise Exit Link Road) (Temporary Prohibition of Traffic) Order 2008 No. 2008/2213. - Enabling power: Road Traffic Regulation Act 1984, s. 14 (1) (a). - Made: 11.08.2008. Coming into force: 16.08.2008. Effect: None. Territorial extent & classification: E. Local *Unpublished*

The M25 Motorway (Junction 9, Anti-Clockwise Entry Slip Road) (Temporary Prohibition of Traffic) Order 2008 No. 2008/2284. - Enabling power: Road Traffic Regulation Act 1984, s. 14 (1) (a). - Made: 18.08.2008. Coming into force: 23.08.2008. Effect: None. Territorial extent & classification: E. Local *Unpublished*

The M25 Motorway (Junction 9, Anti-clockwise Exit Slip Road) (Temporary Prohibition of Traffic) Order 2008 No. 2008/3273. - Enabling power: Road Traffic Regulation Act 1984, s. 14 (1) (a). - Made: 08.12.2008. Coming into force: 03.01.2009. Effect: None. Territorial extent & classification: E. Local *Unpublished*

The M25 Motorway (Junction 11, Anti-Clockwise Carriageway) (Temporary Prohibition of Traffic) Order 2008 No. 2008/1005. - Enabling power: Road Traffic Regulation Act 1984, s. 14 (1) (a). - Made: 17.03.2008. Coming into force: 22.03.2008. Effect: None. Territorial extent & classification: E. Local *Unpublished*

The M25 Motorway (Junction 11, Dedicated Link Roads) (Temporary Prohibition of Traffic) Order 2008 No. 2008/1509. - Enabling power: Road Traffic Regulation Act 1984, s. 14 (1) (a). - Made: 02.06.2008. Coming into force: 09.06.2008. Effect: None. Territorial extent & classification: E. Local. - Revoked by S.I. 2009/2518 (Unpublished) *Unpublished*

The M25 Motorway (Junction 14 and Terminal 5 Spur Roads) (Temporary Prohibition of Traffic) Order 2008 No. 2008/2014. - Enabling power: Road Traffic Regulation Act 1984, s. 14 (1) (a). - Made: 07.07.2008. Coming into force: 17.07.2008. Effect: None. Territorial extent & classification: E. Local *Unpublished*

The M25 Motorway (Junction 18, Anti-clockwise) (Temporary Restriction and Prohibition of Traffic) Order 2008 No. 2008/2185. - Enabling power: Road Traffic Regulation Act 1984, s. 14 (1) (a) (7). - Made: 04.08.2008. Coming into force: 09.08.2008. Effect: None. Territorial extent & classification: E. Local *Unpublished*

The M25 Motorway (Junction 23, Anti-clockwise Entry Slip Road) (Temporary Prohibition of Traffic) Order 2008 No. 2008/276. - Enabling power: Road Traffic Regulation Act 1984, s. 14 (1) (a). - Made: 28.01.2008. Coming into force: 02.02.2008. Effect: None. Territorial extent & classification: E. Local *Unpublished*

The M25 Motorway (Junction 23, Anti-clockwise Exit Slip Road) (Temporary Prohibition of Traffic) Order 2008 No. 2008/3215. - Enabling power: Road Traffic Regulation Act 1984, s. 14 (1) (a). - Made: 24.11.2008. Coming into force: 29.11.2008. Effect: None. Territorial extent & classification: E. Local *Unpublished*

The M25 Motorway (Junction 23, Clockwise Exit Slip Road) (Temporary Prohibition of Traffic) Order 2008 No. 2008/1171. - Enabling power: Road Traffic Regulation Act 1984, s. 14 (1) (a). - Made: 21.04.2008. Coming into force: 26.04.2008. Effect: None. Territorial extent & classification: E. Local *Unpublished*

The M25 Motorway (Junction 23) (Temporary Restriction and Prohibition of Traffic) Order 2008 No. 2008/1688. - Enabling power: Road Traffic Regulation Act 1984, s. 14 (1) (a) (7). - Made: 23.06.2008. Coming into force: 28.06.2008. Effect: None. Territorial extent & classification: E. Local *Unpublished*

The M25 Motorway (Junction 24, Anti-clockwise Entry Slip Road) (Temporary Prohibition of Traffic) Order 2008 No. 2008/35. - Enabling power: Road Traffic Regulation Act 1984, s. 14 (1) (a). - Made: 07.01.2008. Coming into force: 12.01.2008. Effect: None. Territorial extent & classification: E. Local *Unpublished*

The M25 Motorway (Junction 24, Slip Roads) (Temporary Prohibition of Traffic) Order 2008 No. 2008/1110. - Enabling power: Road Traffic Regulation Act 1984, s. 14 (1) (a). - Made: 07.04.2008. Coming into force: 12.04.2008. Effect: None. Territorial extent & classification: E. Local *Unpublished*

The M25 Motorway (Junction 24, Slip Roads) (Temporary Prohibition of Traffic) Order 2008 No. 2008/2535. - Enabling power: Road Traffic Regulation Act 1984, s. 14 (1) (a). - Made: 22.09.2008. Coming into force: 27.09.2008. Effect: None. Territorial extent & classification: E. Local *Unpublished*

The M25 Motorway (Junction 25, Clockwise Entry Slip Road) (Temporary Prohibition of Traffic) Order 2008 No. 2008/2046. - Enabling power: Road Traffic Regulation Act 1984, s. 14 (1) (a). - Made: 14.07.2008. Coming into force: 19.07.2008. Effect: None. Territorial extent & classification: E. Local *Unpublished*

The M25 Motorway (Junction 25, Clockwise Entry Slip Road) (Temporary Prohibition of Traffic) Order 2008 No. 2008/451. - Enabling power: Road Traffic Regulation Act 1984, s. 14 (1) (a). - Made: 18.02.2008. Coming into force: 23.02.2008. Effect: None. Territorial extent & classification: E. Local *Unpublished*

The M25 Motorway (Junction 27, Carriageways) (Temporary Prohibition of Traffic) Order 2008 No. 2008/1564. - Enabling power: Road Traffic Regulation Act 1984, s. 14 (1) (a). - Made: 09.06.2008. Coming into force: 14.06.2008. Effect: None. Territorial extent & classification: E. Local *Unpublished*

Road traffic: Traffic regulation

The M25 Motorway (Junction 27) (Temporary Restriction and Prohibition of Traffic) Order 2008 No. 2008/1175. - Enabling power: Road Traffic Regulation Act 1984, s. 14 (1) (a) (7). - Made: 21.04.2008. Coming into force: 26.04.2008. Effect: None. Territorial extent & classification: E. Local *Unpublished*

The M25 Motorway (Junction 28, Clockwise Carriageway) (Temporary Prohibition of Traffic) Order 2008 No. 2008/1221. - Enabling power: Road Traffic Regulation Act 1984, s. 14 (1) (a). - Made: 21.04.2008. Coming into force: 26.04.2008. Effect: None. Territorial extent & classification: E. Local *Unpublished*

The M25 Motorway (Junction 28, Clockwise) (Temporary Restriction and Prohibition of Traffic) Order 2008 No. 2008/774. - Enabling power: Road Traffic Regulation Act 1984, s. 14 (1) (a) (7). - Made: 25.02.2008. Coming into force: 01.03.2008. Effect: None. Territorial extent & classification: E. Local *Unpublished*

The M25 Motorway (Junction 28, Dedicated Link Road) (Temporary Prohibition of Traffic) Order 2008 No. 2008/902. - Enabling power: Road Traffic Regulation Act 1984, s. 14 (1) (a). - Made: 03.03.2008. Coming into force: 10.03.2008. Effect: None. Territorial extent & classification: E. Local *Unpublished*

The M25 Motorway (Junction 28) (Temporary Restriction and Prohibition of Traffic) Order 2008 No. 2008/2814. - Enabling power: Road Traffic Regulation Act 1984, s. 14 (1) (a) (7). - Made: 20.10.2008. Coming into force: 27.10.2008. Effect: None. Territorial extent & classification: E. Local. - Revoked by S.I. 2009/1004 (Unpublished) *Unpublished*

The M25 Motorway (Junction 29, Clockwise Slip Roads) (Temporary Prohibition of Traffic) Order 2008 No. 2008/1683. - Enabling power: Road Traffic Regulation Act 1984, s. 14 (1) (a). - Made: 23.06.2008. Coming into force: 28.06.2008. Effect: None. Territorial extent & classification: E. Local *Unpublished*

The M25 Motorway (Junction 29, Slip Roads) (Temporary Prohibition of Traffic) Order 2008 No. 2008/2536. - Enabling power: Road Traffic Regulation Act 1984, s. 14 (1) (a). - Made: 22.09.2008. Coming into force: 27.09.2008. Effect: None. Territorial extent & classification: E. Local *Unpublished*

The M25 Motorway (Junction 31 - North of Junction 30, Anti-clockwise) (Temporary Restriction and Prohibition of Traffic) Order 2008 No. 2008/1056. - Enabling power: Road Traffic Regulation Act 1984, s. 14 (1) (a) (7). - Made: 25.02.2008. Coming into force: 01.03.2008. Effect: None. Territorial extent & classification: E. Local *Unpublished*

The M25 Motorway (Junctions 5, 6 and 8, Slip Roads) (Temporary Prohibition of Traffic) Order 2008 No. 2008/452. - Enabling power: Road Traffic Regulation Act 1984, s. 14 (1) (a). - Made: 18.02.2008. Coming into force: 23.02.2008. Effect: None. Territorial extent & classification: E. Local *Unpublished*

The M25 Motorway (Junctions 6 - 10, Slip Roads) (Temporary Prohibition of Traffic) Order 2008 No. 2008/29. - Enabling power: Road Traffic Regulation Act 1984, s. 14 (1) (a). - Made: 07.01.2008. Coming into force: 15.01.2008. Effect: None. Territorial extent & classification: E. Local *Unpublished*

The M25 Motorway (Junctions 17 - 25) (Temporary Prohibition of Traffic) Order 2008 No. 2008/2316. - Enabling power: Road Traffic Regulation Act 1984, s. 14 (1) (a). - Made: 26.08.2008. Coming into force: 01.09.2008. Effect: None. Territorial extent & classification: E. Local. - Revoked by S.I. 2009/2118 (Unpublished) *Unpublished*

The M25 Motorway (Junctions 24 - 25, Clockwise) (Temporary Restriction of Traffic) Order 2008 No. 2008/999. - Enabling power: Road Traffic Regulation Act 1984, s. 14 (1) (a) (7). - Made: 25.03.2008. Coming into force: 29.03.2008. Effect: None. Territorial extent & classification: E. Local *Unpublished*

The M25 Motorway (Junctions 25 - 26) (Temporary Restriction and Prohibition of Traffic) Order 2008 No. 2008/1112. - Enabling power: Road Traffic Regulation Act 1984, s. 14 (1) (a) (7). - Made: 07.04.2008. Coming into force: 12.04.2008. Effect: None. Territorial extent & classification: E. Local *Unpublished*

The M25 Motorway (Junctions 30 - 29, Anti-Clockwise) (Temporary Restriction of Traffic) Order 2008 No. 2008/1234. - Enabling power: Road Traffic Regulation Act 1984, s. 14 (1) (a) (7). - Made: 28.04.2008. Coming into force: 03.05.2008. Effect: None. Territorial extent & classification: E. Local *Unpublished*

The M25 Motorway, the M4 Motorway and the M40 Motorway (M25 Junctions 15 - 16) (Temporary Restriction and Prohibition of Traffic) Order 2008 No. 2008/277. - Enabling power: Road Traffic Regulation Act 1984, s. 14 (1) (a) (7). - Made: 28.01.2008. Coming into force: 07.02.2008. Effect: None. Territorial extent & classification: E. Local *Unpublished*

The M25 Motorway, the M23 Motorway and the M3 Motorway (M25 Junctions 7 - 13, Slip/Link Roads) (Temporary Restriction and Prohibition of Traffic) Order 2008 No. 2008/2518. - Enabling power: Road Traffic Regulation Act 1984, s. 14 (1) (a) (7), sch. 9, para. 27 (1). - Made: 15.09.2008. Coming into force: 22.09.2008. Effect: S.I. 2008/1509 revoked. Territorial extent & classification: E. Local *Unpublished*

The M26 and M20 Motorways (Junctions 2 - 7) (Temporary Restriction and Prohibition of Traffic) Order 2008 No. 2008/2318. - Enabling power: Road Traffic Regulation Act 1984, s. 14 (1) (a). - Made: 26.08.2008. Coming into force: 30.08.2008. Effect: None. Territorial extent & classification: E. Local *Unpublished*

The M26 Motorway (Junction 1, Eastbound) (Temporary Restriction of Traffic) Order 2008 No. 2008/278. - Enabling power: Road Traffic Regulation Act 1984, s. 14 (1) (a) (7). - Made: 28.01.2008. Coming into force: 02.02.2008. Effect: None. Territorial extent & classification: E. Local *Unpublished*

Road traffic: Traffic regulation

The M26 Motorway (Junction 2A, Slip Roads) (Temporary Prohibition of Traffic) Order 2008 No. 2008/1684. - Enabling power: Road Traffic Regulation Act 1984, s. 14 (1) (a). - Made: 23.06.2008. Coming into force: 01.07.2008. Effect: None. Territorial extent & classification: E. Local *Unpublished*

The M27 Motorway (Junction 1, Slip Roads) (Temporary Prohibition of Traffic) Order 2008 No. 2008/1356. - Enabling power: Road Traffic Regulation Act 1984, s. 14 (1) (a). - Made: 12.05.2008. Coming into force: 17.05.2008. Effect: None. Territorial extent & classification: E. Local *Unpublished*

The M27 Motorway (Junction 4, Eastbound Link Road) (Temporary Prohibition of Traffic) Order 2008 No. 2008/1558. - Enabling power: Road Traffic Regulation Act 1984, s. 14 (1) (a). - Made: 09.06.2008. Coming into force: 14.06.2008. Effect: None. Territorial extent & classification: E. Local *Unpublished*

The M27 Motorway (Junction 4, Westbound) (Temporary Prohibition of Traffic) Order 2008 No. 2008/2063. - Enabling power: Road Traffic Regulation Act 1984, s. 14 (1) (a). - Made: 21.07.2008. Coming into force: 26.07.2008. Effect: None. Territorial extent & classification: E. Local *Unpublished*

The M27 Motorway (Junction 8, Westbound Carriageway) (Temporary Prohibition of Traffic) Order 2008 No. 2008/1565. - Enabling power: Road Traffic Regulation Act 1984, s. 14 (1) (a). - Made: 09.06.2008. Coming into force: 14.06.2008. Effect: None. Territorial extent & classification: E. Local *Unpublished*

The M27 Motorway (Junction 10 - Hilsea) (Temporary Restriction of Traffic) Order 2008 No. 2008/31. - Enabling power: Road Traffic Regulation Act 1984, s. 14 (1) (a) (7). - Made: 07.01.2008. Coming into force: 12.01.2008. Effect: None. Territorial extent & classification: E. Local *Unpublished*

The M27 Motorway (Junction 11, Eastbound Entry Slip Road) (Temporary Prohibition of Traffic) Order 2008 No. 2008/872. - Enabling power: Road Traffic Regulation Act 1984, s. 14 (1) (a). - Made: 10.03.2008. Coming into force: 15.03.2008. Effect: None. Territorial extent & classification: E. Local *Unpublished*

The M27 Motorway (Junctions 3 - 5) (Temporary Restriction and Prohibition of Traffic) Order 2008 No. 2008/152. - Enabling power: Road Traffic Regulation Act 1984, s. 14 (1) (a) (7). - Made: 21.01.2008. Coming into force: 26.01.2008. Effect: None. Territorial extent & classification: E. Local *Unpublished*

The M27 Motorway (Junctions 3 - 5) (Temporary Restriction and Prohibition of Traffic) Order 2008 Variation Order 2008 No. 2008/1625. - Enabling power: Road Traffic Regulation Act 1984, s. 14 (1) (a) (7), sch. 9, para. 27 (1). - Made: 16.06.2008. Coming into force: 21.06.2008. Effect: S.I. 2008/152 varied. Territorial extent & classification: E. Local *Unpublished*

The M27 Motorway (Junctions 7, 8 and 9, Slip Roads) (Temporary Prohibition of Traffic) Order 2008 No. 2008/1348. - Enabling power: Road Traffic Regulation Act 1984, s. 14 (1) (a). - Made: 12.05.2008. Coming into force: 17.05.2008. Effect: None. Territorial extent & classification: E. Local *Unpublished*

The M32 Motorway (Junction 1) (Temporary Prohibition of Traffic) Order 2008 No. 2008/2963. - Enabling power: Road Traffic Regulation Act 1984, s. 14 (1) (a). - Made: 05.11.2008. Coming into force: 08.11.2008. Effect: None. Territorial extent & classification: E. Local *Unpublished*

The M32 Motorway (Junction 2) (Temporary Prohibition of Traffic) Order 2008 No. 2008/829. - Enabling power: Road Traffic Regulation Act 1984, s. 14 (1) (a). - Made: 27.02.2008. Coming into force: 01.03.2008. Effect: None. Territorial extent & classification: E. Local *Unpublished*

The M32 Motorway (Junction 2) (Temporary Prohibition of Traffic) Order 2008 No. 2008/1222. - Enabling power: Road Traffic Regulation Act 1984, s. 14 (1) (a) (c). - Made: 25.04.2008. Coming into force: 29.04.2008. Effect: None. Territorial extent & classification: E. Local *Unpublished*

The M32 Motorway (Junctions 1 - 2) (Temporary Restriction of Traffic) Order 2008 No. 2008/1107. - Enabling power: Road Traffic Regulation Act 1984, s. 14 (1) (a) (7). - Made: 09.04.2008. Coming into force: 12.04.2008. Effect: None. Territorial extent & classification: E. Local *Unpublished*

The M32 Motorway (Junctions 2 - 3) (Temporary Prohibition and Restriction of Traffic) Order 2008 No. 2008/1549. - Enabling power: Road Traffic Regulation Act 1984, s. 14 (1) (a) (7). - Made: 05.06.2008. Coming into force: 07.06.2008. Effect: None. Territorial extent & classification: E. Local *Unpublished*

The M32 Motorway (Junctions 2 - 3) (Temporary Prohibition of Traffic) Order 2008 No. 2008/1048. - Enabling power: Road Traffic Regulation Act 1984, s. 14 (1) (a). - Made: 25.03.2008. Coming into force: 29.03.2008. Effect: None. Territorial extent & classification: E. Local *Unpublished*

The M40 and M42 Motorways (Junction 3a, Solihull) (Link Road) (Temporary Prohibition of Traffic) Order 2008 No. 2008/1545. - Enabling power: Road Traffic Regulation Act 1984, s. 14 (1) (a). - Made: 16.05.2008. Coming into force: 23.05.2008. Effect: None. Territorial extent & classification: E. Local *Unpublished*

The M40 Motorway and the A40 Trunk Road (Denham) (Temporary Restriction and Prohibition of Traffic) Order 2008 No. 2008/281. - Enabling power: Road Traffic Regulation Act 1984, s. 14 (1) (a). - Made: 28.01.2008. Coming into force: 02.02.2008. Effect: None. Territorial extent & classification: E. Local *Unpublished*

The M40 Motorway and the A40 Trunk Road
(Denham) (Temporary Restriction and Prohibition of
Traffic) Order 2008 Variation Order 2008 No.
2008/837. - Enabling power: Road Traffic Regulation Act
1984, s. 14 (1) (a). - Made: 03.03.2008. Coming into force:
10.03.2008. Effect: S.I. 2008/281 varied. Territorial extent
& classification: E. Local *Unpublished*

The M40 Motorway and the M25 Motorway (M40
Junction 1a, Eastbound Link Roads) (Temporary
Prohibition of Traffic) Order 2008 No. 2008/2920. -
Enabling power: Road Traffic Regulation Act 1984, s. 14
(1) (a). - Made: 03.11.2008. Coming into force:
08.11.2008. Effect: None. Territorial extent &
classification: E. Local *Unpublished*

The M40 Motorway (Junction 2) Slip Roads
(Temporary Prohibition of Traffic) Order 2008 No.
2008/2730. - Enabling power: Road Traffic Regulation Act
1984, s. 14 (1) (a). - Made: 06.10.2008. Coming into force:
13.10.2008. Effect: None. Territorial extent &
classification: E. Local *Unpublished*

The M40 Motorway (Junction 4, Buckinghamshire and
Junction 9, Oxfordshire) (Temporary Prohibition of
Traffic) Order 2008 No. 2008/1525. - Enabling power:
Road Traffic Regulation Act 1984, s. 14 (1) (a). - Made:
27.05.2008. Coming into force: 03.06.2008. Effect: None.
Territorial extent & classification: E. Local *Unpublished*

The M40 Motorway (Junction 4, Westbound Entry Slip
Road) (Temporary Prohibition of Traffic) Order 2008
No. 2008/1349. - Enabling power: Road Traffic Regulation
Act 1984, s. 14 (1) (a). - Made: 12.05.2008. Coming into
force: 17.05.2008. Effect: None. Territorial extent &
classification: E. Local *Unpublished*

The M40 Motorway (Junction 6) Southbound Entry
Slip Road (Temporary Prohibition of Traffic) Order
2008 No. 2008/1198. - Enabling power: Road Traffic
Regulation Act 1984, s. 14 (1) (a). - Made: 21.04.2008.
Coming into force: 28.04.2008. Effect: None. Territorial
extent & classification: E. Local *Unpublished*

The M40 Motorway (Junction 10) and the A43 Trunk
Road (Cherwell, Oxfordshire) (Temporary Restriction
and Prohibition of Traffic) Order 2008 No. 2008/2013. -
Enabling power: Road Traffic Regulation Act 1984, s. 14
(1) (a). - Made: 01.07.2008. Coming into force:
08.07.2008. Effect: None. Territorial extent &
classification: E. Local *Unpublished*

The M40 Motorway (Junction 10) Northbound and
Southbound Entry Slip Roads (Temporary Prohibition
of Traffic) Order 2008 No. 2008/340. - Enabling power:
Road Traffic Regulation Act 1984, s. 14 (1) (a). - Made:
04.02.2008. Coming into force: 11.02.2008. Effect: None.
Territorial extent & classification: E. Local *Unpublished*

The M40 Motorway (Junction 10) Slip Roads
(Temporary Prohibition of Traffic) Order 2008 No.
2008/2745. - Enabling power: Road Traffic Regulation Act
1984, s. 14 (1) (a). - Made: 07.10.2008. Coming into force:
14.10.2008. Effect: None. Territorial extent &
classification: E. Local *Unpublished*

The M40 Motorway (Junction 15) (Temporary
Prohibition and Restriction of Traffic) Order 2008 No.
2008/2577. - Enabling power: Road Traffic Regulation Act
1984, s. 14 (1) (a) (7). - Made: 12.09.2008. Coming into
force: 19.09.2008. Effect: None. Territorial extent &
classification: E. Local *Unpublished*

The M40 Motorway (Junctions 1 - 15) Slip Roads
(Temporary Prohibition of Traffic) Order 2008 No.
2008/1706. - Enabling power: Road Traffic Regulation Act
1984, s. 14 (1) (a). - Made: 23.06.2008. Coming into force:
30.06.2008. Effect: None. Territorial extent &
classification: E. Local *Unpublished*

The M40 Motorway (Junctions 2 and 3) Westbound
Exit Slip Roads (Temporary Prohibition of Traffic)
Order 2008 No. 2008/2607. - Enabling power: Road
Traffic Regulation Act 1984, s. 14 (1) (a). - Made:
23.09.2008. Coming into force: 30.09.2008. Effect: None.
Territorial extent & classification: E. Local *Unpublished*

The M40 Motorway (Junctions 6 to 8a, Oxfordshire)
(Temporary Restriction and Prohibition of Traffic)
Order 2008 No. 2008/1359. - Enabling power: Road
Traffic Regulation Act 1984, s. 14 (1) (a) (7). - Made:
12.05.2008. Coming into force: 19.05.2008. Effect: None.
Territorial extent & classification: E. Local *Unpublished*

The M42 Motorway and A5 Trunk Road (M42
Junction 10, Tamworth) (Temporary Prohibition and
Restriction of Traffic) Order 2008 No. 2008/2485. -
Enabling power: Road Traffic Regulation Act 1984, s. 14
(1) (a). - Made: 29.08.2008. Coming into force:
05.09.2008. Effect: None. Territorial extent &
classification: E. Local *Unpublished*

The M42 Motorway and M40 Motorway (Junction 3 to
3a, Warwickshire) (Temporary Restriction and
Prohibition of Traffic) Order 2008 No. 2008/245. -
Enabling power: Road Traffic Regulation Act 1984, s. 14
(1) (a) (7). - Made: 25.01.2008. Coming into force:
01.02.2008. Effect: None. Territorial extent &
classification: E. Local *Unpublished*

The M42 Motorway (Junction 3A) (Link Road)
(Temporary Prohibition of Traffic) Order 2008 No.
2008/2006. - Enabling power: Road Traffic Regulation Act
1984, s. 14 (1) (a). - Made: 04.07.2008. Coming into force:
11.07.2008. Effect: None. Territorial extent &
classification: E. Local *Unpublished*

The M42 Motorway (Junction 3) (Northbound Entry
Slip Road) (Temporary Prohibition of Traffic) Order
2008 No. 2008/2041. - Enabling power: Road Traffic
Regulation Act 1984, s. 14 (1) (a). - Made: 11.07.2008.
Coming into force: 18.07.2008. Effect: None. Territorial
extent & classification: E. Local *Unpublished*

The M42 Motorway (Junction 5, Solihull) (Northbound
Entry Slip Road) (Temporary Prohibition of Traffic)
Order 2008 No. 2008/2743. - Enabling power: Road
Traffic Regulation Act 1984, s. 14 (1) (a). - Made:
03.10.2008. Coming into force: 10.10.2008. Effect: None.
Territorial textent & classification: E. Local *Unpublished*

The M42 Motorway (Junction 5, Solihull) (Southbound Entry Slip Road) (Temporary Prohibition of Traffic) Order 2008 No. 2008/1076. - Enabling power: Road Traffic Regulation Act 1984, s. 14 (1) (a). - Made: 21.03.2008. Coming into force: 28.03.2008. Effect: None. Territorial extent & classification: E. Local *Unpublished*

The M42 Motorway (Junction 6) (Northbound Entry Slip Road) (Temporary Prohibition of Traffic) Order 2008 No. 2008/3029. - Enabling power: Road Traffic Regulation Act 1984, s. 14 (1) (a). - Made: 10.11.2008. Coming into force: 17.11.2008. Effect: None. Territorial extent & classification: E. Local *Unpublished*

The M42 Motorway (Junction 6, Solihull) (Temporary Prohibition of Traffic) Order 2008 No. 2008/2618. - Enabling power: Road Traffic Regulation Act 1984, s. 14 (1) (a). - Made: 19.09.2008. Coming into force: 26.09.2008. Effect: None. Territorial extent & classification: E. Local *Unpublished*

The M42 Motorway (Junction 7, Solihull) (Link Road) (Temporary Prohibition of Traffic) Order 2008 No. 2008/2490. - Enabling power: Road Traffic Regulation Act 1984, s. 14 (1) (a). - Made: 29.08.2008. Coming into force: 05.09.2008. Effect: None. Territorial extent & classification: E. Local *Unpublished*

The M42 Motorway (Junction 10, Warwickshire) (Southbound Entry Slip Road) (Temporary Prohibition of Traffic) Order 2008 No. 2008/3357. - Enabling power: Road Traffic Regulation Act 1984, s. 14 (1) (a). - Made: 22.12.2008. Coming into force: 29.12.2008. Effect: None. Territorial extent & classification: E. Local *Unpublished*

The M42 Motorway (Junctions 3 - 2, Worcestershire) (Temporary Prohibition of Traffic) Order 2008 No. 2008/2575. - Enabling power: Road Traffic Regulation Act 1984, s. 14 (1) (a) (7). - Made: 12.09.2008. Coming into force: 19.09.2008. Effect: None. Territorial extent & classification: E. Local *Unpublished*

The M42 Motorway (Junctions 3 - 3a, Warwickshire) (Temporary Prohibition of Traffic) Order 2008 No. 2008/2809. - Enabling power: Road Traffic Regulation Act 1984, s. 14 (1) (a) (7). - Made: 13.10.2008. Coming into force: 20.10.2008. Effect: None. Territorial extent & classification: E. Local *Unpublished*

The M42 Motorway (Junctions 4 - 3A) (Temporary Prohibition of Traffic) Order 2008 No. 2008/2468. - Enabling power: Road Traffic Regulation Act 1984, s. 14 (1) (a). - Made: 08.09.2008. Coming into force: 15.09.2008. Effect: None. Territorial extent & classification: E. Local *Unpublished*

The M45 Motorway (M45/M1 Junction 17, Northamptonshire to Thurlaston, Warwickshire) (Temporary Prohibition of Traffic) Order 2008 No. 2008/256. - Enabling power: Road Traffic Regulation Act 1984, s. 14 (1) (a). - Made: 25.01.2008. Coming into force: 01.02.2008. Effect: None. Territorial extent & classification: E. Local *Unpublished*

The M48 Motorway (Junction 1) (Temporary Prohibition of Traffic) Order 2008 No. 2008/1229. - Enabling power: Road Traffic Regulation Act 1984, s. 14 (1) (a). - Made: 25.04.2008. Coming into force: 29.04.2008. Effect: None. Territorial extent & classification: E. Local *Unpublished*

The M48 Motorway (Junction 2, Severn Bridge) (Temporary Restriction of Traffic) Order 2008 No. 2008/1448. - Enabling power: Road Traffic Regulation Act 1984, s. 14 (1) (a). - Made: 28.05.2008. Coming into force: 31.05.2008. Effect: None. Territorial extent & classification: E. Local *Unpublished*

The M48 Motorway (Junctions 1 - 2, Severn Bridge) (Temporary Prohibition of Traffic) Order 2008 No. 2008/286. - Enabling power: Road Traffic Regulation Act 1984, s. 14 (1) (a). - Made: 30.01.2008. Coming into force: 05.02.2008. Effect: None. Territorial extent & classification: E. Local *Unpublished*

The M48 Motorway (Junctions 1 - 2, Severn Bridge) (Temporary Restriction of Traffic) Order 2008 No. 2008/857. - Enabling power: Road Traffic Regulation Act 1984, s. 14 (1) (b). - Made: 28.02.2008. Coming into force: 01.03.2008. Effect: None. Territorial extent & classification: E. Local *Unpublished*

The M48 Motorway (M4 Junction 21 to M48 Junction 1) (Temporary Prohibition of Traffic) (Number 2) Order 2008 No. 2008/1666. - Enabling power: Road Traffic Regulation Act 1984, s. 14 (1) (a). - Made: 18.06.2008. Coming into force: 21.06.2008. Effect: None. Territorial extent & classification: E. Local *Unpublished*

The M48 Motorway (M4 Junction 21 to M48 Junction 1) (Temporary Prohibition of Traffic) Order 2008 No. 2008/1301. - Enabling power: Road Traffic Regulation Act 1984, s. 14 (1) (a). - Made: 06.05.2008. Coming into force: 08.05.2008. Effect: None. Territorial extent & classification: E. Local *Unpublished*

The M48 Motorway (Severn Bridge, Separate Footways and Cycle Tracks) (Temporary Restriction of Traffic) Order 2008 No. 2008/2914. - Enabling power: Road Traffic Regulation Act 1984, s. 14 (1) (a). - Made: 04.11.2008. Coming into force: 07.11.2008. Effect: None. Territorial extent & classification: E. Local *Unpublished*

The M49 Motorway and M5 Motorway (Junction 18A) (Temporary Prohibition of Traffic) (Number 2) Order 2008 No. 2008/1398. - Enabling power: Road Traffic Regulation Act 1984, s. 14 (1) (a). - Made: 21.05.2008. Coming into force: 24.05.2008. Effect: None. Territorial extent & classification: E. Local *Unpublished*

The M49 Motorway and M5 Motorway (Junction 18A) (Temporary Prohibition of Traffic) Order 2008 No. 2008/1395. - Enabling power: Road Traffic Regulation Act 1984, s. 14 (1) (a). - Made: 20.05.2008. Coming into force: 24.05.2008. Effect: None. Territorial extent & classification: E. Local *Unpublished*

Road traffic: Traffic regulation

The M49 Motorway (M5 Junctions 18A to M4 Junction 22) (Temporary Restriction of Traffic) Order 2008 No. 2008/1218. - Enabling power: Road Traffic Regulation Act 1984, s. 14 (1) (a) (7). - Made: 25.04.2008. Coming into force: 29.04.2008. Effect: None. Territorial extent & classification: E. Local *Unpublished*

The M50 Motorway and the A449 Trunk Road (Junction 2 to 4) (Temporary Prohibition and Restriction of Traffic) Order 2008 No. 2008/1074. - Enabling power: Road Traffic Regulation Act 1984, s. 14 (1) (a). - Made: 24.03.2008. Coming into force: 31.03.2008. Effect: None. Territorial extent & classification: E. Local *Unpublished*

The M50 Motorway (Junction 1 - 2) (Temporary Restriction and Prohibition of Traffic) Order 2008 No. 2008/2456. - Enabling power: Road Traffic Regulation Act 1984, s. 14 (1) (a). - Made: 29.08.2008. Coming into force: 05.09.2008. Effect: None. Territorial extent & classification: E. Local *Unpublished*

The M50 Motorway (Junction 1) (Slip Roads) (Temporary Prohibition of Traffic) Order 2008 No. 2008/1072. - Enabling power: Road Traffic Regulation Act 1984, s. 14 (1) (a). - Made: 31.03.2008. Coming into force: 07.04.2008. Effect: None. Territorial extent & classification: E. Local *Unpublished*

The M50 Motorway (Junction 1 to M5 Junction 8) (Temporary Prohibition of Traffic) Order 2008 No. 2008/58. - Enabling power: Road Traffic Regulation Act 1984, s. 14 (1) (a). - Made: 09.01.2008. Coming into force: 16.01.2008. Effect: None. Territorial extent & classification: E. Local *Unpublished*

The M50 Motorway (Junction 2 - Junction 1) (Temporary Prohibition of Traffic) Order 2008 No. 2008/995. - Enabling power: Road Traffic Regulation Act 1984, s. 14 (1) (a). - Made: 14.03.2008. Coming into force: 21.03.2008. Effect: None. Territorial extent & classification: E. Local *Unpublished*

The M53 Motorway (Bidston Moss Viaduct) (Temporary Restriction of Traffic) Order 2008 No. 2008/2879. - Enabling power: Road Traffic Regulation Act 1984, s. 14 (1) (b). - Made: 10.10.2008. Coming into force: 09.11.2008. Effect: None. Territorial extent & classification: E. Local *Unpublished*

The M53 Motorway (Junction 2, Southbound Entry Slip Road) (Temporary Prohibition of Traffic) Order 2008 No. 2008/3330. - Enabling power: Road Traffic Regulation Act 1984, s. 14 (1) (a). - Made: 15.12.2008. Coming into force: 12.01.2009. Effect: None. Territorial extent & classification: E. Local *Unpublished*

The M53 Motorway (Junction 4, Northbound Entry Slip Road) (Temporary Prohibition of Traffic) Order 2008 No. 2008/1622. - Enabling power: Road Traffic Regulation Act 1984, s. 14 (1) (a). - Made: 06.06.2008. Coming into force: 03.07.2008. Effect: None. Territorial extent & classification: E. Local *Unpublished*

The M53 Motorway (Junction 4, Southbound Exit Slip Road) (Temporary Prohibition of Traffic) Order 2008 No. 2008/2202. - Enabling power: Road Traffic Regulation Act 1984, s. 14 (1) (a). - Made: 04.08.2008. Coming into force: 01.09.2008. Effect: None. Territorial extent & classification: E. Local *Unpublished*

The M53 Motorway (Junction 10 Southbound Entry Slip Road) (Temporary Prohibition of Traffic) Order 2008 No. 2008/2026. - Enabling power: Road Traffic Regulation Act 1984, s. 14 (1) (b). - Made: 07.07.2008. Coming into force: 02.08.2008. Effect: None. Territorial extent & classification: E. Local *Unpublished*

The M53 Motorway (Junction 11, Southbound and Northbound Link Roads to the M56 Eastbound) (Temporary Prohibition of Traffic) Order 2008 No. 2008/2923. - Enabling power: Road Traffic Regulation Act 1984, s. 14 (1) (a). - Made: 21.10.2008. Coming into force: 13.11.2008. Effect: None. Territorial extent & classification: E. Local *Unpublished*

The M53 Motorway (Junctions 2-1, Northbound and Southbound Carriageways) (Junction 2 Northbound Entry Slip Road and Junction 1 Southbound Entry Slip Road and Southbound Entry Slip Road from the A5139) and Moreton Spur (Temporary Prohibition and Restriction of Traffic) Order 2008 No. 2008/3335. - Enabling power: Road Traffic Regulation Act 1984, s. 14 (1) (a) (7). - Made: 30.12.2008. Coming into force: 02.01.2009. Effect: None. Territorial extent & classification: E. Local *Unpublished*

The M53 Motorway (Junctions 7-8, Southbound Carriageway and Junction 7 Southbound Entry Slip Road) (Temporary Prohibition of Traffic) Order 2008 No. 2008/2876. - Enabling power: Road Traffic Regulation Act 1984, s. 14 (1) (a). - Made: 17.10.2008. Coming into force: 11.11.2008. Effect: None. Territorial extent & classification: E. Local *Unpublished*

The M53 Motorway (Junctions 10-11, Northbound and Southbound Carriageways and Junction 10 Link Road and Slip Road) (Temporary Prohibition of Traffic) Order 2008 No. 2008/2465. - Enabling power: Road Traffic Regulation Act 1984, s. 14 (1) (b). - Made: 26.08.2008. Coming into force: 20.09.2008. Effect: None. Territorial extent & classification: E. Local *Unpublished*

The M53 Motorway (Junctions 10 - 11, Northbound and Southbound Carriageways) (Temporary Prohibition of Traffic) Order 2008 No. 2008/1664. - Enabling power: Road Traffic Regulation Act 1984, s. 14 (1) (a). - Made: 16.06.2008. Coming into force: 22.06.2008. Effect: None. Territorial extent & classification: E. Local *Unpublished*

The M54 Motorway and A5 Trunk Road (Cluddley to Preston, Shropshire) (Temporary Prohibition of Traffic) Order 2008 No. 2008/2044. - Enabling power: Road Traffic Regulation Act 1984, s. 14 (1) (a). - Made: 14.07.2008. Coming into force: 21.07.2008. Effect: None. Territorial extent & classification: E. Local *Unpublished*

The M54 Motorway (Junction 2, Staffordshire) (Eastbound Carriageway) (Temporary Prohibition of Traffic) Order 2008 No. 2008/1996. - Enabling power: Road Traffic Regulation Act 1984, s. 14 (1) (a). - Made: 07.07.2008. Coming into force: 14.07.2008. Effect: None. Territorial extent & classification: E. Local *Unpublished*

The M54 Motorway (Junction 2, Staffordshire) (Temporary Prohibition of Traffic) Order 2008 No. 2008/2808. - Enabling power: Road Traffic Regulation Act 1984, s. 14 (1) (a). - Made: 13.10.2008. Coming into force: 20.10.2008. Effect: None. Territorial extent & classification: E. Local *Unpublished*

The M54 Motorway (Junction 3) (Eastbound Exit Slip Road) (Temporary Prohibition of Traffic) Order 2008 No. 2008/2043. - Enabling power: Road Traffic Regulation Act 1984, s. 14 (1) (a). - Made: 14.07.2008. Coming into force: 21.07.2008. Effect: None. Territorial extent & classification: E. Local *Unpublished*

The M54 Motorway (Junctions 2 - 3, Shropshire) (Temporary Prohibition of Traffic) Order 2008 No. 2008/1541. - Enabling power: Road Traffic Regulation Act 1984, s. 14 (1) (b). - Made: 23.05.2008. Coming into force: 30.05.2008. Effect: None. Territorial extent & classification: E. Local *Unpublished*

The M54 Motorway (Junctions 4 - 6, Shropshire) (Temporary Prohibition of Traffic) Order 2008 No. 2008/871. - Enabling power: Road Traffic Regulation Act 1984, s. 14 (1) (a). - Made: 29.02.2008. Coming into force: 07.03.2008. Effect: None. Territorial extent & classification: E. Local *Unpublished*

The M54 Motorway (Junctions 6 - 7) (Temporary Prohibition of Traffic) Order 2008 No. 2008/2122. - Enabling power: Road Traffic Regulation Act 1984, s. 14 (1) (a). - Made: 22.07.2008. Coming into force: 29.07.2008. Effect: None. Territorial extent & classification: E. Local *Unpublished*

The M55 Motorway (Junction 1 Westbound and Eastbound Main Carriageways) (Temporary Prohibition of Traffic) Order 2008 No. 2008/1711. - Enabling power: Road Traffic Regulation Act 1984, s. 14 (1) (a). - Made: 23.06.2008. Coming into force: 20.07.2008. Effect: None. Territorial extent & classification: E. Local *Unpublished*

The M55 Motorway (Junction 3 Westbound and Eastbound Entry and Exit Slip Roads) and the A585 Trunk Road (Temporary Prohibition and Restriction of Traffic) Order 2008 No. 2008/2414. - Enabling power: Road Traffic Regulation Act 1984, s. 14 (1) (a). - Made: 13.08.2008. Coming into force: 16.08.2008. Effect: None. Territorial extent & classification: E. Local *Unpublished*

The M55 Motorway (Junction 4 Westbound Carriageway and Westbound Exit Slip Road) (Temporary Prohibition and Restriction of Traffic) Order 2008 No. 2008/814. - Enabling power: Road Traffic Regulation Act 1984, s. 14 (1) (a). - Made: 25.02.2008. Coming into force: 28.02.2008. Effect: None. Territorial extent & classification: E. Local *Unpublished*

The M55 Motorway (Junctions 1-3, Eastbound and Westbound Carriageways) (Temporary Prohibition of Traffic) Order 2008 No. 2008/1379. - Enabling power: Road Traffic Regulation Act 1984, s. 14 (1) (b). - Made: 13.05.2008. Coming into force: 17.05.2008. Effect: None. Territorial extent & classification: E. Local *Unpublished*

The M55 Motorway (Junctions 1 - 3, Westbound and Eastbound Main Carriageways) (Temporary Restriction of Traffic) Order 2008 No. 2008/126. - Enabling power: Road Traffic Regulation Act 1984, s. 14 (1) (a) (7). - Made: 15.01.2008. Coming into force: 10.02.2008. Effect: None. Territorial extent & classification: E. Local *Unpublished*

The M55 Motorway (Junctions 3 to 1, Eastbound and Westbound Main Carriageways) (Temporary Restriction of Traffic) Order 2008 No. 2008/73. - Enabling power: Road Traffic Regulation Act 1984, s. 14 (1) (a) (7). - Made: 08.01.2008. Coming into force: 03.02.2008. Effect: None. Territorial extent & classification: E. Local *Unpublished*

The M56 Motorway (Junction 1 Eastbound Exit Slip Road to the A34 Northbound) (Temporary Prohibition of Traffic) Order 2008 No. 2008/2235. - Enabling power: Road Traffic Regulation Act 1984, s. 14 (1) (a). - Made: 08.08.2008. Coming into force: 07.09.2008. Effect: None. Territorial extent & classification: E. Local *Unpublished*

The M56 Motorway (Junction 1 Westbound Entry Slip Road from the A34 Southbound) (Temporary Prohibition of Traffic) Order 2008 No. 2008/2236. - Enabling power: Road Traffic Regulation Act 1984, s. 14 (1) (a). - Made: 08.08.2008. Coming into force: 03.09.2008. Effect: None. Territorial extent & classification: E. Local *Unpublished*

The M56 Motorway (Junction 2 Eastbound Entry Slip Road) (Temporary Prohibition of Traffic) Order 2008 No. 2008/2237. - Enabling power: Road Traffic Regulation Act 1984, s. 14 (1) (a). - Made: 08.08.2008. Coming into force: 04.09.2008. Effect: None. Territorial extent & classification: E. Local *Unpublished*

The M56 Motorway (Junction 2) (Sharston Link Road) (Temporary Prohibition of Traffic) Order 2008 No. 2008/3302. - Enabling power: Road Traffic Regulation Act 1984, s. 14 (1) (a). - Made: 08.12.2008. Coming into force: 15.12.2008. Effect: None. Territorial extent & classification: E. Local *Unpublished*

The M56 Motorway (Junction 4 Eastbound Entry Slip Road) (Temporary Prohibition of Traffic) Order 2008 No. 2008/358. - Enabling power: Road Traffic Regulation Act 1984, s. 14 (1) (a). - Made: 21.01.2008. Coming into force: 30.01.2008. Effect: None. Territorial extent & classification: E. Local *Unpublished*

The M56 Motorway (Junction 4 Westbound Exit Slip Road) (Temporary Prohibition of Traffic) Order 2008 No. 2008/2239. - Enabling power: Road Traffic Regulation Act 1984, s. 14 (1) (a). - Made: 11.08.2008. Coming into force: 07.09.2008. Effect: None. Territorial extent & classification: E. Local *Unpublished*

The M56 Motorway (Junction 5 Eastbound Exit Slip Road) (Temporary Prohibition of Traffic) Order 2008 No. 2008/859. - Enabling power: Road Traffic Regulation Act 1984, s. 14 (1) (a). - Made: 25.02.2008. Coming into force: 03.03.2008. Effect: None. Territorial extent & classification: E. Local *Unpublished*

The M56 Motorway (Junction 5 Eastbound Exit Slip Road) (Temporary Prohibition of Traffic) Order 2008 No. 2008/2025. - Enabling power: Road Traffic Regulation Act 1984, s. 14 (1) (a). - Made: 07.07.2008. Coming into force: 30.07.2008. Effect: None. Territorial extent & classification: E. Local *Unpublished*

The M56 Motorway (Junction 5 Westbound Entry Slip Road) (Temporary Prohibition of Traffic) Order 2008 No. 2008/2464. - Enabling power: Road Traffic Regulation Act 1984, s. 14 (1) (a). - Made: 05.09.2008. Coming into force: 30.09.2008. Effect: None. Territorial extent & classification: E. Local *Unpublished*

The M56 Motorway (Junction 6 Eastbound Exit Slip Road) (Temporary Prohibition of Traffic) Order 2008 No. 2008/1150. - Enabling power: Road Traffic Regulation Act 1984, s. 14 (1) (a). - Made: 11.04.2008. Coming into force: 11.05.2008. Effect: None. Territorial extent & classification: E. Local *Unpublished*

The M56 Motorway (Junction 7, Eastbound Main Carriageway and Entry and Exit Slip Roads) (Temporary Prohibition and Restriction of Traffic) Order 2008 No. 2008/1674. - Enabling power: Road Traffic Regulation Act 1984, s. 14 (1) (a) (7). - Made: 09.05.2008. Coming into force: 04.06.2008. Effect: None. Territorial extent & classification: E. Local *Unpublished*

The M56 Motorway (Junction 7 Westbound Exit Slip Road) (Temporary Prohibition of Traffic) Order 2008 No. 2008/3339. - Enabling power: Road Traffic Regulation Act 1984, s. 14 (1) (a). - Made: 29.12.2008. Coming into force: 23.01.2009. Effect: None. Territorial extent & classification: E. Local *Unpublished*

The M56 Motorway (Junction 8, Westbound Entry Slip Road) (Temporary Prohibition of Traffic) Order 2008 No. 2008/2466. - Enabling power: Road Traffic Regulation Act 1984, s. 14 (1) (a). - Made: 05.09.2008. Coming into force: 05.10.2008. Effect: None. Territorial extent & classification: E. Local *Unpublished*

The M56 Motorway (Junction 9, Eastbound and Westbound Link Roads to the M6 Motorway Northbound) (Temporary Prohibition of Traffic) Order 2008 No. 2008/2736. - Enabling power: Road Traffic Regulation Act 1984, s. 14 (1) (a). - Made: 07.10.2008. Coming into force: 12.10.2008. Effect: None. Territorial extent & classification: E. Local *Unpublished*

The M56 Motorway (Junction 11, Eastbound Entry Slip Road) (Temporary Prohibition of Traffic) Order 2008 No. 2008/2748. - Enabling power: Road Traffic Regulation Act 1984, s. 14 (1) (a). - Made: 07.10.2008. Coming into force: 16.10.2008. Effect: None. Territorial extent & classification: E. Local *Unpublished*

The M56 Motorway (Junction 12, Eastbound Entry Slip Road) (Temporary Prohibition of Traffic) Order 2008 No. 2008/1290. - Enabling power: Road Traffic Regulation Act 1984, s. 14 (1) (a). - Made: 28.04.2008. Coming into force: 26.05.2008. Effect: None. Territorial extent & classification: E. Local *Unpublished*

The M56 Motorway (Junction 15, Westbound Carriageway) (Temporary Prohibition of Traffic) Order 2008 No. 2008/2750. - Enabling power: Road Traffic Regulation Act 1984, s. 14 (1) (a). - Made: 07.10.2008. Coming into force: 13.10.2008. Effect: None. Territorial extent & classification: E. Local *Unpublished*

The M56 Motorway (Junctions 6 - 7, Westbound Carriageway) (Temporary Prohibition and Restriction of Traffic) Order 2008 No. 2008/1069. - Enabling power: Road Traffic Regulation Act 1984, s. 14 (1) (a) (7). - Made: 28.03.2008. Coming into force: 24.04.2008. Effect: None. Territorial extent & classification: E. Local *Unpublished*

The M56 Motorway (Junctions 15 to 16, Westbound Carriageway) (Temporary Prohibition of Traffic) Order 2008 No. 2008/3175. - Enabling power: Road Traffic Regulation Act 1984, s. 14 (1) (a). - Made: 25.11.2008. Coming into force: 01.12.2008. Effect: None. Territorial extent & classification: E. Local *Unpublished*

The M56 Motorway (Junctions 16 to 15, Eastbound Carriageway) (Temporary Prohibition of Traffic) Order 2008 No. 2008/989. - Enabling power: Road Traffic Regulation Act 1984, s. 14 (1) (a). - Made: 11.03.2008. Coming into force: 14.03.2008. Effect: None. Territorial extent & classification: E. Local *Unpublished*

The M57 Motorway (A5036 Dunnings Bridge Road) Switch Island (Temporary Restriction of Traffic) Order 2008 No. 2008/76. - Enabling power: Road Traffic Regulation Act 1984, s. 14 (1) (b). - Made: 08.01.2008. Coming into force: 01.02.2008. Effect: None. Territorial extent & classification: E. Local *Unpublished*

The M57 Motorway (Junctions 1 to 2, Northbound and Southbound Carriageways and Junctions 1 and 2 Slip Roads) (Temporary Prohibition of Traffic) Order 2008 No. 2008/2028. - Enabling power: Road Traffic Regulation Act 1984, s. 14 (1) (a). - Made: 08.07.2008. Coming into force: 11.07.2008. Effect: None. Territorial extent & classification: E. Local *Unpublished*

The M58 Motorway (Junction 3, Westbound Carriageway and Westbound Entry Slip Road) (Temporary Prohibition and Restriction of Traffic) Order 2008 No. 2008/1663. - Enabling power: Road Traffic Regulation Act 1984, s. 14 (1) (a) (7). - Made: 18.06.2008. Coming into force: 14.07.2008. Effect: None. Territorial extent & classification: E. Local *Unpublished*

The M58 Motorway (Junction 4 to Junction 5 Eastbound Carriageway) (Temporary Prohibition and Restriction of Traffic) Order 2008 No. 2008/443. - Enabling power: Road Traffic Regulation Act 1984, s. 14 (1) (a) (7). - Made: 11.02.2008. Coming into force: 06.03.2008. Effect: None. Territorial extent & classification: E. Local *Unpublished*

Road traffic: Traffic regulation

The M58 Motorway (Junctions 3-1 Westbound Carriageway) (Temporary Prohibition and Restriction of Traffic) Order 2008 No. 2008/201. - Enabling power: Road Traffic Regulation Act 1984, s. 14 (1) (a) (7). - Made: 14.01.2008. Coming into force: 07.02.2008. Effect: None. Territorial extent & classification: E. Local *Unpublished*

The M60, M66, M56, M6, M65, M62, M53 and M61 Motorways (Various Slip Road Closures) (Temporary Prohibition of Traffic) Order 2008 No. 2008/3281. - Enabling power: Road Traffic Regulation Act 1984, s. 14 (1) (b). - Made: 01.12.2008. Coming into force: 06.12.2008. Effect: None. Territorial extent & classification: E. Local *Unpublished*

The M60 Motorway (Junction 3, Anticlockwise Entry Slip Road from the A34 Northbound) (Temporary Prohibition of Traffic) (No. 2) Order 2008 No. 2008/2900. - Enabling power: Road Traffic Regulation Act 1984, s. 14 (1) (a). - Made: 20.10.2008. Coming into force: 16.11.2008. Effect: None. Territorial extent & classification: E. Local *Unpublished*

The M60 Motorway (Junction 3 Anticlockwise Entry Slip Road from the A34 Northbound) (Temporary Prohibition of Traffic) Order 2008 No. 2008/1021. - Enabling power: Road Traffic Regulation Act 1984, s. 14 (1) (a). - Made: 07.02.2008. Coming into force: 06.04.2008. Effect: None. Territorial extent & classification: E. Local *Unpublished*

The M60 Motorway (Junction 4, Anticlockwise Exit Slip Road) (Temporary Prohibition of Traffic) Order 2008 No. 2008/3331. - Enabling power: Road Traffic Regulation Act 1984, s. 14 (1) (a). - Made: 15.12.2008. Coming into force: 08.01.2009. Effect: None. Territorial extent & classification: E. Local *Unpublished*

The M60 Motorway (Junction 4, Clockwise, Entry Slip Road from A34) (Temporary Prohibition of Traffic) Order 2008 No. 2008/2311. - Enabling power: Road Traffic Regulation Act 1984, s. 14 (1) (a). - Made: 15.08.2008. Coming into force: 15.09.2008. Effect: None. Territorial extent & classification: E. Local *Unpublished*

The M60 Motorway (Junction 5) and the A5103 Trunk Road (Princess Parkway) (Temporary Restriction and Prohibition of Traffic and Temporary Suspension of Statutory Provisions) Order 2008 No. 2008/1984. - Enabling power: Road Traffic Regulation Act 1984, s. 14 (1) (a) (7). - Made: 23.06.2008. Coming into force: 10.07.2008. Effect: None. Territorial extent & classification: E. Local *Unpublished*

The M60 Motorway (Junction 5 Anticlockwise Exit Slip Road) (Temporary Prohibition of Traffic) Order 2008 No. 2008/1045. - Enabling power: Road Traffic Regulation Act 1984, s. 14 (1) (b). - Made: 17.03.2008. Coming into force: 26.03.2008. Effect: None. Territorial extent & classification: E. Local *Unpublished*

The M60 Motorway (Junction 11, Anti-clockwise Entry Slip Road) (Temporary Prohibition of Traffic) Order 2008 No. 2008/471. - Enabling power: Road Traffic Regulation Act 1984, s. 14 (1) (a). - Made: 18.02.2008. Coming into force: 13.03.2008. Effect: None. Territorial extent & classification: E. Local *Unpublished*

The M60 Motorway (Junction 11, Anticlockwise, Exit Slip Road) (Temporary Prohibition of Traffic) Order 2008 No. 2008/2243. - Enabling power: Road Traffic Regulation Act 1984, s. 14 (1) (a). - Made: 11.08.2008. Coming into force: 08.09.2008. Effect: None. Territorial extent & classification: E. Local *Unpublished*

The M60 Motorway (Junction 11, Clockwise Entry Slip Road) (Temporary Prohibition of Traffic) Order 2008 No. 2008/2752. - Enabling power: Road Traffic Regulation Act 1984, s. 14 (1) (a). - Made: 06.10.2008. Coming into force: 03.11.2008. Effect: None. Territorial extent & classification: E. Local *Unpublished*

The M60 Motorway (Junction 12 Anticlockwise Carriageway and Link Roads and Junction 13 Anticlockwise Carriageway and Entry Slip Road) (Temporary Prohibition of Traffic) Order 2008 No. 2008/2949. - Enabling power: Road Traffic Regulation Act 1984, s. 14 (1) (a). - Made: 21.10.2008. Coming into force: 16.11.2008. Effect: None. Territorial extent & classification: E. Local *Unpublished*

The M60 Motorway (Junction 12 Anticlockwise, Link Roads from M602 Westbound and M62 Eastbound) (Temporary Prohibition of Traffic) Order 2008 No. 2008/2242. - Enabling power: Road Traffic Regulation Act 1984, s. 14 (1) (a). - Made: 11.08.2008. Coming into force: 04.09.2008. Effect: None. Territorial extent & classification: E. Local *Unpublished*

The M60 Motorway (Junction 13, Clockwise and Anticlockwise Entry Slip Roads) (Temporary Prohibition of Traffic) Order 2008 No. 2008/2201. - Enabling power: Road Traffic Regulation Act 1984, s. 14 (1) (a). - Made: 04.08.2008. Coming into force: 31.08.2008. Effect: None. Territorial extent & classification: E. Local *Unpublished*

The M60 Motorway (Junction 15 Clockwise and Anticlockwise Carriageways and Link Roads to the M61) (Temporary Prohibition and Restriction of Traffic) Order 2008 No. 2008/1046. - Enabling power: Road Traffic Regulation Act 1984, s. 14 (1) (a) (7). - Made: 19.03.2008. Coming into force: 24.03.2008. Effect: None. Territorial extent & classification: E. Local *Unpublished*

The M60 Motorway (Junction 16, Clockwise, Entry Slip Road) (Temporary Prohibition of Traffic) Order 2008 No. 2008/2312. - Enabling power: Road Traffic Regulation Act 1984, s. 14 (1) (a). - Made: 18.08.2008. Coming into force: 16.09.2008. Effect: None. Territorial extent & classification: E. Local *Unpublished*

The M60 Motorway (Junction 18 Simister Island) (Temporary Prohibition of Traffic) Order 2008 No. 2008/2467. - Enabling power: Road Traffic Regulation Act 1984, s. 14 (1) (a). - Made: 08.09.2008. Coming into force: 02.10.2008. Effect: None. Territorial extent & classification: E. Local *Unpublished*

The M60 Motorway (Junction 19 Anticlockwise Carriageway and Exit Slip Road) (Temporary Prohibition and Restriction of Traffic) Order 2008 No. 2008/357. - Enabling power: Road Traffic Regulation Act 1984, s. 14 (1) (a). - Made: 08.02.2008. Coming into force: 06.03.2008. Effect: None. Territorial extent & classification: E. Local *Unpublished*

The M60 Motorway (Junction 21, Anticlockwise Entry Slip Road from the A663) (Temporary Prohibition of Traffic) Order 2008 No. 2008/2247. - Enabling power: Road Traffic Regulation Act 1984, s. 14 (1) (a). - Made: 07.08.2008. Coming into force: 02.09.2008. Effect: None. Territorial extent & classification: E. Local *Unpublished*

The M60 Motorway (Junction 22 - 23 Clockwise Carriageway) (Temporary Restriction of Traffic) Order 2008 No. 2008/467. - Enabling power: Road Traffic Regulation Act 1984, s. 14 (1) (a). - Made: 15.02.2008. Coming into force: 13.03.2008. Effect: None. Territorial extent & classification: E. Local *Unpublished*

The M60 Motorway (Junction 22-24 Anticlockwise Carriageway and Junction 23 Anticlockwise Exit Slip Road) (Temporary Prohibition and Restriction of Traffic) Order 2008 No. 2008/1846. - Enabling power: Road Traffic Regulation Act 1984, s. 14 (1) (a) (7). - Made: 23.06.2008. Coming into force: 21.07.2008. Effect: None. Territorial extent & classification: E. Local *Unpublished*

The M60 Motorway (Junction 23, Anticlockwise Exit Slip Road) (Temporary Prohibition of Traffic) Order 2008 No. 2008/2526. - Enabling power: Road Traffic Regulation Act 1984, s. 14 (1) (a). - Made: 15.09.2008. Coming into force: 13.10.2008. Effect: None. Territorial extent & classification: E. Local *Unpublished*

The M60 Motorway (Junction 24-25, Clockwise Main Carriageway) (Temporary Restriction of Traffic) Order 2008 No. 2008/1845. - Enabling power: Road Traffic Regulation Act 1984, s. 14 (1) (b). - Made: 25.06.2008. Coming into force: 04.07.2008. Effect: None. Territorial extent & classification: E. Local *Unpublished*

The M60 Motorway (Junction 25, Anticlockwise Entry Slip Road) (Temporary Prohibition of Traffic) (No. 2) Order 2008 No. 2008/2463. - Enabling power: Road Traffic Regulation Act 1984, s. 14 (1) (a). - Made: 08.09.2008. Coming into force: 05.10.2008. Effect: None. Territorial extent & classification: E. Local *Unpublished*

The M60 Motorway (Junction 25, Anticlockwise Entry Slip Road) (Temporary Prohibition of Traffic) Order 2008 No. 2008/359. - Enabling power: Road Traffic Regulation Act 1984, s. 14 (1) (a). - Made: 01.02.2008. Coming into force: 28.02.2008. Effect: None. Territorial extent & classification: E. Local *Unpublished*

The M60 Motorway (Junction 25, Anticlockwise, Entry Slip Road) (Temporary Prohibition of Traffic) Order 2008 No. 2008/2309. - Enabling power: Road Traffic Regulation Act 1984, s. 14 (1) (a). - Made: 15.08.2008. Coming into force: 11.09.2008. Effect: None. Territorial extent & classification: E. Local *Unpublished*

The M60 Motorway (Junction 27, Clockwise Carriageway and Junction 27 Clockwise Entry Slip Road) (Temporary Prohibition and Restriction of Traffic) Order 2008 No. 2008/2154. - Enabling power: Road Traffic Regulation Act 1984, s. 14 (1) (a) (7). - Made: 02.07.2008. Coming into force: 28.07.2008. Effect: None. Territorial extent & classification: E. Local *Unpublished*

The M60 Motorway (Junctions 4-2, Anticlockwise Carriageway and Junction 3 Anticlockwise Entry and Junction 2 Anticlockwise Exit Slip Roads) (Temporary Prohibition and Restriction of Traffic) Order 2008 No. 2008/870. - Enabling power: Road Traffic Regulation Act 1984, s. 14 (1) (a) (7). - Made: 08.02.2008. Coming into force: 04.03.2008. Effect: None. Territorial extent & classification: E. Local *Unpublished*

The M60 Motorway (Junctions 6 to 7 Clockwise Collector-Distributor Road and Junction 6 Clockwise Entry and Junction 7 Clockwise Exit Slip Roads) (Temporary Prohibition of Traffic) Order 2008 No. 2008/564. - Enabling power: Road Traffic Regulation Act 1984, s. 14 (1) (a). - Made: 18.02.2008. Coming into force: 16.03.2008. Effect: None. Territorial extent & classification: E. Local *Unpublished*

The M60 Motorway (Junctions 7 to 8 Clockwise Collector-Distributor Road and Junction 7 Clockwise Entry and Junction 8 Clockwise Exit Slip Roads) (Temporary Prohibition of Traffic) Order 2008 No. 2008/1019. - Enabling power: Road Traffic Regulation Act 1984, s. 14 (1) (a). - Made: 18.02.2008. Coming into force: 18.03.2008. Effect: None. Territorial extent & classification: E. Local *Unpublished*

The M60 Motorway (Junctions 8 to 7 Anticlockwise Collector-Distributor Road and Junction 8 Anticlockwise Entry and Junction 7 Anticlockwise Exit Slip Roads) (Temporary Prohibition of Traffic) Order 2008 No. 2008/1044. - Enabling power: Road Traffic Regulation Act 1984, s. 14 (1) (a). - Made: 18.02.2008. Coming into force: 17.03.2008. Effect: None. Territorial extent & classification: E. Local *Unpublished*

The M60 Motorway (Junctions 12-10, Anticlockwise Carriageway, Junction 11, Anticlockwise Entry Slip Road and Link Roads from the M602 Westbound and M62 Eastbound) (Temporary Prohibition and Restriction of Traffic) Order 2008 No. 2008/3287. - Enabling power: Road Traffic Regulation Act 1984, s. 14 (1) (a) (7). - Made: 09.12.2008. Coming into force: 04.01.2009. Effect: None. Territorial extent & classification: E. Local *Unpublished*

The M60 Motorway (Junctions 14-16 Clockwise Carriageway and Junctions 14 and 15 Clockwise Entry Slip Roads) (Temporary Prohibition and Restriction of Traffic) Order 2008 No. 2008/360. - Enabling power: Road Traffic Regulation Act 1984, s. 14 (1) (a) (7). - Made: 05.02.2008. Coming into force: 15.02.2008. Effect: None. Territorial extent & classification: E. Local *Unpublished*

The M60 Motorway (Junctions 16-18 Anticlockwise Carriageway and Junction 17 Anticlockwise Entry Slip Road) (Temporary Prohibition and Restriction of Traffic) Order 2008 No. 2008/1450. - Enabling power: Road Traffic Regulation Act 1984, s. 14 (1) (a) (7). - Made: 19.05.2008. Coming into force: 12.06.2008. Effect: None. Territorial extent & classification: E. Local *Unpublished*

The M60 Motorway (Junctions 19-21, Clockwise Carriageway and Junction 20 Clockwise Exit Slip Road) (Temporary Prohibition and Restriction of Traffic) Order 2008 No. 2008/1043. - Enabling power: Road Traffic Regulation Act 1984, s. 14 (1) (a). - Made: 14.03.2008. Coming into force: 10.04.2008. Effect: None. Territorial extent & classification: E. Local *Unpublished*

The M60 Motorway (Junctions 21 - 22, Clockwise Carriageway and Junction 21 Clockwise Entry Slip Road) (Temporary Prohibition and Restriction of Traffic) Order 2008 No. 2008/1380. - Enabling power: Road Traffic Regulation Act 1984, s. 14 (1) (a). - Made: 13.05.2008. Coming into force: 15.05.2008. Effect: None. Territorial extent & classification: E. Local *Unpublished*

The M60 Motorway (Junctions 21 - 23, Clockwise Carriageway and Junction 22 Clockwise Entry and Exit Slip Roads) (Temporary Prohibition and Restriction of Traffic) Order 2008 No. 2008/877. - Enabling power: Road Traffic Regulation Act 1984, s. 14 (1) (a). - Made: 29.02.2008. Coming into force: 27.03.2008. Effect: None. Territorial extent & classification: E. Local *Unpublished*

The M60 Motorway (Junctions 23 - 22, Anticlockwise Carriageway and Junction 22 Anticlockwise Exit Slip Road) (Temporary Prohibition and Restriction of Traffic) Order 2008 No. 2008/344. - Enabling power: Road Traffic Regulation Act 1984, s. 14 (1) (a). - Made: 01.02.2008. Coming into force: 28.02.2008. Effect: None. Territorial extent & classification: E. Local *Unpublished*

The M60 Motorway (Junctions 23-25 Anticlockwise Carriageway and Junction 24 Anticlockwise Exit Slip Road) (Temporary Prohibition and Restriction of Traffic) Order 2008 No. 2008/1988. - Enabling power: Road Traffic Regulation Act 1984, s. 14 (1) (a) (7). - Made: 23.06.2008. Coming into force: 20.07.2008. Effect: None. Territorial extent & classification: E. Local *Unpublished*

The M61 Motorway (Junction 2 Southbound Link Road to A580 Eastbound) (Temporary Prohibition of Traffic) Order 2008 No. 2008/2310. - Enabling power: Road Traffic Regulation Act 1984, s. 14 (1) (a). - Made: 18.08.2008. Coming into force: 14.09.2008. Effect: None. Territorial extent & classification: E. Local *Unpublished*

The M61 Motorway (Junction 3 Kearsley Spur Northbound Carriageway) (Temporary Prohibition of Traffic) Order 2008 No. 2008/3288. - Enabling power: Road Traffic Regulation Act 1984, s. 14 (1) (a). - Made: 09.12.2008. Coming into force: 12.12.2008. Effect: None. Territorial extent & classification: E. Local *Unpublished*

The M61 Motorway (Junction 3, Southbound Exit Slip Road) (Temporary Prohibition of Traffic) Order 2008 No. 2008/2238. - Enabling power: Road Traffic Regulation Act 1984, s. 14 (1) (a). - Made: 11.08.2008. Coming into force: 09.09.2008. Effect: None. Territorial extent & classification: E. Local *Unpublished*

The M61 Motorway (Junction 8, Southbound Carriageway) (Temporary Prohibition of Traffic) Order 2008 No. 2008/1530. - Enabling power: Road Traffic Regulation Act 1984, s. 14 (1) (a). - Made: 26.05.2008. Coming into force: 19.06.2008. Effect: None. Territorial extent & classification: E. Local *Unpublished*

The M61 Motorway (Junction 9 Northbound Exit Slip Road to M65 Eastbound) (Temporary Prohibition of Traffic) Order 2008 No. 2008/2899. - Enabling power: Road Traffic Regulation Act 1984, s. 14 (1) (a). - Made: 20.10.2008. Coming into force: 17.11.2008. Effect: None. Territorial extent & classification: E. Local *Unpublished*

The M61 Motorway (Junctions 7 to 8, Bolton West Services, Northbound Entry and Exit Slip Roads) (Temporary Prohibition of Traffic) Order 2008 No. 2008/2241. - Enabling power: Road Traffic Regulation Act 1984, s. 14 (1) (a). - Made: 11.08.2008. Coming into force: 09.09.2008. Effect: None. Territorial extent & classification: E. Local *Unpublished*

The M62/M606 Motorways (Chain Bar Roundabout - Car Share Lane) (Experimental) Order 2008 No. 2008/988. - Enabling power: Road Traffic Regulation Act 1984, ss. 9 (1) to (3), 10 (1) (2). - Made: 04.03.2008. Coming into force: 17.03.2008. Effect: None. Territorial extent & classification: E. Local *Unpublished*

The M62 Motorway (Eastbound Entry Link Road to the M60 Motorway Anticlockwise at Junction 12) (Temporary Prohibition of Traffic) Order 2008 No. 2008/2527. - Enabling power: Road Traffic Regulation Act 1984, s. 14 (1) (a). - Made: 09.09.2008. Coming into force: 04.10.2008. Effect: None. Territorial extent & classification: E. Local *Unpublished*

The M62 Motorway (Junction 6 Roundabout) (Tarbock Interchange) (Temporary Restriction of Traffic) Order 2008 No. 2008/1078. - Enabling power: Road Traffic Regulation Act 1984, s. 14 (1) (a). - Made: 01.04.2008. Coming into force: 06.04.2008. Effect: None. Territorial extent & classification: E. Local *Unpublished*

The M62 Motorway (Junction 6, Westbound Exit Slip Road) (Temporary Prohibition of Traffic) Order 2008 No. 2008/855. - Enabling power: Road Traffic Regulation Act 1984, s. 14 (1) (a). - Made: 29.02.2008. Coming into force: 30.03.2008. Effect: None. Territorial extent & classification: E. Local *Unpublished*

Road traffic: Traffic regulation

The M62 Motorway (Junction 7 to 8 Eastbound Carriageway and Junction 7 Eastbound Entry Slip Road) (Temporary Prohibition and Restriction of Traffic) Order 2008 No. 2008/2152. - Enabling power: Road Traffic Regulation Act 1984, s. 14 (1) (a) (7). - Made: 25.07.2008. Coming into force: 25.08.2008. Effect: None. Territorial extent & classification: E. Local *Unpublished*

The M62 Motorway (Junction 10, Westbound Link Roads) to the M6 Motorway (Northbound and Southbound) (Temporary Prohibition of Traffic) Order 2008 No. 2008/853. - Enabling power: Road Traffic Regulation Act 1984, s. 14 (1) (a). - Made: 25.02.2008. Coming into force: 06.03.2008. Effect: None. Territorial extent & classification: E. Local *Unpublished*

The M62 Motorway (Junction 11, Eastbound Carriageway and Eastbound Entry Slip Road) (Temporary Prohibition and Restriction of Traffic) Order 2008 No. 2008/129. - Enabling power: Road Traffic Regulation Act 1984, s. 14 (1) (a) (7). - Made: 02.01.2008. Coming into force: 10.01.2008. Effect: None. Territorial extent & classification: E. Local *Unpublished*

The M62 Motorway (Junction 11, Eastbound Carriageway and Eastbound Entry Slip Road) (Temporary Prohibition and Restriction of Traffic) Order 2008 No. 2008/1200. - Enabling power: Road Traffic Regulation Act 1984, s. 14 (1) (a) (7). - Made: 14.04.2008. Coming into force: 18.04.2008. Effect: None. Territorial extent & classification: E. Local *Unpublished*

The M62 Motorway (Junction 11, Eastbound Entry Slip Road) (Temporary Prohibition of Traffic) Order 2008 No. 2008/2244. - Enabling power: Road Traffic Regulation Act 1984, s. 14 (1) (a). - Made: 11.08.2008. Coming into force: 04.09.2008. Effect: None. Territorial extent & classification: E. Local *Unpublished*

The M62 Motorway (Junction 11, Eastbound Exit Slip Road) (Temporary Prohibition of Traffic) Order 2008 No. 2008/2240. - Enabling power: Road Traffic Regulation Act 1984, s. 14 (1) (a). - Made: 28.07.2008. Coming into force: 25.08.2008. Effect: None. Territorial extent & classification: E. Local *Unpublished*

The M62 Motorway (Junction 19 to 20 Eastbound Carriageway and Junction 19 Eastbound Entry Slip Road) (Temporary Prohibition and Restriction of Traffic) Order 2008 No. 2008/86. - Enabling power: Road Traffic Regulation Act 1984, s. 14 (1) (a) (7). - Made: 07.01.2008. Coming into force: 14.01.2008. Effect: None. Territorial extent & classification: E. Local *Unpublished*

The M62 Motorway (Junction 19 to 20 Eastbound Carriageway and Junction 20 Eastbound Entry Slip Road) (Temporary Prohibition and Restriction of Traffic) Order 2008 No. 2008/1986. - Enabling power: Road Traffic Regulation Act 1984, s. 14 (1) (a) (7). - Made: 27.06.2008. Coming into force: 27.07.2008. Effect: None. Territorial extent & classification: E. Local *Unpublished*

The M62 Motorway (Junction 19, Westbound Entry Slip Road) (Temporary Prohibition of Traffic) Order 2008 No. 2008/200. - Enabling power: Road Traffic Regulation Act 1984, s. 14 (1) (a). - Made: 21.01.2008. Coming into force: 30.01.2008. Effect: None. Territorial extent & classification: E. Local *Unpublished*

The M62 Motorway (Junction 20, Eastbound Carriageway and Eastbound Entry Slip Road) (Temporary Prohibition and Restriction of Traffic) Order 2008 No. 2008/1061. - Enabling power: Road Traffic Regulation Act 1984, s. 14 (1) (a) (7). - Made: 14.03.2008. Coming into force: 10.04.2008. Effect: None. Territorial extent & classification: E. Local *Unpublished*

The M62 Motorway (Junction 20 to 21, Eastbound Carriageway and Junction 21 Eastbound Exit Slip Road) (Temporary Prohibition and Restriction of Traffic) Order 2008 No. 2008/1310. - Enabling power: Road Traffic Regulation Act 1984, s. 14 (1) (a) (7). - Made: 06.05.2008. Coming into force: 29.05.2008. Effect: None. Territorial extent & classification: E. Local *Unpublished*

The M62 Motorway (Junction 20, Westbound Entry Slip Road) (Temporary Prohibition of Traffic) Order 2008 No. 2008/2761. - Enabling power: Road Traffic Regulation Act 1984, s. 14 (1) (a). - Made: 06.10.2008. Coming into force: 02.11.2008. Effect: None. Territorial extent & classification: E. Local *Unpublished*

The M62 Motorway (Junction 22 to Junction 25) (Temporary Restriction and Prohibition of Traffic) Order 2008 No. 2008/27. - Enabling power: Road Traffic Regulation Act 1984, s. 14 (1) (a) (7). - Made: 03.01.2008. Coming into force: 13.01.2008. Effect: None. Territorial extent & classification: E. Local *Unpublished*

The M62 Motorway (Junction 22 to Junction 26) (Temporary Restriction and Prohibition of Traffic) Order 2008 No. 2008/2205. - Enabling power: Road Traffic Regulation Act 1984, s. 14 (1) (a) (7). - Made: 07.08.2008. Coming into force: 15.08.2008. Effect: None. Territorial extent & classification: E. Local *Unpublished*

The M62 Motorway (Junction 22, Westbound Carriageway and Junction 22 Westbound Entry and Exit Slip Roads) (Temporary Prohibition and Restriction of Traffic) Order 2008 No. 2008/2023. - Enabling power: Road Traffic Regulation Act 1984, s. 14 (1) (a). - Made: 30.06.2008. Coming into force: 24.07.2008. Effect: None. Territorial extent & classification: E. Local *Unpublished*

The M62 Motorway (Junction 22, Westbound Entry Slip Road) (Temporary Prohibition of Traffic) Order 2008 No. 2008/475. - Enabling power: Road Traffic Regulation Act 1984, s. 14 (1) (a). - Made: 18.02.2008. Coming into force: 27.02.2008. Effect: None. Territorial extent & classification: E. Local *Unpublished*

The M62 Motorway (Junction 23, Outlane Interchange) (Temporary Prohibition of Traffic) Order 2008 No. 2008/2651. - Enabling power: Road Traffic Regulation Act 1984, s. 14 (1) (a). - Made: 29.09.2008. Coming into force: 09.10.2008. Effect: None. Territorial extent & classification: E. Local *Unpublished*

The M62 Motorway (Junction 25, Brighouse) (Temporary Prohibition of Traffic) Order 2008 No. 2008/398. - Enabling power: Road Traffic Regulation Act 1984, s. 14 (1) (a). - Made: 11.02.2008. Coming into force: 17.02.2008. Effect: None. Territorial extent & classification: E. Local *Unpublished*

The M62 Motorway (Junction 26, Chain Bar) (Temporary Prohibition of Traffic) Order 2008 No. 2008/2619. - Enabling power: Road Traffic Regulation Act 1984, s. 14 (1) (a). - Made: 25.09.2008. Coming into force: 05.10.2008. Effect: None. Territorial extent & classification: E. Local *Unpublished*

The M62 Motorway (Junction 27 to Junction 28) (Temporary Restriction and Prohibition of Traffic) Order 2008 No. 2008/2895. - Enabling power: Road Traffic Regulation Act 1984, s. 14 (1) (a) (7). - Made: 27.10.2008. Coming into force: 09.11.2008. Effect: None. Territorial extent & classification: E. Local *Unpublished*

The M62 Motorway (Junction 28, Tingley) (Temporary Prohibition of Traffic) Order 2008 No. 2008/2290. - Enabling power: Road Traffic Regulation Act 1984, s. 14 (1) (a). - Made: 18.08.2008. Coming into force: 28.08.2008. Effect: None. Territorial extent & classification: E. Local *Unpublished*

The M62 Motorway (Junction 29 and Junction 30) (Temporary Prohibition of Traffic) Order 2008 No. 2008/1609. - Enabling power: Road Traffic Regulation Act 1984, s. 14 (1) (a). - Made: 12.06.2008. Coming into force: 22.06.2008. Effect: None. Territorial extent & classification: E. Local *Unpublished*

The M62 Motorway (Junction 29 to Junction 28) and the M1 Motorway (Lofthouse Interchange) (Temporary Prohibition of Traffic) Order 2008 No. 2008/2636. - Enabling power: Road Traffic Regulation Act 1984, s. 14 (1) (a). - Made: 29.09.2008. Coming into force: 14.10.2008. Effect: None. Territorial extent & classification: E. Local *Unpublished*

The M62 Motorway (Junction 30, Rothwell) (Temporary Prohibition of Traffic) Order 2008 No. 2008/1224. - Enabling power: Road Traffic Regulation Act 1984, s. 14 (1) (a). - Made: 25.04.2008. Coming into force: 07.05.2008. Effect: None. Territorial extent & classification: E. Local *Unpublished*

The M62 Motorway (Junction 30 to Junction 31) (Temporary Restriction and Prohibition of Traffic) Order 2008 No. 2008/2008. - Enabling power: Road Traffic Regulation Act 1984, s. 14 (1) (a) (7). - Made: 01.07.2008. Coming into force: 13.07.2008. Effect: None. Territorial extent & classification: E. Local *Unpublished*

The M62 Motorway (Junction 32) (Temporary Restriction and Prohibition of Traffic) Order 2008 No. 2008/478. - Enabling power: Road Traffic Regulation Act 1984, s. 14 (1) (a) (7). - Made: 18.02.2008. Coming into force: 24.02.2008. Effect: None. Territorial extent & classification: E. Local *Unpublished*

The M62 Motorway (Junction 35 to Junction 34) (Temporary Restriction and Prohibition of Traffic) Order 2008 No. 2008/2136. - Enabling power: Road Traffic Regulation Act 1984, s. 14 (1) (a) (7). - Made: 28.07.2008. Coming into force: 10.08.2008. Effect: None. Territorial extent & classification: E. Local *Unpublished*

The M62 Motorway (Junction 36, Airmyn) (Temporary Prohibition of Traffic) (No. 2) Order 2008 No. 2008/1612. - Enabling power: Road Traffic Regulation Act 1984, s. 14 (1) (a). - Made: 11.06.2008. Coming into force: 24.08.2008. Effect: None. Territorial extent & classification: E. Local *Unpublished*

The M62 Motorway (Junction 36, Airmyn) (Temporary Prohibition of Traffic) Order 2008 No. 2008/765. - Enabling power: Road Traffic Regulation Act 1984, s. 14 (1) (a). - Made: 20.02.2008. Coming into force: 02.03.2008. Effect: None. Territorial extent & classification: E. Local *Unpublished*

The M62 Motorway (Junction 37, Howden Interchange) (Temporary Prohibition of Traffic) Order 2008 No. 2008/889. - Enabling power: Road Traffic Regulation Act 1984, s. 14 (1) (a). - Made: 12.03.2008. Coming into force: 16.03.2008. Effect: None. Territorial extent & classification: E. Local *Unpublished*

The M62 Motorway (Junction 37 to Junction 38) and the A63 Trunk Road (North Cave Interchange) (Temporary Restriction and Prohibition of Traffic) Order 2008 No. 2008/2652. - Enabling power: Road Traffic Regulation Act 1984, s. 14 (1) (a) (7). - Made: 29.09.2008. Coming into force: 10.10.2008. Effect: None. Territorial extent & classification: E. Local *Unpublished*

The M62 Motorway (Junction 37 to Junction 38) (Temporary Prohibition of Traffic) Order 2008 No. 2008/271. - Enabling power: Road Traffic Regulation Act 1984, s. 14 (1) (a). - Made: 21.01.2008. Coming into force: 03.02.2008. Effect: None. Territorial extent & classification: E. Local *Unpublished*

The M62 Motorway (Junctions 6 to 7, Westbound and Eastbound Carriageways and Junctions 6 and 7 Slip Roads) (Temporary Prohibition of Traffic) Order 2008 No. 2008/1531. - Enabling power: Road Traffic Regulation Act 1984, s. 14 (1) (a). - Made: 12.05.2008. Coming into force: 08.06.2008. Effect: None. Territorial extent & classification: E. Local *Unpublished*

The M62 Motorway (Junctions 9 to 8, Burtonwood Services, Westbound Entry and Exit Slip Roads) (Temporary Prohibition of Traffic) Order 2008 No. 2008/1550. - Enabling power: Road Traffic Regulation Act 1984, s. 14 (1) (b). - Made: 02.06.2008. Coming into force: 27.06.2008. Effect: None. Territorial extent & classification: E. Local *Unpublished*

The M62 Motorway (Junctions 11 to 12 Eastbound and Westbound Carriageways) (Temporary Prohibition and Restriction of Traffic) Order 2008 No. 2008/2522. - Enabling power: Road Traffic Regulation Act 1984, s. 14 (1) (a) (7). - Made: 08.09.2008. Coming into force: 02.10.2008. Effect: None. Territorial extent & classification: E. Local *Unpublished*

Road traffic: Traffic regulation

The M62 Motorway (Junctions 20 to 21 Eastbound Carriageway) (Temporary Prohibition and Restriction of Traffic) Order 2008 No. 2008/470. - Enabling power: Road Traffic Regulation Act 1984, s. 14 (1) (a) (7). - Made: 18.02.2008. Coming into force: 25.02.2008. Effect: None. Territorial extent & classification: E. Local *Unpublished*

The M62 Motorway, the M621 Motorway and the A62 Trunk Road (Gildersome Interchange) (Temporary Restriction and Prohibition of Traffic) Order 2008 No. 2008/270. - Enabling power: Road Traffic Regulation Act 1984, s. 14 (1) (a). - Made: 21.01.2008. Coming into force: 29.01.2008. Effect: None. Territorial extent & classification: E. Local *Unpublished*

The M65 Motorway (Junction 2 Eastbound Entry Slip Road) (Temporary Prohibition of Traffic) Order 2008 No. 2008/2951. - Enabling power: Road Traffic Regulation Act 1984, s. 14 (1) (a). - Made: 13.10.2008. Coming into force: 10.11.2008. Effect: None. Territorial extent & classification: E. Local *Unpublished*

The M65 Motorway (Junction 3 Eastbound Entry Slip Road) (Temporary Prohibition of Traffic) Order 2008 No. 2008/2756. - Enabling power: Road Traffic Regulation Act 1984, s. 14 (1) (a). - Made: 06.10.2008. Coming into force: 30.10.2008. Effect: None. Territorial extent & classification: E. Local *Unpublished*

The M65 Motorway (Junction 3 Westbound Entry Slip Road) (Temporary Prohibition of Traffic) Order 2008 No. 2008/2760. - Enabling power: Road Traffic Regulation Act 1984, s. 14 (1) (a). - Made: 06.10.2008. Coming into force: 03.11.2008. Effect: None. Territorial extent & classification: E. Local *Unpublished*

The M65 Motorway (Junction 4 Eastbound Entry Slip Road) (Temporary Prohibition of Traffic) Order 2008 No. 2008/2735. - Enabling power: Road Traffic Regulation Act 1984, s. 14 (1) (a). - Made: 07.10.2008. Coming into force: 03.11.2008. Effect: None. Territorial extent & classification: E. Local *Unpublished*

The M65 Motorway (Junction 4 Westbound Entry Slip Road) (Temporary Prohibition of Traffic) Order 2008 No. 2008/2753. - Enabling power: Road Traffic Regulation Act 1984, s. 14 (1) (a). - Made: 07.10.2008. Coming into force: 30.10.2008. Effect: None. Territorial extent & classification: E. Local *Unpublished*

The M65 Motorway (Junction 5 Eastbound Entry Slip Road) (Temporary Prohibition of Traffic) Order 2008 No. 2008/2737. - Enabling power: Road Traffic Regulation Act 1984, s. 14 (1) (a). - Made: 07.10.2008. Coming into force: 30.10.2008. Effect: None. Territorial extent & classification: E. Local *Unpublished*

The M65 Motorway (Junction 6 Eastbound and Westbound Entry and Exit Slip Roads) (Temporary Prohibition of Traffic) Order 2008 No. 2008/261. - Enabling power: Road Traffic Regulation Act 1984, s. 14 (1) (a). - Made: 22.01.2008. Coming into force: 24.01.2008. Effect: None. Territorial extent & classification: E. Local *Unpublished*

The M65 Motorway (Junction 8 Westbound Entry Slip Road) (Temporary Prohibition of Traffic) Order 2008 No. 2008/2952. - Enabling power: Road Traffic Regulation Act 1984, s. 14 (1) (a). - Made: 14.10.2008. Coming into force: 09.11.2008. Effect: None. Territorial extent & classification: E. Local *Unpublished*

The M65 Motorway (Junction 8 Westbound Exit Slip Road) (Temporary Prohibition of Traffic) Order 2008 No. 2008/2898. - Enabling power: Road Traffic Regulation Act 1984, s. 14 (1) (a). - Made: 21.10.2008. Coming into force: 17.11.2008. Effect: None. Territorial extent & classification: E. Local *Unpublished*

The M65 Motorway (Junctions 6-7, Eastbound and Westbound Carriageways and Slip Roads) (Temporary Prohibition and Restriction of Traffic) Order 2008 No. 2008/1983. - Enabling power: Road Traffic Regulation Act 1984, s. 14 (1) (a) (7). - Made: 16.06.2008. Coming into force: 13.07.2008. Effect: None. Territorial extent & classification: E. Local *Unpublished*

The M66 Motorway (Junction 3, Northbound and Southbound Entry and Exit Slip Roads) (Temporary Prohibition of Traffic) Order 2008 No. 2008/1225. - Enabling power: Road Traffic Regulation Act 1984, s. 14 (1) (a). - Made: 14.04.2008. Coming into force: 11.05.2008. Effect: None. Territorial extent & classification: E. Local *Unpublished*

The M66 Motorway (Junction 3, Northbound Entry and Exit Slip Roads) (Temporary Prohibition of Traffic) Order 2008 No. 2008/2877. - Enabling power: Road Traffic Regulation Act 1984, s. 14 (1) (a). - Made: 13.10.2008. Coming into force: 09.11.2008. Effect: None. Territorial extent & classification: E. Local *Unpublished*

The M67 Motorway (Junction 1a, Eastbound Exit Slip Road) (Temporary Prohibition of Traffic) Order 2008 No. 2008/2523. - Enabling power: Road Traffic Regulation Act 1984, s. 14 (1) (a). - Made: 12.09.2008. Coming into force: 09.10.2008. Effect: None. Territorial extent & classification: E. Local *Unpublished*

The M67 Motorway (Junction 3 Eastbound Exit Slip Road) (Temporary Prohibition of Traffic) Order 2008 No. 2008/2422. - Enabling power: Road Traffic Regulation Act 1984, s. 14 (1) (a). - Made: 01.09.2008. Coming into force: 05.09.2008. Effect: None. Territorial extent & classification: E. Local *Unpublished*

The M67 Motorway (Junctions 3-4 Eastbound Carriageway and Junction 3 Eastbound Entry Slip Road) (Temporary Prohibition and Restriction of Traffic) (No. 2) Order 2008 No. 2008/1990. - Enabling power: Road Traffic Regulation Act 1984, s. 14 (1) (a). - Made: 30.06.2008. Coming into force: 23.07.2008. Effect: None. Territorial extent & classification: E. Local *Unpublished*

Road traffic: Traffic regulation

The M67 Motorway (Junctions 3-4 Eastbound Carriageway and Junction 3 Eastbound Entry Slip Road) (Temporary Prohibition and Restriction of Traffic) Order 2008 No. 2008/863. - Enabling power: Road Traffic Regulation Act 1984, s. 14 (1) (a) (7). - Made: 25.02.2008. Coming into force: 02.03.2008. Effect: None. Territorial extent & classification: E. Local *Unpublished*

The M69 Motorway (Hinckley to Leicester) (Temporary Restriction and Prohibition of Traffic) Order 2008 No. 2008/3221. - Enabling power: Road Traffic Regulation Act 1984, s. 14 (1) (a) (7). - Made: 21.11.2008. Coming into force: 28.11.2008. Effect: None. Territorial extent & classification: E. Local *Unpublished*

The M69 Motorway (Junction 3, Bedworth) (Slip Road) (Temporary Prohibition of Traffic) Order 2008 No. 2008/2220. - Enabling power: Road Traffic Regulation Act 1984, s. 14 (1) (a) (7). - Made: 01.08.2008. Coming into force: 08.08.2008. Effect: None. Territorial extent & classification: E. Local *Unpublished*

The M69 Motorway (Junctions 4 - 3A) (Temporary Prohibition of Traffic) Order 2008 No. 2008/2471. - Enabling power: Road Traffic Regulation Act 1984, s. 14 (1) (a) (7). - Made: 28.07.2008. Coming into force: 04.08.2008. Effect: None. Territorial extent & classification: E. Local *Unpublished*

The M69 Motorway (Leicestershire) (Temporary Restriction and Prohibition of Traffic) Order 2008 No. 2008/355. - Enabling power: Road Traffic Regulation Act 1984, s. 14 (1) (a) (7). - Made: 28.01.2008. Coming into force: 04.02.2008. Effect: None. Territorial extent & classification: E. Local *Unpublished*

The M180 Motorway (Junction 2, Woodhouse) (Temporary Prohibition of Traffic) Order 2008 No. 2008/269. - Enabling power: Road Traffic Regulation Act 1984, s. 14 (1) (a). - Made: 21.01.2008. Coming into force: 03.02.2008. Effect: None. Territorial extent & classification: E. Local *Unpublished*

The M180 Motorway (Junction 3 Midmoor and Junction 4 Broughton) and the M181 Motorway (Midmoor Interchange) (Temporary Restriction and Prohibition of Traffic) Order 2008 No. 2008/2007. - Enabling power: Road Traffic Regulation Act 1984, s. 14 (1) (a) (7). - Made: 04.07.2008. Coming into force: 11.07.2008. Effect: None. Territorial extent & classification: E. Local *Unpublished*

The M180 Motorway (Junction 5, Barnetby) (Temporary Prohibition of Traffic) Order 2008 No. 2008/268. - Enabling power: Road Traffic Regulation Act 1984, s. 14 (1) (a). - Made: 28.01.2008. Coming into force: 10.02.2008. Effect: None. Territorial extent & classification: E. Local *Unpublished*

The M180 Motorway (Junction 18) (Temporary Prohibition of Traffic) Order 2008 No. 2008/2980. - Enabling power: Road Traffic Regulation Act 1984, s. 14 (1) (a). - Made: 12.11.2008. Coming into force: 16.11.2008. Effect: None. Territorial extent & classification: E. Local *Unpublished*

The M181 Motorway (Frodingham Grange Roundabout to Midmoor Interchange) and the M180 Motorway (Junction 3, Midmoor Interchange) (Temporary Prohibition of Traffic) Order 2008 No. 2008/1993. - Enabling power: Road Traffic Regulation Act 1984, s. 14 (1) (a). - Made: 07.07.2008. Coming into force: 20.07.2008. Effect: None. Territorial extent & classification: E. Local *Unpublished*

The M602 Motorway (Junction 2 Eastbound and Westbound Carriageways and Westbound Entry and Eastbound Exit Slip Roads) (Temporary Prohibition of Traffic) Order 2008 No. 2008/2759. - Enabling power: Road Traffic Regulation Act 1984, s. 14 (1) (a). - Made: 06.10.2008. Coming into force: 02.11.2008. Effect: None. Territorial extent & classification: E. Local *Unpublished*

The M602 Motorway (Westbound Link Road to the M60 Motorway Clockwise at Junction 12) (Temporary Prohibition of Traffic) Order 2008 No. 2008/2313. - Enabling power: Road Traffic Regulation Act 1984, s. 14 (1) (a). - Made: 18.08.2008. Coming into force: 10.09.2008. Effect: None. Territorial extent & classification: E. Local *Unpublished*

The M606 Motorway (Junction 3, Staygate) (Temporary Prohibition of Traffic) Order 2008 No. 2008/2634. - Enabling power: Road Traffic Regulation Act 1984, s. 14 (1) (a). - Made: 18.09.2008. Coming into force: 28.09.2008. Effect: None. Territorial extent & classification: E. Local *Unpublished*

The M621 Motorway (Gildersome Interchange & Junction 1, Beeston) (Temporary Prohibition of Traffic) Order 2008 No. 2008/2052. - Enabling power: Road Traffic Regulation Act 1984, s. 14 (1) (a). - Made: 14.07.2008. Coming into force: 20.07.2008. Effect: None. Territorial extent & classification: E. Local *Unpublished*

The M621 Motorway (Gildersome Interchange) (Temporary Restriction and Prohibition of Traffic) Order 2008 No. 2008/3177. - Enabling power: Road Traffic Regulation Act 1984, s. 14 (1) (a) (7). - Made: 02.12.2008. Coming into force: 06.12.2008. Effect: None. Territorial extent & classification: E. Local *Unpublished*

The M621 Motorway (Junction 1, Beeston) (Temporary Prohibition of Traffic) Order 2008 No. 2008/399. - Enabling power: Road Traffic Regulation Act 1984, s. 14 (1) (a). - Made: 11.02.2008. Coming into force: 24.02.2008. Effect: None. Territorial extent & classification: E. Local *Unpublished*

The M621 Motorway (Junction 1 to Junction 7) (Temporary Prohibition of Traffic) (No. 2) Order 2008 No. 2008/2402. - Enabling power: Road Traffic Regulation Act 1984, s. 14 (1) (a). - Made: 01.09.2008. Coming into force: 14.09.2008. Effect: None. Territorial extent & classification: E. Local *Unpublished*

The M621 Motorway (Junction 1 to Junction 7) (Temporary Prohibition of Traffic) Order 2008 No. 2008/1630. - Enabling power: Road Traffic Regulation Act 1984, s. 14 (1) (a). - Made: 17.06.2008. Coming into force: 27.06.2008. Effect: None. Territorial extent & classification: E. Local *Unpublished*

The M621 Motorway (Junction 4, Hunslet) (Temporary Prohibition of Traffic) (No. 2) Order 2008 No. 2008/1133. - Enabling power: Road Traffic Regulation Act 1984, s. 14 (1) (a). - Made: 01.04.2008. Coming into force: 12.04.2008. Effect: None. Territorial extent & classification: E. Local *Unpublished*

The M621 Motorway (Junction 4, Hunslet) (Temporary Prohibition of Traffic) Order 2008 No. 2008/888. - Enabling power: Road Traffic Regulation Act 1984, s. 14 (1) (a). - Made: 03.03.2008. Coming into force: 13.03.2008. Effect: None. Territorial extent & classification: E. Local *Unpublished*

The M621 Motorway (Junction 7, Stourton) (Temporary Prohibition of Traffic) Order 2008 No. 2008/2979. - Enabling power: Road Traffic Regulation Act 1984, s. 14 (1) (a). - Made: 12.11.2008. Coming into force: 16.11.2008. Effect: None. Territorial extent & classification: E. Local *Unpublished*

Road traffic, England

The A1(M) Motorway and the M62 Motorway (Holmfield Interchange Link Roads) (Speed Limit) Regulations 2008 No. 2008/2262. - Enabling power: Road Traffic Regulation Act 1984, s. 17 (2) (3). - Issued: 02.09.2008. Made: 20.08.2008. Laid: 27.08.2008. Coming into force: 22.09.2008. Effect: None. Territorial extent & classification: E. Local. - 4p.: 30 cm. - 978-0-11-083857-1 £3.00

The A27 Trunk Road (Southerham to Beddingham Improvement) (Banned Turns) Order 2008 No. 2008/2821. - Enabling power: Road Traffic Regulation Act 1984, ss. 1 (1), 2 (1) (2). - Issued: 20.11.2008. Made: 27.10.2008. Coming into force: 10.11.2008. Effect: None. Territorial extent & classification: E. Local. - This statutory instrument has been printed in substitution of the SI of the same number [and ISBN] and is being issued free of charge to all known recipients of that statutory instrument. - 2p.: 30 cm. - 978-0-11-084803-7 £4.00

The A27 Trunk Road (Southerham to Beddingham Improvement) (Derestriction and Revocation) Order 2008 No. 2008/2820. - Enabling power: Road Traffic Regulation Act 1984, ss. 82 (2), 83 (1). - Issued: 20.11.2008. Made: 27.10.2008. Coming into force: 10.11.2008. Effect: S.I. 2004/2085 revoked. Territorial extent & classification: E. Local. - This statutory instrument has been printed in substitution of the SI of the same number [and isbn] and is being issued free of charge to all known recipients of that statutory instrument. - 2p.: 30 cm. - 978-0-11-084789-4 £4.00

The Civil Enforcement of Parking Contraventions (County of Buckinghamshire) (District of Wycombe) Designation Order 2008 No. 2008/2344. - Enabling power: Traffic Management Act 2004, s. 89 (3), sch. 8, para. 8 (1), sch. 10, para. 3 (1). - Issued: 09.09.2008. Made: 01.09.2008. Laid: 04.09.2008. Coming into force: 01.10.2008. Effect: S.I. 1997/56; 1999/1667 revoked. Territorial extent & classification: E. General. - 2p.: 30 cm. - 978-0-11-084009-3 £4.00

The Civil Enforcement of Parking Contraventions (County of Cheshire) (Borough of Macclesfield) Designation Order 2008 No. 2008/1084. - Enabling power: Traffic Management Act 2004, sch. 8, para. 8 (1), sch. 10, para. 3 (1). - Issued: 23.04.2008. Made: 15.04.2008. Laid: 17.04.2008. Coming into force: 14.05.2008. Effect: None. Territorial extent & classification: E. General. - 2p.: 30 cm. - 978-0-11-081376-9 £3.00

The Civil Enforcement of Parking Contraventions (County of Cheshire) (City of Chester and Borough of Ellesmere Port & Neston) Designation Order 2008 No. 2008/3198. - Enabling power: Traffic Management Act 2004, sch. 8, para. 8 (1), sch. 10, para. 3 (1). - Issued: 22.12.2008. Made: 11.12.2008. Laid: 17.12.2008. Coming into force: 08.01.2009. Effect: None. Territorial extent & classification: E. General. - 4p.: 30 cm. - 978-0-11-147188-3 £4.00

The Civil Enforcement of Parking Contraventions (County of Cornwall) Designation Order 2008 No. 2008/1055. - Enabling power: Traffic Management Act 2004, s. 89 (3), sch. 8, para. 8 (1), sch. 10, para. 3 (1). - Issued: 15.04.2008. Made: 05.04.2008. Laid: 10.04.2008. Coming into force: 05.05.2008. Effect: None. Territorial extent & classification: E. General. - 4p.: 30 cm. - 978-0-11-081359-2 £3.00

The Civil Enforcement of Parking Contraventions (County of Devon) Designation Order 2008 No. 2008/1051. - Enabling power: Traffic Management Act 2004, sch. 8, para. 8 (1), sch. 10, para. 3 (1). - Issued: 15.04.2008. Made: 05.04.2008. Laid: 10.04.2008. Coming into force: 05.05.2008. Effect: None. Territorial extent & classification: E. General. - 2p.: 30 cm. - 978-0-11-081357-8 £3.00

The Civil Enforcement of Parking Contraventions (County of East Sussex) (Borough of Eastbourne) Designation Order 2008 No. 2008/2442. - Enabling power: Traffic Management Act 2004, sch. 8, para. 8 (1), sch. 10, para. 3 (1). - Issued: 24.09.2008. Made: 17.09.2008. Laid: 18.09.2008. Coming into force: 13.10.2008. Effect: None. Territorial extent & classification: E. General. - 4p.: 30 cm. - 978-0-11-084227-1 £4.00

The Civil Enforcement of Parking Contraventions (County of Gloucestershire) (Forest of Dean District) Designation Order 2008 No. 2008/1212. - Enabling power: Traffic Management Act 2004, sch. 8, para. 8 (1), sch. 10, para. 3 (1). - Issued: 02.05.2008. Made: 28.04.2008. Laid: 01.05.2008. Coming into force: 26.05.2008. Effect: None. Territorial extent & classification: E. General. - 2p.: 30 cm. - 978-0-11-081423-0 £3.00

The Civil Enforcement of Parking Contraventions (County of Nottinghamshire) Designation Order 2008 No. 2008/1086. - Enabling power: Traffic Management Act 2004, sch. 8, para. 8 (1), sch. 10, para. 3 (1). - Issued: 23.04.2008. Made: 15.04.2008. Laid: 17.04.2008. Coming into force: 12.05.2008. Effect: None. Territorial extent & classification: E. General. - 2p.: 30 cm. - 978-0-11-081378-3 £3.00

The Civil Enforcement of Parking Contraventions (County of Rutland) Designation Order 2008 No. 2008/1211. - Enabling power: Traffic Management Act 2004, sch. 8, para. 8 (1), sch. 10, para. 3 (1). - Issued: 02.05.2008. Made: 28.04.2008. Laid: 01.05.2008. Coming into force: 02.06.2008. Effect: None. Territorial extent & classification: E. General. - 2p.: 30 cm. - 978-0-11-081424-7 £3.00

The Civil Enforcement of Parking Contraventions (County of Wiltshire) (District of West Wiltshire) Designation Order 2008 No. 2008/1340. - Enabling power: Traffic Management Act 2004, sch. 8, para. 8 (1), sch. 10, para. 3 (1). - Issued: 29.05.2008. Made: 21.05.2008. Laid: 23.05.2008. Coming into force: 16.06.2008. Effect: None. Territorial extent & classification: E. General. - 4p.: 30 cm. - 978-0-11-081755-2 £3.00

The Civil Enforcement of Parking Contraventions (Dudley) Designation Order 2008 No. 2008/1764. - Enabling power: Traffic Management Act 2004, sch. 8, para. 8 (1), sch. 10, para. 3 (1). - Issued: 11.07.2008. Made: 04.07.2008. Laid: 04.07.2008. Coming into force: 07.07.2008. Effect: S.I. 2008/1518 revoked. Territorial extent & classification: E. General. - This Statutory Instrument has been made in consequence of a defect in SI 2008/1518 and is being issued free of charge to all known recipients of that Statutory Instrument. - 2p.: 30 cm. - 978-0-11-081972-3 £3.00

The Civil Enforcement of Parking Contraventions (England) General (Amendment) Regulations 2008 No. 2008/1513. - Enabling power: Traffic Management Act 2004, ss. 72, 73 (3), 78, 79, 89. - Issued: 18.06.2008. Made: 11.06.2008. Laid: 12.06.2008. Coming into force: 03.07.2008. Effect: S.I. 2007/3483 amended. Territorial extent & classification: E. General. - Revoked by S.I. 2009/478 (ISBN 9780111475348). - 4p.: 30 cm. - 978-0-11-081841-2 £3.00

The Civil Enforcement of Parking Contraventions (St. Helens) Designation Order 2008 No. 2008/3160. - Enabling power: Traffic Management Act 2004, sch. 8, para. 8 (1), sch. 10, para. 3 (1). - Issued: 17.12.2008. Made: 10.12.2008. Laid: 15.12.2008. Coming into force: 12.01.2009. Effect: None. Territorial extent & classification: E. General. - 4p.: 30 cm. - 978-0-11-147150-0 £4.00

The Civil Enforcement of Parking Contraventions (The Borough Council of Dudley) Designation Order 2008 No. 2008/1518. - Enabling power: Traffic Management Act 2004, sch. 8, para. 8 (1), sch. 10, para. 3 (1). - Issued: 17.06.2008. Made: 11.06.2008. Laid: 13.06.2008. Coming into force: 07.07.2008. Effect: None. Territorial extent & classification: E. General. - Revoked by S.I. 2008/1764 (ISBN 9780110819723). - 2p.: 30 cm. - 978-0-11-081845-0 £3.00

The Civil Enforcement of Parking Contraventions (the County Council of Durham) (Durham District) Designation Order 2008 No. 2008/2567. - Enabling power: Traffic Management Act 2004, sch. 8, para. 8 (1), sch. 10, para. 3 (1). - Issued: 10.10.2008. Made: 01.10.2008. Laid: 06.10.2008. Coming into force: 03.11.2008. Effect: None. Territorial extent & classification: E. General. - 2p.: 30 cm. - 978-0-11-084359-9 £4.00

The Removal and Disposal of Vehicles (Traffic Officers) (England) Regulations 2008 No. 2008/2367. - Enabling power: Road Traffic Regulation Act 1984, s. 99 (1) (2) (3), 101 (3) (7), 101A (1), 103 (3). - Issued: 12.09.2008. Made: 04.09.2008. Laid before Parliament: 09.09.2008. Coming into force: 01.10.2008. Effect: S.I. 1984 c. 27 amended. Territorial extent & classification: E. General. - 12p.: 30 cm. - 978-0-11-084130-4 £5.00

The Removal, Storage and Disposal of Vehicles (Prescribed Sums and Charges) (Amendment) (England) Regulations 2008 No. 2008/3013. - Enabling power: Road Traffic Regulation Act 1984, ss. 102 (2), 102 (2ZA), 103 (3). - Issued: 27.11.2008. Made: 20.11.2008. Laid: 25.11.2008. Coming into force: 17.12.2008. Effect: S.I. 2008/2095 amended. Territorial extent & classification: E. General. - 2p.: 30 cm. - 978-0-11-147036-7 £4.00

The Road User Charging (Enforcement and Adjudication) (London) (Amendment) Regulations 2008 No. 2008/1956. - Enabling power: Greater London Authority Act 1999, sch. 23, paras. 12 (3), 28. - Issued: 24.07.2008. Made: 18.07.2008. Laid: 22.07.2008. Coming into force: 20.08.2008. Effect: S.I. 2001/2313 amended. Territorial extent & classification: E. General. - 2p.: 30 cm. - 978-0-11-083522-8 £3.00

The Traffic Management Act 2004 (Commencement No. 5 and Transitional Provisions) (England) (Amendment) Order 2008 No. 2008/757 (C.35). - Enabling power: Traffic Management Act 2004, s. 99(1), (2) (4). - Issued: 25.03.2008. Made: 17.03.2008. Coming into force: 17.03.2008. Effect: S.I. 2007/2053 (C.78) amended. Territorial extent & classification: E. General. - With correction slip dated June 2009. - 8p.: 30 cm. - 978-0-11-081271-7 £3.00

Road traffic, England and Wales

The Removal, Storage and Disposal of Vehicles (Prescribed Sums and Charges) Regulations 2008 No. 2008/2095. - Enabling power: Road Traffic Regulation Act 1984, ss. 101A (3), 101A (4), 102 (2), 103 (3), 142 (1) & Refuse Disposal (Amenity) Act 1978, ss. 4 (5) (6), 5 (1), 10 (1), 11 (1). - Issued: 07.08.2008. Made: 28.07.2008. Laid: 05.08.2008. Coming into force: 01.10.2008. Effect: S.I. 1989/744 revoked with savings. Territorial extent & classification: E/W. General. - 4p.: 30 cm. - 978-0-11-083703-1 £3.00

The Road Safety Act 2006 (Commencement No. 3) (England and Wales) Order 2008 No. 2008/1862 (C.78). - Enabling power: Road Safety Act 2006, s. 61. Bringing into operation various provisions of the 2006 Act on 30.07.2008. - Issued: 21.07.2008. Made: 14.07.2008. Effect: None. Territorial extent & classification: E/W. General. - 2p.: 30 cm. - 978-0-11-083200-5 £3.00

Road traffic, Wales

The Civil Enforcement Officers (Wearing of Uniforms) (Wales) Regulations 2008 No. 2008/616 (W.68). - Enabling power: Traffic Management Act 2004, 76 (4). - Issued: 31.03.2008. Made: 06.03.2008. Laid before the National Assembly for Wales: 10.03.2008. Coming into force: 31.03.2008. Effect: None. Territorial extent & classification: W. General. - In English and Welsh. Welsh title: Rheoliadau Swyddogion Gorfodi Sifil (Gwisgo Lifrai) (Cymru) 2008. - 4p.: 30 cm. - 978-0-11-091746-7 £3.00

The Civil Enforcement of Parking Contraventions (Approved Devices) (Wales) (No. 2) Order 2008 No. 2008/1215 (W.123). - Enabling power: Traffic Management Act 2004, s. 92 (1). - Issued: 14.05.2008. Made: 29.04.2008 Laid before the National Assembly for Wales: 30.04.2008 Coming into force: 22.05.2008. Effect: S.I. 2008/620 (W.69) revoked. Territorial extent & classification: W. General. - In English and Welsh. Welsh title: Gorchymyn Gorfodi Sifil ar Dramgwyddau Parcio (Dyfeisiadau a Gymeradwyir) (Cymru) (Rhif 2) 2008. - 8p.: 30 cm. - 978-0-11-091814-3 £3.00

The Civil Enforcement of Parking Contraventions (Approved Devices) (Wales) Order 2008 No. 2008/620 (W.69). - Enabling power: Road Traffic Regulation Act 1984, s. 101B. - Issued: 31.03.2008. Made: 06.03.2008. Laid before the National Assembly for Wales: 10.03.2008. Coming into force: 31.03.2008. Effect: None. Territorial extent & classification: W. General. - Revoked by W.S.I. 2008/1215 (W.123) (ISBN 9780110918143). - In English and Welsh. Welsh title: Gorchymyn Gorfodi Sifil ar Dramgwyddau Parcio (Dyfeisiadau a Gymeradwyir) (Cymru) 2008. - 8p.: 30 cm. - 978-0-11-091745-0 £3.00

The Civil Enforcement of Parking Contraventions (General Provisions) (Wales) (No. 2) Regulations 2008 No. 2008/1214 (W.122). - Enabling power: Traffic Management Act 2004, ss. 72, 73 (3), 79, 88, 89. - Issued: 14.05.2008. Made: 29.04.2008. Laid before the National Assembly for Wales: 30.04.2008. Coming into force: 22.05.2008. Effect: 1984 c. 27 modified & S.I. 2008/614 (W.66) revoked. Territorial extent & classification: W. General. - In English and Welsh. Welsh language title: Rheoliadau Gorfodi Sifil ar Dramgwyddau Parcio (Darpariaethau Cyffredinol) (Cymru) (Rhif 2) 2008. - 16p.: 30 cm. - 978-0-11-091815-0 £3.00

The Civil Enforcement of Parking Contraventions (General Provisions) (Wales) Regulations 2008 No. 2008/614 (W.66). - Enabling power: Traffic Management Act 2004, ss. 72, 73 (3), 79, 88, 89. - Issued: 28.03.2008. Made: 06.03.2008. Laid before the National Assembly for Wales: 10.03.2008. Coming into force: 31.03.2008. Effect: 1984 c.27 modified. Territorial extent & classification: W. General. - Revoked by W.S.I. 2008/1214 (W.122) (ISBN 9780110918150). - In English and Welsh. Welsh language title: Rheoliadau Gorfodi Sifil ar Dramgwyddau Parcio (Darpariaethau Cyffredinol) (Cymru) 2008. - 16p.: 30 cm. - 978-0-11-091774-0 £3.00

The Civil Enforcement of Parking Contraventions (Guidelines on Levels of Charges) (Wales) Order 2008 No. 2008/613 (W.65). - Enabling power: Traffic Management Act 2004, sch. 9, para. 8. - Issued: 31.03.2008. Made: 06.03.2008. Laid before the National Assembly for Wales: 10.03.2008. Coming into force: 31.03.2008. Effect: None. Territorial extent & classification: W. General. - In English and Welsh. Welsh title: Gorchymyn Gorfodi Sifil ar Dramgwyddau Parcio (Canllawiau ar LefelauTaliadau) (Cymru) 2008. - 8p.: 30 cm. - 978-0-11-091775-7 £3.00

The Civil Enforcement of Parking Contraventions (Penalty Charge Notices, Enforcement and Adjudication) (Wales) (Amendment) Regulations 2008 No. 2008/913. - Enabling power: Traffic Management Act 2004, ss. 78, 81, 82, 89. - Issued: 02.04.2008. Made: 27.03.2008. Laid: 28.03.2008. Coming into force: 31.03.2008. Effect: SI 2008/609 amended. Territorial extent & classification: W. General. - This instrument has been made to correct a defect in SI 2008/609 and is being issued free of charge to all recipients of the original instrument. - 2p.: 30 cm. - 978-0-11-081312-7 £3.00

The Civil Enforcement of Parking Contraventions (Penalty Charge Notices, Enforcement and Adjudication) (Wales) Regulations 2008 No. 2008/609. - Enabling power: Traffic Management Act 2004, ss. 78, 81, 82, 89. - Issued: 13.03.2008. Made: 06.03.2008. Laid: 10.03.2008. Coming into force: 31.03.2008. Effect: None. Territorial extent & classification: W. General. - 16p.: 30 cm. - 978-0-11-081142-0 £3.00

The Civil Enforcement of Parking Contraventions (Representations and Appeals) Removed Vehicles (Wales) Regulations 2008 No. 2008/615 (W.67). - Enabling power: Road Traffic Regulation Act 1984, s. 101B. - Issued: 28.03.2008. Made: 06.03.2008. Laid before the National Assembly for Wales: 10.03.2008. Coming into force: 31.03.2008. Effect: None. Territorial extent & classification: W. General. - In English and Welsh. Welsh language title: Rheoliadau Gorfodi Sifil ar Dramgwyddau Parcio (Sylwadau ac Apelau) Cerbydau a Symudwyd Ymaith (Cymru) 2008. - 12p.: 30 cm. - 978-0-11-091768-9 £3.00

The Civil Enforcement of Parking Contraventions (Representations and Appeals) (Wales) Regulations 2008 No. 2008/608. - Enabling power: Traffic Management Act 2004, ss. 80, 89. - Issued: 17.03.2008. Made: 06.03.2008. Coming into force: 31.03.2008. Effect: None. Territorial extent & classification: W. General. - 24p.: 30 cm. - 978-0-11-081201-4 £4.00

The Removal and Disposal of Vehicles (Amendment) (Wales) Regulations 2008 No. 2008/612 (W.64). - Enabling power: Road Traffic Regulation Act 1984, s. 99 (1) (2). - Issued: 31.03.2008. Made: 06.03.2008. Laid before the National Assembly for Wales: 10.03.2008. Coming into force: 31.03.2008. Effect: S.I. 1986/183 amended. Territorial extent & classification: W. General. - In English and Welsh. Welsh title: Rheoliadau Symud Ymaith a Gwaredu Cerbydau (Diwygio) (Cymru) 2008. - 8p.: 30 cm. - 978-0-11-091744-3 £3.00

The Road Traffic (Permitted Parking Area and Special Parking Area) (County Borough of Wrexham) Order 2008 No. 2008/226 (W.28). - Enabling power: Road Traffic Act 1991, sch. 3, paras 1 (1), 2 (1) 3 (3). - Issued: 20.02.2008. Made: 05.02.2008. Laid before the National Assembly for Wales: 06.02.2008. Coming into force: 01.03.2008. Effect: 1984 c.27; 1991 c.40 modified in relation to the parking area specified. Territorial extent & classification: W. General. - In English and Welsh. Welsh language title: Gorchymyn Traffig Ffyrdd (Ardal Barcio a Ganiateir ac Ardal Barcio Arbennig) (Bwrdeistref Sirol Wrecsam) 2008. - 12p.: 30 cm. - 978-0-11-091706-1 £3.00

Road traffic, Wales: Speed limits

The A470 Trunk Road (North of Blaenau Ffestiniog, Gwynedd) (40 mph Speed Limit) Order 2008 No. 2008/1442 (W.151). - Enabling power: Road Traffic Regulation Act 1984, ss. 82 (2), 83 (1), 84 (1) (2). - Made: 06.06.2008. Coming into force: 16.06.2008. Effect: None. Territorial extent & classification: W. Local. - In English and Welsh *Unpublished*

Road traffic, Wales: Traffic regulation

The A5 Trunk Road (Carrog, Llidiart Y Parc, Corwen, Denbighshire) (Temporary Traffic Restrictions) Order 2008 No. 2008/418 (W.38). - Enabling power: Road Traffic Regulation Act 1984, s. 14 (1) (4). - Made: 19.02.2008. Coming into force: 04.03.2008. Effect: None. Territorial extent & classification: W. Local. - In English and Welsh *Unpublished*

The A5 Trunk Road (Chirk Bypass between Halton Roundabout and the Wales/England Border, Wrexham County Borough) (Temporary Traffic Restrictions) Order 2008 No. 2008/84 (W.12). - Enabling power: Road Traffic Regulation Act 1984, s. 14 (1) (4). - Made: 11.01.2008. Coming into force: 03.02.2008. Effect: None. Territorial extent & classification: W. Local. - In English and Welsh *Unpublished*

The A5 Trunk Road (Glyndyfrdwy, Denbighshire) (Temporary Traffic Restrictions) Order 2008 No. 2008/2215 (W.194). - Enabling power: Road Traffic Regulation Act 1984, ss. 14 (1) (4). - Made: 18.08.2008. Coming into force: 01.09.2008. Effect: None. Territorial extent & classification: W. Local. - In English and Welsh *Unpublished*

The A5 Trunk Road (Halton Roundabout, Chirk, County Borough of Wrexham) (Temporary Traffic Restrictions) Order 2008 No. 2008/2432 (W.207). - Enabling power: Road Traffic Regulation Act 1984, s. 14 (1) (4). - Made: 09.09.2008. Coming into force: 22.09.2008. Effect: None. Territorial extent & classification: W. Local. - In English and Welsh *Unpublished*

The A5 Trunk Road (Pentrefoelas, Conwy) (Temporary Traffic Restrictions) Order 2008 No. 2008/2216 (W.195). - Enabling power: Road Traffic Regulation Act 1984, ss. 14 (1) (4). - Made: 18.08.2008. Coming into force: 01.09.2008. Effect: None. Territorial extent & classification: W. Local. - In English and Welsh *Unpublished*

The A5 Trunk Road (Pentrefoelas, Conwy to Llangollen, Denbighshire) (Temporary 40 mph Speed Limit) Order 2008 No. 2008/2827 (W.250). - Enabling power: Road Traffic Regulation Act 1984, ss. 14 (1) (4). - Made: 27.10.2008. Coming into force: 03.11.2008. Effect: None. Territorial extent & classification: W. Local. - In English and Welsh *Unpublished*

The A40 Trunk Road (Bancyfelin, Carmarthenshire) (Temporary Traffic Restrictions) Order 2008 No. 2008/366 (W.32). - Enabling power: Road Traffic Regulation Act 1984, s. 14 (1) (4). - Made: 14.02.2008. Coming into force: 22.02.2008. Effect: None. Territorial extent & classification: W. Local. - In English and Welsh *Unpublished*

The A40 Trunk Road (Blackbridge Roundabout, Whitland, Carmarthenshire) (Temporary Traffic Restrictions) Order 2008 No. 2008/368 (W.34). - Enabling power: Road Traffic Regulation Act 1984, s. 14 (1) (4). - Made: 14.02.2008. Coming into force: 22.02.2008. Effect: None. Territorial extent & classification: W. Local. - In English and Welsh *Unpublished*

The A40 Trunk Road (Gibraltar Tunnels, Monmouth, Monmouthshire) (Temporary Traffic Restrictions) Order 2008 No. 2008/2642 (W.232). - Enabling power: Road Traffic Regulation Act 1984, s. 14 (1) (4). - Made: 06.10.2008. Coming into force: 12.10.2008. Effect: None. Territorial extent & classification: W. Local. - In English and Welsh *Unpublished*

The A40 Trunk Road (Llanboidy Road Roundabout, Whitland, Carmarthenshire) (Temporary Traffic Restrictions) Order 2008 No. 2008/369 (W.35). - Enabling power: Road Traffic Regulation Act 1984, s. 14 (1) (4). - Made: 14.02.2008. Coming into force: 22.02.2008. Effect: None. Territorial extent & classification: W. Local. - In English and Welsh *Unpublished*

The A40 Trunk Road (Penblewin to Llandewi Velfrey, Pembrokeshire) (Temporary Traffic Restrictions) Order 2008 No. 2008/365 (W.31). - Enabling power: Road Traffic Regulation Act 1984, s. 14 (1) (4). - Made: 14.02.2008. Coming into force: 22.02.2008. Effect: None. Territorial extent & classification: W. Local. - In English and Welsh *Unpublished*

The A40 Trunk Road (Pensarn, Carmarthenshire) (Temporary Traffic Restrictions) Order 2008 No. 2008/512 (W.47). - Enabling power: Road Traffic Regulation Act 1984, s. 14 (1) (4). - Made: 26.02.2008. Coming into force: 06.03.2008. Effect: None. Territorial extent & classification: W. Local. - In English and Welsh *Unpublished*

The A40 Trunk Road (Raglan to Abergavenny, Monmouthshire) (Temporary Traffic Restrictions) Order 2008 No. 2008/578 (W.57). - Enabling power: Road Traffic Regulation Act 1984, s. 14 (1) (4) (7). - Made: 04.03.2008. Coming into force: 10.03.2008. Effect: None. Territorial extent & classification: W. Local. - In English and Welsh *Unpublished*

The A40 Trunk Road (Redstone Cross, Pembrokeshire) (Temporary Traffic Restrictions) Order 2008 No. 2008/513 (W.48). - Enabling power: Road Traffic Regulation Act 1984, s. 14 (1) (4). - Made: 26.02.2008. Coming into force: 06.03.2008. Effect: None. Territorial extent & classification: W. Local. - In English and Welsh *Unpublished*

The A40 Trunk Road (South of Wolf's Castle, Pembrokeshire) (Temporary Traffic Restrictions) Order 2008 No. 2008/952 (W.103). - Enabling power: Road Traffic Regulation Act 1984, s. 14 (1) (4). - Made: 01.04.2008. Coming into force: 09.04.2008. Effect: None. Territorial extent & classification: W. Local. - In English and Welsh *Unpublished*

The A40 Trunk Road (Travellers Rest, Carmarthenshire) (Temporary Traffic Restrictions) Order 2008 No. 2008/370 (W.36). - Enabling power: Road Traffic Regulation Act 1984, s. 14 (1) (4). - Made: 14.02.2008. Coming into force: 25.02.2008. Effect: None. Territorial extent & classification: W. Local. - In English and Welsh *Unpublished*

The A48 and A483 Trunk Roads and M4 Motorway (Pont Abraham, Carmarthenshire) (Temporary Traffic Restrictions) Order 2008 No. 2008/2032 (W.186). - Enabling power: Road Traffic Regulation Act 1984, ss. 14 (1) (4). - Made: 24.07.2008. Coming into force: 03.08.2008. Effect: None. Territorial extent & classification: W. Local. - In English and Welsh *Unpublished*

The A48 Trunk Road (Chepstow - Wye Bridge County Boundary, Monmouthshire) (Temporary Traffic Restrictions) Order 2008 No. 2008/1039 (W.109). - Enabling power: Road Traffic Regulation Act 1984, ss. 14 (1) (4). - Made: 07.04.2008. Coming into force: 14.04.2008. Effect: None. Territorial extent & classification: W. Local. - In English and Welsh *Unpublished*

The A48 Trunk Road (Nantycaws, Carmarthenshire) (Temporary Traffic Restrictions) Order 2008 No. 2008/1244 (W.125). - Enabling power: Road Traffic Regulation Act 1984, ss. 14 (1) (4). - Made: 30.04.2008. Coming into force: 09.05.2008. Effect: None. Territorial extent & classification: W. Local. - In English and Welsh *Unpublished*

The A48 Trunk Road (Nantycaws, Carmarthen) (Temporary 50 mph Speed Limit) Order 2008 No. 2008/44 (W.9). - Enabling power: Road Traffic Regulation Act 1984, ss. 14 (1) (4). - Made: 10.01.2008. Coming into force: 18.02.2008. Effect: None. Territorial extent & classification: W. Local. - In English and Welsh *Unpublished*

The A48 Trunk Road (Nantycaws Hill, Carmarthenshire) (Temporary No Right Turn) Order 2008 No. 2008/2837 (W.251). - Enabling power: Road Traffic Regulation Act 1984, ss. 14 (1) (4). - Made: 30.10.2008. Coming into force: 10.11.2008. Effect: None. Territorial extent & classification: W. Local. - In English and Welsh *Unpublished*

The A55 Trunk Road (Angelsey) (Temporary 40 MPH Speed Limit) Order 2008 No. 2008/918 (W.85). - Enabling power: Road Traffic Regulation Act 1984, s. 14 (1) (4). - Made: 28.03.2008. Coming into force: 02.04.2008. Effect: None. Territorial extent & classification: W. Local. - In English and Welsh *Unpublished*

The A55 Trunk Road (Broughton, Flintshire) (Temporary Prohibition of Vehicles) Order 2008 No. 2008/1343 (W.142). - Enabling power: Road Traffic Regulation Act 1984, s. 14 (1) (4). - Made: 22.05.2008. Coming into force: 05.06.2008. Effect: None. Territorial extent & classification: W. Local. - In English and Welsh *Unpublished*

The A55 Trunk Road (Conwy Tunnel, Conwy) (Temporary Traffic Restrictions) Order 2008 No. 2008/12 (W.5). - Enabling power: Road Traffic Regulation Act 1984, ss. 14 (1) (4) (7). - Made: 08.01.2008. Coming into force: 20.02.2008. Effect: None. Territorial extent & classification: W. Local. - In English and Welsh *Unpublished*

The A55 Trunk Road (Dobshill, Flintshire) (Temporary Traffic Restrictions) Order 2008 No. 2008/2711 (W.244). - Enabling power: Road Traffic Regulation Act 1984, s. 14 (1) (4). - Made: 10.10.2008. Coming into force: 22.10.2008. Effect: None. Territorial extent & classification: W. Local. - In English and Welsh *Unpublished*

The A55 Trunk Road (Glan Conwy - Conwy Morfa, Conwy County Borough) (Temporary 70 mph Speed Limit) Order 2008 No. 2008/2505 (W.219). - Enabling power: Road Traffic Regulation Act 1984, s. 14 (1) (7). - Made: 24.09.2008. Coming into force: 26.09.2008. Effect: None. Territorial extent & classification: W. Local. - In English and Welsh *Unpublished*

The A55 Trunk Road (Holyhead, Anglesey) (Temporary Traffic Restrictions) (No. 2) Order 2008 No. 2008/1333 (W.139). - Enabling power: Road Traffic Regulation Act 1984, s. 14 (1) (4). - Made: 21.05.2008. Coming into force: 02.06.2008. Effect: None. Territorial extent & classification: W. Local. - In English and Welsh *Unpublished*

The A55 Trunk Road (Holyhead, Anglesey) (Temporary Traffic Restrictions) Order 2008 No. 2008/955 (W.105). - Enabling power: Road Traffic Regulation Act 1984, s. 14 (1) (4). - Made: 01.04.2008. Coming into force: 07.04.2008. Effect: None. Territorial extent & classification: W. Local. - In English and Welsh *Unpublished*

The A55 Trunk Road (Holyhead, Isle of Anglesey to Bangor, Gwynedd) (Temporary 30 MPH & 40 MPH Speed Limits) Order 2008 No. 2008/1191 (W.120). - Enabling power: Road Traffic Regulation Act 1984, s. 14 (1) (4). - Made: 21.04.2008. Coming into force: 01.05.2008. Effect: None. Territorial extent & classification: W. Local. - In English and Welsh *Unpublished*

The A55 Trunk Road (Junction 11, Llys y Gwynt Interchange, Bangor, Gwynedd to the Wales/England Border) and the A494/A550 Trunk Road (Ewoe Interchange) (Temporary Traffic Restrictions) Order 2008 No. 2008/943 (W.102). - Enabling power: Road Traffic Regulation Act 1984, s. 14 (1) (4). - Made: 25.03.2008. Coming into force: 01.04.2008. Effect: None. Territorial extent & classification: W. Local. - In English and Welsh *Unpublished*

The A55 Trunk Road (Junction 16a, Glanyrafon Junction, Dwygyfylchi, Conwy) (Temporary Prohibition of Vehicles) Order 2008 No. 2008/1280 (W.134). - Enabling power: Road Traffic Regulation Act 1984, s. 14 (1) (4). - Made: 12.05.2008. Coming into force: 19.05.2008. Effect: None. Territorial extent & classification: W. Local. - In English and Welsh *Unpublished*

The A55 Trunk Road (Junction 24, Abergele, Conwy County Borough) (Temporary Prohibition of Vehicles and 40 mph Speed Limit) Order 2008 No. 2008/1041 (W.111). - Enabling power: Road Traffic Regulation Act 1984, ss. 14 (1) (4). - Made: 07.04.2008. Coming into force: 21.04.2008. Effect: None. Territorial extent & classification: W. Local. - In English and Welsh *Unpublished*

The A55 Trunk Road (Junction 33, Northop Interchange to Junction 35, Dobshill Interchange, Flintshire) (Temporary Traffic Restrictions) Order 2008 No. 2008/2369 (W.204). - Enabling power: Road Traffic Regulation Act 1984, s. 14 (1) (4). - Made: 08.09.2008. Coming into force: 22.09.2008. Effect: None. Territorial extent & classification: W. Local. - In English and Welsh *Unpublished*

The A55 Trunk Road (Llanddulas, Conwy County Borough) (Temporary Traffic Restrictions) Order 2008 No. 2008/2710 (W.243). - Enabling power: Road Traffic Regulation Act 1984, s. 14 (1) (4). - Made: 10.10.2008. Coming into force: 21.10.2008. Effect: None. Territorial extent & classification: W. Local. - In English and Welsh *Unpublished*

The A55 Trunk Road (Near Bryngwran and Llanfairpwllgwyngyll, Isle of Anglesey) (Temporary Traffic Restrictions) Order 2008 No. 2008/2559 (W.224). - Enabling power: Road Traffic Regulation Act 1984, s. 14 (1) (4). - Made: 29.09.2008. Coming into force: 06.10.2008. Effect: None. Territorial extent & classification: W. Local. - In English and Welsh *Unpublished*

The A55 Trunk Road (Penmaenbach Tunnels, Conwy) (Temporary Traffic Restrictions) Order 2008 No. 2008/2 (W.2). - Enabling power: Road Traffic Regulation Act 1984, ss. 14 (1) (4) (7). - Made: 02.01.2008. Coming into force: 06.01.2008. Effect: None. Territorial extent & classification: W. Local. - In English and Welsh *Unpublished*

The A55 Trunk Road (Penmaenmawr, Conwy) (Temporary Prohibition of Vehicles) Order 2008 No. 2008/1141 (W.117). - Enabling power: Road Traffic Regulation Act 1984, s. 14 (1) (4). - Made: 14.04.2008. Coming into force: 27.04.2008. Effect: None. Territorial extent & classification: W. Local. - In English and Welsh *Unpublished*

The A55 Trunk Road (Penmaenmawr Tunnel East Service Building Lay-by, Conwy) (Temporary Prohibition of Vehicles) Order 2008 No. 2008/1279 (W.133). - Enabling power: Road Traffic Regulation Act 1984, s. 14 (1) (4). - Made: 12.05.2008. Coming into force: 19.05.2008. Effect: None. Territorial extent & classification: W. Local. - In English and Welsh *Unpublished*

The A55 Trunk Road (Pentre Halkyn, between Northop and Holywell) (Temporary Traffic Restrictions) Order 2008 No. 2008/3293 (W.289). - Enabling power: Road Traffic Regulation Act 1984, s. 14 (1) (4). - Made: 19.12.2008. Coming into force: 02.01.2009. Effect: None. Territorial extent & classification: W. Local. - In English and Welsh *Unpublished*

The A55 Trunk Road (Pen-y-clip Tunnel, Conwy) (Temporary Traffic Restrictions) (No. 2) Order 2008 No. 2008/2100 (W.188). - Enabling power: Road Traffic Regulation Act 1984, ss. 14 (1) (4) (7). - Made: 04.08.2008. Coming into force: 08.08.2008. Effect: None. Territorial extent & classification: W. Local. - In English and Welsh *Unpublished*

The A55 Trunk Road (Pen-y-clip Tunnel, Conwy) (Temporary Traffic Restrictions) Order 2008 No. 2008/114 (W.16). - Enabling power: Road Traffic Regulation Act 1984, ss. 14 (1) (4) (7). - Made: 21.01.2008. Coming into force: 03.02.2008. Effect: None. Territorial extent & classification: W. Local. - In English and Welsh *Unpublished*

The A55 Trunk Road (Rhuallt, Denbighshire) (Temporary Traffic Restrictions) Order 2008 No. 2008/2348 (W.200). - Enabling power: Road Traffic Regulation Act 1984, s. 14 (1) (4). - Made: 21.08.2008. Coming into force: 01.09.2008. Effect: None. Territorial extent & classification: W. Local. - In English and Welsh *Unpublished*

The A55 Trunk Road (Various Slip Roads between Abergwyngregyn, Gwynedd and Rhualt, Denbighshire) (Temporary Prohibition of Vehicles) Order 2008 No. 2008/3059 (W.266). - Enabling power: Road Traffic Regulation Act 1984, ss. 14 (1) (4). - Made: 24.11.2008. Coming into force: 08.12.2008. Effect: None. Territorial extent & classification: W. Local. - In English and Welsh *Unpublished*

The A465 Trunk Road (Dukestown to Rassau, Blaenau Gwent) (Temporary Traffic Restrictions) Order 2008 No. 2008/2910 (W.256). - Enabling power: Road Traffic Regulation Act 1984, s. 14 (1) (4). - Made: 07.11.2008. Coming into force: 21.11.2008. Effect: None. Territorial extent & classification: W. Local. - In English and Welsh *Unpublished*

The A465 Trunk Road (Hirwaun Flats Roundabout, Rhondda Cynon Taf) (Temporary Traffic Restrictions) Order 2008 No. 2008/3003 (W.263). - Enabling power: Road Traffic Regulation Act 1984, s. 14 (1) (4). - Made: 13.11.2008. Coming into force: 24.11.2008. Effect: None. Territorial extent & classification: W. Local. - In English and Welsh *Unpublished*

The A465 Trunk Road (Llanfoist-Gilwen, Monmouthshire) (Temporary 30 mph, 40 mph & 50 mph Speed Limits) Order 2008 No. 2008/1274 (W.131). - Enabling power: Road Traffic Regulation Act 1984, ss. 14 (1) (4). - Made: 08.05.2008. Coming into force: 16.05.2008. Effect: None. Territorial extent & classification: W. Local. - In English and Welsh *Unpublished*

The A465 Trunk Road (Llangua, Monmouthshire) (Temporary Traffic Restrictions) Order 2008 No. 2008/2944 (W.261). - Enabling power: Road Traffic Regulation Act 1984, s. 14 (1) (4). - Made: 14.11.2008. Coming into force: 24.11.2008. Effect: None. Territorial extent & classification: W. Local. - In English and Welsh *Unpublished*

The A465 Trunk Road (Upper Triley Mill, Monmouthshire) (Temporary Traffic Restrictions) Order 2008 No. 2008/3057 (W.265). - Enabling power: Road Traffic Regulation Act 1984, s. 14 (1) (4). - Made: 21.11.2008. Coming into force: 01.12.2008. Effect: None. Territorial extent & classification: W. Local. - In English and Welsh *Unpublished*

The A470 Trunk Road (Blaenau Ffestiniog to Cancoed, Gwynedd and Conwy) (Temporary Traffic Restrictions) Order 2008 No. 2008/596 (W.61). - Enabling power: Road Traffic Regulation Act 1984, s. 14 (1) (4). - Made: 04.03.2008. Coming into force: 14.03.2008. Effect: None. Territorial extent & classification: W. Local. - In English and Welsh *Unpublished*

The A470 Trunk Road (Bronaber to Ganllwyd, Gwynedd) (Temporary Traffic Restrictions) Order 2008 No. 2008/2354 (W.202). - Enabling power: Road Traffic Regulation Act 1984, s. 14 (1) (4). - Made: 03.09.2008. Coming into force: 15.09.2008. Effect: None. Territorial extent & classification: W. Local. - In English and Welsh *Unpublished*

The A470 Trunk Road (Bryn Cemlyn to Nant Las, Ganllwyd, Gwynedd) (Temporary Traffic Restrictions) Order 2008 No. 2008/45 (W.10). - Enabling power: Road Traffic Regulation Act 1984, ss. 14 (1) (4). - Made: 10.01.2008. Coming into force: 18.02.2008. Effect: None. Territorial extent & classification: W. Local. - In English and Welsh *Unpublished*

The A470 Trunk Road (Glan Conwy, Conwy County Borough) (Temporary Traffic Restrictions) Order 2008 No. 2008/2255 (W.196). - Enabling power: Road Traffic Regulation Act 1984, ss. 14 (1) (4). - Made: 21.08.2008. Coming into force: 01.09.2008. Effect: None. Territorial extent & classification: W. Local. - In English and Welsh *Unpublished*

The A470 Trunk Road (Llanelltyd Bridge, Llanelltyd, Gwynedd) (Temporary 40 mph Speed Limit) Order 2008 No. 2008/1815 (W.176). - Enabling power: Road Traffic Regulation Act 1984, s. 14 (1) (4). - Made: 26.06.2008. Coming into force: 03.07.2008. Effect: None. Territorial extent & classification: W. Local. - In English and Welsh *Unpublished*

The A470 Trunk Road (Llanrwst to Hafod, Conwy) (Temporary Traffic Restrictions) Order 2008 No. 2008/3254 (W.287). - Enabling power: Road Traffic Regulation Act 1984, s. 14 (1) (4). - Made: 18.12.2008. Coming into force: 01.01.2009. Effect: None. Territorial extent & classification: W. Local. - In English and Welsh *Unpublished*

The A470 Trunk Road (Llwyn Viaduct, Dolgellau, Gwynedd) (Temporary 50 mph Speed Limit) Order 2008 No. 2008/1483 (W.154). - Enabling power: Road Traffic Regulation Act 1984, s. 14 (1) (4). - Made: 09.06.2008. Coming into force: 23.06.2008. Effect: None. Territorial extent & classification: W. Local. - In English and Welsh *Unpublished*

The A470 Trunk Road (North of Dinas Mawddwy, Gwynedd) (Temporary Traffic Restrictions) Order 2008 No. 2008/1475 (W.152). - Enabling power: Road Traffic Regulation Act 1984, s. 14 (1) (4). - Made: 09.06.2008. Coming into force: 23.06.2008. Effect: None. Territorial extent & classification: W. Local. - In English and Welsh *Unpublished*

The A470 Trunk Road (Various Interchanges between Coryton Interchange Cardiff and Abercanaid Roundabout Merthyr Tydfil) (Temporary Prohibition of Vehicles) Order 2008 No. 2008/2158 (W.191). - Enabling power: Road Traffic Regulation Act 1984, s. 14 (1) (4). - Made: 11.08.2008. Coming into force: 25.08.2008. Effect: None. Territorial extent & classification: W. Local. - In English and Welsh *Unpublished*

The A477 Trunk Road (Bageston to Waterloo, Pembroke Dock, Pembrokeshire) (Temporary Traffic Restrictions) Order 2008 No. 2008/2782 (W.249). - Enabling power: Road Traffic Regulation Act 1984, s. 14 (1) (4). - Made: 23.10.2008. Coming into force: 27.10.2008. Effect: None. Territorial extent & classification: W. Local. - In English and Welsh *Unpublished*

The A477 Trunk Road (East of Red Roses, Carmarthenshire) (Temporary 40 MPH Speed Limit) Order 2008 No. 2008/2650 (W.233). - Enabling power: Road Traffic Regulation Act 1984, s. 14 (1) (4). - Made: 07.10.2008. Coming into force: 17.10.2008. Effect: None. Territorial extent & classification: W. Local. - In English and Welsh *Unpublished*

The A477 Trunk Road (West of Amroth Junction, Pembrokeshire) (Temporary Traffic Restrictions) Order 2008 No. 2008/2498 (W.216). - Enabling power: Road Traffic Regulation Act 1984, s. 14 (1) (4). - Made: 22.09.2008. Coming into force: 06.10.2008. Effect: None. Territorial extent & classification: W. Local. - In English and Welsh *Unpublished*

The A477 Trunk Road (West of Llanddowror, nr. St Clears, Carmarthenshire) (Temporary Traffic Restrictions) Order 2008 No. 2008/742 (W.77). - Enabling power: Road Traffic Regulation Act 1984, s. 14 (1) (4). - Made: 13.03.2008. Coming into force: 19.03.2008. Effect: None. Territorial extent & classification: W. Local. - In English and Welsh *Unpublished*

The A483 Trunk Road (Ffairfach Square, Carmarthenshire) (Prohibition of Waiting) Order 2008 No. 2008/98 (W.13). - Enabling power: Road Traffic Regulation Act 1984, s. 1 (1), 2 (1) (2), 4 (2). - Made: 16.01.2008. Coming into force: 28.01.2008. Effect: S.I. 1977/235 revoked. Territorial extent & classification: W. Local. - In English and Welsh *Unpublished*

The A483 Trunk Road (Moors Straight, Nr. Welshpool, Powys) (Temporary 30 mph Speed Limit) Order 2008 No. 2008/3056 (W.264). - Enabling power: Road Traffic Regulation Act 1984, ss. 14 (1) (4). - Made: 21.11.2008. Coming into force: 28.11.2008. Effect: None. Territorial extent & classification: W. Local. - In English and Welsh *Unpublished*

The A483 Trunk Road (Near Rossett, Wrexham) (Temporary Prohibition of Vehicles) Order 2008 No. 2008/3060 (W.267). - Enabling power: Road Traffic Regulation Act 1984, ss. 14 (1) (4). - Made: 24.11.2008. Coming into force: 08.12.2008. Effect: None. Territorial extent & classification: W. Local. - In English and Welsh *Unpublished*

The A483 Trunk Road (Pontardulais Road, Tycroes, Ammanford, Carmarthenshire) (Prohibition of Waiting) Order 2008 No. 2008/2565 (W.225). - Enabling power: Road Traffic Regulation Act 1984, ss. 1 (1), 2 (1) (2), 4 (2). - Made: 01.08.2008. Coming into force: 10.08.2008. Effect: None. Territorial extent & classification: W. Local. - In English and Welsh *Unpublished*

The A483 Trunk Road (Rhosmaen Street, Llandeilo, Carmarthenshire) (Temporary Prohibition of Vehicles) Order 2008 No. 2008/841 (W.84). - Enabling power: Road Traffic Regulation Act 1984, s. 14 (1) (4). - Made: 26.03.2008. Coming into force: 07.04.2008. Effect: None. Territorial extent & classification: W. Local. - In English and Welsh *Unpublished*

The A483 Trunk Road (Ruthin Road Interchange (Junction 4) to the Wales/England Border, Wrexham) (Temporary Prohibition of Vehicles) Order 2008 No. 2008/2351 (W.201). - Enabling power: Road Traffic Regulation Act 1984, s. 14 (1) (4). - Made: 01.09.2008. Coming into force: 08.09.2008. Effect: None. Territorial extent & classification: W. Local. - In English and Welsh *Unpublished*

The A483 Trunk Road (Wrexham County Borough) (Temporary 40 mph Speed Limit) Order 2008 No. 2008/1145 (W.118). - Enabling power: Road Traffic Regulation Act 1984, s. 14 (1) (4). - Made: 17.04.2008. Coming into force: 01.05.2008. Effect: None. Territorial extent & classification: W. Local. - In English and Welsh *Unpublished*

The A487 Trunk Road (Blaenannerch, Ceredigion) (Temporary Prohibition of Vehicles) Order 2008 No. 2008/1574 (W.157). - Enabling power: Road Traffic Regulation Act 1984, s. 14 (1) (4). - Made: 16.06.2008. Coming into force: 23.06.2008. Effect: None. Territorial extent & classification: W. Local. - In English and Welsh *Unpublished*

The A487 Trunk Road (Britannia Bridge, Porthmadog) (Temporary Traffic Restrictions) Order 2008 No. 2008/1260 (W.127). - Enabling power: Road Traffic Regulation Act 1984, ss. 14 (1) (4). - Made: 30.04.2008. Coming into force: 12.05.2008. Effect: None. Territorial extent & classification: W. Local. - In English and Welsh *Unpublished*

The A487 Trunk Road (Constantine Terrace to South Road, Caernarfon, Gwynedd) (Temporary Prohibition of Vehicles) Order 2008 No. 2008/3326 (W.291). - Enabling power: Road Traffic Regulation Act 1984, s. 14 (1) (4). - Made: 23.12.2008. Coming into force: 05.01.2009. Effect: None. Territorial extent & classification: W. Local. - In English and Welsh *Unpublished*

The A487 Trunk Road (East of Fishguard, Pembrokeshire) (Temporary Traffic Restrictions) Order 2008 No. 2008/971 (W.106). - Enabling power: Road Traffic Regulation Act 1984, s. 14 (1) (4). - Made: 02.04.2008. Coming into force: 10.04.2008. Effect: None. Territorial extent & classification: W. Local. - In English and Welsh *Unpublished*

The A487 Trunk Road (Golan to Penmorfa, Gwynedd) (Temporary 40 MPH Speed Limit) Order 2008 No. 2008/1555 (W.156). - Enabling power: Road Traffic Regulation Act 1984, s. 14 (1) (4). - Made: 13.06.2008. Coming into force: 23.06.2008. Effect: None. Territorial extent & classification: W. Local. - In English and Welsh *Unpublished*

The A487 Trunk Road (Porthmadog, Gwynedd) (Temporary Prohibition of Vehicles, Pedestrians & Cyclists) Order 2008 No. 2008/2842 (W.253). - Enabling power: Road Traffic Regulation Act 1984, ss. 14 (1) (4). - Made: 30.10.2008. Coming into force: 01.11.2008. Effect: None. Territorial extent & classification: W. Local. - In English and Welsh *Unpublished*

The A487 Trunk Road (Various Roads, Penrhyndeudraeth, Gwynedd) (Prohibition of Waiting) Order 2008 No. 2008/522 (W.49). - Enabling power: Road Traffic Regulation Act 1984, ss. 1 (1), 2 (1) (2), 4 (2). - Made: 10.01.2008. Coming into force: 31.01.2008. Effect: None. Territorial extent & classification: W. Local. - In English and Welsh *Unpublished*

The A494 & A5 Trunk Roads (Rhug Chapel, Corwen, Denbighshire) (Temporary Traffic Restrictions) Order 2008 No. 2008/2506 (W.220). - Enabling power: Road Traffic Regulation Act 1984, s. 14 (1) (4). - Made: 24.09.2008. Coming into force: 29.09.2008. Effect: None. Territorial extent & classification: W. Local. - In English and Welsh *Unpublished*

The A494/A550 Trunk Road (Deeside, Flintshire) (Temporary 40 mph Speed Limit and Trafficking of Hard Shoulder) Order 2008 No. 2008/197 (W.24). - Enabling power: Road Traffic Regulation Act 1984, ss. 14 (1) (4). - Made: 31.01.2008. Coming into force: 01.02.2008. Effect: None. Territorial extent & classification: W. Local. - In English and Welsh *Unpublished*

The A494/A550 Trunk Road (Garden City Interchange to Deeside Park Interchange, Flintshire) (Temporary Prohibition of Vehicles & Cyclists) Order 2008 No. 2008/2709 (W.242). - Enabling power: Road Traffic Regulation Act 1984, ss. 14 (1) (4). - Made: 10.10.2008. Coming into force: 20.10.2008. Effect: None. Territorial extent & classification: W. Local. - In English and Welsh *Unpublished*

The A494/A550 Trunk Road (Queensferry, Deeside, Flintshire) (Temporary Traffic Restrictions) Order 2008 No. 2008/3079 (W.270). - Enabling power: Road Traffic Regulation Act 1984, s. 14 (1) (4). - Made: 28.11.2008. Coming into force: 07.12.2008. Effect: None. Territorial extent & classification: W. Local. - In English and Welsh *Unpublished*

The A494/A550 Trunk Roads (Deeside Park Interchange, Flintshire) (Temporary Prohibition of Vehicles and Cyclists) Order 2008 No. 2008/2040 (W.187). - Enabling power: Road Traffic Regulation Act 1984, s. 14 (1) (4). - Made: 28.07.2008. Coming into force: 08.08.2008. Effect: None. Territorial extent & classification: W. Local. - In English and Welsh *Unpublished*

The A494 Trunk Road (Bont Newydd and Rhydymain, near Dolgellau, Gwynedd) (Temporary Traffic Restrictions) Order 2008 No. 2008/2695 (W.240). - Enabling power: Road Traffic Regulation Act 1984, s. 14 (1) (4). - Made: 10.10.2008. Coming into force: 27.10.2008. Effect: None. Territorial extent & classification: W. Local. - In English and Welsh *Unpublished*

The A494 Trunk Road (Golwg Hir, Nr. Dolgellau, Gwynedd) (Temporary 40 mph Speed Limit) Order 2008 No. 2008/1658 (W.161). - Enabling power: Road Traffic Regulation Act 1984, s. 14 (1) (4). - Made: 25.06.2008. Coming into force: 03.07.2008. Effect: None. Territorial extent & classification: W. Local. - In English and Welsh *Unpublished*

The A494 Trunk Road (Junction with the Unclassified Road leading to Llanfair Dyffryn Clwyd, South of Ruthin, Denbighshire) (Temporary Traffic Restrictions) Order 2008 No. 2008/1403 (W.143). - Enabling power: Road Traffic Regulation Act 1984, s. 14 (1) (4). - Made: 29.05.2008. Coming into force: 02.06.2008. Effect: None. Territorial extent & classification: W. Local. - In English and Welsh *Unpublished*

The A494 Trunk Road (Lanycil, Gwynedd) (Temporary 30 mph Speed Limit) Order 2008 No. 2008/920 (W.86). - Enabling power: Road Traffic Regulation Act 1984, s. 14 (1) (4). - Made: 28.03.2008. Coming into force: 07.04.2008. Effect: None. Territorial extent & classification: W. Local. - In English and Welsh *Unpublished*

The A494 Trunk Road (Llanbedr Dyffryn Clwyd, Denbighshire) (Temporary Traffic Restrictions) Order 2008 No. 2008/3300 (W.290). - Enabling power: Road Traffic Regulation Act 1984, s. 14 (1) (4). - Made: 29.12.2008. Coming into force: 12.01.2009. Effect: None. Territorial extent & classification: W. Local. - In English and Welsh *Unpublished*

The A494 Trunk Road (Ruthin to Pwllglas, Denbighshire) (Temporary Traffic Restrictions) Order 2008 No. 2008/2433 (W.208). - Enabling power: Road Traffic Regulation Act 1984, s. 14 (1) (4). - Made: 15.09.2008. Coming into force: 29.09.2008. Effect: None. Territorial extent & classification: W. Local. - In English and Welsh *Unpublished*

The A4042 Trunk Road (Llanvihangel Pontymoel to Penperlleni, Monmouthshire) (Temporary 10 mph and 50 mph Speed Limits) Order 2008 No. 2008/38 (W.8). - Enabling power: Road Traffic Regulation Act 1984, ss. 14 (1) (4). - Made: 09.01.2008. Coming into force: 18.02.2008. Effect: None. Territorial extent & classification: W. Local. - In English and Welsh *Unpublished*

The A4076 Trunk Road (North Steynton to South Johnston, Pembrokeshire) (Temporary Traffic Restrictions) Order 2008 No. 2008/367 (W.33). - Enabling power: Road Traffic Regulation Act 1984, s. 14 (1) (4). - Made: 14.02.2008. Coming into force: 22.02.2008. Effect: None. Territorial extent & classification: W. Local. - In English and Welsh *Unpublished*

The A4232 Trunk Road (Northbound Entry Slip Road at Culverhouse Cross, Cardiff) (Temporary Prohibition of Vehicles) Order 2008 No. 2008/3061 (W.268). - Enabling power: Road Traffic Regulation Act 1984, ss. 14 (1) (4). - Made: 25.11.2008. Coming into force: 13.12.2008. Effect: None. Territorial extent & classification: W. Local. - In English and Welsh *Unpublished*

The M4 Motorway and A48 Trunk Road (Junction 41, Pentyla and Sunnycroft Roundabout to Briton Ferry Roundabout, Neath Port Talbot) (Temporary 40 MPH Speed Limit) Order 2008 No. 2008/2571 (W.227). - Enabling power: Road Traffic Regulation Act 1984, s. 14 (1) (4) (7). - Made: 02.10.2008. Coming into force: 13.10.2008. Effect: None. Territorial extent & classification: W. Local. - In English and Welsh *Unpublished*

The M4 Motorway and the A449 Trunk Road (Junction 24, Coldra Roundabout) (Temporary 30 mph & 50 mph Speed Limits) Order 2008 No. 2008/1404 (W.144). - Enabling power: Road Traffic Regulation Act 1984, s. 14 (1) (4). - Made: 29.05.2008. Coming into force: 02.06.2008. Effect: None. Territorial extent & classification: W. Local. - In English and Welsh *Unpublished*

The M4 Motorway and the A4042 Trunk Road (Grove Park Roundabout, Newport) (Temporary Traffic Restrictions) Order 2008 No. 2008/2665 (W.234). - Enabling power: Road Traffic Regulation Act 1984, s. 14 (1) (4). - Made: 06.10.2008. Coming into force: 13.10.2008. Effect: None. Territorial extent & classification: W. Local. - In English and Welsh *Unpublished*

The M4 Motorway and the A4232 Trunk Road (Junction 33, Capel Llanilltern, Cardiff) (Temporary Traffic Restrictions) Order 2008 No. 2008/2931 (W.259). - Enabling power: Road Traffic Regulation Act 1984, s. 14 (1) (4). - Made: 07.11.2008. Coming into force: 20.11.2008. Effect: None. Territorial extent & classification: W. Local. - In English and Welsh *Unpublished*

The M4 Motorway (Brynglas Tunnels, Newport) (Temporary Prohibition of Vehicles & 40mph Speed Limit) (No. 2) Order 2008 No. 2008/2555 (W.223). - Enabling power: Road Traffic Regulation Act 1984, s. 14 (1) (4) (7). - Made: 30.09.2008. Coming into force: 12.10.2008. Effect: None. Territorial extent & classification: W. Local. - In English and Welsh *Unpublished*

The M4 Motorway (Brynglas Tunnels, Newport) (Temporary Prohibition of Vehicles & 40 mph Speed Limit) Order 2008 No. 2008/1 (W.1). - Enabling power: Road Traffic Regulation Act 1984, s. 14 (1) (4) (7). - Made: 02.01.2008. Coming into force: 04.01.2008. Effect: None. Territorial extent & classification: W. Local. - In English and Welsh *Unpublished*

The M4 Motorway (Eastbound Carriageway Between Junctions 47 and 48, Swansea) (Temporary Prohibition of Vehicles & 50 mph Speed Limit) Order 2008 No. 2008/942 (W.101). - Enabling power: Road Traffic Regulation Act 1984, s. 14 (1) (4) (7). - Made: 31.03.2008. Coming into force: 07.04.2008. Effect: None. Territorial extent & classification: W. Local. - In English and Welsh *Unpublished*

The M4 Motorway (Eastbound Entry Slip Road at Junction 42 (Earlswood), Neath Port Talbot) (Temporary Prohibition of Vehicles) Order 2008 No. 2008/2174 (W.193). - Enabling power: Road Traffic Regulation Act 1984, s. 14 (1) (4). - Made: 14.08.2008. Coming into force: 26.08.2008. Effect: None. Territorial extent & classification: W. Local. - In English and Welsh *Unpublished*

The M4 Motorway (Eastsbound Carriageway Between Junction 43 & Junction 42, Neath Port Talbot) (Temporary Prohibition of Vehicles) Order 2008 No. 2008/545 (W.54). - Enabling power: Road Traffic Regulation Act 1984, s. 14 (1) (4). - Made: 28.02.2008. Coming into force: 03.03.2008. Effect: None. Territorial extent & classification: W. Local. - In English and Welsh *Unpublished*

The M4 Motorway (Junction 26, Malpas, Newport) (Temporary Traffic Restrictions) Order 2008 No. 2008/2843 (W.254). - Enabling power: Road Traffic Regulation Act 1984, s. 14 (1) (4) (7). - Made: 30.10.2008. Coming into force: 03.11.2008. Effect: None. Territorial extent & classification: W. Local. - In English and Welsh *Unpublished*

The M4 Motorway (Junction 28 (Tredegar Park) to Junction 32 (Coryton)) (Temporary Traffic Restrictions) (No. 2) Order 2008 No. 2008/2640 (W.230). - Enabling power: Road Traffic Regulation Act 1984, s. 14 (1) (4) (7). - Made: 06.10.2008. Coming into force: 10.10.2008. Effect: None. Territorial extent & classification: W. Local. - In English and Welsh *Unpublished*

The M4 Motorway (Junction 28 (Tredegar Park) to Junction 32 (Coryton)) (Temporary Traffic Restrictions) Order 2008 No. 2008/2509 (W.221). - Enabling power: Road Traffic Regulation Act 1984, s. 14 (1) (4). - Made: 24.09.2008. Coming into force: 26.09.2008. Effect: None. Territorial extent & classification: W. Local. - In English and Welsh *Unpublished*

Road traffic, Wales: Traffic regulation

The M4 Motorway (Junction 38 (Margam) to Junction 40 (Taiback), Neath Port Talbot) (Temporary Traffic Restrictions) Order 2008 No. 2008/1974 (W.184). - Enabling power: Road Traffic Regulation Act 1984, s. 14 (1) (4). - Made: 21.07.2008. Coming into force: 01.08.2008. Effect: None. Territorial extent & classification: W. Local. - In English and Welsh *Unpublished*

The M4 Motorway (Junction 42 (Earlswood) to Junction 43 (Llandarcy), Neath Port Talbot) (Temporary Prohibition of Vehicles) Order 2008 No. 2008/758 (W.79). - Enabling power: Road Traffic Regulation Act 1984, s. 14 (1) (4). - Made: 18.03.2008. Coming into force: 20.03.2008. Effect: None. Territorial extent & classification: W. Local. - In English and Welsh *Unpublished*

The M4 Motorway (Junction 42 (Earlswood) to Junction 44 (Lond Las), Neath Port Talbot) (Temporary Prohibition of Vehicles & 50 MPH Speed Limit) Order 2008 No. 2008/953 (W.104). - Enabling power: Road Traffic Regulation Act 1984, s. 14 (1) (4). - Made: 31.03.2008. Coming into force: 07.04.2008. Effect: None. Territorial extent & classification: W. Local. - In English and Welsh *Unpublished*

The M4 Motorway (Junction 42, Westbound on Slip Road, Earlswood, Neath Port Talbot) (Temporary Prohibition of Vehicles) Order 2008 No. 2008/982 (W.107). - Enabling power: Road Traffic Regulation Act 1984, s. 14 (1) (4). - Made: 01.04.2008. Coming into force: 15.04.2008. Effect: None. Territorial extent & classification: W. Local. - In English and Welsh *Unpublished*

The M4 Motorway (Slip Roads at Junction 30 (Cardiff Gate) and Junction 32 (Coryton), Cardiff) (Temporary Prohibition of Vehicles) Order 2008 No. 2008/2641 (W.231). - Enabling power: Road Traffic Regulation Act 1984, s. 14 (1) (4). - Made: 06.10.2008. Coming into force: 10.10.2008. Effect: None. Territorial extent & classification: W. Local. - In English and Welsh *Unpublished*

The M4 Motorway (Slip Roads at Junction 32, Coryton Interchange and Junction 33, Capel Llanilltern Interchange, Cardiff) (Temporary Prohibition of Vehicles) Order 2008 No. 2008/3088 (W.272). - Enabling power: Road Traffic Regulation Act 1984, s. 14 (1) (4). - Made: 02.12.2008. Coming into force: 13.12.2008. Effect: None. Territorial extent & classification: W. Local. - In English and Welsh *Unpublished*

The M48 Motorway (Rogiet to Newhouse Roundabout Near Chepstow, Monmouthshire) (Temporary Traffic Restrictions) Order 2008 No. 2008/1433 (W.149). - Enabling power: Road Traffic Regulation Act 1984, s. 14 (1) (4). - Made: 30.05.2008. Coming into force: 09.06.2008. Effect: None. Territorial extent & classification: W. Local. - In English and Welsh *Unpublished*

The Temporary Prohibition of Cyclists & Pedestrians on the Cycletrack/Footway between Crymlyn Road Over-bridge, Skewen and the Bowling Club, Llandarcy, Neath Port Talbot Order 2008 No. 2008/784 (W.81). - Enabling power: Road Traffic Regulation Act 1984, s. 14 (1) (4). - Made: 19.03.2008. Coming into force: 01.04.2008. Effect: None. Territorial extent & classification: W. Local. - In English and Welsh *Unpublished*

Savings banks

The National Savings Bank (Amendment) (No. 2) Regulations 2008 No. 2008/1142. - Enabling power: National Savings Bank Act 1971, s. 2 (1). - Issued: 23.04.2008. Made: 21.04.2008. Laid: 21.04.2008. Coming into force: 12.05.2008. Effect: S.I. 1972/764 amended. Territorial extent & classification: E/W/S/NI. General. - 4p.: 30 cm. - 978-0-11-081388-2 *£3.00*

The National Savings Bank (Amendment) (No. 3) Regulations 2008 No. 2008/1164. - Enabling power: National Savings Bank Act 1971, s. 2 (1). - Issued: 28.04.2008. Made: 23.04.2008. Laid: 24.04.2008. Coming into force: 19.05.2008. Effect: S.I.1972/764; 1977/1210 amended. Territorial extent & classification: E/W/S/NI. General. - 4p.: 30 cm. - 978-0-11-081403-2 *£3.00*

The National Savings Bank (Amendment) (No. 4) Regulations 2008 No. 2008/3098. - Enabling power: National Savings Bank Act 1971, s. 2 (1). - Issued: 09.12.2008. Made: 03.12.2008. Laid: 04.12.2008. Coming into force: 06.04.2009 for regs 6 to 9 & 01.01.2009 for all other purposes. Effect: S.I.1972/764 amended. Territorial extent & classification: E/W/S/NI. General. - 4p.: 30 cm. - 978-0-11-147098-5 *£4.00*

The National Savings Bank (Amendment) Regulations 2008 No. 2008/734. - Enabling power: National Savings Bank Act 1971, s. 2 (1). - Issued: 18.03.2008. Made: 13.03.2008. Laid: 14.03.2008. Coming into force: 06.04.2008. Effect:S.I. 1972/764; 1977/1210 amended. Territorial extent & classification: E/W/S/NI. General. - 4p.: 30 cm. - 978-0-11-081239-7 *£3.00*

Scientific research

The Technology Strategy Board (Transfer of Property etc.) Order 2008 No. 2008/1405. - Enabling power: Science and Technology Act 1965, s. 3 (6). - Issued: 03.06.2008. Made: 29.03.2008. Coming into force: 07.06.2008. Effect: None. Territorial extent & classification: E/W/S/NI. General. - 4p.: 30 cm. - 978-0-11-081766-8 *£3.00*

Sea fisheries, England

The Tope (Prohibition of Fishing) Order 2008 No. 2008/691. - Enabling power: Sea Fish (Conservation) Act 1967, ss. 5 (1), 5 (6), 6 (1), 6 (1A), 15 (3). - Issued: 14.03.2008. Made: 09.03.2008. Laid: 13.03.2008. Coming into force: 06.04.2008. Effect: None. Territorial extent & classification: E. General. - 4p.: 30 cm. - 978-0-11-081189-5 £3.00

Sea fisheries, England: Conservation

The Fal & Helford Designated Area (Fishing Restrictions) Order 2008 No. 2008/2360. - Enabling power: Sea Fish (Conservation) Act 1967, ss. 5, 5A, 15 (3). - Issued: 10.09.2008. Made: 01.09.2008. Laid: 08.09.2008. Coming into force: 01.10.2008. Effect: None. Territorial extent & classification: E. General. - 4p.: 30 cm. - 978-0-11-084088-8 £4.00

The Lyme Bay Designated Area (Fishing Restrictions) Order 2008 No. 2008/1584. - Enabling power: Sea Fish (Conservation) Act 1967, ss. 5, 5A, 15 (3). - Issued: 23.06.2008. Made: 17.06.2008. Laid: 19.06.2008. Coming into force: 11.07.2008. Effect: None. Territorial extent & classification: E. General. - 4p.: 30 cm. - 978-0-11-081874-0 £3.00

Sea fisheries, England: Sea fish industry

The Fisheries and Aquaculture Structures (Grants) (England) (Amendment) Regulations 2008 No. 2008/1322. - Enabling power: European Communities Act 1972, s. 2 (2). - Issued: 22.05.2008. Made: 18.05.2008. Laid: 21.05.2008. Coming into force: 20.06.2008. Effect: S.I. 2001/1117 amended. Territorial extent & classification: E. General. - This Statutory Instrument has been made in consequence of a defect in S.I. 2001/1117 and is being issued free of charge to all known recipients of that Statutory Instrument. - 2p.: 30 cm. - 978-0-11-081484-1 £3.00

Sea fisheries, England and Wales

The Sea Fishing (Enforcement of Community Measures) (Penalty Notices) Order 2008 No. 2008/984. - Enabling power: Fisheries Act 1981, s. 30 (2). - Issued: 09.04.2008. Made: 03.04.2008. Laid: 07.04.2008. Coming into force: 28.04.2008. Effect: None. Territorial extent & classification: E/W. General. - 8p.: 30 cm. - 978-0-11-081353-0 £3.00

The Sea Fishing (Recovery Measures) Order 2008 No. 2008/2347. - Enabling power: Fisheries Act 1981, s. 30 (2) & European Communities Act 1972, sch. 2, para. 1A. - Issued: 08.09.2008. Made: 01.09.2008. Laid: 05.09.2008. Coming into force: 30.09.2009. Effect: S.I. 2005/393; 2006/1327, 1796 (W. 191) revoked. Territorial extent & classification: E/W. General. - EC note: This Order makes provision for the enforcement of restrictions and obligations relating to fishing for cod, northern hake, plaice and sole contained in Council Regulation (EC) No 423/2004 (the "Cod Regulation"), Council Regulation (EC) No 811/2004 (the "Hake Regulation"), Council Regulation (EC) No 676/2007 (the "North Sea Place and Sole Regulation") and Council Regulation (EC) No 509/2007- 12p.: 30 cm. - 978-0-11-084013-0 £5.00

Sea fisheries, England and Wales: Shellfish

The Dee Estuary Cockle Fishery Order 2008 No. 2008/1472. - Enabling power: Sea Fisheries (Shellfish) Act 1967, s. 1, 3 (1), 4 (2) (4), sch. 1. - Issued: 13.06.2008. Made: 08.06.2008. Laid: 09.06.2008. Coming into force: 01.07.2008. Effect: None. Territorial extent & classification: E/W. Local. - 8p.: 30 cm. - 978-0-11-081821-4 £3.00

Sea fisheries, Wales

The Tope (Prohibition of Fishing) (Wales) Order 2008 No. 2008/1438 (W.150). - Enabling power: Sea Fish (Conservation) Act 1967, ss. 5 (1) (6), 6 (1) (1A), 15 (3). - Issued: 19.06.2008. Made: 04.06.2008. Laid before the National Assembly for Wales : 06.06.2008. Coming into force: 01.07.2008. Effect: None. Territorial extent & classification: W. General. - In English and Welsh. Welsh title: Gorchymyn Cwn Gleision (Gwahardd eu Pysgota) (Cymru) 2008. - 8p.: 30 cm. - 978-0-11-091793-1 £3.00

Sea fisheries, Wales: Conservation of sea fish

The Shrimp Fishing Nets (Wales) (Amendment) Order 2008 No. 2008/3144 (W.279). - Enabling power: Sea Fish (Conservation) Act 1967, s. 3 (1) & European Communities Act 1972, s. 2 (2), sch. 2, para. 1A. - Issued: 30.12.2008. Made: 08.12.2008. Laid before the National Assembly for Wales: 09.12.2008. Coming into force: 02.01.2009. Effect: S.I. 2008/1811 (W.175) amended. Territorial extent & classification: W. General. - In English & Welsh. Welsh title: Gorchymyn Rhwydi Pysgota Berdys (Cymru) (Diwygio) 2008. - 4p.: 30 cm. - 978-0-11-091914-0 £4.00

The Shrimp Fishing Nets (Wales) Order 2008 No. 2008/1811 (W.175). - Enabling power: Sea Fish (Conservation) Act 1967, ss. 3 (1), 15 (3) & European Communities Act 1972, s. 2 (2), sch. 2, para. 1A. - Issued: 21.07.2008. Made: 08.07.2008. Laid before the National Assembly for Wales: 09.07.2008. Coming into force: 30.07.2008. Effect: S.I. 2003/3035 (W.283) revoked. Territorial extent & classification: W. General. - EC note: This Order regulates the carriage and use of any fishing nets with mesh size between 16 and 31 millimetres, measured in accordance with Commission Regulation (EC) No. 129/2003 laying down detailed rules for determining the mesh size and thickness of twine of fishing nets. This Order sets out the national provisions called for by Article 25 of Council Regulation (EC) No. 850/98 by specifying veil nets and sorting grids as the types of device required to be used. - In English & Welsh. Welsh title: Gorchymyn Rhwydi Pysgota Berdys (Cymru) 2008. - 8p.: 30 cm. - 978-0-11-091819-8 £3.00

Serious crime prevention orders

The Serious Crime Act 2007 (Commencement No.1) Order 2008 No. 2008/219 (C.5). - Enabling power: Serious Crime Act 2007, s. 94 (1). Bringing into operation various provisions of the 2007 Act on 15.02.2008 & 01.03.2008. - Issued: 08.02.2008. Made: 05.02.2008. Effect: None. Territorial extent & classification: E/W/S/NI. General. - 4p.: 30 cm. - 978-0-11-080902-1 £3.00

The Serious Crime Act 2007 (Commencement No. 2 and Transitional and Transitory Provisions and Savings) Order 2008 No. 2008/755 (C.34). - Enabling power: Serious Crime Act 2007, ss. 91 (2), 94 (1). Bringing into operation various provisions of the 2007 Act on 01.04.2008 & 06.04.2008. - Issued: 25.03.2008. Made: 17.03.2008. Effect: None. Territorial extent & classification: E/W/S/NI [part E/W only]. General. - 12p.: 30 cm. - 978-0-11-081264-9 £3.00

Serious crime prevention orders, England and Wales

The Serious Crime Act 2007 (Appeals under Section 24) Order 2008 No. 2008/1863. - Enabling power: Serious Crime Act 2007, ss. 24 (9) (10), 89 (2) (b). - Issued: 17.07.2008. Made: 14.07.2008. Laid: 15.07.2008. Coming into force: 18.08.2008. Effect: None. Territorial extent & classification: E/W/NI. General. - 28p.: 30 cm. - 978-0-11-083174-9 £4.50

Serious crime prevention orders, Northern Ireland

The Serious Crime Act 2007 (Appeals under Section 24) Order 2008 No. 2008/1863. - Enabling power: Serious Crime Act 2007, ss. 24 (9) (10), 89 (2) (b). - Issued: 17.07.2008. Made: 14.07.2008. Laid: 15.07.2008. Coming into force: 18.08.2008. Effect: None. Territorial extent & classification: E/W/NI. General. - 28p.: 30 cm. - 978-0-11-083174-9 £4.50

Serious Organised Crime Agency

The Serious Organised Crime and Police Act 2005 (Disclosure of Information by SOCA) Order 2008 No. 2008/1908. - Enabling power: Serious Organised Crime and Police Act 2005, s. 33 (2) (f). - Issued: 22.07.2008. Made: 17.07.2008. Coming into force: 23.07.2008. Effect: None. Territorial extent & classification: E/W/S/NI. General. - Supersedes draft S.I. (ISBN 9780110814490) issued 13.05.2008. - 2p.: 30 cm. - 978-0-11-083414-6 £3.00

Sex discrimination

The Sex Discrimination Act 1975 (Amendment) Regulations 2008 No. 2008/656. - Enabling power: European Communities Act 1972, s. 2 (2). - Issued: 14.03.2008. Made: 08.03.2008. Laid: 14.03.2008. Coming into force: 06.04.2008. Effect: 1975 c.65 amended. Territorial extent & classification: E/W/S [reg. 22 to E/W only]. - EC note: These Regulations implement in Great Britain Council Directive 2002/73/EC, in part. The Directive concerns the principle of equal treatment of men and women as regards access to employment, vocational training and promotion and working conditions. These Regulations amend the 1975 Act in order to give full effect to the Directive in relation to the definitions of harassment and discrimination on grounds of pregnancy or maternity leave and so far as it relates to terms and condition during maternity leave. - 4p.: 30 cm. - 978-0-11-081169-7 £3.00

The Sex Discrimination (Amendment of Legislation) Regulations 2008 No. 2008/963. - Enabling power: European Communities Act 1972, s. 2 (2). - Issued: 07.04.2008. Made: 01.01.2008. Coming into force: 06.04.2008. Effect: 1936 c. 49; 1975 c. 65 & S.I. 1976/1042 (N.I.15) amended. Territorial extent & classification: E/W/S/NI. General. - Supersedes draft SI (ISBN 9780110811048) issued 10.03.2008. EC note: These Regulations implement in the UK Council Directive 2004/113/EC. - 16p.: 30 cm. - 978-0-11-081347-9 £3.00

Social care

The Appointments Commission (Amendment) Regulations 2008 No. 2008/2792. - Enabling power: Health Act 2006, sch. 4, para. 2 (b) (d). - Issued: 31.10.2008. Made: 26.10.2008. Laid: 31.10.2008. Coming into force: 08.12.2008. Effect: S.I. 2006/2380 amended. Territorial extent & classification: E/W/S/NI [some aspects E. only]. General. - 2p.: 30 cm. - 978-0-11-084743-6 *£4.00*

The Health and Social Care Act 2008 (Commencement No.2) Order 2008 No. 2008/2497 (C.106). - Enabling power: Health and Social Care Act 2008, s. 170 (3) (4). Bringing into operation various provisions of the 2008 Act on 01.10.2008; 01.01.2009. - Issued: 25.09.2008. Made: 19.09.2008. Effect: None. Territorial extent & classification: E/WS/NI [parts E or E/W only]. General. - 4p.: 30 cm. - 978-0-11-084265-3 *£4.00*

The Health and Social Care Act 2008 (Commencement No. 4) Order 2008 No. 2008/2994 (C.129). - Enabling power: Health and Social Care Act 2008, s. 170 (3) (4). Bringing into operation various provisions of the 2008 Act on 01.12.2008, 01.04.2009 in accord. with art. 3. - Issued: 21.11.2008. Made: 15.11.2008. Effect: None. Territorial extent & classification: E/WS/NI (parts E or E/W only). General. - 4p.: 30 cm. - 978-0-11-147028-2 *£4.00*

The Health and Social Care Act 2008 (Consequential Amendments and Transitory Provisions) Order 2008 No. 2008/2250. - Enabling power: Health and Social Care Act 2008, s. 167. - Issued: 28.08.2008. Made: 20.08.2008. Laid: 28.08.2008. Coming into force: 01.10.2008. Effect: 1952 c. 52; 1996 c.16; 1998 c.18; 1999 c. 27; 2000 c.10; c. 43; 2003 c. 39; 2004 c. 23; 2006 c. 40, c. 41 modified & S.I. 1999/260, 2277; 2000/89; 2003/3060; 2005/408, 1447; 2415, 2531; 2006/2380, 3335 amended. Territorial extent & classification: E/W/S/NI. General. - 8p.: 30 cm. - 978-0-11-083849-6 *£3.00*

Social care, England

The Care Quality Commission (Membership) Regulations 2008 No. 2008/2252. - Enabling power: Health and Social Care Act 2008, s. 161 (3) (4), sch. 1, para. 3 (3). - Issued: 03.09.2008. Made: 20.08.2008. Laid: 03.09.2008. Coming into force: 01.10.2008. Effect: None. Territorial extent & classification: E. General. - With correction slip dated September 2009. - 8p.: 30 cm. - 978-0-11-083851-9 *£3.00*

The Fostering Services (Amendment) Regulations 2008 No. 2008/640. - Enabling power: Care Standards Act 2000, ss. 22 (1), 118 (5). - Issued: 13.03.2008. Made: 06.03.2008. Laid: 10.03.2008. Coming into force: 31.03.2008. Effect: S.I. 2002/57 amended. Territorial extent & classification: E. General. - 2p.: 30 cm. - 978-0-11-081143-7 *£3.00*

The Health Act 2006 (Commencement No. 4) Order 2008 No. 2008/1147 (C.50). - Enabling power: Health Act 2006, s. 83 (7) (8). Bringing into operation various provisions of the 2006 Act on 22.04.2008; 28.04.2008; 01.05.2008. - Issued: 25.04.2008. Made: 21.04.2008. Effect: None. Territorial extent & classification: E/S [parts E. only]. General. - 4p.: 30 cm. - 978-0-11-081396-7 *£3.00*

The Local Government and Public Involvement in Health Act 2007 (Commencement No. 4) Order 2008 No. 2008/461 (C.17). - Enabling power: Local Government and Public Involvement in Health Act 2007, s. 245 (5) (6). Bringing into operation various provisions of the 2007 Act on 21.02.2008; 10.03.2008; 01.04.2008; 30.06.2008 in accord. with art. 2. - Issued: 28.02.2008. Made: 19.02.2008. Effect: None. Territorial extent & classification: E. General. - 4p.: 30 cm. - 978-0-11-081004-1 *£3.00*

The Local Involvement Networks (Amendment) Regulations 2008 No. 2008/1877. - Enabling power: Local Government and Public Involvement in Health Act 2007, s. 228 (3). - Issued: 18.07.2008. Made: 11.07.2008. Laid: 18.07.2008. Coming into force: 01.09.2008. Effect: S.I. 2008/528 amended. Territorial extent & classification: E. General. - 2p.: 30 cm. - 978-0-11-083292-0 *£3.00*

The Local Involvement Networks Regulations 2008 No. 2008/528. - Enabling power: Health and Social Care (Community Health and Standards) Act 2003, ss. 113 (1), 175 (1) (2) & National Health Service Act 2006, ss. 13 (4), 89 (1), 94 (1), 104 (1), 109 (1), 121 (1), 126 (2), 243 (8) to (10), 244 (2), 272 (7) (8), sch. 12, paras 2, 3 & Local Government and Public Involvement in Health Act 2007, ss. 223, 224 (1), 226 (6), 228 (3) (4) (5), 229 (2), 240 (10). - Issued: 05.03.2008. Made: 25.02.2008. Laid: 05.03.2008. Coming into force: 01.04.2008. Effect: S.I. 1986/975; 2002/3007, 3038, 3048; 2003/1617, 3006; 2004/291, 627, 1768; 2005/641, 3361, 3373; 2006/552 amended. Territorial extent & classification: E. General. - 20p.: 30 cm. - With correction slip dated August 2008. - 978-0-11-081040-9 *£3.50*

Social care, Wales

The Disqualification from Caring for Children (Wales) (Amendment) Regulations 2008 No. 2008/2691 (W.239). - Enabling power: Children Act 1989, ss. 68 (1) (2), 79C (2) (3), 79M (1) (c), 104 (4), sch. 9A, para. 4. - Issued: 24.10.2008. Made: 08.10.2008. Laid before the National Assembly for Wales: 10.10.2008. Coming into force: 03.11.2008. Effect: S.I. 2004/2695 (W.235) revoked. Territorial extent & classification: W. General. - In English and Welsh. Welsh title: Rheoliadau Datgymhwyso rhag Gofalu am Blant (Cymru) (Diwygio) 2008. - 4p.: 30 cm. - 978-0-11-091861-7 *£4.00*

The Suspension of Day Care Providers and Child Minders (Wales) (Amendment) Regulations 2008 No. 2008/2689 (W.238). - Enabling power: Children Act 1989, ss. 79H (1) (2), 104 (4). - Issued: 24.10.2008. Made: 08.10.2008. Laid before the National Assembly for Wales: 10.10.2008. Coming into force: 03.11.2008. Effect: S.I. 2004/3282 amended. Territorial extent & classification: W. General. - In English and Welsh. Welsh title: Rheoliadau Atal Dros Dro Ddarparwyr Gofal Dydd a Gwarchodwyr Plant (Cymru) (Diwygio) 2008. - 4p.: 30 cm. - 978-0-11-091888-4 £4.00

Social security

The Child Benefit (Rates) (Amendment) Regulations 2008 No. 2008/3246. - Enabling power: Social Security Contributions and Benefits Act 1992, ss. 145 (1) (2), 147 (1) & Social Security Contributions and Benefits (Northern Ireland) Act 1992, ss. 141 (1) (2), 173 (1). - Issued: 23.12.2008. Made: 18.12.2008. Coming into force: 18.12.2008. Effect: S.I. 2006/965 amended. Territorial extent & classification: E/W/S/NI. - Supersedes draft S.I. (ISBN 9780111470732) issued 01.12.2008. - 2p.: 30 cm. - 978-0-11-147218-7 £4.00

The Child Benefit Up-rating Order 2008 No. 2008/797. - Enabling power: Social Security Administration Act 1992, ss. 150 (9), 189 (4) & Social Security Administration (Northern Ireland) Act 1992, ss. 132 (1), 165 (4). - Issued: 01.04.2008. Made: 26.03.2008. Coming into force: 07.04.2008. Effect: S.I. 2006/965 amended. Territorial extent & classification: E/W/S/NI. General. - Supersedes draft S.I. (ISBN 9780110809175) issued on 11.02.2008. - 2p.: 30 cm. - 978-0-11-081294-6 £3.00

The Child Maintenance and Other Payments Act 2008 (Commencement) Order 2008 No. 2008/1476 (C. 67). - Enabling power: Child Maintenance and Other Payments Act 2008, s. 62 (3) (4). Bringing into operation various provisions of 2008 Act are 10.06.2008, 14.07.2008 & 01.10.2008 in accord. with art. 2. - Issued: 13.06.2008. Made: 09.06.2008. Effect: -. Territorial extent & classification: E/W/S. General. - 4p.: 30 cm. - 978-0-11-081825-2 £3.00

The Christmas Bonus (Relevant Week) Order 2008 No. 2008/3064. - Enabling power: Social Security Contributions and Benefits Act 1992, s. 150 (4). - Issued: 27.11.2008. Made: 26.11.2008. Laid: 26.11.2008. Coming into force: 27.11.2008. Effect: None. Territorial extent & classification: E/W/S. General. - 2p.: 30 cm. - 978-0-11-147068-8 £4.00

The Christmas Bonus (Specified Sum) Order 2008 No. 2008/3255. - Enabling power: Social Security Contributions and Benefits Act 1992, ss. 148 (3) (b), 175 (3) (b). - Issued: 22.12.2008. Made: 18.12.2008. Coming into force: 19.12.2008 in accord.with art. 1. Effect: None. Territorial extent & classification: E/W/S. General. - Supersedes draft S.I. (ISBN 9780111470695) issued 01.12.2008. - 2p.: 30 cm. - 978-0-11-147217-0 £4.00

The Companies Act 2006 (Consequential Amendments) (Taxes and National Insurance) Order 2008 No. 2008/954. - Enabling power: Companies Act 2006, ss. 1292, 1294, 1296. - Issued: 07.04.2008. Made: 01.04.2008. Coming into force: 06.04.2008. Effect: 14 acts & 11 SIs amended. Territorial extent & classification: E/W/S/NI. General. - Supersedes draft SI (ISBN 9780110810126) issued 28.02.0008. - 12p.: 30 cm. - 978-0-11-081334-9 £3.00

The Discretionary Financial Assistance (Amendment) Regulations 2008 No. 2008/637. - Enabling power: Child Support, Pensions and Social Security Act 2000, s. 69 (1) (2) (7) & Social Security Administration Act 1992, s. 189 (4) to (6). - Issued: 12.03.2008. Made: 06.03.2008. Laid: 12.03.2008. Coming into force: 07.04.2008. Effect: S.I. 2001/1167 amended. Territorial extent & classification: E/W/S. General- 4p.: 30 cm. - 978-0-11-081161-1 £3.00

The Discretionary Housing Payments (Grants) Amendment Order 2008 No. 2008/1167. - Enabling power: Social Security Administration Act 1992, ss. 140B (1), 140C (1) (4), 189 (4) to (6) and Child Support, Pensions and Social Security Act 2000 s. 70. - Issued: 30.04.2008. Made: 24.04.2008. Laid: 30.04.2008. Coming into force: 22.05.2008. Effect: S.I. 2001/2340 amended. Territorial extent & classification: E/W/S. General. - 2p.: 30 cm. - 978-0-11-081407-0 £3.00

The Employment and Support Allowance (Consequential Provisions) (No. 2) Regulations 2008 No. 2008/1554. - Enabling power: Welfare Reform Act 2007, s. 28 (2). - Issued: 19.06.2008. Made: 12.06.2008. Laid: 19.06.2008. Coming into force: 27.07.2008 for Parts 1 and 4 except reg 21; 27.10.2008 for remainder in accord. with reg. 1. Effect: 35 instruments & 2 Acts amended. Territorial extent & classification: E/W/S General. - 56p.: 30 cm. - 978-0-11-081858-0 £9.00

The Employment and Support Allowance (Consequential Provisions) (No. 3) Regulations 2008 No. 2008/1879. - Enabling power: Welfare Reform Act 2007, s. 28 (2). - Issued: 18.07.2008. Made: 16.07.2008. Laid: 18.07.2008. Coming into force: 27.10.2008. Effect: 1996 c.18 & 38 statutory instruments amended. Territorial extent & classification: E/W/S General. - With correction slip dated September 2009. - 20p.: 30 cm. - 978-0-11-083311-8 £3.50

The Employment and Support Allowance (Consequential Provisions) Regulations 2008 No. 2008/1082. - Enabling power: Social Security Contributions and Benefits Act 1992, ss. 130 (2) to (4), 135 (1), 136 (3), 137 (1) (2) (d) (i), 175 (1) (2) (3) (4) & Social Security Administration Act 1992, ss. 5 (1) (a) (i) (p), 6 (1) (a) (k), 75 (4), 189 (1) (3) (4) to (6), 191 & Social Security Act 1998, ss. 34 (1), 79 (1) (3) (4) (6), 84 & Child Support, Pensions and Social Security Act 2000, sch. 7, paras 4 (6), 20 (1) (b) (3), 23 (1) & Welfare Reform Act 2007, ss. 32 (1), 34 (6). - Issued: 18.04.2008. Made: 14.04.2008. Laid: 18.04.2008. Coming into force: 27.10.2008. Effect: S.I. 2001/1002; 2006/213, 214, 215, 216, 217 amended. Territorial extent & classification: E/W/S. General. - 28p.: 30 cm. - 978-0-11-081375-2 £4.50

The Employment and Support Allowance (Miscellaneous Amendments) Regulations 2008 No. 2008/2428. - Enabling power: Social Security Contributions and Benefits Act 1992, ss. 135 (1), 136 (3), 137 (2) (h), 175 (1) (4) & Child Support, Pensions and Social Security Act 2000, sch. 7, paras 4 (6), 20 (1) (b) (3), 23 (1) & Welfare Reform Act 2007, ss. 2 (1), 3 (2) (3), 4 (2), 5 (3), 8 (1) (2) (a) (b), 9 (1) (2) (a) (b), 17 (1) (2) (3) (b), 18 (4), 24 (1), 25 (1) (2) (3) (5) (a), 28 (2), sch. 1, paras 1 (4), 6, sch. 2, paras 1 (a), 2, 10. - Issued: 17.09.2008. Made: 08.09.2008. Laid: 17.08.2008. Coming into force: 27.10.2008. Effect: 1992 c. 5; S.I. 1983/1598; 1988/664; 2008/794, 795, 1082, 1554 amended. Territorial extent & classification: E/W/S General. - 20p.: 30 cm. - 978-0-11-084204-2 £5.00

The Employment and Support Allowance Regulations 2008 No. 2008/794. - Enabling power: Welfare Reform Act 2007, ss. 2 (1) (a) (c) (4) (a) (c), 3 (1) (c) (2) (b) (d) (3), 4 (2) (a) (3) (6) (a) (c), 5 (2) (3), 8 (1) to (3) (4) (a) (b) (5) (6), 9 (1) to (3) (4) (a) (b), 11 (1) (2) (a) to (g) (3) to (5) (6) (a) (7) (c), 12 (1) (2) (a) to (h) (3) to (7), 14 (1) (2) (a) (b), 16 (2) (a) (4), 17, 18 (1) (2) (4), 20 (2) to (7), 22, 23 (1) (3), 24 (1) (2) (b) (3), 25 (1) to (5), 26 (2), sch. 1, paras 1 (4), 3 (2), 4 (1) (a) (c) (3) (4), 6 (1) (b) (2) to (5) (7) (8), sch. 2, paras 1 to 7, 8 (1), 9, 10, 12, 14 & Social Security Administration Act 1992, s. 5 (1) & Social Security Act 1998, s. 21 (1) (a). - Issued: 01.04.2008. Made: 25.03.2008. Laid: 27.03.2008. Coming into force: In accord. with reg. 1. Effect: 2007 c.5 modified. Territorial extent & classification: E/W/S General. - With correction slip dated July 2008. - 184p.: 30 cm. - 978-0-11-081287-8 £26.00

The Employment and Support Allowance (Transitional Provisions) (Amendment) Regulations 2008 No. 2008/2783. - Enabling power: Welfare Reform Act 2007, ss. 25 (2) (b) (c), 29, sch. 4, paras 2 (a), 3 (b). - Issued: 08.01.2009. Made: 21.10.2008. Laid: 23.10.2008. Coming into force: 26.10.2008. Effect: S.I. 2008/795 amended. Territorial extent & classification: E/W/S General. - This statutory instrument has been made in consequence of a defect in SI 2008/795 (ISBN 9780110812847) and is being issued free of charge to all known recipients of that statutory instrument. Supersedes S.I. of same no. & title (ISBN 9780110847306). - 2p.: 30 cm. - 978-0-11-147244-6 £4.00

The Employment and Support Allowance (Transitional Provisions) (Amendment) Regulations 2008 No. 2008/2783. - Enabling power: Welfare Reform Act 2007, ss. 25 (2) (b) (c), 29, sch. 4, paras 2 (a), 3 (b). - Issued: 27.10.2008. Made: 21.10.2008. Laid: 23.10.2008. Coming into force: 26.10.2008. Effect: S.I. 2008/795 amended. Territorial extent & classification: E/W/S General. - Superseded by S.I. of same no. and title (ISBN 9780111472446). - 2p.: 30 cm. - 978-0-11-084730-6 £4.00

The Employment and Support Allowance (Transitional Provisions) Regulations 2008 No. 2008/795. - Enabling power: Welfare Reform Act 2007, ss. 25 (2) (b) (c), 29, sch. 4, paras 1 (1), 2, 3 (b) (c) (d). - Issued: 01.04.2008. Made: 25.03.2008. Laid: 27.03.2008. Coming into force: 27.07.2008 for regs 2, 3, 4 & 27.10.2008 for reg. 5. Effect: None. Territorial extent & classification: E/W/S General. - This SI has been corrected by SI 2008/2783 (ISBN 9780111472446) which is being issued free of charge to all known recipients of SI 2008/795. - 4p.: 30 cm. - 978-0-11-081284-7 £3.00

The Employment and Support Allowance (Up-rating Modification) (Transitional) Regulations 2008 No. 2008/3270. - Enabling power: Welfare Reform Act 2007, ss. 24 (1), 25 (2) (c) (3) (a) (5), sch. 4, para. 10. - Issued: 29.12.2008. Made: 18.12.2008. Laid: 29.12.2008. Coming into force: 20.01.2009. Effect: 1992 c. 5 modified. Territorial extent & classification: E/W/S General. - 4p.: 30 cm. - 978-0-11-147232-3 £4.00

The Guardian's Allowance Up-rating Order 2008 No. 2008/798. - Enabling power: Social Security Administration Act 1992, ss. 150 (9), 189 (4). - Issued: 01.04.2008. Made: 26.03.2008. Coming into force: 07.04.2008. Effect: 1992 c.4 amended. Territorial extent & classification: E/W/S. General. - Supersedes draft S.I. (ISBN 9780110809090) issued on 08.02.2008. - 2p.: 30 cm. - 978-0-11-081293-9 £3.00

The Guardian's Allowance Up-rating Regulations 2008 No. 2008/840. - Enabling power: Social Security Contributions and Benefits Act 1992, ss. 113 (1), 122 (1), 175 (3) (4) & Social Security Administration Act 1992, ss. 155 (3), 189 (4) (5), 191 & Social Security Contributions and Benefits (Northern Ireland) Act 1992, ss. 113 (1), 121 (1), 171 (3) (4) & Social Security Administration (Northern Ireland) Act 1992, ss. 135 (3), 165 (4) (5), 167 (1). - Issued: 01.04.2008. Made: 26.03.2008. Laid: 27.03.2008. Coming into force: 07.04.2008. Effect: S.I. 2007/1071 superseded. Territorial extent & classification: E/W/S/NI. General. - 4p.: 30 cm. - 978-0-11-081298-4 £3.00

The Health and Social Care Act 2008 (Commencement No. 5) Order 2008 No. 2008/3137 (C.136). - Enabling power: Health and Social Care Act 2008, ss. 170 (3) (4), 171 (5). Bringing into operation various provisions of the 2008 Act on 01.01.2009 in accord. with art. 2. - Issued: 15.12.2008. Made: 09.12.2008. Effect: None. Territorial extent & classification: E/WS/NI. General. - 4p.: 30 cm. - 978-0-11-147140-1 £4.00

The Health and Social Care Act 2008 (Commencement No. 7) Order 2008 No. 2008/3244 (C.148). - Enabling power: Health and Social Care Act 2008, s. 170 (3) (4). Bringing into operation various provisions of the 2008 Act on 01.01.2009 in accord. with arts 2 & 3. - Issued: 23.12.2008. Made: 17.12.2008. Effect: None. Territorial extent & classification: E/W/S/NI. General. - 4p.: 30 cm. - 978-0-11-147209-5 £4.00

The Health in Pregnancy Grant (Entitlement and Amount) Regulations 2008 No. 2008/3108. - Enabling power: Social Security Contributions and Benefits Act 1992, ss. 140A (1) (2) (4) to (6), 140B (1), 175 & Social Security Contributions and Benefits (Northern Ireland) Act 1992, ss. 136A (1) (2) (4) to (6), 136B (1), 171 & Immigration and Asylum Act 1999, ss. 115 (3) (5). - Issued: 12.12.2008. Made: 09.12.2008. Laid:10.12.2008. Coming into force: 01.01.2009. Effect: S.I. 2000/636 amended. Territorial extent & classification: E/W/S/NI. General. - 4p.: 30 cm. - 978-0-11-147125-8 *£4.00*

The Housing Benefit and Council Tax Benefit (Amendment) (No. 2) Regulations 2008 No. 2008/2824. - Enabling power: Social Security Contributions and Benefits Act 1992, ss. 123 (1) (d) (e), 130A (3) (4), 137 (1), 175 (1) to (3) & Social Security Administration Act 1992, ss. 5 (1) (a), 6 (1) (a), 75 (3) (4), 76 (1) to (3), 134 (1A), 189 (1) (3) (4) (6), 191. - Issued: 06.11.2008. Made: 29.10.2008. Laid: 06.11.2008. Coming into force: 27.11.2008 for regs 8 9; 06.04.2009 for remainder. Effect: S.I. 2006/213, 214, 215, 216 amended. Territorial extent & classification: E/W/S. General. - 12p.: 30 cm. - 978-0-11-084775-7 *£5.00*

The Housing Benefit and Council Tax Benefit (Amendment) (No. 3) Regulations 2008 No. 2008/2987. - Enabling power: Social Security Administration Act 1992, ss. 5 (1) (a) (h) (hh), 6 (1) (a) (h) (hh), 189 (1) (4), 191. - Issued: 20.11.2008. Made: 17.11.2008. Laid: 20.11.2008. Coming into force: 22.12.2008. Effect: S.I. 2006/213, 214, 215, 216 amended. Territorial extent & classification: E/W/S. General. - 8p.: 30 cm. - 978-0-11-147013-8 *£5.00*

The Housing Benefit and Council Tax Benefit (Amendment) Regulations 2008 No. 2008/2299. - Enabling power: Social Security Administration Act 1992, ss. 5 (1) (a) (h), 6 (1) (a) (h), 113, 122C (2), 122E (3), 189 (1) (4) to (6), 191. - Issued: 03.09.2008. Made: 27.08.2008. Laid: 03.09.2008. Coming into force: 01.10.2008. Effect: S.I. 2006/213, 214, 215, 216 amended. Territorial extent & classification: E/W/S. General. - With correction slip dated July 2009. - 16p.: 30 cm. - 978-0-11-083868-7 *£5.50*

The Housing Benefit and Council Tax Benefit (Extended Payments) Amendment Regulations 2008 No. 2008/959. - Enabling power: Social Security Contributions and Benefits Act 1992, s. 134 (2) & Social Security Administration Act 1992, ss. 5 (1), 6 (1), 122E (3), 128A & Welfare Reform Act 2007, ss. 32, 33, 34 (6). - Issued: 09.04.2008. Made: 01.04.2008. Laid: 09.04.2008. Coming into force: 06.10.2008. Effect: S.I. 2006/213, 214, 215, 216 amended. Territorial extent & classification: E/W/S. General. - 32p.: 30 cm. - 978-0-11-081337-0 *£5.50*

The Housing Benefit (Local Housing Allowance, Information Sharing and Miscellaneous) Amendment Regulations 2008 No. 2008/586. - Enabling power: Social Security Contributions and Benefits Act 1992, ss. 123 (1) (d), 130A (2) to (4), 137 (1), 175 (1) (3) (4) (6) & Social Security Administration Act 1992, ss. 5 (2A) to (2C), 75 (3) (b), 189 (1) (3) to (6), 191 & Child Support, Pensions and Social Security Act 2000, sch. 7, para. 4 (4A) (6). - Issued: 10.03.2008. Made: 03.03.2008. Laid: 10.03.2008. Coming into force: 07.04.2008. Effect: S.I. 2006/213, 214; 2007/2868, 2869, 2870 amended. Territorial extent & classification: E/W/S. General. - 8p.: 30 cm. - 978-0-11-081106-2 *£3.00*

The Income-related Benefits (Subsidy to Authorities) Amendment (No.3) Order 2008 No. 2008/1649. - Enabling power: Social Security Administration Act 1992, ss. 140B, 140C (1) (4), 140F (2), 189 (1) (4) (7). - Issued: 30.06.2008. Made: 23.06.2008. Laid: 30.06.2008. Coming into force: 25.07.2008. Effect: S.I. 1998/562 amended. Territorial extent & classification: E/W/S. General. - 12p.: 30 cm. - 978-0-11-081907-5 *£3.00*

The Income-related Benefits (Subsidy to Authorities) Amendment Order 2008 No. 2008/196. - Enabling power: Social Security Administration Act 1992, ss. 140B, 140C (1) (4), 140F (2), 189 (1) (4) (5) (7). - Issued: 06.02.2008. Made: 28.01.2008. Laid: 06.02.2008. Coming into force: 28.02.2008. Effect: S.I. 1998/562 amended. Territorial extent & classification: E/W/S. General. - 12p.: 30 cm. - 978-0-11-080886-4 *£3.00*

The Jobseeker's Allowance (Joint Claims) Amendment Regulations 2008 No. 2008/13. - Enabling power: Jobseekers Act 1995, ss. 1 (2C) (4) (b), 35 (1), 36 (2) (4), sch.1, para. 8A. - Issued: 14.01.2008. Made: 08.01.2008. Laid: 14.01.2008. Coming into force: 25.02.2008. Effect: S.I. 1996/207 amended. Territorial extent & classification: E/W/S. General. - 2p.: 30 cm. - 978-0-11-080822-2 *£3.00*

The Mesothelioma Lump Sum Payments (Claims and Reconsiderations) (Amendment) Regulations 2008 No. 2008/2706. - Enabling power: Child Maintenance and Other Payments Act 2008, s. 50 (4). - Issued: 20.10.2008. Made: 13.10.2008. Laid: 15.10.2008. Coming into force: 03.11.2008. Effect: S.I. 2008/1595 amended. Territorial extent & classification: E/W/S. General. - 2p.: 30 cm. - 978-0-11-084646-0 *£4.00*

The Mesothelioma Lump Sum Payments (Claims and Reconsiderations) Regulations 2008 No. 2008/1595. - Enabling power: Child Maintenance and Other Payments Act 2008, ss. 48 (1) to (3), 49 (2), 50 (4), 53 (2). - Issued: 25.06.2008. Made: 18.06.2008. Laid: 25.06.2008. Coming into force: 01.10.2008. Effect: None. Territorial extent & classification: E/W/S. General. - 4p.: 30 cm. - 978-0-11-081888-7 *£3.00*

The Mesothelioma Lump Sum Payments (Conditions and Amounts) Regulations 2008 No. 2008/1963. - Enabling power: Pneumoconiosis etc. (Workers' Compensation) Act 1979, s. 1 (1) & Child Maintenance and Other Payments Act 2008, ss. 46 (3), 47. - Issued: 25.07.2008. Made: 17.07.2008. Coming into force: 01.10.2008. Effect: S.I. 1988/668 amended. Territorial extent & classification: E/W/S. General. - Supersedes draft S.I. (ISBN 9780110818603) issued 26.06.2008. - 8p.: 30 cm. - 978-0-11-083548-8 £3.00

The National Insurance Contributions (Application of Part 7 of the Finance Act 2004) (Amendment) Regulations 2008 No. 2008/2678. - Enabling power: Social Security Administration Act 1992, ss. 132A (1), 189 (4) (5). - Issued: 14.10.2008. Made: 09.10.2008. Laid: 09.10.2008. Coming into force: 01.11.2008. Effect: S.I. 2007/785 amended. Territorial extent & classification: E/W/S/NI. General. - 12p.: 30 cm. - 978-0-11-084549-4 £5.00

The Pneumoconiosis etc. (Workers' Compensation) (Payment of Claims) (Amendment) Regulations 2008 No. 2008/650. - Enabling power: Pneumoconiosis etc. (Workers' Compensation) Act 1979, ss. 1 (1) (2) (4), 7. - Issued: 16.04.2008. Made: 05.03.2008. Coming into force: 01.04.2008. Effect: S.I. 1988/668 amended. Territorial extent & classification: E/W/S. General. - Supersedes draft S.I. (ISBN 9780110808109) issued 14.01.2008. This is a corrected reprint which replaces that published on 13.03.2008 (same ISBN) and is being issued free of charge to all known recipients of the original version. - 12p.: 30 cm. - 978-0-11-081196-3 £3.00

The Rates of Child Benefit (Commencement) Order 2008 No. 2008/3247. - Enabling power: Social Security Contributions and Benefits Act 1992, s. 145 (3) & Social Security Contributions and Benefits (Northern Ireland) Act 1992, s. 141 (3). Bringing into force the different rates of child benefit prescribed in the Child Benefit (Rates) (Amendment) Regulations 2008 (S.I. 2008/3246) on 05.01.2009. - Issued: 23.12.2008. Made: 18.12.2008. Effect: None. Territorial extent & classification: E/W/S/NI. General. - Supersedes draft S.I. (ISBN 9780111470732) issued 01.12.2008. - 2p.: 30 cm. - 978-0-11-147220-0 £4.00

The Rent Officers (Housing Benefit Functions) Amendment Order 2008 No. 2008/587. - Enabling power: Housing Act 1996, s. 122 (1) (6). - Issued: 10.03.2008. Made: 28.02.2008. Laid: 10.03.2008. Coming into force: 07.04.2008. Effect: S.I. 2007/2871 amended. Territorial extent & classification: E/W/S. General. - 2p.: 30 cm. - 978-0-11-081107-9 £3.00

The Social Fund (Applications and Miscellaneous Provisions) Regulations 2008 No. 2008/2265. - Enabling power: Social Security Administration Act 1992, ss. 12, 189 (1) (4) (5) (6), 191. - Issued: 29.08.2008. Made: 21.08.2008. Laid: 29.08.2008. Coming into force: 01.10.2008. Effect: S.I. 1988/524; 1990/1788; 2002/2323 revoked. Territorial extent & classification: E/W/S. General. - With correction slip dated September 2009. - 4p.: 30 cm. - 978-0-11-083860-1 £3.00

The Social Fund Cold Weather Payments (General) Amendment Regulations 2008 No. 2008/2569. - Enabling power: Social Security Contributions and Benefits Act 1992, ss. 138 (2) (4), 175 (1) (3) (4). - Issued: 06.10.2008. Made: 02.10.2008. Laid: 06.10.2008. Coming into force: 27.10.2008, 01.11.2008 in accord. with reg. 1. Effect: S.I. 1988/1724 amended. Territorial extent & classification: E/W/S. General. - 12p.: 30 cm. - 978-0-11-084362-9 £5.00

The Social Fund Winter Fuel Payment (Temporary Increase) Regulations 2008 No. 2008/1778. - Enabling power: Social Security Contributions and Benefits Act 1992, ss. 138 (2) (4), 175 (1) (3) (4). - Issued: 10.07.2008. Made: 03.07.2008. Laid: 10.07.2008. Coming into force: 15.09.2008. Effect: S.I. 2000/729 modified. Territorial extent & classification: E/W/S. General. - Revoked by S.I. 2009/1489 (ISBN 9780111480779). - 2p.: 30 cm. - 978-0-11-081991-4 £3.00

The Social Security Benefits Up-rating Regulations 2008 No. 2008/667. - Enabling power: Social Security Contributions and Benefits Act 1992, ss. 90, 113 (1), 122 (1), 175 (1) (3) & Social Security Administration Act 1992, ss. 55 (1) (p), 155 (3), 189 (1) (4), 191. - Issued: 13.03.2008. Made: 09.03.2008. Laid: 13.03.2008. Coming into force: 07.04.2008. Effect: S.I. 1977/343; 1987/1968 amended & S.I. 2007/775 revoked. Territorial extent & classification: E/W/S. General. - Revoked by S.I. 2009/607 (ISBN 9780111476192). - 4p.: 30 cm. - 978-0-11-081178-9 £3.00

The Social Security (Child Benefit Disregard) Regulations 2008 No. 2008/3140. - Enabling power: Social Security Contributions and Benefits Act 1992, ss. 123 (1) (a) (d) (e), 136 (3) (5) (b), 137 (1), 175 (1) (3) (4) and Jobseekers Act 1995, ss. 12 (1) (4) (b), 35 (1), 36 (1) (2) (4). - Issued: 11.12.2008. Made: 05.12.2008. Laid: 11.12.2008. Coming into force: 05.01.2009. Effect: S.I. 1987/1967; 1996/207; 2006/213, 215 amended. Territorial extent & classification: E/W/S. General. - 4p.: 30 cm. - 978-0-11-147130-2 £4.00

The Social Security (Child Maintenance Amendments) Regulations 2008 No. 2008/2111. - Enabling power: Social Security Contributions and Benefits Act 1992, ss. 123 (1) (a), 136 (3) (5) (b), 137 (1), 175 (1) (2) (4) & Jobseekers Act 1995, ss. 12 (2) (4) (b), 35 (1), 36 (1) (2) (4). - Issued: 08.08.2008. Made: 05.08.2008. Laid: 08.08.2008. Coming into force: In accord. with reg. 1. Effect: S.I. 1987/1967; 1996/207; 2003/455 amended. Territorial extent & classification: E/W/S. General. - 8p.: 30 cm. - 978-0-11-083718-5 £3.00

The Social Security (Claims and Payments) Amendment Regulations 2008 No. 2008/441. - Enabling power: Social Security Administration Act 1992, ss. 1 (1), 189 (1) (3) (4), 191. - Issued: 25.02.2008. Made: 21.02.2008. Laid: 25.02.2008. Coming into force: 17.03.2008. Effect: S.I. 1987/1968 amended. Territorial extent & classification: E/W/S. General. - 2p.: 30 cm. - 978-0-11-080997-7 £3.00

The Social Security (Contributions) (Amendment No. 2) Regulations 2008 No. 2008/607. - Enabling power: Social Security Contributions and Benefits Act 1992, ss. 3 (2) (3), 12 (6), 13 (7), 175 (1A) (5) & Social Security Contributions and Benefits (Northern Ireland) Act 1992, ss. 3 (2) (3), 12 (6), 13 (7), 171 (5). - Issued: 13.03.2008. Made: 06.03.2008. Laid: 06.03.2008. Coming into force: 01.04.2008; 06.04.2008 in accord. with reg. 1. Effect: S.I. 2001/1004 amended. Territorial extent & classification: E/W/S/NI. General. - 4p.: 30 cm. - 978-0-11-081135-2 £3.00

The Social Security (Contributions) (Amendment No. 3) Regulations 2008 No. 2008/636. - Enabling power: Social Security Contributions and Benefits Act 1992, s. 175 (3), sch. 1, paras 6, 7 & Social Security Contributions and Benefits (Northern Ireland) Act 1992, s. 171 (3), sch. 1, paras 6, 7. - Issued: 13.03.2008. Made: 07.03.2008. Laid: 07.03.2008. Coming into force: 01.04.2008; 06.04.2008 in accord. with reg. 1. Effect: S.I. 2001/1004 amended. Territorial extent & classification: E/W/S/NI. General. - With 2 correction slips dated June & September 2008. - 8p.: 30 cm. - 978-0-11-081139-0 £3.00

The Social Security (Contributions) (Amendment No. 4) Regulations 2008 No. 2008/1431. - Enabling power: Social Security Contributions and Benefits Act 1992, ss. 3 (2) (3), 175 (1A) (4) (5). - Issued: 10.06.2008. Made: 05.06.2008. Laid: 06.06.2008. Coming into force: 01.07.2008. Effect: S.I. 2001/1004 amended. Territorial extent & classification: E/W/S. General. - 2p.: 30 cm. - 978-0-11-081788-0 £3.00

The Social Security (Contributions) (Amendment No. 5) Regulations 2008 No. 2008/2624. - Enabling power: Social Security Contributions and Benefits Act 1992, ss. 3 (2) (3), 175 (1A) (4) (5). - Issued: 08.10.2008. Made: 06.10.2008. Laid: 06.10.2008. Coming into force: 27.10.2008. Effect: S.I. 2001/1004 amended. Territorial extent & classification: E/W/S. General. - 2p.: 30 cm. - 978-0-11-084390-2 £4.00

The Social Security (Contributions) (Amendment No.6) Regulations 2008 No. 2008/3099. - Enabling power: Social Security Contributions and Benefits Act 1992, ss. 12 (6), 13 (7) & Social Security Contributions and Benefits (Northern Ireland) Act 1992, ss. 12 (6), 13 (7). - Issued: 09.12.2008. Made: 04.12.2008. Laid: 04.12.2008. Coming into force: 27.12.2008. Effect: S.I. 2001/1004 amended. Territorial extent & classification: E/W/S/NI. General. - 2p.: 30 cm. - 978-0-11-147099-2 £4.00

The Social Security (Contributions) (Amendment) Regulations 2008 No. 2008/133. - Enabling power: Social Security Contributions and Benefits Act 1992, ss. 5, 122 (1), 175 (3) (4) & Social Security Contributions and Benefits (Northern Ireland) Act 1992, ss. 5, 121 (1), 171 (3) (4) (10). - Issued: 28.01.2008. Made: 22.01.2008. Laid: 23.01.2008. Coming into force: 06.04.2008. Effect: S.I. 2001/1004 amended. Territorial extent & classification: E/W/S/NI. General. - 2p.: 30 cm. - 978-0-11-080867-3 £3.00

The Social Security (Contributions) (Re-rating) Consequential Amendment Regulations 2008 No. 2008/703. - Enabling power: Social Security Contributions and Benefits Act 1992, ss. 117 (1), 175 (3) and Social Security Contributions and Benefits (Northern Ireland) Act 1992, ss. 117 (1), 171 (3). - Issued: 13.03.2008. Made: 12.03.2008. Laid: 13.03.2008. Coming into force: 06.04.2008. Effect: S.I. 2001/1004 amended. Territorial extent & classification: E/W/S/NI. General. - 2p.: 30 cm. - 978-0-11-081211-3 £3.00

The Social Security (Contributions) (Re-rating) Order 2008 No. 2008/579. - Enabling power: Social Security Administration Act 1992, ss. 141 (4) (5), 142 (2) (3) & Social Security Administration (Northern Ireland) Act 1992, ss. 129, 165 (11A). - Issued: 07.03.2008. Made: 04.03.2008. Coming into force: 06.04.2008. Effect: 1992 c. 4, c. 7 amended. Territorial extent & classification: E/W/S/NI. General. - 4p.: 30 cm. - 978-0-11-081098-0 £3.00

The Social Security (Housing Costs Special Arrangements) (Amendment and Modification) Regulations 2008 No. 2008/3195. - Enabling power: Social Security Contributions and Benefits Act 1992, ss. 123 (1) (a), 135 (1), 137 (1), 175 (1) (3) (4) & Jobseekers Act 1995, ss. 4 (5), 35 (1), 36 (2) (4) & State Pension Credit Act 2002, ss. 2 (3) (b), 17 (1), 19 (1) & Welfare Reform Act 2007, ss. 4 (2) (a) (3), 24 (1), 25 (2) (3) (5). - Issued: 19.12.2008. Made: 15.12.2008. Laid: 15.12.2008. Coming into force: 05.01.2009 in accord. with reg. 1 (2) (3). Effect: S.I. 1987/1967; 1996/207; 2002/1792; 2008/794 amended. Territorial extent & classification: E/W/S. General. - A defect in this SI has been corrected by SI 2009/3257 (ISBN 9780111489529) which is being issued free of charge to all known recipients of SI 2009/3257. - 12p.: 30 cm. - 978-0-11-147184-5 £5.00

The Social Security (Incapacity Benefit Work-focused Interviews) Regulations 2008 No. 2008/2928. - Enabling power: Social Security Administration Act 1992, ss. 2A (1) (3) to (6) (8), 2B (2) (6) (7), 189 (4) to (6) (7A), 191. - Issued: 14.11.2008. Made: 10.11.2008. Laid: 14.11.2008. Coming into force: 15.12.2008. Effect: S.I. 2000/1926; 2002/1703 amended & S.I. 2003/2439 revoked with savings & S.I. 2005/3, 2604; 2006/536, 3088 revoked. Territorial extent & classification: E/W/S. General- 12p.: 30 cm. - 978-0-11-084997-3 £5.00

The Social Security (Industrial Injuries) (Dependency) (Permitted Earnings Limits) Order 2008 No. 2008/699. - Enabling power: Social Security Contributions and Benefits Act 1992, sch. 7, para. 4 (5). - Issued: 17.03.2008. Made: 11.03.2008. Laid: 17.03.2008. Coming into force: 09.04.2008. Effect: 1992 c. 4 amended. Territorial extent & classification: E/W/S. General. - 2p.: 30 cm. - 978-0-11-081193-2 £3.00

The Social Security (Industrial Injuries) (Prescribed Diseases) Amendment (No. 2) Regulations 2008 No. 2008/1552. - Enabling power: Social Security Contributions and Benefits Act 1992, ss. 108 (2), 122 (1), 175 (1) to (4). - Issued: 18.06.2008. Made: 12.06.2008. Laid: 18.06.2008. Coming into force: 21.07.2008. Effect: S.I. 1985/967 amended. Territorial extent & classification: E/W/S. General. - 2p.: 30 cm. - 978-0-11-081856-6 £3.00

The Social Security (Industrial Injuries) (Prescribed Diseases) Amendment Regulations 2008 No. 2008/14. - Enabling power: Social Security Contributions and Benefits Act 1992, ss. 108 (2), 122 (1), 175 (1) to (3). - Issued: 14.01.2008. Made: 07.01.2008. Laid: 14.01.2008. Coming into force: 07.04.2008. Effect: S.I. 1985/967 amended. Territorial extent & classification: E/W/S. General. - 2p.: 30 cm. - 978-0-11-080826-0 £3.00

The Social Security (Jobcentre Plus Interviews for Partners) Amendment Regulations 2008 No. 2008/759. - Enabling power: Social Security Administration Act 1992, ss. 2AA (1) (4) to (7), 189 (1) (4) to (6), 191. - Issued: 25.03.2008. Made: 18.03.2008. Laid: 25.03.2008. Coming into force: 28.04.2008. Effect: S.I. 2003/1886 amended. Territorial extent & classification: E/W/S. General. - 4p.: 30 cm. - 978-0-11-081265-6 £3.00

The Social Security (Local Authority Investigations and Prosecutions) Regulations 2008 No. 2008/463. - Enabling power: Social Security Administration Act 1992, ss. 110A (1B) (1C) (a), 116A (2) (a), 189 (4) (5), 191. - Issued: 27.02.2008. Made: 20.02.2008. Laid: 27.02.2008. Coming into force: 07.04.2008. Effect: None. Territorial extent & classification: E/W/S. General. - 4p.: 30 cm. - 978-0-11-081010-2 £3.00

The Social Security (Lone Parents and Miscellaneous Amendments) Regulations 2008 No. 2008/3051. - Enabling power: Social Security Administration Act 1992, ss. 2A, 2B, 189 (1) (4) to (6) (7A), 191 & Social Security Contributions and Benefits Act 1992, ss. 123 (1) (a), 124 (1) (e), 137 (1), 175 (1) to (4) & Jobseekers Act 1995, ss. 6 (2) (4), 7 (4), 8 (2) (d) (ii), 19 (8) (a), 36 (2) (4), sch. 1, paras 8, 10 (1) (a) (2) (a) & Welfare Reform Act 2007, ss. 2 (4) (a), 4 (6) (a), 24 (1). - Issued: 27.11.2008. Made: 23.11.2008. Coming into force: In accord. with reg. 1 (2). Effect: S.I. 1987/1967; 1996/207; 2000/1926; 2002/1703; 2008/794 amended. Territorial extent & classification: E/W/S. General. - Supersedes draft S.I. (ISBN 9780110843285) issued 06.10.2008. - For approval by resolution of each House of Parliament. - 20p.: 30 cm. - 978-0-11-147063-3 £5.00

The Social Security (Miscellaneous Amendments) (No.2) Regulations 2008 No. 2008/1042. - Enabling power: Social Security Contributions and Benefits Act 1992, ss. 123 (1) (d) (e), 135 (1), 136 (3) to (5), 136A (3), 137 (1) (2) (f) (h) (i), 175 (1) (3) (4) & Social Security Administration Act 1992, ss. 5 (1) (h) (j), 6 (1) (h) (k), 75 (1) (2) (4), 134, 189 (1) (3) to (6), 191 & Social Security Act 1998, ss. 10 (6), 34(1) (2), 79 (1) (3) (4), 84. - Issued: 11.04.2008. Made: 07.04.2008. Laid: 11.04.2008. Coming into force: 19.05.2008 except for regs 3 (12) (h), 5 (12) (d); 27.10.2008 for regs 3 (12) (h), 5 (12) (d), in accord. with reg. 1. Effect: S.I. 1999/991; 2006/213, 214, 215, 216, 217 amended. Territorial extent & classification: E/W/S. General. - 12p.: 30 cm. - 978-0-11-081354-7 £3.00

The Social Security (Miscellaneous Amendments) (No. 3) Regulations 2008 No. 2008/2365. - Enabling power: Social Security Contributions and Benefits Act 1992, ss. 30C (3), 30DD (4), 30E (1), 171D (2), 171(G) (2), 175 (1), sch. 7, para. 2 (3) & Social Security Administration Act 1992, s. 189 (4) & Social Security (Recovery of Benefits) Act 1997, ss. 1A (3), 30 (4), 57 (2) & Child Maintenance and Other Payments Act 2008, ss. 47 (1) (a) (2) (a) (3) (e), 53. - Issued: 10.09.2008. Made: 04.09.2008. Laid: 10.09.2008. Coming into force: 01.10.2008. Effect: S.I. 1982/1408; 1994/2946; 1995/311; 2008/1963, 1596 amended. Territorial extent & classification: E/W/S. General. - 4p.: 30 cm. - 978-0-11-084113-7 £4.00

The Social Security (Miscellaneous Amendments) (No. 4) Regulations 2008 No. 2008/2424. - Enabling power: Social Security Administration Act 1992, ss. 5 (1) (a), 6 (1) (a), 189 (1) (3) (4) (5), 191 & Social Security Contributions and Benefits Act 1992, ss. 175 (4) & State Pension Credit Act 2002, ss. 1 (5), 17, 19. - Issued: 15.09.2008. Made: 10.09.2008. Laid: 15.09.2008. Coming into force: 06.10.2008. Effect: S.I. 1987/1968; 2002/1792; 2006/213, 214, 215, 216 amended. Territorial extent & classification: E/W/S. General. - 4p.: 30 cm. - 978-0-11-084208-0 £4.00

The Social Security (Miscellaneous Amendments) (No. 5) Regulations 2008 No. 2008/2667. - Enabling power: Social Security Administration Act 1992, ss. 1 (1), 5 (1) (a) (b) (i), 189 (1) (3) (4) (6), 191 & Social Security Act 1998, ss. 9 (1), 10 (3) (6), 79 (1) (3) (4), 84 & Child Support, Pensions and Social Security Act 2000, sch. 7, paras 4 (6), 12, 13 (1) (2) (c) (3) (c), 20 (1) (b). - Issued: 10.10.2008. Made: 07.10.2008. Laid: 09.10.2008. Coming into force: 30.10.2008. Effect: S.I. 1987/1968; 1999/991; 2001/1002; S.I. 2006/213, 214 amended. Territorial extent & classification: E/W/S. General. - 8p.: 30 cm. - 978-0-11-084500-5 £5.00

The Social Security (Miscellaneous Amendments) (No. 6) Regulations 2008 No. 2008/2767. - Enabling power: Social Security Contributions and Benefits Act 1992, ss. 123 (1) (a) (d) (e), 124 (1) (e), 130 (4), 130A (2), 131 (3) (b) (7) (b) (10), 135 (1), 136 (3) (4) (5) (a) to (c), 136A (3), 137 (1) (2) (b) (h), 175 (1) to (4) & Social Security Administration Act 1992, ss. 5 (1) (h) (p), 6 (1) (h) (k), 189 (1) (3) to (5) & Jobseekers Act 1995, ss. 4 (5), 12 (1) to (3) (4) (a) to (c), 35 (1), 36 (1) (2) (4), sch. 1, paras 1 (2) (a) (3) (b), 11 (2) & State Pension Credit Act 2002, ss. 1 (5) (a), 2 (3) (b) (6), 15 (3) (6) (b), 17 (1), 19 (1). - Issued: 24.10.2008. Made: 17.10.2008. Laid: 24.10.2008. Coming into force: 17.11.2008 except for regs 7 (7), 8 (7); 06.04.2009 for regs 7 (7), 8 (7), in accord. with reg. 1. Effect: S.I. 1987/1967, 1968; 1996/207; 2002/1792; 2006/213, 214, 215, 216 amended. Territorial extent & classification: E/W/S. General. - 16p.: 30 cm. - 978-0-11-084708-5 £5.00

The Social Security (Miscellaneous Amendments) (No. 7) Regulations 2008 No. 2008/3157. - Enabling power: Social Security Administration Act 1992, ss.134 (8) (a), 139 (6) (a) & Social Security Contributions and Benefits Act 1992, ss. 123 (1) (a) (d) (e), 130 (2), 136 (1) (3) (4) (5), 136A (3), 137 (1), 175 (1) to (4) & Jobseekers Act 1995, ss. 12 (1) (2) (4), 35 (1), 36 (1) (2) (4) & State Pension Credit Act 2002, ss. 15 (1) (e) (j) (2) to (6), 17 (1), 19 (1) & Welfare Reform Act 2007, ss. 17, 24 (1), 25. - Issued: 15.12.2008. Made: 09 .12.2008. Laid: 15.12.2008. Coming into force: 05.01.2009. Effect: S.I. 1987/1967; 1996/207; 2002/1792; 2006/213, 214, 215, 216, 217; 2007/1619; 2008/794 amended. Territorial extent & classification: E/W/S. General. - 28p.: 30 cm. - 978-0-11-147147-0 £5.00

The Social Security (Miscellaneous Amendments) Regulations 2008 No. 2008/698. - Enabling power: Social Security Contributions and Benefits Act 1992, ss. 123 (1) (a) (d) (e), 124 (1) (d) (e), 135 (1), 136 (3) (5) (a) to (c), 137 (1) (2) (d), 175 (1) to (4) & Social Security Administration Act 1992, ss. 5 (1) (p), 189 (1) (3) to (5) & Jobseekers Act 1995, ss. 4 (5), 12 (2) (4) (a) (b), 35 (1), 36 (1) (2) (4), sch. 1, paras 1 (2) (a), 3(b) & State Pension Credit Act 2002, ss. 2 (3) (b) (6), 17 (1), 19 (1). - Issued: 17.03.2008. Made: 11.03.2008. Laid: 17.03.2008. Coming into force: 07.04.2008 & 14.04.2008. In accord. with reg. 1. Effect: S.I. 1987/1967, 1968; 1996/207; 2002/1792; 2006/213, 215 amended. Territorial extent & classification: E/W/S. General. - 16p.: 30 cm. - 978-0-11-081192-5 £3.00

The Social Security (National Insurance Numbers) Amendment Regulations 2008 No. 2008/223. - Enabling power: Social Security Administration Act 1992, ss. 182C, 189 (1) (4) to (6). - Issued: 08.02.2008. Made: 04.02.2008. Laid: 08.02.2008. Coming into force: 29.02.2008. Effect: S.I. 2001/769 amended. Territorial extent & classification: E/W/S. General. - 4p.: 30 cm. - 978-0-11-080907-6 £3.00

The Social Security Pensions (Home Responsibilities) Amendment Regulations 2008 No. 2008/498. - Enabling power: Social Security Contributions and Benefits Act 1992, s. 175 (3), sch. 3, para. 5 (7) (b) (7A). - Issued: 04.03.2008. Made: 27.02.2008. Laid: 04.03.2008. Coming into force: 06.04.2007. Effect: S.I.1994/704 amended. Territorial extent & classification: E/W/S. General. - 2p.: 30 cm. - 978-0-11-081065-2 £3.00

The Social Security Pensions (Low Earnings Threshold) Order 2008 No. 2008/726. - Enabling power: Social Security Administration Act 1992, s. 148A. - Issued: 18.03.2008. Made: 12.03.2008. Laid: 14.03.2008. Coming into force: 06.04.2008. Effect: None. Territorial extent & classification: E/W/S. General. - 2p.: 30 cm. - 978-0-11-081237-3 £3.00

The Social Security (Recovery of Benefits) (Lump Sum Payments) Regulations 2008 No. 2008/1596. - Enabling power: Social Security Administration Act 1992, s. 189 (4) (6) & Social Security (Recovery of Benefits) Act 1997, ss. 1A, 14 (2) (3) (4), 18, 19, 21 (3), 23 (1) (2) (7), 29, sch. 1, paras 4, 8 & Social Security Act 1998, s. 79 (6) & Child Maintenance and Other Payments Act 2008, s. 53. - Issued: 25.06.2008. Made: 18.06.2008. Laid: 25.06.2008. Coming into force: 01.10.2008. Effect: 1997 c.27 modified & S.I. 1999/991amended. Territorial extent & classification: E/W/S. General. - 20p.: 30 cm. - 978-0-11-081887-0 £3.50

The Social Security Revaluation of Earnings Factors Order 2008 No. 2008/730. - Enabling power: Social Security Administration Act 1992, ss. 148 (3) (4), 189 (1) (4) (5). - Issued: 18.03.2008. Made: 12.03.2008. Laid: 14.03.2008. Coming into force: 06.04.2008. Effect: None. Territorial extent & classification: E/W/S. General. - 4p.: 30 cm. - 978-0-11-081229-8 £3.00

The Social Security (Students and Miscellaneous Amendments) Regulations 2008 No. 2008/1599. - Enabling power: Social Security Contributions and Benefits Act 1992, ss. 123 (1) (a) (d) (e), 136 (3) (4) (5) (b), 137 (1), 175 (1) (3) (4) & Social Security Administration Act 1992, ss. 5 (1) (hh) (j), 189 (1) (4) (6), 191 & Jobseekers Act 1995, ss. 12 (1) to (3) (4) (b), 35 (1), 36 (2) (4) & Welfare Reform Act 2007, ss. 17 (1) (2) (3) (b), 24 (1), 25 (1) (2) (3) (b). - Issued: 26.06.2008. Made: 19.06.2008. Laid: 26.06.2008. Coming into force: In accord. with reg. 1. Effect: S.I. 1987/1967, 1968; 1996/207; 2006/213, 215; 2008/794 amended. Territorial extent & classification: E/W/S. General. - 8p.: 30 cm. - 978-0-11-081895-5 £3.00

The Social Security (Students Responsible for Children or Young Persons) Amendment Regulations 2008 No. 2008/1826. - Enabling power: Social Security Contributions and Benefits Act 1992, ss. 123 (1) (a), 124 (1) (d) (e), 137 (1), 175 (1) (3) & Jobseekers Act 1995, ss. 6 (4), 35 (1), 36 (2) (4). - Issued: 15.07.2008. Made: 08.07.2008. Coming into force: 09.07.2008. Effect: S.I. 1987/1967; 1996/207 amended. Territorial extent & classification: E/W/S. General. - Supersedes draft S.I. (ISBN 9780110814513) issued 14.05.2008. - 4p.: 30 cm. - 978-0-11-083149-7 £3.00

The Statutory Sick Pay (General) Amendment Regulations 2008 No. 2008/1735. - Enabling power: Social Security Contributions and Benefits Act 1992, s. 153 (5) & Social Security Administration Act 1992, s. 130 (2). - Issued: 07.07.2008. Made: 01.07.2008. Laid: 07.07.2008. Coming into force: 27.10.2008. Effect: S.I. 1982/894 amended. Territorial extent & classification: E/W/S. General. - 2p.: 30 cm. - 978-0-11-081951-8 *£3.00*

The Taxes (Interest Rate) (Amendment) Regulations 2008 No. 2008/778. - Enabling power: Finance Act 1989, s. 178 (1) to (3). - Issued: 25.03.2008. Made: 19.03.2008. Laid: 19.03.2008. Coming into force: 06.04.2008. Effect: S.I. 1989/1297 amended. Territorial extent & classification: E/W/S/NI. General. - 2p.: 30 cm. - 978-0-11-081269-4 *£3.00*

The Welfare Reform Act 2007 (Commencement No. 5) Order 2008 No. 2008/411 (C.16). - Enabling power: Welfare Reform Act 2007, s. 70 (2). Bringing into operation various provisions of the 2007 Act on 19.02.2008; 01.04.2008; 07.04.2008; 06.10.2008 in accord. with art. 2. - Issued: 29.02.2008. Made: 18.02.2008. Effect: None. Territorial extent & classification: E/W/S. General. - 4p.: 30 cm. - 978-0-11-081033-1 *£3.00*

The Welfare Reform Act 2007 (Commencement No. 6 and Consequential Provisions) Order 2008 No. 2008/787 (C. 36). - Enabling power: Welfare Reform Act 2007, ss. 68, 70 (2). Bringing into operation various provisions of the 2007 Act on 18.03.2008; 01.04.2008; 27.07.2008; 27.10.2008 in accord. with art. 2. - Issued: 27.03.2008. Made: 17.03.2008. Effect: S.I. 1999/991; 2001/4022 amended. Territorial extent & classification: E/W/S. General. - 8p.: 30 cm. - 978-0-11-081277-9 *£3.00*

The Welfare Reform Act 2007 (Commencement No. 7, Transitional and Savings Provisions) Order 2008 No. 2008/2101 (C.99). - Enabling power: Welfare Reform Act 2007, ss. 68, 70 (2). Bringing into operation various provisions of the 2007 Act on 01.09.2008 & 07.10.2008 in accord. with art. 2. - Issued: 08.08.2008. Made: 04.08.2008. Effect: None. Territorial extent & classification: E/W/S. General. - 8p.: 30 cm. - 978-0-11-083714-7 *£3.00*

The Welfare Reform Act 2007 (Commencement No. 8) Order 2008 No. 2008/2772 (C.121). - Enabling power: Welfare Reform Act 2007, s. 70 (2). Bringing into operation various provisions of the 2007 Act on 27.10.2008. - Issued: 24.10.2008. Made: 20.10.2008. Effect: None. Territorial extent & classification: E/W/S. General. - 8p.: 30 cm. - 978-0-11-084700-9 *£5.00*

The Welfare Reform Act 2007 (Commencement No. 9) Order 2008 No. 2008/3167 (C.142). - Enabling power: Welfare Reform Act 2007, s. 70 (2). Bringing into operation various provisions of the 2007 Act on 11.12.2008. - Issued: 15.12.2008. Made: 10.12.2008. Effect: None. Territorial extent & classification: E/W/S. General. - 8p.: 30 cm. - 978-0-11-147173-9 *£5.00*

The Workmen's Compensation (Supplementation) (Amendment) Scheme 2008 No. 2008/721. - Enabling power: Social Security Contributions and Benefits Act 1992, sch. 8, para. 2 & Social Security Administration Act 1992, sch. 9, para. 1. - Issued: 18.03.2008. Made: 12.03.2008. Laid: 18.03.2008. Coming into force: 09.04.2008. Effect: S.I. 1982/1489 amended. Territorial extent & classification: E/W/S. General. - 4p.: 30 cm. - 978-0-11-081219-9 *£3.00*

Social security: Terms and conditions of employment

The Social Security Benefits Up-rating Order 2008 No. 2008/632. - Enabling power: Social Security Administration Act 1992, ss. 150, 150A, 151, 189 (1) (4) (5). - Issued: 13.03.2008. Made: 06.03.2008. Coming into force: In accord. with art. 1. Effect: 1965, c.51; 1992 c.4 & S.I. 1978/393; 1986/1960; 1987/1967, 1969; 1991/2890; 1994/2946; 1995/310; 1996/207; 2002/1792, 2818; 2005/454; 2006/213, 214, 215, 216 amended & S.I. 2007/688 revoked. Territorial extent & classification: E/W/S. General- Revoked by S.I. 2009/497 (ISBN 9780111475539). Supersedes draft S.I. (9780110808567) issued 29.01.2008. - 52p.: 30 cm. - 978-0-11-081171-0 *£9.00*

Social security, England and Wales

The Health in Pregnancy Grant (Administration) Regulations 2008 No. 2008/3109. - Enabling power: Social Security Administration Act 1992, ss. 5, 12A (1) (5), 189, 191 & Social Security Administration (Northern Ireland) Act 1992, ss. 5, 10A (1) (5), 165, 167 & Health and Social Care Act 2008, ss. 132 (2), 135 (2). - Issued: 15.12.2008. Made: 09.12.2008. Laid: 10.12.2008. Coming into force: 01.01.2009. Effect: None. Territorial extent & classification: E/W/NI. General. - 8p.: 30 cm. - 978-0-11-147139-5 *£5.00*

The Income-related Benefits (Subsidy to Authorities) Amendment (No.2) Order 2008 No. 2008/695. - Enabling power: Social Security Administration Act 1992, ss. 140B, 140F (2), 189 (1) (4) (5) (7). - Issued: 17.03.2008. Made: 10.03.2008. Laid: 11.03.2008. Coming into force: 01.04.2008. Effect: S.I. 1998/562 amended. Territorial extent & classification: E/W. General. - 12p.: 30 cm. - 978-0-11-081187-1 *£3.00*

The Social Security and Child Support (Decisions and Appeals) (Amendment) Regulations 2008 No. 2008/1957. - Enabling power: Social Security Act 1998, s. 6 (3). - Issued: 25.07.2008. Made: 18.07.2008. Laid: 22.07.2008. Coming into force: 20.08.2008. Effect: S.I. 1999/991 amended. Territorial extent & classification: E/W. General. - Revoked by S.I. 2008/2683 (ISBN 9780110846156). - 2p.: 30 cm. - 978-0-11-083531-0 *£3.00*

The Social Security (Use of Information for Housing Benefit and Welfare Services Purposes) Regulations 2008 No. 2008/2112. - Enabling power: Welfare Reform Act 2007, s. 42 (2) (8) (9). - Issued: 08.08.2008. Made: 05.08.2008. Laid: 08.08.2008. Coming into force: 01.09.2008. Effect: None. Territorial extent & classification: E/W. General. - 4p.: 30 cm. - 978-0-11-083719-2 £3.00

The Welfare Reform Act (Relevant Enactment) Order 2008 No. 2008/2114. - Enabling power: Welfare Reform Act 2007, s. 42 (7). - Issued: 08.08.2008. Made: 05.08.2008. Laid: 08.08.2008. Coming into force: 01.09.2008. Effect: None. Territorial extent & classification: E/W. General. - Revoked by S.I. 2009/2162 (ISBN 9780111484418). - 2p.: 30 cm. - 978-0-11-083729-1 £3.00

Social security, Northern Ireland

The Guardian's Allowance Up-rating (Northern Ireland) Order 2008 No. 2008/799. - Enabling power: Social Security Administration (Northern Ireland) Act 1992, ss. 132 (1), 165 (4). - Issued: 01.04.2008. Made: 26.03.2008. Coming into force: 07.04.2008. Effect: 1992, c. 7 amended. Territorial extent & classification: NI. General. - Supersedes draft S.I. (ISBN 9780110809595) issued on 19.02.2008. - 2p.: 30 cm. - 978-0-11-081300-4 £3.00

The Health in Pregnancy Grant (Administration) Regulations 2008 No. 2008/3109. - Enabling power: Social Security Administration Act 1992, ss. 5, 12A (1) (5), 189, 191 & Social Security Administration (Northern Ireland) Act 1992, ss. 5, 10A (1) (5), 165, 167 & Health and Social Care Act 2008, ss. 132 (2), 135 (2). - Issued: 15.12.2008. Made: 09.12.2008. Laid: 10.12.2008. Coming into force: 01.01.2009. Effect: None. Territorial extent & classification: E/W/NI. General. - 8p.: 30 cm. - 978-0-11-147139-5 £5.00

South Atlantic territories

The Falkland Islands Constitution Order 2008 No. 2008/2846. - Enabling power: British Settlements Acts 1887 & 1945. - Issued: 12.11.2008. Made: 05.11.2008. Laid: 12.11.2008. Coming into force: In accord. with art. 1 (3). Effect: S.I. 1985/444; 1997/864, 2974 revoked with effect from the appointed day. Territorial extent & classification: Falkland Islands. General. - 52p.: 30 cm. - 978-0-11-084968-3 £9.00

Sports grounds and sporting events, England and Wales

The Football Spectators (2008 European Championship Control Period) Order 2008 No. 2008/1165. - Enabling power: Football Spectators Act 1989, ss. 14 (6), 22A (2). - Issued: 30.04.2008. Made: 24.04.2008. Laid: 25.04.2008. Coming into force: 19.05.2008. Effect: None. Territorial extent & classification: E/W. General. - 2p.: 30 cm. - 978-0-11-081404-9 £3.00

The Football Spectators (Seating) Order 2008 No. 2008/1749. - Enabling power: Football Spectators Act 1989, s. 11. - Issued: 08.07.2008. Made: 30.06.2008. Laid: 03.07.2008. Coming into force: 25.07.2008. Effect: None. Territorial extent & classification: E/W. General. - 4p.: 30 cm. - 978-0-11-081961-7 £3.00

The Safety of Sports Grounds (Designation) (No.2) Order 2008 No. 2008/1644. - Enabling power: Safety of Sports Grounds Act 1975, s. 1 (1). - Issued: 27.06.2008. Made: 24.06.2008. Laid: 24.06.2008. Coming into force: 18.07.2008. Effect: None. Territorial extent & classification: E/W. General. - 2p.: 30 cm. - 978-0-11-081905-1 £3.00

The Safety of Sports Grounds (Designation) Order 2008 No. 2008/55. - Enabling power: Safety of Sports Grounds Act 1975, ss. 1 (1), 18 (2). - Issued: 18.01.2008. Made: 14.01.2008. Laid: 15.01.2008. Coming into force: 05.02.2008. Effect: S.I. 1985/1064 amended. Territorial extent & classification: E/W/S [but applies to E/W only]. General. - 2p.: 30 cm. - 978-0-11-080839-0 £3.00

Stamp duty

The Stamp Duty and Stamp Duty Reserve Tax (Investment Exchanges and Clearing Houses) (Eurex Clearing AG) (Amendment) Regulations 2008 No. 2008/164. - Enabling power: Finance Act 1991, ss. 116, 117. - Issued: 31.01.2008. Made: 28.01.2008. Laid: 29.01.2008. Coming into force: 19.02.2008. Effect: S.I. 2007/1097 amended. Territorial extent & classification: E/W/S/NI. General. - 4p.: 30 cm. - 978-0-11-080878-9 £3.00

The Stamp Duty and Stamp Duty Reserve Tax (Investment Exchanges and Clearing Houses) Regulations (No. 2) 2008 No. 2008/3235. - Enabling power: Finance Act 1991, ss. 116, 117. - Issued: 22.12.2008. Made: 16.12.2008. Laid: 17.12.2008. Coming into force: 07.01.2009. Effect: None. Territorial extent & classification: E/W/S/NI. General. - 4p.: 30 cm. - 978-0-11-147198-2 £4.00

Stamp duty land tax

The Stamp Duty Land Tax (Exemption of Certain Acquisitions of Residential Property) Regulations 2008 No. 2008/2339. - Enabling power: Finance Act 2003, sch. 3, para. 5. - Issued: 05.09.2008. Made: 02.09.2008. Laid: 02.09.2008. Coming into force: 03.09.2008. Effect: None. Territorial extent & classification: E/W/S/NI. General. - 2p.: 30 cm. - 978-0-11-083994-3 £4.00

The Stamp Duty Land Tax (Open-ended Investment Companies) Regulations 2008 No. 2008/710. - Enabling power: Finance Act 2003, ss. 102, 123 (2) (3). - Issued: 12.03.2008. Made: 12.03.2008. Laid: 12.03.2008. Coming into force: 06.04.2008. Effect: None. Territorial extent & classification: E/W/S/NI. General. - 4p.: 30 cm. - 978-0-11-081208-3 £3.00

The Stamp Duty Land Tax (Variation of Part 4 of the Finance Act 2003) Regulations 2008 No. 2008/2338. - Enabling power: Finance Act 2003, s. 109. - Issued: 06.11.2008. Made: 02.09.2008. Laid: 02.09.2008. Coming into force: 03.09.2008. Effect: 2003 c.14 varied. Territorial extent & classification: E/W/S/NI. General. - Approved by the House of Commons. - 2p.: 30 cm. - 978-0-11-084858-7 £4.00

The Stamp Duty Land Tax (Variation of Part 4 of the Finance Act 2003) Regulations 2008 No. 2008/2338. - Enabling power: Finance Act 2003, s. 109. - Issued: 05.09.2008. Made: 02.09.2008. Laid: 02.09.2008. Coming into force: 03.09.2008. Effect: 2003 ch. 14 amended. Territorial extent & classification: E/W/S/NI. General. - For approval by resolution of the House of Commons within 28 days from the date of being made. - 2p.: 30 cm. - 978-0-11-083985-1 £4.00

The Stamp Duty Land Tax (Zero-Carbon Homes Relief) (Amendment) Regulations 2008 No. 2008/1932. - Enabling power: Finance Act 2003, ss. 58B, 58C & Finance Act 2008, s. 93 (7). - Issued: 28.07.2008. Made: 22.07.2008. Laid: 22.07.2008. Coming into force: 13.08.2008. Effect: S.I. 2007/3437 amended. Territorial extent & classification: E/W/S/NI. General. - With correction slip dated August 2008. - 2p.: 30 cm. - 978-0-11-083536-5 £3.00

Stamp duty reserve tax

The Authorised Investment Funds (Tax) (Amendment No. 3) Regulations 2008 No. 2008/3159. - Enabling power: Finance (No. 2) Act 2005, ss. 17 (3), 18. - Issued: 16.12.2008. Made: 10.12.2008. Laid: 11.12.2008. Coming into force: 01.01.2009. Effect: S.I. 2006/964 amended. Territorial extent & classification: E/W/S/NI. General. - 16p.: 30 cm. - With correction slip dated October 2009 - 978-0-11-147156-2 £5.00

The Stamp Duty and Stamp Duty Reserve Tax (Investment Exchanges and Clearing Houses) (Eurex Clearing AG) (Amendment) Regulations 2008 No. 2008/164. - Enabling power: Finance Act 1991, ss. 116, 117. - Issued: 31.01.2008. Made: 28.01.2008. Laid: 29.01.2008. Coming into force: 19.02.2008. Effect: S.I. 2007/1097 amended. Territorial extent & classification: E/W/S/NI. General. - 4p.: 30 cm. - 978-0-11-080878-9 £3.00

The Stamp Duty and Stamp Duty Reserve Tax (Investment Exchanges and Clearing Houses) Regulations (No. 2) 2008 No. 2008/3235. - Enabling power: Finance Act 1991, ss. 116, 117. - Issued: 22.12.2008. Made: 16.12.2008. Laid: 17.12.2008. Coming into force: 07.01.2009. Effect: None. Territorial extent & classification: E/W/S/NI. General. - 4p.: 30 cm. - 978-0-11-147198-2 £4.00

The Stamp Duty Reserve Tax (Amendment of section 89AA of the Finance Act 1986) Regulations 2008 No. 2008/3236. - Enabling power: Finance Act 1986, s. 89AA (8). - Issued: 22.12.2008. Made: 17.12.2008. Laid: 17.12.2008. Coming into force: 18.12.2008. Effect: 1986 c. 41 amended. Territorial extent & classification: E/W/S/NI. General. - 2p.: 30 cm. - 978-0-11-147222-4 £4.00

The Stamp Duty Reserve Tax (Investment Exchanges and Clearing Houses) (The London Stock Exchange) Regulations 2008 No. 2008/52. - Enabling power: Finance Act 1991, ss. 116 (3) (4), 117. - Issued: 21.01.2008. Made: 14.01.2008. Laid: 14.01.2008. Coming into force: 04.02.2008. Effect: None. Territorial extent & classification: E/W/S/NI. General. - 4p.: 30 cm. - 978-0-11-080843-7 £3.00

Statistics Board

The Statistics and Registration Service Act 2007 (Commencement No. 2 and Transitional Provisions) Order 2008 No. 2008/839 (C.41). - Enabling power: Statistics and Registration Service Act 2007, s. 74. Bringing into operation various provisions of the 2007 Act on 01.04.2008. - Issued: 01.04.2008. Made: 20.03.2008. Effect: None. Territorial extent & classification: E/W/S/NI. General. - 2p.: 30 cm. - 978-0-11-081299-1 £3.00

The Statistics and Registration Service Act 2007 (Delegation of Functions) (Economic Statistics) Order 2008 No. 2008/792. - Enabling power: Statistics and Registration Service Act 2007, s. 24 (1) (4). - Issued: 28.03.2008. Made: 21.03.2008. Coming into force: 01.04.2008 in accord. with art. 1 (2). Effect: None. Territorial extent & classification: E/W/S/NI. General. - 2p.: 30 cm. - 978-0-11-081282-3 £3.00

Statistics of trade

The Statistics of Trade (Customs and Excise) (Amendment) (No. 2) Regulations 2008 No. 2008/2847. - Enabling power: European Communities Act 1972, s. 2 (2). - Issued: 07.11.2008. Made: 03.11.2008. Laid: 04.11.2008. Coming into force: 01.01.2009. Effect: S.I. 1992/2790 amended. Territorial extent & classification: E/W/S/NI. General. - 2p.: 30 cm. - 978-0-11-084868-6 £4.00

The Statistics of Trade (Customs and Excise) (Amendment) Regulations 2008 No. 2008/557. - Enabling power: European Communities Act 1972, s. 2 (2). - Issued: 11.03.2008. Made: 05.03.2008. Laid: 05.03.2008. Coming into force: 01.04.2008. Effect: S.I. 1992/2790 amended. Territorial extent & classification: UK. General. - 8p.: 30 cm. - 978-0-11-081119-2 £3.00

Supreme Court of England and Wales

The Civil Procedure (Amendment No.2) Rules 2008 No. 2008/3085 (L.26). - Enabling power: Counter-Terrorism Act 2008, ss. 66, 67, 72. - Issued: 09.02.2009. Made: 02.12.2008. Laid: 03.12.2008. Coming into force: 04.12.2008. Effect: S.I. 1998/3132 amended. Territorial extent & classification: E/W. General. - Approved by both Houses of Parliament. - 16p.: 30 cm. - 978-0-11-147348-1 £5.00

The Civil Procedure (Amendment No.2) Rules 2008 No. 2008/3085 (L.26). - Enabling power: Counter-Terrorism Act 2008, s. 72. - Issued: 08.12.2008. Made: 02.12.2008. Laid: 03.12.2008. Coming into force: 04.12.2008. Effect: S.I. 1998/3132 amended. Territorial extent & classification: E/W. General. - For approval by resolution of each House of Parliament within 40 days beginning with the day on which these Rules were made, subject to extension for periods of dissolution, prorogation or adjournment for more than four days. - 16p.: 30 cm. - 978-0-11-147091-6 £5.00

The Civil Procedure (Amendment No.3) Rules 2008 No. 2008/3327 (L. 29). - Enabling power: Civil Procedure Act 1997, s. 2. - Issued: 09.01.2009. Made: 29.12.2008. Laid: 07.01.2009. Coming into force: 06.04.2009. Effect: S.I. 1998/3132 amended. Territorial extent & classification: E/W. General. - 8p.: 30 cm. - 978-0-11-147245-3 £5.00

The Civil Procedure (Amendment) Rules 2008 No. 2008/2178 (L.10). - Enabling power: Civil Procedure Act 1997, s. 2. - Issued: 19.08.2008. Made: 07.08.2008. Laid: 15.08.2008. Coming into force: In accord. with rule 1. Effect: S.I. 1998/3132 amended. Territorial extent & classification: E/W. General. - 44p.: 30 cm. - 978-0-11-083831-1 £6.50

The Civil Proceedings Fees (Amendment) Order 2008 No. 2008/2853 (L.19). - Enabling power: Courts Act 2003, s. 92. - Issued: 10.11.2008. Made: 04.11.2008. Laid: 05.11.2008. Coming into force: 26.11.2008. Effect: S.I. 2008/1053 amended. Territorial extent & classification: E/W. General. - 2p.: 30 cm. - 978-0-11-084949-2 £4.00

The Civil Proceedings Fees (Amendment) Order 2008 No. 2008/116 (L.2). - Enabling power: Courts Act 2003, s. 92. - Issued: 28.01.2008. Made: 21.01.2008. Laid: 21.01.2008. Coming into force: 11.02.2008. Effect: S.I. 2004/3121 amended. Territorial extent & classification: E/W. General. - Revoked by S.I. 2008/1053 (L.5) (ISBN 9780110813561). This Statutory Instrument has been made in consequence of defects in S.I. 2007/2176 (ISBN 9780110782829) and is being issued free of charge to all known recipients of that SI. - 2p.: 30 cm. - 978-0-11-080862-8 £3.00

The Civil Proceedings Fees Order 2008 No. 2008/1053 (L.5). - Enabling power: Courts Act 2003, s. 92 & Insolvency Act 1986, ss. 414, 415. - Issued: 11.04.2008. Made: 07.04.2008. Laid: 09.04.2008. Coming into force: 01.05.2008. Effect: S.I. 2004/3121; 2005/473, 3445; 2006/719; 2007/680, 2176, 2801; 2008/116 revoked. Territorial extent & classification: E/W. General. - 20p.: 30 cm. - 978-0-11-081356-1 £3.50

The Contracting Out (Administrative and Other Court Staff) (Amendment) Order 2008 No. 2008/2791. - Enabling power: Courts Act 1971, s. 2 (6). - Issued: 31.10.2008. Made: 23.10.2008. Laid: 28.10.2008. Coming into force: 01.12.2008. Effect: S.I. 2001/3698 amended. Territorial extent & classification: E/W. General. - 2p.: 30 cm. - 978-0-11-084741-2 £4.00

The Criminal Procedure (Amendment No. 2) Rules 2008 No. 2008/3269 (L.28). - Enabling power: Courts Act 2003, s. 69. - Issued: 24.12.2008. Made: 14.12.2008. Laid: 19.12.2008. Coming into force: 06.04.2009. Effect: S.I. 2005/384 amended. Territorial extent and classification: E/W. General. - 24p.: 30 cm. - 978-0-11-147233-0 £5.00

The Criminal Procedure (Amendment) Rules 2008 No. 2008/2076 (L.9). - Enabling power: Courts Act 2003, s. 69. - Issued: 06.08.2008. Made: 21.07.2008. Laid: 31.07.2008. Coming into force: 06.10.2008. Effect: S.I. 2005/384 amended. Territorial extent and classification: E/W. General. - 20p.: 30 cm. - 978-0-11-083658-4 £3.50

The Family Proceedings (Amendment) (No.2) Rules 2008 No. 2008/2861 (L.25). - Enabling power: Matrimonial and Family Proceedings Act 1984, s. 40 (1). - Issued: 12.11.2008. Made: 03.11.2008. Laid: 06.11.2008. Coming into force: 08.12.2008. Effect: S.I. 1991/1247 amended. Territorial extent & classification: E/W. General. - 60p.: 30 cm. - 978-0-11-084967-6 £9.00

The Family Proceedings (Amendment) Rules 2008 No. 2008/2446 (L.11). - Enabling power: Matrimonial and Family Proceedings Act 1984, s. 40 (1) (4) (aa). - Issued: 22.09.2008. Made: 16.09.2008. Laid: 18.09.2008. Coming into force: 03.11.2008 for rules 1, 2, 3(a), 5, 6, 10, 12; 25.11.2008 for remainder, in accord. with rule 1 (2). Effect: S.I. 1991/1247 amended. Territorial extent & classification: E/W. General. - 34p.: 30 cm. - 978-0-11-084250-9 £9.00

The Family Proceedings Fees (Amendment No. 2) Order 2008 No. 2008/3106 (L.27). - Enabling power: Courts Act 2003, s. 92. - Issued: 09.12.2008. Made: 03.12.2008. Laid: 04.12.2008. Coming into force: 05.12.2008. Effect: S.I. 2008/2856 (L.22) amended. Territorial extent & classification: E/W. General. - This Statutory Instrument is made in consequence of a defect in S.I. 2008/2856 and is being issued free of charge to all known recipients of that Statutory Instrument. - 2p.: 30 cm. - 978-0-11-147105-0 *£4.00*

The Family Proceedings Fees (Amendment) Order 2008 No. 2008/2856 (L.22). - Enabling power: Courts Act 2003, s. 92. - Issued: 10.11.2008. Made: 04.11.2008. Laid: 05.11.2008. Coming into force: 26.11.2008 except for art. 5; 08.12.2008 for art. 5. Effect: S.I. 2008/1054 (L.6) amended. Territorial extent & classification: E/W. General. - 4p.: 30 cm. - 978-0-11-084957-7 *£4.00*

The Family Proceedings Fees (Amendment) Order 2008 No. 2008/115 (L.1). - Enabling power: Courts Act 2003, s. 92. - Issued: 28.01.2008. Made: 21.01.2008. Laid: 21.01.2008. Coming into force: 11.02.2008. Effect: S.I. 2004/3114 amended. Territorial extent & classification: E/W. General. - Revoked by S.I. 2008/1054 (L.6) (ISBN 9780110813585). This Statutory Instrument has been made in consequence of defects in S.I. 2007/2175 (ISBN 9780110782836) and is being issued free of charge to all known recipients of that SI. - 2p.: 30 cm. - 978-0-11-080861-1 *£3.00*

The Family Proceedings Fees Order 2008 No. 2008/1054 (L.6). - Enabling power: Courts Act 2003, s. 92. - Issued: 14.04.2008. Made: 07.04.2008. Laid: 09.04.2008. Coming into force: 01.05.2008. Effect: S.I. 2004/3114; 2005/472, 3443; 2006/739; 2007/682, 2175, 2800; 2008/115 revoked. Territorial extent & classification: E/W. General. - 16p.: 30 cm. - 978-0-11-081358-5 *£3.00*

The Maximum Number of Judges Order 2008 No. 2008/1777. - Enabling power: Supreme Court Act 1981, s. 2 (4). - Issued: 16.05.2008. Made: -. Laid:-. Effect: 1981 c. 54 amended. Territorial extent & classification: E/W. General. - Supersedes draft S.I. (ISBN 9780110814605) issued 16.05.2008. - 2p.: 30 cm. - 978-0-11-083135-0 *£3.00*

The Non-Contentious Probate Fees (Amendment) Order 2008 No. 2008/2854 (L.20). - Enabling power: Courts Act 2003, s. 92. - Issued: 10.11.2008. Made: 04.11.2008. Laid: 05.11.2008. Coming into force: 26.11.2008. Effect: S.I. 2004/3120 amended. Territorial extent & classification: E/W. General. - 2p.: 30 cm. - 978-0-11-084948-5 *£4.00*

The Tribunals, Courts and Enforcement Act 2007 (Commencement No. 3) Order 2008 No. 2008/749 (C.31). - Enabling power: Tribunals, Courts and Enforcement Act 2007, s. 148 (5). Bringing into operation, in relation to England, various provisions of the 2007 Act on 06.04.2008. - Issued: 20.03.2008. Made: 14.03.2008. Effect: None. Territorial extent & classification: E/W. General. - 2p.: 30 cm. - 978-0-11-081260-1 *£3.00*

Supreme Court of England and Wales: Jurisdiction

The High Court and County Courts Jurisdiction (Amendment) Order 2008 No. 2008/2934. - Enabling power: Courts and Legal Services Act 1990, ss. 1, 120. - Issued: 17.11.2008. Made: 11.11.2008. Laid: 13.11.2008. Coming into force: 12.12.2008; 01.01.2009; 06.04.2009 in accord. with art. 1. Effect: S.I. 1991/724 amended. Territorial extent & classification: E/W. General. - 4p.: 30 cm. - 978-0-11-146997-2 *£4.00*

Tax credits

The Tax Credits Act 2002 (Transitional Provisions) Order 2008 No. 2008/3151 (C.139). - Enabling power: Tax Credits Act 2002, s. 62 (2). - Issued: 15.12.2008. Made: 09.12.2008. Coming into force: 09.12.2008. Effect: S.I. 2003/962 (C. 51) amended. Territorial extent & classification: E/W/S/NI. General. - 2p.: 30 cm. - 978-0-11-147136-4 *£4.00*

The Tax Credits (Miscellaneous Amendments) (No. 2) Regulations 2008 No. 2008/2169. - Enabling power: Tax Credits Act 2002, ss. 4 (1), 7 (8), 8 (2) (3), 12 (1) to (4), 65 (1) (2) (7), 67. - Issued: 18.08.2008. Made: 13.08.2008. Laid: 14.08.2008. Coming into force: 01.09.2008. Effect: S.I. 2002/2005, 2006, 2007, 2014 amended. Territorial extent & classification: E/W/S/NI. General. - 8p.: 30 cm. - 978-0-11-083789-5 *£3.00*

The Tax Credits (Miscellaneous Amendments) Regulations 2008 No. 2008/604. - Enabling power: Tax Credits Act 2002, ss. 4 (1) (b), 7(8), 12, 24 (7), 65 (1) (2). - Issued: 11.03.2008. Made: -. Coming into force: 10.04.2008 for all other purposes; 06.04.2008 for reg. 2 (2), in accord. with reg. 1. Effect: S.I.2002/2005, 2006, 2014, 2173 amended. Territorial extent & classification: E/W/S/NI. General. - 4p.: 30 cm. - 978-0-11-081121-5 *£3.00*

The Tax Credits Up-rating Regulations 2008 No. 2008/796. - Enabling power: Tax Credits Act 2002, ss. 7 (1) (a), 9, 11, 13, 65 (1). - Issued: 01.04.2008. Made: 26.03.2008. Coming into force: 06.04.2008. Effect: S.I. 2002/2005, 2007, 2008 amended. Territorial extent & classification: E/W/S/NI. General. - Supersedes draft S.I. (ISBN 9780110809168) issued on 15.02.2008. - 4p.: 30 cm. - 978-0-11-081295-3 *£3.00*

Tax credits, Wales

The Tax Credits (Approval of Child Care Providers) (Wales) (Amendment) Scheme 2008 No. 2008/2687 (W.237). - Enabling power: Tax Credits Act 2002, ss. 12 (5) (7) (8), 65 (3) (9). - Issued: 24.10.2008. Made: 08.10.2008. Laid before the National Assembly for Wales: 10.10.2008. Coming into force: 03.11.2008. Effect: S.I. 2007/226 (W.20) amended. Territorial extent & classification: W. General. - In English and Welsh. Welsh title: Cynllun Credydau Treth (Cymeradwyo Darparwyr Gofal Plant) (Cymru) (Diwygio) 2008. - 4p.: 30 cm. - 978-0-11-091890-7 £4.00

Taxes

The Companies Act 2006 (Consequential Amendments) (Taxes and National Insurance) Order 2008 No. 2008/954. - Enabling power: Companies Act 2006, ss. 1292, 1294, 1296. - Issued: 07.04.2008. Made: 01.04.2008. Coming into force: 06.04.2008. Effect: 14 acts & 11 SIs amended. Territorial extent & classification: E/W/S/NI. General. - Supersedes draft SI (ISBN 9780110810126) issued 28.02.0008. - 12p.: 30 cm. - 978-0-11-081334-9 £3.00

The Finance Act 2008, Schedule 38, (Appointed Day) Order 2008 No. 2008/1935 (C.93). - Enabling power: Finance Act 2008, s. 116 (2). Bringing into force various provisions of the 2008 Act on 01.11.2008 in accord. with art. 2. - Issued: 25.07.2008. Made: 22.07.2008. Effect: None. Territorial extent & classification: E/W/S/NI. General. - 2p.: 30 cm. - 978-0-11-083550-1 £3.00

The International Tax Enforcement (Bermuda) Order 2008 No. 2008/1789. - Enabling power: Finance Act 2006, s. 173 (1). - Issued: 15.07.2008. Made: 09.07.2008. Coming into force: 09.07.2008. Effect: None. Territorial extent & classification: E/W/S/NI. General. - Supersedes draft S.I. (ISBN 9780110814667) issued 19.05.2008. - 12p.: 30 cm. - 978-0-11-083136-7 £3.00

The Stamp Duty and Stamp Duty Reserve Tax (Investment Exchanges and Clearing Houses) (European Central Counterparty Limited and the Turquoise Multilateral Trading Facility) Regulations 2008 No. 2008/1814. - Enabling power: Finance Act 1991, ss. 116, 117. - Issued: 14.07.2008. Made: 08.07.2008. Laid: 09.07.2008. Coming into force: 30.07.2008. Effect: None. Territorial extent & classification: E/W/S/NI. General. - 4p.: 30 cm. - 978-0-11-083094-0 £3.00

The Stamp Duty and Stamp Duty Reserve Tax (Investment Exchanges and Clearing Houses) Regulations 2008 No. 2008/2777. - Enabling power: Finance Act 1991, ss. 116, 117. - Issued: 27.10.2008. Made: 22.10.2008. Laid: 23.10.2008. Coming into force: 13.11.2008. Effect: None. Territorial extent & classification: E/W/S/NI. General. - 4p.: 30 cm. - 978-0-11-084710-8 £4.00

The Stamp Duty Reserve Tax (virt-x Exchange Limited) (Amendment) Regulations 2008 No. 2008/914. - Enabling power: Finance Act 1991, ss. 116 (3) (4), 117. - Issued: 02.04.2008. Made: 27.03.2008. Laid: 28.03.2008. Coming into force: 18.04.2008. Effect: S.I. 1995/2051 amended. Territorial extent & classification: E/W/S/NI. General. - 2p.: 30 cm. - 978-0-11-081314-1 £3.00

The Tax Avoidance Schemes (Information) (Amendment) Regulations 2008 No. 2008/1947. - Enabling power: Finance Act 2004, ss. 312 (2) (5), 312A (2) (5). - Issued: 28.07.2008. Made: 22.07.2008. Laid: 22.07.2008. Coming into force: 01.11.2008. Effect: S.I. 2004/1864 amended. Territorial extent & classification: E/W/S/NI. General. - 2p.: 30 cm. - 978-0-11-083577-8 £3.00

The Taxes (Fees for Payment by Internet) Regulations 2008 No. 2008/2991. - Enabling power: Finance Act 2008, s. 136 (1) (3). - Issued: 21.11.2008. Made: 17.11.2008. Laid: 18.11.2008. Coming into force: 09.12.2008. Effect: None. Territorial extent & classification: E/W/S/NI. General. - 2p.: 30 cm. - 978-0-11-147017-6 £4.00

The Taxes (Fees for Payment by Telephone) Regulations 2008 No. 2008/1948. - Enabling power: Finance Act 2008, s. 136 (1) (3). - Issued: 28.07.2008. Made: 22.07.2008. Laid: 22.07.2008. Coming into force: 13.08.2008. Effect: None. Territorial extent & classification: E/W/S/NI. General. - 2p.: 30 cm. - 978-0-11-083573-0 £3.00

The Taxes (Interest Rate) (Amendment) Regulations 2008 No. 2008/778. - Enabling power: Finance Act 1989, s. 178 (1) to (3). - Issued: 25.03.2008. Made: 19.03.2008. Laid: 19.03.2008. Coming into force: 06.04.2008. Effect: S.I. 1989/1297 amended. Territorial extent & classification: E/W/S/NI. General. - 2p.: 30 cm. - 978-0-11-081269-4 £3.00

Taxes: Tonnage tax

The Tonnage Tax (Training Requirement) (Amendment) Regulations 2008 No. 2008/2264. - Enabling power: Finance Act 2000, sch. 22, paras 29, 31, 36. - Issued: 29.08.2008. Made: 20.08.2008. Laid: 27.08.2008. Coming into force: 01.10.2008. Effect: S.I. 2000/2129 amended. Territorial extent & classification: E/W/S/NI. General. - Revoked by S.I. 2009/2304 (ISBN 9780111484838). With correction slip dated September 2009. - 2p.: 30 cm. - 978-0-11-083859-5 £3.00

Terms and conditions of employment

The Employment Rights (Increase of Limits) Order 2008 No. 2008/3055. - Enabling power: Employment Relations Act 1999, s. 34. - Issued: 01.12.2008. Made: 24.11.2008. Laid: 26.11.2008. Coming into force: 01.02.2009. Effect: S.I. 2007/3570 revoked with saving. Territorial extent & classification: E/W/S. General. - 8p.: 30 cm. - 978-0-11-147066-4 £5.00

The Fixed-term Employees (Prevention of Less Favourable Treatment) (Amendment) Regulations 2008 No. 2008/2776. - Enabling power: Employment Act 2002, ss. 45, 51 (1). - Issued: 27.10.2008. Made: 22.10.2008. Coming into force: 27.10.2008. Effect: S.I. 2002/2034 amended. Territorial extent & classification: E/W/S. General. - Supersedes draft S.I. (ISBN 9780110819259) issued 02.07.2008. - 2p.: 30 cm. - 978-0-11-084711-5 £4.00

The Maternity and Parental Leave etc. and the Paternity and Adoption Leave (Amendment) Regulations 2008 No. 2008/1966. - Enabling power: Employment Rights Act 1996, ss. 47C (1) (2), 73 (4) (6) (7), 75 (2), 75B (4) (7) (8), 75D (2), 99 (1) (2). - Issued: 29.07.2008. Made: 22.07.2008. Coming into force: 23.07.2008. Effect: S.I. 1999/3312; 2002/2788 amended. Territorial extent & classification: E/W/S. General. - Supersedes draft S.I. (ISBN 9780110819341) issued 03.07.2008. - 8p.: 30 cm. - 978-0-11-083593-8 £3.00

The National Minimum Wage Regulations 1999 (Amendment) Regulations 2008 No. 2008/1894. - Enabling power: National Minimum Wage Act 1998, s. 51 (5). - Issued: 23.07.2008. Made: 16.07.2008. Coming into force: 17.07.2008 for regs, 1, 4, 7; 01.10.2008 for remainder, in accord. with reg. 1. Effect: S.I. 1999/584 amended & S.I. 2007/2318 partially revoked. Territorial extent & classification: E/W/S/NI. General. - Partially revoked by S.I. 2009/1902 (ISBN 9780111482995). - 4p.: 30 cm. - 978-0-11-083395-8 £3.00

The Public Interest Disclosure (Prescribed Persons) (Amendment) Order 2008 No. 2008/531. - Enabling power: Employment Rights Act 1996, s. 43F. - Issued: 04.03.2008. Made: 26.02.2008. Laid: 29.02.2008. Coming into force: 06.04.2008. Effect: S.I. 1999/1549 amended. Territorial extent & classification: E/W/S. General. - 4p.: 30 cm. - 978-0-11-081044-7 £3.00

The Statutory Sick Pay (General) Amendment Regulations 2008 No. 2008/1735. - Enabling power: Social Security Contributions and Benefits Act 1992, s. 153 (5) & Social Security Administration Act 1992, s. 130 (2). - Issued: 07.07.2008. Made: 01.07.2008. Laid: 07.07.2008. Coming into force: 27.10.2008. Effect: S.I. 1982/894 amended. Territorial extent & classification: E/W/S. General. - 2p.: 30 cm. - 978-0-11-081951-8 £3.00

Town and country planning, England

The Crossrail (Fees for Requests for Planning Approval) Regulations 2008 No. 2008/2175. - Enabling power: Crossrail Act 2008, s. 12, sch. 7, para. 30 (5). - Issued: 21.08.2008. Made: 14.08.2008. Laid: 18.08.2008. Coming into force: 10.09.2008. Effect: None. Territorial extent & classification: E. General. - 8p.: 30 cm. - With correction slip dated September 2009. - 978-0-11-083825-0 £3.00

The Crossrail (Planning Appeals) (Written Representations Procedure) (England) Regulations 2008 No. 2008/2908. - Enabling power: Crossrail Act 2008, sch. 7, paras 30 (1), 34, 35 (1). - Issued: 12.11.2008. Made: 10.11.2008. Laid: 10.11.2008. Coming into force: 01.12.2008. Effect: None. Territorial extent & classification: E. General. - With correction slip dated September 2009. - 16p.: 30 cm. - 978-0-11-084992-8 £5.00

The Planning (Listed Buildings and Conservation Areas) (Amendment) (England) Regulations 2008 No. 2008/551. - Enabling power: Planning (Listed Buildings and Conservation Areas) Act 1990, ss. 10 (3) (4), 11 (1). - Issued: 10.03.2008. Made: 26.02.2008. Laid: 10.03.2008. Coming into force: 06.04.2008. Effect: S.I. 1990/1519 amended in relation to England. Territorial extent & classification: E. General. - With correction slip dated March 2008 and 2nd correction slip dated October 2009. - 4p.: 30 cm. - 978-0-11-081097-3 £3.00

The Town and Country Planning (Determination of Appeals by Appointed Persons) (Prescribed Classes) (Amendment) (England) Regulations 2008 No. 2008/595. - Enabling power: Town and Country Planning Act 1990, s. 333, sch. 6, para. 1 & Planning (Listed Buildings and Conservation Areas) Act 1990, s. 93, sch. 3, para. 1 & Planning (Hazardous Substances) Act 1990, s. 40, sch., para. 1. - Issued: 12.03.2008. Made: 05.03.2008. Laid: 12.03.2008. Coming into force: 06.04.2008. Effect: S.I. 1997/420 amended. Territorial extent & classification: E. General. - 4p.: 30 cm. - 978-0-11-081115-4 £3.00

The Town and Country Planning (Environmental Impact Assessment) (Amendment) (England) Regulations 2008 No. 2008/2093. - Enabling power: European Communities Act 1972, s. 2 (2) & Town and Country Planning Act 1990, s. 333, sch. 6, para. 1. - Issued: 07.08.2008. Made: 30.07.2008. Laid: 07.08.2008. Coming into force: 01.09.2008. Effect: S.I. 1997/420; 1999/293; 2008/1556 amended. Territorial extent & classification: E. General. - EC note: The Town and Country Planning (Environmental Impact Assessment) (England and Wales) Regulations 1999 (S.I.1999/293) ("the 1999 regulations") implemented, in England and Wales, Council Directive 85/337/EEC ("the EIA Directive") on the assessment of the effects of certain public and private projects on the environment as amended by Council Directive 97/11/EC. The EIA Directive was also amended by Council Directive 2003/35/EC. The Town and Country Planning (Environmental Impact Assessment) (England and Wales) (Amendment) Regulations 2000 (S.I. 2000/2867) ("the 2000 Regulations") implemented the Directives in respect of ROMP applications (applications made to mineral planning authorities to determine the conditions to which a mineral planning permission is subject under Schedule 2 to the Planning and Compensation Act 1991 (c.34) and Schedules 13 and 14 to the Environment Act 1995 (c.25) made after the commencement of the 2000 Regulations (15 November 2000). The Town and Country Planning (Environmental Impact Assessment) (Minerals Permissions and Amendment)(England) Regulations 2008 (S.I. 2008/1556) ("the 2008 Regulations") applied the 1999 Regulations, with modifications, to ROMP applications made before 15

November 2000 which were undetermined on 22 July 2008 and contained provisions applying to all ROMP applications. These Regulations amend the 1999 Regulations to implement the Directives in respect of applications for approval of reserved matters and applications for approval of conditions attached to the grant of planning permissions ("subsequent applications") and applications for approval of conditions attached to the grant of minerals permissions ("ROMP subsequent applications"). - 16p.: 30 cm. - 978-0-11-083710-9 £3.00

The Town and Country Planning (Environmental Impact Assessment) (Mineral Permissions and Amendment) (England) Regulations 2008 No. 2008/1556. - Enabling power: European Communities Act 1972, s. 2 (2). - Issued: 19.06.2008. Made: 12.06.2008. Laid: 19.06.2008. Coming into force: 22.07.2008. Effect: S.I.1999/293 amended. Territorial extent & classification: E. General. - 12p.: 30 cm. - With correction slip dated September 2009. - 978-0-11-081859-7 £3.00

The Town and Country Planning (Fees for Applications and Deemed Applications) (Amendment) (England) Regulations 2008 No. 2008/958. - Enabling power: Town and Country Planning Act 1990, s. 303. - Issued: 04.04.2008. Made: 02.04.2008. Coming into force: 06.04.2008. Effect: S.I. 1989/193 amended in relation to England & S.I. 2005/843 revoked. Territorial extent & classification: E. General. - Supersedes draft SI (ISBN 9780110809892) issued 27.02.2008. - 8p.: 30 cm. - 978-0-11-081335-6 £3.00

The Town and Country Planning (General Development Procedure) (Amendment) (England) Order 2008 No. 2008/550. - Enabling power: Town and Country Planning Act 1990, ss. 59, 61 (1), 62, 65, 74, 78 (2), 193, 333 (7). - Issued: 10.03.2008. Made: 26.02.2008. Laid: 10.03.2008. Coming into force: 06.04.2008. Effect: S.I. 1995/419 amended. Territorial extent & classification: E. General. - 8p.: 30 cm. - 978-0-11-081090-4 £3.00

The Town and Country Planning (General Permitted Development) (Amendment) (England) Order 2008 No. 2008/675. - Enabling power: Town and Country Planning Act 1990, ss. 59, 60, 61, 333 (7). - Issued: 13.03.2008. Made: 10.03.2008. Laid: 13.03.2008. Coming into force: 06.04.2008. Effect: S.I. 1995/418 amended. Territorial extent & classification: E. General. - 4p.: 30 cm. - 978-0-11-081181-9 £3.00

The Town and Country Planning (General Permitted Development) (Amendment) (No. 2) (England) Order 2008 No. 2008/2362. - Enabling power: Town and Country Planning Act 1990, ss. 59, 60, 61, 333 (7). - Issued: 10.09.2008. Made: 04.09.2008. Laid: 10.09.2008. Coming into force: 01.10.2008. Effect: S.I. 1995/416 amended. Territorial extent & classification: E. General. - With correction slip dated September 2008. - 12p.: 30 cm. - 978-0-11-084095-6 £5.00

The Town and Country Planning (Local Development) (England) Regulations 2008 No. 2008/1371. - Enabling power: Planning and Compulsory Act 2004, ss. 14 (3), 15 (2) (g) (3) (6A) (b) (6B) (7) (c) (8B) (b) (8C), 17 (1) (a), 20(3), 24 (3), 36, 122 (3). - Issued: 02.06.2008. Made: 19.05.2008. Laid: 02.06.2008. Coming into force: 27.06.2008. Effect: S.I. 2004/2204 amended. Territorial extent & classification: E. General. - 20p.: 30 cm. - 978-0-11-081762-0 £3.50

The Town and Country Planning (Mayor of London) Order 2008 No. 2008/580. - Enabling power: Town and Country Planning Act 1990, ss. 2A, 2D, 2F, 59 (1), 74. - Issued: 11.03.2008. Made: 04.03.2008. Laid: 11.03.2008. Coming into force: 06.04.2008. Effect: S.I. 2000/1493 revoked with savings. Territorial extent & classification: E. General. - 12p.: 30 cm. - 978-0-11-081111-6 £3.00

The Town and Country Planning (Trees) (Amendment) (England) Regulations 2008 No. 2008/2260. - Enabling power: Town and Country Planning Act 1990, ss. 198 (8), 199 (2) (3), 323, 333 (1). - Issued: 29.08.2008. Made: 21.08.2008. Laid: 29.08.2008. Coming into force: 01.10.2008. Effect: S.I. 1999/1892 amended. Territorial extent & classification: E. General. - 8p.: 30 cm. - 978-0-11-083854-0 £3.00

The Town and Country Planning (Trees) (Amendment No. 2) (England) Regulations 2008 No. 2008/3202. - Enabling power: Town and Country Planning Act 1990, ss. 199 (2) (3), 323, 333 (1). - Issued: 22.12.2008. Made: 15.12.2008. Laid: 22.12.2008. Coming into force: 26.01.2009. Effect: S.I. 1999/1892 amended. Territorial extent & classification: E. General. - This Statutory Instrument has been printed to correct errors in SI 2008/2260 and is being issued free of charge to all known recipients of that Statutory Instrument. - 2p.: 30 cm. - 978-0-11-147193-7 £4.00

The West Northamptonshire Joint Committee Order 2008 No. 2008/1572. - Enabling power: Planning and Compulsory Purchase Act 2004, s. 29. - Issued: 19.06.2008. Made: 11.06.2008. Laid: 19.06.2008. Coming into force: 25.07.2008. Effect: None. Territorial extent & classification: E. General. - 8p.: 30 cm. - 978-0-11-081862-7 £3.00

Town and country planning, England and Wales

The Crossrail (Qualifying Authorities) Order 2008 No. 2008/2034. - Enabling power: Crossrail Act 2008, sch. 7, para. 1. - Issued: 31.07.2008. Made: 23.07.2008. Coming into force: 24.07.2008. Effect: None. Territorial extent & classification: E/W. General. - 2p.: 30 cm. - 978-0-11-083643-0 £3.00

Town and country planning, Scotland

The Planning (National Security Directions and Appointed Representatives) (Scotland) Rules 2008 No. 2008/1590 (S.5). - Enabling power: Town and Country Planning (Scotland) Act 1997, s. 265A (6) (a) & Planning (Listed Buildings and Conservation Areas) (Scotland) Act 1997, sch. 3, para. 6 (7) & Planning (Hazardous Substances) (Scotland) Act 1997, sch. para. 6 (7). - Issued: 25.06.2008. Made: 19.06.2008. Laid: 23.06.2008. Coming into force: 14.07.2008. Effect: None. Territorial extent & classification: S. General. - 12p.: 30 cm. - 978-0-11-082046-0 £3.00

The Planning (National Security Directions and Appointed Representatives) (Scotland) Rules 2008 No. 2008/1590 (S.5). - Enabling power: Town and Country Planning (Scotland) Act 1997, s. 265A (6) (a) & Planning (Listed Buildings and Conservation Areas) (Scotland) Act 1997, sch. 3, para. 6 (7) & Planning (Hazardous Substances) (Scotland) Act 1997, sch., para. 6 (7). - Issued: 21.07.2008. Made: 19.06.2008. Laid: 23.06.2008. Coming into force: 14.07.2008. Effect: None. Territorial extent & classification: S. General. - This Statutory Instrument has been printed to correct an error in the S.I. of the same number (but different ISBN - 9780110820460) and is being issued free of charge to all known recipients of that Statutory Instrument. - 12p.: 30 cm. - 978-0-11-082018-7 £3.00

Town and country planning, Wales

The Planning and Compulsory Purchase Act 2004 (Commencement No.4 and Consequential, Transitional and Savings Provisions) (Wales) (Amendment No.1) Order 2008 No. 2008/10 (W.4). - Enabling power: Planning and Compulsory Purchase Act 2004, ss. 121 (5), 122 (3). - Issued: 14.01.2008. Made: 08.01.2008. Coming into force: 29.01.2008. Effect: S.I. 2005/2722 (W.193) (C.110) amended. Territorial extent & classification: W. General. - In English and Welsh. Welsh language title: Gorchymyn Diwygio Deddf Cynllunio a Phrynu Gorfodol 2004 (Cychwyn Rhif 4 a Darpariaethau Canlyniadol a Throsiannol a Darpariaethau Arbed) (Cymru) (Diwygio Rhif 1) 2008. - 4p.: 30 cm. - 978-0-11-091727-6 £3.00

The Planning and Compulsory Purchase Act 2004 (Commencement No.4 and Consequential, Transitional and Savings Provisions) (Wales) (Amendment No. 2) Order 2008 No. 2008/2162 (W.192). - Enabling power: Planning and Compulsory Purchase Act 2004, ss. 121 (5), 122 (3). - Issued: 03.09.2008. Made: 12.08.2008. Coming into force: 02.09.2008. Effect: S.I. 2005/2722 (W.193) (C.110) amended. Territorial extent & classification: W. General. - In English and Welsh. Welsh language title: Gorchymyn Diwygio Deddf Cynllunio a Phrynu Gorfodol 2004 (Cychwyn Rhif 4 a Darpariaethau Canlyniadol a Throsiannol a Darpariaethau Arbed) (Cymru) (Diwygio Rhif 2) 2008. - 4p.: 30 cm. - 978-0-11-091833-4 £3.00

The Town and Country Planning (Environmental Impact Assessment) (Amendment) (Wales) Regulations 2008 No. 2008/2335 (W.198). - Enabling power: European Communities Act 1972, s. 2 (2) & Town and Country Planning Act 1990, s. 333, sch. 6, para. 1. - Issued: 01.10.2008. Made: 31.08.2008. Laid: 02.09.2008. Coming into force: 06.10.2008. Effect: S.I. 1997/420; 1999/293 amended in relation to Wales. Territorial extent & classification: W. General. - EC note: The Town and Country Planning (Environmental Impact Assessment) (England and Wales) Regulations 1999 (S.I.1999/293) implemented, in England and Wales, Council Directive 85/337/EEC on the assessment of the effects of certain public and private projects on the environment as amended by Council Directive 97/11/ECThe EIA Directive was also amended by Council Directive 2003/35/EC. These Regulations amend the 1999 Regulations to implement the Directives in respect of applications. - In English and Welsh. Welsh title: Rheoliadau Cynllunio Gwlad a Thref (Asesu Effeithiau Amgylcheddol) (Diwygio) (Cymru) 2008. - 16p.: 30 cm. - 978-0-11-091877-8 £5.00

The Town and Country Planning (General Development Procedure) (Amendment) (Wales) Order 2008 No. 2008/2336 (W.199). - Enabling power: Town and Country Planning Act 1990, ss. 59, 61 (1), 62 (1), 333 (7). - Issued: 15.09.2008. Made: 31.08.2008. Laid before the National Assembly for Wales: 02.09.2008. Coming into force: 06.10.2008. Effect: S.I. 1995/419 amended in relation to Wales. Territorial extent & classification: W. General. - In English and Welsh. Welsh language title: Gorchymyn Cynllunio Gwlad a Thref (Gweithdrefn Datblygu Cyffredinol) (Diwygio) (Cymru) 2008. - 8p.: 30 cm. - 978-0-11-091834-1 £5.00

The Town and Country Planning (General Permitted Development) (Amendment) (Wales) Order 2008 No. 2008/502 (W.43). - Enabling power: Town and Country Planning Act 1990, ss. 59, 60, 333 (7). - Issued: 20.03.2008. Made: 25.02.2008. Laid: 26.02.2008. Coming into force: 21.03.2008. Effect: S.I. 1995/418 amended in relation to Wales. Territorial extent & classification: W. General. - In English and Welsh. Welsh language title: Gorchymyn Cynllunio Gwlad a Thref (Datblygu Cyffredinol a Ganiateir) (Diwygio) (Cymru) 2008. - 4p.: 30 cm. - 978-0-11-091763-4 £3.00

Trade descriptions

The Business Protection from Misleading Marketing Regulations 2008 No. 2008/1276. - Enabling power: European Communities Act 1972, s. 2 (2). - Issued: 16.05.2008. Made: 08.05.2008. Coming into force: 26.05.2008. Effect: None. Territorial extent & classification: E/W/S/NI. General. - Supersedes draft SI (ISBN 9780110811475) issued 13.03.2008. EC note: These Regulations implement Directive 2006/114/EC concerning misleading and comparative advertising. The Directive replaces Council Directive 84/450/EEC concerning misleading and comparative advertising and codifies the amendments made to that directive. Council Directive 84/450/EEC was implemented by the Control of Misleading Advertising Regulations 1988 (S.I. 1988/915).

Those Regulations are revoked by the Consumer Protection from Unfair Trading Regulations 2008- 16p.: 30 cm. - 978-0-11-081459-9 *£3.00*

The Textile Products (Determination of Composition) Regulations 2008 No. 2008/15. - Enabling power: European Communities Act 1972, s. 2 (2), sch. 2, para 1A. - Issued: 16.01.2008. Made: 08.01.2008. Laid: 11.01.2008. Coming into force: 02.02.2008. Effect: S.I. 2006/3298 revoked. Territorial extent & classification: E/W/S/NI. General. - EC note: These Regulations implement Council Directive 73/44/EEC on the quantitative analysis of ternary fibre mixtures and Council Directive 96/73/EC on certain methods for the quantitative analysis of binary textile fibre mixtures as amended by Directives 2006/2/EC and 2007/4/EC. - 4p.: 30 cm. - 978-0-11-080820-8 *£3.00*

The Textile Products (Indications of Fibre Content) (Amendment) Regulations 2008 No. 2008/6. - Enabling power: European Communities Act 1972, s. 2 (2), sch. 2, para. 1A. - Issued: 16.01.2008. Made: 08.01.2008. Laid: 11.01.2008. Coming into force: 02.02.2008. Effect: S.I.1986/26 amended. Territorial extent & classification: E/W/S/NI. General. - EC note: These Regulations amend the Textile Products (Indications of Fibre Content) Regulations 1986 which implement Directive 96/74/EC on textile names. The Regulations set the names to be used for different types of textile fibres and fibre descriptions and the percentage allowances to apply to the anhydrous mass of each fibre when determining composition of mixtures by weight. They also provide that the references to Annex I and Annex II to Directive 96/74/EC are to those annexes as amended from time to time. - 4p.: 30 cm. - 978-0-11-080821-5 *£3.00*

Trade marks

The Community Trade Mark (Amendment) Regulations 2008 No. 2008/1959. - Enabling power: Trade Marks Act 1994, s. 52. - Issued: 29.07.2008. Made: 21.07.2008. Laid: 23.07.2008. Coming into force: 01.10.2008. Effect: S.I. 2006/1027 amended. Territorial extent & classification: E/W/S/NI. General. - 2p.: 30 cm. - 978-0-11-083530-3 *£3.00*

The Trade Marks (Amendment) Rules 2008 No. 2008/2300. - Enabling power: Trade Marks Act 1994, s. 78. - Issued: 03.09.2008. Made: 28.08.2008. Laid: 01.09.2008. Coming into force: 01.10.2008. Effect: S.I. 2008/1797 amended. Territorial extent & classification: E/W/S/NI. General. - This Statutory Instrument has been made in consequence of a defect in SI 2008/1797 (ISBN 9780110819921) and is being issued free of charge to all known recipients of that Statutory Instrument. - 2p.: 30 cm. - 978-0-11-083874-8 *£4.00*

The Trade Marks and Trade Marks (Fees) (Amendment) Rules 2008 No. 2008/11. - Enabling power: Trade Marks Act 1994, ss. 78, 79 & S.I. 1988/93. - Issued: 14.01.2008. Made: 08.01.2008. Laid: 10.01.2008. Coming into force: 06.04.2008. Effect: S.I. 2000/136, 137 amended. Territorial extent & classification: E/W/S/NI. General. - Revoked by S.I. 2008/1958 (ISBN 9780110835266). - 4p.: 30 cm. - 978-0-11-080816-1 *£3.00*

The Trade Marks (Earlier Trade Marks) Regulations 2008 No. 2008/1067. - Enabling power: European Communities Act 1972, s. 2 (2). - Issued: 16.04.2008. Made: 09.04.2008. Laid: 14.04.2008. Coming into force: 10.05.2008. Effect: 1994 c.26 amended. Territorial extent & classification: E/W/S/NI. General. - This Statutory Instrument has been made in consequence of defects in SI 2004/946 (ISBN 9780110490274) and SI 2004/2332 (ISBN 9780110497969) and is being issued free of charge to all known recipients of those Statutory Instruments. - 4p.: 30 cm. - 978-0-11-081371-4 *£3.00*

The Trade Marks (Fees) (Revocation) Rules 2008 No. 2008/2207. - Enabling power: Trade Marks Act 1994, ss. 54, 79. - Issued: 26.08.2008. Made: 13.08.2008. Laid: 19.08.2008. Coming into force: 01.10.2008. Effect: S.I. 2000/137 revoked (with saving). Territorial extent & classification: E/W/S/NI. General. - 2p.: 30 cm. - 978-0-11-083842-7 *£3.00*

The Trade Marks (Fees) Rules 2008 No. 2008/1958. - Enabling power: Trade Marks Act 1994, s. 79 & S.I.1988/93. - Issued: 29.07.2008. Made: 21.07.2008. Laid: 23.07.2008. Coming into force: 01.10.2008. Effect: S.I. 2000/137 revoked with saving & S.I. 2007/2077; 2008/11 revoked. Territorial extent & classification: E/W/S/NI. General. - 4p.: 30 cm. - 978-0-11-083526-6 *£3.00*

The Trade Marks (International Registration) Order 2008 No. 2008/2206. - Enabling power: Trade Marks Act 1994, s. 54. - Issued: 26.08.2008. Made: 13.08.2008. Laid: 19.08.2008. Coming into force: 01.10.2008. Effect: S.I. 1996/714; 2000/138; 2002/692; 2004/948; 2006/763, 1080 revoked. Territorial extent & classification: E/W/S/NI. General. - 20p.: 30 cm. - 978-0-11-083840-3 *£3.50*

The Trade Marks Rules 2008 No. 2008/1797. - Enabling power: Trade Marks Act 1994, ss. 4 (4), 13 (2), 25 (1) (5) (6), 34 (1), 35 (5), 38 (1) (2), 39 (3), 40 (4), 41 (1) (3), 43 (2) (3) (5) (6), 44 (3), 45 (2), 63 (2) (3), 64 (4), 65 (1) (2), 66 (2), 67 (1) (2), 68 (1) (3), 69, 76 (1), 78, 80 (3), 81, 82, 88, sch. 1, para. 6(2), sch. 2, para. 7(2). - Issued: 14.07.2008. Made: 07.07.2008. Laid: 08.07.2008. Coming into force: 01.10.2008. Effect: S.I. 2006/760; 2008/11 amended & S.I. 2000/136; 2001/3832; 2004/947; 2006/1029, 3039; 2007/2076 revoked. Territorial extent & classification: E/W/S/NI. General. - 36p.: 30 cm. - 978-0-11-081992-1 *£6.50*

Transport

The Cross-border Railway Services (Working Time) Regulations 2008 No. 2008/1660. - Enabling power: European Communities Act 1972, s. 2 (2). - Issued: 03.07.2008. Made: 25.06.2008. Laid: 01.07.2008. Coming into force: 27.07.2008. Effect: 1996 c.17, c.18; 2002 c.22; S.I. 1998/1833 amended. Territorial extent & classification: E/W/S. General. - EC note: These Regulations implement the provisions of Council Directive 2005/47/EC on the Agreement between the Community of European Railways (CER) and the European Transport Workers' Federation (ETF) on certain aspects of the working conditions of mobile workers engaged in interoperable cross-border services in the railway sector. - 20p.: 30 cm. - 978-0-11-081916-7 £3.50

The Crossrail (Nomination) Order 2008 No. 2008/2036. - Enabling power: Crossrail Act 2008, s. 39 (1). - Issued: 04.08.2008. Made: 23.07.2008. Coming into force: 24.07.2008. Effect: None. Territorial extent & classification: E/W/S/NI. General. - 4p.: 30 cm. - 978-0-11-083650-8 £3.00

The Rail Vehicle Accessibility (B2007 Vehicles) Exemption Order 2008 No. 2008/925. - Enabling power: Disability Discrimination Act 1995, ss. 47(1) (1A) (3) (4), 67 (2). - Issued: 03.04.2008. Made: 30.03.2008. Coming into force: 31.03.2008. Effect: None. Territorial extent & classification: E/W/S. General. - Supersedes draft SI (ISBN 9780110808970) issued 07.02.2008. - 8p.: 30 cm. - 978-0-11-081321-9 £3.00

The Rail Vehicle Accessibility (Interoperable Rail System) Regulations 2008 No. 2008/1746. - Enabling power: European Communities Act 1972, s. 2 (2) & Disability Discrimination Act 1995, s. 46 (1) & Transport Act 2000, s. 247. - Issued: 10.07.2008. Made: 02.07.2008. Coming into force: In accord. with reg. 1. Effect: 2005 c.13 & S.I. 1998/2456; 2006/397 amended. Territorial extent & classification: E/W/S/NI. General. - EC note: These Regulations pave the way for the introduction on the 1st July 2008 of European accessibility standards for passenger rail vehicles on the "interoperable rail system". Supersedes draft S.I. (ISBN 9780110817477) issued 28.05.2008. - 8p.: 30 cm. - 978-0-11-081967-9 £3.00

The Transport Tribunal (Amendment) Rules 2002 No. 2008/2142. - Enabling power: Transport Act 1985, para. 11 (1). - Issued: 12.08.2008. Made: 05.08.2008. Laid: 08.08.2008. Coming into force: 01.09.2008. Effect: S.I. 2000/3226 amended. Territorial extent & classification: E/W/S. General. - 4p.: 30 cm. - 978-0-11-083736-9 £3.00

The Rail Vehicle Accessibility (London Underground Victoria Line 09TS Vehicles) Exemption Order 2008 No. 2008/2969. - Enabling power: Disability Discrimination Act 1995, ss. 47 (1) (1A) (3) (a) (4), 67 (2). - Issued: 24.11.2008. Made: 14.11.2008. Coming into force: 15.11.2008. Effect: None. Territorial extent & classification: E/W/S. General. - Supersedes draft S.I. (ISBN 9780110845579) issued 14.10.2008. - 4p.: 30 cm. - 978-0-11-147011-4 £4.00

Transport: Railways

The Channel Tunnel Rail Link (Nomination) Order 2008 No. 2008/3076. - Enabling power: Channel Tunnel Rail Link Act 1996, s. 34 (1) (4). - Issued: 04.12.2008. Made: 28.11.2008. Coming into force: 30.11.2008. Effect: S.I. 1999/391 revoked. Territorial extent & classification: E/W/S/NI. General. - 4p.: 30 cm. - 978-0-11-147083-1 £4.00

Transport and works, England

The Felixstowe Branch Line and Ipswich Yard Improvement Order 2008 No. 2008/2512. - Enabling power: Transport and Works Act 1992, ss. 1, 5. - Issued: 01.10.2008. Made: 23.09.2008. Coming into force: 14.10.2008. Effect: None. Territorial extent & classification: E. General. - 53p.: 30 cm. - 978-0-11-084308-7 £9.00

The Network Rail (Thameslink) (Land Acquisition) Order 2008 No. 2008/3163. - Enabling power: Transport and Works Act 1992, ss. 1, 5, sch. 1, paras 3 to 5, 7, 11, 16. - Issued: 18.12.2008. Made: 05.12.2008. Coming into force: 29.12.2008. Effect: None. Territorial extent & classification: E. General. - 8p.: 30 cm. - 978-0-11-147165-4 £5.00

The River Humber (Upper Burcom Tidal Stream Generator) Order 2008 No. 2008/969. - Enabling power: Transport and Works Act 1992, ss. 3, 5 of, sch. 1, paras 1 to 5, 7, 8, 10, 11, 15 to 17- Issued: 09.04.2008. Made: 02.04.2008. Coming into force: In accord. with art. 1. Effect: None. Territorial extent & classification: E. General. - 16p.: 30 cm. - 978-0-11-081348-6 £3.00

The Teesport (Land Acquisition) Order 2008 No. 2008/1238. - Enabling power: Transport and Works Act 1992, ss. 3, 5, sch. 1, paras 3 to 5, 7, 8, 11, 16. - Issued: 06.05.2008. Made: 30.04.2008. Coming into force: 21.05.2008. Effect: None. Territorial extent & classification: E. General. - 12p.: 30 cm. - 978-0-11-081430-8 £3.00

Transport, England

The Felixstowe Branch Line and Ipswich Yard Improvement Order 2008 No. 2008/2512. - Enabling power: Transport and Works Act 1992, ss. 1, 5. - Issued: 01.10.2008. Made: 23.09.2008. Coming into force: 14.10.2008. Effect: None. Territorial extent & classification: E. General. - 53p.: 30 cm. - 978-0-11-084308-7 £9.00

The Local Authorities (Elected Mayors) (England) Regulations 2008 No. 2008/3112. - Enabling power: Local Government Act 2000, ss. 39 (5B). - Issued: 11.12.2008. Made: 03.12.2008. Laid: 09.12.2008. Coming into force: 31.12.2008. Effect: None. Territorial extent & classification: E. General. - With correction slip dated October 2009. - 2p.: 30 cm. - 978-0-11-147120-3 £4.00

The Network Rail (Thameslink) (Land Acquisition) Order 2008 No. 2008/3163. - Enabling power: Transport and Works Act 1992, ss. 1, 5, sch. 1, paras 3 to 5, 7, 11, 16. - Issued: 18.12.2008. Made: 05.12.2008. Coming into force: 29.12.2008. Effect: None. Territorial extent & classification: E. General. - 8p.: 30 cm. - 978-0-11-147165-4 £5.00

The Teesport (Land Acquisition) Order 2008 No. 2008/1238. - Enabling power: Transport and Works Act 1992, ss. 3, 5, sch. 1, paras 3 to 5, 7, 8, 11, 16. - Issued: 06.05.2008. Made: 30.04.2008. Coming into force: 21.05.2008. Effect: None. Territorial extent & classification: E. General. - 12p.: 30 cm. - 978-0-11-081430-8 £3.00

Transport, Wales

The Regional Transport Planning (Wales) (Amendment) Order 2008 No. 2008/1286 (W.135). - Enabling power: Transport Act 2000, s. 109C. - Issued: 29.05.2008. Made: 13.05.2008. Laid before the National Assembly for Wales: 14.05.2008. Coming into force: 12.06.2008. Effect: S.I. 2006/2993 (W.280) amended. Territorial extent & classification: W. General. - In English and Welsh. Welsh title: Gorchymyn Cynllunio Trafnidiaeth Rhanbarthol (Cymru) (Diwygio) 2008. - 4p.: 30 cm. - 978-0-11-091785-6 £3.00

Tribunals and inquiries

The Appeals (Excluded Decisions) (Amendment) Order 2008 No. 2008/2780. - Enabling power: Tribunals, Courts and Enforcement Act 2007, s. 11 (5) (f). - Issued: 28.10.2008. Made: 21.10.2008. Laid: 24.10.2008. Coming into force: 03.11.2008. Effect: S.I. 2008/2707 amended. Territorial extent & classification: E/W/S/NI. General. - Revoked by S.I. 2009/275 (ISBN 9780111474020). This statutory instrument has been made to correct an error in S.I. 2008/2707 (ISBN 9780110846477) and is being issued free of charge to all known recipients of that statutory instrument. - 2p.: 30 cm. - 978-0-11-084720-7 £4.00

The Appeals (Excluded Decisions) Order 2008 No. 2008/2707. - Enabling power: Tribunals, Courts and Enforcement Act 2007, s. 11 (5) (f). - Issued: 20.10.2008. Made: 13.10.2008. Laid: 15.10.2008. Coming into force: 03.11.2008. Effect: None. Territorial extent & classification: E/W/S/NI. General. - 2p.: 30 cm. - 978-0-11-084647-7 £4.00

The Charity Tribunal Rules 2008 No. 2008/221. - Enabling power: Charities Act 1993, s. 2B. - Issued: 08.02.2008. Made: 04.02.2008. Laid: 05.02.2008. Coming into force: 27.02.2008. Effect: None. Territorial extent & classification: E/W. General. - Revoked by S.I. 2009/1834 (ISBN 9780111482452). With 2 correction slips dated February 2008 & October 2009. - 20p.: 30 cm. - 978-0-11-080903-8 £3.50

The Consumer Credit Appeals Tribunal Rules 2008 No. 2008/668. - Enabling power: Consumer Credit Act 1974, ss. 40A(3), 41A(6), sch. A1, para. 10. - Issued: 14.03.2008. Made: 10.03.2008. Laid: 11.03.2008. Coming into force: 06.04.2008. Effect: None. Territorial extent & classification: E/W/S/NI. General. - Revoked by S.I. 2009/1835 (ISBN 9780111482476). - 16p.: 30 cm. - 978-0-11-081176-5 £3.00

The First-tier Tribunal and Upper Tribunal (Chambers) Order 2008 No. 2008/2684. - Enabling power: Tribunals, Courts and Enforcement Act 2007, s. 7 (1) (9). - Issued: 20.10.2008. Made: 13.10.2008. Laid: 15.10.2008. Coming into force: 03.11.2008. Effect: None. Territorial extent & classification: E/W/S/NI. General. - 4p.: 30 cm. - 978-0-11-084657-6 £4.00

The First-tier Tribunal and Upper Tribunal (Composition of Tribunal) Order 2008 No. 2008/2835. - Enabling power: Tribunals, Courts and Enforcement Act 2007, s. 145 (1), sch. 4, para. 15. - Issued: 04.11.2008. Made: 29.10.2008. Coming into force: 03.11.2008. Effect: None. Territorial extent & classification: E/W/S/NI. General. - 2p.: 30 cm. - 978-0-11-084834-1 £4.00

The Judicial Appointments Order 2008 No. 2008/2995. - Enabling power: Tribunals, Courts and Enforcement Act 2007, s. 51 & Social Security Act 1998, s. 7 (6A) (6B). - Issued: 21.11.2008. Made: 17.11.2008. Coming into force: 18.11.2008 except for art. 7 (b); 30.11.2010 for art. 7 (b) in accord. with art. 1 (2). Effect: None. Territorial extent & classification: E/W/S/NI. General. - Supersedes draft S.I. (ISBN 9780110843360) issued 06.10.2008. - 4p.: 30 cm. - 978-0-11-147020-6 £4.00

The Membership of the Tribunal Procedure Committee Transitional Order 2008 No. 2008/1149. - Enabling power: Tribunals, Courts and Enforcement Act 2007, sch. 9, para. 2. - Issued: 24.04.2008. Made: 18.04.2008. Laid: 22.04.2008. Coming into force: 19.05.2008. Effect: None. Territorial extent & classification: E/W/S/NI. General. - 2p.: 30 cm. - 978-0-11-081397-4 £3.00

The Mesothelioma Lump Sum Payments (Claims and Reconsiderations) (Amendment) Regulations 2008 No. 2008/2706. - Enabling power: Child Maintenance and Other Payments Act 2008, s. 50 (4). - Issued: 20.10.2008. Made: 13.10.2008. Laid: 15.10.2008. Coming into force: 03.11.2008. Effect: S.I. 2008/1595 amended. Territorial extent & classification: E/W/S. General. - 2p.: 30 cm. - 978-0-11-084646-0 £4.00

The Qualifications for Appointment of Members to the First-tier Tribunal and Upper Tribunal Order 2008 No. 2008/2692. - Enabling power: Tribunals, Courts and Enforcement Act 2007, sch. 2, para. 2 (2), sch. 3, para. 2 (2). - Issued: 20.10.2008. Made: 15.10.2008. Laid: 15.10.2008. Coming into force: 03.11.2008. Effect: None. Territorial extent & classification: E/W/S/NI. General. - 2p.: 30 cm. - 978-0-11-084656-9 £4.00

The Transfer of Tribunal Functions Order 2008 No. 2008/2833. - Enabling power: Tribunals, Courts and Enforcement Act 2007, ss. 30 (1) (4), 31 (1) (2) (9), 32 (3) (5), 33 (2) (3), 34 (2) (3), 37 (1), 38, 145, sch. 5, para. 30. - Issued: 04.11.2008. Made: 29.10.2008. Coming into force: 03.11.2008. Effect: 51 acts amended or partially repealed & 4 S.I.s partially revoked & S.I. 2003/2589; 2007/2185 revoked. Territorial extent & classification: E/W/S/NI. General. - Supersedes draft S.I. (ISBN 9780110817828) issued 10.06.2008. - 52p.: 30 cm. - 978-0-11-084825-9 £9.00

The Tribunal Procedure (First-tier Tribunal) (Social Entitlement Chamber) Rules 2008 No. 2008/2685 (L.13). - Enabling power: Social Security Act 1998, s. 20 (2) (3) & Tribunals, Courts and Enforcement Act 2007, ss. 9 (3), 22, 29 (3), sch. 5. - Issued: 20.10.2008. Made: 09.10.2008. Laid: 15.10.2008. Coming into force: 03.11.2008. Effect: None. Territorial extent & classification: E/W/S/NI. General. - 24p.: 30 cm. - 978-0-11-084675-0 £5.00

The Tribunal Procedure (Upper Tribunal) Rules 2008 No. 2008/2698 (L.15). - Enabling power: Tribunals, Courts and Enforcement Act 2007, ss. 10 (3), 16 (9), 22, 29 (3) (4), sch. 5. - Issued: 20.10.2008. Made: 09.10.2008. Laid: 15.10.2008. Coming into force: 03.11.2008. Effect: None. Territorial extent & classification: E/W/S/NI. General. - 28p.: 30 cm. - With correction slip dated September 2009. - 978-0-11-084671-2 £5.00

The Tribunals, Courts and Enforcement Act 2007 (Commencement No. 5 and Transitional Provisions) Order 2008 No. 2008/1653 (C.73). - Enabling power: Tribunals, Courts and Enforcement Act 2007, s. 145, 148 (5). Bringing into operation various provisions of the 2007 Act on 21.07.2008. - Issued: 01.07.2008. Made: 23.06.2008. Laid: 26.06.2008. Effect: None. Territorial extent & classification: E/W/S/NI. General. - 4p.: 30 cm. - 978-0-11-081912-9 £3.00

The Tribunals, Courts and Enforcement Act 2007 (Commencement No. 6 and Transitional Provisions) Order 2008 No. 2008/2696 (C.117). - Enabling power: Tribunals, Courts and Enforcement Act 2007, ss. 31 (9), 148 (5). Bringing into operation various provisions of the 2007 Act on 03.11.2008 & 01.04.2009 in accord. with art. 2. - Issued: 20.10.2008. Made: 09.10.2008. Laid: 15.10.2008. Effect: None. Territorial extent & classification: E/W/S/NI. General. - 8p.: 30 cm. - 978-0-11-084610-1 £5.00

The Tribunals, Courts and Enforcement Act 2007 (Transitional and Consequential Provisions) Order 2008 No. 2008/2683. - Enabling power: Tribunals, Courts and Enforcement Act 2007, s. 31 (9), 145, sch. 5, para. 30. - Issued: 20.10.2008. Made: 09.10.2008. Laid: 15.10.2008. Coming into force: 03.11.2008. Effect: 108 SIs amended and 30 SIs revoked. Territorial extent & classification: E/W/S/NI. General. - 52p.: 30 cm. - 978-0-11-084615-6 £9.00

The Tribunals, Courts and Enforcement Act 2007 (Transitional Judicial Pensions Provisions) Regulations 2008 No. 2008/2697. - Enabling power: Tribunals, Courts and Enforcement Act 2007, sch. 9, para. 12 (2). - Issued: 20.10.2008. Made: 09.10.2008. Laid: 15.10.2008. Coming into force: 03.11.2008. Effect: None. Territorial extent & classification: E/W/S/NI. General. - 2p.: 30 cm. - 978-0-11-084618-7 £4.00

Tribunals and inquiries, England and Wales

The Appeals from the Upper Tribunal to the Court of Appeal Order 2008 No. 2008/2834. - Enabling power: Tribunals, Courts and Enforcement Act 2007, s. 13 (6). - Issued: 04.11.2008. Made: 29.10.2008. Coming into force: 03.11.2008 in accord. with art. 1. Effect: None. Territorial extent & classification: E/W/NI. General. - Supersedes draft S.I. (ISBN 9780110817897) issued 09.06.2008. - 2p.: 30 cm. - 978-0-11-084828-0 £4.00

The Mental Health Review Tribunal for Wales Rules 2008 No. 2008/2705 (L.17). - Enabling power: Mental Health Act 1983, s. 78. - Issued: 16.10.2008. Made: 13.10.2008. Laid: 13.10.2008. Coming into force: 03.11.2008. Effect: S.I. 1983/942; 1996/314; 1998/1189 revoked. Territorial extent & classification: E/W. General. - 20p.: 30 cm. - With correction sip dated September 2009. - 978-0-11-084642-2 £5.00

The Tribunal Procedure (First-tier Tribunal) (Health, Education and Social Care Chamber) Rules 2008 No. 2008/2699 (L.16). - Enabling power: Tribunals, Courts and Enforcement Act 2007, ss. 9 (3), 22, 29 (3) (4), sch. 5. - Issued: 20.10.2008. Made: 09.10.2008. Laid: 15.10.2008. Coming into force: 03.11.2008. Effect: None. Territorial extent & classification: E/W. General. - With correction slip dated September 2009. - 28p.: 30 cm. - 978-0-11-084619-4 £5.00

The Tribunal Procedure (First-tier Tribunal) (War Pensions and Armed Forces Compensation Chamber) Rules 2008 No. 2008/2686 (L.14). - Enabling power: Tribunals, Courts and Enforcement Act 2007, ss. 9 (3), 22, 29 (3), sch. 5. - Issued: 20.10.2008. Made: 09.10.2008. Laid: 15.10.2008. Coming into force: 03.11.2008. Effect: None. Territorial extent & classification: E/W. General. - 20p.: 30 cm. - With correction slip dated September 2009. - 978-0-11-084630-9 £5.00

Tribunals and inquiries, Northern Ireland

The Appeals from the Upper Tribunal to the Court of Appeal Order 2008 No. 2008/2834. - Enabling power: Tribunals, Courts and Enforcement Act 2007, s. 13 (6). - Issued: 04.11.2008. Made: 29.10.2008. Coming into force: 03.11.2008 in accord. with art. 1. Effect: None. Territorial extent & classification: E/W/NI. General. - Supersedes draft S.I. (ISBN 9780110817897) issued 09.06.2008. - 2p.: 30 cm. - 978-0-11-084828-0 £4.00

Trustees, England and Wales

The Public Trustee (Fees) Order 2008 No. 2008/611. - Enabling power: Public Trustee Act 1906, s. 9 (1). - Issued: 12.03.2008. Made: 05.03.2008. Coming into force: 01.04.2008. Effect: S.I. 1999/855; 2002/2232; 2003/690; 2004/799; 2005/351; 2007/681 revoked. Territorial extent & classification: E/W. General. - 12p.: 30 cm. - 978-0-11-081131-4 *£3.00*

United Nations

The United Nations Arms Embargoes (Dependent Territories) (Amendment) Order 2008 No. 2008/3123. - Enabling power: United Nations Act 1946, s. 1. - Issued: 16.12.2008. Made: 10.12.2008. Laid: 11.12.2008. Coming into force: 12.12.2008. Effect: S.I. 1995/1032 amended. Territorial extent & classification: Anguilla, Bermuda, British Antarctic Territory, British Indian Ocean Territory, Cayman Islands, Falkland Islands, Gibraltar, Montserrat, Pitcairn, Henderson, Ducie and Oeno Islands, St. Helena and its Dependencies, South Georgia and South Sandwich Islands, The Sovereign Base areas of Akrotiri and Dhekelia, Turks and Caicos Islands and Virgin Islands. General. - 2p.: 30 cm. - 978-0-11-147151-7 *£4.00*

The United Nations Arms Embargoes (Rwanda) (Amendment) Order 2008 No. 2008/3128. - Enabling power: United Nations Act 1946, s. 1. - Issued: 16.12.2008. Made: 10.12.2008. Laid: 11.12.2008. Coming into force: 12.12.2008. Effect: S.I. 1993/1787 amended. Territorial extent & classification: UK. General. - 2p.: 30 cm. - 978-0-11-147148-7 *£4.00*

Value added tax

The Travellers' Allowances (Amendment) Order 2008 No. 2008/3058. - Enabling power: Customs and Excise Duties (General Reliefs) Act 1979, s. 13 (1) (3). - Issued: 23.01.2009. Made: 28.11.2008. Laid: 28.11.2008. Coming into force: 01.12.2008. Effect: S.I. 1994/955 amended & S.I. 1995/3044 revoked. Territorial extent & classification: E/W/S/NI. General. - Approved by the House of Commons- 4p.: 30 cm. - 978-0-11-147302-3 *£4.00*

The Travellers' Allowances (Amendment) Order 2008 No. 2008/3058. - Enabling power: Customs and Excise Duties (General Reliefs) Act 1979, s. 13 (1) (3). - Issued: 04.12.2008. Made: 28.11.2008. Laid: 28.11.2008. Coming into force: 01.12.2008. Effect: S.I. 1994/955 amended & S.I. 1995/3044 revoked. Territorial extent & classification: E/W/S/NI. General. - For approval by that House before the end of the period of 28 days beginning with the day on which it was made, no account being taken of any time during which Parliament is dissolved or prorogued or during which the House of Commons is adjourned for more than 4 days. - 4p.: 30 cm. - 978-0-11-147084-8 *£4.00*

The Value Added Tax (Amendment) (No. 2) Regulations 2008 No. 2008/3021. - Enabling power: Value Added Tax Act 1994, ss. 26B, 88(5), sch. 11, paras 2 (1) (10, 2A. - Issued: 25.11.2008. Made: 24.11.2008. Laid: 24.11.2008. Coming into force: 01.12.2008. Effect: S.I. 1995/2518 amended. Territorial extent & classification: E/W/S/NI. General. - 4p.: 30 cm. - 978-0-11-147053-4 *£4.00*

The Value Added Tax (Amendment) Regulations 2008 No. 2008/556. - Enabling power: Value Added Tax Act 1994, sch. 11, paras 2 (3). - Issued: 11.03.2008. Made: 05.03.2008. Laid: 05.03.2008. Coming into force: 01.04.2008. Effect: S.I. 1995/2518 amended. Territorial extent & classification: E/W/S/NI. General. - 4p.: 30 cm. - 978-0-11-081118-5 *£3.00*

The Value Added Tax (Buildings and Land) Order 2008 No. 2008/1146. - Enabling power: Finance Act 2006, s. 17 (1) to (5). - Issued: 25.04.2008. Made: 21.04.2008. Laid: 22.04.2008. Coming into force: 01.06.2008. Effect: 1994 c.23 amended. Territorial extent & classification: E/W/S/NI. General. - For approval by resolution of that House within twenty-eight days beginning with the day on which the Order was made, subject to extension for periods of dissolution, prorogation or adjournment for more than four days. - 36p.: 30 cm. - 978-0-11-081395-0 *£6.50*

The Value Added Tax (Buildings and Land) Order 2008 No. 2008/1146. - Enabling power: Finance Act 2006, s. 17 (1) to (5). - Issued: 20.05.2008. Made: 21.04.2008. Laid: 22.04.2008. Coming into force: 01.06.2008. Effect: 1994 c.23 amended. Territorial extent & classification: E/W/S/NI. General. - Approved by the House of Commons. Supersedes SI of same no. (ISBN 9780110813950) issued 24.04.2008. - 36p.: 30 cm. - With correction slip dated July 2009. - 978-0-11-081473-5 *£6.50*

The Value Added Tax (Change of Rate) Order 2008 No. 2008/3020. - Enabling power: Value Added Tax Act 1994, ss. 2 (2), 21 (7). - Issued: 25.11.2008. Made: 24.11.2008. Laid: 24.11.2008. Coming into force: 01.12.2008. Effect: 1994 c. 23 amended. Territorial extent & classification: E/W/S/NI. General. - 2p.: 30 cm. - 978-0-11-147052-7 *£4.00*

The Value Added Tax (Consideration for Fuel Provided for Private Use) Order 2008 No. 2008/722. - Enabling power: Value Added Tax Act 1994, s. 57(4) to (4G). - Issued: 19.03.2008. Made: 12.03.2008. Laid: 13.03.2008. Coming into force: 01.04.2008. Effect: 1994 c. 23 amended. Territorial extent & classification: E/W/S/NI. General. - 4p.: 30 cm. - 978-0-11-081258-8 *£3.00*

The Value Added Tax, etc (Correction of Errors, etc) Regulations 2008 No. 2008/1482. - Enabling power: Value Added Tax Act 1994, sch. 11, paras 2 (1) (10) (11) & Finance Act 1994, ss. 38 (1), 42 (2), 54, 74 (7) (8) & Finance Act 1996, ss. 49, 71 (8) (9) & Finance Act 2000, sch. 6, paras 41(1) (2), 146 (7) & Finance Act 2001, ss. 25 (1) (2), 45 (5). - Issued: 18.06.2008. Made: 09.06.2008. Laid: 10.06.2008. Coming into force: 01.07.2008. Effect: S.I. 1994/1738, 1774; 1995/2518; 1996/1527; 2001/838; 2002/761 amended. Territorial extent & classification: E/W/S/NI. General. - 12p.: 30 cm. - 978-0-11-081855-9 *£3.00*

The Value Added Tax (Finance) (No. 2) Order 2008 No. 2008/2547. - Enabling power: Value Added Tax Act 1994, ss. 31 (2), 96 (9). - Issued: 02.10.2008. Made: 29.09.2008. Laid: 29.09.2008. Coming into force: 30.09.2008 for art. 2; 01.10.2008 for remainder in accord. with art. 1. Effect: 1994 c. 23 amended and S.I. 2008/1892 revoked (30.09.2008). Territorial extent & classification: E/W/S/NI. General. - For approval by resolution of the House of Commons within twenty-eight days beginning with the date on which the Order was made, subject to extension for periods of dissolution, prorogation or adjournment for more than four days. This Statutory Instrument has been made in consequence of a defect in S.I. 2008/1892 and is being issued free of charge to all known recipients of that Statutory Instrument. - 4p.: 30 cm. - 978-0-11-084323-0 £4.00

The Value Added Tax (Finance) (No. 2) Order 2008 No. 2008/2547. - Enabling power: Value Added Tax Act 1994, ss. 31 (2), 96 (9). - Issued: 28.10.2008. Made: 29.09.2008. Laid: 29.09.2008. Coming into force: 30.09.2008 for art. 2 & 01.10.2008 for remainder in accord. with art. 1. Effect: 1994 c. 23 amended and S.I. 2008/1892 revoked. Territorial extent & classification: E/W/S/NI. General. - Approved by the House of Commons. With correction slip dated August 2009. - 4p.: 30 cm. - 978-0-11-084714-6 £4.00

The Value Added Tax (Finance) Order 2008 No. 2008/1892. - Enabling power: Value Added Tax Act 1994, ss. 31 (2), 96 (9). - Issued: 23.07.2003. Made: 17.07.2003. Laid: 17.07.2008. Coming into force: 01.08.2008. Effect: 1994 c. 23 amended. Territorial extent & classification: E/W/S/NI. General. - Revoked by S.I. 2008/2547 (ISBN 9780110847146). For approval by resolution of the House of Commons within twenty-eight days beginning with the date on which the Order was made, subject to extension for periods of dissolution, prorogation or adjournment for more than four days. - 4p.: 30 cm. - 978-0-11-083386-6 £3.00

The Value Added Tax (Increase of Registration Limits) Order 2008 No. 2008/707. - Enabling power: Value Added Tax Act 1994, sch. 1, para. 15; sch. 3, para. 9. - Issued: 13.03.2008. Made: 12.03.2008. Laid: 13.03.2008. Coming into force: 01.04.2008. Effect: 1994 c.23 amended. Territorial extent & classification: E/W/S/NI. General. - 2p.: 30 cm. - 978-0-11-081209-0 £3.00

The Value Added Tax (Reduced Rate) (Smoking Cessation Products) Order 2008 No. 2008/1410. - Enabling power: Value Added Tax Act 1994, s. 29A. - Issued: 10.06.2008. Made: 02.06.2008. Laid: 03.06.2008. Coming into force: 30.06.2008. Effect: 1994 c.23 amended. Territorial extent & classification: E/W/S/NI. General. - 2p.: 30 cm. - 978-0-11-081770-5 £3.00

The Value Added Tax (Reduced Rate) (Supplies of Domestic Fuel or Power) Order 2008 No. 2008/2676. - Enabling power: Value Added Tax Act, 1994, ss. 29A, 96 (9). - Issued: 14.10.2008. Made: 08.10.2008. Laid: 09.10.2008. Coming into force: 01.11.2008. Effect: 1994 c. 23 amended. Territorial extent & classification: E/W/S/NI. General. - 2p.: 30 cm. - 978-0-11-084539-5 £4.00

The Value Added Tax (Refund of Tax to Museums and Galleries) (Amendment) Order 2008 No. 2008/1339. - Enabling power: Value Added Tax Act 1994, s. 33A (9). - Issued: 28.05.2008. Made: 21.05.2008. Laid: 22.05.2008. Coming into force: 01.07.2008. Effect: S.I. 2001/2879 amended. Territorial extent & classification: E/W/S/NI. General. - 4p.: 30 cm. - 978-0-11-081754-5 £3.00

Veterinary surgeons

The Veterinary Surgeons and Veterinary Practitioners (Registration) (Amendment) Regulations Order of Council 2008 No. 2008/2933. - Enabling power: Veterinary Surgeons Act 1966, s. 11. - Issued: 17.11.2008. Made: 07.11.2008. Coming into force: 01.04.2009. Effect: S.I. 2005/3517 amended. Territorial extent & classification: E/W/S/NI. General. - 4p.: 30 cm. - 978-0-11-146998-9 £4.00

The Veterinary Surgeons (Examination of Commonwealth and Foreign Candidates) (Amendment) Regulations Order of Council 2008 No. 2008/2501. - Enabling power: Veterinary Surgeons Act 1966, s. 25 (1). - Issued: 01.10.2008. Made: 13.09.2008. Coming into force: 01.10.2008. Effect: S.I. 2005/3240 amended. Territorial extent & classification: E/W/S/NI. General. - 4p.: 30 cm. - 978-0-11-084291-2 £4.00

The Veterinary Surgeons' Qualifications (European Recognition) Regulations 2008 No. 2008/1824. - Enabling power: European Communities Act 1972, s. 2 (2). - Issued: 16.07.2008. Made: 08.07.2008. Laid: 11.07.2008. Coming into force: 06.08.2008. Effect: 1966 c. 36 amended & S.I. 2003/2919 part revoked & S.I. 2007/1348 revoked. Territorial extent & classification: E/W/S/NI. General. - EC note: These regulations give effect to Directive 2005/36/EC. - 24p.: 30 cm. - 978-0-11-083104-6 £4.00

Water, England

The Nitrate Pollution Prevention Regulations 2008 No. 2008/2349. - Enabling power: European Communities Act 1972, s. 2 (2). - Issued: 09.09.2008. Made: 01.09.2008. Laid: 04.09.2008. Coming into force: 01.01.2009 except reg. 22 (1) and Part 7; 01.01.2012 for reg. 22 (1) and Part 7, in accord. with reg. 3. Effect: S.I. 1994/1729; 1995/1708, 2095; 1996/888, 3105; 1997/990; 1998/79, 1202, 2138; 2002/744, 2614; 2003/562; 2006/1289 revoked in relation to England. Territorial extent & classification: E. General. - EC note: They continue to implement in England Council Directive 91/676/EEC concerning the protection of waters against pollution by nitrates from agricultural sources- 24p.: 30 cm. - 978-0-11-084012-3 £5.00

The Water Act 2003 (Commencement No. 8) Order 2008 No. 2008/1922 (C.87). - Enabling power: Water Act 2003, s. 105 (3) to (6). Bringing into operation various provisions of the 2003 Act on 01.08.2008. - Issued: 24.07.2008. Made: 17.07.2008. Effect: None. Territorial extent & classification: E. General. - 8p.: 30 cm. - 978-0-11-083466-5 £3.00

Water industry, England and Wales

The Water Supply and Sewerage Services (Customer Service Standards) Regulations 2008 No. 2008/594. - Enabling power: Water Industry Act 1991, ss. 38 (2) to (4), 95 (2) to (4), 213 (2A) (a) (b) (c) (2B), para. (2) (d) (e). - Issued: 11.03.2008. Made: 04.03.2008. Laid: 10.03.2008. Coming into force: 01.04.2008. Effect: S.I. 1989/1159, 1383; 1993/500; 1996/3065; 2000/2301 revoked. Territorial extent & classification: E/W. General. - 12p.: 30 cm. - 978-0-11-081112-3 *£3.00*

Water resources

The Bathing Water Regulations 2008 No. 2008/1097. - Enabling power: European Communities Act 1972, s. 2 (2). - Issued: 23.04.2008. Made: 16.04.2008. Laid: 21.04.2008. Laid before the National Assembly for Wales: 21.04.2008. Coming into force: 14.05.2008; 24.03.2012; 24.03.2015 in accord. with reg. 1. Effect: 1991 c. 57, 1995 c. 25; S.I. 2003/3242; 2004/99 amended; and S.I. 1991/1597 transitionally amended and then revoked (24.03.2015) & S.I. 2003/1238 revoked (24.03.2015). Territorial extent & classification: E/W [though any amendment or revocation made by these Regulations has the same extent as the enactment being amended or revoked]. General. - EC note: These Regulations make provision for the purpose of implementing, in England and Wales, Directive 2006/7/EC concerning the management of bathing water quality and repealing Directive 76/160/EEC. - 20p.: 30 cm. - 978-0-11-081385-1 *£3.50*

Water resources, England and Wales

The Water Resources (Abstraction and Impounding) (Amendment) Regulations 2008 No. 2008/165. - Enabling power: Water Resources Act 1991, ss. 37 (4) (6), 51 (1C) (b) (1D) (3), 189, 219 (2) (d) (e) (f), 221 (1). - Issued: 01.02.2008. Made: 26.01.2008. Laid: 31.01.2008. Coming into force: 29.02.2008. Effect: S.I. 2006/641 amended. Territorial extent & classification: E/W. General. - This Statutory Instrument has been made in consequence of a defect SI 2006/641 and is being issued free of charge to all known recipients of that Statutory Instrument. - 4p.: 30 cm. - 978-0-11-080879-6 *£3.00*

Water, Wales

The Nitrate Pollution Prevention (Wales) Regulations 2008 No. 2008/3143 (W.278). - Enabling power: European Communities Act 1972, s. 2 (2), sch. 2, para. 1A. - Issued: 31.12.2008. Made: 06.12.2008. Laid before the National Assembly for Wales: 09.12.2008. Coming into force: 01.01.2009 (other than reg. 22 (1) and part 7); 01.01.2012 for reg. 22 (1) and part 7, in accord. with reg. 3. Effect: S.I. 1996/888; 1998/1202; 2002/2297 (W. 226); 2006/1289 revoked insofar as they apply in relation to Wales. Territorial extent & classification: W. General. - In English and Welsh. Welsh title: Rheoliadau Atal Llygredd Nitradau (Cymru) 2008. - 40p.: 30 cm. - 978-0-11-091916-4 *£9.00*

Weights and measures

The Measuring Instruments (EC Requirements) (Amendment) Regulations 2008 No. 2008/1267. - Enabling power: European Communities Act 1972, s. 2 (2). - Issued: 12.05.2008. Made: 07.05.2008. Laid: 08.05.2008. Coming into force: 01.06.2008. Effect: S.I. 1988/186 amended. Territorial extent & classification: E/W/S/NI. General. - EC note: These Regulations update the Measuring Instruments (EEC Requirements) Regulations 1988 (S.I. 1988/186). The 1988 Regulations implement Council Directive 71/316/EEC. For new designs of certain instrument types, Directive 71/316/EEC has been superseded by the Measuring Instruments Directive (2004/22/EC), but it remains relevant for a number of older instruments which are still manufactured. When an instrument has been granted pattern approval or has successfully undergone initial verification under Directive 71/316/EEC, it must be marked in such a way as to indicate, amongst other things, by which Member State the approval has been granted or in which Member State the verification has taken place as the case may be. The Directive specified the form of these marks, based on stylised versions of the distinguishing letters of the Member States. This instrument shows the new marks based on stylised versions of the distinguishing letters of the new Member States. - 8p.: 30 cm. - 978-0-11-081438-4 *£3.00*

The Non-automatic Weighing Instruments (Amendment) Regulations 2008 No. 2008/738. - Enabling power: European Communities Act 1972, s. 2 (2) & Weights and Measures Act 1985, ss. 15 (1), 86 (1). - Issued: 20.03.2008. Made: 06.03.2008. Laid: 14.03.2008. Coming into force: 06.04.2008. Effect: S.I. 2000/3236 amended. Territorial extent & classification: E/W/S/NI [except for part III which does not apply to NI]. General. - EC note: These Regulations amend the enforcement provisions of the Non-automatic Weighing Instruments Regulations 2000 (S.I. 2000/3236) which have two purposes. First, they implement Council Directive 90/384/EEC (as amended by Council Directive 93/68/EEC) on the harmonisation of the laws of the member States relating to non-automatic weighing instruments ("instruments"). Secondly, Part III of the principal Regulations contains provisions in relation to instruments which are used for trade within the meaning of the Weights and Measures Act 1985. - 8p.: 30 cm. - 978-0-11-081251-9 £3.00

Welsh language

The Welsh Language Schemes (Public Bodies) Order 2008 No. 2008/1890 (W.179). - Enabling power: Welsh Language Act 1993, s. 6 (1). - Issued: 21.08.2008. Made: 16.07.2008. Laid before the National Assembly for Wales: 17.07.2008. Coming into force: 11.08.2008. Effect: None. Territorial extent & classification: W. General. - In English and Welsh. Welsh title: Gorchymyn Cynlluniau Iaith Gymraeg (Cyrff Cyhoeddus) 2008. - 4p.: 30 cm. - 978-0-11-091830-3 £3.00

Wildlife, England

The Wildlife and Countryside Act 1981 (Variation of Schedule 4) (England) Order 2008 No. 2008/2356. - Enabling power: Wildlife and Countryside Act 1981, s. 21 (1). - Issued: 09.09.2008. Made: 01.09.2008. Laid: 05.09.2008. Coming into force: 01.10.2008. Effect: 1981 c. 69 amended & S.I. 1994 /1151 partially revoked. Territorial extent & classification: E/W but applies to England only. General. - 4p.: 30 cm. - 978-0-11-084063-5 £4.00

The Wildlife and Countryside Act 1981 (Variation of Schedule 5) (England) Order 2008 No. 2008/431. - Enabling power: Wildlife and Countryside Act 1981, s. 22 (3). - Issued: 27.02.2008. Made: 21.02.2008. Laid: 26.02.2008. Coming into force: 06.04.2008. Effect: 1981 c.69 amended. Territorial extent & classification: E/W but applies substantively in relation to England only. General. - 4p.: 30 cm. - 978-0-11-081008-9 £3.00

The Wildlife and Countryside (Registration and Ringing of Certain Captive Birds) (Amendment) (England) Regulations 2008 No. 2008/2357. - Enabling power: Wildlife and Countryside Act 1981, s. 7 (1) (2). - Issued: 12.09.2008. Made: 01.09.2008. Laid: 05.09.2008. Coming into force: 01.10.2008. Effect: S.I. 1982/1221 amended. Territorial extent & classification: E. General. - 4p.: 30 cm. - 978-0-11-084164-9 £4.00

Wildlife, England and Wales

The Conservation (Natural Habitats, &c.) (Amendment) (England and Wales) Regulations 2008 No. 2008/2172. - Enabling power: European Communities Act 1972, s. 2 (2). - Issued: 20.08.2008. Made: 12.08.2008. Laid: 20.08.2008. Coming into force: 01.10.2008. Effect: 1981 c. 69 & S.I. 1994/2716 amended. Territorial extent & classification: E/W. General. - EC note: These Regulations amend the 1994 Regulations on the Conservation of Natural Habitats, which make provision implementing Council Directive 92/43/EEC on the conservation of natural habitats and of wild flora and fauna. - 4p.: 30 cm. - 978-0-11-083803-8 £3.00

Wildlife, Wales

The Wildlife and Countryside Act 1981 (Variation of Schedule 5) (Wales) Order 2008 No. 2008/1927 (W.183). - Enabling power: Wildlife and Countryside Act 1981, s. 22 (3). - Issued: 15.08.2008. Made: 17.07.2008. Laid before the National Assembly for Wales: 21.07.2008. Coming into force: 12.08.2008. Effect: 1981 c. 69 amended in relation to Wales. Territorial extent & classification: W. General. - In English and Welsh. Welsh title: Gorchymyn Deddf Bywyd Gwyllt a Chefn Gwlad 1981 (Amrywio Atodlen 5) (Cymru) 2008. - 4p.: 30 cm. - 978-0-11-091828-0 £3.00

Young offender institutions, England and Wales

The Young Offender Institution (Amendment) Rules 2008 No. 2008/599. - Enabling power: Prison Act 1952, s. 47. - Issued: 11.03.2008. Made: 04.03.2008. Laid: 05.03.2008. Coming into force: 01.04.2008. Effect: S.I. 2000/3371 amended. Territorial extent & classification: E/W. General. - With correction slip dated July 2009. - 4p.: 30 cm. - 978-0-11-081113-0 £3.00

Statutory Instruments

Arranged by Number

1 (W.1)	Road traffic, Wales
2 (W.2)	Road traffic, Wales
3	Insolvency
	Fees
4	Education, England
5	Immigration
	Police
6	Trade descriptions
7 (W.3)	Rating and valuation, Wales
8	Immigration
	Police
	Revenue and customs
9	Environmental protection
10 (W.4)	Town and country planning, Wales
11	Trade marks
12 (W.5)	Road traffic, Wales
13	Social security
14	Social security
15	Trade descriptions
16	Children and young persons, England and Wales
	Protection of vulnerable adults, England and Wales
17 (W.6) (C.1)	Children and young persons, Wales
18 (W.7)	Education, Wales
19	Betting, gaming and lotteries
20	Road traffic
21	Road traffic
22	Road traffic
23	Road traffic
24	Road traffic
25	Road traffic
26	Road traffic
27	Road traffic
28	Road traffic
29	Road traffic
30	Road traffic
31	Road traffic
32	Road traffic
33	Road traffic
34	Road traffic
35	Road traffic
36	Road traffic
37	Environmental protection
38 (W.8)	Road traffic, Wales
39	Pensions
40	Legal Services Commission, England and Wales
41	Environmental protection
42	Food, England
43	Local government, England
44 (W.9)	Road traffic, Wales
45 (W.10)	Road traffic, Wales
46	Education, England
47	Education, England
48 (S.1)	Representation of the people
49	Education, England
50	Education, England
51	Agriculture, England
52	Stamp duty reserve tax
53	Education, England
54	Education, England
55	Sports grounds and sporting events, England and Wales
56 (W.11)	Food, Wales
57	Road traffic
58	Road traffic
59	Road traffic
60	Road traffic
61	Road traffic
62	Road traffic
63	Road traffic
64	Road traffic
65	Road traffic
66	Road traffic
67	Road traffic
68	Road traffic
69	Road traffic
70	Road traffic
71	Road traffic
72	Road traffic
73	Road traffic
74	Road traffic
75	Road traffic
76	Road traffic
77	Road traffic
78	Criminal law, England and Wales
79	National Health Service, England
80	Agriculture, England
81	Legal profession, England and Wales
	Legal profession, Northern Ireland

82	Police, England and Wales	124	Road traffic
83	National Health Service, England	125	Road traffic
84 (W.12)	Road traffic, Wales	126	Road traffic
85	Food, England	127	Road traffic
86	Road traffic	128	Road traffic
87	Road traffic	129	Road traffic
88	Road traffic	130 (W.17)	Animals, Wales
89	Road traffic	131	Customs and excise
90	Road traffic	132	Immigration
91	Environmental protection	133	Social security
92	Road traffic	134	Road traffic
93	Road traffic	135	British nationality
94	Road traffic	136 (W.18)	Education, Wales
95	Road traffic	137 (W.19)	Food, Wales
96	Road traffic	138 (W.20)	Food, Wales
97	Environmental protection	139	Electronic communications
98 (W.13)	Road traffic, Wales	140	Education, England
99 (C.2)	Immigration	141	Road traffic
100	Education, England	142	Road traffic
101 (W.14)	Highways, Wales	143	Road traffic
102 (W.15)	Highways, Wales	144	Road traffic
103	Road traffic	145	Road traffic
104	Road traffic	146	Road traffic
105	Road traffic	147	Road traffic
106	Road traffic	148	Road traffic
107	Road traffic	149	Road traffic
108	Road traffic	150	Road traffic
109	Road traffic	151	Road traffic
110	Road traffic	152	Road traffic
111	Road traffic	153	Road traffic
112	Road traffic	154	Road traffic
113 (C.3)	London government	155	Road traffic
114 (W.16)	Road traffic, Wales	156	Road traffic
115 (L.1)	Family proceedings, England and Wales	157	Road traffic
	Supreme Court of England and Wales	158	Road traffic
		159	Road traffic
	County courts, England and Wales	160	Road traffic
116 (L.2)	Supreme Court of England and Wales	161	Road traffic
		162	Road traffic
	County courts, England and Wales	163	Merchant shipping
117 (L.3)	Magistrates' courts, England and Wales	164	Stamp duty
			Stamp duty reserve tax
118	Education, England	165	Water resources, England and Wales
119	Education, England	166	Immigration
120	Civil aviation	167	Police, England and Wales
121	Civil aviation	168 (W.21)	Education, Wales
122	Civil aviation	169 (W.22)	Children and young persons, Wales
123	Civil aviation		

170 (W.23)	Children and young persons, Wales		Pensions, England
171	Pensions	215 (W.26)	Education, Wales
172 (C.4)	Local government, England	216	Rating and valuation, England
173	Local government, England	217	Pensions
174	Local government, England	218	Immigration
175	Local government, England		Nationality
176	Local government, England	219 (C.5)	Disclosure of information
177	Local government, England		Investigatory powers
178	Local government, England		Proceeds of crime
179	Local government, England		Public audit
180	Local government, England		Revenue and customs
			Serious crime prevention orders
181	Civil aviation	220 (W.27)	Local government, Wales
182	Civil aviation	221	Tribunals and inquiries
183	Civil aviation	222 (C.6)	Legal services, England and Wales
184	Civil aviation	223	Social security
185	Civil aviation	224	National Health Service, England
186	Civil aviation	225	Petroleum
187	Civil aviation	226 (W.28)	Road traffic, Wales
188	Electricity	227	Local government, England
	Gas	228	Education, England
189	Road traffic	229	Pensions
190	Road traffic	230	Harbours, docks, piers and ferries
191	Road traffic	231	Highways, England
192	Road traffic	232	Highways, England
193	Road traffic	233	Highways, England
194	Road traffic	234	Highways, England
195	Road traffic	235	Education, England
196	Social security	236	Electronic communications
197 (W.24)	Road traffic, Wales	237	Electronic communications
198	Road traffic	238	Pensions, England and Wales
199 (W.25)	Fire and rescue services, Wales	239	Pensions, England and Wales
200	Road traffic	240	Road traffic
201	Road traffic	241	Road traffic
202	Road traffic	242	Road traffic
203	Road traffic	243	Road traffic
204	Road traffic	244	Road traffic
205	Road traffic	245	Road traffic
206	Road traffic	246	Road traffic
207	Road traffic	247	Road traffic
208	Road traffic	248	Road traffic
209	Road traffic	249	Road traffic
210	Road traffic	250	Road traffic
211	Copyright	251	Road traffic
212	Immigration, England and Wales	252	National Health Service, England and Wales
213	Fire and rescue services, England		
	Pensions, England	253 (W.29)	Landlord and tenant, Wales
214	Fire and rescue services, England	254 (W.30)	Housing, Wales

255	National lottery
	Olympic games and paralympic games
256	Road traffic
257	Road traffic
258	Road traffic
259	Road traffic
260	Road traffic
261	Road traffic
262	Road traffic
263	Road traffic
264	Road traffic
265	Road traffic
266	Road traffic
267	Road traffic
268	Road traffic
269	Road traffic
270	Road traffic
271	Road traffic
272	Road traffic
273	Police, England and Wales
274	Road traffic
275	Road traffic
276	Road traffic
277	Road traffic
278	Road traffic
279	Road traffic
280	Road traffic
281	Road traffic
282	Road traffic
283	Road traffic
284	Road traffic
285	Road traffic
286	Road traffic
287	Road traffic
288	Road traffic
289	Road traffic
290	Local government, England
291	Road traffic
292	Road traffic
293	Road traffic
294	Road traffic
295	Dangerous drugs
296	Dangerous drugs
297	European Communities
298	Proceeds of crime
299	Defence
300	Judicial Committee
301	European Communities
302	Proceeds of crime
303	Local government, England
304	Local government, England
305 (S.2)	Representation of the people
306 (C.7)	Police, England and Wales
307 (S.3)	Constitutional law
	Devolution, Scotland
308 (C.8)	Countryside, England
309 (C.9)	Immigration
310 (C.10)	Immigration
311 (C.11)	Police, England and Wales
312	Police, England and Wales
313 (C.12)	Education, England
314	Environmental protection, England
315	Council tax, England
316	Council tax, England
317	Civil aviation
318	Civil aviation
319	Civil aviation
320	Civil aviation
321	Civil aviation
322	Civil aviation
323	Road traffic
324	Road traffic
325	Road traffic
326	Road traffic
327	Road traffic
328	Road traffic
329	Road traffic
330	Road traffic
331	Road traffic
332	Road traffic
333	Road traffic
334	Road traffic
335	Road traffic
336	Road traffic
337 (C.13)	Local government, England
338	Road traffic
339	Road traffic
340	Road traffic
341	Road traffic
342	Highways, England
343	Road traffic
344	Road traffic
345	Road traffic

346	Financial services and markets	391	Road traffic
347	Road traffic	392	Road traffic
348	Road traffic	393	Companies
349	Road traffic	394	Road traffic
350	Road traffic	395	Road traffic
351	Road traffic	396	Criminal law
352	Road traffic	397	Road traffic
353	Road traffic	398	Road traffic
354	Road traffic	399	Road traffic
355	Road traffic	400	Road traffic
356	Road traffic	401 (C.15)	Criminal law
357	Road traffic	402	Road traffic
358	Road traffic	403	Revenue and customs Disclosure of information
359	Road traffic		
360	Road traffic	404	Road traffic
361	Road traffic	405	Road traffic
362	Civil aviation	406	Road traffic
363	Civil aviation	407	Road traffic
364	Education, England	408	Food
365 (W.31)	Road traffic, Wales	409	Companies
366 (W.32)	Road traffic, Wales	410	Companies
367 (W.33)	Road traffic, Wales	411 (C.16)	Social security
368 (W.34)	Road traffic, Wales	412	National Health Service, England
369 (W.35)	Road traffic, Wales	413	Environmental protection
370 (W.36)	Road traffic, Wales	414	Local government, England
371 (W.37)	Housing, Wales	415	National Health Service, England
372	Local government, England	416	National Health Service, England
373	Companies	417	Public passenger transport, England
374	Companies	418 (W.38)	Road traffic, Wales
375	Environmental protection, England	419	Road traffic
376	Local government, England	420 (W.39)	Agriculture, Wales
377	Education, England	421	Local government, England
378	Northern Ireland	422	Local government, England
379 (C. 14)	Corporation tax	423	Local government, England
380	Road traffic	424	Local government, England
381	Corporation tax	425	Local government, England
382	Road traffic	426	Local government, England
383	Income tax Corporation tax	427	Local government, England
		428	Rating and valuation, England
384	Road traffic	429	Rating and valuation, England
385	Road traffic	430	National Health Service, England
386	Rating and valuation, England	431	Wildlife, England
387	Council tax, England Rating and valuation, England	432	Banks and banking
		433	Civil aviation
388	Road traffic	434	Civil aviation
389	Road traffic	435	Civil aviation
390	Road traffic	436	Civil aviation

437	Civil aviation	478	Road traffic
438	Food	479	Road traffic
439	Food, England	480	Road traffic
440	National Health Service, England	481	Road traffic
441	Social security	482	Road traffic
442	Highways, England	483	Road traffic
443	Road traffic	484	Road traffic
444	Road traffic	485	Road traffic
445	Road traffic	486	Road traffic
446	Road traffic	487	Road traffic
447	Food, England	488	Road traffic
448	Road traffic	489	Companies
449	Road traffic	490	Local government, England
450 (W.40)	Fire and rescue services, Wales	491	Local government, England
451	Road traffic	492	Local government, England
452	Road traffic	493	Local government, England
453	Road traffic	494	Local government, England
454	Road traffic	495	Companies
455	Road traffic	496	Companies
456	Road traffic	497	Companies
457	Road traffic	498	Social security
458	Road traffic	499	Companies
459	Road traffic		Auditors
460	Road traffic	500	Local government, England
461 (C.17)	National Health Service, England Social care, England	501	Local government, England
		502 (W.43)	Town and country planning, Wales
462	Health care and associated professions	503 (W.44)	Local government, Wales
		504 (C.18)	Probation, England and Wales Prisons, England and Wales
463	Social security		
464	Medicines	505	Immigration
465	Animals, England	506	Road traffic
466 (W.41)	Highways, Wales	507	London government
467	Road traffic	508	Road traffic
468	Road traffic	509 (W.45)	Education, Wales
469	Betting, gaming and lotteries	510 (W.46)	Education, Wales
470	Road traffic	511	Income tax
471	Road traffic	512 (W.47)	Road traffic, Wales
472	Road traffic	513 (W.48)	Road traffic, Wales
473	Children and young persons, England and Wales Protection of vulnerable adults, England and Wales	514	Clean air, England
		515	Clean air, England
		516	Local government, England
474	Children and young persons, England and Wales Protection of vulnerable adults, England and Wales	517	Food, England
		518	Civil aviation
		519	National Health Service, England
475	Road traffic	520	Environmental protection, England
476 (W.42)	Local government, Wales	521	Environmental protection, Wales
477	Road traffic	522 (W.49)	Road traffic, Wales

523	Proceeds of crime, England and Wales	559	Prevention and suppression of terrorism
	Proceeds of crime, Northern Ireland	560	Plant health, England
524 (W.50)	Animals, Wales	561 (C.19)	Income tax
525	Fees and charges	562	Income tax
	Health and safety	563	Government trading funds
526	National Health Service, England	564	Road traffic
527	Charities, England and Wales	565	Insurance
528	National Health Service, England	566	Fire and rescue services, England
	Social care, England	567	Banks and banking
529	Education, England and Wales	568 (C.20)	Revenue and customs
	Education, Northern Ireland	569	Partnership
530	Fees and charges	570	Police, England and Wales
531	Terms and conditions of employment		Registration of births, deaths and marriages, etc., England and Wales
532	Education, England	571	National Health Service, England
533	Housing, England	572	Housing, England and Wales
534	Employment and training	573	Employment and training
535	Employment and training	574	Proceeds of crime
536	Family law	575	Proceeds of crime, England and Wales
537	Legal services, England and Wales		
538 (W.51)	Education, Wales		Proceeds of crime, Northern Ireland
539	Immigration	576	Agriculture
	Police	577 (W.56)	National Health Service, Wales
	Revenue and customs	578 (W.57)	Road traffic, Wales
540 (W.52)	Highways, Wales	579	Social security
541	Education, England and Wales	580	Town and country planning, England
542	Criminal law, Northern Ireland		
543 (W.53)	Food, Wales	581	Pensions
544	Immigration	582 (C.21)	London government
	Nationality	583	Companies
545 (W.54)	Road traffic, Wales	584 (W.58)	Local government, Wales
546	Education	585	Highways, England
547	National Health Service, England	586	Social security
548	Medicines	587	Social security
549	Local government, England	588 (W.59)	Local government, Wales
550	Town and country planning, England	589	Highways, England
		590	Government trading funds
551	Town and country planning, England	591 (W.60)(C.22)	Local government, Wales
		592	Pensions
552	Medicines	593	National assistance services, England
	Fees and charges		
	Consumer protection	594	Water industry, England and Wales
553	National Health Service, England	595	Town and country planning, England
554	Health care and associated professions		
		596 (W.61)	Road traffic, Wales
555 (W.55)	Education, Wales	597	Prisons, England and Wales
556	Value added tax	598	Probation, England and Wales
557	Statistics of trade	599	
558	National Health Service, England		

	Young offender institutions, England and Wales	642	Road traffic
600 (W.62)	Highways, Wales	643	Electronic communications Broadcasting
601 (W.63)	Food, Wales	644	Plant health
602	Local government, England	645	Consumer credit
603	Local government, England	646	Farriers
604	Tax credits	647	Building and buildings, England and Wales
605	Inheritance tax		
606	Inheritance tax	648	Defence
607	Social security	649	Pensions
608	Road traffic, Wales	650	Social security
609	Road traffic, Wales	651	Companies
610 (C.23)	Representation of the people	652	Animals, England
611	Trustees, England and Wales	653	National Health Service, England and Wales
612 (W.64)	Road traffic, Wales	654	National Health Service, England and Wales
613 (W.65)	Road traffic, Wales		
614 (W.66)	Road traffic, Wales	655	National Health Service, England and Wales
615 (W.67)	Road traffic, Wales		
616 (W.68)	Road traffic, Wales	656	Sex discrimination
617 (C. 24)	Police, England and Wales	657	Education, England
618	Animals, England	658	Legal Services Commission, England and Wales
619	Police, England and Wales	659	Local government, England and Wales
620 (W.69)	Road traffic, Wales		
621	Criminal law, England and Wales		Police, England and Wales
622	Agriculture, England Food, England	660 (W.70)	National Health Service, Wales
		661	Pensions
623	Companies	662 (S.4)	Insolvency, Scotland
624	Pensions	663 (W.71)	Environmental protection, Wales
625	Local government, England	664	Pensions
626	Council tax, England Local government, England	665	Agriculture, England and Wales Pesticides, England and Wales
627 (C.25)	Pensions	666	Legal services, England and Wales
628	Government trading funds	667	Social security
629	Charities, England and Wales	668	Tribunals and inquiries
630	Police, England and Wales	669	Civil aviation
631	Police, England and Wales	670	Insolvency, England and Wales
632	Social security	671	Building and buildings, England and Wales
633	Education, England		
634	Local government, England	672	Insolvency Insolvency
635	Defence		
636	Social security	673	Income tax
637	Social security	674 (C. 26)	Companies
638	Employment	675	Town and country planning, England
639	Customs		
640	Social care, England Children and young persons, England	676	Diplomatic Service
		677	Copyright Rights in performances
641	Disabled persons	678	Ministers of the Crown

679	Pensions	721	Social security
680	Immigration	722	Value added tax
681	Education, England Children and young persons, England	723	Legal Services Commission, England and Wales
		724	London government
682	Financial services and markets	725	Legal Services Commission, England and Wales
683	National Health Service, England	726	Social security
684	Immigration	727	National Health Service, England
685 (W.72)	Food, Wales	728	European Communities
686	Electronic communications	729	Companies
687	Electronic communications	730	Social security
688	Electronic communications	731	Pensions
689	Electronic communications	732	Fees and charges
690	Companies	733	Financial services and markets
691	Sea fisheries, England	734	Savings banks
692 (C. 27)	Criminal law, Northern Ireland	735	Medical profession, England
693	Broadcasting	736	Health and safety
694 (C.28)	Criminal law, Northern Ireland	737	Insolvency, England and Wales
695	Social security, England and Wales	738	Weights and measures
696	Gas	739	Companies
697 (C.29)	Criminal law, Northern Ireland	740	Income tax
698	Social security	741	Education, England
699	Social security	742 (W.77)	Road traffic, Wales
700	Police, Northern Ireland Registration of births, deaths and marriages, etc., Northern Ireland	743 (W.78)	National assistance, Wales
		744	Local government, England
		745 (C.30)	Mental health, England and Wales
701	London government	746	Local government, England
702	Plant health	747	Local government, England
703	Social security	748	Local government, England
704	Income tax	749 (C.31)	Supreme Court of England and Wales
705	Income tax Corporation tax Capital gains tax	750	Land drainage, England
		751 (C.32)	Charities, England and Wales
706	Income tax	752 (C.33)	Children and young persons, England
707	Value added tax		
708	Capital gains tax	753	Excise
709	Income tax	754	Excise
710	Stamp duty land tax	755 (C.34)	Police, England and Wales Proceeds of crime Public audit Serious crime prevention orders
711	Pensions		
712 (W.73)	National Health Service, Wales		
713 (W.74)	Food, Wales		
714	Insolvency, England and Wales	756	Local government, England
715	Gender recognition	757 (C.35)	Road traffic, England
716 (W.75)	National Health Service, Wales	758 (W.79)	Road traffic, Wales
717 (W.76)	National Health Service, Wales	759	Social security
718	Banks and banking	760	Immigration
719	Companies	761	Road traffic
720	Income tax	762	Road traffic

763	Road traffic	804	Civil aviation
764	Road traffic	805	Civil aviation
765	Road traffic	806	Civil aviation
766	Road traffic	807	Civil aviation
767	Road traffic	808	Civil aviation
768	Road traffic	809	Civil aviation
769	Road traffic	810	Civil aviation
770	Landfill tax	811	Civil aviation
771	Road traffic	812	Education, England
772	Road traffic	813	Road traffic
773	Road traffic	814	Road traffic
774	Road traffic	815	Road traffic
775	Road traffic	816	Road traffic
776	Road traffic	817	Government resources and accounts
777	Road traffic	818	Road traffic
778	Taxes Social security	819	Road traffic
		820	Road traffic
779	Road traffic	821	Road traffic
780	Road traffic, Wales	822	Road traffic
781 (W.80)	Agriculture, Wales Food, Wales	823	Road traffic
		824	Road traffic
782	Income tax	825	Road traffic
783	Education, England	826	Road traffic
784 (W.81)	Road traffic, Wales	827	Road traffic
785 (C.35)	Children and young persons, England	828	Road traffic
		829	Road traffic
786	Immigration	830	Road traffic
787 (C. 36)	Social security	831 (C.40)	Consumer credit
788 (W.82)	Local government, Wales	832	Road traffic
789 (W.83)	Animals, Wales	833	Road traffic
790 (C.37)	Police, England and Wales Police, Northern Ireland	834	Road traffic
		835	Road traffic
791 (C.38)	Criminal law, England and Wales Criminal law, Northern Ireland	836	Income tax
		837	Road traffic
792	Disclosure of information Statistics Board	838	Income tax
		839 (C.41)	Disclosure of information Official statistics Registration of births, deaths and marriages, etc. Statistics Board
793	Children and young persons, England		
794	Social security		
795	Social security		
796	Tax credits	840	Social security
797	Social security	841 (W.84)	Road traffic, Wales
798	Social security	842	Ecclesiastical law, England and Wales
799	Social security, Northern Ireland		
800 (C.39)	Mental health, England and Wales	843	National Health Service, England
801	Civil aviation	844	Road traffic
802	Civil aviation	845	Road traffic
803	Civil aviation	846	Road traffic

847	Road traffic	894	National Health Service, England
848	Road traffic	895	National Health Service, England
849	Road traffic	896	Road traffic
850	Road traffic	897	Road traffic
851	Road traffic	898 (C.42)	Housing, England and Wales
852	Road traffic	899	Road traffic
853	Road traffic	900	Road traffic
854	Road traffic	901	Road traffic
855	Road traffic	902	Road traffic
856	Road traffic	903	Road traffic
857	Road traffic	904	Road traffic
858	Road traffic	905 (C.43)	Consumer protection Estate agents
859	Road traffic	906	National Health Service, England and Wales
860	Road traffic	907	Local government, England
861	Road traffic	908	Fees and charges
862	Road traffic	909	Pensions
863	Road traffic	910	Pensions
864	Road traffic	911	Pensions
865	Road traffic	912	Probation
866	Road traffic	913	Road traffic, Wales
867	Road traffic	914	Taxes
868	Road traffic	915	National Health Service, England
869	Road traffic	916	Food, England
870	Road traffic	917 (C.44)	Local government, England and Wales
871	Road traffic	918 (W.85)	Road traffic, Wales
872	Road traffic	919	Museums and galleries
873	Road traffic	920 (W.86)	Road traffic, Wales
874	Road traffic	921	International development
875	Road traffic	922 (W.87)	National Health Service, Wales
876	Road traffic	923	Education, England and Wales Education, Northern Ireland
877	Road traffic	924 (W.88)	National Health Service, Wales
878	Road traffic	925	Disabled persons Transport
879	Road traffic	926 (W.89)	National Health Service, Wales
880	Road traffic	927 (W.90)	National Health Service, Wales
881	Road traffic	928	Official statistics
882	Road traffic	929	Local government, Wales
883	Road traffic	930 (C.45)	Children and young persons, Northern Ireland Protection of vulnerable adults, Northern Ireland
884	Road traffic		
885	Road traffic		
886	Road traffic		
887	Road traffic		
888	Road traffic		
889	Road traffic		
890	Road traffic	931 (W.91)	National Health Service, Wales
891	Road traffic	932 (W.92)	National Health Service, Wales
892	Road traffic	933 (W.93)	National Health Service, Wales
893	Road traffic	934 (W.94)	National Health Service, Wales

935 (W.95)	National Health Service, Wales		Children and young persons, England
936 (W.96)	National Health Service, Wales	975	Children and young persons, England
937 (W.97)	National Health Service, Wales		
938 (W.98)	National Health Service, Wales	976	Children and young persons, England
939 (W.99)	National Health Service, Wales		
940 (W.100)	National Health Service, Wales	977	Prisons, England and Wales
941	Medicines	978	Prisons, England and Wales
942 (W.101)	Road traffic, Wales	979	Children and young persons, England
943 (W.102)	Road traffic, Wales		
944	Animals, England	980	Local government, England
945 (C.46)	Charities	981	Local government finance, England
946	Proceeds of crime	982 (W.107)	Road traffic, Wales
947	Proceeds of crime	983 (W.108)(C.48)	Education, Wales
948	Companies	984	Sea fisheries, England and Wales
949	Proceeds of crime	985	Road traffic
950	Defence	986	Road traffic
951	Local government, England	987	Road traffic
952 (W.103)	Road traffic, Wales	988	Road traffic
953 (W.104)	Road traffic, Wales	989	Road traffic
954	Taxes	990	Road traffic
	Social security	991	Road traffic
955 (W.105)	Road traffic, Wales	992	Road traffic
956 (C. 47)	Environmental protection, England and Wales	993	Road traffic
		994	Road traffic
957	Legal Services Commission, England and Wales	995	Road traffic
		996	Road traffic
958	Town and country planning, England	997	Road traffic
		998	Road traffic
959	Social security	999	Road traffic
960	Regulatory reform	1000	Road traffic
	Health and safety	1001	Road traffic
961	Children and young persons, England	1002	Road traffic
		1003	Road traffic
962	Animals, England	1004	Road traffic
963	Sex discrimination	1005	Road traffic
964	Civil aviation	1006	Road traffic
965	Civil aviation	1007	Road traffic
966	Civil aviation	1008	Road traffic
967	Civil aviation	1009	Road traffic
968	Civil aviation	1010	Road traffic
969	Transport and works, England	1011	Road traffic
	Offshore installations, England	1012	Road traffic
	Electricity, England	1013	Road traffic
970	Civil aviation	1014	Road traffic
971 (W.106)	Road traffic, Wales	1015	Road traffic
972	Evidence, England and Wales	1016	Road traffic
973	Criminal law, England and Wales	1017	Road traffic
	Criminal law, Northern Ireland		
974			

1018	Road traffic		County courts, England and Wales
1019	Road traffic	1055	Road traffic, England
1020	Road traffic	1056	Road traffic
1021	Road traffic	1057	Road traffic
1022	Road traffic	1058	Road traffic
1023	Road traffic	1059	Road traffic
1024	Road traffic	1060	Road traffic
1025	Road traffic	1061	Road traffic
1026	Road traffic	1062	Children and young persons, England and Wales
1027	Road traffic		Protection of vulnerable adults, England and Wales
1028	Road traffic		
1029	Road traffic	1063 (W.112)	Plant health, Wales
1030	Road traffic	1064 (W.113)	Animals, Wales
1031	Road traffic	1065 (C.49)	Education, England and Wales
1032	Road traffic	1066	Animals, England
1033	Road traffic	1067	Trade marks
1034	Ministers of the Crown	1068	Pensions
1035	Constitutional law	1069	Road traffic
	Devolution, Scotland	1070	Road traffic
	Agriculture	1071	Road traffic
	Animals	1072	Road traffic
	Animals	1073	Road traffic
	Poultry		
1036	Constitutional law	1074	Road traffic
	Devolution, Wales	1075	Road traffic
1037	Health care and associated professions	1076	Road traffic
		1077	Road traffic
1038	Road traffic	1078	Road traffic
1039 (W.109)	Road traffic, Wales	1079	Agriculture, England
1040 (W.110)	Agriculture, Wales		Food, England
1041 (W.111)	Road traffic, Wales	1080 (W.114)	Agriculture, Wales
1042	Social security	1081 (W.115)	Agriculture, Wales
1043	Road traffic	1082	Social security
1044	Road traffic	1083	Pensions, England and Wales
1045	Road traffic	1084	Road traffic, England
1046	Road traffic	1085	Local government, England
1047	Road traffic	1086	Road traffic, England
1048	Road traffic	1087	Health and safety
1049	Road traffic	1088 (L.7)	Immigration
1050	Pensions	1089 (L.8)	Immigration
1051	Road traffic, England	1090 (W.116)	Animals, Wales
1052 (L.4)	Magistrates' courts, England and Wales	1091	Civil aviation
		1092	Civil aviation
1053 (L.5)	Supreme Court of England and Wales	1093	Civil aviation
		1094	Civil aviation
	County courts, England and Wales	1095	Civil aviation
1054 (L.6)	Family proceedings, England and Wales	1096	Civil aviation
	Supreme Court of England and Wales	1097	Water resources

1098	Customs	1145 (W.118)	Road traffic, Wales
1099	Road traffic	1146	Value added tax
1100	Road traffic	1147 (C.50)	National Health Service, England
1101	Road traffic		National Health Service, Scotland
1102	Road traffic		Social care, England
1103	Road traffic	1148	National Health Service, England
1104	Road traffic	1149	Tribunals and inquiries
1105	Road traffic	1150	Road traffic
1106	Road traffic	1151	Road traffic
1107	Road traffic	1152	Road traffic
1108	Road traffic	1153	Road traffic
1109	Road traffic	1154	Road traffic
1110	Road traffic	1155	Road traffic
1111	Road traffic	1156	Road traffic
1112	Road traffic	1157	Road traffic
1113	Road traffic	1158 (C.51)	Cultural objects, England and Wales
1114	Road traffic		Cultural objects, Northern Ireland
1115	Road traffic	1159	Cultural objects
1116	Road traffic	1160	Harbours, docks, piers and ferries
1117	Road traffic	1161	Medicines
1118	Road traffic	1162	Medicines
1119	Road traffic	1163	Electricity
1120	Road traffic		Gas
1121	Road traffic	1164	Savings banks
1122	Road traffic	1165	Sports grounds and sporting events, England and Wales
1123	Road traffic	1166	Armorial bearings, ensigns and flags
1124	Road traffic	1167	Social security
1125	Road traffic	1168	Road traffic
1126	Road traffic	1169	Road traffic
1127	Road traffic	1170	Road traffic
1128	Road traffic	1171	Road traffic
1129	Road traffic	1172	Road traffic
1130	Road traffic	1173	Road traffic
1131	Road traffic	1174	Road traffic
1132	Road traffic	1175	Road traffic
1133	Road traffic	1176	Road traffic
1134	Road traffic	1177	Road traffic
1135	Road traffic	1178	Road traffic
1136	Road traffic	1179	Road traffic
1137	Road traffic	1180	Animals, England
1138	Road traffic	1181	Public health
1139	Agriculture, England	1182 (W.119)	Animals, Wales
1140	Friendly societies	1183	Immigration
1141 (W.117)	Road traffic, Wales	1184	Mental health, England
1142	Savings banks	1185	National Health Service, England
1143	Building societies	1186	National Health Service, England
1144	Friendly societies	1187	National Health Service, England

1188	Food, England	1233	Road traffic
1189	Housing, England	1234	Road traffic
1190	Housing, England	1235	Road traffic
1191 (W.120)	Road traffic, Wales	1236	Road traffic
1192	Road traffic	1237 (W.124)	Food, Wales
1193	Road traffic	1238	Transport and works, England
1194	Road traffic		Transport, England
1195	Road traffic	1239	Civil aviation
1196	Road traffic	1240	British nationality
1197	Road traffic	1241	Northern Ireland
1198	Road traffic	1242	Northern Ireland
1199	Road traffic		Northern Ireland
1200	Road traffic	1243	Merchant shipping
1201	Road traffic	1244 (W.125)	Road traffic, Wales
1202	Maintenance of dependants	1245	Civil aviation
1203	Maintenance of dependants, England and Wales	1246	Road traffic
		1247	Road traffic
	Maintenance of dependants, Northern Ireland	1248	Road traffic
		1249	Road traffic
1204	Mental health, England and Wales	1250	Road traffic
1205	Mental health, England	1251	Road traffic
1206	Mental health, England	1252	Road traffic
1207	Mental health, England	1253	Road traffic
1208	Government trading funds	1254	Road traffic
1209	National Health Service, England	1255	Road traffic
1210 (C.52)	Mental health, England and Wales	1256	Health care and associated professions
1211	Road traffic, England	1257	Civil aviation
1212	Road traffic, England	1258	Education, England
1213 (W.121)	Highways, Wales	1259 (W.126)	Education, Wales
1214 (W.122)	Road traffic, Wales	1260 (W.127)	Road traffic, Wales
1215 (W.123)	Road traffic, Wales	1261	Harbours, docks, piers and ferries
1216 (NI.1)	Northern Ireland	1262 (C.53)	Consumer protection
1217	Road traffic	1263	Probation, England and Wales
1218	Road traffic	1264	Civil aviation
1219	Road traffic	1265 (C.54)	Local government, England and Wales
1220	Road traffic		
1221	Road traffic	1266	Housing, England and Wales
1222	Road traffic	1267	Weights and measures
1223	Road traffic	1268 (W.128)	Food, Wales
1224	Road traffic	1269	National Health Service, England
1225	Road traffic	1270 (W.129)	Animals, Wales
1226	Road traffic	1271	Freedom of information
1227	Road traffic	1272	Industrial development
1228	Road traffic	1273 (W.130)	Education, Wales
1229	Road traffic	1274 (W.131)	Road traffic, Wales
1230	Road traffic	1275 (W.132)	Animals, Wales
1231	Road traffic	1276	Trade descriptions
1232	Road traffic		

1277	Consumer protection	1321	Local government, England
1278	Education, England	1322	Sea fisheries, England
1279 (W.133)	Road traffic, Wales		Fish farming, England
1280 (W.134)	Road traffic, Wales	1323	National Health Service, England
1281	Customs	1324 (W.137)	Education, Wales
1282	Income tax	1325 (C. 58)	Defence
1283	Local government, England	1326 (C.59)	Betting, gaming and lotteries
1284	Consumer protection	1327	Betting, gaming and lotteries
1285	Local government, England	1328	Legal Services Commission, England and Wales
1286 (W.135)	Transport, Wales	1329 (W.138)	National Health Service, Wales
1287	Food, England	1330	Betting, gaming and lotteries
1288	Road traffic	1331	Architects
1289	Road traffic	1332	Road traffic
1290	Road traffic	1333 (W.139)	Road traffic, Wales
1291	Road traffic	1334 (C.60)	Public health, Scotland
1292	Road traffic		Public health, Northern Ireland
1293	Road traffic	1335	Disabled persons
1294	Road traffic	1336	Disabled persons
1295	Road traffic	1337	Immigration
1296	Road traffic		Nationality
1297	Road traffic	1338 (W.140)	Medical profession, Wales
1298	Road traffic	1339	Value added tax
1299	Road traffic	1340	Road traffic, England
1300	Road traffic	1341 (W.141)	Food, Wales
1301	Road traffic	1342	European Communities, England
1302	Road traffic	1343 (W.142)	Road traffic, Wales
1303	Road traffic	1344	Banks and banking
1304	Road traffic	1345	Road traffic
1305	Road traffic	1346	Road traffic
1306	Road traffic	1347	Road traffic
1307	Road traffic	1348	Road traffic
1308	Road traffic	1349	Road traffic
1309	Road traffic	1350	Road traffic
1310	Road traffic	1351	Road traffic
1311	Road traffic	1352	Road traffic
1312	Road traffic	1353	Road traffic
1313	Local government, England	1354	Road traffic
1314 (W.136)	Animals, Wales	1355	Road traffic
1315	Mental capacity, England	1356	Road traffic
1316 (C.55)	Representation of the people	1357	Road traffic
1317	Food, England	1358	Road traffic
1318 (C.56)	Northern Ireland	1359	Road traffic
1319	Political parties	1360	Road traffic
1320 (C.57)	Children and young persons, England and Wales	1361	Road traffic
		1362	Road traffic
	Protection of vulnerable adults, England and Wales	1363	Road traffic
	Data protection	1364	Road traffic

1365	Road traffic	1411	Civil aviation
1366	Road traffic	1412	Civil aviation
1367	Road traffic	1413	Civil aviation
1368	Road traffic	1414	Civil aviation
1369	Road traffic	1415	Civil aviation
1370	Fire and rescue services, England	1416	Civil aviation
1371	Town and country planning, England	1417	Civil aviation
		1418	Education, England
1372 (C.61)	London government	1419	Local government, England
1373	Highways, England	1420	Broadcasting
1374	Road traffic	1421	Broadcasting
1375	Road traffic	1422	Land drainage, England
1376	Road traffic	1423	Land drainage, England
1377	Road traffic	1424 (C. 63)	Criminal law, England and Wales
1378	Road traffic	1425 (W.147)	National Health Service, Wales
1379	Road traffic	1426	Animals, England
1380	Road traffic	1427	Building societies
1381	Road traffic	1428	Agriculture, England
1382	Road traffic	1429 (W.148)(C.64)	Education, Wales
1383	Road traffic	1430	Local government, England and Wales
1384	Road traffic		
1385	Road traffic		Police, England and Wales
1386	Road traffic		Fees and charges, England and Wales
1387	Road traffic	1431	Social security
1388	Road traffic	1432	Pensions
1389	Road traffic	1433 (W.149)	Road traffic, Wales
1390	Road traffic	1434	Designs
1391	Road traffic	1435	Road traffic
1392	Road traffic	1436 (C.65)	Legal services, England and Wales
1393	Road traffic	1437	Children and young persons, England
1394	Road traffic		
1395	Road traffic	1438 (W.150)	Sea fisheries, Wales
1396	Road traffic	1439	Financial services and markets
1397	Road traffic	1440	Government resources and accounts
1398	Road traffic	1441	Consumer protection, England and Wales
1399	Road traffic		
1400	Road traffic	1442 (W.151)	Road traffic, Wales
1401	Road traffic	1443	Road traffic
1402	Road traffic	1444	Road traffic
1403 (W.143)	Road traffic, Wales	1445	Road traffic
1404 (W.144)	Road traffic, Wales	1446	Road traffic
1405	Scientific research	1447	Road traffic
1406	Criminal law, England and Wales	1448	Road traffic
1407 (C. 62)	Criminal law, England and Wales	1449	Road traffic
1408 (W.145)	Education, Wales	1450	Road traffic
1409 (W.146)	Education, Wales	1451	Road traffic
1410	Value added tax	1452	Road traffic

1453	Road traffic	1490	Road traffic
1454	Road traffic	1491	Road traffic
1455	Road traffic	1492	Road traffic
1456	Road traffic	1493	Road traffic
1457	Road traffic	1494	Road traffic
1458	Public passenger transport	1495	Road traffic
1459	Disabled persons	1496	Road traffic
1460	Road traffic	1497	Children and young persons, England and Wales
1461	Road traffic		Protection of vulnerable adults, England and Wales
1462	Road traffic		
1463	Income tax	1498	Road traffic
	Corporation tax	1499	Road traffic
	Capital gains tax	1500	Road traffic
1464	Income tax	1501	Road traffic
1465	Public passenger transport	1502	Road traffic
1466 (C. 66)	Prisons, England and Wales	1503	Road traffic
1467	Financial services and markets	1504	Road traffic
1468	Financial services and markets	1505	Road traffic
1469	Financial services and markets	1506	Road traffic
1470	Public passenger transport, England and Wales	1507	Road traffic
1471	National Health Service, England	1508	Road traffic
1472	Sea fisheries, England and Wales	1509	Road traffic
1473	Public passenger transport	1510	Road traffic
1474	Road traffic	1511	Road traffic
1475 (W.152)	Road traffic, Wales	1512 (W.155)	Commissioner for Older People in Wales
1476 (C. 67)	Family law	1513	Road traffic, England
	Social security	1514	National Health Service, England
1477	Education, England and Wales	1515	Road traffic
1478	Education, England	1516	Road traffic
1479	Education, England and Wales	1517	Road traffic
1480 (W.153)	National Health Service, Wales	1518	Road traffic, England
1481	Income tax	1519	Building societies
1482	Value added tax	1520	Corporation tax
	Insurance premium tax	1521 (C.68)	Corporation tax
	Excise	1522	Offshore installations
	Landfill tax	1523	Agriculture, England
	Climate change levy	1524	Road traffic
	Aggregates levy	1525	Road traffic
1483 (W.154)	Road traffic, Wales	1526	Road traffic
1484	Education, England	1527	Road traffic
	Children and young persons, England	1528	Road traffic
1485	Health care and associated professions	1529	Road traffic
1486	Representation of the people	1530	Road traffic
1487	Civil aviation	1531	Road traffic
1488	Defence	1532	Road traffic
1489	Road traffic	1533	Road traffic

1534	Road traffic	1579	Corporation tax
1535	Road traffic	1580	Road traffic
1536	Road traffic	1581	Road traffic
1537	Road traffic	1582	Education, England and Wales
1538	Road traffic		Education, Northern Ireland
1539	Road traffic	1583 (W.158)	Animals, Wales
1540	Road traffic	1584	Sea fisheries, England
1541	Road traffic	1585	Defence
1542	Road traffic	1586 (C.69)	Criminal law, England and Wales
1543	Road traffic		Criminal law, Northern Ireland
1544	Road traffic		Criminal procedure, England and Wales
1545	Road traffic		Criminal procedure, Northern Ireland
1546	Road traffic		Legal Services Commission, England and Wales
1547	Road traffic		Police, England and Wales
1548	Road traffic		Prisons, England and Wales
1549	Road traffic		Prisons, Northern Ireland
1550	Road traffic	1587	Criminal law, England and Wales
1551	Road traffic		Criminal law, Northern Ireland
1552	Social security		Prisons
1553	Health care and associated professions	1588	Capital gains tax
			Corporation tax
1554	Social security	1589	Extradition
1555 (W.156)	Road traffic, Wales	1590 (S.5)	Town and country planning, Scotland
1556	Town and country planning, England	1591 (C.70)	Legal services, England and Wales
1557	Road traffic	1592 (C.71)	Data protection
1558	Road traffic	1593	Education, England
1559	Road traffic	1594	Education, England
1560	Road traffic	1595	Social security
1561	Road traffic	1596	Social security
1562	Road traffic	1597	Health and safety
1563	Road traffic	1598	Acquisition of land, England
1564	Road traffic		Compensation, England
1565	Road traffic	1599	Social security
1566	Road traffic	1600	Civil aviation
1567	Road traffic	1601	Civil aviation
1568	Road traffic	1602	Civil aviation
1569	Road traffic	1603	Civil aviation
1570	Road traffic	1604	Civil aviation
1571	Road traffic	1605	Civil aviation
1572	Town and country planning, England	1606	Civil aviation
		1607	Civil aviation
1573	Local government, England	1608	Civil aviation
1574 (W.157)	Road traffic, Wales	1609	Road traffic
1575	Education, England	1610	Civil aviation
1576	Road traffic	1611	Civil aviation
1577	Public passenger transport	1612	Road traffic
1578	Road traffic		

1613	Road traffic		Political parties
1614	Road traffic	1657	National Health Service, England
1615	Road traffic	1658 (W.161)	Road traffic, Wales
1616	Road traffic	1659	Companies
1617	Road traffic	1660	Transport
1618	Road traffic	1661	Road traffic
1619	Road traffic	1662	Road traffic
1620	Road traffic	1663	Road traffic
1621	Road traffic	1664	Road traffic
1622	Road traffic	1665	Road traffic
1623	Road traffic	1666	Road traffic
1624	Road traffic	1667	Road traffic
1625	Road traffic	1668	Road traffic
1626	Road traffic	1669	Road traffic
1627	Road traffic	1670	Road traffic
1628	Road traffic	1671	Road traffic
1629	Road traffic	1672	Road traffic
1630	Road traffic	1673	Road traffic
1631	Road traffic	1674	Road traffic
1632	Road traffic	1675	Road traffic
1633	Road traffic	1676	Road traffic
1634	Road traffic	1677	Road traffic
1635	Road traffic	1678	Road traffic
1636	Road traffic	1679	Road traffic
1637	Road traffic	1680	Road traffic
1638	Road traffic	1681	Road traffic
1639	Employment and training	1682 (W.162)	Food, Wales
1640	Education, England	1683	Road traffic
1641	Financial services and markets	1684	Road traffic
1642	Food, England	1685	Road traffic
1643	Education, England	1686	Road traffic
1644	Sports grounds and sporting events, England and Wales	1687	Road traffic
		1688	Road traffic
1645	Prevention and suppression of terrorism	1689	Road traffic
		1690	Road traffic
1646 (W.159)	Agriculture, Wales	1691	Road traffic
	Food, Wales	1692	Medicines
1647	European Communities	1693	Immigration
1648 (W.160)	National Health Service, Wales	1694	Defence
1649	Social security	1695	Immigration
1650 (C.72)	Defence		Nationality
1651	Defence	1696	Defence
1652	Coroners, England and Wales	1697	National Health Service, England
1653 (C.73)	Tribunals and inquiries	1698	Defence
	Judicial appointments and discipline	1699	Defence
1654	Consumer protection	1700	National Health Service, England
1655	Education, England	1701	Education, England
1656 (C. 74)	Northern Ireland		

1702	Road traffic
1703	Road traffic
1704	Road traffic
1705	Road traffic
1706	Road traffic
1707	Road traffic
1708	Road traffic
1709	Road traffic
1710	Road traffic
1711	Road traffic
1712	Estate agents
1713	Estate agents
1714	Financial services and markets
1715	Road traffic
1716 (W.163)	Children and young persons, Wales
1717 (W.164)	National Health Service, Wales
1718	Food, England
1719 (W.165)	National Health Service, Wales
1720 (W.166)	National Health Service, Wales
1721 (W.167)	National Health Service, Wales
1722	Children and young persons, England
1723	Education, England
1724	Children and young persons, England
1725	Financial services and markets
1726	Representation of the people
1727	Education, England
1728 (W.168) (C.75)	Education, Wales
1729	Children and young persons, England
1730	Land registration, England and Wales
1731	Land registration, England and Wales
1732 (W.169)	Education, Wales
1733	Education, England
1734	Education, England
1735	Social security Terms and conditions of employment
1736 (W.170)	Education, Wales
1737	Political parties
1738	Companies
1739 (W.171)	Education, Wales
1740	Children and young persons, England
1741	Representation of the people
1742 (W.172)	Animals, Wales
1743	Children and young persons, England
1744	Education, England Children and young persons, England
1745	Prevention and suppression of terrorism
1746	Disabled persons Transport
1747	Education, England
1748	Land registration, England and Wales
1749	Sports grounds and sporting events, England and Wales
1750	Land registration, England and Wales
1751	Consumer credit
1752	Education, England
1753	Education, England
1754	Education, England
1755	Education, England
1756	Education, England
1757	Education, England
1758	Education, England
1759	Education, England
1760	Education, England
1761	Education, England
1762	Education, England
1763	Education, England
1764	Road traffic, England
1765	Insurance
1766	Education, England
1767	Energy
1768	Immigration Housing, England Housing, Scotland Housing, Northern Ireland
1769 (NI. 2)	Northern Ireland
1770	Capital gains tax Corporation tax Income tax
1771	Education, England
1772	Education, England
1773	Education, England
1774	Health care and associated professions
1775	National Health Service, England
1776	Constitutional law Devolution, Scotland Environmental protection
1777	

	Supreme Court of England and Wales	1808	Children and young persons, England and Wales
1778	Social security		Children and young persons, Northern Ireland
1779	Northern Ireland	1809	Children and young persons, England and Wales
1780	Defence		
1781	Parliament		Children and young persons, Northern Ireland
1782	Civil aviation		
1783	Cinema and films	1810	Pensions
1784	Education, England	1811 (W.175)	Sea fisheries, Wales
	Children and young persons, England	1812	National Health Service, England
		1813	Financial services and markets
1785	Constitutional law	1814	Taxes
	Devolution, Wales	1815 (W.176)	Road traffic, Wales
1786	Constitutional law	1816	Consumer protection
	Devolution, Wales	1817	Harbours, docks, piers and ferries
1787 (W.173)	Education, Wales	1818 (C.77)	Immigration
1788	Constitutional law	1819	Immigration
	Devolution, Scotland	1820	Competition
	Criminal law	1821	Income tax
1789	Taxes	1822	Health care and associated professions
1790	Education, England		
1791	Representation of the people		Dentists
1792	European Communities	1823	Health care and associated professions
1793	Income tax		
	Corporation tax		Professions complementary to dentistry
	Capital gains tax		
1794	Merchant shipping	1824	Veterinary surgeons
1795	Capital gains tax	1825	Environmental protection
	Corporation tax	1826	Social security
	Income tax	1827	Road traffic
1796	Income tax	1828	Road traffic
	Corporation tax	1829	Road traffic
	Capital gains tax	1830	Road traffic
1797	Trade marks	1831	Road traffic
1798 (C.76)	Children and young persons, England and Wales	1832	Road traffic
		1833	Road traffic
	Children and young persons, Northern Ireland	1834	Road traffic
1799	Legal services, England and Wales	1835	Road traffic
1800	Education, England	1836	Road traffic
1801	Education, England	1837	Road traffic
1802	Children and young persons, England and Wales	1838	Road traffic
		1839	Road traffic
1803	Betting, gaming and lotteries	1840	Road traffic
1804	Children and young persons, England	1841	Road traffic
		1842	Road traffic
1805	Customs	1843	Road traffic
1806 (W.174)	Agriculture, Wales	1844	Road traffic
1807	Children and young persons, England and Wales	1845	Road traffic
		1846	Road traffic
	Children and young persons, Northern Ireland		

1847	Road traffic		Devolution, Scotland
1848 (W.177)	Local government, Wales		Housing
1849	Defence	1890 (W.179)	Welsh language
1850	Council tax, England	1891	Pensions
1851	Civil aviation	1892	Value added tax
1852	Civil aviation	1893	Income tax
1853	Civil aviation	1894	Terms and conditions of employment
1854	Civil aviation	1895	Road traffic
1855	Civil aviation	1896 (W.180)	Highways, Wales
1856	Civil aviation	1897	Companies
1857	Civil aviation	1898	Electricity
1858	Mental capacity, England		Gas
1859	National Health Service, England	1899 (W.181)	Education, Wales
1860	Companies, England and Wales	1900 (C.84)	Mental health, England and Wales
1861	Companies	1901	Representation of the people
1862 (C.78)	Road traffic, England and Wales	1902	National Health Service, England
1863	Serious crime prevention orders, England and Wales	1903	Pensions
	Serious crime prevention orders, Northern Ireland	1904 (W.182)(C.85)	Children and young persons, Wales
		1905	Corporation tax
1864 (C. 79)	Road traffic	1906	Corporation tax
1865	Legal services, England and Wales	1907	Government resources and accounts
1866 (W.178)	Education, Wales	1908	Serious Organised Crime Agency
1867	Education, England	1909	Proceeds of crime
1868	Education, England	1910	Highways, England
1869	Education, England	1911	Limited liability partnerships
1870	Education, England	1912	Limited liability partnerships
1871	Education, England	1913	Limited liability partnerships
1872	Education, England	1914	Representation of the people
1873	Education, England	1915	Companies
1874	Education, England	1916	Income tax
1875	Education, England		Corporation tax
1876	Education, England	1917	Income tax
1877	National Health Service, England		Corporation tax
	Social care, England	1918 (C.86)	Road traffic
1878 (C. 80)	Income tax	1919	Land registration, England and Wales
1879	Social security	1920	Commonhold, England and Wales
1880 (C. 81)	Income tax	1921	Land registration, England and Wales
1881	Animals, England	1922 (C.87)	Water, England
1882 (C.82)	Pensions	1923	Corporation tax
1883	Education, England	1924	Corporation tax
1884	Education, England	1925 (C.88)	Corporation tax
1885	Excise	1926	Corporation tax
1886 (C.83)	Companies	1927 (W.183)	Wildlife, Wales
1887	Police, England and Wales	1928 (C. 89)	Corporation tax
	Pensions, England and Wales	1929 (C. 90)	Corporation tax
1888	Electricity		
1889	Constitutional law		

1930 (C. 91)	Corporation tax	1968	Ecclesiastical law, England and Wales
1931	Prevention and suppression of terrorism	1969	Ecclesiastical law, England and Wales
1932	Stamp duty land tax	1970	Ecclesiastical law, England and Wales
1933 (C. 92)	Corporation tax	1971 (C. 95)	Education, England
1934	Income tax	1972 (C. 96)	National Health Service, England
1935 (C.93)	Taxes	1973	Health and safety
1936	Revenue and customs	1974 (W.184)	Road traffic, Wales
1937	Corporation tax	1975	Prisons, Northern Ireland
1938	National Health Service, England and Wales	1976 (W.185)	Public health, Wales
	National Health Service, Scotland	1977	Clerk of the Crown in Chancery
	Health and personal social services, Northern Ireland	1978	Proceeds of crime, England and Wales
1939	Environmental protection		Proceeds of crime, Northern Ireland
1940	Health care and associated professions	1979	Pensions
	Opticians	1980	Road traffic
1941	Environmental protection	1981	Road traffic
1942	Corporation tax	1982	Road traffic
1943	Civil aviation	1983	Road traffic
1944	Corporation tax	1984	Road traffic
1945	Insurance premium tax	1985	Road traffic
1946	Income tax	1986	Road traffic
1947	Taxes	1987	Road traffic
1948	Taxes	1988	Road traffic
1949	Excise	1989	Road traffic
1950	Insurance	1990	Road traffic
1951	Highways, England	1991	Road traffic
1952	Children and young persons, England	1992	Road traffic
1953	Children and young persons, England	1993	Road traffic
		1994	Road traffic
1954	Representation of the people	1995	Road traffic
1955	Family law, England and Wales	1996	Road traffic
1956	London government	1997	Road traffic
	Road traffic, England	1998	Road traffic
1957	Social security, England and Wales	1999	Road traffic
	Family law, England and Wales	2000	Road traffic
1958	Trade marks	2001	Road traffic
1959	Trade marks	2002	Road traffic
1960 (C. 94)	Commons, England	2003	Road traffic
1961	Commons, England	2004	Road traffic
1962	Commons, England	2005	Road traffic
1963	Social security	2006	Road traffic
1964	Customs	2007	Road traffic
1965	Road traffic	2008	Road traffic
1966	Terms and conditions of employment	2009	Road traffic
1967	Freedom of information	2010	Road traffic

2011	Environmental protection	2056	Road traffic
2012	Road traffic	2057	Road traffic
2013	Road traffic	2058	Road traffic
2014	Road traffic	2059	Police
2015	Road traffic	2060	Road traffic
2016	Road traffic	2061	Road traffic
2017	Road traffic	2062	Road traffic
2018	Road traffic	2063	Road traffic
2019	Road traffic	2064	Road traffic
2020	Road traffic	2065	Road traffic
2021	Road traffic	2066	Road traffic
2022	Road traffic	2067	Road traffic
2023	Road traffic	2068	Road traffic
2024	Road traffic	2069	Road traffic
2025	Road traffic	2070	Road traffic
2026	Road traffic	2071	Road traffic
2027	Road traffic	2072	Agriculture, England
2028	Road traffic	2073	Civil aviation
2029	Road traffic	2074	Civil aviation
2030	Road traffic	2075	Civil aviation
2031	Road traffic	2076 (L.9)	Supreme Court of England and Wales
2032 (W.186)	Road traffic, Wales		Magistrates' courts, England and Wales
2033 (C.97)	Family law		
2034	Town and country planning, England and Wales	2077	Immigration
		2078	Education, England
2035	Education, England	2079	Education, England
2036	Transport	2080	Education, England
2037 (C.98)	London government	2081	Education, England
2038	London government	2082	Education, England
2039	Criminal law, England and Wales Criminal law, Northern Ireland	2083	Education, England
		2084	Education, England
2040 (W.187)	Road traffic, Wales	2085	Education, England
2041	Road traffic	2086	International development
2042	Road traffic	2087	Education, England
2043	Road traffic	2088	International development
2044	Road traffic	2089	International development
2045	Road traffic	2090	International development
2046	Road traffic	2091	Public passenger transport, England
2047	Road traffic	2092	Education, England
2048	Road traffic	2093	Town and country planning
2049	Road traffic	2094	Education, England
2050	Road traffic	2095	Road traffic, England and Wales
2051	Road traffic	2096	Police, England and Wales
2052	Road traffic	2097	Road traffic
2053	Road traffic	2098	Lord Chief Justice Judicial appointments and discipline
2054	Road traffic		
2055	Road traffic	2099	Education, England

2100 (W.188)	Road traffic, Wales	2147	Road traffic
2101 (C.99)	Social security	2148	Road traffic
2102	Highways, England	2149	Road traffic
2103	Public health	2150	Road traffic
2104	Electronic communications	2151	Road traffic
2105	Electronic communications	2152	Road traffic
2106	Electronic communications	2153	Road traffic
2107	Highways, England	2154	Road traffic
2108	Health and safety	2155	Education, England and Wales
2109	Highways, England	2156	Criminal law, England and Wales
2110	Highways, England		Criminal law, Northern Ireland
2111	Social security	2157	Offshore installations
2112	Social security, England and Wales	2158 (W.191)	Road traffic, Wales
2113	Local government, England	2159	Disabled persons
2114	Social security, England and Wales	2160	Pensions
2115	Road traffic	2161	Competition
2116	Road traffic		Consumer protection
2117	Road traffic	2162 (W.192)	Town and country planning, Wales
2118	Road traffic	2163	Criminal law, England and Wales
2119	Road traffic	2164	Environmental protection
2120	Road traffic	2165	Merchant shipping
2121	Road traffic	2166	Merchant shipping
2122	Road traffic	2167	Excise
2123	Road traffic	2168	Excise
2124	Road traffic	2169	Tax credits
2125	Road traffic	2170	Income tax
2126	Road traffic	2171	Highways, England
2127	Road traffic	2172	Wildlife, England and Wales
2128	Road traffic		Countryside, England and Wales
2129	Road traffic	2173	Consumer protection
2130	Road traffic	2174 (W.193)	Road traffic, Wales
2131	Road traffic	2175	Town and country planning, England
2132	Road traffic	2176	Local government, England
2133	Road traffic	2177	Road traffic
2134	Road traffic	2178 (L.10)	Supreme Court of England and Wales
2135	Road traffic		County courts, England and Wales
2136	Road traffic	2179	Road traffic
2137	Road traffic	2180	Road traffic
2138	Road traffic	2181	Road traffic
2139	Road traffic	2182	Road traffic
2140 (W.189)	Education, Wales	2183	Road traffic
2141 (W.190)	Agriculture, Wales	2184	Road traffic
2142	Transport	2185	Road traffic
2143	Police, England and Wales	2186	Road traffic
2144	Road traffic	2187	Road traffic
2145	Road traffic	2188	Road traffic
2146	Road traffic		

2189	Road traffic	2235	Road traffic
2190	Road traffic	2236	Road traffic
2191	Road traffic	2237	Road traffic
2192	Road traffic	2238	Road traffic
2193	Road traffic	2239	Road traffic
2194	Road traffic	2240	Road traffic
2195	Road traffic	2241	Road traffic
2196	Road traffic	2242	Road traffic
2197	Road traffic	2243	Road traffic
2198	Road traffic	2244	Road traffic
2199	Road traffic	2245	Road traffic
2200	Road traffic	2246	Road traffic
2201	Road traffic	2247	Road traffic
2202	Road traffic	2248	Road traffic
2203	Road traffic	2249	Road traffic
2204	Road traffic	2250	National Health Service Public health Social care
2205	Road traffic		
2206	Trade marks	2251	National Health Service, England
2207	Trade marks	2252	National Health Service, England Social care, England Public health, England
2208	Road traffic		
2209	Road traffic		
2210	Road traffic	2253	Highways, England
2211	Road traffic	2254	Highways, England
2212	Road traffic	2255 (W.196)	Road traffic, Wales
2213	Road traffic	2256	Public procurement, England and Wales Public procurement, Northern Ireland
2214 (C.100)	Health care and associated professions		
2215 (W.194)	Road traffic, Wales		
2216 (W.195)	Road traffic, Wales	2257	Civil aviation
2217	Road traffic	2258	Civil aviation
2218	Road traffic	2259	Civil aviation
2219	Road traffic	2260	Town and country planning, England
2220	Road traffic		
2221	Road traffic	2261 (C.101)	Children and young persons, England
2222	Road traffic	2262	Road traffic, England
2223	Road traffic	2263	National Health Service, England and Wales
2224	Road traffic		
2225	Road traffic	2264	Taxes
2226	Road traffic	2265	Social security
2227	Road traffic	2266	Road traffic
2228	Road traffic	2267	Consumer protection Postal services
2229	Road traffic		
2230	Road traffic	2268	Consumer protection Electricity Gas
2231	Road traffic		
2232	Road traffic	2269	Animals, England
2233	Road traffic	2270	Animals, England
2234	Road traffic	2271	Road traffic

2272	Road traffic
2273	Road traffic
2274	Road traffic
2275	Road traffic
2276	Road traffic
2277	Road traffic
2278	Road traffic
2279	Road traffic
2280	Road traffic
2281	Road traffic
2282	Road traffic
2283	Road traffic
2284	Road traffic
2285	Road traffic
2286	Road traffic
2287	Road traffic
2288	Road traffic
2289	Road traffic
2290	Road traffic
2291	Road traffic
2292	Road traffic
2293	Road traffic
2294	Road traffic
2295	Road traffic
2296	Road traffic
2297	Medicines
2298 (W.197)	Fire and rescue services, Wales
2299	Social security
2300	Trade marks
2301	Pensions
2302 (C. 102)	Excise
2303	Civil aviation
2304	Civil aviation
2305	Civil aviation
2306	Road traffic
2307	Road traffic
2308	Road traffic
2309	Road traffic
2310	Road traffic
2311	Road traffic
2312	Road traffic
2313	Road traffic
2314	Road traffic
2315	Road traffic
2316	Road traffic
2317	Road traffic
2318	Road traffic
2319	Road traffic
2320	Road traffic
2321	Road traffic
2322	Road traffic
2323	Health and safety
2324	Road traffic
2325	Road traffic
2326	Road traffic
2327	Road traffic
2328	Road traffic
2329	Road traffic
2330	Road traffic
2331	Road traffic
2332	Rating and valuation, England
2333	Rating and valuation, England
2334	Building and buildings, England and Wales
2335 (W.198)	Town and country planning, Wales
2336 (W.199)	Town and country planning, Wales
2337	Health and safety
2338	Stamp duty land tax
2339	Stamp duty land tax
2340	Education, England
2341	Legal services, Scotland
2342	Clean air, England
2343	Clean air, England
2344	Road traffic, England
2345	Housing, England
2346	Housing, England
2347	Sea fisheries, England and Wales
2348 (W.200)	Road traffic, Wales
2349	Agriculture, England Water, England
2350	Highways, England
2351 (W.201)	Road traffic, Wales
2352	Public health, England
2353	Disclosure of information, England and Wales Disclosure of information, Northern Ireland
2354 (W.202)	Road traffic, Wales
2355	Postal services
2356	Wildlife, England
2357	Wildlife, England
2358 (C. 103)	Housing, England
2359	Harbours, docks, piers and ferries
2360	Sea fisheries, England
2361	Housing, England

2362	Town and country planning, England	2407	Road traffic
2363	Building and buildings, England and Wales	2408	Road traffic
		2409	Road traffic
2364 (W.203)	National Health Service, Wales	2410	Road traffic
2365	Social security	2411	Plant health, England
2366	Channel Tunnel	2412	Road traffic
2367	Road traffic, England	2413	Road traffic
2368	Mental capacity, England	2414	Road traffic
2369 (W.204)	Road traffic, Wales	2415	Road traffic
2370 (W.205)	Housing, Wales	2416	Road traffic
2371 (C.104)	Regulatory reform	2417	Road traffic
2372	Road traffic	2418	Road traffic
2373	Highways, England	2419	Road traffic
2374	Highways, England	2420	Road traffic
2375	Gas	2421	Road traffic
2376	Electricity	2422	Road traffic
2377 (W.206)	Housing, Wales	2423	Road traffic
2378	Road traffic	2424	Social security
2379	Road traffic	2425	Pensions, England and Wales
2380	Road traffic	2426	Electronic communications
2381	Road traffic	2427	Electronic communications
2382	Road traffic	2428	Social security
2383	Road traffic	2429	Civil aviation
2384	Road traffic	2430	Legal Services Commission, England and Wales
2385	Road traffic	2431	National Health Service, England
2386	Road traffic	2432 (W.207)	Road traffic, Wales
2387	Road traffic	2433 (W.208)	Road traffic, Wales
2388	Road traffic	2434 (C. 105)	National Health Service, England
2389	Road traffic	2435	Local government, England
2390	Road traffic	2436 (W.209)	Mental health, Wales
2391	Road traffic	2437 (W.210)	Mental health, Wales
2392	Road traffic	2438 (W.211)	National Health Service, Wales
2393	Road traffic	2439 (W.212)	Mental health, Wales
2394	Road traffic	2440 (W.213)	Mental health, Wales
2395	Road traffic	2441 (W.214)	Mental health, Wales
2396	Road traffic	2442	Road traffic, England
2397	Road traffic	2443 (W.215)	National Health Service, Wales
2398	Road traffic	2444 (C.105)	Consumer credit
2399	Road traffic	2445	Food, England
2400	Road traffic	2446 (L.11)	Family proceedings, England and Wales
2401	Road traffic		
2402	Road traffic		Supreme Court of England and Wales
2403	Road traffic		County courts, England and Wales
2404	Road traffic	2447 (L. 12)	Family proceedings, England and Wales
2405	Road traffic		
2406	Road traffic	2448	Criminal law, England and Wales

2449	National Health Service, England	2496	National Health Service, England
2450	Pensions	2497 (C.106)	Health care and associated professions
2451	Road traffic		Hearing Aid Council
2452	Road traffic		Social care
2453	Road traffic		National Health Service, England
2454	Offshore installations		Public health, England
2455	Road traffic	2498 (W.216)	Road traffic, Wales
2456	Road traffic	2499 (W.217)	Rating and valuation, Wales
2457	Road traffic	2500 (W.218)	Agriculture, Wales
2458	Road traffic	2501	Veterinary surgeons
2459	Road traffic	2502	Highways, England
2460	Road traffic	2503 (C.107)	Police, England and Wales
2461	Road traffic		Police, Northern Ireland
2462	Road traffic	2504 (C. 108)	Criminal law, England and Wales
2463	Road traffic		Criminal law, Northern Ireland
2464	Road traffic		Disclosure of information, England and Wales
2465	Road traffic		Disclosure of information, Northern Ireland
2466	Road traffic		
2467	Road traffic	2505 (W.219)	Road traffic, Wales
2468	Road traffic	2506 (W.220)	Road traffic, Wales
2469	Road traffic	2507	Education, England
2470	Ecclesiastical law, England	2508	Road traffic
2471	Road traffic	2509 (W.221)	Road traffic, Wales
2472	Road traffic	2510	Highways, England
2473	Road traffic	2511	Highways, England
2474	Road traffic	2512	Transport and works, England
2475	Road traffic		Transport, England
2476	Road traffic	2513	Road traffic
2477	Road traffic	2514	Road traffic
2478	Road traffic	2515	Road traffic
2479	Road traffic	2516	Road traffic
2480	Road traffic	2517	Road traffic
2481	Road traffic	2518	Road traffic
2482	Road traffic	2519	Road traffic
2483	Road traffic	2520	Road traffic
2484	Road traffic	2521	Road traffic
2485	Road traffic	2522	Road traffic
2486	Road traffic	2523	Road traffic
2487	Road traffic	2524	Road traffic
2488	Road traffic	2525	Road traffic
2489	Road traffic	2526	Road traffic
2490	Road traffic	2527	Road traffic
2491	Road traffic	2528	Road traffic
2492	Road traffic	2529	Road traffic
2493	Road traffic	2530	Road traffic
2494	Road traffic	2531	Road traffic
2495	Road traffic	2532	Road traffic

2533	Road traffic	2574	Road traffic
2534	Road traffic	2575	Road traffic
2535	Road traffic	2576	Road traffic
2536	Road traffic	2577	Road traffic
2537	Road traffic	2578	Road traffic
2538	Road traffic	2579	Road traffic
2539	Road traffic	2580	Road traffic
2540	Road traffic	2581	Road traffic
2541	Road traffic	2582	Road traffic
2542	Road traffic	2583	Road traffic
2543	Family law	2584	Road traffic
2544	Family law	2585	Road traffic
2545 (C.109)	Family law	2586	Road traffic
2546	Banks and banking	2587	Road traffic
2547	Value added tax	2588	Road traffic
2548 (C.110)	Family law	2589	Road traffic
2549	Environmental protection, England and Wales	2590	Road traffic
		2591	Road traffic
2550 (C.111)	Consumer protection	2592	Road traffic
2551	Family law	2593	National Health Service, England
2552 (W.222)	National Health Service, Wales	2594	Road traffic
2553	Health care and associated professions	2595	Road traffic
		2596	Road traffic
2554	Health care and associated professions	2597 (C.114)	Judicial appointments and discipline, England and Wales
2555 (W.223)	Road traffic, Wales	2598	Environmental protection, England
2556 (C.112)	Health care and associated professions	2599	Excise
2557	Electronic communications Broadcasting	2600	Excise
		2601	Income tax
2558	National Health Service, England	2602 (W.228)	Food, Wales
2559 (W.224)	Road traffic, Wales	2603	Income tax
2560	Mental health, England	2604	Road traffic
2561 (C.113)	Mental health, England and Wales	2605	Road traffic
2562	Civil aviation	2606	Road traffic
2563	Education, England Children and young persons, England	2607	Road traffic
		2608	Road traffic
2564	European Communities	2609	Road traffic
2565 (W.225)	Road traffic, Wales	2610	Road traffic
2566	Consumer protection	2611	Road traffic
2567	Road traffic, England	2612	Road traffic
2568 (W.226)	National Health Service, Wales	2613	Road traffic
2569	Social security	2614	Road traffic
2570	Agriculture, England and Wales Pesticides, England and Wales	2615	Road traffic
		2616	Road traffic
2571 (W.227)	Road traffic, Wales	2617	Road traffic
2572	Road traffic	2618	Road traffic
2573	Road traffic	2619	Road traffic

2620	Road traffic
2621	Road traffic
2622	Road traffic
2623	Road traffic
2624	Social security
2625	Corporation tax
2626	Income tax
2627	Corporation tax
2628	Income tax
2629 (W.229)	Education, Wales
2630	Road traffic
2631	Road traffic
2632	Road traffic
2633	Road traffic
2634	Road traffic
2635	Road traffic
2636	Road traffic
2637	Road traffic
2638	Police, England and Wales
2639	Companies Auditors
2640 (W.230)	Road traffic, Wales
2641 (W.231)	Road traffic, Wales
2642 (W.232)	Road traffic, Wales
2643	Corporation tax
2644	Banks and banking
2645	Competition
2646	Corporation tax
2647	Corporation tax
2648	Medicines
2649	Corporation tax
2650 (W.233)	Road traffic, Wales
2651	Road traffic
2652	Road traffic
2653	Road traffic
2654	Road traffic
2655	Road traffic
2656	Family law
2657	Road traffic
2658	Road traffic
2659	Road traffic
2660	Road traffic
2661	Road traffic
2662	Road traffic
2663	Road traffic
2664 (C. 115)	Education, England
2665 (W.234)	Road traffic, Wales
2666	Banks and banking
2667	Social security
2668	Banks and banking
2669	Landfill tax
2670	Corporation tax
2671 (W.235)	Rating and valuation, Wales
2672 (W.236)	Rating and valuation, Wales
2673	Corporation tax
2674	Banks and banking
2675 (C.116)	Family law
2676	Value added tax
2677	National Health Service, England
2678	Social security
2679	Corporation tax
2680	Legal services, England and Wales
2681	Income tax
2682	Income tax
2683	Tribunals and inquiries
2684	Tribunals and inquiries
2685 (L.13)	Tribunals and inquiries
2686 (L.14)	Tribunals and inquiries, England and Wales
2687 (W.237)	Tax credits, Wales
2688	Income tax
2689 (W.238)	Social care, Wales Children and young persons, Wales
2690	Health care and associated professions
2691 (W.239)	Social care, Wales Children and young persons, Wales
2692	Tribunals and inquiries
2693	Excise Insurance premium tax Landfill tax Climate change levy Aggregates levy
2694	Local government, England
2695 (W.240)	Road traffic, Wales
2696 (C.117)	Tribunals and inquiries Judicial appointments and discipline
2697	Tribunals and inquiries
2698 (L.15)	Tribunals and inquiries
2699 (L.16)	Tribunals and inquiries, England and Wales
2700	Lord Chancellor Lord Chief Justice Judges
2701 (W.241)	Highways, Wales
2702	Civil aviation

2703	Legal Services Commission, England and Wales
2704	Legal Services Commission, England and Wales
2705 (L.17)	Tribunals and inquiries, England and Wales
2706	Social security
	Tribunals and inquiries
2707	Tribunals and inquiries
2708	Landlord and tenant, England
2709 (W.242)	Road traffic, Wales
2710 (W.243)	Road traffic, Wales
2711 (W.244)	Road traffic, Wales
2712 (C.118)	Criminal law, England and Wales
	Criminal law, Northern Ireland
	Criminal procedure, England and Wales
	Criminal procedure, Northern Ireland
	Magistrates' courts, England and Wales
	Police, England and Wales
	Anti-Social behaviour, England and Wales
2713	Criminal law, England and Wales
2714 (C.119)	Medicines
2715	Education
2716 (W.245)	Animals, Wales
2717 (C.120)	Health care and associated professions
2718	Road traffic
2719	Road traffic
2720	Road traffic
2721	Road traffic
2722	Road traffic
2723	Road traffic
2724	Road traffic
2725	Road traffic
2726	Road traffic
2727	Road traffic
2728	Road traffic
2729	Road traffic
2730	Road traffic
2731	Road traffic
2732	Road traffic
2733	Road traffic
2734	Road traffic
2735	Road traffic
2736	Road traffic
2737	Road traffic
2738	Road traffic
2739	Local government, England
2740	Local government, England
2741	Road traffic
2742	Road traffic
2743	Road traffic
2744	Road traffic
2745	Road traffic
2746	Road traffic
2747	Road traffic
2748	Road traffic
2749	Road traffic
2750	Road traffic
2751	Road traffic
2752	Road traffic
2753	Road traffic
2754	Civil aviation
2755	Civil aviation
2756	Road traffic
2757	Road traffic
2758	Road traffic
2759	Road traffic
2760	Road traffic
2761	Road traffic
2762	Road traffic
2763	Road traffic
2764	Road traffic
2765	Plant health, England
2766	Banks and banking
2767	Social security
2768	Criminal law, England and Wales
2769	National Health Service, England
2770 (W.246)	Rating and valuation, Wales
2771	Employment tribunals
2772 (C.121)	Social security
2773	Education, England
2774 (W.247)	Animals, Wales
2775	Protection of wrecks, England
2776	Terms and conditions of employment
2777	Taxes
2778	Civil aviation
2779 (C.122)	Family law, England and Wales
2780	Tribunals and inquiries
2781 (W.248)	Plant health, Wales
2782 (W.249)	Road traffic, Wales
2783	Social security
2784	National Health Service, England

2785 (C.123)	Police, England and Wales	2824	Social security
2786	National Health Service, England	2825	Road traffic
2787	Local government, England	2826	Regulatory reform
2788 (C.124)	Mental health, England and Wales	2827 (W.250)	Road traffic, Wales
2789	Medicines	2828	Mental health
2790	Immigration	2829	Betting, gaming and lotteries
	Nationality	2830	Immigration
2791	Contracting out, England and Wales	2831	Housing, England and Wales
	Supreme Court of England and Wales	2832	Excise
	Mental capacity, England and Wales	2833	Tribunals and inquiries
	County courts, England and Wales	2834	Tribunals and inquiries, England and Wales
	Magistrates' courts, England and Wales		Tribunals and inquiries, Northern Ireland
2792	Public health		
	National Health Service, England	2835	Tribunals and inquiries
	Social care	2836 (L. 18)	Family law, England and Wales
2793	Criminal law, England and Wales	2837 (W.251)	Road traffic, Wales
2794	Electronic communications	2838 (W.252)	Rating and valuation, Wales
2795	Customs	2839	Housing, England and Wales
	Animals	2840	Local government, England and Wales
2796	Civil aviation		
2797	Road traffic		Regulatory reform
2798	Road traffic	2841	Cremation, England and Wales
2799	Road traffic	2842 (W.253)	Road traffic, Wales
2800	Road traffic	2843 (W.254)	Road traffic, Wales
2801	Road traffic	2844	Road traffic
2802	Road traffic	2845 (W.255)	Acquisition of land, Wales
2803	Road traffic	2846	South Atlantic territories
2804	Road traffic	2847	Statistics of trade
2805	Road traffic	2848	Public procurement, England and Wales
2806	Road traffic		Public procurement, Northern Ireland
2807	Road traffic		
2808	Road traffic	2849	Road traffic
2809	Road traffic	2850	Road traffic
2810	Road traffic	2851	Merchant shipping
2811	Road traffic	2852	Consumer protection
2812	Road traffic		Environmental protection
2813	Road traffic		Health and safety
2814	Road traffic	2853 (L.19)	Supreme Court of England and Wales
2815	Road traffic		County courts, England and Wales
2816	Road traffic	2854 (L.20)	Supreme Court of England and Wales
2817	Road traffic		
2818	Road traffic	2855 (L.21)	Magistrates' courts, England and Wales
2819	Road traffic	2856 (L.22)	Family proceedings, England and Wales
2820	Road traffic, England		
2821	Road traffic, England		Supreme Court of England and Wales
2822 (C.125)	Immigration		
2823	CANCELLED		County courts, England and Wales
		2857	Local government, England

2858 (L.23)	Magistrates' courts, England and Wales
2859 (L.24)	Magistrates' courts, England and Wales
2860 (C.126)	Companies
2861 (L.25)	Family proceedings, England and Wales
	Supreme Court of England and Wales
	County courts, England and Wales
2862	Police, England and Wales
2863	Police, England and Wales
2864	Police, England and Wales
2865	Police, England and Wales
2866	Police, England and Wales
2867	Local government, England
2868	National Health Service, England
2869	Political parties
2870 (C.127)	Children and young persons, England and Wales
2871	Recovery of taxes
2872	Land registration, England and Wales
2873	Road traffic
2874	Road traffic
2875	Road traffic
2876	Road traffic
2877	Road traffic
2878	Road traffic
2879	Road traffic
2880	Road traffic
2881	Road traffic
2882	Road traffic
2883	Road traffic
2884	Road traffic
2885	Road traffic
2886	Road traffic
2887	Road traffic
2888	Education, England
2889	Education, England
2890	Road traffic
2891	Road traffic
2892	Road traffic
2893	Road traffic
2894	Road traffic
2895	Road traffic
2896	Road traffic
2897	Road traffic
2898	Road traffic
2899	Road traffic
2900	Road traffic
2901	Road traffic
2902	Road traffic
2903	Road traffic
2904	Road traffic
2905	Road traffic
2906	Road traffic
2907	Road traffic
2908	Town and country planning, England
2909	Housing, England
2910 (W.256)	Road traffic, Wales
2911	Civil aviation
2912	Civil aviation
2913 (W.257)	Plant health, Wales
2914	Road traffic
2915	Road traffic
2916	Road traffic
2917	Road traffic
2918	Road traffic
2919	Road traffic
2920	Road traffic
2921	Road traffic
2922	Road traffic
2923	Road traffic
2924	Marine pollution
2925	Road traffic
2926	Road traffic
2927	Health care and associated professions
2928	Social security
2929 (W.258)	Rating and valuation, Wales
2930	Legal Services Commission, England and Wales
2931 (W.259)	Road traffic, Wales
2932	Industrial organisation and development
2933	Veterinary surgeons
2934	County courts, England and Wales
	Supreme Court of England and Wales
2935	Road traffic
2936	Consumer protection
2937	Road traffic
2938	Local government, England
2939	Education, England
2940	Children and young persons, England

2941	CANCELLED		Private international law, England and Wales
2942	Pensions		
2943 (W.260)	Children and young persons, Wales		Private international law, Northern Ireland
2944 (W.261)	Road traffic, Wales	2987	Social security
2945	Education, England	2988	Highways, England
2946	Medicines	2989	Pensions, England and Wales
2947	Pensions, England	2990	Income tax
2948	Education, England	2991	Taxes
2949	Road traffic	2992	Education, England
2950	Road traffic	2993 (C.128)	Criminal law, England and Wales
2951	Road traffic		Criminal law, Northern Ireland
2952	Road traffic		Anti-Social behaviour, England and Wales
2953	Road traffic		Police, England and Wales
2954	Road traffic	2994 (C.129)	Human rights
2955	Road traffic		National Health Service, England
2956	Road traffic		Public health, England
2957	Road traffic		Social care
2958	Road traffic	2995	Tribunals and inquiries
2959	Road traffic		Judicial appointments and discipline
2960	Road traffic	2996	Companies
2961	Road traffic	2997 (W.262)	Rating and valuation, Wales
2962	Road traffic	2998	Official statistics
2963	Road traffic	2999	Food
2964	Road traffic	3000	Companies
2965	Road traffic	3001	Regulatory reform
2966	Road traffic	3002	Housing, England and Wales
2967	Road traffic		Housing, Northern Ireland
2968	Road traffic	3003 (W.263)	Road traffic, Wales
2969	Disabled persons Transport	3004	Local loans
		3005	Education, England
2970	CANCELLED	3006	Companies
2971	Road traffic	3007	Companies
2972	Road traffic	3008	Race relations
2973	Road traffic	3009 (C.130)	Criminal law
2974	Road traffic		Road traffic
2975	Disabled persons	3010	Road traffic
2976	Road traffic	3011	Offshore installations
2977	Road traffic	3012	Civil contingencies, England
2978	Road traffic	3013	Road traffic, England
2979	Road traffic	3014	Companies
2980	Road traffic	3015	Housing, England
2981	Road traffic	3016	Education, England
2982	Road traffic	3017	Immigration Nationality
2983	Road traffic		
2984	Road traffic	3018	Excise
2985	Road traffic	3019	Excise
2986		3020	Value added tax
		3021	Value added tax

3022	Local government, England
3023	Income tax
3024	Income tax
3025	Income tax
3026	Excise
3027	Road traffic
3028	Road traffic
3029	Road traffic
3030	Road traffic
3031	Road traffic
3032	Road traffic
3033	Road traffic
3034	Road traffic
3035	Road traffic
3036	Road traffic
3037	Road traffic
3038	Road traffic
3039	Road traffic
3040	Road traffic
3041	Road traffic
3042	Road traffic
3043	Road traffic
3044	Road traffic
3045	Electricity, England and Wales
3046	Electricity, England and Wales
3047	Health care and associated professions
3048	Immigration
3049	Immigration
3050	Children and young persons, England and Wales
	Protection of vulnerable adults, England and Wales
3051	Social security
3052	Immigration
3053	Financial services
3054	Education, England
3055	Terms and conditions of employment
3056 (W.264)	Road traffic, Wales
3057 (W.265)	Road traffic, Wales
3058	Value added tax
	Excise
3059 (W.266)	Road traffic, Wales
3060 (W.267)	Road traffic, Wales
3061 (W.268)	Road traffic, Wales
3062	Excise
3063	Customs
3064	Social security
3065 (C.131)	Criminal law, Northern Ireland
3066	Antarctica
3067	Human tissue, England and Wales
	Human tissue, Northern Ireland
3068 (C.132)	Housing, England and Wales
3069	Pensions
3070	Pensions
3071	Children and young persons, England
3072	Education, England
3073	Banks and banking
3074	Legal services, England and Wales
3075 (W.269)	Rating and valuation, Wales
3076	Transport
3077 (C.133)	Education, England and Wales
3078	Rating and valuation, England
3079 (W.270)	Road traffic, Wales
3080	National Health Service, England
3081	Education, England
3082 (W.271)	Education, Wales
3083	Education, England
3084	Education, England
3085 (L.26)	Supreme Court of England and Wales
3086	Education, England
3087	Atomic energy and radioactive substances
3088 (W.272)	Road traffic, Wales
3089	Education, England
3090	Education, England
3091	Education, England
3092	Education, England
3093	Education, England
3094 (W.273)	Animals, Wales
3095	Local government, England
3096	Corporation tax
3097	Medicines
3098	Savings banks
3099	Social security
3100 (W.274)	Clean air, Wales
3101 (W.275)	Clean air, Wales
3102	Representation of the people
3103	National lottery, England
3104	Housing, England
3105	Betting, gaming and lotteries
3106 (L.27)	Family proceedings, England and Wales

	Supreme Court of England and Wales	3143 (W.278)	Agriculture, Wales
	County courts, England and Wales		Water, Wales
3107	Housing, England and Wales	3144 (W.279)	Sea fisheries, Wales
3108	Social security	3145	Merchant shipping
3109	Social security, England and Wales	3146	Police, England and Wales
	Social security, Northern Ireland	3147	Education, England
3110 (C.134)	Local government, England and Wales	3148	Health care and associated professions
		3149 (C.137)	Legal services, England and Wales
3111	Housing, England	3150 (C.138)	Health care and associated professions
3112	Local government, England		
	Transport, England	3151 (C.139)	Tax credits
3113	Health care and associated professions	3152 (W.280)	Local government, Wales
		3153 (W.281)	Animals, Wales
3114 (W.276)	Education, Wales	3154 (W.282)	Animals, Wales
3115	Parliamentary Commissioner	3155	Criminal law, England and Wales
3116	European Communities	3156	Housing
3117	European Communities	3157	Social security
3118	Education, Wales	3158	Immigration
3119	Civil aviation	3159	Income tax
3120	Civil aviation		Corporation tax
3121	Civil aviation		Capital gains tax
3122	Companies		Stamp duty reserve tax
3123	United Nations	3160	Road traffic, England
3124	International immunities and privileges	3161	Customs
		3162	Administration of estates, England and Wales
3125	Civil aviation		
3126	Education, England	3163	Transport and works, England
	Children and young persons, England		Transport, England
		3164 (C.140)	Road traffic
3127	Caribbean and North Atlantic territories	3165 (C. 141)	Income tax
		3166	Mental health, England
3128	United Nations	3167 (C.142)	Social security
3129	Defence	3168 (C.143)	National Health Service, England
3130	Dangerous drugs	3169	Civil aviation
3131	Health care and associated professions	3170 (W.283)	Education, Wales
		3171 (W.284) (C.144)	National Health Service, Wales
3132	Constitutional law		
	Devolution, Wales	3172	Road traffic
3133	Civil aviation	3173	Road traffic
3134	Ministers of the Crown	3174	Road traffic
3135	International criminal court	3175	Road traffic
3136 (C.135)	Immigration	3176	Road traffic
3137 (C.136)	Social security	3177	Road traffic
3138 (W.277)	Highways, Wales	3178	Road traffic
3139	Pensions, England and Wales	3179	Road traffic
3140	Social security	3180	Road traffic
3141	Local government, England	3181	Road traffic
3142	Local government, England	3182	Road traffic
		3183	Road traffic

3184	Road traffic	3227	Road traffic
3185	Road traffic	3228	Road traffic
3186	Road traffic	3229	Companies
3187	Road traffic	3230	Agriculture, England
3188	Road traffic	3231	Customs
3189	Road traffic	3232 (C.146)	Employment
3190	Electronic communications	3233	Plant health, England
3191	Electronic communications	3234	Revenue and customs
3192	Electronic communications	3235	Stamp duty
3193	Electronic communications		Stamp duty reserve tax
3194	CANCELLED	3236	Stamp duty reserve tax
3195	Social security	3237	Corporation tax
3196	Animals, England	3238	Healthcare and associated professions
3197	Electronic communications		Health care and associated professions
3198	Road traffic, England	3239 (W.286)	Dangerous drugs, Wales
3199	Highways, England	3240	Employment tribunals
3200 (W.285)	Landlord and tenant, Wales	3241 (C.147)	Pensions
3201	Land registration, England and Wales	3242	Magistrates' courts, England and Wales
3202	Town and country planning, England	3243	Environmental protection, England and Wales
3203	Agriculture, England	3244 (C.148)	Social security
3204 (C.145)	Children and young persons, England	3245	Pensions, England and Wales
	Protection of vulnerable adults, England	3246	Social security
3205	Road traffic	3247	Social security
3206	Food	3248	Housing, England
3207	Road traffic	3249	Banks and banking
3208	Road traffic	3250	Banks and banking
3209	Road traffic	3251	Banks and banking
3210	Road traffic	3252	Agriculture, England
3211	Road traffic	3253	Education, England
3212	Road traffic	3254 (W.287)	Road traffic, Wales
3213	Road traffic	3255	Social security
3214	Road traffic	3256	Education, England
3215	Road traffic	3257	Marine pollution
3216	Road traffic	3258	National Health Service, England and Wales
3217	Road traffic		National Health Service, Scotland
3218	Road traffic		Health and personal social services, Northern Ireland
3219	Road traffic	3259	Rehabilitation of offenders, England and Wales
3220	Road traffic		
3221	Road traffic	3260 (C.149)	Rehabilitation of offenders, England and Wales
3222	Road traffic		Police, England and Wales
3223	Road traffic		Criminal law, England
3224	Road traffic	3261	Local government, England
3225	Road traffic	3262	Regulatory reform
3226	Road traffic		

3263	Highways, England	3303	Road traffic
3264	Council tax, England	3304	Road traffic
	Rating and valuation, England	3305	Road traffic
3265	Children and young persons, England and Wales	3306	Road traffic
		3307	Road traffic
	Protection of vulnerable adults, England and Wales	3308	Road traffic
3266 (W.288)	Animals, Wales	3309	Road traffic
3267 (C.150)	Charities, England and Wales	3310	Road traffic
3268	Charities, England and Wales	3311	Road traffic
3269 (L.28)	Supreme Court of England and Wales	3312	Road traffic
		3313	Road traffic
	Magistrates' courts, England and Wales	3314	Road traffic
3270	Social security	3315	Road traffic
3271	Road traffic	3316	Road traffic
3272	Road traffic	3317	Road traffic
3273	Road traffic	3318	Road traffic
3274	Road traffic	3319	Road traffic
3275	Road traffic	3320	Road traffic
3276	Road traffic	3321	Road traffic
3277	Road traffic	3322	Road traffic
3278	Road traffic	3323	Road traffic
3279	Road traffic	3324	Road traffic
3280	Road traffic	3325	Highways, England
3281	Road traffic	3326 (W.291)	Road traffic, Wales
3282	Road traffic	3327 (L. 29)	Supreme Court of England and Wales
3283	Road traffic		
3284	Road traffic		County courts, England and Wales
3285	Road traffic	3328	*CANCELLED*
3286	Road traffic	3329	Road traffic
3287	Road traffic	3330	Road traffic
3288	Road traffic	3331	Road traffic
3289	Road traffic	3332	Road traffic
3290	Road traffic	3333	Road traffic
3291	Highways, England	3334	Road traffic
3292	Highways, England	3335	Road traffic
3293 (W.289)	Road traffic, Wales	3336	Road traffic
3294	Defence	3337	Road traffic
3295	Animals, England	3338	Road traffic
3296 (C.151)	Prevention and suppression of terrorism	3339	Road traffic
		3340	Road traffic
3297	Criminal law, England and Wales	3341	Road traffic
	Police, England and Wales	3342	Road traffic
3298	Highways, England	3343	Road traffic
3299	Civil aviation	3344	Road traffic
3300 (W.290)	Road traffic, Wales	3345	Road traffic
3301	Road traffic	3346	Road traffic
3302	Road traffic	3347	Road traffic

3348	Road traffic
3349	Road traffic
3350	Road traffic
3351	Road traffic
3352	Road traffic
3353	Road traffic
3354	Road traffic
3355	Road traffic
3356	Road traffic
3357	Road traffic
3358	Road traffic
3359	Road traffic
3360	Road traffic
3361	Road traffic
3362	Road traffic
3363	Road traffic
3364	Road traffic
3365	Road traffic
3366	Road traffic
3367	Road traffic
3368	Road traffic
3369	Road traffic
3370	Road traffic
3371	Road traffic

Subsidiary Numbers

Commencement orders (bring an act or part of an act into operation)

17 (W.6) (C.1)
99 (C.2)
113 (C.3)
172 (C.4)
219 (C.5)
222 (C.6)
306 (C.7)
308 (C.8)
309 (C.9)
310 (C.10)
311 (C.11)
313 (C.12)
337 (C.13)
379 (C.14)
401 (C.15)
411 (C.16)
461 (C.17)
504 (C.18)
561 (C.19)
568 (C.20)
582 (C.21)
591 (W.60)(C.22)
610 (C.23)
617 (C.24)
627 (C.25)
674 (C.26)
692 (C.27)
694 (C.28)
697 (C.29)
745 (C.30)
749 (C.31)
751 (C.32)
752 (C.33)
755 (C.34)
757 (C.35)
785 (C.35)
787 (C.36)
790 (C.37)
791 (C.38)
800 (C.39)
831 (C.40)
839 (C.41)
898 (C.42)
905 (C.43)
917 (C.44)
930 (C.45)
945 (C.46)
956 (C. 47)
983 (W.108)(C.48)
1065 (C.49)
1147 (C.50)
1158 (C.51)
1210 (C.52)
1262 (C.53)
1265 (C.54)
1316 (C.55)
1318 (C.56)
1320 (C.57)
1325 (C.58)
1326 (C.59)
1334 (C.60)
1372 (C.61)
1407 (C.62)

1424 (C.63)	2550 (C.111)
1429 (W.148)(C.64)	2556 (C.112)
1436 (C.65)	2561 (C.113)
1466 (C.66)	2597 (C.114)
1476 (C.67)	2664 (C.115)
1521 (C.68)	2675 (C.116)
1586 (C.69)	2696 (C.117)
1591 (C.70)	2712 (C.118)
1592 (C.71)	2714 (C.119)
1650 (C.72)	2717 (C.120)
1653 (C.73)	2772 (C.121)
1656 (C.74)	2779 (C.122)
1728 (W.168) (C.75)	2785 (C.123)
1798 (C.76)	2788 (C.124)
1818 (C.77)	2822 (C.125)
1862 (C.78)	2860 (C.126)
1864 (C.79)	2870 (C.127)
1878 (C.80)	2993 (C.128)
1880 (C.81)	2994 (C.129)
1882 (C.82)	3009 (C.130)
1886 (C.83)	3065 (C.131)
1900 (C.84)	3068 (C.132)
1904 (W.182)(C.85)	3077 (C.133)
1918 (C.86)	3110 (C.134)
1922 (C.87)	3136 (C.135)
1925 (C.88)	3137 (C.136)
1928 (C.89)	3149 (C.137)
1929 (C.90)	3150 (C.138)
1930 (C.91)	3151 (C.139)
1933 (C.92)	3164 (C.140)
1935 (C.93)	3165 (C.141)
1960 (C.94)	3167 (C.142)
1971 (C.95)	3168 (C.143)
1972 (C.96)	3171 (W.284) (C.144)
2033 (C.97)	3204 (C.145)
2037 (C.98)	3232 (C.146)
2101 (C.99)	3241 (C.147)
2214 (C.100)	3244 (C.148)
2261 (C.101)	3260 (C.149)
2302 (C.102)	3267 (C.150)
2358 (C.103)	3296 (C.151)
2371 (C.104)	
2434 (C.105)	
2444 (C.105)	
2497 (C.106)	
2503 (C.107)	
2504 (C.108)	
2545 (C.109)	
2548 (C.110)	

Instruments relating to fees or procedure in courts in England and Wales

115 (L.1)
116 (L.2)
117 (L.3)
1052 (L.4)

1053 (L.5)
1054 (L.6)
1088 (L.7)
1089 (L.8)
2076 (L.9)
2178 (L.10)
2446 (L.11)
2447 (L.12)
2685 (L.13)
2686 (L.14)
2698 (L.15)
2699 (L.16)
2705 (L.17)
2836 (L 18)
2853 (L.19)
2854 (L.20)
2855 (L.21)
2856 (L.22)
2858 (L.23)
2859 (L.24)
2861 (L.25)
3085 (L.26)
3106 (L.27)
3269 (L.28)
3327 (L.29)

Certain orders in Council relating to Northern Ireland

1216 (NI.1)
1769 (NI. 2)

Instruments that extend only to Scotland

48 (S.1)
305 (S.2)
307 (S.3)
662 (S.4)
1590 (S.5)

Instruments that extend only to Wales

1 (W.1)
2 (W.2)
7 (W.3)
10 (W.4)
12 (W.5)
17 (W.6) (C.1)
18 (W.7)
38 (W.8)
44 (W.9)
45 (W.10)
56 (W.11)
84 (W.12)
98 (W.13)
101 (W.14)
102 (W.15)
114 (W.16)
130 (W.17)
136 (W.18)
137 (W.19)
138 (W.20)
168 (W.21)
169 (W.22)
170 (W.23)
197 (W.24)
199 (W.25)
215 (W.26)
220 (W.27)
226 (W.28)
253 (W.29)
254 (W.30)
365 (W.31)
366 (W.32)
367 (W.33)
368 (W.34)
369 (W.35)
370 (W.36)
371 (W.37)
418 (W.38)
420 (W.39)
450 (W.40)
466 (W.41)
476 (W.42)
502 (W.43)
503 (W.44)
509 (W.45)
510 (W.46)
512 (W.47)
513 (W.48)
522 (W.49)
524 (W.50)
538 (W.51)
540 (W.52)
543 (W.53)
545 (W.54)
555 (W.55)
577 (W.56)
578 (W.57)

584 (W.58)
588 (W.59)
591 (W.60)(C.22)
596 (W.61)
600 (W.62)
601 (W.63)
612 (W.64)
613 (W.65)
614 (W.66)
615 (W.67)
616 (W.68)
620 (W.69)
660 (W.70)
663 (W.71)
685 (W.72)
712 (W.73)
713 (W.74)
716 (W.75)
717 (W.76)
742 (W.77)
743 (W.78)
758 (W.79)
781 (W.80)
784 (W.81)
788 (W.82)
789 (W.83)
841 (W.84)
918 (W.85)
920 (W.86)
922 (W.87)
924 (W.88)
926 (W.89)
927 (W.90)
931 (W.91)
932 (W.92)
933 (W.93)
934 (W.94)
935 (W.95)
936 (W.96)
937 (W.97)
938 (W.98)
939 (W.99)
940 (W.100)
942 (W.101)
943 (W.102)
952 (W.103)
953 (W.104)
955 (W.105)
971 (W.106)

982 (W.107)
983 (W.108)(C.48)
1039 (W.109)
1040 (W.110)
1041 (W.111)
1063 (W.112)
1064 (W.113)
1080 (W.114)
1081 (W.115)
1090 (W.116)
1141 (W.117)
1145 (W.118)
1182 (W.119)
1191 (W.120)
1213 (W.121)
1214 (W.122)
1215 (W.123)
1237 (W.124)
1244 (W.125)
1259 (W.126)
1260 (W.127)
1268 (W.128)
1270 (W.129)
1273 (W.130)
1274 (W.131)
1275 (W.132)
1279 (W.133)
1280 (W.134)
1286 (W.135)
1314 (W.136)
1324 (W.137)
1329 (W.138)
1333 (W.139)
1338 (W.140)
1341 (W.141)
1343 (W.142)
1403 (W.143)
1404 (W.144)
1408 (W.145)
1409 (W.146)
1425 (W.147)
1429 (W.148)(C.64)
1433 (W.149)
1438 (W.150)
1442 (W.151)
1475 (W.152)
1480 (W.153)
1483 (W.154)
1512 (W.155)

1555 (W.156)
1574 (W.157)
1583 (W.158)
1646 (W.159)
1648 (W.160)
1658 (W.161)
1682 (W.162)
1716 (W.163)
1717 (W.164)
1719 (W.165)
1720 (W.166)
1721 (W.167)
1728 (W.168) (C.75)
1732 (W.169)
1736 (W.170)
1739 (W.171)
1742 (W.172)
1787 (W.173)
1806 (W.174)
1811 (W.175)
1815 (W.176)
1848 (W.177)
1866 (W.178)
1890 (W.179)
1896 (W.180)
1899 (W.181)
1904 (W.182)(C.85)
1927 (W.183)
1974 (W.184)
1976 (W.185)
2032 (W.186)
2040 (W.187)
2100 (W.188)
2140 (W.189)
2141 (W.190)
2158 (W.191)
2162 (W.192)
2174 (W.193)
2215 (W.194)
2216 (W.195)
2255 (W.196)
2298 (W.197)
2335 (W.198)
2336 (W.199)
2348 (W.200)
2351 (W.201)
2354 (W.202)
2364 (W.203)

2369 (W.204)
2370 (W.205)
2377 (W.206)
2432 (W.207)
2433 (W.208)
2436 (W.209)
2437 (W.210)
2438 (W.211)
2439 (W.212)
2440 (W.213)
2441 (W.214)
2443 (W.215)
2498 (W.216)
2499 (W.217)
2500 (W.218)
2505 (W.219)
2506 (W.220)
2509 (W.221)
2552 (W.222)
2555 (W.223)
2559 (W.224)
2565 (W.225)
2568 (W.226)
2571 (W.227)
2602 (W.228)
2629 (W.229)
2640 (W.230)
2641 (W.231)
2642 (W.232)
2650 (W.233)
2665 (W.234)
2671 (W.235)
2672 (W.236)
2687 (W.237)
2689 (W.238)
2691 (W.239)
2695 (W.240)
2701 (W.241)
2709 (W.242)
2710 (W.243)
2711 (W.244)
2716 (W.245)
2770 (W.246)
2774 (W.247)
2781 (W.248)
2782 (W.249)
2827 (W.250)
2837 (W.251)

2838 (W.252)	3088 (W.272)
2842 (W.253)	3094 (W.273)
2843 (W.254)	3100 (W.274)
2845 (W.255)	3101 (W.275)
2910 (W.256)	3114 (W.276)
2913 (W.257)	3138 (W.277)
2929 (W.258)	3143 (W.278)
2931 (W.259)	3144 (W.279)
2943 (W.260)	3152 (W.280)
2944 (W.261)	3153 (W.281)
2997 (W.262)	3154 (W.282)
3003 (W.263)	3170 (W.283)
3056 (W.264)	3171 (W.284) (C.144)
3057 (W.265)	3200 (W.285)
3059 (W.266)	3239 (W.286)
3060 (W.267)	3254 (W.287)
3061 (W.268)	3266 (W.288)
3075 (W.269)	3293 (W.289)
3079 (W.270)	3300 (W.290)
3082 (W.271)	3326 (W.291)

Scottish Legislation

Acts of the Scottish Parliament

Acts of the Scottish Parliament 2008

Abolition of Bridge Tolls (Scotland) Act 2008: 2008 asp 1. - 4p.: 30 cm. - Royal assent, 24th January 2008. An Act of the Scottish Parliament to abolish tolls on road bridges. Explanatory notes to assist in the understanding of this Act are available separately (ISBN 9780105911098). - 978-0-10-590127-3 £3.00

Budget (Scotland) Act 2008: 2008 asp 2. - [3], 20, [1]p.: 30 cm. - Royal assent, 12th March 2008. An Act of the Scottish Parliament to make provision, for financial year 2008/09, for the use of resources by the Scottish Administration and certain bodies whose expenditure is payable out of the Scottish Consolidated Fund, for authorising the payment of sums out of the Fund and for the maximum amounts of borrowing by certain statutory bodies; to make provision, for financial year 2009/10, for authorising the payment of sums out of the Fund on a temporary basis. - 978-0-10-590128-0 £4.50

Glasgow Commonwealth Games Act 2008: 2008 asp 4. - [3], 19, [1]p.: 30 cm. - Royal assent, 10th June 2008. An Act of the Scottish Parliament to make provision in relation to the Commonwealth Games that are to be held principally in Glasgow in 2014. Explanatory notes to assist in the understanding of this Act are available separately (ISBN 9780105911142). - 978-0-10-590130-3 £4.00

Graduate Endowment Abolition (Scotland) Act 2008: 2008 asp 3. - [8]p.: 30 cm. - Royal assent, 4th April 2008. An Act of the Scottish Parliament to abolish the graduate endowment. Explanatory notes have been produced to assist in the understanding of this Act and will be available separately. - 978-0-10-590129-7 £3.00

Judiciary and Courts (Scotland) Act 2008: 2008 asp 6. - iv, 55p.: 30 cm. - Royal assent, 29 October 2008. An Act of the Scottish Parliament to make provision about the judiciary and the courts; to establish the Scottish Court Service. Explanatory notes have been produced to assist in the understanding of this Act and are available separately (ISBN 9780105911166). - 978-0-10-590132-7 £9.00

Public Health etc (Scotland) Act 2008: 2008 asp 5. - vi, 100p.: 30 cm. - Royal assent, 16th July 2008. An Act of the Scottish Parliament to restate and amend the law on public health; to make provision about mortuaries and the disposal of bodies; to enable the Scottish Ministers to implement their obligations under the International Health Regulations; to make provision relating to the use, sale or hire of sunbeds; to amend the law on statutory nuisances. Explanatory notes have been produced to assist in the understanding of this Act are available separately (ISBN 9780105911159). - 978-0-10-590131-0 £13.50

Scottish Register of Tartans Act 2008: 2008 asp 7. - [2], 9p.: 30 cm. - Royal assent, 13th November 2008. An Act of the Scottish Parliament to establish a register of tartans. Explanatory notes have been produced to assist in the understanding of the Act and are available separately (ISBN 9780105911173). - 978-0-10-590133-4 £5.00

Acts of the Scottish Parliament - Explanatory notes 2008

Glasgow Commonwealth Games Act 2008 (asp 4): explanatory notes. - [18]p.: 30 cm. - These notes relate to the Glasgow Commonwealth Games Act 2008 (asp 4) (ISBN 9780105901303) which received Royal assent on 10 June 2008. - 978-0-10-591114-2 £3.50

Graduate Endowment Abolition (Scotland) Act 2008 (asp 3): explanatory notes. - [4]p.: 30 cm. - These notes relate to the Graduate Endowment Abolition (Scotland) Act 2008 (asp 3) (ISBN 9780105901297) which received Royal assent on 4 April 2008. - 978-0-10-591111-1 £3.00

Judiciary and Courts (Scotland) Act 2008 (asp 6): explanatory notes. - 37p.: 30 cm. - These Notes relate to the Judiciary and Courts (Scotland) Act 2008 (asp 6) (ISBN 9780105901327) which received Royal Assent on 29 October 2008. - 978-0-10-591116-6 £9.00

Public Health etc. (Scotland) Act 2008 (asp 5): explanatory notes. - 47p.: 30 cm. - These notes relate to the Public Health etc. (Scotland) Act 2008 (asp 5) (ISBN 9780105901310) which received Royal assent on 16 July 2008. - 978-0-10-591115-9 £7.50

Scottish Register of Tartans Act 2008 (asp 7): explanatory notes. - [12]p.: 30 cm. - These Notes relate to the Scottish Register of Tartans Act 2008 (asp 7) (ISBN 9780105901334) which received Royal Assent on 13 November 2008. - 978-0-10-591117-3 £5.00

Other statutory publications

Office of the Queen's Printer for Scotland.

The acts of the Scottish Parliament 2007: with lists of the acts, tables and index. - 1205p.: hdbk: 31 cm. - 978-0-11-840452-5 £96.00

Scottish statutory instruments 2007. - 4v. (xv, 3566p.): hdbk: 31 cm. - Contents: Vol 1 Introduction, List of instruments, General Instrument Nos 1 to 159; Vol 2 Nos 160 to 256; Vol 3 Nos 257 to 471; Vol. 4 Nos to 472 to 577, selected Local SSIs, selected instruments not registered as SSIs, Classified list of Local Instruments,

Office of the Queen's Printer for Scotland.

Table of effects, Numerical and issue list, Index. - 978-0-11-840466-2 £360.00 for 4 vols not sold sep.

Scottish Statutory Instruments
By Subject Heading

Adult support

The Adult Support and Protection (Scotland) Act 2007 (Adults with Incapacity) (Consequential Provisions) Order 2008 No. 2008/50. - Enabling power: Adult Support and Protection (Scotland) Act 2007, s. 76 (1) (a). - Issued: 26.02.2008. Made: 20.02.2008. Laid before the Scottish Parliament: 21.02.2008. Coming into force: 01.04.2008. Effect: S.S.I. 2002/494 amended & S.S.I. 2001/78 revoked. Territorial extent & classification: S. General. - 4p.: 30 cm. - 978-0-11-081517-6 £3.00

The Adult Support and Protection (Scotland) Act 2007 (Commencement No. 2 and Transitional Provisions) Amendment Order 2008 No. 2008/116 (C.11). - Enabling power: Adult Support and Protection (Scotland) Act 2007, s. 79 (3) (4). Bringing into operation various provisions of the 2007 Act on 01.10.2008, in accord. with art. 2. - Issued: 19.03.2008. Made: 13.03.2008. Effect: S.S.I. 2008/49 amended. Territorial extent & classification: S. General. - This SSI has been made in consequence of a defect in S.S.I. 2008/49 (ISBN 978011081569) and is being issued free of charge to all known recipients of that instrument. - 4p.: 30 cm. - 978-0-11-081579-4 £3.00

The Adult Support and Protection (Scotland) Act 2007 (Commencement No. 2 and Transitional Provisions) Order 2008 No. 2008/49 (C.6). - Enabling power: Adult Support and Protection (Scotland) Act 2007, s. 79 (3) (4). Bringing into operation various provisions of the 2007 Act on 01.04.2008 and 01.10.2008. - Issued: 26.02.2008. Made: 20.02.2008. Effect: None. Territorial extent & classification: S. General. - 4p.: 30 cm. - 978-0-11-081516-9 £3.00

The Adult Support and Protection (Scotland) Act 2007 (Commencement No. 3 and Related Amendments) Order 2008 No. 2008/314 (C. 28). - Enabling power: Adult Support and Protection (Scotland) Act 2007, s. 79 (3). Bringing into operation various provisions of the 2007 Act on 29.10.2008, in accord. with art. 2. - Issued: 23.09.2008. Made: 16.09.2008. Effect: S.S.I. 2008/49 amended. Territorial extent & classification: S. General. - 4p.: 30 cm. - 978-0-11-084491-6 £4.00

The Adult Support and Protection (Scotland) Act 2007 (Restriction on the Authorisation of Council Officers) Order 2008 No. 2008/306. - Enabling power: Adult Support and Protection (Scotland) Act 2007, ss. 52 (1), 76 (1). - Issued: 16.09.2008. Made: 10.09.2008. Laid before the Scottish Parliament: 11.09.2008. Coming into force: 29.10.2008. Effect: None. Territorial extent & classification: S. General. - 4p.: 30 cm. - 978-0-11-084477-0 £4.00

Adults with incapacity

The Adult Support and Protection (Scotland) Act 2007 (Adults with Incapacity) (Consequential Provisions) Order 2008 No. 2008/50. - Enabling power: Adult Support and Protection (Scotland) Act 2007, s. 76 (1) (a). - Issued: 26.02.2008. Made: 20.02.2008. Laid before the Scottish Parliament: 21.02.2008. Coming into force: 01.04.2008. Effect: S.S.I. 2002/494 amended & S.S.I. 2001/78 revoked. Territorial extent & classification: S. General. - 4p.: 30 cm. - 978-0-11-081517-6 £3.00

The Adult Support and Protection (Scotland) Act 2007 (Commencement No. 2 and Transitional Provisions) Order 2008 No. 2008/49 (C.6). - Enabling power: Adult Support and Protection (Scotland) Act 2007, s. 79 (3) (4). Bringing into operation various provisions of the 2007 Act on 01.04.2008 and 01.10.2008. - Issued: 26.02.2008. Made: 20.02.2008. Effect: None. Territorial extent & classification: S. General. - 4p.: 30 cm. - 978-0-11-081516-9 £3.00

The Adults with Incapacity (Accounts and Funds) (Scotland) Regulations 2008 No. 2008/51. - Enabling power: Adults with Incapacity (Scotland) Act 2000, ss. 24D(7), 27B, 27E(2). - Issued: 26.02.2008. Made: 20.02.2008. Laid before the Scottish Parliament: 21.02.2008. Coming into force: 01.04.2008. Effect: S.S.I. 2001/76 revoked. Territorial extent & classification: S. General. - 8p.: 30 cm. - 978-0-11-081518-3 £3.00

The Adults with Incapacity (Certificates in Relation to Powers of Attorney) (Scotland) Regulations 2008 No. 2008/56. - Enabling power: Adults with Incapacity (Scotland) Act 2000, ss. 7 (1) (c), 15 (3) (c), 16 (3) (c), 22A (2) (b). - Issued: 26.02.2008. Made: 20.02.2008. Laid before the Scottish Parliament: 21.02.2008. Coming into force: 01.04.2008. Effect: S.S.I. 2001/80 revoked with saving. Territorial extent & classification: S. General. - 8p.: 30 cm. - 978-0-11-081523-7 £3.00

The Adults with Incapacity (Electronic Communications) (Scotland) Order 2008 No. 2008/380. - Enabling power: Electronic Communications Act 2000, ss. 8, 9. - Issued: 26.11.2008. Made: 30.10.2008. Coming into force: 31.10.2008. Effect: 2000 asp 4 amended. Territorial extent & classification: S. General. - Supersedes draft S.S.I. (ISBN 9780110839615) issued 11.09.2008. - 4p.: 30 cm. - 978-0-11-100086-1 £4.00

The Adults with Incapacity (Public Guardian's Fees) (Scotland) Amendment Regulations 2008 No. 2008/238. - Enabling power: Adults with Incapacity (Scotland) Act 2000, s. 7 (2). - Issued: 16.06.2008. Made: 06.06.2008. Laid before the Scottish Parliament: 06.06.2008. Coming into force: in accord. with reg. 1. Effect: S.S.I. 2008/52 amended. Territorial extent & classification: S. General. - 12p.: 30 cm. - 978-0-11-082031-6 £3.00

The Adults with Incapacity (Public Guardian's Fees) (Scotland) Regulations 2008 No. 2008/52. - Enabling power: Adults with Incapacity (Scotland) Act 2000, ss. 7 (2), 86 (2). - Issued: 26.02.2008. Made: 20.02.2008. Laid before the Scottish Parliament: 21.02.2008. Coming into force: 01.04.2008. Effect: S.S.I. 2001/725 revoked. Territorial extent & classification: S. General. - 8p.: 30 cm. - 978-0-11-081519-0 £3.00

The Adults with Incapacity (Recall of Guardians' Powers) (Scotland) Amendment Regulations 2008 No. 2008/53. - Enabling power: Adults with Incapacity (Scotland) Act 2000, s. 73 (5). - Issued: 26.02.2008. Made: 20.02.2008. Laid before the Scottish Parliament: 21.02.2008. Coming into force: 01.04.2008. Effect: S.S.I. 2002/97 amended. Territorial extent & classification: S. General. - 4p.: 30 cm. - 978-0-11-081520-6 £3.00

The Adults with Incapacity (Reports in Relation to Guardianship and Intervention Orders) (Scotland) Amendment Regulations 2008 No. 2008/55. - Enabling power: Adults with Incapacity (Scotland) Act 2000, ss. 57 (3), 60 (3), 86 (2). - Issued: 26.02.2008. Made: 20.02.2008. Laid before the Scottish Parliament: 21.02.2008. Coming into force: 01.04.2008. Effect: S.S.I. 2002/96 amended. Territorial extent & classification: S. General. - 16p.: 30 cm. - 978-0-11-081522-0 £3.00

Agriculture

The Action Programme for Nitrate Vulnerable Zones (Scotland) Amendment Regulations 2008 No. 2008/298. - Enabling power: European Communities Act 1972, s. 2 (2). - Issued: 12.09.2008. Made: 04.09.2008. Laid before the Scottish Parliament: 08.09.2008. Coming into force: 01.01.2009. Effect: S.S.I. 2003/51 (with saving), 169 revoked. Territorial extent & classification: S. General. - 36p.: 30 cm. - 978-0-11-083973-8 £9.00

The Action Programme for Nitrate Vulnerable Zones (Scotland) Amendment Regulations 2008 No. 2008/394. - Enabling power: European Communities Act 1972, s. 2 (2). - Issued: 02.12.2008. Made: 26.11.2008. Laid before the Scottish Parliament: 27.11.2008. Coming into force: 01.01.2009. Effect: S.S.I. 2008/298 amended. Territorial extent & classification: S. General. - This Scottish Statutory Instrument has been made to correct errors in S.S.I. 2008/298 and is being issued free of charge to all known recipients of that instrument. - 4p.: 30 cm. - 978-0-11-100098-4 £4.00

The Agricultural Processing, Marketing and Co-operation Grants (Scotland) Regulations 2008 No. 2008/64. - Enabling power: European Communities Act 1972, s. 2 (2), sch. 2, para 1A. - Issued: 04.03.2008. Made: 25.02.2008. Laid before the Scottish Parliament: 28.02.2008. Coming into force: 24.03.2008. Effect: None. Territorial extent & classification: S. General. - EC note: These Regulations introduce measures to supplement Council Regulation No. 1698/2005. They also implement Article 74(1) of the Council Regulation and Article 9(1) of Council Regulation (No. 1290/2005. - 8p.: 30 cm. - 978-0-11-081534-3 £3.00

The Beef and Veal Labelling (Scotland) Regulations 2008 No. 2008/418. - Enabling power: European Communities Act 1972, s. 2 (2), sch. 2, para. 1A. - Issued: 22.12.2008. Made: 16.12.2008. Laid before the Scottish Parliament: 17.12.2008. Coming into force: 25.01.2009. Effect: S.S.I. 2001/252 revoked. Territorial extent & classification: S. General. - EC note: These Regulations continue to enforce Title II of Regulation (EC) No. 1760/2000 establishing a system for the identification and registration of bovine animals and regarding the labelling of beef and beef products and subsidiary Commission Regulations. They also enforce the provisions relating to veal of Council Regulation (EC) No. 1234/2007 establishing a common organisation of agricultural markets and on specific provisions for certain agricultural products as well as the provisions Commission Regulation (EC) No. 566/2008 laying down detailed rules for the application of Council Regulation (EC) No. 1234/2007 as regards the marketing of the meat of bovine animals aged 12 months or less. - 8p.: 30 cm. - 978-0-11-100142-4 £5.00

The Common Agricultural Policy (Single Farm Payment and Support Schemes and Cross-Compliance) (Scotland) Amendment Regulations 2008 No. 2008/184. - Enabling power: European Communities Act 1972, s. 2 (2). - Issued: 19.05.2008. Made: 13.05.2008. Laid before the Scottish Parliament: 14.05.2008. Coming into force: 15.05.2008. Effect: S.I. 2005/218; S.S.I. 2004/381, 518; 2005/143; amended. Territorial extent & classification: S. General. - EC note: These Regulations implement Council Regulation (EC) No. 146/2008 which, among other things, amends Council Regulation (EC) No. 1782/2003 establishing common rules for direct support schemes under the common agricultural policy. They also implement Commission Regulation (EC) No. 319/2008, which amends Commission Regulation (EC) No. 795/2004 laying down detailed rules for the implementation of the single payment scheme provided for in Council Regulation (EC) No. 1782/2003, and Commission Regulation (EC) No. 796/2004 laying down detailed rules for the implementation of cross-compliance, modulation and the integrated administration and control system provided for in Council Regulation (EC) No. 1782/2003. - 8p.: 30 cm. - 978-0-11-081643-2 £3.00

The Feed (Hygiene and Enforcement) (Scotland) Amendment Regulations 2008 No. 2008/201. - Enabling power: European Communities Act 1972, s. 2 (2) & Agriculture Act 1970, ss. 66 (1), 74A, 78 (6), 79 (1) (2) (9), 84. - Issued: 03.06.2008. Made: 28.05.2008. Laid before the Scottish Parliament: 29.05.2008. Coming into force: 20.06.2008. Effect: S.S.I. 2005/522, 608 amended. Territorial extent & classification: S. General. - 4p.: 30 cm. - 978-0-11-081667-8 £3.00

The Feeding Stuffs (Scotland) Amendment Regulations 2008 No. 2008/215. - Enabling power: Agriculture Act 1970, ss. 66 (1), 68 (1), 74A, 84. - Issued: 09.06.2008. Made: 03.06.2008. Laid before the Scottish Parliament: 04.06.2008. Coming into force: 30.07.2008. Effect: S.S.I. 2005/605 amended. Territorial extent & classification: S. General. - EC note: These Regulations provide for the implementation of Commission Directive 2008/4/EC amending Directive 94/39/EC as regards feedingstuffs intended for the reduction of the risk of milk fever (O.J. No. L6, 10.1.2008, p.4) (as corrected by a Corrigendum. Directive 2008/4/EC permits, subject to specified labelling requirements, two additional types of dietetic feed to be marketed for the reduction of milk fever in dairy cows. - 4p.: 30 cm. - 978-0-11-081678-4 £3.00

The Guar Gum (Restriction on First Placing on the Market) (Scotland) Regulations 2008 No. 2008/176. - Enabling power: European Communities Act 1972, s. 2 (2). - Issued: 09.05.2008. Made: 02.05.2008. Laid before the Scottish Parliament: 02.05.2008. Coming into force: 05.05.2008. Effect: None. Territorial extent & classification: S. General. - EC note: These Regulations implement, in Scotland, Commission Decision 2008/352/EC imposing special conditions governing guar gum originating in or consigned from India due to contamination risk of those products by pentachlorophenal and dioxins. - 4p.: 30 cm. - 978-0-11-081635-7 £3.00

The Land Managers Skills Development Grants (Scotland) Regulations 2008 No. 2008/162. - Enabling power: European Communities Act 1972, s. 2 (2), sch. 2, para 1A. - Issued: 28.04.2008. Made: 22.04.2008. Laid before the Scottish Parliament: 23.04.2008. Coming into force: 18.05.2008. Effect: None Territorial extent & classification: S. General. - EC note: These regs supplement Council Regulation (EC) No. 1698/2005 which lays down general rules governing Community support for rural development, financed by the European Agricultural Fund for Rural Development established by Council Regulation (EC) No. 1290/2005. They also implement Article 74(1) of Council Regulation (EC) No. 1698/2005 and Article 9(1) of Council Regulation (EC) No. 1290/2005, which require Member States to adopt legislative and administrative provisions to ensure that the Community's financial interests in relation to expenditure on rural development are effectively protected. - 12p.: 30 cm. - 978-0-11-081624-1 £3.00

The Leader Grants (Scotland) Regulations 2008 No. 2008/66. - Enabling power: European Communities Act 1972, s. 2 (2). - Issued: 05.03.2008. Made: 28.02.2008. Laid before the Scottish Parliament: 29.02.2008. Coming into force: 22.03.2008. Effect: S.S.I. 2004/381 amended. Territorial extent & classification: S. - EC note: These Regulations make provision for the purposes of implementation of Council Regulation (EC) No. 1698/2005 on support for rural development from the European Agricultural Fund for Rural Development and Commission Regulations (EC) Nos. 1974/2006 and 1975/2006 laying down detailed rules for the application of Council Regulation No. 1698/2005. The Instrument provides for LEADER funding being made available by the Scottish Ministers from the Scotland Rural Development Programme 2007-13 to local action groups. - 16p.: 30 cm. - 978-0-11-081536-7 £3.00

The Less Favoured Area Support Scheme (Scotland) Amendment Regulations 2008 No. 2008/294. - Enabling power: European Communities Act 1972, s. 2 (2). - Issued: 09.09.2008. Made: 03.09.2008. Laid before the Scottish Parliament: 04.09.2008. Coming into force: 26.09.2008. Effect: S.S.I. 2004/381; 2007/439 amended. Territorial extent & classification: S. General. - 4p.: 30 cm. - 978-0-11-083937-0 £4.00

The Official Feed and Food Controls (Scotland) Amendment Regulations 2008 No. 2008/218. - Enabling power: European Communities Act 1972, s. 2 (2). - Issued: 09.06.2008. Made: 04.06.2008. Laid before the Scottish Parliament: 06.06.2008. Coming into force: 01.07.2008. Effect: S.S.I. 2007/522 amended. Territorial extent & classification: S. General. - This Scottish Statutory Instrument has been made in consequence of a defect in S.S.I. 2008/176 and is being issued free of charge to all known recipients of that instrument. - 4p.: 30 cm. - 978-0-11-081681-4 £3.00

The Pesticides (Maximum Residue Levels in Crops, Food and Feeding Stuffs) (Scotland) Amendment Regulations 2008 No. 2008/65. - Enabling power: European Communities Act 1972, s. 2 (2). - Issued: 05.02.2008. Made: 28.02.2008. Laid before the Scottish Parliament: 29.02.2008. Coming into force: 28.03.2008 except for reg 4 (15.03.2008) and reg 5 (15.09.2008). Effect: S.S.I. 2005/599 amended. Territorial extent & classification: S. General. - Revoked by S.S.I. 2008/342 (ISBN 9780111000489). EC note: These Regulations implement Commission Directive 2007/73/EC. - 24p.: 30 cm. - 978-0-11-081535-0 £4.00

The Pesticides (Maximum Residue Levels) (Scotland) Regulations 2008 No. 2008/342. - Enabling power: European Communities Act 1972, s. 2 (2), sch. 2, para. 1A. - Issued: 23.10.2008. Made: 15.10.2008. Laid before the Scottish Parliament: 20.10.2008. Coming into force: 18.11.2008. Effect: S.S.I. 2005/599; 2006/151, 312, 548; 2007/142, 306, 481, 523; 2008/65 revoked. Territorial extent & classification: S. General. - EC note: These Regulations enforce the provisions of Regulation 396/2005 on maximum residue levels in or on food and feed of plant and animal origin and amending Council Directive 91/41/EEC. - 8p.: 30 cm. - 978-0-11-100048-9 £5.00

The Quality Meat Scotland Order 2008 No. 2008/77. - Enabling power: Natural Environment and Rural Communities Act 2006, ss. 87, 88, 89, 90, 96, 97, sch. 8, paras 5 to 11, sch. 9, sch. 10. - Issued: 10.03.2008. Made: 28.02.2008. Coming into force: 01.04.2008. Effect: None. Territorial extent & classification: S. General. - 12p.: 30 cm. - 978-0-11-081540-4 £3.00

The Rice Products from the United States of America (Restriction on First Placing on the Market) (Scotland) Regulations 2008 No. 2008/87. - Enabling power: European Communities Act 1972, s. 2 (2). - Issued: 11.03.2008. Made: 05.03.2008. Laid before the Scottish Parliament: 06.03.2008. Coming into force: 07.03.2008. Effect: S.S.I. 2006/542 revoked. Territorial extent & classification: S. General. - EC note: These Regulations implement, in relation to Scotland, Commission Decision 2006/601/EC as amended by Commission Decision 2006/754/EC amending Decision 2006/601/EC and by Commission Decision 2008/162/EC amending Decision 2006/601/EC. - 4p.: 30 cm. - 978-0-11-081554-1 £3.00

The Rural Development Contracts (Land Managers Options) (Scotland) Regulations 2008 No. 2008/159. - Enabling power: European Communities Act 1972, s. 2 (2), sch. 2, para. 1A. - Issued: 07.05.2008. Made: 17.04.2008. Laid before the Scottish Parliament: 21.04.2008. Coming into force: 15.05.2008. Effect: S.S.I. 2004/381 amended. Territorial extent & classification: S. General. - Corrected reprint which is being issued free of charge to all known recipients of original version published on 25.04.2008. - EC note: These Regulations introduce measures to supplement Council Regulation No. 1698/2005 (the Council Regulation) and Commission Regulations Nos. 1974/2006 and 1975/2006. They also implement Article 74 (1) of the Council Regulation and Article 9 (1) of Council Regulation No. 1290/2005. - 40p.: 30 cm. - 978-0-11-081621-0 £7.50

The Rural Development Contracts (Rural Priorities) (Scotland) Amendment Regulations 2008 No. 2008/233. - Enabling power: European Communities Act 1972, s. 2 (2). - Issued: 11.06.2008. Made: 05.06.2008. Laid before the Scottish Parliament: 06.06.2008. Coming into force: 28.06.2008. Effect: S.S.I. 2008/100 amended. Territorial extent & classification: S. General. - EC note: These Regulations amend the Rural Development Contracts (Rural Priorities) (Scotland) Regulations 2008 which introduce measures to supplement Council Regulation (EC) No. 1698/2005 which lays down general rules governing Community support for rural development (financed by the European Agricultural Fund for Rural Development established by Council Regulation (EC) No. 1290/2005) and Commission Regulation (EC) Nos. 1974/2006 and 1975/2006 laying down detailed rules for the application of the Council Regulation. - 8p.: 30 cm. - 978-0-11-081688-3 £3.00

The Rural Development Contracts (Rural Priorities) (Scotland) Regulations 2008 No. 2008/100. - Enabling power: European Communities Act 1972, s. 2 (2), sch. 2, para. 1A. - Issued: 17.03.2008. Made: 06.03.2008. Laid before the Scottish Parliament: 07.03.2088. Coming into force: 29.03.2008. Effect: S.S.I. 2004/381 amended. Territorial extent & classification: S. General. - EC note: These Regulations introduce measures to supplement Council Regulation (EC) No. 1698/2005 which lays down general rules governing Community support for rural development (financed by the European Agricultural Fund for Rural Development established by Council Regulation (EC) No. 1290/2005) and Commission Regulations (EC) Nos. 1974/2006 and 1975/2006 laying down detailed rules for the application of the Council Regulation. They also implement Article 74(1) of the Council Regulation and Article 9(1) of Council Regulation (EC) No. 1290/2005. - 144p.: 30 cm. - 978-0-11-081564-0816920 £19.50

The Specified Products from China (Restriction on First Placing on the Market) (Scotland) Regulations 2008 No. 2008/148. - Enabling power: European Communities Act 1972, s. 2 (2). - Issued: 17.04.2008. Made: 14.04.2008. Laid before the Scottish Parliament: 14.04.2008. Coming into force: 15.04.2008. Effect: None. Territorial extent & classification: S. General. - EC note: These Regulations implement, in Scotland, Commission Decision 2008/289/EC on emergency measures regarding the unauthorised genetically modified organism 'Bt 63' in rice products. - 4p.: 30 cm. - 978-0-11-081607-4 £3.00

Agriculture: Livestock industries

The Horses (Zootechnical Standards) (Scotland) Regulations 2008 No. 2008/99. - Enabling power: European Communities Act 1972, s. 2 (2). - Issued: 12.03.2008. Made: 06.03.2008. Laid before the Scottish Parliament: 07.03.2008. Coming into force: 01.04.2008. Effect: S.S.I. 1992/3045 revoked. Territorial extent & classification: S. General. - 8p.: 30 cm. - 978-0-11-081562-6 £3.00

Animals: Animal health

The Animals and Animal Products (Import and Export) (Scotland) Amendment Regulations 2008 No. 2008/155. - Enabling power: European Communities Act 1972, s. 2 (2). - Issued: 22.04.2008. Made: 15.04.2008. Laid before the Scottish Parliament: 17.04.2008. Coming into force: 09.05.2008. Effect: S.S.I. 2007/194 amended. Territorial extent & classification: S. General. - EC note: These Regulations amend the Animals and Animal Products (Import and Export) (Scotland) Regulations 2007, to take account of Commission Regulation (EC) No. 1266/2007 on implementing rules for Council Directive 2000/75/EC as regards the control, monitoring, surveillance and restrictions on movements of certain animals of susceptible species in relation to bluetongue. - 4p.: 30 cm. - 978-0-11-081613-5 £3.00

The Bluetongue (Scotland) Amendment (No. 2) Order 2008 No. 2008/327. - Enabling power: Animal Health Act 1981, ss. 1, 8 (1), 17 (1), 23, 28, 87 (2). - Issued: 08.10.2008. Made: 02.10.2008. Coming into force: 04.10.2008. Effect: S.S.I. 2008/11 amended. Territorial extent & classification: S. General. - 8p.: 30 cm. - 978-0-11-100025-0 £5.00

The Bluetongue (Scotland) Amendment Order 2008 No. 2008/234. - Enabling power: Animal Health Act 1981, ss. 1, 8 (1), 17 (1), 23, 28. - Issued: 11.06.2008. Made: 05.06.2008. Coming into force: 06.06.2008. Effect: S.S.I. 2008/11 amended. Territorial extent & classification: S. General. - EC note: This Order continues to implement Council Directive 2000/75/EC laying down specific provisions for the control and eradication of Bluetongue. It revokes and remakes the Bluetongue (Scotland) Order 2003 in order also to enforce Commission Regulation (EC) No. 1266/2007. - 8p.: 30 cm. - 978-0-11-081692-0 *£3.00*

The Bluetongue (Scotland) Order 2008 No. 2008/11. - Enabling power: European Communities Act 1972, s. 2 (2), sch. 2, para. 1A & Animal Health Act 1981, ss. 1, 7 (1), 8 (1), 15 (4), 17 (1), 23, 25, 28, 32 (2), 35, 72, 83 (2), 88 (2). - Issued: 23.01.2008. Made: 16.01.2008. Laid before the Scottish Parliament: 18.01.2008. Coming into force: 11.02.2008. Effect: S.S.I. 2003/91 revoked. Territorial extent & classification: S. General. - EC note: This Order continues to implement Council Directive 2000/75/EC laying down specific provisions for the control and eradication of Bluetongue. It revokes and remakes the Bluetongue (Scotland) Order 2003 in order also to enforce Commission Regulation (EC) No. 1266/2007. - 12p.: 30 cm. - 978-0-11-080221-3 *£3.00*

The Control of Salmonella in Poultry (Scotland) Order 2008 No. 2008/266. - Enabling power: Animal Health Act 1981, s. 1, 8 (1) & European Communities Act 1972, s. 2 (2), sch. 2, para. 1A. - Issued: 02.07.2008. Made: 25.06.2008. Laid before the Scottish Parliament: 27.06.2008. Coming into force: 22.07.2008. Effect: S.S.I. 2007/254 revoked. Territorial extent & classification: S. General. - Revoked by S.S.I. 2009/229 (ISBN 97801110056757). EC note: These regs. enforce Commission Regulation (EC) No. 1003/2005, Commission Regulation (EC) No. 1168/2006 and Commission Regulation (EC) No. 1177/2006. - 8p.: 30 cm. - 978-0-11-082013-2 *£3.00*

The Control of Salmonella in Poultry (Scotland) Order 2008 No. 2008/266 Cor.. - Correction slip (to ISBN 9780110820132) dated August 2009. - 1 sheet: 30 cm. *Free*

The Diseases of Animals (Approved Disinfectants) (Scotland) Order 2008 No. 2008/219. - Enabling power: Animal Health Act 1981, s. 1. - Issued: 10.06.2008. Made: 02.06.2008. Coming into force: 23.06.2008. Effect: S.S.I. 2006/44, 336 amended & S.I. 1978/32; 1999/919 revoked in so far as they relate to Scotland and not already revoked & S.S.I. 2001/45; 2003/334 (revoked in so far as not already revoked) & S.S.I. 2006/352 revoked. Territorial extent & classification: S. General. - 8p.: 30 cm. - 978-0-11-081682-1 *£3.00*

The Pigs (Records, Identification and Movement) Amendment (Scotland) Order 2008 No. 2008/369. - Enabling power: Animal Health Act 1981, s. 1. - Issued: 17.11.2008. Made: 11.11.2008. Coming into force: 05.12.2008. Effect: S.I. 1995/11 amended in relation to Scotland. Territorial extent & classification: S. General. -EC note: This Order amends the Pigs (Records, Identification and Movement) Order 1995 by replacing the reference to Council Directive 92/102/EEC on the identification and registration of animals with a reference to Council Directive 2008/71/EC on the identification and registration of pigs. - 2p.: 30 cm. - 978-0-11-100073-1 *£4.00*

The Products of Animal Origin (Disease Control) (Scotland) Order 2008 No. 2008/158. - Enabling power: Animal Health Act 1981, ss. 1, 7 (1) (2), 8 (1), 11, 15 (4) (5), 23 (c) to (g), 28, 35 (1) (3), 64, 83 (2), 87 (2), 88 (2). - Issued: 23.04.2008. Made: 17.04.2008. Coming into force: 12.05.2008. Effect: None. Territorial extent & classification: S. General. - EC note: This Order transposes in Scotland Articles 3 and 4 of Council Directive 2002/99/EC laying down the animal health rules governing the production, processing, distribution and introduction of products of animal origin for human consumption. This Order also transposes, insofar as it applies to Newcastle disease, Commission Decision 2007/118/EC establishing an alternative health mark pursuant to Directive 2002/99/EC. - 16p.: 30 cm. - 978-0-11-081619-7 *£3.00*

The Sheep and Goats (Identification and Traceability) (Scotland) Amendment Regulations 2008 No. 2008/368. - Enabling power: European Communities Act 1972, s. 2 (2). - Issued: 17.11.2008. Made: 11.11.2008. Laid before the Scottish Parliament: 12.11.2008. Coming into force: 05.12.1008. Effect: S.S.I. 2006/73 amended. Territorial extent & classification: S. General. - EC note: These Regulations amend the Sheep and Goats (Identification and Traceability) (Scotland) Regulations 2006 (S.S.I. 2006/73) to remove references to Council Directive 92/102/EEC which has been repealed, and to provide for minor administrative changes in the form of the movement document set out in Schedule 2 to the 2006 Regulations. - 4p.: 30 cm. - 978-0-11-100072-4 *£4.00*

Animals: Animal health

The Transmissible Spongiform Encephalopathies (Scotland) Amendment (No. 2) Regulations 2008 No. 2008/417. - Enabling power: European Communities Act 1972, s. 2 (2). - Issued: 22.12.2008. Made: 16.12.2008. Laid before the Scottish Parliament: 17.12.2008. Coming into force: 01.01.2009. Effect: S.S.I. 1995/614; 2006/530 amended. Territorial extent & classification: S. General. - EC note: These Regulations further amend the Transmissible Spongiform Encephalopathies (Scotland) Regulations 2006, which provide for the enforcement in Scotland of Regulation (EC) No. 999/2001 laying down rules for the prevention, control and eradication of certain transmissible spongiform encephalopathies as amended. They give effect in Scotland to Commission Decision 2008/908/EC which authorises certain Member States (including the UK) to revise the annual monitoring programmes provided for by Article 6 of the Community TSE Regulation, by providing in paragraph 5 for the testing at slaughterhouses of brain stems that must be tested in accordance with the Community TSE Regulation as read with that Decision. - 12p.: 30 cm. - 978-0-11-100140-0 *£5.00*

The Transmissible Spongiform Encephalopathies (Scotland) Amendment Regulations 2008 No. 2008/166. - Enabling power: European Communities Act 1972, s. 2 (2). - Issued: 30.04.2008. Made: 24.04.2008. Laid before the Scottish Parliament: 25.04.2008. Coming into force: 26.04.2008. Effect: S.S.I. 2006/530 amended and S.S.I. 1999/186 revoked. Territorial extent & classification: S. General. - EC note: These Regulations further amend the Transmissible Spongiform Encephalopathies (Scotland) Regulations 2006, which provide for the enforcement in Scotland of Regulation (EC) No. 999/2001 laying down rules for the prevention, control and eradication of certain transmissible spongiform encephalopathies as amended. - 12p.: 30 cm. - 978-0-11-081629-6 *£3.00*

The Zoonoses and Animal By-Products (Fees) (Scotland) Amendment (No. 2) Regulations 2008 No. 2008/423. - Enabling power: Finance Act 1973, s. 56 (1) (2). - Issued: 23.12.2008. Made: 17.12.2008. Laid before the Scottish Parliament: 18.12.2008. Coming into force: 25.01.2009. Effect: S.S.I. 2007/577 amended. Territorial extent & classification: S. General. - Revoked by S.S.I. 2009/230 (ISBN 9780111005514) with saving. - 4p.: 30 cm. - 978-0-11-100163-9 *£4.00*

The Zoonoses and Animal By-Products (Fees) (Scotland) Amendment Regulations 2008 No. 2008/378. - Enabling power: Finance Act 1973, s. 56 (1) (2). - Issued: 25.11.2008. Made: 19.11.2008. Laid before the Scottish Parliament: 20.11.2008. Coming into force: 12.12.2008. Effect: S.S.I. 2007/577 amended. Territorial extent & classification: S. General. - Revoked by S.S.I. 2009/230 (ISBN 9780111005514) with saving. - 4p.: 30 cm. - 978-0-11-100084-7 *£4.00*

Animals: Dangerous wild animals

The Dangerous Wild Animals Act 1976 (Modification) (Scotland) Order 2008 No. 2008/302. - Enabling power: Dangerous Wild Animals Act 1976, s. 8 (1). - Issued: 16.09.2008. Made: 09.09.2008. Laid before the Scottish Parliament: 09.09.2008. Coming into force: 01.10.2008. Effect: 1976 c. 38 modified & S.I. 1984/1111 revoked in relation to Scotland. Territorial extent & classification: S. General. - 8p.: 30 cm. - 978-0-11-084476-3 *£5.00*

Armorial bearings, ensigns and flags

The Lyon Court and Office Fees (Variation) (No. 2) Order 2008 No. 2008/168. - Enabling power: Public Expenditure and Receipts Act 1968, s. 5. - Issued: 01.05.2008. Made: 24.04.2008. Laid before the Scottish Parliament: 28.04.2008. Coming into force: In accord. with art. 1 (1). Effect: 1867 c. 17 amended. Territorial extent & classification: S. General. - 4p.: 30 cm. - 978-0-11-081631-9 *£3.00*

Bankruptcy

The Bankruptcy and Diligence etc. (Scotland) Act 2007 (Commencement No. 3, Savings and Transitionals) Order 2008 No. 2008/115 (C.10). - Enabling power: Bankruptcy and Diligence etc. (Scotland) Act 2007, ss. 224 (2), 227 (3) (4). Bringing into operation various provisions of the 2007 Act on 01.04.2008, in accord. with art. 3. - Issued: 19.03.2008. Made: 12.03.2008. Effect: None. Territorial extent & classification: S. General. - 16p.: 30 cm. - 978-0-11-081578-7 *£3.00*

The Bankruptcy (Scotland) Act 1985 (Low Income, Low Asset Debtors etc.) Regulations 2008 No. 2008/81. - Enabling power: Bankruptcy (Scotland) Act 1985, ss. 5A, 39A (4) (a). - Issued: 10.03.2008. Made: 04.03.2008. Coming into force: 01.04.2008. Effect: 1985 c.66 amended. Territorial extent & classification: S. General. - 4p.: 30 cm. - 978-0-11-081545-9 *£3.00*

The Bankruptcy (Scotland) Amendment Regulations 2008 No. 2008/334. - Enabling power: Bankruptcy (Scotland) Act 1985, ss. 5(4C)(a) (b), 72(1), 73(1). - Issued: 10.10.2008. Made: 06.10.2008. Laid before the Scottish Parliament: 07.10.2008. Coming into force: 14.11.2008. Effect: S.S.I. 2008/82 amended. Territorial extent & classification: S. General. - 16p.: 30 cm. - 978-0-11-100041-0 *£5.00*

The Bankruptcy (Scotland) Regulations 2008 No. 2008/82. - Enabling power: Bankruptcy (Scotland) Act 1985, ss. 5 (4C), 6 (7), 7 (1) (d), 8 (2), 11 (1), 15 (6), 19 (1), 22 (2) (a) (6), 23 (1) (a), 25 (6) (b), 45 (3) (a), 48 (7), 49 (3), 51 (7) (a), 54 (2), 67 (8), 69, 73, 74 & Bankruptcy and Diligence (Scotland) Act 2007, s. 225 (1). - Issued: 11.03.2008. Made: 04.03.2008. Laid before the Scottish Parliament: 05.03.2008. Coming into force: 01.04.2008. Effect: 1985 c.66 amended & S.I. 1985/1925 revoked with savings. Territorial extent & classification: S. General. - 96p.: 30 cm. - 978-0-11-081546-6 *£13.50*

The Protected Trust Deeds (Scotland) Regulations 2008 No. 2008/143. - Enabling power: Bankruptcy (Scotland) Act 1985, s. 72, sch. 5, para. 5 (1). - Issued: 07.04.2008. Made: 28.03.2008. Coming into force: 01.04.2008. Effect: None. Territorial extent & classification: S. General. - 28p.: 30 cm. - 978-0-11-081603-6 *£4.50*

Building and buildings

The Building (Fees) (Scotland) Amendment Regulations 2008 No. 2008/397. - Enabling power: Building (Scotland) Act 2003, s. 38. - Issued: 03.12.2008. Made: 27.11.2008. Laid before the Scottish Parliament: 27.11.2008. Coming into force: 04.01.2009. Effect: S.S.I. 2004/508 amended. Territorial extent & classification: S. General. - 4p.: 30 cm. - 978-0-11-100109-7 *£4.00*

The Building (Scotland) Amendment Regulations 2008 No. 2008/310. - Enabling power: Building (Scotland) Act 2003, ss. 1, 8 (8). - Issued: 23.09.2008. Made: 16.09.2008. Laid before the Scottish Parliament: 18.09.2008. Coming into force: 04.01.2009. Effect: S.S.I. 2004/406 amended. Territorial extent & classification: S. General. - 4p.: 30 cm. - 978-0-11-084486-2 *£4.00*

The Energy Performance of Buildings (Scotland) Amendment Regulations 2008 No. 2008/389. - Enabling power: European Communities Act 1972, s. 2 (2). - Issued: 01.12.2008. Made: 25.11.2008. Laid before the Scottish Parliament: 26.11.2008. Coming into force: 31.12.2008. Effect: S.S.I. 2008/309 amended. Territorial extent & classification: S. General. - 4p.: 30 cm. - 978-0-11-100095-3 *£4.00*

The Energy Performance of Buildings (Scotland) Regulations 2008 No. 2008/309. - Enabling power: European Communities Act 1972, s. 2 (2). - Issued: 23.09.2008. Made: 16.09.2008. Laid before the Scottish Parliament: 18.09.2008. Coming into force: 04.01.2009. Effect: None. Territorial extent & classification: S. General. - EC note: These Regulations further transpose Article 7 (energy performance certificates) and partially transpose Article 4(3) of Directive 2002/91/EC. - 12p.: 30 cm. - 978-0-11-084481-7 *£5.00*

Canals and inland waterways

The Transport and Works (Scotland) Act 2007 (Access to Land by the Scottish Ministers) Order 2008 No. 2008/200. - Enabling power: Transport and Works (Scotland) Act 2007, ss. 18 (1) (b) (2) (b) (c), 28 (6). - Issued: 29.05.2008. Made: 21.05.2008. Coming into force: 22.05.2008. Effect: None. Territorial extent & classification: S. General. - Supersedes draft SSI (ISBN 9780110816111) issued 21.04.2008. - 12p.: 30 cm. - 978-0-11-081666-1 *£3.00*

The Transport and Works (Scotland) Act 2007 (Access to Land on Application) Order 2008 No. 2008/199. - Enabling power: Transport and Works (Scotland) Act 2007, ss. 18 (1) (a) (2) (a) (c), 28 (6). - Issued: 28.05.2008. Made: 21.05.2008. Coming into force: 22.05.2008. Effect: None. Territorial extent & classification: S. General. - Supersedes draft S.S.I. (ISBN 9780110816128) issued 21.04.2008. - 12p.: 30 cm. - 978-0-11-081665-4 *£3.00*

Charities

The Charities References in Documents (Scotland) Amendment Regulations 2008 No. 2008/59. - Enabling power: Charities and Trustee Investment (Scotland) Act 2005, s. 15. - Issued: 27.02.2008. Made: 21.02.2008. Laid before the Scottish Parliament: 22.02.2008. Coming into force: 01.04.2008. Effect: S.S.I. 2007/203 amended. Territorial extent & classification: S. General. - 2p.: 30 cm. - 978-0-11-081527-5 *£3.00*

The Charity Test (Specified Bodies) (Scotland) Order 2008 No. 2008/268. - Enabling power: Charities and Trustee Investment (Scotland) Act 2005, s. 7 (5). - Issued: 03.07.2008. Made: 26.06.2008. Coming into force: 27.06.2008. Effect: None. Territorial extent & classification: S. General. - Supersedes draft S.S.I. (ISBN 9780110816586) issued 27.05.2008. - 4p.: 30 cm. - 978-0-11-082014-9 *£3.00*

The Further and Higher Education (Scotland) Act 1992 Modification Order 2008 No. 2008/262. - Enabling power: Charities and Trustee Investment (Scotland) Act 2005, s. 102 (a). - Issued: 02.07.2008. Made: 24.06.2008. Coming into force: 01.08.2008. Effect: 1992 c.37 modified. Territorial extent & classification: S. General. - Supersedes draft S.S.I. (ISBN 9780110816548) issued 21.05.2008. - 2p.: 30 cm. - 978-0-11-082008-8 *£3.00*

The Protection of Charities Assets (Exemption) and the Charity Test (Specified Bodies) (Scotland) Amendment Order 2008 No. 2008/413. - Enabling power: Charities and Trustee Investment (Scotland) Act 2005, ss. 7 (5), 19 (8) (9). - Issued: 19.12.2008. Made: 12.12.2008. Coming into force: 25.01.2009, for art. 3 & 01.01.2009, for remainder. Effect: S.S.I. 2006/220; 2008/268 amended. Territorial extent & classification: S. General. - Supersedes draft SI (ISBN 9780111000540) published 06.11.2008. - 4p.: 30 cm. - 978-0-11-100133-2 *£4.00*

Children and young persons

The Adoption and Children (Scotland) Act 2007 (Commencement No. 1) Order 2008 No. 2008/130 (C.12). - Enabling power: Adoption and Children Act 2007, s. 121 (2) (3). Bringing into operation various provisions of the 2007 Act on 07.04.2008. - Issued: 26.03.2008. Made: 19.03.2008. Effect: None. Territorial extent & classification: S. General. - 4p.: 30 cm. - 978-0-11-081592-3 *£3.00*

The Adoption and Children (Scotland) Act 2007 (Commencement No. 2) Order 2008 No. 2008/282 (C.23). - Enabling power: Adoption and Children Act 2007, s. 121 (2). Bringing into operation various provisions of the 2007 Act on 01.09.2008. - Issued: 22.08.2008. Made: 18.08.2008. Effect: None. Territorial extent & classification: S. General. - 4p.: 30 cm. - 978-0-11-082021-7 *£3.00*

The Adoptions with a Foreign Element (Special Restrictions on Adoptions from Abroad) (Scotland) Regulations 2008 No. 2008/303. - Enabling power: Adoption and Children (Scotland) Act 2007, ss. 64 (3), 65 (1), 117 (2) (a) (3). - Issued: 16.09.2008. Made: 10.09.2008. Laid before the Scottish Parliament: 11.09.2008. Coming into force: 07.10.2008. Effect: None. Territorial extent & classification: S. General. - 4p.: 30 cm. - 978-0-11-083981-3 *£4.00*

The Intensive Support and Monitoring (Scotland) Regulations 2008 No. 2008/75. - Enabling power: Children (Scotland) Act 1995, ss. 17, 31, 70 (12) (13) (14) (17), 103. - Issued: 07.03.2008. Made: 04.03.2008. Laid before the Scottish Parliament: 05.03.2008. Coming into force: 01.04.2008. Effect: S.S.I. 2006/15 revoked. Territorial extent & classification: S. General. - 8p.: 30 cm. - 978-0-11-081539-8 *£3.00*

The Protection of Children (Scotland) Act 2003 (Amendment of the Definition of Child Care Position) Order 2008 No. 2008/260. - Enabling power: Protection of Children (Scotland) Act 2003, s. 21 (2), sch. 2, para. 13. - Issued: 01.07.2008. Made: 25.06.2008. Coming into force: 01.07.2008. Effect: 2003 asp 5 amended. Territorial extent & classification: S. General. - Supersedes draft S.S.I. (ISBN 9780110816449) issued 20.05.2008. - 4p.: 30 cm. - 978-0-11-082006-4 *£3.00*

The Special Restrictions on Adoptions from Cambodia (Scotland) Order 2008 No. 2008/304. - Enabling power: Adoption and Children (Scotland) Act 2007, s. 62 (3). - Issued: 16.09.2008. Made: 10.09.2008. Laid before the Scottish Parliament: 11.09.2008. Coming into force: 07.10.2008. Effect: None. Territorial extent & classification: S. General. - 2p.: 30 cm. - 978-0-11-084474-9 *£4.00*

The Special Restrictions on Adoptions from Guatemala (Scotland) Order 2008 No. 2008/305. - Enabling power: Adoption and Children (Scotland) Act 2007, s. 62 (3). - Issued: 16.09.2008. Made: 10.09.2008. Laid before the Scottish Parliament: 11.09.2008. Coming into force: 07.10.2008. Effect: None. Territorial extent & classification: S. General. - 2p.: 30 cm. - 978-0-11-084475-6 *£4.00*

Clean air

The Smoke Control Areas (Authorised Fuels) (Scotland) (No. 2) Regulations 2008 No. 2008/295. - Enabling power: Clean Air Act 1993, ss. 20 (6), 63 (1). - Issued: 09.09.2008. Made: 03.09.2008. Laid before the Scottish Parliament: 04.09.2008. Coming into force: 01.10.2008. Effect: S.S.I. 2008/154 revoked. Territorial extent & classification: S. General. - 16p.: 30 cm. - 978-0-11-083942-4 *£5.00*

The Smoke Control Areas (Authorised Fuels) (Scotland) Regulations 2008 No. 2008/154. - Enabling power: Clean Air Act 1993, ss. 20 (6), 63 (1). - Issued: 22.04.2008. Made: 16.04.2008. Laid before the Scottish Parliament: 17.04.2008. Coming into force: 09.05.2008. Effect: S.S.I. 2001/433; 2002/527; 2005/614; 2007/56 revoked. Territorial extent & classification: S. General. - Revoked by S.S.I. 2008/295 (ISBN 9780110839424). - 16p.: 30 cm. - 978-0-11-081616-6 *£3.00*

The Smoke Control Areas (Exempt Fireplaces) (Scotland) (No. 2) Order 2008 No. 2008/296. - Enabling power: Clean Air Act 1993, s. 21. - Issued: 10.09.2008. Made: 03.09.2008. Laid before the Scottish Parliament: 04.09.2008. Coming into force: 01.10.2008. Effect: S.S.I. 2008/157 revoked. Territorial extent & classification: S. General. - Revoked by S.S.I. 2009/214 (ISBN 9780111005538). - 24p.: 30 cm. - 978-0-11-083953-0 *£5.00*

The Smoke Control Areas (Exempt Fireplaces) (Scotland) Order 2008 No. 2008/157. - Enabling power: Clean Air Act 1993, s. 21. - Issued: 22.04.2008. Made: 16.04.2008. Laid before the Scottish Parliament: 17.04.2008. Coming into force: 09.05.2008. Effect: S.S.I. 2007/55 revoked. Territorial extent & classification: S. General. - Revoked by S.S.I. 2008/296 (ISBN 9780110839530). - 16p.: 30 cm. - 978-0-11-081618-0 *£3.00*

Companies

The Companies Act 2006 (Scottish public sector companies to be audited by the Auditor General for Scotland) Order 2008 No. 2008/144. - Enabling power: Companies Act 2006, s. 483 (1) to (3). - Issued: 08.04.2008. Made: 31.03.2008. Coming into force: 06.04.2008. Effect: None. Territorial extent & classification: S. General. - Supersedes draft SSI (ISBN 9780110815008) issued 19.02.2008. - 4p.: 30 cm. - 978-0-11-081604-3 *£3.00*

The Insolvency (Scotland) Rules 1986 Amendment Rules 2008 No. 2008/393. - Enabling power: Insolvency Act 1986, s. 411. - Issued: 02.12.2008. Made: 26.11.2008. Laid before the Scottish Parliament: 27.11.2008. Coming into force: 20.12.2008. Effect: S.I. 1986/1915 amended. Territorial extent & classification: S. General. - 4p.: 30 cm. - 978-0-11-100096-0 *£4.00*

Countryside

The Conservation (Natural Habitats, &c.) Amendment (No. 2) (Scotland) Regulations 2008 No. 2008/425. - Enabling power: European Communities Act 1972, s. 2 (2) & Wildlife and Countryside Act 1981, s. 26A. - Issued: 24.12.2008. Made: 18.12.2008. Laid before the Scottish Parliament: 19.12.2008. Coming into force: 26.01.2009. Effect: S.I. 1994/2716 amended in relation to Scotland. Territorial extent & classification: S. General. - EC note: These Regulations make further provision for the transposition of Council Directive 92/43/EEC on the conservation of natural habitats and of wild flora and fauna. - 4p.: 30 cm. - 978-0-11-100164-6 £4.00

The Conservation (Natural Habitats, &c.) Amendment (Scotland) Regulations 2008 No. 2008/17. - Enabling power: European Communities Act 1972, s. 2 (2) & Wildlife and Countryside Act 1981, s. 26A. - Issued: 29.01.2008. Made: 23.01.2008. Laid before the Scottish Parliament: 24.01.2008. Coming into force: 25.02.2008. Effect: S.I. 1994/2716 amended in relation to Scotland. Territorial extent & classification: S. General. - EC note: These Regulations make further provision for the transposition of Council Directive 92/43/EEC on the conservation of natural habitats and of wild flora and fauna. - 4p.: 30 cm. - 978-0-11-080231-2 £3.00

The National Scenic Areas (Scotland) Regulations 2008 No. 2008/202. - Enabling power: European Communities Act 1972, s. 2 (2) & Electricity Act 1989, ss. 37 (2) (c), 60 & Town and Country Planning (Scotland) Act 1997, s. 40. - Issued: 03.06.2008. Made: 28.05.2008. Laid before the Scottish Parliament: 29.05.2008. Coming into force: 20.06.2008. Effect: 1964 c.40 & S.I. 1990/2035; 1999/1672 amended in relation to Scotland & S.S.I. 1999/1, 43; 2000/320; 2006/582 amended. Territorial extent & classification: S. General. - 4p.: 30 cm. - 978-0-11-081668-5 £3.00

Court of Session

Act of Sederunt (Fees of Messengers-at-Arms) 2008 No. 2008/431. - Enabling power: Execution of Diligence (Scotland) Act 1926, s. 6 & Court of Session Act 1988, s. 5. - Issued: 29.12.2008. Made: 17.12.2008. Coming into force: 12.01.2009. Effect: S.S.I. 2002/566 amended. Territorial extent & classification: S. General. - 8p.: 30 cm. - 978-0-11-100177-6 £5.00

Act of Sederunt (Fees of Messengers-at-Arms) (EC Service Regulation) 2008 No. 2008/366. - Enabling power: Debtors (Scotland) Act 1987, s. 75. - Issued: 14.11.2008. Made: 07.11.2008. Coming into force: 13.11.2008. Effect: None. Territorial extent & classification: S. General. - 2p.: 30 cm. - 978-0-11-100071-7 £4.00

Act of Sederunt (Rules of the Court of Session Amendment) (Fees of Solicitors) 2008 No. 2008/39. - Enabling power: Court of Session Act 1988, s. 5. - Issued: 21.02.2008. Made: 15.02.2008. Coming into force: 01.04.2008. Effect: S.I. 1994/1443 amended. Territorial extent & classification: S. General. - 8p.: 30 cm. - 978-0-11-081504-6 £3.00

Act of Sederunt (Rules of the Court of Session Amendment No. 2) (Fees of Shorthand Writers) 2008 No. 2008/120. - Enabling power: Court of Session Act 1988, s. 5. - Issued: 25.03.2008. Made: 13.03.2008. Coming into force: 05.05.2008. Effect: S.I. 1994/1443 amended. Territorial extent & classification: S. General. - 4p.: 30 cm. - 978-0-11-081586-2 £3.00

Act of Sederunt (Rules of the Court of Session Amendment No. 3) (Bankruptcy and Diligence etc. (Scotland) Act 2007) 2008 No. 2008/122. - Enabling power: Court of Session Act 1988, s. 5 & Bankruptcy (Scotland) Act 1985, s. 28A (3) & Debtors (Scotland) Act 1987, ss. 15D (2) (a), 15L (2) (a) & Debt Arrangement and Attachment (Scotland) Act 2002, ss. 9C (2) (a), 9F (3) (a) (i), 9L (5) (a), 9M (3) (a), 9N (2) (a). - Issued: 25.03.2008. Made: 13.03.2008. Coming into force: 01.04.2008. Effect: S.I. 1994/1443 amended. Territorial extent & classification: S. General. - 8p.: 30 cm. - 978-0-11-081591-6 £3.00

Act of Sederunt (Rules of the Court of Session Amendment No. 4) (Miscellaneous) 2008 No. 2008/123. - Enabling power: Court of Session Act 1988, s. 5 & Scottish Commission for Human Rights Act 2006, s. 14. - Issued: 25.03.2008. Made: 13.03.2008. Coming into force: 01.04.2008. Effect: S.I. 1994/1443 amended. Territorial extent & classification: S. General. - 8p.: 30 cm. - 978-0-11-081589-3 £3.00

Act of Sederunt (Rules of the Court of Session Amendment No. 5) (Miscellaneous) 2008 No. 2008/349. - Enabling power: Court of Session Act 1988, s. 5 & European Communities Act 1972, sch. 2, para. 1A. - Issued: 10.11.2008. Made: 24.10.2008. Coming into force: 03.11.2008 for paras 7, 9; 13.11.2008 for para. 5; 01.12.2008 for remainder, in accord. with para. 1 (1) (2) (3). Effect: S.I. 1994/1443 amended. Territorial extent & classification: S. General. - 8p.: 30 cm. - 978-0-11-100060-1 £5.00

Act of Sederunt (Rules of the Court of Session Amendment No. 6) (Counter-Terrorism Act 2008) 2008 No. 2008/401. - Enabling power: Court of Session Act 1988, s. 5 & Counter-Terrorism Act 2008, ss. 66, 67. - Issued: 08.12.2008. Made: 02.12.2008. Coming into force: 04.12.2008. Effect: S.I. 1994/1443 amended. Territorial extent & classification: S. General. - 8p.: 30 cm. - 978-0-11-100113-4 £5.00

Act of Sederunt (Transfer of Judicial Review Applications from the Court of Session) 2008 No. 2008/357. - Enabling power: Tribunals, Courts and Enforcement Act 2007, s. 20 (3). - Issued: 10.11.2008. Made: 31.10.2008. Coming into force: 10.11.2008. Effect: None. Territorial extent & classification: S. General. - 2p.: 30 cm. - 978-0-11-100058-8 £4.00

The Court of Session etc. Fees Amendment Order 2008 No. 2008/236. - Enabling power: Courts of Law Fees (Scotland) Act 1895, s. 2. - Issued: 17.06.2008. Made: 06.06.2008. Laid before the Scottish Parliament: 06.06.2008. Coming into force: In accord. with art. 1. Effect: S.I. 1997/688 amended. Territorial extent & classification: S. General. - 32p.: 30 cm. - 978-0-11-082030-9 £5.50

Criminal law

The Crime (International Co-operation) Act 2003 (Designation of Participating Countries) (Scotland) Order 2008 No. 2008/264. - Enabling power: Crime (International Co-operation) Act 2003, s. 51 (2) (b). - Issued: 02.07.2008. Made: 24.06.2008. Coming into force: 25.06.2008 in accord with art. 1. Effect: None. Territorial extent & classification: S. General. - Supersedes draft S.S.I. (ISBN 9780110816524) issued 21.05.2008. - 2p.: 30 cm. - 978-0-11-082011-8 £3.00

The Criminal Procedure (Scotland) Act 1995 Compensation Offer (Maximum Amount) Order 2008 No. 2008/7. - Enabling power: Criminal Procedure (Scotland) Act 1995, s. 302A (8). - Issued: 21.01.2008. Made: 15.01.2008. Laid before the Scottish Parliament: 16.01.2008. Coming into force: 10.03.2008. Effect: None. Territorial extent & classification: S. General. - 2p.: 30 cm. - 978-0-11-080214-5 £3.00

The Criminal Procedure (Scotland) Act 1995 Fixed Penalty Order 2008 No. 2008/108. - Enabling power: Criminal Procedure (Scotland) Act 1995, s. 302 (7) (8). - Issued: 13.03.2008. Made: 05.03.2008. Coming into force: 10.03.2008. Effect: S.I. 1996/617 revoked with savings. Territorial extent & classification: S. General. - Supersedes draft S.I. (ISBN 9780110802176) issued on 21.01.2008. - 4p.: 30 cm. - 978-0-11-081572-5 £3.00

The Criminal Proceedings etc. (Reform) (Scotland) Act 2007 (Commencement No. 3 and Savings) Order 2008 No. 2008/42 (C.4). - Enabling power: Criminal Proceedings etc. (Reform) (Scotland) Act 2007, s. 84 (1) (2). Bringing various provisions of the 2007 Act into operation on 10.03.2008. - Issued: 25.02.2008. Made: 19.02.2008. Effect: None. Territorial extent & classification: S. General. - 12p.: 30 cm. - 978-0-11-081507-7 £3.00

The Criminal Proceedings etc. (Reform) (Scotland) Act 2007 (Commencement No. 4) Order 2008 No. 2008/192 (C.19). - Enabling power: Criminal Proceedings etc. (Reform) (Scotland) Act 2007, s. 84 (1) (2). Bringing various provisions of the 2007 Act into operation on 02.06.2008. - Issued: 26.05.2008. Made: 20.05.2008. Effect: None. Territorial extent & classification: S. General. - 12p.: 30 cm. - 978-0-11-081657-9 £3.00

The Criminal Proceedings etc. (Reform) (Scotland) Act 2007 (Commencement No. 5) Order 2008 No. 2008/329 (C.29). - Enabling power: Criminal Proceedings etc. (Reform) (Scotland) Act 2007, s. 84 (1) (2). Bringing various provisions of the 2007 Act into operation on 08.12.2008, in accord. with reg. 3. - Issued: 08.10.2008. Made: 02.10.2008. Effect: None. Territorial extent & classification: S. General. - 12p.: 30 cm. - 978-0-11-100032-8 £5.00

The Criminal Proceedings etc. (Reform) (Scotland) Act 2007 (Commencement No. 6) Order 2008 No. 2008/362 (C.30). - Enabling power: Criminal Proceedings etc. (Reform) (Scotland) Act 2007, s. 84 (1) (2). Bringing various provisions of the 2007 Act into operation on 23.02.2009. - Issued: 12.11.2008. Made: 06.11.2008. Effect: None. Territorial extent & classification: S. General. - 12p.: 30 cm. - 978-0-11-100066-3 £5.00

The Criminal Proceedings etc. (Reform) (Scotland) Act 2007 (Supplemental Provisions) Order 2008 No. 2008/109. - Enabling power: Criminal Proceedings etc. (Reform) (Scotland) Act 2007, s. 82. - Issued: 13.03.2008. Made: 05.03.2008. Coming into force: 10.03.2008. Effect: 1995 c. 46 amended. Territorial extent & classification: S. General. - Supersedes draft S.I. (ISBN 9780110802190) issued on 22.01.2008. - 2p.: 30 cm. - 978-0-11-081573-2 £3.00

The Emergency Workers (Scotland) Act 2005 (Modification) Order 2008 No. 2008/37. - Enabling power: Emergency Workers (Scotland) Act 2005, s. 8 (1). - Issued: 19.02.2008. Made: 31.01.2008. Coming into force: 01.04.2008. Effect: 2005 asp 2 modified. Territorial extent & classification: S. General. - Supersedes draft S.S.I. (ISBN 9780110801810) issued 13.12.2007. - 4p.: 30 cm. - 978-0-11-081501-5 £3.00

The Enforcement of Fines (Diligence) (Scotland) Regulations 2008 No. 2008/104. - Enabling power: Criminal Procedure (Scotland) Act 1995, s. 226F (6) (7). - Issued: 12.03.2008. Made: 06.03.2008. Laid before the Scottish Parliament: 07.03.2008. Coming into force: 01.04.2008. Effect: 1892 c.17 (55 & 56 Vict.); 1926 c.16 (16 & 17 Geo. 5); 1987 c.18 modified. Territorial extent & classification: S. General. - 4p.: 30 cm. - 978-0-11-081567-1 £3.00

The Enforcement of Fines (Seizure and Disposal of Vehicles) (Scotland) Regulations 2008 No. 2008/103. - Enabling power: Criminal Procedure (Scotland) Act 1995, s. 226D (12). - Issued: 12.03.2008. Made: 06.03.2008. Laid before the Scottish Parliament: 07.03.2008. Coming into force: 01.04.2008. Effect: None. Territorial extent & classification: S. General. - 12p.: 30 cm. - 978-0-11-081565-7 £3.00

The Home Detention Curfew Licence (Prescribed Standard Conditions) (Scotland) (No. 2) Order 2008 No. 2008/125. - Enabling power: Prisoners and Criminal Proceedings (Scotland) Act 1993, s. 12AA (3) (5). - Issued: 25.03.2008. Made: 18.03.2008. Laid before the Scottish Parliament: 18.03.2008. Coming into force: 21.03.2008. Effect: S.S.I. 2006/315 revoked. Territorial extent & classification: S. General. - 8p.: 30 cm. - 978-0-11-081588-6 £3.00

The Home Detention Curfew Licence (Prescribed Standard Conditions) (Scotland) Order 2008 No. 2008/36. - Enabling power: Prisoners and Criminal Proceedings (Scotland) Act 1993, s. 12AA (3) (5). - Issued: 15.02.2008. Made: 11.02.2008. Laid before the Scottish Parliament: 12.02.2008. Coming into force: 21.03.2008. Effect: S.S.I. 2006/315 revoked. Territorial extent & classification: S. General. - Revoked by S.S.I. 2008/124 (ISBN 9780110815879). - 8p.: 30 cm. - 978-0-11-081499-5 £3.00

The Home Detention Curfew Licence (Prescribed Standard Conditions) (Scotland) Revocation Order 2008 No. 2008/124. - Enabling power: S.I. 1999/1096, art. 11 (4) (b). - Issued: 25.03.2008. Made: 18.03.2008. Coming into force: 20.03.2008. Effect: S.S.I. 2008/36 revoked. Territorial extent & classification: S. General. - 2p.: 30 cm. - 978-0-11-081587-9 £3.00

The Management of Offenders etc. (Scotland) Act 2005 (Commencement No. 4) Order 2008 No. 2008/21 (C.2). - Enabling power: Management of Offenders etc. (Scotland) Act 2005, s. 24 (2) (3). Bringing into operation various provisions of the 2005 Act on 11.02.2008 & 21.03.2008. - Issued: 04.02.2008. Made: 28.01.2008. Effect: None. Territorial extent & classification: S. General. - 4p.: 30 cm. - 978-0-11-080237-4 £3.00

The Management of Offenders etc. (Scotland) Act 2005 (Commencement No. 5) Order 2008 No. 2008/149 (C.13). - Enabling power: Management of Offenders etc. (Scotland) Act 2005, s. 24 (2) (3). Bringing into operation various provisions of the 2005 Act on 30.04.2008. - Issued: 18.04.2008. Made: 14.04.2008. Effect: None. Territorial extent & classification: S. General. - 4p.: 30 cm. - 978-0-11-081608-1 £3.00

The Management of Offenders etc. (Scotland) Act 2005 (Members' Remuneration and Supplementary Provisions) Order 2008 No. 2008/30. - Enabling power: Management of Offenders etc. (Scotland) Act 2005, ss. 3 (1), 22 (1) (2). - Issued: 12.02.2008. Made: 05.02.2008. Coming into force: 31.03.2008. Effect: S.S.I. 2006/182 amended. Territorial extent & classification: S. - Supersedes draft SI (9780110801896) issued 21.12.2007. - 4p.: 30 cm. - 978-0-11-080244-2 £3.00

The Offenders Assisting Investigations and Prosecutions (Substituted Sentences) (Scotland) Order 2008 No. 2008/232. - Enabling power: Police, Public Order and Criminal Justice (Scotland) Act 2006, s. 94 (3). - Issued: 11.06.2008. Made: 05.06.2008. Laid before the Scottish Parliament: 06.06.2008. Coming into force: 30.06.2008. Effect: None. Territorial extent & classification: S. General. - 4p.: 30 cm. - 978-0-11-081687-6 £3.00

The Restriction of Liberty Order (Scotland) Amendment Regulations 2008 No. 2008/307. - Enabling power: Criminal Procedure (Scotland) Act 1995, s. 245C (3). - Issued: 22.09.2008. Made: 16.09.2008. Laid before the Scottish Parliament: 17.09.2008. Coming into force: 20.10.2008. Effect: S.I. 2006/8 amended. Territorial extent & classification: S. General. - 4p.: 30 cm. - 978-0-11-084478-7 £4.00

The Sexual Offences Act 2003 (Prescribed Police Stations) (Scotland) Regulations 2008 No. 2008/128. - Enabling power: Sexual Offences Act 2003, s. 87 (1) (a). - Issued: 26.03.2008. Made: 19.03.2008. Laid: 20.03.2008. Coming into force: 06.05.2008. Effect: S.S.I. 2004/137; 370; 2005/9, 156; 2007/72 revoked. Territorial extent & classification: S. General. - 8p.: 30 cm. - 978-0-11-081593-0 £3.00

The Stipendiary Magistrates (Specified Day) (Sheriffdom of Glasgow and Strathkelvin) Order 2008 No. 2008/330. - Enabling power: Criminal Proceedings etc. (Reform) (Scotland) Act 2007, ss. 74 (12), 81 (2). - Issued: 08.10.2008. Made: 02.10.2008. Laid before the Scottish Parliament: 03.10.2008. Coming into force: 08.12.2008. Effect: None. Territorial extent & classification: S. General. - 2p.: 30 cm. - 978-0-11-100035-9 £4.00

The Victim Notification Scheme (Scotland) Order 2008 No. 2008/185. - Enabling power: Criminal Justice (Scotland) Act 2003, s. 16 (4) (a) (b). - Issued: 20.05.2008. Made: 12.05.2008. Coming into force: 15.05.2008. Effect: 2003 asp 7 amended. Territorial extent & classification: S. General. - Supersedes draft SSI (ISBN 9780110815817) issued 20.03.2008. - 4p.: 30 cm. - 978-0-11-081646-3 £3.00

Crofters, cottars and small landholders

The Crofting Counties Agricultural Grants (Scotland) Amendment Scheme 2008 No. 2008/58. - Enabling power: European Communities Act 1972, s. 2 (2). - Issued: 27.02.2008. Made: 21.02.2008. Laid before the Scottish Parliament: 22.02.2008. Coming into force: 17.03.2008. Effect: S.S.I. 2004/381; 2006/24 amended. Territorial extent & classification: S. General. - 8p.: 30 cm. - 978-0-11-081525-1 £3.00

Cultural objects

The Tribunals, Courts and Enforcement Act 2007 (Commencement) (Scotland) Order 2008 No. 2008/150 (C.14). - Enabling power: Tribunals, Courts and Enforcement Act 2007, s.148 (4). Bringing into operation various provisions of the 2007 Act on 21.04.2008. - Issued: 18.04.2008. Made: 14.04.2008. Effect: None. Territorial extent & classification: S. General. - 2p.: 30 cm. - 978-0-11-081609-8 £3.00

Debt

The Bankruptcy and Diligence etc. (Scotland) Act 2007 (Commencement No. 3, Savings and Transitionals) Order 2008 No. 2008/115 (C.10). - Enabling power: Bankruptcy and Diligence etc. (Scotland) Act 2007, ss. 224 (2), 227 (3) (4). Bringing into operation various provisions of the 2007 Act on 01.04.2008, in accord. with art. 3. - Issued: 19.03.2008. Made: 12.03.2008. Effect: None. Territorial extent & classification: S. General. - 16p.: 30 cm. - 978-0-11-081578-7 £3.00

Diligence

The Bankruptcy and Diligence etc. (Scotland) Act 2007 (Commencement No. 3, Savings and Transitionals) Order 2008 No. 2008/115 (C.10). - Enabling power: Bankruptcy and Diligence etc. (Scotland) Act 2007, ss. 224 (2), 227 (3) (4). Bringing into operation various provisions of the 2007 Act on 01.04.2008, in accord. with art. 3. - Issued: 19.03.2008. Made: 12.03.2008. Effect: None. Territorial extent & classification: S. General. - 16p.: 30 cm. - 978-0-11-081578-7 *£3.00*

Education

The Academic Awards and Distinctions (Additional Powers of the University of Aberdeen) Order of Council 2008 No. 2008/220. - Enabling power: Further and Higher Education (Scotland) Act 1992, ss. 48, 60. - Issued: 10.06.2008. Made: 04.06.2008. Laid before the Scottish Parliament: 06.06.2008. Coming into force: 01.09.2008. Effect: None. Territorial extent & classification: S. General. - 4p.: 30 cm. - 978-0-11-081683-8 *£3.00*

The Academic Awards and Distinctions (UHI Millennium Institute) (Scotland) Order of Council 2008 No. 2008/212. - Enabling power: Further and Higher Education (Scotland) Act 1992, ss. 48, 60. - Issued: 06.06.2008. Made: 02.06.2008. Laid before the Scottish Parliament: 06.06.2008. Coming into force: 01.08.2008. Effect: None. Territorial extent & classification: S. - 4p.: 30 cm. - 978-0-11-081675-3 *£3.00*

The Central Institutions (Recognition) (Scotland) Revocation Regulations 2008 No. 2008/178. - Enabling power: Education (Scotland) Act 1980, s. 135 (1). - Issued: 15.05.2008. Made: 08.05.2008. Laid before the Scottish Parliament: 09.05.2008. Coming into force: 01.06.2008. Effect: S.I. 1990/2386 revoked. Territorial extent & classification: S. General. - This Scottish Statutory Instrument has been made in consequence of a defect in S.S.I. 2008/163 and is being issued free of charge to all known recipients of that instrument. - 2p.: 30 cm. - 978-0-11-081641-8 *£3.00*

The Designation of Institutions of Higher Education (The Scottish Agricultural College) (Scotland) (No. 2) Order 2008 No. 2008/177. - Enabling power: Further and Higher Education (Scotland) Act 1992, ss. 44 (1), 60 (3). - Issued: 15.05.2008. Made: 08.05.2008. Laid before the Scottish Parliament: 09.05.2008. Coming into force: 31.05.2008 for arts 1 & 3; 01.06.2008 for art. 2. Effect: S.S.I. 2008/163 revoked (31.05.2008). Territorial extent & classification: S. General. - This Order supersedes S.S.I. 2008/163 published on 29th April 2008 and is being issued free of charge to all known recipients of that instrument. - 4p.: 30 cm. - 978-0-11-081640-1 *£3.00*

The Designation of Institutions of Higher Education (The Scottish Agricultural College) (Scotland) Order 2008 No. 2008/163. - Enabling power: Further and Higher Education (Scotland) Act 1992, ss. 44 (1), 60 (3) & Education (Scotland) Act 1980, s. 135 (1). - Issued: 28.04.2008. Made: 21.04.2008. Laid before the Scottish Parliament: 23.04.2008. Coming into force: 01.06.2008. Effect: S.I. 1990/2386 revoked. Territorial extent & classification: S. General. - Revoked by S.S.I. 2008/177 (ISBN 9780110816401). - 4p.: 30 cm. - 978-0-11-081626-5 *£3.00*

The Edinburgh Napier University Order of Council 2008 No. 2008/388. - Enabling power: Further and Higher Education (Scotland) Act 1992, ss. 45, 60. - Issued: 01.12.2008. Made: 21.11.2008. Laid before the Scottish Parliament: 02.12.2008. Coming into force: 25.01.2009. Effect: S.I. 1985/1163; 1993/557 amended. Territorial extent & classification: S. General. - 4p.: 30 cm. - 978-0-11-100090-8 *£4.00*

The Education (Assisted Places) (Scotland) Amendment Regulations 2008 No. 2008/213. - Enabling power: Education (Scotland) Act 1980, ss. 75A (9) (10), 75B. - Issued: 09.06.2008. Made: 30.05.2008. Laid before the Scottish Parliament: 04.06.2008. Coming into force: 01.08.2008. Effect: S.S.I. 2001/222 amended. Territorial extent & classification: S. General. - 4p.: 30 cm. - 978-0-11-081676-0 *£3.00*

The Education (Means Testing) (Scotland) Amendment Regulations 2008 No. 2008/206. - Enabling power: Education (Scotland) Act 1980, ss. 73 (f), 74 (1). - Issued: 05.06.2008. Made: 29.05.2008. Laid before the Scottish Parliament: 02.06.2008. Coming into force: 01.08.2008. Effect: S.S.I. 2007/151, 153, 154 amended. Territorial extent & classification: S. General. - 4p.: 30 cm. - 978-0-11-081674-6 *£3.00*

The Education (Student Loans) (Scotland) Regulations 2008 No. 2008/205. - Enabling power: Education (Scotland) Act 1980, ss. 73 (f), 74 (1). - Issued: 04.06.2008. Made: 29.05.2008. Laid before the Scottish Parliament: 02.06.2008. Coming into force: 01.08.2008. Effect: S.S.I. 2007/154 amended. Territorial extent & classification: S. General. - 4p.: 30 cm. - 978-0-11-081671-5 *£3.00*

The Fundable Bodies (Scotland) Order 2008 No. 2008/412. - Enabling power: Further and Higher Education (Scotland) Act 2005, s. 7 (1). - Issued: 19.12.2008. Made: 12.12.2008. Coming into force: 25.01.2009 for art. 2 (c) (d) & 01.01.2009 for the remainder. Effect: 2005 asp 6 modified. Territorial extent & classification: S. General. - 4p.: 30 cm. - 978-0-11-100132-5 *£4.00*

The Fundable Bodies (The Scottish Agricultural College) (Scotland) Order 2008 No. 2008/241. - Enabling power: Further and Higher Education (Scotland) Act 2005, s. 7 (1) (a). - Issued: 13.06.2008. Made: 04.06.2008. Coming into force: 01.08.2008. Effect: 2005 asp 6 modified. Territorial extent & classification: S. General. - 2p.: 30 cm. - 978-0-11-082028-6 *£3.00*

The Graduate Endowment (Scotland) Regulations 2008 No. 2008/235. - Enabling power: Education (Scotland) Act 1980, ss. 73 (f), 73B. - Issued: 12.06.2008. Made: 06.06.2008. Laid before the Scottish Parliament: 06.06.2008. Coming into force: 30.06.2008. Effect: None. Territorial extent & classification: S. General. - 8p.: 30 cm. - 978-0-11-082026-2 £3.00

The Individual Learning Account (Scotland) Amendment (No. 2) Regulations 2008 No. 2008/204. - Enabling power: Education and Training (Scotland) Act 2000, ss. 1, 2, 3 (2). - Issued: 04.06.2008. Made: 29.06.2008. Laid before the Scottish Parliament: 02.06.2008. Coming into force: 27.10.2008; for reg. 5 (5) (b); 01.01.2009; for reg. 8 (a); 30.06.2008 for the remainder. Effect: S.S.I. 2004/83 amended. Territorial extent & classification: S. General. - 4p.: 30 cm. - 978-0-11-081670-8 £3.00

The Individual Learning Account (Scotland) Amendment Regulations 2008 No. 2008/1. - Enabling power: Education and Training (Scotland) Act 2000, ss. 1, 3 (2). - Issued: 15.01.2008. Made: 08.01.2008. Laid before the Scottish Parliament: 09.01.2008. Coming into force: 31.01.2008. Effect: S.S.I. 2004/83 amended. Territorial extent & classification: S. General. - 4p.: 30 cm. - 978-0-11-080204-6 £3.00

The Nutritional Requirements for Food and Drink in Schools (Scotland) Regulations 2008 No. 2008/265. - Enabling power: Education (Scotland) Act 1980, ss. 56A, 56B, 56D. - Issued: 02.07.2008. Made: 26.06.2008. Coming into force: 04.08.2008 & 03.08.2009 in accord. with reg. 1. Effect: None. Territorial extent & classification: S. General. - Supersedes draft S.S.I. (ISBN 9780110816456) issued 23.05.2008. - 12p.: 30 cm. - 978-0-11-082012-5 £3.00

The Provision of School Lunches (Disapplication of the Requirement to Charge) (Scotland) Order 2008 No. 2008/400. - Enabling power: Local Government in Scotland Act 2003, s. 57 (1) (3). - Issued: 04.12.2008. Made: 28.11.2008. Coming into force: 01.12.2008. Effect: S.S.I. 2007/451 revoked. Territorial extent & classification: S. General. - Supersedes draft S.S.I. (ISBN 9780111000090) issued 06.10.2008. - 4p.: 30 cm. - 978-0-11-100111-0 £4.00

The Schools (Health Promotion and Nutrition) (Scotland) Act 2007 (Commencement No. 2) Order 2008 No. 2008/171 (C.17). - Enabling power: Schools (Health Promotion and Nutrition) Act 2007, s. 11 (2) (3). Bringing into operation various provisions of the 2007 Act on 12.05.2008, 04.08.2008, in accord. with reg. 2. - Issued: 08.05.2008. Made: 01.05.2008. Effect: None. Territorial extent & classification: S. General. - 2p.: 30 cm. - 978-0-11-081634-0 £3.00

The St Mary's Music School (Aided Places) (Scotland) Amendment Regulations 2008 No. 2008/214. - Enabling power: Education (Scotland) Act 1980, ss. 73 (f), 74 (1). - Issued: 09.06.2008. Made: 30.05.2008. Laid before the Scottish Parliament: 04.06.2008. Coming into force: 01.08.2008. Effect: S.S.I. 2001/223 amended. Territorial extent & classification: S. General. - 4p.: 30 cm. - 978-0-11-081677-7 £3.00

Electricity

The Electricity Works (Environmental Impact Assessment) (Scotland) Amendment Regulations 2008 No. 2008/246. - Enabling power: European Communities Act 1972, s. 2 (2). - Issued: 18.06.2008. Made: 12.06.2008. Laid before the Scottish Parliament: 13.06.2008. Coming into force: 08.09.2008. Effect: S.S.I. 2000/320 amended. Territorial extent & classification: S. General. - EC note: Implement amendments to Council Directive 85/337/EEC made by Directive 2003/35/EC. - 12p.: 30 cm. - 978-0-11-082037-8 £3.00

The Renewables Obligation (Scotland) Amendment Order 2008 No. 2008/132. - Enabling power: Electricity Act 1989, ss. 32 to 32A. - Issued: 28.03.2008. Made: 18.03.2008. Coming into force: 01.04.2008. Effect: S.S.I. 2007/267 amended. Territorial extent & classification: S. General. - Revoked by S.S.I. 2009/140 (ISBN 9780111004715) with savings. Supersedes draft SSI (ISBN 9780110802350) issued 01.02.2008. - 4p.: 30 cm. - 978-0-11-081596-1 £3.00

Electronic communications

The Adults with Incapacity (Electronic Communications) (Scotland) Order 2008 No. 2008/380. - Enabling power: Electronic Communications Act 2000, ss. 8, 9. - Issued: 26.11.2008. Made: 30.10.2008. Coming into force: 31.10.2008. Effect: 2000 asp 4 amended. Territorial extent & classification: S. General. - Supersedes draft S.S.I. (ISBN 9780110839615) issued 11.09.2008. - 4p.: 30 cm. - 978-0-11-100086-1 £4.00

Energy conservation

The Home Energy Efficiency Scheme (Scotland) Amendment Regulations 2008 No. 2008/38. - Enabling power: Social Security Act 1990, s. 15. - Issued: 20.02.2008. Made: 13.02.2008. Laid before the Scottish Parliament: 15.02.2008. Coming into force: 06.04.2008. Effect: S.S.I. 2006/570 amended & S.S.I. 2007/85 revoked. Territorial extent & classification: S. General. - 2p.: 30 cm. - 978-0-11-081502-2 £3.00

Environmental protection

The Action Programme for Nitrate Vulnerable Zones (Scotland) Amendment Regulations 2008 No. 2008/298. - Enabling power: European Communities Act 1972, s. 2 (2). - Issued: 12.09.2008. Made: 04.09.2008. Laid before the Scottish Parliament: 08.09.2008. Coming into force: 01.01.2009. Effect: S.S.I. 2003/51 (with saving), 169 revoked. Territorial extent & classification: S. General. - 36p.: 30 cm. - 978-0-11-083973-8 £9.00

The Action Programme for Nitrate Vulnerable Zones (Scotland) Amendment Regulations 2008 No. 2008/394. - Enabling power: European Communities Act 1972, s. 2 (2). - Issued: 02.12.2008. Made: 26.11.2008. Laid before the Scottish Parliament: 27.11.2008. Coming into force: 01.01.2009. Effect: S.S.I. 2008/298 amended. Territorial extent & classification: S. General. - This Scottish Statutory Instrument has been made to correct errors in S.S.I. 2008/298 and is being issued free of charge to all known recipients of that instrument. - 4p.: 30 cm. - 978-0-11-100098-4 *£4.00*

The Bathing Waters (Scotland) Regulations 2008 No. 2008/170. - Enabling power: European Communities Act 1972, s. 2 (2). - Issued: 08.05.2008. Made: 30.04.2008. Laid before the Scottish Parliament: 01.05.2008. Coming into force: In accord. with reg. 1. Effect: S.S.I. 2005/348 amended and S.I. 1991/1609 revoked with savings (01.01.2015). Territorial extent & classification: S. General. - These Regulations make provision for the purpose of implementing, in Scotland, Directive 2006/7/EC concerning the management of bathing water quality and repealing Directive 76/160/EEC. - 24p.: 30 cm. - 978-0-11-081632-6 *£4.00*

The Pollution Prevention and Control (Designation of Batteries Directive) (Scotland) Order 2008 No. 2008/86. - Enabling power: Pollution Prevention and Control Act 1999, sch. 1, para. 20 (2) (c). - Issued: 10.03.2008. Made: 28.02.2008. Coming into force: 17.03.2008. Effect: None. Territorial extent & classification: S. General. - 2p.: 30 cm. - 978-0-11-081550-3 *£3.00*

The Pollution Prevention and Control (Scotland) Amendment Regulations 2008 No. 2008/410. - Enabling power: Pollution Prevention and Control Act 1999, s. 2. - Issued: 16.12.2008. Made: 10.12.2008. Laid before the Scottish Parliament: 11.12.2008. Coming into force: 19.01.2009. Effect: S.S.I. 2000/323 amended. Territorial extent & classification: S. General. - 4p.: 30 cm. - 978-0-11-100123-3 *£4.00*

The Water Environment and Water Services (Scotland) Act 2003 (Commencement No. 8) Order 2008 No. 2008/269 (C.22). - Enabling power: Water Environment and Water Services (Scotland) Act 2003, s. 38 (1). Bringing into operation various provisions of the 2003 Act on 10.07.2008. - Issued: 03.07.2008. Made: 30.06.2008. Effect: None. Territorial extent & classification: S. General. - 2p.: 30 cm. - 978-0-11-082015-6 *£3.00*

The Water Environment (Diffuse Pollution) (Scotland) Regulations 2008 No. 2008/54. - Enabling power: Water Environment and Water Services (Scotland) Act 2003, ss. 20, 36 (3). - Issued: 26.02.2008. Made: 20.02.2008. Laid before the Scottish Parliament: 21.02.2008. Coming into force: 01.04.2008. Effect: S.S.I. 2003/531; 2005/348 amended. Territorial extent & classification: S. General. - 12p.: 30 cm. - 978-0-11-081521-3 *£3.00*

The Water Environment (Relevant Enactments and Designation of Responsible Authorities and Functions) Order 2008 No. 2008/263. - Enabling power: Water Environment and Water Services (Scotland) Act 2003, s. 2 (8). - Issued: 02.07.2008. Made: 26.06.2008. Laid before the Scottish Parliament: 27.06.2008. Coming into force: 22.09.2008. Effect: S.S.I. 2006/126., 554 revoked. Territorial extent & classification: S. General. - 8p.: 30 cm. - 978-0-11-082009-5 *£3.00*

European Communities

The European Communities (Service of Judicial and Extrajudicial Documents) (Scotland) Amendment Regulations 2008 No. 2008/372. - Enabling power: European Communities Act 1972, s. 2 (2). - Issued: 18.11.2008. Made: 13.11.2008. Laid: 13.11.2008. Coming into force: 05.12.2008. Effect: S.S.I. 2001/172. amended. Territorial extent & classification: S. General. - EC note: These regs amend the 2001 regulations which implemented Council Regulation (EC) No. 1348/2000 on the service in the Member States of judicial and extrajudicial documents in civil or commercial matters. EC Reg 1348/2000 was repealed and replaced by Regulation (EC) No. 1393/2007. - 4p.: 30 cm. - 978-0-11-100076-2 *£4.00*

Family law

The Divorce etc. (Pensions) (Scotland) Amendment Regulations 2008 No. 2008/293. - Enabling power: Family Law (Scotland) Act 1985, s. 10 (8) (8A). - Issued: 08.09.2008. Made: 28.08.2008. Laid before the Scottish Parliament: 03.09.2008. Coming into force: 01.10.2008. Effect: S.S.I. 2000/112 amended. Territorial extent & classification: S. General. - 4p.: 30 cm. - 978-0-11-083936-3 *£4.00*

Fire services

The Firefighters' Pension Scheme Amendment (Scotland) Order 2008 No. 2008/161. - Enabling power: Fire Services Act 1947, s. 26 (1) to (5) & Superannuation Act 1972, ss. 12, 16. - Issued: 28.04.2008. Made: 21.04.2008. Laid: 22.04.2008. Coming into force: 14.05.2008. Effect: S.I. 1992/129 amended in relation to Scotland. Territorial extent & classification: S. General. - 8p.: 30 cm. - 978-0-11-081623-4 *£3.00*

The Firefighters' Pension Scheme (Scotland) Order 2007 Amendment Order 2008 No. 2008/160. - Enabling power: Fire and Rescue Services Act 2004, ss. 34 (1) to (4), 60 (2). - Issued: 28.04.2008. Made: 21.04.2008. Laid: 22.04.2008. Coming into force: 14.05.2008. Effect: S.S.I. 2007/199 amended. Territorial extent & classification: S. General. - 12p.: 30 cm. - 978-0-11-081622-7 *£3.00*

Fish farming

The Fish Farming Businesses (Record Keeping) (Scotland) Order 2008 No. 2008/326. - Enabling power: Aquaculture and Fisheries (Scotland) Act 2007, s. 1. - Issued: 08.10.2008. Made: 02.10.2008. Laid before the Scottish Parliament: 03.10.2008. Coming into force: 10.11.2008. Effect: None. Territorial extent & classification: S. General. - 8p.: 30 cm. - 978-0-11-100017-5 *£5.00*

Food

The Beef and Veal Labelling (Scotland) Regulations 2008 No. 2008/418. - Enabling power: European Communities Act 1972, s. 2 (2), sch. 2, para. 1A. - Issued: 22.12.2008. Made: 16.12.2008. Laid before the Scottish Parliament: 17.12.2008. Coming into force: 25.01.2009. Effect: S.S.I. 2001/252 revoked. Territorial extent & classification: S. General. - EC note: These Regulations continue to enforce Title II of Regulation (EC) No. 1760/2000 establishing a system for the identification and registration of bovine animals and regarding the labelling of beef and beef products and subsidiary Commission Regulations. They also enforce the provisions relating to veal of Council Regulation (EC) No. 1234/2007 establishing a common organisation of agricultural markets and on specific provisions for certain agricultural products as well as the provisions Commission Regulation (EC) No. 566/2008 laying down detailed rules for the application of Council Regulation (EC) No. 1234/2007 as regards the marketing of the meat of bovine animals aged 12 months or less. - 8p.: 30 cm. - 978-0-11-100142-4 *£5.00*

The Condensed Milk and Dried Milk (Scotland) Amendment Regulations 2008 No. 2008/12. - Enabling power: Food Safety Act 1990, ss. 16 (1) (a) (e), 17 (1), 48 (1). - Issued: 25.01.2008. Made: 21.01.2008. Laid before the Scottish Parliament: 22.01.2008. Coming into force: 22.02.2008. Effect: S.I. 1995/3124, 3187 amended in relation to Scotland & S.S.I. 2003/311 amended. Territorial extent and classification: S. General. - EC note: These Regulations implement Council Directive 2007/61/EC. - 4p.: 30 cm. - 978-0-11-080224-4 *£3.00*

The Eggs and Chicks (Scotland) (No. 2) Regulations 2008 No. 2008/395. - Enabling power: European Communities Act 1972, s. 2 (2), sch. 2, para. 1A & Food Safety Act 1990, ss. 6 (4), 16 (1), 17, 26 (2) (3), 48 (1). - Issued: 03.12.2008. Made: 26.11.2008. Laid before the Scottish Parliament: 27.11.2008. Coming into force: 19.12.2008. Effect: S.I. 1995/3124; 1996/1499 & S.S.I. 2006/3, 336, 337 amended & S.S.I. 2008/129 revoked. Territorial extent & classification: S. General. - EC note: These Regulations revoke and remake, with modifications, the Eggs and Chicks (Scotland) Regulations 2008 ("the 2008 Regulations") following the adoption of Council Regulation No. 1234/2007 establishing a common organisation of agricultural markets and on specific provisions for certain agricultural products (Single CMO Regulation) and two Commission Regulations adopted under that Regulation, Commission Regulation No. 617/2008 and Commission Regulation No. 589/2008 (as amended by Commission Regulation (EC) No. 598/2008. The 2008 regulations made provision for the enforcement or continued enforcement of certain provisions of Regulations (EEC) 2782/75, 1868/77, 1028/2006 and (EC) 557/2007 which are now repealed. - 28p.: 30 cm. - 978-0-11-100100-4 *£5.00*

The Eggs and Chicks (Scotland) Regulations 2008 No. 2008/129. - Enabling power: European Communities Act 1972, s. 2 (2) & Food Safety Act 1990, ss. 6 (4), 16 (1), 17, 26 (2) (3), 48 (1). - Issued: 31.03.2008. Made: 19.03.2008. Laid before the Scottish Parliament: 20.03.2008. Coming into force: 27.04.2008. Effect: 1990 c. 16 modified & S.I. 1995/3124; 1996/1499 amended in relation to Scotland & S.S.I. 2006/3, 336, 337 amended & S.S.I. 2005/332 revoked. Territorial extent & classification: S. General. - Revoked by S.S.I. 2008/395 (ISBN 9780111001004). EC note: Thee regulations make provision for the enforcement or continued enforcement of certain provisions of Regulations (EEC) 2782/75, 1868/77, 1028/2006 and (EC) 557/2007. - 28p.: 30 cm. - 978-0-11-081598-5 *£4.50*

The Food Labelling (Declaration of Allergens) (Scotland) Regulations 2008 No. 2008/180. - Enabling power: Food Safety Act 1990, ss. 16 (1) (e), 17 (1), 26 (1) (a), 48 (1). - Issued: 14.05.2008. Made: 08.05.2008. Laid before the Scottish Parliament: 09.05.2008. Coming into force: 31.05.2008. Effect: S.I. 1996/1499 amended in relation to Scotland; S.S.I. 2004/472 partially revoked & S.S.I. 2005/542; 2007/534 revoked. Territorial extent & classification: S. General. - EC note: These Regulations implement, in Scotland, Commission Directive No. 2007/68/EC amending Annex IIIa of Directive 2000/13/EC listing the ingredients which must under all circumstances appear on the labelling of foodstuffs. The ingredients in question are those that are likely to cause an allergic reaction in some consumers. - 4p.: 30 cm. - 978-0-11-081638-8 *£3.00*

The Guar Gum (Restriction on First Placing on the Market) (Scotland) Regulations 2008 No. 2008/176. - Enabling power: European Communities Act 1972, s. 2 (2). - Issued: 09.05.2008. Made: 02.05.2008. Laid before the Scottish Parliament: 02.05.2008. Coming into force: 05.05.2008. Effect: None. Territorial extent & classification: S. General. - EC note: These Regulations implement, in Scotland, Commission Decision 2008/352/EC imposing special conditions governing guar gum originating in or consigned from India due to contamination risk of those products by pentachlorophenal and dioxins. - 4p.: 30 cm. - 978-0-11-081635-7 *£3.00*

The Infant Formula and Follow-on Formula (Scotland) Amendment Regulations 2008 No. 2008/322. - Enabling power: Food Safety Act 1990, ss. 16 (1) (e), 17 (1), 26 (1) (a) (3), 48 (1). - Issued: 30.09.2008. Made: 24.09.2008. Laid before the Scottish Parliament: 25.09.2008. Coming into force: 04.11.2008. Effect: S.S.I. 2000/130; 2007/549 amended. Territorial extent & classification: S. General. - 8p.: 30 cm. - 978-0-11-100007-6 *£5.00*

The Meat (Official Controls Charges) (Scotland) Regulations 2008 No. 2008/98. - Enabling power: European Communities Act 1972, s. 2 (2), sch. 2, para. 1A. - Issued: 12.03.2008. Made: 06.03.2008. Laid before the Scottish Parliament: 07.03.2008. Coming into force: 31.03.2008. Effect: S.S.I. 2007/537 amended & S.S.I. 2007/538 revoked. Territorial extent & classification: S. General. - Revoked by S.S.I. 2009/262 (ISBN 9780111005927). - 16p.: 30 cm. - 978-0-11-081561-9 *£3.00*

The Official Feed and Food Controls (Scotland) Amendment Regulations 2008 No. 2008/218. - Enabling power: European Communities Act 1972, s. 2 (2). - Issued: 09.006.2008. Made: 04.06.2008. Laid before the Scottish Parliament: 06.06.2008. Coming into force: 01.07.2008. Effect: S.S.I. 2007/522 amended. Territorial extent & classification: S. General. - This Scottish Statutory Instrument has been made in consequence of a defect in S.S.I. 2008/176 and is being issued free of charge to all known recipients of that instrument. - 4p.: 30 cm. - 978-0-11-081681-4 *£3.00*

The Plastic Materials and Articles in Contact with Food (Scotland) Amendment Regulations 2008 No. 2008/261. - Enabling power: Food Safety Act 1990, ss. 16 (2), 17 (1) (2), 26 (1) (a), 48 (1). - Issued: 02.07.2008. Made: 26.06.2008. Laid before the Scottish Parliament: 27.06.2008. Coming into force: 30.06.2008 for reg. 2 (3); 01.07.2008 for remainder, in accord. with reg. 1. Effect: S.S.I. 2007/433, 471; 2008/127 amended. Territorial extent & classification: S. General. - EC note: These regs provide for enforcement of Commission Regulation (EC) No. 597/2008 amending Commission Regulation (EC) No. 372/2007 laying down transitional migration limits for plasticisers in gaskets in lids intended to come into contact with foods and extends the application of Commission Regulation (EC) No. 372/2007 until 30th April 2009. - 4p.: 30 cm. - 978-0-11-082007-1 *£3.00*

The Plastic Materials and Articles in Contact with Food (Scotland) Regulations 2008 No. 2008/127. - Enabling power: Food Safety Act 1990, ss. 16 (2), 17 (1) (2), 26 (1) (a) (2) (a) (3), 31, 48 (1). - Issued: 27.03.2008. Made: 19.03.2008. Laid before the Scottish Parliament: 20.03.2008. Coming into force: 01.05.2008 except for reg. 26 (c); 01.07.2008 for reg. 26 (c). Effect: S.I. 1990/2463; S.S.I. 2007/471 amended and S.S.I. 2006/517; 2007/433 revoked. Territorial extent & classification: S. General. - Revoked by S.S.I. 2009/30 (ISBN 9780111002285). EC note: The principal Directives implemented by these Regulations are: (a) Council Directive 82/711/EEC laying down the basic rules necessary for testing migration of the constituents of plastic materials and articles intended to come into contact with foodstuffs, as amended by Commission Directives 93/8/EEC and 97/48/EC; (b) Council Directive 85/572/EEC laying down the list of simulants to be used for testing migration of constituents of plastic materials and articles intended to come into contact with foodstuffs; (c) Commission Directive 2002/72/EC) relating to plastic materials and articles intended to come into contact with foodstuffs, as amended by Commission Directives 2004/1/EC, 2004/19/EC, 2005/79/EC and 2007/19/EC. - 36p.: 30 cm. - 978-0-11-081594-7 *£6.50*

The Rice Products from the United States of America (Restriction on First Placing on the Market) (Scotland) Regulations 2008 No. 2008/87. - Enabling power: European Communities Act 1972, s. 2 (2). - Issued: 11.03.2008. Made: 05.03.2008. Laid before the Scottish Parliament: 06.03.2008. Coming into force: 07.03.2008. Effect: S.S.I. 2006/542 revoked. Territorial extent & classification: S. General. - EC note: These Regulations implement, in relation to Scotland, Commission Decision 2006/601/EC as amended by Commission Decision 2006/754/EC amending Decision 2006/601/EC and by Commission Decision 2008/162/EC amending Decision 2006/601/EC. - 4p.: 30 cm. - 978-0-11-081554-1 *£3.00*

The Specified Products from China (Restriction on First Placing on the Market) (Scotland) Regulations 2008 No. 2008/148. - Enabling power: European Communities Act 1972, s. 2 (2). - Issued: 17.04.2008. Made: 14.04.2008. Laid before the Scottish Parliament: 14.04.2008. Coming into force: 15.04.2008. Effect: None. Territorial extent & classification: S. General. - EC note: These Regulations implement, in Scotland, Commission Decision 2008/289/EC on emergency measures regarding the unauthorised genetically modified organism 'Bt 63' in rice products. - 4p.: 30 cm. - 978-0-11-081607-4 *£3.00*

The Spreadable Fats, Milk and Milk Products (Scotland) Regulations 2008 No. 2008/216. - Enabling power: Food Safety Act 1990, ss. 6 (4), 16 (1), 17 (2), 26 (1) (3), 48 (1). - Issued: 09.06.2008. Made: 03.06.2008. Laid before the Scottish Parliament: 04.06.2008. Coming into force: 01.07.2008. Effect: S.I. 1990/816; S.S.I. 1999/34; 2007/303 revoked. Territorial extent & classification: S. General. - EC note: These Regulations, which extend to Scotland only, provide for the execution and enforcement of certain provisions of Council Regulation (EC) No. 1234/2007 establishing a common organisation of agricultural markets and on specific provisions for certain agricultural products (Single CMO Regulation). The provisions contained in that Council Regulation as regards spreadable fats are supplemented by Commission Regulation (EC) No. 445/2007. - 8p.: 30 cm. - 978-0-11-081679-1 £3.00

Food: Composition and labelling

The Meat Products (Scotland) Amendment Regulations 2008 No. 2008/97. - Enabling power: Food Safety Act 1990, ss. 16 (1) (e), 48 (1). - Issued: 12.03.2008. Made: 06.03.2008. Laid before the Scottish Parliament: 07.03.2008. Coming into force: 06.04.2008. Effect: S.S.I. 2004/6 amended. Territorial extent & classification: S. General. - 4p.: 30 cm. - 978-0-11-081560-2 £3.00

Forestry

The Forestry Challenge Funds (Scotland) Regulations 2008 No. 2008/135. - Enabling power: European Communities Act 1972, s. 2 (2), sch. 2, para. 1A. - Issued: 02.04.2008. Made: 26.03.2008. Laid before the Scottish Parliament: 28.03.2008. Coming into force: 07.05.2008. Effect: None. Territorial extent & classification: S. General. - 12p.: 30 cm. - 978-0-11-081599-2 £3.00

Freedom of information

The Freedom of Information (Relaxation of Statutory Prohibitions on Disclosure of Information) (Scotland) Orders 2008 No. 2008/339. - Enabling power: Freedom of Information (Scotland) Act 2002, s. 64 (1) (3). - Issued: 15.10.2008. Made: 09.10.2008. Coming into force: 13.10.2008. Effect: 1961 c. 34; 1963 c. 41; 1968 c. 67; 1974 c. 37; 1983 c. 30 amended. Territorial extent & classification: S. General. - Supersedes draft S.S.I. (ISBN 9780110839233) issued 04.09.2008. - 4p.: 30 cm. - 978-0-11-100046-5 £4.00

The Freedom of Information (Scotland) Act 2002 (Scottish Public Authorities) Amendment Order 2008 No. 2008/297. - Enabling power: Freedom of Information (Scotland) Act 2002, s. 4 (1). - Issued: 11.09.2008. Made: 01.09.2008. Laid before the Scottish Parliament: 05.09.2008. Coming into force: 13.10.2008. Effect: 2002 asp 13 amended. Territorial extent & classification: S. General. - 4p.: 30 cm. - 978-0-11-083956-1 £4.00

Harbours, docks, piers and ferries

The Caledonian Maritime Assets Limited (Largs) Harbour Revision Order 2008 No. 2008/182. - Enabling power: Harbours Act 1964, s. 14 (2) (b). - Issued: 19.05.2008. Made: 06.05.2008. Coming into force: 07.05.2008. Effect: 1832 c.xliv; 1899 c.ccxxii; 1933 c.lv partially repealed. Territorial extent & classification: S. General. - 24p.: 30 cm. - 978-0-11-081642-5 £16.80

The Dumfries and Galloway Council (Garlieston) Harbour Empowerment Order 2008 No. 2008/190. - Enabling power: Harbours Act 1964, s. 16. - Issued: 22.05.2008. Made: 14.05.2008. Coming into force: 23.05.2008. Effect: None. Territorial extent & classification: S. General. - 28p.: 30 cm. - 978-0-11-081651-7 £4.50

The Dumfries and Galloway Council (Isle of Whithorn) Harbour Empowerment Order 2008 No. 2008/189. - Enabling power: Harbours Act 1964, s. 16. - Issued: 22.05.2008. Made: 14.05.2008. Coming into force: 23.05.2008. Effect: None. Territorial extent & classification: S. General. - 28p.: 30 cm. - 978-0-11-081650-0 £4.50

The Dumfries and Galloway Council (Port William) Harbour Empowerment Order 2008 No. 2008/188. - Enabling power: Harbours Act 1964, s. 16. - Issued: 22.05.2008. Made: 14.05.2008. Coming into force: 23.05.2008. Effect: None. Territorial extent & classification: S. General. - 28p.: 30 cm. - 978-0-11-081649-4 £4.50

The Peterhead Port Authority Harbour Revision Order 2008 No. 2008/331. - Enabling power: Harbours Act 1964, s. 14. - Issued: 09.10.2008. Made: 02.10.2008. Coming into force: 03.10.2008. Effect: None. Territorial extent & classification: S. Local. - 8p.: 30 cm. - 978-0-11-100037-3 £5.00

The Stornoway Harbour Revision (Constitution) Order 2008 No. 2008/422. - Enabling power: Harbours Act 1964, s. 14. - Issued: 23.12.2008. Made: 17.12.2008. Coming into force: 18.12.2008. Effect: 1976 c.xxi; S.I. 2003/435 amended. Territorial extent & classification: S. Local. - 12p.: 30 cm. - 978-0-11-100150-9 £5.00

The Whiteness Marina Harbour Revision Order 2008 No. 2008/361. - Enabling power: Harbours Act 1964, s. 14. - Issued: 12.11.2008. Made: 06.11.2008. Coming into force: 07.11.2008. Effect: 1975 c.xxiv repealed. Territorial extent & classification: S. Local. - 16p.: 30 cm. - 978-0-11-100064-9 £5.00

High Court of Justiciary

Act of Adjournal (Criminal Procedure Rules Amendment) (Criminal Proceedings etc. (Reform) (Scotland) Act 2007) 2008 No. 2008/61. - Enabling power: Criminal Procedure (Scotland) Act 1995, ss. 156 (5) (b) (i), 226F (1), 305. - Issued: 03.03.2008. Made: 20.02.2008. Coming into force: 10.03.2008. Effect: S.I. 1996/513 amended. Territorial extent & classification: S. General. - 20p.: 30 cm. - 978-0-11-081529-9 £3.50

The High Court of Justiciary Fees Amendment Order 2008 No. 2008/237. - Enabling power: Courts of Law Fees (Scotland) Act 1895, s. 2. - Issued: 16.06.2008. Made: 06.06.2008. Laid before the Scottish Parliament: 06.06.2008. Coming into force: In accord. with art. 1. Effect: S.I. 1984/252 amended. Territorial extent & classification: S. General. - 4p.: 30 cm. - 978-0-11-082033-0 £3.00

Housing

The Homelessness etc. (Scotland) Act 2003 (Commencement No. 3) Order 2008 No. 2008/313 (C. 27). - Enabling power: Homelessness etc. (Scotland) Act 2003, s. 14 (1) (2). Bringing into operation various provisions of the 2003 Act on 02.10.2008 & 01.04.2009 in accord. with art. 2- Issued: 23.09.2008. Made: 18.09.2008. Effect: None. Territorial extent and classification: S. General. - 2p.: 30 cm. - 978-0-11-084488-6 £4.00

The Housing Grants (Application Forms) (Scotland) Amendment Regulations 2008 No. 2008/283. - Enabling power: Housing (Scotland) Act 1987, ss. 237, 330. - Issued: 29.08.2008. Made: 22.08.2008. Laid before the Scottish Parliament: 27.08.2008. Coming into force: 27.10.2008. Effect: S.I. 2003/420 amended. Territorial extent & classification: S. General. - 4p.: 30 cm. - 978-0-11-082022-4 £3.00

The Housing Grants (Assessment of Contributions) (Scotland) Amendment Regulations 2008 No. 2008/336. - Enabling power: Housing (Scotland) Act 1987, s. 240A. - Issued: 10.10.2008. Made: 04.10.2008. Coming into force: 27.10.2008. Effect: S.S.I. 2003/461 amended. Territorial extent & classification: S. General. - Supersedes draft S.S.I. (ISBN 9780110820231) issued 29.08.2008. - 4p.: 30 cm. - 978-0-11-100045-8 £4.00

The Housing Revenue Account General Fund Contribution Limits (Scotland) Order 2008 No. 2008/34. - Enabling power: Housing (Scotland) Act 1987, s. 204. - Issued: 14.02.2008. Made: 06.02.2008. Laid: 11.02.2008. Coming into force: 12.03.2008. Effect: None. Territorial extent & classification: S. General. - 2p.: 30 cm. - 978-0-11-080249-7 £3.00

The Housing (Scotland) Act 2001 (Alteration of Housing Finance Arrangements) Order 2008 No. 2008/28. - Enabling power: Housing (Scotland) Act 2001, ss. 94 (1) (2) (3), 109 (2). - Issued: 08.02.2008. Made: 31.01.2008. Laid before the Scottish Parliament: 05.02.2008. Coming into force: 01.04.2008. Effect: None. Territorial extent & classification: S. General. - 4p.: 30 cm. - 978-0-11-080241-1 £3.00

The Housing (Scotland) Act 2006 (Commencement No. 6 and Transitional Provision) Order 2008 No. 2008/308 (C.25). - Enabling power: Housing (Scotland) Act 2006, ss. 191 (2), 195 (3). Bringing into operation various provisions of the 2006 Act on 29.09.2008, 01.12.2008 in accord. with art. 3. - Issued: 22.09.2008. Made: 16.09.2008. Effect: None. Territorial extent & classification: S. General. - 4p.: 30 cm. - 978-0-11-084479-4 £4.00

The Housing (Scotland) Act 2006 (Prescribed Documents) Regulations 2008 No. 2008/76. - Enabling power: Housing (Scotland) Act 2006, ss. 99 (2), 104 (1) to (3), 105. - Issued: 10.03.2008. Made: 21.02.2008. Coming into force: 01.10.2008. Effect: None. Territorial extent & classification: S. General. - 40p., col. ill.: 30 cm. - 978-0-11-081541-1 £11.35

The Housing (Scotland) Act 2006 (Scheme of Assistance) Regulations 2008 No. 2008/406. - Enabling power: Housing (Scotland) Act 2006, ss. 73 (3), 77 (1), 79 (6). - Issued: 10.12.2008. Made: 02.12.2008. Coming into force: 01.04.2009. Effect: None. Territorial extent & classification: S. General. - Supersedes draft S.S.I. (ISBN 9780111000182) issued 08.10.2008. - 4p.: 30 cm. - 978-0-11-100119-6 £4.00

The Housing Support Grant (Scotland) Order 2008 No. 2008/133. - Enabling power: Housing (Scotland) Act 1987, ss. 191, 192. - Issued: 31.03.2008. Made: 17.03.2008. Coming into force: 01.04.2008. Effect: None. Territorial extent & classification: S. General. - Supersedes draft SSI (ISBN 9780110802459) issued 13.02.2008. - 4p.: 30 cm. - 978-0-11-081597-8 £3.00

The Notice to Local Authorities (Scotland) Regulations 2008 No. 2008/324. - Enabling power: Homelessness (Scotland) etc. Act 2003, s. 11 (3) (4). - Issued: 07.10.2008. Made: 02.10.2008. Laid before the Scottish Parliament: 03.10.2008. Coming into force: 01.04.2009. Effect: None. Territorial extent & classification: S. General. - 8p.: 30 cm. - 978-0-11-100010-6 £5.00

The Private Landlord Registration (Advice and Assistance) (Scotland) Amendment Regulations 2008 No. 2008/402. - Enabling power: Antisocial Behaviour etc. (Scotland) Act 2004, s. 99. - Issued: 09.12.2008. Made: 03.12.2008. Laid before the Scottish Parliament: 04.12.2008. Coming into force: 12.02.2009. Effect: S.S.I. 2005/557 amended. Territorial extent & classification: S. General. - 2p.: 30 cm. - 978-0-11-100114-1 £4.00

The Private Landlord Registration (Information and Fees) (Scotland) Amendment Regulations 2008 No. 2008/403. - Enabling power: Antisocial Behaviour etc. (Scotland) Act 2004, ss. 83 (3), 87 (4). - Issued: 09.12.2008. Made: 03.12.2008. Laid before the Scottish Parliament: 04.12.2008. Coming into force: 12.02.2009. Effect: S.S.I. 2005/558 amended. Territorial extent & classification: S. General. - 4p.: 30 cm. - 978-0-11-100115-8 £4.00

Human rights

The Scottish Commission for Human Rights Act 2006 (Commencement No. 2) Order 2008 No. 2008/112 (C.9). - Enabling power: Scottish Commission for Human Rights Act 2006, s. 22 (3). Bringing various provisions of the 2006 Act on 01.04.2008, in accord. with art. 2. - Issued: 18.03.2008. Made: 12.03.2008. Effect: None. Territorial extent & classification: S. General. - 2p.: 30 cm. - 978-0-11-081577-0 £3.00

The Scottish Commission for Human Rights (Specification) Order 2008 No. 2008/355. - Enabling power: Scottish Commission for Human Rights Act 2006, s. 9 (6) (d). - Issued: 11.11.2008. Made: 05.11.2008. Coming into force: 06.11.2008 in accord. with art. 1. Effect: None. Territorial extent & classification: S. General. - Supersedes draft S.S.I. (ISBN 9780110839677) issued 11.09.2008. - 4p.: 30 cm. - 978-0-11-100063-2 £4.00

Human tissue

The Human Tissue (Scotland) Act 2006 (Consequential Amendment) Order 2008 No. 2008/259. - Enabling power: Human Tissue (Scotland) Act 2006, s. 58 (1) (2). - Issued: 30.06.2008. Made: 23.06.2008. Coming into force: 24.06.2008. Effect: 2004 c.19 amended. Territorial extent & classification: S. General. - Supersedes draft S.S.I. (ISBN 9780110816562) issued 22.05.2008. - 2p.: 30 cm. - 978-0-11-082048-4 £3.00

Insolvency

The Bankruptcy and Diligence etc. (Scotland) Act 2007 (Commencement No. 3, Savings and Transitionals) Order 2008 No. 2008/115 (C.10). - Enabling power: Bankruptcy and Diligence etc. (Scotland) Act 2007, ss. 224 (2), 227 (3) (4). Bringing into operation various provisions of the 2007 Act on 01.04.2008, in accord. with art. 3. - Issued: 19.03.2008. Made: 12.03.2008. Effect: None. Territorial extent & classification: S. General. - 16p.: 30 cm. - 978-0-11-081578-7 £3.00

The Insolvency (Scotland) Rules 1986 Amendment Rules 2008 No. 2008/393. - Enabling power: Insolvency Act 1986, s. 411. - Issued: 02.12.2008. Made: 26.11.2008. Laid before the Scottish Parliament: 27.11.2008. Coming into force: 20.12.2008. Effect: S.I. 1986/1915 amended. Territorial extent & classification: S. General. - 4p.: 30 cm. - 978-0-11-100096-0 £4.00

Insolvency: Bankruptcy

The Bankruptcy and Diligence etc. (Scotland) Act 2007 (Commencement No. 2 and Saving) Order 2008 No. 2008/45 (C.5). - Enabling power: Bankruptcy and Diligence etc. (Scotland) Act 2007, ss. 224 (2), 227 (3). Bringing into operation various provisions of the 2007 Act on 19.02.2008. - Issued: 25.02.2008. Made: 18.02.2008. Effect: None. Territorial extent & classification: S. General. - 2p.: 30 cm. - 978-0-11-081510-7 £3.00

The Bankruptcy Fees (Scotland) Amendment (No. 2) Regulations 2008 No. 2008/79. - Enabling power: Bankruptcy (Scotland) Act 1985, ss. 69A, 72, 73 (1) & Bankruptcy and Diligence (Scotland) Act 2007, s. 225 (1). - Issued: 10.03.2008. Made: 04.03.2008. Laid before the Scottish Parliament: 05.03.2008. Coming into force: 01.04.2008. Effect: S.I. 1993/486 amended. Territorial extent & classification: S. General. - 4p.: 30 cm. - 978-0-11-081543-5 £3.00

The Bankruptcy Fees (Scotland) Amendment Regulations 2008 No. 2008/5. - Enabling power: Bankruptcy (Scotland) Act 1985, ss. 69A, 72, 73 (1). - Issued: 16.01.2008. Made: 10.01.2008. Laid before the Scottish Parliament: 10.01.2008. Coming into force: 01.02.2008. Effect: S.I. 1993/486; 1999/752; 2007/220 amended. Territorial extent & classification: S. General. - 8p.: 30 cm. - 978-0-11-080208-4 £3.00

Justice of the Peace courts

Act of Adjournal (Criminal Procedure Rules Amendment) (Criminal Proceedings etc. (Reform) (Scotland) Act 2007) 2008 No. 2008/61. - Enabling power: Criminal Procedure (Scotland) Act 1995, ss. 156 (5) (b) (i), 226F (1), 305. - Issued: 03.03.2008. Made: 20.02.2008. Coming into force: 10.03.2008. Effect: S.I. 1996/513 amended. Territorial extent & classification: S. General. - 20p.: 30 cm. - 978-0-11-081529-9 £3.50

Act of Adjournal (Criminal Procedure Rules Amendment No. 2) (Miscellaneous) 2008 No. 2008/62. - Enabling power: Criminal Procedure (Scotland) Act 1995, s. 302. - Issued: 28.02.2008. Made: 20.02.2008. Coming into force: 10.03.2008; 01.04.2008 in accord. with para. 1 (2) (3). Effect: S.I. 1996/513; S.S.I. 2005/188, 574; 2006/76. amended. Territorial extent & classification: S. General. - 8p.: 30 cm. - 978-0-11-081531-2 £3.00

Act of Adjournal (Criminal Procedure Rules Amendment No. 3) (Seizure and Disposal of Vehicles) 2008 No. 2008/275. - Enabling power: Criminal Procedure (Scotland) Act 1995, s. 305. - Issued: 29.07.2008. Made: 18.07.2008. Coming into force: 15.08.2008. Effect: S.I. 1996/513 amended. Territorial extent & classification: S. General. - 4p.: 30 cm. - 978-0-11-082020-0 £3.00

The Justice of the Peace Court (Sheriffdom of Glasgow and Strathkelvin) Amendment Order 2008 No. 2008/374. - Enabling power: Criminal Proceedings etc. (Reform) (Scotland) Act 2007, ss. 64 (1, 65 (5). - Issued: 19.11.2008. Made: 13.11.2008. Laid before the Scottish Parliament: 14.11.2008. Coming into force: 08.12.2008. Effect: S.S.I. 2008/328 amended. Territorial extent & classification: S. General. - 4p.: 30 cm. - 978-0-11-100077-9 £4.00

The Justice of the Peace Court (Sheriffdom of Glasgow and Strathkelvin) Order 2008 No. 2008/328. - Enabling power: Criminal Proceedings etc. (Reform) (Scotland) Act 2007, ss. 59 (2), 64 (1) (4), 65 (1), 81 (2), 82 (1). - Issued: 08.10.2008. Made: 02.10.2008. Laid before the Scottish Parliament: 03.10.2008. Coming into force: 10.11.2008 for arts 1, 4, 6, 7 (9) (10); 08.12.2008 for remainder. Effect: 1975 c. 20 partial repeal. Territorial extent & classification: S. General. - 8p.: 30 cm. - 978-0-11-100027-4 £5.00

The Justice of the Peace Courts (Sheriffdom of Grampian, Highland and Islands) Amendment Order 2008 No. 2008/179. - Enabling power: Criminal Proceedings etc. (Reform) (Scotland) Act 2007, ss. 64 (1), 65 (1), 65 (5). - Issued: 14.05.2008. Made: 08.05.2008. Laid before the Scottish Parliament: 09.05.2008. Coming into force: 02.06.2008. Effect: S.S.I. 2008/93 amended. Territorial extent & classification: S. General. - 4p.: 30 cm. - 978-0-11-081637-1 £3.00

The Justice of the Peace Courts (Sheriffdom of Grampian, Highland and Islands) Order 2008 No. 2008/93. - Enabling power: Criminal Proceedings etc. (Reform) (Scotland) Act 2007, ss. 59 (2), 64 (1) (4), 81 (2). - Issued: 11.03.20008. Made: 05.03.2008. Laid before the Scottish Parliament: 06.03.2008. Coming into force: 31.03.2008 for arts 1& 5; 02.06.2008 for remainder. Effect: 1975 c. 20 partially repealed. Territorial extent & classification: S. General. - 8p.: 30 cm. - 978-0-11-081556-5 £3.00

The Justice of the Peace Courts (Sheriffdom of Lothian and Borders) etc. Order 2008 No. 2008/31. - Enabling power: Criminal Proceedings etc. (Reform) (Scotland) Act 2007, ss. 59 (2), 64 (1) (4), 65 (1) (5), 81 (2). - Issued: 13.02.2008. Made: 07.02.2008. Laid before the Scottish Parliament: 08.02.2008. Coming into force: 10.03.2008. Effect: 1975 c. 20 partially repealed. Territorial extent & classification: S. General. - With correction slip dated May 2008. Subject heading Criminal Law should be deleted and replaced with Justice of the Peace Court. - 8p.: 30 cm. - 978-0-11-080246-6 £3.00

The Justice of the Peace Courts (Sheriffdom of Tayside, Central and Fife) Order 2008 No. 2008/363. - Enabling power: Criminal Proceedings etc. (Reform) (Scotland) Act 2007, ss. 59 (2), 64 (1) (4), 65 (1), 81 (2). - Issued: 12.11.2008. Made: 06.11.2008. Laid before the Scottish Parliament: 07.11.2008. Coming into force: 01.12.2008 for arts 1, 4, 6 & 23.02.2009 for remainder. Effect: 1975 c. 20 partial repeal. Territorial extent & classification: S. General. - 8p.: 30 cm. - 978-0-11-100067-0 £5.00

Legal aid and advice

The Advice and Assistance (Financial Conditions) (Scotland) Regulations 2008 No. 2008/137. - Enabling power: Legal Aid (Scotland) Act 1986, ss. 11 (2), 36 (2) (b). - Issued: 07.04.2008. Made: 27.03.2008. Coming into force: 07.04.2008. Effect: 1986 c.47 amended & S.S.I. 2007/247 revoked with savings. Territorial extent & classification: S. General. - Revoked by S.S.I. 2009/143 (ISBN 9780111004746) with savings. Supersedes draft SSI (ISBN 9780110815114) issued 25.02.2008. - 4p.: 30 cm. - 978-0-11-081601-2 £3.00

The Advice and Assistance (Limits, Conditions and Representation) (Scotland) Regulations 2008 No. 2008/251. - Enabling power: Legal Aid (Scotland) Act 1986, ss. 9, 11 (2), 36 (2) (b). - Issued: 23.06.2008. Made: 06.06.2008. Coming into force: 30.06.2008. Effect: S.I. 1993/3187; S.S.I. 2008/137 amended. Territorial extent & classification: S. - Supersedes draft S.S.I. (ISBN 9780110816302) issued 01.05.2008. - 8p.: 30 cm. - 978-0-11-082041-5 £3.00

The Advice and Assistance (Scotland) Amendment Regulations 2008 No. 2008/47. - Enabling power: Legal Aid (Scotland) Act 1986, s. 12 (3). - Issued: 26.02.2008. Made: 20.02.2008. Laid before the Scottish Parliament: 21.02.2008. Coming into force: 07.04.2008. Effect: S.I. 1996/2447 amended. Territorial extent & classification: S. General. - Revoked by S.S.I. 2009/49 (ISBN 9780111002728). - 2p.: 30 cm. - 978-0-11-081514-5 £3.00

The Assistance by Way of Representation (District Court Financial Limit) (Scotland) Order 2008 No. 2008/416. - Enabling power: Criminal Proceedings etc. (Reform) (Scotland) Act 2007, s. 64 (5). - Issued: 22.12.2008. Made: 16.12.2008. Laid before the Scottish Parliament: 17.12.2008. Coming into force: 12.02.2009. Effect: None. Territorial extent & classification: S. General. - 2p.: 30 cm. - 978-0-11-100139-4 £4.00

The Civil Legal Aid (Financial Conditions) (Scotland) Regulations 2008 No. 2008/138. - Enabling power: Legal Aid (Scotland) Act 1986, s. 36 (2) (b). - Issued: 07.04.2008. Made: 27.03.2008. Coming into force: 07.04.2008. Effect: 1986 c.47 amended & S.S.I. 2007/249 revoked with savings. Territorial extent & classification: S. General. - Revoked by S.S.I. 2009/143 (ISBN 9780111004746) with savings. Supersedes draft SSI (ISBN 9780110815121) issued 27.02.2008. - 4p.: 30 cm. - 978-0-11-081602-9 £3.00

The Civil Legal Aid (Scotland) Amendment Regulations 2008 No. 2008/48. - Enabling power: Legal Aid (Scotland) Act 1986, ss. 17 (2B), 36 (1). - Issued: 26.02.2008. Made: 20.02.2008. Laid before the Scottish Parliament: 21.02.2008. Coming into force: 07.04.2008. Effect: S.S.I. 2002/494 amended. Territorial extent & classification: S. General. - Revoked by S.S.I. 2009/49 (ISBN 9780111002728). - 2p.: 30 cm. - 978-0-11-081515-2 £3.00

The Criminal Legal Assistance (Fees and Information etc.) (Scotland) Regulations 2008 No. 2008/240. - Enabling power: Legal Aid (Scotland) Act 1986, ss. 12 (3), 33, 36 (1) (2) (a) (e) (g), 41A. - Issued: 16.06.2008. Made: 06.06.2008. Laid before the Scottish Parliament: 06.06.2008. Coming into force: 30.06.2008. Effect: S.I. 1989/1491; 1996/2447; 1999/491 amended and S.S.I. 2006/233 revoked. Territorial extent & classification: S. - 16p.: 30 cm. - 978-0-11-082029-3 £3.00

Legal profession

The Legal Profession and Legal Aid (Scotland) Act 2007 (Abolition of the Scottish legal services ombudsman) Order 2008 No. 2008/352. - Enabling power: Legal Profession and Legal Aid (Scotland) Act 2007, s. 26 (1). - Issued: 04.11.2008. Made: 29.10.2008. Coming into force: 16.11.2008. Effect: None. Territorial extent & classification: S. General. - 2p.: 30 cm. - 978-0-11-100052-6 £4.00

The Legal Profession and Legal Aid (Scotland) Act 2007 (Commencement No. 5) Order 2008 No. 2008/311 (C.26). - Enabling power: Legal Profession and Legal Aid (Scotland) Act 2007, s. 82 (2). Bringing various provisions of the 2007 Act on 23.11.2007, in accord. with art. 2. - Issued: 01.10.2008. Made: 17.09.2008. Effect: None. Territorial extent & classification: S. General. - 8p.: 30 cm. - 978-0-11-084484-8 £5.00

The Legal Profession and Legal Aid (Scotland) Act 2007 (Handling Complaints and Specification of Interest Rates) Order 2008 No. 2008/428. - Enabling power: Legal Profession and Legal Aid (Scotland) Act 2007, ss. 23 (4) (b), 27 (3) (b), 28 (3) (b). - Issued: 29.12.2008. Made: 18.12.2008. Laid before the Scottish Parliament: 22.12.2008. Coming into force: 30.01.2009. Effect: None. Territorial extent & classification: S. General. - 4p.: 30 cm. - 978-0-11-100173-8 £4.00

The Legal Profession and Legal Aid (Scotland) Act 2007 (Transitional, Savings and Consequential Provisions) Order 2008 No. 2008/332. - Enabling power: Legal Profession and Legal Aid (Scotland) Act 2007, s. 78. - Issued: 09.10.2008. Made: 30.09.2008. Coming into force: 01.10.2008. Effect: 1980 c.46; 1990 c.40 amended & S.S.I. 2002/32 revoked with savings. Territorial extent & classification: S. General. - Supersedes draft SSI (ISBN 9780110820439) issued 24.06.2008. - 4p.: 30 cm. - 978-0-11-100038-0 £4.00

Licensing (liquor)

The Licensing (Scotland) Act 2005 (Commencement No. 5) Order 2008 No. 2008/292 (C. 24). - Enabling power: Licensing (Scotland) Act 2005, ss. 146 (2), 150 (2). Bringing into operation various provisions of the 2005 Act on 05.09.2008, in accord. with art. 2. - Issued: 05.09.2008. Made: 01.09.2008. Effect: None. Territorial extent & classification: S. General. - 2p.: 30 cm. - 978-0-11-083933-2 £4.00

The Licensing (Transitional Provisions) (Scotland) Order 2008 No. 2008/194. - Enabling power: Licensing (Scotland) Act 2005, s. 145. - Issued: 28.05.2008. Made: 21.05.2008. Laid before the Scottish Parliament: 22.05.2008. Coming into force: 18.06.2008. Effect: 1976 c. 66 modified. Territorial extent & classification: S. General. - 2p.: 30 cm. - 978-0-11-081659-3 £3.00

Local government

The Business Improvement Districts (Scotland) Amendment Regulations 2008 No. 2008/359. - Enabling power: Planning etc. (Scotland) Act 2006, s. 46. - Issued: 11.11.2008. Made: 05.11.2008. Laid before the Scottish Parliament: 06.11.2008. Coming into force: 01.01.2009. Effect: S.S.I. 2007/202 amended. Territorial extent & classification: S. General. - 2p.: 30 cm. - 978-0-11-100061-8 £4.00

The Dumfries and Galloway (Electoral Arrangements) Amendment Order 2008 No. 2008/325. - Enabling power: Local Government (Scotland) Act 1973, ss. 26, 233. - Issued: 07.10.2008. Made: 01.10.2008. Coming into force: 22.10.2008. Effect: S.S.I. 2006/434 amended. Territorial extent & classification: S. General. - 2p.: 30 cm. - 978-0-11-100014-4 £4.00

The Local Governance (Scotland) Act 2004 (Remuneration) Amendment Regulations 2008 No. 2008/415. - Enabling power: Local Government and Housing Act 1989, s. 18 & Local Governance (Scotland) Act 2004, ss. 11, 16 (2). - Issued: 19.12.2008. Made: 16.12.2008. Laid before the Scottish Parliament: 16.12.2008. Coming into force: 10.02.2009. Effect: S.I. 2007/183 amended. Territorial extent & classification: S. General. - 4p.: 30 cm. - 978-0-11-100137-0 £4.00

The Local Government (Allowances and Expenses) (Scotland) Amendment Regulations 2008 No. 2008/414. - Enabling power: Local Government (Scotland) Act 1973, s. 50 & Local Government and Housing Act 1989, s. 18 & Local Governance (Scotland) Act 2004, ss. 11, 16. - Issued: 19.12.2008. Made: 16.12.2008. Laid before the Scottish Parliament: 16.12.2008. Coming into force: 10.02.2009. Effect: S.S.I. 2007/108 amended. Territorial extent & classification: S. General. - 4p.: 30 cm. - 978-0-11-100136-3 £4.00

The Local Government Finance (Scotland) Order 2008 No. 2008/33. - Enabling power: Local Government Finance Act 1992, sch. 12, paras 1, 9 (4). - Issued: 14.02.2008. Made: 23.01.2008. Laid before the Scottish Parliament: 24.01.2008. Coming into force: 08.02.2008. Effect: S.S.I. 2007/65 partially revoked. Territorial extent & classification: S. General. - Partially revoked by S.S.I. 2009/50 (ISBN 9780111002797). Supersedes draft SSI (ISBN 9780110802336) issued 29.01.2008. - 8p.: 30 cm. - 978-0-11-080248-0 £3.00

The Local Government Finance (Scotland) Order 2008 No. 2008/136. - Enabling power: Local Government Finance Act 1992, sch. 12, paras 1, (4). - Issued: 02.04.2008. Made: 12.03.2008. Laid before the Scottish Parliament: 13.03.2008. Coming into force: 28.03.2008. Effect: S.S.I. 2008/33 amended. Territorial extent & classification: S. General. - 4p.: 30 cm. - 978-0-11-081600-5 £3.00

The Private Landlord Registration (Advice and Assistance) (Scotland) Amendment Regulations 2008 No. 2008/402. - Enabling power: Antisocial Behaviour etc. (Scotland) Act 2004, s. 99. - Issued: 09.12.2008. Made: 03.12.2008. Laid before the Scottish Parliament: 04.12.2008. Coming into force: 12.02.2009. Effect: S.S.I. 2005/557 amended. Territorial extent & classification: S. General. - 2p.: 30 cm. - 978-0-11-100114-1 £4.00

The Private Landlord Registration (Information and Fees) (Scotland) Amendment Regulations 2008 No. 2008/403. - Enabling power: Antisocial Behaviour etc. (Scotland) Act 2004, ss. 83 (3), 87 (4). - Issued: 09.12.2008. Made: 03.12.2008. Laid before the Scottish Parliament: 04.12.2008. Coming into force: 12.02.2009. Effect: S.S.I. 2005/558 amended. Territorial extent & classification: S. General. - 4p.: 30 cm. - 978-0-11-100115-8 £4.00

The Provision of School Lunches (Disapplication of the Requirement to Charge) (Scotland) Order 2008 No. 2008/400. - Enabling power: Local Government in Scotland Act 2003, s. 57 (1) (3). - Issued: 04.12.2008. Made: 28.11.2008. Coming into force: 01.12.2008. Effect: S.S.I. 2007/451 revoked. Territorial extent & classification: S. General. - Supersedes draft S.S.I. (ISBN 9780111000090) issued 06.10.2008. - 4p.: 30 cm. - 978-0-11-100111-0 £4.00

Mental health

The Adult Support and Protection (Scotland) Act 2007 (Commencement No. 2 and Transitional Provisions) Amendment Order 2008 No. 2008/116 (C.11). - Enabling power: Adult Support and Protection (Scotland) Act 2007, s. 79 (3) (4). Bringing into operation various provisions of the 2007 Act on 01.10.2008, in accord. with art. 2. - Issued: 19.03.2008. Made: 13.03.2008. Effect: S.S.I. 2008/49 amended. Territorial extent & classification: S. General. - This Scottish Statutory Instrument has been made in consequence of a defect in S.S.I. 2008/49 (ISBN 978011081569) and is being issued free of charge to all known recipients of that instrument. - 4p.: 30 cm. - 978-0-11-081579-4 £3.00

The Adult Support and Protection (Scotland) Act 2007 (Commencement No. 2 and Transitional Provisions) Order 2008 No. 2008/49 (C.6). - Enabling power: Adult Support and Protection (Scotland) Act 2007, s. 79 (3) (4). Bringing into operation various provisions of the 2007 Act on 01.04.2008 and 01.10.2008. - Issued: 26.02.2008. Made: 20.02.2008. Effect: None. Territorial extent & classification: S. General. - 4p.: 30 cm. - 978-0-11-081516-9 £3.00

The Adult Support and Protection (Scotland) Act 2007 (Commencement No. 3 and Related Amendments) Order 2008 No. 2008/314 (C. 28). - Enabling power: Adult Support and Protection (Scotland) Act 2007, s. 79 (3). Bringing into operation various provisions of the 2007 Act on 29.10.2008, in accord. with art. 2. - Issued: 23.09.2008. Made: 16.09.2008. Effect: S.S.I. 2008/49 amended. Territorial extent & classification: S. General. - 4p.: 30 cm. - 978-0-11-084491-6 £4.00

The Mental Health (Absconding Patients from Other Jurisdictions) (Scotland) Regulations 2008 No. 2008/333. - Enabling power: Mental Health (Care and Treatment) (Scotland) Act 2003, ss. 309, 326 (2). - Issued: 10.10.2008. Made: 01.10.2008. Coming into force: 02.10.2008 in accord. with reg. 1 (1). Effect: 2003 asp 13 modified. Territorial extent & classification: S. General. - Supersedes draft S.S.I. (ISBN 9780110820422) issued 23.06.2008. - 8p.: 30 cm. - 978-0-11-100039-7 £5.00

The Mental Health (Certificates for Medical Treatment) (Scotland) Amendment Regulations 2008 No. 2008/316. - Enabling power: Mental Health (Care and Treatment) (Scotland) Act 2003, ss. 245 (2), 246 (1), 325. - Issued: 24.09.2008. Made: 18.09.2008. Laid before the Scottish Parliament: 19.09.2008. Coming into force: 12.10.2008. Effect: S.S.I. 2005/443 amended. Territorial extent & classification: S. General. - 12p.: 30 cm. - 978-0-11-100002-1 £5.00

The Mental Health (Cross-border Visits) (Scotland) Regulations 2008 No. 2008/181. - Enabling power: Mental Health (Care and Treatment) (Scotland) Act 2003, s. 309A. - Issued: 14.05.2008. Made: 06.05.2008. Coming into force: 07.05.2008 in accord. with reg. 1 (1). Effect: 2003 asp 13 modified. Territorial extent & classification: S. General. - Supersedes draft S.S.I. (ISBN 9780110815824) issued 20.03.2008. - 4p.: 30 cm. - 978-0-11-081639-5 £3.00

The Mental Health (England and Wales Cross-border transfer: patients subject to requirements other than detention) (Scotland) Regulations 2008 No. 2008/356. - Enabling power: Mental Health (Care and Treatment) (Scotland) Act 2003, ss. 289, 326. - Issued: 07.11.2008. Made: 02.11.2008. Coming into force: 03.11.2008. Effect: S.S.I. 2005/463 amended. Territorial extent & classification: S. General. - 16p.: 30 cm. - 978-0-11-100055-7 £5.00

The Mental Health Tribunal for Scotland (Practice and Procedure) (No. 2) Amendment Rules 2008 No. 2008/396. - Enabling power: Mental Health (Care and Treatment) (Scotland) Act 2003, ss. 21 (4), 326 (2), sch. 2, para. 10. - Issued: 03.12.2008. Made: 27.11.2008. Laid before the Scottish Parliament: 27.11.2008. Coming into force: 20.12.2008. Effect: S.S.I. 2005/519 amended. Territorial extent & classification: S. General. - 4p.: 30 cm. - 978-0-11-100103-5 £4.00

National assistance services

The National Assistance (Assessment of Resources) Amendment (Scotland) Regulations 2008 No. 2008/13. - Enabling power: National Assistance Act 1948, s. 22 (5). - Issued: 25.01.2008. Made: 21.01.2008. Laid: 23.01.2008. Coming into force: 07.04.2008. Effect: S.I. 1992/2977 amended in relation to Scotland & S.S.I. 2007/102 partially revoked. Territorial extent & classification: S. General. - Revoked by S.S.I. 2009/72 (ISBN 9780111003183). - 4p.: 30 cm. - 978-0-11-080225-1 £3.00

The National Assistance (Sums for Personal Requirements) (Scotland) Regulations 2008 No. 2008/14. - Enabling power: National Assistance Act 1948, s. 22 (4). - Issued: 25.01.2008. Made: 21.01.2008. Laid before the Scottish Parliament: 23.01.2008. Coming into force: 07.04.2008. Effect: S.S.I. 2007/103 revoked. Territorial extent & classification: S. General. - Revoked by S.S.I. 2009/73 (ISBN 9780111003213). - 4p.: 30 cm. - 978-0-11-080226-8 *£3.00*

National Health Service

The National Health Service (Charges for Drugs and Appliances) (Scotland) Amendment Regulations 2008 No. 2008/105. - Enabling power: National Health Service (Scotland) Act 1978, ss. 27 (1) (2), 69 (1) (2), 75A, 105 (7), 108 (1). - Issued: 12.03.2008. Made: 06.03.2008. Laid before the Scottish Parliament: 07.03.2008. Coming into force: 01.04.2008. Effect: S.S.I. 2008/27 amended. Territorial extent & classification: S. General. - This Scottish Statutory Instrument has been made to correct errors in S.S.I. 2008/27 (ISBN 9780110802404) and is being issued free of charge to all known recipients of that instrument. - 4p.: 30 cm. - 978-0-11-081568-8 *£3.00*

The National Health Service (Charges for Drugs and Appliances) (Scotland) Regulations 2008 No. 2008/27. - Enabling power: National Health Service (Scotland) Act 1978, ss. 17E, 17K, 17N, 17P, 25 (2), 27 (1) (2), 28 (1), 69 (1) (2), 75 (a), 75A, 105 (7), 108 (1). - Issued: 07.02.2008. Made: 31.01.2008. Laid before the Scottish Parliament: 01.02.2008. Coming into force: 01.04.2008. Effect: S.I. 1995/414; 2003/460; 2004/114, 115, 116 amended & S.S.I. 2007/389 revoked with savings. Territorial extent & classification: S. General. - With correction slip dated June 2008. - 24p.: 30 cm. - 978-0-11-080240-4 *£4.00*

The National Health Service (Charges for Drugs and Appliances) (Scotland) Regulations 2008 (Correction slip) No. 2008/27 Cor.. - Correction slip (to ISBN 9780110802404) dated June 2008. - 2p.: 30 cm. *Free*

The National Health Service (Charges to Overseas Visitors) (Scotland) Amendment Regulations 2008 No. 2008/290. - Enabling power: National Health Service (Scotland) Act 1978, ss. 98, 105 (7), 108 (1). - Issued: 04.09.2008. Made: 27.08.2008. Laid before the Scottish Parliament: 01.09.2008. Coming into force: 06.10.2008. Effect: S.I. 1989/364 amended. Territorial extent & classification: S. General. - 4p.: 30 cm. - 978-0-11-083916-5 *£4.00*

The National Health Service (Clinical Negligence and Other Risks Indemnity Scheme) (Scotland) Amendment Regulations 2008 No. 2008/60. - Enabling power: National Health Service (Scotland) Act 1978, ss. 2 (5), 85B, 105 (7), 108 (1). - Issued: 27.02.2008. Made: 19.02.2008. Laid before the Scottish Parliament: 22.02.2008. Coming into force: 17.03.2008. Effect: S.S.I. 2000/54 amended. Territorial extent & classification: S. General. - 4p.: 30 cm. - 978-0-11-081528-2 *£3.00*

The National Health Service (Functions of the Common Services Agency) (Scotland) Order 2008 No. 2008/312. - Enabling power: National Health Service (Scotland) Act 1978, ss. 10 (3) (4), 105 (6) (7). - Issued: 23.09.2008. Made: 11.09.2008. Coming into force: 01.10.2008. Effect: S.I. 1974/467; 1991/900; S.S.I. 2000/224; 2003/159, 306; 2006/603 revoked. Territorial extent & classification: S. General. - 8p.: 30 cm. - 978-0-11-084487-9 *£5.00*

The National Health Service (Optical Charges and Payments) (Scotland) Amendment (No. 2) Regulations 2008 No. 2008/289. - Enabling power: National Health Service (Scotland) Act 1978, ss. 70 (1), 105 (7), 108 (1), sch. 11, paras 2, 2A. - Issued: 03.09.2008. Made: 27.08.2008. Laid before the Scottish Parliament: 01.09.2008. Coming into force: 27.10.2008. Effect: S.I. 1998/642 amended. Territorial extent & classification: S. General. - 4p.: 30 cm. - 978-0-11-083915-8 *£3.00*

The National Health Service (Optical Charges and Payments) (Scotland) Amendment Regulations 2008 No. 2008/106. - Enabling power: National Health Service (Scotland) Act 1978, ss. 26, 70 (1), 73 (a), 74 (a), 105 (7), 108 (1), sch. 11, paras 2, 2A. - Issued: 12.03.2008. Made: 06.03.2008. Laid before the Scottish Parliament: 07.03.2008. Coming into force: 01.04.2008. Effect: S.I. 1998/642 amended. Territorial extent & classification: S. General. - 8p.: 30 cm. - 978-0-11-081569-5 *£3.00*

The National Health Service Pension Scheme (Scotland) Regulations 2008 No. 2008/224. - Enabling power: Superannuation Act 1972, ss. 10, 12, sch. 3. - Issued: 19.06.2008. Made: 04.06.2008. Laid before the Scottish Parliament: 06.06.2008. Coming into force: 28.06.2008. Effect: None. Territorial extent & classification: S. General. - 204p.: 30 cm. - 978-0-11-082027-9 *£26.00*

The National Health Service (Recognition of Health Service Bodies) (Scotland) Order 2008 No. 2008/315. - Enabling power: National Health Service (Scotland) Act 1978, ss. 88 (1) (e), 88 (2) (d), 105 (7). - Issued: 23.09.2008. Made: 17.09.2008. Laid before the Scottish Parliament: 18.09.2008. Coming into force: 13.10.2008. Effect: None. Territorial extent & classification: S. General. - 4p.: 30 cm. - 978-0-11-084493-0 *£4.00*

The National Health Service Superannuation Scheme (Additional Voluntary Contributions, Injury Benefits and Compensation for Premature Retirement) (Scotland) Amendment Regulations 2008 No. 2008/225. - Enabling power: Superannuation Act 1972, ss. 10, 12, 24, sch. 3. - Issued: 11.06.2008. Made: 04.06.2008. Laid before the Scottish Parliament: 05.06.2008. Coming into force: 28.06.2008. Effect: S.I. 1998/1451, 1594 & S.S.I. 2003/344 amended. Territorial extent & classification: S. General. - 12p.: 30 cm. - 978-0-11-081689-0 *£3.00*

The National Health Service (Superannuation Scheme, Injury Benefits, Additional Voluntary Contributions and Compensation for Premature Retirement) (Scotland) Amendment Regulations 2008 No. 2008/92. - Enabling power: Superannuation Act 1972, ss. 10, 12, 24, sch. 3. - Issued: 11.03.2008. Made: 04.03.2008. Laid before the Scottish Parliament: 06.03.2008. Coming into force: 31.03.2008. Effect: S.I. 1995/365; 1998/1451, 1594 & S.S.I. 2003/344 amended. Territorial extent & classification: S. General. - 12p.: 30 cm. - 978-0-11-081555-8 £3.00

The National Health Service Superannuation Scheme (Scotland) Amendment Regulations 2008 No. 2008/226. - Enabling power: Superannuation Act 1972, ss. 10, 12, sch. 3. - Issued: 12.06.2008. Made: 04.06.2008. Laid before the Scottish Parliament: 05.06.2008. Coming into force: 28.06.2008. Effect: S.I. 1995/365 amended. Territorial extent & classification: S. General. - 64p.: 30 cm. - 978-0-11-081690-6 £10.50

The National Health Service (Travelling Expenses and Remission of Charges) (Scotland) Amendment (No. 2) Regulations 2008 No. 2008/288. - Enabling power: National Health Service (Scotland) Act 1978, ss. 75A, 105 (7), 108 (1). - Issued: 03.09.2008. Made: 27.08.2008. Laid before the Scottish Parliament: 01.09.2008. Coming into force: 27.10.2008. Effect: S.S.I. 2003/460 amended. Territorial extent & classification: S. General. - 4p.: 30 cm. - 978-0-11-082024-8 £3.00

The National Health Service (Travelling Expenses and Remission of Charges) (Scotland) Amendment (No. 3) Regulations 2008 No. 2008/390. - Enabling power: National Health Service (Scotland) Act 1978, ss. 75A, 105 (7), 108 (1). - Issued: 01.12.2008. Made: 25.11.2008. Laid before the Scottish Parliament: 26.11.2008. Coming into force: 19.12.2008. Effect: S.S.I. 2003/460 amended. Territorial extent & classification: S. General. - 8p.: 30 cm. - 978-0-11-100094-6 £5.00

The National Health Service (Travelling Expenses and Remission of Charges) (Scotland) Amendment Regulations 2008 No. 2008/147. - Enabling power: National Health Service (Scotland) Act 1978, ss. 75A, 105 (7), 108 (1). - Issued: 17.04.2008. Made: 11.04.2008. Laid before the Scottish Parliament: 14.04.2008. Coming into force: 06.05.2008. Effect: S.S.I. 2003/460 amended. Territorial extent & classification: S. General. - 4p.: 30 cm. - 978-0-11-081606-7 £3.00

The Personal Injuries (NHS Charges) (Amounts) (Scotland) Amendment Regulations 2008 No. 2008/96. - Enabling power: Health and Social Care (Community Health and Standards) Act 2003, ss. 153 (2) (5), 168, 195 (1) (2). - Issued: 12.03.2008. Made: 06.03.2008. Laid before the Scottish Parliament: 07.03.2008. Coming into force: 01.04.2008. Effect: S.S.I. 2006/588 amended. Territorial extent & classification: S. General. - 4p.: 30 cm. - 978-0-11-081559-6 £3.00

Nature conservation

The Nature Conservation (Scotland) Act 2004 (Commencement No. 3) Order 2008 No. 2008/193 (C.20). - Enabling power: Nature Conservation (Scotland) Act 2004, ss. 53 (2), 59 (2). Bringing into operation various provisions of the 2004 Act on 02.06.2008 & 30.06.2008 in accord. with art. 2. - Issued: 28.05.2008. Made: 20.05.2008. Effect: None. Territorial extent & classification: S. General. - 2p.: 30 cm. - 978-0-11-081660-9 £3.00

The Register of Sites of Special Scientific Interest (Scotland) Regulations 2008 No. 2008/221. - Enabling power: Nature Conservation (Scotland) Act 2004, ss. 22 (3), 53 (2). - Issued: 10.06.2008. Made: 04.06.2008. Laid before the Scottish Parliament: 05.06.2008. Coming into force: 27.06.2008. Effect: None. Territorial extent & classification: S. General. - 4p.: 30 cm. - 978-0-11-081684-5 £3.00

Official statistics

The Official Statistics (Scotland) Order 2008 No. 2008/131. - Enabling power: Statistics and Registration Service Act 2007, s. 6 (1) (b) (ii) (2). - Issued: 28.03.2008. Made: 18.03.2008. Coming into force: 19.03.2008 in accord. with art. 1 (1). Effect: None. Territorial extent & classification: S. General. - Supersedes draft SSI (ISBN 9780110815039) issued 21.02.2008. - 4p.: 30 cm. - 978-0-11-081595-4 £3.00

The Pre-release Access to Official Statistics (Scotland) Order 2008 No. 2008/399. - Enabling power: Statistics and Registration Service Act 2007, s. 11(2) (4) (5). - Issued: 04.12.2008. Made: 27.11.2008. Coming into force: 01.12.2008. Effect: None. Territorial extent & classification: S. General. - Supersedes draft S.S.I. (ISBN 9780111000236) issued 08.10.2008. - 8p.: 30 cm. - 978-0-11-100110-3 £5.00

Pensions

The Firefighters' Pension Scheme Amendment (Scotland) Order 2008 No. 2008/161. - Enabling power: Fire Services Act 1947, s. 26 (1) to (5) & Superannuation Act 1972, ss. 12, 16. - Issued: 28.04.2008. Made: 21.04.2008. Laid: 22.04.2008. Coming into force: 14.05.2008. Effect: S.I. 1992/129 amended in relation to Scotland. Territorial extent & classification: S. General. - 8p.: 30 cm. - 978-0-11-081623-4 £3.00

The Firefighters' Pension Scheme (Scotland) Order 2007 Amendment Order 2008 No. 2008/160. - Enabling power: Fire and Rescue Services Act 2004, ss. 34 (1) to (4), 60 (2). - Issued: 28.04.2008. Made: 21.04.2008. Laid: 22.04.2008. Coming into force: 14.05.2008. Effect: S.S.I. 2007/199 amended. Territorial extent & classification: S. General. - 12p.: 30 cm. - 978-0-11-081622-7 £3.00

The Local Government Pension Scheme (Administration) (Scotland) Regulations 2008 No. 2008/228. - Enabling power: Superannuation Act 1972, s. 7, sch. 3. - Issued: 12.06.2008. Made: 04.06.2008. Laid before the Scottish Parliament: 06.06.2008. Coming into force: 01.04.2009. Effect: None. Territorial extent & classification: S. General. - 72p.: 30 cm. - 978-0-11-081693-7 £10.50

The Local Government Pension Scheme (Benefits, Membership and Contributions) (Scotland) Regulations 2008 No. 2008/230. - Enabling power: Superannuation Act 1972, ss. 7, 12, sch. 3. - Issued: 11.06.2008. Made: 04.06.2008. Laid before the Scottish Parliament: 06.06.2008. Coming into force: 01.04.2009 except for reg 4 (3); 01.04.2010 for reg. 4 (3). Effect: None. Territorial extent & classification: S. General. - 20p.: 30 cm. - 978-0-11-082025-5 £3.50

The Local Government Pension Scheme (Transitional Provisions) (Scotland) Regulations 2008 No. 2008/229. - Enabling power: Superannuation Act 1972, ss. 7, 12, sch. 3. - Issued: 11.06.2008. Made: 04.06.2008. Laid before the Scottish Parliament: 06.06.2008. Coming into force: 01.04.2009. Effect: S.I. 1998/366 amended and 33 instruments revoked. Territorial extent & classification: S. General. - 16p.: 30 cm. - 978-0-11-081694-4 £3.00

The Police Pensions (Amendment) (Scotland) Regulations 2008 No. 2008/387. - Enabling power: Police Pensions Act 1976, s. 1. - Issued: 01.12.2008. Made: 24.11.2008. Laid before the Scottish Parliament: 26.11.2008. Coming into force: 19.12.2008. Effect: S.I. 1987/257, 2215 & S.S.I. 2007/68, 201 amended. Territorial extent & classification: S. General. - 12p.: 30 cm. - 978-0-11-100088-5 £5.00

The Teachers' Superannuation (Scotland) Amendment Regulations 2008 No. 2008/227. - Enabling power: Superannuation Act 1972, ss. 9, 12, 24, sch. 3. - Issued: 11.06.2008. Made: 04.06.2008. Laid before the Scottish Parliament: 05.06.2008. Coming into force: 01.07.2008. Effect: S.I. 1995/2814; 1996/2317; S.S.I. 2005/393 amended. Territorial extent & classification: S. General. - 16p.: 30 cm. - 978-0-11-081691-3 £3.00

Pesticides

The Pesticides (Maximum Residue Levels in Crops, Food and Feeding Stuffs) (Scotland) Amendment Regulations 2008 No. 2008/65. - Enabling power: European Communities Act 1972, s. 2 (2). - Issued: 05.02.2008. Made: 28.02.2008. Laid before the Scottish Parliament: 29.02.2008. Coming into force: 28.03.2008 except for reg 4 (15.03.2008) and reg 5 (15.09.2008). Effect: S.S.I. 2005/599 amended. Territorial extent & classification: S. General. - Revoked by S.S.I. 2008/342 (ISBN 9780111000489). EC note: These Regulations implement Commission Directive 2007/73/EC. - 24p.: 30 cm. - 978-0-11-081535-0 £4.00

The Pesticides (Maximum Residue Levels) (Scotland) Regulations 2008 No. 2008/342. - Enabling power: European Communities Act 1972, s. 2 (2), sch. 2, para. 1A. - Issued: 23.10.2008. Made: 15.10.20008. Laid before the Scottish Parliament: 20.10.2008. Coming into force: 18.11.2008. Effect: S.S.I. 2005/599; 2006/151, 312, 548; 2007/142, 306, 481, 523; 2008/65 revoked. Territorial extent & classification: S. General. - EC note: These Regulations enforce the provisions of Regulation 396/2005 on maximum residue levels in or on food and feed of plant and animal origin and amending Council Directive 91/41/EEC. - 8p.: 30 cm. - 978-0-11-100048-9 £5.00

Plant health

The Plant Health Fees (Scotland) Regulations 2008 No. 2008/153. - Enabling power: European Communities Act 1972, s. 2 (2). - Issued: 22.04.2008. Made: 15.04.2008. Laid before the Scottish Parliament: 17.04.2008. Coming into force: 01.06.2008. Effect: S.I. 1996/1784 (S. 148) & S.S.I. 2004/249; 2005/555; 2007/314 revoked. Territorial extent & classification: S. General. - 8p.: 30 cm. - 978-0-11-081614-2 £3.00

The Plant Health (Scotland) Amendment (No. 2) Order 2008 No. 2008/350. - Enabling power: Plant Health Act 1967, ss. 2, 3, 4 (1) & European Communities Act 1972, s. 2 (2), sch. 2, para. 1A. - Issued: 04.11.2008. Made: 29.10.2008. Laid before the Scottish Parliament: 30.10.2008. Coming into force: 21.11.2008. Effect: S.S.I. 2005/613; 2008/300 amended. Territorial extent & classification: S. General. - EC note: This Order amends the Plant Health (Scotland) Order 2005 (S.S.I. 2005/613) to implement certain import restrictions on certain plant species, other than seeds, intended for planting, originating in any third country to prevent the introduction into Scotland of Anoplophora chinensis (Forster) (the citrus longhorn beetle). - 8p.: 30 cm. - 978-0-11-100051-9 £5.00

The Plant Health (Scotland) Amendment Order 2008 No. 2008/300. - Enabling power: Plant Health Act 1967, ss. 2, 3, 4 (1) & European Communities Act 1972, s. 2 (2), sch. 2, para. 1A. - Issued: 12.09.2008. Made: 05.09.2008. Laid before the Scottish Parliament: 09.09.2008. Coming into force: 01.10.2008. Effect: S.S.I. 2005/613 amended. Territorial extent & classification: S. General. - EC note: This SSI amends SSI 2005/613 so as to implement the following: Commission Directive 2008/61/EC (a codification of Directive 95/44/EC as amended), 2008/64/EC amending annexes I to IV to Council Directive 2000/29/EC; Commission Decision No 1/2008; and Corrigendum 15528/07 to Council Directive 2000/29/EC- 8p.: 30 cm. - 978-0-11-083978-3 £5.00

The Potatoes Originating in Poland (Notification) (Scotland) Amendment Order 2008 No. 2008/299. - Enabling power: Plant Health Act 1967, ss. 2, 3, 4 (1). - Issued: 12.09.2008. Made: 05.09.2008. Laid before the Scottish Parliament: 09.09.2008. Coming into force: 01.10.2008. Effect: S.S.I. 2004/255 amended & S.S.I. 2001/333; 2005/73 revoked. Territorial extent & classification: S. General. - 4p.: 30 cm. - 978-0-11-083974-5 £4.00

Police

The Police Act 1997 (Criminal Records) (Scotland) Amendment Regulations 2008 No. 2008/6. - Enabling power: Police Act 1997, ss. 113B (2) (b) (5A) (9) (11) (c), 118 (2A) (e), 119 (7). - Issued: 21.01.2008. Made: 14.01.2008. Laid before the Scottish Parliament: 15.01.2008. Coming into force: 06.02.2008. Effect: S.S.I. 2006/96 amended. Territorial extent & classification: S. General. - 4p.: 30 cm. - 978-0-11-080213-8 £3.00

The Police Grant (Scotland) Order 2008 No. 2008/46. - Enabling power: Police (Scotland) Act 1967, s. 32 (3) (5). - Issued: 26.02.2008. Made: 19.02.2008. Laid before the Scottish Parliament: 21.02.2008. Coming into force: 01.04.2008. Effect: None. Territorial extent & classification: S. General. - 4p.: 30 cm. - 978-0-11-081513-8 £3.00

The Police Grant (Variation) (Scotland) Order 2008 No. 2008/20. - Enabling power: Police (Scotland) Act 1967, s. 32 (3) (5). - Issued: 21.02.2008. Made: 29.01.2008. Laid before the Scottish Parliament: 30.01.2008. Coming into force: 07.03.2008. Effect: S.S.I. 2007/109 amended. Territorial extent & classification: S. General. - This Scottish Statutory Instrument had been printed in substitution of the S.S.I. of the same number (published 04.02.2008, same ISBN) and is being issued free of charge to all known recipients of that instrument. - 4p.: 30 cm. - 978-0-11-080236-7 £3.00

The Police (Special Constables) (Scotland) Regulations 2008 No. 2008/117. - Enabling power: Police (Scotland) Act 1967, ss. 3 (4), 7 (1), 16, 26, 48 (1) & Police Reform Act 2002, s. 82 (4). - Issued: 20.03.2008. Made: 13.03.2008. Laid before the Scottish Parliament: 17.03.2008. Coming into force: 12.05.2008. Effect: S.I. 1966/97 (with savings); 1994/3039; S.S.I. 2003/21 revoked. Territorial extent & classification: S. General. - 20p.: 30 cm. - 978-0-11-081580-0 £3.50

Prisons

The Discontinuance of Legalised Police Cells (Scotland) Revocation Rules 2008 No. 2008/35. - Enabling power: Prisons (Scotland) Act 1989, ss. 14, 39. - Issued: 15.02.2008. Made: 07.02.2008. Laid before the Scottish Parliament: 12.02.2008. Coming into force: 19.02.2008. Effect: S.S.I. 2008/8 revoked. Territorial extent & classification: S. General. - 2p.: 30 cm. - 978-0-11-081498-8 £3.00

The Discontinuance of Legalised Police Cells (Scotland) Rules 2008 No. 2008/8. - Enabling power: Prisons (Scotland) Act 1989, ss. 14, 39. - Issued: 21.01.2008. Made: 14.01.2008. Laid before the Scottish Parliament: 16.01.2008. Coming into force: 20.02.2008. Effect: S.R. & O. 1893 p. 477, p. 479; 1927/600; 1940/1658; S.I. 1954/16 revoked. Territorial extent & classification: S. General. - Revoked by S.S.I. 2008/35 (ISBN 9780110814988). - 4p.: 30 cm. - 978-0-11-080215-2 £3.00

The Home Detention Curfew Licence (Amendment of Specified Days) (Scotland) Order 2008 No. 2008/126. - Enabling power: Prisoners and Criminal Proceedings (Scotland) Act 1993, s. 3AA (6) (c). - Issued: 25.03.2008. Made: 18.03.2008. Laid before the Scottish Parliament: 18.03.2008. Coming into force: 21.03.2008. Effect: 1993 c.9 amended. Territorial extent & classification: S. General. - 2p.: 30 cm. - 978-0-11-081590-9 £3.00

The Prisons and Young Offenders Institutions (Scotland) Amendment Rules 2008 No. 2008/377. - Enabling power: Prisons (Scotland) Act 1989, s. 39. - Issued: 24.11.2008. Made: 18.11.2008. Laid before the Scottish Parliament: 19.11.2008. Coming into force: 11.12.2008. Effect: S.S.I. 2006/94 amended. Territorial extent & classification: S. General. - 4p.: 30 cm. - 978-0-11-100082-3 £4.00

Private international law

The Law Applicable to Non-Contractual Obligations (Scotland) Regulations 2008 No. 2008/404. - Enabling power: European Communities Act 1972, s. 2 (2). - Issued: 09.12.2008. Made: 03.12.2008. Laid before the Scottish Parliament: 04.12.2008. Coming into force: 11.01.2009. Effect: 1995 c.42. amended. Territorial extent & classification: S. - 4p.: 30 cm. - 978-0-11-100116-5 £4.00

Proceeds of crime

The Serious Crime Act 2007 (Commencement No. 1) (Scotland) Order 2008 No. 2008/152 (C.15). - Enabling power: Serious Crime Act 2007, s. 94 (3) (4) (c). Bringing into operation various provisions of the 2007 Act on 28.04.2008. - Issued: 21.04.2008. Made: 14.04.2008. Effect: None. Territorial extent & classification: S. General. - 2p.: 30 cm. - 978-0-11-081610-4 £3.00

Public bodies

The Public Appointments and Public Bodies etc. (Scotland) Act 2003 (Amendment of Specified Authorities) Order 2008 No. 2008/348. - Enabling power: Public Appointments and Public Bodies etc. (Scotland) Act 2003, s. 3 (2) (a). - Issued: 31.10.2008. Made: 21.10.2008. Coming into force: 22.10.2008. Effect: 2003 asp 4 amended. Territorial extent & classification: S General. - 4p.: 30 cm. - 978-0-11-100049-6 £4.00

Public finance and accountability

The Budget (Scotland) Act 2007 Amendment Order 2008 No. 2008/107. - Enabling power: Budget (Scotland) Act 2007, s. 7 (1). - Issued: 13.03.2008. Made: 04.03.2008. Coming into force: 05.03.2008 in accord. with art. 1. Effect: 2007 asp 9 amended. Territorial extent & classification: S. General. - Supersedes draft S.S.I. (ISBN 9780110802329) issued 29.01.2008. - 4p.: 30 cm. - 978-0-11-081570-1 £3.00

The Budget (Scotland) Act 2008 Amendment Order 2008 No. 2008/424. - Enabling power: Budget (Scotland) Act 2008, s. 7 (1). - Issued: 23.12.2008. Made: 17.12.2008. Coming into force: 18.12.2008 in accord. with art. 1. Effect: 2008 asp 2 amended. Territorial extent & classification: S. General. - Supersedes draft S.S.I. (ISBN 9780111000502) issued 03.11.2008. - 8p.: 30 cm. - 978-0-11-100155-4 £5.00

Public health: Contamination of food

The Food Protection (Emergency Prohibitions) (Radioactivity in Sheep) Partial Revocation (Scotland) Order 2008 No. 2008/63. - Enabling power: Food and Environment Protection Act 1985, ss. 1 (1) (2), 24 (3). - Issued: 04.03.2008. Made: 27.02.2008. Laid before the Scottish Parliament: 28.02.2008. Coming into force: 29.02.2008. Effect: S.I. 1991/20 partially revoked in relation to Scotland. Territorial extent & classification: S. General. - 4p.: 30 cm. - 978-0-11-081532-9 £3.00

Public passenger transport

The Public Service Vehicles (Registration of Local Services) (Scotland) Amendment Regulations 2008 No. 2008/253. - Enabling power: Public Passenger Vehicles Act 1981, ss. 52 (1), 60 (1) (e) (1A). - Issued: 24.06.2008. Made: 17.06.2008. Laid before the Scottish Parliament: 20.06.2008. Coming into force: 15.09.2008. Effect: S.S.I. 2001/219 amended. Territorial extent & classification: S. General. - 2p.: 30 cm. - 978-0-11-082045-3 £3.00

The Public Service Vehicles (Traffic Regulation Conditions) Amendment (Scotland) Regulations 2008 No. 2008/2. - Enabling power: Public Passenger Vehicles Act 1981, s. 60 and Transport Act 1985, s. 7 (6) (d). - Issued: 15.01.2008. Made: 09.01.2008. Laid before the Scottish Parliament: 09.01.2008. Coming into force: 31.01.2008. Effect: S.I. 1986/1030 amended. Territorial extent & classification: S. General. - 4p.: 30 cm. - 978-0-11-080205-3 £3.00

Public procurement

The Public Contracts and Utilities Contracts (Common Procurement Vocabulary Codes) Amendment (Scotland) Regulations 2008 No. 2008/291. - Enabling power: European Communities Act 1972, s. 2 (2). - Issued: 04.09.2008. Made: 28.08.2008. Laid before the Scottish Parliament: 01.09.2008. Coming into force: 23.09.2008. Effect: S.S.I. 2006/1, 2 amended. Territorial extent & classification: S. General. - EC note: These regulations amend the 2006 regulations to reflect the amendments made by Commission Regulation (EC) 213/2008 to Directives 2004/17/EC and 2004/18/EC. - 16p.: 30 cm. - 978-0-11-083918-9 £5.00

The Public Contracts and Utilities Contracts (Postal Services and Common Procurement Vocabulary Codes) Amendment (Scotland) Regulations 2008 No. 2008/376. - Enabling power: European Communities Act 1972, s. 2 (2). - Issued: 21.11.2008. Made: 17.11.2008. Laid before the Scottish Parliament: 18.11.2008. Coming into force: 12.12.2008. Effect: S.S.I. 2006/1, 2 amended. Territorial extent & classification: S. General. - EC note: These regs implement Article 6 of Council Directive 2004/17/EC concerning the co-ordination of procurement procedures of entities operating in the water, energy, transport and postal service sectors. Most of the provisions of that Directive are already implemented by the Utilities Contracts Regulations. Article 71 of the Directive allowed an additional period for the implementation of article 6. They also reflect amendments to the scope of Council Directive 2004/18/EC concerning the co-ordination of procedures for the award of public works contracts, public supply contracts and public services contracts. - 8p.: 30 cm. - 978-0-11-100079-3 £5.00

The Public Contracts and Utilities Contracts (Scotland) Amendment Regulations 2008 No. 2008/94. - Enabling power: European Communities Act 1972, s. 2 (2). - Issued: 12.03.2008. Made: 26.02.2008. Laid before the Scottish Parliament: 07.03.2008. Coming into force: 31.03.2008. Effect: S.S.I. 2006/1, 2 amended. Territorial extent & classification: S. General. - These regs relate to the implementation of Directive 2004/18/EC concerning the co-ordination of the procedures for the award of public works contracts, public supply contracts and public services contracts and Directive 2004/17/EC concerning the co-ordination of procurement procedures of entities operating in the water, energy, transport and postal service sectors. - 12p.: 30 cm. - 978-0-11-081557-2 £3.00

Rating and valuation

The Non-Domestic Rate (Scotland) Order 2008 No. 2008/32. - Enabling power: Local Government (Scotland) Act 1975, ss. 7B (1), 37 (1). - Issued: 13.02.2008. Made: 07.02.2008. Laid before the Scottish Parliament: 08.02.2008. Coming into force: 01.04.2008. Effect: None. Territorial extent & classification: S. General. - 2p.: 30 cm. - 978-0-11-080247-3 £3.00

The Non-Domestic Rates (Levying) (Scotland) Regulations 2008 No. 2008/85. - Enabling power: Local Government etc. (Scotland) Act 1994, s. 153. - Issued: 10.03.2008. Made: 04.03.2008. Laid before the Scottish Parliament: 05.03.2008. Coming into force: 01.04.2008. Effect: S.S.I. 2007/216 revoked with savings. Territorial extent & classification: S. General. - Revoked by S.I. 2009/42 (ISBN 9780111002629) with savings. - 8p.: 30 cm. - 978-0-11-081549-7 £3.00

The Non-Domestic Rating (Rural Areas and Rateable Value Limits) (Scotland) Amendment Order 2008 No. 2008/370. - Enabling power: Local Government and Rating Act 1997, sch., 2, para. 1 (3) (c). - Issued: 18.11.2008. Made: 05.11.2008. Laid before the Scottish Parliament: 12.11.2008. Coming into force: 01.04.2009. Effect: S.S.I. 2005/103 amended & S.S.I. 2007/36 revoked. Territorial extent & classification: S. General. - 8p.: 30 cm. - 978-0-11-100074-8 £5.00

The Non-Domestic Rating (Rural Areas and Rateable Value Limits) (Scotland) Amendment Order 2009 Amendment Order 2008 No. 2008/371. - Enabling power: Local Government and Rating Act 1997, sch., 2, para. 1 (3) (c). - Issued: 18.11.2008. Made: 12.11.2008. Laid before the Scottish Parliament: 13.11.2008. Coming into force: 12.12.2008. Effect: S.S.I. 2008/370 amended. Territorial extent & classification: S. General. - This Scottish Statutory Instrument has been made in consequence of a defect in S.S.I. 2008/370 and is being issued free of charge to all known recipients of that instrument. - 2p.: 30 cm. - 978-0-11-100075-5 £4.00

The Non-Domestic Rating (Telecommunications and Canals) (Scotland) Amendment Order 2008 No. 2008/84. - Enabling power: Valuation and Rating (Scotland) Act 1956, s. 6A. - Issued: 10.03.2008. Made: 04.03.2008. Laid before the Scottish Parliament: 05.03.2008. Coming into force: 31.03.2008. Effect: S.I. 1995/239 amended. Territorial extent & classification: S. General. - 2p.: 30 cm. - 978-0-11-081548-0 £3.00

The Non-Domestic Rating (Unoccupied Property) (Scotland) Amendment Regulations 2008 No. 2008/83. - Enabling power: Local Government (Scotland) Act 1966, ss. 24 (2), 24A (4). - Issued: 10.03.2008. Made: 04.03.2008. Laid before the Scottish Parliament: 05.03.2008. Coming into force: 01.04.2008. Effect: S.I. 1994/3200 amended. Territorial extent & classification: S. General. - 4p.: 30 cm. - 978-0-11-081547-3 £3.00

The Valuation and Rating (Exempted Classes) (Scotland) Order 2008 No. 2008/80. - Enabling power: Valuation and Rating (Exempted Classes) (Scotland) Act 1976, s.1. - Issued: 10.03.2008. Made: 04.03.2008. Coming into force: 01.04.2008. Effect: None. Territorial extent & classification: S. General. - Supersedes draft (ISBN 9780110802114) issued 18.01.2008. - 4p.: 30 cm. - 978-0-11-081544-2 £3.00

The Valuation for Rating (Plant and Machinery) (Scotland) Amendment Regulations 2008 No. 2008/360. - Enabling power: Lands Valuation (Scotland) Act 1854, s. 42. - Issued: 11.11.2008. Made: 05.11.2008. Laid: 06.11.2008. Coming into force: 01.01.2009. Effect: S.S.I. 2000/58 amended. Territorial extent & classification: S. General. - 4p.: 30 cm. - 978-0-11-100062-5 £4.00

Registration of births, deaths, marriages, etc.

The Book of Scottish Connections Regulations 2008 No. 2008/386. - Enabling power: Local Electoral Administration and Registration Services (Scotland) Act 2006, ss. 54 (6) (b) (c), 55 (2) (6) (9), 61 (2)(a). - Issued: 01.12.2008. Made: 24.11.2008. Laid before the Scottish Parliament: 25.11.2008. Coming into force: 05.01.2009. Effect: None. Territorial extent & classification: S. General. - 24p.: 30 cm. - 978-0-11-100087-8 £5.00

The Local Electoral Administration and Registration Services (Scotland) Act 2006 (Commencement No. 4) Order 2008 No. 2008/405 (C.31). - Enabling power: Local Electoral Administration and Registration Services (Scotland) Act 2006, s. 63 (2). Bringing into operation various provisions of the 2006 Act on 05.01.2009. - Issued: 12.12.2008. Made: 04.12.2008. Effect: None. Territorial extent & classification: S. General. - 2p.: 30 cm. - 978-0-11-100122-6 £4.00

The National Health Service Central Register (Scotland) Amendment Regulations 2008 No. 2008/358. - Enabling power: Local Electoral Administration and Registration Services (Scotland) Act 2006, s. 57 (3) (i) (4) (6). - Issued: 10.11.2008. Made: 04.11.2008. Laid before the Scottish Parliament: 05.11.2008. Coming into force: 01.12.2008. Effect: S.S.I. 2006/484 amended. Territorial extent & classification: S. General. - 4p.: 30 cm. - 978-0-11-100059-5 £4.00

River: Salmon and freshwater fisheries

The Annual Close Time (Permitted Periods of Fishing) (River Dee (Aberdeenshire) Salmon Fishery District) Order 2008 No. 2008/19. - Enabling power: Salmon and Freshwater Fisheries (Consolidation) (Scotland) Act 2003, s. 37 (3). - Issued: 01.02.2008. Made: 24.01.2008. Coming into force: 01.02.2008 (and ceases to have effect on 16 October 2011). Effect: None. Territorial extent & classification: S. General. - 4p.: 30 cm. - 978-0-11-080234-3 £3.00

The Freshwater Fish Conservation (Prohibition on Fishing for Eels) (Scotland) Regulations 2008 No. 2008/419. - Enabling power: Salmon and Freshwater Fisheries (Consolidation) (Scotland) Act 2003, s. 51A. - Issued: 23.12.2008. Made: 15.12.2008. Laid before the Scottish Parliament: 18.12.2008. Coming into force: 26.01.2009. Effect: None. Territorial extent & classification: S. General. - EC note: These Regulations are made in implementation of Council Regulation (EC) No. 1100/2007 establishing measures for the recovery of the stock of European eel (Anguilla Anguilla). - 2p.: 30 cm. - 978-0-11-100144-8 £4.00

The Registration of Fish Farming and Shellfish Farming Businesses Amendment (Scotland) Order 2008 No. 2008/222. - Enabling power: Diseases of Fish Act 1983, s. 7 (1) (2) (3). - Issued: 10.06.2008. Made: 04.06.2008. Laid before the Scottish Parliament: 05.06.2008. Coming into force: 27.06.2008. Effect: S.I. 1985/1391 amended. Territorial extent & classification: S. General. - 8p.: 30 cm. - 978-0-11-081685-2 £3.00

Roads and bridges

The A9 Trunk Road (Bankfoot Junction Improvement) (Side Roads) Order 2008 No. 2008/337. - Enabling power: Roads (Scotland) Act 1984, ss. 12 (1) (5), 70 (1), 145. - Made: 06.10.2008. Coming into force: 17.10.2008. Effect: S.S.I. 2003/186 revoked. Territorial extent & classification: S. Local *Unpublished*

The A9 Trunk Road (Bankfoot Junction Improvement) (Slip Roads) Order 2008 No. 2008/338. - Enabling power: Roads (Scotland) Act 1984, s. 5 (2). - Made: 06.10.2008. Coming into force: 17.10.2008. Effect: None. Territorial extent & classification: S. Local *Unpublished*

The A76 Trunk Road (Newbridge Drive, Dumfries to Newbridge Village) (Redetermination of Means of Exercise of Public Right of Passage) Order 2008 No. 2008/211. - Enabling power: Roads (Scotland) Act 1984, ss. 2 (1), 152 (2). - Made: 30.05.2008. Coming into force: 06.06.2008. Effect: None. Territorial extent & classification: S. Local *Unpublished*

The A77 Trunk Road (Park End to Bennane Improvement) (Side Roads) Order 2008 No. 2008/231. - Enabling power: Roads (Scotland) Act 1984, ss. 12 (1) (5), 70 (1). - Made: 03.06.2008. Coming into force: 10.06.2008. Effect: None. Territorial extent & classification: S. Local *Unpublished*

The A835 Trunk Road (Tore to Maryburgh Cycle Track) (Redetermination of Means of Exercise of Public Right of Passage) Order 2008 No. 2008/145. - Enabling power: Roads (Scotland) Act 1984, ss. 2 (1), 152 (2). - Made: 02.04.2008. Coming into force: 15.04.2008. Effect: None. Territorial extent & classification: S. Local *Unpublished*

The Abolition of Bridge Tolls (Scotland) Act 2008 (Commencement) Order 2008 No. 2008/22 (C.3). - Enabling power: Abolition of Bridge Tolls (Scotland) Act 2008, s. 4 (2). Bringing various provisions of the 2008 Act into operation on 11.02.2008. - Issued: 05.02.2008. Made: 30.01.2008. Effect: None. Territorial extent & classification: S. General. - 2p.: 30 cm. - 978-0-11-080239-8 £3.00

The Roads (Scotland) Act 1984 (Fixed Penalty) Regulations 2008 No. 2008/243. - Enabling power: Roads (Scotland) Act 1984, sch. 8B, paras 2, 4 (1), 5 (2), 12 (2), 13 (b) (c) & New Roads and Street Works Act 1991, s. 156. - Issued: 17.06.2008. Made: 11.06.2008. Laid before the Scottish Parliament: 12.06.2008. Coming into force: 01.10.2008. Effect: 1984 c. 54 modified. Territorial extent & classification: S. General. - 8p.: 30 cm. - 978-0-11-082034-7 £3.00

The Road Works (Fixed Penalty) (Scotland) Regulations 2008 No. 2008/244. - Enabling power: New Roads and Street Works Act 1991, ss. 108 (5), 156 (1) (2), sch. 6B, paras 2, 4 (1), 5 (2), 12 (2), 13 (2) (3). - Issued: 17.06.2008. Made: 11.06.2008. Laid before the Scottish Parliament: 12.06.2008. Coming into force: 01.10.2008. Effect: 1991 c. 22 modified. Territorial extent & classification: S. General. - 8p.: 30 cm. - 978-0-11-082035-4 £3.00

The Road Works (Inspection Fees) (Scotland) Amendment Regulations 2008 No. 2008/43. - Enabling power: New Roads and Street Works Act 1991, s. 134. - Issued: 25.02.2008. Made: 19.02.2008. Laid before the Scottish Parliament: 20.02.2008. Coming into force: 01.04.2008. Effect: S.S.I. 2003/415 amended & S.S.I. 2007/4 revoked. Territorial extent & classification: S. General. - Revoked by S.S.I. 2009/74 (ISBN 9780111003244). - 4p.: 30 cm. - 978-0-11-081508-4 £3.00

The Road Works (Scottish Road Works Register, Notices, Directions and Designations) (Scotland) Regulations 2008 No. 2008/88. - Enabling power: New Roads and Street Works Act 1991, ss. 108 (5), 112A (2), 112B, 113 (1) (2) (3A), 114 (1) (2) (3A) (7), 115 (2), 115A (4), 116 (3A), 117 (1) (5), 121 (1), 122 (2), 123 (1) (2), 129 (5A), 131 (3) (3A), 149 (2) (2A), 156 (1) (2), 163 (1) (3). - Issued: 12.03.2008. Made: 05.03.2008. Laid before the Scottish Parliament: 06.03.2008. Coming into force: 01.04.2008. Effect: S.I. 1992/2991; 1997/1505; 1998/2254 revoked. Territorial extent & classification: S. General. - 20p.: 30 cm. - 978-0-11-081551-0 £3.50

The Road Works (Settlement of Disputes and Appeals against Directions) (Scotland) Regulations 2008 No. 2008/89. - Enabling power: New Roads and Street Works Act 1991, ss. 115 (2A), 115A (5), 117 (7), 120 (6), 121 (5), 133 (2), 143 (3), 155 (3), 157A, 163 (1), sch. 6, paras 2 (1), 12 (2) & Transport (Scotland) Act 2005, s. 18 (3). - Issued: 11.03.2008. Made: 05.03.2008. Laid before the Scottish Parliament: 06.03.2008. Coming into force: 01.04.2008. Effect: None. Territorial extent & classification: S. General. - 4p.: 30 cm. - 978-0-11-081552-7 £3.00

The Scottish Road Works Register (Prescribed Fees and Amounts) Regulations 2008 No. 2008/16. - Enabling power: New Roads and Street Works Act 1991, ss. 112A (4), 163 (1). - Issued: 28.01.2008. Made: 22.01.2008. Laid before the Scottish Parliament: 23.01.2008. Coming into force: 29.02.2008. Effect: None. Territorial extent & classification: S. General. - Partially revoked by S.S.I. 2009/26 (ISBN 9780111002209). - 8p.: 30 cm. - 978-0-11-080229-9 £3.00

Road traffic

The Local Authorities' Traffic Orders (Procedure) (Scotland) Amendment Regulations 2008 No. 2008/3. - Enabling power: Road Traffic Regulation Act 1984, s. 124, sch. 9, Part III. - Issued: 15.01.2008. Made: 07.01.2008. Laid before the Scottish Parliament: 10.01.2008. Coming into force: 08.02.2008. Effect: S.I. 1999/614 amended. Territorial extent & classification: S. General. - 4p.: 30 cm. - 978-0-11-080206-0 £3.00

The School Crossing Patrol Sign (Scotland) Regulations 2008 No. 2008/4. - Enabling power: Road Traffic Regulation Act 1984, s. 28 (4). - Issued: 15.01.2008. Made: 07.01.2008. Laid before the Scottish Parliament: 10.01.2008. Coming into force: 08.02.2008 except for reg. 2; 01.01.2011 for reg. 2. Effect: S.S.I. 2002/549 revoked. Territorial extent & classification: S. General. - 8p., col. ill: 30 cm. - 978-0-11-080207-7 £9.35

Road traffic: Speed limits

The A68 Trunk Road (Dalkeith) (30 mph Speed Limit and St David's Primary School part-time 20 mph Speed Limit) Order 2008 No. 2008/367. - Enabling power: Road Traffic Regulation Act 1984, ss. 82 (2) (a), 83 (1), 84 (1) (a) (c), 124 (1) (d). - Made: 07.11.2008. Coming into force: 14.11.2008. Effect: S.S.I. 2004/540; 2006/563 revoked. Territorial extent & classification: S. Local *Unpublished*

The A68 Trunk Road (Pathhead) (30mph Speed Limit) Order 2008 No. 2008/364. - Enabling power: Road Traffic Regulation Act 1984, ss. 84 (1) (a), 124 (1) (d). - Made: 06.11.2008. Coming into force: 17.11.2008. Effect: S.S.I. 1992/2747; 2006/258 revoked. Territorial extent & classification: S. Local *Unpublished*

The A77 Trunk Road (Bogend to Dutchhouse) (50 mph Speed Limit) Order 2008 No. 2008/67. - Enabling power: Road Traffic Regulation Act 1984, s. 84 (1). - Made: 25.02.2008. Coming into force: 10.03.2008. Effect: None. Territorial extent & classification: S. Local *Unpublished*

The A82 Trunk Road (Ballachulish) (50mph Speed Limit) Order 2008 No. 2008/398. - Enabling power: Road Traffic Regulation Act 1984, s. 84 (1) (a). - Made: 25.02.2008. Coming into force: 10.03.2008. Effect: None. Territorial extent & classification: S. Local *Unpublished*

The A82 Trunk Road (Glencoe Village) (40 mph Speed Limit) Order 2008 No. 2008/169. - Enabling power: Road Traffic Regulation Act 1984, s. 84 (1) (a). - Made: 25.04.2008. Coming into force: 03.05.2008. Effect: None. Territorial extent & classification: S. Local *Unpublished*

The A84/A85 Trunk Road (Strathyre) (30mph and 40mph Speed Limits) Order 2008 No. 2008/280. - Enabling power: Road Traffic Regulation Act 1984, ss. 84 (1) (a), 124 (1) (d). - Made: 13.08.2008. Coming into force: 21.08.2008. Effect: S.I. 1975/440 varied & S.I. 1981/1680; 1995/1270 revoked. Territorial extent & classification: S. Local *Unpublished*

The A85 Trunk Road (Dalmally) (40mph Speed Limit) Order 2008 No. 2008/407. - Enabling power: Road Traffic Regulation Act 1984, s. 84 (1) (a). - Made: 04.12.2008. Coming into force: 15.12.2008. Effect: S.I. 1995/1346 revoked. Territorial extent & classification: S. Local *Unpublished*

The A977 Trunk Road (Kincardine) (30mph and 40mph Speed Limits) Order 2008 No. 2008/250. - Enabling power: Road Traffic Regulation Act 1984, s. 84 (1) (a). - Made: 13.06.2008. Coming into force: 27.06.2008. Effect: None. Territorial extent & classification: S. Local *Unpublished*

Road traffic: Traffic regulation

The A7 Trunk Road (Auchenrivock Improvement) (Temporary Prohibition of Traffic, Temporary Prohibition of Overtaking and Temporary Speed Restriction) Order 2008 No. 2008/421. - Enabling power: Road Traffic Regulation Act 1984, ss. 14 (1) (4), 2 (1) (2), 4 (1). - Made: 05.12.2008. Coming into force: 20.12.2008. Effect: None. Territorial extent & classification: S. Local *Unpublished*

The A9 Trunk Road (Aberuthven to Loaninghead) (Temporary Prohibition of Specified Turns) Order 2008 No. 2008/252. - Enabling power: Road Traffic Regulation Act 1984, s. 14 (1) (a). - Made: 13.06.2008. Coming into force: 30.06.2008. Effect: None. Territorial extent & classification: S. Local *Unpublished*

The A9 Trunk Road (Scrabster) (Prohibition of Waiting) Order 2008 No. 2008/91. - Enabling power: Road Traffic Regulation Act 1984, ss. 1 (1), 124 (1) (d). - Made: 20.02.2008. Coming into force: 10.03.2008. Effect: S.I. 1982/646 revoked. Territorial extent & classification: S. Local *Unpublished*

The A68 Trunk Road (Dalkeith Northern Bypass) (Temporary Prohibition of Traffic, Temporary Prohibition of Overtaking and Temporary Speed Restriction) (No. 2) Order 2008 No. 2008/340. - Enabling power: Road Traffic Regulation Act 1984, ss. 14 (1) (4), 2 (1) (2), 4 (1). - Made: 07.10.2008. Coming into force: 16.10.2008. Effect: None. Territorial extent & classification: S. Local *Unpublished*

The A68 Trunk Road (Dalkeith Northern Bypass) (Temporary Prohibition of Traffic, Temporary Prohibition of Overtaking and Temporary Speed Restriction) Order 2008 No. 2008/323. - Enabling power: Road Traffic Regulation Act 1984, ss. 14 (1) (4), 2 (1) (2), 4 (1). - Made: 22.09.2008. Coming into force: 29.09.2008. Effect: None. Territorial extent & classification: S. Local *Unpublished*

The A68 Trunk Road (Station Bar, Jedburgh) (Temporary Width Restriction of Traffic) Order 2008 No. 2008/354. - Enabling power: Road Traffic Regulation Act 1984, ss. 14 (1) (4), 2 (1) (2), 4 (1). - Made: 30.10.2008. Coming into force: 08.11.2008. Effect: None. Territorial extent & classification: S. Local *Unpublished*

The A76 Trunk Road (Glenairlie Improvement) (Temporary Prohibition of Traffic, Temporary Prohibition of Overtaking and Temporary Speed Restriction) Order 2008 No. 2008/408. - Enabling power: Road Traffic Regulation Act 1984, ss. 14 (1) (4), 2 (1) (2), 4 (1). - Made: 26.11.2008. Coming into force: 04.12.2008. Effect: None. Territorial extent & classification: S. Local *Unpublished*

The A77 Trunk Road (Dalrymple Street, Girvan) (Special Event) (Temporary Prohibition of Traffic) Order 2008 No. 2008/392. - Enabling power: Road Traffic Regulation Act 1984, s. 16A. - Made: 24.11.2008. Coming into force: 28.11.2008. Effect: None. Territorial extent & classification: S. Local *Unpublished*

The A82 Trunk Road (Invermoriston to Fort Augustus, Portclair) (Temporary Prohibition of Traffic, Temporary Prohibition of Overtaking and Temporary Speed Restriction) Order 2008 No. 2008/353. - Enabling power: Road Traffic Regulation Act 1984, ss. 14 (1) (4), 2 (1) (2) (3), 4 (1). - Made: 30.10.2008. Coming into force: 10.11.2008. Effect: None. Territorial extent & classification: S. Local *Unpublished*

The A82 Trunk Road (Scottish Open Golf Tournament, Loch Lommond) (Special Event) (Temporary Restriction of Speed) Order 2008 No. 2008/271. - Enabling power: Road Traffic Regulation Act 1984, s. 88 (1) (a) (2). - Made: 01.07.2008. Coming into force: 09.07.2008. Effect: None. Territorial extent & classification: S. Local *Unpublished*

The A90 Trunk Road (B957 Tannadice Junction) (Temporary Prohibition of Specified Turns) Order 2008 No. 2008/281. - Enabling power: Road Traffic Regulation Act 1984, s. 14 (1) (a). - Made: 14.08.2008. Coming into force: 28.08.2008. Effect: None. Territorial extent & classification: S. Local *Unpublished*

The A90 Trunk Road (Glendoick) (Temporary Prohibition of Specified Turns) Order 2008 No. 2008/242. - Enabling power: Road Traffic Regulation Act 1984, s. 14 (1) (a). - Made: 06.06.2008. Coming into force: 23.06.2008. Effect: None. Territorial extent & classification: S. Local *Unpublished*

The A90 Trunk Road (North Anderson Drive, Aberdeen) (Prohibition of Specified Turns) Order 2008 No. 2008/341. - Enabling power: Road Traffic Regulation Act 1984, s. 1 (1), 2 (1) (2). - Made: 10.10.2008. Coming into force: 24.10.2008. Effect: None. Territorial extent & classification: S. Local *Unpublished*

The A90 Trunk Road (Oatyhill) (Temporary Prohibition of Specified Turns) Order 2008 No. 2008/113. - Enabling power: Road Traffic Regulation Act 1984, s. 14 (1) (a). - Made: 06.03.2008. Coming into force: 22.03.2008. Effect: None. Territorial extent & classification: S. Local *Unpublished*

The A92/A972 Trunk Road (Cadham Road and Car Wash Facility) (Prohibition of Specified Turns) Order 2008 No. 2008/18. - Enabling power: Road Traffic Regulation Act 1984, s. 1 (1). - Made: 18.01.2008. Coming into force: 01.02.2008. Effect: None. Territorial extent & classification: S. Local *Unpublished*

The A92/A972 Trunk Road (Kingsway East, Dundee) (Temporary Prohibition of Specified Turns) Order 2008 No. 2008/183. - Enabling power: Road Traffic Regulation Act 1984, s. 14 (1) (a). - Made: 09.05.2008. Coming into force: 19.05.2008. Effect: None. Territorial extent & classification: S. Local *Unpublished*

The A92/A972 Trunk Road (Scott Fyffe Roundabout, Dundee to Pitkerro Roundabout, Dundee) (Temporary Prohibition of Specified Turns) Order 2008 No. 2008/272. - Enabling power: Road Traffic Regulation Act 1984, s. 14 (1) (a). - Made: 18.07.2008. Coming into force: 01.08.2008. Effect: None. Territorial extent & classification: S. Local *Unpublished*

The A92 Trunk Road (B969 Western Avenue Junction, Glenrothes) (Temporary Prohibition of Specified Turns) Order 2008 No. 2008/134. - Enabling power: Road Traffic Regulation Act 1984, s. 14 (1) (a). - Made: 25.03.2008. Coming into force: 05.04.2008. Effect: None. Territorial extent & classification: S. Local *Unpublished*

The A96 Trunk Road (Church Road, Keith) (Special Event) (Temporary Prohibition of Traffic) Order 2008 No. 2008/347. - Enabling power: Road Traffic Regulation Act 1984, s. 16A. - Made: 22.10.2008. Coming into force: 09.11.2008. Effect: None. Territorial extent & classification: S. Local *Unpublished*

The A96 Trunk Road (Moss Street, Keith) (Prohibition of Waiting and Loading) Order 2008 No. 2008/373. - Enabling power: Road Traffic Regulation Act 1984, ss. 1, 2 (1) (2). - Made: 11.11.2008. Coming into force: 21.11.2008. Effect: None. Territorial extent & classification: S. Local *Unpublished*

The A96 Trunk Road (Moss Street, Keith) (Temporary Prohibition of Specified Turns) Order 2008 No. 2008/274. - Enabling power: Road Traffic Regulation Act 1984, s. 14 (1) (a). - Made: 18.07.2008. Coming into force: 01.08.2008. Effect: None. Territorial extent & classification: S. Local *Unpublished*

The A96 Trunk Road (West Road, Elgin) (Prohibition of Waiting) Order 2008 No. 2008/114. - Enabling power: Road Traffic Regulation Act 1984, ss. 1 (1), 2 (2). - Made: 07.03.2008. Coming into force: 21.03.2008. Effect: S.I. 1982/646 revoked. Territorial extent & classification: S. Local *Unpublished*

The A702 Trunk Road (Biggar High Street, Biggar) (Special Event) (Temporary Prohibition of Traffic) Order 2008 No. 2008/420. - Enabling power: Road Traffic Regulation Act 1984, ss. 16A. - Made: 11.12.2008. Coming into force: 30.12.2008. Effect: None. Territorial extent & classification: S. Local *Unpublished*

The A720 Trunk Road (Edinburgh City Bypass) (Temporary Prohibition of Traffic, Temporary Prohibition of Overtaking and Temporary Speed Restriction) Order 2008 No. 2008/167. - Enabling power: Road Traffic Regulation Act 1984, s. 14 (1) (4), 2 (1) (2), 4 (1). - Made: 17.04.2008. Coming into force: 24.04.2008. Effect: None. Territorial extent & classification: S. Local *Unpublished*

The A737/A738 Trunk Road (Howgate, Kilwinning to Cockenzie Road, Dalvargen) (Temporary Width and Wieght Restriction of Traffic) Order 2008 No. 2008/270. - Enabling power: Road Traffic Regulation Act 1984, ss. 14 (1) (4), 2 (1) (2), 4 (1). - Made: 27.06.2008. Coming into force: 07.07.2008. Effect: None. Territorial extent & classification: S. Local *Unpublished*

The A737/A738 Trunk Road (Park Lane, Old Woodwynd Road, The Meadows, Claremont Crescent, Kilwinning) (Temporary Prohibition of Specified Turns) Order 2008 No. 2008/249. - Enabling power: Road Traffic Regulation Act 1984, s. 14 (1) (a). - Made: 12.06.2008. Coming into force: 26.06.2008. Effect: None. Territorial extent & classification: S. Local *Unpublished*

The A830 Trunk Road (Arisaig to Loch nan Uamh Improvement) (Temporary Prohibition of Traffic, Temporary Prohibition of Overtaking and Temporary Speed Restriction) Order 2008 No. 2008/381. - Enabling power: Road Traffic Regulation Act 1984, ss. 14 (1) (4), 2 (1) (2), 4 (1). - Made: 18.11.2008. Coming into force: 21.06.2008. Effect: None. Territorial extent & classification: S. Local *Unpublished*

The M8 Motorway (Junction 21, Paisley Road) (Temporary Prohibition of Traffic) Order 2008 No. 2008/441. - Enabling power: Road Traffic Regulation Act 1984, s. 14 (1) (a) (4), 2 (1) (2), 4 (1). - Made: 30.12.2008. Coming into force: 12.01.2009. Effect: None. Territorial extent & classification: S. Local *Unpublished*

The M9/A9 Trunk Road (Olrig Street, Traill Street & Sir George's Street, Thurso) (Prohibition of Waiting and Loading) Order 2008 No. 2008/301. - Enabling power: Road Traffic Regulation Act 1984, ss. 1 (1), 2 (1) (2), 124 (1) (d). - Made: 14.05.2008. Coming into force: 24.05.2008. Effect: S.I. 1974/1818; 1992/2411 revoked. Territorial extent & classification: S. Local *Unpublished*

The M9/A9 Trunk Road (Scrabster) (Prohibition of Waiting) Order 2008 No. 2008/409. - Enabling power: Road Traffic Regulation Act 1984, s. 1 (1). - Made: 05.12.2008. Coming into force: 19.12.2008. Effect: None. Territorial extent & classification: S. Local *Unpublished*

The M9/A9 Trunk Road (Temporary Width Restriction of Traffic) Order 2008 No. 2008/95. - Enabling power: Road Traffic Regulation Act 1984, ss. 14 (1) (4), 2 (1), 4 (1). - Made: 29.02.2008. Coming into force: 07.03.2008. Effect: None. Territorial extent & classification: S. Local *Unpublished*

The M77/A77 Trunk Road (Bellfield to Dutchhouse) (Temporary Prohibition of Specified Turns) Order 2008 No. 2008/146. - Enabling power: Road Traffic Regulation Act 1984, s. 14 (1) (a). - Made: 002.04.2008. Coming into force: 16.04.2008. Effect: None. Territorial extent & classification: S. Local *Unpublished*

The M77/A77 Trunk Road (Bogend Toll) (Temporary Prohibition of Specified Turns) Order 2008 No. 2008/254. - Enabling power: Road Traffic Regulation Act 1984, s. 14 (1) (a). - Made: 10.06.2008. Coming into force: 23.06.2008. Effect: None. Territorial extent & classification: S. Local *Unpublished*

The M80/A80 Trunk Road (Temporary Width Restriction of Traffic) Order 2008 No. 2008/73. - Enabling power: Road Traffic Regulation Act 1984, s. 14 (1) (4), 2 (1) (2), 4 (1). - Made: 01.02.2008. Coming into force: 07.02.2008. Effect: None. Territorial extent & classification: S. Local *Unpublished*

The M90/A90 Trunk Road (Bruntland Road Junction, Portlethen) (Temporary Prohibition of Specified Turns) Order 2008 No. 2008/273. - Enabling power: Road Traffic Regulation Act 1984, s. 14 (1) (a). - Made: 18.07.2008. Coming into force: 03.08.2008. Effect: None. Territorial extent & classification: S. Local *Unpublished*

The M90/A90 Trunk Road (Powrie Brae) (Temporary Prohibition of Specified Turns) Order 2008 No. 2008/351. - Enabling power: Road Traffic Regulation Act 1984, s. 14 (1) (a). - Made: 23.10.2008. Coming into force: 10.11.2008. Effect: None. Territorial extent & classification: S. Local *Unpublished*

The M90 Trunk Road (Gairneybridge to Milnathort) (Temporary 50mph Speed Limit) Order 2008 No. 2008/267. - Enabling power: Road Traffic Regulation Act 1984, s. 14 (1). - Made: 23.06.2008. Coming into force: 09.07.2008. Effect: None. Territorial extent & classification: S. Local *Unpublished*

The North East Unit Trunk Roads Area (Temporary Prohibitions of Traffic, Temporary Prohibitions of Overtaking and Temporary Speed Restrictions) (No. 2) Order 2008 No. 2008/68. - Enabling power: Road Traffic Regulation Act 1984, s. 14 (1) (4), 2 (1) (2), 4 (1). - Made: 28.02.2008. Coming into force: 01.03.2008. Effect: None. Territorial extent & classification: S. Local *Unpublished*

The North East Unit Trunk Roads Area (Temporary Prohibitions of Traffic, Temporary Prohibitions of Overtaking and Temporary Speed Restrictions) (No. 3) Order 2008 No. 2008/142. - Enabling power: Road Traffic Regulation Act 1984, s. 14 (1) (4), 2 (1) (2), 4 (1). - Made: 20.03.2008. Coming into force: 01.04.2008. Effect: None. Territorial extent & classification: S. Local *Unpublished*

The North East Unit Trunk Roads Area (Temporary Prohibitions of Traffic, Temporary Prohibitions of Overtaking and Temporary Speed Restrictions) (No. 4) Order 2008 No. 2008/174. - Enabling power: Road Traffic Regulation Act 1984, s. 14 (1) (4), 2 (1) (2), 4 (1). - Made: 18.04.2008. Coming into force: 01.05.2008. Effect: None. Territorial extent & classification: S. Local *Unpublished*

The North East Unit Trunk Roads Area (Temporary Prohibitions of Traffic, Temporary Prohibitions of Overtaking and Temporary Speed Restrictions) (No. 5) Order 2008 No. 2008/210. - Enabling power: Road Traffic Regulation Act 1984, s. 14 (1) (4), 2 (1) (2), 4 (1). - Made: 20.05.2008. Coming into force: 01.06.2008. Effect: None. Territorial extent & classification: S. Local *Unpublished*

The North East Unit Trunk Roads Area (Temporary Prohibitions of Traffic, Temporary Prohibitions of Overtaking and Temporary Speed Restrictions) (No. 6) Order 2008 No. 2008/258. - Enabling power: Road Traffic Regulation Act 1984, s. 14 (1) (4), 2 (1) (2), 4 (1). - Made: 19.06.2008. Coming into force: 01.07.2008. Effect: None. Territorial extent & classification: S. Local *Unpublished*

The North East Unit Trunk Roads Area (Temporary Prohibitions of Traffic, Temporary Prohibitions of Overtaking and Temporary Speed Restrictions) (No. 7) Order 2008 No. 2008/279. - Enabling power: Road Traffic Regulation Act 1984, s. 14 (1) (4), 2 (1) (2), 4 (1). - Made: 22.07.2008. Coming into force: 01.08.2008. Effect: None. Territorial extent & classification: S. Local *Unpublished*

The North East Unit Trunk Roads Area (Temporary Prohibitions of Traffic, Temporary Prohibitions of Overtaking and Temporary Speed Restrictions) (No. 8) Order 2008 No. 2008/287. - Enabling power: Road Traffic Regulation Act 1984, s. 14 (1) (4), 2 (1) (2), 4 (1). - Made: 20.08.2008. Coming into force: 01.09.2008. Effect: None. Territorial extent & classification: S. Local *Unpublished*

The North East Unit Trunk Roads Area (Temporary Prohibitions of Traffic, Temporary Prohibitions of Overtaking and Temporary Speed Restrictions) (No. 9) Order 2008 No. 2008/320. - Enabling power: Road Traffic Regulation Act 1984, s. 14 (1) (4), 2 (1) (2), 4 (1). - Made: 19.09.2008. Coming into force: 01.10.2008. Effect: None. Territorial extent & classification: S. Local *Unpublished*

The North East Unit Trunk Roads Area (Temporary Prohibitions of Traffic, Temporary Prohibitions of Overtaking and Temporary Speed Restrictions) (No. 10) Order 2008 No. 2008/343. - Enabling power: Road Traffic Regulation Act 1984, s. 14 (1) (4), 2 (1) (2), 4 (1). - Made: 22.10.2008. Coming into force: 01.11.2008. Effect: None. Territorial extent & classification: S. Local *Unpublished*

The North East Unit Trunk Roads Area (Temporary Prohibitions of Traffic, Temporary Prohibitions of Overtaking and Temporary Speed Restrictions) (No. 11) Order 2008 No. 2008/385. - Enabling power: Road Traffic Regulation Act 1984, s. 14 (1) (4), 2 (1) (2), 4 (1). - Made: 19.11.2008. Coming into force: 01.12.2008. Effect: None. Territorial extent & classification: S. Local *Unpublished*

The North East Unit Trunk Roads Area (Temporary Prohibitions of Traffic, Temporary Prohibitions of Overtaking and Temporary Speed Restrictions) (No. 12) Order 2008 No. 2008/437. - Enabling power: Road Traffic Regulation Act 1984, ss. 14 (1) (4), 2 (1) (2), 4 (1). - Made: 19.12.2008. Coming into force: 01.01.2009. Effect: None. Territorial extent & classification: S. Local *Unpublished*

The North East Unit Trunk Roads Area (Temporary Prohibitions of Traffic, Temporary Prohibitions of Overtaking and Temporary Speed Restrictions) Order 2008 No. 2008/26. - Enabling power: Road Traffic Regulation Act 1984, s. 14 (1) (4), 2 (1) (2), 4 (1). - Made: 30.01.2008. Coming into force: 01.02.2008. Effect: None. Territorial extent & classification: S. Local *Unpublished*

The North West Unit Trunk Roads Area (Temporary Prohibitions of Traffic, Temporary Prohibitions of Overtaking and Temporary Speed Restrictions) (No. 2) Order 2008 No. 2008/69. - Enabling power: Road Traffic Regulation Act 1984, s. 14 (1) (4), 2 (1) (2), 4 (1). - Made: 28.02.2008. Coming into force: 01.03.2008. Effect: None. Territorial extent & classification: S. Local *Unpublished*

The North West Unit Trunk Roads Area (Temporary Prohibitions of Traffic, Temporary Prohibitions of Overtaking and Temporary Speed Restrictions) (No. 3) Order 2008 No. 2008/141. - Enabling power: Road Traffic Regulation Act 1984, s. 14 (1) (4), 2 (1) (2), 4 (1). - Made: 20.03.2008. Coming into force: 01.04.2008. Effect: None. Territorial extent & classification: S. Local *Unpublished*

The North West Unit Trunk Roads Area (Temporary Prohibitions of Traffic, Temporary Prohibitions of Overtaking and Temporary Speed Restrictions) (No. 4) Order 2008 No. 2008/175. - Enabling power: Road Traffic Regulation Act 1984, s. 14 (1) (4), 2 (1) (2), 4 (1). - Made: 18.04.2008. Coming into force: 01.05.2008. Effect: None. Territorial extent & classification: S. Local *Unpublished*

The North West Unit Trunk Roads Area (Temporary Prohibitions of Traffic, Temporary Prohibitions of Overtaking and Temporary Speed Restrictions) (No. 5) Order 2008 No. 2008/209. - Enabling power: Road Traffic Regulation Act 1984, s. 14 (1) (4), 2 (1) (2), 4 (1). - Made: 20.05.2008. Coming into force: 01.06.2008. Effect: None. Territorial extent & classification: S. Local *Unpublished*

The North West Unit Trunk Roads Area (Temporary Prohibitions of Traffic, Temporary Prohibitions of Overtaking and Temporary Speed Restrictions) (No. 6) Order 2008 No. 2008/257. - Enabling power: Road Traffic Regulation Act 1984, s. 14 (1) (4), 2 (1) (2), 4 (1). - Made: 19.06.2008. Coming into force: 01.07.2008. Effect: None. Territorial extent & classification: S. Local *Unpublished*

The North West Unit Trunk Roads Area (Temporary Prohibitions of Traffic, Temporary Prohibitions of Overtaking and Temporary Speed Restrictions) (No. 7) Order 2008 No. 2008/277. - Enabling power: Road Traffic Regulation Act 1984, s. 14 (1) (4), 2 (1) (2), 4 (1). - Made: 22.07.2008. Coming into force: 01.08.2008. Effect: None. Territorial extent & classification: S. Local *Unpublished*

The North West Unit Trunk Roads Area (Temporary Prohibitions of Traffic, Temporary Prohibitions of Overtaking and Temporary Speed Restrictions) (No. 8) Order 2008 No. 2008/286. - Enabling power: Road Traffic Regulation Act 1984, s. 14 (1) (4), 2 (1) (2), 4 (1). - Made: 20.08.2008. Coming into force: 01.09.2008. Effect: None. Territorial extent & classification: S. Local *Unpublished*

The North West Unit Trunk Roads Area (Temporary Prohibitions of Traffic, Temporary Prohibitions of Overtaking and Temporary Speed Restrictions) (No. 9) Order 2008 No. 2008/321. - Enabling power: Road Traffic Regulation Act 1984, s. 14 (1) (4), 2 (1) (2), 4 (1). - Made: 19.09.2008. Coming into force: 01.10.2008. Effect: None. Territorial extent & classification: S. Local *Unpublished*

The North West Unit Trunk Roads Area (Temporary Prohibitions of Traffic, Temporary Prohibitions of Overtaking and Temporary Speed Restrictions) (No. 10) Order 2008 No. 2008/344. - Enabling power: Road Traffic Regulation Act 1984, s. 14 (1) (4), 2 (1) (2), 4 (1). - Made: 22.10.2008. Coming into force: 01.11.2008. Effect: None. Territorial extent & classification: S. Local *Unpublished*

The North West Unit Trunk Roads Area (Temporary Prohibitions of Traffic, Temporary Prohibitions of Overtaking and Temporary Speed Restrictions) (No. 11) Order 2008 No. 2008/384. - Enabling power: Road Traffic Regulation Act 1984, s. 14 (1) (4), 2 (1) (2), 4 (1). - Made: 19.11.2008. Coming into force: 01.12.2008. Effect: None. Territorial extent & classification: S. Local *Unpublished*

Road traffic: Traffic regulation

The North West Unit Trunk Roads Area (Temporary Prohibitions of Traffic, Temporary Prohibitions of Overtaking and Temporary Speed Restrictions) (No. 12) Order 2008 No. 2008/438. - Enabling power: Road Traffic Regulation Act 1984, s. 14 (1) (4), 2 (1) (2), 4 (1). - Made: 19.12.2008. Coming into force: 01.01.2009. Effect: None. Territorial extent & classification: S. Local *Unpublished*

The North West Unit Trunk Roads Area (Temporary Prohibitions of Traffic, Temporary Prohibitions of Overtaking and Temporary Speed Restrictions) Order 2008 No. 2008/25. - Enabling power: Road Traffic Regulation Act 1984, s. 14 (1) (4), 2 (1) (2), 4 (1). - Made: 30.01.2008. Coming into force: 01.02.2008. Effect: None. Territorial extent & classification: S. Local *Unpublished*

The South East Unit Trunk Roads Area (Temporary Prohibitions of Traffic, Temporary Prohibitions of Overtaking and Temporary Speed Restrictions) (No. 2) Order 2008 No. 2008/70. - Enabling power: Road Traffic Regulation Act 1984, s. 14 (1) (4), 2 (1) (2), 4 (1). - Made: 28.02.2008. Coming into force: 01.03.2008. Effect: None. Territorial extent & classification: S. Local *Unpublished*

The South East Unit Trunk Roads Area (Temporary Prohibitions of Traffic, Temporary Prohibitions of Overtaking and Temporary Speed Restrictions) (No. 3) Order 2008 No. 2008/140. - Enabling power: Road Traffic Regulation Act 1984, s. 14 (1) (4), 2 (1) (2), 4 (1). - Made: 20.03.2008. Coming into force: 01.04.2008. Effect: None. Territorial extent & classification: S. Local *Unpublished*

The South East Unit Trunk Roads Area (Temporary Prohibitions of Traffic, Temporary Prohibitions of Overtaking and Temporary Speed Restrictions) (No. 4) Order 2008 No. 2008/173. - Enabling power: Road Traffic Regulation Act 1984, s. 14 (1) (4), 2 (1) (2), 4 (1). - Made: 18.04.2008. Coming into force: 01.05.2008. Effect: None. Territorial extent & classification: S. Local *Unpublished*

The South East Unit Trunk Roads Area (Temporary Prohibitions of Traffic, Temporary Prohibitions of Overtaking and Temporary Speed Restrictions) (No. 5) Order 2008 No. 2008/208. - Enabling power: Road Traffic Regulation Act 1984, s. 14 (1) (4), 2 (1) (2), 4 (1). - Made: 20.05.2008. Coming into force: 01.06.2008. Effect: None. Territorial extent & classification: S. Local *Unpublished*

The South East Unit Trunk Roads Area (Temporary Prohibitions of Traffic, Temporary Prohibitions of Overtaking and Temporary Speed Restrictions) (No. 6) Order 2008 No. 2008/256. - Enabling power: Road Traffic Regulation Act 1984, s. 14 (1) (4), 2 (1) (2), 4 (1). - Made: 19.06.2008. Coming into force: 01.07.2008. Effect: None. Territorial extent & classification: S. Local *Unpublished*

The South East Unit Trunk Roads Area (Temporary Prohibitions of Traffic, Temporary Prohibitions of Overtaking and Temporary Speed Restrictions) (No. 7) Order 2008 No. 2008/278. - Enabling power: Road Traffic Regulation Act 1984, s. 14 (1) (4), 2 (1) (2), 4 (1). - Made: 22.07.2008. Coming into force: 01.08.2008. Effect: None. Territorial extent & classification: S. Local *Unpublished*

The South East Unit Trunk Roads Area (Temporary Prohibitions of Traffic, Temporary Prohibitions of Overtaking and Temporary Speed Restrictions) (No. 8) Order 2008 No. 2008/285. - Enabling power: Road Traffic Regulation Act 1984, s. 14 (1) (4), 2 (1) (2), 4 (1). - Made: 20.08.2008. Coming into force: 01.09.2008. Effect: None. Territorial extent & classification: S. Local *Unpublished*

The South East Unit Trunk Roads Area (Temporary Prohibitions of Traffic, Temporary Prohibitions of Overtaking and Temporary Speed Restrictions) (No. 9) Order 2008 No. 2008/319. - Enabling power: Road Traffic Regulation Act 1984, s. 14 (1) (4), 2 (1) (2), 4 (1). - Made: 19.09.2008. Coming into force: 01.10.2008. Effect: None. Territorial extent & classification: S. Local *Unpublished*

The South East Unit Trunk Roads Area (Temporary Prohibitions of Traffic, Temporary Prohibitions of Overtaking and Temporary Speed Restrictions) (No. 10) Order 2008 No. 2008/345. - Enabling power: Road Traffic Regulation Act 1984, s. 14 (1) (4), 2 (1) (2), 4 (1). - Made: 22.10.2008. Coming into force: 01.11.2008. Effect: None. Territorial extent & classification: S. Local *Unpublished*

The South East Unit Trunk Roads Area (Temporary Prohibitions of Traffic, Temporary Prohibitions of Overtaking and Temporary Speed Restrictions) (No. 11) Order 2008 No. 2008/383. - Enabling power: Road Traffic Regulation Act 1984, s. 14 (1) (4), 2 (1) (2), 4 (1). - Made: 19.11.2008. Coming into force: 01.12.2008. Effect: None. Territorial extent & classification: S. Local *Unpublished*

The South East Unit Trunk Roads Area (Temporary Prohibitions of Traffic, Temporary Prohibitions of Overtaking and Temporary Speed Restrictions) (No. 12) Order 2008 No. 2008/439. - Enabling power: Road Traffic Regulation Act 1984, s. 14 (1) (4), 2 (1) (2), 4 (1). - Made: 19.12.2008. Coming into force: 01.01.2009. Effect: None. Territorial extent & classification: S. Local *Unpublished*

The South East Unit Trunk Roads Area (Temporary Prohibitions of Traffic, Temporary Prohibitions of Overtaking and Temporary Speed Restrictions) Order 2008 No. 2008/24. - Enabling power: Road Traffic Regulation Act 1984, s. 14 (1) (4), 2 (1) (2), 4 (1). - Made: 30.01.2008. Coming into force: 01.02.2008. Effect: None. Territorial extent & classification: S. Local *Unpublished*

The South West Unit Trunk Roads Area (Temporary Prohibitions of Traffic, Temporary Prohibitions of Overtaking and Temporary Speed Restrictions) (No. 2) Order 2008 No. 2008/71. - Enabling power: Road Traffic Regulation Act 1984, s. 14 (1) (4), 2 (1) (2), 4 (1). - Made: 28.02.2008. Coming into force: 01.03.2008. Effect: None. Territorial extent & classification: S. Local *Unpublished*

The South West Unit Trunk Roads Area (Temporary Prohibitions of Traffic, Temporary Prohibitions of Overtaking and Temporary Speed Restrictions) (No. 3) Order 2008 No. 2008/139. - Enabling power: Road Traffic Regulation Act 1984, s. 14 (1) (4), 2 (1) (2), 4 (1). - Made: 20.03.2008. Coming into force: 01.04.2008. Effect: None. Territorial extent & classification: S. Local *Unpublished*

The South West Unit Trunk Roads Area (Temporary Prohibitions of Traffic, Temporary Prohibitions of Overtaking and Temporary Speed Restrictions) (No. 4) Order 2008 No. 2008/172. - Enabling power: Road Traffic Regulation Act 1984, s. 14 (1) (4), 2 (1) (2), 4 (1). - Made: 18.04.2008. Coming into force: 01.05.2008. Effect: None. Territorial extent & classification: S. Local *Unpublished*

The South West Unit Trunk Roads Area (Temporary Prohibitions of Traffic, Temporary Prohibitions of Overtaking and Temporary Speed Restrictions) (No. 5) Order 2008 No. 2008/207. - Enabling power: Road Traffic Regulation Act 1984, s. 14 (1) (4), 2 (1) (2), 4 (1). - Made: 20.05.2008. Coming into force: 01.06.2008. Effect: None. Territorial extent & classification: S. Local *Unpublished*

The South West Unit Trunk Roads Area (Temporary Prohibitions of Traffic, Temporary Prohibitions of Overtaking and Temporary Speed Restrictions) (No. 6) Order 2008 No. 2008/255. - Enabling power: Road Traffic Regulation Act 1984, s. 14 (1) (4), 2 (1) (2), 4 (1). - Made: 19.06.2008. Coming into force: 01.07.2008. Effect: None. Territorial extent & classification: S. Local *Unpublished*

The South West Unit Trunk Roads Area (Temporary Prohibitions of Traffic, Temporary Prohibitions of Overtaking and Temporary Speed Restrictions) (No. 7) Order 2008 No. 2008/276. - Enabling power: Road Traffic Regulation Act 1984, s. 14 (1) (4), 2 (1) (2), 4 (1). - Made: 22.07.2008. Coming into force: 01.08.2008. Effect: None. Territorial extent & classification: S. Local *Unpublished*

The South West Unit Trunk Roads Area (Temporary Prohibitions of Traffic, Temporary Prohibitions of Overtaking and Temporary Speed Restrictions) (No. 8) Order 2008 No. 2008/284. - Enabling power: Road Traffic Regulation Act 1984, s. 14 (1) (4), 2 (1) (2), 4 (1). - Made: 20.08.2008. Coming into force: 01.09.2008. Effect: None. Territorial extent & classification: S. Local *Unpublished*

The South West Unit Trunk Roads Area (Temporary Prohibitions of Traffic, Temporary Prohibitions of Overtaking and Temporary Speed Restrictions) (No. 9) Order 2008 No. 2008/318. - Enabling power: Road Traffic Regulation Act 1984, s. 14 (1) (4), 2 (1) (2), 4 (1). - Made: 19.09.2008. Coming into force: 01.10.2008. Effect: None. Territorial extent & classification: S. Local *Unpublished*

The South West Unit Trunk Roads Area (Temporary Prohibitions of Traffic, Temporary Prohibitions of Overtaking and Temporary Speed Restrictions) (No. 10) Order 2008 No. 2008/346. - Enabling power: Road Traffic Regulation Act 1984, s. 14 (1) (4), 2 (1) (2), 4 (1). - Made: 22.10.2008. Coming into force: 01.11.2008. Effect: None. Territorial extent & classification: S. Local *Unpublished*

The South West Unit Trunk Roads Area (Temporary Prohibitions of Traffic, Temporary Prohibitions of Overtaking and Temporary Speed Restrictions) (No. 11) Order 2008 No. 2008/382. - Enabling power: Road Traffic Regulation Act 1984, s. 14 (1) (4), 2 (1) (2), 4 (1). - Made: 19.11.2008. Coming into force: 01.12.2008. Effect: None. Territorial extent & classification: S. Local *Unpublished*

The South West Unit Trunk Roads Area (Temporary Prohibitions of Traffic, Temporary Prohibitions of Overtaking and Temporary Speed Restrictions) (No. 12) Order 2008 No. 2008/340. - Enabling power: Road Traffic Regulation Act 1984, s. 14 (1) (4), 2 (1) (2), 4 (1). - Made: 19.12.2008. Coming into force: 01.01.2009. Effect: None. Territorial extent & classification: S. Local *Unpublished*

The South West Unit Trunk Roads Area (Temporary Prohibitions of Traffic, Temporary Prohibitions of Overtaking and Temporary Speed Restrictions) Order 2008 No. 2008/23. - Enabling power: Road Traffic Regulation Act 1984, s. 14 (1) (4), 2 (1) (2), 4 (1). - Made: 30.01.2008. Coming into force: 01.02.2008. Effect: None. Territorial extent & classification: S. Local *Unpublished*

The Trunk Roads (Route A84 (Callander)) (Prohibition of Waiting and Loading) (Variation) Order 2008 No. 2008/110. - Enabling power: Road Traffic Regulation Act 1984, s. 1 (1). - Made: 16.01.2008. Coming into force: 30.01.2008. Effect: S.I. 1981/1601; 1993/3117 & S.S.I. 2003/327 varied. Territorial extent & classification: S. Local *Unpublished*

Sea fisheries

The Aquaculture and Fisheries (Scotland) Act 2007 (Fixed Penalty Notices) Order 2008 No. 2008/101. - Enabling power: Aquaculture and Fisheries (Scotland) Act 2007, ss. 25 (2) (b), 26 (5), 27 (1) (3), 29 (2) (b), 43 (1) (b). - Issued: 12.03.2008. Made: 06.03.2008. Laid: 07.03.2008. Coming into force: 01.04.2008. Effect: None. Territorial extent & classification: S. General. - 12p.: 30 cm. - 978-0-11-081563-3 *£3.00*

The Inshore Fishing (Prohibition on Fishing) (Lamlash Bay) (Scotland) Order 2008 No. 2008/317. - Enabling power: Inshore Fishing (Scotland) Act 1984, ss. 1, 2A. - Issued: 24.09.2008. Made: 18.09.2008. Laid before the Scottish Parliament: 19.09.2008. Coming into force: 20.09.2008. Effect: None. Territorial extent & classification: S. General. - 4p., col. map: 30 cm. - 978-0-11-100006-9 *£9.15*

The Sea Fishing (Control Procedures for Herring, Mackerel and Horse Mackerel) (Scotland) Amendment Order 2008 No. 2008/156. - Enabling power: Fisheries Act 1981, s. 30 (2) & European Communities Act 1972, sch. 2, para. 1A. - Issued: 22.04.2008. Made: 16.04.2008. Laid before the Scottish Parliament: 17.04.2008. Coming into force: 09.05.2008. Effect: S.S.I. 2008/102 amended. Territorial extent & classification: S. General. - This Scottish Statutory Instrument has been made in consequence of a defect in S.S.I. 2008/102 (ISBN 9780110815664) and is being issued free to all known recipients of that instrument. - 4p.: 30 cm. - 978-0-11-081617-3 *£3.00*

The Sea Fishing (Control Procedures for Herring, Mackerel and Horse Mackerel) (Scotland) Order 2008 No. 2008/102. - Enabling power: Fisheries Act 1981, s. 30 (2) & European Communities Act 1972, sch. 2, para. 1A. - Issued: 12.03.2008. Made: 06.03.2008. Laid before the Scottish Parliament: 07.03.2008. Coming into force: 01.04.2008. Effect: S.S.I. 2007/127 amended. Territorial extent & classification: S. General. - 16p.: 30 cm. - 978-0-11-081566-4 £3.00

The Sea Fishing (Enforcement of Community Quota and Third Country Fishing Measures and Restriction on Days at Sea) (Scotland) Order 2008 No. 2008/151. - Enabling power: Fisheries Act 1981, s. 30 (2) & Aquaculture and Fisheries (Scotland) Act 2007, s. 25 (2) (b). - Issued: 24.04.2008. Made: 15.04.2008. Laid before the Scottish Parliament: 15.04.2008. Coming into force: 16.04.2008. Effect: S.S.I. 2000/18; 2008/101 amended & S.S.I. 2007/40, 127 revoked. Territorial extent & classification: S. General. - Partially revoked by S.S.I. 2009/317 (ISBN 9780111006368). EC note: This Order, which forms part of the law of Scotland only, makes provision for the enforcement of Council Regulation (EC) No. 40/2008. - 28p.: 30 cm. - 978-0-11-081620-3 £4.50

The Shrimp Fishing Nets (Scotland) Amendment Order 2008 No. 2008/10. - Enabling power: Sea Fish (Conservation) Act 1967, s. 3 (1). - Issued: 23.01.2008. Made: 17.01.2008. Laid before the Scottish Parliament: 18.01.2008. Coming into force: 07.02.2008. Effect: S.S.I. 2004/261 amended. Territorial extent & classification: S. General. - 2p.: 30 cm. - 978-0-11-080220-6 £3.00

Sea fisheries: Conservation of sea fish

The Sea Fish (Prohibited Methods of Fishing) (Firth of Clyde) Order 2008 No. 2008/29. - Enabling power: Sea Fish (Conservation) Act 1967, ss. 5 (1) (c), 15 (3). - Issued: 11.02.2008. Made: 04.02.2008. Laid before the Scottish Parliament: 05.02.2008. Coming into force: 14.02.2008. Effect: S.S.I. 2007/63 revoked. Territorial extent & classification: S. General. - Revoked by S.S.I. 2009/38 (ISBN 9780111002582). This Order shall remain in force until the end of 30th April 2008. EC note: This Order is made pursuant to Article 46 of Council Regulation (EC) No. 850/98 for the conservation of fishery resources through technical measures for the protection of juveniles of marine organisms. - 8p., map: 30 cm. - 978-0-11-080243-5 £3.00

Sheriff Court

Act of Adjournal (Criminal Procedure Rules Amendment) (Criminal Proceedings etc. (Reform) (Scotland) Act 2007) 2008 No. 2008/61. - Enabling power: Criminal Procedure (Scotland) Act 1995, ss. 156 (5) (b) (i), 226F (1), 305. - Issued: 03.03.2008. Made: 20.02.2008. Coming into force: 10.03.2008. Effect: S.I. 1996/513 amended. Territorial extent & classification: S. General. - 20p.: 30 cm. - 978-0-11-081529-9 £3.50

Act of Adjournal (Criminal Procedure Rules Amendment No. 2) (Miscellaneous) 2008 No. 2008/62. - Enabling power: Criminal Procedure (Scotland) Act 1995, s. 302. - Issued: 28.02.2008. Made: 20.02.2008. Coming into force: 10.03.2008; 01.04.2008 in accord. with para. 1 (2) (3). Effect: S.I. 1996/513; S.S.I. 2005/188, 574; 2006/76. amended. Territorial extent & classification: S. General. - 8p.: 30 cm. - 978-0-11-081531-2 £3.00

Act of Adjournal (Criminal Procedure Rules Amendment No. 3) (Seizure and Disposal of Vehicles) 2008 No. 2008/275. - Enabling power: Criminal Procedure (Scotland) Act 1995, s. 305. - Issued: 29.07.2008. Made: 18.07.2008. Coming into force: 15.08.2008. Effect: S.I. 1996/513 amended. Territorial extent & classification: S. General. - 4p.: 30 cm. - 978-0-11-082020-0 £3.00

Act of Sederunt (Fees of Sheriff Officers) 2008 No. 2008/430. - Enabling power: Sheriff Courts (Scotland) Act 1907, s. 40 & Execution of Diligence (Scotland) Act 1926, s. 6. - Issued: 29.12.2008. Made: 17.12.2008. Laid before the Scottish Parliament: 22.12.2008. Coming into force: 26.01.2009. Effect: S.S.I. 2002/567 amended. Territorial extent & classification: S. General. - 8p.: 30 cm. - 978-0-11-100176-9 £5.00

Act of Sederunt (Fees of Shorthand Writers in the Sheriff Court) (Amendment) 2008 No. 2008/118. - Enabling power: Sheriff Courts (Scotland) Act 1907, s. 40. - Issued: 20.03.2008. Made: 13.03.2008. Laid: 17.03.2008. Coming into force: 05.05.2008. Effect: S.I. 1992/1878 amended. Territorial extent & classification: S. General. - 4p.: 30 cm. - 978-0-11-081583-1 £3.00

Act of Sederunt (Fees of Solicitors in the Sheriff Court) (Amendment) 2008 No. 2008/40. - Enabling power: Sheriff Courts (Scotland) Act 1907, s. 40. - Issued: 22.02.2008. Made: 15.02.2008. Laid before the Scottish Parliament: 19.02.2008. Coming into force: 01.04.2008. Effect: S.I. 1993/3080 amended. Territorial extent & classification: S. General. - 12p.: 30 cm. - 978-0-11-081505-3 £3.00

Act of Sederunt (Fees of Solicitors in the Sheriff Court) (Amendment No. 2) 2008 No. 2008/72. - Enabling power: Sheriff Courts (Scotland) Act 1907, s. 40. - Issued: 07.03.2008. Made: 29.02.2008. Laid before the Scottish Parliament: 04.03.2008. Coming into force: 31.03.2008. Effect: S.I. 2008/40 amended. Territorial extent & classification: S. General. - This Scottish Statutory Instrument has been made in consequence of a defect in S.S.I. 2008/40 (ISBN 9780110815053) and is being issued free of charge to all known recipients of that instrument. - 2p.: 30 cm. - 978-0-11-081537-4 £3.00

Act of Sederunt (Sheriff Court Bankruptcy Rules) 2008 No. 2008/119. - Enabling power: Sheriff Courts (Scotland) Act 1971, s. 32 & Bankruptcy (Scotland) Act 1985, ss. 1A (1) (b), 14 (4), 62 (2), sch. 5, para. 2 & European Communities Act 1972. sch. 2, para. 1A. - Issued: 25.03.2008. Made: 13.03.2008. Coming into force: 01.04.2008. Effect: S.I. 1996/2507 revoked with saving. Territorial extent & classification: S. General. - 28p.: 30 cm. - 978-0-11-081584-8 £4.50

Act of Sederunt (Sheriff Court European Order for Payment Procedure Rules) 2008 No. 2008/436. - Enabling power: Sheriff Courts (Scotland) Act 1971, s. 32. - Issued: 31.12.2008. Made: 19.12.2008. Coming into force: 12.01.2009. Effect: None. Territorial extent & classification: S. General. - 8p.: 30 cm. - 978-0-11-100186-8 £5.00

Act of Sederunt (Sheriff Court European Small Claims Procedure Rules) 2008 No. 2008/435. - Enabling power: Sheriff Courts (Scotland) Act 1971, s. 32. - Issued: 31.12.2008. Made: 19.12.2008. Coming into force: 12.01.2009. Effect: None. Territorial extent & classification: S. General. - 12p.: 30 cm. - 978-0-11-100185-1 £5.00

Act of Sederunt (Sheriff Court Rules Amendment) (Diligence) 2008 No. 2008/121. - Enabling power: Debtors (Scotland) Act 1987, ss. 15D (2) (a), 15L (2) (a) & Sheriff Courts (Scotland) Act 1971, s. 32 & Debt Arrangement and Attachment (Scotland) Act 2002, ss. 9C (2) (a), 9F (3) (a) (i), 9L (5) (a), 9M (3) (a), 9N (2) (a). - Issued: 25.03.2008. Made: 13.03.2008. Coming into force: 01.04.2008. Effect: 1907 c.51 amended & S.I. 1988/2013 & S.S.I. 2002/132, 560 amended. Territorial extent & classification: S. General. - 24p.: 30 cm. - 978-0-11-081585-5 £4.00

Act of Sederunt (Sheriff Court Rules) (Miscellaneous Amendments) 2008 No. 2008/223. - Enabling power: Sheriff Courts (Scotland) Act 1971, s. 32; Scottish Commission for Human Rights Act 2006, s. 14 (7) and Judicial Factors (Scotland) Act 1880, s. 5. - Issued: 11.06.2008. Made: 03.06.2008. Coming into force: 01.07.2008. Effect: 1907 c.51; S.I. 1986/2297; 1992/272; 1999/929; S.S.I. 2002/132, 133 amended. Territorial extent & classification: S. General. - 32p.: 30 cm. - 978-0-11-081686-9 £5.50

Act of Sederunt (Sheriff Court Rules) (Miscellaneous Amendments) (No. 2) 2008 No. 2008/365. - Enabling power: Sheriff Courts (Scotland) Act 1971, s. 32; UK Borders Act 2007, 11 (6). - Issued: 14.11.2008. Made: 07.11.2008. Coming into force: 13.11.2008 except for paras 2-6; 25.11.2008 for para 6; 01.12.2008 for paras 2-5. Effect: 1907 c.51; S.I. 1999/929; S.S.I. 2002/132, 133 amended. Territorial extent & classification: S. General. - 8p.: 30 cm. - 978-0-11-100069-4 £5.00

Act of Sederunt (Summary Applications, Statutory Applications and Appeals etc. Rules) Amendment (Adult Support and Protection (Scotland) Act 2007) 2008 No. 2008/111. - Enabling power: Sheriff Courts (Scotland) Act 1971, s. 32. - Issued: 13.03.2008. Made: 04.03.2008. Coming into force: 01.04.2008. Effect: S.I. 1999/929 amended. Territorial extent & classification: S. General. - 4p.: 30 cm. - 978-0-11-081574-9 £3.00

Act of Sederunt (Summary Applications, Statutory Applications and Appeals etc. Rules) Amendment (Adult Support and Protection (Scotland) Act 2007) (No.2) 2008 No. 2008/335. - Enabling power: Sheriff Courts (Scotland) Act 1971, s. 32 & Adult Support and Protection (Scotland) Act 2007, ss. 21 (3), 25 (2) (a), 26 (2), 27 (1) (2). - Issued: 10.10.2008. Made: 03.10.2008. Coming into force: 29.10.2008. Effect: S.I. 1999/929 amended. Territorial extent & classification: S. General. - 8p.: 30 cm. - 978-0-11-100044-1 £5.00

Act of Sederunt (Summary Applications, Statutory Applications and Appeals etc. Rules) Amendment (Adult Support and Protection (Scotland) Act 2007) (No. 3) 2008 No. 2008/375. - Enabling power: Sheriff Courts (Scotland) Act 1971, s. 32 & Adult Support and Protection (Scotland) Act 2007, ss. 26 (2), 27 (1) (2). - Issued: 19.11.2008. Made: 13.11.2008. Coming into force: 20.11.2008. Effect: S.I. 1999/929 amended. Territorial extent & classification: S. General. - 8p.: 30 cm. - 978-0-11-100078-6 £5.00

Act of Sederunt (Summary Applications, Statutory Applications and Appeals etc. Rules) Amendment (Licensing (Scotland) Act 2005) 2008 No. 2008/9. - Enabling power: Sheriff Courts (Scotland) Act 1971, s. 32 & Licensing (Scotland) Act 2005, s. 132 (9). - Issued: 21.01.2008. Made: 15.01.2008. Coming into force: 01.02.2008. Effect: S.I. 1999/929 amended. Territorial extent & classification: S. General. - 8p.: 30 cm. - 978-0-11-080218-3 £3.00

Act of Sederunt (Summary Applications, Statutory Applications and Appeals etc. Rules) Amendment (Registration Appeals) 2008 No. 2008/41. - Enabling power: Sheriff Courts (Scotland) Act 1971, s. 32. - Issued: 21.02.2008. Made: 14.02.2008. Coming into force: 17.03.2008. Effect: S.I. 1999/929 amended. Territorial extent & classification: S. General. - 4p.: 30 cm. - 978-0-11-081506-0 £3.00

The Sheriff Court Fees Amendment Order 2008 No. 2008/239. - Enabling power: Courts of Law Fees (Scotland) Act 1895, s. 2. - Issued: 17.06.2008. Made: 06.06.2008. Laid before the Scottish Parliament: 06.06.2008. Coming into force: In accord. with art. 1. Effect: S.I. 1997/687 amended. Territorial extent & classification: S. General. - 24p.: 30 cm. - 978-0-11-082032-3 £4.00

The Vulnerable Witnesses (Scotland) Act 2004 (Commencement No. 7, Savings and Transitional Provisions) Order 2008 No. 2008/57 (C.7). - Enabling power: Vulnerable Witnesses (Scotland) Act 2004. s. 25. Bringing into operation various provisions of the 2004 Act on 01.04.2008. - Issued: 27.02.2008. Made: 20.02.2008. Effect: None. Territorial extent & classification: S. General. - 4p.: 30 cm. - 978-0-11-081524-4 £3.00

Social care

The Adult Support and Protection (Scotland) Act 2007 (Restriction on the Authorisation of Council Officers) Order 2008 No. 2008/306. - Enabling power: Adult Support and Protection (Scotland) Act 2007, ss. 52 (1), 76 (1). - Issued: 16.09.2008. Made: 10.09.2008. Laid before the Scottish Parliament: 11.09.2008. Coming into force: 29.10.2008. Effect: None. Territorial extent & classification: S. General. - 4p.: 30 cm. - 978-0-11-084477-0 £4.00

The Community Care (Personal Care and Nursing Care) (Scotland) Amendment Regulations 2008 No. 2008/78. - Enabling power: Community Care and Health (Scotland) Act 2002, ss. 1 (2) (a), 2, 23 (4). - Issued: 10.03.2008. Made: 03.03.2008. Coming into force: 01.04.2008. Effect: S.S.I. 2002/303 amended. Territorial extent & classification: S. General. - Supersedes draft (ISBN 9780110802220) issued 23.01.2008. - 2p.: 30 cm. - 978-0-11-081542-8 £3.00

Sports grounds and sporting events

The Glasgow Commonwealth Games Act 2008 (Commencement No. 1) Order 2008 No. 2008/245 (C.21). - Enabling power: Glasgow Commonwealth Games Act 2008, s. 49 (2). Bringing into operation various provisions of the 2008 Act on 20.06.2008. - Issued: 17.06.2008. Made: 11.06.2008. Effect: None. Territorial extent & classification: S. General. - 2p.: 30 cm. - 978-0-11-082036-1 £3.00

The Sports Grounds and Sporting Events (Designation) (Scotland) Amendment Order 2008 No. 2008/379. - Enabling power: Criminal Law (Consolidation) (Scotland) Act 1995, s. 18. - Issued: 25.11.2008. Made: 20.11.2008. Laid before the Scottish Parliament: 20.11.2008. Coming into force: 12.12.2008. Effect: S.S.I. 2004/356 amended. Territorial extent & classification: S. General. - 2p.: 30 cm. - 978-0-11-100085-4 £4.00

Title conditions

The Title Conditions (Scotland) Act 2003 (Conservation Bodies) Amendment Order 2008 No. 2008/217. - Enabling power: Title Conditions (Scotland) Act 2003, s. 38 (4). - Issued: 09.06.2008. Made: 03.06.2008. Laid before the Scottish Parliament: 06.06.2008. Coming into force: 30.06.2008. Effect: S.S.I. 2003/453 amended. Territorial extent & classification: S. General. - 2p.: 30 cm. - 978-0-11-081680-7 £3.00

The Title Conditions (Scotland) Act 2003 (Rural Housing Bodies) Amendment Order 2008 No. 2008/391. - Enabling power: Title Conditions (Scotland) Act 2003, s. 43 (5). - Issued: 01.12.2008. Made: 25.11.2008. Laid before the Scottish Parliament: 26.11.2008. Coming into force: 01.01.2009. Effect: S.S.I. 2004/477 amended. Territorial extent & classification: S. General. - 2p.: 30 cm. - 978-0-11-100092-2 £4.00

Town and country planning

The Planning etc. (Scotland) Act 2006 (Commencement No. 3) Order 2008 No. 2008/164 (C.16). - Enabling power: Planning etc. (Scotland) Act 2006, s. 59 (2). Bringing into operation various provisions of the 2006 Act on 19.05.2008 & 25.06.2008, in accord. with art. 2. - Issued: 28.04.2008. Made: 22.04.2008. Effect: None. Territorial extent & classification: S. General. - 4p.: 30 cm. - 978-0-11-081625-8 £3.00

The Planning etc. (Scotland) Act 2006 (Commencement No. 4) Order 2008 No. 2008/191 (C.18). - Enabling power: Planning etc. (Scotland) Act 2006, s. 59 (2). Bringing into operation various provisions of the 2006 Act on 01.06.2008. - Issued: 21.05.2008. Made: 15.05.2008. Coming into force: 16.05.2008. Effect: S.S.I. 2008/164 amended. Territorial extent & classification: S. General. - 2p.: 30 cm. - 978-0-11-081655-5 £3.00

The Planning etc. (Scotland) Act 2006 (Commencement No. 5) Order 2008 No. 2008/411 (C.32). - Enabling power: Planning etc. (Scotland) Act 2006, s. 59 (2). Bringing into operation various provisions of the 2006 Act on 12.12.2008. - Issued: 17.12.2008. Made: 11.12.2008. Effect: None. Territorial extent & classification: S. General. - 2p.: 30 cm. - 978-0-11-100129-5 £4.00

The Planning etc. (Scotland) Act 2006 (Development Planning) (Saving Provisions) Order 2008 No. 2008/165. - Enabling power: Planning etc. (Scotland) Act 2006, s. 58 (1). - Issued: 28.04.2008. Made: 22.04.2008. Laid before the Scottish Parliament: 23.04.2008. Coming into force: 19.05.2008. Effect: None. Territorial extent & classification: S. General. - 2p.: 30 cm. - 978-0-11-081627-2 £3.00

The Planning etc. (Scotland) Act 2006 (Development Planning) (Saving, Transitional and Consequential Provisions) Order 2008 No. 2008/427. - Enabling power: Planning etc. (Scotland) Act 2006, s. 58 (1) (2)- Issued: 24.12.2008. Made: 18.12.2008. Laid before the Scottish Parliament: 19.12.2008. Coming into force: 28.02.2008. Effect: S.I. 1992/223; 1994/2716 (in relation to Scotland) amended & S.I. 1983/1590; 1995/3002 revoked with savings. Territorial extent & classification: S. General. - This SSI has been corrected by SSI 2009/18 (ISBN 9780111002070) which is being issued free of charge to all known recipients of 2008/427. - 8p.: 30 cm. - 978-0-11-100170-7 £5.00

The Strategic Development Planning Authority Designation (No. 1) (Scotland) Order 2008 No. 2008/195. - Enabling power: Town and Country Planning (Scotland) Act 1997, s. 4 (1). - Issued: 28.05.2008. Made: 21.05.2008. Laid before the Scottish Parliament: 22.05.2008. Coming into force: 25.06.2008. Effect: None. Territorial extent & classification: S. General. - 2p.: 30 cm. - 978-0-11-081661-6 £3.00

The Strategic Development Planning Authority Designation (No. 2) (Scotland) Order 2008 No. 2008/196. - Enabling power: Town and Country Planning (Scotland) Act 1997, s. 4 (1). - Issued: 28.05.2008. Made: 21.05.2008. Laid before the Scottish Parliament: 22.05.2008. Coming into force: 25.06.2008. Effect: None. Territorial extent & classification: S. General. - 2p.: 30 cm. - 978-0-11-081662-3 £3.00

The Strategic Development Planning Authority Designation (No. 3) (Scotland) Order 2008 No. 2008/197. - Enabling power: Town and Country Planning (Scotland) Act 1997, s. 4 (1). - Issued: 28.05.2008. Made: 21.05.2008. Laid before the Scottish Parliament: 22.05.2008. Coming into force: 25.06.2008. Effect: None. Territorial extent & classification: S. General. - 2p.: 30 cm. - 978-0-11-081663-0 £3.00

The Strategic Development Planning Authority Designation (No. 4) (Scotland) Order 2008 No. 2008/198. - Enabling power: Town and Country Planning (Scotland) Act 1997, s. 4 (1). - Issued: 28.05.2008. Made: 21.05.2008. Laid before the Scottish Parliament: 22.05.2008. Coming into force: 25.06.2008. Effect: None. Territorial extent & classification: S. General. - 2p.: 30 cm. - 978-0-11-081664-7 £3.00

The Town and Country Planning (Appeals) (Scotland) Regulations 2008 No. 2008/434. - Enabling power: Town and Country Planning (Scotland) Act 1997, ss. 47 (2) (3), 130 (3), 131 (1). - Issued: 31.12.2008. Made: 22.12.2008. Laid before the Scottish Parliament: 23.12.2008. Coming into force: 03.08.2009. Effect: None. Territorial extent & classification: S. General. - 20p.: 30 cm. - 978-0-11-100187-5 £5.00

The Town and Country Planning (Development Management Procedure) (Scotland) Regulations 2008 No. 2008/432. - Enabling power: Town and Country Planning (Scotland) Act 1997, ss. 27A (1), 27C, 30 (1) (3), 32, 34, 35 (1) (2) (3) (7), 35A (1), 35B (4) (5), 35C (2), 36, 36A (1) (2) (b), 38 (2) (b), 38A (1), 43, 59, 152, 275. - Issued: 31.12.2008. Made: 22.12.2008. Laid before the Scottish Parliament: 23.12.2008. Coming into force: 06.04.2009 for parts 1, 2, 10 & 03.08.2009 for remainder in accord. with reg. 1 (2) (3). Effect: S.I. 1992/224 revoked with savings (03.08.2009). Territorial extent & classification: S. General. - 40p.: 30 cm. - 978-0-11-100182-0 £9.00

The Town and Country Planning (Development Planning) (Scotland) Regulations 2008 No. 2008/426. - Enabling power: Town and Country Planning (Scotland) Act 1997, ss. 7 (2) (a), 8 (1) (b), 9 (4) (c), 9 (6), 10 (1) (d) (7), 12 (3), 12A (8), 15 (3) (4) (a), 16 (2) (b), 17 (4) (b) (6), 18 (1) (d) (e) (4) (b) (5), 19 (5) (10) (b), 19A (8), 20B (7), 21 (7), 22 (2), 23A (1), 23D, 275. - Issued: 24.12.2008. Made: 18.12.2008. Laid before the Scottish Parliament: 19.12.2008. Coming into force: 28.02.2008. Effect: None. Territorial extent & classification: S. General. - 20p.: 30 cm. - 978-0-11-100169-1 £5.00

The Town and Country Planning (General Permitted Development) (Avian Influenza) (Scotland) Amendment Order 2008 No. 2008/74. - Enabling power: Town and Country Planning (Scotland) Act 1997, ss. 30, 31, 275. - Issued: 07.03.2008. Made: 03.03.2008. Laid before the Scottish Parliament: 04.03.2008. Coming into force: 26.03.2008. Effect: S.I. 1992/223 amended. Territorial extent & classification: S. General. - 2p.: 30 cm. - 978-0-11-081538-1 £3.00

The Town and Country Planning (General Permitted Development) (Scotland) Amendment Order 2008 No. 2008/203. - Enabling power: Town and Country Planning (Scotland) Act 1997, ss. 30, 31, 275 (8). - Issued: 03.06.2008. Made: 28.05.2008. Laid before the Scottish Parliament: 29.05.2008. Coming into force: 20.06.2008. Effect: S.I. 1992/223 amended. Territorial extent & classification: S. General. - 2p.: 30 cm. - 978-0-11-081669-2 £3.00

The Town and Country Planning (Schemes of Delegation and Local Review Procedure) (Scotland) Regulations 2008 No. 2008/433. - Enabling power: Town and Country Planning (Scotland) Act 1997, ss. 43A (1) (a) (ii) (4) (10) (11) (13) (17), 275, 275A. - Issued: 31.12.2008. Made: 22.12.2008. Laid before the Scottish Parliament: 23.12.2008. Coming into force: 06.04.2009 for parts 1, 2 & 03.08.2009 for remainder, in accord. with reg. 1 (2) (3). Effect: None. Territorial extent & classification: S. General. - 16p.: 30 cm. - 978-0-11-100183-7 £5.00

Transport

The Abolition of Bridge Tolls (Scotland) Act 2008 (Commencement) Order 2008 No. 2008/22 (C.3). - Enabling power: Abolition of Bridge Tolls (Scotland) Act 2008, s. 4 (2). Bringing various provisions of the 2008 Act into operation on 11.02.2008. - Issued: 05.02.2008. Made: 30.01.2008. Effect: None. Territorial extent & classification: S. General. - 2p.: 30 cm. - 978-0-11-080239-8 £3.00

The Mobility and Access Committee for Scotland Revocation Regulations 2008 No. 2008/187. - Enabling power: Transport (Scotland) Act 2001, ss. 72, 81 (2). - Issued: 20.05.2008. Made: 14.05.2008. Laid before the Scottish Parliament: 15.05.2008. Coming into force: 01.07.2008. Effect: S.S.I. 2002/69; 2005/589 revoked. Territorial extent & classification: S. General. - Revoked by S.S.I. 2008/247 (ISBN 9780110820392). - 2p.: 30 cm. - 978-0-11-081648-7 £3.00

The Mobility and Access Committee for Scotland Revocation Regulations 2008 Revocation Regulations 2008 No. 2008/247. - Enabling power: Transport (Scotland) Act 2001, ss. 72, 81 (2). - Issued: 18.06.2008. Made: 12.06.2008. Laid before the Scottish Parliament: 13.06.2008. Coming into force: 14.06.2008. Effect: S.S.I. 2008/187 revoked. Territorial extent & classification: S. General. - 2p.: 30 cm. - 978-0-11-082039-2 £3.00

The Public Transport Users' Committee for Scotland Amendment Order 2008 No. 2008/186. - Enabling power: Transport (Scotland) Act 2005, s. 41 (1) (2) (a). - Issued: 20.05.2008. Made: 14.05.2008. Laid before the Scottish Parliament: 15.05.2008. Coming into force: 01.07.2008. Effect: S.S.I. 2006/250 amended. Territorial extent & classification: S. General. - Revoked by S.S.I. 2008/248 (ISBN 9780110820408). - 2p.: 30 cm. - 978-0-11-081647-0 £3.00

The Public Transport Users' Committee for Scotland Amendment Order 2008 Revocation Order 2008 No. 2008/248. - Enabling power: Transport (Scotland) Act 2005, s. 41 (1) (2) (a). - Issued: 18.06.2008. Made: 12.06.2008. Laid before the Scottish Parliament: 13.06.2008. Coming into force: 14.06.2008. Effect: S.S.I. 2008/186 revoked. Territorial extent & classification: S. General. - 2p.: 30 cm. - 978-0-11-082040-8 £3.00

The Transport and Works (Scotland) Act 2007 (Access to Land by the Scottish Ministers) Order 2008 No. 2008/200. - Enabling power: Transport and Works (Scotland) Act 2007, ss. 18 (1) (b) (2) (b) (c), 28 (6). - Issued: 29.05.2008. Made: 21.05.2008. Coming into force: 22.05.2008. Effect: None. Territorial extent & classification: S. General. - Supersedes draft SSI (ISBN 9780110816111) issued 21.04.2008. - 12p.: 30 cm. - 978-0-11-081666-1 £3.00

The Transport and Works (Scotland) Act 2007 (Access to Land on Application) Order 2008 No. 2008/199. - Enabling power: Transport and Works (Scotland) Act 2007, ss. 18 (1) (a) (2) (a) (c), 28 (6). - Issued: 28.05.2008. Made: 21.05.2008. Coming into force: 22.05.2008. Effect: None. Territorial extent & classification: S. General. - Supersedes draft S.S.I. (ISBN 9780110816128) issued 21.04.2008. - 12p.: 30 cm. - 978-0-11-081665-4 £3.00

The Transport (Scotland) Act 2005 (Commencement No. 4) Amendment Order 2008 No. 2008/90 (C. 8). - Enabling power: Transport (Scotland) Act 2005, ss. 52 (4), 54 (2). Various provisions of the 2005 Act brought into operation on 01.04.2008 & 01.10.2008. - Issued: 11.03.2008. Made: 05.03.2008. Effect: S.S.I 2008/15 (C.1) amended. Territorial extent & classification: S. General. - 4p.: 30 cm. - 978-0-11-081553-4 £3.00

The Transport (Scotland) Act 2005 (Commencement No. 4) Order 2008 No. 2008/15 (C.1). - Enabling power: Transport (Scotland) Act 2005, ss. 52 (4), 54 (2). Bringing various provisions of the 2005 Act into operation on 29.02.2008, 01.04.2008 and 01.10.2008. - Issued: 28.01.2008. Made: 22.01.2008. Effect: None. Territorial extent & classification: S. General. - 4p.: 30 cm. - 978-0-11-080228-2 £3.00

Transport and works

The Transport and Works (Scotland) Act 2007 (Access to Land by the Scottish Ministers) Order 2008 No. 2008/200. - Enabling power: Transport and Works (Scotland) Act 2007, ss. 18 (1) (b) (2) (b) (c), 28 (6). - Issued: 29.05.2008. Made: 21.05.2008. Coming into force: 22.05.2008. Effect: None. Territorial extent & classification: S. General. - Supersedes draft SSI (ISBN 9780110816111) issued 21.04.2008. - 12p.: 30 cm. - 978-0-11-081666-1 £3.00

The Transport and Works (Scotland) Act 2007 (Access to Land on Application) Order 2008 No. 2008/199. - Enabling power: Transport and Works (Scotland) Act 2007, ss. 18 (1) (a) (2) (a) (c), 28 (6). - Issued: 28.05.2008. Made: 21.05.2008. Coming into force: 22.05.2008. Effect: None. Territorial extent & classification: S. General. - Supersedes draft S.S.I. (ISBN 9780110816128) issued 21.04.2008. - 12p.: 30 cm. - 978-0-11-081665-4 £3.00

Water

The Action Programme for Nitrate Vulnerable Zones (Scotland) Amendment Regulations 2008 No. 2008/298. - Enabling power: European Communities Act 1972, s. 2 (2). - Issued: 12.09.2008. Made: 04.09.2008. Laid before the Scottish Parliament: 08.09.2008. Coming into force: 01.01.2009. Effect: S.S.I. 2003/51 (with saving), 169 revoked. Territorial extent & classification: S. General. - 36p.: 30 cm. - 978-0-11-083973-8 £9.00

The Action Programme for Nitrate Vulnerable Zones (Scotland) Amendment Regulations 2008 No. 2008/394. - Enabling power: European Communities Act 1972, s. 2 (2). - Issued: 02.12.2008. Made: 26.11.2008. Laid before the Scottish Parliament: 27.11.2008. Coming into force: 01.01.2009. Effect: S.S.I. 2008/298 amended. Territorial extent & classification: S. General. - This Scottish Statutory Instrument has been made to correct errors in S.S.I. 2008/298 and is being issued free of charge to all known recipients of that instrument. - 4p.: 30 cm. - 978-0-11-100098-4 £4.00

The Bathing Waters (Scotland) Regulations 2008 No. 2008/170. - Enabling power: European Communities Act 1972, s. 2 (2). - Issued: 08.05.2008. Made: 30.04.2008. Laid before the Scottish Parliament: 01.05.2008. Coming into force: In accord. with reg. 1. Effect: S.S.I. 2005/348 amended and S.I. 1991/1609 revoked with savings (01.01.2015). Territorial extent & classification: S. General. - These Regulations make provision for the purpose of implementing, in Scotland, Directive 2006/7/EC concerning the management of bathing water quality and repealing Directive 76/160/EEC. - 24p.: 30 cm. - 978-0-11-081632-6 £4.00

The Water Environment and Water Services (Scotland) Act 2003 (Commencement No. 8) Order 2008 No. 2008/269 (C.22). - Enabling power: Water Environment and Water Services (Scotland) Act 2003, s. 38 (1). Bringing into operation various provisions of the 2003 Act on 10.07.2008. - Issued: 03.07.2008. Made: 30.06.2008. Effect: None. Territorial extent & classification: S. General. - 2p.: 30 cm. - 978-0-11-082015-6 £3.00

The Water Environment (Diffuse Pollution) (Scotland) Regulations 2008 No. 2008/54. - Enabling power: Water Environment and Water Services (Scotland) Act 2003, ss. 20, 36 (3). - Issued: 26.02.2008. Made: 20.02.2008. Laid before the Scottish Parliament: 21.02.2008. Coming into force: 01.04.2008. Effect: S.S.I. 2003/531; 2005/348 amended. Territorial extent & classification: S. General. - 12p.: 30 cm. - 978-0-11-081521-3 £3.00

Water industry

The Water and Sewerage Services Undertaking (Lending by the Scottish Ministers) Order 2008 No. 2008/44. - Enabling power: Water Services etc. (Scotland) Act 2005, s. 14 (2). - Issued: 25.02.2008. Made: 19.02.2008. Laid before the Scottish Parliament: 20.02.2008. Coming into force: 17.03.2008. Effect: None. Territorial extent & classification: S. General. - 2p.: 30 cm. - 978-0-11-081509-1 £3.00

Water supply

The Scottish Water (Loch of Boardhouse) Water Order 2008 No. 2008/429. - Enabling power: Water (Scotland) Act 1980, ss. 17 (2), 29 (1), 107 (1) (b). - Issued: 29.12.2008. Made: 16.12.2008. Coming into force: 18.12.2008. Effect: S.I. 1958/738 (S.33); 1989/1676 (S.129) revoked. Territorial extent & classification: S. General. - 8p.: 30 cm. - 978-0-11-100175-2 £5.00

Wildlife

The Conservation (Natural Habitats, &c.) Amendment (No. 2) (Scotland) Regulations 2008 No. 2008/425. - Enabling power: European Communities Act 1972, s. 2 (2) & Wildlife and Countryside Act 1981, s. 26A. - Issued: 24.12.2008. Made: 18.12.2008. Laid before the Scottish Parliament: 19.12.2008. Coming into force: 26.01.2009. Effect: S.I. 1994/2716 amended in relation to Scotland. Territorial extent & classification: S. General. - EC note: These Regulations make further provision for the transposition of Council Directive 92/43/EEC on the conservation of natural habitats and of wild flora and fauna. - 4p.: 30 cm. - 978-0-11-100164-6 £4.00

The Conservation (Natural Habitats, &c.) Amendment (Scotland) Regulations 2008 No. 2008/17. - Enabling power: European Communities Act 1972, s. 2 (2) & Wildlife and Countryside Act 1981, s. 26A. - Issued: 29.01.2008. Made: 23.01.2008. Laid before the Scottish Parliament: 24.01.2008. Coming into force: 25.02.2008. Effect: S.I. 1994/2716 amended in relation to Scotland. Territorial extent & classification: S. General. - EC note: These Regulations make further provision for the transposition of Council Directive 92/43/EEC on the conservation of natural habitats and of wild flora and fauna. - 4p.: 30 cm. - 978-0-11-080231-2 £3.00

Young offender institutions

The Prisons and Young Offenders Institutions (Scotland) Amendment Rules 2008 No. 2008/377. - Enabling power: Prisons (Scotland) Act 1989, s. 39. - Issued: 24.11.2008. Made: 18.11.2008. Laid before the Scottish Parliament: 19.11.2008. Coming into force: 11.12.2008. Effect: S.S.I. 2006/94 amended. Territorial extent & classification: S. General. - 4p.: 30 cm. - 978-0-11-100082-3 £4.00

Scottish Statutory Instruments

Arranged by Number

1	Education
2	Public passenger transport
3	Road traffic
4	Road traffic
5	Insolvency
6	Police
7	Criminal law
8	Prisons
9	Sheriff Court
10	Sea fisheries
11	Animals
12	Food
13	National assistance services
14	National assistance services
15 (C.1)	Transport
16	Roads and bridges
17	Wildlife
	Countryside
18	Road traffic
19	River
20	Police
21 (C.2)	Criminal law
22 (C.3)	Transport
	Roads and bridges
23	Road traffic
24	Road traffic
25	Road traffic
26	Road traffic
27	National Health Service
28	Housing
29	Sea fisheries
30	Criminal law
31	Justice of the Peace Court
32	Rating and valuation
33	Local government
34	Housing
35	Prisons
36	Criminal law
37	Criminal law
38	Energy conservation
39	Court of Session
40	Sheriff Court
41	Sheriff Court
42 (C.4)	Criminal law
43	Roads and bridges
44	Water industry
45 (C.5)	Insolvency
46	Police
47	Legal aid and advice
48	Legal aid and advice
49 (C.6)	Mental health
	Adults with incapacity
	Adult support
50	Adult support
	Adults with incapacity
51	Adults with incapacity
52	Adults with incapacity
53	Adults with incapacity
54	Environmental protection
	Water
55	Adults with incapacity
56	Adults with incapacity
57 (C.7)	Sheriff Court
58	Crofters, cottars and small landholders
59	Charities
60	National Health Service
61	High Court of Justiciary
	Sheriff Court
	Justice of the peace courts
62	Sheriff Court
	Justice of the Peace Court
63	Public health
64	Agriculture
65	Agriculture
	Pesticides
66	Agriculture
67	Road traffic
68	Road traffic
69	Road traffic
70	Road traffic
71	Road traffic
72	Sheriff Court
73	Road traffic
74	Town and country planning
75	Children and young persons
76	Housing
77	Agriculture
78	Social care
79	Insolvency
80	Rating and valuation

81	Bankruptcy	124	Criminal law
82	Bankruptcy	125	Criminal law
83	Rating and valuation	126	Prisons
84	Rating and valuation	127	Food
85	Rating and valuation	128	Criminal law
86	Environmental protection	129	Food
87	Agriculture Food	130 (C.12)	Children and young persons
88	Roads and bridges	131	Official statistics
89	Roads and bridges	132	Electricity
90 (C. 8)	Transport	133	Housing
91	Road traffic	134	Road traffic
92	National Health Service	135	Forestry
93	Justice of the peace courts	136	Local government
94	Public procurement	137	Legal aid and advice
95	Road traffic	138	Legal aid and advice
96	National Health Service	139	Road traffic
97	Food	140	Road traffic
98	Food	141	Road traffic
99	Agriculture	142	Road traffic
100	Agriculture	143	Bankruptcy
101	Sea fisheries	144	Companies
102	Sea fisheries	145	Roads and bridges
103	Criminal law	146	Road traffic
104	Criminal law	147	National Health Service
105	National Health Service	148	Agriculture Food
106	National Health Service	149 (C.13)	Criminal law
107	Public finance and accountability	150 (C.14)	Cultural objects
108	Criminal law	151	Sea fisheries
109	Criminal law	152 (C.15)	Proceeds of crime
110	Road traffic	153	Plant health
111	Sheriff Court	154	Clean air
112 (C.9)	Human rights	155	Animals
113	Road traffic	156	Sea fisheries
114	Road traffic	157	Clean air
115 (C.10)	Insolvency Bankruptcy Debt Diligence	158	Animals
		159	Agriculture
		160	Fire services Pensions
116 (C.11)	Mental health Adult support	161	Fire services Pensions
117	Police	162	Agriculture
118	Sheriff Court	163	Education
119	Sheriff Court	164 (C.16)	Town and country planning
120	Court of Session	165	Town and country planning
121	Sheriff Court	166	Animals
122	Court of Session	167	Road traffic
123	Court of Session		

168	Armorial bearings, ensigns and flags	210	Road traffic
169	Road traffic	211	Roads and bridges
170	Environmental protection	212	Education
	Water	213	Education
171 (C.17)	Education	214	Education
172	Road traffic	215	Agriculture
173	Road traffic	216	Food
174	Road traffic	217	Title conditions
175	Road traffic	218	Agriculture
176	Agriculture		Food
	Food	219	Animals
177	Education	220	Education
178	Education	221	Nature conservation
179	Justice of the Peace courts	222	River
180	Food	223	Sheriff Court
181	Mental health	224	National Health Service
182	Harbours, docks, piers and ferries	225	National Health Service
183	Road traffic	226	National Health Service
184	Agriculture	227	Pensions
185	Criminal law	228	Pensions
186	Transport	229	Pensions
187	Transport	230	Pensions
188	Harbours, docks, piers and ferries	231	Roads and bridges
189	Harbours, docks, piers and ferries	232	Criminal law
190	Harbours, docks, piers and ferries	233	Agriculture
191 (C.18)	Town and country planning	234	Animals
192 (C.19)	Criminal law	235	Education
193 (C.20)	Nature conservation	236	Court of Session
194	Licensing (liquor)	237	High Court of Justiciary
195	Town and country planning	238	Adults with incapacity
196	Town and country planning	239	Sheriff Court
197	Town and country planning	240	Legal aid and advice
198	Town and country planning	241	Education
199	Transport and works	242	Road traffic
	Transport	243	Roads and bridges
	Canals and inland waterways	244	Roads and bridges
200	Transport and works	245 (C.21)	Sports grounds and sporting events
	Transport	246	Electricity
	Canals and inland waterways	247	Transport
201	Agriculture	248	Transport
202	Countryside	249	Road traffic
203	Town and country planning	250	Road traffic
204	Education	251	Legal aid and advice
205	Education	252	Road traffic
206	Education	253	Public passenger transport
207	Road traffic	254	Road traffic
208	Road traffic	255	Road traffic
209	Road traffic		

256	Road traffic	300	Plant health
257	Road traffic	301	Road traffic
258	Road traffic	302	Animals
259	Human tissue	303	Children and young persons
260	Children and young persons	304	Children and young persons
261	Food	305	Children and young persons
262	Charities	306	Adult support
263	Environmental protection		Social care
264	Criminal law	307	Criminal law
265	Education	308 (C.25)	Housing
266	Animals	309	Building and buildings
267	Road traffic	310	Building and buildings
268	Charities	311 (C.26)	Legal profession
269 (C.22)	Environmental protection	312	National Health Service
	Water	313 (C. 27)	Housing
270	Road traffic	314 (C. 28)	Mental health
271	Road traffic		Adult support
272	Road traffic	315	National Health Service
273	Road traffic	316	Mental health
274	Road traffic	317	Sea fisheries
275	Sheriff Court	318	Road traffic
	Justice of the Peace Court	319	Road traffic
276	Road traffic	320	Road traffic
277	Road traffic	321	Road traffic
278	Road traffic	322	Food
279	Road traffic	323	Road traffic
280	Road traffic	324	Housing
281	Road traffic	325	Local government
282 (C.23)	Children and young persons	326	Fish farming
283	Housing	327	Animals
284	Road traffic	328	Justice of the Peace courts
285	Road traffic	329 (C.29)	Criminal law
286	Road traffic	330	Criminal law
287	Road traffic	331	Harbours, docks, piers and ferries
288	National Health Service	332	Legal profession
289	National Health Service	333	Mental health
290	National Health Service	334	Bankruptcy
291	Public procurement	335	Sheriff Court
292 (C. 24)	Licensing (liquor)	336	Housing
293	Family law	337	Roads and bridges
294	Agriculture	338	Roads and bridges
295	Clean air	339	Freedom of information
296	Clean air	340	Road traffic
297	Freedom of information	341	Road traffic
298	Environmental protection	342	Agriculture
	Agriculture		Pesticides
	Water	343	Road traffic
299	Plant health		

344	Road traffic	388	Education
345	Road traffic	389	Building and buildings
346	Road traffic	390	National Health Service
347	Road traffic	391	Title conditions
348	Public bodies	392	Road traffic
349	Court of Session	393	Insolvency
350	Plant health		Companies
351	Road traffic	394	Environmental protection
352	Legal profession		Agriculture
353	Road traffic		Water
354	Road traffic	395	Food
355	Human rights	396	Mental health
356	Mental health	397	Building and buildings
357	Court of Session	398	Road traffic
358	Registration of births, deaths, marriages, etc.	399	Official statistics
		400	Local government
359	Local government		Education
360	Rating and valuation	401	Court of Session
361	Harbours, docks, piers and ferries	402	Housing
			Local government
362 (C.30)	Criminal law	403	Housing
363	Justice of the Peace courts		Local government
364	Road traffic	404	Private international law
365	Sheriff Court	405 (C.31)	Registration of births, deaths, marriages, etc.
366	Court of Session		
367	Road traffic	406	Housing
368	Animals	407	Road traffic
369	Animals	408	Road traffic
370	Rating and valuation	409	Road traffic
371	Rating and valuation	410	Environmental protection
372	European Communities	411 (C.32)	Town and country planning
373	Road traffic	412	Education
374	Justice of the Peace courts	413	Charities
375	Sheriff Court	414	Local government
376	Public procurement	415	Local government
377	Prisons	416	Legal aid and advice
	Young offender institutions	417	Animals
378	Animals	418	Food
379	Sports grounds and sporting events		Agriculture
380	Adults with incapacity	419	River
	Electronic communications	420	Road traffic
381	Road traffic	421	Road traffic
382	Road traffic	422	Harbours, docks, piers and ferries
383	Road traffic	423	Animals
384	Road traffic	424	Public finance and accountability
385	Road traffic	425	Wildlife
386	Registration of births, deaths, marriages, etc.		Countryside
		426	Town and country planning
387	Pensions		

427	Town and country planning	90 (C. 8)
428	Legal profession	112 (C.9)
429	Water supply	115 (C.10)
430	Sheriff Court	116 (C.11)
431	Court of Session	130 (C.12)
432	Town and country planning	149 (C.13)
433	Town and country planning	150 (C.14)
434	Town and country planning	152 (C.15)
435	Sheriff Court	164 (C.16)
436	Sheriff Court	171 (C.17)
437	Road traffic	191 (C.18)
438	Road traffic	192 (C.19)
439	Road traffic	193 (C.20)
440	Road traffic	245 (C.21)
441	Road traffic	269 (C.22)

List of Scottish Commencement Orders

15 (C.1)
21 (C.2)
22 (C.3)
42 (C.4)
45 (C.5)
49 (C.6)
57 (C.7)

282 (C.23)
292 (C.24)
308 (C.25)
311 (C.26)
313 (C.27)
314 (C.28)
329 (C.29)
362 (C.30)
405 (C.31)
411 (C.32)

Northern Ireland Legislation

Acts of the Northern Ireland Assembly

Acts of the Northern Ireland Assembly 2008

Budget Act (Northern Ireland) 2008: chapter 3. - 35p.: 30 cm. - An Act to authorise the issue out of the Consolidated Fund of certain sums for the service of the years ending 31st March 2008 and 2009; to appropriate those sums for specified purposes; to authorise the Department of Finance and Personnel to borrow on the credit of the appropriated sums; to authorise the use for the public service of certain resources for the years ending 31st March 2008 and 2009; and to revise the limits on the use of certain accruing resources in the year ending 31st March 2008. Explanatory notes are available separately (ISBN 9780105960409). - 978-0-10-595047-9 £6.50

Mesothelioma, etc., Act (Northern Ireland) 2008: chapter 9. - [1], 7p.: 30 cm. - Royal assent 2nd July 2008. An Act to make lump sum payments to or in respect of persons with diffuse mesothelioma. Explanatory notes to the Act are available separately (ISBN 9780105960485). - 978-0-10-595054-7 £3.00

Pensions Act (Northern Ireland) 2008: chapter 1. - iii, 60p.: 30 cm. - An Act to make provision about pensions and other benefits payable to persons in connection with bereavement or by reference to pensionable age; to make provision about the functions of the Personal Accounts Delivery Authority. Royal assent, 11th February 2008. Explanatory notes to the Act are available separately (ISBN 9780105960379). - 978-0-10-595045-5 £10.50

Pensions (No. 2) Act (Northern Ireland) 2008: chapter 13. - vi, 128p.: 30 cm. - Royal assent, 15th December 2008. An Act to make provision relating to pensions. Explanatory notes to the Act are available separately (ISBN 9780105960515). - 978-0-10-595058-5 £18.00

Commission for Victims and Survivors Act (Northern Ireland) 2008: chapter 6. - [12]p.: 30 cm. - Royal assent 23rd May 2008. An Act to replace the Commissioner for Victims and Survivors for Northern Ireland established by the Victims and Survivors (Northern Ireland) Order 2006 with a Commission for Victims and Survivors for Northern Ireland. Explanatory notes to the Act are available separately (ISBN 9780105960454). - 978-0-10-595051-6 £3.00

Budget (No. 2) Act (Northern Ireland) 2008: chapter 11. - [1], 20p.: 30 cm. - An Act to authorise the issue out of the Consolidated Fund of certain sums for the service of the year ending 31st March 2009; to appropriate those sums for specified purposes; to authorise the Department of Finance and Personnel to borrow on the credit of the appropriated sums; to authorise the use for the public service of certain resources (including accruing resources) for the year ending 31st March 2009; to authorise the issue out of the Consolidated Fund on an excess cash sum for the year ending 31st March 2007; and to repeal certain spent provisions. Explanatory notes to the Act are available separately (ISBN 9780105960478). - 978-0-10-595056-1 £4.50

Local Government (Boundaries) Act (Northern Ireland) 2008: chapter 7. - [8]p.: 30 cm. - Royal assent 23rd May 2008. An Act to provide for 11 local government districts in Northern Ireland, for the division of those districts into wards, for the appointment of a Local Government Boundaries Commissioner to recommend the boundaries and names of those districts and wards and the number of wards in each district. Explanatory notes to the Act are available separately (ISBN 9780105960447). - 978-0-10-595050-9 £3.00

Public Health (Amendment) Act (Northern Ireland) 2008: chapter 5. - [8]p.: 30 cm. - Royal assent 6th May 2008. An Act to amend section 2A of the Public Health Act (Northern Ireland) 1967. Explanatory notes to the Act are available separately (ISBN 9780105960430). - 978-0-10-595049-3 £3.00

Taxis Act (Northern Ireland) 2008: chapter 4. - iii, 42p.: 30 cm. - Royal Assent 21st April 2008. An Act to make provision regulating taxi operators and taxi drivers. Explanatory notes are available separately (ISBN 9780105960416). - 978-0-10-595048-6 £7.50

Libraries Act (Northern Ireland) 2008: chapter 8. - [1], 16p.: 30 cm. - Royal assent 17th June 2008. An Act to provide for the establishment and functions of the Northern Library Authority; to enable the Department of Culture, Arts and Leisure to make grants in connection with the provision of library services. Explanatory notes to the Act are available separately (ISBN 9780105960461). - 978-0-10-595052-3 £4.00

Charities Act (Northern Ireland) 2008: chapter 12. - vii, 178p.: 30 cm. - Royal assent, 9th September 2008. An Act to provide for the establishment and functions of the Charity Commission for Northern Ireland and the Charity Tribunal for Northern Ireland; to make provision about the law of charities, including provision about charitable incorporated organisations; to make further provision about public charitable collections and other fund-raising carried on in connection with charities and other institutions. Explanatory notes to the Act are available separately (ISBN 9780105960508). - 978-0-10-595057-8 £26.00

Health (Miscellaneous Provisions) Act (Northern Ireland) 2008: chapter 2. - ii, [2], 21p.: 30 cm. - An Act to amend the Health and Personal Social Services (Northern Ireland) Order 1972 in relation to the provision of health care. Royal assent, 25th February 2008. Explanatory notes are available separately (ISBN 9780105960386). - 978-0-10-595046-2 £4.50

Child Maintenance Act (Northern Ireland) 2008: chapter 10. - ii, 51p.: 30 cm. - Royal assent 2nd July 2008. An Act to amend the law relating to child support. Explanatory notes to the Act are available separately (ISBN 9780105960492). - 978-0-10-595055-4 £8.50

Acts of the Northern Ireland Assembly - Explanatory notes 2008

Libraries Act (Northern Ireland) 2008: chapter 8; explanatory notes. - [8]p.: 30 cm. - These notes refer to the Libraries Act (Northern Ireland) 2008 (c. 8) (ISBN 9780105950523) which received Royal assent on 18th June 2008. - With correction slip dated August 2008 amending the date of Royal assent from 17th to 18th June 2008. - 978-0-10-596046-1 £3.00

Mesothelioma, etc., Act (Northern Ireland) 2008: chapter 9; explanatory notes. - 8p.: 30 cm. - These notes refer to the Mesothelioma, etc., Act (Northern Ireland) 2008 (c. 9) (ISBN 9780105950485) which received Royal assent on 2nd July 2008. - 978-0-10-596048-5 £3.00

Budget Act (Northern Ireland) 2008: chapter 3; explanatory notes. - 5p.: 30 cm. - These notes refer to the Budget Act (Northern Ireland) 2008 (c. 3) (ISBN 9780105950479) which received Royal assent on 12 March 2008. - 978-0-10-596040-9 £3.00

Libraries Act (Northern Ireland) 2008: chapter 8; explanatory notes (correction slip). - 1 sheet: 30 cm. - Correction slip (to ISBN 9780105960461) dated August 2008, correcting the date of Royal assent from 17th to 18th June 2008. - 978-9-99-906080-6 *Free*

Pensions Act (Northern Ireland) 2008: chapter 1; explanatory notes. - 25p.: 30 cm. - These notes refer to the Pensions Act (Northern Ireland) 2008 (c. 1) (ISBN 9780105950455) which received Royal assent on 11 February 2008. - 978-0-10-596037-9 £5.50

Public Health (Amendment) Act (Northern Ireland) 2008: chapter 5; explanatory notes. - [8]p.: 30 cm. - These notes refer to the Public Health (Amendment) Act (Northern Ireland) 2008 (c. 5) (ISBN 9780105950493) which received Royal assent on 6 May 2008. - 978-0-10-596043-0 £3.00

Local Government (Boundaries) Act (Northern Ireland) 2008: chapter 7; explanatory notes. - [6]p.: 30 cm. - These notes refer to the Local Government (Boundaries) Act (Northern Ireland) 2008 (c. 7) (ISBN 9780105950509) which received Royal assent on 23rd May 2008. - 978-0-10-596044-7 £3.00

Pensions (No. 2) Act (Northern Ireland) 2008: chapter 13; explanatory notes. - 52p.: 30 cm. - These notes refer to the Pensions (No. 2) Act (Northern Ireland) 2008 (c. 13) (ISBN 9780105950585) which received Royal assent on 15th December 2008. - 978-0-10-596051-5 £9.00

Charities Act (Northern Ireland) 2008: chapter 12; explanatory notes. - [8]p.: 30 cm. - These notes refer to the Charities Act (Northern Ireland) 2008 (c. 12) (ISBN 9780105950578) which received Royal assent on 9th September 2008. - 978-0-10-596050-8 £5.00

Budget (No. 2) Act (Northern Ireland) 2008: chapter 11; explanatory notes. - 4p.: 30 cm. - These notes refer to the Budget (No. 2) Act (Northern Ireland) 2008 (c. 11) (ISBN 9780105950561) which received Royal assent on 2 July 2008. - 978-0-10-596047-8 £3.00

Taxis Act (Northern Ireland) 2008: chapter 4; explanatory notes. - 8p.: 30 cm. - These notes refer to the Taxis Act (Northern Ireland) 2008 (c. 4) (ISBN 9780105950486) which received Royal assent on 21st April 2008. - 978-0-10-596041-6 £3.00

Child Maintenance Act (Northern Ireland) 2008: chapter 10; explanatory notes. - 45p.: 30 cm. - These notes refer to the Child Maintenance Act (Northern Ireland) 2008 (c. 10) (ISBN 9780105950554) which received Royal assent on 2nd July 2008. - 978-0-10-596049-2 £7.50

Commission for Victims and Survivors (Northern Ireland) Act 2008: chapter 6; explanatory notes. - [8]p.: 30 cm. - These Notes refer to the Commission For Victims And Survivors Act (Northern Ireland) 2008 (c.6) (ISBN 9780105950516) which received Royal Assent 23 May 2008. - 978-0-10-596045-4 £3.00

Health (Miscellaneous Provisions) Act (Northern Ireland) 2008: chapter 2; explanatory notes. - 6p.: 30 cm. - These notes refer to the Health (Miscellaneous Provisions) Act (Northern Ireland) 2008 (c. 2) (ISBN 9780105950462) which received Royal assent on 25 February 2008. - 978-0-10-596038-6 £3.00

Other statutory publications

Statutory Publications Office.

Chronological table of statutory rules Northern Ireland : covering the legislation to 31 December 2006. - 3rd ed. - [approx. 780 pages]: looseleaf with binder holes: 30 cm. - 978-0-337-08982-4 £90.00

Chronological table of statutory rules Northern Ireland : covering the legislation to 31 December 2007. - 4th ed. - ca. 840 pages: looseleaf with binder holes: 30 cm. - Supersedes 3rd edition (ISBN 9780337089824). - 978-0-337-09029-5 £100.00

Chronological table of statutory rules Northern Ireland: covering the legislation to 31 December 2008. - 5th ed. - ca. 888 pages: looseleaf with binder holes: 30 cm. - Supersedes 4th edition (ISBN 9780337090295). - 978-0-337-09563-4 *£115.00*

Chronological table of the statutes Northern Ireland: covering the legislation to 31 December 2007. - 34th ed. - x, 1324p.: looseleaf with binder holes: 30 cm. - 978-0-337-09178-0 *£130.00*

The statutes revised: Northern Ireland. - Cumulative supplement vols A-D (1537 - 1920) to 31 December 2006. - 2nd ed. - x, 66p.: looseleaf with binder holes: 25 cm. - The material held in the main updated Statutes revised has been integrated into the UK Statute Law Database, available online at www.statutelaw.gov.uk. However, pre-1921 legislation published in vols A to D and amended since is not currently covered by the Statute Law Database, so printed supplements will continue to be issued for amendments made to that legislation. - 978-0-337-09062-2 *£20.00*

The statutes revised. - Cumulative supplement vols A-D (1537 - 1920) to 31 December 2007. - 2nd ed. - x, 66p.: looseleaf with binder holes: 25 cm. - The material held in the main updated Statutes revised has been integrated into the UK Statute Law Database, available online at www.statutelaw.gov.uk. However, pre-1921 legislation published in vols A to D and amended since is not currently covered by the Statute Law Database, so printed supplements will continue to be issued for amendments made to that legislation. - 978-0-337-09183-4 *£20.00*

The statutory rules of Northern Ireland 2007

Part 4: Nos. 451-509. - xxxvi, p. 3193-3642: hdbk: 31 cm. - 978-0-337-09608-2 *£275.00*

The statutory rules of Northern Ireland 2008

Part 1: Nos. 1-150. - xiv, p. 1-619: hdbk: 31 cm. - 978-0-337-09609-9 *£360.00*

Part 2. Sections 1 & 2: Nos. 151-251; 252-300. - 2v. (xiv, p. 621-1232; xiv p. 1233-1839) : hdbk: 31 cm. - 978-0-337-09610-5 *£710.00*

The statutory rules of Northern Ireland 2009

Part 1: Nos. 1-150. - 2 vol. (xiv, p. 1-1171): hdbk: 31 cm. - 978-0-337-09613-6 *£625.00*

Part 2: Nos. 151-300. - xiv, p. 1173-1934: hdbk: 31 cm. - 978-0-337-09614-3 *£440.00*

Title page and index to Northern Ireland statutes volume 2007. - 14p.: looseleaf with binder holes: 30 cm. - 978-0-337-09061-5 *£5.00*

Title page and index to Northern Ireland statutes volume 2008. - 14p.: looseleaf with binder holes: 30 cm. - 978-0-337-09179-7 *£5.00*

Statutory Rules of Northern Ireland

By Subject Heading

Agriculture

Agriculture (Student Fees) (Amendment) Regulations (Northern Ireland) 2008 No. 2008/389. - Enabling power: Agriculture Act (Northern Ireland) 1949, s. 5A (1) (2). - Issued: 26.09.2008. Made: 22.09.2008. Coming into operation: 20.10.2008. Effect: S.R. 2007/54 amended; S.R. 2007/410 revoked. - Partially revoked by S.R. 2009/321 (ISBN 9780337978692). - 4p: 30 cm. - 978-0-337-97521-9 *£4.00*

The Common Agricultural Policy Single Payment and Support Schemes (Amendment) Regulations (Northern Ireland) 2008 No. 2008/194. - Enabling power: European Communities Act 1972, s. 2 (2). - Issued: 07.05.2008. Made: 30.04.2008. Coming into operation: 31.05.2008. Effect: S.R. 2005/256 amended. - EC note: These Regs relate to provision in Northern Ireland for the administration of Council Regulation (EC) No. 1782/2003 and a number of other EC instruments relating to the system of direct support schemes (including the Single Payment Scheme) which was introduced under the Common Agricultural Policy in 2005. - 4p.: 30 cm. - 978-0-337-97376-5 *£3.00*

Countryside Management Regulations (Northern Ireland) 2008 No. 2008/174. - Enabling power: European Communities Act 1972, s. 2 (2). - Issued: 18.04.2008. Made: 14.04.2008. Coming into operation: 14.05.2008. Effect: S.R. 2005/268, 276, 277 revoked. - EC note: These Regulations supplement certain provisions of Council Regulation No. 1698/2005 on support for rural development from the European Agricultural Fund for Rural Development and also include provisions to meet the requirements of Commission Regulation No. 1975/2006. - 12p: 30 cm. - 978-0-337-97360-4 *£3.00*

The Environmental Impact Assessment (Agriculture) (Amendment) Regulations (Northern Ireland) 2008 No. 2008/278. - Enabling power: European Communities Act 1972, s. 2 (2). - Issued: 04.07.2008. Made: 01.07.2008. Coming into operation: 31.07.2008. Effect: S.R. 2007/421 amended. - 4p.: 30 cm. - 978-0-337-97441-0 *£3.00*

Farm Modernisation Programme Regulations (Northern Ireland) 2008 No. 2008/295. - Enabling power: European Communities Act 1972, s. 2 (2). - Issued: 29.07.2008. Made: 17.07.2008. Coming into operation: 21.08.2008. Effect: None. - EC note: These Regs supplement previous regulations and also implement art. 74 (1) of Council Regulation 1698/2005 and art. 9 (1) of Council Regulation 1290/2005 which require Member States to adopt legislative and administrative provisions to ensure that the Community financial interests in relation to expenditure on rural development are effectively protected. - 8p.: 30 cm. - 978-0-337-97468-7 *£3.00*

The Feeding Stuffs (Amendment) Regulations (Northern Ireland) 2008 No. 2008/260. - Enabling power: Agriculture Act 1970, ss. 66 (1), 68 (1), 74A, 84. - Issued: 30.06.2008. Made: 23.06.2008. Coming into operation: 30.07.2008. Effect: S.R. 2005/545 amended. - EC note: These Regs provide for the implementation of Commission Directive 2008/4/EC amending Directive 94/39/EC as regards feedingstuffs intended for the reduction of the risk of milk fever. - 8p: 30 cm. - 978-0-337-97431-1 £3.00

The Financial Assistance for Young Farmers Scheme (Amendment) Order (Northern Ireland) 2008 No. 2008/186. - Enabling power: S.I. 2004/3080 (N.I. 21), art. 3 (1) to (4) (7). - Issued: 30.04.2008. Made: 24.04.2008. Coming into operation: 02.06.2008. Effect: S.R. 2005/69 amended. - 4p.: 30 cm. - 978-0-337-97370-3 £3.00

The Less Favoured Area Compensatory Allowances (No. 2) Regulations (Northern Ireland) 2008 No. 2008/473. - Enabling power: European Communities Act 1972, s. 2 (2). - Issued: 08.12.2008. Made: 27.11.2008. Coming into operation: 01.01.2009. Effect: S.R. 2001/391 amended. - EC note: These Regulations provide for the implementation of Articles 13(a), 14(1), 14(2) first and second indents, 15 of Council Regulation (EC) No. 1257/1999 together with Articles 36(a)(ii) and 51(1) of Council Regulation (EC) No. 1698/2005, in so far as those Council Regulations relate to less favoured areas. - 12p.: 30 cm. - 978-0-337-97589-9 £5.00

Less Favoured Area Compensatory Allowances Regulations (Northern Ireland) 2008 No. 2008/34. - Enabling power: European Communities Act 1972, s. 2 (2). - Issued: 08.02.2008. Made: 30.01.2008. Coming into operation: 25.02.2008. Effect: S.R. 2001/391; 2007/361 amended & S.R. 2007/27 partially revoked. - EC note: These Regulations provide for the implementation of Arts 13(a), 14(1), 14(2) first and second indents, and 15 of Council Regulation No. 1257/1999 as last amended by Council Regulation No. 1698/2005. They also provide for the implementation of Measure 2.1 of the Northern Ireland Rural Development Programme approved by Commission Decision C(2007) 4411. - 12p.: 30 cm. - 978-0-337-97250-8 £3.00

Milk and Milk Products (Pupils in Educational Establishments) Regulations (Northern Ireland) 2008 No. 2008/323. - Enabling power: European Communities Act 1972, s. 2 (2), sch. 2, para. 1A. - Issued: 01.08.2008. Made: 28.07.2008. Coming into operation: 25.08.2008. Effect: S.R. 2001/129; 2007/490 revoked. - EC note: These Regulations provide that references to Council Regulation No 1234/2007 establishing a common organisation of agricultural markets and on specific provisions for certain agricultural products (Single CMO Regulation) and to Commission Regulation (EC) No 657/2008 laying down detailed rules for applying Council Regulation No 1234/2007 as regards Community aid for supplying milk and certain milk products to pupils in educational establishments are references to those Regulations as amended from time to time. These Regulations provide that, in the making of any national "top-up" aid payments as permitted by art. 102(2) of Regulation 1234/2007, such payments shall be subject to the same rules, requirements and conditions as apply to Community aid under art. 102(1) of that Council Regulation, and which are contained in Commission Regulation (EC) No 657/2008 (regulation 3). - 4p.: 30 cm. - 978-0-337-97473-1 £3.00

The Organic Farming (Amendment) Regulations (Northern Ireland) 2008 No. 2008/435. - Enabling power: European Communities Act 1972, s. 2 (2). - Issued: 12.11.2008. Made: 06.11.2008. Coming into operation: 01.01.2009. Effect: S.R. 2008/172 amended. - EC note: These Regulations amend S.R. 2008/172 by amending the interpretation of the Council Regulation to take account of the introduction of Council Regulation 834/2007 which repeals and replaces Council Regulation 2092/91 from 1 January 2009. - 4p: 30 cm. - 978-0-337-97564-6 £4.00

Organic Farming Regulations (Northern Ireland) 2008 No. 2008/172. - Enabling power: European Communities Act 1972, s. 2 (2). - Issued: 17.04.2008. Made: 10.04.2008. Coming into operation: 08.05.2008. Effect: S.R. 2001/5 revoked. - EC note: These Regulations provide for the payment of grant to farmers who agree to introduce organic farming methods and comply with the statutory management requirements and standards of good agricultural and environmental condition provided for in Articles 4 and 5 of and Annexes III and IV to Council Regulation (EC) No 1782/2003 (otherwise known as "cross compliance"). Grant paid under these Regulations is part of the Northern Ireland Rural Development Programme submitted by the United Kingdom to the European Commission in accordance with Article 18 of Council Regulation (EC) No. 1698/2005 on support for rural development by the European Agricultural Fund for Rural Development (EAFRD), and approved by the Commission on 24th July 2007. - 12p: 30 cm. - 978-0-337-97359-8 £3.00

The Pesticides (Maximum Residue Levels) Regulations (Northern Ireland) 2008 No. 2008/433. - Enabling power: European Communities Act 1972, s. 2 (2). - Issued: 11.11.2008. Made: 05.11.2008. Coming into operation: 08.12.2008. Effect: S.R. 2006/220, 501; 2007/428, 465; 2008/195 revoked. - EC note: These regs enforce the provisions of Regulation (EC) No 396/2005 on maximum residue levels of pesticides in or on food and feed of plant and animal origin and amending Council Directive 91/41/EEC. - 8p.: 30 cm. - 978-0-337-97562-2 £5.00

Pig Production Development (Levy) Revocation (No 2) Order (Northern Ireland) 2008 No. 2008/83. - Enabling power: Pig Production Development Act (Northern Ireland) 1964, s. 5 (1) (2) (3). - Issued: 10.03.2008. Made: 05.03.2008. Coming into operation: 01.04.2008. Effect: S.R. 1996/502; 2008/25 revoked. - This Statutory Rule has been made in consequence of a defect in SR 2008 No. 25 (ISBN 9780337972386) and is being issued free of charge to all known recipients of that Statutory Rule. - 2p.: 30 cm. - 978-0-337-97283-6 £3.00

Pig Production Development (Levy) Revocation Order (Northern Ireland) 2008 No. 2008/25. - Enabling power: Pig Production Development Act (Northern Ireland) 1964, s. 11 (1). - Issued: 29.01.2008. Made: 24.01.2008. Coming into operation: 01.04.2008. Effect: S.R. (N.I.) 1996/502 revoked. - With correction slip dated February 2008. Revoked by S.R. 2008/83 (ISBN 9780337972836). - 2p.: 30 cm. - 978-0-337-97238-6 £3.00

Pig Production Development (Levy) Revocation Order (Northern Ireland) 2008 (Correction slip) No. 2008/25 Cor.. - Correction slip (to ISBN 9780337972386) dated February 2008. - 1 sheet: 30 cm. *Free*

Reporting of Prices of Milk Products Regulations (Northern Ireland) 2008 No. 2008/240. - Enabling power: European Communities Act 1972, s. 2 (2), sch. 2, para. 1A. - Issued: 09.06.2008. Made: 03.06.2008. Coming into operation: 01.07.2008. Effect: S.R. 2005/286 revoked. - EC note: These Regulations implement Article 6 of Commission Regulation (EC) No. 562/2005 laying down rules for the implementation of Council Regulation (EC) No 1255/1999 as regards communications between the Member States and the Commission in the milk and milk products sector, as amended from time to time. - 4p: 30 cm. - 978-0-337-97408-3 £3.00

The Rice Products from the United States of America (Restriction on First Placing on the Market) Regulations (Northern Ireland) 2008 No. 2008/99. - Enabling power: European Communities Act 1972, s. 2 (2). - Issued: 14.03.2008. Made: 10.03.2008. Coming into operation: 12.03.2008. Effect: S.R. 2006/443 revoked. - EC note: These Regulations implement Commission Decision 2006/601/EC on emergency measures regarding the non-authorised genetically modified organism "LL RICE 601" in rice products as last amended by Commission Decision 2008/162/EC. - 4p.: 30 cm. - 978-0-337-97299-7 £3.00

Rural Development (Financial Assistance) Regulations (Northern Ireland) 2008 No. 2008/380. - Enabling power: European Communities Act 1972, s. 2 (2). - Issued: 26.09.2008. Made: 11.09.2008. Coming into operation: 15.10.2008. Effect: S.R. 2001/332 revoked with savings. - EC note: These regs supplement the Community legislation listed in the Schedule which inter alia provides for assistance to be paid from the European Agricultural Fund for Rural Development (EAFRD) towards operations which promote rural development by facilitating the improvement of the quality of life in rural areas and diversification of the rural economy. They also provide for the use of local action groups to assist with the delivery of rural development. The Northern Ireland Rural Development Programme 2007-2013 is co-funded by the EAFRD and the UK Exchequer. The Regulations also implement Article 74(1) of Council Regulation (EC) No. 1698/2005 and Article 9(1) of Council Regulation (EC) No. 1290/2005, which requires Member States to adopt legislative and administrative provisions to ensure that the Community's financial interests in relation to expenditure on rural development are effectively protected. - 12p.: 30 cm. - 978-0-337-97518-9 £5.00

The Seed Potatoes (Levy) (Revocation) Order (Northern Ireland) 2008 No. 2008/496. - Enabling power: S.I. 1984/702 (N.I. 2), art. 3(1) (2) (4) (6). - Issued: 17.12.2008. Made: 11.12.2008. Coming into operation: 01.05.2009. Effect: S.R. 1985/1; 1987/89; 1990/323; 2004/70 revoked. - 4p.: 30 cm. - 978-0-337-97602-5 £4.00

The Specified Products from China (Restriction on First Placing on the Market) Regulations (Northern Ireland) 2008 No. 2008/171. - Enabling power: European Communities Act 1972, s. 2 (2). - Issued: 17.04.2008. Made: 11.04.2008. Coming into operation: 15.04.2008. Effect: None. - EC note: These Regulations implement, in Northern Ireland, Commission Decision 2008/289/EC on emergency measures regarding the unauthorised genetically modified organism 'Bt 63' in rice products. - 4p.: 30 cm. - 978-0-337-97358-1 £3.00

Supply Chain Development Programme Grant Regulations (Northern Ireland) 2008 No. 2008/296. - Enabling power: European Communities Act 1972, s. 2 (2). - Issued: 29.07.2008. Made: 17.07.2008. Coming into operation: 21.08.2008. Effect: None. - EC note: These Regs supplement previous regulations and also implement art. 74 (1) of Council Regulation 1698/2005 and art. 9 (1) of Council Regulation 1290/2005 which require Member States to adopt legislative and administrative provisions to ensure that the Community financial interests in relation to expenditure on rural development are effectively protected. - 8p.: 30 cm. - 978-0-337-97469-4 £3.00

Agriculture

Vocational Training and Information Actions Grant Regulations (Northern Ireland) 2008 No. 2008/297. - Enabling power: European Communities Act 1972, s. 2 (2). - Issued: 29.07.2008. Made: 17.07.2008. Coming into operation: 21.08.2008. Effect: None. - EC note: These Regs supplement previous regulations and also implement art. 74 (1) of Council Regulation 1698/2005 and art. 9 (1) of Council Regulation 1290/2005 which require Member States to adopt legislative and administrative provisions to ensure that the Community financial interests in relation to expenditure on rural development are effectively protected. - 8p.: 30 cm. - 978-0-337-97467-0 £3.00

Agriculture: Pesticides

Pesticides (Maximum Residue Levels in Crops, Food and Feeding Stuffs) (Amendment) Regulations (Northern Ireland) 2008 No. 2008/195. - Enabling power: European Communities Act 1972, s. 2 (2). - Issued: 09.05.2008. Made: 01.05.2008. Coming into operation: 16.06.2008. Effect: S.R. 2006/220 amended. - Revoked by S.R. 2008/433 (ISBN 9780337975622). EC note: These regs implement Commission Directives 2007/27/EC; 2007/28/EC; 2007/39/EC; 2007/56/EC; and 2007/73/EC (in relation to Deltamethrin only). - 32p.: 30 cm. - 978-0-337-97378-9 £5.50

Airports

The Airports (Designation) (Power to Detain and Sell Aircraft) Order (Northern Ireland) 2008 No. 2008/13. - Enabling power: S.I. 1994/426 (N.I. 1), art. 23 (1). - Issued: 16.01.2008. Made: 10.01.2007. Coming into operation: 11.02.2008. Effect: None. - 2p.: 30 cm. - 978-0-337-97225-6 £3.00

Animal health

The Transmissible Spongiform Encephalopathies Regulations (Northern Ireland) 2008 No. 2008/508. - Enabling power: European Communities Act 1972, s. 2 (2). - Issued: 09.01.2009. Made: 22.12.2008. Coming into operation: 01.01.2009. Effect: S.R. 2005/515; 2006/202; 2007/307; 2008/188 revoked. - EC note: These Regulations revoke and remake with amendments The Transmissible Spongiform Encephalopathies Regulations (Northern Ireland) 2006 (S.R. 2006 No. 202 as amended), which enforced Regulation (EC) No 999/2001 laying down rules for the prevention, control and eradication of certain transmissible spongiform encephalopathies as amended. These Regulations implement Commission Decision 2007/411 prohibiting the placing on the market of products derived from bovine animals born or reared within the United Kingdom before 1st August 1996 for any purpose and exempting such animals from certain control and eradication measures laid down in Regulation (EC) No. 999/2001 and repealing Decision 2005/598. - 48p.: 30 cm. - 978-0-337-97616-2 £9.00

Animals

The Animals and Animal Products (Import and Export) (Amendment) Regulations (Northern Ireland) 2008 No. 2008/53. - Enabling power: European Communities Act 1972, s. 2 (2) & Finance Act 1973, s. 56 (1) (2) (5). - Issued: 14.02.2008. Made: 08.02.2008. Coming into operation: 10.03.2008. Effect: S.R. 2006/401 amended. - Partially revoked by S.R. 2009/86 (ISBN 9780337976933). EC note: These regs take account of Commission Regulation No. 1266/2007 on implementing rules for Council Directive 2000/75/EC as regards the control, monitoring, surveillance and restrictions on movements of certain animals of susceptible species in relation to bluetongue. - 4p: 30 cm. - 978-0-337-97262-1 £3.00

The Zootechnical Standards (Amendment) Regulations (Northern Ireland) 2008 No. 2008/37. - Enabling power: European Communities Act 1972, s. 2 (2). - Issued: 08.02.2008. Made: 01.02.2008. Coming into operation: 22.02.2008. Effect: S.R. 1992/438 amended. - EC note: These regs give effect to the amendments to Council Directive 87/328/EEC on the acceptance for breeding purposes of pure-bred breeding animals of the bovine species made by Council Directive 2005/24/EC with regard to the use of ova and embryos and storage centres for semen from pure-bred breeding animals of the bovine species. - 4p: 30 cm. - 978-0-337-97247-8 £3.00

Animals: Animal health

The Avian Influenza (Miscellaneous Amendments) Regulations (Northern Ireland) 2008 No. 2008/197. - Enabling power: European Communities Act 1972, s. 2 (2). - Issued: 09.05.2008. Made: 02.05.2008. Coming into operation: 29.05.2008. Effect: S.R. 2007/70, 207, 208 amended. - This statutory rule has been made in consequence of a defect in S.R. 2007 nos. 70 (ISBN 9780337968549), 207 (ISBN 9780337969706) & 208 (ISBN 9780337969713) and is being issued free of charge to all known recipients of those statutory rules- 4p: 30 cm. - 978-0-337-97380-2 £3.00

The Bluetongue (Amendment) Order (Northern Ireland) 2008 No. 2008/59. - Enabling power: European Communities Act 1972, s. 2 (2), sch. 2, para. 1A & S.I.1981/1115 (N.I.22), arts 5 (1), 10 (6), 12 (1), 14, 19, 20, 44, 46 (7A), 60 (1). - Issued: 21.02.2008. Made: 15.02.2008. Coming into operation: 16.02.2008. Effect: S.R. 2008/38 amended. - 2p: 30 cm. - 978-0-337-97265-2 £3.00

The Bluetongue Order (Northern Ireland) Order 2008 No. 2008/38. - Enabling power: European Communities Act 1972, sch. 2, para. 1A & S.I. 1981/1115 (N.I. 22) arts 5 (1), 10 (6), 12 (1), 14, 19, 20, 44, 46 (7A), 60 (1). - Issued: 08.02.2008. Made: 01.02.2008. Coming into operation: 22.02.2008. Effect: S.R. 2003/55 revoked. - Revoked by S.R. 2008/275 (ISBN 9780337974380). EC note: This Order continues to implement Council Directive 2000/75/EC laying down specific provisions for the control and eradication of bluetongue. It revokes and remakes the Bluetongue Order (Northern Ireland) 2003 in order to enforce Commission Regulation (EC) No. 1266/2007. - 12p: 30 cm. - 978-0-337-97248-5 *£3.00*

The Bluetongue Regulations (Northern Ireland) 2008 No. 2008/275. - Enabling power: European Communities Act 1972, s. 2 (2), sch. 2, para. 1A. - Issued: 04.07.2008. Made: 30.06.2008. Coming into operation: 21.07.2008. Effect: S.R. 2008/38 revoked. - EC note: These Regulations implement Council Directive 2000/75/EC and enforce Commission Regulation (EC) 1266/2007. - 12p: 30 cm. - 978-0-337-97438-0 *£3.00*

The Control of Salmonella in Poultry Scheme Order (Northern Ireland) 2008 No. 2008/263. - Enabling power: S.I. 1981/1115 (N.I. 22), art. 8 (1) (2). - Issued: 01.07.2008. Made: 25.06.2008. Coming into operation: 28.07.2008. Effect: S.R. 2007/209 revoked. - EC note: These Regulations enforce Commission Regulation (EC) No 1003/2005, Commission Regulation (EC) No 1168/2006 and Commission Regulation (EC) No 1177/2006. - This Statutory Rule has been printed to correct errors in the SR of the same number and ISBN (issued 01.07.2008) and is being issued free of charge to all known recipients of the original version. - 12p.: 30 cm. - 978-0-337-97434-2 *£3.00*

The Products of Animal Origin (Disease Control) Regulations (Northern Ireland) 2008 No. 2008/431. - Enabling power: European Communities Act 1972, s. 2 (2). - Issued: 31.10.2008. Made: 27.10.2008. Coming into operation: 21.11.2008. Effect: None. - EC note: These Regulations partially transpose in Northern Ireland Articles 3 and 4 of Council Directive 2002/99/EC laying down the animal health rules governing the production, processing, distribution and introduction of products of animal origin for human consumption. These Regulations also transpose, insofar as they apply to Newcastle disease, the Commission Decision 2007/118/EC establishing an alternative health mark pursuant to Directive 2002/99/EC. - 16p: 30 cm. - 978-0-337-97558-5 *£5.00*

The Specified Animal Pathogens Order (Northern Ireland) 2008 No. 2008/336. - Enabling power: S.I. 1981/1115 (N.I. 22), arts. 2 (3), 5 (1), 19, 30 (1), 60 (1). - Issued: 12.08.2008. Made: 06.08.2008. Coming into force: 30.08.2008. Effect: S.R. 1999/436 revoked. - 12p.: 25 cm. - 978-0-337-97480-9 *£3.00*

The Transmissible Spongiform Encephalopathies (Amendment) Regulations (Northern Ireland) 2008 No. 2008/188. - Enabling power: European Communities Act 1972, s. 2 (2). - Issued: 01.05.2008. Made: 24.04.2008. Coming into operation: 26.04.2008. Effect: S.R. 2006/202 amended & S.R. 1997/540; 1999/495 revoked. - Revoked by S.R. 2008/508 (ISBN 9780337976162). EC note: These Regulations provide for the enforcement of Regulation (EC) No. 999/2001laying down rules for the prevention, control and eradication of certain transmissible spongiform encephalopathies, as amended. - 12p.: 30 cm. - 978-0-337-97371-0 *£3.00*

The Welfare of Animals (Slaughter or Killing) (Amendment) Regulations (Northern Ireland) 2008 No. 2008/277. - Enabling power: European Communities Act, s. 2 (2). - Issued: 04.07.20008. Made: 30.06.2008. Coming into operation: 31.07.2008. Effect: S.R. 1996/558 amended. - EC note: These Regulations insert a new Schedule 7A into the 1996 Regulations, which implement Directive 93/119/EC on the protection of animals at the time of slaughter or killing, and also give effect to amendments to that Directive made by Regulation (EC) 1/2005 on the protection of animals during transport. - 8p: 30 cm. - 978-0-337-97440-3 *£3.00*

The Zoonoses and Animal By-Products (Fees) Regulations (Northern Ireland) 2008 No. 2008/359. - Enabling power: European Communities Act 1972, s. 2 (2) & Finance Act 1973, s. 56 (1) (2) (5). - Issued: 05.09.2008. Made: 01.09.2008. Coming into operation: 26.09.2008. Effect: S.R. 2004/146 revoked. - EC note: These Regulations make provision for the Department to charge fees for activities required under Commission Regulation (EC) 1003/2005. - 4p.: 30 cm. - 978-0-337-97498-4 *£4.00*

The Zoonoses (Monitoring) Regulations (Northern Ireland) 2008 No. 2008/340. - Enabling power: European Communities Act 1972, s. 2 (2). - Issued: 13.08.2008. Made: 07.08.2008. Coming into operation: 31.08.2008. Effect: None. - EC note: These Regulations provide inspectors with powers of entry to monitor for zoonoses and antimicrobial resistance to zoonotic agents and other agents that pose a threat to public health, as required by Directive 2003/99/EC (on the monitoring of zoonoses and zoonotic agents, amending Council Decision 90/424/EEC and repealing Council Directive 92/117/EEC) (regulation 4). - 8p.: 30 cm. - 978-0-337-97482-3 *£3.00*

Animals: Diseases

The Diseases of Animals (Approval of Disinfectants) Order (Northern Ireland) 2008 No. 2008/272. - Enabling power: S.I. 1981 No.1115 (N.I.22), arts 5, 19, 60 (1). - Issued: 03.07.2008. Made: 27.06.2008. Coming into operation: 28.07.2008. Effect: S.R. 1972/16; 1975/69; 1995/467 revoked. - 8p: 30 cm. - 978-0-337-97437-3 *£3.00*

Audit and accountability

The Companies (Public Sector Audit) Order (Northern Ireland) 2008 No. 2008/264. - Enabling power: S.I. 2003/418 (N.I. 5), arts 5 (3) (4). - Issued: 01.07.2008. Made: 25.06.2008. Coming into operation: 01.07.2008. Effect: None. - Supersedes draft S.R. (ISBN 9780337973741) issued 02.05.2008. - 2p.: 30 cm. - 978-0-337-97435-9 £3.00

Institutions of Further Education (Public Sector Audit) Order (Northern Ireland) 2008 No. 2008/511. - Enabling power: S.I. 2003/418 (N.I. 5), art. 5 (3) (4). - Issued: 09.01.2009. Made: 09.12.2008. Coming into operation: 09.12.2008. Effect: SI 1997/1772 (N.I. 15) amended. - Supersedes draft S.R. (ISBN 9780337975806) issued 02.12.2008. - 4p.: 30 cm. - 978-0-337-97619-3 £4.00

Child support

The Child Support (Consequential Provisions) Regulations (Northern Ireland) 2008 No. 2008/404. - Enabling power: Child Maintenance Act (Northern Ireland) 2008, s. 38 (2). - Issued: 08.10.2008. Made: 02.10.2008. Coming into operation: 27.10.2008. Effect: S.R. 1992/340; 1995/162, 475; 1996/289, 317, 358, 503, 541; 1999/162, 167, 246 (C.20); 2001/17, 18, 19, 20, 21; 2002/164; 2003/84, 469; 2005/125 amended. - Partially revoked by S.R. 2009/133 (ISBN 9780337977275). - 8p.: 30 cm. - 978-0-337-97533-2 £5.00

The Child Support Information Regulations (Northern Ireland) 2008 No. 2008/403. - Enabling power: S.I. 1991/2628 (NI. 23), ss. 7 (4), 16 (1) (3), 46 (5), 47 (1), 48 (4), 50 (1) (2), sch. 1, para. 16 (11). - Issued: 08.10.2008. Made: 02.10.2008. Coming into operation: 27.10.2008. Effect: S.R. 1994/65; 1995/19, 162, 475; 1996/317, 541; 1998/8; 1999/152, 246 (C.20); 2001/16; 2002/164; 2004/428; 2005/536; 2006/273; 2007/347; 2008/119 amended and S.R. 1992/339; 2003/522 revoked. - 12p.: 30 cm. - 978-0-337-97532-5 £5.00

The Child Support, Pensions and Social Security (2000 Act) (Commencement No. 11) Order (Northern Ireland) 2008 No. 2008/402 (C.23). - Enabling power: Child Support, Pensions and Social Security Act (Northern Ireland) 2000, s. 68 (2) (a). Bringing into operation various provisions of the 2000 Act on 03.10.2008 and 27.10.2008, in accord. with art. 2. - Issued: 08.10.2008. Made: 02.10.2008. Effect: None. - 4p.: 30 cm. - 978-0-337-97531-8 £4.00

Clean air

The Smoke Control Areas (Authorised Fuels) Regulations (Northern Ireland) 2008 No. 2008/415. - Enabling power: S.I. 1981/158 (N.I. 4), art. 2 (2). - Issued: 10.10.2008. Made: 03.10.2008. Coming into operation: 07.10.2008. Effect: S.R. 2003/450 revoked & 2007/17 revoked with savings. - 16p: 30 cm. - 978-0-337-97543-1 £5.00

The Smoke Control Areas (Exempted Fireplaces) (Amendment) Regulations (Northern Ireland) 2008 No. 2008/282. - Enabling power: S.I. 1981/158 (N.I. 4), art. 17 (7). - Issued: 08.07.2008. Made: 02.07.2008. Coming into operation: 04.08.2008. Effect: S.R. 1999/289 amended. - Revoked by S.R. 2009/257 (ISBN 9780337978289). - 12p.: 30 cm. - 978-0-337-97444-1 £3.00

Companies

The Companies (1986 Order) (Annual Return) and Companies (Principal Business Activities) (Amendment) Regulations (Northern Ireland) 2008 No. 2008/379. - Enabling power: S.I. 1986/1032 (N.I. 6), arts 372 (3), 373 (1), 681 (1). - Issued: 22.09.2008. Made: 16.09.2008. Coming into operation: 01.10.2008. Effect: S.I. 1986/1032 (N.I. 6) & S.R. 1991/399 amended. - 8p: 30 cm. - 978-0-337-97514-1 £5.00

The Companies (Late Filing Penalties) Regulations (Northern Ireland) 2008 No. 2008/133. - Enabling power: S.I. 1986/1032 (N.I. 6), art. 265 (1). - Issued: 31.03.2008. Made: 19.03.2008. Coming into operation: 06.04.2008. Effect: S.I. 1986/1032 (N.I.6) amended. - 4p.: 30 cm. - 978-0-337-97329-1 £3.00

The Companies (Tables A to F) (Amendment) Regulations (Northern Ireland) 2008 No. 2008/161. - Enabling power: S.I. 1986/1032 (N.I. 6), arts. 119 (4) (a) (c), 681 (1). - Issued: 10.04.2008. Made: 07.04.2008. Coming into operation: 01.05.2008. Effect: S.R. 1986/264 amended. - 2p.: 30 cm. - 978-0-337-97353-6 £3.00

The Insolvency (Amendment) Rules (Northern Ireland) 2008 No. 2008/118. - Enabling power: S.I. 1989/2405 (N.I. 19), art. 359. - Issued: 15.04.2008. Made: 12.03.2008. Coming into operation: 06.04.2008. Effect: S.R. 1991/364 amended. - 20p: 30 cm. - 978-0-337-97315-4 £3.50

The Limited Liability Partnerships (Filing Periods and Late Filing Penalties) Regulations (Northern Ireland) 2008 No. 2008/134. - Enabling power: Limited Liability Partnerships Act (Northern Ireland) 2002, s. 11 (a). - Issued: 31.03.2008. Made: 19.03.2008. Coming into operation: 06.04.2008. Effect: S.R. 2004/307 amended. - 4p.: 30 cm. - 978-0-337-97331-4 £3.00

Coroners

The Coroners (Practice and Procedure) (Amendment) Rules (Northern Ireland) 2008 No. 2008/32. - Enabling power: Coroners Act (Northern Ireland) Act 1959, s. 36 (1) (b), (1B) (1C). - Issued: 08.02.2008. Made: 29.01.2008. Coming into operation: 01.03.2008. Effect: S.R. 1963/199 amended. - 4p: 30 cm. - 978-0-337-97245-4 £3.00

County courts

The County Court (Amendment) Rules (Northern Ireland) 2008 No. 2008/199. - Enabling power: S.I. 1980/397 (N.I.3), art. 47. - Issued: 12.05.2008. Made: 03.05.2008. Coming into operation: 30.05.2008. Effect: S.R. 1981/225 amended. - 4p: 30 cm. - 978-0-337-97382-6 *£3.00*

The Family Proceedings (Amendment No. 2) Rules (Northern Ireland) 2008 No. 2008/259. - Enabling power: S.I. 1993/1576 (N.I. 6), art. 12. - Issued: 27.06.2008. Made: 20.06.2008. Coming into operation: 05.09.2008. Effect: S.R. 1996/322 amended. - 4p.: 30 cm. - 978-0-337-97428-1 *£3.00*

The Family Proceedings (Amendment No. 3) Rules (Northern Ireland) 2008 No. 2008/466. - Enabling power: S.I. 1993/1576 (N.I. 6), art. 12. - Issued: 28.11.2008. Made: 20.11.2008. Coming into operation: 22.12.2008. Effect: S.R. 1996/322 amended. - 16p.: 30 cm. - 978-0-337-97579-0 *£5.00*

The Family Proceedings (Amendment) Rules (Northern Ireland) 2008 No. 2008/24. - Enabling power: S.I. 1993/1576 (N.I. 6), art. 12. - Issued: 07.02.2008. Made: 22.01.2008. Coming into operation: 25.02.2008. Effect: S.R. 1996/322 amended. - 4p.: 30 cm. - 978-0-337-97237-9 *£3.00*

Criminal justice

Juvenile Justice Centre Rules (Northern Ireland) 2008 No. 2008/427. - Enabling power: S.I. 1998/1504 (NI. 9), art. 52 (1). - Issued: 30.10.2008. Made: 20.10.2008. Coming into operation: 12.11.2008. Effect: S.R. 1999/28 revoked. - 20p.: 30 cm. - 978-0-337-97557-8 *£5.00*

Criminal law

The Criminal Justice (Northern Ireland) Order 2004 (Commencement No. 3) Order 2008 No. 2008/471 (C.27). - Enabling power: S.I. 2004/1500 (N.I. 9), art. 1 (3). Bringing various provisions of the 2004 Order into operation on 02.02.2009 in accord. with art. 2. - Issued: 01.12.2008. Made: 20.11.2008. Coming into operation: -. Effect: None. - 2p.: 30 cm. - 978-0-337-97581-3 *£4.00*

Criminal Justice (Northern Ireland) Order 2008 (Commencement No.1 and Savings and Transitory Provisions) Order 2008 No. 2008/217 (C.8). - Enabling power: S.I. 2008/1216 (N.I. 1), arts 1 (4), 100 (4). Bringing various provisions of the 2008 Order into operation on 15.05.2008 in accord. with art. 2. - Issued: 21.05.2008. Made: 15.05.2008. Coming into operation: -. Effect: None. - 8p.: 30 cm. - 978-0-337-97391-8 *£3.00*

Criminal Justice (Northern Ireland) Order 2008 (Commencement No. 2) Order 2008 No. 2008/293 (C.16). - Enabling power: S.I. 2008/1216 (N.I. 1), arts 1 (4), 100 (4). Bringing various provisions of the 2008 Order into operation on 16.07.2008 in accord. with art. 2. - Issued: 16.07.2008. Made: 25.06.2008. Coming into operation: -. Effect: None. - 4p.: 30 cm. - 978-0-337-97453-3 *£3.00*

Criminal Justice (Northern Ireland) Order 2008 (Commencement No. 3 and Transitional Provisions) Order 2008 No. 2008/383 (C. 20). - Enabling power: S.I. 2008/1216 (N.I. 1), arts 1 (4), 100 (4). Bringing various provisions of the 2008 Order into operation on 06.10.2008 in accord. with art. 2. - Issued: 24.09.2008. Made: 17.09.2008. Coming into operation: -. Effect: None. - 4p.: 30 cm. - 978-0-337-97517-2 *£4.00*

Criminal Justice (Northern Ireland) Order 2008 (Commencement No. 4) Order 2008 No. 2008/472 (C.28). - Enabling power: S.I. 2008/1216 (N.I. 1), art. 1 (4). Bringing various provisions of the 2008 Order into operation in accord. with art. 2. - Issued: 01.12.2008. Made: 20.11.2008. Coming into operation: -. Effect: None. - 4p.: 30 cm. - 978-0-337-97582-0 *£4.00*

The Criminal Justice (Northern Ireland) Order 2008 (Retention and Disposal of Seized Motor Vehicles) Regulations (Northern Ireland) 2008 No. 2008/495. - Enabling power: S.I. 2008/1216 (N.I. 1), art. 66. - Issued: 19.12.2008. Made: 11.12.2008. Laid: 16.12.2008. Coming into operation: 06.01.2009. Effect: None. - 8p.: 30 cm. - 978-0-337-97606-3 *£5.00*

Sexual Offences (Northern Ireland) Order 2008 (Commencement) Order 2008 No. 2008/510 (C.30). - Enabling power: S.I. 2008/1769 (N.I. 2), art. 1 (3). Bringing various provisions of the 2008 Order into operation on 02.02.2009. - Issued: 09.01.2009. Made: 24.12.2008. Coming into operation: -. Effect: None. - 2p.: 30 cm. - 978-0-337-97618-6 *£4.00*

Disabled persons

The Disability Discrimination Act 1995 (Commencement No. 10) Order (Northern Ireland) 2008 No. 2008/236 (C.12). - Enabling power: Disability Discrimination Act 1995, s. 70 (3). Bringing into operation various provisions of the 1995 Act on 03.06.2008. - Issued: 06.06.2008. Made: 02.06.2008. Coming into operation: -. Effect: None. - 8p: 30 cm. - 978-0-337-97404-5 *£3.00*

The Disability Discrimination (Guidance on the Definition of Disability) (Appointed Day) Order (Northern Ireland) 2008 No. 2008/141. - Enabling power: Disability Discrimination Act 1995, ss. 3 (9), 67 (2) (3) (a). Bringing "Guidance on matters to be taken into account in determining questions relating to the definition of disability" (as laid before the Assembly in draft on 11th December 2007 and issued under section 3(8) of the 1995 Act on 21st March 2008) into operation on 21.04.2008. - Issued: 01.04.2008. Made: 21.03.2008. Coming into operation: -. Effect: None. - 4p: 30 cm. - 978-0-337-97335-2 *£3.00*

The Disability Discrimination (Guidance on the Definition of Disability) (Revocation) Order (Northern Ireland) 2008 No. 2008/140. - Enabling power: Disability Discrimination Act 1995, ss. 3 (11) (b), 67 (2) (3) (a). - Issued: 01.04.2008. Made: 21.03.2008. Coming into operation: 21.04.2008. Effect: Guidance on matters to be taken into account in determining questions relating to the definition of disability (ISBN No. 0-337-09436-5, referred to in S.R. 1996/549) revoked with saving. - 4p: 30 cm. - 978-0-337-97336-9 £3.00

The Disability Discrimination (Private Clubs, etc.) Regulations (Northern Ireland) 2008 No. 2008/81. - Enabling power: Disability Discrimination Act 1995, ss. 21F (6), 21G (5) (7), 21H (1) (2), 67 (2) (3), 68 (1). - Issued: 10.03.2008. Made: 04.03.2008. Coming into operation: 05.03.2008 in accord. with reg. 1. Effect: None. - Supersedes draft (ISBN 9780337972225) issued 04.01.2008. - 12p.: 30 cm. - 978-0-337-97281-2 £3.00

The Disability Discrimination (Private Hire Vehicles) (Carrying of Guide Dogs etc.) Regulations (Northern Ireland) 2008 No. 2008/19. - Enabling power: Disability Discrimination Act 1995, s. 37A (8) (b) (9). - Issued: 23.01.2008. Made: 16.01.2008. Coming into operation: 28.02.2008 for reg. 2 (1) & 01.06.2008 for remainder, in accord. with reg. 1 (1). Effect: None. - 4p.: 30 cm. - 978-0-337-97229-4 £3.00

Education

The Education (Student Loans) (Amendment) Regulations (Northern Ireland) 2008 No. 2008/255. - Enabling power: S.I. 1990/1506 (N.I. 11), art. 3 (5), sch. 2, para. 1 (1). - Issued: 26.06.2008. Made: 16.06.2008. Coming into operation: 01.08.2008. Effect: S.R. 1998/58; 2007/329 amended. - 4p.: 30 cm. - 978-0-337-97421-2 £3.00

The Education (Student Loans) (Repayment) (Amendment) Regulations (Northern Ireland) 2008 No. 2008/129. - Enabling power: S.I.1998/1760 (N.I. 14), arts 3 (2), 8 (4). - Issued: 26.03.2008. Made: 13.03.2008. Coming into operation: 01.04.2008. Effect: S.R. 2000/121 amended. - Revoked by S.R. 2009/128 (ISBN 9780337977237). - 4p.: 30 cm. - 978-0-337-97326-0 £3.00

The Education (Student Support) Regulations (Northern Ireland) 2008 No. 2008/250. - Enabling power: S.I. 1998/1760 (N.I. 14), arts 3, 8 (4). - Issued: 26.06.2008. Made: 16.06.2008. Coming into operation: 17.07.2008. Effect: S.R. 2007/195 amended and then revoked with saving; 2007/293, 363 revoked (both on 01.09.2008 in accord. with art. 4). - Revoked by S.R. 2009/37 (ISBN 9780337976407). - 128p.: 30 cm. - 978-0-337-97416-8 £17.50

The Further Education (Student Support) (Eligibility) Regulations (Northern Ireland) 2008 No. 2008/324. - Enabling power: S.I. 1998/1760 (N.I. 14), arts 3 (2), 8 (4). - Issued: 01.08.2008. Made: 25.07.2008. Coming into operation: 01.09.2008. Effect: S.R. 2007/342 revoked. - Revoked by S.R. 2009/211 (ISBN 9780337977862). - 12p.: 30 cm. - 978-0-337-97474-8 £3.00

Grammar Schools (Charges) (Amendment) Regulations (Northern Ireland) 2008 No. 2008/376. - Enabling power: S.I. 1989/2406 (N.I. 20), art. 132 (2) (3). - Issued: 16.09.2008. Made: 09.09.2008. Coming into operation: 01.11.2008. Effect: S.R. 1992/171 amended & S.R. 2006/511 revoked. - 2p.: 30 cm. - 978-0-337-97511-0 £4.00

The Special Educational Needs and Disability (2005 Order) (Amendment) (General Qualifications Bodies) (Alteration of Premises and Enforcement) Regulations (Northern Ireland) 2008 No. 2008/177. - Enabling power: S.I. 2005/1117 (N.I. 6), arts 38 (1) (2) (5) (6), 49 (4). - Issued: 23.04.2008. Made: 16.04.2008. Coming into operation: 23.04.2008. Effect: S.I. 2005/1117 (N.I. 6) amended. - Supersedes Draft SR (ISBN 9780337973024) issued 26.03.2008. - 12p.: 30 cm. - 978-0-337-97362-8 £3.00

The Special Educational Needs and Disability (General Qualifications Bodies) (Relevant Qualifications, Reasonable Steps and Physical Features) Regulations (Northern Ireland) 2008 No. 2008/79. - Enabling power: S.I. 2005/1117 (N.I. 6), arts 34 (4), 37 (6) (c) (d) (f), 38 (7), 49 (4). - Issued: 11.03.2008. Made: 03.03.2008. Coming into operation: 01.04.2008. Effect: None. - 4p.: 30 cm. - 978-0-337-97280-5 £3.00

The Student Fees (Amounts) (Amendment) Regulations (Northern Ireland) 2008 No. 2008/455. - Enabling power: S.I. 2005/1116 (N.I. 5), arts. 4 (8), 14 (4). - Issued: 25.11.2008. Made: 19.11.2008. Coming into operation: 01.09.2009. Effect: S.R. 2005/290 amended & S.R. 2007/442 revoked. - 2p.: 30 cm. - 978-0-337-97573-8 £4.00

Students Awards (Amendment) Regulations (Northern Ireland) 2008 No. 2008/254. - Enabling power: S.I. 1986/594 (N.I. 3), arts 50 (1) (2), 134 (1). - Issued: 26.06.2008. Made: 16.06.2008. Coming into operation: 01.08.2008. Effect: S.R. 2003/459 amended & S.R. 2007/336 partially revoked. - 4p.: 30 cm. - 978-0-337-97420-5 £3.00

The Teachers' Pensions (Miscellaneous Amendments) Regulations (Northern Ireland) 2008 No. 2008/50. - Enabling power: S.I. 1972/1073 (N.I. 10), arts. 11 (1) (2) (3) (3A), 14 (1), sch. 3, paras 1, 3, 4, 5, 6, 8, 11, 13. - Issued: 14.02.2008. Made: 07.03.2008. Coming into operation: 01.03.2008. Effect: S.R. 1996/260; 1998/333 amended. - 2p.: 30 cm. - 978-0-337-97261-4 £3.00

Electricity

Electricity (Guarantees of Origin of Electricity Produced from Renewable Energy Sources) (Amendment) Regulations (Northern Ireland) 2008 No. 2008/507. - Enabling power: European Communities Act 1972, s. 2 (2). - Issued: 08.01.2009. Made: 19.12.2008. Coming into operation: 02.02.2009. Effect: S.R. 2003/470 amended. - 4p.: 30 cm. - 978-0-337-97615-5 £4.00

Electricity (Offshore Wind and Water Driven Generating Stations) (Permitted Capacity) Order (Northern Ireland) 2008 No. 2008/54. - Enabling power: S.I. 1992/231 (N.I. 1), art. 39 (3). - Issued: 14.02.2008. Made: 07.02.2008. Coming into operation: 05.03.2008. Effect: S.I. 1992/231 (N.I. 1) amended. - 2p: 30 cm. - 978-0-337-97263-8 £3.00

The Energy Order 2003 (Supply of Information) Regulations (Northern Ireland) 2008 No. 2008/3. - Enabling power: S.I. 2003/419 (N.I.6), art. 27 (1), 66 (3). - Issued: 14.01.2008. Made: 07.01.2008. Coming into operation: 15.02.2008. Effect: None. - 8p.: 30 cm. - 978-0-337-97227-0 £3.00

The Guarantees of Origin of Electricity Produced from High-efficiency Cogeneration Regulations (Northern Ireland) 2008 No. 2008/287. - Enabling power: European Communities Act 1972, s. 2 (2). - Issued: 11.07.2008. Made: 30.06.2008. Coming into operation: 22.09.2008. Effect: None. - These Regulations implement as respects Northern Ireland Article 5 of the Directive 2004/8/EC on the promotion of cogeneration based on a useful heat demand in the internal energy market and amending Directive 92/42/EEC. That article provides for the issue of guarantees of origin of electricity from high-efficiency cogeneration. The cogeneration of electricity is more commonly referred to in the United Kingdom as electricity produced from combined heat and power or CHP. - 8p: 30 cm. - 978-0-337-97447-2 £3.00

The Offshore Electricity Development (Environmental Impact Assessment) Regulations (Northern Ireland) 2008 No. 2008/55. - Enabling power: European Communities Act 1972, s. 2 (2). - Issued: 14.02.2008. Made: 07.02.2008. Coming into operation: 05.03.2008. Effect: None. - EC note: These Regulations are concerned with the implementation in Northern Ireland of Council Directive 85/337/EEC as amended by Council Directive 97/11/EC on the assessment of the effects of certain public and private developments on the environment. - 16p: 30 cm. - 978-0-337-97264-5 £3.00

Employment

The Conduct of Employment Agencies and Employment Businesses (Amendment) Regulations (Northern Ireland) 2008 No. 2008/76. - Enabling power: S.I. 1981/839 (N.I. 20), arts 6 (1), 7 (1), 10 (1). - Issued: 05.03.2008. Made: 28.02.2008. Coming into operation: 06.04.2008. Effect: S.R. 2005/395 amended. - 4p.: 30 cm. - 978-0-337-97278-2 £3.00

The Employment Rights (Increase of Limits) Order (Northern Ireland) 2008 No. 2008/47. - Enabling power: S.I. 1999/2790 (N.I. 9), arts 33 (2) (3), 39 (3). - Issued: 12.02.2008. Made: 06.02.2008. Coming into operation: 02.03.2008. Effect: S.R. 2007/22 revoked. - Revoked by S.R. 2009/45 (ISBN 9780337976483). - 8p: 30 cm. - 978-0-337-97256-0 £3.00

The Fixed-term Employees (Prevention of Less Favourable Treatment) (Amendment) (No. 2) Regulations (Northern Ireland) 2008 No. 2008/416. - Enabling power: Employment Act 2002, s. 46. - Issued: 13.10.2008. Made: 08.10.2008. Coming into operation: 27.10.2008. Effect: S.R. 2008/326 amended. - 4p.: 30 cm. - 978-0-337-97544-8 £4.00

The Fixed-term Employees (Prevention of Less Favourable Treatment) (Amendment) Regulations (Northern Ireland) 2008 No. 2008/326. - Enabling power: Employment Act 2002, s. 46. - Issued: 01.08.2008. Made: 28.07.2008. Coming into operation: 27.10.2008. Effect: S.R. 2002/298 amended. - Subject to affirmative resolution of the Assembly. - 4p.: 30 cm. - 978-0-337-97475-5 £3.00

The Maternity and Parental Leave etc. and the Paternity and Adoption Leave (Amendment) Regulations (Northern Ireland) 2008 No. 2008/374. - Enabling power: S.I. 1996/1919 (N.I. 16), arts 70C (2), 105 (4) (6) (7), 107B (4) (7) (8), 131 (1). - Issued: 12.12.2008. Made: 01.09.2008. Coming into operation: 01.10.2008. Effect: S.R. 1999/471; 2002/377 amended. - Approved by resolution of the Assembly on 10th November 2008. Supersedes previous version (ISBN 9780337975097). - 8p.: 30 cm. - 978-0-337-97598-1 £4.00

The Maternity and Parental Leave etc. and the Paternity and Adoption Leave (Amendment) Regulations (Northern Ireland) 2008 No. 2008/374. - Enabling power: S.I. 1996/1919 (N.I. 16), arts 70C (2), 105 (4) (6) (7), 107B (4) (7) (8), 131 (1). - Issued: 15.09.2008. Made: 01.09.2008. Coming into operation: 01.10.2008. Effect: S.R. 1999/471; 2002/377amended. - For approval of the Assembly before the expiration of six months from the date of their coming into operation. Superseded by S.R. of the same number (ISBN 9780337975981). - 8p.: 30 cm. - 978-0-337-97509-7 £5.00

The Social Security Benefits Up-rating Order (Northern Ireland) 2008 No. 2008/92. - Enabling power: Social Security Administration (Northern Ireland) Act 1992, ss. 132, 132A, 165 (1) (4) (5). - Issued: 15.04.2008. Made: 07.03.2008. Coming into operation: In accord. with art. 1. Effect: 1966 c. 6 (N.I.); 1992 c. 7; S.R. 1987/459; 1992/32; 1994/461; 1995/35; 1996/198; 2003/28; 2006/405, 406 amended & S.R. 2007/153 revoked. - Revoked by S.R. 2009/89 (ISBN 9780337976902). For approval of the Northern Ireland Assembly before the expiration of six months from the date of its coming into operation. - 36p.: 30 cm. - 978-0-337-97291-1 £6.50

The Social Security Benefits Up-rating Order (Northern Ireland) 2008 No. 2008/92. - Enabling power: Social Security Administration (Northern Ireland) Act 1992, ss. 132, 132A, 165 (1) (4) (5). - Issued: 27.06.2008. Made: 07.03.2008. Coming into operation: In accord. with art. 1. Effect: 1966 c. 6 (N.I.); 1992 c. 7; S.R. 1987/459; 1992/32; 1994/461; 1995/35; 1996/198; 2002/380; 2003/28; 2006/405, 406 amended & S.R. 2007/153 revoked (10.04.2008). - Affirmed by resolution of the Assembly on 23.06.08. Supersedes SI of same number (ISBN 9780337972911) issued 15.04.2008. - 40p.: 30 cm. - 978-0-337-97429-8 £6.50

Energy conservation

The Domestic Energy Efficiency Grants (Amendment) Regulations (Northern Ireland) 2008 No. 2008/67. - Enabling power: S.I. 1990/1511 (N.I. 15), art. 17 (1) (2) (3) (4). - Issued: 28.02.2008. Made: 13.02.2008. Coming into operation: 01.04.2008. Effect: S.R. 2002/56 amended. - 2p.: 30 cm. - 978-0-337-97271-3 £3.00

Environmental protection

The Deposits in the Sea (Exemptions) (Amendment) Order (Northern Ireland) 2008 No. 2008/20. - Enabling power: Food and Environment Protection Act 1985, s. 7 (1) (2), 25 (3). - Issued: 24.01.2008. Made: 18.01.2008. Coming into operation: 08.02.2008. Effect: S.R. 1995/234 amended and S.R. 2007/51 revoked. - 4p.: 30 cm. - 978-0-337-97234-8 £3.00

The Nitrates Action Programme (Amendment) Regulations (Northern Ireland) 2008 No. 2008/196. - Enabling power: European Communities Act 1972, s. 2 (2). - Issued: 09.05.2008. Made: 02.05.2008. Coming into operation: 09.06.2008. Effect: S.R. 2006/489 amended. - EC note: These Regulations implement Commission Decision 2007/863/EC granting derogation to Northern Ireland pursuant to Council Directive 91/676/EC concerning the protection of waters against pollution caused by nitrates from agricultural sources. - 8p.: 30 cm. - 978-0-337-97379-6 £3.00

The Quality of Bathing Water Regulations (Northern Ireland) 2008 No. 2008/231. - Enabling power: European Communities Act 1972, s. 2 (2). - Issued: 04.06.2008. Made: 28.05.2008. Coming into operation: In accord. with reg. 1. Effect: S.R. 1993/205 revoked (30.09.2015). - 16p.: 30 cm. - 978-0-337-97399-4 £3.00

The Waste (Amendment) (2007 Order) (Commencement No.2) Order (Northern Ireland) 2008 No. 2008/75 (C.2). - Enabling power: S.I. 2007/611 (N.I. 3), art. 1 (3). Bringing various provisions of the 2007 Order into operation on 07.04.2008. - Issued: 04.03.2008. Made: 27.02.2008. Coming into operation: -. Effect: None. - 2p.: 30 cm. - 978-0-337-97277-5 £3.00

The Waste and Contaminated Land (1997 Order) (Commencement No. 8) Order (Northern Ireland) 2008 No. 2008/138 (C.6). - Enabling power: S.I. 1997/2778 (N.I. 19), art. 1 (2). Bringing various provisions of the 1997 Order into operation on 03.04.2008. - Issued: 31.03.2008. Made: 20.03.2008. Coming into operation: -. Effect: None. - 8p.: 30 cm. - 978-0-337-97332-1 £3.00

The Waste Management Licences (Consultation and Compensation) Regulations (Northern Ireland) 2008 No. 2008/160. - Enabling power: S.I. 1997/2778 (N.I.19), arts 7 (3) (4), 9 (5) (b), 11 (6) (b). - Issued: 10.04.2008. Made: 04.04.2008. Coming into operation: 19.05.2008. Effect: None. - 8p.: 30 cm. - 978-0-337-97352-9 £3.00

The Waste Management (Miscellaneous Provisions) Regulations (Northern Ireland) 2008 No. 2008/18. - Enabling power: S.I. 1997/2778 (N.I.19), art. 4 (3) & S.I.1981/158 (N.I.4), art. 4 (3). - Issued: 23.01.2008. Made: 17.01.2008. Coming into operation: 13.02.2007. Effect: S.R. 1981/340; 2003/493 amended. - EC note: These regs amend the 2003 Regulations which implement (in part), in relation to Northern Ireland, Council Directive 75/442/EEC on waste and Council Directive 1999/31/EC on the landfill of waste. - 4p.: 30 cm. - 978-0-337-97233-1 £3.00

European Communities

The Animals and Animal Products (Import and Export) (Amendment) Regulations (Northern Ireland) 2008 No. 2008/53. - Enabling power: European Communities Act 1972, s. 2 (2) & Finance Act 1973, s. 56 (1) (2) (5). - Issued: 14.02.2008. Made: 08.02.2008. Coming into operation: 10.03.2008. Effect: S.R. 2006/401 amended. - Partially revoked by S.R. 2009/86 (ISBN 9780337976933). EC note: These regs take account of Commission Regulation No. 1266/2007 on implementing rules for Council Directive 2000/75/EC as regards the control, monitoring, surveillance and restrictions on movements of certain animals of susceptible species in relation to bluetongue. - 4p: 30 cm. - 978-0-337-97262-1 £3.00

The Energy Performance of Buildings (Certificates and Inspections) (Amendment) Regulations (Northern Ireland) 2008 No. 2008/241. - Enabling power: European Communities Act 1972, s. 2 (2). - Issued: 10.06.2008. Made: 06.06.2008. Coming into operation: 30.06.2008. Effect: S.R. 2008/170 amended. - This Statutory Rule has been made in consequence of a defect in SR 2008/170 (ISBN 9780337973574) and is being issued free of charge to all known recipients of that SR. - 4p.: 30 cm. - 978-0-337-97409-0 £3.00

The Energy Performance of Buildings (Certificates and Inspections) Regulations (Northern Ireland) 2008 No. 2008/170. - Enabling power: European Communities Act 1972, s. 2 (2). - Issued: 25.04.2008. Made: 10.04.2008. Coming into operation: 30.06.2008. Effect: S.R. 2000/389 amended. - EC note: These Regulations implement in Northern Ireland Articles 7 (energy performance certificate), 9 (inspection of air-conditioning systems) and 10 (independent experts) of the Energy Performance of Buildings Directive, 2002/91/EC ("the Directive") which lays down requirements for the production of energy performance certificates when buildings are constructed, sold or rented out, display of display energy certificates in large public buildings providing a public service, and regular inspections of air-conditioning systems. - 24p.: 30 cm. - 978-0-337-97357-4 £4.00

The Energy Performance of Buildings (Certificates and Inspections) Regulations (Northern Ireland) 2008 (correction slipi) No. 2008/170 Cor.. - Correction slip (to ISBN 9780337973574) dated May 2008. - 1 sheet: 30 cm. *Free*

The Olive Oil (Marketing Standards) Regulations (Northern Ireland) 2008 No. 2008/189. - Enabling power: European Communities Act 1972, s. 2 (2). - Issued: 02.05.2008. Made: 23.04.2008. Coming into operation: 20.06.2008. Effect: S.R. 1998/383 amended & S.R. 1987/431 revoked with savings. - EC note: These Regulations provide for the application of: Article 4 of Regulation No. 865/2004 on the establishment of a common organisation of the market in olive oil and table olives; and Commission Regulation (EC) No. 1019/2002 on marketing standards for olive oil as last amended by Commission Regulation (EC) No. 1044/2006. - 8p.: 30 cm. - 978-0-337-97372-7 £3.00

European Communities: Animals

The Scrapie (Fees) Regulations (Northern Ireland) 2008 No. 2008/456. - Enabling power: European Communities Act 1972, s. 2 (2) & Finance Act 1973, s. 56 (1) (2) (5). - Issued: 25.11.2008. Made: 19.11.2008. Coming into operation: 01.01.2009. Effect: None. - 4p: 30 cm. - 978-0-337-97574-5 £4.00

Explosives

The Explosives (Amendment) Regulations (Northern Ireland) 2008 No. 2008/491. - Enabling power: Explosives Act (Northern Ireland) 1970, s. 3. - Issued: 09.01.2009. Made: 25.11.2008. Coming into operation: 01.04.2009. Effect: S.R. & O. (N.I.) 1970/110; S.R. 1976/369; 1977/128 amended. - 4p.: 30 cm. - 978-0-337-97597-4 £4.00

Fair employment

The Fair Employment (Specification of Public Authorities) (Amendment) Order (Northern Ireland) 2008 No. 2008/480. - Enabling power: S.I. 1998/3162 (N.I. 21), arts 50, 51. - Issued: 08.12.2008. Made: 02.12.2008. Coming into operation: 01.01.2009. Effect: S.R. 2004/494 amended. - 2p: 30 cm. - 978-0-337-97591-2 £4.00

Family law

The Child Support (Consequential Provisions) Regulations (Northern Ireland) 2008 No. 2008/404. - Enabling power: Child Maintenance Act (Northern Ireland) 2008, s. 38 (2). - Issued: 08.10.2008. Made: 02.10.2008. Coming into operation: 27.10.2008. Effect: S.R. 1992/340; 1995/162, 475; 1996/289, 317, 358, 503, 541; 1999/162, 167, 246 (C.20); 2001/17, 18, 19, 20, 21; 2002/164; 2003/84, 469; 2005/125 amended. - Partially revoked by S.R. 2009/133 (ISBN 9780337977275). - 8p.: 30 cm. - 978-0-337-97533-2 £5.00

The Child Support Information Regulations (Northern Ireland) 2008 No. 2008/403. - Enabling power: S.I. 1991/2628 (NI. 23), ss. 7 (4), 16 (1) (3), 46 (5), 47 (1), 48 (4), 50 (1) (2), sch. 1, para. 16 (11). - Issued: 08.10.2008. Made: 02.10.2008. Coming into operation: 27.10.2008. Effect: S.R. 1994/65; 1995/19, 162, 475; 1996/317, 541; 1998/8; 1999/152, 246 (C.20); 2001/16; 2002/164; 2004/428; 2005/536; 2006/273; 2007/347; 2008/119 amended and S.R. 1992/339; 2003/522 revoked. - 12p.: 30 cm. - 978-0-337-97532-5 £5.00

The Child Support, Pensions and Social Security (2000 Act) (Commencement No. 11) Order (Northern Ireland) 2008 No. 2008/402 (C.23). - Enabling power: Child Support, Pensions and Social Security Act (Northern Ireland) 2000, s. 68 (2) (a). Bringing into operation various provisions of the 2000 Act on 03.10.2008 and 27.10.2008, in accord. with art. 2. - Issued: 08.10.2008. Made: 02.10.2008. Effect: None. - 4p.: 30 cm. - 978-0-337-97531-8 £4.00

The Forced Marriage (Civil Protection) Act 2007 (Commencement No. 1) Order (Northern Ireland) 2008 No. 2008/446 (C.26). - Enabling power: Forced Marriage (Civil Protection) Act 2007, s. 4 (4). Bringing various provisions of the 2007 Act into operation on 25.11.2008 with art. 2. - Issued: 24.11.2008. Made: 13.11.2008. Coming into operation: -. Effect: None. - 2p.: 30 cm. - 978-0-337-97572-1 £4.00

Family law: Child support

The Child Maintenance (2008 Act) (Commencement No. 1) Order (Northern Ireland) 2008 No. 2008/291 (C.15). - Enabling power: Child Maintenance Act (Northern Ireland) 2008, s. 41 (1) (2). Bringing into operation various provisions of the 2008 Act on 09.07.2008 & 14.07.2008 in accord. with reg. 2. - Issued: 16.07.2008. Made: 08.07.2008. Coming into operation: -. Effect: None. - 4p.: 30 cm. - 978-0-337-97450-2 £3.00

The Child Maintenance (2008 Act) (Commencement No. 2) Order (Northern Ireland) 2008 No. 2008/331 (C.17). - Enabling power: Child Maintenance Act (Northern Ireland) 2008, s. 41 (1). Bringing into operation various provisions of the 2008 Act on 05.08.2008 in accord. with reg. 2. - Issued: 05.08.2008. Made: 31.07.2008. Coming into operation: -. Effect: None. - 2p.: 30 cm. - 978-0-337-97477-9 £3.00

The Child Maintenance (2008 Act) (Commencement No. 3 and Transitional and Savings Provisions) Order (Northern Ireland) 2008 No. 2008/399 (C.22). - Enabling power: Child Maintenance Act (Northern Ireland) 2008, s. 41 (1) (2). Bringing into operation various provisions of the 2008 Act on 29.09.2008 & 27.10.2008 in accord. with reg. 2. - Issued: 02.10.2008. Made: 26.09.2008. Coming into operation: -. Effect: None. - 4p.: 30 cm. - 978-0-337-97528-8 £4.00

The Child Maintenance (2008 Act) (Commencement No. 4) Order (Northern Ireland) 2008 No. 2008/419 (C.24). - Enabling power: Child Maintenance Act (Northern Ireland) 2008, s. 41 (1). Bringing into operation various provisions of the 2008 Act on 27.10.2008 & 01.11.2008 in accord. with regs. 2 & 3. - Issued: 23.10.2008. Made: 17.10.2008. Coming into operation: -. Effect: None. - 4p.: 30 cm. - 978-0-337-97547-9 £4.00

The Child Maintenance (2008 Act) (Commencement No. 5) Order (Northern Ireland) 2008 No. 2008/489 (C.29). - Enabling power: Child Maintenance Act (Northern Ireland) 2008, s. 41 (1). Bringing into operation various provisions of the 2008 Act on 05.12.2008 in accord. with reg. 2. - Issued: 10.12.2008. Made: 04.2.2008. Coming into operation: -. Effect: None. - 2p.: 30 cm. - 978-0-337-97595-0 £4.00

The Child Support and Social Security (Miscellaneous Amendments) Regulations (Northern Ireland) 2008 No. 2008/409. - Enabling power: S.I. 1991/2628 (N.I. 23), arts. 29 (2) (4) (6) (7), 32 (2) (bb), 47 (1) (2) (b), 48 (4), sch. 1, paras 10 (1) (2), 11. - Issued: 08.10.2008. Made: 03.10.2008. Coming into operation: 27.10.2008. Effect: S.R. 1992/340, 390; 1999/162; 2001/17, 18, 19 amended. - 8p.: 30 cm. - 978-0-337-97538-7 £5.00

The Child Support (Miscellaneous Amendments) Regulations (Northern Ireland) 2008 No. 2008/119. - Enabling power: S.I. 1991/2628 (N.I. 23), arts. 16 (1), 32 (1) (3) (a) (8) (9). - Issued: 20.03.2008. Made: 13.03.2008. Coming into operation: 06.04.2008. Effect: S.R. 1992/339, 390 amended. - 4p.: 30 cm. - 978-0-337-97316-1 £3.00

Family proceedings

The Family Proceedings (Amendment No. 2) Rules (Northern Ireland) 2008 No. 2008/259. - Enabling power: S.I. 1993/1576 (N.I. 6), art. 12. - Issued: 27.06.2008. Made: 20.06.2008. Coming into operation: 05.09.2008. Effect: S.R. 1996/322 amended. - 4p.: 30 cm. - 978-0-337-97428-1 £3.00

The Family Proceedings (Amendment No. 3) Rules (Northern Ireland) 2008 No. 2008/466. - Enabling power: S.I. 1993/1576 (N.I. 6), art. 12. - Issued: 28.11.2008. Made: 20.11.2008. Coming into operation: 22.12.2008. Effect: S.R. 1996/322 amended. - 16p.: 30 cm. - 978-0-337-97579-0 £5.00

The Family Proceedings (Amendment) Rules (Northern Ireland) 2008 No. 2008/24. - Enabling power: S.I. 1993/1576 (N.I. 6), art. 12. - Issued: 07.02.2008. Made: 22.01.2008. Coming into operation: 25.02.2008. Effect: S.R. 1996/322 amended. - 4p.: 30 cm. - 978-0-337-97237-9 £3.00

Fire and rescue services: Pensions

The Firefighters' Compensation Scheme (Amendment) Order (Northern Ireland) 2008 No. 2008/238. - Enabling power: S.I. 1984/1821 (N.I. 11), art. 10 (1) (3) (4) (5). - Issued: 09.06.2008. Made: 03.06.2008. Coming into operation: 04.07.2008. Effect: S.R. 2007/143 amended. - 16p.: 30 cm. - 978-0-337-97406-9 £3.00

The Firefighters' Pension Scheme (Amendment) Order (Northern Ireland) 2008 No. 2008/382. - Enabling power: S.I. 1984/1821 (N.I. 11), art. 10 (1) (3) (4) (5). - Issued: 24.09.2008. Made: 17.09.2008. Coming into operation: 16.10.2008. Effect: S.R. 2007/144 amended. - 8p.: 30 cm. - 978-0-337-97516-5 £5.00

The New Firefighters' Pension Scheme (Amendment) Order (Northern Ireland) 2008 No. 2008/381. - Enabling power: S.I. 1984/1821 (N.I. 11), art. 10 (1) (3) (4) (5). - Issued: 24.09.2008. Made: 17.09.2008. Coming into operation: 16.10.2008. Effect: S.R. 2007/215 amended. - 12p.: 30 cm. - 978-0-337-97515-8 £5.00

Fisheries

Eel Fishing (Licence Duties) Regulations (Northern Ireland) 2008 No. 2008/476. - Enabling power: Fisheries Act (Northern Ireland) 1966, ss. 15 (1), 19 (1). - Issued: 03.12.2008. Made: 27.11.2008. Coming into operation: 01.01.2009. Effect: S.R. 2007/472 revoked. - 4p: 30 cm. - 978-0-337-97586-8 £4.00

The European Fisheries Fund (Grants) (Amendment) Regulations (Northern Ireland) 2008 No. 2008/500. - Enabling power: European Communities Act 1972, s. 2 (2). - Issued: 19.12.2008. Made: 15.12.2008. Coming into operation: 09.01.2009. Effect: S.R. 2008/394 amended. - This Statutory Rule has been made to correct a drafting error in S.R. 2008 No.394 and is being issued free of charge to all known recipients of that Statutory Rule. - 2p.: 30 cm. - 978-0-337-97608-7 £4.00

The European Fisheries Fund (Grants) Regulations (Northern Ireland) 2008 No. 2008/394. - Enabling power: European Communities Act 1972, s. 2 (2), sch. 2, para. 1A. - Issued: 29.09.2008. Made: 23.09.2008. Coming into operation: 20.10.2008. Effect: None. - 8p.: 30 cm. - 978-0-337-97523-3 £5.00

Fisheries (Amendment) Byelaws (Northern Ireland) 2008 No. 2008/318. - Enabling power: Fisheries Act (Northern Ireland) 1966, s. 26 (1). - Issued: 08.08.2008. Made: 24.07.2008. Coming into operation: 15.09.2008. Effect: S.R. 2003/525 amended. - 4p: 30 cm. - 978-0-337-97471-7 £3.00

Fisheries (Amendment No. 2) Byelaws (Northern Ireland) 2008 No. 2008/475. - Enabling power: Fisheries Act (Northern Ireland) 1966, ss. 26 (1), 37, 115 (1) (b). - Issued: 03.12.2008. Made: 27.11.2008. Coming into operation: 01.01.2009. Effect: S.R. 2003/525; 2007/471 amended. - 8p: 30 cm. - 978-0-337-97585-1 £4.00

Fisheries (Conservation of Coarse Fish) Byelaws (Northern Ireland) 2008 No. 2008/319. - Enabling power: Fisheries Act (Northern Ireland) 1966, s. 26 (1). - Issued: 08.08.2008. Made: 24.07.2008. Coming into operation: 15.09.2008. Effect: None. - 4p: 30 cm. - 978-0-337-97472-4 *£3.00*

Fish Health (Amendment) Regulations (Northern Ireland) 2008 No. 2008/183. - Enabling power: European Communities Act 1972, s. 2 (2). - Issued: 25.04.2008. Made: 22.04.2008. Coming into operation: 23.04.2008. Effect: S.R. 1998/310 amended. - Revoked by S.R. 2009/129 (ISBN 9780337977244). - 4p.: 30 cm. - 978-0-337-97365-9 *£3.00*

The Foyle and Carlingford Fisheries (2007 Order) (Commencement No. 1) Order (Northern Ireland) 2008 No. 2008/232 (C.10). - Enabling power: S.I. 2007/915 (N.I. 9), art. 1 (3). Bringing into operation various provisions of the 2007 Order on 01.06.2008. - Issued: 05.06.2008. Made: 29.05.2008. Coming into operation: -. Effect: None. - 4p.: 30 cm. - 978-0-337-97400-7 *£3.00*

Foyle Area and Carlingford Area (Angling) (Amendment) Regulations 2008 No. 2008/33. - Enabling power: Foyle Fisheries Act 1952, s. 13 (1) & Foyle Fisheries Act (Northern Ireland) 1952, s. 13 (1). - Issued: 11.02.2008. Made: 24.01.2008. Coming into operation: 29.02.2008. Effect: S.R. 2001/158 amended. - 4p.: 30 cm. - 978-0-337-97244-7 *£3.00*

The Foyle Area and Carlingford Area (Prohibition of Sale of Salmon and Sea Trout Caught by Rod and Line) Regulations 2008 No. 2008/302. - Enabling power: Foyle Fisheries Act 1952, s. 13 (1) & Foyle Fisheries Act (Northern Ireland) 1952, s. 13 (1). - Issued: 21.07.2008. Made: 10.07.2008. Coming into operation: 31.07.2008. Effect: None. - 4p.: 30 cm. - 978-0-337-97459-5 *£3.00*

The Foyle Area (Control of Oyster Fishing) Regulations 2008 No. 2008/298. - Enabling power: Foyle Fisheries Act 1952, s. 13 (1) & Foyle Fisheries Act (Northern Ireland) 1952, s. 13 (1). - Issued: 21.07.2008. Made: 10.07.2008. Coming into operation: 31.07.2008. Effect: None. - 4p.: 30 cm. - 978-0-337-97455-7 *£3.00*

The Foyle Area (Landing Areas for Oysters) Regulations 2008 No. 2008/299. - Enabling power: Foyle Fisheries Act 1952, s. 13 (1) & Foyle Fisheries Act (Northern Ireland) 1952, s. 13 (1). - Issued: 21.07.2008. Made: 10.07.2008. Coming into operation: 31.07.2008. Effect: None. - 4p.: 30 cm. - 978-0-337-97456-4 *£3.00*

The Foyle Area (Licensing of Oyster Fishing) Regulations 2008 No. 2008/300. - Enabling power: Foyle Fisheries Act 1952, s. 13 (1) (2) & Foyle Fisheries Act (Northern Ireland) 1952, s. 13 (1) (2). - Issued: 21.07.2008. Made: 10.07.2008. Coming into operation: 31.07.2008. Effect: None. - 4p.: 30 cm. - 978-0-337-97457-1 *£3.00*

The Foyle Area (Oyster Logbook and Identification Tagging) Regulations 2008 No. 2008/301. - Enabling power: Foyle Fisheries Act 1952, s. 13 (1) & Foyle Fisheries Act (Northern Ireland) 1952, s. 13 (1). - Issued: 29.07.2008. Made: 10.07.2008. Coming into operation: 31.07.2008. Effect: None. - 8p.: 30 cm. - 978-0-337-97458-8 *£3.00*

The Sea Fishing (Enforcement of Community Measures) (Penalty Notices) (Northern Ireland) Order 2008 No. 2008/492. - Enabling power: Fisheries Act 1981, s. 30 (2). - Issued: 16.12.2008. Made: 10.12.2008. Coming into operation: 05.01.2009. Effect: None. - 8p.: 30 cm. - 978-0-337-97600-1 *£4.00*

The Sea Fishing (Marking and Identification of Passive Fishing Gear and Beam Trawls) Order (Northern Ireland) 2008 No. 2008/484. - Enabling power: Fisheries Act 1981, s. 30 (2). - Issued: 08.12.2008. Made: 03.12.2008. Coming into operation: 31.12.2008. Effect: None. - EC note: Provides, in Northern Ireland, for the enforcement of Community restrictions and other obligations relating to the marking and identification of passive gear and beam trawls deployed by fishing vessels as set out in Commission Regulation 356/2005 as amended. - 8p.: 30 cm. - 978-0-337-97592-9 *£4.00*

Food

The Condensed Milk and Dried Milk (Amendment) Regulations (Northern Ireland) 2008 No. 2008/42. - Enabling power: S.I. 1991/762 (N.I. 7), arts 15 (1) (a) (e), 16 (1), 47 (2). - Issued: 08.02.2008. Made: 01.02.2008. Coming into operation: 07.03.2008. Effect: S.R. 1996/49, 50; 2003/300 amended. - EC note: These regs make provision for the implementation of Council Directive 2007/61/EC amending Directive 2001/114/EC relating to certain partly or wholly dehydrated preserved milk for human consumption. - 4p.: 30 cm. - 978-0-337-97252-2 *£3.00*

Dairy Produce Quotas (Amendment) Regulations (Northern Ireland) 2008 No. 2008/70. - Enabling power: European Communities Act 1972, s. 2 (2). - Issued: 03.03.2008. Made: 25.02.2008. Coming into operation: 01.04.2008. Effect: S.R. 2005/70; 2007/33 amended. - EC note: These regs amend the 2005 Regulations which implemented Council Regulation (EC) No 1788/2003. Council Regulation (EC) No 1788/2003 is repealed on 1st April 2008 and replaced by Articles 55(1)(a) and 55(2) and Section III of Chapter III of Part II (Articles 65 to 84) of Council Regulation (EC) No 1234/2007 establishing a common organisation of agricultural markets and on specific provisions for certain agricultural products (Single CMO Regulation). - 8p: 30 cm. - 978-0-337-97275-1 *£3.00*

The Drinking Milk Regulations (Northern Ireland) 2008 No. 2008/237. - Enabling power: S.I. 1991/762 (N.I.7), arts 15 (1), 16 (2), 25 (1) (3), 26 (3), 47 (2) & European Communities Act 1972, sch. 2, para. 1A. - Issued: 09.06.2008. Made: 02.06.2008. Coming into operation: 01.07.2008. Effect: SR 1996/383 amended & S.R. 1998/359 revoked. - EC note: These Regulations make provision for the enforcement of Article 114(2) of, and Annex XIII to, Council Regulation (EC) No 1234/2007 establishing a common organisation of agricultural markets and on specific provisions for certain agricultural products (Single CMO Regulation). - 4p: 30 cm. - 978-0-337-97405-2 *£3.00*

The Eggs and Chicks (No. 2) Regulations (Northern Ireland) 2008 No. 2008/451. - Enabling power: European Communities Act 1972, s. 2 (2), sch. 2, para. 1A & S.I. 1991/762 (N.I. 7), arts 15 (1),16, 25 (2) (3), 26 (3), 47 (2). - Issued: 24.11.2008. Made: 18.11.2008. Coming into operation: 22.12.2008. Effect: S.R. 2008/98 revoked. - EC note: These Regulations revoke and remake, with modifications, the Eggs and Chicks Regulations(Northern Ireland) 2008 (S.R. 2008 No. 98) following the adoption of Council Regulation No. 1234/2007 establishing a common organisation of agricultural markets and on specific provisions for certain agricultural products (Single CMO Regulation) and two Commission Regulations adopted under that Regulation, Commission Regulation No. 617/2008 and Commission Regulation No. 589/2008. Regulations 2782/75, 1028/2006, 1868/77 and 557/2007 have been repealed by various other Regulations. - 24p: 30 cm. - 978-0-337-97570-7 £5.00

The Eggs and Chicks Regulations (Northern Ireland) 2008 No. 2008/98. - Enabling power: European Communities Act 1972, s. 2 (2), sch. 2, para. 1A & S.I. 1991/762 (N.I. 7), arts 15 (1),16, 25 (2) (3), 26 (3) (f), 47 (2). - Issued: 14.03.2008. Made: 10.03.2008. Coming into operation: 14.03.2008. Effect: S.R. 1995/382; 1997/108, 451; 1998/269; 2006/287 revoked. - Revoked by S.R. 2008/451 (ISBN 9780337975707). EC note: These regs replace the 1995 Regulations, as amended, which made provision for the enforcement of certain provisions of Regulation (EEC) No. 2782/75 on the production and marketing of eggs for hatching and of farmyard poultry chicks Regulation (EEC) No. 1868/77 laying down detailed rules of application for Regulation (EEC) No. 2782/75. They also made provision for the enforcement of certain provisions of Regulation (EEC) No. 1907/90 on certain marketing standards for eggs and Commission Regulation (EC) No. 2295/2003 introducing detailed rules for implementing Regulation (EEC) No. 1907/90Council Regulation (EEC) No. 1907/90 and Commission Regulation (EC) No. 2295/2003 have been revoked and replaced by Council Regulation (EC) No. 1028/2006 and Commission Regulation (EC) No. 557/2007. These Regulations make provision for the continued enforcement of certain provisions of Council Regulation (EEC) No. 2782/75 and the continued enforcement of certain provisions of Commission Regulation (EEC) No. 1868/77, as from time to time amended, and also for the enforcement of certain provisions of Council Regulation (EC) No. 1028/2006, as from time to time amended, and Commission Regulation (EC) No. 557/2007, as from time to time amended. - 24p: 30 cm. - 978-0-337-97298-0 £4.00

The Food Labelling (Declaration of Allergens) Regulations (Northern Ireland) 2008 No. 2008/198. - Enabling power: S.I. 1991/762 (N.I.7), arts 15 (1) (e), 16 (1), 25 (1) (a), 47 (2). - Issued: 12.05.2008. Made: 02.05.2008. Coming into operation: 31.05.2008. Effect: SR 1996/383 amended & S.R. 2005/396, 475; 2007/498 revoked. - EC note: These Regulations implement in Northern Ireland Commission Directive No. 2007/68/EC amending Annex IIIa to Directive 2000/13/EC as regards certain food ingredients. The ingredients in question are those that are likely to cause an allergic reaction in some consumers. - 8p: 30 cm. - 978-0-337-97381-9 £3.00

The Healthy Start Scheme and Day Care Food Scheme (Amendment) Regulations (Northern Ireland) 2008 No. 2008/131. - Enabling power: S.I. 1988/594 (N.I. 2), art. 13 (1) to (4) (6) (8) & Social Security Contributions and Benefits (Northern Ireland) Act 1992, s. 171 (2) to (5). - Issued: 03.04.2008. Made: 14.03.2008. Coming into operation: 06.04.2008. Effect: S.R. 2006/478 amended. - 4p.: 30 cm. - 978-0-337-97337-6 £3.00

The Honey (Amendment) Regulations (Northern Ireland) 2008 No. 2008/126. - Enabling power: S.I. 1991/762 (N.I. 7), arts. 15 (1) (e), 16 (1), 25 (1), 47 (2). - Issued: 20.03.2008. Made: 13.03.2008. Coming into operation: 14.04.2008. Effect: S.R. 2003/383 amended. - EC note: These Regs implement the corrigendum to Council Directive 2001/110/EC which corrected an error in Annex II to this Directive. - 4p.: 30 cm. - 978-0-337-97321-5 £3.00

The Infant Formula and Follow-on Formula (Amendment) Regulations (Northern Ireland) 2008 No. 2008/405. - Enabling power: S.I. 1991/762 (NI. 7), arts. 15 (1) (e), 16 (1), 25 (1) (a) (3), 47 (2). - Issued: 08.10.2008. Made: 02.10.2008. Coming into force: 04.11.2008. Effect: S.R. 2000/187; 2007/506 amended. - EC note: The 2007 Regulations fail to comply with Commission Directive 2006/141/EC on infant formulae and follow-on formulae and amending Directive 1999/21/EC to the extent that they prohibit as from 11 January 2008 (instead of as from 31 December 2009) trade in infant formula and follow-on formula whose labelling satisfies the labelling requirements of the Infant Formula and Follow-on Formula Regulations (Northern Ireland) 1995 (S.R. 1995 No. 85, as amended) but does not satisfy the labelling requirements of the 2007 Regulations. These amend the 2007 regulations accordingly. - 8p.: 30 cm. - 978-0-337-97534-9 £4.00

The Meat (Official Controls Charges) Regulations (Northern Ireland) 2008 No. 2008/89. - Enabling power: European Communities Act 1972, s. 2 (2), sch. 2, para. 1A. - Issued: 12.03.2008. Made: 06.03.2008. Coming into operation: 30.03.2008. Effect: S.R. 2007/496 revoked. - Revoked by S.R. 2009/247 (ISBN 9780337978180). EC note: These Regulations provide for the execution and enforcement of Articles 26 and 27 of Regulation (EC) No. 882/2004 (as revised) on official controls performed to ensure the verification of compliance with feed and food law, animal health and animal welfare rules. - 16p: 30 cm. - 978-0-337-97288-1 £3.00

The Meat Products (Amendment) Regulations (Northern Ireland) 2008 No. 2008/82. - Enabling power: S.I. 1991/762 (N.I.7), arts 15 (1) (e), 47 (2). - Issued: 10.03.2008. Made: 03.03.2008. Coming into operation: 06.04.2008. Effect: S.R. 2004/13 amended. - 4p.: 30 cm. - 978-0-337-97282-9 *£3.00*

The Miscellaneous Food Additives (Amendment) Regulations (Northern Ireland) 2008 No. 2008/41. - Enabling power: S.I. 1991/762 (N.I. 7), arts 15 (1) (a), 16 (1), 47 (2), sch. 1, para. 1. - Issued: 08.02.2008. Made: 01.02.2008. Coming into operation: 07.03.2008. Effect: S.R. 1996/50 amended. - This Statutory Rule has been made in consequence of a defect in SR 2007 No. 325 (ISBN 9780337970740) and is being issued free of charge to all known recipients of that Statutory Rule. - 4p.: 30 cm. - 978-0-337-97251-5 *£3.00*

The Olive Oil (Marketing Standards) Regulations (Northern Ireland) 2008 No. 2008/189. - Enabling power: European Communities Act 1972, s. 2 (2). - Issued: 02.05.2008. Made: 23.04.2008. Coming into operation: 20.06.2008. Effect: S.R. 1998/383 amended & S.R. 1987/431 revoked with savings. - EC note: These Regulations provide for the application of: Article 4 of Regulation No. 865/2004 on the establishment of a common organisation of the market in olive oil and table olives; and Commission Regulation (EC) No. 1019/2002 on marketing standards for olive oil as last amended by Commission Regulation (EC) No. 1044/2006. - 8p.: 30 cm. - 978-0-337-97372-7 *£3.00*

The Plastic Materials and Articles in Contact with Food (Amendment) Regulations (Northern Ireland) 2008 No. 2008/271. - Enabling power: S.I. 1991/762 (N.I.7), arts 15 (2), 16 (1) (2), 25 (1) (a) (2) (a) (3), 32, 47 (2). - Issued: 02.07.2008. Made: 26.06.2008. Coming into operation: 30.06.2008 for the purposes of reg. 6; 01.07.2008 for all other purposes. Effect: S.R. 1991/198; 2007/419; 2008/167 amended. - EC note: These Regulations provide for the execution and enforcement in Northern Ireland of Commission Regulation (EC) No. 597/2008 amending Commission Regulation (EC) No. 372/2007 laying down transitional migration limits for plasticisers in gaskets in lids intended to come into contact with foods, ('the new Commission Regulation'). The new Commission Regulation extends the relevant deadline for such materials and articles to 30th April 2009. - 24p.: 30 cm. - 978-0-337-97436-6 *£4.00*

The Plastic Materials and Articles in Contact with Food Regulations (Northern Ireland) 2008 No. 2008/167. - Enabling power: S.I. 1991/762 (N.I.7), arts 15 (2), 16 (1) (2), 25 (1) (a) (2) (a) (3), 32, 47 (2). - Issued: 30.04.2008. Made: 10.04.2008. Coming into operation: 05.05.2008 except for reg. 27 (c); 01.07.2008 for reg. 27 (c). Effect: S.R. 2007/434 amended & S.R. 2006/420; 2007/419 revoked. - Revoked by S.R. 2009/56 (ISBN 9780337976544). EC note: These regs provide for a) the implementation of the further amendments made to Commission Directive 2002/72/EC and to Council Directive 85/572/EEC by Commission Dir. 2007/19/EC (corrected version at OJ No. L 97, 12.4.2007, p.50), which introduces new specifications and restrictions relating to plastic multi-layer materials and articles and to substances used in the manufacture of plastic materials and articles in contact with food in general, and amends certain specifications relating to migration testing in fatty foods; and b) provision that a reference in these Regulations to an Annex to Commission Directive 2002/72/EC is to be construed as a reference to that Annex as it may be amended from time to time. The principal Directives implemented by these Regulations are: Council Directive 82/711/EEC laying down the basic rules necessary for testing migration of the constituents of plastic materials and articles intended to come into contact with foodstuffs, as amended by Commission Directives 93/8/EEC and 97/48/EC; Council Directive 85/572/EEC laying down the list of simulants to be used for testing migration of constituents of plastic materials and articles intended to come into contact with foodstuffs, as amended by 2007/19/EC; Commission Directive 2002/72/EC relating to plastic materials and articles intended to come into contact with foodstuffs, as amended by Commission Directives 2004/1/EC, 2004/19/EC and 2005/79/EC, and 2007/19/EC. - 36p.: 30 cm. - 978-0-337-97355-0 *£6.50*

The Rice Products from the United States of America (Restriction on First Placing on the Market) Regulations (Northern Ireland) 2008 No. 2008/99. - Enabling power: European Communities Act 1972, s. 2 (2). - Issued: 14.03.2008. Made: 10.03.2008. Coming into operation: 12.03.2008. Effect: S.R. 2006/443 revoked. - EC note: These Regulations implement Commission Decision 2006/601/EC on emergency measures regarding the non-authorised genetically modified organism "LL RICE 601" in rice products as last amended by Commission Decision 2008/162/EC. - 4p.: 30 cm. - 978-0-337-97299-7 *£3.00*

The Specified Products from China (Restriction on First Placing on the Market) Regulations (Northern Ireland) 2008 No. 2008/171. - Enabling power: European Communities Act 1972, s. 2 (2). - Issued: 17.04.2008. Made: 11.04.2008. Coming into operation: 15.04.2008. Effect: None. - EC note: These Regulations implement, in Northern Ireland, Commission Decision 2008/289/EC on emergency measures regarding the unauthorised genetically modified organism 'Bt 63' in rice products. - 4p.: 30 cm. - 978-0-337-97358-1 *£3.00*

The Spreadable Fats (Marketing Standards) and the Milk and Milk Products (Protection of Designations) Regulations (Northern Ireland) 2008 No. 2008/239. - Enabling power: S.I. 1991/762 (N.I.7), arts 15 (1), 16 (2), 25 (1) (3), 47 (2). - Issued: 09.06.2008. Made: 02.06.2008. Coming into operation: 01.07.2008. Effect: S.R. 1990/103; 1999/383; 2007/304 revoked. - EC note: These Regulations provide for the execution and enforcement, of certain provisions of Council Regulation (EC) No. 1234/2007 establishing a common organisation of agricultural markets and on specific provisions for certain agricultural products. - 8p: 30 cm. - 978-0-337-97407-6 £3.00.

Game

Game Preservation (Special Protection for Irish Hares) Order (Northern Ireland) 2008 No. 2008/407. - Enabling power: Game Preservation Act (Northern Ireland) 1928, ss. 7C (1), 7F (1) (2). - Issued: 08.10.2008. Made: 02.10.2008. Coming into operation: 01.11.2008. Effect: None. - 2p: 30 cm. - 978-0-337-97536-3 £4.00

Gas

The Energy Order 2003 (Supply of Information) Regulations (Northern Ireland) 2008 No. 2008/3. - Enabling power: S.I. 2003/419 (N.I.6), art. 27 (1), 66 (3). - Issued: 14.01.2008. Made: 07.01.2008. Coming into operation: 15.02.2008. Effect: None. - 8p.: 30 cm. - 978-0-337-97227-0 £3.00

Government resources and accounts

The Whole of Government Accounts (Designation of Bodies) Order (Northern Ireland) 2008 No. 2008/191. - Enabling power: Government Resources and Accounts Act (Northern Ireland) 2001, s. 15 (1). - Issued: 02.05.2008. Made: 28.04.2008. Coming into operation: 23.05.2008. Effect: None. - 8p.: 30 cm. - 978-0-337-97373-4 £3.00

Harbours

Donaghadee (Harbour Area) Order (Northern Ireland) 2008 No. 2008/143. - Enabling power: Harbours Act (Northern Ireland) 1970, s. 1 (1), sch. 1. - Issued: 02.04.2008. Made: 27.04.2008. Coming into operation: In accord. with art. 1. Effect: None. - Subject to affirmative resolution of the Assembly. Superseded by affirmed rei-issue (ISBN 9780337974229). - 4p., map: 30 cm. - 978-0-337-97341-3 £3.00

Donaghadee (Harbour Area) Order (Northern Ireland) 2008 No. 2008/143. - Enabling power: Harbours Act (Northern Ireland) 1970, s. 1 (1), sch. 1. - Issued: 24.06.2008. Made: 27.03.2008. Coming into operation: 18.06.2008 in accord. with art. 1. Effect: None. - Affirmed by resolution of the Assembly 17.06.2008. Supersedes S.R. of same number (ISBN 9780337973413). - 4p., map: 30 cm. - 978-0-337-97422-9 £3.00

Health and personal social services

The Care Tribunal (Amendment) Regulations (Northern Ireland) 2008 No. 2008/249. - Enabling power: S.I. 2003/431 (N.I. 9), arts. 44 (2) (3), 48 (2). - Issued: 16.06.2008. Made: 10.06.2008. Coming into operation: 21.07.2008. Effect: S.R. 2005/178 amended. - 8p.: 30 cm. - 978-0-337-97415-1 £3.00

The Charges for Drugs and Appliances (Amendment) Regulations (Northern Ireland) 2008 No. 2008/488. - Enabling power: S.I 1972/1265 (N.I. 14), arts, 98, 106, sch. 15. - Issued: 09.12.2008. Made: 03.12.2008. Coming into operation: 01.01.2009. Effect: S.R. 1997/382 amended. - 4p.: 30 cm. - 978-0-337-97594-3 £4.00

The Establishment and Agencies (Fitness of Workers) Regulations (Northern Ireland) 2008 No. 2008/346. - Enabling power: S.I. 2003/431 (N.I. 9), arts 23 (1) (2) (b) (f) (h) (7) (c), 48 (2). - Issued: 15.08.2008. Made: 12.08.2008. Coming into operation: 13.08.2008. Effect: S.R. 2005/160 amended. - Partially revoked by S.R. 2009/28 (ISBN 9780337976339). - 12p.: 30 cm. - 978-0-337-97487-8 £3.00

General Dental Services (Amendment) Regulations (Northern Ireland) 2008 No. 2008/395. - Enabling power: S.I. 1972/1265 (N.I. 14), arts 61 (1) (2) (2AA), 106, 107 (6). - Issued: 30.09.2008. Made: 19.09.2008. Coming into operation: 17.10.2008. Effect: S.R. 1993/326 amended. - 4p.: 30 cm. - 978-0-337-97525-7 £4.00

The Health and Personal Social Services (Assessment of Resources) (Amendment) Regulations (Northern Ireland) 2008 No. 2008/91. - Enabling power: S.I. 1972/1265 (N.I. 14), arts 36 (6), 99 (5). - Issued: 12.03.2008. Made: 07.03.2008. Coming into operation: 07.04.2008. Effect: S.R. 1993/127 amended. - 4p.: 30 cm. - 978-0-337-97290-4 £3.00

The Health and Personal Social Services (Joint Committee for Commissioning) (Amendment) Order (Northern Ireland) 2008 No. 2008/139. - Enabling power: S.I. 1972/1265 (N.I. 14), art. 19. - Issued: 31.03.2008. Made: 21.03.2008. Coming into operation: 14.04.2008. Effect: S.R. 2007/14 amended. - 2p: 30 cm. - 978-0-337-97334-5 £3.00

The Health and Personal Social Services (Primary Medical Services Performers Lists) (Amendment) Regulations (Northern Ireland) 2008 No. 2008/434. - Enabling power: S.I. 1972/1265 (N.I. 14), arts 57G, 106 (b), 107 (6), sch. 11, para. 1 (8) (a). - Issued: 12.11.2008. Made: 06.11.2008. Coming into operation: 08.12.2008. Effect: S.R. 2004/149 amended. - 12p.: 30 cm. - 978-0-337-97563-9 £5.00

The Health and Personal Social Services
(Superannuation) (Additional Voluntary Contributions,
Injury Benefits and Compensation for Premature
Retirement) (Amendment) Regulations (Northern
Ireland) 2008 No. 2008/350. - Enabling power: S.I.
1972/1073 (N.I. 10), arts 12, 14, 19 (1) (3) (4), sch. 3. -
Issued: 26.08.2008. Made: 19.08.2008. Coming into
operation: 09.09.2008. Effect: S.R. 1983/155; 1999/294;
2001/367 amended. - 12p.: 30 cm. - 978-0-337-97490-8
£3.00.

The Health and Personal Social Services
(Superannuation) (Amendment) Regulations (Northern
Ireland) 2008 No. 2008/163. - Enabling power: S.I.
1972/1073 (N.I. 10), arts 12, 14 (1) (3A), sch. 3. - Issued:
16.04.2008. Made: 08.04.2008. Coming into operation:
09.04.2008. Effect: S.R. 1995/95 amended. - 60p: 30 cm. -
978-0-337-97354-3 £9.00

The Health and Personal Social Services
(Superannuation Scheme and Compensation for
Premature Retirement) (Amendment) Regulations
(Northern Ireland) 2008 No. 2008/96. - Enabling power:
S.I. 1972/1073 (N.I. 10), arts 12, 14, 19, sch. 3. - Issued:
13.03.2008. Made: 06.03.2008. Coming into operation:
30.03.2008. Effect: S.R. 1983/155; 1995/95 amended. - 8p:
30 cm. - 978-0-337-97295-9 £3.00

The Health and Personal Social Services
(Superannuation Scheme, Injury Benefits, Additional
Voluntary Contributions and Compensation for
Premature Retirement) (Amendment) Regulations
(Northern Ireland) 2008 No. 2008/130. - Enabling power:
S.I. 1972/1073 (N.I. 10), arts 12, 14, sch. 3. - Issued:
31.03.2008. Made: 14.03.2008. Coming into operation:
31.03.2008. Effect: S.R. 1983/155; 1995/95; 1999/294;
2001/367 amended. - 8p.: 30 cm. - 978-0-337-97333-8
£3.00

The Health and Social Care (Pension Scheme)
Regulations (Northern Ireland) 2008 No. 2008/256. -
Enabling power: S.I. 1972/1073 (N.I. 10), arts 12, 14 (1),
sch. 3. - Issued: 27.06.2008. Made: 17.06.2008. Coming
into operation: 01.07.2008. Effect: None. - 188p.: 30 cm. -
978-0-337-97424-3 £26.00

The Health and Social Services Trusts (Establishment)
(Amendment) Order (Northern Ireland) 2008 No.
2008/426. - Enabling power: S.I. 1991/194 (N.I. 1), art. 10
(1), sch. 3, paras 3 (1) (b), 3A. - Issued: 29.10.2008. Made:
22.10.2008. Coming into operation: 24.10.2008. Effect:
S.R. 1995/143; 2006/292, 293, 294, 295, 296 amended. -
4p: 30 cm. - 978-0-337-97553-0 £4.00

The Health and Social Services Trusts (Originating
Capital) Order (Northern Ireland) 2008 No. 2008/142. -
Enabling power: S.I. 1991/194 (N.I. 1), art. 14 (1). -
Issued: 02.04.2008. Made: 21.03.2008. Coming into
operation: 21.03.2008. Effect: S.R. 1996/125 amended &
S.R. 1994/303; 1995/124, 144; 1997/186; 1999/165, 414
revoked. - 4p.: 30 cm. - 978-0-337-97342-0 £3.00

The Optical Charges and Payments (Amendment No. 2)
Regulations (Northern Ireland) 2008 No. 2008/423. -
Enabling power: S.I 1972/1265 (N.I. 14), arts 62, 98, 106,
107 (6), sch. 15. - Issued: 24.10.2008. Made: 20.10.2008.
Coming into operation: 27.10.2008. Effect: S.R. 1997/191
amended. - 4p.: 30 cm. - 978-0-337-97549-3 £4.00

The Optical Charges and Payments (Amendment)
Regulations (Northern Ireland) 2008 No. 2008/128. -
Enabling power: S.I 1972/1265 (N.I. 14), arts 62, 98, 106,
107 (6), sch. 15. - Issued: 26.03.2008. Made: 18.03.2008.
Coming into operation: 01.04.2008. Effect: S.R. 1997/191
amended. - 8p.: 30 cm. - 978-0-337-97325-3 £3.00

Provision of Health Services to Persons not Ordinarily
Resident (Amendment) Regulations (Northern Ireland)
2008 No. 2008/377. - Enabling power: S.I. 1972/1265 (N.I.
14), arts 42 (1) to (3), 106 (b), 107 (b). - Issued:
18.09.2008. Made: 11.09.2008. Coming into operation:
06.10.2008. Effect: S.R. 2005/551 amended. - 4p.: 30 cm. -
978-0-337-97512-7 £4.00

The Travelling Expenses and Remission of Charges
(Amendment No.2) Regulations (Northern Ireland)
2008 No. 2008/292. - Enabling power: S.I. 1972/1265 (N.I.
14), arts 45, 98, 106, 107 (6), sch. 15, paras 1 (b), 1B. -
Issued: 16.07.2008. Made: 08.07.2008. Coming into
operation: 01.08.2008. Effect: S.R. 2004/91 amended. -
4p.: 30 cm. - 978-0-337-97452-6 £3.00

The Travelling Expenses and Remission of Charges
(Amendment No. 3) Regulations (Northern Ireland)
2008 No. 2008/391. - Enabling power: S.I. 1972/1265 (N.I.
14), arts 45, 98, 106, 107 (6), sch. 15, paras 1(b), 1B. -
Issued: 29.09.2008. Made: 19.09.2008. Coming into
operation: 27.10.2008. Effect: S.R. 2004/91 amended. -
4p.: 30 cm. - 978-0-337-97522-6 £4.00

The Travelling Expenses and Remission of Charges
(Amendment) Regulations (Northern Ireland) 2008 No.
2008/39. - Enabling power: S.I. 1972/1265 (N.I. 14), arts
45, 98, 106, 107 (6), sch. 15, paras 1 (b), 1B. - Issued:
08.02.2008. Made: 01.02.2008. Coming into operation:
27.02.2008. Effect: S.R. 2004/91 amended. - 4p.: 30 cm. -
978-0-337-97249-2 £3.00

Health and safety

The Chemicals (Hazard Information and Packaging for
Supply) (Amendment) Regulations (Northern Ireland)
2008 No. 2008/424. - Enabling power: European
Communities Act 1972, s. 2 (2) & S.I. 1978/1039 (N.I. 9),
arts. 17 (1) to (6), 55 (2), sch. 3, paras 1 (1) (4) (5), 2 (2),
14 (1), 15. - Issued: 27.10.2008. Made: 22.10.2008.
Coming into operation: 28.11.2008. Effect: S.R. 2000/93;
2002/301 amended. - Revoked by S.R. 2009/238 (ISBN
9780337978081). EC note: These Regulations correct
certain errors in the Chemicals (Hazard Information and
Packaging for Supply) Regulations (Northern Ireland)
2002 (S.R. 2002 No. 301, as amended) in transposing
provisions of (a) Council Directive 1992/32/EEC
amending for the 7th time Council Directive 67/548/EEC
relating to the classification, packaging and labelling of
dangerous substances; and (b) Council Directive

1999/45/EC on the classification, packaging and labelling of dangerous preparations concerning the labelling of single receptacles and receptacles in outer packagings where the national and international transport rules also apply. - 12p.: 30 cm. - 978-0-337-97551-6 £5.00

The Equipment and Protective Systems Intended for Use in Potentially Explosive Atmospheres (Amendment) Regulations (Northern Ireland) 2008 No. 2008/422. - Enabling power: European Communities Act 1972, s. 2 (2). - Issued: 23.10.2008. Made: 20.10.2008. Coming into operation: 01.12.2008. Effect: S.R. 1996/247; 1999/305; 2000/85 amended & S.R. 1999/124 revoked. - EC note: These Regs amend the principal Regulations which implemented DIR 94/9/EC to give effect to corrigenda to the ATEX Directive which makes typographical changes (reg 3 (3) (5) (8), (10) - (16)). - 8p: 30 cm. - 978-0-337-97548-6 £4.00

The Health and Safety (Fees) Regulations (Northern Ireland) 2008 No. 2008/21. - Enabling power: European Communities Act 1972, s. 2 (2) & S.I. 1978/1039 (N.I. 9), arts 40 (2) (4), 49, 55 (2). - Issued: 28.01.2008. Made: 21.01.2008. Coming into operation: 10.03.2008. Effect: S.R. 2007/247 partially revoked & S.R. 2007/62 revoked with savings. - Revoked by S.R. 2009/132 (ISBN 9780337977268) with savings. - 28p: 30 cm. - 978-0-337-97235-5 £4.50

Health services charges

The Recovery of Health Services Charges (Amounts) (Amendment) Regulations (Northern Ireland) 2008 No. 2008/90. - Enabling power: S.I. 2006/1944 (N.I. 13), arts 2, 5 (2) (5), 19 (3). - Issued: 12.03.2008. Made: 06.03.2008. Coming into operation: 01.04.2008. Effect: S.R. 2006/507 amended. - 2p: 30 cm. - 978-0-337-97289-8 £3.00

Housing

The Housing Benefit (Amendment No. 2) Regulations (Northern Ireland) 2008 No. 2008/504. - Enabling power: Social Security Administration (Northern Ireland) Act 1992, ss. 5 (1) (a), 73 (3) (4), 165 (1) (4) (6). - Issued: 24.12.2008. Made: 19.12.2008. Coming into operation: 27.01.2009 for reg. 3 (2), 4; 06.04.2009 for remainder. Effect: S.R. 2006/405, 406 amended & S.R. 2008/410 partially revoked. - 8p.: 30 cm. - 978-0-337-97612-4 £4.00

The Housing Benefit (Amendment) Regulations (Northern Ireland) 2008 No. 2008/371. - Enabling power: Social Security Administration (Northern Ireland) Act 1992, ss. 5 (1) (a) (h), 107, 165 (1) (4) to (6). - Issued: 12.09.2008. Made: 08.09.2008. Coming into operation: 01.10.2008. Effect: S.R. 2006/405, 406, 462 amended. - 8p.: 30 cm. - 978-0-337-97506-6 £5.00

The Housing Benefit (Employment and Support Allowance Consequential Provisions) Regulations (Northern Ireland) 2008 No. 2008/378. - Enabling power: Welfare Reform Act (Northern Ireland) 2007, s. 28 (2). - Issued: 19.09.2008. Made: 15.09.2008. Coming into operation: 27.10.2008. Effect: S.R. 2001/213; 2006/405, 406, 407 amended. - 16p.: 30 cm. - 978-0-337-97513-4 £5.00

The Housing Benefit (Executive Determinations) (Amendment) Regulations (Northern Ireland) 2008 No. 2008/506. - Enabling power: Social Security Contributions and Benefits (Northern Ireland) Act 1992, ss. 122 (1) (d), 129A (2), 171 (1) (3) to (5). - Issued: 08.01.2009. Made: 22.12.2008. Coming into operation: 05.01.2009. Effect: S.R. 2008/100 amended. - 2p.: 30 cm. - 978-0-337-97614-8 £4.00

The Housing Benefit (Executive Determinations) Regulations (Northern Ireland) 2008 No. 2008/100. - Enabling power: Social Security Contributions and Benefits (Northern Ireland) Act 1992, ss. 122 (1) (d), 129A (2), 171 (1) (3) to (5). - Issued: 18.03.2008. Made: 11.03.2008. Coming into operation: 20.03.2008. Effect: None. - 8p.: 30 cm. - 978-0-337-97303-1 £3.00

The Housing Benefit (Extended Payments) (Amendments) Regulations (Northern Ireland) 2008 No. 2008/285. - Enabling power: Social Security Contributions and Benefits (Northern Ireland) Act 1992, s. 130 (2) & Social Security Administration (Northern Ireland) 1992, s. 5 (1) & Welfare Reform Act (Northern Ireland) 2007, ss. 32, 33. - Issued: 10.07.2008. Made: 04.07.2008. Coming into operation: 06.10.2008. Effect: S.R. 2006/405, 406 amended. - 12p.: 30 cm. - 978-0-337-97446-5 £3.00

The Housing Benefit (Local Housing Allowance) (Amendment) Regulations (Northern Ireland) 2008 No. 2008/101. - Enabling power: Social Security Contributions and Benefits (Northern Ireland) Act 1992, ss. 122 (1) (d), 129 (2), 129A (2) to (5), 171 (1) (3) to (5) & Social Security Administration (Northern Ireland) Act 1992, ss. 5 (1) (q) (5), 165 (1) (4) to (6). - Issued: 18.03.2008. Made: 11.03.2008. Coming into operation: 07.04.2008 in accord.with reg. 1. Effect: S.R. 2006/405; 2007/196, 266 amended. - 16p.: 30 cm. - 978-0-337-97304-8 £3.00

The Housing Benefit (Local Housing Allowance) (Miscellaneous and Consequential Amendments) Regulations (Northern Ireland) 2008 No. 2008/103. - Enabling power: Social Security Contributions and Benefits (Northern Ireland) Act 1992, ss. 129A (2) (3), 171 (1) (3) (4) & Child Support, Pensions and Social Security Act (Northern Ireland) 2000, sch. 7, para. 4 (3A). - Issued: 18.03.2008. Made: 11.03.2008. Coming into operation: 07.04.2008 in accord.with reg. 1. Effect: S.R. 1987/465; 2001/213, 216; 2004/8, 144; 2006/407 amended. - 12p.: 30 cm. - 978-0-337-97306-2 £3.00

The Housing Benefit (State Pension Credit) (Local Housing Allowance) (Amendment) Regulations (Northern Ireland) 2008 No. 2008/102. - Enabling power: Social Security Contributions and Benefits (Northern Ireland) Act 1992, ss. 122 (1) (d), 129 (2), 129A (2) to (5), 171 (1) (3) to (5) & Social Security Administration (Northern Ireland) Act 1992, ss. 5 (1) (q) (5), 165 (1) (4) to (6). - Issued: 18.03.2008. Made: 11.03.2008. Coming into operation: 07.04.2008 in accord.with reg. 1. Effect: S.R. 2006/406; 2007/196, 266 amended. - 16p.: 30 cm. - 978-0-337-97305-5 £3.00

The Social Security Benefits Up-rating Order (Northern Ireland) 2008 No. 2008/92. - Enabling power: Social Security Administration (Northern Ireland) Act 1992, ss. 132, 132A, 165 (1) (4) (5). - Issued: 15.04.2008. Made: 07.03.2008. Coming into operation: In accord. with art. 1. Effect: 1966 c. 6 (N.I.); 1992 c. 7; S.R. 1987/459; 1992/32; 1994/461; 1995/35; 1996/198; 2003/28; 2006/405, 406 amended & S.R. 2007/153 revoked. - Revoked by S.R. 2009/89 (ISBN 9780337976902). For approval of the Northern Ireland Assembly before the expiration of six months from the date of its coming into operation. - 36p.: 30 cm. - 978-0-337-97291-1 £6.50

The Social Security Benefits Up-rating Order (Northern Ireland) 2008 No. 2008/92. - Enabling power: Social Security Administration (Northern Ireland) Act 1992, ss. 132, 132A, 165 (1) (4) (5). - Issued: 27.06.2008. Made: 07.03.2008. Coming into operation: In accord. with art. 1. Effect: 1966 c. 6 (N.I.); 1992 c. 7; S.R. 1987/459; 1992/32; 1994/461; 1995/35; 1996/198; 2002/380; 2003/28; 2006/405, 406 amended & S.R. 2007/153 revoked (10.04.2008). - Affirmed by resolution of the Assembly on 23.06.08. Supersedes SI of same number (ISBN 9780337972911) issued 15.04.2008. - 40p.: 30 cm. - 978-0-337-97429-8 £6.50

The Social Security (Child Benefit Disregard) Regulations (Northern Ireland) 2008 No. 2008/497. - Enabling power: Social Security Contributions and Benefits (Northern Ireland) Act 1992, ss. 122 (1) (a) (d), 132 (3) (4) (b), 171 (1) (3) (4) & S.I. 1995/2705 (N.I. 15), arts 14(1) (4) (b), 36 (2)- Issued: 17.12.2008. Made: 11.12.2008. Coming into operation: 05.01.2009. Effect: S.R. 1987/459; 1996/198; 2006/45 amended. - 8p.: 30 cm. - 978-0-337-97603-2 £4.00

The Social Security (Miscellaneous Amendments No. 2) Regulations (Northern Ireland) 2008 No. 2008/179. - Enabling power: Social Security Contributions and Benefits (Northern Ireland) Act 1992, ss. 122 (1) (d), 131 (1), 132 (3) (4) (a) (b), 133 (2) (f) (h) (i), 171 (1) (3) (4) & S.I. 1998/1506 (N.I. 10), arts 11 (6), 74 (1) (3). - Issued: 24.04.2008. Made: 18.04.2008. Coming into operation: In accord. with reg. 1. Effect: S.R. 1999/162; 2006/405, 406, 407 amended & S.R. 2007/306, 392 partially revoked. - Partially revoked by S.R. 2008/417 (ISBN 9780337975455). - 8p.: 30 cm. - 978-0-337-97364-2 £3.00

The Social Security (Miscellaneous Amendments No. 3) Regulations (Northern Ireland) 2008 No. 2008/410. - Enabling power: Social Security Contributions and Benefits (Northern Ireland) Act 1992, ss. 171 (4) & Social Security Administration (Northern Ireland) Act 1992, ss. 5 (1) (a), 165 (1) (3) to (5). - Issued: 08.10.2008. Made: 03.10.2008. Coming into operation: 06.10.2008. Effect: S.R. 1987/465; 2003/28, 421; 2004/304; 2006/128, 405, 406 amended. - 4p.: 30 cm. - 978-0-337-97539-4 £4.00

The Social Security (Miscellaneous Amendments No. 4) Regulations (Northern Ireland) 2008 No. 2008/417. - Enabling power: Social Security Administration (Northern Ireland) Act 1992, ss. 1 (1), 5 (1) (a) (b) (j), 165 (1) (3) (4) (6) & S.I. 1998/1506 (N.I. 10), arts 10 (1), 11 (3) (6), 74 (1) (3) & Child Support, Pensions and Social Security Act (Northern Ireland) 2000, sch. 7, paras 4 (5), 12, 13 (1) (2) (c) (3) (c), 20 (1) (b). - Issued: 14.10.2008. Made: 09.10.2008. Coming into operation: 30.10.2008. Effect: S.R. 1987/465; 1999/162; 2001/213; 2006/405, 406 amended & S.R. 2000/215; 2006/365; 2007/392; 2008/179 partially revoked. - 8p.: 30 cm. - 978-0-337-97545-5 £5.00

The Social Security (Miscellaneous Amendments No. 5) Regulations (Northern Ireland) 2008 No. 2008/428. - Enabling power: Social Security Contributions and Benefits (Northern Ireland) Act 1992, ss. 122 (1) (a) (d), 123 (1) (e), 129A (2), 131 (1), 132 (3) (4) (a) to (c), 132A (3), 133 (2) (h), 171 (1) to (4) & Social Security Administration (Northern Ireland) Act 1992, ss. 5 (1) (h) (q), 165 (1) (3) to (5) & S.I. 1995/2705 (N.I. 15), arts 6 (5), 14 (1) to (3) (4)(a) to (c), 36 (2), sch. 1, para. 3(b) & State Pension Credit Act (Northern Ireland) 2002, ss. 2 (3) (b) (6), 15 (3) (6) (b), 19 (1) (2) (a) (3). - Issued: 29.10.2008. Made: 23.10.2008. Coming into operation: 17.11.2008 except for reg. 7 (5); 06.04.2009 for reg. 7 (5). Effect: S.R. 1987/459, 465; 1988/205; 1993/120, 195; 1996/198, 503; 2002/222; 2003/28; 2006/405, 406; 2007/382 amended. - 12p.: 30 cm. - 978-0-337-97554-7 £5.00

The Social Security (Miscellaneous Amendments No. 7) Regulations (Northern Ireland) 2008 No. 2008/498. - Enabling power: Social Security Contributions and Benefits (Northern Ireland) Act 1992, ss. 122 (1) (a) (d), 123 (1) (d), 132 (1) (3) (4), 132A (3), 171 (1) to (4) & S.I. 1995/2705 (N.I. 15), arts 14 (4), 36 (2), sch. 1, para. 8 (a) & State Pension Credit Act (Northern Ireland) 2002, ss. 15 (1) (e) (j) (2) (6), 19 (1) to (3) & Welfare Reform Act (Northern Ireland) 2007, ss. 17, 25, 28 (2). - Issued: 17.12.2008. Made: 11.12.2008. Coming into operation: 05.01.2009. Effect: S.R. 1987/459; 1993/120; 1994/77; 1995/367, 481; 1996/198, 449; 2000/260; 2002/128; 2003/28; 2005/98, 536; 2006/405, 406, 407; 2007/306; 2008/179, 280, 286 amended or partially revoked. - Partially revoked by S.R. 2009/338 (ISBN 9780337978821). - 16p.: 30 cm. - 978-0-337-97604-9 £5.00

The Social Security (Miscellaneous Amendments) Regulations (Northern Ireland) 2008 No. 2008/112. - Enabling power: Social Security Contributions and Benefits (Northern Ireland) Act 1992, ss. 122 (1) (a) (d), 123 (1) (d), 131 (1), 132 (3) (4) (a) to (c), 133 (2) (d), 171 (1) to (4) & Social Security Administration (Northern Ireland) Act 1992, ss. 5 (1) (q), 165 (1) (3) to (5) & S.I. 1995/2705 (N.I. 15), arts 6 (5), 14 (2) (4) (a) (b), 36 (2), sch. 1, paras 1 (2) (a), 3 (b) & State Pension Credit Act (Northern Ireland) 2002, ss. 2 (3) (b) (6), 19 (1) to (3). - Issued: 19.03.2008. Made: 12.03.2008. Coming into operation: In accord. with reg. 1. Effect: S.R. 1987/459, 465; 1988/146; 1989/249, 365; 1996/198, 199; 1998/2; 1999/371 (C.28); 2001/151; 2003/28, 195, 338; 2005/319 (C.23); 2006/405; 2007/396 amended. - 16p.: 30 cm. - 978-0-337-97309-3 *£3.00*

The Social Security (Students and Miscellaneous Amendments) Regulations (Northern Ireland) 2008 No. 2008/262. - Enabling power: Social Security Contributions and Benefits (Northern Ireland) Act 1992, ss. 122 (1) (a) (d), 132 (3) (4) (b), 171 (1) (3) (4) & Social Security Administration (Northern Ireland) Act 1992, ss. 5 (1) (hh) (k), 165 (1) (4) (6) & S.I. 1995/2705 (N.I. 15), arts 14 (1) to (3) (4) (b), 36 (2). - Issued: 01.07.2008. Made: 23.06.2008. Coming into operation: In accord. with reg. 1. Effect: S.R. 1987/459, 465; 1996/198; 2006/405 amended. - Partly revoked by S.R. 2009/261 (ISBN 9780337978319). - 8p.: 30 cm. - 978-0-337-97433-5 *£3.00*

The Social Security (Use of Information for Housing Benefit and Welfare Services Purposes) Regulations (Northern Ireland) 2008 No. 2008/343. - Enabling power: Welfare Reform Act (Northern Ireland) 2007, ss. 39 (2) (8) (9). - Issued: 14.08.2008. Made: 08.08.2008. Coming into operation: 01.09.2008. Effect: None. - 4p.: 30 cm. - 978-0-337-97484-7 *£3.00*

Industrial training

The Industrial Training Levy (Construction Industry) Order (Northern Ireland) 2008 No. 2008/294. - Enabling power: S.I. 1984/1159 (N.I. 9), arts 23 (2) (3), 24 (3) (4). - Issued: 17.07.2008. Made: 08.07.2008. Coming into operation: 31.08.2008. Effect: None. - 8p.: 30 cm. - 978-0-337-97454-0 *£3.00*

Insolvency

The Insolvency (Amendment) Rules (Northern Ireland) 2008 No. 2008/118. - Enabling power: S.I. 1989/2405 (N.I. 19), art. 359. - Issued: 15.04.2008. Made: 12.03.2008. Coming into operation: 06.04.2008. Effect: S.R. 1991/364 amended. - 20p: 30 cm. - 978-0-337-97315-4 *£3.50*

The Insolvency (Company Arrangement or Administration Provisions for an Industrial and Provident Society) Order (Northern Ireland) 2008 No. 2008/445. - Enabling power: S.I. 2005/1455 (N.I. 10), art. 10 (2) (3) (5) (6). - Issued: 20.11.2008. Made: 14.11.2008. Coming into operation: 14.11.2008. Effect: None. - 4p: 30 cm. - 978-0-337-97569-1 *£4.00*

The Insolvency (Disqualification from Office: General) Order (Northern Ireland) 2008 No. 2008/94. - Enabling power: S.I. 2005/1455 (N.I. 10), art. 24. - Issued: 21.05.2008. Made: 06.03.2008. Coming into operation: 12.05.2008 in accord. with art. 1. Effect: 1967 c.21 (N.I.) & S.I. 1986/2232 (N.I. 25); 1995/1622 (N.I. 7), 1623 (N.I. 8); 1995/3213 (N.I. 22); 1998/261 (N.I. 2) & S.R. 1993/115, 326; 1994/63; 2001/313; 2002/386; 2004/37 amended. - Affirmed by resolution of the Assembly on 12.05.2008. - 8p: 30 cm. - 978-0-337-97390-1 *£3.00*

The Insolvency (Disqualification from Office: General) Order (Northern Ireland) 2008 No. 2008/94. - Enabling power: S.I. 2005/1455 (N.I. 10), art. 24. - Issued: 16.04.2008. Made: 06.03.2008. Coming into operation: On the day after the day on which it is affirmed by resolution of the Assembly. Effect: None. - This Statutory Rule has been printed in substitution of the SR of the same number and ISBN (previously issued 14.03.2008) and is being issued free of charge to all known recipients of that Statutory Rule. Order laid before the Assembly under Article 24 of the Insolvency (Northern Ireland) Order 2005 and subject to affirmative resolution procedure of the Assembly. - 8p: 30 cm. - 978-0-337-97293-5 *£3.00*

The Insolvency (Voluntary Winding Up) (Forms) Regulations (Northern Ireland) 2008 No. 2008/261. - Enabling power: S.I. 1989/2405 (N.I. 19), art. 95 (1). - Issued: 01.07.2008. Made: 24.06.2008. Coming into operation: 01.08.2008. Effect: S.R. 1991/412 amended. - 4p: 30 cm. - 978-0-337-97432-8 *£3.00*

Judicature

The Court Funds (Amendment) Rules (Northern Ireland) 2008 No. 2008/156. - Enabling power: Judicature (Northern Ireland) Act 1978, s. 82 (1). - Issued: 10.04.2008. Made: 02.04.2008. Coming into operation: 19.05.2008. Effect: S.R. 1979/105 amended. - 4p.: 30 cm. - 978-0-337-97350-5 *£3.00*

Judiciary

The District Judge (Magistrates' Courts) Order (Northern Ireland) 2008 No. 2008/154. - Enabling power: Courts Act 2003, s. 102 (1) (2) (5). - Issued: 07.04.2008. Made: 31.03.2008. Coming into operation: 02.06.2008. Effect: None. - 4p.: 30 cm. - 978-0-337-97349-9 *£3.00*

Justice

Victims of Mentally Disordered Offenders Information (Northern Ireland) Scheme 2008 No. 2008/457. - Enabling power: Justice (Northern Ireland) Act 2002, s. 69A. - Issued: 26.11.2008. Made: 17.11.2008. Coming into operation: 15.12.2008. Effect: None. - 4p.: 30 cm. - 978-0-337-97576-9 *£4.00*

Lands Tribunal

Lands Tribunal (Salaries) Order (Northern Ireland) 2008 No. 2008/432. - Enabling power: Administration and Financial Provisions Act (Northern Ireland) 1962, s. 18 & Lands Tribunal and Compensation Act (Northern Ireland) 1964, s. 2 (5). - Issued: 11.11.2008. Made: 05.11.2008. Coming into operation: 05.11.2008. Effect: S.R. 2007/255 revoked. - Revoked by S.R. 2009/253 (ISBN 9780337978241). - Laid before the Assembly in draft. - 2p.: 30 cm. - 978-0-337-97561-5 *£4.00*

Legal aid and advice

Legal Advice and Assistance (Amendment) Regulations (Northern Ireland) 2008 No. 2008/106. - Enabling power: S.I. 1981/228 (N.I. 8), arts 7 (2), 22, 27. - Issued: 02.04.2008. Made: 08.03.2008. Coming into operation: 07.04.2008. Effect: S.R. 1981/366 amended & S.R. 2007/173 revoked. - Revoked by S.R. 2009/102 (ISBN 9780337977299). - 4p.: 30 cm. - 978-0-337-97338-3 *£3.00*

Legal Advice and Assistance (Financial Conditions) Regulations (Northern Ireland) 2008 No. 2008/107. - Enabling power: S.I. 1981/228 (N.I. 8), arts 3 (2), 7 (3), 22, 27. - Issued: 02.04.2008. Made: 08.03.2008. Coming into operation: 07.04.2008. Effect: S.I. 1981/228 (N.I. 8) amended & S.R. 2007/174 revoked. - Revoked by S.R. 2009/103 (ISBN 9780337977305). - 4p.: 30 cm. - 978-0-337-97339-0 *£3.00*

Legal Aid (Financial Conditions) Regulations (Northern Ireland) 2008 No. 2008/108. - Enabling power: S.I. 1981/228 (N.I. 8), arts 9 (2), 12 (2), 22, 27. - Issued: 02.04.2008. Made: 08.03.2008. Coming into operation: 07.04.2008. Effect: S.I. 1981/228 (N.I. 8) amended & S.R. 2007/175 revoked with saving. - Revoked by S.R. 2009/104 (ISBN 9780337977312). - 4p.: 30 cm. - 978-0-337-97340-6 *£3.00*

The Legal Aid in Criminal Proceedings (Costs) (Amendment) Rules (Northern Ireland) 2008 No. 2008/248. - Enabling power: S.I. 1981/228 (N.I. 8), art. 36 (3). - Issued: 12.06.2008. Made: 03.06.2008. Coming into operation: 01.07.2008. Effect: S.R. 1992/314 amended. - 2p.: 30 cm. - 978-0-337-97414-4 *£3.00*

Libraries

The Libraries (2008 Act) (Commencement No 1) Order (Northern Ireland) 2008 No. 2008/396 (C.21). - Enabling power: Libraries Act (Northern Ireland) 2008, s. 12 (2). Bringing various provisions of the 2008 Act into operation on 01.10.2008. - Issued: 02.10.2008. Made: 25.09.2008. Coming into operation: -. Effect: None. - 2p.: 30 cm. - 978-0-337-97527-1 *£4.00*

Local government

The Local Government (Constituting a Joint Committee a Body Corporate) Order (Northern Ireland) 2008 No. 2008/310. - Enabling power: Local Government Act (Northern Ireland) 1972, s. 19 (9). - Issued: 28.07.2008. Made: 22.07.2008. Coming into operation: 20.08.2008. Effect: None. - 4p.: 30 cm. - 978-0-337-97464-9 *£3.00*

Magistrates' courts

The Magistrates' Courts (Amendment No. 2) Rules (Northern Ireland) 2008 No. 2008/361. - Enabling power: S.I. 1981/1675 (N.I. 26), art. 13 & S.I. 1999/2789 (N.I. 8), art. 39 (1) & S.I. 2004/1500 (N.I. 9), art. 14 & S.I. 2004/1501 (N.I. 10), arts. 16, 35. - Issued: 09.09.2008. Made: 03.09.2008. Coming into operation: In accord. with rules1 and 2. Effect: S.R. 1984/225 amended. - 16p.: 30 cm. - 978-0-337-97502-8 *£5.00*

The Magistrates' Courts (Amendment) Rules (Northern Ireland) 2008 No. 2008/251. - Enabling power: S.I. 1981/1675 (N.I. 26), art. 13. - Issued: 23.06.2008. Made: 16.06.2008. Coming into operation: In accord. with rule 1. Effect: S.R. 1984/225 amended. - 28p.: 30 cm. - 978-0-337-97418-2 *£4.50*

The Magistrates' Courts (Amendment) Rules (Northern Ireland) 2008 (correction slip) No. 2008/251 Cor.. - Correction slip (to ISBN 970337974182) dated July 2008. - 1 sheet: 30 cm. *Free*

The Magistrates' Courts (Anti-social Behaviour Orders) (Amendment) Rules (Northern Ireland) 2008 No. 2008/253. - Enabling power: S.I. 1981/1675 (N.I. 26), art. 13 & S.I. 2004/1988 (N.I. 12), art. 6C (4). - Issued: 23.06.2008. Made: 16.06.2008. Coming into operation: 16.07.2008. Effect: S.R. 2004/324 amended. - 12p.: 30 cm. - 978-0-337-97419-9 *£3.00*

The Magistrates' Courts (Children (Northern Ireland) Order 1995) (Amendment No. 2) Rules (Northern Ireland) 2008 No. 2008/225. - Enabling power: S.I. 1981/1675 (N.I. 26), art. 13 & S.I. 1995/755 (N.I. 2), art. 165. - Issued: 28.05.2008. Made: 20.05.2008. Coming into operation: 23.06.2008. Effect: S.R. 1996/323 amended. - 2p.: 30 cm. - 978-0-337-97394-9 *£3.00*

The Magistrates' Courts (Children (Northern Ireland) Order 1995) (Amendment) Rules (Northern Ireland) 2008 No. 2008/35. - Enabling power: S.I. 1981/1675 (N.I. 26), art. 13 & S.I. 1995/755 (N.I. 2), art. 165. - Issued: 08.02.2008. Made: 31.01.2008. Coming into operation: 10.03.2008. Effect: S.R. 1996/323 amended. - 2p.: 30 cm. - 978-0-337-97246-1 *£3.00*

The Magistrates' Courts (Costs in Criminal Cases) (Amendment) Rules (Northern Ireland) 2008 No. 2008/363. - Enabling power: S.I. 1981/1675 (N.I. 26), art. 13 & Costs in Criminal Cases Act (Northern Ireland) 1968, s. 7. - Issued: 09.09.2008. Made: 03.09.2008. Coming into operation: 01.10.2008. Effect: S.R. 1988/136 amended. - 2p.: 30 cm. - 978-0-337-97504-2 *£4.00*

The Magistrates' Courts (Criminal Justice (Children)) (Amendment) Rules (Northern Ireland) 2008 No. 2008/252. - Enabling power: S.I. 1981/1675 (N.I. 26), art. 13. - Issued: 23.06.2008. Made: 16.06.2008. Coming into operation: In accord. with rule 1. Effect: S.R. 1999/7 amended. - 8p.: 30 cm. - 978-0-337-97417-5 £3.00

The Magistrates' Courts (Detention and Forfeiture of Seized Cash) (Amendment) Rules (Northern Ireland) 2008 No. 2008/362. - Enabling power: S.I. 1981/1675 (N.I. 26), art. 13. - Issued: 09.09.2008. Made: 03.09.2008. Coming into operation: 01.10.2008. Effect: S.R. 2003/17 amended. - 4p.: 30 cm. - 978-0-337-97503-5 £4.00

Northern Ireland Departments

The Departments (Transfer of Functions) Order (Northern Ireland) 2008 No. 2008/46. - Enabling power: S.I.1999/283 (NI 1), art. 8. - Issued: 15.02.2008. Made: 06.02.2008. Coming into operation: 01.04.2008, in accord. with 1 (2). Effect: None. - Order made by the First Minister and deputy First Minister acting jointly under Article 8 of the Departments (Northern Ireland) Order 1999 and subject to affirmative resolution of the Assembly. - 4p: 30 cm. - 978-0-337-97255-3 £3.00

The Departments (Transfer of Functions) Order (Northern Ireland) 2008 No. 2008/46. - Enabling power: S.I.1999/283 (NI 1), art. 8. - Issued: 14.03.2008. Made: 06.02.2008. Coming into operation: 01.04.2008, in accord. with 1 (2). Effect: None. - Affirmed by resolution of the Assembly 10.03.2008. Supersedes version presented for affirmation (ISBN 9780337972553). - 4p: 30 cm. - 978-0-337-97297-3 £3.00

Pensions

The Guaranteed Minimum Pensions Increase Order (Northern Ireland) 2008 No. 2008/84. - Enabling power: Pension Schemes (Northern Ireland) Act 1993, s. 105. - Issued: 11.03.2008. Made: 05.03.2008. Coming into operation: 06.04.2008. Effect: None. - 2p.: 30 cm. - 978-0-337-97284-3 £3.00

The Occupational and Personal Pension Schemes (General Levy) (Amendment) Regulations (Northern Ireland) 2008 No. 2008/97. - Enabling power: Pension Schemes (Northern Ireland) Act 1993, ss. 170, 177 (2). - Issued: 13.03.2008. Made: 10.03.2008. Coming into operation: 01.04.2008. Effect: S.R. 2005/92 amended. - 4p: 30 cm. - 978-0-337-97296-6 £3.00

The Occupational and Personal Pension Schemes (Transfer Values) (Amendment) Regulations (Northern Ireland) 2008 No. 2008/388. - Enabling power: Pension Schemes (Northern Ireland) Act 1993, ss. 93 (1) (2) (b), 97AF (1) (3) (b) (4) (b), 177 (2) to (4), 178. - Issued: 26.09.2008. Made: 22.09.2008. Coming into operation: 13.10.2008. Effect: S.R. 1987/290; 1996/619; 2006/49 amended. - 4p: 30 cm. - 978-0-337-97520-2 £4.00

The Occupational Pension Schemes (Employer Debt and Miscellaneous Amendments) Regulations (Northern Ireland) 2008 No. 2008/132. - Enabling power: S.I. 1995/3213 (N.I. 22), arts 68 (2)(e), 75 (1) (b) (5) (10), 75A (1) to (8), 115 (1) (a) (b), 116, 122 (3), 166 (2) (3) & S.I. 2005/255 (N.I. 1), arts 2 (5) (a), 64 (2) (a) (3) (a), 88 (2) (q), 110 (5), 211, 280 (1) (b), 287 (1) to (3), sch. 1, para. 2 (d). - Issued: 31.03.2008. Made: 18.03.2008. Coming into operation: 06.04.2008. Effect: S.R. 2005/91, 126, 168, 378, 568 amended & S.R. 2005/387; 2007/64 partially revoked. - 36p: 30 cm. - 978-0-337-97328-4 £6.50

The Occupational Pension Schemes (Employer Debt: Apportionment Arrangements) (Amendment) Regulations (Northern Ireland) 2008 No. 2008/178. - Enabling power: S.I. 1995/3213 (N.I. 22), arts 68 (2) (e), 75 (5), 75A (1) to (8), 166 (1) to (3). - Issued: 24.04.2008. Made: 17.04.2008. Coming into operation: 18.04.2008. Effect: S.R. 2005/168 amended. - This statutory rule has been made in consequence of defects in S.R. 2008 no. 132 (ISBN 9780337973284) and is being issued free of charge to all known recipients of that statutory rule. - 4p: 30 cm. - 978-0-337-97363-5 £3.00

The Occupational Pension Schemes (Internal Dispute Resolution Procedures) (Consequential and Miscellaneous Amendments) Regulations (Northern Ireland) 2008 No. 2008/116. - Enabling power: Pension Schemes (Northern Ireland) Act 1993, ss. 109 (1) (d), 177 (2) to (4) & S.I. 1995/3213 (N.I. 22), arts 50 (8) (c) (9) (c), 166 (1) to (3). - Issued: 20.03.2008. Made: 13.03.2008. Coming into operation: 06.04.2008. Effect: S.R. 1997/39; 1999/486; 2001/119; 2005/536 amended & S.R. 1996/203 revoked. - 8p: 30 cm. - 978-0-337-97313-0 £3.00

The Occupational Pension Schemes (Levies) (Amendment) Regulations (Northern Ireland) 2008 No. 2008/145. - Enabling power: S.I. 2005/255 (N.I. 1), art. 103 (1) (3). - Issued: 27.06.2008. Made: 28.03.2008. Coming into operation: 01.04.2008. Effect: S.R. 2005/147 amended & S.R. 2007/210 partially revoked. - Affirmed by resolution of the Assembly on 23.06.2008. Supersedes SI of same number (ISBN 9780337973444) issued 02.04.2008. - 4p.: 30 cm. - 978-0-337-97430-4 £3.00

The Occupational Pension Schemes (Levies) (Amendment) Regulations (Northern Ireland) 2008 No. 2008/145. - Enabling power: S.I. 2005/255 (N.I. 1), art. 103 (1) (3). - Issued: 02.04.2008. Made: 28.03.2008. Coming into operation: 01.04.2008. Effect: S.R. 2005/147; 2007/210 amended. - For approval of the Assembly before the expiration of six months from the date of their coming into operation. - 4p.: 30 cm. - 978-0-337-97344-4 £3.00

The Occupational Pension Schemes (Levy Ceiling) Order (Northern Ireland) 2008 No. 2008/144. - Enabling power: S.I. 2005/255 (N.I. 1), arts. 161, 287 (3). - Issued: 02.04.2008. Made: 28.03.2008. Coming into operation: 31.03.2008. Effect: S.R. 2007/212 revoked. - Revoked by S.R. 2009/139 (ISBN 9780337977343). - 2p.: 30 cm. - 978-0-337-97343-7 £3.00

The Occupational Pension Schemes (Non-European Schemes Exemption) Regulations (Northern Ireland) 2008 No. 2008/117. - Enabling power: S.I. 2005/255 (N.I. 1), art. 230 (5). - Issued: 20.03.2008. Made: 13.03.2008. Coming into operation: 06.04.2008. Effect: None. - 2p: 30 cm. - 978-0-337-97314-7 £3.00

The Occupational Pension Schemes (Transfer Values) (Amendment) Regulations (Northern Ireland) 2008 No. 2008/370. - Enabling power: 1993 c. 49, ss. 23 (3), 89A (2), 91 (2) (d), 93(1) (2) (b) (3) (c) (4), 97AC (2) (a), 97AF (1) (3) (b) (4) (b) (5) (a), 97H (2) (3), 97I, 97L, 109(1) (3), 177(2) to (4), 178 & S.I.1995/3213 (N.I. 22), arts 67D(4), 166(1) to (3) & S.I. 1999/3147(N.I. 11), ss. 21 (1) (b), 27, 38 (1) (2), 73(4), sch. 5, paras 5(b), 8(1) (2). - Issued: 10.09.2008. Made: 05.09.2008. Coming into operation: 01.10.2008. Effect: S.R. 1987/290; 1996/619; 1997/56; 2000/142, 143, 144, 145, 146; 2006/49, 149 amended & S.R. 1988/107; 1994/300; 1997/160; 2000/335; 2005/114, 171, 568; 2007/64 partially revoked & S.R. 1988/214; 2003/337; 2005/114 revoked. - 28p.: 30 cm. - 978-0-337-97505-9 £5.00

The Occupational Pensions (Revaluation) Order (Northern Ireland) 2008 No. 2008/485. - Enabling power: Pension Schemes (Northern Ireland) Act 1993, sch. 2, para. 2 (1). - Issued: 09.12.2008. Made: 03.12.2008. Coming into operation: 01.01.2009. Effect: None. - 2p.: 30 cm. - 978-0-337-97593-6 £4.00

The Pension Protection Fund (Entry Rules) (Amendment) Regulations (Northern Ireland) 2008 No. 2008/303. - Enabling power: S.I. 2005/255 (N.I.1), art. 110 (3). - Issued: 21.07.2008. Made: 11.07.2008. Coming into operation: 02.08.2008. Effect: S.R. 2005/126 amended. - 2p.: 30 cm. - 978-0-337-97460-1 £3.00

The Pension Protection Fund (Pension Compensation Cap) Order (Northern Ireland) 2008 No. 2008/146. - Enabling power: S.I. 2005/255 (N.I. 1), art. 287 (3), sch. 6, paras 26 (7), 27. - Issued: 02.04.2008. Made: 28.03.2008. Coming into operation: 01.04.2008. Effect: S.R. 2007/211 revoked. - Revoked by S.R. 2009/140 (ISBN 9780337977350). - 2p: 30 cm. - 978-0-337-97345-1 £3.00

The Pensions (2005 Order) (Code of Practice) (Dispute Resolution) (Appointed Day) Order (Northern Ireland) 2008 No. 2008/305. - Enabling power: S.I. 2005/255 (N.I. 1), art. 86 (7). Appoints 28.07.2008 as the date for the coming into effect of Pensions Regulator Code of practice No. 11: Dispute resolution - reasonable periods. - Issued: 22.07.2008. Made: 16.07.2008. Coming into operation: -. Effect: None. - 2p.: 30 cm. - 978-0-337-97463-2 £3.00

The Pensions (2005 Order) (Commencement No. 11) Order (Northern Ireland) 2008 No. 2008/104 (C. 4). - Enabling power: S.I. 2005/255 (N.I. 1), arts. 1 (2). Bringing into operation various provisions of the 2005 Order on 12.03.2008; 06.04.2008 in accord. with art 2. - Issued: 14.03.2008. Made: 11.03.2008. Coming into operation: -. Effect: None. - 8p: 30 cm. - 978-0-337-97300-0 £3.00

The Pensions (2008 Act) (Actuarial Guidance) (Consequential Provisions) Order (Northern Ireland) 2008 No. 2008/365. - Enabling power: Pensions Act (Northern Ireland) 2008, s. 19 (1). - Issued: 09.09.2008. Made: 03.09.2008. Coming into operation: 01.10.2008. Effect: S.R. 1987/288; 1996/493, 585, 621; 1997/98; 2000/262; 2005/568 amended & S.R. 2002/410; 2007/64 partially revoked. - 4p: 30 cm. - 978-0-337-97501-1 £4.00

The Pensions (2008 Act) (Commencement No. 1) Order (Northern Ireland) 2008 No. 2008/65 (C.1). - Enabling power: Pensions Act (Northern Ireland) 2008, s. 21 (1). Bringing into operation various provisions of the 2008 Act on 29.02.2008. - Issued: 26.02.2008. Made: 21.02.2008. Coming into operation: -. Effect: None. - 2p: 30 cm. - 978-0-337-97268-3 £3.00

Pensions Appeal Tribunals (Northern Ireland) (Amendment) Rules 2008 No. 2008/444. - Enabling power: Pensions Appeals Tribunals Act 1943, s. 6, sch., para. 5. - Issued: 21.11.2008. Made: 11.11.2008. Coming into operation: 15.12.2008. Effect: S.R. 1981/231 amended. - 4p.: 30 cm. - 978-0-337-97567-7 £4.00

Pensions Increase (Review) Order (Northern Ireland) 2008 No. 2008/123. - Enabling power: S.I. 1975/1503 (N.I. 15), art. 69 (1) (2) (5) (5ZA). - Issued: 02.04.2008. Made: 14.03.2008. Coming into operation: 07.04.2008. Effect: None. - 8p: 30 cm. - 978-0-337-97327-7 £3.00

The Personal and Occupational Pension Schemes (Amendment) Regulations (Northern Ireland) 2008 No. 2008/364. - Enabling power: Pension Schemes (Northern Ireland) Act 1993, ss. 5 (5) (a), 22, 24 (5), 177 (2) to (4). - Issued: 09.09.2008. Made: 03.09.2008. Coming into operation: 01.10.2008. Effect: S.R. 1997/56, 139 amended & S.R. 2001/118; 2002/109; 2003/256 partially revoked & S.R. 2006/20 revoked. - 4p: 30 cm. - 978-0-337-97500-4 £4.00

Pesticides

The Pesticides (Maximum Residue Levels) Regulations (Northern Ireland) 2008 No. 2008/433. - Enabling power: European Communities Act 1972, s. 2 (2). - Issued: 11.11.2008. Made: 05.11.2008. Coming into operation: 08.12.2008. Effect: S.R. 2006/220, 501; 2007/428, 465; 2008/195 revoked. - EC note: These regs enforce the provisions of Regulation (EC) No 396/2005 on maximum residue levels of pesticides in or on food and feed of plant and animal origin and amending Council Directive 91/41/EEC. - 8p.: 30 cm. - 978-0-337-97562-2 £5.00

Plant Protection Products (Amendment No 2) Regulations (Northern Ireland) 2008 No. 2008/499. - Enabling power: European Communities Act 1972, s. 2 (2). - Issued: 19.12.2008. Made: 15.12.2008. Coming into operation: 12.01.2009. Effect: S.R. 2005/526 amended & S.R. 2008/85 revoked. - EC note: These Regulations amend the Plant Protection Products Regulations (Northern Ireland) 2005 (S.R. 2005 No. 526) which implement in Northern Ireland Council Directive 91/414/EEC to be read with the Corrigenda published in O.J. No. L170, 25.6.92, p. 40 concerning the placing of plant protection products on the market as amended. - 4p: 30 cm. - 978-0-337-97607-0 £4.00

Plant Protection Products (Amendment) Regulations (Northern Ireland) 2008 No. 2008/85. - Enabling power: European Communities Act 1972, s. 2 (2). - Issued: 11.03.2008. Made: 05.03.2008. Coming into operation: 17.04.2008. Effect: S.R. 2005/526 amended & S.R. 2007/251 revoked. - Revoked by S.R. 2008/499 (ISBN 9780337976070). EC note: These Regulations amend the Plant Protection Products Regulations (Northern Ireland) 2005 (S.R. 2005 No. 526) (the principal Regulations) which implement in Northern Ireland Council Directive 91/414/EEC concerning the placing of plant protection products on the market (the Directive), as amended. Schedule 1 is replaced by the Schedule to these Regulations. In consequence the list of active substances which can be used in products capable of being approved under regulations 5 and 6 of the principal Regulations for placing on the market is extended accordingly. - 8p: 30 cm. - 978-0-337-97285-0 £3.00

Pharmacy

The European Qualifications (Pharmacy) Regulations (Northern Ireland) 2008 No. 2008/192. - Enabling power: European Communities Act 1972, s. 2 (2). - Issued: 06.05.2008. Made: 29.04.2008. Coming into operation: 22.05.2008. Effect: 1968 c. 67; 2006 c. 28; S.I. 1976/1213 (N.I. 22); 2004/1031 amended. - EC note: These regs implement, in part, Directive 2005/36/EC which concerns the recognition of professional qualifications. The essential aim of the Directive is to facilitate free movement of persons between member States of the European Community, by setting out principles and procedures which member States are to apply in determining the rights of migrants to pursue professions which require professional qualifications. - 16p.: 30 cm. - 978-0-337-97375-8 £3.00

The Pharmaceutical Society of Northern Ireland (General) (Amendment) Regulations (Northern Ireland) 2008 No. 2008/222. - Enabling power: S.I. 1976/1213 (N.I. 22), art. 5. - Issued: 30.05.2008. Made: 15.05.2008. Coming into operation: 01.06.2008. Effect: S.R. 1994/202 amended. - 2p.: 30 cm. - 978-0-337-97395-6 £3.00

Registration of Pharmaceutical Chemists (Exempt Persons) Regulations (Northern Ireland) 2008 No. 2008/193. - Enabling power: S.I.1976/1213 (N.I.22), art. 5 (1). - Issued: 07.05.2008. Made: 30.04.2008. Coming into operation: 23.05.2008. Effect: None. - 4p.: 30 cm. - 978-0-337-97377-2 £3.00

Planning

The Planning (Avian Influenza) (Special Development) Order (Northern Ireland) 2008 No. 2008/235. - Enabling power: S.I.1991/1220 (N.I. 11), art. 13. - Issued: 06.06.2008. Made: 02.06.2008. Coming into operation: 01.07.2008. Effect: None. - 4p.: 30 cm. - 978-0-337-97403-8 £3.00

The Planning (Environmental Impact Assessment) (Amendment No.2) Regulations (Northern Ireland) 2008 No. 2008/372. - Enabling power: European Communities Act 1972, s. 2 (2). - Issued: 12.09.2008. Made: 09.09.2008. Coming into operation: 01.10.2008. Effect: S.R. 1999/73 amended. - 8p.: 30 cm. - 978-0-337-97507-3 £5.00

The Planning (Environmental Impact Assessment) (Amendment) Regulations (Northern Ireland) 2008 No. 2008/17. - Enabling power: European Communities Act 1972, s. 2 (2). - Issued: 22.01.2008. Made: 16.01.2008. Coming into operation: 12.02.2008. Effect: S.R. 1999/73 amended. - 8p.: 30 cm. - 978-0-337-97231-7 £3.00

Plant health

The Plant Health (Amendment No.2) Order (Northern Ireland) 2008 No. 2008/442. - Enabling power: Plant Health Act (Northern Ireland) 1967, ss. 2, 3 & European Communities Act 1972, sch. 2, para. 1A. - Issued: 17.11.2008. Made: 12.11.2008. Coming into operation: 04.12.2008. Effect: S.R. 2006/82 amended & S.R. 2002/7; 2004/289; 2005/296 revoked. - EC note: This Order amends the Plant Health Order (Northern Ireland) 2006 (S.I. 2006/82) so as to implement; Commission Directive 2008/64/EC amending Council Directive 2000/29/EC; Commission Directive 2008/61/EC; Commission Directive 2008/86/EC, being Decision No. 1/2008 of the Joint Committee on Agriculture set up by the Agreement between the European Community and the Swiss Confederation on Trade in Agriculture Products, which makes changes to the list of relevant material originating in Switzerland which may be landed or moved within Northern Ireland if accompanied by a Swiss plant passport. - 8p: 30 cm. - 978-0-337-97566-0 £4.00

The Plant Health (Amendment No.3) Order (Northern Ireland) 2008 No. 2008/493. - Enabling power: Plant Health Act (Northern Ireland) 1967, s. 2. - Issued: 16.12.2008. Made: 11.12.2008. Coming into operation: 12.12.2008. Effect: S.R. 2006/82 amended. - EC note: This Order amends the Plant Health Order (Northern Ireland) 2006 (S.I. 2006/82) so as to implement; Commission Directive 2008/840/EC putting in place certain import restrictions of plants, other than seeds, of Acer spp., intended for planting, originating in any third country so as to prevent the introduction into Northern Ireland of Anoplophora chinensis (Forster) (the citrus longhorn beetle). - 4p: 30 cm. - 978-0-337-97601-8 *£4.00*

The Plant Health (Amendment) Order (Northern Ireland) 2008 No. 2008/205. - Enabling power: Plant Health Act (Northern Ireland) 1967, ss. 2, 3 (1) & European Communities Act 1972, sch. 2, para. 1A. - Issued: 14.05.2008. Made: 07.05.2008. Coming into operation: 30.06.2008. Effect: S.R. 2006/82 amended. - EC note: This Order amends the Plant Health Order (Northern Ireland) 2006 (S.I. 2006/82) so as to implement emergency measures to prevent the introduction, into and the spread within the Community of Rhynchophorus ferrugineus (Olivier) (Commission Decision 2007/365/EC); of Gibberella circinata Nirenberg (Decision 2007/433/EC); of Potato spindle tuber viroid (Decision 2007/410/EC). It also implements Decision 2004/416/EC (as amended) on temporary emergency measures in respect of certain citrus fruits originating in Argentina or Brazil, and Directive 2007/41/EC amending certain Annexes to Council Directive 2000/29/EC on protective measures against the introduction into the Community of organisms harmful to plants or plant products and against their spread within the Community. - 8p: 30 cm. - 978-0-337-97387-1 *£3.00*

The Plant Health (Import Inspection Fees) (Amendment) Regulations (Northern Ireland) 2008 No. 2008/60. - Enabling power: European Communities Act 1972, s. 2 (2) & Finance Act 1973, s. 56 (1) (2) (5). - Issued: 22.02.2008. Made: 18.02.2008. Coming into operation: 31.03.2008. Effect: S.R. 2005/373 amended. - EC note: These Regulations amend the 2005 Regs which implemented Article 13(d) of Council Directive 2000/29/EC as amended by Directive 2002/89/EC. - 8p: 30 cm. - 978-0-337-97267-6 *£3.00*

The Potatoes Originating in Egypt (Amendment) Regulations (Northern Ireland) 2008 No. 2008/125. - Enabling power: European Communities Act 1972, s. 2 (2). - Issued: 20.03.2008. Made: 14.03.2008. Coming into operation: 25.04.2008. Effect: S.R. 2004/183 amended & S.R. 2006/512 revoked. - Revoked by S.R. 2009/30 (ISBN 9780337976353). EC note: These regulations amend the definition of the "decision" in the principal Regulations so as to include the amendments effected by Commission Decision 2007/842/EC. - 4p.: 30 cm. - 978-0-337-97320-8 *£3.00*

Police

The Police and Criminal Evidence (Northern Ireland) Order 1989 (Codes of Practice) (No. 4) Order 2008 No. 2008/408. - Enabling power: S.I. 1989/1341 (N.I. 12), art. 66 (4) (5). - Issued: 14.10.2008. Made: 02.10.2008. Laid: 13.10.2008. Coming into operation: 10.11.2008. Effect: None. - 4p.: 30 cm. - 978-0-337-97537-0 *£4.00*

Police Powers for Designated Staff (Code of Ethics) Order (Northern Ireland) 2008 No. 2008/243. - Enabling power: Police (Northern Ireland) Act 2003, s. 37. - Issued: 11.06.2008. Made: 04.06.2008. Coming into operation: 01.07.2008. Effect: None. - 4p.: 30 cm. - 978-0-337-97412-0 *£3.00*

Police Powers for Designated Staff (Complaints and Misconduct) Regulations (Northern Ireland) 2008 No. 2008/242. - Enabling power: Police (Northern Ireland) Act 2003, s. 34. - Issued: 13.06.2008. Made: 04.06.2008. Coming into operation: 01.07.2008. Effect: None. - 40p.: 30 cm. - 978-0-337-97411-3 *£6.50*

Police Service of Northern Ireland and Police Service of Northern Ireland Reserve (Full-Time) (Severance) (Amendment) Regulations 2008 No. 2008/439. - Enabling power: Police (Northern Ireland) Act 1998, ss. 25 (1) (2) (k), 26 (1) (2) (g), 72 (2) & Police (Northern Ireland) Act 2000, s. 49. - Issued: 01.12.2008. Made: 27.10.2008. Coming into operation: 22.12.2008. Effect: S.R. 2003/60; 2006/313 amended. - 4p.: 30 cm. - 978-0-337-97565-3 *£4.00*

Police Service of Northern Ireland (Conduct) (Amendment) Regulations 2008 No. 2008/56. - Enabling power: Police (Northern Ireland) Act 1998, ss. 25, 26. - Issued: 21.02.2008. Made: 01.02.2008. Coming into operation: 10.03.2008. Effect: S.R. 2000/315, 320 amended. - 12p: 30 cm. - 978-0-337-97266-9 *£3.00*

The Police Service of Northern Ireland (Promotion) Regulations 2008 No. 2008/477. - Enabling power: Police (Northern Ireland) Act 1998, ss. 25, 72 (2). - Issued: 10.12.2008. Made: 01.12.2008. Coming into operation: 31.12.2008. Effect: S.R. 1995/120 revoked. - 8p.: 30 cm. - 978-0-337-97588-2 *£5.00*

The Police Support Staff (Transfer of Employment) Regulations (Northern Ireland) 2008 No. 2008/360. - Enabling power: Police (Northern Ireland) Act 2000, ss. 5 (1), 76 (2). - Issued: 11.09.2008. Made: 22.08.2008. Coming into operation: 01.10.2008. Effect: None. - 4p.: 30 cm. - 978-0-337-97499-1 *£4.00*

Police (Testing for Substance Misuse) Regulations (Northern Ireland) 2008 No. 2008/325. - Enabling power: Police (Northern Ireland) Act 1998, ss. 25, 26 & Police (Northern Ireland) Act 2000, ss. 41, 44. - Issued: 05.08.2008. Made: 24.07.2008. Coming into operation: 01.09.2008. Effect: S.R. 1996/564; 2001/369; 2004/2, 3, 122; 2005/547 amended. - 8p.: 30 cm. - 978-0-337-97476-2 *£3.00*

Police Trainee (Amendment) Regulations (Northern Ireland) 2008 No. 2008/314. - Enabling power: Police (Northern Ireland) Act 2000, ss. 41, 44. - Issued: 01.08.2008. Made: 14.07.2008. Laid: 24.07.2008. Coming into operation: 18.08.2008. Effect: S.R. 2001/140, 369 amended. - 8p.: 30 cm. - 978-0-337-97470-0 £3.00

Prisons

The Prison and Young Offenders Centre (Amendment) Rules (Northern Ireland) 2008 No. 2008/452. - Enabling power: Prison Act (Northern Ireland) 1953, ss. 13 (1), 34 (6) (as extended by the Treatment of Offenders Act (Northern Ireland) 1968, s. 2). - Issued: 05.12.2008. Made: 17.11.2008. Laid: 26.11.2008. Coming into operation: 19.12.2008. Effect: S.R. 1995/8 amended. - 4p.: 30 cm. - 978-0-337-97571-4 £4.00

Procedure

The Crown Court (Amendment) Rules (Northern Ireland) 2008 No. 2008/505. - Enabling power: Judicature (Northern Ireland) Act 1978, ss. 52 (1), 53A & S.I. 1999/2789 (N.I. 8), art. 39 (1) & S.I. 2004/1500 (N.I. 9), art. 14. - Issued: 14.01.2009. Made: 18.12.2008. Coming into operation: 02.02.2009. Effect: S.R. 1979/90 amended. - 16p.: 30 cm. - 978-0-337-97613-1 £5.00

Public health

The Children and Young Persons (Sale of Tobacco etc.) Regulations (Northern Ireland) 2008 No. 2008/306. - Enabling power: S.I. 2006/2957 (N.I. 20), arts 14, 15 (1). - Issued: 06.08.2008. Made: 17.07.2008. Coming into operation: 01.09.2008 in accord. with reg. 1. Effect: S.I. 1978/1907 (N.I. 26); 1991/2872 (N.I. 25) amended. - Laid before the Assembly in draft. Supersedes draft S.R. (ISBN 9780337974267) issued on 26.06.2008. - 8p.: 30 cm. - 978-0-337-97465-6 £3.00

The Producer Responsibility Obligations (Packaging Waste) (Amendment No. 2) Regulations (Northern Ireland) 2008 No. 2008/373. - Enabling power: European Communities Act 1972, s. 2 (2) & S.I. 1998/1762 (N.I. 16), arts. 3 to 5. - Issued: 12.09.2008. Made: 09.09.2008. Coming into operation: 13.10.2008. Effect: S.R. 2007/198 amended. - 4p.: 30 cm. - 978-0-337-97508-0 £4.00

The Producer Responsibility Obligations (Packaging Waste) (Amendment) Regulations (Northern Ireland) 2008 No. 2008/77. - Enabling power: European Communities Act 1972, s. 2 (2) & S.I. 1998/1762 (N.I. 16), arts. 3 to 5. - Issued: 07.03.2008. Made: 29.02.2008. Coming into operation: 06.04.2008. Effect: S.R. 2007/198 amended. - EC note: These Regulations correct an error in the 2007 Regulations in respect of the definition of the Waste Directive. These Regulations increase the recovery and recycling targets imposed on producers by the 2007 Regulations. - 4p.: 30 cm. - 978-0-337-97279-9 £3.00

The Public Health (Aircraft) Regulations (Northern Ireland) 2008 No. 2008/436. - Enabling power: Public Health Act (Northern Ireland) 1967, ss. 2A (1) to (4), 2B (1). - Issued: 25.11.2008. Made: 05.11.2008. Coming into operation: 11.12.2008. Effect: S.R. 1971/182 revoked. - 20p.: 30 cm. - 978-0-337-97575-2 £5.00

The Public Health (Ships) Regulations (Northern Ireland) 2008 No. 2008/333. - Enabling power: Public Health Act (Northern Ireland) 1967, s. 2A (1) to (4). - Issued: 20.08.2008. Made: 31.07.2008. Coming into operation: 21.08.2008. Effect: S.R. & O. (N.I.) 1971/183 revoked. - 24p.: 30 cm. - 978-0-337-97489-2 £4.00

The Smoke-free (Exemptions, Vehicles, Penalties and Discounted Amounts) (Amendment) Regulations (Northern Ireland) 2008 No. 2008/307. - Enabling power: S.I. 2006/2957 (N.I. 20), arts 4, 6, 10 (3), 15 (1), sch. 1, paras 5, 8. - Issued: 06.08.2008. Made: 17.07.2008. Coming into operation: 01.09.2008. Effect: S.R. 2007/138 amended. - Laid before the assembly in draft. Supersedes draft S.R. (ISBN 9780337974274) issued on 26.06.2008. - 2p.: 30 cm. - 978-0-337-97466-3 £3.00

Rates

The Housing Benefit (Amendment No. 2) Regulations (Northern Ireland) 2008 No. 2008/504. - Enabling power: Social Security Administration (Northern Ireland) Act 1992, ss. 5 (1) (a), 73 (3) (4), 165 (1) (4) (6). - Issued: 24.12.2008. Made: 19.12.2008. Coming into operation: 27.01.2009 for reg. 3 (2), 4; 06.04.2009 for remainder. Effect: S.R. 2006/405, 406 amended & S.R. 2008/410 partially revoked. - 8p.: 30 cm. - 978-0-337-97612-4 £4.00

The Housing Benefit (Amendment) Regulations (Northern Ireland) 2008 No. 2008/371. - Enabling power: Social Security Administration (Northern Ireland) Act 1992, ss. 5 (1) (a) (h), 107, 165 (1) (4) to (6). - Issued: 12.09.2008. Made: 08.09.2008. Coming into operation: 01.10.2008. Effect: S.R. 2006/405, 406, 462 amended. - 8p.: 30 cm. - 978-0-337-97506-6 £5.00

The Housing Benefit (Employment and Support Allowance Consequential Provisions) Regulations (Northern Ireland) 2008 No. 2008/378. - Enabling power: Welfare Reform Act (Northern Ireland) 2007, s. 28 (2). - Issued: 19.09.2008. Made: 15.09.2008. Coming into operation: 27.10.2008. Effect: S.R. 2001/213; 2006/405, 406, 407 amended. - 16p.: 30 cm. - 978-0-337-97513-4 £5.00

The Housing Benefit (Extended Payments) (Amendments) Regulations (Northern Ireland) 2008 No. 2008/285. - Enabling power: Social Security Contributions and Benefits (Northern Ireland) Act 1992, s. 130 (2) & Social Security Administration (Northern Ireland) 1992, s. 5 (1) & Welfare Reform Act (Northern Ireland) 2007, ss. 32, 33. - Issued: 10.07.2008. Made: 04.07.2008. Coming into operation: 06.10.2008. Effect: S.R. 2006/405, 406 amended. - 12p.: 30 cm. - 978-0-337-97446-5 £3.00

The Housing Benefit (Local Housing Allowance) (Miscellaneous and Consequential Amendments) Regulations (Northern Ireland) 2008 No. 2008/103. - Enabling power: Social Security Contributions and Benefits (Northern Ireland) Act 1992, ss. 129A (2) (3), 171 (1) (3) (4) & Child Support, Pensions and Social Security Act (Northern Ireland) 2000, sch. 7, para. 4 (3A). - Issued: 18.03.2008. Made: 11.03.2008. Coming into operation: 07.04.2008 in accord.with reg. 1. Effect: S.R. 1987/465; 2001/213, 216; 2004/8, 144; 2006/407 amended. - 12p.: 30 cm. - 978-0-337-97306-2 £3.00

The New NAV List (Time of Valuation) Order (Northern Ireland) 2008 No. 2008/15. - Enabling power: S.I. 1977/2157 (N.I. 28), art. 39A (1). - Issued: 23.01.2008. Made: 11.01.2008. Coming into operation: 01.04.2008. Effect: None. - 2p: 30 cm. - 978-0-337-97232-4 £3.00

The Rate Relief (Lone Pensioner Allowance) Regulations (Northern Ireland) 2008 No. 2008/124. - Enabling power: S.I. 1977/2157 (N.I. 28), art. 30A. - Issued: 20.03.2008. Made: 14.03.2008. Coming into operation: 01.04.2008. Effect: None. - 8p.: 30 cm. - 978-0-337-97319-2 £3.00

The Rate Relief (Qualifying Age) (Amendment) Regulations (Northern Ireland) 2008 No. 2008/68. - Enabling power: S.I. 1977/2157 (N.I. 28), art. 30A. - Issued: 28.02.2008. Made: 25.02.2008. Coming into operation: 01.04.2008. Effect: S.R. 2007/203 amended. - 2p.: 30 cm. - 978-0-337-97273-7 £3.00

The Rates (Industrial Hereditaments) (Amendment) Order (Northern Ireland) 2008 No. 2008/49. - Enabling power: S.I. 1977/2157 (N.I. 28), art. 17 (2), sch. 7, para 4 (5). - Issued: 13.02.2008. Made: 07.02.2008. Coming into operation: In accord. with art. 1. Effect: S.I. 1977/2157 (N.I. 28) amended. - Subject to affirmative resolution procedure of the Assembly. Superseded by S.R. of the same number (ISBN 9780337973246) issued on and affirmed by resolution of the Assembly. - 2p.: 30 cm. - 978-0-337-97258-4 £3.00

The Rates (Industrial Hereditaments) (Amendment) Order (Northern Ireland) 2008 No. 2008/49. - Enabling power: S.I. 1977/2157 (N.I. 28), art. 17 (2), sch. 7, para 4 (5). - Issued: 20.03.2008. Made: 07.02.2008. Coming into operation: In accord. with art. 1. Effect: S.I. 1977/2157 (N.I. 28) amended. - Affirmed by resolution of the Assembly on 03.03.2008. - 2p.: 30 cm. - 978-0-337-97324-6 £3.00

The Rates (Regional Rates) Order (Northern Ireland) 2008 No. 2008/48. - Enabling power: S.I. 1977/2157 (N.I. 28), art. 7 (1) (2). - Issued: 20.03.2008. Made: 07.02.2008. Coming into operation: In accord. with art. 1. Effect: None. - Affirmed by resolution of the Assembly on 03.03.2008. - 2p.: 30 cm. - 978-0-337-97323-9 £3.00

The Rates (Regional Rates) Order (Northern Ireland) 2008 No. 2008/48. - Enabling power: S.I. 1977/2157 (N.I. 28), art. 7 (1) (3). - Issued: 13.02.2008. Made: 07.02.2008. Coming into operation: In accord. with art. 1. Effect: None. - Subject to affirmative resolution procedure of the Assembly. Superseded by S.R. of the same number (ISBN 9780337973239) and affirmed by resolution of the Assembly. - 2p.: 30 cm. - 978-0-337-97257-7 £3.00

The Social Security Benefits Up-rating Order (Northern Ireland) 2008 No. 2008/92. - Enabling power: Social Security Administration (Northern Ireland) Act 1992, ss. 132, 132A, 165 (1) (4) (5). - Issued: 15.04.2008. Made: 07.03.2008. Coming into operation: In accord. with art. 1. Effect: 1966 c. 6 (N.I.); 1992 c. 7; S.R. 1987/459; 1992/32; 1994/461; 1995/35; 1996/198; 2003/28; 2006/405, 406 amended & S.R. 2007/153 revoked. - For approval of the Northern Ireland Assembly before the expiration of six months from the date of its coming into operation. - 36p.: 30 cm. - 978-0-337-97291-1 £6.50

The Social Security Benefits Up-rating Order (Northern Ireland) 2008 No. 2008/92. - Enabling power: Social Security Administration (Northern Ireland) Act 1992, ss. 132, 132A, 165 (1) (4) (5). - Issued: 27.06.2008. Made: 07.03.2008. Coming into operation: In accord. with art. 1. Effect: 1966 c. 6 (N.I.); 1992 c. 7; S.R. 1987/459; 1992/32; 1994/461; 1995/35; 1996/198; 2002/380; 2003/28; 2006/405, 406 amended & S.R. 2007/153 revoked (10.04.2008). - Affirmed by resolution of the Assembly on 23.06.08. Supersedes SR of same number (ISBN 9780337972911) issued 15.04.2008. Revoked by S.R. 2009/89 (ISBN 9780337976902). - 40p.: 30 cm. - 978-0-337-97429-8 £6.50

The Social Security (Child Benefit Disregard) Regulations (Northern Ireland) 2008 No. 2008/497. - Enabling power: Social Security Contributions and Benefits (Northern Ireland) Act 1992, ss. 122 (1) (a) (d), 132 (3) (4) (b), 171 (1) (3) (4) & S.I. 1995/2705 (N.I. 15), arts 14(1) (4) (b), 36 (2). - Issued: 17.12.2008. Made: 11.12.2008. Coming into operation: 05.01.2009. Effect: S.R. 1987/459; 1996/198; 2006/45 amended. - 8p.: 30 cm. - 978-0-337-97603-2 £4.00

The Social Security (Miscellaneous Amendments No. 2) Regulations (Northern Ireland) 2008 No. 2008/179. - Enabling power: Social Security Contributions and Benefits (Northern Ireland) Act 1992, ss. 122 (1) (d), 131 (1), 132 (3) (4) (a) (b), 133 (2) (f) (h) (i), 171 (1) (3) (4) & S.I. 1998/1506 (N.I. 10), arts 11 (6), 74 (1) (3). - Issued: 24.04.2008. Made: 18.04.2008. Coming into operation: In accord. with reg. 1. Effect: S.R. 1999/162; 2006/405, 406, 407 amended & S.R. 2007/306, 392 partially revoked. - Partially revoked by S.R. 2008/417 (ISBN 9780337975455). - 8p.: 30 cm. - 978-0-337-97364-2 £3.00

The Social Security (Miscellaneous Amendments No. 3) Regulations (Northern Ireland) 2008 No. 2008/410. - Enabling power: Social Security Contributions and Benefits (Northern Ireland) Act 1992, ss. 171 (4) & Social Security Administration (Northern Ireland) Act 1992, ss. 5 (1) (a), 165 (1) (3) to (5). - Issued: 08.10.2008. Made: 03.10.2008. Coming into operation: 06.10.2008. Effect: S.R. 1987/465; 2003/28, 421; 2004/304; 2006/128, 405, 406 amended. - 4p.: 30 cm. - 978-0-337-97539-4 £4.00

The Social Security (Miscellaneous Amendments No. 4) Regulations (Northern Ireland) 2008 No. 2008/417. - Enabling power: Social Security Administration (Northern Ireland) Act 1992, ss. 1 (1), 5 (1) (a) (b) (j), 165 (1) (3) (4) (6) & S.I. 1998/1506 (N.I. 10), arts 10 (1), 11 (3) (6), 74 (1) (3) & Child Support, Pensions and Social Security Act (Northern Ireland) 2000, sch. 7, paras 4 (5), 12, 13 (1) (2) (c) (3) (c), 20 (1) (b). - Issued: 14.10.2008. Made: 09.10.2008. Coming into operation: 30.10.2008. Effect: S.R. 1987/465; 1999/162; 2001/213; 2006/405, 406 amended & S.R. 2000/215; 2006/365; 2007/392; 2008/179 partially revoked. - 8p.: 30 cm. - 978-0-337-97545-5 £5.00

The Social Security (Miscellaneous Amendments No. 5) Regulations (Northern Ireland) 2008 No. 2008/428. - Enabling power: Social Security Contributions and Benefits (Northern Ireland) Act 1992, ss. 122 (1) (a) (d), 123 (1) (e), 129A (2), 131 (1), 132 (3) (4) (a) to (c), 132A (3), 133 (2) (h), 171 (1) to (4) & Social Security Administration (Northern Ireland) Act 1992, ss. 5 (1) (h) (q), 165 (1) (3) to (5) & S.I. 1995/2705 (N.I. 15), arts 6 (5), 14 (1) to (3) (4)(a) to (c), 36 (2), sch. 1, para. 3(b) & State Pension Credit Act (Northern Ireland) 2002, ss. 2 (3) (b) (6), 15 (3) (6) (b), 19 (1) (2) (a) (3). - Issued: 29.10.2008. Made: 23.10.2008. Coming into operation: 17.11.2008 except for reg. 7 (5); 06.04.2009 for reg. 7 (5). Effect: S.R. 1987/459, 465; 1988/205; 1993/120, 195; 1996/198, 503; 2002/222; 2003/28; 2006/405, 406; 2007/382 amended. - 12p.: 30 cm. - 978-0-337-97554-7 £5.00

The Social Security (Miscellaneous Amendments No. 7) Regulations (Northern Ireland) 2008 No. 2008/498. - Enabling power: Social Security Contributions and Benefits (Northern Ireland) Act 1992, ss. 122 (1) (a) (d), 123 (1) (d), 132 (1) (3) (4), 132A (3), 171 (1) to (4) & S.I. 1995/2705 (N.I. 15), arts 14 (4), 36 (2), sch. 1, para. 8 (a) & State Pension Credit Act (Northern Ireland) 2002, ss. 15 (1) (e) (j) (2) (6), 19 (1) to (3) & Welfare Reform Act (Northern Ireland) 2007, ss. 17, 25, 28 (2). - Issued: 17.12.2008. Made: 11.12.2008. Coming into operation: 05.01.2009. Effect: S.R. 1987/459; 1993/120; 1994/77; 1995/367, 481; 1996/198, 449; 2000/260; 2002/128; 2003/28; 2005/98, 536; 2006/405, 406, 407; 2007/306; 2008/179, 280, 286 amended or partially revoked. - Partially revoked by S.R. 2009/338 (ISBN 9780337978821). - 16p.: 30 cm. - 978-0-337-97604-9 £5.00

The Social Security (Miscellaneous Amendments) Regulations (Northern Ireland) 2008 No. 2008/112. - Enabling power: Social Security Contributions and Benefits (Northern Ireland) Act 1992, ss. 122 (1) (a) (d), 123 (1) (d), 131 (1), 132 (3) (4) (a) to (c), 133 (2) (d), 171 (1) to (4) & Social Security Administration (Northern Ireland) Act 1992, ss. 5 (1) (q), 165 (1) (3) to (5) & S.I. 1995/2705 (N.I. 15), arts 6 (5), 14 (2) (4) (a) (b), 36 (2), sch. 1, paras 1 (2) (a), 3 (b) & State Pension Credit Act (Northern Ireland) 2002, ss. 2 (3) (b) (6), 19 (1) to (3). - Issued: 19.03.2008. Made: 12.03.2008. Coming into operation: In accord. with reg. 1. Effect: S.R. 1987/459, 465; 1988/146; 1989/249, 365; 1996/198, 199; 1998/2; 1999/371 (C.28); 2001/151; 2003/28, 195, 338; 2005/319 (C.23); 2006/405; 2007/396 amended. - 16p.: 30 cm. - 978-0-337-97309-3 £3.00

The Social Security (Students and Miscellaneous Amendments) Regulations (Northern Ireland) 2008 No. 2008/262. - Enabling power: Social Security Contributions and Benefits (Northern Ireland) Act 1992, ss. 122 (1) (a) (d), 132 (3) (4) (b), 171 (1) (3) (4) & Social Security Administration (Northern Ireland) Act 1992, ss. 5 (1) (hh) (k), 165 (1) (4) (6) & S.I. 1995/2705 (N.I. 15), arts 14 (1) to (3) (4) (b), 36 (2). - Issued: 01.07.2008. Made: 23.06.2008. Coming into operation: In accord. with reg. 1. Effect: S.R. 1987/459, 465; 1996/198; 2006/405 amended. - Partly revoked by S.R. 2009/261 (ISBN 9780337978319). - 8p.: 30 cm. - 978-0-337-97433-5 £3.00

The Social Security (Use of Information for Housing Benefit and Welfare Services Purposes) Regulations (Northern Ireland) 2008 No. 2008/343. - Enabling power: Welfare Reform Act (Northern Ireland) 2007, ss. 39 (2) (8) (9). - Issued: 14.08.2008. Made: 08.08.2008. Coming into operation: 01.09.2008. Effect: None. - 4p.: 30 cm. - 978-0-337-97484-7 £3.00

The Valuation Tribunal (Amendment) Rules (Northern Ireland) 2008 No. 2008/153. - Enabling power: S.I. 1977/2157 (N.I. 28), art. 36A (3), sch. 9B, paras 7 to 13. - Issued: 07.04.2008. Made: 31.03.2008. Coming into operation: 05.05.2008. Effect: S.R. 2007/182 amended. - 8p.: 30 cm. - 978-0-337-97348-2 £3.00

The Valuation (Water Undertaking) Regulations (Northern Ireland) 2008 No. 2008/226. - Enabling power: S.I. 1977/2157 (N.I. 28), art. 37 (4). - Issued: 02.06.2008. Made: 23.05.2008. Coming into operation: 07.07.2008. Effect: S.R. 2003/186 revoked. - 4p.: 30 cm. - 978-0-337-97396-3 £3.00

Registration of vital events

General Register Office (Fees) Order (Northern Ireland) 2008 No. 2008/219. - Enabling power: S.I. 1976/1041 (N.I. 14), art. 47 (1) (2) & S.I. 2003/413 (N.I. 3), arts 3 (3) (b), 19 (1) (a), 35 (3), 36 (1) (b) (3), 37 & Civil Partnership Act 2004, s. 157 (1). - Issued: 22.05.2008. Made: 19.05.2008. Laid: - Coming into operation: 01.06.2008. Effect: S.R. 2005/478 revoked. - 8p.: 30 cm. - 978-0-337-97392-5 £3.00

Road and railway transport

Penalty Fares (Increase) Order (Northern Ireland) 2008 No. 2008/281. - Enabling power: Transport Act (Northern Ireland) 1967, sch. 1B. para. 4 (2). - Issued: 08.07.2008. Made: 02.07.2008. Coming into operation: 11.08.2008. Effect: 1967 c.37 (N.I.) amended. - 2p.: 30 cm. - 978-0-337-97443-4 £3.00

Roads

M2/A26 (Ballee Road East link) Order (Northern Ireland) 2008 No. 2008/14. - Enabling power: S.I. 1993/3160 (N.I. 15), arts 14 (1), 15 (1), 16 (1) (2), 68 (1) (3). - Issued: 12.03.2008. Made: 06.03.2008. Coming into operation: 18.04.2008. Effect: None. - 4p.: 30 cm. - 978-0-337-97286-7 £3.00

The Motorways Traffic Regulations (Northern Ireland) 2008 No. 2008/135. - Enabling power: S.I. 1993/3160 (N.I.15), art. 20 (3). - Issued: 31.03.2008. Made: 19.03.2008. Coming into operation: 28.05.2008. Effect: S.R. 1984/160; 1997/468; 1999/297; 2004/336; 2006/83; 2007/242 revoked. - 8p.: 30 cm. - 978-0-337-97330-7 £3.00

The Street Works (Inspection Fees) (Amendment) Regulations (Northern Ireland) 2008 No. 2008/40. - Enabling power: S.I. 1995/3210 (N.I. 19), art. 35. - Issued: 11.02.2008. Made: 04.02.2008. Coming into operation: 01.04.2008. Effect: S.R. 2005/259 amended. - 2p: 30 cm. - 978-0-337-97253-9 £3.00

The Westlink (Busways) Regulations (Northern Ireland) 2008 No. 2008/328. - Enabling power: S.I. 1993/3160 (N.I.15), art. 20 (3). - Issued: 06.08.2008. Made: 31.07.2008. Coming into operation: 24.10.2008. Effect: None. - 8p.: 30 cm. - 978-0-337-97478-6 £3.00

Road traffic

The Mutual Recognition of Driving Disqualifications (Northern Ireland and Ireland) Regulations (Northern Ireland) 2008 No. 2008/458. - Enabling power: Crime (International Co-operation) Act 2003, ss. 57 (2) (b) (4) (b), 73 (3). - Issued: 27.11.2008. Made: 21.11.2008. Coming into operation: In accord. with reg. 1 (1). Effect: None. - 4p: 30 cm. - 978-0-337-97577-6 £4.00

Road traffic and vehicles

The Disabled Persons (Badges for Motor Vehicles) (Amendment) Regulations (Northern Ireland) 2008 No. 2008/501. - Enabling power: Chronically Sick and Disabled Persons (Northern Ireland) Act 1978, s. 14. - Issued: 23.12.2008. Made: 17.12.2008. Coming into operation: 01.04.2009. Effect: S.R. 1993/202 amended. - 8p.: 30 cm. - 978-0-337-97609-4 £5.00

The Disclosure of Vehicle Insurance Information Regulations (Northern Ireland) 2008 No. 2008/234. - Enabling power: S.I. 2007/916 (N.I. 10), art. 81. - Issued: 05.06.2008. Made: 30.05.2008. Coming into operation: 14.07.2008. Effect: None. - 4p.: 30 cm. - 978-0-337-97402-1 £3.00

The Motor Hackney Carriages (Belfast) (Amendment) By-Laws (Northern Ireland) 2008 No. 2008/245. - Enabling power: S.I. 1981/154 (N.I. 1), art. 65 (1) (2). - Issued: 12.06.2008. Made: 05.06.2008. Coming into operation: 01.08.2008. Effect: By-laws relating to Motor Hackney Carriages standing or plying for hire made by the Council of the County Borough of Belfast on 04.06.1951 amended & S.R. 2006/284 amended & 2006/450 revoked. - 4p.: 30 cm. - 978-0-337-97413-7 £3.00

The Motor Vehicles (Driving Licences) (Amendment) Regulations (Northern Ireland) 2008 No. 2008/418. - Enabling power: S.I. 1981/154 (N.I. 1), arts 5 (1) (3) (4) (5), 19C (1), 218 (1). - Issued: 22.10.2008. Made: 17.10.2008. Coming into operation: 24.11.2008. Effect: S.R. 1996/542 amended. - 12p: 30 cm. - 978-0-337-97546-2 £5.00

The Motor Vehicles (Speed Limits) (Amendment) Regulations (Northern Ireland) 2008 No. 2008/344. - Enabling power: S.I. 1997/276 (N.I. 2), art. 39 (1). - Issued: 15.08.2008. Made: 11.08.2008. Coming into operation: In accord. with reg. 1. Effect: S.R. 1989/203 amended. - Subject to affirmative resolution procedure of the Assembly. Superseded by affirmed version (ISBN 9780337975592). - 4p.: 30 cm. - 978-0-337-97486-1 £3.00

The Motor Vehicles (Speed Limits) (Amendment) Regulations (Northern Ireland) 2008 No. 2008/344. - Enabling power: S.I. 1997/276 (N.I. 2), art. 39 (1). - Issued: 31.10.2008. Made: 11.08.2008. Coming into operation: 22.10.2008 in accord. with reg. 1. Effect: S.R. 1989/203 amended. - Affirmed by resolution of the Assembly on 21st October 2008. Supersedes pre-affirmed version (ISBN 9780337974861). - 4p.: 30 cm. - 978-0-337-97559-2 £4.00

The Motor Vehicles (Taxi Drivers' Licences) (Fees) (Amendment) Regulations (Northern Ireland) 2008 No. 2008/387. - Enabling power: S.I. 1981/154 (N.I. 1), arts 79A (2), 218 (1). - Issued: 25.09.2008. Made: 18.09.2008. Coming into operation: 31.10.2008. Effect: S.R. 1991/454 amended. - 2p.: 30 cm. - 978-0-337-97519-6 £4.00

The Motor Vehicles (Wearing of Seat Belts) (Amendment) Regulations (Northern Ireland) 2008 No. 2008/29. - Enabling power: S.I. 1995/2994 (N.I. 18), arts 23 (1) (2), 110 (4). - Issued: 30.01.2008. Made: 24.01.2008. Coming into operation: 01.05.2008. Effect: S.R. 1993/362 amended. - Subject to affirmative resolution of the Assembly. - 4p.: 30 cm. - 978-0-337-97242-3 £3.00

The Motor Vehicles (Wearing of Seat Belts) (Amendment) Regulations (Northern Ireland) 2008 No. 2008/29. - Enabling power: S.I. 1995/2994 (N.I. 18), arts 23 (1) (2), 110 (4). - Issued: 22.04.2008. Made: 24.01.2008. Coming into operation: 01.05.2008. Effect: S.R. 1993/362 amended. - Affirmed by resolution of the Assembly on 10.03.2008. - 4p.: 30 cm. - 978-0-337-97361-1 £3.00

The Motor Vehicle Testing (Amendment) Regulations (Northern Ireland) 2008 No. 2008/109. - Enabling power: S.I. 1995/2994 (N.I. 18), arts. 61 (2) (6), 62, 110 (2). - Issued: 18.03.2008. Made: 11.03.2008. Coming into operation: 01.05.2008. Effect: S.R. 2003/303 amended. - 4p: 30 cm. - 978-0-337-97397-0 £3.00

The Motorways Traffic Regulations (Northern Ireland) 2008 No. 2008/135. - Enabling power: S.I. 1993/3160 (N.I.15), art. 20 (3). - Issued: 31.03.2008. Made: 19.03.2008. Coming into operation: 28.05.2008. Effect: S.R. 1984/160; 1997/468; 1999/297; 2004/336; 2006/83; 2007/242 revoked. - 8p.: 30 cm. - 978-0-337-97330-7 £3.00

The Penalty Charges (Additional Contravention) Regulations (Northern Ireland) 2008 No. 2008/78. - Enabling power: S.I. 2005/1964 (N.I. 14), art. 4 (3). - Issued: 21.05.2008. Made: 29.02.2008. Coming into operation: 30.04.2008. Effect: S.I. 2005/1964 (N.I. 14) amended. - 4p.: 30 cm. - 978-0-337-97389-5 £3.00

The Road Traffic (2007 Order) (Commencement No. 3 and Amendment) Order (Northern Ireland) 2008 No. 2008/223 (C.9). - Enabling power: S.I. 2007/916 (N.I. 10), art. 1 (3) (4) (b). Bringing into operation various provisions of the 2007 Order on 26.05.2008. - Issued: 28.05.2008. Made: 20.05.2008. Coming into operation: -. Effect: S.R. 2000/331 amended. - 4p.: 30 cm. - 978-0-337-97393-2 £3.00

The Road Traffic (2007 Order) (Commencement No. 4 and Amendment) Order (Northern Ireland) 2008 No. 2008/244 (C.13). - Enabling power: S.I. 2007/916 (N.I. 10), art. 1 (3) (4) (b). Bringing into operation various provisions of the 2007 Order on 09.06.2008. - Issued: 10.06.2008. Made: 04.06.2008. Coming into operation: -. Effect: S.I. 2007/916 (N.I. 10) amended. - 4p.: 30 cm. - 978-0-337-97410-6 £3.00

The Road Traffic (Northern Ireland) Order 1981 (Retention and Disposal of Seized Motor Vehicles) Regulations (Northern Ireland) 2008 No. 2008/494. - Enabling power: S.I. 1981/154 (N.I. 1), art. 180C. - Issued: 19.12.2008. Made: 11.12.2008. Laid: 16.12.2008. Coming into force: 06.01.2009. Effect: None. - 8p.: 30 cm. - 978-0-337-97605-6 £5.00

The Road Traffic (Traffic Wardens) (Revocation) Order (Northern Ireland) 2008 No. 2008/341. - Enabling power: S.I. 1997/276 (NI. 2), art. 44. - Issued: 14.08.2008. Made: 08.08.2008. Coming into force: In accord. with art. 1. Effect: S.R. 1999/410 revoked. - Subject to affirmative resolution procedure of the Assembly. Superseded by affirmed re-issue (ISBN 9780337975608). - 2p.: 25 cm. - 978-0-337-97485-4 £3.00

The Road Traffic (Traffic Wardens) (Revocation) Order (Northern Ireland) 2008 No. 2008/341. - Enabling power: S.I. 1997/276 (N.I. 2), art. 44. - Issued: 31.10.2008. Made: 08.08.2008. Coming into force: 22.10.2008 in accord. with art. 1. Effect: S.R. 1999/410 revoked. - Affirmed by resolution of the Assembly on 21.10.2008. Supersedes pre-affirmed version (ISBN 9780337974854). - 2p.: 30 cm. - 978-0-337-97560-8 £4.00

The Taxis (Antrim) Bye-Laws (Northern Ireland) 2008 No. 2008/230. - Enabling power: S.I. 1981/154 (N.I. 1), art. 65 (1) (2). - Issued: 04.06.2008. Made: 28.05.2008. Coming into operation: 15.09.2008. Effect: S.R. 1994/451 revoked. - 4p.: 30 cm. - 978-0-337-97398-7 £3.00

The Taxis (Enniskillen) (Revocation) Bye-Laws (Northern Ireland) 2008 No. 2008/257. - Enabling power: S.I. 1981/154 (N.I. 1), art. 65 (1) (2). - Issued: 24.06.2008. Made: 18.06.2008. Coming into operation: 25.07.2008. Effect: S.R. 2006/73 revoked. - 2p.: 30 cm. - 978-0-337-97423-6 £3.00

The Traffic Signs (Amendment) Regulations (Northern Ireland) 2008 No. 2008/63. - Enabling power: S.I. 1997/276 (N.I. 2), art. 28 (2). - Issued: 05.03.2008. Made: 20.02.2008. Coming into operation: 16.05.2008. Effect: S.R. 1997/386 amended. - 8p.: 30 cm. - 978-0-337-97270-6 £3.00

The Westlink (Busways) Regulations (Northern Ireland) 2008 No. 2008/328. - Enabling power: S.I. 1993/3160 (N.I.15), art. 20 (3). - Issued: 06.08.2008. Made: 31.07.2008. Coming into operation: 24.10.2008. Effect: None. - 8p.: 30 cm. - 978-0-337-97478-6 £3.00

Safeguarding vulnerable groups

The Safeguarding Vulnerable Groups (2007 Order) (Commencement No. 1) Order (Northern Ireland) 2008 No. 2008/127 (C.5). - Enabling power: S.I. 2007/1351 (N.I. 11), art. 1 (3). Bringing into operation various provisions of the 2007 Order on 14.03.2008 & 14.04.2008. - Issued: 20.03.2008. Made: 14.03.2008. Coming into operation: -. Effect: None. - 4p.: 30 cm. - 978-0-337-97322-2 £3.00

The Safeguarding Vulnerable Groups (2007 Order) (Commencement No. 2) Order (Northern Ireland) 2008 No. 2008/233 (C. 11). - Enabling power: S.I. 2007/1351 (N.I. 11), art. 1 (3). Bringing into operation various provisions of the 2007 Order on 29.05.2008. - Issued: 05.06.2008. Made: 29.05.2008. Coming into operation: -. Effect: None. - 8p.: 30 cm. - 978-0-337-97401-4 £3.00

The Safeguarding Vulnerable Groups (Barred List Prescribed Information) Regulations (Northern Ireland) 2008 No. 2008/202. - Enabling power: S.I. 2007/1351 (N.I. 11), arts 6 (5), 61 (1). - Issued: 29.05.2008. Made: 06.05.2008. Coming into operation: 16.06.2008. Effect: None. - 4p: 30 cm. - 978-0-337-97385-7 £3.00

The Safeguarding Vulnerable Groups (Barring Procedure) Regulations (Northern Ireland) 2008 No. 2008/203. - Enabling power: S.I. 2007/1351 (N.I. 11), art 61 (1), sch. 1, paras 15 (1) (2), 18 (3) (b) (6). - Issued: 29.05.2008. Made: 06.05.2008. Coming into operation: 16.06.2008. Effect: None. - 8p: 30 cm. - 978-0-337-97386-4 £3.00

The Safeguarding Vulnerable Groups (Prescribed Criteria) (Transitional Provisions) Regulations (Northern Ireland) 2008 No. 2008/201. - Enabling power: S.I. 2007/1351 (N.I. 11), art. 61 (1), sch. 1, paras 1 (1), 7 (1), 24 (1) to (3). - Issued: 29.05.2008. Made: 06.05.2008. Coming into operation: 16.06.2008. Effect: None. - 8p: 30 cm. - 978-0-337-97384-0 £3.00

The Safeguarding Vulnerable Groups (Transitional Provisions) Order (Northern Ireland) 2008 No. 2008/200. - Enabling power: S.I. 2007/1351 (N.I. 11), art. 61 (1), sch. 6, paras 2, 3. - Issued: 29.05.2008. Made: 06.05.2008. Coming into operation: 16.06.2008. Effect: None. - 8p: 30 cm. - 978-0-337-97383-3 £3.00

Salaries

The Salaries (Assembly Ombudsman and Commissioner for Complaints) Order (Northern Ireland) 2008 No. 2008/26. - Enabling power: S.I. 1996/1298 (N.I.8), art. 5 (1) (2) & S.I. 1996/1297 (N.I.7), art. 4 (1) (2). - Issued: 30.01.2008. Made: 24.01.2008. Coming into operation: 01.03.2008. Effect: S.R. 2006/442 revoked. - Revoked by S.R. 2008/397 (ISBN 9780337975264). - 2p.: 30 cm. - 978-0-337-97240-9 £3.00

The Salaries (Assembly Ombudsman and Commissioner for Complaints) Order (Northern Ireland) 2008 No. 2008/397. - Enabling power: S.I. 1996/1298 (N.I.8), art. 5 (1) (2) & S.I. 1996/1297 (N.I.7), art. 4 (1) (2). - Issued: 01.10.2008. Made: 25.09.2008. Coming into operation: 03.11.2008. Effect: S.R. 2008/26 revoked. - Revoked by S.R. 2009/335 (ISBN 9780337978791). - 2p.: 30 cm. - 978-0-337-97526-4 £4.00

Sea fisheries

Conservation of Scallops Regulations (Northern Ireland) 2008 No. 2008/430. - Enabling power: Fisheries Act (Northern Ireland) 1966, ss. 19 (1), 124 (1) (2), 127 (1). - Issued: 29.10.2008. Made: 24.10.2008. Coming into force: 17.11.2008. Effect: S.R.1983/417; 1997/89; 2000/39 revoked. - 4p.: 30 cm. - 978-0-337-97556-1 £4.00

The Inshore Fishing (Prohibition of Fishing and Fishing Methods) (Amendment) Regulations (Northern Ireland) 2008 No. 2008/304. - Enabling power: Fisheries Act (Northern Ireland) 1966, ss. 19 (1), 124 (1) (2) (2A). - Issued: 22.07.2008. Made: 11.07.2008. Coming into operation: 11.07.2008. Effect: S.R. 1993/155; 1998/414 amended. - 4p.: 30 cm. - 978-0-337-97461-8 £3.00

The Unlicensed Fishing for Crabs and Lobster Regulations (Northern Ireland) 2008 No. 2008/185. - Enabling power: Fisheries Act (Northern Ireland) 1966, s. 124 (1) (2). - Issued: 30.04.2008. Made: 24.04.2008. Coming into operation: 30.05.2008. Effect: None. - 4p.: 30 cm. - 978-0-337-97369-7 £3.00

Seeds

The Seed Potatoes (Crop Fees) (Amendment) Regulations (Northern Ireland) 2008 No. 2008/184. - Enabling power: Seeds Act (Northern Ireland) 1965, s. 1. - Issued: 29.04.2008. Made: 23.04.2008. Coming into operation: 01.05.2008. Effect: S.R. 2006/186 amended. - Revoked by S.R. 2009/59 (ISBN 9780337976575). - 4p.: 30 cm. - 978-0-337-97368-0 £3.00

Seeds (Miscellaneous Amendments) Regulations (Northern Ireland) 2008 No. 2008/114. - Enabling power: Seeds Act (Northern Ireland) 1965, ss. 1 (1) (2A), 2. - Issued: 19.03.2008. Made: 12.03.2008. Coming into operation: 30.04.2008. Effect: S.R. 1994/250, 251, 252, 254, 255 amended. - EC note: These Regulations implement as respects Northern Ireland - Council Directive 2004/117/EC amending Council Directives 66/401/EEC, 66/402/EEC, 2002/54/EC, 2002/55/EC and 2002/57/EC; Commission Directive 2006/55/EC amending Annex III to Council Directive 66/402/EEC; Commission Directive 2006/124/EC amending Council Directive 2002/55/EC on the marketing of vegetable seeds and Commission Decision 2007/321/EC. - 12p.: 30 cm. - 978-0-337-97311-6 £3.00

Sex discrimination

Sex Discrimination Order 1976 (Amendment) Regulations (Northern Ireland) 2008 No. 2008/159. - Enabling power: European Communities Act 1972, s. 2 (2). - Issued: 10.04.2008. Made: 04.04.2008. Coming into operation: 06.04.2008. Effect: S.I. 1976/1042 (N.I. 15) amended. - EC note: These Regulations implement in Northern Ireland Council Directive 2002/73/EC in part. The Directive concerns the principle of equal treatment of men and women as regards access to employment, vocational training and promotion and working conditions. - 4p.: 30 cm. - 978-0-337-97351-2 £3.00

Social security

The Christmas Bonus (Relevant Week) Order (Northern Ireland) 2008 No. 2008/474. - Enabling power: Social Security Contributions and Benefits (Northern Ireland) Act 1992, s. 146 (4). - Issued: 03.12.2008. Made: 27.11.2008. Coming into operation: 28.11.2008. Effect: None. - 2p.: 30 cm. - 978-0-337-97584-4 £4.00

The Christmas Bonus (Specified Sum) Order (Northern Ireland) 2008 No. 2008/502. - Enabling power: Social Security Contributions and Benefits (Northern Ireland) Act 1992, ss. 144 (3) (b), 171 (3) (b). - Issued: 24.02.2009. Made: 18.12.2008. Coming into operation: 19.12.2008. Effect: None. - Approved by resolution of the Assembly on 17.02.2009. Supersedes version published 23.12.2008 (ISBN 9780337976117). - 2p.: 30 cm. - 978-0-337-97653-7 £4.00

The Christmas Bonus (Specified Sum) Order (Northern Ireland) 2008 No. 2008/502. - Enabling power: Social Security Contributions and Benefits (Northern Ireland) Act 1992, ss. 144 (3) (b), 171 (3) (b). - Issued: 23.12.2008. Made: 18.12.2008. Coming into operation: 19.12.2008. Effect: None. - 2p.: 30 cm. - 978-0-337-97611-7 £4.00

The Discretionary Financial Assistance Regulations (Northern Ireland) 2008 No. 2008/111. - Enabling power: Child Support, Pensions and Social Security Act (Northern Ireland) 2000, s. 60 (1) (2) & S.I. 1998/1506 (N.I. 10), art. 74 (4) to (6). - Issued: 19.03.2008. Made: 12.03.2008. Coming into operation: 07.04.2008. Effect: S.R. 2001/216 amended. - 4p.: 30 cm. - 978-0-337-97308-6 £3.00

The Employment and Support Allowance (Consequential Provisions No. 2) Regulations (Northern Ireland) 2008 No. 2008/412. - Enabling power: Welfare Reform Act (Northern Ireland) 2007, ss. 25 (2), 28 (2). - Issued: 10.10.2008. Made: 06.10.2008. Coming into operation: 27.10.2008. Effect: S.I. 1981/228 (N.I. 8); 1996/1919 (N.I. 16); 1999/584; 2000/704; 2002/2008; 2006/223; SR. 1981/189, 366; 1996/438; 2000/121; 2006/478; S.I. 2006/758 amended. - 8p: 30 cm. - 978-0-337-97541-7 £4.00

The Employment and Support Allowance (Consequential Provisions) Regulations (Northern Ireland) 2008 No. 2008/286. - Enabling power: Welfare Reform Act (Northern Ireland) 2007, ss. 25 (2), 28 (2). - Issued: 17.07.2008. Made: 04.07.2008. Coming into operation: 27.07.2008 for regs 13(1) to (12), (14) to (20), 22; 27.10.2008 for all other purposes, in accord. with reg. 1, 27.10.2008. Effect: 43 instruments amended. - Partially revoked by S.R. 2009/133 (ISBN 9780337977275) and partially revoked by S.R. 2009/261 (ISBN 9780337978319). - 52p: 30 cm. - 978-0-337-97451-9 £9.00

The Employment and Support Allowance (Miscellaneous Amendments) Regulations (Northern Ireland) 2008 No. 2008/413. - Enabling power: Welfare Reform Act (Northern Ireland) 2007, ss. 2 (1) (c), 3 (2) (b) (d) (3), 4 (2) (a), 5 (3), 8 (1) (2) (a) (b), 17 (1) (2) (3) (b), 25 (2) (a), 28 (2), sch. 1, paras. 1 (4), 6 (1) (b) (2) to (5) (8), sch. 2, paras. 1 (a), 2, 10. - Issued: 10.10.2008. Made: 06.10.2008. Coming into operation: 27.10.2008. Effect: 1992 c.8; S.R. 1984/245; 1987/465; 1995/150; 2008/280, 283, 286 amended. - Partly revoked by S.R. 2009/261 (ISBN 9780337978319) & Partially revoked by S.R. 2009/338 (ISBN 9780337978821). - 12p: 30 cm. - 978-0-337-97542-4 £5.00

The Employment and Support Allowance Regulations (Northern Ireland) 2008 No. 2008/280. - Enabling power: Social Security Administration (Northern Ireland) Act 1992, s. 5 (1) & S.I. 1998/1506 (N.I. 10), art. 21 (1) (a) & Welfare Reform Act (Northern Ireland) 2007, ss. 2 (1) (a) (c) (4) (a) (c), 3 (1) (c) (2) (b) (d) (3), 4 (2) (a) (3) (6) (a) (c), 5 (2) (3), 8 (1) to (3) (4) (a) (b) (5) (6), 9 (1) to (3) (4) (a) (b), 11 (1) (2) (a) to (g) (3) to (5) (6)(a) (7) (c), 12 (1) (2) (a) to (h) (3) to (7), 14 (1) (2) (a) (b), 16 (2) (a) (4), 17, 18 (1) (2) (4), 20 (2) to (7), 23 (1) (3), 24 (1) (2) (b) (3), 25 (1) (2), 26(1), sch. 1, paras 1 (4), 3 (2), 4 (1) (a) (c) (3) (4), 6 (1) (b) (2) to (5) (7) (8), sch. 2, paras 1 to 7, 8 (1), 9, 10, 12, 14. - Issued: 10.07.2008. Made: 01.07.2008. Coming into operation: In accord. with reg. 1. Effect: 2007 c. 2 (NI) modified. - 176p: 30 cm. - 978-0-337-97442-7 £24.00

The Employment and Support Allowance (Transitional Provisions) (Amendment) Regulations (Northern Ireland) 2008 No. 2008/429. - Enabling power: Welfare Reform Act (Northern Ireland) 2007, ss. 25 (2), sch. 4, paras 2 (a), 3 (b). - Issued: 29.10.2008. Made: 24.10.2008. Coming into operation: 26.10.2008. Effect: S.R. 2008/283 amended. - 2p.: 30 cm. - 978-0-337-97555-4 £4.00

The Employment and Support Allowance (Transitional Provisions) Regulations (Northern Ireland) 2008 No. 2008/283. - Enabling power: Welfare Reform Act (Northern Ireland) 2007, ss. 25 (2), sch. 4, paras 1(1), 2, 3 (b) to (d). - Issued: 10.07.2008. Made: 03.07.2008. Coming into operation: 27.07.2008 except for reg. 5; 27.10.2008 for reg. 5 in accord. with reg. 1. Effect: None. - 4p: 30 cm. - 978-0-337-97445-8 £3.00

The Housing Benefit (Local Housing Allowance) (Miscellaneous and Consequential Amendments) Regulations (Northern Ireland) 2008 No. 2008/103. - Enabling power: Social Security Contributions and Benefits (Northern Ireland) Act 1992, ss. 129A (2) (3), 171 (1) (3) (4) & Child Support, Pensions and Social Security Act (Northern Ireland) 2000, sch. 7, para. 4 (3A). - Issued: 18.03.2008. Made: 11.03.2008. Coming into operation: 07.04.2008 in accord.with reg. 1. Effect: S.R. 1987/465; 2001/213, 216; 2004/8, 144; 2006/407 amended. - 12p.: 30 cm. - 978-0-337-97306-2 £3.00

The Jobseeker's Allowance (Joint Claims) (Amendment) Regulations (Northern Ireland) 2008 No. 2008/16. - Enabling power: S.I. 1995/2705 (N.I. 15), arts 3 (2C) (4) (b), 36 (2),sch. 1, para. 8A. - Issued: 22.01.2008. Made: 15.01.2008. Coming into operation: 25.02.2008. Effect: S.R. 1996/198 amended. - 2p.: 30 cm. - 978-0-337-97230-0 £3.00

The Mesothelioma, etc. (2008 Act) (Commencement) Order (Northern Ireland) 2008 No. 2008/351 (C. 19). - Enabling power: Mesothelioma, etc., Act (Northern Ireland) 2008, s. 12 (1). - Issued: 02.09.2008. Made: 26.08.2008. Coming into operation: In accord. with sch., 27.08.2008. Effect: None. - 2p.: 30 cm. - 978-0-337-97491-5 £3.00

The Mesothelioma Lump Sum Payments (Claims and Reconsiderations) Regulations (Northern Ireland) 2008 No. 2008/353. - Enabling power: Mesothelioma, etc., Act (Northern Ireland) 2008, ss. 3 (1) to (3), 4 (2), 5 (4) (c), 9 (2). - Issued: 02.09.2008. Made: 27.08.2008. Coming into operation: 01.10.2008. Effect: None. - 4p.: 30 cm. - 978-0-337-97493-9 *£3.00*

The Mesothelioma Lump Sum Payments (Conditions and Amounts) Regulations (Northern Ireland) 2008 No. 2008/354. - Enabling power: Mesothelioma, etc., Act (Northern Ireland) 2008, ss. 1 (3), 2 (1) (b) (c) (2) (b) (c) (3) (e) (4) (d). - Issued: 02.09.2008. Made: 27.08.2008. Coming into operation: 01.10.2008. Effect: None. - For approval of the Assembly before the expiration of six months from the date of their coming into operation. - 8p.: 30 cm. - 978-0-337-97494-6 *£3.00*

The Mesothelioma Lump Sum Payments (Conditions and Amounts) Regulations (Northern Ireland) 2008 No. 2008/354. - Enabling power: Mesothelioma, etc., Act (Northern Ireland) 2008, ss. 1 (3), 2 (1) (b) (c) (2) (b) (c) (3) (e) (4) (d). - Issued: 24.02.2009. Made: 27.08.2008. Coming into operation: 01.10.2008. Effect: None. - Approved by resolution of the Assembly on 17.02.2009. Supersedes version issued 02.09.2008 (ISBN 9780337974946). - 8p.: 30 cm. - 978-0-337-97652-0 *£4.00*

The Pneumoconiosis, etc., (Workers' Compensation) (Payment of Claims) (Amendment No. 2) Regulations (Northern Ireland) 2008 No. 2008/352. - Enabling power: S.I. 1979/925 (N.I.9), arts. 3 (3), 11 (1). - Issued: 02.09.2008. Made: 27.08.2008. Coming into operation: In accord. with reg. 1. Effect: S.R. 1988/242 amended. - Subject to affirmative resolution of the Assembly. - 2p: 30 cm. - 978-0-337-97492-2 *£3.00*

The Pneumoconiosis, etc., (Workers' Compensation) (Payment of Claims) (Amendment No. 2) Regulations (Northern Ireland) 2008 No. 2008/352. - Enabling power: S.I. 1979/925 (N.I.9), arts. 3 (3), 11 (1). - Issued: 03.10.2008. Made: 27.08.2008. Coming into operation: 01.10.2008 in accord. with reg. 1 (1). Effect: S.R. 1988/242 amended. - Affirmed by resolution of the Assembly on 30.09.2008. - 2p: 30 cm. - 978-0-337-97529-5 *£4.00*

The Pneumoconiosis, etc., (Workers' Compensation) (Payment of Claims) (Amendment) Regulations (Northern Ireland) 2008 No. 2008/73. - Enabling power: S.I. 1979/925 (N.I.9), arts. 3 (3), 4 (3), 11 (1) (4). - Issued: 03.03.2008. Made: 27.02.2008. Coming into operation: In accord. with reg. 1 (1). Effect: S.R. 1988/242 amended. - Subject to affirmative resolution of the Assembly. - 8p: 30 cm. - 978-0-337-97276-8 *£3.00*

The Pneumoconiosis, etc., (Workers' Compensation) (Payment of Claims) (Amendment) Regulations (Northern Ireland) 2008 No. 2008/73. - Enabling power: S.I. 1979/925 (N.I.9), arts. 3 (3), 4 (3), 11 (1) (4). - Issued: 04.04.2008. Made: 27.02.2008. Coming into operation: In accord. with reg. 1 (1). Effect: S.R. 1988/242 amended. - Affirmed by resolution of the Assembly on 31.03.2008. - 8p: 30 cm. - 978-0-337-97347-5 *£3.00*

The Social Fund (Applications and Miscellaneous Provisions) Regulations (Northern Ireland) 2008 No. 2008/357. - Enabling power: Social Security Administration (Northern Ireland) Act 1992, ss. 10, 165 (1) (4) (5) (6). - Issued: 03.09.2008. Made: 26.08.2008. Coming into operation: 01.10.2008. Effect: S.R. 1988/130; 1990/327; 2002/284 revoked. - 4p.: 30 cm. - 978-0-337-97497-7 *£3.00*

The Social Fund (Cold Weather Payments) (General) (Amendment) Regulations (Northern Ireland) 2008 No. 2008/411. - Enabling power: Social Security Contributions and Benefits (Northern Ireland) Act 1992, ss. 134 (2), 171 (1) (3) (4). - Issued: 09.10.2008. Made: 03.10.2008. Coming into operation: 27.10.2008 for regs 1 & 2; 01.11.2008 for reg. 3, in accord. with reg. 1. Effect: S.R. 1988/368 amended. - 2p.: 30 cm. - 978-0-337-97540-0 *£4.00*

The Social Fund Winter Fuel Payment (Temporary Increase) Regulations (Northern Ireland) 2008 No. 2008/289. - Enabling power: Social Security Contributions and Benefits (Northern Ireland) Act 1992, ss. 134 (2), 171 (1) (3) (4). - Issued: 16.07.2008. Made: 08.07.2008. Coming into operation: 15.09.2008. Effect: S.R. 2000/91 modified. - Revoked by S.R. 2009/233 (ISBN 9780337978050). - 2p.: 30 cm. - 978-0-337-97448-9 *£3.00*

The Social Security Benefits Up-rating Order (Northern Ireland) 2008 No. 2008/92. - Enabling power: Social Security Administration (Northern Ireland) Act 1992, ss. 132, 132A, 165 (1) (4) (5). - Issued: 15.04.2008. Made: 07.03.2008. Coming into operation: In accord. with art. 1. Effect: 1966 c. 6 (N.I.); 1992 c. 7; S.R. 1987/459; 1992/32; 1994/461; 1995/35; 1996/198; 2003/28; 2006/405, 406 amended & S.R. 2007/153 revoked. - Revoked by S.R. 2009/89 (ISBN 9780337976902). For approval of the Northern Ireland Assembly before the expiration of six months from the date of its coming into operation. - 36p.: 30 cm. - 978-0-337-97291-1 *£6.50*

The Social Security Benefits Up-rating Order (Northern Ireland) 2008 No. 2008/92. - Enabling power: Social Security Administration (Northern Ireland) Act 1992, ss. 132, 132A, 165 (1) (4) (5). - Issued: 27.06.2008. Made: 07.03.2008. Coming into operation: In accord. with art. 1. Effect: 1966 c. 6 (N.I.); 1992 c. 7; S.R. 1987/459; 1992/32; 1994/461; 1995/35; 1996/198; 2002/380; 2003/28; 2006/405, 406 amended & S.R. 2007/153 revoked (10.04.2008). - Affirmed by resolution of the Assembly on 23.06.08. Supersedes SI of same number (ISBN 9780337972911) issued 15.04.2008. - 40p.: 30 cm. - 978-0-337-97429-8 *£6.50*

The Social Security Benefits Up-rating Regulations (Northern Ireland) 2008 No. 2008/105. - Enabling power: Social Security Contributions and Benefits (Northern Ireland) Act 1992, ss. 90, 113 (1) (a), 171 (1) (3) & Social Security Administration (Northern Ireland) Act 1992, ss. 5 (1) (q), 135 (3), 165 (1) (4). - Issued: 14.03.2008. Made: 11.03.2008. Coming into operation: 07.04.2008. Effect: S.R. 1977/74; 1987/465 amended & S.R. 2007/155 revoked. - Revoked by S.R. 2009/100 (ISBN 9780337977039). - 4p.: 30 cm. - 978-0-337-97301-7 *£3.00*

Social security

The Social Security (Child Benefit Disregard) Regulations (Northern Ireland) 2008 No. 2008/497. - Enabling power: Social Security Contributions and Benefits (Northern Ireland) Act 1992, ss. 122 (1) (a) (d), 132 (3) (4) (b), 171 (1) (3) (4) & S.I. 1995/2705 (N.I. 15), arts 14(1) (4) (b), 36 (2). - Issued: 17.12.2008. Made: 11.12.2008. Coming into operation: 05.01.2009. Effect: S.R. 1987/459; 1996/198; 2006/45 amended. - 8p.: 30 cm. - 978-0-337-97603-2 *£4.00*

The Social Security (Child Maintenance Amendments) Regulations (Northern Ireland) 2008 No. 2008/406. - Enabling power: Social Security Contributions and Benefits (Northern Ireland) Act 1992, ss. 122 (1) (a), 132 (3) (4) (b), 171 (1) (2) (4) & S.I. 1995/2705 (N.I. 15), arts. 14 (2) (4) (b), 36 (2). - Issued: 08.10.2008. Made: 02.10.2008. Coming into operation: 27.10.2008, in acc. with reg. 1. Effect: S.R. 1987/459; 1988/146; 1990/346; 1996/198, 202, 288, 405, 503; 2000/367; 2001/25, 29; 2003/195 amended. - Partially revoked by S.R. 2009/338 (ISBN 9780337978821). - 12p.: 30 cm. - 978-0-337-97535-6 *£5.00*

The Social Security (Claims and Payments) (Amendment) Regulations (Northern Ireland) 2008 No. 2008/69. - Enabling power: Social Security Administration (Northern Ireland) Act 1992, ss. 1 (1), 165 (1) (4). - Issued: 28.02.2008. Made: 25.02.2008. Coming into operation: 17.03.2008. Effect: S.R. 1987/465 amended. - 2p.: 30 cm. - 978-0-337-97272-0 *£3.00*

The Social Security (Housing Costs Special Arrangements) (Amendment and Modification) Regulations (Northern Ireland) 2008 No. 2008/503. - Enabling power: Social Security Contributions and Benefits (Northern Ireland) Act 1992, ss. 122 (1) (a), 131 (1), 171 (1) (3) (4) & S.I. 1995/2705 (N.I. 15), arts 6 (5), 36 (2) & State Pension Credit Act (Northern Ireland) 2002, ss. 2 (3) (b), 19 (1) to (3) & Welfare Reform Act (Northern Ireland) 2007, ss. 4 (2) (a) (3), 25 (2). - Issued: 23.12.2008. Made: 18.12.2008. Coming into operation: In accord. with reg. 1. Effect: S.R. 1987/459; 1996/198; 2008/280 amended. - 12p.: 30 cm. - 978-0-337-97610-0 *£5.00*

The Social Security (Incapacity Benefit Work-focused Interviews) Regulations (Northern Ireland) 2008 No. 2008/465. - Enabling power: Social Security Administration (Northern Ireland) Act 1992, ss. 2A (1) (3) to (6) (8), 2B (6) (7), 165 (4) to (6) (7A). - Issued: 27.11.2008. Made: 21.11.2008. Coming into operation: 15.12.2008. Effect: S.R. 2005/443 amended & S.R. 2005/414 revoked with savings & 2006/167, 398; 2007/129 revoked. - 12p.: 30 cm. - 978-0-337-97578-3 *£5.00*

The Social Security (Incapacity) (Miscellaneous Amendments) Regulations (Northern Ireland) 2008 No. 2008/375. - Enabling power: Social Security Contributions and Benefits (Northern Ireland) Act 1992, ss. 30C (3), 30DD (4), 30E (1), 167D, 171 (1), sch. 7, para. 2 (3). - Issued: 15.09.2008. Made: 09.09.2008. Coming into operation: 01.10.2008. Effect: S.R. 1984/92; 1994/461; 1995/41 amended & S.R. 2007/396 partially revoked. - 4p.: 30 cm. - 978-0-337-97510-3 *£4.00*

The Social Security (Industrial Injuries) (Dependency) (Permitted Earnings Limits) Order (Northern Ireland) 2008 No. 2008/113. - Enabling power: Social Security Contributions and Benefits (Northern Ireland) Act 1992, sch. 7, para. 4 (5). - Issued: 19.03.2008. Made: 12.03.2008. Coming into operation: 09.04.2008. Effect: 1992 c.7 amended & S.R. 2007/156 revoked. - Revoked by S.R. 2009/101 (ISBN 9780337977046). - 2p.: 30 cm. - 978-0-337-97310-9 *£3.00*

The Social Security (Industrial Injuries) (Prescribed Diseases) (Amendment No. 2) Regulations (Northern Ireland) 2008 No. 2008/258. - Enabling power: Social Security Contributions and Benefits (Northern Ireland) Act 1992, ss. 108 (2), 171 (1) (3) (4). - Issued: 26.06.2008. Made: 20.06.2008. Coming into operation: 21.07.2008. Effect: S.R. 1986/179 amended & S.R. 1997/158 partially revoked. - 4p.: 30 cm. - 978-0-337-97425-0 *£3.00*

The Social Security (Industrial Injuries) (Prescribed Diseases) (Amendment) Regulations (Northern Ireland) 2008 No. 2008/45. - Enabling power: Social Security Contributions and Benefits (Northern Ireland) Act 1992, ss. 108 (2), 171 (1) to (3). - Issued: 11.02.2008. Made: 05.02.2008. Coming into operation: 07.04.2008. Effect: S.R. 1986/179 amended. - 2p.: 30 cm. - 978-0-337-97254-6 *£3.00*

The Social Security (Lone Parents and Miscellaneous Amendments) Regulations (Northern Ireland) 2008 No. 2008/478. - Enabling power: Social Security Contributions and Benefits (Northern Ireland) Act 1992, 122 (1) (a), 123 (1) (e), 171 (1) to (4) & Social Security Administration (Northern Ireland) Act 1992, ss. 2A, 2B, 165 (1) (4) to (6) (7A) & S.I. 1995/2705 (N.I. 15), arts 8 (2) (4), 9 (4), 10 (2) (d) (ii), 21 (8) (a), 36 (2), sch. 1, paras 8, 10 (1) (a) (2) (a) & Welfare Reform Act (Northern Ireland) 2007, ss. 2 (4) (a), 4 (6) (a). - Issued: 02.06.2009. Made: 01.12.2008. Coming into operation: 02.12.2008; 26.10.2009; & 25.10.2010 in accord. with reg. 1 (1). Effect: S.R. 1987/459; 1996/198; 2001/152; 2003/274; 2005/443; 2006/234; 2008/280 amended. - Approved by resolution of the Assembly on 26th May 2009. - 20p.: 30 cm. - 978-0-337-97787-9 *£5.50*

The Social Security (Lone Parents and Miscellaneous Amendments) Regulations (Northern Ireland) 2008 No. 2008/478. - Enabling power: Social Security Contributions and Benefits (Northern Ireland) Act 1992, 122 (1) (a), 123 (1) (e), 171 (1) to (4) & Social Security Administration (Northern Ireland) Act 1992, ss. 2A, 2B, 165 (1) (4) to (6) (7A) & S.I. 1995/2705 (N.I. 15), arts 8 (2) (4), 9 (4), 10 (2) (d) (ii), 21 (8) (a), 36 (2), sch. 1, paras 8, 10 (1) (a) (2) (a) & Welfare Reform Act (Northern Ireland) 2007, ss. 2 (4) (a), 4 (6) (a). - Issued: 05.12.2008. Made: 01.12.2008. Coming into operation: 02.12.2008; 26.10.2009; & 25.10.2010 in accord. with reg. 1 (1). Effect: S.R. 1987/459; 1996/198; 2001/152; 2003/274; 2005/443; 2006/234; 2008/280 amended. - For approval of the Assembly before the expiration of 6 months from the coming into operation date. - 20p.: 30 cm. - 978-0-337-97587-5 *£5.00*

The Social Security (Miscellaneous Amendments No. 2) Regulations (Northern Ireland) 2008 No. 2008/179. - Enabling power: Social Security Contributions and Benefits (Northern Ireland) Act 1992, ss. 122 (1) (d), 131 (1), 132 (3) (4) (a) (b), 133 (2) (f) (h) (i), 171 (1) (3) (4) & S.I. 1998/1506 (N.I. 10), arts 11 (6), 74 (1) (3). - Issued: 24.04.2008. Made: 18.04.2008. Coming into operation: In accord. with reg. 1. Effect: S.R. 1999/162; 2006/405, 406, 407 amended & S.R. 2007/306, 392 partially revoked. - Partially revoked by S.R. 2008/417 (ISBN 9780337975455). - 8p.: 30 cm. - 978-0-337-97364-2 *£3.00*

The Social Security (Miscellaneous Amendments No. 3) Regulations (Northern Ireland) 2008 No. 2008/410. - Enabling power: Social Security Contributions and Benefits (Northern Ireland) Act 1992, ss. 171 (4) & Social Security Administration (Northern Ireland) Act 1992, ss. 5 (1) (a), 165 (1) (3) to (5). - Issued: 08.10.2008. Made: 03.10.2008. Coming into operation: 06.10.2008. Effect: S.R. 1987/465; 2003/28, 421; 2004/304; 2006/128, 405, 406 amended. - 4p.: 30 cm. - 978-0-337-97539-4 *£4.00*

The Social Security (Miscellaneous Amendments No. 4) Regulations (Northern Ireland) 2008 No. 2008/417. - Enabling power: Social Security Administration (Northern Ireland) Act 1992, ss. 1 (1), 5 (1) (a) (b) (j), 165 (1) (3) (4) (6) & S.I. 1998/1506 (N.I. 10), arts 10 (1), 11 (3) (6), 74 (1) (3) & Child Support, Pensions and Social Security Act (Northern Ireland) 2000, sch. 7, paras 4 (5), 12, 13 (1) (2) (c) (3) (c), 20 (1) (b). - Issued: 14.10.2008. Made: 09.10.2008. Coming into operation: 30.10.2008. Effect: S.R. 1987/465; 1999/162; 2001/213; 2006/405, 406 amended & S.R. 2000/215; 2006/365; 2007/392; 2008/179 partially revoked. - 8p.: 30 cm. - 978-0-337-97545-5 *£5.00*

The Social Security (Miscellaneous Amendments No. 5) Regulations (Northern Ireland) 2008 No. 2008/428. - Enabling power: Social Security Contributions and Benefits (Northern Ireland) Act 1992, ss. 122 (1) (a) (d), 123 (1) (e), 129A (2), 131 (1), 132 (3) (4) (a) to (c), 132A (3), 133 (2) (h), 171 (1) to (4) & Social Security Administration (Northern Ireland) Act 1992, ss. 5 (1) (h) (q), 165 (1) (3) to (5) & S.I. 1995/2705 (N.I. 15), arts 6 (5), 14 (1) to (3) (4)(a) to (c), 36 (2), sch. 1, para. 3(b) & State Pension Credit Act (Northern Ireland) 2002, ss. 2 (3) (b) (6), 15 (3) (6) (b), 19 (1) (2) (a) (3). - Issued: 29.10.2008. Made: 23.10.2008. Coming into operation: 17.11.2008 except for reg. 7 (5); 06.04.2009 for reg. 7 (5). Effect: S.R. 1987/459, 465; 1988/205; 1993/120, 195; 1996/198, 503; 2002/222; 2003/28; 2006/405, 406; 2007/382 amended. - 12p.: 30 cm. - 978-0-337-97554-7 *£5.00*

The Social Security (Miscellaneous Amendments No. 6) Regulations (Northern Ireland) 2008 No. 2008/490. - Enabling power: Welfare Reform Act (Northern Ireland) 2007, s. 28 (2) & Mesothelioma, etc., Act (Northern Ireland) 2008, ss. 5 (4) (b), 9 (3). - Issued: 10.12.2008. Made: 05.12.2008. Coming into operation: 05.01.2009. Effect: S.R. 1999/162, 242; 2000/215; 2008/353 amended/partially revoked. - 4p.: 30 cm. - 978-0-337-97596-7 *£4.00*

The Social Security (Miscellaneous Amendments No. 7) Regulations (Northern Ireland) 2008 No. 2008/498. - Enabling power: Social Security Contributions and Benefits (Northern Ireland) Act 1992, ss. 122 (1) (a) (d), 123 (1) (d), 132 (1) (3) (4), 132A (3), 171 (1) to (4) & S.I. 1995/2705 (N.I. 15), arts 14 (4), 36 (2), sch. 1, para. 8 (a) & State Pension Credit Act (Northern Ireland) 2002, ss. 15 (1) (e) (j) (2) (6), 19 (1) to (3) & Welfare Reform Act (Northern Ireland) 2007, ss. 17, 25, 28 (2). - Issued: 17.12.2008. Made: 11.12.2008. Coming into operation: 05.01.2009. Effect: S.R. 1987/459; 1993/120; 1994/77; 1995/367, 481; 1996/198, 449; 2000/260; 2002/128; 2003/28; 2005/98, 536; 2006/405, 406, 407; 2007/306; 2008/179, 280, 286 amended or partially revoked. - Partially revoked by S.R. 2009/338 (ISBN 9780337978821). - 16p.: 30 cm. - 978-0-337-97604-9 *£5.00*

The Social Security (Miscellaneous Amendments) Regulations (Northern Ireland) 2008 No. 2008/112. - Enabling power: Social Security Contributions and Benefits (Northern Ireland) Act 1992, ss. 122 (1) (a) (d), 123 (1) (d), 131 (1), 132 (3) (4) (a) to (c), 133 (2) (d), 171 (1) to (4) & Social Security Administration (Northern Ireland) Act 1992, ss. 5 (1) (q), 165 (1) (3) to (5) & S.I. 1995/2705 (N.I. 15), arts 6 (5), 14 (2) (4) (a) (b), 36 (2), sch. 1, paras 1 (2) (a), 3 (b) & State Pension Credit Act (Northern Ireland) 2002, ss. 2 (3) (b) (6), 19 (1) to (3). - Issued: 19.03.2008. Made: 12.03.2008. Coming into operation: In accord. with reg. 1. Effect: S.R. 1987/459, 465; 1988/146; 1989/249, 365; 1996/198, 199; 1998/2; 1999/371 (C.28); 2001/151; 2003/28, 195, 338; 2005/319 (C.23); 2006/405; 2007/396 amended. - 16p.: 30 cm. - 978-0-337-97309-3 *£3.00*

The Social Security (National Insurance Numbers) (Amendment) Regulations (Northern Ireland) 2008 No. 2008/51. - Enabling power: Social Security Administration (Northern Ireland) Act 1992, ss. 158C, 165 (1) (4) to (6). - Issued: 13.02.2008. Made: 07.02.2008. Coming into operation: 29.02.2008. Effect: S.R. 2001/102 amended. - 4p.: 30 cm. - 978-0-337-97259-1 *£3.00*

The Social Security Pensions (Home Responsibilities) (Amendment) Regulations (Northern Ireland) 2008 No. 2008/88. - Enabling power: Social Security Contributions and Benefits (Northern Ireland) Act 1992, ss. 171 (3) (5), sch. 3, para. 5 (7) (b) (7A). - Issued: 13.03.2008. Made: 06.03.2008. Coming into operation: 06.04.2008. Effect: S.R. 1994/89 amended. - 4p.: 30 cm. - 978-0-337-97287-4 *£3.00*

The Social Security Pensions (Low Earnings Threshold) Order (Northern Ireland) 2008 No. 2008/120. - Enabling power: Social Security Administration (Northern Ireland) Act 1992, ss. 130A. - Issued: 20.03.2008. Made: 13.03.2008. Coming into operation: 06.04.2008. Effect: None. - 2p.: 30 cm. - 978-0-337-97317-8 *£3.00*

The Social Security (Recovery of Benefits) (Lump Sum Payments) Regulations (Northern Ireland) 2008 No. 2008/355. - Enabling power: Social Security Administration (Northern Ireland) Act 1992, s. 165 (4) (6) & S.I. 1997/ 1183 (N.I. 12), arts. 3A, 16 (2) to (4), 20, 21, 23 (3), 25 (1) (2) (7), sch. 1, para. 4, 8 & Mesothelioma, etc. Act (Northern Ireland) 2008, s. 9. - Issued: 02.09.2008. Made: 27.08.2008. Coming into operation: 01.10.2008. Effect: S.R.1999/162 amended. - 20p: 30 cm. - 978-0-337-97495-3 £3.50

The Social Security Revaluation of Earnings Factors Order (Northern Ireland) 2008 No. 2008/121. - Enabling power: Social Security Administration (Northern Ireland) Act 1992, ss. 130, 165 (1) (4) (5). - Issued: 20.03.2008. Made: 13.03.2008. Coming into operation: 06.04.2008. Effect: None. - 4p.: 30 cm. - 978-0-337-97318-5 £3.00

The Social Security (Students and Miscellaneous Amendments) Regulations (Northern Ireland) 2008 No. 2008/262. - Enabling power: Social Security Contributions and Benefits (Northern Ireland) Act 1992, ss. 122 (1) (a) (d), 132 (3) (4) (b), 171 (1) (3) (4) & Social Security Administration (Northern Ireland) Act 1992, ss. 5 (1) (hh) (k), 165 (1) (4) (6) & S.I. 1995/2705 (N.I. 15), arts 14 (1) to (3) (4) (b), 36 (2). - Issued: 01.07.2008. Made: 23.06.2008. Coming into operation: In accord. with reg. 1. Effect: S.R. 1987/459, 465; 1996/198; 2006/405 amended. - Partly revoked by S.R. 2009/261 (ISBN 9780337978319). - 8p.: 30 cm. - 978-0-337-97433-5 £3.00

The Social Security (Students Responsible for Children or Young Persons) (Amendment) Regulations (Northern Ireland) 2008 No. 2008/290. - Enabling power: Social Security Contributions and Benefits (Northern Ireland) Act 1992, ss. 122 (1) (a), 123 (1) (d) (e), 171 (1) (3) & S.I. 1995/2705 (N.I. 15), arts 8 (4), 36 (2). - Issued: 16.07.2008. Made: 08.07.2008. Coming into operation: 09.07.2008. Effect: S.R. 1987/459; 1996/198 amended. - For approval of the Assembly before the end of 6 months from date of coming into operation. - 4p.: 30 cm. - 978-0-337-97449-6 £3.00

The Social Security (Students Responsible for Children or Young Persons) (Amendment) Regulations (Northern Ireland) 2008 No. 2008/290. - Enabling power: Social Security Contributions and Benefits (Northern Ireland) Act 1992, ss. 122 (1) (a), 123 (1) (d) (e), 171 (1) (3) & S.I. 1995/2705 (N.I. 15), arts 8 (4), 36 (2). - Issued: 27.10.2008. Made: 08.07.2008. Coming into operation: 09.07.2008. Effect: S.R. 1987/459; 1996/198 amended. - Approved by resolution of the Assembly on 14th October 2008. - 4p.: 30 cm. - 978-0-337-97550-9 £4.00

The Social Security (Use of Information for Housing Benefit and Welfare Services Purposes) Regulations (Northern Ireland) 2008 No. 2008/343. - Enabling power: Welfare Reform Act (Northern Ireland) 2007, ss. 39 (2) (8) (9). - Issued: 14.08.2008. Made: 08.08.2008. Coming into operation: 01.09.2008. Effect: None. - 4p.: 30 cm. - 978-0-337-97484-7 £3.00

The Social Security (Work-focused Interviews for Partners) (Amendment) Regulations (Northern Ireland) 2008 No. 2008/169. - Enabling power: Social Security Administration (Northern Ireland) Act 1992, ss. 2AA (1) (4) to (7), 165 (1) (4) to (6). - Issued: 16.04.2008. Made: 11.04.2008. Coming into operation: 28.04.2008. Effect: S.R. 2003/405 amended. - 4p.: 30 cm. - 978-0-337-97356-7 £3.00

The Welfare Reform (2007 Act) (Commencement No. 3) Order (Northern Ireland) 2008 No. 2008/93 (C.3). - Enabling power: Welfare Reform Act (Northern Ireland) 2007, s. 60 (1). Bringing into operation various provisions of the 2007 Act on 10.03.2008 & 07.04.2008, in accord. with art. 2. - Issued: 13.03.2008. Made: 07.03.2008. Coming into operation: -. Effect: None. - 2p.: 30 cm. - 978-0-337-97292-8 £3.00

The Welfare Reform (2007 Act) (Commencement No. 4 and Consequential Provisions) Order (Northern Ireland) 2008 No. 2008/147 (C.7). - Enabling power: Welfare Reform Act (Northern Ireland) 2007, ss. 59, 60 (1). Bringing into operation various provisions of the 2007 on 01.04.2008 in accord. with art. 2. - Issued: 02.04.2008. Made: 28.03.2008. Coming into operation: -. Effect: S.R. 1999/162 amended. - 4p.: 30 cm. - 978-0-337-97346-8 £3.00

The Welfare Reform (2007 Act) (Commencement No. 5) Order (Northern Ireland) 2008 No. 2008/276 (C.14). - Enabling power: Welfare Reform Act (Northern Ireland) 2007, s. 60 (1). Bringing into operation various provisions of the 2007 Act in accord. with art. 2. - Issued: 04.07.2008. Made: 30.06.2008. Coming into operation: -. Effect: None. - 4p.: 30 cm. - 978-0-337-97439-7 £3.00

The Welfare Reform (2007 Act) (Commencement No. 6 and Transitional and Savings Provisions) Order (Northern Ireland) 2008 No. 2008/339 (C.18). - Enabling power: Welfare Reform Act (Northern Ireland) 2007, ss. 59, 60 (1). Bringing into operation various provisions of the 2007 Act on 08.08.2008; 01.09.2008; 07.10.2008 in accord. with art. 2. - Issued: 13.08.2008. Made: 07.08.2008. Coming into operation: -. Effect: None. - 4p.: 30 cm. - 978-0-337-97481-6 £3.00

The Welfare Reform (2007 Act) (Commencement No. 7) Order (Northern Ireland) 2008 No. 2008/425 (C.25). - Enabling power: Welfare Reform Act (Northern Ireland) 2007, s. 60 (1). Bringing into operation various provisions of the 2007 Act on 27.10.2008 in accord. with art. 2. - Issued: 29.10.2008. Made: 23.10.2008. Coming into operation: -. Effect: None. - 4p.: 30 cm. - 978-0-337-97552-3 £4.00

The Welfare Reform Act (Relevant Statutory Provision) Order (Northern Ireland) 2008 No. 2008/342. - Enabling power: Welfare Reform Act (Northern Ireland) 2007, s. 39 (7). - Issued: 14.08.2008. Made: 08.08.2008. Coming into operation: 01.09.2008. Effect: None. - 2p.: 30 cm. - 978-0-337-97483-0 £3.00

The Workmen's Compensation (Supplementation) (Amendment) Regulations (Northern Ireland) 2008 No. 2008/115. - Enabling power: Social Security Contributions and Benefits (Northern Ireland) Act 1992, s. 171 (4), sch. 8, para. 2 & Social Security Administration (Northern Ireland) Act 1992, sch. 6, para. 1. - Issued: 20.03.2008. Made: 12.03.2008. Coming into operation: 09.04.2008. Effect: S.R. 1983/101 amended & S.R. 2007/172 revoked. - 8p.: 30 cm. - 978-0-337-97312-3 £3.00

Statutory maternity pay

The Social Security Benefits Up-rating Order (Northern Ireland) 2008 No. 2008/92. - Enabling power: Social Security Administration (Northern Ireland) Act 1992, ss. 132, 132A, 165 (1) (4) (5). - Issued: 15.04.2008. Made: 07.03.2008. Coming into operation: In accord. with art. 1. Effect: 1966 c. 6 (N.I.); 1992 c. 7; S.R. 1987/459; 1992/32; 1994/461; 1995/35; 1996/198; 2003/28; 2006/405, 406 amended & S.R. 2007/153 revoked. - Revoked by S.R. 2009/89 (ISBN 9780337976902). For approval of the Northern Ireland Assembly before the expiration of six months from the date of its coming into operation. - 36p.: 30 cm. - 978-0-337-97291-1 £6.50

The Social Security Benefits Up-rating Order (Northern Ireland) 2008 No. 2008/92. - Enabling power: Social Security Administration (Northern Ireland) Act 1992, ss. 132, 132A, 165 (1) (4) (5). - Issued: 27.06.2008. Made: 07.03.2008. Coming into operation: In accord. with art. 1. Effect: 1966 c. 6 (N.I.); 1992 c. 7; S.R. 1987/459; 1992/32; 1994/461; 1995/35; 1996/198; 2002/380; 2003/28; 2006/405, 406 amended & S.R. 2007/153 revoked (10.04.2008). - Affirmed by resolution of the Assembly on 23.06.08. Supersedes SI of same number (ISBN 9780337972911) issued 15.04.2008. - 40p.: 30 cm. - 978-0-337-97429-8 £6.50

Statutory sick pay

The Social Security Benefits Up-rating Order (Northern Ireland) 2008 No. 2008/92. - Enabling power: Social Security Administration (Northern Ireland) Act 1992, ss. 132, 132A, 165 (1) (4) (5). - Issued: 15.04.2008. Made: 07.03.2008. Coming into operation: In accord. with art. 1. Effect: 1966 c. 6 (N.I.); 1992 c. 7; S.R. 1987/459; 1992/32; 1994/461; 1995/35; 1996/198; 2003/28; 2006/405, 406 amended & S.R. 2007/153 revoked. - Revoked by S.R. 2009/89 (ISBN 9780337976902). For approval of the Northern Ireland Assembly before the expiration of six months from the date of its coming into operation. - 36p.: 30 cm. - 978-0-337-97291-1 £6.50

The Social Security Benefits Up-rating Order (Northern Ireland) 2008 No. 2008/92. - Enabling power: Social Security Administration (Northern Ireland) Act 1992, ss. 132, 132A, 165 (1) (4) (5). - Issued: 27.06.2008. Made: 07.03.2008. Coming into operation: In accord. with art. 1. Effect: 1966 c. 6 (N.I.); 1992 c. 7; S.R. 1987/459; 1992/32; 1994/461; 1995/35; 1996/198; 2002/380; 2003/28; 2006/405, 406 amended & S.R. 2007/153 revoked (10.04.2008). - Affirmed by resolution of the Assembly on 23.06.08. Supersedes SI of same number (ISBN 9780337972911) issued 15.04.2008. - 40p.: 30 cm. - 978-0-337-97429-8 £6.50

The Statutory Sick Pay (General) (Amendment) Regulations (Northern Ireland) 2008 No. 2008/356. - Enabling power: Social Security Contributions and Benefits (Northern Ireland) Act 1992, s. 149 (5) & Social Security Administration (Northern Ireland) Act 1992, s. 122 (2). - Issued: 03.09.2008. Made: 27.08.2008. Coming into operation: 27.10.2008. Effect: S.R. 1982/263 amended & S.R. 1986/83; 1987/248; 1996/108 partially revoked. - 4p.: 30 cm. - 978-0-337-97496-0 £3.00

Street works

The Street Works (Inspection Fees) (Amendment) Regulations (Northern Ireland) 2008 No. 2008/40. - Enabling power: S.I. 1995/3210 (N.I. 19), art. 35. - Issued: 11.02.2008. Made: 04.02.2008. Coming into operation: 01.04.2008. Effect: S.R. 2005/259 amended. - 2p: 30 cm. - 978-0-337-97253-9 £3.00

Supreme Court

The Family Proceedings (Amendment No. 2) Rules (Northern Ireland) 2008 No. 2008/259. - Enabling power: S.I. 1993/1576 (N.I. 6), art. 12. - Issued: 27.06.2008. Made: 20.06.2008. Coming into operation: 05.09.2008. Effect: S.R. 1996/322 amended. - 4p.: 30 cm. - 978-0-337-97428-1 £3.00

The Family Proceedings (Amendment No. 3) Rules (Northern Ireland) 2008 No. 2008/466. - Enabling power: S.I. 1993/1576 (N.I. 6), art. 12. - Issued: 28.11.2008. Made: 20.11.2008. Coming into operation: 22.12.2008. Effect: S.R. 1996/322 amended. - 16p.: 30 cm. - 978-0-337-97579-0 £5.00

The Family Proceedings (Amendment) Rules (Northern Ireland) 2008 No. 2008/24. - Enabling power: S.I. 1993/1576 (N.I. 6), art. 12. - Issued: 07.02.2008. Made: 22.01.2008. Coming into operation: 25.02.2008. Effect: S.R. 1996/322 amended. - 4p.: 30 cm. - 978-0-337-97237-9 £3.00

Supreme Court: Procedure

The Rules of the Supreme Court (Northern Ireland) (Amendment) 2008 No. 2008/22. - Enabling power: Judicature (Northern Ireland) Act 1978, ss. 55, 55A. - Issued: 07.02.2008. Made: 21.01.2008. Coming into operation: 25.02.2008. Effect: S.R. 1980/346 amended. - 8p.: 30 cm. - 978-0-337-97236-2 £3.00

Supreme Court, Northern Ireland

The Crown Court (Amendment) Rules (Northern Ireland) 2008 No. 2008/505. - Enabling power: Judicature (Northern Ireland) Act 1978, ss. 52 (1), 53A & S.I. 1999/2789 (N.I. 8), art. 39 (1) & S.I. 2004/1500 (N.I. 9), art. 14. - Issued: 14.01.2009. Made: 18.12.2008. Coming into operation: 02.02.2009. Effect: S.R. 1979/90 amended. - 16p.: 30 cm. - 978-0-337-97613-1 £5.00

Supreme Court, Northern Ireland: Counter-terrorism

The Rules of the Supreme Court (Northern Ireland) (Amendment No. 3) 2008 No. 2008/479. - Enabling power: Judicature (Northern Ireland) Act 1978, s. 55 & Counter-Terrorism Act 2008, ss. 66, 67. - Issued: 10.02.2009. Made: 02.12.2008. Laid: 03.12.2008. Coming into operation: 04.12.2008. Effect: S.R. 1980/346 amended. - Approved by both Houses of Parliament. - 20p.: 30 cm. - 978-0-337-97638-4 £5.00

The Rules of the Supreme Court (Northern Ireland) (Amendment No. 3) 2008 No. 2008/479. - Enabling power: Judicature (Northern Ireland) Act 1978, s. 55 & Counter-Terrorism Act 2008, ss. 66, 67. - Issued: 05.12.2008. Made: 02.12.2008. Coming into operation: 04.12.2008. Effect: S.R. 1980/346 amended. - For approval of each House of Parliament within 40 days. - 20p.: 30 cm. - 978-0-337-97590-5 £5.00

Supreme Court, Northern Ireland: Procedure

The Criminal Appeal (Offenders Assisting Investigations and Prosecutions) Rules (Northern Ireland) 2008 No. 2008/23. - Enabling power: Judicature (Northern Ireland) Act 1978, ss. 55, 55A. - Issued: 07.02.2008. Made: 21.01.2008. Coming into operation: 25.02.2008. Effect: None. - 20p.: 30 cm. - 978-0-337-97239-3 £3.50

The Rules of the Supreme Court (Northern Ireland) (Amendment) 2008 (Correction Slip) No. 2008/22 Cor. - Correction slip (to ISBN 9780337972362) dated February 2008. - 1 sheet: 30 cm. *Free*

The Rules of the Supreme Court (Northern Ireland) (Amendment No. 2) 2008 No. 2008/401. - Enabling power: Judicature (Northern Ireland) Act 1978, ss. 55, 55A. - Issued: 07.10.2008. Made: 26.09.2008. Coming into operation: 03.11.2008. Effect: S.R. 1980/346 amended. - 4p.: 30 cm. - 978-0-337-97530-1 £4.00

Trade unions

Certification Officer (Fees) Regulations (Northern Ireland) 2008 No. 2008/95. - Enabling power: S.I. 1992/807 (N.I. 5), arts 5 (4), 6 (2), 107 (3) & S.I. 1995/1980 (N.I. 12), art. 89 (1). - Issued: 13.03.2008. Made: 05.03.2008. Coming into operation: 06.04.2008. Effect: S.R. 1997/367 revoked. - 4p.: 30 cm. - 978-0-337-97294-2 £3.00

Transport

The Cross-border Railway Services (Working Time) Regulations (Northern Ireland) 2008 No. 2008/315. - Enabling power: European Communities Act 1972, s. 2 (2). - Issued: 12.08.2008. Made: 23.07.2008. Coming into operation: 01.10.2008. Effect: S.I. 1996/1921 (N.I. 18), 1919 (N.I. 16); 1998 No. 386; 2003/2902 (N.I. 15). - EC note: These Regulations implement the provisions of Council Directive 2005/47/EC on the Agreement between the Community of European Railways (CER) and the European Transport Workers' Federation (ETF) on certain aspects of the working conditions of mobile workers engaged in interoperable cross-border services in the railway sector. - 16p.: 30 cm. - 978-0-337-97479-3 £3.00

Treatment of offenders

The Prison and Young Offenders Centre (Amendment) Rules (Northern Ireland) 2008 No. 2008/452. - Enabling power: Prison Act (Northern Ireland) 1953, ss. 13 (1), 34 (6) (as extended by the Treatment of Offenders Act (Northern Ireland) 1968, s. 2). - Issued: 05.12.2008. Made: 17.11.2008. Laid: 26.11.2008. Coming into operation: 19.12.2008. Effect: S.R. 1995/8 amended. - 4p.: 30 cm. - 978-0-337-97571-4 £4.00

Weights and measures

The Measuring Instruments (Use for Trade) (Amendment) Regulations (Northern Ireland) 2008 No. 2008/52. - Enabling power: S.I. 1981/231 (N.I. 10), art. 13 (1). - Issued: 13.02.2008. Made: 08.02.2008. Coming into operation: 17.03.2008. Effect: S.R. 2007/383, 384, 385, 386, 387, 388, 389, 390 amended. - This Statutory Rule has been made in consequence of a defect in S.R. 2007 Nos. 383 to 390 and is being issued free of charge to all known recipients of those Statutory Rules. - 4p: 30 cm. - 978-0-337-97260-7 £3.00

Statutory Rules of Northern Ireland

Arranged by Number

1	*
2	*
3	Electricity
	Gas
4	*
5	*
6	*
7	*
8	*
9	*
10	*
11	*
12	*
13	Airports
14	Roads
15	Rates
16	Social security
17	Planning
18	Environmental protection
19	Disabled persons
20	Environmental protection
21	Health and safety
22	Supreme Court
23	Supreme Court, Northern Ireland
24	Family proceedings
	Supreme Court
	County courts
25	Agriculture
26	Salaries
27	*
28	*
29	Road traffic and vehicles
30	*
31	*
32	Coroners
33	Fisheries
34	Agriculture
35	Magistrates' courts
36	*
37	Animals
38	Animals
39	Health and personal social services
40	Roads
	Street works
41	Food
42	Food
43	*
44	*
45	Social security
46	Northern Ireland Departments
47	Employment
48	Rates
49	Rates
50	Education
51	Social security
52	Weights and measures
53	European Communities
	Animals
54	Electricity
55	Electricity
56	Police
57	*
58	*
59	Animals
60	Plant health
61	*
62	*
63	Road traffic and vehicles
64	*
65 (C.1)	Pensions
66	*
67	Energy conservation
68	Rates
69	Social security
70	Food
71	*
72	*
73	Social security
74	*
75 (C.2)	Environmental protection
76	Employment
77	Public health
78	Road traffic and vehicles
79	Education
80	*
81	Disabled persons
82	Food
83	Agriculture
84	Pensions

85	Pesticides	123	Pensions
86	*	124	Rates
87	*	125	Plant health
88	Social security	126	Food
89	Food	127 (C.5)	Safeguarding vulnerable groups
90	Health services charges	128	Health and personal social services
91	Health and personal social services	129	Education
92	Social security Statutory maternity pay Statutory sick pay Employment Housing Rates	130	Health and personal social services
		131	Food
		132	Pensions
		133	Companies
		134	Companies
		135	Roads Road traffic and vehicles
93 (C.3)	Social security		
94	Insolvency	136	*
95	Trade unions	137	*
96	Health and personal social services	138 (C.6)	Environmental protection
97	Pensions	139	Health and personal social services
98	Food	140	Disabled persons
99	Agriculture Food	141	Disabled persons
		142	Health and personal social services
100	Housing	143	Harbours
101	Housing	144	Pensions
102	Housing	145	Pensions
103	Housing Rates Social security	146	Pensions
		147 (C.7)	Social security
104 (C. 4)	Pensions	148	*
105	Social security	149	*
106	Legal aid and advice	150	*
107	Legal aid and advice	151	*
108	Legal aid and advice	152	*
109	Road traffic and vehicles	153	Rates
110	*	154	Judiciary
111	Social security	155	*
112	Housing Rates Social security	156	Judicature
		157	*
		158	*
113	Social security	159	Sex discrimination
114	Seeds	160	Environmental protection
115	Social security	161	Companies
116	Pensions	162	*
117	Pensions	163	Health and personal social services
118	Insolvency Companies	164	*
		165	*
119	Family law	166	*
120	Social security	167	Food
121	Social security	168	*
122	*		

169	Social security	212	*
170	European Communities	213	*
171	Agriculture Food	214	*
		215	*
172	Agriculture	216	*
173	*	217 (C.8)	Criminal law
174	Agriculture	218	*
175	*	219	Registration of vital events
176	*	220	*
177	Education	221	*
178	Pensions	222	Pharmacy
179	Housing Rates Social security	223 (C.9)	Road traffic and vehicles
		224	*
		225	Magistrates' courts
180	*	226	Rates
181	*	227	*
182	*	228	*
183	Fisheries	229	*
184	Seeds	230	Road traffic and vehicles
185	Sea fisheries	231	Environmental protection
186	Agriculture	232 (C.10)	Fisheries
187	*	233 (C.11)	Safeguarding vulnerable groups
188	Animals	234	Road traffic and vehicles
189	European Communities Food	235	Planning
		236 (C.12)	Disabled persons
190	*	237	Food
191	Government resources and accounts	238	Fire and rescue services
192	Pharmacy	239	Food
193	Pharmacy	240	Agriculture
194	Agriculture	241	European Communities
195	Agriculture	242	Police
196	Environmental protection	243	Police
197	Animals	244 (C.13)	Road traffic and vehicles
198	Food	245	Road traffic and vehicles
199	County courts	246	*
200	Safeguarding vulnerable groups	247	*
201	Safeguarding vulnerable groups	248	Legal aid and advice
202	Safeguarding vulnerable groups	249	Health and personal social services
203	Safeguarding vulnerable groups	250	Education
204	*	251	Magistrates' courts
205	Plant health	252	Magistrates' courts
206	*	253	Magistrates' courts
207	*	254	Education
208	*	255	Education
209	*	256	Health and personal social services
210	*	257	Road traffic and vehicles
211	*	258	Social security

259	Family proceedings	302	Fisheries
	Supreme Court	303	Pensions
	County courts	304	Sea fisheries
260	Agriculture	305	Pensions
261	Insolvency	306	Public health
262	Housing	307	Public health
	Rates	308	*
	Social security	309	*
263	Animals	310	Local government
264	Audit and accountability	311	*
265	*	312	*
266	*	313	*
267	*	314	Police
268	*	315	Transport
269	*	316	*
270	*	317	*
271	Food	318	Fisheries
272	Animals	319	Fisheries
273	*	320	*
274	*	321	*
275	Animals	322	*
276 (C.14)	Social security	323	Agriculture
277	Animals	324	Education
278	Agriculture	325	Police
279	*	326	Employment
280	Social security	327	*
281	Road and railway transport	328	Roads
282	Clean air		Road traffic and vehicles
283	Social security	329	*
284	*	330	*
285	Housing	331 (C.17)	Family law
	Rates	332	*
286	Social security	333	Public health
287	Electricity	334	*
288	*	335	*
289	Social security	336	Animals
290	Social security	337	*
291 (C.15)	Family law	338	*
292	Health and personal social services	339 (C.18)	Social security
293 (C.16)	Criminal law	340	Animals
294	Industrial training	341	Road traffic and vehicles
295	Agriculture	342	Social security
296	Agriculture	343	Social security
297	Agriculture		Housing
298	Fisheries		Rates
299	Fisheries	344	Road traffic and vehicles
300	Fisheries	345	*
301	Fisheries		

346	Health and personal social services	391	Health and personal social services
347	*	392	*
348	*	393	*
349	*	394	Fisheries
350	Health and personal social services	395	Health and personal social services
351 (C. 19)	Social security	396 (C.21)	Libraries
352	Social security	397	Salaries
353	Social security	398	*
354	Social security	399 (C.22)	Family law
355	Social security	400	*
356	Statutory sick pay	401	Supreme Court, Northern Ireland
357	Social security	402 (C.23)	Family law Child support
358	*	403	Family law Child support
359	Animals		
360	Police	404	Family law Child support
361	Magistrates' courts		
362	Magistrates' courts	405	Food
363	Magistrates' courts	406	Social security
364	Pensions	407	Game
365	Pensions	408	Police
366	*	409	Family law
367	*	410	Housing Rates Social security
368	*		
369	*		
370	Pensions	411	Social security
371	Housing Rates	412	Social security
		413	Social security
372	Planning	414	*
373	Public health	415	Clean air
374	Employment	416	Employment
375	Social security	417	Social security Housing Rates
376	Education		
377	Health and personal social services		
378	Housing Rates	418	Road traffic and vehicles
		419 (C.24)	Family law
379	Companies	420	*
380	Agriculture	421	*
381	Fire and rescue services	422	Health and safety
382	Fire and rescue services	423	Health and personal social services
383 (C. 20)	Criminal law	424	Health and safety
384	*	425 (C.25)	Social security
385	*	426	Health and personal social services
386	*	427	Criminal justice
387	Road traffic and vehicles	428	Housing Social security Rates
388	Pensions		
389	Agriculture		
390	*	429	Social security

430	Sea fisheries	474	Social security
431	Animals	475	Fisheries
432	Lands Tribunal	476	Fisheries
433	Agriculture Pesticides	477	Police
		478	Social security
434	Health and personal social services	479	Supreme Court, Northern Ireland
435	Agriculture	480	Fair employment
436	Public health	481	*
437	*	482	*
438	*	483	*
439	Police	484	Fisheries
440	*	485	Pensions
441	*	486	*
442	Plant health	487	*
443	*	488	Health and personal social services
444	Pensions	489 (C.29)	Family law
445	Insolvency	490	Social security
446 (C.26)	Family law	491	Explosives
447	*	492	Fisheries
448	*	493	Plant health
449	*	494	Road traffic and vehicles
450	*	495	Criminal law
451	Food	496	Agriculture
452	Prisons Treatment of offenders	497	Housing Rates Social security
453	*	498	Housing Rates Social security
454	*		
455	Education		
456	European Communities	499	Pesticides
457	Justice	500	Fisheries
458	Road traffic	501	Road traffic and vehicles
459	*	502	Social security
460	*	503	Social security
461	*	504	Housing Rates
462	*		
463	*	505	Supreme Court, Northern Ireland Procedure
464	*		
465	Social security	506	Housing
466	Family proceedings Supreme Court County courts	507	Electricity
		508	Animal health
		509	*
467	*	510 (C.30)	Criminal law
468	*	511	Audit and accountability
469	*		
470	*		

List of Commencement Orders

471 (C.27)	Criminal law
472 (C.28)	Criminal law

65 (C.1)

473	Agriculture

75 (C.2)

93 (C.3)	331 (C.17)
104 (C. 4)	339 (C.18)
127 (C.5)	351 (C. 19)
138 (C.6)	383 (C. 20)
147 (C.7)	396 (C.21)
217 (C.8)	399 (C.22)
223 (C.9)	402 (C.23)
232 (C.10)	419 (C.24)
233 (C. 11)	425 (C.25)
236 (C.12)	446 (C.26)
244 (C.13)	471 (C.27)
276 (C.14)	472 (C.28)
291 (C.15)	489 (C.29)
293 (C.16)	510 (C.30)

Alphabetical Index

A

Abertawe Bro Morgannwg University National Health Service Trust: Establishment: Wales 128
Abertawe Bro Morgannwg University National Health Service Trust: Transfer of property, rights & liabilities: Wales . . 129
Abolition of Bridge Tolls (Scotland) Act 2008: Commencements: Scotland 354, 364
Abortion: England 118
Abortion: Wales 118
Academic awards & distinctions: UHI Millennium Institute: Scotland 337
Accident hazard: Major accident hazard: Control 88
Accounting standards: Prescribed body: Companies 34
Accounts: Dormant: Banks & building societies: Acts 5
Acquisition of land: Home loss payments: Prescribed amounts: England 9, 37
Acquisition of land: Home loss payments: Prescribed amounts: Wales 10
Act of Adjournal: Criminal procedure rules: Amendments: Criminal Proceedings etc. (Reform) (Scotland) Act 2007: Scotland 342, 344, 361
Act of Adjournal: Criminal procedure rules: Amendments: Scotland 344, 361
Act of Sederunt: Bankruptcy & Diligence etc. (Scotland) Act 2007: Court of Session: Rules: Amendments: Scotland . . . 334
Act of Sederunt: Court of Session: Judicial review applications: Transfers: Scotland 334
Act of Sederunt: Court of Session: Messengers-at-Arms: Fees: EC service regulation: Scotland 334
Act of Sederunt: Court of Session: Messengers-at-Arms: Fees: Scotland 334
Act of Sederunt: Court of Session: Rules: Counter-Terrorism Act 2008: Scotland 334
Act of Sederunt: Court of Session: Rules: Miscellaneous: Scotland 334
Act of Sederunt: Court of Session: Rules: Solicitors: Fees: Scotland 334
Act of Sederunt: Court of Session: Shorthand writers: Fees: Scotland 334
Act of Sederunt: Sheriff Court: Bankruptcy Rules: Scotland 361
Act of Sederunt: Sheriff Court: European order for payment: Procedure: Rules: Scotland 362
Act of Sederunt: Sheriff Court: European small claims: Procedure: Rules: Scotland 362
Act of Sederunt: Sheriff Court: Rules: Amendments: Diligence: Scotland 362
Act of Sederunt: Sheriff Court: Rules: Amendments: Scotland 362
Act of Sederunt: Sheriff Court: Sheriff officers: Fees: Scotland 361
Act of Sederunt: Sheriff Court: Shorthand writers: Fees: Scotland 361
Act of Sederunt: Sheriff Court: Solicitors: Fees: Scotland 361
Act of Sederunt: Summary & statutory applications & appeals etc.: Rules: Adult Support & Protection (Scotland) Act 2007: Sheriff Court: Scotland 362
Act of Sederunt: Summary & statutory applications & appeals etc.: Rules: Amendments: Licensing (Scotland) Act 2005: Scotland 362
Act of Sederunt: Summary & statutory applications & appeals etc.: Rules: Registration appeals: Scotland 362
Actuarial guidance: Pensions : Northern Ireland 397
Additional voluntary contributions: Health & personal social services: Northern Ireland 391
Additives: Food: England 82
Additives: Food: Northern Ireland 389
Additives: Food: Wales 84
Adoption & Children Act 2002: Commencements: Scotland 332
Adoption & Children Act 2007: Commencements: Scotland 333
Adoption & paternity leave 268
Adoption & paternity leave: Northern Ireland 383
Adoption: Family procedure 77
Adoption: From abroad: Restrictions 24, 25
Adoption: From abroad: Restrictions: Scotland 333
Adoption: From Cambodia: Restrictions 25, 26
Adoption: From Cambodia: Restrictions: Scotland 333
Adoption: From Guatemala: Restrictions 25, 26
Adoption: From Guatemala: Restrictions: Scotland 333
Adult Support & Protection (Scotland) Act 2007: Adults with incapacity: Consequential provisions: Scotland 326
Adult Support & Protection (Scotland) Act 2007: Commencements: Scotland 326, 347
Adult Support & Protection (Scotland) Act 2007: Council officers: Authorisation: Restrictions: Scotland 326, 363
Adult Support & Protection (Scotland) Act 2007: Sheriff Court: Summary & statutory applications & appeals etc.: Rules: Act of Sederunt: Scotland 362
Adults with incapacity: Accounts & funds: Scotland 326

Adults with incapacity: Adult Support & Protection (Scotland) Act 2007: Commencements: Scotland 326, 347
Adults with incapacity: Adult Support & Protection (Scotland) Act 2007: Consequential provisions: Scotland 326
Adults with incapacity: Electronic communications: Scotland 326, 338
Adults with incapacity: Guardian's powers: Recall: Scotland 327
Adults with incapacity: Guardianship & intervention orders: Reports: Scotland 327
Adults with incapacity: Powers of attorney: Certificates: Scotland 326
Adults with incapacity: Public Guardians: Fees: Scotland 326, 327
Adults: Safeguarding Vulnerable Groups: 2007 Order: Commencements: Northern Ireland 404
Adults: Vulnerable adults: Protection: Care Standards Tribunal: England & Wales 24
Adventure activities: Licensing: Amendments 87
Advice & assistance: Financial conditions: Scotland 345
Advice & assistance: Limits, conditions & representation: Scotland 345
Advice & assistance: Scotland 345
Aerodromes: Designation: Chargeable air services 27
African Development Bank: African Development Fund: Eleventh replenishment 104
African Development Fund: Multilateral debt relief initiative 105
Age discrimination: Employment & training 70
Aggregates levy: Amusement machines: Licencing: Duties 10, 33, 74, 104, 106
Aggregates levy: Value added tax: Correction of errors 10, 33, 76, 104, 106, 275
Agricultural grants: Crofting counties: Scotland 336
Agricultural holdings: Units of production: England 107
Agricultural holdings: Units of production: Wales 107
Agriculture & Horticulture Development Board 10
Agriculture: Animals: Welfare: Mutilations: Permitted procedures 15
Agriculture: Beef & veal: Labelling: England 10
Agriculture: Bovine semen: Wales 13
Agriculture: Common Agricultural Policy: Single payment & support schemes: Cross-compliance: England 10
Agriculture: Common Agricultural Policy: Single payment & support schemes: Cross-compliance: Northern Ireland . . . 375
Agriculture: Common Agricultural Policy: Single payment & support schemes: Cross-compliance: Scotland 327
Agriculture: Common Agricultural Policy: Single payment & support schemes: England 10
Agriculture: Common Agricultural Policy: Single payment & support schemes: Wales 12
Agriculture: Countryside: Management: Northern Ireland 375
Agriculture: Environmental impact assessment: Northern Ireland 375
Agriculture: Farm modernisation programme: Northern Ireland 375
Agriculture: Feed & food: Official controls: Scotland 328, 341
Agriculture: Feed: Hygiene & enforcement: Scotland 327
Agriculture: Feeding stuffs: England 11
Agriculture: Feeding stuffs: Northern Ireland 376
Agriculture: Feeding stuffs: Scotland 328
Agriculture: Feeding stuffs: Wales 12
Agriculture: Financial assistance for young farmers scheme: Northern Ireland 376
Agriculture: Guar gum: Marketing: Restrictions: Scotland 328, 341
Agriculture: Heath & grass: Burning: Wales 13
Agriculture: Hill farm allowance: England 11
Agriculture: Horses: Zootechnical standards: Scotland 329
Agriculture: Labelling: Beef & veal: Scotland 327, 340
Agriculture: Land managers: Skills development grants: Scotland 328
Agriculture: Leader grants: Scotland 328
Agriculture: Less favoured area support scheme: Scotland 328
Agriculture: Less favoured areas: Compensatory allowances: Northern Ireland 376
Agriculture: Milk & milk products: Educational establishments: Pupils: England 11
Agriculture: Milk & milk products: Educational establishments: Pupils: Northern Ireland 376
Agriculture: Milk products: Prices: Reporting: England 11
Agriculture: Milk products: Prices: Reporting: Northern Ireland 377
Agriculture: Nitrate pollution: Prevention 11, 276
Agriculture: Nitrate pollution: Prevention: Wales 12, 277
Agriculture: Nitrate vulnerable zones: Action programmes: Scotland 327, 339, 365
Agriculture: Organic farming: Northern Ireland 376
Agriculture: Pesticides: Maximum residue levels: Crops, food & feeding stuffs: England & Wales 12, 138
Agriculture: Pesticides: Maximum residue levels: Crops, food & feeding stuffs: Northern Ireland 378
Agriculture: Pesticides: Maximum residue levels: Crops, food & feeding stuffs: Scotland 328, 350
Agriculture: Pesticides: Maximum residue levels: England & Wales 11, 138
Agriculture: Pesticides: Maximum residue levels: Northern Ireland 377, 397
Agriculture: Pesticides: Maximum residue levels: Scotland 328, 350
Agriculture: Pig production development: Levy: Northern Ireland 377

Agriculture: Processing, marketing & co-operation grants : Scotland 327
Agriculture: Products of animal origin: Third country imports: England 11
Agriculture: Quality Meat Scotland: Establishment: Scotland 329
Agriculture: Rice products: From United States: Marketing: Restrictions: England. 11, 82
Agriculture: Rice products: From United States: Marketing: Restrictions: Northern Ireland. 377, 389
Agriculture: Rice products: From United States: Marketing: Restrictions: Scotland 329, 341
Agriculture: Rice products: From United States: Marketing: Restrictions: Wales. 12, 85
Agriculture: Rural Development Contracts: Land managers options: Scotland 329
Agriculture: Rural Development Contracts: Rural priorities: Scotland. 329
Agriculture: Rural development: Financial assistance: Northern Ireland. 377
Agriculture: School milk: Wales 12, 13
Agriculture: Scotland Act 1998: Agency arrangements: Specification 10, 13, 38, 45, 53, 143
Agriculture: Seed potatoes: Levies: Northern Ireland. 377
Agriculture: Specified products: From China: Marketing: Restrictions: England 11, 82
Agriculture: Specified products: From China: Marketing: Restrictions: Northern Ireland 377, 389
Agriculture: Specified products: From China: Marketing: Restrictions: Scotland 329, 341
Agriculture: Specified products: From China: Marketing: Restrictions: Wales 13
Agriculture: Student fees: Northern Ireland. 375
Agriculture: Supply chain development programme grant: Northern Ireland 377
Agriculture: Vocational training & information actions grant: Northern Ireland. 378
Agriculture: Welsh Levy Board 13
Air Force Act 1955: Part 1: Amendments 51
Air Force Discipline Act: Continuation 51
Air Force: Court-martial: Rules. 52
Air Force: Disablement & death: Service pensions 135
Air Force: Service complaints 51
Air Force: Service Discipline Acts: Alignment. 51
Air navigation. 27
Air navigation: Civil aviation: Guernsey. 27
Air navigation: Civil aviation: Jersey. 27
Air navigation: Dangerous goods. 27
Air navigation: Environmental standards: Non-EASA aircraft. 27
Air navigation: Flying restrictions: Abingdon 27
Air navigation: Flying restrictions: Bacton. 27
Air navigation: Flying restrictions: Biggin Hill Air Fair 28
Air navigation: Flying restrictions: Biggin Hill, Air Fair. 28
Air navigation: Flying restrictions: Bournemouth Air Festival 28
Air navigation: Flying restrictions: Bow, East London. 28
Air navigation: Flying restrictions: Bruntingthorpe 28
Air navigation: Flying restrictions: Chelmsford Prison 28
Air navigation: Flying restrictions: Cheltenham 28
Air navigation: Flying restrictions: Chilbolton. 28
Air navigation: Flying restrictions: City of Manchester Stadium 28
Air navigation: Flying restrictions: Coombe Abbey 28
Air navigation: Flying restrictions: Copdock. 28
Air navigation: Flying restrictions: Coventry. 28, 29
Air navigation: Flying restrictions: Dover Straights 29
Air navigation: Flying restrictions: Dunsfold. 29
Air navigation: Flying restrictions: Duxford 29
Air navigation: Flying restrictions: Eastbourne 29
Air navigation: Flying restrictions: Enniskillen 29
Air navigation: Flying restrictions: Farnborough Airshow. 29
Air navigation: Flying restrictions: Farnborough Flypast 29
Air navigation: Flying restrictions: Glastonbury festival. 29
Air navigation: Flying restrictions: Her Majesty The Queen's 82nd Birthday Flypast 29
Air navigation: Flying restrictions: Ipswich 29
Air navigation: Flying restrictions: Jet Formation Display Teams. 29, 30
Air navigation: Flying restrictions: Kemble 30
Air navigation: Flying restrictions: Labour Party Conference Manchester 30
Air navigation: Flying restrictions: Lowestoft 30
Air navigation: Flying restrictions: Nacton. 30
Air navigation: Flying restrictions: North Sea, Britannia Oil Rig 30
Air navigation: Flying restrictions: Nuclear installations 30
Air navigation: Flying restrictions: Orpington 30
Air navigation: Flying restrictions: Remembrance Sunday 30

Air navigation: Flying restrictions: Royal Air Force 90th Anniversary Flypast 30
Air navigation: Flying restrictions: Royal Air Force Colour Presentation 30
Air navigation: Flying restrictions: Royal Air Force Leuchars. 30
Air navigation: Flying restrictions: Royal Air Force Role Demonstration 30
Air navigation: Flying restrictions: Royal Air Force Waddington 30
Air navigation: Flying restrictions: Royal Albert Hall 30
Air navigation: Flying restrictions: Royal International Air Tattoo RAF Fairford. 31
Air navigation: Flying restrictions: Rutland Water. 31
Air navigation: Flying restrictions: Scottish Highlands 31
Air navigation: Flying restrictions: Shenington, Oxfordshire 31
Air navigation: Flying restrictions: Silverstone & Turweston 31
Air navigation: Flying restrictions: South Wales. 31
Air navigation: Flying restrictions: Southend 31
Air navigation: Flying restrictions: Southport 31
Air navigation: Flying restrictions: State Opening of Parliament 31
Air navigation: Flying restrictions: Stonehenge 31
Air navigation: Flying restrictions: Sunderland 31
Air navigation: Flying restrictions: Trooping of the Colour Ceremony 31
Air navigation: Flying restrictions: Usk Reservoir 31
Air navigation: Flying restrictions: Visit by the President of the United States of America 31
Air navigation: Flying restrictions: Waddington 31
Air navigation: Flying restrictions: Walney Island 31
Air navigation: Flying restrictions: West Wales Airport 32
Air navigation: Flying restrictions: Weston Park 32
Air navigation: Flying restrictions: Weston-super-Mare 32
Air navigation: Flying restrictions: Whittlesey 32
Air navigation: Flying restrictions: Wycombe Air Park, Aero Expo. 32
Air navigation: Flying restrictions: Yeovilton 32
Air navigation: Isle of Man 27
Air navigation: Overseas territories. 27
Air navigation: Rules of the air: Civil aviation 32
Air pollution: Ships: Prevention. 118
Aircraft: Power to detain & sell: Northern Ireland 378
Aircraft: Public health: Northern Ireland 400
Airports: Designation: Power to detain & sell aircraft: Northern Ireland. 378
Airports: Economic regulation: Designation 32
Alcoholic liquor: Duties: Surcharges 74
Alcoholic liquor: Spirits duty: Surcharges 74
All Saints CE (Aided) Primary School: Religious character: Designation 56
All Saints CofE School: Religious character: Designation 56
Allergens: Declaration: Food: Labelling: Northern Ireland 388
Allergens: Food: Labelling: Declaration: Scotland 340
Alnwick: Parishes: Local government 110
Amusement machines: Licence duties 10, 33, 74, 104, 106
Angling: Foyle & Carlingford areas: Northern Ireland 387
Animal by-products: Zoonoses: Fees:: England 15
Animal by-products: Zoonoses: Fees:: Northern Ireland 379
Animal by-products: Zoonoses: Fees:: Scotland 331
Animal by-products: Zoonoses: Fees:: Wales 16, 17
Animal health: Animals & animal products: Import & export 10
Animal health: Animals & animal products: Import & export: Northern Ireland 378, 384
Animal health: Animals & animal products: Import & export: Scotland 329
Animal health: Avian influenza: Northern Ireland 378
Animal health: Bluetongue: England 13
Animal health: Bluetongue: Northern Ireland 378, 379
Animal health: Bluetongue: Scotland 330
Animal health: Bluetongue: Wales 15
Animal health: Brucellosis 14
Animal health: Disease control: England 14
Animal health: Disease control: Wales 15
Animal health: Diseases: Approved disinfectants: Fees: England 14
Animal health: Pathogens: Specified: England 14
Animal health: Pathogens: Specified: Northern Ireland. 379
Animal health: Pathogens: Specified: Wales 16
Animal health: Pigs: Records, identification & movement: Scotland 330

Animal health: Pigs: Records, identification & movement: Wales. 15
Animal health: Poultry: Salmonella: Control: Northern Ireland 379
Animal health: Poultry: Salmonella: Control: Scotland. 330
Animal health: Poultry: Salmonella: Control: Wales. 15
Animal health: Products of animal origin: Disease control: Northern Ireland 379
Animal health: Products of animal origin: Disease control: Wales 15
Animal health: Sheep & goats: Identification & traceability: Scotland. 330
Animal health: Sheep & goats: Records, identification & movement: Wales 16
Animal health: Transmissible spongiform encephalopathies: England 14
Animal health: Transmissible spongiform encephalopathies: Northern Ireland. 378, 379
Animal health: Transmissible spongiform encephalopathies: Scotland. 331
Animal health: Transmissible spongiform encephalopathies: Wales. 16
Animal health: Transport: Cleansing & disinfection: Wales. 16
Animal health: Tuberculosis: Testing & powers of entry: Wales 16
Animal health: Zoonoses & animal by-products: Fees: England. 15
Animal health: Zoonoses & animal by-products: Fees: Northern Ireland 379
Animal health: Zoonoses & animal by-products: Fees: Scotland. 331
Animal health: Zoonoses & animal by-products: Fees: Wales. 16, 17
Animal health: Zoonoses: Monitoring: Northern Ireland 379
Animal health: Zootechnical standards. 17
Animal welfare: Mutilations: Permitted procedures: Wales 17
Animals & animal products: Import & export 10
Animals & animal products: Import & export: Northern Ireland 378, 384
Animals & animal products: Import & export: Scotland 329
Animals: Cat & dog fur: Control of import, export & placing on the market 13, 49
Animals: Dangerous Wild Animals Act 1976: Modifications: Scotland 331
Animals: Diseases: Disinfectants: Approval: Northern Ireland 379
Animals: Diseases: Disinfectants: Approved: Scotland. 330
Animals: Products of animal origin: Disease control: England 14
Animals: Products of animal origin: Disease control: Scotland. 330
Animals: Products of animal origin: Third country imports: England 11
Animals: Scotland Act 1998: Agency arrangements: Specification 10, 13, 38, 45, 53, 143
Animals: Scrapie: Fees: Northern Ireland. 385
Animals: Welfare: Mutilations: Permitted procedures 15
Animals: Welfare: Slaughter or killing: Northern Ireland 379
Animals: Zootechnical standards: Northern Ireland. 378
Annuities: Purchased: Income tax. 102
Antarctic: Regulations 17
Anti-social behaviour orders: Magistrates' courts: Rules: Northern Ireland 395
Anti-Social behaviour: Criminal Justice & Immigration Act 2008: Commencements 17, 46, 47, 48, 49, 117, 140
Appointments Commission: National Health Service 123, 147, 254
Appropriation: Acts 4
Aquaculture & Fisheries (Scotland) Act 2007: Fixed penalty notices: Scotland 360
Architects: European qualifications: Recognition 17
Area support schemes: Less favoured: Agriculture: Scotland 328
Armed Forces Act 2006: Commencements. 51
Armed Forces: Compensation schemes 134, 135
Armed Forces: Criminal Procedure & Investigations Act 1996: Application 52
Armed Forces: Criminal Procedure & Investigations Act 1996: Code of practice. 52
Armed Forces: Discipline Act: Continuation. 51
Armed Forces: Entry, search & seizure. 51
Armed Forces: Gurkha pensions 135
Armed forces: Service Discipline Acts: Alignment 51
Armed Forces: Service inquiries 51
Armorial bearings, ensigns & flags: Lyon Court & Office: Fees: Variation. 17
Armorial bearings, ensigns & flags: Lyon Court & Office: Fees: Variation: Scotland. 331
Arms decommissioning: Amnesty period: Northern Ireland 133
Army Discipline Act: Continuation. 51
Army: Court-martial: Rules. 52
Army: Disablement & death: Service pensions 135
Army: Service complaints 51
Army: Service Discipline Acts: Alignment. 51
Army: Terms of service. 52
Arnot St Mary CE Primary School: Religious character: Designation. 56
Art & design: National curriculum: Attainment targets & programmes of study: Key stage 3: England 58

ASBOs: Magistrates' courts: Rules: Northern Ireland 395
Assembly learning grants & loans: Higher education: Wales 65
Assembly learning grants: European Institutions: Wales. 65
Assembly Ombudsman: Salaries: Northern Ireland. 405
Assets Recovery Agency: Abolition 146
Assistance by way of representation: Financial limit: District Court: Scotland 345
Asylum & Immigration Tribunal: Fast track procedures. 97
Asylum & Immigration Tribunal: Procedure. 97
Asylum: Immigration, Asylum & Nationality Act 2006: Commencements 98
Asylum: Immigration, Asylum & Nationality Act 2006: Data Sharing: Code of practice 98, 139, 154
Asylum: Immigration, Asylum & Nationality Act 2006: Information: Duty to share & disclosure for security purposes . . 98, 140, 154
Asylum: Immigration: Information supply: To Secretary of State, Home Office 99
Asylum: Immigration: Isle of Man 98
Asylum: Immigration: Police: Passenger, crew & service information. 98, 139
Asylum: Support 97
Atcham: Shrewsbury & Atcham: Parishes: Local government 113
Atomic energy & radioactive substances: Radioactive waste & spent fuel: Transfrontier shipments 18
Audit & accountability: Companies: Public sector audit: Northern Ireland 380
Audit & accountability: Public sector audit: Institutions of further education: Northern Ireland. 380
Auditors: Remuneration: Disclosure 35
Auditors: Statutory & third country 18, 36, 37
Auditors: Statutory: Delegation of functions 37
Authorised Investment Funds: Taxes 21, 40, 41, 99, 100, 264
Avian influenza: Amendments: Northern Ireland. 378
Avian influenza: Planning: Northern Ireland 398
Avian influenza: Town & country planning: General permitted development: Scotland. 364
Aviation: Civil: Air navigation 27
Aviation: Civil: Air navigation: Environmental standards: Non-EASA aircraft. 27
Aviation: Civil: Air navigation: Isle of Man 27
Aviation: Civil: Rules of the air 32
Awdurdod Gwasanaethau Busnes y GIG: NHS Business Services Authority: Counter fraud & security management: Delegation of functions 125

B

B2007 Vehicles: Accessibility: Exemptions 54, 272
Badges: Motor vehicles: Disabled persons: Northern Ireland. 403
Bail: Electronic monitoring: Responsible officers: England & Wales 46
Bail: Remand: Disapplication of credit period 47
Bank accounts: EC Directive 18
Banking: Special provisions: Acts 4
Bankruptcy & Diligence etc. (Scotland) Act 2007: Commencements: Scotland 331, 336, 337, 344
Bankruptcy (Scotland) Act 1985: Low income, low asset debtors etc.: Scotland 331
Bankruptcy & Diligence etc. (Scotland) Act 2007: Court of Session: Rules: Amendments: Act of Sederunt: Scotland. . . 334
Bankruptcy Rules: Sheriff Court: Act of Sederunt: Scotland 361
Bankruptcy: Fees: Scotland 344
Bankruptcy: Scotland 331
Bankruptcy: Trust deeds: Protected: Scotland 332
Banks & banking: Bank accounts: EC Directive 18
Banks & banking: Bradford & Bingley plc: Compensation scheme 18
Banks & banking: Bradford & Bingley plc: Transfer of securities & property 18
Banks & banking: Cash ratio deposits: Value bands & ratios 18
Banks & banking: Heritable Bank plc: Compensation: Determination 18
Banks & banking: Heritable Bank plc: Transfer of certain rights & liabilities. 18
Banks & banking: Kaupthing Singer & Friedlander Ltd.: Compensation: Determination. 18
Banks & banking: Kaupthing Singer & Friedlander Ltd.: Transfer of certain rights & liabilities 18
Banks & banking: Landsbanki: Freezing. 19
Banks & banking: Northern Rock plc: Compensation schemes 19
Banks & banking: Northern Rock plc: Transfer to public ownership 19
Banks & banking: Takeover code: Concert parties. 19
Banks & banking: Transfer of rights & liabilities: ING order 19
Banks: Dormant accounts: Acts 5
Barrow-in-Furness (Borough): Electoral changes. 110
Basingstoke & Deane (Borough): Electoral changes 110

Bathing water 277
Bathing water: Quality: Northern Ireland 384
Bathing water: Scotland 339, 365
Batteries & accumulators: Market: Placing: Environmental protection 70
Batteries: Pollution: Prevention & control: Directives: Designation: Scotland 339
Beam trawls & fishing gear (passive): Sea fishing: Marking & identification: Northern Ireland 387
Bede Sixth Form College, Billingham: Dissolution 56
Bedfordshire: Local government: Structural changes 110
Beef: Labelling: Declaration: Scotland 327, 340
Beef: Labelling: England 10
Beer: Excise 74
Bellefield Primary & Nursery School: Religious character: Designation 56
Bermuda: International tax: Enforcement 267
Berwick-upon-Tweed (Borough): Parish electoral arrangements & electoral changes: Local government 110
Berwick-upon-Tweed: Parishes: Local government 110
Best value performance indicators: Local government: Wales 115
Better off in Work Credit: Government pilot schemes: Taxation of benefits 102
Better regulation: Local Better Regulation Office: Establishment: Acts 7
Better regulation: Local Better Regulation Office: Establishment: Acts: Explanatory notes 8
Betting, gaming & lotteries: Casinos: Categories 19
Betting, gaming & lotteries: Gambling Act 2005: Commencements 19
Betting, gaming & lotteries: Gambling Act 2005: Foreign gambling: Advertising 19
Betting, gaming & lotteries: Gambling: Casinos: Premises licences: Geographical distribution 19
Betting, gaming & lotteries: Gambling: Casinos: Premises licences: Inviting competing applications 20
Betting, gaming & lotteries: Gambling: Operating licences & single-machine permit fees 20
Bioblend: Private pleasure-flying & craft: Payment of rebate 75
Biofuels & other fuel substitutes: Determination of composition of a substance 75
Biometric registration: Civil penalty: Code of practice: Immigration 98
Biometric registration: Immigration 98
Biometric registration: Pilot: Immigration 98
Bird flu *see* Avian influenza: Northern Ireland
Birds: Captive: Registration & ringing: England 278
Birds: Influenza see Avian influenza: Northern Ireland 378
Black Sluice Internal Drainage Board 106
Blood tests: Evidence: Paternity 74
Blood: Safety & quality 78, 87
Bluetongue: England 13
Bluetongue: Northern Ireland 378, 379
Bluetongue: Scotland 330
Bluetongue: Wales 15
Bonds: Regulated covered bonds 79, 80
Borders Sheriffdom: Justice of the peace courts: Scotland 345
Bovine semen: Wales 13
Bovines: Tuberculosis: Animal health: Testing & powers of entry: Wales 16
Bradford & Bingley plc: Compensation scheme 18
Bradford & Bingley: Transfer of securities & property 18
Bradford District Care Trust: National Health Service Trust 123
Bradford: Electoral changes: Local government 110
Bridge tolls: Abolition: Acts: Scotland 325
Bristol: North Bristol National Health Service Trust 127
British citizenship: Designated service 20
British nationality: British citizenship: Designated service 20
British overseas territories: Citizenship: Designated service 20
Bro Morgannwg National Health Service Trust: Dissolution: Wales 129
Bro Morgannwg National Health Service Trust: Transfer of Staff, property, rights & liabilities: Wales 129
Broadcasting: Digital Switchover (Disclosure of Information) Act 2007: Disclosure of information: Prescription of
information 20, 68
Broadcasting: S4C: Investment activities: Approval 20
Broadcasting: Television licensing 20, 68
Broadcasting: Television multiplex services: Digital capacity: Reservation 20
Broadcasting: Television multiplex services: Licences: Gaelic programming 20
Broadcasts: Educational recording: Copyright: Educational Recording Agency Limited: Licensing scheme: Certification . 40
Brucellosis 14
Buckinghamshire (County): Wycombe (District): Parking contraventions: Civil enforcement 241
Budget (Scotland) Act 2007: Amendments: Scotland 351

Budget (Scotland) Act 2008: Amendments: Scotland. 352
Budget: Acts: Explanatory notes: Northern Ireland. 374
Budget: Acts: Northern Ireland 373
Budget: Acts: Scotland 325
Budget: Northern Ireland: Acts 373
Budget: Northern Ireland: Acts: Explanatory notes. 374
Budgets: Schools: Shares: Prescribed purposes: Wales 67
Building & buildings: Amendments: Scotland 332
Building & buildings: Energy performance: Certificates & inspections: England & Wales. 20, 21
Building & buildings: Energy performance: Scotland 332
Building & buildings: Fees: Amendments: Scotland 332
Building regulations: Electronic communications: Building. 20
Building societies: Accounts & related provisions 21
Building societies: Accounts, audit & EEA state amendments. 21
Building societies: Dormant accounts: Acts 5
Building societies: Financial assistance 21
Building societies: Income tax: Interest payments 101
Building: Electronic communications 20
Building: England & Wales. 20
Buildings & land: Value added tax 275
Buildings: Energy performance: Certificates & inspections: European Communities: Northern Ireland 384
Buildings: Listed: Conservation areas: Planning: England 268
Burma: Export: Control. 49
Bus services: Community bus services 148
Bus travel: Concessionary bus travel: Permits 149
Business improvement districts: Scotland. 346
Business protection: From misleading marketing. 271
Business transfer schemes: Insurance: Corporation tax acts: Amendments 42

C

Caledonian Maritime Assets Limited (Largs): Harbour revision: Scotland. 342
Cambridgeshire & Peterborough Mental Health Partnership National Health Service Trust. 123
Cambridgeshire: South Cambridgeshire: Electoral changes: Local government 113
Canals & inland waterways: Transport & Works (Scotland) Act 2007: Access to land by the Scottish Ministers: Scotland 332, 365
Canals & inland waterways: Transport & Works (Scotland) Act 2007: Access to land on application: Scotland . . . 332, 365
Cannock Chase Technical College: Dissolution 62
Canon Peter Hall Church of England Primary School: Religious character: Designation 56
Canon Sharples Church of England Primary School & Nursery: Religious character: Designation. 56
Capital allowances: Energy-saving plant & machinery. 41, 100
Capital allowances: Environmentally beneficial plant & machinery 41, 100
Capital finance & accounting: Wales 115
Capital gains tax: Annual exempt amount 21
Capital gains tax: Authorised Investment Funds. 21, 40, 41, 99, 100, 264
Capital gains tax: Chargeable gains: Gilt-edged securities. 22, 43
Capital gains tax: Double taxation: Relief & international enforcement: Moldova. 21, 41, 100
Capital gains tax: Double taxation: Relief & international enforcement: New Zealand 21, 41, 100
Capital gains tax: Double taxation: Relief & international enforcement: Saudi Arabia 21, 41, 100
Capital gains tax: Double taxation: Relief & international enforcement: Slovenia. 21, 41, 100
Car fuel: Benefit. 100
Carbon emissions: Electricity & gas: Reduction 67, 86
Carbon emissions: Zero-carbon homes: Tax relief 264
Cardiothoracic Centre-Liverpool: National Health Service Trust. 123
Care quality commission: Membership. 123, 148, 254
Care Standards Tribunal: Children & vulnerable adults: Protection: England & Wales. 24
Care Tribunal: Regulations: Amendments: Northern Ireland. 390
Caribbean & north Atlantic territories: Cayman Islands: Constitution. 22
Carlingford & Foyle: Fisheries: 2007 Order: Commencements: Northern Ireland 387
Carlingford Area: Angling: Northern Ireland. 387
Carlingford Area: Salmon & Sea Trout: Caught by rod & line: Prohibition of sale: Northern Ireland. 387
Carmarthenshire National Health Service Trust: Dissolution: Wales. 129
Carmarthenshire National Health Service Trust: Transfer of Staff, property, rights & liabilities: Wales 129
Cars: Motor cars: Driving instruction 155
Case tribunals: England 110

Cash ratio deposits: Value bands & ratios 18
Casinos: Categories. 19
Casinos: Premises licences: Geographical distribution. 19
Casinos: Premises licences: Inviting competing applications 20
Cat & dog fur: Control of import, export & placing on the market 13, 49
Cayman Islands: Constitution. 22
Central institutions: Recognition: Education: Scotland 337
Central rating list: England 150
Central rating list: Wales 150
Ceredigion & Mid Wales National Health Service Trust: Dissolution: Wales 129
Ceredigion & Mid Wales National Health Service Trust: Transfer of Staff, property, rights & liabilities: Wales 129
Certification officer: Fees: Trade unions: Northern Ireland. 412
Chancellor of the Exchequer: Transfer of functions: To Secretary of State for the Home Department: Registration 123
Channel Tunnel Rail Link: Supplementary provisions: Acts 4
Channel Tunnel Rail Link: Supplementary provisions: Acts: Explanatory notes 7
Channel Tunnel: International arrangements 22
Channel Tunnel: Rail link: Nomination 272
Charities Act 2006: Commencements 22
Charities: Accounts & reports 22
Charities: Acts: Explanatory notes: Northern Ireland 374
Charities: Acts: Northern Ireland 373
Charities: Charitable companies audit & group accounts provisions: England & Wales 22
Charities: Charity test: Specified bodies: Scotland 332
Charities: Further & Higher Education (Scotland) Act 1992: Modification: Scotland 332
Charities: Protection of assets: Exemption: Scotland 332
Charities: References in documents: Scotland 332
Charities: Registration: Exceptions 22
Charities: Tribunal rules. 273
Charity: Prescribed: Legal Services Act 2007. 109
Chemicals: Dangerous chemicals: Export & import: Health & safety 88
Chemicals: Hazard information & packaging for supply. 87
Chemicals: Hazard information & packaging for supply: Northern Ireland 392
Cheshire (County): Chester (City): Ellesmere Port & Neston (Borough): Parking contraventions: Civil enforcement . . . 241
Cheshire (County): Macclesfield (Borough): Parking contraventions: Civil enforcement 241
Cheshire: Local government: Structural changes 110
Chester (City): Ellesmere Port & Neston (Borough): Cheshire (County): Parking contraventions: Civil enforcement . . . 241
Chicks: Marketing standards: England 81
Chicks: Northern Ireland 388
Child benefit: Disregard: Northern Ireland 393, 401, 408
Child benefit: Rates: Amendments 255
Child benefit: Rates: Commencements 258
Child benefits: Disregard 258
Child benefits: Up-rating 255
Child care providers: Tax credits: Approval 267
Child Maintenance & Enforcement Commission: Establishment: Acts. 4
Child Maintenance & Enforcement Commission: Establishment: Acts: Explanatory notes 7
Child Maintenance & Other Payments Act 2008: Commencements 76, 255
Child Maintenance Act 2008 Act: Commencements: Northern Ireland 385, 386
Child maintenance: Acts 4
Child maintenance: Acts: Explanatory notes 7
Child maintenance 258
Child maintenance: Northern Ireland 408
Child minders: Day care providers: Suspension: Wales 26, 255
Child Support, Pensions & Social Security Act 2000: Commencement 77
Child support, pensions & social security: 2000 Act: Commencement: Northern Ireland 380, 385
Child support: Acts 4
Child support: Acts: Explanatory notes 7
Child support: Acts: Explanatory notes: Northern Ireland 374
Child support: Acts: Northern Ireland 374
Child support: Amendments 260
Child support: Child Maintenance & Other Payments Act 2008: Commencements 76, 255
Child support: Commissioners: Procedures 77
Child support: Consequential provisions: Northern Ireland 380, 385
Child support: Family law 77
Child support: Family law: Consequential provisions 76, 77

Child support: Family law: Information 76
Child support: Family law: Information: Northern Ireland 380, 385
Child support: Northern Ireland. 386
Child support: Social security & child support: Decisions & appeals 77, 262
Child support: Social security: Northern Ireland 386
Child tax credit: Up-rating. 266
Childcare Act 2006: Commencements: England. 22
Childcare Act 2006: Commencements: Wales 26
Childcare Act 2006: Information: Provision 26
Childcare: Disqualification 22
Childcare: Early years & general childcare registers: Common provisions 23
Childcare: Early years register 23
Childcare: Fees: England 23
Childcare: General childcare register 23
Childcare: Income tax: Qualifying 102
Childcare: Information: Supply & disclosure. 23
Childcare: Inspections 23
Childcare: Registration: Exemptions 23
Childcare: Up-Front Childcare Fund: Government pilot schemes: Taxation of benefits 102
Childcare: Voluntary registration. 23
Childcare: Young children: Information provision: England. 23
Children & Adoption Act 2006: Commencements. 24, 25
Children & young persons: Acts 4
Children & young persons: Adoption & Children Act 2002: Commencements: Scotland 332
Children & young persons: Adoption & Children Act 2007: Commencements: Scotland 333
Children & young persons: Adoption: From abroad: Restrictions 24, 25
Children & young persons: Adoption: From abroad: Restrictions: Scotland 333
Children & young persons: Adoption: From Cambodia: Restrictions 25, 26
Children & young persons: Adoption: From Cambodia: Restrictions: Scotland 333
Children & young persons: Adoption: From Guatemala: Restrictions 25, 26
Children & young persons: Adoption: From Guatemala: Restrictions: Scotland 333
Children & young persons: Care: Acts: Explanatory notes 7
Children & young persons: Child maintenance: Acts: Explanatory notes: Northern Ireland. 374
Children & young persons: Child maintenance: Acts: Northern Ireland 374
Children & young persons: Childcare Act 2006: Commencements: England 22
Children & young persons: Childcare Act 2006: Commencements: Wales 26
Children & young persons: Childcare Act 2006: Information: Provision 26
Children & young persons: Childcare: Disqualification 22
Children & young persons: Childcare: Early years & general childcare registers: Common provisions 23
Children & young persons: Childcare: Early years register 23
Children & young persons: Childcare: Fees: England 23
Children & young persons: Childcare: General childcare register 23
Children & young persons: Childcare: Inspections. 23
Children & young persons: Childcare: Registration: Exemptions 23
Children & young persons: Childcare: Voluntary registration. 23
Children & young persons: Childcare: Young children: Information provision: England. 23
Children & young persons: Children Act 1989: Contact activity: Directions & conditions: Financial assistance. 23
Children & young persons: Children Act 2004: Commencements: England. 23
Children & young persons: Children Act 2004: Commencements: Wales. 26
Children & young persons: Day care providers & child minders: Suspension: Wales 26, 255
Children & young persons: Early Years Foundation Stage: Learning & development requirements 23
Children & young persons: Early Years Foundation Stage: Learning & development requirements: Exemptions 23
Children & young persons: Early Years Foundation Stage: Welfare requirements 24
Children & young persons: Education, Children's Services & Skills: Inspectors: Appointments: England. 24, 61
Children & young persons: Fostering services: England 24, 254
Children & young persons: Information: Supply & disclosure. 23
Children & young persons: Intensive support & monitoring: Scotland 333
Children & young persons: Local authorities: Early years provision: Free: Duty 24
Children & young persons: Magistrates' courts: Children Act 1989: Contact orders: Enforcement 117
Children & young persons: Protection of Children & Vulnerable Adults & Care Standards Tribunal: Children's & adults' barred lists. 25, 146
Children & young persons: Protection of Children (Scotland) Act 2003: Child care position: Definition: Amendments: Scotland 333
Children & young persons: Protection: Care Standards Tribunal: England & Wales 24
Children & young persons: Qualifications & Curriculum Authority: Additional functions 24, 62

Children & young persons: Safeguarding Vulnerable Groups Act 2006: Barred list prescribed information: England & Wales 25, 147
Children & young persons: Safeguarding Vulnerable Groups Act 2006: Barring procedure: England & Wales 25, 147
Children & young persons: Safeguarding Vulnerable Groups Act 2006: Commencements: England 24, 146
Children & young persons: Safeguarding Vulnerable Groups Act 2006: Commencements: England & Wales ... 25, 51, 147
Children & young persons: Safeguarding Vulnerable Groups Act 2006: Commencements: Northern Ireland 26, 147
Children & young persons: Safeguarding Vulnerable Groups Act 2006: Prescribed criteria: Foreign offices: England & Wales 25, 147
Children & young persons: Safeguarding Vulnerable Groups Act 2006: Prescribed criteria: Transitional provisions: England & Wales 25, 147
Children & young persons: Safeguarding Vulnerable Groups Act 2006: Prescribed information: England & Wales .. 25, 147
Children & young persons: Safeguarding Vulnerable Groups Act 2006: Transitional provisions: England & Wales .. 25, 147
Children & young persons: Tobacco: Sale: Northern Ireland 400
Children & young persons: Well-being: Local authorities: Targets 24
Children Act 1989: Contact activity: Directions & conditions: Financial assistance 23
Children Act 1989: Contact activity: Directions & conditions: Financial assistance: Wales 26
Children Act 1989: Contact orders: Enforcement: Magistrates' courts 117
Children Act 1989: Family proceedings courts: Amendments 117
Children Act 2004: Commencements: England 23
Children Act 2004: Commencements: Wales 26
Children: Caring: Disqualification: Wales 26, 254
Children: Criminal justice: Magistrates' courts: Rules: Northern Ireland 396
Children: Magistrates' courts: Northern Ireland 395
Children: Safeguarding Vulnerable Groups: 2007 Order: Commencements: Northern Ireland 404
Chiropractors: General Chiropractic Council: Constitution 89
Christ the King Catholic & Church of England (VA) Centre for Learning: Religious character: Designation 56
Christmas bonus: Relevant week: Northern Ireland 405
Christmas bonus: Specified sum 255
Christmas bonus: Specified sum: Northern Ireland 406
Chronological tables: Statutes 8
Church of England: General Synod: Measures 8
Church of England: General Synod: Measures: Bound volumes 9
Church of England: General Synod: Measures: Tables & index 9
CHURCH, Ian 9
Churches Conservation Trust: Grants to 55
Churches Conservation Trust: Payments 55
Cider: Excise 74
Cinema & films: Films: Co-Production agreements 27
Citizenship: National curriculum: Attainment targets & programmes of study: Key stage 3 & 4: England 58
Civil aviation: Aerodromes: Designation: Chargeable air services 27
Civil aviation: Air navigation 27
Civil aviation: Air navigation: Dangerous goods 27
Civil aviation: Air navigation: Environmental standards: Non-EASA aircraft 27
Civil aviation: Air navigation: Guernsey 27
Civil aviation: Air navigation: Isle of Man 27
Civil aviation: Air navigation: Jersey 27
Civil aviation: Air navigation: Overseas territories 27
Civil aviation: Airports: Economic regulation: Designation 32
Civil aviation: Flying restrictions 27, 28, 29, 30, 31, 32
Civil aviation: Overseas territories: Gibraltar 32
Civil aviation: Rules of the air 32
Civil Contingencies Act 2004: List of responders: Amendments 32
Civil enforcement officers: Wearing of uniforms: Wales 243
Civil enforcement: Parking contraventions: England 242
Civil legal aid: Financial conditions: Scotland 345
Civil legal aid: Scotland 345
Civil procedure: Rules: England & Wales 44, 265
Civil proceedings: Fees: England & Wales 44, 265
Civil recovery proceedings: Legal expenses:: Proceeds of Crime Act 2002 146
Civil Service: Government departments & solicitors: Authorised: Lists 8
Civil Service: Solicitors: Authorised: Lists 8
Cleadon Village Church of England VA Primary School: Religious character: Designation 56
Clean air: Smoke control areas: Authorised fuels: England 32
Clean air: Smoke control areas: Authorised fuels: Northern Ireland 380
Clean air: Smoke control areas: Authorised fuels: Scotland 333

Clean air: Smoke control areas: Authorised fuels: Wales 33
Clean air: Smoke control areas: Fireplaces: Exempt: England 33
Clean air: Smoke control areas: Fireplaces: Exempt: Northern Ireland 380
Clean air: Smoke control areas: Fireplaces: Exempt: Scotland 333
Clean air: Smoke control areas: Fireplaces: Exempt: Wales 33
Clean Neighbourhoods & Environment Act 2005: Commencements 72
Clerk of the Crown in Chancery: Crown Office: Fees 33
Climate Change & Sustainable Energy Act 2006: Energies & technologies: Sources 70
Climate change levy: Amusement machines: Licencing: Duties 10, 33, 74, 104, 106
Climate change levy: Value added tax: Correction of errors 10, 33, 76, 104, 106, 275
Climate change: Acts 4
Climate change: Acts: Explanatory notes 7
Clubs: Private clubs: Disabled persons: Discrimination: Northern Ireland 382
Coarse fishing: Byelaws: Conservation: Northern Ireland 387
Cold weather payments: Social fund 258
Cold weather payments: Social fund: Northern Ireland 407
Collective investment schemes: Financial Services & Markets Act 2000 79
Commission for Healthcare Audit and Inspection: Defence Medical Services 148
Commission for Victims & Survivors: Acts: Explanatory notes: Northern Ireland 374
Commission for Victims & Survivors: Acts: Northern Ireland 373
Commissioner for Complaints: Salaries: Northern Ireland 405
Commissioner for Older People in Wales 33
Common Agricultural Policy: Single payment & support schemes: Cross-compliance: England 10
Common Agricultural Policy: Single payment & support schemes: Cross-compliance: Northern Ireland . . . 375
Common Agricultural Policy: Single payment & support schemes: Cross-compliance: Scotland 327
Common Agricultural Policy: Single payment & support schemes: England 10
Common Agricultural Policy: Single payment & support schemes: Wales 12
Common land: Commons registration: England 34
Commonhold: Land registration: England & Wales 34
Commons Act 2006: Commencements 34
Commons registration: England 34
Commons Services Agency: National Health Service: Functions: Scotland 348
Commons: Dartmoor Commons: Authorised severance 34
Commonwealth Games: Glasgow: Acts: Explanatory notes: Scotland 325
Commonwealth Games: Glasgow: Acts: Scotland 325
Communications hereditaments: Valuation, alteration of lists & appeals & material day: Non-domestic rating: Wales . . 150
Communications: Television licensing 20, 68
Community bus services 148
Community care: Personal care & nursing care: Scotland 363
Community emissions trading scheme: Allocation of allowances for payment 72
Community investment: Tax relief: Community development finance institutions: Accreditation 41, 100
Community Legal Service: Financial: Amendments 108
Community Legal Service: Funding: Amendments 108
Community Legal Service: Funding: Amendments: England & Wales 108
Community Legal Service: Funding: Counsel: Family proceedings: England & Wales 109
Companies Act 1985: Annual return & Companies (Principal Business Activities) 34
Companies Act 2006: Accounts & reports: Amendments 34
Companies Act 2006: Annual return & service addresses 34
Companies Act 2006: Commencements 34
Companies Act 2006: Consequential amendments 35
Companies Act 2006: Consequential amendments: Taxes & national insurance 255, 267
Companies Act 2006: Public sector companies: Audited by the Auditor General for Scotland: Scotland 333
Companies Act 2006: Takeover panel provisions: Extension: Isle of Man 35
Companies: 1986 Order: Annual return: Northern Ireland 380
Companies: Accounting standards: Prescribed body 34
Companies: Accounts & reports: Supervision: Prescribed body 35
Companies: Annual return & service addresses 34
Companies: Auditor remuneration & liability limitation agreements: Disclosure 35
Companies: Authorised minimum 35
Companies: Capital: Reduction: Creditor protection 36
Companies: Charges: Particulars 36
Companies: Cross-border mergers 35
Companies: Defective accounts & directors' reports: Authorised person 35
Companies: Defective accounts & reports: Revision 36
Companies: European grouping of territorial co-operation 73

Companies: Forms ... 35
Companies: Insolvency ... 103
Companies: Insolvency: Rules ... 103
Companies: Insolvency: Scotland ... 104, 333, 344
Companies: Large & medium-sized companies & groups: Accounts & reports ... 36
Companies: Late filing penalties ... 35
Companies: Late filing penalties: Northern Ireland ... 380
Companies: Model articles ... 35
Companies: Names: Adjudicator ... 36
Companies: Principal business activities ... 34
Companies: Principal business activities: Northern Ireland ... 380
Companies: Public companies: Mergers & divisions ... 35
Companies: Public sector audit: Northern Ireland ... 380
Companies: Records ... 35
Companies: Records: Inspection: Fees ... 35
Companies: Registration ... 36
Companies: Share capital: Reduction ... 36
Companies: Small companies & groups: Accounts & Directors' reports ... 36
Companies: Summary financial statements ... 36
Companies: Tables A to F ... 36
Companies: Tables A to F: Northern Ireland ... 380
Companies: Trading disclosures ... 36
Companies: Trading disclosures: Insolvency ... 36
Companies: Welsh language forms ... 37
Compensation: Claims management services ... 40
Compensation: Consumers, Estate Agents & Redress Act 2007: Commencements ... 39, 73
Compensation: Home loss payments: Prescribed amounts: England ... 9, 37
Competition Act 1998: Public policy exclusions ... 37
Competition: Enterprise Act 2002: Section 58: Specification of additional consideration ... 37
Competition: Enterprise Act 2002: Super-complaints: Designated bodies ... 37, 39
Concessionary bus travel: Permits ... 149
Congo (Democratic Republic): Export: Control ... 49, 50
Conservation areas: Listed buildings: Planning: England ... 268
Conservation: Natural habitats: England & Wales ... 44, 278
Conservation: Natural habitats: Scotland ... 334, 366
Conservation: Scallops: Northern Ireland ... 405
Consolidated Fund: Acts ... 4
Constables: Special constables: Scotland ... 351
Constitutional law: Housing (Scotland) Act 2006: Consequential provisions ... 37, 52, 94
Constitutional law: National Assembly for Wales: Legislative competence: Education & training ... 37, 53
Constitutional law: National Assembly for Wales: Legislative competence: Social welfare ... 37, 38, 53
Constitutional law: National Assembly for Wales: Legislative competence: Social welfare: Wales ... 38, 53
Constitutional law: Scotland Act 1998: Agency arrangements: Specification ... 10, 13, 38, 45, 53, 143
Constitutional law: Scotland Act 1998: Transfer of functions ... 38, 53, 71
Constitutional law: Scottish Parliament: Elections ... 38, 53
Constitutional law: Welsh Ministers: Transfer of functions: Wales ... 38, 53
Constitutional Reform Act 2005: Commencements ... 106
Construction industry scheme: Income tax: Amendments ... 101
Construction Industry Training Board: Industrial training levy ... 70
Construction industry: Industrial training levy: Northern Ireland ... 394
Consular fees ... 53
Consumer Credit Act 2006: Commencements ... 38
Consumer credit: Exempt agreements ... 38
Consumer credit: Information requirements Licenses & charges: Duration ... 38
Consumer credit: Legislative reform ... 152
Consumer protection: Compensation: Claims management services ... 40
Consumer protection: Contracts: Made in consumer's home or place of work: Cancellation ... 38
Consumer protection: Cosmetic products: Safety ... 39
Consumer protection: Enterprise Act 2002: Super-complaints: Designated bodies ... 37, 39
Consumer protection: From unfair trading ... 39
Consumer protection: Gas & electricity: Regulated providers: Redress schemes ... 39, 68, 86
Consumer protection: Magnetic toys: Safety ... 39
Consumer protection: Medical devices ... 40
Consumer protection: Medicines: Human use: Fees ... 40, 78, 119
Consumer protection: Postal services: Regulated providers: Redress schemes ... 40, 143

Consumer protection: REACH: Enforcement 40, 71, 88
Consumers, Estate Agents & Redress Act 2007: Commencements 39, 73
Contaminated land: Radioactive contaminated land: Enactments: Modification: England 72
Contaminated land: Radioactive contaminated land: Enactments: Modification: Wales 73
Contracting out: Court staff: Contracting out. 40, 44, 117, 120, 265
Contracts: Made in consumer's home or place of work: Cancellation 38
Controlled drugs: Management & use: Supervision: Wales 51
Conwy & Denbighshire National Health Service Trust: Dissolution: Wales 129
Conwy & Denbighshire National Health Service Trust: Transfer of Staff, property, rights & liabilities: Wales 129
Copyright & performances: Application to other countries. 40, 154
Copyright: Broadcasts: Educational recording: Educational Recording Agency Limited: Licensing scheme: Certification . 40
Cornwall (County): Parking contraventions: Civil enforcement 241
Cornwall Partnership National Health Service Trust 124
Cornwall: Local government: Structural changes. 111
Coroners: Practice & procedure: Northern Ireland 380
Coroners: Rules. 40
Corporate Manslaughter & Corporate Homicide Act 2007: Commencements. 45
Corporate Manslaughter & Corporate Homicide Act 2007: Schedule 1: Amendments 45
Corporation tax *see also* taxes
Corporation tax: Acts: Amendments: Insurance business transfer schemes 42
Corporation tax: Acts: Modification: Friendly societies 42
Corporation tax: Acts: Modification: Friendly societies: Transfers of other business 42
Corporation tax: Authorised Investment Funds 21, 40, 41, 99, 100, 264
Corporation tax: Capital allowances: Energy-saving plant & machinery. 41, 100
Corporation tax: Capital allowances: Environmentally beneficial plant & machinery 41, 100
Corporation tax: Chargeable gains: Gilt-edged securities 22, 43
Corporation tax: Community investment: Tax relief: Community development finance institutions: Accreditation . . 41, 100
Corporation tax: Double taxation: Relief & international enforcement: Moldova 21, 41, 100
Corporation tax: Double taxation: Relief & international enforcement: New Zealand 21, 41, 100
Corporation tax: Double taxation: Relief & international enforcement: Saudi Arabia 21, 41, 100
Corporation tax: Double taxation: Relief & international enforcement: Slovenia 21, 41, 100
Corporation tax: Energy-saving items 41
Corporation tax: European single currency: Taxes. 41
Corporation tax: Finance Act 2007: Schedule 9 41
Corporation tax: Finance Act 2007: Section 17 (2): Energy-saving items: Deduction: Appointed day 42
Corporation tax: Finance Act 2008: Section 26: Appointed day 42
Corporation tax: Finance Act 2008: Section 27: Appointed day 42
Corporation tax: Finance Act 2008: Section 28: Appointed day 42
Corporation tax: Finance Act 2008: Section 29: Appointed day 42
Corporation tax: Finance Act 2008: Section 30: Appointed day 42
Corporation tax: Instalment payments 41
Corporation tax: Insurance companies: Amendments 42, 43
Corporation tax: Insurance companies: Overseas life assurance business: Compliance 43
Corporation tax: Insurance companies: Overseas life assurance business: Excluded business 43
Corporation tax: Insurance companies: Reinsurance business 43
Corporation tax: Insurance companies: Reserves. 43
Corporation tax: Insurance companies: Taxation: Special purpose vehicles 43
Corporation tax: Insurance: Financing-arrangement-funded transfers to shareholders 42
Corporation tax: Insurance: Non-resident companies: General insurance business 43
Corporation tax: Loan relationships & derivative contracts: Accounting practice: Changes 43
Corporation tax: Mergers Directive: Implementation 41
Corporation tax: Non-resident insurance companies: Overseas losses: Group relief: Corporation Tax Acts: Modification . 42
Corporation tax: Overseas life insurance companies 43
Cosmetic products: Safety 39
Cotswold: Parishes: Local government 111
Council for Healthcare Regulatory Excellence: Appointment procedure 88
Council tax benefit: Amendments 257, 260, 261
Council tax benefit: Housing benefit: Extended payments 257
Council tax: Electronic communications: England. 44
Council tax: Limitation: Maximum amounts. 44
Council tax: Non-domestic rating: Demand notices: England 43, 150
Council tax: Valuations, alteration of lists & appeals: England 44
Counter-Terrorism Act 2008: Commencements 143
Counter-Terrorism Act 2008: Court of Session: Rules: Act of Sederunt: Scotland. 334
Counter-terrorism: Acts 5

Counter-terrorism: Acts: Explanatory notes...7
Countryside & Rights of Way Act 2000: Commencements...44
Countryside: Birds: Captive: Registration & ringing: England..278
Countryside: Conservation: Natural habitats: England & Wales..44, 278
Countryside: Conservation: Natural habitats: Scotland...334, 366
Countryside: Management: Northern Ireland...375
Countryside: National scenic areas: Scotland...334
Countryside: Wildlife & Countryside Act 1981: Schedule 5: Variation: Wales..........................278
County courts: Civil procedure rules: England & Wales..44, 265
County courts: Civil procedure: Rules: England & Wales..44, 265
County courts: Civil proceedings: Fees: England & Wales...44, 265
County courts: Family proceedings..44, 45, 77, 265
County courts: Family proceedings: Fees: England & Wales.......................................45, 77, 78, 266
County courts: Family proceedings: Rules: Northern Ireland.......................................381, 386, 411
County courts: Jurisdiction: England & Wales...45, 266
County courts: Rules: Northern Ireland...381
County courts: Staff: Contracting out...40, 44, 117, 120, 265
Court funds: Rules: Northern Ireland..394
Court of Session: Fees: Scotland...335
Court of Session: Judicial review applications: Transfers: Act of Sederunt: Scotland................334
Court of Session: Messengers-at-Arms: Fees: Act of Sederunt: Scotland..................................334
Court of Session: Messengers-at-Arms: Fees: EC service regulation: Act of Sederunt: Scotland...334
Court of Session: Rules: Amendments: Bankruptcy and Diligence etc. (Scotland) Act 2007: Act of Sederunt: Scotland..334
Court of Session: Rules: Counter-Terrorism Act 2008: Act of Sederunt: Scotland......................334
Court of Session: Rules: Miscellaneous: Act of Sederunt: Scotland..334
Court of Session: Rules: Solicitors: Fees: Act of Sederunt: Scotland..334
Court of Session: Shorthand writers: Fees: Act of Sederunt: Scotland......................................334
Court-martial: Royal Navy, Army & Royal Air Force: Rules..52
Courts & Legal Services Act 1990: Licensed conveyancers: Modification of power to make rules about: England & Wales
....109
Courts: County courts: Civil proceedings: Fees: England & Wales.......................................44, 265
Courts: County courts: Family proceedings: Fees: England & Wales...............................45, 77, 78, 266
Courts: Judiciary: Acts: Explanatory notes: Scotland...325
Courts: Judiciary: Acts: Scotland...325
Crabs & lobsters: Unlicensed fishing: Northern Ireland...405
Cremation: England & Wales..45
Crime & Disorder Act 1998: Additional authorities..46
Crime & Disorder Act 1998: Responsible authorities: England & Wales....................................46
Crime & disorder: Prescribed information: England & Wales..46
Crime (International Co-operation) Act 2003: Commencements...45, 154
Crime (International Co-operation) Act 2003: Participating countries: Designation.................46, 47
Crime (International Co-operation) Act 2003: Participating countries: Designation: United States: Scotland.........335
Crime: Prisoners: Fixed-term: Eligibility period: Amendment..144
Crime: Prisoners: Short-term & long-term: Requisite period: Amendment...............................144
Crime: Proceeds of Crime Act 2002: Investigations: United Kingdom......................................145
Crime: Proceeds of Crime Act 2002: Prosecutors: Investigative powers: Code of Practice: England, Wales & Northern
Ireland..146
Crime: Proceeds of crime: Assets Recovery Agency: Abolition..146
Crime: Serious Crime Act 2007: Commencements...54, 105, 142, 145, 147, 154, 253
Crime: Serious Crime Act 2007: Commencements: Scotland...351
Crime: Serious Crime Act 2007: Section 24: Appeals..253
Criminal appeals: Offenders assisting investigations & prosecutions: Supreme Court, Northern Ireland: Northern Ireland 412
Criminal cases: Costs: England & Wales..46
Criminal Defence Service: Defence costs orders: Recovery..108
Criminal Defence Service: Financial eligibility..108
Criminal Defence Service: Funding: England & Wales..108
Criminal Defence Service: General..108
Criminal Defence Service: High cost cases: England & Wales..108
Criminal evidence: Witness anonymity: Acts..5
Criminal evidence: Witness anonymity: Acts: Explanatory notes...7
Criminal Justice & Immigration Act 2008: Commencements............17, 46, 47, 48, 49, 109, 117, 140, 144, 152
Criminal Justice & Immigration Act 2008: Transitory provisions......................................47, 48, 144
Criminal Justice (Northern Ireland) Order 2004: Commencements: Northern Ireland...............381
Criminal Justice (Northern Ireland) Order 2008: Commencements: Northern Ireland...............381
Criminal Justice (Northern Ireland) Order 2008: Seized motor vehicles: Retention & disposal: Northern Ireland.....381

Criminal Justice Act 1988: Offensive weapons ... 46, 47
Criminal Justice Act 2003: Commencements ... 46
Criminal Justice Act 2003: Commencements: Northern Ireland ... 48
Criminal justice: Acts ... 5
Criminal justice: Acts: Explanatory notes ... 7
Criminal justice: Children: Magistrates' courts: Rules: Northern Ireland ... 396
Criminal justice: Juvenile justice centres: Rules: Northern Ireland ... 381
Criminal justice: Northern Ireland ... 133
Criminal justice: Sentencing: Curfew conditions ... 47
Criminal law: Bail: Bail: Electronic monitoring: Responsible officers: England & Wales ... 46
Criminal law: Bail: Remand: Disapplication of credit period ... 47
Criminal law: Corporate Manslaughter & Corporate Homicide Act 2007: Commencements ... 45
Criminal law: Corporate Manslaughter & Corporate Homicide Act 2007: Schedule 1: Amendments ... 45
Criminal law: Crime & Disorder Act 1998: Additional authorities ... 46
Criminal law: Crime & Disorder Act 1998: Responsible authorities: England & Wales ... 46
Criminal law: Crime & disorder: Prescribed information: England & Wales ... 46
Criminal law: Crime (International Co-operation) Act 2003: Commencements ... 45, 154
Criminal law: Crime (International Co-operation) Act 2003: Participating countries: Designation ... 46, 47
Criminal law: Crime (International Co-operation) Act 2003: Participating countries: Designation: United States: Scotland 335
Criminal law: Criminal cases: Costs: England & Wales ... 46
Criminal law: Criminal Justice & Immigration Act 2008: Commencements ... 17, 46, 47, 48, 49, 109, 117, 140, 144, 152
Criminal law: Criminal Justice & Immigration Act 2008: Transitory provisions ... 47, 48, 144
Criminal law: Criminal Justice (Northern Ireland) Order 2004: Commencements: Northern Ireland ... 381
Criminal law: Criminal Justice (Northern Ireland) Order 2008: Commencements: Northern Ireland ... 381
Criminal law: Criminal Justice (Northern Ireland) Order 2008: Seized motor vehicles: Retention & disposal: Northern Ireland ... 381
Criminal law: Criminal Justice Act 1988: Offensive weapons ... 46, 47
Criminal law: Criminal Justice Act 2003: Commencements ... 46
Criminal law: Criminal Justice Act 2003: Commencements: Northern Ireland ... 48
Criminal law: Criminal justice: Northern Ireland ... 133
Criminal law: Criminal justice: Sentencing: Curfew conditions ... 47
Criminal law: Criminal Procedure & Investigations Act 1996: Code of practice: Armed Forces ... 52
Criminal law: Criminal Procedure (Scotland) Act 1995: Compensation offer: Maximum amount: Scotland ... 335
Criminal law: Criminal Procedure (Scotland) Act 1995: Fixed penalties: Scotland ... 335
Criminal law: Criminal Proceedings etc. (Reform) (Scotland) Act 2007: Commencements: Scotland ... 335
Criminal law: Criminal Proceedings etc. (Reform) (Scotland) Act 2007: Supplemental provisions: Scotland ... 335
Criminal law: Disorderly behaviour: Penalties: Amount: England & Wales ... 47, 140
Criminal law: Domestic Violence, Crime & Victims Act 2004: Commencements: Northern Ireland ... 48
Criminal law: Emergency Workers (Scotland) Act 2005: Modification: Scotland ... 335
Criminal law: Fines: Discharge: Unpaid work: Pilot scheme ... 47
Criminal law: Fines: Enforcement: Diligence: Scotland ... 335
Criminal law: Fines: Enforcement: Seizure & disposal of vehicles: Scotland ... 335
Criminal law: Home Detention Curfew Licence: Prescribed specified conditions: Scotland ... 335, 336
Criminal law: Justice of the Peace courts: Sheriffdom of Glasgow & Strathkelvin: Scotland ... 344
Criminal law: Justice of the Peace courts: Sheriffdom of Highland & Islands: Scotland ... 345
Criminal law: Justice of the Peace courts: Sheriffdom of Tayside, Central & Fife: Scotland ... 345
Criminal law: Liberty: Restriction: Scotland ... 336
Criminal law: Management of Offenders etc. (Scotland) Act 2005: Commencements: Scotland ... 336
Criminal law: Management of Offenders etc. (Scotland) Act 2005: Members' remuneration & supplementary provisions: Scotland ... 336
Criminal law: Offenders: Assisting investigations & prosecutions: Substituted sentences: Scotland ... 336
Criminal law: Police & Justice Act 2006: Commencements ... 141
Criminal law: Police Act 1997: Commencements: Northern Ireland ... 48
Criminal law: Police Act 1997: Criminal records: Disclosure: Northern Ireland ... 48
Criminal law: Serious Crime Act 2007: Commencements ... 47, 48, 55
Criminal law: Serious Organised Crime & Police Act 2005: Commencements: Northern Ireland ... 48
Criminal law: Sexual Offences Act 2003: Prescribed police stations: Scotland ... 336
Criminal law: Sexual offences: 2008 Order: Commencements: Northern Ireland ... 381
Criminal law: Sheriffdom of Glasgow & Strathkelvin: Scotland ... 336
Criminal law: Victim notification scheme: Scotland ... 336
Criminal law: Violent Crime Reduction Act 2006: Commencements ... 47, 48
Criminal law: Youth Justice Board for England & Wales ... 47
Criminal legal assistance: Fees & information: Scotland ... 345
Criminal Procedure (Scotland) Act 1995: Compensation offer: Maximum amount: Scotland ... 335

Criminal Procedure (Scotland) Act 1995: Fixed penalties: Scotland 335
Criminal Procedure & Investigations Act 1996: Application: Armed Forces 52
Criminal procedure rules: Amendments: Act of Adjournal: Scotland. 344, 361
Criminal procedure rules: Amendments: Criminal Proceedings etc. (Reform) (Scotland) Act 2007: Act of Adjournal: Scotland. 342, 344, 361
Criminal procedure: Criminal Justice & Immigration Act 2008: Commencements 17, 46, 48, 49, 109, 117, 140, 144
Criminal procedure: Rules: England & Wales. 117, 265
Criminal Proceedings etc. (Reform) (Scotland) Act 2007: Commencements: Scotland 335
Criminal Proceedings etc. (Reform) (Scotland) Act 2007: Criminal procedure rules: Amendments: Act of Adjournal: Scotland. 342, 344, 361
Criminal Proceedings etc. (Reform) (Scotland) Act 2007: Supplemental provisions: Scotland 335
Criminal proceedings: Costs: Legal aid & advice: Northern Ireland 395
Criminal records: Police Act 1997: Scotland 351
Crofters, cottars & small landholders: Crofting counties: Agricultural grants scheme: Scotland 336
Crofting counties: Agricultural grants scheme: Scotland 336
Crops, food & feeding stuffs: Pesticides: Maximum residue levels: England & Wales 12, 138
Crops, food & feeding stuffs: Pesticides: Maximum residue levels: Northern Ireland 378
Crops, food & feeding stuffs: Pesticides: Maximum residue levels: Scotland 328, 350
Crops: Seed potatoes: Crop fees: Northern Ireland 405
Cross-border railway services: Working time. 272
Cross-border railway services: Working time: Northern Ireland 412
Crossrail: Acts 5
Crossrail: Acts: Explanatory notes. 7
Crossrail: Nomination 272
Crossrail: Planning approval: Planning appeals: Written representations procedure 268
Crossrail: Planning approval: Request fees 268
Crossrail: Qualifying authorities 269
Crown Agents Holding & Realisation Board: Property, rights, liabilities & obligations: Transfer: Prescribed day 105
Crown Court: Rules: Northern Ireland. 400, 412
Crown Office: Fees. 33
Crown Proceedings Act 1947: Government departments & solicitors: Authorised: Lists. 8
Cultural objects: On loan: Protection: Information: Publication & provision 49
Cultural objects: Tribunals, Courts & Enforcement Act 2007: Commencements: Scotland 336
Cultural objects: Tribunals, Courts & Enforcement Act 2007: Commencements: Wales & Northern Ireland 49
Cumbria: North Cumbria Acute Hospitals: National Health Service Trust 127
Currency: European single: Taxes 41
Curriculum: National: Attainment targets & programmes of study: Art & design: Key stage 3: England 58
Curriculum: National: Attainment targets & programmes of study: Citizenship: Key stage 3 & 4: England 58
Curriculum: National: Attainment targets & programmes of study: Design & technology: Key stage 3: England 58
Curriculum: National: Attainment targets & programmes of study: English: Key stage 3 & 4: England 58
Curriculum: National: Attainment targets & programmes of study: Geography: Key stage 3: England. 58
Curriculum: National: Attainment targets & programmes of study: History: Key stage 3: England 58
Curriculum: National: Attainment targets & programmes of study: Information & communication technology: Key stage 3 & 4: England. 59
Curriculum: National: Attainment targets & programmes of study: Mathematics: Key stage 3 & 4: England 59
Curriculum: National: Attainment targets & programmes of study: Modern foreign languages: Key stage 3: England . . . 58
Curriculum: National: Attainment targets & programmes of study: Music: Key stage 3: England 58
Curriculum: National: Attainment targets & programmes of study: Physical education: Key stage 3 & 4: England 59
Curriculum: National: Attainment targets & programmes of study: Science: Key stage 3: England 58
Curriculum: National: Key stage 3: Assessment arrangements: England 59
Curriculum: National: Modern foreign languages: England 59
Curriculum: Wales 67
Customs & excise duties: Travellers' allowances. 76, 275
Customs & excise: Export: Control: Congo (Democratic Republic). 49, 50
Customs & excise: Trade: Statistics. 265
Customs: Cat & dog fur: Control of import, export & placing on the market 13, 49
Customs: Export of goods, technology transfer & technical assistance provision: Control 50
Customs: Export: Control. 50
Customs: Export: Control: Burma 49
Customs: Export: Control: Iran 49
Customs: Security & para-military goods 50
Customs: Trade: Goods: Control 50
Cwm Taf National Health Service Trust: Establishment: Wales 129
Cycletrack/footway: Llandarcy, Neath Port Talbot 251

D

Dairy produce: Quotas: England 81
Dairy produce: Quotas: General provisions 80
Dairy produce: Quotas: Northern Ireland 387
Dairy produce: Quotas: Wales 83
Dangerous chemicals: Export & import: Health & safety 88
Dangerous drugs: Controlled drugs: Management & use: Supervision: Wales 51
Dangerous drugs: Controlled drugs: Precursors: Community external trade. 50
Dangerous drugs: Controlled drugs: Precursors: Intra-community trade. 51
Dangerous drugs: Misuse of Drugs Act 1971: Amendment 51
Dangerous goods: Air navigation. 27
Dangerous Wild Animals Act 1976: Modifications: Scotland 331
Dartford - Thurrock Crossing charging scheme: A282. 91
Dartford - Thurrock Crossing: Amendments 92
Dartmoor Commons: Authorised severance 34
Dartmouth-Kingswear Floating Bridge: Vehicle classifications & revision of charges 92
Data Protection Act 1998: Commencements 51
Data protection: Safeguarding Vulnerable Groups Act 2006: Commencements: England 24, 146
Data protection: Safeguarding Vulnerable Groups Act 2006: Commencements: England & Wales 25, 51, 147
Data sharing: Code of practice: Immigration, Asylum & Nationality Act 2006. . . . . 98, 139, 154
Daventry: Parishes: Local government 111
Day care food scheme: Healthy start scheme: Northern Ireland 388
Day care providers & child minders: Suspension: Wales 26, 255
Deane: Basingstoke & Deane (Borough): Electoral changes 110
Deaths: Register: Supply of information: England & Wales 142, 152
Deaths: Register: Supply of information: Northern Ireland 142, 152
Dee Estuary Cockle Fishery: England. 252
Defence Aviation Repair Agency Trading Fund 86
Defence Aviation Repair Agency Trading Fund: Revocation 87
Defence costs orders: Recovery: Criminal Defence Service 108
Defence Medical Services: Commission for Healthcare Audit and Inspection 148
Defence Support Group Trading Fund 87
Defence: Armed Forces Act 2006: Commencements 51
Defence: Armed Forces, Army, Air Force & Naval Discipline Acts: Continuation 51
Defence: Armed Forces: Service Discipline Acts: Alignment 51
Defence: Armed Forces: Service inquiries 51
Defence: Armed Forces: Terms of service 52
Defence: Courts-martial: Royal Navy, Army & Royal Air Force: Rules 52
Defence: Criminal Procedure & Investigations Act 1996: Application: Armed Forces 52
Defence: Criminal Procedure & Investigations Act 1996: Code of practice: Armed Forces 52
Defence: Naval Medical Compassionate Fund 52
Defence: Protection of Military Remains Act 1986: Vessels & controlled sites: Designations 52
Defence: Royal Air Force: Air Force Act 1955: Part 1: Amendments 51
Defence: Serious Organised Crime & Police Act 2005: Commencements 52
Defence: Service complaints 51
Defence: Visiting forces 52
Denbighshire & Conwy: National Health Service Trust: Dissolution: Wales 129
Denbighshire & Conwy: National Health Service Trust: Transfer of Staff, property, rights & liabilities: Wales 129
Dental charges: National Health Service 125
Dental services: General: Northern Ireland 390
Dentistry: Complementary professions: General Dental Council: Continuing Professional Development 89, 146
Dentistry: Private: Wales 148
Dentists: General Dental Council: Constitution: Amendments 89, 90
Dentists: General Dental Council: Continuing Professional Development 52, 88
Departments: Transfer of functions: Northern Ireland 396
Dependants: Maintenance orders: Reciprocal enforcement: Reciprocating countries: Designation 117
Dependent territories: United Nations: Arms embargoes 275
Derwen: Pembrokeshire & Derwen National Health Service Trust: Transfer of Staff, property, rights & liabilities: Wales 131
Derwentside: Parish electoral arrangements: Local government 111
Design & technology: National curriculum: Attainment targets & programmes of study: Key stage 3: England 58
Design right: Semiconductor topographies 52
Devolution, Scotland: Housing (Scotland) Act 2006: Consequential provisions 37, 52, 94
Devolution, Scotland: Scotland Act 1998: Agency arrangements: Specification 10, 13, 38, 45, 53, 143
Devolution, Scotland: Scottish Parliament: Elections 38, 53

Devolution, Wales: National Assembly for Wales: Legislative competence: Education & training. 37, 53
Devolution, Wales: National Assembly for Wales: Legislative competence: Social welfare 37, 38, 53
Devolution, Wales: National Assembly for Wales: Legislative competence: Social welfare: Wales 38, 53
Devolution, Wales: Welsh Ministers: Transfer of functions: Wales. 38, 53
Devolution: Scotland Act 1998: Transfer of functions 38, 53, 71
Devon (County): Parking contraventions: Civil enforcement. 241
Devon: East Devon College, Tiverton: Dissolution 57
Devon: South Devon Healthcare NHS Foundation Trust 127
Dewsbury College: Dissolution. 56
Digital capacity: Reservation: Television multiplex services 20
Digital Switchover (Disclosure of Information) Act 2007: Disclosure of information: Prescription of information . . . 20, 68
Diocese of Carlisle: Educational endowments 57
Diocese of Chelmsford: Educational endowments 57
Diocese of Chester: Educational endowments 57
Diocese of Coventry: Educational endowments 57
Diocese of Lichfield: Educational endowments 57
Diplomatic Service: Consular fees 53
Disability Discrimination Act 1995: Commencements: Northern Ireland 381
Disability Discrimination Code of Practice: Trade organisations, qualifications bodies & general qualifications bodies:
Commencement. 54
Disability Discrimination Code of Practice: Trade organisations, qualifications bodies: Revocation 53
Disability discrimination *see also* Disabled persons: Northern Ireland
Disability discrimination: General qualification bodies: Relevant qualifications, reasonable steps & physical features . . . 54
Disability discrimination: Public authorities: Statutory duties 54
Disability: Definition: Guidance: Northern Ireland 381, 382
Disability: General qualifications bodies: Relevant qualifications, reasonable steps & physical features: Northern Ireland 382
Disabled facilities: Housing: Grants: Maximum amounts & additional purposes: England 94
Disabled facilities: Housing: Grants: Maximum amounts & additional purposes: Wales 96
Disabled persons: Definition: Guidance: Northern Ireland 381, 382
Disabled persons: Disability Discrimination Act 1995: Commencements: Northern Ireland 381
Disabled persons: Disability Discrimination Code of Practice: Trade organisations, qualifications bodies & general
qualifications bodies: Commencement 54
Disabled persons: Disability Discrimination Code of Practice: Trade organisations, qualifications bodies: Revocation . . . 53
Disabled persons: Disability discrimination: General qualification bodies: Relevant qualifications, reasonable steps &
physical features 54
Disabled persons: Disability discrimination: Public authorities: Statutory duties 54
Disabled persons: Discrimination: Private clubs: Northern Ireland. 382
Disabled persons: Discrimination: Private hire vehicles: Carrying of guide dogs, etc.: Northern Ireland 382
Disabled persons: Motor vehicles: Badges: Northern Ireland. 403
Disabled persons: Public service vehicles: Accessibility 54
Disabled persons: Rail vehicles: Accessiblity: B2007 Vehicles: Accessibility: Exemptions. 54, 272
Disabled persons: Rail vehicles: Accessibility: Exemption orders: Parliamentary procedures 54
Disabled persons: Rail vehicles: Accessibility: Interoperable rail system 54, 272
Disabled persons: Rail vehicles: Accessibility: London Underground Victoria Line 09TS vehicles: Exemptions . . . 54, 272
Disablement & death: Navy, Army & Air Force: Service pensions 135
Disaster or emergency: Finance Act 2008: Section 135 154
Disclosure of information: Revenue & Customs: Serious Crime Act 2007. 54, 154
Disclosure of information: Serious Crime Act 2007: Anti-fraud organisations 55
Disclosure of information: Serious Crime Act 2007: Commencements. 47, 48, 54, 55, 105, 145, 147, 154, 253
Disclosure of information: Statistics & Registration Service Act 2007: Commencements 54, 134, 151, 264
Disclosure of information: Statistics & Registration Service Act 2007: Delegation of functions: Economic statistics . 54, 264
Discretionary financial assistance: Social security 255
Discretionary financial assistance: Social security: Northern Ireland. 406
Discrimination: Age: Employment & training 70
Discrimination: Disability Discrimination Act 1995: Commencements: Northern Ireland. 381
Discrimination: Disability Discrimination Code of Practice: Trade organisations, qualifications bodies & general
qualifications bodies: Commencement 54
Discrimination: Disability Discrimination Code of Practice: Trade organisations, qualifications bodies: Revocation 53
Discrimination: Disability discrimination: Private clubs: Northern Ireland 382
Discrimination: Disability discrimination: Private hire vehicles: Carrying of guide dogs, etc.: Northern Ireland 382
Discrimination: Disability: General qualification bodies: Relevant qualifications, reasonable steps & physical features . . 54
Disease control: Animal health: England. 14
Disease control: Animal health: Wales. 15
Disorderly behaviour: Penalties: Amount: England & Wales. 47, 140
Divorce etc.: Pensions: Scotland 339

Doctors: General Medical Council: Constitution..90
Doctors: General Medical Council: Fitness to practice: Standard of proof: Amendments..................90
Doctors: Medical Act 1983: Qualifying examinations....................................90
Doctors: Postgraduate Medical Education & Training Board: Fees: Rules..................90
Dog & cat fur: Control of import, export & placing on the market..........................13, 49
Domestic fuel or power: Supplies: Reduced rate: Value added tax..........................276
Domestic Violence, Crime & Victims Act 2004: Commencements: Northern Ireland..........................48
Donaghadee harbour area: Northern Ireland..........................390
Donaghee harbour area: Northern Ireland..........................390
Dormant accounts: Banks & building societies: Acts..........................5
Dorset: National Health Service Primary Care Trust..........................124
Double taxation: Relief: Relievable tax: Within a group: Surrender..........................100
Driver licensing: Fees..........................78
Drivers: Passenger & goods vehicles: Drivers: Training: Certificates of professional competence..........................157
Drivers: Vehicle drivers: Professional competence: Certificates: Amendments..........................157
Driving licences: Motor vehicles: Northern Ireland..........................403
Driving: Disqualifications: Mutual recognition: Great Britain & Ireland..........................156
Driving: Disqualifications: Mutual recognition: Northern Ireland & Ireland..........................403
Drugs & appliances: Charges: National Health Service: England..........................125
Drugs & appliances: Charges: National Health Service: Scotland..........................348
Drugs & appliances: Charges: Northern Ireland..........................390
Drugs: Controlled drugs: Management & use: Supervision: Wales..........................51
Drugs: Controlled drugs: Precursors: Community external trade..........................50
Drugs: Controlled drugs: Precursors: Intra-community trade..........................51
Drugs: Misuse of Drugs Act 1971: Amendment..........................51
Dudley & Walsall Mental Health Partnership: National Health Service Trust: Establishment..........................124
Dudley (Borough): Parking contraventions: Civil enforcement..........................242
Dudley: Parking contraventions: Civil enforcement..........................242
Dumfries & Galloway Council: Garlieston: Harbour: Empowerment: Scotland..........................342
Dumfries & Galloway Council: Isle of Whithorn: Harbour: Empowerment: Scotland..........................342
Dumfries & Galloway Council: Port William: Harbour: Empowerment: Scotland..........................342
Dumfries & Galloway: Electoral arrangements: Scotland..........................346
Durham (County): Local government: Structural changes..........................111
Durham (District): Parking contraventions: Civil enforcement..........................242
Duties: Interest rates: Amendments..........................154

E

Early Years Foundation Stage: Learning & development requirements..........................23
Early Years Foundation Stage: Learning & development requirements: Exemptions..........................23
Early Years Foundation Stage: Welfare requirements..........................24
East Devon College, Tiverton: Dissolution..........................57
East Kent Hospitals: National Health Service Trust..........................124
East Kent Hospitals: National Health Service Trusts: Trust property: Transfer..........................124
East Suffolk Internal Drainage Board..........................106
East Sussex (County): Eastbourne (Borough): Parking contraventions: Civil enforcement..........................241
Eastbourne (Borough): East Sussex (County): Parking contraventions: Civil enforcement..........................241
Eccles & Salford Colleges: Dissolution..........................57
Ecclesiastical law: Churches Conservation Trust: Grants to..........................55
Ecclesiastical law: Churches Conservation Trust: Payments..........................55
Ecclesiastical law: Judges, legal officers & others: Fees..........................55
Ecclesiastical law: Legal officers: Annual fees..........................55
Ecclesiastical law: Parochial fees..........................55
Economic statistics: Statistics & Registration Service Act 2007: Delegation of functions..........................54, 264
Edinburgh Napier University: Scotland..........................337
Education & Inspections Act 2006: Commencements: England..........................57
Education & Inspections Act 2006: Commencements: Wales..........................66
Education & Skills Act 2008: Commencements: England & Wales..........................63
Education & skills: Acts..........................5
Education & skills: Acts: Explanatory notes..........................7
Education & training: Inspectors: Wales..........................66
Education Act 2002: Commencements..........................66
Education authorities performance targets: Education: England..........................59
Education, Children's Services & Skills: Inspectors: Appointments: England..........................24, 61
Education: Academic awards & distinctions: UHI Millennium Institute: Scotland..........................337

Education: Admission arrangements: Variation: England 62
Education: Admissions appeals arrangements: England 57
Education: Aided places: St Mary's Music School: Scotland. 338
Education: Assembly learning grants: European Institutions: Wales 65
Education: Assisted places: England 57
Education: Assisted places: Incidental expenses: England. 57
Education: Assisted places: Incidental expenses: Wales 66
Education: Assisted places: Scotland 337
Education: Assisted places: Wales 66
Education: Bede Sixth Form College, Billingham: Dissolution 56
Education: Budget statements: England 57
Education: Central institutions: Recognition: Scotland 337
Education: Curriculum: Wales 67
Education: Designation institutions. 57
Education: Dewsbury College: Dissolution 56
Education: Diocese of Carlisle: Educational endowments 57
Education: Diocese of Chelmsford: Educational endowments 57
Education: Diocese of Chester: Educational endowments 57
Education: Diocese of Coventry: Educational endowments 57
Education: Diocese of Lichfield: Educational endowments 57
Education: Disability: General qualifications bodies: Relevant qualifications, reasonable steps & physical features: Northern Ireland 382
Education: East Devon College, Tiverton: Dissolution 57
Education: Eccles & Salford Colleges: Dissolution 57
Education: Edinburgh Napier University: Scotland. 337
Education: Fees & awards: Wales 66
Education: Financial reporting: Consistent 56
Education: Fundable bodies: Scotland 337
Education: Further Education & Training Act 2007: Commencements 60
Education: Further Education & Training Act 2007: Commencements: England & Wales 64
Education: Further Education & Training Act 2007: Commencements: Wales 67
Education: Further education: Assembly learning grant: Wales 64
Education: Further education: Student support: Eligibility: Northern Ireland 382
Education: General Teaching Council for England: Disciplinary functions 60
Education: General Teaching Council for England: Provisional registration: Eligibility 60
Education: Graduate endowments: Scotland 338
Education: Grammar schools: Charges: Northern Ireland 382
Education: Higher education: Assembly learning grants & loans: Wales 65
Education: Higher education: Institutions: Designation: Scottish Agricultural College: Scotland 337
Education: Independent schools: Inspection fees & publication: England 57
Education: Independent schools: Standards: England 58
Education: Individual learning accounts: Scotland 338
Education: Information: Individual pupils: England 58
Education: Institutions of further education: Public sector audit: Northern Ireland 380
Education: Leeds City College: Government. 61
Education: Leeds City College: Incorporation 61
Education: Listed bodies: England 58
Education: London Skills & Employment Board: Establishment 61
Education: London Skills & Employment Board: Specified functions. 61
Education: Maintained schools & further education bodies: Collaboration arrangements: Wales. 65
Education: Manchester College of Arts & Technology and City College, Manchester: Dissolution 61
Education: Manchester College: Government 61
Education: Manchester College: Incorporation. 61
Education: Mandatory awards 64
Education: Means testing: Scotland 337
Education: National curriculum: Attainment targets & programmes of study: Art & design: Key stage 3: England 58
Education: National curriculum: Attainment targets & programmes of study: Citizenship: Key stage 3 & 4: England. . . . 58
Education: National curriculum: Attainment targets & programmes of study: Design & technology: Key stage 3: England. 58
Education: National curriculum: Attainment targets & programmes of study: English: Key stage 3 & 4: England. 58
Education: National curriculum: Attainment targets & programmes of study: Geography: Key stage 3: England 58
Education: National curriculum: Attainment targets & programmes of study: History: Key stage 3: England 58
Education: National curriculum: Attainment targets & programmes of study: Information & communication technology: Key stage 3 & 4: England 59
Education: National curriculum: Attainment targets & programmes of study: Mathematics: Key stage 3 & 4: England . . . 59

Education: National curriculum: Attainment targets & programmes of study: Modern foreign languages: Key stage 3: England... 58
Education: National curriculum: Attainment targets & programmes of study: Music: Key stage 3: England.......... 58
Education: National curriculum: Attainment targets & programmes of study: Physical education: Key stage 3 & 4: England 59
Education: National curriculum: Attainment targets & programmes of study: Science: Key stage 3: England......... 58
Education: National curriculum: Foundations stage: Wales... 66, 67
Education: National curriculum: Key stage 1: Dissaplication: Wales... 66
Education: National curriculum: Key stage 3: Assessment arrangements: England.............................. 59
Education: National curriculum: Modern foreign languages: England... 59
Education: National curriculum: Modern foreign languages: Wales... 67
Education: National curriculum: Study: Attainment targets & programmes: Wales.............................. 66
Education: Outturn statements: England.. 59
Education: Penwith College, Penzance: Dissolution.. 62
Education: Provision: Information: England... 60
Education: Pupil exclusions & appeals: Pupil referral units... 59
Education: Pupil information: England... 59
Education: Pupils: Milk & milk products: England... 11
Education: QCA levy... 64
Education: Qualifications & Curriculum Authority: Additional functions................................. 24, 62
Education: Recognised bodies: England.. 59
Education: Regional Learning & Skills Councils... 62
Education: Rochdale Sixth Form College: Government... 62
Education: Rochdale Sixth Form College: Incorporation.. 62
Education: Rodbaston College, Cannock Chase Technical College & Tamworth & Lichfield College: Dissolution..... 62
Education: Rural primary schools: Designation: England... 56
Education: School & local education authority performance targets: England............................... 59
Education: School admission appeals code: Appointed day: England... 62
Education: School day & school year: Wales... 67
Education: School food: Nutritional standards & requirements: England.................................... 59
Education: School lunches: Charging: Requirement: Dissapplication: Scotland...................... 338, 347
Education: School teachers: Incentive payments: England.. 63
Education: School teachers: Pay & conditions: England & Wales.. 64
Education: School teachers: Qualifications: Wales.. 67
Education: Schools (Health Promotion & Nutrition) Act 2007: Commencements: Scotland..................... 338
Education: Schools budget: Shares: Prescribed purposes: Wales.. 67
Education: Schools forums: England... 63
Education: Schools: Admission arrangements: England.. 62
Education: Schools: Admissions: Co-ordination of arrangements: England................................... 62
Education: Schools: Admissions: Local authority reports & admission forums: England...................... 62
Education: Schools: All Saints CE (Aided) Primary School: Religious character: Designation................ 56
Education: Schools: All Saints CofE School: Religious character: Designation.............................. 56
Education: Schools: Arnot St Mary CE Primary School: Religious character: Designation..................... 56
Education: Schools: Bellefield Primary & Nursery School: Religious character: Designation................. 56
Education: Schools: Canon Peter Hall Church of England Primary School: Religious character: Designation.... 56
Education: Schools: Canon Sharples Church of England Primary School & Nursery: Religious character: Designation... 56
Education: Schools: Christ the King Catholic & Church of England (VA) Centre for Learning: Religious character: Designation... 56
Education: Schools: Cleadon Village Church of England VA Primary School: Religious character: Designation..... 56
Education: Schools: Finance: England... 62
Education: Schools: Hackleton Church of England Primary School: Religious character: Designation........... 60
Education: Schools: Hawthorn Church of England Controlled First School: Religious character: Designation.... 60
Education: Schools: Hazardous equipment & materials: Restrictions: Removal: England...................... 57
Education: Schools: Information: England... 62
Education: Schools: Inspection: England.. 59
Education: Schools: King's Stanley CofE Primary School: Religious character: Designation.................. 61
Education: Schools: Krishna-Avanti Primary School: Religious character: Designation....................... 61
Education: Schools: Maintained schools: Collaboration: Wales... 65
Education: Schools: Manor CE VC Primary: Religious character: Designation................................. 61
Education: Schools: Meals: North Yorkshire County Council.. 62
Education: Schools: Norham St Ceolwulfs CofE Controlled First School: Religious character: Designation..... 61
Education: Schools: Nutritional requirements: Food & drink: Scotland..................................... 338
Education: Schools: Performance information: England... 59, 60
Education: Schools: Premises: Control: Wales... 65, 66
Education: Schools: Religious character: Designation: England.. 56
Education: Schools: Religious character: Designation: Independent schools: England....................... 56

Education: Schools: St Gregory's Catholic Primary School: Religious character: Designation 63
Education: Schools: St Saviour's Catholic Primary School: Religious character: Designation 63
Education: Schools: Thatcham Park Church of England Primary School: Religious character: Designation 63
Education: Schools: Towcester CofE Primary School: Religious character: Designation 63
Education: Schools: Trinity Anglican-Methodist Primary School: Religious character: Designation 63
Education: Schools: William Parker School: Religious character: Designation 63
Education: Schools: Wylye Valley Church of England Voluntary Aided Primary School: Religious character: Designation 63
Education: Scottish Agricultural College: Fundable bodies: Scotland 337
Education: South Staffordshire College: Government 63
Education: South Staffordshire College: Incorporation 63
Education: Special Educational Needs & Disability: 2005 Order: Amendment: General qualifications bodies: Alteration of premises & enforcement: Northern Ireland 382
Education: Special Educational Needs (Information) Act 2008: Commencements 63
Education: Special educational needs: England 60
Education: Special educational needs: Information: Acts 7
Education: Specified work & registration: Amendments: England 60
Education: Student awards: Northern Ireland 382
Education: Student fees: Amounts: England 63
Education: Student fees: Amounts: Northern Ireland 382
Education: Student fees: Qualifying courses & persons: England 63
Education: Student loans: England & Wales 64
Education: Student loans: Northern Ireland 382
Education: Student loans: Repayment 55
Education: Student loans: Repayment: Northern Ireland 382
Education: Student loans: Sale: Acts 7
Education: Student loans: Sale: Acts: Explanatory notes 8
Education: Student loans: Scotland 337
Education: Student support 60, 64
Education: Student support: European Institutions 60
Education: Student support: Northern Ireland 382
Education: Teachers: Induction arrangements: England 58
Education: Teachers: Pensions 64
Education: Teachers: Pensions: Northern Ireland 382
Education: University of Aberdeen: Academic awards & distinctions: Additional powers: Scotland 337
Educational establishments: Pupils: Milk & milk products: Northern Ireland 376
Educational Recording Agency Limited: Broadcasts: Educational recording: Licensing scheme: Certification 40
Eel fishing: Licence duties: Northern Ireland 386
Eel fishing: Prohibition: Scotland 353
Eggs & chicks: Food: Scotland 340
Eggs & chicks: Scotland 340
Eggs: Marketing standards: England 81
Eggs: Northern Ireland 388
Elderly persons: Commissioner for Older People in Wales 33
Elections: Councils: Local authorities: England 112
Electoral Administration Act 2006: Commencements 153
Electoral Administration Act 2006: Commencements: Northern Ireland 133, 142
Electoral Administration Act 2006: Loans: Regulation: Northern Ireland 143
Electoral changes: Barrow-in-Furness (Borough) 110
Electoral changes: Basingstoke & Deane (Borough) 110
Electoral changes: Bradford 110
Electoral changes: Isle of Wight 111
Electoral changes: Maidstone 112
Electoral changes: South Cambridgeshire 113
Electoral changes: South Lakeland (District) 111
Electoral changes: Uttlesford 114
Electoral changes: Welwyn Hatfield (Borough) 110
Electrical & electronic equipment: Hazardous substances: Use restriction 71
Electricity works: Environmental impact assessment: Scotland 338
Electricity: Applications for licences, modifications of an area & extensions & restrictions of licences 67
Electricity: Billing 67, 86
Electricity: Carbon emissions: Reduction 67, 86
Electricity: Consumer complaints: Handling Standards 68, 86
Electricity: Energy: 2003 Order: Information supply: Northern Ireland 383, 390
Electricity: From high-efficiency cogeneration: Guarantees of origin: Northern Ireland 383
Electricity: Generation: Licence requirement: Exemption: Gunfleet Sands II: England & Wales 68

Electricity: Generation: Licence requirement: Exemption: Little Cheyne Court: England & Wales 68
Electricity: Offshore development: Environmental impact assessment: Northern Ireland 383
Electricity: Offshore wind & water driven generating stations: Permitted capacity: Northern Ireland. 383
Electricity: Regulated providers: Redress schemes. 39, 68, 86
Electricity: Renewable energy sources: Guarantees of origin: Northern Ireland 382
Electricity: Renewables (Origin of): Gas & Electricity Markets Authority: Power to act: Northern Ireland Authority for
Utility Rregulation 68
Electricity: Renewables obligation: Scotland 338
Electricity: River Humber: Upper Burcom Tidal Stream Generator. 68, 134, 272
Electronic communications: 3400-3800 MHz frequency band: Management 68
Electronic communications: Adults with incapacity: Scotland 326, 338
Electronic communications: Building 20
Electronic communications: Council tax: England 44
Electronic communications: Digital Switchover (Disclosure of Information) Act 2007: Disclosure of information:
Prescription of information 20, 68
Electronic communications: Television licensing 20, 68
Electronic communications: Wireless telegraphy: Automotive short range radar: Exemptions 68
Electronic communications: Wireless telegraphy: Exemptions 68
Electronic communications: Wireless telegraphy: Licence awards 69
Electronic communications: Wireless telegraphy: Licence awards: Cardiff 68
Electronic communications: Wireless telegraphy: Licence awards: Manchester 69
Electronic communications: Wireless telegraphy: Licence charges 69
Electronic communications: Wireless telegraphy: Mobile communication services on aircraft: Exemptions 69
Electronic communications: Wireless telegraphy: Register 69
Electronic communications: Wireless telegraphy: Spectrum access: Licences: Number limitation 69
Electronic communications: Wireless telegraphy: Spectrum trading 69
Ellesmere Port & Neston (Borough): Chester (City): Cheshire (County) Parking contraventions: Civil enforcement. . . . 241
Ellesmere Port & Neston: Parishes: Local government 111
Embryology: Acts 6
Embryology: Acts: Explanatory notes 8
Emergency Workers (Scotland) Act 2005: Modification: Scotland. 335
Emissions trading: Community scheme: Allocation of allowances for payment. 72
Employees: Fixed-term: Less favourable treatment: Prevention 268
Employees: Fixed-term: Less favourable treatment: Prevention: Northern Ireland 383
Employers' liability: Compulsory insurance 104
Employment & support allowance 255, 256
Employment & support allowance: Consequential provisions 255
Employment & support allowance: Northern Ireland 406
Employment & support allowance: Transitional provisions 256
Employment & support allowance: Up-rating modification 256
Employment & training: Age discrimination 70
Employment & training: Industrial training levy: Construction Industry Training Board 70
Employment & training: Industrial training levy: Engineering Construction Industry Training Board 70
Employment & training: Industrial training levy: Reasonable steps 70
Employment Act 2008: Commencements 69
Employment rights: Increase of limits: Northern Ireland 383
Employment rights: Limits: Increase 267
Employment tribunals: Constitution & rules of procedure 70
Employment: Acts 5
Employment: Acts: Explanatory notes 7
Employment: Agencies & businesses: Conduct: Northern Ireland 383
Employment: Companies: Cross-border mergers 35
Employment: Fixed-term employees: Less favourable treatment: Prevention: Northern Ireland 383
Employment: Gangmasters: Licensing conditions 70
Employment: Maternity & parental leave: Paternity & adoption leave: Northern Ireland 383
Employment: Social security: Benefits: Up-rating: Northern Ireland 383, 393, 401, 407, 411
Employment: Statutory sick pay: General 262, 268
Employment: Terms & conditions: Maternity, parental, paternity & adoption leave 268
Employment: Terms & conditions: Social security: Benefits up-rating 262
Endowment: Graduate endowment: Abolition: Acts: Explanatory notes: Scotland 325
Endowment: Graduate endowment: Abolition: Acts: Scotland 325
Energy conservation: Domestic energy: Efficiency grants: Northern Ireland 384
Energy conservation: Home energy efficiency scheme: Scotland 338
Energy performance: Buildings: Certificates & inspections: European Communities: Northern Ireland 384
Energy performance: Buildings: Scotland. 332

Energy performance: Certificates & inspections: Building & buildings: England & Wales. 20, 21
Energy saving items: Corporation tax 41
Energy: 2003 Order: Information supply: Northern Ireland. 383, 390
Energy: Acts. 5
Energy: Acts: Explanatory notes. 7
Energy: Climate Change & Sustainable Energy Act 2006: Energies & technologies: Sources 70
Energy: Planning: Acts. 6
Engineering Construction Industry Training Board: Industrial training levy 70
England: Plant & machinery: Rating & valuation. 150
English: National curriculum: Attainment targets & programmes of study: Key stage 3 & 4: England. 58
Enterprise Act 2002: Section 58: Specification of additional consideration 37
Enterprise Act 2002: Super-complaints: Designated bodies 37, 39
Enterprise management: Incentives: Income tax: Limits 101
Environment: Climate change: Acts 4
Environment: Climate change: Acts: Explanatory notes. 7
Environment: Taxes: Landfill tax 106
Environmental impact assessment: Agriculture: Northern Ireland 375
Environmental impact assessment: Planning: Northern Ireland 398
Environmental impact assessment: Town & country planning: Wales 270
Environmental impact: Electricity works: Scotland. 338
Environmental offences: Fixed penalties: Wales. 73
Environmental protection: Waste & contaminated land: 1997 Order: Commencements: Northern Ireland. 384
Environmental protection: Bathing water: Quality: Northern Ireland 384
Environmental protection: Bathing water: Scotland. 339, 365
Environmental protection: Batteries & accumulators: Market: Placing 70
Environmental protection: Clean Neighbourhoods & Environment Act 2005: Commencements. 72
Environmental protection: Environmental offences: Fixed penalties: Wales 73
Environmental protection: Financial assistance: England & Wales 72
Environmental protection: Genetically modified organisms: England. 72
Environmental protection: Greenhouse gases: Fluorinated. 70
Environmental protection: Hazardous substances: Use restriction: Electrical & electronic equipment 71
Environmental protection: Mobile machinery: Non-road: Gaseous & particulate pollutants: Emissions 71
Environmental protection: Nitrates Action Programme: Northern Ireland 384
Environmental protection: Noise: England. 72
Environmental protection: Ozone depleting substances: Controls 70
Environmental protection: Ozone depleting substances: Qualifications 71
Environmental protection: Pollution: Prevention & control: Batteries: Directives: Designation: Scotland 339
Environmental protection: Pollution: Prevention & control: Designation of directives: England & Wales 72
Environmental protection: Pollution: Prevention & control: Scotland 339
Environmental protection: Producer responsibility & obligations: Packaging waste 71
Environmental protection: Radioactive contaminated land: Enactments: Modification: England. 72
Environmental protection: Radioactive contaminated land: Enactments: Modification: Wales 73
Environmental protection: REACH: Enforcement 40, 71, 88
Environmental protection: Scotland Act 1998: Transfer of functions 38, 53, 71
Environmental protection: Sea: Deposits: Exemptions: Northern Ireland 384
Environmental protection: Site waste management plans: England 72
Environmental protection: Waste management: Licences: Consultation & compensation : Northern Ireland 384
Environmental protection: Waste management: Northern Ireland 384
Environmental protection: Waste: 2007 Amendment Order: Commencements: Northern Ireland. 384
Environmental protection: Waste: Transfrontier shipments 72
Environmental protection: Water Environment & Water Services (Scotland) Act 2003: Commencements: Scotland . 339, 366
Environmental protection: Water environment: Relevant enactments: Scotland 339
Equality: Employment: Age discrimination 70
Equality: Sex discrimination: Legislation: Amendments 253
Establishments & agencies: Fitness of workers: Northern Ireland 390
Estate agents: Consumers, Estate Agents & Redress Act 2007: Commencements 39, 73
Estate agents: Redress scheme 73
Estate agents: Redress scheme: Penalty charges 73
Eurex Clearing AG: Stamp duty & stamp duty reserve tax: Investment exchanges & clearing houses. 263, 264
European Central Counterparty Ltd: Stamp duty & stamp duty reserve tax: Investment exchanges & clearing houses . . . 267
European Championship: Control period: 2008. 263
European Communities: Animals & animal products: Import & export: Northern Ireland 378, 384
European Communities: Buildings: Energy performance: Certificates & inspections: Northern Ireland 384
European Communities: Community trade marks 271
European Communities: Controlled drugs: Precursors: External trade 50

European Communities: Controlled drugs: Precursors: Intra-community trade 51
European Communities: Definition of treaties: European Economic Area: Enlargement: Agreements 73
European Communities: Definition of treaties: International Tropical Timber Agreement 2006 73
European Communities: Designation. 73
European Communities: European grouping of territorial co-operation 73
European Communities: Finance: Acts 5
European Communities: Finance: Acts: Explanatory notes 7
European Communities: Financial instrument: Definition 79
European Communities: Judicial & extrajudicial documents: Service of: Scotland 339
European Communities: Lawyer's practice & services 108
European Communities: Non-contractual obligations: Law: England, Wales & Northern Ireland. 144
European Communities: Olive oil: Marketing standards: Northern Ireland 385, 389
European Communities: Scrapie: Fees: Northern Ireland. 385
European Fisheries Fund: Grants: Northern Ireland 386
European Parliament: House of Lords: Disqualification 74
European Parliament: Number of MEPs & distribution between electoral regions: United Kingdom & Gibraltar 153
European Parliamentary elections: Poll: Appointed day 153
European Parliamentary elections: Returning officers 153
European qualifications: Health & social care professions. 88
European qualifications: Pharmacy: Northern Ireland 398
European Regional Development Fund: London Operational Programme: Implementation 74
European single currency: Taxes 41
European Union: Treaties: Amendments: Acts 6
European Union: Treaties: Amendments: Acts: Explanatory notes 7
Excise duty: Immobilisation, removal & disposal of vehicles 157
Excise warehousing. 75
Excise: Alcoholic liquor: Spirits duty: Surcharges. 74
Excise: Amusement machines: Licencing: Duties. 10, 33, 74, 104, 106
Excise: Beer, cider & perry, wine & made-wine 74
Excise: Biofuels & other fuel substitutes: Determination of composition of a substance 75
Excise: Customs & excise duties: Travellers' allowances 76, 275
Excise: Duties: Alcoholic liquor & tobacco products 74
Excise: Duties: Heavy oil: Rebated: Supply: Payment of rebate. 75
Excise: Duties: Hydrocarbon oils & bioblend: Private pleasure-flying & pleasure craft: Payment of rebate 75
Excise: Duties: Surcharges or rebates: Hydrocarbon oils 75
Excise: Finance Act 1998: Drawback: Assessments 75
Excise: Gaming: Duty 75
Excise: Hydrocarbon oil: Determination of composition of a substance. 75
Excise: Other fuel substitutes: Excise duties: Rates 76
Excise: Road fuel gas: Reliefs 74, 75
Excise: Value added tax: Correction of errors 10, 33, 76, 104, 106, 275
Explosive atmospheres (potentially): Equipment & protective systems: Intended for Use: Northern Ireland 392
Explosives: Northern Ireland 385
Export control: Iran. 49
Export: Cat & dog fur: Control of import, export & placing on the market 13, 49
Export: Control 50
Export: Control: Burma. 49
Export: Control: Congo (Democratic Republic) 49, 50
Export: Control: Security & para-military goods. 50
Export: Goods: Technology: Transfer: Technical assistance: Provision: Control: Customs. 50
Extradition Act 2003: Designations: Amendments. 76

F

Fair employment: Public authorities: Specification: Northern Ireland 385
Fal & Helford: Fishing restrictions 252
Falkland Islands: Constitution. 263
Family intervention tenancies: Local authority decisions: Reviews: England 94
Family law: Proceedings: Allocation: England & Wales 77
Family law: Child Maintenance & Other Payments Act 2008: Commencements 76, 255
Family law: Child support 77
Family law: Child Support, Pensions & Social Security Act 2000: Commencement 77
Family law: Child support, pensions & social security: 2000 Act: Commencement: Northern Ireland. 380, 385
Family law: Child support: Amendments. 77
Family law: Child support: Child Maintenance Act 2008 Act: Commencements: Northern Ireland 385, 386

Family law: Child support: Commissioners: Procedures. 77
Family law: Child support: Consequential provisions 76, 77
Family law: Child support: Consequential provisions: Northern Ireland 380, 385
Family law: Child support: Information 76
Family law: Child support: Information: Northern Ireland 380, 385
Family law: Child support: Northern Ireland 386
Family law: Divorce etc.: Pensions: Scotland. 339
Family law: Forced Marriage (Civil Protection) Act 2007: Commencements 77
Family law: Forced Marriage (Civil Protection) Act 2007: Commencements: Northern Ireland 385
Family law: Social security & child support: Decisions & appeals. 77, 262
Family law: Social security & child support: Northern Ireland. 386
Family procedure: Adoption 77
Family proceedings 44, 45, 77, 265
Family proceedings courts: Children Act 1989: Amendments 117
Family proceedings: Fees. 45, 78, 266
Family proceedings: Fees: England & Wales. 45, 77, 78, 266
Family proceedings: Rules: Northern Ireland 381, 386, 411
Farm modernisation programme: Agriculture: Northern Ireland 375
Farmers: Financial assistance for young farmers scheme: Northern Ireland 376
Farriers: Qualifications: European recognition. 78
Fats: Spreadable fats: Marketing standards: England 83
Fats: Spreadable fats: Marketing standards: Northern Ireland 390
Fats: Spreadable fats: Marketing standards: Wales. 85
Fats: Spreadable fats: Scotland 342
FCO Services Trading Fund 87
Feed: Hygiene & enforcement: Scotland 327
Feed: Official controls: Scotland. 328, 341
Feeding stuffs, crops & food: Pesticides: Maximum residue levels: England & Wales 12, 138
Feeding stuffs, crops & food: Pesticides: Maximum residue levels: Northern Ireland. 378
Feeding stuffs, crops & food: Pesticides: Maximum residue levels: Scotland 328, 350
Feeding stuffs: England. 11
Feeding stuffs: Northern Ireland 376
Feeding stuffs: Scotland. 328
Feeding stuffs: Wales. 12
Fees & charges: Driver licensing & vehicle registration: Fees. 78
Fees & charges: Local authorities: Alcohol disorder zones 79, 114, 140
Fees & charges: Measuring instruments: EEC requirements. 78
Fees & charges: Medical devices. 78
Fees & charges: Medicines: Human use: Fees 40, 78, 119
Felixstowe branch line: Ipswich Yard improvements. 272
Films: Co-Production agreements 27
Finance Act 1998: Drawback: Assessments 75
Finance Act 2004: Part 7: Application: National insurance: Contributions. 258
Finance Act 2006: Section 28: Appointed day 100
Finance Act 2007: Schedule 24: Commencements 154
Finance Act 2007: Schedule 9 41
Finance Act 2007: Section 17 (2): Corporation tax: Energy-saving items: Deduction: Appointed day 42
Finance Act 2007: Section 46: Commencements. 100
Finance Act 2007: Section 50: Appointed day 101
Finance Act 2008. 6
Finance Act 2008: Schedule 38: Appointed day 267
Finance Act 2008: Section 135: Disaster or emergency 154
Finance Act 2008: Section 26: Appointed day 42
Finance Act 2008: Section 27: Appointed day 42
Finance Act 2008: Section 28: Appointed day 42
Finance Act 2008: Section 29: Appointed day 42
Finance Act 2008: Section 30: Appointed day 42
Finance Act 2008: Section 31: Specified tax year. 101
Finance arrangements: Alternative: Community investment tax relief. 99
Finance At 2004: Part 4: Variation: Stamp duty land tax 264
Finance: Banking: Special provisions: Acts 4
Financial assistance for young farmers scheme: Northern Ireland 376
Financial assistance scheme: Amendments: Pensions 135
Financial assistance: Environmental purposes: England & Wales. 72
Financial assistance: Industry: Limit: Increases. 103

Financial instrument: Definition: European Communities 79
Financial Services & Markets Act 2000: Business transfers: Control 79
Financial Services & Markets Act 2000: Business transfers: Control: Lloyds. 79
Financial Services & Markets Act 2000: Collective investment schemes 79
Financial Services & Markets Act 2000: Consequential amendments 79
Financial Services & Markets Act 2000: Exemption. 79
Financial Services & Markets Act 2000: Market abuse 79
Financial Services & Markets Act 2000: Part 7: Amendments. 79
Financial Services & Markets Act 2000: Section 323: Amendments 79
Financial Services & Markets Act 2000: Taxes: Consequential amendments 42
Financial services & markets: Regulated covered bonds. 79, 80
Financial services: Financial instrument: Definition: European Communities. 79
Financing-arrangement-funded transfers to shareholders: Insurance: Corporation tax 42
Fines: Discharge: Unpaid work: Pilot scheme 47
Fines: Enforcement: Diligence: Scotland 335
Fines: Enforcement: Seizure & disposal of vehicles: Scotland 335
Fire & rescue authorities: Best value performance indicators: Wales 80
Fire & rescue authorities: Improvement plans: Wales 80
Fire & rescue services: Fire & rescue authorities: Best value performance indicators: Wales. 80
Fire & rescue services: Fire & rescue authorities: Improvement plans: Wales 80
Fire & rescue services: Firefighters' pension scheme: England 80, 137
Fire & rescue services: Firefighters' pension scheme: Northern Ireland 386
Fire & rescue services: National framework: England. 80
Fire & rescue services: National framework: Wales 80
Fire & rescue services: Tyne & Wear Fire & Rescue Authority: Members: Increase 80
Fire services: Pensions: Compensation scheme: Northern Ireland 386
Firefighters: Pension schemes: Amendment : Scotland 339, 349
Firefighters: Pensions: Compensation scheme: Northern Ireland. 386
Firefighters' pension scheme: England 80, 137
Firefighters' pension scheme: Northern Ireland. 386
Firefighters' pension scheme: Scotland 339, 349
Fireplaces: Exempt: Smoke control areas: England 33
Fireplaces: Exempt: Smoke control areas: Northern Ireland 380
Fireplaces: Exempt: Smoke control areas: Scotland 333
Fireplaces: Exempt: Smoke control areas: Wales 33
Fish farming: Businesses: Record keeping: Scotland 340
Fish farming: Businesses: Registration: Scotland. 354
Fish farming: Fisheries & aquaculture structures: Grants: England 80, 252
Fisheries & aquaculture structures: Grants: England 80, 252
Fisheries: Aquaculture & Fisheries (Scotland) Act 2007: Fixed penalty notices: Scotland 360
Fisheries: Byelaws: Amendments: Northern Ireland 386
Fisheries: Byelaws: Coarse fish: Conservation: Northern Ireland 387
Fisheries: Eel fishing: Licence duties: Northern Ireland 386
Fisheries: Fish health: Northern Ireland. 387
Fisheries: Foyle & Carlingford areas: Northern Ireland. 387
Fisheries: Foyle & Carlingford Areas: Salmon & Sea Trout: Caught by rod & line: Prohibition of sale: Northern Ireland . 387
Fisheries: Foyle & Carlingford: 2007 Order: Commencements: Northern Ireland 387
Fisheries: Foyle Area: Oyster fishing: Control: Northern Ireland. 387
Fisheries: Foyle Area: Oyster fishing: Licensing: Northern Ireland 387
Fisheries: Foyle Area: Oyster logbook & identification tagging: Northern Ireland 387
Fisheries: Foyle Area: Oysters: Landing areas: Northern Ireland. 387
Fisheries: Salmon & freshwater: Fish & shellfish farming: Businesses: Registration: Scotland 354
Fisheries: Salmon & freshwater: River Dee, Aberdeenshire: Salmon Fishery District: Annual close time: Scotland 353
Fisheries: Sea fishing: Community measures: Enforcement: Penalty notices: Northern Ireland 387
Fisheries: Sea fishing: Passive Fishing gear & beam trawls: Marking & identification: Northern Ireland. . . . 387
Fisheries: Shrimp fishing nets: Scotland 361
Fisheries: Shrimp fishing nets: Wales 252, 253
Fishing gear (passive) & beam trawls: Sea fishing: Marking & identification: Northern Ireland 387
Fishing vessels: Lifting operations & equipment 122
Fishing vessels: Work equipment: Provision & use. 122
Fishing: Crabs & lobsters: Unlicensed fishing: Northern Ireland. 405
Fishing: Eels: Prohibition: Scotland. 353
Fishing: Inshore fishing: Methods: Prohibition: Northern Ireland 405
Fishing: Prohibited methods: Firth of Clyde: Scotland 361
Fishing: Prohibition: Lamlash Bay: Scotland 360

Fishing: Sea fishing: Community measures: Enforcement: Penalty notices: Northern Ireland. 387
Fixed-term employees: Less favourable treatment: Prevention. 268
Fixed-term employees: Less favourable treatment: Prevention: Northern Ireland 383
Fluorinated greenhouse gases. 70
Food labelling: Allergens: Declaration: Wales. 83
Food protection: Emergency prohibitions: Sheep: Radioactivity: Scotland 352
Food, feeding stuffs & crops: Pesticides: Maximum residue levels: England & Wales 12, 138
Food, feeding stuffs & crops: Pesticides: Maximum residue levels: Northern Ireland 378
Food, feeding stuffs & crops: Pesticides: Maximum residue levels: Scotland 328, 350
Food: Additives: England. 82
Food: Additives: Northern Ireland 389
Food: Additives: Wales. 84
Food: Dairy produce: Quotas: England. 81
Food: Dairy produce: Quotas: General provisions 80
Food: Dairy produce: Quotas: Northern Ireland 387
Food: Dairy produce: Quotas: Wales. 83
Food: Drinking milk: Northern Ireland 387
Food: Eggs & chicks: Marketing standards: England 81
Food: Eggs & chicks: Northern Ireland 388
Food: Eggs & chicks: Scotland 340
Food: Guar gum: Marketing: Restrictions: Scotland 328, 341
Food: Healthy start scheme & welfare food 81
Food: Healthy start scheme: Day care food scheme: Northern Ireland 388
Food: Honey: Northern Ireland 388
Food: Honey: Wales 83
Food: Infant & follow-on formula: England 81
Food: Infant & follow-on formula: Northern Ireland 388
Food: Infant & follow-on formula: Scotland 341
Food: Infant formula & follow-on formula: Wales. 83
Food: Labelling: Allergens: Declaration: England. 81
Food: Labelling: Allergens: Declaration: Northern Ireland. 388
Food: Labelling: Allergens: Declaration: Scotland 340
Food: Labelling: Beef & veal: Scotland 327, 340
Food: Meat products: England 83
Food: Meat products: Northern Ireland 389
Food: Meat products: Scotland 342
Food: Meat products: Wales 85
Food: Meat: Official controls: Charges: England 82
Food: Meat: Official controls: Charges: Northern Ireland 388
Food: Meat: Official controls: Charges: Scotland. 341
Food: Meat: Official controls: Charges: Wales. 83
Food: Milk & milk products: Designations: Protection: England 83
Food: Milk & milk products: Designations: Protection: Northern Ireland 390
Food: Milk & milk products: Designations: Protection: Wales 85
Food: Milk & milk products: Scotland 342
Food: Milk: Condensed & dried milk: England 81
Food: Milk: Condensed & dried milk: Northern Ireland 387
Food: Milk: Condensed & dried milk: Scotland 340
Food: Milk: Condensed & dried milk: Wales 83
Food: Milk: Drinking milk: England 81
Food: Official controls: Scotland 328, 341
Food: Olive oil: Marketing standards: Northern Ireland. 385, 389
Food: Plastic materials & articles: Contact: England. 82
Food: Plastic materials & articles: Contact: Lid gaskets: Wales. 84
Food: Plastic materials & articles: Contact: Northern Ireland 389
Food: Plastic materials & articles: Contact: Scotland. 341
Food: Plastic materials & articles: Contact: Wales. 84
Food: Residues surveillance: Charges 80
Food: Rice products: From United States: Marketing: Restrictions: England 11, 82
Food: Rice products: From United States: Marketing: Restrictions: Northern Ireland 377, 389
Food: Rice products: From United States: Marketing: Restrictions: Scotland 329, 341
Food: Rice products: From United States: Marketing: Restrictions: Wales 12, 85
Food: Specified products: From China: Marketing: Restrictions: England 11, 82
Food: Specified products: From China: Marketing: Restrictions: Northern Ireland. 377, 389
Food: Specified products: From China: Marketing: Restrictions: Scotland. 329, 341

Food: Specified products: From China: Marketing: Restrictions: Wales 13
Food: Spirit drinks 81
Food: Spreadable fats: Marketing standards: England 83
Food: Spreadable fats: Marketing standards: Northern Ireland 390
Food: Spreadable fats: Marketing standards: Wales 85
Food: Spreadable fats: Scotland 342
Food: Sweeteners: Northern Ireland 389
Food: Sweeteners: Wales 84
Football spectators: 2008 European Championship: Control period 263
Football spectators: Seating: Sports grounds & sporting events 263
Forced Marriage (Civil Protection) Act 2007: Commencements 77
Forced Marriage (Civil Protection) Act 2007: Commencements: Northern Ireland 385
Forestry: Challenge funds: Scotland 342
Forestry: Plant health 138
Forestry: Plant health: Fees 138
Fostering services: England 24, 254
Foundation stage: National curriculum: Wales 66, 67
Foyle & Carlingford: Fisheries: 2007 Order: Commencements: Northern Ireland 387
Foyle Area: Angling: Northern Ireland 387
Foyle Area: Oyster fishing: Control: Northern Ireland 387
Foyle Area: Oyster fishing: Licensing: Northern Ireland 387
Foyle Area: Oyster logbook & identification tagging: Northern Ireland 387
Foyle Area: Oysters: Landing areas: Northern Ireland 387
Foyle Area: Salmon & Sea Trout: Caught by rod & line: Prohibition of sale: Northern Ireland . . . 387
Freedom of information: Disclosure: Statutory prohibitions: Relaxation: Scotland 342
Freedom of information: Parliament & National Assembly for Wales 85
Freedom of information: Public authorities: Additional 85
Freedom of information: Scottish public bodies: Scotland 342
Friendly societies: Accounts & related provisions: Amendments 85
Friendly societies: Accounts, audit & EEA state amendments 86
Friendly societies: Corporation tax acts: Modification 42
Friendly societies: Transfers of other business: Corporation tax: Acts: Modification 42
Fuel: Car fuel: Benefits 100
Fuel: Private use: Consideration: Value added tax 275
Fuels: Authorised fuels: Smoke control areas: England 32
Fuels: Authorised fuels: Smoke control areas: Northern Ireland 380
Fuels: Authorised fuels: Smoke control areas: Wales 33
Fuels: Biofuels & other fuel substitutes: Determination of composition of a substance 75
Fuels: Other fuel substitutes: Excise duties: Rates 76
Fundable bodies: Education: Scotland 337
Fundable bodies: Scottish Agricultural College: Education: Scotland 337
Further & Higher Education (Scotland) Act 1992: Modification: Scotland 332
Further Education & Training Act 2007: Commencements 60
Further Education & Training Act 2007: Commencements: England & Wales 64
Further Education & Training Act 2007: Commencements: Wales 67
Further education bodies: Maintained schools: Collaboration arrangements: Wales 65
Further education: Assembly learning grant: Wales 64
Further education: Student support: Eligibility: Northern Ireland 382

G

Gaelic programming: Television multiplex services: Licences 20
Galleries & museums: Value added tax: Refund 276
Galloway: Dumfries & Galloway: Electoral arrangements: Scotland 346
Gambling Act 2005: Commencements 19
Gambling Act 2005: Foreign gambling: Advertising 19
Gambling: Casinos: Categories 19
Gambling: Casinos: Premises licences: Geographical distribution 19
Gambling: Casinos: Premises licences: Inviting competing applications 20
Gambling: Operating licences & single-machine permit fees 20
Game preservation: Irish hares: Special protection: Northern Ireland 390
Gaming: Duty 75
Gangmasters: Licensing conditions 70
Garlieston: Dumfries & Galloway Council: Harbour: Empowerment: Scotland 342
Gas: Applications for licences & extensions & restrictions of licences 86

Gas: Billing ... 67, 86
Gas: Carbon emissions: Reduction ... 67, 86
Gas: Consumer complaints: Handling standards ... 68, 86
Gas: Energy: 2003 Order: Information supply: Northern Ireland ... 383, 390
Gas: Performance standards ... 86
Gas: Regulated providers: Redress schemes ... 39, 68, 86
Gender recognition: Application fees ... 86
General Chiropractic Council: Constitution ... 89
General Dental Council: Constitution: Amendments ... 89, 90
General Dental Council: Continuing Professional Development ... 52, 88, 89, 146
General Medical Council: Constitution ... 90
General Medical Council: Fitness to practice: Standard of proof: Amendments ... 90
General medical services: National Health Service: Contracts ... 130
General ophthalmic services: Contracts: National Health Service ... 124
General ophthalmic services: National Health Service: Wales ... 130
General Optical Council: Committee constitution: Rules ... 90
General Optical Council: Fitness to practise: Rules ... 90
General Optical Council: Therapeutics & contact lens specialties ... 89, 134
General Register Office: Fees: Northern Ireland ... 402
General Synod of the Church of England: Measures ... 8
General Synod of the Church of England: Measures: Bound volumes ... 9
General Synod of the Church of England: Measures: Tables & index ... 9
General Teaching Council for England: Disciplinary functions ... 60
General Teaching Council for England: Provisional registration: Eligibility ... 60
Generation: Electricity: Licence requirement: Exemption: Gunfleet Sands II: England & Wales ... 68
Generation: Electricity: Licence requirement: Exemption: Little Cheyne Court: England & Wales ... 68
Genetically modified organisms: England ... 72
Geography: National curriculum: Attainment targets & programmes of study: Key stage 3: England ... 58
Gibraltar: Civil aviation: Overseas territories ... 32
Gibraltar: Merchant Shipping (Liner Conferences) Act 1982: Repeals ... 122
Gilt-edged securities: Chargeable gains: Capital gains tax ... 22, 43
Glamorgan: North Glamorgan National Health Service Trust: Dissolution: Wales ... 131
Glamorgan: North Glamorgan National Health Service Trust: Transfer of Staff, property, rights & liabilities: Wales ... 131
Glasgow & Strathkelvin Sheriffdom: Justice of the Peace courts: Scotland ... 344
Glasgow & Strathkelvin Sheriffdom: Stipendiary magistrates: Scotland ... 336
Glasgow Commonwealth Games Act 2008: Commencements: Scotland ... 363
Glasgow Commonwealth Games: Acts: Explanatory notes: Scotland ... 325
Glasgow Commonwealth Games: Acts: Scotland ... 325
Gloucestershire (County): Forest of Dean (District): Parking contraventions: Civil enforcement ... 241
Goats & sheep: Records, identification & movement: Wales ... 16
Goats: Identification & traceability: Scotland ... 330
Goods vehicles: International journeys: Authorisation: Fees ... 154
Goods vehicles: Operator licensing: Fees ... 154
Goods vehicles: Plating & testing ... 155
Goods vehicles: Recording equipment: Downloading & retention of data ... 156
Goods vehicles: Recording equipment: Fitters & workshops: Approval: Fees ... 156
Goods: International carriage: Dangerous goods: Road transport: Fees ... 155
Goods: International transport: TIR carnets: Fees ... 155
Goods: Trade: Control ... 50
Government Resources & Accounts Act 2000: Audit of public bodies ... 86
Government resources & accounts: Whole of government: Accounts: Bodies: Designation ... 86
Government resources & accounts: Whole of government: Accounts: Bodies: Designation: Northern Ireland ... 390
Government Trading Funds: Defence Aviation Repair Agency ... 86
Government Trading Funds: Defence Aviation Repair Agency: Revocation ... 87
Government trading funds: Defence Support Group Trading Fund ... 87
Government Trading Funds: FCO Services ... 87
Government: Whole of government: Accounts: Bodies: Designation ... 86
Government: Whole of government: Accounts: Bodies: Designation: Northern Ireland ... 390
Graduate endowment: Abolition: Acts: Explanatory notes: Scotland ... 325
Graduate endowment: Abolition: Acts: Scotland ... 325
Graduate endowments: Scotland ... 338
Grammar schools: Charges: Northern Ireland ... 382
Grampian, Highland & Islands Sheriffdom: Justice of the Peace courts: Scotland ... 345
Grass: Burning: Wales ... 13
Greater London Authority Act 2007: Commencements ... 116

Greater London Authority Act 2007: Election addresses 116
Greater London Authority: Mayor of London: Appointments 116
Greater London Authority: Salaries: Limitation 116
Greenhouse gases: Fluorinated 70
Guar gum: Marketing restrictions: Scotland 328, 341
Guardian's allowance: Up-rating 256
Guardian's allowance: Up-rating: Northern Ireland 263
Guernsey: Air navigation: Civil aviation 27
Gurkhas: Pensions: Armed Forces 135

H

H.M. Land Registry: Adjudicator: Practice & procedure 107
H5N1 *see* Avian influenza
Hackleton Church of England Primary School: Religious character: Designation 60
Halton: Parish electoral arrangements: Local government 111
Hammersmith Hospitals Transfer of trust property 127
Hansard: Centenary volume 1909-2009: Great speeches: Anthologies 9
Harbours, docks, piers & ferries: Caledonian Maritime Assets Limited (Largs) : Harbour revision: Scotland 342
Harbours, docks, piers & ferries: Garlieston: Dumfries & Galloway Council: Harbour: Empowerment: Scotland 342
Harbours, docks, piers & ferries: Harwich Haven: Harbour revision 87
Harbours, docks, piers & ferries: Isle of Whithorn: Dumfries & Galloway Council: Harbour: Empowerment: Scotland . . 342
Harbours, docks, piers & ferries: London Gateway: Port harbour empowerment 87
Harbours, docks, piers & ferries: Peterhead Port Authority: Harbour revision: Scotland 342
Harbours, docks, piers & ferries: Port of Tyne Harbour: Harbour revision 87
Harbours, docks, piers & ferries: Port of Weston Harbour: Harbour revision 87
Harbours, docks, piers & ferries: Port William: Dumfries & Galloway Council: Harbour: Empowerment: Scotland . . . 342
Harbours, docks, piers & ferries: Stornoway: Harbour revision constitution: Scotland 342
Harbours, docks, piers & ferries: Teesport: Harbour revision 87
Harbours, docks, piers & ferries: Whiteness Marina: Harbour revision: Scotland 342
Harbours: Donaghadee harbour area: Northern Ireland 390
Harbours: Donaghee harbour area: Northern Ireland 390
Hares: Irish: Special protection: Game preservation: Northern Ireland 390
Harwich Haven: Harbour revision 87
Hawthorn Church of England Controlled First School: Religious character: Designation 60
Hazardous equipment & materials: Schools: Restrictions: Removal: England 57
Hazardous substances: Use restriction: Electrical & electronic equipment 71
Health & personal social services trusts: Originating capital: Northern Ireland 391
Health & personal social services: Care Tribunal: Regulations: Amendments: Northern Ireland . . . 390
Health & personal social services: Drugs & appliances: Charges: Northern Ireland 390
Health & personal social services: Establishments & agencies: Fitness of workers: Northern Ireland . . . 390
Health & personal social services: General dental services: Northern Ireland 390
Health & personal social services: Health & social care: Pension schemes: Northern Ireland 391
Health & personal social services: Joint Committee for Commissioning: Northern Ireland 390
Health & personal social services: Optical charges & payments: Northern Ireland 391
Health & personal social services: Premature retirement: Compensation: Northern Ireland 391
Health & personal social services: Primary medical services: Performers lists: Northern Ireland . . . 390
Health & personal social services: Provision: Persons not ordinarily resident: Northern Ireland . . . 391
Health & personal social services: Resources: Assessment: Northern Ireland 390
Health & personal social services: Superannuation scheme, injury benefits, additional voluntary contributions & compensation for premature retirement: Northern Ireland 391
Health & personal social services: Superannuation scheme: Northern Ireland 391
Health & personal social services: Superannuation: Northern Ireland 391
Health & personal social services: Travelling expenses & remission of charges: Northern Ireland . . 391
Health & Safety Executive: Legislative reform 88, 152
Health & safety: Adventure activities: Licensing: Amendments 87
Health & safety: Blood 78, 87
Health & safety: Chemicals: Hazard information & packaging for supply 87
Health & safety: Chemicals: Hazard information & packaging for supply: Northern Ireland 392
Health & safety: Dangerous chemicals: Export & import 88
Health & safety: Enforcing authority for railways & other guided transport systems 88
Health & safety: Explosive atmospheres (potentially): Equipment & protective systems: Intended for Use: Northern Ireland
. . . . 392
Health & safety: Fees 88
Health & safety: Fees: Northern Ireland 392

Health & safety: Machinery: Supply 88
Health & safety: Major accident hazard: Control. 88
Health & safety: Offences 7
Health & safety: Offences: Acts 6
Health & safety: Offshore installations: Safety zones. 134
Health & safety: REACH: Enforcement 40, 71, 88
Health & Social Care (Community Health & Standards) Act 2003: Commencements. 148
Health & Social Care Act 2008: Commencements 89, 91, 96, 124, 148, 254, 256
Health & Social Care Act 2008: Consequential amendments 123, 148, 254
Health & Social Care Information Centre: Transfer of staff, property & liabilities 124
Health & social care professions: European qualifications. 88
Health & social care: Pension schemes: Northern Ireland 391
Health & Social Services Trusts: Establishment: Amendment: Northern Ireland 391
Health Act 2006: Commencements 118, 124, 128, 254
Health Act 2006: Commencements: Wales 130
Health care & associated professions: Amendments 89
Health care & associated professions: Amendments order: Commencements 89
Health care & associated professions: Council for Healthcare Regulatory Excellence: Appointment procedure 88
Health care & associated professions: Doctors: General Medical Council: Constitution 90
Health care & associated professions: General Dental Council: Continuing Professional Development 52, 88, 89, 146
Health care & associated professions: General Medical Council: Fitness to practice: Standard of proof: Amendments . . . 90
Health care & associated professions: General Optical Council: Therapeutics & contact lens specialties 89, 134
Health care & associated professions: Health & Social Care Act 2008: Commencements 89, 91, 124, 148, 254
Health care & associated professions: Medical Act 1983: Qualifying examinations 90
Health care & associated professions: Medical profession: Amendments 89
Health care & associated professions: Nurse & midwives: Nursing & Midwifery Council: Constitution. 90
Health care & associated professions: Nursing & Midwifery Council: Midwifery & Practice Committees: Constitution . . 90
Health care & associated professions: Postgraduate Medical Education & Training Board: Fees: Rules 90
Health care & associated professions: Royal Pharmaceutical Society of Great Britain: Registration rules: Order of Council 90
Health care: Private & voluntary: England 148
Health in pregnancy grant: Administration 262, 263
Health in pregnancy grant: Entitlement & amount 257
Health service: Local involvement networks: Duty of services-providers to allow entry 125
Health service: Medicines: Branded medicines: Prices control: Information supply. 87, 128
Health Service: National Trusts. 123, 124, 126, 127, 128, 129, 130, 131, 132
Health Service: National: District Care Trusts 123
Health Service: National: Primary Care Trusts 127
Health services: Charges: Recovery: Amounts: Northern Ireland 392
Health: Acts 6
Health: Acts: Explanatory notes 7
Health: Acts: Explanatory notes: Northern Ireland 374
Health: Acts: Northern Ireland 374
Health: Human fertilisation & embryology: Acts 6
Health: Human fertilisation & embryology: Acts: Explanatory notes. 8
Health: Local Government & Public Involvement in Health Act 2007: Commencements 112, 114, 124, 125, 254
Health: Mesothelioma: Acts: Explanatory notes: Northern Ireland. 374
Health: Mesothelioma: Acts: Northern Ireland 373
Health: Public health: Acts: Explanatory notes: Northern Ireland 374
Health: Public health: Acts: Explanatory notes: Scotland. 325
Health: Public health: Acts: Northern Ireland. 373
Health: Public health: Acts: Scotland 325
Health: Public: Aircraft: Northern Ireland 400
Health: Public: Ships: Northern Ireland 400
Health: Schools (Health Promotion & Nutrition) Act 2007: Commencements: Scotland 338
Healthcare & associated professions: General Dental Council: Constitution: Amendments. 89, 90
Healthy Start Scheme 81
Healthy start scheme: Day care food scheme: Northern Ireland 388
Hearing Aid Council: Health & Social Care Act 2008: Commencements 89, 91, 124, 148, 254
Heather: Burning: Wales 13
Heritable Bank plc: Compensation: Determination 18
Heritable Bank plc: Transfer of certain rights & liabilities. 18
Herring: Sea fishing: Control procedures: Scotland 360, 361
Hertmere: Parishes: Local government 111
Hertsmere: Parish electoral arrangements: Local government 111

High Court of Justiciary: Act of Adjournal: Criminal procedure rules: Amendments: Criminal Proceedings etc. (Reform) (Scotland) Act 2007: Scotland 342, 344, 361
High Court of Justiciary: Fees: Scotland 343
High court: Jurisdiction: England & Wales 45, 266
High Peak: Parishes: Local government. 111
Higher education: Assembly learning grants & loans: Wales 65
Higher education: Assembly learning grants: European Institutions: Wales. 65
Higher education: Institutions: Designation: Scottish Agricultural College: Scotland 337
Higher education: Student loans: Sale: Acts 7
Higher education: Student loans: Sale: Acts: Explanatory notes 8
Highways: A282: Dartford - Thurrock Crossing charging scheme. 91
Highways: Countryside & Rights of Way Act 2000: Commencements 44
Highways: Dartford - Thurrock Crossing: Amendments. 92
Highways: Dartmouth-Kingswear Floating Bridge: Vehicle classifications & revision of charges 92
Highways: England 91, 92, 93
Highways: Kent County Council: Milton Creek Bridge No. 2 scheme: Confirmation. 92
Highways: Kingston upon Hull City Council: Scale Lane Bridge: Scheme 2008: Confirmation instrument 92
Highways: Motorways: England 92
Highways: Public rights of way: Combined orders: England 92
Highways: Severn Bridges: Tolls. 92
Highways: Street works: Fixed penalty: Wales. 93
Highways: Street works: Inspection fees: England 93
Highways: Street works: Inspection fees: Wales. 93
Highways: Street works: Registers, notices, directions & designations: Wales 93, 94
Highways: Wakefield City Council: Wakefield Waterfront Hepworth Gallery footbridge scheme 92
Highways: Wales 93
Hill farm allowance: England. 11
History: National curriculum: Attainment targets & programmes of study: Key stage 3: England 58
Home Detention Curfew Licence: Prescribed specified conditions: Scotland. 335, 336
Home Detention Curfew Licence: Specified days: Scotland 351
Home energy efficiency scheme: Scotland 338
Home loss payments: Prescribed amounts: England. 9, 37
Home loss payments: Prescribed amounts: Wales 10
Homelessness etc. (Scotland) Act 2003: Commencement: Scotland 343
Homelessness: Housing authority accommodation: Immigration control 95, 96, 99
Honey: Northern Ireland. 388
Honey: Wales. 83
Horse mackerel: Sea fishing: Control procedures: Scotland. 360, 361
Horses: Zootechnical standards: Scotland. 329
House of Commons: Hansard: Centenary volume 1909-2009: Great speeches: Anthologies. 9
Housing & Regeneration Act 2008: Commencements 94, 95
Housing & Regeneration Act 2008: Consequential provisions. 95, 96
Housing & regeneration: Acts 6
Housing & regeneration: Acts: Explanatory notes. 7
Housing (Scotland) Act 2001: Housing finance arrangements: Alteration: Scotland. 343
Housing (Scotland) Act 2006: Commencements: Scotland. 343
Housing (Scotland) Act 2006: Consequential provisions 37, 52, 94
Housing (Scotland) Act 2006: Prescribed documents: Scotland 343
Housing (Scotland) Act 2006: Scheme of assistance: Scotland. 343
Housing Act 2004: Commencements. 95
Housing benefit: Amendments 257, 260, 261
Housing benefit: Council tax benefit: Extended payments 257
Housing benefit: Employment & support allowance: Consequential provisions: Northern Ireland. 392, 400
Housing benefit: Executive determinations: Northern Ireland 392
Housing benefit: Extended payments: Northern Ireland. 392, 400
Housing benefit: Functions: Rent officers: Amendments. 94, 258
Housing benefit: Local housing allowance: Information sharing: Amendments 257
Housing benefit: Local housing allowance: Northern Ireland 392, 401, 406
Housing benefit: Northern Ireland. 392, 400
Housing benefit: Social security: Information: Use. 263
Housing benefit: State pension credit: Local housing allowance: Northern Ireland 393
Housing corporations: Functions: Transfer. 96
Housing costs special arrangements: Social security: Amendments & modifications 259
Housing grants: Application forms: Scotland. 343
Housing payments: Discretionary: Grants. 255

Housing renewal grants: Wales. 96
Housing Revenue Account: General Fund Contribution: Limits: Scotland. 343
Housing: Allocation: Family intervention tenancies: England. 94
Housing: Authority accommodation: Homelessness: Immigration control 95, 96, 99
Housing: Child benefit: Disregard: Northern Ireland. 393, 401, 408
Housing: Costs: Social security: Special arrangements: Northern Ireland 408
Housing: Disabled facilities: Grants: Maximum amounts & additional purposes: England 94
Housing: Disabled facilities: Grants: Maximum amounts & additional purposes: Wales 96
Housing: Family intervention tenancies: Local authority decisions: Reviews: England. 94
Housing: Grants: Contributions: Assessment of: Amendments: Scotland 343
Housing: Home information packs: England & Wales. 95
Housing: Homelessness etc. (Scotland) Act 2003: Commencement: Scotland. 343
Housing: Houses in multiple occupation: Specified educational establishments 94
Housing: Housing & Regeneration Act 2008: Commencements. 94, 95
Housing: Housing & Regeneration Act 2008: Consequential provisions 95
Housing: Landlords: Private: Registration: Advice & assistance: Scotland. 343, 347
Housing: Landlords: Private: Registration: Information & fees: Scotland 343, 347
Housing: Local authorities: Notices: Scotland 343
Housing: Local authorities: Property searches: Charges: Disapplication: England 95
Housing: Local authorities: Property searches: Charges: England. 95
Housing: Renewal grants: England. 94
Housing: Rent: Repayment orders: Supplementary provisions: Wales 96
Housing: Right to buy: Priority of charges: Wales. 26, 96
Housing: Right to buy: Service charges: England 94
Housing: Right to manage: England 95
Housing: Rural housing bodies: Title Conditions (Scotland) Act 2003: Scotland 363
Housing: Social security: Amendments: Northern Ireland 393, 394, 401, 402, 409
Housing: Social security: Benefits: Up-rating: Northern Ireland 383, 393, 401, 407, 411
Housing: Student accommodation: Approval 94
Housing: Students: Amendments: Northern Ireland 394, 402, 410
Housing: Support grant: Scotland. 343
Human fertilisation & embryology: Acts 6
Human fertilisation & embryology: Acts: Explanatory notes 8
Human rights: Health & Social Care Act 2008: Commencements. 96, 124, 148, 254
Human rights: Scottish Commission for Human Rights Act 2006: Commencements: Scotland. 343
Human rights: Scottish Commission for Human Rights: Specifications: Scotland. 344
Human Tissue (Scotland) Act 2006: Consequential amendments: Scotland 344
Human Tissue Act 2004: Transplants: Ethical approval, exceptions from licensing & supply of information 96, 97
Hydrocarbon oil: Determination of composition of a substance 75
Hydrocarbon oils: Excise: Duties: Surcharges or rebates 75
Hydrocarbon oils: Heavy oil: Rebates: Supply: Excise: Payment of rebate 75
Hydrocarbon oils: Private pleasure-flying & craft: Payment of rebate. 75
Hywel Dda National Health Service Trust: Establishment: Wales 130

I

Immigration & nationality: Cost recovery fees 97, 132
Immigration & nationality: Fees 97, 132
Immigration control: Persons subject to: Housing authority accommodation: Homelessness. 95, 96, 99
Immigration Services Commissioner: Designated professional body: Fees 99
Immigration, Asylum & Nationality Act 2006: Commencements 98
Immigration, Asylum & Nationality Act 2006: Data sharing: Code of practice. 98, 139, 154
Immigration, Asylum & Nationality Act 2006: Information: Duty to share & disclosure for security purposes . . 98, 140, 154
Immigration: Acts 5
Immigration: Acts: Explanatory notes 7
Immigration: Asylum & Immigration Tribunal: Fast track procedures 97
Immigration: Asylum & Immigration Tribunal: Procedure 97
Immigration: Asylum: Support 97
Immigration: Biometric registration 98
Immigration: Biometric registration: Civil penalty: Code of practice 98
Immigration: Biometric registration: Pilot 98
Immigration: Employment of adults subject to immigration control: Maximum penalty 98
Immigration: Independent Police Complaints Commission: Immigration & asylum enforcement functions: England & Wales
. . . . 99
Immigration: Information supply: To Secretary of State, Home Office 99

Immigration: Isle of Man ... 98
Immigration: Notices ... 98
Immigration: Police: Passenger, crew & service information ... 98, 139
Immigration: Property: Disposal ... 98
Immigration: Registration cards ... 99
Immigration: Travel bans: Designation ... 98
Immigration: UK Borders Act 2007: Children: Code of practice ... 99
Immigration: UK Borders Act 2007: Commencements ... 99
Imperial College Healthcare: National Health Service Trusts: Trust funds: Trustees appointment ... 124
Import: Cat & dog fur: Control of import, export & placing on the market ... 13, 49
Incapacity benefit: Work-focused interviews ... 259
Incapacity benefit: Work-focused interviews: Northern Ireland ... 408
Incapacity: Adults with incapacity: Accounts & funds: Scotland ... 326
Incapacity: Adults with incapacity: Adult Support & Protection (Scotland) Act 2007: Commencements: Scotland ... 326, 347
Incapacity: Adults with incapacity: Adult Support & Protection (Scotland) Act 2007: Consequential provisions: Scotland ... 326
Incapacity: Adults with incapacity: Electronic communications: Scotland ... 326, 338
Incapacity: Adults with incapacity: Guardian's powers: Recall: Scotland ... 327
Incapacity: Adults with incapacity: Guardianship & intervention orders: Reports: Scotland ... 327
Incapacity: Adults with incapacity: Powers of attorney: Certificates: Scotland ... 326
Incapacity: Adults with incapacity: Public Guardians: Fees: Scotland ... 326, 327
Incapacity: Social security: Northern Ireland ... 408
Income tax: Authorised Investment Funds ... 21, 40, 41, 99, 100, 264
Income tax: Capital allowances: Energy-saving plant & machinery ... 41, 100
Income tax: Capital allowances: Environmentally beneficial plant & machinery ... 41, 100
Income tax: Car fuel benefit ... 100
Income tax: Childcare: Qualifying ... 102
Income tax: Community investment: Tax relief: Community development finance institutions: Accreditation ... 41, 100
Income tax: Construction industry scheme: Amendments ... 101
Income tax: Deposit-takers & building societies: Interest payments ... 101
Income tax: Double taxation: Relief & international enforcement: Moldova ... 21, 41, 100
Income tax: Double taxation: Relief & international enforcement: New Zealand ... 21, 41, 100
Income tax: Double taxation: Relief & international enforcement: Saudi Arabia ... 21, 41, 100
Income tax: Double taxation: Relief & international enforcement: Slovenia ... 21, 41, 100
Income tax: Double taxation: Relief: Relievable tax: Within a group: Surrender ... 100
Income tax: Finance Act 2006: Section 28: Appointed day ... 100
Income tax: Finance Act 2007: Section 46: Commencements ... 100
Income tax: Finance Act 2007: Section 50: Appointed day ... 101
Income tax: Finance Act 2008: Section 31: Specified tax year ... 101
Income tax: Finance arrangements: Alternative: Community investment tax relief ... 99
Income tax: Indexation ... 101
Income tax: Individual savings accounts ... 102
Income tax: Insurance companies: Profits: Calculation: Policy holders' tax ... 42
Income tax: Interest payments: Information powers ... 101
Income tax: Limits: Enterprise management: Incentives ... 101
Income tax: Overseas insurers: Tax representatives ... 102
Income tax: PAYE: Amendments ... 101
Income tax: Payments on account ... 101
Income tax: Pension schemes: Registered: Provision of information ... 102
Income tax: Pension schemes: Transitional provisions ... 102
Income tax: Professional fees ... 101
Income tax: Purchased life annuities ... 102
Income tax: Registered pension schemes: Transfer of sums & assets ... 102
Income tax: Taxation of benefits: Government pilot schemes: Better off in Work Credit ... 102
Income tax: Taxation of benefits: Government pilot schemes: Up-Front Childcare Fund ... 102
Income tax: Venture capital trusts ... 103
Income-related benefits: Students: Amendments: Northern Ireland ... 394, 402, 410
Income-related benefits: Subsidy to authorities ... 257
Income-related benefits: Subsidy to authorities: England & Wales ... 257, 262
Independent Police Complaints Commission: Immigration & asylum enforcement functions: England & Wales ... 99
Individual learning accounts: Education: Scotland ... 338
Individual savings accounts: Income tax ... 102
Industrial & provident society: Company arrangement or administration provisions for: Insolvency: Northern Ireland ... 394
Industrial development: Financial assistance: Limit: Increases ... 103
Industrial hereditaments: Rates: Northern Ireland ... 401
Industrial injuries: Dependency: Permitted earnings limits ... 259

Industrial injuries: Dependency: Permitted earnings limits: Northern Ireland 408
Industrial injuries: Prescribed diseases 260
Industrial injuries: Prescribed diseases: Northern Ireland. 408
Industrial organisation & development: Wool textile industry: Export promotion levy: Revocation 103
Industrial training levy: Construction Industry Training Board 70
Industrial training levy: Construction industry: Northern Ireland. 394
Industrial training levy: Engineering Construction Industry Training Board 70
Industrial training levy: Reasonable steps 70
Infant & follow-on formula: England. 81
Infant & follow-on formula: Northern Ireland 388
Infant & follow-on formula: Scotland. 341
Infant formula & follow-on formula: Wales 83
Information & communication technology: National curriculum: Attainment targets & programmes of study: Key stage 3 & 4: England. 59
Information: Duty to share & disclosure for security purposes: Immigration, Asylum & Nationality Act 2006 . . 98, 140, 154
Infrastructure: Planning: Acts 6
Infrastructure: Planning: Acts: Explanatory notes 8
Inheritance tax: Accounts: Delivery: Excepted settlements. 103
Inheritance tax: Accounts: Delivery: Excepted transfers & terminations. 103
Injury benefits: Health & personal social services: Northern Ireland. 391
Injury benefits: National Health Service: England & Wales 128
Inshore fishing: Methods: Prohibition: Northern Ireland 405
Insolvency practitioners & insolvency services account: Fees 78, 103
Insolvency: Bankruptcy & Diligence etc. (Scotland) Act 2007: Commencements: Scotland 331, 336, 337, 344
Insolvency: Bankruptcy: Fees: Scotland 344
Insolvency: Companies 103
Insolvency: Companies: Scotland 104, 333, 344
Insolvency: Companies: Trading disclosures. 36
Insolvency: Industrial & provident society: Company arrangement or administration provisions: Northern Ireland 394
Insolvency: Northern Ireland. 380, 394
Insolvency: Office: Disqualification from: General: Northern Ireland 394
Insolvency: Practitioners & services account: Fees 103
Insolvency: Proceedings: Fees 103
Insolvency: Rules: Companies 103
Insolvency: Voluntary winding up: Forms: Northern Ireland. 394
Insurance accounts: EC Directive 104
Insurance companies: Corporation tax acts: Amendments 42, 43
Insurance companies: Overseas life assurance business: Compliance 43
Insurance companies: Overseas life assurance business: Excluded business 43
Insurance companies: Profits: Calculation of: Policy holders' tax 42
Insurance companies: Reinsurance business: Taxation. 43
Insurance companies: Reserves: Taxation 43
Insurance companies: Taxation: Special purpose vehicles 43
Insurance premium tax 104
Insurance premium tax: Amusement machines: Licencing: Duties 10, 33, 74, 104, 106
Insurance premium tax: Value added tax: Correction of errors 10, 33, 76, 104, 106, 275
Insurance: Accounts directive: Lloyd's syndicate & aggregate accounts. 104
Insurance: Business transfer schemes: Corporation tax acts: Amendments 42
Insurance: Corporation tax: Financing-arrangement-funded transfers to shareholders 42
Insurance: Employers' liability: Compulsory insurance 104
Insurance: Life: Overseas companies: Income tax 43
Insurance: Non-resident companies: General insurance business 43
Insurance: Non-resident insurance companies: Overseas losses: Group relief: Corporation Tax Acts: Modification 42
Insurers: Life assurance & other policies: Information & duties 102
Interest payments: Information powers: Income tax 101
International carriage: Dangerous goods: Road transport: Fees. 155
International criminal court: Remand time 104
International Development Association: Fifteenth replenishment 105
International Development Association: Multilateral debt relief initiative 105
International development: African Development Bank: African Development Fund: Eleventh replenishment. 104
International development: African Development Fund: Multilateral debt relief initiative 105
International development: Crown Agents Holding & Realisation Board: Property, rights, liabilities & obligations: Transfer: Prescribed day 105
International development: International Development Association: Fifteenth replenishment. 105
International immunities & privileges: International Organization for Migration: Immunities & privileges 105

International journeys: Goods vehicles: Authorisation: Fees 154
International Organization for Migration: Immunities & privileges 105
Intestate succession: Interest & capitalisation: England & Wales 10
Investigatory powers: Serious Crime Act 2007: Commencements 54, 105, 145, 147, 154, 253
Investment companies: Open-ended: Stamp duty land tax 264
Investment exchanges & clearing houses: Stamp duty & stamp duty reserve tax 263, 264, 267
Investment: Collective investment schemes: Financial Services & Markets Act 2000 79
Iran: Export control 49
Irish hares: Special protection: Game preservation: Northern Ireland 390
Isle of Whithorn: Dumfries & Galloway Council: Harbour: Empowerment: Scotland 342
Isle of Wight: Electoral changes 111
Isle of Wight: Parishes: Local government 111

J

Jersey: Air navigation: Civil aviation 27
Jobcentre Plus: Interviews for partners 260
Jobseeker's allowance: Joint claims 257
Jobseeker's allowance: Joint claims: Northern Ireland 406
Joint Committee for Commissioning: Health & personal social services: Northern Ireland 390
Judges, legal officers & others: Fees: Ecclesiastical law 55
Judges: Discipline 105, 116, 117
Judges: Maximum number 266
Judicature: Court funds: Rules: Northern Ireland 394
Judicial & extrajudicial documents: Service of: European Communities: Scotland 339
Judicial appointments & discipline 105, 273
Judicial appointments & discipline: Constitutional Reform Act 2005: Commencements 106
Judicial appointments & discipline: Judicial discipline: Prescribed procedures: Amendments 105, 117
Judicial appointments & discipline: Tribunals, Courts & Enforcement Act 2007: Commencements 105, 274
Judicial Committee: General appellate jurisdiction 106
Judicial discipline: Prescribed procedures: Amendments 105, 117
Judicial Pensions & Retirement Act 1993: Qualifying judicial offices 135, 137
Judiciary & courts: Acts: Explanatory notes: Scotland 325
Judiciary & courts: Acts: Scotland 325
Judiciary: Magistrates' courts: District judge: Northern Ireland 394
Justice of the Peace Court: Act of Adjournal: Criminal procedure rules: Amendments: Criminal Proceedings etc. (Reform)
(Scotland) Act 2007: Scotland 342, 344, 361
Justice of the Peace Court: Act of Adjournal: Criminal procedure rules: Amendments: Scotland 344, 361
Justice of the Peace Court: Act of Adjournal: Criminal procedure rules: Seizure & disposal of vehicles: Scotland . . 344, 361
Justice of the Peace courts: Sheriffdom of Glasgow & Strathkelvin: Scotland 344
Justice of the Peace courts: Sheriffdom of Grampian, Highland & Islands: Scotland 345
Justice of the peace courts: Sheriffdom of Lothian & Borders: Scotland 345
Justice of the Peace courts: Sheriffdom of Tayside, Central & Fife: Scotland 345
Justice: Victims: Mentally disordered offenders: Information: Schemes: Northern Ireland 394
Juvenile justice centres: Rules: Northern Ireland 381

K

Kaupthing Singer & Friedlander Ltd.: Compensation: Determination 18
Kaupthing Singer & Friedlander Ltd.: Transfer of certain rights & liabilities 18
Kent County Council: Milton Creek Bridge No. 2 scheme: Confirmation 92
Kent: East Kent Hospitals: National Health Service Trust 124
Kettering: Parishes: Local government 111
King's Stanley CofE Primary School: Religious character: Designation 61
Kingston upon Hull City Council: Scale Lane Bridge: Scheme 2008: Confirmation instrument 92
Krishna-Avanti Primary School: Religious character: Designation 61

L

Land & buildings: Value added tax 275
Land drainage: Black Sluice Internal Drainage Board 106
Land drainage: East Suffolk Internal Drainage Board 106
Land drainage: Welland & Deepings Internal Drainage Board 106
Land managers: Skills development grants: Scotland 328
Land Registration Act 2002: Amendments 107

Land registration: Amendments: England & Wales. 107
Land registration: Commonhold: England & Wales 34
Land registration: Electronic conveyancing: England & Wales 107
Land registration: H.M. Land Registry: Adjudicator: Practice & procedure 107
Land registration: Network access: England & Wales 107
Land registration: Proper office: England & Wales. 107
Land: Acquisition: Home loss payments: Prescribed amounts: England 9, 37
Land: Common land: Commons registration: England. 34
Land: Radioactive contaminated land: Enactments: Modification: England. 72
Land: Radioactive contaminated land: Enactments: Modification: Wales. 73
Landfill tax 106
Landfill tax: Contaminated land: Exemption phase out. 106
Landfill tax: Value added tax: Correction of errors 10, 33, 76, 104, 106, 275
Landlord & tenant: Agricultural holdings: Units of production: England 107
Landlord & tenant: Agricultural holdings: Units of production: Wales. 107
Landlords: Private: Registration: Advice & assistance: Scotland 343, 347
Landlords: Private: Registration: Information & fees: Scotland. 343, 347
Lands Tribunal: Salaries: Northern Ireland 395
Landsbanki: Freezing. 19
Languages: Modern foreign: National curriculum: England 59
Law: Family law: Child support, pensions & social security: 2000 Act: Commencement: Northern Ireland. 380, 385
Law: Family law: Child support: Consequential provisions: Northern Ireland 380, 385
Law: Family law: Child support: Information: Northern Ireland 380, 385
Law: Family law: Divorce etc.: Pensions: Scotland. 339
Law: Family proceedings: Allocation: England & Wales 77
Law: Non-contractual obligations: Scotland 351
Law: Statute law: Repeals: Acts 7
Lawyer's practice & services: European Communities. 108
Leader grants: Agriculture: Scotland 328
Learning accounts: Individual: Education: Scotland 338
Learning grants & loans: Higher education: Wales 65
Learning grants: European Institutions: Wales. 65
Leeds City College: Government. 61
Leeds City College: Incorporation 61
Leeds: Parishes: Local government 111
Legal advice & assistance: Financial conditions: Northern Ireland. 395
Legal advice & assistance: Northern Ireland 395
Legal aid & advice: Advice & assistance: Financial conditions: Scotland 345
Legal aid & advice: Advice & assistance: Limits, conditions & representation: Scotland 345
Legal aid & advice: Advice & assistance: Scotland. 345
Legal aid & advice: Assistance by way of representation: Financial limit: District Court: Scotland. 345
Legal aid & advice: Civil legal aid: Financial conditions: Scotland 345
Legal aid & advice: Civil legal aid: Scotland 345
Legal aid & advice: Criminal legal assistance: Fees & information: Scotland 345
Legal aid & advice: Criminal proceedings: Costs: Northern Ireland 395
Legal aid & advice: Financial conditions: Northern Ireland 395
Legal aid & advice: Legal advice & assistance: Financial conditions: Northern Ireland. 395
Legal aid & advice: Legal advice & assistance: Northern Ireland 395
Legal aid: Legal Profession & Legal Aid (Scotland) Act 2007: Commencements: Scotland 346
Legal aid: Legal Profession & Legal Aid (Scotland) Act 2007: Handling complaints & specification of interest rates: Scotland 346
Legal aid: Legal Profession & Legal Aid (Scotland) Act 2007: Scottish legal services ombudsman: Abolition: Scotland . 346
Legal aid: Legal Profession & Legal Aid (Scotland) Act 2007: Transitional, savings & consequential provisions: Scotland 346
Legal expenses: Civil recovery proceedings: Proceeds of Crime Act 2002 146
Legal officers: Annual fees: Ecclesiastical law. 55
Legal Profession & Legal Aid (Scotland) Act 2007: Commencements: Scotland 346
Legal Profession & Legal Aid (Scotland) Act 2007: Handling complaints & specification of interest rates: Scotland . . . 346
Legal Profession & Legal Aid (Scotland) Act 2007: Scottish legal services ombudsman: Abolition: Scotland 346
Legal Profession & Legal Aid (Scotland) Act 2007: Transitional, savings & consequential provisions: Scotland 346
Legal Services Act 2007: Commencements. 109
Legal Services Act 2007: Designated regulators: Functions 109
Legal Services Act 2007: Prescribed charity 109
Legal Services Act 2007: Transitional, savings & consequential provisions: Scotland 110
Legal Services Act 2007: Transitory provisions 109
Legal Services Commission: Community Legal Service: Financial: Amendments 108

Legal Services Commission: Community Legal Service: Funding: Amendments 108
Legal Services Commission: Community Legal Service: Funding: Amendments: England & Wales 108
Legal Services Commission: Criminal Defence Service: Defence costs orders: Recovery. 108
Legal Services Commission: Criminal Defence Service: Financial eligibility 108
Legal Services Commission: Criminal Defence Service: Funding: England & Wales 108
Legal Services Commission: Criminal Defence Service: General 108
Legal Services Commission: Criminal Defence Service: High cost cases: England & Wales 108
Legal Services Commission: Criminal Justice & Immigration Act 2008: Commencements 46, 48, 49, 109, 140, 144
Legal services: Community Legal Service: Funding: Counsel: Family proceedings: England & Wales. 109
Legal services: Courts & Legal Services Act 1990: Licensed conveyancers: Modification of power to make rules about:
England & Wales 109
Legal services: Probate services: Approved services: England & Wales 109
Legislative reform: Weighing & measuring equipment: Verfication 152
Liability limitation agreements: Disclosure 35
Liberty: Restriction: Criminal law: Scotland 336
Libraries: 2008 Act: Commencements: Northern Ireland 395
Libraries: Acts: Explanatory notes: Northern Ireland 374
Libraries: Acts: Northern Ireland 373
Licencing: Duties: Amusement machines 10, 33, 74, 104, 106
Licensing (Scotland) Act 2005: Act of Sederunt: Summary & statutory applications & appeals etc.: Amendments: Scotland
. . . . 362
Licensing (Scotland) Act 2005: Commencements: Scotland 346
Licensing: Liquor: Scotland 346
Lichfield: Parishes: Local government 111
Life assurance: Insurers: Information & duties 102
Life insurance: Overseas companies: Income tax 43
Limited liability partnerships: Companies Act 2006: Accounts & audit 110
Limited liability partnerships: Filing periods & late filing penalties 35
Limited liability partnerships: Large & medium-sized limited liability partnerships: Accounts 110
Limited liability partnerships: Small limited liability partnerships: Accounts 110
Liner Conferences: Merchant Shipping (Liner Conferences) Act 1982: Gibraltar: Repeals 122
Liquor: Licensing (Scotland) Act 2005: Commencements: Scotland 346
Liquor: Licensing: Scotland 346
Listed buildings: Conservation areas: Planning: England 268
Listed buildings: Planning: Appointed persons: Determination of appeals: Prescribed classes: England 268
Livestock industries: Bovine semen: Wales 13
Livestock: Horses: Zootechnical standards: Scotland 329
Lloyd's: Legislative reform 152
Lloyd's: Syndicate & aggregate accounts: Accounts directive 104
Loan relationships & derivative contracts: Accounting practice: Changes. 43
Local authorities *see also* Local government
Local authorities: Alcohol disorder zones 79, 114, 140
Local authorities: Capital finance & accounting: England 111
Local authorities: Capital finance & accounting: Wales 115
Local authorities: Consent requirements: Legislative reform: England & Wales 114, 152
Local authorities: Early years provision: Free: Duty 24
Local authorities: Elected mayors: England 111, 272
Local authorities: Elections: Councils: England 112
Local authorities: Family intervention tenancies: Decisions: Reviews: England 94
Local authorities: Functions & responsibilities: England 112
Local authorities: Model code of conduct: Wales 115
Local authorities: Notices: Scotland 343
Local authorities: Parishes & parish councils 112
Local authorities: Property searches: Charges: Disapplication: England 95
Local authorities: Property searches: Charges: England 95
Local authorities: Requisite calculations: Alteration: England 114
Local authorities: Requisite calculations: Alteration: Wales 116
Local authorities: Social security: Investigations & prosecutions 260
Local authorities: Targets: Well-being of young children 24
Local authorities: Traffic orders: Procedure: Scotland 354
Local Better Regulation Office: Establishment: Acts 7
Local Better Regulation Office: Establishment: Acts: Explanatory notes 8
Local Electoral Administration & Registration Services (Scotland) Act 2006: Commencements: Scotland 353
Local Governance (Scotland) Act 2004: Remuneration: Amendments: Scotland 346
Local Government & Public Involvement in Health Act 2007: Commencements 112, 114, 124, 125, 254

Local Government & Public Involvement in Health Act 2007: Commencements: Wales 115
Local Government & Public Involvement in Health Act 2007: Consequential provisions 125, 254
Local Government & Public Involvement in Health Act 2007: Local involvement networks: Amendments. 125, 254
Local government *see also* Local authorities
Local government: Allowances & expenses: Amendments: Scotland 346
Local government: Best value performance indicators: Wales 115
Local government: Boundaries: Acts: Explanatory notes: Northern Ireland 374
Local government: Boundaries: Acts: Northern Ireland 373
Local government: Business improvement districts: Scotland 346
Local government: Case tribunals: England. 110
Local government: Dumfries & Galloway: Electoral arrangements: Scotland 346
Local government: Electoral changes: Barrow-in-Furness 110
Local government: Electoral changes: Basingstoke & Deane (Borough). 110
Local government: Electoral changes: Bradford 110
Local government: Electoral changes: Isle of Wight 111
Local government: Electoral changes: Maidstone 112
Local government: Electoral changes: South Cambridgeshire 113
Local government: Electoral changes: South Lakeland (District) 111
Local government: Electoral changes: Uttlesford. 114
Local government: Electoral changes: Welwyn Hatfield (Borough) 110
Local government: Finance: New parishes 44, 112
Local government: Finance: Penalties: Substitution: England 115
Local government: Finance: Scotland. 346
Local government: Joint committee as body corporate: Constituting: Northern Ireland 395
Local government: Landlords: Private: Registration: Advice & assistance: Scotland. 343, 347
Local government: Landlords: Private: Registration: Information & fees: Scotland 343, 347
Local government: Local authorities: Capital finance & accounting: England. 111
Local government: Local authorities: Capital finance & accounting: Wales. 115
Local government: Local authorities: Elected mayors: England 111, 272
Local government: Local Governance (Scotland) Act 2004: Remuneration: Amendments: Scotland 346
Local government: Non-domestic rating: Amendments: England 150
Local government: Overview & scrutiny: Reference by councillors: Excluded matters: England. 113
Local government: Parish councils: Power to promote well-being: Prescribed conditions. 113
Local government: Parish electoral arrangements & electoral changes: Berwick-upon-Tweed (Borough) 110
Local government: Parish electoral arrangements & electoral changes: Stratford-on-Avon 114
Local government: Parish electoral arrangements & electoral changes: Stroud 114
Local government: Parish electoral arrangements: Derwentside 111
Local government: Parish electoral arrangements: Halton 111
Local government: Parish electoral arrangements: Hertsmere 111
Local government: Parish electoral arrangements: Newark & Sherwood Forest. 113
Local government: Parish electoral arrangements: Oxford. 113
Local government: Parish electoral arrangements: Sevenoaks 113
Local government: Parish electoral arrangements: Tewkesbury (Borough) 110
Local government: Parishes: Alnwick. 110
Local government: Parishes: Berwick-upon-Tweed 110
Local government: Parishes: Cotswold 111
Local government: Parishes: Daventry 111
Local government: Parishes: Ellesmere Port & Neston. 111
Local government: Parishes: Hertmere 111
Local government: Parishes: High Peak. 111
Local government: Parishes: Isle of Wight 111
Local government: Parishes: Leeds 111
Local government: Parishes: Lichfield 111
Local government: Parishes: Newark & Sherwood. 113
Local government: Parishes: North Dorset. 113
Local government: Parishes: North Norfolk 113
Local government: Parishes: North Wiltshire. 113
Local government: Parishes: Oxford 113
Local government: Parishes: Pendle 113
Local government: Parishes: Restormel 111, 113
Local government: Parishes: Salisbury 113
Local government: Parishes: Sevenoaks 113
Local government: Parishes: Shrewsbury & Atcham. 113
Local government: Parishes: St Helens 114
Local government: Pension schemes 138

Local government: Pension schemes: Administration 137
Local government: Pension schemes: Administration: Scotland 350
Local government: Pension schemes: Amendments 137
Local government: Pension schemes: Benefits, membership & contributions: Scotland. 350
Local government: Pension schemes: Scotland. 350
Local government: Pension schemes: Transitional provisions 138
Local government: Police authorities: Best value: Performance indicators 115, 141
Local government: Politically restricted posts: Wales 115
Local government: Powys: Communities 115
Local government: Recreation grounds: Parish Council byelaws: Revocation: England. 113
Local government: Referendums: Conduct: Wales 115
Local government: Relevant authorities: Code of conduct: Prescribed period for undertakings: Wales 115
Local government: Rhondda Cynon Taf: Llanharan, Llanharry, Llantrisant & Pont-y-clun Communities 115
Local government: School lunches: Charging: Requirement: Dissapplication: Scotland 338, 347
Local government: Standards Committee 114
Local government: Structural & boundary changes: Staffing. 112
Local government: Structural changes: Bedfordshire 110
Local government: Structural changes: Cheshire 110
Local government: Structural changes: Cornwall 111
Local government: Structural changes: Durham (County) 111
Local government: Structural changes: Finance 114
Local government: Structural changes: Functions, property, rights & liabilities 112
Local government: Structural changes: Northumberland 113
Local government: Structural changes: Shropshire 113
Local government: Structural changes: Transitional arrangements 112
Local government: Structural changes: Wiltshire 114
Local government: Sustainable communities: England 114
Local housing allowance: Information sharing: Amendments: Housing benefit 257
Local involvement networks 125, 254
Local involvement networks: Amendments 125, 254
Local involvement networks: National Health Service: Duty of services-providers to allow entry 125
Local involvement networks: National Health Service: England 125
Local loans: Increase of limit 116
Local transport: Acts 6
Local transport: Acts: Explanatory notes 8
Loch of Boardhouse: Scottish Water: Scotland 366
London Gateway: Port harbour empowerment 87
London government: Greater London Authority Act 2007: Commencements 116
London government: Greater London Authority Act 2007: Election addresses 116
London government: London Waste & Recycling Board 116
London government: Road user charging: Enforcement & adjudication 116, 242
London Local Authorities: Transport: Local acts 8
London Operational Programme: European Regional Development Fund: Implementation 74
London Skills & Employment Board: Establishment 61
London Skills & Employment Board: Specified functions 61
London Stock Exchange: Stamp duty & stamp duty reserve tax: Investment exchanges & clearing houses 264
London Underground Victoria Line 09TS vehicles: Accessibility: Exemptions 54, 272
London Waste & Recycling Board 116
London: Railways: Crossrail: Acts 5
London: Railways: Crossrail: Acts: Explanatory notes 7
London: Transport for London Act 2008: Local acts 8
Lone parents: Miscellaneous amendments: Northern Ireland 408
Lone parents: Social security: Northern Ireland 408
Lord Chancellor: Judges: Discipline 105, 116, 117
Lord Chief Justice: Judges: Discipline 105, 116, 117
Lord Chief Justice: Judicial discipline: Prescribed procedures: Amendments 105, 117
Lothian & Borders Sheriffdom: Justice of the peace courts: Scotland 345
Lotteries: National lottery: Parks for People: Joint scheme: Authorisation: England 133
Lyme Bay: Fishing restrictions 252
Lyon Court & Office: Fees: Variation 17
Lyon Court & Office: Fees: Variation: Scotland 331

M

M2/A26: Ballee Road East link: Northern Ireland 403

Macclesfield (Borough): Cheshire (County): Parking contraventions: Civil enforcement 241
Machinery: Supply: Safety 88
Mackerel: Sea fishing: Control procedures: Scotland 360, 361
Magistrates' courts: Anti-social behaviour orders: Rules: Northern Ireland 395
Magistrates' courts: Children Act 1989: Contact orders: Enforcement 117
Magistrates' courts: Children: Northern Ireland 395
Magistrates' courts: Criminal Justice & Immigration Act 2008: Commencements 17, 46, 48, 49, 117, 140
Magistrates' courts: Criminal justice: Children: Rules: Northern Ireland 396
Magistrates' courts: Criminal procedure: Rules: England & Wales 117, 265
Magistrates' courts: District judge: Northern Ireland 394
Magistrates' courts: Family proceedings courts: Children Act 1989: Amendments 117
Magistrates' courts: Fees: England & Wales 117
Magistrates' courts: Fines: Information disclosure: Prescribed benefits: Collection 117
Magistrates' courts: Rules: Northern Ireland 395
Magistrates' courts: Seized cash: Detention & forfeiture: Northern Ireland 396
Magistrates' courts: Staff: Contracting out 40, 44, 117, 120, 265
Magnetic toys: Safety 39
Maidstone: Electoral changes: Local government 112
Maintained schools: Further education bodies: Collaboration arrangements: Wales 65
Maintenance orders: Enforcement facilities 118
Maintenance orders: Reciprocal enforcement: Reciprocating countries: Designation 117
Major accident hazard: Control 88
Management of Offenders etc. (Scotland) Act 2005: Commencements: Scotland 336
Management of Offenders etc. (Scotland) Act 2005: Members' remuneration & supplementary provisions: Scotland . . . 336
Manchester College of Arts & Technology and City College, Manchester: Dissolution 61
Manchester College: Government 61
Manchester College: Incorporation 61
Manor CE VC Primary: Religious character: Designation 61
Marine environment: Sea: Deposits: Exemptions: Northern Ireland 384
Marine pollution: Prevention: Merchant shipping 118
Market abuse: Financial Services & Markets Act 2000 79
Marketing: Misleading: Business protection from 271
Markets: St Austell: Local acts 8
Marriage: Church of England: General Synod: Measures 8
Maternity & parental leave 268
Maternity & parental leave: Northern Ireland 383
Mathematics: National curriculum: Attainment targets & programmes of study: Key stage 3 & 4: England 59
Mayor of London: Appointments: Greater London Authority 116
Mayor of London: Town & country planning 269
Mayors: Elected: Local authorities: England 111, 272
Measuring instruments: EC requirements 277
Measuring instruments: EEC requirements: Fees 78
Measuring instruments: Non-automatic weighing instruments 278
Measuring instruments: Use for trade: Northern Ireland 412
Meat products: England 83
Meat products: Northern Ireland 389
Meat products: Scotland 342
Meat products: Wales 85
Meat: Official controls: Charges: England 82
Meat: Official controls: Charges: Northern Ireland 388
Meat: Official controls: Charges: Scotland 341
Meat: Official controls: Charges: Wales 83
Medical Act 1983: Qualifying examinations 90
Medical devices: Consumer protection 40
Medical devices: Fees 78
Medical profession: Abortion: England 118
Medical profession: Abortion: Wales 118
Medical profession: Amendments 89
Medical services, general: National Health Service: Contracts: Wales 130
Medical services: Primary 130
Medical services: Primary: Performers lists: Northern Ireland 390
Medicines: Branded medicines: Prices control: Information supply: National Health Service 87, 128
Medicines: Health Act 2006: Commencements 118
Medicines: Human use: Clinical trials 118
Medicines: Human use: Fees 40, 78, 119

Medicines: Human use: Marketing Authorisations: Amendments 118
Medicines: Human use: Prescribing. 119
Medicines: Human use: Prescription: EEA practitioners 119
Medicines: Human use: Prohibition: Senecio & amendments 119
Medicines: Pharmacies: Applications for registration & fees. 119
Medicines: Pharmacies: Responsible pharmacist 119
Medicines: Prescription only: Human use. 119
Medicines: Sale or supply 119
Medicines: Veterinary medicines 119
Mental capacity: Liberty: Deprivation: Relevant person's representative: Appointment: England 119
Mental capacity: Liberty: Deprivation: Standard authorisations, assessments & ordinary residence: England 120
Mental Health Act 2007: Commencements 120, 121
Mental Health Act 2007: Consequential amendments 120
Mental Health Review Tribunal for Wales: Rules 274
Mental Health Tribunal for Scotland: Practice & procedure: Scotland 347
Mental health: Absconding patients from other jurisdictions: Scotland 347
Mental health: Adult Support & Protection (Scotland) Act 2007: Commencements: Scotland 326, 347
Mental health: Approved mental health professionals: Wales 121
Mental health: Approved professionals: Approval: England 120
Mental health: Conflicts of interest: England 120
Mental health: Conflicts of interest: Wales 121
Mental health: Cross-border transfer: Patients subject to requirements other than detention: Scotland 347
Mental health: Cross-border visits: Scotland 347
Mental health: Hospitals, guardianship & treatment: England 120
Mental health: Hospitals, guardianship, community treatment & consent to treatment 121
Mental health: Independent advocates: Wales 121
Mental health: Independent mental health advocates: England 120
Mental health: Medical treatment: Certificates: Scotland 347
Mental health: Mutual recognition: England & Wales 121
Mental health: Nurses: England 120
Mental health: Nurses: Wales 121
Mentally disordered offenders: Information: Victims: Schemes: Northern Ireland 394
Merchant Shipping (Liner Conferences) Act 1982: Gibraltar: Repeals. 122
Merchant Shipping (Liner Conferences) Act 1982: Repeals 122
Merchant shipping: Air pollution: Prevention. 118
Merchant shipping: Fishing vessels: Lifting operations & equipment 122
Merchant shipping: Fishing vessels: Work equipment: Provision & use 122
Merchant shipping: Marine pollution: Prevention: Sewage & garbage. 118
Merchant shipping: Relevant British possessions: Registries: Categorisation 122
Merchant shipping: Training & certification 122
Merchant shipping: Vessel traffic: Monitoring & reporting requirements 122
Mergers Directive: Implementation: Corporation tax 41
Mergers: Companies: Cross-border mergers 35
Mergers: Public companies: Mergers & divisions 35
Mesothelioma: Acts: Explanatory notes: Northern Ireland 374
Mesothelioma: Acts: Northern Ireland 373
Mesothelioma: Commencements: Northern Ireland 406
Mesothelioma: Diffuse: Payments: Acts. 4
Mesothelioma: Diffuse: Payments: Acts: Explanatory notes 7
Mesothelioma: Lump sum payments: Claims & reconsiderations. 257, 273
Mesothelioma: Lump sum payments: Claims & reconsiderations: Northern Ireland. 407
Mesothelioma: Lump sum payments: Conditions & amounts 258
Mesothelioma: Lump sum payments: Conditions & amounts: Northern Ireland 407
Messengers-at-Arms: Fees: Court of Session: Act of Sederunt: Scotland 334
Messengers-at-Arms: Fees: Court of Session: EC service regulation: Act of Sederunt: Scotland 334
Metropolitan Police Authority. 140
Mid Wales: Ceredigion & Mid Wales National Health Service Trust: Dissolution: Wales 129
Mid Wales: Ceredigion & Mid Wales National Health Service Trust: Transfer of Staff, property, rights & liabilities: Wales
. . . . 129
Midwives: Nursing & Midwifery Council: Constitution 90
Midwives: Nursing & Midwifery Council: Midwifery & Practice Committees: Constitution. 90
Milk & milk products: Designations: Protection: England 83
Milk & milk products: Designations: Protection: Northern Ireland. 390
Milk & milk products: Designations: Protection: Wales 85
Milk & milk products: Educational establishments: Pupils: England 11

Milk & milk products: Educational establishments: Pupils: Northern Ireland 376
Milk & milk products: Scotland. 342
Milk products: Prices: Reporting: England. 11
Milk products: Prices: Reporting: Northern Ireland. 377
Milk: Condensed & dried milk: England 81
Milk: Condensed & dried milk: Northern Ireland. 387
Milk: Condensed & dried milk: Scotland 340
Milk: Condensed & dried milk: Wales 83
Milk: Drinking milk: England 81
Milk: Drinking milk: Northern Ireland 387
Milk: School: Wales 13
Ministerial & other salaries 134
Ministers of the Crown: Chancellor of the Exchequer: Transfer of functions: To Secretary of State for the Home Department:
Registration 123
Ministers of the Crown: Functions: Transfer 122
Ministers of the Crown: Functions: Transfer: Rent Officer Service: Administration: England 122
Ministry of Defence: Police: Appeal tribunals 140
Misuse of Drugs Act 1971: Amendment 51
Mobile machinery: Non-road: Gaseous & particulate pollutants: Emissions 71
Mobility & Access Committee for Scotland: Revocation: Scotland 364
Modern foreign languages: National curriculum: Attainment targets & programmes of study: Key stage 3: England 58
Modern foreign languages: National curriculum: England. 59
Modern foreign languages: National curriculum: Wales. 67
Moldova: Double taxation: Relief & international enforcement 21, 41, 100
Motor cars: Driving instruction 155
Motor cycles: Single vehicle approval: Fees 155
Motor hackney carriages: Belfast: Byelaws: Amendments: Northern Ireland 403
Motor vehicles: Approval: Fees. 155
Motor vehicles: Disabled persons: Badges: Northern Ireland. 403
Motor vehicles: Driving licences 155
Motor vehicles: Driving licences: Northern Ireland. 403
Motor vehicles: EC type approval. 155
Motor vehicles: Seat belts: Wearing: Northern Ireland 403, 404
Motor vehicles: Seized vehicles: Retention & disposal. 156
Motor vehicles: Seized: Retention & disposal: Criminal Justice (Northern Ireland) Order 2008: Northern Ireland 381
Motor vehicles: Seized: Retention & disposal: Road traffic & vehicles: Northern Ireland. 404
Motor vehicles: Speed limits: Northern Ireland. 403
Motor vehicles: Taxi Drivers' licences: Fees: Amendments: Northern Ireland. 403
Motor vehicles: Testing: Northern Ireland 404
Motor vehicles: Tests 155, 156
Motorways: A1(M) 159, 160, 161
Motorways: A1(M)/A1. . . . . 159, 161
Motorways: A1(M)/A1/A195(M) 159
Motorways: A1(M)/A1/A66. 161
Motorways: A1(M)/A167 159
Motorways: A1(M)/M1 208
Motorways: A1(M)/M62 241
Motorways: A1: Dishforth to Barton Section 91
Motorways: A194(M). 199
Motorways: A195(M)/A1(M)/A1. 159
Motorways: A404(M) 201
Motorways: A556(M): M6 to M56 link & connecting roads scheme: Revocation 91
Motorways: A556(M): M6 to M56 link supplementary connecting roads scheme: Revocation. 91
Motorways: A627(M). 205
Motorways: A66(M). 195
Motorways: A66(M)/A66 195
Motorways: M1 . . . . 205, 206, 207, 208, 209
Motorways: M1/A1(M) 208
Motorways: M1/A42 206
Motorways: M1/A421. 207
Motorways: M1/A46 209
Motorways: M1/M62. . . . . 207, 208, 238
Motorways: M1/M62 207
Motorways: M1: Junction 13 & connecting roads 92
Motorways: M10 207

Motorways: M11	222, 223
Motorways: M11/A120	222
Motorways: M11/A14/A1307	222
Motorways: M11/M25	225
Motorways: M18	223
Motorways: M18/M180	223
Motorways: M180	240
Motorways: M180/M18	223
Motorways: M180/M181	240
Motorways: M181/M180	240
Motorways: M1-A1 link road	93
Motorways: M2	209
Motorways: M2/A2	167, 209
Motorways: M2/A26	403
Motorways: M20	224
Motorways: M20/A20	176, 223, 224
Motorways: M20/M25/A20	225
Motorways: M20/M26	227
Motorways: M23	224, 225
Motorways: M23/A23	177
Motorways: M23/M25	224
Motorways: M23/M3/M25	227
Motorways: M25	225, 226, 227
Motorways: M25/A2/A282	225
Motorways: M25/A21	225
Motorways: M25/A282	225
Motorways: M25/A3	225
Motorways: M25/A30	179
Motorways: M25/M11	225
Motorways: M25/M20/A20	225
Motorways: M25/M23	224
Motorways: M25/M23/M3	227
Motorways: M25/M26	225
Motorways: M25/M3	210
Motorways: M25/M4	225
Motorways: M25/M4/M40	227
Motorways: M25/M40	224, 229
Motorways: M26	227, 228
Motorways: M26/M20	227
Motorways: M26/M25	225
Motorways: M27	228
Motorways: M3	210
Motorways: M3/A316	209, 210
Motorways: M3/M25	210
Motorways: M3/M25/M23	227
Motorways: M32	228
Motorways: M32/M4	211
Motorways: M4	210, 211, 212, 245, 250, 251
Motorways: M4/A4042	250
Motorways: M4/A4232	250
Motorways: M4/A449	250
Motorways: M4/A48	250
Motorways: M4/M25	225
Motorways: M4/M32	211
Motorways: M4/M40/M25	227
Motorways: M4/M5	213
Motorways: M40	215, 229
Motorways: M40/A40	228, 229
Motorways: M40/A43	229
Motorways: M40/M25	224, 229
Motorways: M40/M25/M4	227
Motorways: M40/M42	228, 229
Motorways: M42	215, 229, 230
Motorways: M42/A5	229
Motorways: M42/M40	228, 229

Motorways: M42/M5	212
Motorways: M42/M6	215
Motorways: M42/M6 Toll/M6	215
Motorways: M45	230
Motorways: M48	230, 251
Motorways: M49	215, 231
Motorways: M49/M5	230
Motorways: M5	179, 212, 213, 214, 215
Motorways: M5/A38	212
Motorways: M5/A4	213
Motorways: M5/A40	213
Motorways: M5/A4123	206
Motorways: M5/M4	213
Motorways: M5/M42	212
Motorways: M5/M49	230
Motorways: M50	231
Motorways: M50/A449	231
Motorways: M53	231
Motorways: M54	231, 232
Motorways: M54/M6 Toll/M6	215
Motorways: M54/M6/A5	217
Motorways: M55	232
Motorways: M55/A585	232
Motorways: M55/M6	221
Motorways: M56	232, 233
Motorways: M57	233
Motorways: M58	233, 234
Motorways: M6	215, 216, 217, 218, 219, 220, 221
Motorways: M6 Toll	215, 222
Motorways: M6 Toll/A38	184
Motorways: M6 toll/M42/M6	215
Motorways: M6 Toll/M6/M42	215
Motorways: M6 Toll/M6/M54	215
Motorways: M6/A500	202
Motorways: M6/M40/M42/M6	215
Motorways: M6/M42	215
Motorways: M6/M42/M6 Toll/A42	215
Motorways: M6/M54/A5	217
Motorways: M6/M54/M6 Toll	215
Motorways: M6/M55	221
Motorways: M6/M6 Toll	217
Motorways: M6/M6 toll/M42	215
Motorways: M6/M6 Toll/M42/M69	215
Motorways: M60	234, 235, 236
Motorways: M60 etc.	234
Motorways: M60/A5103	234
Motorways: M602	240
Motorways: M606	240
Motorways: M606/M62	236
Motorways: M61	236
Motorways: M62	236, 237, 238, 239
Motorways: M62/A63	194, 238
Motorways: M62/M1	207, 208, 238
Motorways: M62/M606	236
Motorways: M62/M621/A62	239
Motorways: M62: A1(M)	241
Motorways: M62	92
Motorways: M621	240, 241
Motorways: M621/A62/M62	239
Motorways: M65	193, 239
Motorways: M66	239
Motorways: M67	239, 240
Motorways: M69	240
Motorways: M69/A46	187
Motorways: M8: Scotland	357

Motorways: Road traffic: Northern Ireland 403, 404
Museums & galleries: Tate Gallery Board: Additional members. 123
Museums & galleries: Value added tax: Refund 276
Music: National curriculum: Attainment targets & programmes of study: Key stage 3: England 58
Mutilations: Permitted procedures: Wales 17

N

National Assembly for Wales: Freedom of information 85
National Assembly for Wales: Legislative competence: Social welfare 37, 38, 53
National Assembly for Wales: Legislative competence: Social welfare: Wales 38, 53
National assistance services: Personal requirements: Sums: England 123
National assistance services: Personal requirements: Sums: Scotland 348
National assistance services: Personal requirements: Sums: Wales. 123
National assistance services: Resources: Assessment: England 123
National assistance services: Resources: Assessment: Scotland 347
National assistance services: Resources: Assessment: Wales. 123
National Child Measurement Programme: England. 125
National curriculum: Attainment targets & programmes of study: Art & design: Key stage 3: England 58
National curriculum: Attainment targets & programmes of study: Citizenship: Key stage 3 & 4: England. 58
National curriculum: Attainment targets & programmes of study: Design & technology: Key stage 3: England. 58
National curriculum: Attainment targets & programmes of study: English: Key stage 3 & 4: England. 58
National curriculum: Attainment targets & programmes of study: Geography: Key stage 3: England 58
National curriculum: Attainment targets & programmes of study: History: Key stage 3: England 58
National curriculum: Attainment targets & programmes of study: Mathematics: Key stage 3 & 4: England 59
National curriculum: Attainment targets & programmes of study: Modern foreign languages: Key stage 3: England 58
National curriculum: Attainment targets & programmes of study: Music: Key stage 3: England. 58
National curriculum: Attainment targets & programmes of study: Physical education: Key stage 3 & 4: England. 59
National curriculum: Attainment targets & programmes of study: Science: Key stage 3: England 58
National curriculum: Foundation stage: Wales. 66, 67
National curriculum: Key stage 1: Disapplication: Wales 66
National curriculum: Key stage 3: Assessment arrangements: England 59
National curriculum: Modern foreign languages: England. 59
National curriculum: Modern foreign languages: Wales. 67
National curriculum: Study: Attainment targets & programmes: Wales 66
National Health Service District Care Trusts: Bradford. 123
National Health Service Foundation Trusts: South Devon Healthcare 127
National Health Service Foundation Trusts: Trust funds: Trustees appointment: England. 126
National Health Service Primary Care Trusts: Dorset 124
National Health Service Primary Care Trusts: Surrey 127
National Health Service Trusts: Abertawe Bro Morgannwg University: Establishment: Wales 128
National Health Service Trusts: Abertawe Bro Morgannwg University: Transfer of property, rights & liabilities: Wales . 129
National Health Service Trusts: Bro Morgannwg: Dissolution: Wales 129
National Health Service Trusts: Bro Morgannwg: Transfer of Staff, property, rights & liabilities: Wales 129
National Health Service Trusts: Cambridgeshire & Peterborough Mental Health Partnership. 123
National Health Service Trusts: Cardiothoracic Centre-Liverpool 123
National Health Service Trusts: Carmarthenshire: Dissolution: Wales 129
National Health Service Trusts: Carmarthenshire: Transfer of Staff, property, rights & liabilities: Wales 129
National Health Service Trusts: Ceredigion & Mid Wales: Dissolution: Wales 129
National Health Service Trusts: Ceredigion & Mid Wales: Transfer of Staff, property, rights & liabilities: Wales 129
National Health Service Trusts: Conwy & Denbighshire: Dissolution: Wales 129
National Health Service Trusts: Conwy & Denbighshire: Transfer of Staff, property, rights & liabilities: Wales. 129
National Health Service Trusts: Cornwall Partnership 124
National Health Service Trusts: Cwm Taf: Establishment: Wales 129
National Health Service Trusts: Dudley & Walsall Mental Health Partnership: National Health Service Trust: Establishment
. . . . 124
National Health Service Trusts: East Kent Hospitals 124
National Health Service Trusts: East Kent Hospitals: Trust property: Transfer 124
National Health Service Trusts: Hammersmith Hospitals: Transfer of trust property 127
National Health Service Trusts: Hywel Dda: Establishment: Wales 130
National Health Service Trusts: Imperial College Healthcare: Trust funds: Trustees appointment 124
National Health Service Trusts: NHS Direct 126
National Health Service Trusts: North Bristol 127
National Health Service Trusts: North Cumbria Acute Hospitals. 127
National Health Service Trusts: North East Wales: Dissolution: Wales 131

National Health Service Trusts: North East Wales: Transfer of Staff, property, rights & liabilities: Wales 131
National Health Service Trusts: North Glamorgan: Dissolution: Wales 131
National Health Service Trusts: North Glamorgan: Transfer of Staff, property, rights & liabilities: Wales 131
National Health Service Trusts: North Primary Care Trust. 127
National Health Service Trusts: North Wales. 131
National Health Service Trusts: North Wales: Transfer of property, rights & liabilities: Wales 131
National Health Service Trusts: Northumberland, Tyne & Wear. 127
National Health Service Trusts: Originating capital: England 126
National Health Service Trusts: Pembrokeshire & Derwen: Dissolution: Wales. 131
National Health Service Trusts: Pembrokeshire & Derwen: Transfer of Staff, property, rights & liabilities: Wales 131
National Health Service Trusts: Pontypridd & Rhondda: Dissolution: Wales 131
National Health Service Trusts: Pontypridd & Rhondda: Transfer of Staff, property, rights & liabilities: Wales 132
National Health Service Trusts: St Mary's: Trust property: Transfer. 127
National Health Service Trusts: Swansea: Dissolution: Wales 132
National Health Service Trusts: Swansea: Transfer of Staff, property, rights & liabilities: Wales. 132
National Health Service: Appointments Commission 123, 147, 254
National Health Service: Care quality commission: Membership 123, 148, 254
National Health Service: Central Register: Scotland 353
National Health Service: Charges: Overseas visitors: Wales 130
National Health Service: Charges: Personal injuries: Amounts. 128
National Health Service: Clinical negligence & other risks: Indemnity scheme: Scotland. 348
National Health Service: Common Services Agency: Functions: Scotland. 348
National Health Service: Dental charges 125
National Health Service: Drugs & appliances: Charges: England 125
National Health Service: Drugs & appliances: Charges: Scotland 348
National Health Service: General medical services contracts. 130
National Health Service: General ophthalmic services: Contracts 124
National Health Service: General ophthalmic services: Wales 130
National Health Service: Health & Social Care Act 2008: Commencements 89, 91, 96, 124, 148, 254
National Health Service: Health & Social Care Act 2008: Consequential amendments 123, 148, 254
National Health Service: Health & Social Care Information Centre: Transfer of staff, property & liabilities 124
National Health Service: Health Act 2006: Commencements 124, 128, 254
National Health Service: Health service bodies: Recognition: Scotland 348
National Health Service: Injury benefits: England & Wales 128
National Health Service: Involvement arrangements: Directions by Strategic Health Authorities to Primary Care Trusts . 126
National Health Service: Involvement arrangements: Strategic Health Authorities: Primary Care Trusts 126
National Health Service: Local Government & Public Involvement in Health Act 2007: Commencements . . . 124, 125, 254
National Health Service: Local Government & Public Involvement in Health Act 2007: Consequential provisions. . 125, 254
National Health Service: Local involvement networks 125, 254
National Health Service: Local involvement networks: Duty of services-providers to allow entry 125
National Health Service: Local involvement networks: England. 125
National Health Service: Medicines: Branded medicines: Prices control: Information supply. 87, 128
National Health Service: National Child Measurement Programme: England 125
National Health Service: National Information Governance Board. 126
National Health Service: NHS Professionals Special Health Authority: Establishment & constitution 127
National Health Service: Optical charges & payments: England 126
National Health Service: Optical charges & payments: Scotland. 348
National Health Service: Optical charges & payments: Wales 130
National Health Service: Overseas visitors: Charges 125
National Health Service: Overseas visitors: Charges: Scotland. 348
National Health Service: Pension scheme: Additional voluntary contributions, injury benefits & compensation for premature
retirement 128
National Health Service: Pension scheme: England & Wales 128
National Health Service: Pension scheme: Scotland 348
National Health Service: Performers lists: England. 126
National Health Service: Personal injuries: Charges: Amounts: Scotland 349
National Health Service: Pharmaceutical services: England 126
National Health Service: Primary care trusts: Membership & procedure: England 127
National Health Service: Primary medical services & performers lists. 130
National Health Service: Primary ophthalmic services 127
National Health Service: Primary ophthalmic services: Amendment, transitional & consequential provisions 127
National Health Service: Primary ophthalmic services: Optical charges & payments: England 127
National Health Service: Primary ophthalmic services: Transitional provisions 127
National Health Service: Strategic health authorities & primary care trusts: Functions: England 126

National Health Service: Superannuation scheme, injury benefits, additional voluntary contributions & compensation for premature retirement: Scotland ... 348, 349
National Health Service: Superannuation scheme: Scotland ... 349
National Health Service: Travelling expenses & remission of charges: England ... 125, 126
National Health Service: Travelling expenses & remission of charges: Scotland ... 349
National Health Service: Travelling expenses & remission of charges: Wales ... 130, 131
National Health Service: Trusts: Membership & procedure: England ... 127
National Information Governance Board ... 126
National insurance numbers: Social security ... 261
National insurance numbers: Social security: Northern Ireland ... 409
National insurance: Companies Act 2006: Consequential amendments ... 35, 255, 267
National insurance: Contributions: Acts ... 6
National insurance: Contributions: Acts: Explanatory notes ... 8
National insurance: Contributions: Application of part 7 of the Finance Act 2004 ... 258
National lottery: Olympic Lottery Distribution Fund: Payments to ... 132, 134
National lottery: Parks for People: Joint scheme: Authorisation: England ... 133
National Minimum Wage Regulations 1999: Amendment ... 268
National Savings Bank ... 251
National scenic areas: Countryside: Scotland ... 334
Nationality & immigration: Cost recovery fees ... 97, 132
Nationality & immigration: Fees ... 97, 132
Nationality: Immigration, Asylum & Nationality Act 2006: Commencements ... 98
Nationality: Immigration, Asylum & Nationality Act 2006: Data Sharing: Code of practice ... 98, 139, 154
Nationality: Immigration, Asylum & Nationality Act 2006: Information: Duty to share & disclosure for security purposes 98, 140, 154
Nationality: Immigration: Isle of Man ... 98
Nationality: Immigration: Police: Passenger, crew & service information ... 98, 139
Natural habitats: Conservation: England & Wales ... 44, 278
Nature Conservation (Scotland) Act 2004: Commencements: Scotland ... 349
Nature conservation: Sites of special scientific interest: Register: Scotland ... 349
NAV list: Valuation: Time: Northern Ireland ... 401
Naval Discipline Act: Continuation ... 51
Naval Medical Compassionate Fund ... 52
Navy: Court-martial: Rules ... 52
Navy: Disablement & death: Service pensions ... 135
Navy: Service complaints ... 51
Navy: Service Discipline Acts: Alignment ... 51
Network access: Land registration: England & Wales ... 107
Network Rail: Thameslink: Land acquisition ... 272, 273
New Zealand: Double taxation: Relief & international enforcement ... 21, 41, 100
Newark & Sherwood Forest: Parish electoral arrangements: Local government ... 113
Newark & Sherwood: Parishes: Local government ... 113
NHS Business Services Authority: Counter fraud & security management: Delegation of functions ... 125
NHS Direct: National Health Service Trust ... 126
NHS Professionals Special Health Authority: Establishment & constitution ... 127
Nitrate pollution: Agriculture: Water: Prevention ... 11, 276
Nitrate pollution: Prevention: Wales ... 12, 277
Nitrate vulnerable zones: Action programmes: Scotland ... 327, 338, 339, 365
Nitrates Action Programme: Environmental protection: Northern Ireland ... 384
Noise: Environment: England ... 72
Non-automatic weighing instruments ... 278
Non-contentious probate: Fees ... 266
Non-contractual obligations: Law: England, Wales & Northern Ireland ... 144
Non-domestic rates: Levying: Scotland ... 352
Non-domestic rates: Scotland ... 352
Non-domestic rating: Communications hereditaments: England ... 150
Non-domestic rating: Communications hereditaments: Valuation, alteration of lists & appeals & material day: Wales ... 150
Non-domestic rating: Contributions: England ... 150
Non-domestic rating: Contributions: Wales ... 151
Non-domestic rating: Demand notices: Council tax: England ... 43, 150
Non-domestic rating: Demand notices: Wales ... 151
Non-domestic rating: Local government: Amendments: England ... 150
Non-domestic rating: Rural areas & rateable value limits: Scotland ... 353
Non-domestic rating: Small business relief: Wales ... 151
Non-domestic rating: Telecommunications & canals: Scotland ... 353

Non-domestic rating: Unoccupied property: England. 150
Non-domestic rating: Unoccupied property: Scotland 353
Non-domestic rating: Unoccupied property: Wales. 151
Norfolk: North Norfolk: Parishes: Local government. 113
Norham St Ceolwulfs CofE Controlled First School: Religious character: Designation. 61
North Bristol National Health Service Trust 127
North Cumbria Acute Hospitals: National Health Service Trust 127
North Dorset: Parishes: Local government 113
North East Wales National Health Service Trust: Dissolution: Wales 131
North East Wales National Health Service Trust: Transfer of Staff, property, rights & liabilities: Wales 131
North Glamorgan National Health Service Trust: Dissolution: Wales 131
North Glamorgan National Health Service Trust: Transfer of Staff, property, rights & liabilities: Wales 131
North Norfolk: Parishes: Local government 113
North Tees Primary Care Trust: National Health Service Trust 127
North Wales National Health Service Trust: Establishment: Wales 131
North Wales National Health Service Trust: Transfer of property, rights & liabilities: Wales. 131
North Wiltshire: Parishes: Local government. 113
North Yorkshire County Council: Schools: Meals 62
Northern Ireland (Miscellaneous Provisions) Act 2006: Commencements. 133
Northern Ireland (Sentences) Act 1998: Specified organisations 144
Northern Ireland Act 1998: Modifications 133
Northern Ireland Arms Decommissioning Act 1997: Amnesty period 133
Northern Ireland: Statutes: Chronological tables 375
Northern Ireland: Statutory rules: Annual volumes. 375
Northern Ireland: Statutory rules: Chronological tables 374, 375
Northern Rock plc: Compensation schemes 19
Northern Rock plc: Transfer to public ownership 19
Northumberland, Tyne & Wear: National Health Service Trust 127
Northumberland: Local government: Structural changes. 113
Nottinghamshire (County): Parking contraventions: Civil enforcement 241
Nuclear installations: Air navigation: Flying restrictions 30
Nurses & midwives: Nursing & midwifery. 90
Nurses: Mental health: Wales 121
Nurses: Nursing & Midwifery Council: Constitution 90
Nurses: Nursing & Midwifery Council: Midwifery & Practice Committees: Constitution 90
Nursing & midwifery. 90
Nursing & Midwifery Council: Constitution 90
Nursing & Midwifery Council: Midwifery & Practice Committees: Constitution. 90
Nutrition: Schools (Health Promotion & Nutrition) Act 2007: Commencements: Scotland 338
Nutrition: Standards: School food: England 59
Nutritional requirements: Food & drink: Schools: Scotland 338

O

Occupational & personal pension schemes 137
Occupational & personal pension schemes: General levy 135
Occupational & personal pension schemes: General levy: Northern Ireland 396
Occupational & personal pension schemes: Transfer values 135
Occupational pension schemes: Amendment: Northern Ireland 397
Occupational pension schemes: Employer debt. 135
Occupational pension schemes: Employer debt: Apportionment arrangements 136
Occupational pension schemes: Employer debt: Apportionment arrangements: Northern Ireland. 396
Occupational pension schemes: Employer debt: Northern Ireland 396
Occupational pension schemes: Internal dispute resolution procedures & amendments: Northern Ireland 396
Occupational pension schemes: Internal dispute resolution procedures: Amendments. 136
Occupational pension schemes: Levies 136
Occupational pension schemes: Levies: Northern Ireland 396
Occupational pension schemes: Levy ceiling. 135
Occupational pension schemes: Levy ceiling: Earnings percentage increase. 136
Occupational pension schemes: Levy ceiling: Northern Ireland 396
Occupational pension schemes: Non-European schemes: Exemption 136
Occupational pension schemes: Non-European schemes: Exemptions: Northern Ireland 397
Occupational pension schemes: Transfer values 136
Occupational pension schemes: Transfer values: Northern Ireland 396, 397
Occupational pensions: Revaluation 136

Occupational pensions: Revaluation: Northern Ireland 397
Offender Management Act 2007: Approved premises 145
Offender Management Act 2007: Commencements. 144, 145
Offender Management Act 2007: Consequential amendments 145
Offender Management Act 2007: Probation trusts: Establishment 145
Offenders: Assisting investigations & prosecutions: Substituted sentences: Scotland 336
Offenders: Rehabilitation of Offenders Act 1974: Exceptions: Amendments: England & Wales 152
Offenders: Road traffic: Prescribed devices. 156
Offensive weapons: Criminal Justice Act 1988 . . . . 46, 47
Official statistics. 133
Official statistics: Pre-release access: Scotland 349
Official statistics: Scotland 349
Official statistics: Statistics & Registration Service Act 2007: Commencements 54, 134, 151, 264
Offshore electricity: Development: Environmental assessment: Northern Ireland 383
Offshore installations: River Humber: Upper Burcom Tidal Stream Generator. 68, 134, 272
Offshore installations: Safety zones. 134
Offshore wind & water driven generating stations: Permitted capacity: Northern Ireland 383
Ofsted: Inspectors: Appointments: England 24, 61
Olive oil: Marketing standards: Northern Ireland 385, 389
Olympic & paralympic games: Olympic Lottery Distribution Fund: Payments to 132, 134
Olympic Lottery Distribution Fund: Payments to 132, 134
Ophthalmic services: General: Contracts: National Health Service. 124
Ophthalmic services: Primary: National Health Service 127
Ophthalmic services: Primary: National Health Service: Amendment, transitional & consequential provisions 127
Ophthalmic services: Primary: Optical charges & payments: National Health Service: England 127
Ophthalmic services: Primary: Transitional provisions: National Health Service 127
Optical charges & payments: National Health Service: England 126
Optical charges & payments: National Health Service: Scotland. 348
Optical charges & payments: National Health Service: Wales 130
Optical charges & payments: Northern Ireland 391
Opticians: General Optical Council: Committee constitution: Rules. 90
Opticians: General Optical Council: Fitness to practise: Rules 90
Opticians: General Optical Council: Therapeutics & contact lens specialties 89, 134
Organic farming: Northern Ireland 376
Overseas insurers: Tax representatives: Income tax 102
Overseas life insurance companies: Income tax 43
Overseas territories: Merchant Shipping (Liner Conferences) Act 1982: Gibraltar: Repeals. 122
Oxford: Parish electoral arrangements: Local government 113
Oxford: Parishes: Local government 113
Ozone depleting substances: Controls 70
Ozone depleting substances: Qualifications 71

P

Packaging waste: Producer responsibility & obligations. 71
Packaging waste: Producer responsibility & obligations: Northern Ireland 400
Parental & maternity leave 268
Parental & maternity leave: Northern Ireland 383
Parents: Lone: Social security. 260
Parish councils: Power to promote well-being: Prescribed conditions 113
Parish electoral arrangements & electoral changes: Berwick-upon-Tweed (Borough). 110
Parish electoral arrangements & electoral changes: Stratford-on-Avon 114
Parish electoral arrangements & electoral changes: Stroud. 114
Parish electoral arrangements: Derwentside 111
Parish electoral arrangements: Halton. 111
Parish electoral arrangements: Hertsmere. 111
Parish electoral arrangements: Newark & Sherwood Forest 113
Parish electoral arrangements: Oxford 113
Parish electoral arrangements: Sevenoaks. 113
Parish electoral arrangements: Tewkesbury (Borough). 110
Parishes & parish councils. 112
Parishes: Alnwick 110
Parishes: Berwick-upon-Tweed 110
Parishes: Cotswold 111
Parishes: Daventry. 111

Parishes: Ellesmere Port & Neston 111
Parishes: Finance: Local government 44, 112
Parishes: Hertmere. 111
Parishes: High Peak 111
Parishes: Isle of Wight. 111
Parishes: Kettering. 111
Parishes: Leeds 111
Parishes: Lichfield 111
Parishes: Newark & Sherwood 113
Parishes: North Dorset. 113
Parishes: North Norfolk 113
Parishes: North Wiltshire 113
Parishes: Oxford. 113
Parishes: Pendle 113
Parishes: Restormel 113
Parishes: Salisbury. 113
Parishes: Sevenoaks 113
Parishes: Shrewsbury & Atcham 113
Parishes: St Helens 114
Parking contraventions: Civil enforcement: Approved devices: Wales. 243
Parking contraventions: Civil enforcement: Buckinghamshire (County): Wycombe (District) 241
Parking contraventions: Civil enforcement: Charges: Guidelines: Wales 243
Parking contraventions: Civil enforcement: Cheshire (County): Chester (City): Ellesmere Port & Neston (Borough) . . . 241
Parking contraventions: Civil enforcement: Cheshire (County): Macclesfield (Borough) 241
Parking contraventions: Civil enforcement: Cornwall (County) 241
Parking contraventions: Civil enforcement: Devon (County). 241
Parking contraventions: Civil enforcement: Dudley 242
Parking contraventions: Civil enforcement: Dudley (Borough) 242
Parking contraventions: Civil enforcement: Durham (District). 242
Parking contraventions: Civil enforcement: East Sussex (County): Eastbourne (Borough) 241
Parking contraventions: Civil enforcement: Gloucestershire (County): Forest of Dean (District) 241
Parking contraventions: Civil enforcement: Nottinghamshire (County) 241
Parking contraventions: Civil enforcement: Representations & appeals: Removed vehicles: Wales. 243
Parking contraventions: Civil enforcement: Representations & appeals: Wales 244
Parking contraventions: Civil enforcement: Rutland (County) 242
Parking contraventions: Civil enforcement: St. Helens 242
Parking contraventions: Civil enforcement: Swansea: Wales 93
Parking contraventions: Civil enforcement: Wales 243
Parking contraventions: Civil enforcement: Wiltshire (County): West Wiltshire (District) 242
Parking contraventions: Penalty charge notices, enforcement & adjudication: Wales 243
Parks: For people: Joint scheme: Authorisation: England 133
Parliament: Freedom of information 85
Parliament: House of Commons: Hansard: Centenary volume 1909-2009: Great speeches: Anthologies 9
Parliament: Ministerial & other salaries. 134
Parliamentary Commissioner 134
Parliamentary constituencies & Assembly electoral regions: Wales 153
Parliamentary constituencies: Redistribution of seats & review of election arrangements: Northern Ireland 154
Parliamentary elections: European: Returning officers 153
Parliamentary elections: European: Returning officers: Poll: Appointed day 153
Parochial fees 55
Partnership: Limited liability partnerships: Companies Act 2006: Accounts & audit 110
Partnerships: Accounts 134
Partnerships: Large & medium-sized limited liability partnerships: Accounts 110
Partnerships: Limited liability: Filing periods & late filing penalties 35
Partnerships: Small limited liability partnerships: Accounts 110
Passenger & goods vehicles: Drivers: Training: Certificates of professional competence 157
Passenger vehicles: Recording equipment: Downloading & retention of data 156
Passenger vehicles: Recording equipment: Fitters & workshops: Approval: Fees 156
Passive fishing gear & beam trawls: Sea fishing: Marking & identification: Northern Ireland 387
Paternity & adoption leave 268
Paternity & adoption leave: Northern Ireland. 383
Paternity: Evidence: Blood tests 74
Pathogens: Animals: Specified: England 14
Pathogens: Animals: Specified: Northern Ireland 379
Pathogens: Animals: Specified: Wales 16

Patient & public involvement: Local Government & Public Involvement in Health Act 2007: Commencements 112, 114, 124, 125, 254
Pay as You Earn *see* PAYE
PAYE: Income tax: Amendments. 101
Pembrokeshire & Derwen National Health Service Trust: Dissolution: Wales. 131
Pembrokeshire & Derwen National Health Service Trust: Transfer of Staff, property, rights & liabilities: Wales 131
Penalties: Amount: Disorderly behaviour: England & Wales. 47, 140
Penalty charges: Additional contravention: Northern Ireland. 404
Pendle: Parishes: Local government 113
Pension credit: Amendments. 260, 261
Pension Protection Fund: Entry rules 136
Pension Protection Fund: Entry rules: Northern Ireland 397
Pension Protection Fund: Pension compensation cap. 136
Pension Protection Fund: Pension compensation cap: Northern Ireland 397
Pension Protection Fund: Prescribed payments 136
Pension schemes: Registered: Provision of information 102
Pensioner allowance: Lone: Rate relief: Northern Ireland 401
Pensions Act 2004: Code of Practice: Dispute resolution: Appointed Day 136
Pensions Act 2004: Commencements. 136
Pensions Act 2007: Actuarial guidance 137
Pensions Act 2008: Commencements. 137
Pensions Appeal Tribunals: Northern Ireland: Northern Ireland 397
Pensions *see also* Pension Protection Fund 136
Pensions: 2005 Order: Codes of practice: Appointed days: Northern Ireland 397
Pensions: 2005 Order: Commencements: Northern Ireland. 397
Pensions: 2008 Act: Commencements: Northern Ireland 397
Pensions: Acts 6
Pensions: Acts: Explanatory notes: Northern Ireland 374
Pensions: Acts: Northern Ireland 373
Pensions: Actuarial guidance: Northern Ireland. 397
Pensions: Armed & Reserve Forces: Compensation 135
Pensions: Armed Forces: Reserve Forces: Compensation schemes 134, 135
Pensions: Christmas bonus: Relevant week 255
Pensions: Family law: Divorce etc.: Scotland. 339
Pensions: Financial assistance scheme: Amendments 135
Pensions: Fire services: Compensation scheme: Northern Ireland 386
Pensions: Firefighters' pension scheme: England. 80, 137
Pensions: Firefighters' pension scheme: Northern Ireland 386
Pensions: Firefighters' pension scheme: Scotland 339, 349
Pensions: Guaranteed minimum increase 135
Pensions: Guaranteed minimum increase: Northern Ireland 396
Pensions: Gurkhas: Armed Forces 135
Pensions: Home responsibilities: Northern Ireland 409
Pensions: Increase: Review 137
Pensions: Increase: Review: Northern Ireland 397
Pensions: Judicial Pensions & Retirement Act 1993: Qualifying judicial offices 135, 137
Pensions: Local government schemes: Administration: Scotland. 350
Pensions: Local government schemes: Benefits, membership & contributions: Scotland 350
Pensions: Local government schemes: Scotland 350
Pensions: Local government: Pension schemes 138
Pensions: Local government: Pension schemes: Administration 137
Pensions: Local government: Pension schemes: Amendments 137
Pensions: Local government: Pension schemes: Transitional provisions 138
Pensions: National Health Service: Pension scheme: Additional voluntary contributions, injury benefits & compensation for premature retirement 128
Pensions: National Health Service: Pension scheme: England & Wales 128
Pensions: Navy, army & air force: Disablement & death: Service pensions 135
Pensions: Occupational & personal pension schemes: General levy 135
Pensions: Occupational & personal pension schemes: General levy: Northern Ireland 396
Pensions: Occupational & personal pension schemes: Transfer values 135
Pensions: Occupational pension schemes: Employer debt 135
Pensions: Occupational pension schemes: Employer debt: Apportionment arrangements 136
Pensions: Occupational pension schemes: Employer debt: Apportionment arrangements: Northern Ireland 396
Pensions: Occupational pension schemes: Employer debt: Northern Ireland. 396
Pensions: Occupational pension schemes: Internal dispute resolution procedures & amendments: Northern Ireland 396

Pensions: Occupational pension schemes: Internal dispute resolution procedures Amendments 136
Pensions: Occupational pension schemes: Levies. 136
Pensions: Occupational pension schemes: Levies: Northern Ireland 396
Pensions: Occupational pension schemes: Levy ceiling 135
Pensions: Occupational pension schemes: Levy ceiling: Earnings percentage increase 136
Pensions: Occupational pension schemes: Levy ceiling: Northern Ireland 396
Pensions: Occupational pension schemes: Non-European schemes: Exemption 136
Pensions: Occupational pension schemes: Non-European schemes: Exemptions: Northern Ireland 397
Pensions: Occupational pension schemes: Transfer values 136
Pensions: Occupational pension schemes: Transfer values: Northern Ireland 397
Pensions: Occupational pensions: Revaluation: Northern Ireland 397
Pensions: Occupational: Revaluation 136
Pensions: Pension Protection Fund: Entry rules: Northern Ireland 397
Pensions: Pension schemes: Income tax: Transitional provisions 102
Pensions: Personal & occupational pension schemes 137
Pensions: Personal & occupational pension schemes: Northern Ireland 397
Pensions: Personal & occupational pension schemes: Transfer values: Amendment: Northern Ireland 396
Pensions: Personal injuries: Civilians 137
Pensions: Police 138, 142
Pensions: Police: Scotland. 350
Pensions: Registered pension schemes: Transfer of sums & assets 102
Pensions: Social security: Home responsibilities 261
Pensions: Social security: Low earnings threshold 261
Pensions: Social security: Low earnings threshold: Northern Ireland 409
Pensions: Superannuation Act 1972: Schedule 1: Admission. 137
Pensions: Teachers: Superannuation: Scotland 350
Pensions: Teachers' pensions. 64
Pensions: Teachers' pensions: Northern Ireland 382
Penwith College, Penzance: Dissolution 62
Perry: Excise 74
Personal & occupational pension schemes 137
Personal Accounts Delivery Authority: Pensions: Acts: Explanatory notes: Northern Ireland. 374
Personal Accounts Delivery Authority: Pensions: Acts: Northern Ireland 373
Personal care & nursing care: Community care: Scotland 363
Personal injuries: Civilians 137
Personal injuries: National Health Service: Charges: Amounts: Scotland 349
Personal injuries: NHS charges: Amounts 128
Personal pension schemes: Amendment: Northern Ireland 397
Personal pension schemes: Transfer values: Northern Ireland 396
Pesticides: Maximum residue levels: Crops, food & feeding stuffs: England & Wales 12, 138
Pesticides: Maximum residue levels: Crops, food & feeding stuffs: Northern Ireland 378
Pesticides: Maximum residue levels: Crops, food & feeding stuffs: Scotland 328, 350
Pesticides: Maximum residue levels: England & Wales 11, 138
Pesticides: Maximum residue levels: Northern Ireland 377, 397
Pesticides: Maximum residue levels: Scotland 328, 350
Pesticides: Plant protection products: Northern Ireland. 398
Peterborough: Cambridgeshire & Peterborough Mental Health Partnership National Health Service Trust. 123
Peterhead Port Authority: Harbour revision: Scotland 342
Petroleum: Licensing: Production: Seaward areas 138
Pharmaceutical chemists: Registration: Exempt persons: Northern Ireland 398
Pharmaceutical services: National Health Service: England 126
Pharmaceutical Society of Northern Ireland: General: Northern Ireland 398
Pharmacies: Applications for registration & fees 119
Pharmacies: Responsible pharmacist 119
Pharmacists: Royal Pharmaceutical Society of Great Britain: Registration rules: Order of Council 90
Pharmacy: European qualifications: Northern Ireland 398
Pharmacy: Pharmaceutical chemists: Registration: Exempt persons: Northern Ireland 398
Physical education: National curriculum: Attainment targets & programmes of study: Key stage 3 & 4: England. 59
Pig production development: Levy: Northern Ireland. 377
Pigs: Animal health: Records, identification & movement: Wales. 15
Pigs: Records, identification & movement: Scotland 330
Planning & Compulsory Purchase Act 2004: Commencements: Wales 270
Planning etc. (Scotland) Act 2006: Commencements: Scotland 363
Planning etc. (Scotland) Act 2006: Development planning: Saving provisions: Scotland 363
Planning etc. (Scotland) Act 2006: Development planning: Saving, transitional & consequential provisions: Scotland .. 363

Planning *see also* Town & country planning
Planning: Acts 6
Planning: Acts: Explanatory notes 8
Planning: Appointed persons: Determination of appeals: Prescribed classes: England 268
Planning: Avian influenza: General permitted development: Scotland 364
Planning: Avian influenza: Northern Ireland 398
Planning: Energy: Acts 6
Planning: Environmental impact assessment: Northern Ireland 398
Planning: Listed buildings: Conservation areas: England 268
Planning: Mayor of London 269
Planning: National security directions & appointed representatives: Scotland 270
Planning: Regional transport planning: Wales 273
Planning: Town & country planning: Environmental impact assessment: England 269
Planning: Town & country planning: General development procedure 269
Planning: Town & country planning: General permitted development: England 269
Planning: Town & country planning: General permitted development: Scotland 364
Planning: Town & country planning: General permitted development: Wales 270
Planning: Town & country planning: General permitted procedure: Wales 270
Planning: Town & country: Applications & deemed applications: Fees: England 269
Planning: Town & country: Environmental impact assessment: Wales 270
Planning: Town & country: Trees 269
Plant & machinery: Environmentally beneficial: Capital allowances 41, 100
Plant & machinery: Rating & valuation: England 150
Plant & machinery: Valuation for rating: Scotland 353
Plant health: Amendments: England 138, 139
Plant health: Amendments: Northern Ireland 398, 399
Plant health: Amendments: Scotland 350
Plant health: Fees: Forestry 138
Plant health: Fees: Scotland 350
Plant health: Forestry 138
Plant health: Import inspection fees: England 139
Plant health: Import inspection fees: Northern Ireland 399
Plant health: Potatoes: Originating in Egypt: Northern Ireland 399
Plant health: Potatoes: Originating in Poland: Notification: Scotland 350
Plant health: Seed potatoes: England 139
Plant health: Seed potatoes: Wales 139
Plant health: Wales 139
Plant protection products: Northern Ireland 398
Plastic materials & articles: Food: Contact: England 82
Plastic materials & articles: Food: Contact: Lid gaskets: Wales 84
Plastic materials & articles: Food: Contact: Northern Ireland 389
Plastic materials & articles: Food: Contact: Scotland 341
Plastic materials & articles: Food: Contact: Wales 84
Pneumoconiosis etc.: Workers' compensation: Claims: Payments 258
Pneumoconiosis etc.: Workers' compensation: Claims: Payments: Northern Ireland 407
Poland: Potatoes: Originating in Poland: Notification: Scotland 350
Police & Criminal Evidence Act 1984: Codes of practice: England & Wales 140, 141
Police & Justice Act 2006: Commencements 141, 142
Police & Justice Act 2006: Supplementary & transitional provisions 141
Police Act 1997: Commencements: Northern Ireland 48
Police Act 1997: Criminal records 140
Police Act 1997: Criminal records: Disclosure: Northern Ireland 48
Police Act 1997: Criminal records: Scotland 351
Police authorities: Best value: Performance indicators 115, 141
Police authorities: Particular functions & transitional provisions: England & Wales 141
Police Authority 141
Police cells: Legalised: Discontinuance: Scotland 351
Police Service of Northern Ireland Reserve: Full-time: Severance: Northern Ireland 399
Police Service of Northern Ireland: Conduct: Northern Ireland 399
Police Service of Northern Ireland: Full-time: Severance: Northern Ireland 399
Police Service of Northern Ireland: Promotion: Northern Ireland 399
Police: Amendments 140
Police: Appeals tribunals 141
Police: Complaints & misconduct 141
Police: Conduct 141

Police: Criminal Justice & Immigration Act 2008: Commencements 17, 46, 47, 48, 49, 109, 117, 140, 144, 152
Police: Deaths: Register: Supply of information: England & Wales 142, 152
Police: Deaths: Register: Supply of information: Northern Ireland 142, 152
Police: Disorderly behaviour: Penalties: Amount: England & Wales. 47, 140
Police: Grants: Scotland 351
Police: Immigration, Asylum & Nationality Act 2006: Data Sharing: Code of practice 98, 139, 154
Police: Immigration, Asylum & Nationality Act 2006: Duty to share & disclosure for security purposes 98, 140, 154
Police: Immigration: Passenger, crew & service information. 98, 139
Police: Local authorities: Alcohol disorder zones 79, 114, 140
Police: Metropolitan Police Authority. 140
Police: Ministry of Defence: Appeal tribunals 140
Police: Pensions 138, 142
Police: Pensions: Scotland. 350
Police: Performance 142
Police: Powers for designated staff: Code of ethics: Northern Ireland 399
Police: Powers for designated staff: Complaints & misconduct: Northern Ireland 399
Police: Promotion: England & Wales 142
Police: Serious Crime Act 2007: Commencements 142, 145, 147, 253
Police: Serious Organised Crime & Police Act 2005: Commencements: England & Wales 142
Police: Special constables: Scotland 351
Police: Substance misuse: Testing for: Northern Ireland 399
Police: Support staff: Transfer of employment: Northern Ireland 399
Police: Terrorism Act 2000: Detention, treatment & questioning: Code of practice: Northern Ireland 399
Police: Trainees: Northern Ireland: Northern Ireland 400
Police: Vehicles: Retention & disposal: England & Wales 142
Policing plans: England & Wales 142
Political donations & regulated transactions: Anonymous electors. 143
Political Parties, Elections & Referendums Act 2000: Northern Ireland political parties 143
Political parties: Donations & regulated transactions: Anonymous electors 143
Political parties: Electoral Administration Act 2006: Commencements: Northern Ireland 133, 142
Political parties: Electoral Administration Act 2006: Loans: Regulation: Northern Ireland 143
Pollution: Air pollution: Ships: Prevention 118
Pollution: Marine pollution: Prevention: Merchant shipping: Sewage & garbage 118
Pollution: Nitrate pollution: Prevention: Wales. 12, 277
Pollution: Nitrate: Agriculture: Water: Prevention 11, 276
Pollution: Nitrates Action Programme: Northern Ireland 384
Pollution: Prevention & control: Batteries: Directives: Designation: Scotland 339
Pollution: Prevention & control: Designation of directives: England & Wales 72
Pollution: Prevention & control: Scotland 339
Pollution: Water environment: Scotland 339, 366
Pontypridd & Rhondda National Health Service Trust: Dissolution: Wales 131
Pontypridd & Rhondda National Health Service Trust: Transfer of Staff, property, rights & liabilities: Wales 132
Port William: Dumfries & Galloway Council: Harbour: Empowerment: Scotland. 342
Postal services: Consumer complaints handling standards 143
Postal services: Regulated providers: Redress schemes. 40, 143
Postgraduate Medical Education & Training Board: Fees: Rules 90
Potatoes: Originating in Egypt: Northern Ireland 399
Potatoes: Originating in Poland: Notification: Scotland 350
Potatoes: Seed potatoes: England 139
Potatoes: Seed potatoes: Wales 139
Potatoes: Seed: Levies: Northern Ireland 377
Poultry: Salmonella: Control: Northern Ireland. 379
Poultry: Salmonella: Control: Scotland 330
Poultry: Salmonella: Control: Wales 15
Poultry: Scotland Act 1998: Agency arrangements: Specification 10, 13, 38, 45, 53, 143
Powys: Communities: Local government 115
PPF see Pension Protection Fund 136
Pregnancy: Health in pregnancy grant: Entitlement & amount 257
Prevention & suppression of terrorism: Counter-Terrorism Act 2008: Commencements 143
Prevention & suppression of terrorism: Terrorism Act 2000: Proscribed organisations 143
Prevention & suppression of terrorism: Terrorism Act 2006: Section 25: Disapplication 143
Prevention of Terrorism Act 2005: Sections 1 to 9: Continuance. 143
Primary care trusts & strategic health authorities: Functions: National Health Service 126
Primary medical services 130
Primary medical services: Performers lists: Northern Ireland 390

Primary ophthalmic services: National Health Service 127
Primary ophthalmic services: National Health Service: Amendment, transitional & consequential provisions 127
Primary ophthalmic services: Optical charges & payments: National Health Service: England 127
Primary ophthalmic services: Transitional provisions: National Health Service 127
Primary schools: Rural: Designation: England 56
Prisoners: Fixed-term: Eligibility period: Amendment 144
Prisoners: Short-term & long-term: Requisite period: Amendment 144
Prisons & young offenders centres: Northern Ireland 400, 412
Prisons: Criminal Justice & Immigration Act 2008: Commencements 46, 48, 49, 109, 140, 144
Prisons: Criminal Justice & Immigration Act 2008: Transitory provisions 47, 48, 144
Prisons: England & Wales 144
Prisons: Home Detention Curfew Licence: Specified days: Scotland 351
Prisons: Northern Ireland (Sentences) Act 1998: Specified organisations 144
Prisons: Offender Management Act 2007: Commencements 144, 145
Prisons: Police cells: Legalised: Discontinuance: Scotland 351
Prisons: Young offender institutions: Amendments: Scotland 351, 366
Private & voluntary health care: England 148
Private hire vehicles: Carrying of guide dogs, etc.: Disabled persons: Discrimination: Northern Ireland 382
Private international law: Non-contractual obligations: Scotland 351
Probate services: Approved bodies: England & Wales 109
Probate: Non-contentious: Fees 266
Probation trusts: Establishment: Offender Management Act 2007 145
Probation: Offender Management Act 2007: Approved premises 145
Probation: Offender Management Act 2007: Commencements 144, 145
Probation: Offender Management Act 2007: Consequential amendments 145
Procedure: Supreme Court, Northern Ireland: Crown Court: Rules: Amendments: Northern Ireland 400, 412
Proceeds of Crime Act 2002: Amendment 145
Proceeds of Crime Act 2002: Cash searches: Code of practice 145
Proceeds of Crime Act 2002: External requests & Orders 145
Proceeds of Crime Act 2002: Information: Disclosure 145
Proceeds of Crime Act 2002: Investigations: Code of practice: England, Wales & Northern Ireland 145
Proceeds of Crime Act 2002: Investigations: United Kingdom 145
Proceeds of Crime Act 2002: Legal expenses: Civil recovery proceedings 146
Proceeds of Crime Act 2002: Prosecutors: Investigative powers: Code of Practice: England, Wales & Northern Ireland . 146
Proceeds of crime: Assets Recovery Agency: Abolition 146
Proceeds of crime: Serious Crime Act 2007: Commencements 54, 105, 142, 145, 147, 154, 253
Proceeds of crime: Serious Crime Act 2007: Commencements: Scotland 351
Producer responsibility & obligations: Packaging waste 71
Producer responsibility & obligations: Packaging waste: Northern Ireland 400
Products of animal origin: Disease control: England 14
Products of animal origin: Disease control: Scotland 330
Products of animal origin: Disease control: Wales 15
Products of animal origin: Third country imports: England 11
Profits: Calculation of: Policy holders' tax: Insurance companies 42
Property: Unoccupied property: Non-domestic rating: Wales 151
Protection of Children & Vulnerable Adults & Care Standards Tribunal: Children's & adults' barred lists 25, 146
Protection of Children (Scotland) Act 2003: Child care position: Definition: Amendments: Scotland 333
Protection of Military Remains Act 1986: Vessels & controlled sites: Designations 52
Protection of vulnerable adults: Protection of Children & Vulnerable Adults & Care Standards Tribunal: Children's & adults'
barred lists 25, 146
Protection of vulnerable adults: Safeguarding Vulnerable Groups Act 2006: Barred list prescribed information: England &
Wales 25, 147
Protection of vulnerable adults: Safeguarding Vulnerable Groups Act 2006: Barring procedure: England & Wales . . 25, 147
Protection of vulnerable adults: Safeguarding Vulnerable Groups Act 2006: Commencements: England 24, 146
Protection of vulnerable adults: Safeguarding Vulnerable Groups Act 2006: Commencements: England & Wales. 25, 51, 147
Protection of vulnerable adults: Safeguarding Vulnerable Groups Act 2006: Commencements: Northern Ireland . . . 26, 147
Protection of vulnerable adults: Safeguarding Vulnerable Groups Act 2006: Prescribed criteria: Foreign offices: England &
Wales 25, 147
Protection of vulnerable adults: Safeguarding Vulnerable Groups Act 2006: Prescribed criteria: Transitional provisions:
England & Wales 25, 147
Protection of vulnerable adults: Safeguarding Vulnerable Groups Act 2006: Prescribed information: England & Wales 25, 147
Protection of vulnerable adults: Safeguarding Vulnerable Groups Act 2006: Transitional provisions: England & Wales . . 25, 147
Protection of wrecks: Designation: England 147
Public & utilities contracts: Public procurement 149

Public Appointments & Public Bodies etc. (Scotland) Act 2003: Specified authorities: Amendments: Scotland 351
Public audit: Serious Crime Act 2007: Commencements 54, 105, 142, 145, 147, 154, 253
Public authorities: Fair employment: Specification: Northern Ireland 385
Public authorities: Statutory duties: Disability discrimination 54
Public bodies: Audit: Government Resources & Accounts Act 2000 86
Public bodies: Welsh language schemes 278
Public contracts: Postal services & common procurement vocabulary codes: Scotland 352
Public contracts: Public procurement: Postal services 149
Public contracts: Scotland 352
Public finance & accountability: Budget (Scotland) Act 2007: Amendments: Scotland 351
Public finance & accountability: Budget (Scotland) Act 2008: Amendments: Scotland 352
Public general acts: Bound volumes 9
Public general acts: Tables & index 9
Public health: Acts: Explanatory notes: Northern Ireland 374
Public health: Acts: Explanatory notes: Scotland 325
Public health: Acts: Northern Ireland 373
Public health: Acts: Scotland 325
Public health: Aircraft: Northern Ireland 400
Public health: Appointments Commission 123, 147, 254
Public health: Care quality commission: Membership 123, 148, 254
Public health: Children & young persons: Tobacco: Sale: Northern Ireland 400
Public health: Contamination of food: Scotland 352
Public health: Dentistry: Private: Wales 148
Public health: Health & Social Care (Community Health & Standards) Act 2003: Commencements 148
Public health: Health & Social Care Act 2008: Commencements 89, 91, 96, 124, 148, 254
Public health: Health & Social Care Act 2008: Consequential amendments 123, 148, 254
Public health: Health Act 2006: Commencements: Wales 130
Public health: Private & voluntary health care: England 148
Public health: Producer responsibility & obligations: Packaging waste: Northern Ireland 400
Public health: Ships: Northern Ireland 400
Public health: Smoke-free: Exemptions, vehicles, penalties & discounted amounts: Northern Ireland 400
Public health: Vaccine damage payments: Specified diseases 148
Public interest: Disclosure: Prescribed persons 268
Public involvement: Local Government & Public Involvement in Health Act 2007: Commencements . . 112, 114, 124, 125, 254
Public passenger transport: Community bus services 148
Public passenger transport: Concessionary bus travel: Permits 149
Public passenger transport: International passenger services 149
Public passenger transport: Public service vehicles: Fitness, equipment, use & certification 149
Public passenger transport: Public service vehicles: Local services: Registration: England & Wales 149
Public passenger transport: Public service vehicles: Local services: Registration: Scotland 352
Public passenger transport: Public service vehicles: Operators' licences: Fees 149
Public passenger transport: Public service vehicles: Traffic regulation conditions: Scotland 352
Public procurement: Public & utilities contracts 149
Public procurement: Public & utilities contracts: Postal services 149
Public procurement: Public & utilities contracts: Postal services & common procurement vocabulary codes: Scotland . . 352
Public procurement: Public & utilities contracts: Scotland 352
Public rights of way: Combined orders: England 92
Public sector audit: Institutions of further education: Northern Ireland 380
Public service vehicles: Accessibility 54
Public service vehicles: Fitness, equipment, use & certification 149
Public service vehicles: Local services: Registration: England & Wales 149
Public service vehicles: Local services: Registration: Scotland 352
Public service vehicles: Operators' licences: Fees 149
Public service vehicles: Traffic regulation conditions: Scotland 352
Public Transport Users' Committee for Scotland 365
Public trustees: Fees 275
Pupils: Education: Information: Individual pupils: England 58
Pupils: Information: England 59
Purchased life annuities 102

Q

QCA levy: Education 64
Qualifications & Curriculum Authority: Additional functions 24, 62

Qualifications: General qualification bodies: Relevant qualifications, reasonable steps & physical features: Disabled persons: Disability discrimination 54
Quality Meat Scotland: Establishment: Scotland 329

R

Race Relations Act 1976: Amendment 150
Radio: 3400-3800 MHz frequency band: Management 68
Radioactive contaminated land: Enactments: Modification: England 72
Radioactive contaminated land: Enactments: Modification: Wales 73
Radioactive waste & spent fuel: Transfrontier shipments 18
Rail vehicles: Accessibility: B2007 Vehicles: Exemptions 54, 272
Rail vehicles: Accessibility: Exemption orders: Parliamentary procedures 54
Rail vehicles: Accessibility: Interoperable rail system 54, 272
Rail vehicles: Accessibility: London Underground Victoria Line 09TS vehicles: Exemptions 54, 272
Railway services: Cross-border: Working time 272
Railway: Road & railway transport: Penalty fares: Increases: Northern Ireland 403
Railways: Channel Tunnel Rail Link: Supplementary provisions: Acts 4
Railways: Channel Tunnel Rail Link: Supplementary provisions: Acts: Explanatory notes 7
Railways: Channel Tunnel: International arrangements 22
Railways: Channel Tunnel: Rail link: Nomination 272
Railways: Cross-border railway services: Working time: Northern Ireland 412
Railways: Crossrail: Acts 5
Railways: Crossrail: Acts: Explanatory notes 7
Railways: Felixstowe branch line: Ipswich Yard improvements 272
Railways: Health & safety: Enforcing authorities 88
Rates: Child benefit: Disregard: Northern Ireland 393, 401, 408
Rates: Housing benefit: Employment & support allowance: Consequential provisions: Northern Ireland 392, 400
Rates: Housing benefit: Extended payments: Northern Ireland 392, 400
Rates: Housing benefit: Local housing allowance: Northern Ireland 392, 401, 406
Rates: Housing benefit: Northern Ireland 392, 400
Rates: Industrial hereditaments: Northern Ireland 401
Rates: NAV list: Valuation: Time: Northern Ireland 401
Rates: Rate relief: Lone pensioner allowance: Northern Ireland 401
Rates: Rate relief: Qualifying age: Northern Ireland 401
Rates: Regional rates: Northern Ireland 401
Rates: Social security: Amendments: Northern Ireland 393, 394, 401, 402, 409
Rates: Social security: Benefits: Up-rating: Northern Ireland 383, 393, 401, 407, 411
Rates: Students: Amendments: Northern Ireland 394, 402, 410
Rates: Valuation tribunal: Northern Ireland 402
Rates: Valuation: Water undertakings: Northern Ireland 402
Rating & valuation: Central rating list: England 150
Rating & valuation: Central rating list: Wales 150
Rating & valuation: Council tax: Non-domestic rating: Demand notices: England 43, 150
Rating & valuation: Exempted classes: Scotland 353
Rating & valuation: Local government: Non-domestic rating: Amendments: England 150
Rating & valuation: Non-domestic rates: Levying: Scotland 352
Rating & valuation: Non-domestic rates: Scotland 352
Rating & valuation: Non-domestic rating: Communications hereditaments: England 150
Rating & valuation: Non-domestic rating: Contributions: England 150
Rating & valuation: Non-domestic rating: Contributions: Wales 151
Rating & valuation: Non-domestic rating: Rural areas & rateable value limits: Scotland 353
Rating & valuation: Non-domestic rating: Small business relief: Wales 151
Rating & valuation: Non-domestic rating: Telecommunications & canals: Scotland 353
Rating & valuation: Non-domestic rating: Unoccupied property: England 150
Rating & valuation: Non-domestic rating: Unoccupied property: Scotland 353
Rating & valuation: Plant & machinery: England 150
Rating & valuation: Plant & machinery: Valuation for rating: Scotland 353
Rating & valuation: Rating lists: Valuation date: England 150
Rating lists: Valuation date: England 150
Rating: Non-domestic: Communications hereditaments: Valuation, alteration of lists & appeals & material day: Wales . . 150
Rating: Non-domestic: Demand notes: Wales 151
Recovery of health services charges: Amounts: Northern Ireland 392
Recovery of taxes: Due in other member states: Finance Act 2002: Section 134: Amendments 151
Recreation grounds: Parish Council byelaws: Revocation: England 113

Recycling: London Waste & Recycling Board ... 116
Regeneration: Housing: Acts. ... 6
Regeneration: Housing: Acts: Explanatory notes ... 7
Regional Learning & Skills Councils. ... 62
Regional transport planning: Wales. ... 273
Registration of births, deaths & marriages, etc.: Local Electoral Administration & Registration Services (Scotland) Act 2006: Commencements: Scotland ... 353
Registration of births, deaths & marriages, etc.: Statistics & Registration Service Act 2007: Commencements . 54, 134, 151, 264
Registration of births, deaths, marriages, etc.: Deaths: Supply of information: Northern Ireland. ... 142, 152
Registration of births, deaths, marriages, etc.: England & Wales ... 142, 152
Registration of births, deaths, marriages, etc.: National Health Service Central Register: Scotland ... 353
Registration of vital events: General Register Office: Fees: Northern Ireland ... 402
Registration, Evaluation, Authorisation & Restriction of Chemicals see REACH. ... 40, 71, 88
Registration: Chancellor of the Exchequer: Transfer of functions: To Secretary of State for the Home Department ... 123
Regulation: Regulatory enforcement: Sanctions: Acts. ... 7
Regulation: Regulatory enforcement: Sanctions: Acts: Explanatory notes ... 8
Regulatory Enforcement & Sanctions Act 2008: Commencements ... 152
Regulatory enforcement: Sanctions: Acts ... 7
Regulatory enforcement: Sanctions: Acts: Explanatory notes. ... 8
Regulatory reform: Consumer credit: Legislative reform. ... 152
Regulatory reform: Health & Safety Executive: Legislative reform ... 88, 152
Regulatory reform: Lloyd's: Legislative reform ... 152
Regulatory reform: Local authorities: Consent requirements: Legislative reform: England & Wales ... 114, 152
Regulatory reform: Regulatory Enforcement & Sanctions Act 2008: Commencements ... 152
Regulatory reform: Weighing & measuring equipment: Verfication ... 152
Rehabilitation of Offenders Act 1974: Exceptions: Amendments: England & Wales ... 152
Rehabilitation of offenders: Criminal Justice & Immigration Act 2008: Commencements. ... 46, 140, 152
Relevant authorities: Local government: Code of conduct: Prescribed period for undertakings: Wales ... 115
Remand time: International criminal court ... 104
Renewable energy sources: Electricity: Guarantees of origin: Northern Ireland ... 382
Renewables (Origin of): Electricity: Gas & Electricity Markets Authority: Power to act: Northern Ireland Authority for Utility Regulation. ... 68
Renewables obligation: Electricity: Scotland ... 338
Rent Officer Service: Administration: Functions: Transfer: England. ... 122
Rent officers: Housing benefit functions: Amendments ... 94, 258
Rent: Repayment orders: Supplementary provisions: Wales. ... 96
Representation of the people ... 153
Representation of the people: Absent voting ... 152
Representation of the people: Amendments: Scotland ... 153
Representation of the people: Electoral Administration Act 2006: Commencements ... 153
Representation of the people: European Parliament: Number of MEPs & distribution between electoral regions: United Kingdom & Gibraltar ... 153
Representation of the people: European Parliamentary elections: Poll: Appointed day ... 153
Representation of the people: European Parliamentary elections: Returning officers ... 153
Representation of the People: Northern Ireland. ... 153
Representation of the people: Parliamentary constituencies & Assembly electoral regions: Wales ... 153
Representation of the people: Parliamentary constituencies: Redistribution of seats & review of election arrangements: Northern Ireland. ... 154
Representation of the people: Service voters: Registration period: Northern Ireland. ... 153
Reserve Forces: Compensation schemes. ... 134, 135
Restormel: Parishes: Local government. ... 113
Retirement: Premature retirement: Compensation: Health & personal social services: Northern Ireland ... 391
Revenue & Customs: Disclosure of information: Serious Crime Act 2007. ... 54, 154
Revenue & customs: Finance Act 2007: Schedule 24: Commencements. ... 154
Revenue & customs: Finance Act 2008: Section 135: Disaster or emergency ... 154
Revenue & customs: Immigration, Asylum & Nationality Act 2006: Data sharing: Code of practice ... 98, 139, 154
Revenue & customs: Immigration, Asylum & Nationality Act 2006: Duty to share & disclosure for security purposes 98, 140, 154
Revenue & customs: Serious Crime Act 2007: Commencements. ... 54, 105, 145, 147, 154, 253
Revenue & customs: Taxes & duties: Interest rates: Amendments. ... 154
Rhondda Cynon Taf: Llanharan, Llanharry, Llantrisant & Pont-y-clun Communities: Local government ... 115
Rhondda: Pontypridd & Rhondda National Health Service Trust: Dissolution: Wales. ... 131
Rhondda: Pontypridd & Rhondda National Health Service Trust: Transfer of Staff, property, rights & liabilities: Wales . 132
Rice products: From United States: Marketing: Restrictions: England ... 11, 82

Rice products: From United States: Marketing: Restrictions: Northern Ireland. 377, 389
Rice products: From United States: Marketing: Restrictions: Scotland 329, 341
Rice products: From United States: Marketing: Restrictions: Wales. 12, 85
Rice products: Specified products: From China: Marketing: Restrictions: England. 11, 82
Rice products: Specified products: From China: Marketing: Restrictions: Northern Ireland 377, 389
Rice products: Specified products: From China: Marketing: Restrictions: Scotland 329, 341
Rice products: Specified products: From China: Marketing: Restrictions: Wales 13
Rights in performances: Copyright & performances: Application to other countries. 40, 154
River Dee, Aberdeenshire: Salmon Fishery District: Annual close time: Scotland. 353
River Humber: Upper Burcom Tidal Stream Generator 68, 134, 272
River: Eels: Fishing: Prohibition: Scotland 353
River: Salmon & freshwater fisheries: Fish & shellfish farming: Businesses: Registration: Scotland 354
River: Salmon & freshwater fisheries: River Dee, Aberdeenshire: Salmon Fishery District: Annual close time: Scotland . 353
Road & railway transport: Penalty fares: Increases: Northern Ireland 403
Road fuel gas: Excise: Reliefs 74, 75
Road Safety Act 2006: Commencements 156, 243
Road traffic & vehicles: Disabled persons: Motor vehicles: Badges: Northern Ireland 403
Road traffic & vehicles: Motor hackney carriages: Belfast: Byelaws: Amendments: Northern Ireland 403
Road traffic & vehicles: Motor vehicles: Driving licences: Northern Ireland 403
Road traffic & vehicles: Motor vehicles: Taxi Drivers' licences: Fees: Amendments: Northern Ireland 403
Road traffic & vehicles: Motor vehicles: Testing: Northern Ireland 404
Road traffic & vehicles: Motorways: Northern Ireland 403, 404
Road traffic & vehicles: Penalty charges: Additional contravention: Northern Ireland 404
Road traffic & vehicles: Road traffic: 2007 Order: Commencements: Northern Ireland. 404
Road traffic & vehicles: Seat belts: Wearing: Northern Ireland. 403, 404
Road traffic & vehicles: Seized motor vehicles: Retention & disposal: Northern Ireland 404
Road traffic & vehicles: Speed limits: Northern Ireland 403
Road traffic & vehicles: Taxis: Antrim: Bye-laws: Northern Ireland. 404
Road traffic & vehicles: Taxis: Enniskillen: Bye-laws: Northern Ireland 404
Road traffic & vehicles: Traffic signs: Northern Ireland 404
Road traffic & vehicles: Traffic wardens: Northern Ireland 404
Road traffic & vehicles: Vehicle insurance information: Disclosure: Northern Ireland 403
Road traffic & vehicles: Westlink: Busways: Northern Ireland. 403, 404
Road traffic: 2007 Order: Commencements: Northern Ireland 404
Road traffic: A27: Southerham to Beddingham improvment: Banned turns 241
Road traffic: A27: Southerham to Beddingham improvment: Derestriction & revocation 241
Road traffic: Civil enforcement officers: Wearing of uniforms: Wales. 243
Road traffic: Civil enforcement: Parking contraventions: England. 242
Road traffic: Crime (International Co-operation) Act 2003: Commencements. 45, 154
Road traffic: Driving: Disqualifications: Mutual recognition: Great Britain & Ireland 156
Road traffic: Driving: Disqualifications: Mutual recognition: Northern Ireland & Ireland. 403
Road traffic: England 241
Road traffic: Goods vehicles: Operator licensing: Fees. 154
Road traffic: Goods vehicles: Plating & testing. 155
Road traffic: International carriage: Dangerous goods: Road transport: Fees 155
Road traffic: Motor cars: Driving instruction 155
Road traffic: Motor vehicles: Approval: Fees. 155
Road traffic: Motor vehicles: Driving licences 155
Road traffic: Motor vehicles: EC type approval. 155
Road traffic: Motor vehicles: Single vehicle approval: Fees 155
Road traffic: Motor vehicles: Tests 155, 156
Road traffic: Offenders: Prescribed devices. 156
Road traffic: Parking contraventions: Civil enforcement: Approved devices: Wales 243
Road traffic: Parking contraventions: Civil enforcement: Buckinghamshire (County): Wycombe (District) 241
Road traffic: Parking contraventions: Civil enforcement: Charges: Guidelines: Wales 243
Road traffic: Parking contraventions: Civil enforcement: Cheshire (County): Chester (City): Ellesmere Port & Neston
(Borough) 241
Road traffic: Parking contraventions: Civil enforcement: Cheshire (County): Macclesfield (Borough) 241
Road traffic: Parking contraventions: Civil enforcement: Cornwall (County) 241
Road traffic: Parking contraventions: Civil enforcement: Devon (County) 241
Road traffic: Parking contraventions: Civil enforcement: Dudley 242
Road traffic: Parking contraventions: Civil enforcement: Dudley (Borough) 242
Road traffic: Parking contraventions: Civil enforcement: Durham (District). 242
Road traffic: Parking contraventions: Civil enforcement: East Sussex (County): Eastbourne (Borough) 241
Road traffic: Parking contraventions: Civil enforcement: Gloucestershire (County): Forest of Dean (District) 241

Road traffic: Parking contraventions: Civil enforcement: Nottinghamshire (County) ... 241
Road traffic: Parking contraventions: Civil enforcement: Representations & appeals: Removed vehicles: Wales ... 243
Road traffic: Parking contraventions: Civil enforcement: Representations & appeals: Wales ... 244
Road traffic: Parking contraventions: Civil enforcement: Rutland (County) ... 242
Road traffic: Parking contraventions: Civil enforcement: St. Helens ... 242
Road traffic: Parking contraventions: Civil enforcement: Swansea: Wales ... 93
Road traffic: Parking contraventions: Civil enforcement: Wales ... 243
Road traffic: Parking contraventions: Civil enforcement: Wiltshire (County): West Wiltshire (District) ... 242
Road traffic: Parking contraventions: Penalty charge notices, enforcement & adjudication: Wales ... 243
Road traffic: Passenger & goods vehicles: Drivers: Training: Certificates of professional competence ... 157
Road traffic: Passenger & goods vehicles: Recording equipment: Downloading & retention of data ... 156
Road traffic: Passenger & goods vehicles: Recording equipment: Fitters & workshops: Approval: Fees ... 156
Road traffic: Road Safety Act 2006: Commencements ... 156, 243
Road traffic: Road user charging: Enforcement & adjudication: London ... 116, 242
Road traffic: Road vehicles: Construction & use ... 156
Road traffic: Road vehicles: Registration & licensing: Amendments ... 156
Road traffic: Road vehicles: Registration marks: Sale ... 157
Road traffic: School crossings: Patrol sign: Scotland ... 355
Road traffic: Seized motor vehicles: Retention & disposal ... 156
Road traffic: Speed limits ... 157, 158, 159
Road traffic: Speed limits: Scotland ... 355
Road traffic: TIR carnets: Goods: International transport: Fees ... 155
Road traffic: Tractors: EC type-approval ... 157
Road traffic: Traffic Management Act 2004: Commencements ... 242
Road traffic: Traffic orders: Local authorities: Procedure: Scotland ... 354
Road traffic: Traffic regulation 159, 160, 161, 162, 163, 164, 165, 166, 167, 168, 169, 170, 171, 172, 173, 174, 175, 176, 177, 178, 179, 180, 181, 182, 183, 184, 185, 186, 187, 188, 189, 190, 191, 192, 193, 194, 195, 196, 197, 198, 199, 200, 201, 202, 203, 204, 205, 206, 207, 208, 209, 210, 211, 212, 213, 214, 215, 216, 217, 218, 219, 220, 221, 222, 223, 224, 225, 226, 227, 228, 229, 230, 231, 232, 233, 234, 235, 236, 237, 238, 239, 240, 241
Road traffic: Traffic regulation: Scotland ... 355, 356, 357, 358, 359, 360
Road traffic: Traffic regulation: Wales ... 244, 245, 246, 247, 248, 249, 250, 251
Road traffic: Traffic signs: Amendments ... 157
Road traffic: Trunk roads: A470: Wales ... 93
Road traffic: Vehicle drivers: Professional competence: Certificates: Amendments ... 157
Road traffic: Vehicle excise duty: Immobilisation, removal & disposal of vehicles ... 157
Road traffic: Vehicles: Crime: Registration plate suppliers: Registration ... 157
Road traffic: Vehicles: Registration marks: Retention ... 156
Road traffic: Vehicles: Removal & disposal: Traffic officers: England ... 242
Road traffic: Vehicles: Removal & disposal: Wales ... 244
Road traffic: Vehicles: Removal, storage & disposal: Prescribed sums & charges: England ... 242
Road traffic: Vehicles: Removal, storage & disposal: Prescribed sums & charges: England & Wales ... 242
Road traffic: Wrexham (County Borough): Permitted & special parking areas: Wales ... 244
Road transport: International passenger services ... 149
Road user charging: Enforcement & adjudication: London ... 116, 242
Road vehicles: Construction & use ... 156
Road vehicles: Registration & licensing: Amendments ... 156
Road vehicles: Registration marks: Sale ... 157
Road works: Disputes & appeals against directions: Settlements: Scotland ... 354
Road works: Fixed penalty: Scotland ... 354
Road works: Inspection fees: Scotland ... 354
Road works: Scottish Road Works Register, notices, directions & designations: Scotland ... 354
Roads & bridges: Abolition of Bridge Tolls (Scotland) Act 2008: Commencements: Scotland ... 354, 364
Roads & bridges: Road works: Disputes & appeals against directions: Settlements: Scotland ... 354
Roads & bridges: Road works: Fixed penalty: Scotland ... 354
Roads & bridges: Road works: Inspection fees: Scotland ... 354
Roads & bridges: Road works: Scottish Road Works Register, notices, directions & designations: Scotland ... 354
Roads & bridges: Scotland ... 354
Roads (Scotland) Act 1984: Fixed penalty: Scotland ... 354
Roads works: Inspection fees: Northern Ireland ... 403, 411
Rochdale Sixth Form College: Government ... 62
Rochdale Sixth Form College: Incorporation ... 62
Rodbaston College: Dissolution ... 62
Royal Air Force: Air Force Act 1955: Part 1: Amendments ... 51
Royal Pharmaceutical Society of Great Britain: Registration rules: Order of Council ... 90
Rules of the air: Civil aviation ... 32

Rural Development Contracts: Land managers options: Scotland 329
Rural Development Contracts: Rural priorities: Scotland. 329
Rural development: Financial assistance: Northern Ireland. 377
Rural housing bodies: Title Conditions (Scotland) Act 2003: Scotland 363
Rural primary schools: Designation: England 56
Rutland (County): Parking contraventions: Civil enforcement 242
Rwanda: United Nations: Arms embargoes. 275

S

S4C: Investment activities: Approval. 20
Safeguarding Vulnerable Groups Act 2006: Barred list prescribed information: England & Wales 25, 147
Safeguarding Vulnerable Groups Act 2006: Barring procedure: England & Wales 25, 147
Safeguarding Vulnerable Groups Act 2006: Commencements: England. 24, 146
Safeguarding Vulnerable Groups Act 2006: Commencements: England & Wales. 25, 51, 147
Safeguarding Vulnerable Groups Act 2006: Commencements: Northern Ireland 26, 147
Safeguarding Vulnerable Groups Act 2006: Prescribed criteria: Foreign Offences: England & Wales 25, 147
Safeguarding Vulnerable Groups Act 2006: Prescribed criteria: Transitional provisions: England & Wales 25, 147
Safeguarding Vulnerable Groups Act 2006: Prescribed information: England & Wales. 25, 147
Safeguarding Vulnerable Groups Act 2006: Protection of Children & Vulnerable Adults & Care Standards Tribunal:
Children's & adults' barred lists. 25, 146
Safeguarding Vulnerable Groups Act 2006: Transitional provisions: England & Wales. 25, 147
Safeguarding Vulnerable Groups: 2007 Order: Commencements: Northern Ireland. 404
Safeguarding vulnerable groups: Barred list: Prescribed information: Northern Ireland 404
Safeguarding vulnerable groups: Barring procedure: Northern Ireland. 405
Safeguarding vulnerable groups: Prescribed criteria: Transitional provisions: Northern Ireland. 405
Safeguarding vulnerable groups: Transitional provisions: Northern Ireland 405
Safety: Machinery: Supply 88
Salaries: Assembly Ombudsman & Commissioner for Complaints: Northern Ireland 405
Salford & Eccles Colleges: Dissolution 57
Salisbury: Parishes: Local government 113
Salmon & freshwater fisheries: Eels: Fishing: Prohibition: Scotland. 353
Salmon & freshwater fisheries: Fish & shellfish farming: Businesses: Registration: Scotland. 354
Salmon & freshwater fisheries: River Dee, Aberdeenshire: Salmon Fishery District: Annual close time: Scotland. . . . 353
Salmon & Sea Trout: Caught by rod & line: Prohibition of sale: Foyle & Carlingford Areas: Northern Ireland 387
Salmonella: Control: Poultry: Northern Ireland. 379
Salmonella: Control: Poultry: Wales 15
Salmonella: Poultry: Control: Scotland 330
Sanctions: Civil: Regulatory offences: Acts 7
Sanctions: Civil: Regulatory offences: Acts: Explanatory notes 8
Saudi Arabia: Double taxation: Relief & international enforcement 21, 41, 100
Savings banks: National Savings Bank 251
Scallops: Conservation: Northern Ireland 405
Scenic areas: National: Countryside: Scotland 334
School admission appeals code: Appointed day: England 62
School crossings: Patrol sign: Scotland 355
School day & school year: Wales. 67
School food: Nutritional standards & requirements: England 59
School lunches: Charging: Requirement: Disapplication: Scotland 338, 347
School milk: Wales. 12, 13
School teachers: Incentive payments: England. 63
School teachers: Pay & conditions: England & Wales 64
Schools (Health Promotion & Nutrition) Act 2007: Commencements: Scotland. 338
Schools forums: England 63
Schools: Admission arrangements: England 62
Schools: Admissions: Co-ordination of arrangements: England 62
Schools: Admissions: Local authority reports & admission forums: England 62
Schools: All Saints CE (Aided) Primary School: Religious character: Designation 56
Schools: All Saints CofE School: Religious character: Designation 56
Schools: Arnot St Mary CE Primary School: Religious character: Designation 56
Schools: Bellefield Primary & Nursery School: Religious character: Designation 56
Schools: Budgets: Shares: Prescribed purposes: Wales 67
Schools: Canon Peter Hall Church of England Primary School: Religious character: Designation 56
Schools: Canon Sharples Church of England Primary School & Nursery: Religious character: Designation 56
Schools: Christ the King Catholic & Church of England (VA) Centre for Learning: Religious character: Designation . . . 56

Schools: Cleadon Village Church of England VA Primary School: Religious character: Designation 56
Schools: Curriculum: Wales 67
Schools: Finance: England 62
Schools: Hackleton Church of England Primary School: Religious character: Designation. 60
Schools: Hawthorn Church of England Controlled First School: Religious character: Designation. 60
Schools: Independent: Inspection fees & publication: Education: England 57
Schools: Independent: Standards: Education: England. 58
Schools: Information: England 62
Schools: Inspection: England 59
Schools: King's Stanley CofE Primary School: Religious character: Designation 61
Schools: Krishna-Avanti Primary School: Religious character: Designation 61
Schools: Maintained schools: Collaboration: Wales 65
Schools: Maintained schools: Further education bodies: Collaboration arrangements: Wales 65
Schools: Manor CE VC Primary: Religious character: Designation 61
Schools: Meals: North Yorkshire County Council 62
Schools: Norham St Ceolwulfs CofE Controlled First School: Religious character: Designation. 61
Schools: Nutritional requirements: Food & drink: Scotland 338
Schools: Performance information: England 59, 60
Schools: Performance targets: Education: England 59
Schools: Premises: Control: Wales 65, 66
Schools: Religious character: Designation: England 56
Schools: Religious character: Designation: Independent schools: England 56
Schools: Rural primary schools: Designation: England 56
Schools: St Gregory's Catholic Primary School: Religious character: Designation 63
Schools: St Saviour's Catholic Primary School: Religious character: Designation 63
Schools: Teacher qualifications: Wales. 67
Schools: Teachers: Induction arrangements: England 58
Schools: Thatcham Park Church of England Primary School: Religious character: Designation 63
Schools: Towcester CofE Primary School: Religious character: Designation 63
Schools: Trinity Anglican-Methodist Primary School: Religious character: Designation 63
Schools: William Parker School: Religious character: Designation 63
Schools: Wylye Valley Church of England Voluntary Aided Primary School: Religious character: Designation 63
Science: National curriculum: Attainment targets & programmes of study: Key stage 3: England 58
Scientific research: Technology Strategy Board: Transfer of property 251
Scotland Act 1998: Agency arrangements: Specification. 10, 13, 38, 45, 53, 143
Scotland Act 1998: Transfer of functions 38, 53, 71
Scottish Agricultural College: Fundable bodies: Scotland 337
Scottish Agricultural College: Higher education: Institutions: Designation: Scotland 337
Scottish Commission for Human Rights Act 2006: Commencements: Scotland. 343
Scottish Commission for Human Rights: Specifications: Scotland 344
Scottish connections: Book: Scotland 353
Scottish legal services ombudsman: Abolition: Scotland 346
Scottish Parliament: Acts: Bound volumes 325
Scottish Parliament: Elections 38, 53
Scottish Road Works Register, notices, directions & designations: Scotland 354
Scottish Road Works Register: Prescribed fees & amounts: Scotland 354
Scottish statutory instruments: Annual volumes 325
Scottish Water: Loch of Boardhouse: Scotland 366
Scrapie: Fees: Northern Ireland 385
Sea fisheries: Community measures: Enforcement: Penalty notices 252
Sea fisheries: Community quota, third country fishing measures & restriction of days at sea: Enforcement: Scotland . . . 361
Sea fisheries: Conservation of sea fish: Shrimp fishing nets: Wales 252, 253
Sea fisheries: Conservation: Scallops: Northern Ireland 405
Sea fisheries: Crabs & lobsters: Unlicensed fishing: Northern Ireland 405
Sea fisheries: Fal & Helford: Fishing restrictions 252
Sea fisheries: Fisheries & aquaculture structures: Grants: England 80, 252
Sea fisheries: Fishing: Prohibition: Lamlash Bay: Scotland 360
Sea fisheries: Inshore fishing: Methods: Prohibition: Northern Ireland 405
Sea fisheries: Lyme Bay: Fishing restrictions 252
Sea fisheries: Prohibited methods of fishing: Firth of Clyde: Scotland 361
Sea fisheries: Recovery measures 252
Sea fisheries: Shellfish: Dee Estuary Cockle Fishery: England 252
Sea fisheries: Shrimp fishing nets: Scotland 361
Sea fisheries: Tope: Fishing: Prohibition: England 252
Sea fisheries: Tope: Fishing: Prohibition: Wales 252

Sea fishing: Community measures: Enforcement: Penalty notices: Northern Ireland 387
Sea fishing: Herring, mackerel & horse mackerel: Control procedures: Scotland. 360, 361
Sea fishing: Passive fishing gear & beam trawls: Marking & identification: Northern Ireland 387
Sea Trout & Salmon: Caught by rod & line: Prohibition of sale: Foyle & Carlingford Areas: Northern Ireland 387
Sea: Deposits: Exemptions: Northern Ireland. 384
Secretary of State for the Home Department: Transfer of functions: From the Chancellor of the Exchequer: Registration . 123
Security & para-military goods: Export: Control. 50
Seed potatoes: Crop fees: Northern Ireland 405
Seed potatoes: England 139
Seed potatoes: Levies: Northern Ireland 377
Seed potatoes: Wales 139
Seeds: Miscellaneous amendments: Northern Ireland 405
Semiconductor topographies: Design right. 52
Senecio: Medicines: Human use: Prohibition 119
Sentencing: Criminal justice: Curfew conditions. 47
Serious Crime Act 2007: Anti-fraud organisations. 55
Serious Crime Act 2007: Commencements 47, 48, 54, 55, 105, 142, 145, 147, 154, 253
Serious Crime Act 2007: Commencements: Scotland 351
Serious Crime Act 2007: Consequential & supplementary amendments 146
Serious Crime Act 2007: Disclosure of information: Revenue & Customs. 54, 154
Serious Crime Act 2007: Proceeds of Crime Act 2002: Amendment. 145
Serious Crime Act 2007: Section 24: Appeals 253
Serious crime prevention orders: Serious Crime Act 2007: Commencements 54, 105, 142, 145, 147, 154, 253
Serious crime prevention orders: Serious Crime Act 2007: Section 24: Appeals. 253
Serious Organised Crime & Police Act 2005: Commencements. 52
Serious Organised Crime & Police Act 2005: Commencements: England & Wales 142
Serious Organised Crime & Police Act 2005: Commencements: Northern Ireland 48
Serious Organised Crime & Police Act 2005: Consequential & supplementary amendments 146
Serious Organised Crime & Police Act 2005: Information: Disclosure: Serious Organised Crime Agency 253
Service voters: Registration period: Northern Ireland. 153
Sevenoaks: Parish electoral arrangements: Local government 113
Sevenoaks: Parishes: Local government 113
Severn Bridges: Tolls. 92
Sex Discrimination Act 1975: Amendments 253
Sex discrimination: 1976 Order: Amendment: Northern Ireland 405
Sex discrimination: Legislation: Amendments 253
Sexual Offences Act 2003: Prescribed police stations: Scotland 336
Sexual offences: 2008 Order: Commencements: Northern Ireland 381
Sexual offences: Northern Ireland. 133
Sheep & goats: Records, identification & movement: Wales 16
Sheep: Identification & traceability: Scotland 330
Sheep: Radioactivity: Food protection: Scotland 352
Shellfish farming: Businesses: Registration: Scotland 354
Sheriff Court: Act of Adjournal: Criminal procedure rules: Amendments: Criminal Proceedings etc. (Reform) (Scotland) Act
2007: Scotland 342, 344, 361
Sheriff Court: Act of Adjournal: Criminal procedure rules: Amendments: Scotland 344, 361
Sheriff Court: Act of Adjournal: Criminal procedure rules: Seizure & disposal of vehicles: Scotland 344, 361
Sheriff Court: Act of Sederunt: Bankruptcy Rules: Scotland 361
Sheriff Court: European order for payment: Procedure: Rules: Act of Sederunt: Scotland 362
Sheriff Court: European small claims: Procedure: Rules: Act of Sederunt: Scotland 362
Sheriff Court: Fees: Scotland 362
Sheriff Court: Rules: Amendments: Act of Sederunt: Scotland. 362
Sheriff Court: Rules: Amendments: Diligence: Act of Sederunt: Scotland. 362
Sheriff Court: Sheriff officers: Fees: Act of Sederunt: Scotland 361
Sheriff Court: Shorthand writers: Fees: Act of Sederunt: Scotland. 361
Sheriff Court: Solicitors: Fees: Act of Sederunt: Scotland 361
Sheriff Court: Summary & statutory applications & appeals etc.: Rules: Adult Support & Protection (Scotland) Act 2007: Act
of Sederunt: Scotland 362
Sheriff Court: Summary & statutory applications & appeals etc.: Rules: Amendments: Licensing (Scotland) Act 2005: Act of
Sederunt: Scotland. 362
Sheriff Court: Summary & statutory applications & appeals etc.: Rules: Registration appeals: Act of Sederunt: Scotland . 362
Sheriff Court: Vulnerable Witnesses (Scotland) Act 2004: Commencements: Scotland 362
Sheriffdom of Glasgow & Strathkelvin: Justice of the Peace courts: Scotland 344
Sheriffdom of Glasgow & Strathkelvin: Stipendiary magistrates: Scotland 336
Sheriffdom of Grampian, Highland & Islands: Justice of the Peace courts: Scotland 345

Sheriffdom of Lothian & Borders: Justice of the peace courts: Scotland 345
Sheriffdom of Tayside, Central & Fife: Justice of the Peace courts: Scotland 345
Sherwood Forest & Newark: Parish electoral arrangements: Local government 113
Ships: Air pollution: Prevention. 118
Ships: Public health: Northern Ireland 400
Shorthand writers: Fees: Court of Session: Act of Sederunt: Scotland 334
Shorthand writers: Fees: Sheriff Court: Act of Sederunt: Scotland. 361
Shrewsbury & Atcham: Parishes: Local government 113
Shrimp fishing nets: Scotland 361
Shrimp fishing nets: Wales. 252, 253
Shropshire: Local government: Structural changes 113
Site waste management plans: England 72
Sites of special scientific interest: Register: Scotland. 349
Skills & education: Acts 5
Skills & education: Acts: Explanatory notes. 7
Skills: Regional Learning & Skills Councils 62
Slovenia: Double taxation: Relief & international enforcement 21, 41, 100
Smoke control areas: Authorised fuels: England. 32
Smoke control areas: Authorised fuels: Northern Ireland. 380
Smoke control areas: Authorised fuels: Scotland 333
Smoke control areas: Authorised fuels: Wales 33
Smoke control areas: Fireplaces: Exempt: England 33
Smoke control areas: Fireplaces: Exempt: Northern Ireland 380
Smoke control areas: Fireplaces: Exempt: Scotland 333
Smoke control areas: Fireplaces: Exempt: Wales 33
Smoke-free: Exemptions, vehicles, penalties & discounted amounts: Northern Ireland 400
Smoking cessation products: Value added tax: Reduced rate. 276
Social care: Acts 6
Social care: Acts: Explanatory notes. 7
Social care: Adult Support & Protection (Scotland) Act 2007: Council officers: Authorisation: Restrictions: Scotland . 326, 363
Social care: Appointments Commission 123, 147, 254
Social care: Care quality commission: Membership 123, 148, 254
Social care: Children: Caring: Disqualification: Wales. 26, 254
Social care: Community care: Personal care & nursing care: Scotland. 363
Social care: Day care providers & child minders: Suspension: Wales 26, 255
Social care: Fostering services: England 24, 254
Social care: Health & Social Care Act 2008: Commencements 89, 91, 96, 124, 148, 254
Social care: Health & Social Care Act 2008: Consequential amendments. 123, 148, 254
Social care: Health Act 2006: Commencements 124, 128, 254
Social care: Local Government & Public Involvement in Health Act 2007: Commencements 112, 124, 254
Social care: Local Government & Public Involvement in Health Act 2007: Consequential provisions 125, 254
Social care: Local involvement networks 125, 254
Social fund: Applications & miscellaneous provisions 258
Social fund: Applications & miscellaneous provisions: Northern Ireland 407
Social fund: Cold weather payments 258
Social fund: Cold weather payments: Northern Ireland. 407
Social fund: Winter fuel payments 258
Social fund: Winter fuel payments: Temporary increase: Northern Ireland 407
Social security & child support: Decisions & appeals 77, 262
Social security: Amendments 260, 261
Social security: Amendments: Northern Ireland. 393, 394, 401, 402, 409
Social security: Benefits up-rating 258
Social security: Benefits up-rating: Northern Ireland 407
Social security: Benefits up-rating: Terms & conditions of employment. 262
Social security: Benefits: Recovery: Lump sum payments 261
Social security: Benefits: Recovery: Northern Ireland 410
Social security: Benefits: Up-rating: Northern Ireland 383, 393, 401, 407, 411
Social security: Child benefit: Disregard: Northern Ireland 393, 401, 408
Social security: Child benefit: Rates: Amendments. 255
Social security: Child benefit: Rates: Commencements 258
Social security: Child benefits: Disregard. 258
Social security: Child benefits: Up-rating. 255
Social security: Child Maintenance & Other Payments Act 2008: Commencements 76, 255
Social security: Child maintenance: 258

Social security: Child maintenance: Northern Ireland 408
Social security: Child support: Northern Ireland 386
Social security: Christmas bonus: Relevant week: Northern Ireland 405
Social security: Christmas bonus: Specified sum 255
Social security: Christmas bonus: Specified sum: Northern Ireland 406
Social security: Claims & payments 258
Social security: Claims & payments: Northern Ireland 408
Social security: Companies Act 2006: Consequential amendments 35
Social security: Companies Act 2006: Consequential amendments: Taxes & national insurance 255, 267
Social security: Contributions 259
Social security: Contributions: Re-rating 259
Social security: Contributions: Re-rating: Consequential amendments 259
Social security: Council tax benefit: Amendments 257
Social security: Council tax benefit: Extended payments 257
Social security: Discretionary financial assistance 255
Social security: Discretionary financial assistance: Northern Ireland 406
Social security: Earnings factors: Revaluation 261
Social security: Earnings factors: Revaluation: Northern Ireland 410
Social security: Employment & support allowance 255, 256
Social security: Employment & support allowance: Consequential provisions 255
Social security: Employment & support allowance: Northern Ireland 406
Social security: Employment & support allowance: Transitional provisions 256
Social security: Employment & support allowance: Up-rating modification 256
Social security: Guardian's allowance: Up-rating 256
Social security: Guardian's allowance: Up-rating: Northern Ireland 263
Social security: Health & Social Care Act 2008: Commencements 256
Social security: Health in pregnancy grant: Administration 262, 263
Social security: Health in pregnancy grant: Entitlement & amount 257
Social security: Housing benefit: Amendments 257
Social security: Housing benefit: Extended payments 257
Social security: Housing benefit: Local housing allowance: Information sharing: Amendments 257
Social security: Housing benefit: Local housing allowance: Northern Ireland 392, 401, 406
Social security: Housing costs special arrangements: Amendments & modifications 259
Social security: Housing costs: Special arrangements: Northern Ireland 408
Social security: Housing payments: Discretionary: Grants 255
Social security: Incapacity benefit: Work-focused interviews 259
Social security: Incapacity benefit: Work-focused interviews: Northern Ireland 408
Social security: Incapacity: Northern Ireland 408
Social security: Income-related benefits: Subsidy to authorities 257
Social security: Income-related benefits: Subsidy to authorities: England & Wales 262
Social security: Industrial injuries: Dependency: Permitted earnings limits 259
Social security: Industrial injuries: Dependency: Permitted earnings limits: Northern Ireland 408
Social security: Industrial injuries: Prescribed diseases 260
Social security: Industrial injuries: Prescribed diseases: Northern Ireland 408
Social security: Information: Use: Housing benefit & welfare services purposes 263
Social security: Information: Use: Housing benefit & welfare services purposes: Northern Ireland 394, 402, 410
Social security: Jobcentre Plus: Interviews for partners 260
Social security: Jobseeker's allowance: Joint claims 257
Social security: Jobseeker's allowance: Joint claims: Northern Ireland 406
Social security: Local authorities: Investigations & prosecutions 260
Social security: Lone parents 260
Social security: Lone parents: Northern Ireland 408
Social security: Mesothelioma: Commencements: Northern Ireland 406
Social security: Mesothelioma: Lump sum payments: Claims & reconsiderations 257, 273
Social security: Mesothelioma: Lump sum payments: Claims & reconsiderations: Northern Ireland 407
Social security: Mesothelioma: Lump sum payments: Conditions & amounts 258
Social security: Mesothelioma: Lump sum payments: Conditions & amounts: Northern Ireland 407
Social security: National Insurance numbers 261
Social security: National Insurance numbers: Northern Ireland 409
Social security: National insurance: Contributions: Application of part 7 of the Finance Act 2004 258
Social security: Northern Ireland Act 1998: Modifications 133
Social security: Pensions: Home responsibilities 261
Social security: Pensions: Home responsibilities: Northern Ireland 409
Social security: Pensions: Low earnings threshold 261
Social security: Pensions: Low earnings threshold: Northern Ireland 409

Social security: Rent officers: Housing benefit functions: Amendments..................94, 258
Social security: Social fund: Applications & miscellaneous provisions........................258
Social security: Social fund: Applications & miscellaneous provisions: Northern Ireland...................407
Social security: Social fund: Cold weather payments........................258
Social security: Social fund: Cold weather payments: Northern Ireland........................407
Social security: Social fund: Winter fuel payments........................258
Social security: Social fund: Winter fuel payments: Temporary increase: Northern Ireland...................407
Social security: Statutory sick pay: General........................262, 268
Social security: Students responsible for children or young persons........................261
Social security: Students.......................261
Social security: Students: Northern Ireland......................394, 402, 410
Social security: Students: Responsible for children or young persons: Social security: Northern Ireland..........410
Social security: Taxes: Interest rate........................262, 267
Social security: Welfare Reform Act 2007: Commencements........................262
Social security: Welfare Reform Act 2007: Relevant enactments........................263
Social security: Workers' compensation: Pneumoconiosis etc.: Claims: Payments........................258
Social security: Workers' compensation: Pneumoconiosis etc.: Claims: Payment: Northern Ireland...........407
Social security: Workers' compensation: Supplementation........................262
Social security: Workers' compensation: Supplementation: Northern Ireland........................411
Social security: Work-focused Interviews: Partners: Northern Ireland........................410
Social services: Children & young persons: Acts........................4
Social services: Children & young persons: Acts: Explanatory notes........................7
Solicitors: Authorised: Civil Service: Lists........................8
South Atlantic territories: Falkland Islands: Constitution........................263
South Cambridgeshire: Electoral changes: Local government........................113
South Devon Healthcare NHS Foundation Trust........................127
South Lakeland (District): Electoral changes........................111
South Staffordshire College: Government........................63
South Staffordshire College: Incorporation........................63
Special constables: Scotland........................351
Special Educational Needs (Information) Act 2008: Commencements........................63
Special educational needs: Disability: 2005 Order: Amendment: General qualifications bodies: Alteration of premises & enforcement: Northern Ireland........................382
Special educational needs: Disability: General qualifications bodies: Relevant qualifications, reasonable steps & physical features: Northern Ireland........................382
Special educational needs: England........................60
Special educational needs: Information: Acts........................7
Spectrum trading: Wireless telegraphy: Electronic communications........................69
Speeches: Hansard: Centenary volume 1909-2009: Anthologies........................9
Spirit drinks........................81
Spirits duty: Alcoholic liquor: Surcharges........................74
Sports grounds & sporting events: Designations: Scotland........................363
Sports grounds & sporting events: Football spectators: 2008 European Championship: Control period..........263
Sports grounds & sporting events: Football spectators: Seating........................263
Sports grounds & sporting events: Glasgow Commonwealth Games Act 2008: Commencements: Scotland........363
Sports grounds: Safety: Designation........................263
Spreadable fats: Marketing standards: England........................83
Spreadable fats: Marketing standards: Northern Ireland........................390
Spreadable fats: Marketing standards: Wales........................85
Spreadable fats: Scotland........................342
St Austell: Markets: Local acts........................8
St Gregory's Catholic Primary School: Religious character: Designation........................63
St Helens: Parishes: Local government........................114
St Helens: Parking contraventions: Civil enforcement........................242
St Mary's Music School: Aided places: Scotland........................338
St Mary's: National Health Service Trusts: Trust property: Transfer........................127
St Saviour's Catholic Primary School: Religious character: Designation........................63
Staffordshire: South Staffordshire College: Government........................63
Staffordshire: South Staffordshire College: Incorporation........................63
Stamp duty & stamp duty reserve tax: Investment exchanges & clearing houses..................263, 264, 267
Stamp duty & stamp duty reserve tax: Investment exchanges & clearing houses: Eurex Clearing AG..........263, 264
Stamp duty & stamp duty reserve tax: Investment exchanges & clearing houses: European Central Counterparty Ltd & Turquoise Multilateral Trading Facility........................267
Stamp duty & stamp duty reserve tax: Investment exchanges & clearing houses: London Stock Exchange..........264
Stamp duty land tax: Finance Act 2003: Part 4: Variation........................264

Stamp duty land tax: Finance Act 2004: Part 4 264
Stamp duty land tax: Open-ended investment companies. 264
Stamp duty land tax: Residential property: Exemptions 264
Stamp duty land tax: Zero-carbon homes relief. 264
Stamp duty reserve tax: Authorised Investment Funds 21, 40, 100, 264
Stamp duty reserve tax: Finance Act 1986: Section 89AA: Amendments 264
Stamp duty reserve tax: virt-x Exchange Ltd.. 267
Standards Committee: Local government. 114
State pension credit: Local housing allowance: Housing benefit: Northern Ireland 393
Statistics & Registration Service Act 2007: Commencements 54, 134, 151, 264
Statistics & Registration Service Act 2007: Delegation of functions: Economic statistics. 54, 264
Statistics Board: Statistics & Registration Service Act 2007: Commencements. 54, 134, 151, 264
Statistics Board: Statistics & Registration Service Act 2007: Delegation of functions: Economic statistics. 54, 264
Statistics of trade: Customs & excise 265
Statistics: Official statisitics. 133
Statistics: Official statistics: Access: Pre-release 133
Statistics: Official statistics: Pre-release access: Scotland 349
Statistics: Official statistics: Scotland. 349
Statute law: Repeals: Acts 7
Statutes: Chronological tables 8
Statutes: Chronological tables: Northern Ireland 375
Statutes: Northern Ireland. 375
Statutes: Title page & index: Northern Ireland 375
Statutory & third country auditors 18, 36, 37
Statutory auditors: Delegation of functions. 37
Statutory instruments: Annual volumes 9
Statutory instruments: National Assembly for Wales: Annual volumes. 9
Statutory maternity pay: Social security: Benefits: Up-rating: Northern Ireland 383, 393, 401, 407, 411
Statutory rules (Northern Ireland): Annual volumes 375
Statutory rules (Northern Ireland): Chronological tables: Northern Ireland. 374, 375
Statutory rules: Chronological tables: Northern Ireland 374
Statutory sick pay: General 262, 268
Statutory sick pay: Northern Ireland 411
Statutory sick pay: Social security: Benefits: Up-rating: Northern Ireland 383, 393, 401, 407, 411
Stipendiary magistrates: Sheriffdom of Glasgow & Strathkelvin: Scotland 336
Stornoway: Harbour revision constitution: Scotland 342
Strategic Development Planning Authority: Designation: Scotland. 363, 364
Strategic health authorities & primary care trusts: Functions: National Health Service 126
Stratford-on-Avon: Parish electoral arrangements & electoral changes: Local government 114
Street works: Fixed penalty: Wales. 93
Street works: Inspection fees: England 93
Street works: Inspection fees: Northern Ireland. 403, 411
Street works: Inspection fees: Wales. 93
Street works: Registers, notices, directions & designations: Wales 93, 94
Stroud: Parish electoral arrangements & electoral changes: Local government 114
Student accommodation: Codes of management practice: Approval. 94
Student awards: Northern Ireland 382
Student fees: Agriculture: Northern Ireland. 375
Student fees: Amounts: England 63
Student fees: Amounts: Northern Ireland 382
Student fees: Qualifying courses & persons: England 63
Student loans: England & Wales. 64
Student loans: Northern Ireland. 382
Student loans: Repayment 55
Student loans: Repayment: Northern Ireland 382
Student loans: Sale: Acts. 7
Student loans: Sale: Acts: Explanatory notes 8
Student loans: Scotland 337
Student support 60, 64
Student support: Eligibility: Further education: Northern Ireland 382
Student support: European Institutions. 60
Student support: Northern Ireland. 382
Students: Responsible for children or young persons: Social security 261
Students: Responsible for children or young persons: Social security: Northern Ireland. 410
Students: Social security: Amendments. 261

Students: Social security: Amendments: Northern Ireland. 394, 402, 410
Substance misuse: Testing for: Police: Northern Ireland 399
Superannuation Act 1972: Schedule 1: Admission 137
Superannuation schemes: Health & personal social services: Northern Ireland 391
Superannuation: Health & personal social services: Northern Ireland 391
Supply chain development programme grant: Agriculture: Northern Ireland 377
Supreme Court of England & Wales: Civil procedure: Rules. 44, 265
Supreme Court of England & Wales: Civil proceedings: Fees 44, 265
Supreme Court of England & Wales: Criminal procedure: Rules. 117, 265
Supreme Court of England & Wales: Family proceedings 44, 45, 77, 265
Supreme Court of England & Wales: Family proceedings: Fees 45, 77, 78, 266
Supreme Court of England & Wales: Judges: Maximum number 266
Supreme Court of England & Wales: Jurisdiction 45, 266
Supreme Court of England & Wales: Probate: Non-contentious: Fees 266
Supreme Court of England & Wales: Staff: Contracting out. 40, 44, 117, 120, 265
Supreme Court of England & Wales: Tribunals, Courts & Enforcement Act 2007: Commencements 266
Supreme Court, Northern Ireland: Counter-terrorism: Rules: Northern Ireland 412
Supreme Court, Northern Ireland: Criminal appeals: Offenders assisting investigations & prosecutions: Northern Ireland 412
Supreme Court, Northern Ireland: Family proceedings: Rules: Northern Ireland 381, 386, 411
Supreme Court, Northern Ireland: Procedure: Crown Court: Rules: Amendments: Northern Ireland 400, 412
Supreme Court, Northern Ireland: Rules: Northern Ireland. 412
Surrey: National Health Service Primary Care Trust 127
Surrogacy: Arrangements: Acts 6
Surrogacy: Arrangements: Acts: Explanatory notes 8
Survivors & victims: Commission: Acts: Explanatory notes: Northern Ireland 374
Sussex: East Sussex (County): Eastbourne (Borough): Parking contraventions: Civil enforcement. 241
Sustainable communities: England 114
Swansea National Health Service Trust: Dissolution: Wales. 132
Swansea National Health Service Trust: Transfer of Staff, property, rights & liabilities: Wales. 132
Swansea: Parking contraventions: Civil enforcement: Wales 93
Sweeteners: Food: Northern Ireland. 389
Sweeteners: Food: Wales. 84

T

Takeover code: Concert parties. 19
Tamworth & Lichfield College: Dissolution 62
Tartans register: Acts: Explanatory notes: Scotland 325
Tartans register: Acts: Scotland 325
Tate Gallery Board: Additional members. 123
Tax credits. 266
Tax Credits Act 2002: Transitional provisions 266
Tax credits: Child care providers: Approval 267
Tax credits: Up-rating 266
Tax relief: Community development finance institutions: Accreditation 41, 100
Taxes *see also* Corporation tax
Taxes *see also* Income tax
Taxes *see also* Value added tax
Taxes: Authorised Investment Funds 21, 40, 41, 99, 100, 264
Taxes: Avoidance schemes: Information: Amendments 267
Taxes: Capital gains tax: Annual exempt amount 21
Taxes: Car fuel: Benefits 100
Taxes: Chargeable gains: Gilt-edged securities 22, 43
Taxes: Companies Act 2006: Consequential amendments 255, 267
Taxes: Corporation tax acts: Amendments: Insurance business transfer schemes 42
Taxes: Corporation tax: Instalment payments 41
Taxes: Corporation tax: Insurance companies: Amendments 42, 43
Taxes: Double taxation: Relief & international enforcement: Moldova 21, 41, 100
Taxes: Double taxation: Relief & international enforcement: New Zealand 21, 41, 100
Taxes: Double taxation: Relief & international enforcement: Saudi Arabia 21, 41, 100
Taxes: Double taxation: Relief & international enforcement: Slovenia 21, 41, 100
Taxes: Double taxation: Relief: Relievable tax: Within a group: Surrender 100
Taxes: Due in other member states: Finance Act 2002: Section 134: Amendments 151
Taxes: European single currency. 41
Taxes: Finance Act 2008: Schedule 38: Appointed day 267

Taxes: Financial Services & Markets Act 2000: Consequential amendments 42
Taxes: Income & corporation: Community investment: Tax relief: Community development finance institutions:
Accreditation 41, 100
Taxes: Income tax: Benefits: Government pilot schemes: Better off in Work Credit 102
Taxes: Income tax: Benefits: Government pilot schemes: Up-Front Childcare Fund 102
Taxes: Income tax: Childcare: Qualifying 102
Taxes: Income tax: Deposit-takers & building societies: Interest payments 101
Taxes: Income tax: Finance arrangements: Alternative: Community investment tax relief 99
Taxes: Income tax: Indexation 101
Taxes: Income tax: Overseas insurers: Tax representatives. 102
Taxes: Income tax: Payments on account 101
Taxes: Income tax: Professional fees 101
Taxes: Income tax: Registered pension schemes: Transfer of sums & assets. 102
Taxes: Inheritance tax: Accounts: Delivery: Excepted settlements 103
Taxes: Inheritance tax: Accounts: Delivery: Excepted transfers & terminations 103
Taxes: Insurance companies: Overseas life assurance business: Excluded business. 43
Taxes: Insurance companies: Profits: Calculation of: Policy holders' tax 42
Taxes: Insurance companies: Reinsurance business 43
Taxes: Insurance companies: Reserves. 43
Taxes: Insurance companies: Special purpose vehicles 43
Taxes: Insurance premium tax. 104
Taxes: Interest rate 262, 267
Taxes: Interest rates: Amendments 154
Taxes: International tax: Enforcement: Bermuda 267
Taxes: Landfill tax. 106
Taxes: Landfill tax: Contaminated land: Exemption phase out 106
Taxes: Life assurance & other policies: Insurers: Information & duties 102
Taxes: Limits: Enterprise management: Incentives 101
Taxes: Loan relationships & derivative contracts: Accounting practice: Changes. 43
Taxes: Non-resident insurance companies: Overseas losses: Group relief: Corporation Tax Acts: Modification 42
Taxes: Payment by telephone: Fees 267
Taxes: Pension schemes: Transitional provisions. 102
Taxes: Purchased life annuities 102
Taxes: Stamp duty & stamp duty reserve tax: Investment exchanges & clearing houses 263, 264, 267
Taxes: Stamp duty & stamp duty reserve tax: Investment exchanges & clearing houses: Amendments. 264
Taxes: Stamp duty & stamp duty reserve tax: Investment exchanges & clearing houses: Eurex Clearing AG 263, 264
Taxes: Stamp duty & stamp duty reserve tax: Investment exchanges & clearing houses: European Central Counterparty Ltd
& Turquoise Multilateral Trading Facility 267
Taxes: Stamp duty & stamp duty reserve tax: Investment exchanges & clearing houses: London Stock Exchange 264
Taxes: Stamp duty land tax: Finance Act 2003: Part 4: Variation 264
Taxes: Stamp duty land tax: Finance Act 2004: Part 4 264
Taxes: Stamp duty land tax: Residential property: Exemptions 264
Taxes: Stamp duty land tax: Zero-carbon homes relief. 264
Taxes: Stamp duty reserve tax: virt-x Exchange Ltd. 267
Taxes: Stamp duty: Open-ended investment companies 264
Taxes: Tax Credits Act 2002: Transitional provisions 266
Taxes: Tonnage tax: Training requirements. 267
Taxes: Value added tax: Buildings & land 275
Taxes: Value added tax: Finance 276
Taxes: Value added tax: Fuel: Private use: Consideration 275
Taxes: Value added tax: Registration limits: Increase 276
Taxis: Acts: Explanatory notes: Northern Ireland. 374
Taxis: Acts: Northern Ireland 373
Taxis: Antrim: Bye-laws: Northern Ireland 404
Taxis: Enniskillen: Bye-laws: Northern Ireland. 404
Tayside, Central & Fife Sheriffdom: Justice of the Peace courts: Scotland 345
Teachers: General Teaching Council for England: Provisional registration: Eligibility 60
Teachers: Induction arrangements: England 58
Teachers: Pensions 64
Teachers: Pensions: Northern Ireland 382
Teachers: Qualifications: Wales 67
Teachers: Superannuation: Scotland 350
Technical assistance: Provision: Control: Export: Goods: Customs 50
Technology Strategy Board: Transfer of property 251
Technology: Transfer: Control: Export: Goods: Customs 50

Teesport: Harbour revision 87
Teesport: Land acquisition 272, 273
Telecommunications & canals: Non-domestic rating: Scotland 353
Television multiplex services: Digital capacity: Reservation 20
Television multiplex services: Licences: Gaelic programming 20
Tenancies: Family intervention tenancies: Housing: Allocation: England 94
Tenancies: Family intervention tenancies: Local authority decisions: Reviews: England 94
Terms & conditions of employment: Employment rights: Limits: Increase 267
Terms & conditions of employment: Fixed-term employees: Less favourable treatment: Prevention 268
Terms & conditions of employment: Maternity, parental, paternity & adoption leave 268
Terms & conditions of employment: National Minimum Wage Regulations 1999: Amendment 268
Terms & conditions of employment: Public interest: Disclosure: Prescribed persons 268
Terms & conditions of employment: Statutory sick pay: General 262, 268
Terrorism Act 2000: Detention, treatment & questioning: Code of practice: Northern Ireland 399
Terrorism Act 2000: Proscribed organisations 143
Terrorism Act 2006: Section 25: Disapplication 143
Terrorism: Acts 5
Terrorism: Acts: Explanatory notes 7
Tewkesbury (Borough): Parish electoral arrangements: Local government 110
Textile products: Composition: Determination 271
Textile products: Fibre content: Trade descriptions 271
Thameslink: Network Rail: Land acquisition 272, 273
Thatcham Park Church of England Primary School: Religious character: Designation 63
TIR carnets: Goods: International transport: Fees 155
Title Conditions (Scotland) Act 2003: Conservation bodies: Scotland 363
Title Conditions (Scotland) Act 2003: Rural housing bodies: Scotland 363
Tobacco products: Duties 74
Tobacco: Sale: Children & young persons: Northern Ireland 400
Tolls: Severn Bridges 92
Tonnage tax: Training requirements 267
Tope: Fishing: Prohibition: England 252
Tope: Fishing: Prohibition: Wales 252
Towcester CofE Primary School: Religious character: Designation 63
Town & country planning: Acts 6
Town & country planning: Acts: Explanatory notes 8
Town & country planning: Appeals: Scotland 364
Town & country planning: Applications & deemed applications: Fees: England 269
Town & country planning: Appointed persons: Determination of appeals: Prescribed classes: England 268
Town & country planning: Avian influenza: General permitted development: Scotland 364
Town & country planning: Crossrail: Planning appeals: Written representations procedure 268
Town & country planning: Crossrail: Planning approval: Request fees 268
Town & country planning: Crossrail: Qualifying authorities 269
Town & country planning: Delegation & local review procedures: Scotland 364
Town & country planning: Development management procedure: Scotland 364
Town & country planning: Development planning: Scotland 364
Town & country planning: Energy: Acts 6
Town & country planning: Environmental impact assessment: England 269
Town & country planning: Environmental impact assessment: Wales 270
Town & country planning: General development procedure 269
Town & country planning: General permitted development: England 269
Town & country planning: General permitted development: Scotland 364
Town & country planning: General permitted development: Wales 270
Town & country planning: General permitted procedure: Wales 270
Town & country planning: Listed buildings: Conservation areas: England 268
Town & country planning: Local development: England 269
Town & country planning: Mayor of London 269
Town & country planning: Mineral permissions: Environmental impact assessment: England 269
Town & country planning: National security directions & appointed representatives: Scotland 270
Town & country planning: Planning & Compulsory Purchase Act 2004: Commencements: Wales 270
Town & country planning: Planning etc. (Scotland) Act 2006: Commencements: Scotland 363
Town & country planning: Planning etc. (Scotland) Act 2006: Development planning: Saving provisions: Scotland . . . 363
Town & country planning: Planning etc. (Scotland) Act 2006: Development planning: Saving, transitional & consequential provisions: Scotland 363
Town & country planning: Strategic Development Planning Authority: Designation: Scotland 363, 364
Town & country planning: Trees 269

Town & country planning: West Northamptonshire Joint Committee 269
Toys: Magnetic toys: Safety 39
Tractors: EC type-approval 157
Trade descriptions: Misleading marketing: Business protection from 271
Trade descriptions: Textile products: Composition: Determination 271
Trade descriptions: Textile products: Fibre content. 271
Trade marks 271
Trade marks: Earlier trade marks 271
Trade marks: European Communities 271
Trade marks: Fees 271
Trade marks: International registration 271
Trade unions: Certification officer: Fees: Northern Ireland. 412
Trade: Goods: Control 50
Trade: Statistics: Customs & excise. 265
Trading disclosures: Companies 36
Trading disclosures: Companies: Insolvency. 36
Trading: Unfair: Consumer protection 39
Traffic Management Act 2004: Commencements 242
Traffic officers: Vehicles: Removal & disposal: England 242
Traffic orders: Local authorities: Procedure: Scotland 354
Traffic regulation conditions: Public service vehicles: Scotland 352
Traffic signs: Amendments 157
Traffic signs: Northern Ireland 404
Traffic wardens: Northern Ireland. 404
Training: Education & skills: Acts. 5
Training: Education & skills: Acts: Explanatory notes 7
Training: Education: Inspectors: Wales 66
Training: Regional Learning & Skills Councils 62
Transfer of rights & liabilities: ING order 19
Transmissible spongiform encephalopathies: England. 14
Transmissible spongiform encephalopathies: Northern Ireland. 378, 379
Transmissible spongiform encephalopathies: Scotland 331
Transmissible spongiform encephalopathies: Wales 16
Transplants: Ethical approval, exceptions from licensing & supply of information 96, 97
Transport & Works (Scotland) Act 2007: Access to land by the Scottish Ministers: Scotland . . . 332, 365
Transport & Works (Scotland) Act 2007: Access to land on application: Scotland. 332, 365
Transport & works: Felixstowe branch line: Ipswich Yard improvements 272
Transport & works: Network Rail: Thameslink: Land acquisition 272, 273
Transport & works: River Humber: Upper Burcom Tidal Stream Generator 68, 134, 272
Transport & works: Teesport: Land acquisition 272, 273
Transport (Scotland) Act 2005: Commencements: Scotland 365
Transport for London Act 2008: Local acts 8
Transport tribunal: Amendment. 272
Transport: Abolition of Bridge Tolls (Scotland) Act 2008: Commencements: Scotland 354, 364
Transport: Animals: Cleansing & disinfection: Wales 16
Transport: Cross-border railway services: Working time. 272
Transport: Cross-border railway services: Working time: Northern Ireland 412
Transport: Crossrail: Nomination 272
Transport: International: Goods: TIR carnets: Fees. 155
Transport: Local transport: Acts 6
Transport: Local transport: Acts: Explanatory notes. 8
Transport: London Local Authorities: Local acts 8
Transport: Mayors: Elected: Local authorities: England. 111, 272
Transport: Mobility & Access Committee for Scotland: Revocation: Scotland 364
Transport: Public passenger transport: Public service vehicles: Fitness, equipment, use & certification 149
Transport: Public service vehicles: Traffic regulation conditions: Scotland 352
Transport: Public Transport Users' Committee for Scotland 365
Transport: Rail vehicles: Accessibility: B2007 Vehicles: Exemptions 54, 272
Transport: Rail vehicles: Accessibility: Exemption orders: Parliamentary procedures 54
Transport: Rail vehicles: Accessibility: Interoperable rail system 54, 272
Transport: Rail vehicles: Accessibility: London Underground Victoria Line 09TS vehicles: Exemptions 54, 272
Transport: Railways: Crossrail: Acts. 5
Transport: Railways: Crossrail: Acts: Explanatory notes 7
Transport: Railways: Felixstowe branch line: Ipswich Yard improvements 272
Transport: Regional transport planning: Wales. 273

Transport: Road & railway transport: Penalty fares: Increases: Northern Ireland 403
Travelling expenses & remission of charges: Health & personal social services: Northern Ireland 391
Travelling expenses & remission of charges: National Health Service: England 125, 126
Travelling expenses & remission of charges: National Health Service: Scotland 349
Travelling expenses & remission of charges: National Health Service: Wales 130, 131
Treatment of offenders: Prisons & young offenders centres: Northern Ireland 400, 412
Trees: Town & country planning 269
Tribunal Procedure Committee: Membership. 273
Tribunals & inquiries. 105, 273
Tribunals & inquiries: Appeals: Excluded decisions 273
Tribunals & inquiries: Charities: Tribunal rules 273
Tribunals & inquiries: Consumer Credit Appeals Tribunal: Rules 273
Tribunals & inquiries: First-tier & Upper tribunals: Chambers. 273
Tribunals & inquiries: First-tier & Upper tribunals: Composition of tribunal 273
Tribunals & inquiries: First-tier & Upper tribunals: Members: Appointment: Qualifications 273
Tribunals & inquiries: First-tier tribunal: Health, education & social care chamber: England & Wales 274
Tribunals & inquiries: First-tier tribunal: Social Entitlement Chamber. 274
Tribunals & inquiries: First-tier tribunal: War pensions & armed forces compensation chamber: England & Wales 274
Tribunals & inquiries: Mental Health Review Tribunal for Wales: Rules 274
Tribunals & inquiries: Mesothelioma: Lump sum payments: Claims & reconsiderations 257, 273
Tribunals & inquiries: Tribunal Procedure Committee: Membership 273
Tribunals & inquiries: Tribunal procedure: Upper tribunal. 274
Tribunals & inquiries: Tribunals, Courts & Enforcement Act 2007: Transitional & consequential provisions 274
Tribunals & inquiries: Tribunals, Courts & Enforcement Act 2007: Transitional judicial pensions provisions 274
Tribunals & inquiries: Tribunals: Functions: Transfer 274
Tribunals & inquiries: Upper Tribunal: Appeals: To Court of Appeal 274
Tribunals, Courts & Enforcement Act 2007: Commencements. 105, 274
Tribunals, Courts & Enforcement Act 2007: Commencements: England & Wales 266
Tribunals, Courts & Enforcement Act 2007: Commencements: Scotland 336
Tribunals, Courts & Enforcement Act 2007: Commencements: Wales & Northern Ireland. 49
Tribunals, Courts & Enforcement Act 2007: Transitional & consequential provisions 274
Tribunals, Courts & Enforcement Act 2007: Transitional judicial pensions provisions 274
Tribunals: Case: England 110
Tribunals: Functions: Transfer 274
Trinity Anglican-Methodist Primary School: Religious character: Designation. 63
Trunk roads: A1 . . . . 160, 161, 162, 163, 164, 165, 166, 167
Trunk roads: A1: Dishforth to Barton Section 91
Trunk roads: A1/A1(M) 159, 161
Trunk roads: A1/A19 175
Trunk roads: A1/A195(M)/A1(M) 159
Trunk roads: A1/A47 159
Trunk roads: A1/A66 162
Trunk roads: A1/A66/A1(M). 161
Trunk roads: A1089 . . . . 205, 206
Trunk roads: A1089/A13. . . . . 157, 173
Trunk roads: A11. . . . . 171, 172
Trunk roads: A12. . . . . 172, 173
Trunk roads: A12/A120 172
Trunk roads: A12/A14. 173
Trunk roads: A120. 198
Trunk roads: A120/A12 172
Trunk roads: A120/M11. 222
Trunk roads: A13 173
Trunk roads: A13/A1089. . . . . 157, 173
Trunk roads: A1307/A14/M11 222
Trunk roads: A14. . . . . 173, 174, 175
Trunk roads: A14/A12. 173
Trunk roads: A14/A1307/M11 222
Trunk roads: A160 . . . . 198, 199
Trunk roads: A160/A180 198
Trunk roads: A167/A1(M) 159
Trunk roads: A168. 199
Trunk roads: A174. 199
Trunk roads: A180. 199
Trunk roads: A180/A160 198

Trunk roads: A184.	199
Trunk roads: A19.	158, 175, 176
Trunk roads: A19/A1.	175
Trunk roads: A19/A1058/A191.	176
Trunk roads: A19/A1068/A1058.	175
Trunk roads: A2.	167, 168
Trunk roads: A2/A282/M25.	225
Trunk roads: A2/M2.	167, 209
Trunk roads: A20.	176, 177, 224
Trunk roads: A20/M20.	176, 223, 224
Trunk roads: A20/M25/M20.	225
Trunk roads: A2070.	206
Trunk roads: A21.	177
Trunk roads: A21/M25.	225
Trunk roads: A23.	177, 178
Trunk roads: A23/A27.	177
Trunk roads: A23/M23.	177
Trunk roads: A249.	199
Trunk roads: A259.	199, 200
Trunk roads: A27.	178, 179
Trunk roads: A27/A23.	177
Trunk roads: A27: Southerham to Beddingham improvment: Banned turns.	241
Trunk roads: A27: Southerham to Beddingham improvment: Derestriction & revocation.	241
Trunk roads: A282.	158, 200
Trunk roads: A282/M25.	225
Trunk roads: A282/M25/A2.	225
Trunk roads: A282: Dartford - Thurrock Crossing charging scheme.	91
Trunk roads: A3.	168, 169
Trunk roads: A3/M25.	225
Trunk roads: A30.	179, 180, 181
Trunk roads: A30/A303.	179
Trunk roads: A30/M25.	179
Trunk roads: A303.	200
Trunk roads: A303/A30.	179
Trunk roads: A31.	181
Trunk roads: A316/M3.	209, 210
Trunk roads: A34.	181, 182
Trunk roads: A35.	182
Trunk roads: A36.	183
Trunk roads: A38.	183, 184, 185, 186
Trunk roads: A38/A5148.	185
Trunk roads: A38/M5.	212
Trunk roads: A38/M6 Toll.	184
Trunk roads: A38: Langley Mill, Warwickshire/Birmingham: Detrunking.	91
Trunk roads: A38: Weeford, Staffordshire to Minworth, Birmingham: Detrunking.	91
Trunk roads: A4.	169, 215
Trunk roads: A4/M5.	213
Trunk roads: A4: Bath to Bristol: Detrunking.	91
Trunk roads: A40.	158, 186, 244, 245
Trunk roads: A40/A49.	186
Trunk roads: A40/M40.	228, 229
Trunk roads: A40/M5.	213
Trunk roads: A40: Penblewin to Slebech Park improvement.	93
Trunk roads: A404.	201
Trunk roads: A4042.	249
Trunk roads: A4042/M4.	250
Trunk roads: A405.	201
Trunk roads: A4076.	250
Trunk roads: A4123.	92, 206
Trunk roads: A4123/M5.	206
Trunk roads: A4146/A5.	170
Trunk roads: A417.	201
Trunk roads: A417/A419.	201
Trunk roads: A419.	158, 201
Trunk roads: A419/A417.	201

Trunk roads: A42 215
Trunk roads: A42/M1 206
Trunk roads: A42/M6/M42/M6 Toll 215
Trunk roads: A421 . . . . 201, 202
Trunk roads: A421/M1 207
Trunk roads: A421: M1 junction 13 to Bedford improvements: Detrunking 91
Trunk roads: A421: MI Junction 13 improvements 91
Trunk roads: A4232 250
Trunk roads: A4232/M4 250
Trunk roads: A428 202
Trunk roads: A43 . . . . 158, 186
Trunk roads: A43/M40 229
Trunk roads: A435/A46 187
Trunk roads: A449 202
Trunk roads: A449/M4 250
Trunk roads: A449/M50 231
Trunk roads: A45 . . . . 186, 187
Trunk roads: A453 202
Trunk roads: A456 202
Trunk roads: A456: Detrunking 91
Trunk roads: A46 . . . . 187, 188, 189
Trunk roads: A46/A435 187
Trunk roads: A46/A52 187
Trunk roads: A46/M1 209
Trunk roads: A46/M69 187
Trunk roads: A465 247
Trunk roads: A465: Llangua Bridge to A49/A465 Belmont Roundabout: Detrunking 91
Trunk roads: A47 . . . . 189, 190
Trunk roads: A47/A1 159
Trunk roads: A470 . . . . 244, 247
Trunk roads: A470: Penloyn to Tan Lan Improvement: Wales 93
Trunk roads: A477 248
Trunk roads: A48 245
Trunk roads: A48/M4 250
Trunk roads: A483 . . . . 202, 245, 248
Trunk roads: A487 . . . . 248, 249
Trunk roads: A49 . . . . 158, 190
Trunk roads: A49/A40 186
Trunk roads: A49/A5 170
Trunk roads: A494 249
Trunk roads: A494/A5 249
Trunk roads: A494/A550 . . . . 158, 249
Trunk roads: A494/A550/A55 246
Trunk roads: A5 . . . . 157, 170, 171, 231, 244
Trunk roads: A5/A4146 170
Trunk roads: A5/A49 170
Trunk roads: A5/A494 249
Trunk roads: A5/M42 229
Trunk roads: A5/M6/M54 217
Trunk roads: A50 . . . . 190, 191, 192
Trunk roads: A500 . . . . 202, 203
Trunk roads: A500/M6 202
Trunk roads: A5006 206
Trunk roads: A5036 206
Trunk roads: A5103 206
Trunk roads: A5103/M60 234
Trunk roads: A5111/A52 192
Trunk roads: A5117 206
Trunk roads: A5148/A38 185
Trunk roads: A52 192
Trunk roads: A52/A46 187
Trunk roads: A52/A5111 192
Trunk roads: A55 . . . . 192, 245, 246, 247
Trunk roads: A55/A494/A550 246
Trunk roads: A550 203

Trunk roads: A550/A494. . . . . 158, 249
Trunk roads: A550/A55/A494. 246
Trunk roads: A556 . . . . 158, 203
Trunk roads: A556: Church Farm - Turnpike Wood, Over Tabley 91
Trunk roads: A556: Turnpike Wood, Over Tabley - A56 Bowden roundabout: Detrunking 92
Trunk roads: A56 193
Trunk roads: A57 193
Trunk roads: A570. 203
Trunk roads: A570: Detrunking 92
Trunk roads: A585 . . . . 178, 203
Trunk roads: A585/M55. 232
Trunk roads: A590 . . . . 203, 204, 205
Trunk roads: A595 . . . . 158, 159, 205
Trunk roads: A616. 205
Trunk roads: A62 193
Trunk roads: A62/M62/M621. 239
Trunk roads: A628. 205
Trunk roads: A63. . . . . 193, 194
Trunk roads: A63/M62. . . . . 194, 238
Trunk roads: A631. 205
Trunk roads: A64 . . . . 158, 194, 195
Trunk roads: A65. . . . . 158, 195
Trunk roads: A65: Junction 36 to roundabout junction with A59: Detrunking 91
Trunk roads: A66. . . . . 195, 196, 197, 198, 205
Trunk roads: A66/A1 162
Trunk roads: A66/A1/A1(M) 161
Trunk roads: A66/A66(M) 195
Trunk roads: A68: Scotland 198, 355
Trunk roads: A69. . . . . 158, 198
Trunk roads: A7: Scotland. 355
Trunk roads: A702: Scotland 356
Trunk roads: A720: Scotland 356
Trunk roads: A737/A738: Scotland 356
Trunk roads: A738/A737: Scotland 356
Trunk roads: A76: Scotland 354, 355
Trunk roads: A77/M77: Scotland 357
Trunk roads: A77: Scotland 354, 355
Trunk roads: A82: Scotland 355, 356
Trunk roads: A830: Scotland 357
Trunk roads: A835: Scotland 354
Trunk roads: A84 (Route): Scotland 360
Trunk roads: A84/A85: Scotland 355
Trunk roads: A85: Scotland 355
Trunk roads: A9/M9: Scotland 357
Trunk roads: A9: Scotland 354, 355
Trunk roads: A90/M90: Scotland 357
Trunk roads: A90: Scotland 356
Trunk roads: A92/A972: Scotland. 356
Trunk roads: A92: Scotland 356
Trunk roads: A96: Scotland 356
Trunk roads: A977: Scotland 355
Trunk roads: M1-A1 link road 93
Trunk roads: M2/A26: Ballee Road east link: Northern Ireland 403
Trunk roads: M77/A77: Scotland 357
Trunk roads: M80/A80: Scotland 357
Trunk roads: M9/A9: Scotland 357
Trunk roads: M90/A90: Scotland 357
Trunk roads: M90: Scotland. 357
Trunk roads: North east unit trunk roads area: Scotland. 357, 358
Trunk roads: North west unit trunk roads area: Scotland 358, 359
Trunk roads: South east unit trunk roads area: Scotland 359
Trunk roads: South west unit trunk roads area: Scotland 359, 360
Trust deeds: Protected: Scotland 332
Trustees: Public trustees: Fees. 275
TSE *see* Transmissible spongiform encephalopathies

Tuberculosis: Animal health: Testing & powers & entry: Wales ... 16
Turquoise Multilateral Trading Facility.: Stamp duty & stamp duty reserve tax: Investment exchanges & clearing houses 267
Tyne & Wear Fire & Rescue Authority: Members: Increase. ... 80
Tyne Harbour Port: Harbour revision. ... 87

U

UHI Millennium Institute: Academic awards & distinctions: Scotland. ... 337
UK Borders Act 2007: Children: Code of practice ... 99
UK Borders Act 2007: Commencements. ... 99
Unfair trading: Consumer protection ... 39
United Nations: Dependent territories: Arms embargoes ... 275
United Nations: Rwanda: Arms embargoes ... 275
University of Aberdeen: Academic awards & distinctions: Additional powers: Scotland ... 337
Up-Front Childcare Fund: Government pilot schemes: Taxation of benefits. ... 102
Upper Burcom Tidal Stream Generator: River Humber ... 68, 134, 272
Upper Tribunal: Appeals: To Court of Appeal ... 274
Urban regeneration: Housing: Acts ... 6
Urban regeneration: Housing: Acts: Explanatory notes ... 7
Utilities contracts: Postal services & common procurement vocabulary codes: Scotland ... 352
Utilities contracts: Public procurement ... 149
Utilities contracts: Public procurement: Postal services ... 149
Utilities contracts: Scotland ... 352
Uttlesford: Electoral changes: Local government ... 114

V

Vaccine damage payments: Specified diseases ... 148
Valuation tribunal: Northern Ireland ... 402
Valuation: Plant & machinery: Valuation for rating: Scotland ... 353
Valuation: Water undertakings: Northern Ireland. ... 402
Value added tax: Amendments ... 275
Value added tax: Buildings & land ... 275
Value added tax: Correction of errors ... 10, 33, 76, 104, 106, 275
Value added tax: Customs & excise duties: Travellers' allowances ... 76, 275
Value added tax: Domestic fuel or power: Supplies: Reduced rate. ... 276
Value added tax: Finance ... 276
Value added tax: Fuel: Private use: Consideration ... 275
Value added tax: Rate: Changes. ... 275
Value added tax: Reduced rate: Smoking cessation products. ... 276
Value added tax: Refund: Museums & galleries ... 276
Value added tax: Registration limits: Increase ... 276
Veal: Labelling: Declaration: Scotland ... 327, 340
Veal: Labelling: England. ... 10
Vehicle drivers: Professional competence: Certificates: Amendments ... 157
Vehicle excise duty: Immobilisation, removal & disposal of vehicles ... 157
Vehicle registration: Fees. ... 78
Vehicles: Crime: Registration plate suppliers: Registration ... 157
Vehicles: Goods vehicles: International journeys: Authorisation: Fees. ... 154
Vehicles: Goods vehicles: Operator licensing: Fees ... 154
Vehicles: Goods vehicles: Plating & testing ... 155
Vehicles: Insurance information: Disclosure: Northern Ireland ... 403
Vehicles: Motor vehicles: Approval: Fees ... 155
Vehicles: Motor vehicles: Driving licences. ... 155
Vehicles: Motor vehicles: Driving licences: Northern Ireland ... 403
Vehicles: Motor vehicles: EC type approval ... 155
Vehicles: Motor vehicles: Taxi Drivers' licences: Fees: Amendments: Northern Ireland ... 403
Vehicles: Motor vehicles: Testing: Northern Ireland ... 404
Vehicles: Motor vehicles: Tests ... 155, 156
Vehicles: Passenger & goods vehicles: Drivers: Training: Certificates of professional competence. ... 157
Vehicles: Passenger & goods vehicles: Recording equipment: Downloading & retention of data ... 156
Vehicles: Passenger & goods vehicles: Recording equipment: Fitters & workshops: Approval: Fees. ... 156
Vehicles: Public service vehicles: Accessibility ... 54
Vehicles: Public service vehicles: Fitness, equipment, use & certification. ... 149
Vehicles: Public service vehicles: Local services: Registration: England & Wales ... 149

Vehicles: Public service vehicles: Operators' licences: Fees 149
Vehicles: Registration marks: Retention 156
Vehicles: Removal & disposal: Traffic officers: England 242
Vehicles: Removal & disposal: Wales 244
Vehicles: Removal, storage & disposal: Prescribed sums & charges: England. 242
Vehicles: Removal, storage & disposal: Prescribed sums & charges: England & Wales. 242
Vehicles: Removed vehicles: Parking contraventions: Civil enforcement: Representations & appeals: Wales 243
Vehicles: Retention & disposal: Police: England & Wales 142
Vehicles: Road vehicles: Registration & licensing: Amendments 156
Vehicles: Road vehicles: Registration marks: Sale 157
Vehicles: Seized motor vehicles: Retention & disposal. 156
Vehicles: Seizure & disposal: Act of Adjournal: Criminal procedure rules: Amendments: Scotland. 344, 361
Vehicles: Special purpose vehicles: Insurance: Taxation 43
Venture capital trusts 103
Veterinary medicines 119
Veterinary surgeons & practitioners: Registration: Amendments. 276
Veterinary surgeons: Commonwealth & foreign candidates: Examinations 276
Veterinary surgeons: Qualifications: European recognition 276
Victim notification scheme: Scotland. 336
Victims & survivors: Commission: Acts: Explanatory notes: Northern Ireland 374
Victims & survivors: Commission: Acts: Northern Ireland. 373
Victims: Mentally disordered offenders: Information: Schemes: Northern Ireland 394
Violent Crime Reduction Act 2006: Commencements. 47, 48
virt-x Exchange Ltd.: Stamp duty reserve tax. 267
Visiting forces 52
Vocational training & information actions grant: Agriculture: Northern Ireland. 378
Voting: Absent voting. 152
Vulnerable adults: Protection of Children & Vulnerable Adults & Care Standards Tribunal: Children's & adults' barred lists
. . . . 25, 146
Vulnerable adults: Protection: Care Standards Tribunal: England & Wales. 24
Vulnerable adults: Safeguarding Vulnerable Groups Act 2006: Barred list prescribed information: England & Wales . 25, 147
Vulnerable adults: Safeguarding Vulnerable Groups Act 2006: Barring procedure: England & Wales 25, 147
Vulnerable adults: Safeguarding Vulnerable Groups Act 2006: Commencements: England. 24, 146
Vulnerable adults: Safeguarding Vulnerable Groups Act 2006: Commencements: England & Wales. 25, 51, 147
Vulnerable adults: Safeguarding Vulnerable Groups Act 2006: Commencements: Northern Ireland 26, 147
Vulnerable adults: Safeguarding Vulnerable Groups Act 2006: Prescribed criteria: Foreign offices: England & Wales 25, 147
Vulnerable adults: Safeguarding Vulnerable Groups Act 2006: Prescribed criteria: Transitional provisions: England & Wales
. . . . 25, 147
Vulnerable adults: Safeguarding Vulnerable Groups Act 2006: Prescribed information: England & Wales. 25, 147
Vulnerable adults: Safeguarding Vulnerable Groups Act 2006: Transitional provisions: England & Wales 25, 147
Vulnerable groups: Adults: Safeguarding Vulnerable Groups: 2007 Order: Commencements: Northern Ireland 404
Vulnerable groups: Safeguarding Vulnerable Groups: 2007 Order: Commencements: Northern Ireland 404
Vulnerable Witnesses (Scotland) Act 2004: Commencements: Scotland. 362

W

Wakefield City Council: Wakefield Waterfront Hepworth Gallery footbridge scheme 92
Wales: North Wales National Health Service Trust: Establishment: Wales 131
Waste & contaminated land: 1997 Order: Commencements: Northern Ireland 384
Waste management: Environmental protection: Northern Ireland 384
Waste management: Licences: Consultation & compensation: Northern Ireland. 384
Waste management: Site plans: England. 72
Waste: 2007 Amendment Order: Commencements: Northern Ireland 384
Waste: Landfill tax 106
Waste: London Waste & Recycling Board 116
Waste: Packaging waste: Producer responsibility & obligations. 71
Waste: Radioactive waste & spent fuel: Transfrontier shipments 18
Waste: Transfrontier shipments. 72
Water & sewerage services: Undertaking: Lending by the Scottish Ministers: Scotland. 366
Water Act 2003: Commencements 276
Water Environment & Water Services (Scotland) Act 2003: Commencements: Scotland 339, 366
Water environment: Diffuse pollution: Scotland 339, 366
Water industry: Supply & sewerage services: Customer service standards. 277
Water resources: Abstraction & impounding 277
Water resources: Bathing water 277

Water supply: Loch of Boardhouse: Scottish Water: Scotland 366
Water undertakings: Valuation: Northern Ireland. 402
Water: Bathing water: Quality: Northern Ireland 384
Water: Bathing water: Scotland 339, 365
Water: Nitrate pollution: Prevention 11, 276
Water: Nitrate pollution: Prevention: Wales 12, 277
Water: Nitrate vulnerable zones: Action programmes: Scotland 327, 338, 339, 365
Water: Water environment: Controlled activities: Relevant enactments: Scotland. 339
Wear: Tyne & Wear Fire & Rescue Authority: Members: Increase 80
Weighing & measuring equipment: Verfication: Legislative reform 152
Weights & measures: Measuring instruments: EC requirements 277
Weights & measures: Measuring instruments: Use for trade: Northern Ireland 412
Weights & measures: Non-automatic weighing instruments 278
Welfare food 81
Welfare Reform Act 2007: Commencements. 262
Welfare Reform Act 2007: Commencements: Northern Ireland 410
Welfare Reform Act 2007: Relevant enactments 263
Welfare Reform Act 2007: Relevant statutory provisions: Northern Ireland 410
Welfare services: Social security: Information: Use 263
Welland & Deepings Internal Drainage Board 106
Welsh language schemes: Public bodies 278
Welsh Levy Board 13
Welsh Ministers: Transfer of functions: Wales. 38, 53
Welsh Statutory instruments: National Assembly for Wales: Annual volumes 9
Welwyn Hatfield (Borough): Electoral changes 110
West Northamptonshire Joint Committee. 269
West Wiltshire (District): Wiltshire (County): Parking contraventions: Civil enforcement 242
Westlink: Busways: Northern Ireland 403, 404
Weston Harbour Port: Harbour revision 87
Whiteness Marina: Harbour revision: Scotland 342
Wildlife & Countryside Act 1981: Schedule 4: Variation: England 278
Wildlife & Countryside Act 1981: Schedule 5: Variation: England 278
Wildlife & Countryside Act 1981: Schedule 5: Variation: Wales 278
Wildlife & countryside: Birds: Captive: Registration & ringing: England 278
Wildlife: Conservation: Natural habitats: England & Wales 44, 278
Wildlife: Conservation: Natural habitats: Scotland 334, 366
William Parker School: Religious character: Designation 63
Wiltshire (County): West Wiltshire (District): Parking contraventions: Civil enforcement 242
Wiltshire: Local government: Structural changes. 114
Wine & made-wine: Excise. 74
Winter fuel payments: Social fund 258
Winter fuel payments: Social fund: Temporary increase: Northern Ireland 407
Wireless telegraphy: Automotive short range radar: Exemptions 68
Wireless telegraphy: Exemptions. 68
Wireless telegraphy: Licence awards. 68, 69
Wireless telegraphy: Licence charges 69
Wireless telegraphy: Mobile communication services on aircraft: Exemptions 69
Wireless telegraphy: Register. 69
Wireless telegraphy: Spectrum access: Licences: Number limitation 69
Wireless telegraphy: Spectrum trading 69
Witness anonymity: Criminal evidence: Acts 5
Witness anonymity: Criminal evidence: Acts: Explanatory notes. 7
Wool textile industry: Export promotion levy: Revocation. 103
Work credit: Better off in Work Credit: Government pilot schemes: Taxation of benefits. 102
Workers: Fixed-term employees: Less favourable treatment: Prevention 268
Workers: Fixed-term employees: Less favourable treatment: Prevention: Northern Ireland 383
Workers' compensation: Pneumoconiosis etc.: Claims: Payments 258
Workers' compensation: Pneumoconiosis etc.: Claims: Payment: Northern Ireland 407
Workers' compensation: Supplementation 262
Workers' compensation: Supplementation: Northern Ireland. 411
Work-focused interviews: Incapacity benefit 259
Work-focused Interviews: Partners: Northern Ireland 410
Working tax credit: Up-rating. 266
Wrecks: Protection: Designation: England 147
Wrexham (County Borough): Permitted & special parking areas: Wales 244

Wycombe (District): Buckinghamshire (County): Parking contraventions: Civil enforcement 241
Wylye Valley Church of England Voluntary Aided Primary School: Religious character: Designation 63

Y

Young offender institutions 278
Young offender institutions: Prisons: Amendments: Scotland 351, 366
Youth Justice Board for England & Wales 47

Z

Zoonoses & animal by-products: Fees: England 15
Zoonoses & animal by-products: Fees: Northern Ireland 379
Zoonoses & animal by-products: Fees: Scotland 331
Zoonoses & animal by-products: Fees: Wales 16, 17
Zoonoses: Monitoring: Northern Ireland 379
Zootechnical standards 17
Zootechnical standards: Horses: Scotland 329
Zootechnical standards: Northern Ireland 378